W9-AOR-222

PROFESSIONAL
C# 7 AND .NET CORE 2.0

Continues

PROFESSIONAL

C# 7 and .NET Core 2.0

PROFESSIONAL

C# 7 and .NET Core 2.0

Christian Nagel

wrox™

A Wiley Brand

Professional C# 7 and .NET Core 2.0

Published by
John Wiley & Sons, Inc.
10475 Crosspoint Boulevard
Indianapolis, IN 46256
www.wiley.com

Copyright © 2018 by John Wiley & Sons, Inc., Indianapolis, Indiana

Published simultaneously in Canada

ISBN: 978-1-119-44927-0
ISBN: 978-1-119-44924-9 (ebk)
ISBN: 978-1-119-44926-3 (ebk)
Manufactured in the United States of America

10 9 8 7 6 5 4 3 2 1

For general information on our other products and services please contact our Customer Care Department within the United States at (877) 762-2974, outside the United States at (317) 572-3993 or fax (317) 572-4002.

Wiley publishes in a variety of print and electronic formats and by print-on-demand. Some material included with standard print versions of this book may not be included in e-books or in print-on-demand. If this book refers to media such as a CD or DVD that is not included in the version you purchased, you may download this material at http://booksupport.wiley.com. For more information about Wiley products, visit www.wiley.com.

Library of Congress Control Number: 2018931434

This book is dedicated to my family—Angela, Stephanie, Matthias, and Katharina—I love you all!

ABOUT THE AUTHOR

CHRISTIAN NAGEL is Microsoft MVP for Visual Studio and Development Technologies and has been Microsoft Regional Director for more than 15 years. Christian founder of CN innovation, where he offers coaching, training, code reviews, and assistance with architecting and developing solutions using Microsoft technologies. He draws on more than 25 years of software development experience.

Christian started his computing career with PDP 11 and VAX/VMS systems at Digital Equipment Corporation, covering a variety of languages and platforms. Since 2000, when .NET was just a technology preview, he has been working with various technologies to build .NET solutions. Currently, he mainly coaches people on development and architecting Windows apps, ASP.NET Core web applications, and Xamarin and helps them use several Microsoft Azure service offerings.

Even after many years in software development, Christian still loves learning and using new technologies and teaching others how to use the new technologies in various forms. Using his profound knowledge of Microsoft technologies, he has written numerous books and is certified as Microsoft Certified Trainer and Certified Solution Developer. Christian speaks at international conferences such as Microsoft Ignite (previously named TechEd), BASTA! and TechDays. He founded INETA Europe to support .NET user groups. You can contact Christian via his website www.cninnovation.com, read his blog at https://csharp .christiannagel.com, and follow his tweets at @christiannagel.

ABOUT THE TECHNICAL EDITOR

 **ISTVÁN NOVÁK** is an associate and the chief technology consultant with SoftwArt, a small Hungarian IT consulting company. He works as a software architect and community evangelist. In the last 25 years, he has participated in more than 50 enterprise software development projects. In 2002, he co-authored the first Hungarian book about .NET development. In 2007, he was awarded the Microsoft Most Valuable Professional (MVP) title, and in 2011 he became a Microsoft Regional Director. István co-authored *Visual Studio 2010 and .NET 4 Six-in-One* (Wiley, 2010) and *Beginning Windows 8 Application Development* (Wiley, 2012), and he authored *Beginning Visual Studio LightSwitch Development* (Wiley, 2011). István holds a master's degree from the Technical University of Budapest, Hungary and also has a doctoral degree in software technology. He lives in Dunakeszi, Hungary, with his wife and two daughters. He is a passionate scuba diver. You may have a good chance of meeting him underwater at the Red Sea in any season of the year.

CREDITS

ACKNOWLEDGMENTS

I WANT TO THANK Charlotte Kughen, who made my text so much more readable. Often I was working late at night writing while .NET Core was continuously evolving. Charlotte was of enormous help to change my ideas into great readable text. She also invested many weekends to help bring this book out fast. Special thanks also goes to István Novák, who has authored several great books. Despite all the issues we had with the fast evolving .NET Core and the interim builds I was using while working on the book, István challenged me to enhance the code samples that allow you—the reader—to better follow the flow. Thank you, Charlotte and István—you've been of great help for the quality of this book.

I also would like to thank Richard Lander from the .NET Core team. We had a great discussion in Redmond on the content and directions for the 11th edition of the book. Rich also found the time to give me good advice on a few chapters of the book.

I also would like to thank Kenyon Brown and everyone else at Wiley who helped to get edition 11 of this great book published. I also want to thank my wife and children for supporting my writing. You've been enormously helpful and understanding while I was working on the book for many nights, weekends, and winter holidays. Angela, Stephanie, Matthias, and Katharina—you are my loved ones. This would not have been possible without you.

CONTENTS

CHAPTER 16: REFLECTION, METADATA, AND DYNAMIC PROGRAMMING

PART II: .NET CORE AND THE WINDOWS RUNTIME

CHAPTER 19: LIBRARIES, ASSEMBLIES, PACKAGES, AND NUGET   539

CHAPTER 20: DEPENDENCY INJECTION   559

CHAPTER 21: TASKS AND PARALLEL PROGRAMMING 583

CHAPTER 26: ENTITY FRAMEWORK CORE 769

PART III: WEB APPLICATIONS AND SERVICES

CHAPTER 30: ASP.NET CORE   923

PART IV: APPS

CHAPTER 33: WINDOWS APPS   1083

ONLINE CHAPTERS

BONUS CHAPTER 1: COMPOSITION   OC1

INTRODUCTION

AFTER SO MANY YEARS, .NET has a new momentum. The .NET Framework has a young sibling: .NET Core! The .NET Framework was closed source and available on Windows systems only. Now, .NET Core is open source, is available on Linux, and uses modern patterns. We can see many great improvements in the .NET ecosystem.

> **NOTE** *Because of the recent changes, C# is within the top 10 of the most loved programming languages, and .NET Core is holds position 3 of the most loved frameworks. Among web and desktop developers, C# holds rank 3 among the most popular languages. You can see the details at* https://insights.stackoverflow.com/survey/2017.

By using C# and ASP.NET Core, you can create web applications and services that run on Windows, Linux, and Mac. You can use the Windows Runtime to create native Windows apps (also known as the Universal Windows Platform, UWP) using C# and XAML, as well as .NET Core. With Xamarin, you can use C# and XAML to create apps that run on Android and iOS devices. With the help of the .NET Standard, you can create libraries that you can share between ASP.NET Core, Windows apps, Xamarin; you also can create traditional Windows Forms and WPF applications. All this is covered in the book.

Most of the samples of the book are built on a Windows system with Visual Studio. Many of the samples are also tested on Linux and run on Linux and the Mac. Except for the Windows apps samples, you can also use Visual Studio Code or Visual Studio for the Mac as the developer environment.

THE WORLD OF .NET CORE

.NET has a long history, but .NET Core is very young. .NET Core 2.0 got many new APIs coming from the .NET Framework to make it easier to move existing .NET Framework applications to the new world of .NET Core.

As an easy move, you can create libraries that use .NET Standard 2.0, which can be used from .NET Framework applications starting with .NET Framework 4.6.1, .NET Core 2.0 applications, and Windows apps starting with Build 16299.

Nowadays, there are not many reasons to not use ASP.NET Core from the backend. With the easy move to the .NET Standard, more and more libraries can be used from .NET Core. From a high-level view, ASP.NET Core MVC looks very similar to its older brother ASP.NET MVC. However, ASP.NET Core MVC is a lot more flexible, easier to work with when using the .NET Core patterns, and easier to extend.

For creating new web applications, using the new technology Razor Pages might be all you need. If the application grows, Razor Pages can be easily extended to the Model-View-Controller pattern using ASP.NET Core MVC.

At the time of writing, a .NET Core version for SignalR, a technology for real-time communication, is near to being released.

ASP.NET Core works great in combination with JavaScript technologies like Angular and React/Redux. There are even templates to create projects with these technologies in combination with ASP.NET Core for the backend services.

> **NOTE** *You can access the source code of .NET Core at* `https://github.com/ dotnet/corefx`. *The .NET Core command line is available at* `https://github .com/dotnet/cli`. *At* `https://github.com/aspnet` *you can find many repositories for ASP.NET Core. Among them are ASP.NET Core MVC, Razor, SignalR, EntityFrameworkCore, and many others.*

Here's a summary of some of the features of .NET Core:

➤ .NET Core is open source.

➤ .NET Core uses modern patterns.

➤ .NET Core supports development on multiple platforms.

➤ ASP.NET Core can run on Windows and Linux.

As you work with .NET Core, you'll see that this technology is the biggest change for .NET since the first version. .NET Core is a new start. From here we can continue our journey on new developments in a fast pace.

THE WORLD OF C#

When C# was released in the year 2002, it was a language developed for the .NET Framework. C# was designed with ideas from C++, Java, and Pascal. Anders Hejlsberg had come to Microsoft from Borland and brought experience with language development of Delphi. At Microsoft, Hejlsberg worked on Microsoft's version of Java, named J++, before creating C#.

> **NOTE** *Today, Anders Hejlsberg has moved to TypeScript (while he still influences C#) and Mads Torgersen is the project lead for C#. C# improvements are discussed openly at* `https://github.com/dotnet/csharplang`. *Here you can read C# language proposals and event meeting notes. You can also submit your own proposals for C#.*

C# started not only as an object-oriented general-purpose programming language but was a component-based programming language that supported properties, events, attributes (annotations), and building assemblies (binaries including metadata).

Over time, C# was enhanced with generics, Language Integrated Query (LINQ), lambda expressions, dynamic features, and easier asynchronous programming. C# is not an easy programming language because of the many features it offers, but it's continuously evolving with features that are practical to use. With this, C# is more than an object-oriented or component-based language; it also includes ideas of functional programming—things that are of practical use for a general-purpose language developing all kind of applications.

With C# 6, the source code of the compiler was completely rewritten. It's more than that the new compiler pipeline can be used from custom programs; Microsoft also got new sources where changes do not break other parts of the program. Thus, it was becoming a lot easier to enhance the compiler.

C# 7 again adds many new features that come from a functional programming background, such as local functions, tuples, and pattern matching.

WHAT'S NEW IN C# 7

The C# 6 extensions included `static using`, expression-bodied methods and properties, auto-implemented property initializers, read-only auto properties, the `nameof` operator, the null conditional operator, string interpolation, dictionary initializers, exception filters, and await in catch. What are the changes of C# 7?

Digit Separators

The digit separators make the code more readable. You can add _ to separate numbers when declaring variables. The compiler just removes the _. The following code snippet looks a lot more readable with C# 7:

In C# 6

```
long n1 = 0x1234567890ABCDEF;
```

In C# 7

```
long n2 = 0x1234_5678_90AB_CDEF;
```

With C# 7.2, you can also put the _ at the beginning.

In C# 7.2

```
long n2 = 0x_1234_5678_90AB_CDEF;
```

Digit separators are covered in Chapter 2, "Core C#."

Binary Literals

C# 7 offers a new literal for binaries. Binaries can have only the values 0 and 1. Now the digit separator becomes especially important:

In C# 7

```
uint binary1 = 0b1111_0000_1010_0101_1111_0000_1010_0101;
```

Binary literals are covered in Chapter 2.

Expression-Bodied Members

C# 6 allows expression-bodied methods and properties. With C# 7, expression bodies can be used with constructors, destructors, local functions, property accessors, and more. Here you can see the difference with property accessors between C# 6 and C# 7:

In C# 6

```
private string _firstName;
public string FirstName
```

```
{
  get { return _firstName; }
  set { Set(ref _firstName, value); }
}
```

In C# 7

```
private string _firstName;
public string FirstName
{
  get => _firstName;
  set => Set(ref _firstName, value);
}
```

Expression-bodied members are covered in Chapter 3, "Objects and Types."

Out Var

Before C# 7, out variables had to be declared before its use. With C# 7, the code is reduced by one line because the variable can be declared on use:

In C# 6

```
string n = "42";
int result;
if (string.TryParse(n, out result)
{
  Console.WriteLine($"Converting to a number was successful: {result}");
}
```

In C# 7

```
string n = "42";
if (string.TryParse(n, out var result)
{
  Console.WriteLine($"Converting to a number was successful: {result}");
}
```

This feature is covered in Chapter 3.

Non-Trailing Named Arguments

C# supports named arguments that are required with optional arguments but can support readability in any cases. With C# 7.2, non-trailing named arguments are supported. Argument names can be added to any argument with C# 7.2:

In C# 7.0

```
if (Enum.TryParse(weekdayRecommendation.Entity, ignoreCase: true,
  result: out DayOfWeek weekday))
{
  reservation.Weekday = weekday;
}
```

In C# 7.2

```
if (Enum.TryParse(weekdayRecommendation.Entity, ignoreCase: true,
  out DayOfWeek weekday))
{
  reservation.Weekday = weekday;
}
```

Named arguments are covered in Chapter 3.

Readonly Struct

Structures should be read-only (with some exceptions). Using C# 7.2 it's possible to declare the struct with the `readonly` modifier, so the compiler verifies that the struct is not changed. This guarantee can also be used by the compiler to not copy a struct that passes it as a parameter but instead passes it as a reference:

In C# 7.2

```
public readonly struct Dimensions
{
  public double Length { get; }
  public double Width { get; }

  public Dimensions(double length, double width)
  {
    Length = length;
    Width = width;
  }

  public double Diagonal => Math.Sqrt(Length * Length + Width * Width);
}
```

The `readonly` struct is covered in Chapter 3.

In Parameters

C# 7.2 also allows the `in` modifier with parameters. This guarantees that a passed value type is not changed, and it can be passed by reference to avoid a copy:

In C# 7.2

```
static void CantChange(in AStruct s)
{
  // s can't change
}
```

`ref`, `in`, and `out` modifiers are covered in Chapter 3.

Private Protected

C# 7.2 adds a new access modifier: `private protected`. The access modifier `protected internal` allows access to the member if it's used from a type in the same assembly, or from a type from another assembly that derives from the class. With private protected, it's an AND instead of an OR—access is only allowed if the class derives from the base class *and* is in the same assembly.

Access modifiers are covered in Chapter 4, "Object-Oriented Programming with C#."

Target-Typed Default

With C# 7.1, a default literal is defined that allows a shorter syntax compared to the default operator. The default operator always requires the repetition of the type, which is now not needed anymore. This is practical with complex types:

In C# 7.0

```
int x = default(int);
ImmutableArray<int> arr = default(ImmutableArray<int>);
```

In C# 7.1

```
int x = default;
ImmutableArray<int> arr = default;
```

The default literal is covered in Chapter 5, "Generics."

Local Functions

Before C# 7, it was not possible to declare a function within a method. You could create a lambda expression and invoke it as shown here in the C# 6 code snippet:

In C# 6

```
public void SomeFunStuff()
{
  Func<int, int, int> add = (x, y) => x + y;

  int result = add(38, 4);
  Console.WriteLine(result);
}
```

With C# 7, a local function can be declared within a method. The local function is only accessible within the scope of the method:

In C# 7

```
public void SomeFunStuff()
{
  int add(int x, int y) => x + y;

  int result = add(38, 4);
  Console.WriteLine(result);
}
```

Local functions are explained in Chapter 13, "Functional Programming." You see it in different uses in several chapters of the book.

Tuples

Tuples allow combining objects of different types. Before C# 7, tuples have been part of the .NET Framework with the `Tuple` class. The members of the tuple can be accessed with `Item1`, `Item2`, `Item3`, and so on. In C# 7, tuples are part of the language, and you can define the names of the members:

In C# 6

```
var t1 = Tuple.Create(42, "astring");
int i1 = t1.Item1;
string s1 = t1.Item2;
```

In C# 7

```
var t1 = (n: 42, s: "magic");
int i1 = t1.n;
string s1 = t1.s;
```

Other than that, the new tuples are value types (`ValueTuple`) whereas the `Tuple` type is a reference type. All the changes with tuples are covered in Chapter 13.

Inferred Tuple Names

C# 7.1 extends tuples by automatically inferring tuple names, similar to anonymous types. With C# 7.0, the members of the tuple always need to be named. In case the tuple member should have the same name as the property or field you assign to it, with C# 7.1, if the name is not supplied, it has the same name as the assigned member:

In C# 7.0

```
var t1 = (FirstName: racer.FirstName, Wins: racer.Wins);
int wins = t1.Wins;
```

In C# 7.1

```
var t1 = (racer.FirstName, racer.Wins);
int wins = t1.Wins;
```

Deconstructors

No, this is not a typo. Deconstructors are not destructors. A tuple can be deconstructed to separate variables, such as the following:

In C# 7

```
(int n, string s) = (42, "magic");
```

It's also possible to deconstruct a `Person` object, if a `Deconstruct` method is defined:

In C# 7

```
var p1 = new Person("Tom", "Turbo");
(string firstName, string lastName) = p1;
```

Deconstruction is covered in Chapter 13.

Pattern Matching

With pattern matching, the `is` operator and the `switch` statement have been enhanced with three kinds of patterns: the const pattern, the type pattern, and the var pattern. The following code snippet shows patterns with the `is` operator. The first check for a match matches the constant 42, the second match checks for a `Person` object, and the third match checks every object with the var pattern. Using the type and the var pattern, a variable can be declared for strongly typed access:

In C# 7

```csharp
public void PatternMatchingWithIsOperator(object o)
{
  if (o is 42)
  {
  }
  if (o is Person p)
  {
  }
  if (o is var v1)
  {
  }
}
```

Using the `switch` statement, you can use the same patterns with the `case` clause. You can also declare a variable to be strongly typed in case the pattern matches. You can also use `when` to filter the pattern on a condition:

In C# 7

```csharp
public void PatternMatchingWithSwitchStatement(object o)
{
  swtich (o)
  {
    case 42:
      break;
    case Person p when p.FirstName == "Katharina":
      break;
    case Person p:
      break;
    case var v:
      break;
  }
}
```

Pattern matching is covered in Chapter 13.

Throw Expressions

Throwing exceptions was only possible with a statement; it wasn't possible in an expression. Thus, when receiving a parameter with a constructor, extra checks for null were necessary to throw an `ArgumentNullException`. With C# 7, exceptions can be thrown in expressions, thus it is possible to throw the `ArgumentNullException` when the left side is null—using the coalescing operator.

In C# 6

```csharp
private readonly IBooksService _booksService;
public BookController(BooksService booksService)
```

```
{
  if (booksService == null)
  {
    throw new ArgumentNullException(nameof(b));
  }

  _booksService = booksService;
}
```

In C# 7

```
private readonly IBooksService _booksService;
public BookController(BooksService booksService)
{
  _booksService = booksService ?? throw new ArgumentNullException(nameof(b));
}
```

Throwing expressions is covered in Chapter 14, "Errors and Exceptions."

Async Main

Before C# 7.1, the Main method always needed to be declared of type void. With C# 7.1, the Main method can also be of type Task and use the async and await keywords:

In C# 7.0

```
static void Main()
{
  SomeMethodAsync().Wait();
}
```

In C# 7.1

```
async static Task Main()
{
  await SomeMethodAsync();
}
```

Asynchronous programming is covered in Chapter 15, "Asynchronous Programming."

Reference Semantics

.NET Core has a big focus on enhancing the performance. Additions to C# features for reference semantics help increase the performance. Before C# 7, the ref keyword could be used with parameters to pass value types by reference. Now it's also possible to use the ref keyword with the return type and with local variables.

The following code snippet declares the method GetNumber to return a reference to an int. This way, the caller has direct access to the element in the array and can change its content:

In C# 7.0

```
int[] _numbers = { 3, 7, 11, 15, 21 };
public ref int GetNumber(int index)
{
  return ref _numbers[index];
}
```

With C# 7.2, the `readonly` modifier can be added to `ref` returns. This way the caller can't change the content of the returned value, but still reference semantics is used, and a copy of the value type when returning the result can be avoided. The caller receives a reference but isn't allowed to change it:

In C# 7.2

```
int[] _numbers = { 3, 7, 11, 15, 21 };
public ref readonly int GetNumber(int index)
{
    return ref _numbers[index];
}
```

Before C# 7.2, C# could create reference types (a class) and value types (a struct). However, the struct could also be stored on the heap when boxing took place. With C# 7.2, a type can be declared that is only allowed on the stack: `ref struct`:

In C# 7.2

```
ref struct OnlyOnTheStack
{
}
```

The new features for references are covered in Chapter 17, "Managed and Unmanaged Memory."

WHAT'S NEW IN ASP.NET CORE

With .NET Core and Visual Studio 2017, we have a new project file. The .NET Core tools that were in preview with Visual Studio 2015 are released with Visual Studio 2017. The tools switched to the MSBuild environment with `csproj` files, so now we have `csproj` files both with .NET Framework as well as .NET Core applications. However, it's not the `csproj` you know from previous generations. `csproj` files are a lot shorter and simplified, and you can also modify them by using a simple text editor.

.NET Core 2.0 is enhanced with classes and methods defined in the .NET Standard 2.0, which makes it easier to bring existing .NET Framework applications to .NET Core.

Creating an ASP.NET Core project, not only the `csproj` file gets simplified, but also the C# source code. When you use the default `WebHostBuilder`, a lot more is predefined. Configuration and logging providers are added without you needing to add them yourself. With ASP.NET Core MVC, small improvements have been made—for example, view components can now be used from a tag helper.

There's also a new technology—Razor Pages—which is easier to learn than ASP.NET Core MVC. Some apps don't need the abstraction from the Model-View-Controller pattern; this is where Razor Pages has its place.

WHAT'S NEW WITH THE UNIVERSAL WINDOWS PLATFORM

Two times a year we get updates with Windows 10. (If you are in the Windows Insiders program, you get the updates more often, but that's not the norm for most users.) Every update of Windows releases a new SDK. The latest two updates have been the Creators Update (build 15063, March 2017) and the Fall Creators Update (build 16299, October 2017).

Microsoft continues to offer new design features that are integrated in the Windows controls. The new design is named Fluent Design, which is incorporated in standard controls and is also directly accessible—for example, with the acrylic and reveal brushes. The `ParallaxView` has been added for a parallax effect in your apps.

Features are also added to enhance productivity. You can use the Windows Template Studio—an extension in Visual Studio—to have a template editor to create many pages and use services pre-generated.

XAML has been enhanced with conditional XAML to make it easier to support multiple Windows 10 versions but use new features not available in older Windows 10 editions.

The `InkCanvas` control offers new rulers that can be easily incorporated in your apps. The `NavigationView` makes it easy to create adaptive menus with a hamburger button and a `SplitView`. You can read about all these new features and many more in the fourth part of the book.

WHAT YOU NEED TO WRITE AND RUN C# CODE

.NET Core runs on Windows, Linux, and Mac operating systems. You can create and build your programs on any of these operating systems using Visual Studio Code (`https://code.visualstudio.com`).

The best developer tool to use, and the tool used with this book, is Visual Studio 2017. You can use Visual Studio Community 2017 edition (`https://www.visualstudio.com`), but some features shown are available only with the Enterprise edition of Visual Studio. It will be mentioned where the Enterprise edition is needed. Visual Studio 2017 requires the Windows 10 build 1507 or higher, Windows 8.1, Windows Server 2012 R2, or Windows 7 SP1. To build and run the Windows apps (Universal Windows Platform) shown in this book, you need Windows 10.

For creating and building Xamarin apps for iOS, you also need a Mac for the build system. Without the Mac, you can still create Xamarin apps for Windows and Android.

For developing apps on the Mac, you can use Visual Studio for Mac: `https://www.visualstudio.com/vs/visual-studio-mac/`. You can use this tool to create ASP.NET Core and Xamarin apps, but you can't create and test Windows apps.

WHAT THIS BOOK COVERS

This book starts by reviewing the overall architecture of .NET in Chapter 1 to give you the background you need to write managed code. You'll get an overview about the different application types and learn how to compile with the new development environment CLI, as well as see the most important parts for a start in Visual Studio. After that, the book is divided into sections that cover both the C# language and its application in a variety of areas.

Part I: The C# Language

This section gives a good grounding in the C# language. This section doesn't presume knowledge of any particular language, although it does assume you are an experienced programmer. You start by looking at C#'s basic syntax and data types and then explore the object-oriented programming before you look at more advanced C# programming topics like delegates, lambda expressions, and Language Integrated Query (LINQ).

As C# contains many features that come from functional programming, you learn the foundation of functional programming among tuples and pattern matching. Asynchronous programming and the new language features for the reference semantics are covered. This section concludes with a tour through many Visual Studio 2017 features. You also learn foundations of Docker as well as how Visual Studio 2017 supports Docker out of the box.

Part II: .NET Core and the Windows Runtime

Chapters 19 to 29 cover topics from .NET Core and the Windows Runtime that are independent of application types. This section starts with creating libraries and NuGet packages in Chapter 19, "Libraries, Assemblies, Packages, and NuGet." You learn how to use the .NET Standard in the best way.

Dependency injection (DI) is used with .NET Core no matter where you look: services are injected with Entity Framework Core and ASP.NET Core. ASP.NET Core MVC uses hundreds of services. DI makes it easy to use the same code across WPF, UWP, and Xamarin. Chapter 20, "Dependency Injection," is dedicated to the foundations of DI, and you also learn advanced features from the `Microsoft.Extensions` `.DependencyInjection` DI container, including adapting non-Microsoft containers. Many of the other chapters use DI as well.

Chapter 21, "Tasks and Parallel Programming," covers parallel programming using the Task Parallel Library (TPL) as well as various objects for synchronization.

In Chapter 22, "Files and Streams," you read about accessing the file system and reading files and directories. You learn about using both streams from the `System.IO` namespace and streams from the Windows Runtime for programming Windows apps.

Chapter 23, "Networking," covers the core foundation of networking using sockets, as well as using higher-level abstractions like the `HttpClient`.

Chapter 24, "Security," makes use of streams when you learn about security and how to encrypt data and allow for secure conversion. This chapter also covers some topics you need to know when creating web applications, such as issues with SQL injection and Cross-Site Request Forgery attacks.

Chapters 25 and 26 show you how to access the database. Chapter 25 uses ADO.NET directly, explains transactions, and covers using ambient transactions with .NET Core. Chapter 26 goes through all the new features offered by Entity Framework Core 2.0. EF Core 2.0 has many features that were not available with the older Entity Framework 6.x technology.

In Chapter 27, "Localization," you learn to localize applications using techniques that are important both for Windows and web applications.

When you're creating functionality with C# code, don't skip the step of creating unit tests. It takes more time in the beginning, but over time you'll see advantages when you add functionality and maintain code. Chapter 28, "Testing," covers creating unit tests, including Live Unit Testing with Visual Studio 2017, web tests, and coded UI tests.

Finally, Chapter 29, "Tracing, Logging, and Analytics," covers the logging facility from .NET Core as well as using Visual Studio AppCenter for analytic information.

Part III: Web Applications and Services

In this section you look at web applications and services. You should start this section with Chapter 30, "ASP.NET Core," to give you the foundation of ASP.NET Core. Creating web applications with the MVC pattern, including the new technology Razor Pages, is covered in Chapter 31, "ASP.NET Core MVC." Chapter 32 covers the REST service features of ASP.NET Core: Web API.

Part IV: Apps

This section is about building apps with XAML—both Universal Windows apps and Xamarin. You learn about the foundation of Windows Apps including the foundation of XAML in Chapter 33, "Windows Apps," with the XAML syntax, dependency properties, and markup extensions where you can create your own XAML syntax. The chapter covers the different categories of Windows controls and the foundation of data binding with XAML.

A big focus on the MVVM (model-view-view model) pattern is in Chapter 34, "Patterns with XAML Apps." Here you learn to take advantage of the data-binding features of XAML-based applications, which allow sharing a lot of code between Windows apps, WPF, and Xamarin. You also can share a lot of code developing for the iOS and Android platforms. Creating WPF applications is not covered in the book itself— this technology didn't get many improvements in the recent years, and you should think about a switch to the Universal Windows Platform, which can be done easier if you use the knowledge you learn in Chapter 34. WPF applications still need to be maintained. For a deeper coverage of WPF, you should read the previous edition of this book, *Professional C# 6 and .NET Core 1.0*.

In Chapter 35, "Styling Windows Apps," you learn about styling your XAML-based apps. Chapter 36, "Advanced Windows Apps," goes into advanced features of creating Windows apps with the Universal Windows Platform. You learn about App Services, inking, the `AutoSuggest` control, advanced compiled binding features, and more.

Chapter 37, "Xamarin.Forms," helps you start Xamarin development for Windows, Android, and iPhone, and shows what happens behind the scenes. You learn the differences between Xamarin.Android, Xamarin.iOS, and what's covered with Xamarin.Forms. You'll see the how the Xamarin.Forms controls differ from the Windows controls for making a faster move from Windows development to Xamarin. A larger sample from this chapter uses the same MVVM libraries done for the Windows apps from Chapter 34.

Bonus Chapters

Five bonus chapters are available for download at www.wrox.com. Search for the book's ISBN (978-1-119-44927-0) to find the PDFs.

Bonus Chapter 1, "Composition," covers Microsoft Composition that allows creating independence between containers and parts. In Bonus Chapter 2, "XML and JSON," you learn about serializing objects into XML and JSON, as well as different techniques for reading and writing XML.

Publish and subscribe technologies for web applications, in the form of using the ASP.NET Core technologies technologies WebHooks and SignalR, are covered in Bonus Chapter 3. Bonus Chapter 4 gives you a new look into creating apps using Bot Services and Azure Cognitive Services.

Bonus Chapter 5, "More Windows Apps Features", covers some extra topics related to Windows apps: using the camera, geolocation to access your current location information, the `MapControl` to display maps in various formats, and several sensors (such as those that give information about the light and measure g-forces).

CONVENTIONS

To help you get the most from the text and keep track of what's happening, I use some conventions throughout the book.

> **WARNING** *Warnings hold important, not-to-be-forgotten information that is directly relevant to the surrounding text.*

> **NOTE** *Notes indicate notes, tips, hints, tricks, and/or asides to the current discussion.*

As for styles in the text:

➤ We *highlight* new terms and important words when we introduce them.

➤ We show keyboard strokes like this: Ctrl+A.

➤ We show filenames, URLs, and code within the text like so: `persistence.properties`.

We present code in two different ways:

```
We use a monofont type with no highlighting for most code examples.
We use bold to emphasize code that's particularly important in the present context or
to show changes from a previous code snippet.
```

SOURCE CODE

As you work through the examples in this book, you may choose either to type in all the code manually or to use the source code files that accompany the book. All the source code used in this book is available for download at `www.wrox.com`. When at the site, simply locate the book's title (either by using the Search box or by using one of the title lists) and click the Download Code link on the book's detail page to obtain all the source code for the book.

> **NOTE** *Because many books have similar titles, you may find it easiest to search by ISBN; this book's ISBN is 978-1-119-44927-0.*

After you download the code, just decompress it with your favorite compression tool. Alternatively, you can go to the main Wrox code download page at `http://www.wrox.com/dynamic/books/download.aspx` to see the code available for this book and all other Wrox books.

GITHUB

The source code is also available on GitHub at `https://www.github.com/ProfessionalCSharp/ProfessionalCSharp7`. With GitHub, you can also open each source code file with a web browser. When you use the website, you can download the complete source code in a zip file. You can also clone the source code to a local directory on your system. Just install the git tools, which you can do with Visual Studio or by downloading the git tools from `https://git-scm.com/downloads` for Windows, Linux, and Mac. To clone the source code to a local directory, use git clone:

```
> git clone https://www.github.com/ProfessionalCSharp/ProfessionalCSharp7
```

With this command, the complete source code is copied to the subdirectory `ProfessionalCSharp7`. From there, you can start working with the source files.

As updates of Visual Studio become available, and libraries such as SignalR will be released, the source code will be updated on GitHub. If the source code changes after you cloned it, you can pull the latest changes after changing your current directory to the directory of the source code:

```
> git pull
```

In case you've made some changes on the source code, `git pull` might result in an error. If this happens, you can stash away your changes, and pull again:

```
> git stash
> git pull
```

The complete list of git commands is available at `https://git-scm.com/docs`.

In case you have problems with the source code, you can report an issue in the repository. Just open `https://github.com/ProfessionalCSharp/ProfessionalCSharp7` in the browser, click the Issues tab, and click the New Issue button. This opens an editor as shown in Figure 1. Just be as descriptive as possible to describe your issue.

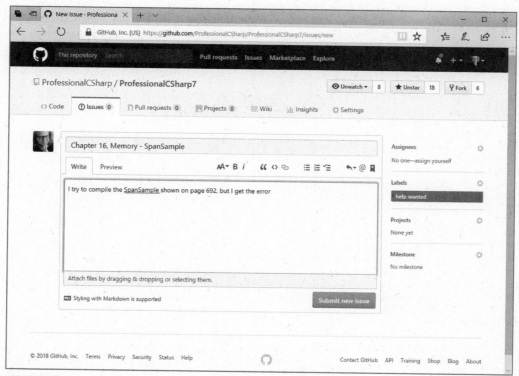

FIGURE 1

For reporting issues, you need a GitHub account. If you have a GitHub account, you can also fork the source code repository to your account. For more information on using GitHub, check `https://guides` `.github.com/activities/hello-world`.

> **NOTE** *You can read the source code and issues and clone the repository without joining GitHub. For posting issues and creating your own repositories on GitHub, you need your own GitHub account.*

ERRATA

We make every effort to ensure that there are no errors in the text or in the code. However, no one is perfect, and mistakes do occur. If you find an error in one of our books, like a spelling mistake or faulty piece of code, we would be grateful for your feedback. By sending in errata you may save another reader hours of frustration, and at the same time you can help provide even higher-quality information.

To find the errata page for this book, go to `http://www.wrox.com` and locate the title using the Search box or one of the title lists. Then, on the book details page, click the Book Errata link. On this page you can view all errata that have been submitted for this book and posted by Wrox editors. A complete book list including links to each book's errata is also available at `www.wrox.com/misc-pages/booklist.shtml`.

If you don't spot "your" error on the Book Errata page, go to `www.wrox.com/contact/techsupport` `.shtml` and complete the form there to send us the error you have found. We'll check the information and, if appropriate, post a message to the book's errata page and fix the problem in subsequent editions of the book.

PROFESSIONAL

C# 7 and .NET Core 2.0

PART I
The C# Language

1

.NET Applications and Tools

WROX.COM CODE DOWNLOADS FOR THIS CHAPTER

The wrox.com code downloads for this chapter are found at www.wrox.com on the Download Code tab. The source code is also available at https://github.com/ProfessionalCSharp/ProfessionalCSharp7 in the directory HelloWorld.

The code for this chapter is divided into the following major examples:

➤ HelloWorld
➤ WebApp
➤ SelfContained HelloWorld

CHOOSING YOUR TECHNOLOGIES

.NET has been a great technology for creating applications on the Windows platform. Now .NET is a great technology for creating applications on Windows, Linux, and the Mac.

The creation of .NET Core has been the biggest change for .NET since its invention. Now .NET code is open-source code, you can create apps for other platforms, and .NET uses modern patterns. .NET Core and NuGet packages allow Microsoft to provide faster update cycles for delivering new features. It's not easy to decide what technology should be used for creating applications. This chapter helps you with that. It gives you information about the different technologies available for creating Windows and web apps and services, offers guidance on what to choose for database access, and highlights the differences between the .NET Framework and .NET Core.

REVIEWING .NET HISTORY

To better understand what is available with .NET and C#, it is best to know something about its history. The following table shows the version of the .NET Framework in relation to the Common Language Runtime (CLR), the version of C#, and the Visual Studio edition that gives some idea about the year when the corresponding versions have been released. Besides knowing what technology to use, it's also good to know what technology is not recommended because there's a replacement.

.NET FRAMEWORK	CLR	C#	VISUAL STUDIO
1.0	1.0	1.0	2002
1.1	1.1	1.2	2003
2.0	2.0	2.0	2005
3.0	2.0	2.0	2005 + Extensions
3.5	2.0	3.0	2008
4.0	4.0	4.0	2010
4.5	4.0	5.0	2012
4.5.1	4.0	5.0	2013
4.6	4.0	6	2015
4.7	4.0	7	2017

When you create applications with .NET Core, it's important to know the timeframe for the support level. *LTS* (Long Time Support) has a longer support length than *Current*, but Current gets new features faster. LTS is supported for three years after the release or 12 months after the next LTS version, whichever is shorter. So, .NET Core 1.0 is supported until June 27, 2019 if the next LTS version is not released before June 27, 2018. In case the next LTS version is released earlier, .NET Core 1.0 is supported one year after the release of the next LTS.

.NET Core 1.1 originally was a Current release, but it changed to LTS with the same support length as .NET Core 1.0.

.NET Core 2.0 is a release with the support level Current. This means it is supported for 3 years, 12 months after the next LTS, or 3 months after the next Current release—whichever is shorter. It can be assumed that the last option will be the case, and .NET Core 2.0 will be supported 3 months after .NET Core 2.1 is available.

The next table lists .NET Core versions, their release dates, and the support level.

.NET CORE VERSION	RELEASE DATE	SUPPORT LEVEL
1.0	June 27, 2016	LTS
1.1	Nov 16, 2016	LTS*
2.0	Aug 14, 2017	Current

The following sections cover the details of these tables and the progress of C# and .NET.

C# 1.0—A New Language

C# 1.0 was a completely new programming language designed for the .NET Framework. At the time it was developed, the .NET Framework consisted of about 3,000 classes and the CLR.

After Microsoft was not allowed by a court order (filed by Sun, the company that created Java) to make changes to the Java code, Anders Hejlsberg designed C#. Before working for Microsoft, Hejlsberg had his roots at Borland where he designed the Delphi programming language (an Object Pascal dialect). At Microsoft he was responsible for J++ (Microsoft's version of the Java programming language). Given Hejlsberg's background, the C# programming language was mainly influenced by C++, Java, and Pascal.

Because C# was created later than Java and C++, Microsoft analyzed typical programming errors that happened with the other languages and did some things differently to avoid these errors. Some differences include the following:

➤ With `if` statements, Boolean expressions are required (C++ allows an integer value here as well).

➤ It's permissible to create value and reference types using the `struct` and `class` keywords (Java only allows creating custom reference types; with C++ the distinction between `struct` and `class` is only the default for the access modifier).

➤ Virtual and non-virtual methods are allowed (this is like C++; Java always creates virtual methods).

Of course, there are a lot more changes as you'll see reading this book.

At this time, C# was not only a pure object-oriented programming language with features for inheritance, encapsulation, and polymorphism. Instead, C# also offered component-based programming enhancements such as delegates and events.

Before .NET and the CLR, every programming language had its own runtime. With C++, the C++ Runtime is linked with every C++ program. Visual Basic 6 had its own runtime with VBRun. The runtime of Java is the Java Virtual Machine—which can be compared to the CLR. The CLR is a runtime that is used by every .NET programming language. At the time the CLR appeared on the scene, Microsoft offered JScript.NET, Visual Basic .NET, and Managed C++ in addition to C#. JScript.NET was Microsoft's JavaScript compiler that was to be used with the CLR and .NET classes. Visual Basic.NET was the name for Visual Basic that offered .NET support. Nowadays it's just called Visual Basic again. Managed C++ was the name for a language that mixed native C++ code with Managed .NET Code. The newer C++ language used today with .NET is C++/CLR.

A compiler for a .NET programming language generates *Intermediate Language* (IL) code. The IL code looks like object-oriented machine code and can be checked by using the tool ildasm.exe to open DLL or EXE files that contain .NET code. The CLR contains a just-in-time (JIT) compiler that generates native code out of the IL code when the program starts to run.

> **NOTE** *IL code is also known as* managed code.

Other parts of the CLR are a garbage collector (GC), which is responsible for cleaning up managed memory that is no longer referenced; a security mechanism that uses code access security to verify what code is allowed to do; an extension for the debugger to allow a debug session between different programming languages (for example, starting a debug session with Visual Basic and continuing to debug within a C# library); and a threading facility that is responsible for creating threads on the underlying platform.

The .NET Framework was already huge with version 1. The classes are organized within namespaces to help facilitate navigating the 3,000 available classes. Namespaces are used to group classes and to solve conflicts by allowing the same class name in different namespaces. Version 1 of the .NET Framework allowed creating Windows desktop applications using Windows Forms (namespace System.Windows.Forms), creating web applications with ASP.NET Web Forms (System.Web), communicating with applications and web services using ASP.NET Web Services, communicating more quickly between .NET applications using .NET Remoting, and creating COM+ components for running in an application server using Enterprise Services.

ASP.NET Web Forms was the technology for creating web applications with the goal for the developer to not need to know something about HTML and JavaScript. Server-side controls that worked similarly to Windows Forms itself created HTML and JavaScript.

C# 1.2 and .NET 1.1 were mainly a bug fix release with minor enhancements.

> **NOTE** *Inheritance is discussed in Chapter 4, "Object-Oriented Programming with C#"; delegates and events are covered in Chapter 8, "Delegates, Lambdas, and Events."*

> **NOTE** *Every new release of .NET has been accompanied by a new version of the book* Professional C#. *With .NET 1.0, the book was already in the second edition as the first edition had been published with Beta 2 of .NET 1.0. You're holding the 11th edition of this book in your hands.*

C# 2 and .NET 2 with Generics

C# 2 and .NET 2 were a huge update. With this version, a change to both the C# programming language and the IL code had been made; that's why a new CLR was needed to support the IL code additions. One big change was *generics*. Generics make it possible to create types without needing to know what inner types are used. The inner types used are defined at instantiation time, when an instance is created.

This advance in the C# programming language also resulted in many new types in the Framework—for example, new generic collection classes found in the namespace System.Collections.Generic. With this, the older collection classes defined with 1.0 are rarely used with newer applications. Of course, the older classes still work nowadays, even with .NET Core.

> **NOTE** *Generics are used all through the book, but they're explained in detail in Chapter 5, "Generics." Chapter 10, "Collections," covers generic collection classes.*

.NET 3—Windows Presentation Foundation

With the release of .NET 3.0 no new version of C# was needed. 3.0 was only a release offering new libraries, but it was a huge release with many new types and namespaces. Windows Presentation Foundation (WPF) was probably the biggest part of the new Framework for creating Windows desktop applications. Windows Forms wrapped the native Windows controls and was based on pixels, whereas WPF was based on DirectX to draw every control on its own. The vector graphics in WPF allow seamless resizing of every form. The templates in WPF also allow for complete custom looks. For example, an application for the Zurich airport can include a button that looks like a plane. As a result, applications can look very different from the traditional Windows applications that had been developed up to that time. Everything below the namespace System.Windows belongs to WPF, except for System.Windows.Forms. With WPF the user interface can be designed using an XML syntax: XML for Applications Markup Language (XAML).

Before .NET 3, ASP.NET Web Services and .NET Remoting were used for communicating between applications. Message Queuing was another option for communicating. The various technologies had different advantages and disadvantages, and all had different APIs for programming. A typical enterprise application had to use more than one communication API, and thus it was necessary to learn several of them. This was solved with Windows Communication Foundation (WCF). WCF combined all the options of the other APIs into the one API. However, to support all the features WCF has to offer, you need to configure WCF.

The third big part of the .NET 3.0 release was Windows Workflow Foundation (WF) with the namespace System.Workflow. Instead of creating custom workflow engines for several different applications (and Microsoft itself created several workflow engines for different products), a workflow engine was available as part of .NET.

With .NET 3.0, the class count of the Framework increased from 8,000 types in .NET 2.0 to about 12,000 types.

> **NOTE** *To read about WPF and WCF, you need the previous edition of the book,* Professional C# 6 and .NET Core 1.0.

C# 3 and .NET 3.5—LINQ

.NET 3.5 came together with a new release of C# 3. The major enhancement was a query syntax defined with C# that allows using the same syntax to filter and sort object lists, XML files, and the database. The language enhancements didn't require any change to the IL code as the C# features used here are just syntax sugar. All the enhancements could have been done with the older syntax as well; just a lot more code would be necessary. The C# language makes it easy to do these queries. With LINQ and lambda expressions, it's possible to use the same query syntax and access object collections, databases, and XML files.

For accessing the database and creating LINQ queries, LINQ to SQL was released as part of .NET 3.5. With the first update to .NET 3.5, the first version of Entity Framework was released. Both LINQ to SQL and Entity Framework offered mapping of hierarchies to the relations of a database and a LINQ provider. Entity Framework was more powerful, but LINQ to SQL was simpler. Over time, features of LINQ to SQL have been implemented in Entity Framework, and now this one is here to stay. The new version of Entity Framework, Entity Framework Core (EF Core) looks very different from the first version released.

Another technology introduced as part of .NET 3.5 was the System.AddIn namespace, which offers an add-in model. This model offers powerful features that run add-ins even out of process, but it is also complex to use.

> **NOTE** *LINQ is covered in detail in Chapter 12, "Language Integrated Query." The newest version of the Entity Framework is very different from the .NET 3.5.1 release; it's described in Chapter 26, "Entity Framework Core."*

C# 4 and .NET 4—Dynamic and TPL

The theme of C# 4 was dynamic—integrating scripting languages and making it easier to use COM integration. C# syntax has been extended with the `dynamic` keyword, named and optional parameters, and enhancements to co- and contra-variance with generics.

Other enhancements have been made within the .NET Framework. With multi-core CPUs, parallel programming had become more and more important. The Task Parallel Library (TPL), with abstractions of threads using `Task` and `Parallel` classes, make it easier to create parallel running code.

Because the workflow engine created with .NET 3.0 didn't fulfill its promises, a completely new Windows Workflow Foundation was part of .NET 4.0. To avoid conflicts with the older workflow engine, the newer one is defined in the `System.Activity` namespace.

The enhancements of C# 4 also required a new version of the runtime. The runtime version skipped from 2 to 4.

With the release of Visual Studio 2010, a new technology shipped for creating web applications: ASP.NET MVC 2.0. Unlike ASP.NET Web Forms, this technology has a focus on the Model-View-Controller (MVC) pattern, which is enforced by the project structure. This technology also has a focus on programming HTML and JavaScript. HTML and JavaScript gained a great push in the developer community with the release of HTML 5. As this technology was very new as well as being out of band (OOB) to Visual Studio and .NET, ASP.NET MVC was updated regularly.

> **NOTE** *The `dynamic` keyword of C# 4 is covered in Chapter 16, "Reflection, Metadata, and Dynamic Programming." The Task Parallel Library is covered in Chapter 21, "Tasks and Parallel Programming."*
>
> *The next generation of ASP.NET, ASP.NET Core is covered in Chapter 30, "ASP .NET Core." Chapter 31, "ASP.NET Core MVC," covers the ASP.NET Core version of ASP.NET Core MVC.*

C# 5 and Asynchronous Programming

C# 5 had only two new keywords: `async` and `await`. However, they made programming of asynchronous methods a lot easier. As touch became more significant with Windows 8, it also became a lot more important to not block the UI thread. Using the mouse, users are accustomed to scrolling taking some time. However, using fingers on a touch interface that is not responsive is really annoying.

Windows 8 also introduced a new programming interface for Windows Store apps (also known as Modern apps, Metro apps, Universal Windows apps, and, more recently, Windows apps): the Windows Runtime. This is a native runtime that looks like .NET by using language projections. Many of the WPF controls have been redone for the new runtime, and a subset of the .NET Framework can be used with such apps.

As the `System.AddIn` framework was much too complex and slow, a new composition framework was created with .NET 4.5: Managed Extensibility Framework with the namespace `System.Composition`.

A new version of platform-independent communication is offered by the ASP.NET Web API. Unlike WCF, which offers stateful and stateless services as well as many different network protocols, the ASP.NET Web API is a lot simpler and based on the Representational State Transfer (REST) software architecture style.

> **NOTE** *The* `async` *and* `await` *keywords of C# 5 are discussed in detail in Chapter 15, "Asynchronous Programming." This chapter also shows the different asynchronous patterns that have been used over time with .NET.*
>
> *Managed Extensibility Framework (MEF) is covered in Bonus Chapter 1, "Composition." Windows apps are covered in Chapters 33 to 36, and the Web API with ASP.NET Core MVC is covered in Chapter 32, "Web API."*

C# 6 and .NET Core 1.0

C# 6 doesn't involve the huge improvements that were made by generics, LINQ, and async, but there are a lot of small and practical enhancements in the language that can reduce the code length in several places. The many improvements have been made possible by a new compiler engine code named Roslyn or the .NET Compiler Platform.

The full .NET Framework is not the only .NET version that was in use in recent years. Some scenarios required smaller frameworks. In 2007, the first version of Microsoft Silverlight was released (code named WPF/E, WPF Everywhere). Silverlight was a web browser plug-in that allowed dynamic content. The first version of Silverlight supported programming only via JavaScript. The second version included a subset of the .NET Framework. Of course, server-side libraries were not needed because Silverlight was always running on the client, but the Framework shipped with Silverlight also removed classes and methods from the core features to make it lightweight and portable to other platforms. The last version of Silverlight for the desktop (version 5) was released in December 2011. Silverlight had also been used for programming for the Windows Phone. Silverlight 8.1 made it into Windows Phone 8.1, but this version of Silverlight is also different from the version on the desktop.

On the Windows desktop, where there is such a huge framework with .NET and the need for faster and faster development cadences, big changes were also required. In a world of DevOps where developers and operations work together or are even the same people to bring applications and new features continuously to the user, there's a need to have new features available in a fast way. Creating new features or making bug fixes is a not-so-easy task with a huge framework and many dependencies.

With several smaller .NET versions available (e.g. Silverlight, Silverlight for the Windows Phone), it became important to share code between the desktop version of .NET and a smaller version. A technology to share code between different .NET versions was the portable library. Over time, with many different .NET Frameworks and versions, the management of the portable library has become a nightmare.

With all these issues, a new version of .NET is a necessity. (Yes, it's really a requirement to solve these issues.) The new version of the Framework is invented with the name *.NET Core.* .NET Core is smaller with modular NuGet packages, has a runtime that's distributed with every application, is open source, and is available not only for the desktop version of Windows but also for many different Windows devices, as well as for Linux and OS X.

For creating web applications, ASP.NET Core 1.0 was a complete rewrite of ASP.NET. This release is not completely backward compatible with older versions and requires some changes to existing ASP.NET MVC code (with ASP.NET Core MVC). However, it also has a lot of advantages when compared with the older versions, such as a lower overhead with every network request—which results in better performance—and it can also run on Linux. ASP.NET Web Forms is not part of this release because ASP.NET Web Forms was not designed for best performance; it was designed for developer friendliness based on patterns known by Windows Forms application developers.

Of course, not all applications can be changed easily to make use of .NET Core. That's why the huge framework received improvements as well—even if those improvements are not completed at as fast a pace as .NET Core. The new version of the full .NET Framework is 4.6. Small updates for ASP.NET Web Forms are available on the full .NET stack.

> **NOTE** *The changes to the C# language are covered in all the language chapters in Part I—for example, read-only properties are in Chapter 3, "Objects and Types"; the* nameof *operator and null propagation are in Chapter 6, "Operators and Casts"; string interpolation is in Chapter 9, "Strings and Regular Expressions"; and exception filters are in Chapter 14, "Errors and Exceptions."*

C# 7 and .NET Core 2.0

C# has been updated to have a faster pace. Major version 7.0 was released in March 2017, and the minor versions 7.1 and 7.2 soon after in August 2017 and December 2017. With a project setting, you can select the compiler version to use.

C# 7 introduces many new features (these are outlined in the Introduction.) The most significant of these features come from functional programming: *pattern matching* and *tuples*.

> **NOTE** *Pattern matching and tuples are covered in Chapter 13, "Functional Programming with C#."*

.NET Core 2.0 is focused on making it easier to bring existing applications written with the .NET Framework to .NET Core. Types that haven't been available with .NET Core but are still in use with many .NET Framework applications and libraries are now available with .NET Core. More than 20,000 APIs have been added to .NET Core 2.0. For example, binary serialization, and the DataSet are back, and you can use these features also on Linux. Another feature that helps bring legacy applications to .NET Core is the Windows Compatibility Pack (Microsoft.Windows.Compatibility). This NuGet package defines APIs for WCF, registry access, cryptography, directory services, drawing, and more. See https://github .com/dotnet/designs/blob/master/accepted/compat-pack/compat-pack.md for a current state.

The .NET Standard is a spec that defines which APIs should be available on any platform that supports the standard. The higher the standard version, the more APIs are available. .NET Standard 2.0 extended the standard by more than 20,000 APIs and is supported by .NET Framework 4.6.1, .NET Core 2.0, and the Universal Windows Platform (Windows Apps) starting with build 16299 (the Fall Creators Update of Windows 10).

> **NOTE** *The .NET Standard is covered in detail in Chapter 19, "Libraries, Assemblies, Packages, and NuGet."*

To check whether your application can easily be ported to .NET Core, you can use the .NET Portability Analyzer. You can install this tool as an extension to Visual Studio. It analyzes your binaries. You can configure the portability information for what versions and frameworks you would like to get, and you can select portability information for .NET Core, .NET Framework, .NET Standard, Mono, Silverlight, Windows, Xamarin, and more. The result can be JSON, HTML, and Excel.

Figure 1-1 shows the summary report after selecting a .NET Framework binary that is 100% compatible with the .NET Framework, 96.67% with .NET Core, and just 69.7% with Windows Apps. Figure 1-2 shows detail information about the problematic APIs.

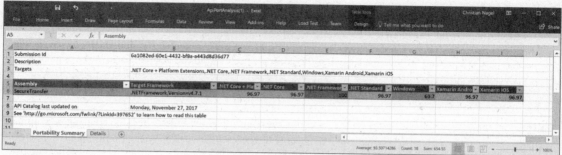

FIGURE 1-1

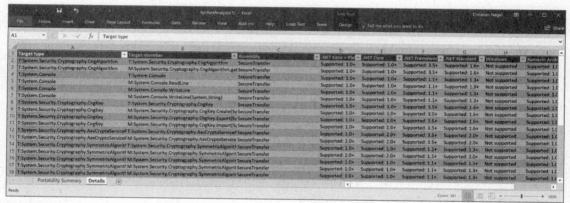

FIGURE 1-2

Choosing Technologies and Going Forward

When you know the reason for competing technologies within the Framework, it's easier to select a technology to use for programming applications. For example, if you're creating new Windows applications it's not a good idea to bet on Windows Forms. Instead, you should use a XAML-based technology, such as the Universal Windows Platform (UWP). Of course, there are still good reasons to use other technologies. Do you need to support Windows 7 clients? In that case, UWP is not an option, but WPF is. You still can create your WPF applications in a way that make it easy to switch to other technologies, such as UWP and Xamarin.

> **NOTE** *Read Chapter 34, "Patterns with XAML Apps," for information about how to design your app to share as much code as possible between WPF, UWP, and Xamarin.*

If you're creating web applications, a safe bet is to use ASP.NET Core with ASP.NET Core MVC. Making this choice rules out using ASP.NET Web Forms. If you're accessing a database, you should use Entity Framework Core, and you should opt for the Managed Extensibility Framework instead of System.AddIn.

Legacy applications still use Windows Forms and ASP.NET Web Forms and some other older technologies. It doesn't make sense to change existing applications just to use new technologies. There must be a huge advantage to making the change—for example, when maintenance of the code is already a nightmare and a lot of refactoring is needed to change to faster release cycles that are being demanded by customers, or when using a new technology allows for reducing the coding time for updates. Depending on the type of legacy application, it might not be worthwhile to switch to a new technology. You can allow the application to still be based on older technologies because Windows Forms and ASP.NET Web Forms will still be supported for many years to come.

The content of this book is based on the newer technologies to show what's best for creating new applications. In case you still need to maintain legacy applications, you can refer to older editions of this book, which cover ASP.NET Web Forms, WCF, Windows Forms, System.AddIn, Workflow Foundation, and other legacy technologies that are still part of and available with the .NET Framework.

.NET TERMS

What are the current .NET technologies? Figure 1-3 gives an overall picture of how the .NET Framework, .NET Core, and Mono relate to each other. All .NET Framework apps, .NET Core apps, and Xamarin apps can use the same libraries if they are built with the .NET Standard. These technologies share the same compiler platform, programming languages, and runtime components. They do not share the same runtime, but they do share components within their runtime. For example, the just-in-time (JIT) compiler RyuJIT is used by the .NET Framework and .NET Core.

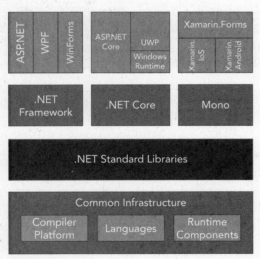

FIGURE 1-3

With the .NET Framework, you can create Windows Forms, WPF, and legacy ASP.NET applications that run on Windows.

Using .NET Core, you can create ASP.NET Core and console apps that run on different platforms. .NET Core is also used by the Universal Windows Platform (UWP), but this doesn't make UWP available on Linux. UWP also makes use of the Windows Runtime, which is available only on Windows.

Xamarin offers Xamarin.IoS and Xamarin.Android, libraries that enable you to develop C# apps for the iPhone and for Android. With Xamarin.Forms, you have a library to share the user interface between the two mobile platforms. Xamarin is currently still based on the Mono framework, a .NET variant developed by Xamarin. At some point, this might change to .NET Core. However, what's important is that all these technologies can use the same libraries created for the .NET Standard.

In the lower part of Figure 1-3, you can see there's also some sharing going on between .NET Framework, .NET Core, and Mono. *Runtime components*, such as the code for the garbage collector and the RyuJIT (this is a new JIT compiler to compile IL code to native code) are shared. The garbage collector is used by CLR, CoreCLR, and .NET Native. The RyuJIT just-in-time compiler is used by CLR and CoreCLR. The .NET Compiler Platform (also known as Roslyn) and the programming languages are used by all these platforms.

.NET Framework

NET Framework 4.7 is the .NET Framework that has been continuously enhanced in the past 15 years. Many of the technologies that have been discussed in the history section are based on this framework. This framework is used for creating Windows Forms and WPF applications. .NET Framework 4.7 still offers enhancements for Windows Forms, such as support for High DPI.

If you want to continue working with ASP.NET Web Forms, ASP.NET 4.7 with .NET Framework 4.7 is the way to go. Otherwise, you need to rewrite some code to move to .NET Core. Depending on the quality of the source code and the need to add new features, rewriting the code might be worthwhile.

.NET Core

.NET Core is the new .NET that is used by all new technologies and has a big focus in this book. This framework is *open source*—you can find it at `http://www.github.com/dotnet`. The runtime is the *CoreCLR* repository; the framework containing collection classes, file system access, console, XML, and a lot more is in the *CoreFX* repository.

Unlike the .NET Framework, where the specific version you needed for the application had to be installed on the system, with .NET Core 1.0 the framework, including the runtime, is delivered with the application. Previously there were times when you might have had problems deploying an ASP.NET web application to a shared server because the provider had older versions of .NET installed; those times are gone. Now you can deliver the runtime with the application and are not dependent on the version installed on the server.

.NET Core is designed in a modular approach. The framework splits up into a large list of NuGet packages. So that you don't have to deal with all the packages, metapackages are used that reference the smaller packages that work together. Metapackages even improved with .NET Core 2.0 and ASP.NET Core 2.0. With ASP.NET Core 2.0, you just need to reference `Microsoft.AspNetCore.All` to get all the packages you typically need with ASP.NET Core web applications.

.NET Core can be updated at a fast pace. Even updating the runtime doesn't influence existing applications because the runtime can be installed with the applications. Now Microsoft can improve .NET Core, including the runtime, with faster release cycles.

> **NOTE** *For developing apps using .NET Core, Microsoft created new command-line utilities named .NET Core Command line (CLI). These tools are introduced later in this chapter through a "Hello World!" application in the section "Using the .NET Core CLI."*

.NET Standard

The .NET Standard is not an implementation; it's a contract. This contract specifies what APIs need to be implemented. .NET Framework, .NET Core, and Xamarin implement this standard.

The standard is versioned. With every version additional APIs are added. Depending on the APIs you need, you can choose the standard version for a library. You need to check whether your platform of choice supports the standard of the needed version.

You can find a detailed table for the platform support for the .NET Standard at `https://docs.microsoft` `.com/en-us/dotnet/standard/net-standard`. The following are the most important parts you need to know:

➤ .NET Core 1.1 supports .NET Standard 1.6; .NET Core 2.0 supports .NET Standard 2.0.

➤ .NET Framework 4.6.1 supports .NET Standard 2.0.

➤ UWP build 16299 and later supports .NET Standard 2.0; older versions support only .NET Standard 1.4.

➤ With Xamarin to use .NET Standard 2.0 you need Xamarin.iOS 10.14 and Xamarin.Android 8.0.

> **NOTE** *Read detailed information on the .NET Standard in Chapter 19.*

NuGet Packages

In the early days, assemblies were reusable units with applications. That use is still possible (and necessary with some assemblies) when you're adding a reference to an assembly for using the public types and methods from your own code. However, using libraries can mean a lot more than just adding a reference and using it. Using libraries can also mean some configuration changes, or scripts that can be used to take advantage of some features. This is one of the reasons to package assemblies within NuGet packages.

A NuGet package is a zip file that contains the assembly (or multiple assemblies) as well as configuration information and PowerShell scripts.

Another reason for using NuGet packages is that they can be found easily; they're available not only from Microsoft but also from third parties. NuGet packages are easily accessible on the NuGet server at `http://` `www.nuget.org`.

From the references within a Visual Studio project, you can open the NuGet Package Manager (see Figure 1-4). There you can search for packages and add them to the application. This tool enables you to search for packages that are not yet released (include prerelease option) and define the NuGet server where the packages should be searched. One place to search for packages is your own shared directory where your internal used packages are placed.

> **NOTE** *When you use third-party packages from the NuGet server, you're always at risk if a package is available later. You also need to check about the support availability of the package. Always check for project links with information about the package before using it. With the package source, you can select Microsoft and .NET to only get packages supported by Microsoft. Third-party packages are also included in the Microsoft and .NET section, but they are third-party packages that are supported by Microsoft.*

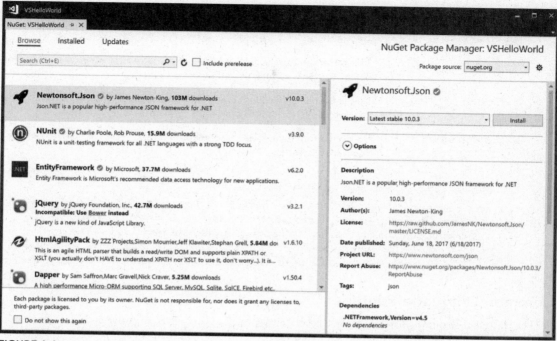

FIGURE 1-4

> **NOTE** *More information about the NuGet Package Manager is covered in Chapter 17, "Visual Studio 2015."*

Namespaces

The classes available with .NET are organized in namespaces whose names start with the System. To give you an idea about the hierarchy, the following table describes a few of the namespaces.

NAMESPACE	DESCRIPTION
System.Collections	This is the root namespace for collections. Collections are also found within subnamespaces, such as System.Collections.Concurrent and System.Collections.Generic.
System.Data	This is the namespace for accessing databases. System.Data.SqlClient contains classes to access the SQL Server.
System.Diagnostics	This is the root namespace for diagnostics information, such as event logging and tracing (in the namespace System.Diagnostics.Tracing).
System.Globalization	This is the namespace that contains classes for globalization and localization of applications.

continues

(continued)

NAMESPACE	DESCRIPTION
`System.IO`	This is the namespace for File IO, which are classes to access files and directories. Readers, writers, and streams are here.
`System.Net`	This is the namespace for core networking, such as accessing DNS servers and creating sockets with `System.Net.Sockets`.
`System.Threading`	This is the root namespace for threads and tasks. Tasks are defined within `System.Threading.Tasks`.

> **NOTE** *Many of the new .NET classes use namespaces that start with the name* `Microsoft` *instead of* `System`, *like* `Microsoft.EntityFrameworkCore` *for the Entity Framework Core and* `Microsoft.Extensions.DependencyInjection` *for the new dependency injection framework.*

Common Language Runtime

The Universal Windows Platform makes use of Native .NET to compile IL to native code with an AOT Compiler. This is like Xamarin.iOS. With all other scenarios, with both applications using the .NET Framework and applications using .NET Core 1.0, a *Common Language Runtime* (CLR) is needed. .NET Core uses the CoreCLR whereas the .NET Framework uses the CLR. So, what's done by a CLR?

Before an application can be executed by the CLR, any source code that you develop (in C# or some other language) needs to be compiled. Compilation occurs in two steps in .NET:

1. Compilation of source code to Microsoft Intermediate Language (IL)
2. Compilation of IL to platform-specific native code by the CLR

The IL code is available within a .NET assembly. During runtime, a Just-In-Time (JIT) compiler compiles IL code and creates the platform-specific native code.

The new CLR and the CoreCLR include the JIT compiler named *RyuJIT*. The new JIT compiler is not only faster than the previous one; it also has better support for the Edit & Continue feature while debugging with Visual Studio. The Edit & Continue feature enables you to edit the code while debugging, and you can continue the debug session without the need to stop and restart the process.

The runtime also includes a type system with a type loader that is responsible for loading types from assemblies. Security infrastructure with the type system verifies whether certain type system structures are permitted—for example, with inheritance.

After creating instances of types, the instances also need to be destroyed and memory needs to be recycled. Another feature of the runtime is the garbage collector. The garbage collector cleans up memory from the managed heap that isn't referenced anymore.

The runtime is also responsible for threading. Creating a managed thread from C# is not necessarily a thread from the underlying operating system. Threads are virtualized and managed by the runtime.

> **NOTE** *How threads can be created and managed from C# is covered in Chapter 21, "Tasks and Parallel Programming," and in Chapter 22, "Task Synchronization." Chapter 17, "Managed and Unmanaged Memory," gives information about the garbage collector and how to clean up memory.*

Windows Runtime

Starting with Windows 8, the Windows operating system offers another framework: the Windows Runtime. This runtime is used by the Windows Universal Platform and was version 1 with Windows 8, version 2 with Windows 8.1, and version 3 with Windows 10.

Unlike the .NET Framework, this framework was created using native code. When it's used with .NET apps, the types and methods contained just look like .NET. With the help of language projection, the Windows Runtime can be used with the JavaScript, C++, and .NET languages, and it looks like it's native to the programming environment. Methods are not only behaving differently regarding case sensitivity; the methods and types can also have different names depending on where they are used.

The Windows Runtime offers an object hierarchy organized in namespaces that start with Windows. Looking at these classes, there's not a lot with duplicate functionality to the .NET types; instead, extra functionality is offered that is available for apps running on the Universal Windows Platform.

NAMESPACE	DESCRIPTION
`Windows.ApplicationModel`	This namespace and its subnamespaces, such as `Windows.ApplicationModel.Contracts`, define classes to manage the app lifecycle and communication with other apps.
`Windows.Data`	`Windows.Data` defines subnamespaces to work with Text, JSON, PDF, and XML data.
`Windows.Devices`	Geolocation, smartcards, point of service devices, printers, scanners, and other devices can be accessed with subnamespaces of `Windows.Devices`.
`Windows.Foundation`	`Windows.Foundation` defines core functionality. Interfaces for collections are defined with the namespace `Windows.Foundation.Collections`. You will not find concrete collection classes here. Instead, interfaces of .NET collection types map to the Windows Runtime types.
`Windows.Media`	`Windows.Media` is the root namespace for playing and capturing video and audio, accessing playlists, and doing speech output.
`Windows.Networking`	This is the root namespace for socket programming, background transfer of data, and push notifications.
`Windows.Security`	Classes from `Windows.Security.Credentials` offer a safe store for passwords; `Windows.Security.Credentials.UI` offers a picker to get credentials from the user.

continues

(continued)

NAMESPACE	DESCRIPTION
`Windows.Services.Maps`	This namespace contains classes for location services and routing.
`Windows.Storage`	With `Windows.Storage` and its subnamespaces, it is possible to access files and directories as well as use streams and compression.
`Windows.System`	The `Windows.System` namespace and its subnamespaces give information about the system and the user, but they also offer a `Launcher` to launch other apps.
`Windows.UI.Xaml`	In this namespace, you can find a ton of types for the user interface.

USING THE .NET CORE CLI

For many chapters in this book you don't need Visual Studio; you can use any editor and a command line. For creating and compiling your applications, you can use the .NET Core Command Line Interface (CLI). Let's have a look how to set up your system and how you can use this tool.

Setting Up the Environment

In case you have Visual Studio 2017 with the latest updates installed, you can immediately start with the CLI tools. As previously mentioned, you can set up a system without Visual Studio 2017. You also can use most of the samples on Linux and OS X. To download the applications for your environment, just go to `https://dot.net` and click the Get Started button. From there, you can download the .NET SDK for Windows, Linux, and macOS.

For Windows, you can download an executable that installs the SDK. With Linux, you need to select the Linux distribution to get the corresponding command:

➤   With Red Hat and CentOS, install the .NET SDK using `yum`.

➤   With Ubuntu and Debian, use `apt-get`.

➤   With Fedora, use `dnf install`.

➤   With SLES/openSUSE, use `zipper install`.

➤   To install the .NET SDK on the Mac, you can download a `.pkg` file.

With Windows, different versions of .NET Core runtimes as well as NuGet packages are installed in the user profile. As you work with .NET, this folder increases in size. Over time as you create multiple projects, NuGet packages are no longer stored in the project itself; they're stored in this user-specific folder. This has the advantage that you do not need to download NuGet packages for every different project. After you have this NuGet package downloaded, it's on your system. Just as different versions of the NuGet packages as well as the runtime are available, all the different versions are stored in this folder. From time to time it might be interesting to check this folder and delete old versions you no longer need.

Installing .NET Core CLI tools, you have the dotnet tools as an entry point to start all these tools. Just start

```
> dotnet --help
```

to see all the different options of the dotnet tools available. Many of the options have a shorthand notation. For help, you can type

```
> dotnet -h
```

Creating the Application

The dotnet tools offer an easy way to create a "Hello World!" application. Just enter this command:

```
> dotnet new console --output HelloWorld
```

This command creates a new `HelloWorld` directory and adds the source code file `Program.cs` and the project file `HelloWorld.csproj`. Starting with .NET Core 2.0, this command also includes a `dotnet restore` where all NuGet packages are downloaded. To see a list of dependencies and versions of libraries used by the application, you can check the file `project.assets.json` in the `obj` subdirectory. Without using the option `--output` (or `-o` as shorthand), the files would be generated in the current directory.

The generated source code looks like the following code snippet (code file `HelloWorld/Program.cs`):

```
using System;

namespace HelloWorld
{
  class Program
  {
    static void Main(string[] args)
    {
      Console.WriteLine("Hello World!");
    }
  }
}
```

Since the 1970s, when Brian Kernighan and Dennis Ritchie wrote the book *The C Programming Language*, it's been a tradition to start learning programming languages using a "Hello World!" application. With the .NET Core CLI, this program is automatically generated.

Let's get into the syntax of this program. The `Main` method is the entry point for a .NET application. The CLR invokes a static `Main` method on startup. The `Main` method needs to be put into a class. Here, the class is named `Program`, but you could call it by any name.

`Console.WriteLine` invokes the `WriteLine` method of the `Console` class. You can find the `Console` class in the `System` namespace. You don't need to write `System.Console.WriteLine` to invoke this method; the `System` namespace is opened with the `using` declaration on top of the source file.

After writing the source code, you need to compile the code to run it.

The created project configuration file is named `HelloWorld.csproj`. Compared to older `csproj` files, the new project file is reduced to a few lines with several defaults:

```
<Project Sdk="Microsoft.NET.Sdk">
  <PropertyGroup>
    <OutputType>Exe</OutputType>
    <TargetFramework>netcoreapp2.0</TargetFramework>
  </PropertyGroup>
</Project>
```

With the project file, the `OutputType` defines the type of the output. With a console application, this is `Exe`. The `TargetFramework` specifies the framework and the version that is used to build the application. With the sample project, the application is built using .NET Core 2.0. You can change this element to `TargetFrameworks` and specify multiple frameworks, such as `netcoreapp2.0;net47` to build applications both for .NET Framework 4.7 and .NET Core 2.0 (project file `HelloWorld/HelloWorld.csproj`):

```
<Project Sdk="Microsoft.NET.Sdk">
  <PropertyGroup>
    <OutputType>Exe</OutputType>
    <TargetFrameworks>netcoreapp2.0;net47</TargetFrameworks>
  </PropertyGroup>
</Project>
```

The Sdk attribute specifies the SDK that is used by the project. Microsoft ships two main SDKs: Microsoft.NET.Sdk for console applications, and Microsoft.NET.Sdk.Web for ASP.NET Core web applications.

You don't need to add source files to the project. Files with the .cs extension in the same directory and subdirectories are automatically added for compilation. Resource files with the .resx extension are automatically added for embedding the resource. You can change the default behavior and exclude/include files explicitly.

You also don't need to add the .NET Core package. By specifying the target framework netcoreapp2.0, the metapackage Microsoft.NetCore.App that references many other packages is automatically included.

Building the Application

To build the application, you need to change the current directory to the directory of the application and start dotnet build. When you compile for .NET Core 2.0 and .NET Framework 4.7, you see output like the following:

```
> dotnet build
Microsoft (R) Build Engine version 15.5.179.9764 for .NET Core
Copyright (C) Microsoft Corporation. All rights reserved.

  Restore completed in 19.8 ms for
    C:\procsharp\Intro\HelloWorld\HelloWorld.csproj.
  HelloWorld -> C:\procsharp\Intro\HelloWorld\bin\Debug\net47\HelloWorld.exe
  HelloWorld ->
    C:\procsharp\Intro\HelloWorld\bin\Debug\netcoreapp2.0\HelloWorld.dll

Build succeeded.
    0 Warning(s)
    0 Error(s)

Time Elapsed 00:00:01.58
```

> **NOTE** *The commands* dotnet new *and* dotnet build *now include restoring NuGet packages. You can also explicitly restore NuGet packages with* dotnet restore.

Because of the compilation process, you find the assembly containing the IL code of the Program class within the bin/debug/[netcoreapp2.0|net47] folders. If you compare the build of .NET Core with .NET 4.7, you will find a DLL containing the IL code with .NET Core, and an EXE containing the IL code with .NET 4.7. The assembly generated for .NET Core has a dependency to the System.Console assembly, whereas the .NET 4.6 assembly finds the Console class in the mscorlib assembly.

To build release code, you need to specify the option --Configuration Release (shorthand -c Release):

```
> dotnet build --configuration Release
```

Some of the code samples in the following chapters make use of features offered by C# 7.1 or C# 7.2. By default, the latest major version of the compiler is used, which is C# 7.0. To enable newer versions of C#, you need to specify this in the project file as shown with the following project file section. Here, the latest version of the C# compiler is configured.

```
<PropertyGroup>
  <LangVersion>latest</LangVersion>
</PropertyGroup>
```

Running the Application

To run the application, you can use the dotnet run command

```
> dotnet run
```

In case the project file targets multiple frameworks, you need to tell the `dotnet run` command which framework to use to run the app by using the option `--framework`. This framework must be configured with the `csproj` file. With the sample application, you can see output like the following after the restore information:

```
> dotnet run --framework netcooreapp2.0
Microsoft (R) Build Engine version 15.5.179.9764 for .NET Core
Copyright (C) Microsoft Corporation. All rights reserved.

  Restore completed in 20.65 ms for
    C:\procsharp\Intro\HelloWorld\HelloWorld.csproj.
Hello World!
```

On a production system, you don't use `dotnet run` to run the application. Instead, you use `dotnet` with the name of the library:

```
> dotnet bin/debug/netcoreapp2.0/HelloWorld.dll
```

You can also create an executable, but executables are platform specific. How this is done is shown later in this chapter in the section "Packaging and Publishing the Application."

> **NOTE** *As you've seen building and running the "Hello World!" app on Windows, the dotnet tools work the same on Linux and OS X. You can use the same dotnet commands on either platform.*
>
> *The focus of this book is on Windows, as Visual Studio 2017 offers a more powerful development platform than is available on the other platforms, but many code samples from this book are based on .NET Core, and you will be able to run them on other platforms as well. You can also use Visual Studio Code, a free development environment, to develop applications directly on Linux and OS X. See the section "Developer Tools" later in this chapter for more information about different editions of Visual Studio.*

Creating a Web Application

You also can use the .NET Core CLI to create a web application. When you start `dotnet new`, you can see a list of templates available (see Figure 1-5).

```
Developer Command Prompt for VS 2017                                    —  □  ×

Templates                         Short Name   Language      Tags
--------------------------------------------------------------------------------
Console Application               console      [C#], F#, VB  Common/Console
Class library                     classlib     [C#], F#, VB  Common/Library
Unit Test Project                 mstest       [C#], F#, VB  Test/MSTest
xUnit Test Project                xunit        [C#], F#, VB  Test/xUnit
ASP.NET Core Empty                web          [C#], F#      Web/Empty
ASP.NET Core Web App (Model-View-Controller)  mvc  [C#], F#  Web/MVC
ASP.NET Core Web App              razor        [C#]          Web/MVC/Razor Pages
ASP.NET Core with Angular         angular      [C#]          Web/MVC/SPA
ASP.NET Core with React.js        react        [C#]          Web/MVC/SPA
ASP.NET Core with React.js and Redux  reactredux  [C#]       Web/MVC/SPA
ASP.NET Core Web API              webapi       [C#], F#      Web/WebAPI
global.json file                  globaljson                 Config
NuGet Config                      nugetconfig                Config
Web Config                        webconfig                  Config
Solution File                     sln                        Solution
Razor Page                        page                       Web/ASP.NET
MVC ViewImports                   viewimports                Web/ASP.NET
MVC ViewStart                     viewstart                  Web/ASP.NET

Examples:
    dotnet new mvc --auth Individual
    dotnet new mstest
    dotnet new --help
```

FIGURE 1-5

The command

```
> dotnet new mvc -o WebApp
```

creates a new ASP.NET Core web application using ASP.NET Core MVC. After changing to the WebApp folder, build and run the program using

```
> dotnet build
> dotnet run
```

starts the Kestrel server of ASP.NET Core to listen on port 5000. You can open a browser to access the pages returned from this server, as shown in Figure 1-6.

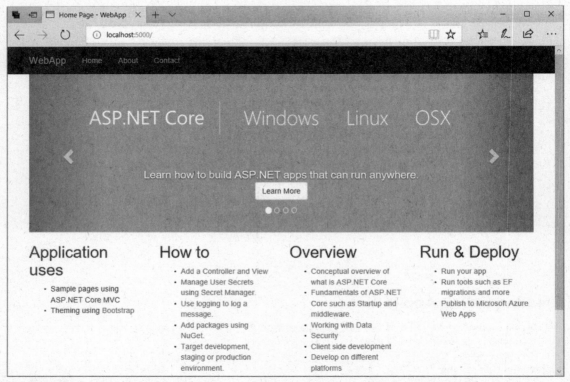

FIGURE 1-6

Publishing the Application

With the dotnet tool you can create a NuGet package and publish the application for deployment. Let's first create a framework-dependent deployment of the application. This reduces the files needed with publishing.

Using the previously created console application, you just need the following command to create the files needed for publishing. The framework is selected by using -f, and the release configuration is selected by using -c:

```
> dotnet publish -f netcoreapp2.0 -c Release
```

The files needed for publishing are put into the bin/Release/netcoreapp2.0/publish directory.

Using these files for publishing on the target system, the runtime is needed as well. You can find the runtime downloads and installation instructions at https://www.microsoft.com/net/download/.

Contrary to the .NET Framework where the same installed runtime can be used by different .NET Framework versions (for example, the .NET Framework 4.0 runtime with updates can be used from .NET Framework 4.7, 4.6, 4.5, 4.0… applications), with .NET Core, to run the application, you need the same runtime version.

> **NOTE** *In case your application uses additional NuGet packages, these need to be referenced in the* csproj *file, and the libraries need to be delivered with the application. Read Chapter 19 for more information.*

Self-Contained Deployments

Instead of needing to have the runtime installed on the target system, the application can deliver the runtime with it. This is known as *self-contained deployment.*

Depending on the platform, the runtime differs. Thus, with self-contained deployment you need to specify the platforms supported by specifying RuntimeIdentifiers in the project file, as shown in the following project file. Here, the runtime identifiers for Windows 10, MacOS, and Ubuntu Linux are specified (project file SelfContainedHelloWorld/SelfContainedHelloWorld.csproj):

```xml
<Project Sdk="Microsoft.NET.Sdk">
  <PropertyGroup>
    <OutputType>Exe</OutputType>
    <TargetFramework>netcoreapp2.0</TargetFramework>
  </PropertyGroup>
  <PropertyGroup>
    <RuntimeIdentifiers>
      win10-x64;ubuntu-x64;osx.10.11-x64;
    </RuntimeIdentifiers>
  </PropertyGroup>
</Project>
```

> **NOTE** *Get all the runtime identifiers for different platforms and versions from the .NET Core Runtime Identifier (RID) catalog at* https://docs.microsoft.com/en-us/dotnet/core/rid-catalog.

Now you can create publish files for all the different platforms:

```
> dotnet publish -c Release -r win10-x64
> dotnet publish -c Release -r osx.10.11-x64
> dotnet publish -c Release -r ubuntu-x64
```

After running these commands, you can find the files needed for publishing in the Release/[win10-x64|osx.10.11-x64|ubuntu-x64]/publish directories. As .NET Core 2.0 is a lot larger, the size needed for publishing was growing. In these directories, you can find platform-specific executables that you can start directly without using the dotnet command.

> **NOTE** *Chapter 19 gives more details on working with the .NET Core CLI and adding NuGet packages, adding projects, creating libraries, working with solution files, and more.*

USING VISUAL STUDIO 2017

Next, let's get into using Visual Studio 2017 instead of the command line. In this section, the most important parts of Visual Studio are covered to get you started. More features of Visual Studio are covered in Chapter 18, "Visual Studio 2017."

Installing Visual Studio 2017

Visual Studio 2017 offers a new installer that should make it easier to install the products you need. With the installer, you can select the Workloads you need for developing applications (see Figure 1-7). To cover all the chapters of the book, install these workloads:

➤ Universal Windows Platform development

➤ .NET Desktop development

➤ ASP.NET and web development

➤ Azure development

➤ Mobile development with .NET

➤ .NET Core cross-platform development

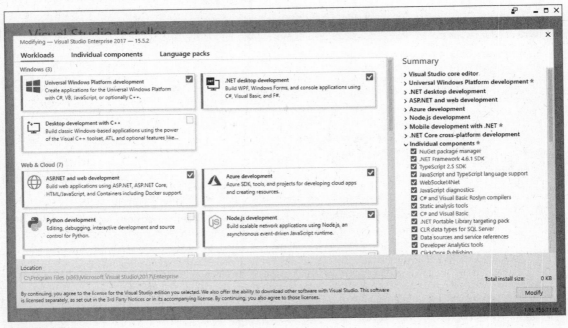

FIGURE 1-7

Creating a Project

You might be overwhelmed by the huge number of menu items and the many options in Visual Studio. To create simple apps in the first chapters of this book, you need only a small subset of the features of Visual Studio. Also, this complete book covers only a part of all the things you can do with Visual Studio. Many features within Visual Studio are offered for legacy applications, as well as for other programming languages.

The first thing you do after starting Visual Studio is create a new project. Select the menu File ⇨ New ⇨ Project. The dialog shown in Figure 1-8 opens. You see a list of project items that you can use to create new projects.

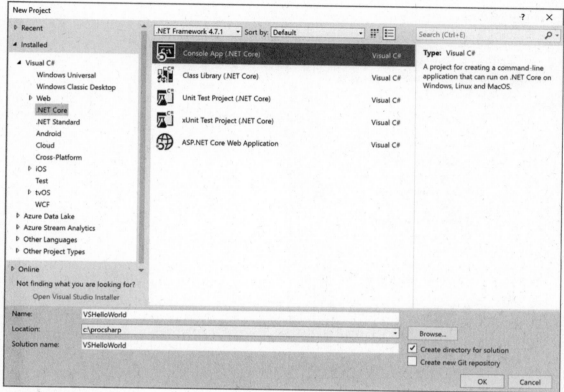

FIGURE 1-8

For this book, you're interested in a subset of the Visual C# project items. With the first chapters of this book, you select the .NET Core category and the project template Console App (.NET Core). On top of the dialog shown in Figure 1-8 you can see where .NET Framework version is selected. Don't be confused, this selection does not apply to .NET Core projects.

In the lower part of this dialog, you can enter the name of the application, chose the folder where to store the project, and enter a name for the solution. Solutions can contain multiple projects.

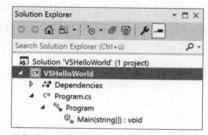

Clicking the OK button creates a "Hello World!" application.

Working with Solution Explorer

In the Solution Explorer (see Figure 1-9), you can see the solution, the projects belonging to the solution, and the files in the project. You can select a source code file you can get into the classes and class members.

FIGURE 1-9

When you select an item in the Solution Explorer and click the right mouse key or press the application key on the keyboard, you open the context menu for the item, as shown in Figure 1-10. The available menus depend on the item you selected and on the features installed with Visual Studio.

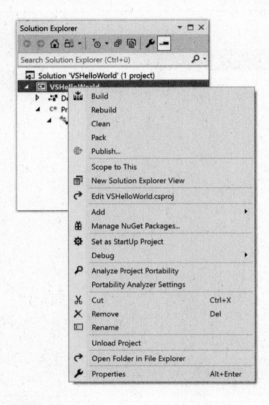

FIGURE 1-10

When you open the context menu for the project, one menu item is to edit the project file. This option opens the project file `VSHelloWorld.csproj` with the same content you've already seen earlier when using the .NET Core CLI.

Configuring Project Properties

You can configure the project properties by selecting the context menu of the project in the Solution Explorer and clicking Properties, or by selecting Project ➪ VSHelloWorld Properties. This opens the view shown in Figure 1-11. Here, you can configure different settings of the project, such as the .NET Core version to use (if you have multiple frameworks installed), build settings, commands that should be invoked during the build process, package configuration, and arguments and environmental variables used while debugging the application. As previously mentioned, with some code samples, C# 7.0 is not enough. You can configure a different version of the C# compiler with the Build category. Clicking the Advanced button opens the Advanced Build Settings dialog (see Figure 1-12). Here, you can configure the version of the C# compiler. This selection goes into the `csproj` project configuration file.

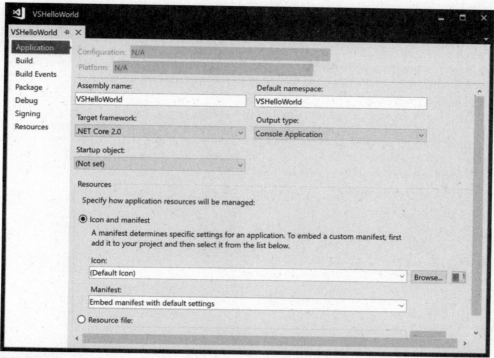

FIGURE 1-11

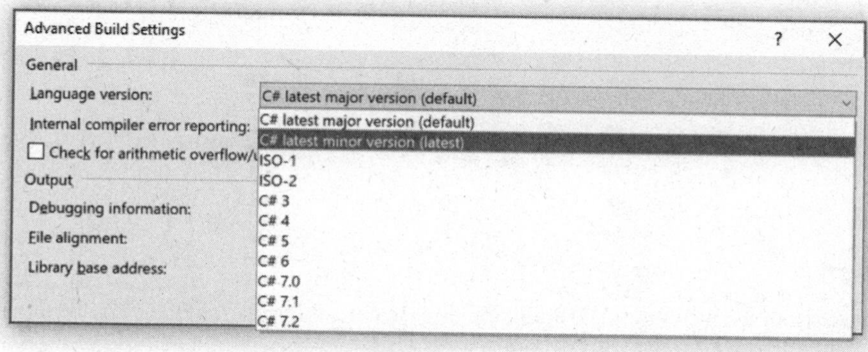

FIGURE 1-12

NOTE *When making a change with the project properties, you need to make sure to select the correct Configuration at the top of the dialog. If you change the version of the C# compiler only with the Debug configuration, building release code will fail when you use newer C# language features. For settings you would like to have with all configurations, select the configuration All Configurations.*

Getting to Know the Editor

The Visual Studio editor is extremely powerful. It offers IntelliSense to offer you available options to invoke methods and properties and completes your typing as you press the Tab button. Compilation takes place while you type, so you can immediately see syntax errors with underlined code. Hovering the mouse pointer over the underlined text brings up a small box that contains the description of the error.

One great productivity feature from the code editor is code snippets. They reduce how much you need to type. Just by typing `cw` and pressing Tab twice in the editor, the editor creates `Console .WriteLine();`. Visual Studio comes with many code snippets that you can see when you select Tools ⇨ Code Snippets Manager to open the Code Snippets Manager (see Figure 1-13), where you can select CSharp in the Language field for the code snippets defined with the C# language; select the group Visual C# to see all predefined code snippets for C#.

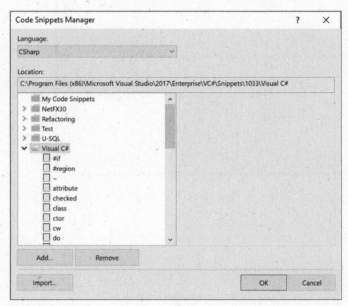

FIGURE 1-13

Building a Project

You compile the project from the menu Build ⇨ Build Solution. In case of errors, the Error List window shows errors and warnings. However, the Output window (see Figure 1-14) is more reliable than the Error List. Sometimes the Error List contains older cached information, or it is not that easy to find the error when the list is large. The Output window usually gives great information for many different tools. You open the Output window by selecting View ⇨ Output.

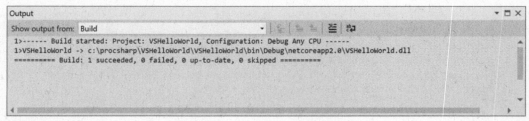

FIGURE 1-14

Running an Application

To run the application, select Debug ➪ Start Without Debugging. This starts the application and keeps the console window opened until you close it.

Remember, you can configure application arguments in the Project Properties selecting the Debug category.

Debugging

To debug an application, you can click the left gray area in the editor to create breakpoints (see Figure 1-15). With breakpoints in place, you can start the debugger by selecting Debug ➪ Start Debugging. When you hit a breakpoint, you can use the Debug toolbar (see Figure 1-16) to step into, over, or out of methods, or you can show the next statement. Hover over variables to see the current values. You also can check the Locals and Watch windows for variables set, and you can change values while the application runs.

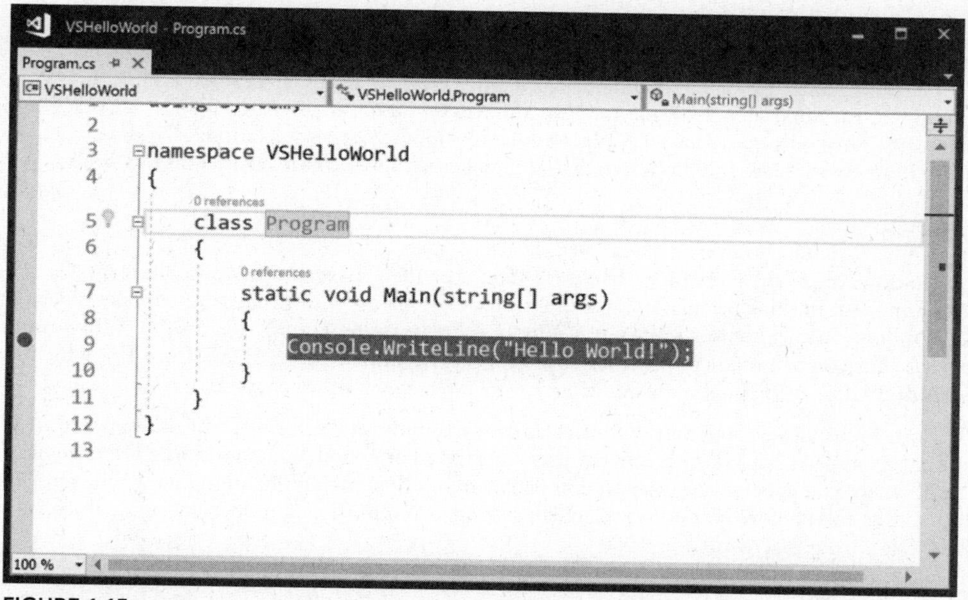

VSHelloWorld - Program.cs
Program.cs
VSHelloWorld
VSHelloWorld.Program
Main(string[] args)
namespace VSHelloWorld
{
0 references
class Program
{
0 references
static void Main(string[] args)
{
Console.WriteLine("Hello World!");
}
}
}
100 %

FIGURE 1-15

Now you've seen the parts of Visual Studio that are most important for helping you to survive the first chapters in this book. Chapter 18 takes a deeper look at Visual Studio 2017.

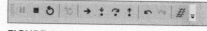

FIGURE 1-16

APPLICATION TYPES AND TECHNOLOGIES

You can use C# to create console applications; with most samples in the first chapters of this book you'll do that exact thing. For many programs, console applications are not used that often. You can use C# to create applications that use many of the technologies associated with .NET. This section gives you an overview of the different types of applications that you can write in C#.

Data Access

Before having a look at the application types, let's look at technologies that are used by all application types: access to data.

Files and directories can be accessed by using simple API calls; however, the simple API calls are not flexible enough for some scenarios. With the stream API you have a lot of flexibility, and the streams offer many more features such as encryption or compression. Readers and writers make using streams easier. All the different options available here are covered in Chapter 22, "Files and Streams." It's also possible to serialize complete objects in XML or JSON format. Bonus Chapter 2, "XML and JSON," (which you can find online) discusses these options.

To read and write to databases, you can use ADO.NET directly (see Chapter 25, "ADO.NET and Transactions"), or you can use an abstraction layer, Entity Framework Core (Chapter 26, "Entity Framework Core"). Entity Framework Core offers a mapping of object hierarchies to the relations of a database.

Entity Framework Core 1.0 is a complete redesign of Entity Framework, as is reflected with the new name. Code needs to be changed to migrate applications from older versions of Entity Framework to the new version. Older mapping variants, such as Database First and Model First, have been dropped, as Code First is a better alternative. The complete redesign was also done to support not only relational databases but also NoSQL. Entity Framework Core 2.0 has a long list of new features, which are covered in this book.

Windows Apps

For creating Windows apps, the technology of choice should be the Universal Windows Platform. Of course, there are restrictions when this option is not available—for example, if you still need to support older O/S versions like Windows 7. In this case you can use Windows Presentation Foundation (WPF). WPF is not covered in this book, but you can read the previous edition, *Professional C# 6 and .NET Core 1.0*, which has five chapters dedicated to WPF, plus some additional WPF coverage in other chapters.

This book has one focus: developing apps with the Universal Windows Platform (UWP). Compared to WPF, UWP offers a more modern XAML to create the user interface. For example, data binding offers a compiled binding variant where you get errors at compile time instead of not showing the bound data. The application is compiled to native code before it's run on the client systems. And it offers a modern design, which is now called Fluent Design from Microsoft.

> **NOTE** *Creating UWP apps is covered in Chapter 33, "Windows Apps," along with an introduction to XAML, the different XAML controls, and the lifetime of apps. You can create apps with WPF, UWP, and Xamarin by using as much common code as possible by supporting the MVVM pattern. This pattern is covered in Chapter 34, "Patterns with XAML Apps." To create cool looks and style the app, be sure to read Chapter 35, "Styling Windows Apps." Chapter 36, "Advanced Windows Apps," dives into some advanced features of UWP.*

Xamarin

It would have been great if Windows had been a bigger player in the mobile phone market. Then Universal Windows Apps would run on the mobile phones as well. Reality turned out differently, and Windows on the phone is (currently) a thing of the past. However, with Xamarin you can use C# and XAML to create apps on the iPhone and Android. Xamarin offers APIs to create apps on Android and libraries to create apps on iPhone—using the C# code you are used to.

With Android, a mapping layer using Android Callable Wrappers (ACW) and Managed Callable Wrappers (MCW) are used to interop between .NET code and Android's Java runtime. With iOS, an Ahead of Time (AOT) compiler compiles the managed code to native code.

Xamarin.Forms offers XAML code to create the user interface and share as much of the user interface as possible between Android, iOS, Windows, and Linux. XAML only offers UI controls that can be mapped to all platforms. For using specific controls from a platform, you can create platform-specific renderers.

> **NOTE** *Developing with Xamarin and Xamarin.Forms is covered in Chapter 37, "Xamarin.Forms."*

Web Applications

The original introduction of ASP.NET fundamentally changed the web programming model. ASP.NET Core changed it again. ASP.NET Core allows the use of .NET Core for high performance and scalability, and it not only runs on Windows but also on Linux systems.

With ASP.NET Core, ASP.NET Web Forms is no longer covered (ASP.NET Web Forms can still be used and is updated with .NET 4.7).

ASP.NET Core MVC is based on the well-known Model-View-Controller (MVC) pattern for easier unit testing. It also allows a clear separation for writing user interface code with HTML, CSS, and JavaScript, and it uses C# on the backend.

> **NOTE** *Chapter 30 covers the foundation of ASP.NET Core. Chapter 31 continues building on the foundation and adds using the ASP.NET Core MVC framework.*

Web API

SOAP and WCF fulfilled their duty in the past, and they're not needed anymore. Modern apps make use of REST (Representational State Transfer) and the Web API. Using ASP.NET Core to create a Web API is an option that is a lot easier for communication and fulfills more than 90 percent of requirements by distributed applications. This technology is based on REST, which defines guidelines and best practices for stateless and scalable web services.

The client can receive JSON or XML data. JSON and XML can also be formatted in a way to make use of the Open Data specification (OData).

The features of this new API make it easy to consume from web clients using JavaScript, the Universal Windows Platform, and Xamarin.

Creating a Web API is a good approach for creating microservices. The approach to build microservices defines smaller services that can run and be deployed independently, having their own control of a data store.

To describe the services, a new standard was defined: the OpenAPI (`https://www.openapis.org`). This standard has its roots with Swagger (`https://swagger.io/`).

> **NOTE** *The ASP.NET Core Web API, Swagger, and more information on microservices are covered in Chapter 32.*

WebHooks and SignalR

For real-time web functionality and bidirectional communication between the client and the server, WebHooks and SignalR are ASP.NET Core technologies available with .NET Core 2.1.

SignalR allows pushing information to connected clients as soon as information is available. SignalR makes use of the WebSocket technology to push information.

WebHooks allows you to integrate with public services, and these services can call into your public ASP .NET Core created Web API service. WebHooks is a technology to receive push notification from services such as GitHub or Dropbox and many other services.

> **NOTE** *The foundation of SignalR connection management, grouping of connections, and authorization and integration of WebHooks are discussed in Bonus Chapter 3, "WebHooks and SignalR," which you can find online.*

Microsoft Azure

Nowadays you can't ignore the cloud when considering the development picture. Although there's not a dedicated chapter on cloud technologies, Microsoft Azure is referenced in several chapters in this book.

Microsoft Azure offers Software as a Service (SaaS), Infrastructure as a Service (IaaS), Platform as a Service (PaaS), and Functions as a Service (FaaS), and sometimes offerings are in between these categories. Let's have a look at some Microsoft Azure offerings.

Software as a Service

SaaS offers complete software; you don't have to deal with management of servers, updates, and so on. Office 365 is one of the SaaS offerings for using e-mail and other services via a cloud offering. A SaaS offering that's relevant for developers is *Visual Studio Team Services*. Visual Studio Team Services is the Team Foundation Server in the cloud that can be used as a private code repository, for tracking bugs and work items, and for build and testing services. Chapter 18 explains DevOps features that can be used from Visual Studio.

Infrastructure as a Service

Another service offering is *IaaS*. Virtual machines are offered by this service offering. You are responsible for managing the operating system and maintaining updates. When you create virtual machines, you can decide between different hardware offerings starting with shared Cores up to 128 cores (at the time of this writing, but things change quickly). 128 cores, 2 TB RAM, and 4 TB local SSD belong to the "M-Series" of machines.

With preinstalled operating systems you can decide between Windows, Windows Server, Linux, and operating systems that come preinstalled with SQL Server, BizTalk Server, SharePoint, and Oracle, and many other products.

I use virtual machines often for environments that I need only for several hours a week, as the virtual machines are paid on an hourly basis. In case you want to try compiling and running .NET Core programs on Linux but don't have a Linux machine, installing such an environment on Microsoft Azure is an easy task.

Platform as a Service

For developers, the most relevant part of Microsoft Azure is PaaS. You can access services for storing and reading data, use computing and networking capabilities of app services, and integrate developer services within the application.

For storing data in the cloud, you can use a relational data store SQL Database. SQL Database is nearly the same as the on-premise version of SQL Server. There are also some NoSQL solutions such as Cosmos DB with different store options like JSON data, relationships, or table storage, and Azure Storage that stores blobs (for example, for images or videos).

App Services can be used to host your web apps and API apps that you are creating with ASP.NET Core.

Microsoft also offers Developer Services in Microsoft Azure. Part of the Developer Services is Visual Studio Team Services. Visual Studio Team Services allows you to manage the source code, automatic builds, tests, and deployments—continuous integration (CI).

Part of the Developer Services is Application Insights. With faster release cycles, it's becoming more and more important to get information about how the user uses the app. What menus are never used because the users probably don't find them? What paths in the app is the user taking to fulfill his or her tasks? With Application Insights, you can get good anonymous user information to find out the issues users have with the application, and with DevOps in place you can do quick fixes.

You also can use *Cognitive Services* that offer functionality to process images, use Bing Search APIs, understand what users say with language services, and more.

Functions as a Service

FaaS is a new concept for cloud service, also known as a *serverless computing* technology. Of course, behind the scenes there's always a server. You just don't pay for reserved CPU and memory as you do with App Services that are used from web apps. Instead the amount you pay is based on consumption—on the number of calls done with some limitations on the memory and time needed for the activity. Azure Functions is one technology that can be deployed using FaaS.

> **NOTE** *In Chapter 29, "Tracing, Logging, and Analytics," you can read about tracing features and learn how to use the Application Insights offering of Microsoft Azure. Chapter 32, "Web API," not only covers creating Web APIs with ASP.NET Core MVC but also shows how the same service functionality can be used from an Azure Function. The Microsoft Bot service as well as Cognitive Services are explained in Bonus Chapter 4, "Bot Framework and Cognitive Services," which you can find online.*

DEVELOPER TOOLS

This final part of the chapter, before we switch to a lot of C# code in the next chapter, covers developer tools and editions of Visual Studio 2017.

Visual Studio Community

This edition of Visual Studio is a free edition with features that the Professional edition previously had. There's a license restriction for when it can be used. It's free for open-source projects and training and to academic and small professional teams. Unlike the Express editions of Visual Studio that previously have been the free editions, this product allows using extensions with Visual Studio.

Visual Studio Professional

This edition includes more features than the Community edition, such as the CodeLens and Team Foundation Server for source code management and team collaboration. With this edition, you also get an MSDN subscription that includes several server products from Microsoft for development and testing.

Visual Studio Enterprise

Unlike the Professional edition, this edition contains a lot of tools for testing, such as Web Load & Performance Testing, Unit Test Isolation with Microsoft Fakes, and Coded UI Testing. (Unit testing is part of all Visual Studio editions.) With Code Clone you can find code clones in your solution. Visual Studio Enterprise also contains architecture and modeling tools to analyze and validate the solution architecture.

> **NOTE** *Be aware that with a Visual Studio subscription you're entitled to free use of Microsoft Azure up to a specific monthly amount that is contingent on the type of Visual Studio subscription you have.*

> **NOTE** *Chapter 18 includes details on using several features of Visual Studio 2017. Chapter 28, "Testing," gets into details of unit testing, web testing, and creating Coded UI tests.*

> **NOTE** *For some of the features in the book—for example, the Coded UI Tests —you need Visual Studio Enterprise. You can work through most parts of the book with the Visual Studio Community edition.*

Visual Studio for Mac

Visual Studio for Mac originates in the Xamarin Studio, but now it offers a lot more than the earlier product. For example, the editor shares code with Visual Studio, so you're soon familiar with it. With Visual Studio for Mac you can not only create Xamarin apps, but you also can create ASP.NET Core apps that run on Windows, Linux, and the Mac. With many chapters of this book, you can use Visual Studio for Mac. Exceptions are the chapters covering the Universal Windows Platform, which requires Windows to run the app and also to develop the app.

Visual Studio Code

Visual Studio Code is a completely different development tool compared to the other Visual Studio editions. While Visual Studio 2017 offers project-based features with a rich set of templates and tools, Visual Studio is a code editor with little project management support. However, Visual Studio Code runs not only on Windows, but also on Linux and OS X.

With many chapters of this book, you can use Visual Studio Code as your development editor. What you can't do is create UWP and Xamarin applications, and you also don't have access to the features covered in Chapter 18, "Visual Studio 2017." You can use Visual Studio Code for .NET Core console applications, and ASP.NET Core 1.0 web applications using .NET Core.

You can download Visual Studio Code from `http://code.visualstudio.com`.

SUMMARY

This chapter covered a lot of ground to review important technologies and changes with technologies. Knowing about the history of some technologies helps you decide which technology should be used with new applications and what you should do with existing applications.

You read about the differences between .NET Framework and .NET Core, and you saw how to create and run a Hello World application with all these environments with and without using Visual Studio.

You've seen the functions of the Common Language Runtime (CLR) and looked at technologies for accessing the database and creating Windows apps. You also reviewed the advantages of ASP.NET Core.

Chapter 2 dives fast into the syntax of C#. You learn variables, implement program flows, organize your code into namespaces, and more.

2

Core C#

WROX.COM CODE DOWNLOADS FOR THIS CHAPTER

The Wrox.com code downloads for this chapter are found at www.wrox.com on the Download Code tab. The source code is also available at https://github.com/ProfessionalCSharp/ProfessionalCSharp7 in the directory CoreCSharp.

The code for this chapter is divided into the following major examples:

FUNDAMENTALS OF C#

Now that you understand more about what C# can do, you need to know how to use it. This chapter gives you a good start in that direction by providing a basic understanding of the fundamentals of C# programming, which is built on in subsequent chapters. By the end of this chapter, you will know enough C# to write simple programs (though without using inheritance or other object-oriented features, which are covered in later chapters).

Hello, World!

Chapter 1, ".NET Application Architectures and Tools," shows how to create a Hello, World! application using the .NET Core CLI tools, Visual Studio, Visual Studio for Mac, and Visual Studio Code. Now let's concentrate on the C# source code. First, I have a few general comments about C# syntax. In C#, as in other C-style languages, statements end in a semicolon (;) and can continue over multiple lines without needing a continuation character. Statements can be joined into blocks using curly braces ({}). Single-line comments begin with two forward slash characters (//), and multiline comments begin with a slash and an asterisk (/*) and end with the same combination reversed (*/). In these aspects, C# is identical to C++ and Java but different from Visual Basic. It is the semicolons and curly braces that give C# code such a different visual appearance from Visual Basic code. If your background is predominantly Visual Basic, take extra care to remember the semicolon at the end of every statement. Omitting this is usually the biggest single cause of compilation errors among developers who are new to C-style languages. Another thing to remember is that C# is case sensitive. That means the variables named `myVar` and `MyVar` are two different variables.

The first few lines in the previous code example are related to *namespaces* (mentioned later in this chapter), which is a way to group associated classes. The `namespace` keyword declares the namespace with which your class should be associated. All code within the braces that follow it is regarded as being within that namespace. The `using` declaration specifies a namespace that the compiler should look at to find any classes that are referenced in your code but aren't defined in the current namespace. This serves the same purpose as the `import` statement in Java and the `using namespace` statement in C++ (code file `HelloWorldApp/Program.cs`):

```
using System;
namespace Wrox.HelloWorldApp
{
```

The reason for the presence of the `using System;` declaration in the `Program.cs` file is that you are going to use the class `Console` from the namespace `System`: `System.Console`. The `using System;` declaration enables you to refer to this class without adding the namespace. You can invoke the `WriteLine` method using the following class:

```
using System;
// ...
Console.WriteLine("Hello World!");
```

> **NOTE** *Namespaces are explained in detail later in this chapter in the section "Getting Organized with Namespaces."*

With the `using static` declaration you can open not only a namespace, but all static members of a class. Declaring `using static System.Console`, you can invoke the `WriteLine` method of the `Console` class without the class name:

```
using static System.Console;
// ...
WriteLine("Hello World!");
```

Omitting the complete `using` declaration, you need to add the namespace name invoking the `WriteLine` method:

```
System.Console.WriteLine("Hello World!");
```

The standard `System` namespace is where the most commonly used .NET types reside. It is important to realize that everything you do in C# depends on .NET base classes. In this case, you are using the `Console` class within the `System` namespace to write to the console window. C# has no built-in keywords of its own for input or output; it is completely reliant on the .NET classes.

Within the source code, a class called `Program` is declared. However, because it has been placed in a namespace called `Wrox.HelloWorldApp`, the fully qualified name of this class is `Wrox.HelloWorldApp.Program` (code file `HelloWorldApp/Program.cs`):

```
namespace Wrox.HelloWorldApp
{
    class Program
    {
```

All C# code must be contained within a class. The class declaration consists of the `class` keyword, followed by the class name and a pair of curly braces. All code associated with the class should be placed between these braces.

The class `Program` contains a method called `Main`. Every C# executable (such as console applications, Windows applications, Windows services, and web applications) must have an entry point—the `Main` method (note the capital `M`).

```
static void Main()
{
```

The method is called when the program is started. This method must return either nothing (`void`) or an integer (`int`). Note the format of method definitions in C#:

```
[modifiers] return_type MethodName([parameters])
{
    // Method body. NB. This code block is pseudo-code.
}
```

Here, the first square brackets represent certain optional keywords. Modifiers are used to specify certain features of the method you are defining, such as from where the method can be called. In this case the `Main` method doesn't have a public access modifier applied. You can do this in case you need a unit test for the `Main` method. The runtime doesn't need the public access modifier applied, and it still can invoke the method. The static modifier is required as the runtime invokes the method without creating an instance of the class. The return type is set to `void`, and in the example parameters are not included.

Finally, we come to the code statement themselves:

```
Console.WriteLine("Hello World!");
```

In this case, you simply call the `WriteLine` method of the `System.Console` class to write a line of text to the console window. `WriteLine` is a `static` method, so you don't need to instantiate a `Console` object before calling it.

Now that you have had a taste of basic C# syntax, you are ready for more detail. Because it is virtually impossible to write any nontrivial program without *variables*, we start by looking at variables in C#.

WORKING WITH VARIABLES

You declare variables in C# using the following syntax:

```
datatype identifier;
```

For example:

```
int i;
```

This statement declares an `int` named `i`. The compiler won't actually let you use this variable in an expression until you have initialized it with a value.

After it has been declared, you can assign a value to the variable using the assignment operator, `=`:

```
i = 10;
```

You can also declare the variable and initialize its value at the same time:

```
int i = 10;
```

If you declare and initialize more than one variable in a single statement, all the variables will be of the same data type:

```
int x = 10, y =20; // x and y are both ints
```

To declare variables of different types, you need to use separate statements. You cannot assign different data types within a multiple-variable declaration:

```
int x = 10;
bool y = true; // Creates a variable that stores true or false
int x = 10, bool y = true; // This won't compile!
```

Notice the `//` and the text after it in the preceding examples. These are comments. The `//` character sequence tells the compiler to ignore the text that follows on this line because it is included for a human to better understand the program; it's not part of the program itself. Comments are explained further later in this chapter in the "Using Comments" section.

Initializing Variables

Variable initialization demonstrates an example of C#'s emphasis on safety. Briefly, the C# compiler requires that any variable be initialized with some starting value before you refer to that variable in an operation. Most modern compilers will flag violations of this as a warning, but the ever-vigilant C# compiler treats such violations as errors.

C# has two methods for ensuring that variables are initialized before use:

➤ Variables that are fields in a class or struct, if not initialized explicitly, are by default zeroed out when they are created (classes and structs are discussed later).

➤ Variables that are local to a method must be explicitly initialized in your code prior to any statements in which their values are used. In this case, the initialization doesn't have to happen when the variable is declared, but the compiler checks all possible paths through the method and flags an error if it detects any possibility of the value of a local variable being used before it is initialized.

For example, you can't do the following in C#:

```
static int Main()
{
  int d;
  Console.WriteLine(d); // Can't do this! Need to initialize d before use
  return 0;
}
```

Notice that this code snippet demonstrates defining `Main` so that it returns an `int` instead of `void`.

If you attempt to compile the preceding lines, you receive this error message:

```
Use of unassigned local variable 'd'
```

Consider the following statement:

```
Something objSomething;
```

In C#, this line of code would create only a *reference* for a `Something` object, but this reference would not yet actually refer to any object. Any attempt to call a method or property against this variable would result in an error.

To instantiate a reference object in C#, you must use the `new` keyword. You create a reference as shown in the previous example and then point the reference at an object allocated on the heap using the `new` keyword:

```
objSomething = new Something(); // This creates a Something object on the heap
```

Using Type Inference

Type inference makes use of the `var` keyword. The syntax for declaring the variable changes by using the `var` keyword instead of the real type. The compiler "infers" what the type of the variable is by what the variable is initialized to. For example:

```
var someNumber = 0;
```

becomes:

```
int someNumber = 0;
```

Even though `someNumber` is never declared as being an `int`, the compiler figures this out and `someNumber` is an `int` for as long as it is in scope. Once compiled, the two preceding statements are equal.

Here is a short program to demonstrate (code file `VariablesSample/Program.cs`):

```
using System;
namespace Wrox
{
  class Program
  {
    static void Main()
    {
      var name = "Bugs Bunny";
      var age = 25;
      var isRabbit = true;
      Type nameType = name.GetType();
      Type ageType = age.GetType();
      Type isRabbitType = isRabbit.GetType();
      Console.WriteLine($"name is of type {nameType}");
      Console.WriteLine($"age is of type {ageType}");
      Console.WriteLine($"isRabbit is of type {isRabbitType}");
    }
  }
}
```

The output from this program is as follows:

```
name is of type System.String
age is of type System.Int32
isRabbit is of type System.Boolean
```

There are a few rules that you need to follow:

➤ The variable must be initialized. Otherwise, the compiler doesn't have anything from which to infer the type.

➤ The initializer cannot be null.

➤ The initializer must be an expression.

➤ You can't set the initializer to an object unless you create a new object in the initializer.

Chapter 3, "Objects and Types," examines these rules more closely in the discussion of anonymous types.

After the variable has been declared and the type inferred, the variable's type cannot be changed. When established, the variable's type strong typing rules that any assignment to this variable must follow the inferred type.

Understanding Variable Scope

The *scope* of a variable is the region of code from which the variable can be accessed. In general, the scope is determined by the following rules:

➤ A *field* (also known as a member variable) of a class is in scope for as long as a local variable of this type is in scope.

➤ A *local variable* is in scope until a closing brace indicates the end of the block statement or method in which it was declared.

➤ A local variable that is declared in a `for`, `while`, or similar statement is in scope in the body of that loop.

Scope Clashes for Local Variables

It's common in a large program to use the same variable name for different variables in different parts of the program. This is fine as long as the variables are scoped to completely different parts of the program so that there is no possibility for ambiguity. However, bear in mind that local variables with the same name can't be declared twice in the same scope. For example, you can't do this:

```
int x = 20;
// some more code
int x = 30;
```

Consider the following code sample (code file `VariableScopeSample/Program.cs`):

```
using System;
namespace VariableScopeSample
{
  class Program
  {
    static int Main()
    {
      for (int i = 0; i < 10; i++)
      {
        Console.WriteLine(i);
      } // i goes out of scope here

      // We can declare a variable named i again, because
      // there's no other variable with that name in scope
      for (int i = 9; i >= 0; i -)
      {
        Console.WriteLine(i);
      } // i goes out of scope here.

      return 0;
    }
  }
}
```

This code simply prints out the numbers from 0 to 9, and then back again from 9 to 0, using two `for` loops. The important thing to note is that you declare the variable `i` twice in this code, within the same method. You can do this because `i` is declared in two separate loops, so each `i` variable is local to its own loop.

Here's another example (code file `VariableScopeSample2/Program.cs`):

```
static int Main()
{
  int j = 20;
  for (int i = 0; i < 10; i++)
```

```
    {
      int j = 30; // Can't do this — j is still in scope
      Console.WriteLine(j + i);
    }
    return 0;
  }
```

If you try to compile this, you'll get an error like the following:

```
error CS0136: A local variable named 'j' cannot be declared in
this scope because that name is used in an enclosing local scope
to define a local or parameter
```

This occurs because the variable j, which is defined before the start of the for loop, is still in scope within the for loop and won't go out of scope until the Main method has finished executing. Although the second j (the illegal one) is in the loop's scope, that scope is nested within the Main method's scope. The compiler has no way to distinguish between these two variables, so it won't allow the second one to be declared.

Scope Clashes for Fields and Local Variables

In certain circumstances, however, you can distinguish between two identifiers with the same name (although not the same fully qualified name) and the same scope, and in this case the compiler allows you to declare the second variable. That's because C# makes a fundamental distinction between variables that are declared at the type level (fields) and variables that are declared within methods (local variables).

Consider the following code snippet (code file VariableScopeSample3/Program.cs):

```
using System;
namespace Wrox
{
  class Program
  {
    static int j = 20;
    static void Main()
    {
      int j = 30;
      Console.WriteLine(j);
      return;
    }
  }
}
```

This code will compile even though you have two variables named j in scope within the Main method: the j that was defined at the class level and doesn't go out of scope until the class Program is destroyed (when the Main method terminates and the program ends), and the j defined within Main. In this case, the new variable named j that you declare in the Main method *hides* the class-level variable with the same name, so when you run this code, the number 30 is displayed.

What if you want to refer to the class-level variable? You can actually refer to fields of a class or struct from outside the object, using the syntax object.fieldname. In the previous example, you are accessing a static field (you find out what this means in the next section) from a static method, so you can't use an instance of the class; you just use the name of the class itself:

```
// ...
static void Main()
{
  int j = 30;
  Console.WriteLine(j);
  Console.WriteLine(Program.j);
}
// ...
```

If you are accessing an instance field (a field that belongs to a specific instance of the class), you need to use the `this` keyword instead.

Working with Constants

As the name implies, a constant is a variable whose value cannot be changed throughout its lifetime. Prefixing a variable with the `const` keyword when it is declared and initialized designates that variable as a constant:

```
const int a = 100; // This value cannot be changed.
```

Constants have the following characteristics:

➤ They must be initialized when they are declared. After a value has been assigned, it can never be overwritten.

➤ The value of a constant must be computable at compile time. Therefore, you can't initialize a constant with a value taken from a variable. If you need to do this, you must use a read-only field (this is explained in Chapter 3).

➤ Constants are always implicitly static. However, notice that you don't have to (and, in fact, are not permitted to) include the `static` modifier in the constant declaration.

At least three advantages exist for using constants in your programs:

➤ Constants make your programs easier to read by replacing magic numbers and strings with readable names whose values are easy to understand.

➤ Constants make your programs easier to modify. For example, assume that you have a `SalesTax` constant in one of your C# programs, and that constant is assigned a value of 6 percent. If the sales tax rate changes later, you can modify the behavior of all tax calculations simply by assigning a new value to the constant; you don't have to hunt through your code for the value .06 and change each one, hoping you will find all of them.

➤ Constants help prevent mistakes in your programs. If you attempt to assign another value to a constant somewhere in your program other than at the point where the constant is declared, the compiler flags the error.

USING PREDEFINED DATA TYPES

Now that you have seen how to declare variables and constants, let's take a closer look at the data types available in C#. As you will see, C# is much stricter about the types available and their definitions than some other languages.

Value Types and Reference Types

Before examining the data types in C#, it is important to understand that C# distinguishes between two categories of data type:

➤ Value types
➤ Reference types

The next few sections look in detail at the syntax for value and reference types. Conceptually, the difference is that a *value type* stores its value directly, whereas a *reference type* stores a reference to the value.

These types are stored in different places in memory; value types are stored in an area known as the *stack*, and reference types are stored in an area known as the *managed heap*. It is important to be aware of whether a type is a value type or a reference type because of the different effect each assignment has.

For example, int is a value type, which means that the following statement results in two locations in memory storing the value 20:

```
// i and j are both of type int
i = 20;
j = i;
```

However, consider the following example. For this code, assume you have defined a class called Vector and that Vector is a reference type and has an int member variable called Value:

```
Vector x, y;
x = new Vector();
x.Value = 30; // Value is a field defined in Vector class
y = x;
Console.WriteLine(y.Value);
y.Value = 50;
Console.WriteLine(x.Value);
```

The crucial point to understand is that after executing this code, there is only one Vector object: x and y both point to the memory location that contains this object. Because x and y are variables of a reference type, declaring each variable simply reserves a reference—it doesn't instantiate an object of the given type. In neither case is an object actually created. To create an object, you have to use the new keyword, as shown. Because x and y refer to the same object, changes made to x will affect y and vice versa. Hence, the code will display 30 and then 50.

If a variable is a reference, it is possible to indicate that it does not refer to any object by setting its value to null:

```
y = null;
```

If a reference is set to null, then it is not possible to call any nonstatic member functions or fields against it; doing so would cause an exception to be thrown at runtime.

> **NOTE** *Non-nullable reference types are planned for C# 8. Variables of these types require initialization with non-null. Reference types that allow* null *explicitly require declaration as a nullable reference type.*

In C#, basic data types such as bool and long are value types. This means that if you declare a bool variable and assign it the value of another bool variable, you will have two separate bool values in memory. Later, if you change the value of the original bool variable, the value of the second bool variable does not change. These types are copied by value.

In contrast, most of the more complex C# data types, including classes that you yourself declare, are reference types. They are allocated upon the heap, have lifetimes that can span multiple function calls, and can be accessed through one or several aliases. The CLR implements an elaborate algorithm to track which reference variables are still reachable and which have been orphaned. Periodically, the CLR destroys orphaned objects and returns the memory that they once occupied back to the operating system. This is done by the garbage collector.

C# has been designed this way because high performance is best served by keeping primitive types (such as int and bool) as value types, and larger types that contain many fields (as is usually the case with classes) as reference types. If you want to define your own type as a value type, you should declare it as a struct.

> **NOTE** *The layout of primitive data types typically aligns with native layouts. This makes it possible to share the same memory between managed and native code.*

.NET Types

The C# keywords for data types—such as `int`, `short`, and `string`—are mapped from the compiler to .NET data types. For example, when you declare an `int` in C#, you are actually declaring an instance of a .NET struct: `System.Int32`. This might sound like a small point, but it has a profound significance: It means that you can treat all the primitive data types syntactically, as if they are classes that support certain methods. For example, to convert an `int` `i` to a `string`, you can write the following:

```
string s = i.ToString();
```

It should be emphasized that behind this syntactical convenience, the types really are stored as primitive types, so absolutely no performance cost is associated with the idea that the primitive types are notionally represented by C# structs.

The following sections review the types that are recognized as built-in types in C#. Each type is listed, along with its definition and the name of the corresponding .NET type. C# has 15 predefined types, 13 value types, and 2 (`string` and `object`) reference types.

Predefined Value Types

The built-in .NET value types represent primitives, such as integer and floating-point numbers, character, and Boolean types.

Integer Types

C# supports eight predefined integer types, shown in the following table.

NAME	.NET TYPE	DESCRIPTION	RANGE (MIN:MAX)	
sbyte	System.SByte	8-bit signed integer	$-128{:}127$ $(-2^7{:}2^7-1)$	
short	System.Int16	16-bit signed integer	$-32,768{:}32,767$ $(-2^{15}{:}2^{15}-1)$	
int	System.Int32	32-bit signed integer	$-2,147,483,648{:}2,147,483,647$ $(-2^{31}{:}2^{31}-1)$	
long	System.Int64	64-bit signed integer	$-9,223,372,036,854,775,808{:}$ $9,223,372,036,854,775,807$ $(-2^{63}{:}2^{63}-1)$	
byte	System.Byte	8-bit unsigned integer	$0{:}255$ $(0{:}2^8-1)$	
ushort	System.UInt16	16-bit unsigned integer	$0{:}65,535$ $(0{:}2^{16}-1)$	
uint	System.UInt32	32-bit unsigned integer	$0{:}4,294,967,295$ $(0{:}2^{32}-1)$	
ulong	System.UInt64	64-bit unsigned integer	$0{:}18,446,744,073,709,551,615$ $(0{:}2^{64}-1)$	

Some C# types have the same names as C++ and Java types but have different definitions. For example, in C# an `int` is always a 32-bit signed integer. In C++ an `int` is a signed integer, but the number of bits is platform-dependent (32 bits on Windows). In C#, all data types have been defined in a platform-independent manner to allow for the possible future porting of C# and .NET to other platforms.

A `byte` is the standard 8-bit type for values in the range 0 to 255 inclusive. Be aware that, in keeping with its emphasis on type safety, C# regards the `byte` type and the `char` type as completely distinct types, and any programmatic conversions between the two must be explicitly requested. Also, be aware that unlike the other types in the integer family, a `byte` type is by default unsigned. Its signed version bears the special name `sbyte`.

With .NET, a short is no longer quite so short; it is 16 bits long. The int type is 32 bits long. The long type reserves 64 bits for values. All integer-type variables can be assigned values in decimal, hex, or binary notation. Binary notation requires the 0b prefix; hex notation requires the 0x prefix:

```
long x = 0x12ab;
```

Binary notation is discussed later in the section "Working with Binary Values."

If there is any ambiguity about whether an integer is int, uint, long, or ulong, it defaults to an int. To specify which of the other integer types the value should take, you can append one of the following characters to the number:

```
uint ui = 1234U;
long l = 1234L;
ulong ul = 1234UL;
```

You can also use lowercase u and l, although the latter could be confused with the integer 1 (one).

Digit Separators

C# 7 offers digit separators. These separators help with readability and don't add any functionality. For example, you can add underscores to numbers, as shown in the following code snippet (code file UsingNumbers/Program.cs):

```
long l1 = 0x123_4567_89ab_cedf;
```

The underscores used as separators are ignored by the compiler. With the preceding sample, reading from the right every 16 bits (or four hexadecimal characters) a digit separator is added. The result is a lot more readable than the alternative:

```
long l2 = 0x123456789abcedf;
```

Because the compiler just ignores the underscores, you are responsible for ensuring readability. You can put the underscores at any position, you need to make sure it helps readability, not as shown in this example:

```
long l3 = 0x12345_6789_abc_ed_f;
```

It's useful to have it allowed on any position as this allows for different use cases—for example, to work with hexadecimal or octal values, or to separate different bits needed for a protocol (as shown in the next section).

> **NOTE** *Digit separators are new with C# 7. C# 7.0 doesn't allow leading digit separators, having the separator before the value (and after the prefix). Leading digit separators can be used with C# 7.2.*

Working with Binary Values

Besides offering digit separators, C# 7 also makes it easier to assign binary values to integer types. If you prefix the variable value with the 0b literal, it's only allowed to use 0 and 1. Only binary values are allowed to assign to the variable, as you can see in the following code snippet (code file UsingNumbers/Program.cs):

```
uint binary1 = 0b1111_1110_1101_1100_1011_1010_1001_1000;
```

This preceding code snippet uses an unsigned int with 32 bits available. Digit separators help a lot with readability in binary values. This snippet makes a separation every four bits. Remember, you can write this in the hex notation as well:

```
uint hex1 = 0xfedcba98;
```

Using the separator every three bits helps when you're working with the octal notation, where characters are used between 0 (000 binary) and 7 (111 binary).

```
uint binary2 = 0b111_110_101_100_011_010_001_000;
```

The following example shows how to define values that could be used in a binary protocol where two bits define the rightmost part, six bits are in the next section, and the last two sections have four bits to complete 16 bits:

```
ushort binary3 = 0b1111_0000_101010_11;
```

Remember to use the correct integer type for the number of bits needed: `ushort` for 16, `uint` for 32, and `ulong` for 64 bits.

> **NOTE** *Read Chapter 6, "Operators and Casts," and Chapter 11, "Special Collections," for additional information on working with binary data.*

> **NOTE** *Binary literals are new with C# 7.*

Floating-Point Types

Although C# provides a plethora of integer data types, it supports floating-point types as well.

NAME	.NET TYPE	DESCRIPTION	SIGNIFICANT FIGURES	RANGE (APPROXIMATE)
float	System.Single	32-bit, single-precision floating point	7	$\pm1.5 \times 10^{245}$ to $\pm3.4 \times 10^{38}$
double	System.Double	64-bit, double-precision floating point	15/16	$\pm5.0 \times 10^{2324}$ to $\pm1.7 \times 10^{308}$

The `float` data type is for smaller floating-point values, for which less precision is required. The `double` data type is bulkier than the `float` data type but offers twice the precision (15 digits).

If you hard-code a non-integer number (such as 12.3), the compiler will normally assume that you want the number interpreted as a `double`. To specify that the value is a `float`, append the character F (or f) to it:

```
float f = 12.3F;
```

The Decimal Type

The `decimal` type represents higher-precision floating-point numbers, as shown in the following table.

NAME	.NET TYPE	DESCRIPTION	SIGNIFICANT FIGURES	RANGE (APPROXIMATE)
decimal	System.Decimal	128-bit, high-precision decimal notation	28	$\pm1.0 \times 10^{228}$ to $\pm7.9 \times 10^{28}$

One of the great things about the .NET and C# data types is the provision of a dedicated `decimal` type for financial calculations. How you use the 28 digits that the decimal type provides is up to you. In other words, you can track smaller dollar amounts with greater accuracy for cents or larger dollar amounts with more rounding in the fractional portion. Bear in mind, however, that decimal is not implemented under the hood as a primitive type, so using decimal has a performance effect on your calculations.

To specify that your number is a decimal type rather than a double, a float, or an integer, you can append the M (or m) character to the value, as shown here:

```
decimal d = 12.30M;
```

The Boolean Type

The C# bool type is used to contain Boolean values of either true or false.

NAME	.NET TYPE	DESCRIPTION	SIGNIFICANT FIGURES	RANGE
bool	System.Boolean	Represents true or false	NA	true or false

You cannot implicitly convert bool values to and from integer values. If a variable (or a function return type) is declared as a bool, you can only use values of true and false. You get an error if you try to use zero for false and a nonzero value for true.

The Character Type

For storing the value of a single character, C# supports the char data type.

NAME	.NET TYPE	VALUES
char	System.Char	Represents a single 16-bit (Unicode) character

Literals of type char are signified by being enclosed in single quotation marks—for example, 'A'. If you try to enclose a character in double quotation marks, the compiler treats the character as a string and throws an error.

As well as representing chars as character literals, you can represent them with four-digit hex Unicode values (for example, '\u0041'), as integer values with a cast (for example, (char) 65), or as hexadecimal values (for example,'\x0041'). You can also represent them with an escape sequence, as shown in the following table.

ESCAPE SEQUENCE	CHARACTER
\'	Single quotation mark
\"	Double quotation mark
\\	Backslash
\0	Null
\a	Alert
\b	Backspace
\f	Form feed
\n	Newline
\r	Carriage return
\t	Tab character
\v	Vertical tab

Literals for Numbers

The following table summarizes the literals that can be used for numbers. The table repeats the literals from the preceding sections so they're all collected in one place.

LITERAL	POSITION	DESCRIPTION
U	Postfix	unsigned int
L	Postfix	long
UL	Postfix	unsigned long
F	Postfix	float
M	Postfix	decimal (money)
0x	Prefix	Hexadecimal number; values from 0 to F are allowed
0b	Prefix	Binary number; only 0 and 1 are allowed
true	NA	Boolean value
False	NA	Boolean value

Predefined Reference Types

C# supports two predefined reference types, `object` and `string`, described in the following table.

NAME	.NET TYPE	DESCRIPTION
object	System.Object	The root type. All other types (including value types) are derived from object.
string	System.String	Unicode character string

The object Type

Many programming languages and class hierarchies provide a root type, from which all other objects in the hierarchy are derived. C# and .NET are no exception. In C#, the `object` type is the ultimate parent type from which all other intrinsic and user-defined types are derived. This means that you can use the `object` type for two purposes:

➤ You can use an `object` reference to bind to an object of any particular subtype. For example, in Chapter 6, "Operators and Casts," you see how you can use the `object` type to box a value object on the stack to move it to the heap; `object` references are also useful in reflection, when code must manipulate objects whose specific types are unknown.

➤ The `object` type implements a number of basic, general-purpose methods, which include `Equals`, `GetHashCode`, `GetType`, and `ToString`. Responsible user-defined classes might need to provide replacement implementations of some of these methods using an object-oriented technique known as *overriding*, which is discussed in Chapter 4, "Object Oriented Programming with C#." When you override `ToString`, for example, you equip your class with a method for intelligently providing a string representation of itself. If you don't provide your own implementations for these methods in your classes, the compiler picks up the implementations in `object`, which might or might not be correct or sensible in the context of your classes.

You examine the `object` type in more detail in subsequent chapters.

The string Type

C# recognizes the `string` keyword, which under the hood is translated to the .NET class, `System.String`. With it, operations like string concatenation and string copying are a snap:

```
string str1 = "Hello ";
string str2 = "World";
string str3 = str1 + str2; // string concatenation
```

Despite this style of assignment, `string` is a reference type. Behind the scenes, a `string` object is allocated on the heap, not the stack; and when you assign one string variable to another string, you get two references to the same string in memory. However, `string` differs from the usual behavior for reference types. For example, strings are immutable. Making changes to one of these strings creates an entirely new string object, leaving the other string unchanged. Consider the following code (code file `StringSample/Program.cs`):

```
using System;

class Program
{
  static void Main()
  {
    string s1 = "a string";
    string s2 = s1;
    Console.WriteLine("s1 is " + s1);
    Console.WriteLine("s2 is " + s2);
    s1 = "another string";
    Console.WriteLine("s1 is now " + s1);
    Console.WriteLine("s2 is now " + s2);
  }
}
```

The output from this is as follows:

```
s1 is a string
s2 is a string
s1 is now another string
s2 is now a string
```

Changing the value of `s1` has no effect on `s2`, contrary to what you'd expect with a reference type! What's happening here is that when `s1` is initialized with the value a `string`, a new string object is allocated on the heap. When `s2` is initialized, the reference points to this same object, so `s2` also has the value a `string`. However, when you now change the value of `s1`, instead of replacing the original value, a new object is allocated on the heap for the new value. The `s2` variable still points to the original object, so its value is unchanged. Under the hood, this happens as a result of operator overloading, a topic that is explored in Chapter 6. In general, the `string` class has been implemented so that its semantics follow what you would normally intuitively expect for a string.

String literals are enclosed in double quotation marks (`" . "`); if you attempt to enclose a string in single quotation marks, the compiler takes the value as a `char` and throws an error. C# strings can contain the same Unicode and hexadecimal escape sequences as `char`s. Because these escape sequences start with a backslash, you can't use this character unescaped in a string. Instead, you need to escape it with two backslashes (`\\`):

```
string filepath = "C:\\ProCSharp\\First.cs";
```

> **WARNING** *Be aware that using backslash (\) for directories and using* `C:` *restricts the application to the Windows operating system. Both Windows and Linux can use the forward slash (/) to separate directories. Chapter 22, "Files and Streams," gives you details about how to work with files and directories both on Windows and Linux.*

Even if you are confident that you can remember to do this all the time, typing all those double backslashes can prove annoying. Fortunately, C# gives you an alternative. You can prefix a string literal with the at character (@) and all the characters after it are treated at face value; they aren't interpreted as escape sequences:

```
string filepath = @"C:\ProCSharp\First.cs";
```

This even enables you to include line breaks in your string literals:

```
string jabberwocky = @"'Twas brillig and the slithy toves
Did gyre and gimble in the wabe.";
```

In this case, the value of `jabberwocky` would be this:

```
'Twas brillig and the slithy toves
Did gyre and gimble in the wabe.
```

C# defines a string interpolation format that is marked by using the $ prefix. You've previously seen this prefix in the section "Working with Variables." You can change the earlier code snippet that demonstrated string concatenation to use the string interpolation format. Prefixing a string with $ enables you to put curly braces into the string that contains a variable—or even a code expression. The result of the variable or code expression is put into the string at the position of the curly braces:

```
public static void Main()
{
  string s1 = "a string";
  string s2 = s1;
  Console.WriteLine($"s1 is {s1}");
  Console.WriteLine($"s2 is {s2}");
  s1 = "another string";
  Console.WriteLine($"s1 is now {s1}");
  Console.WriteLine($"s2 is now {s2}");
}
```

> **NOTE** *Note Strings and the features of string interpolation are covered in detail in Chapter 9, "Strings and Regular Expressions."*

CONTROLLING PROGRAM FLOW

This section looks at the real nuts and bolts of the language: the statements that allow you to control the *flow* of your program rather than execute every line of code in the order it appears in the program.

Conditional Statements

Conditional statements enable you to branch your code depending on whether certain conditions are met or what the value of an expression is. C# has two constructs for branching code: the `if` statement, which tests whether a specific condition is met, and the `switch` statement, which compares an expression with several different values.

The if Statement

For conditional branching, C# inherits the C and C++ `if..else` construct. The syntax should be fairly intuitive for anyone who has done any programming with a procedural language:

```
if (condition)
   statement(s)
else
   statement(s)
```

If more than one statement is to be executed as part of either condition, these statements need to be joined into a block using curly braces ({ . }). (This also applies to other C# constructs where statements can be joined into a block, such as the for and while loops):

```
bool isZero;
if (i == 0)
{
  isZero = true;
  Console.WriteLine("i is Zero");
}
else
{
  isZero = false;
  Console.WriteLine("i is Non-zero");
}
```

If you want to, you can use an if statement without a final else statement. You can also combine else if clauses to test for multiple conditions (code file IfStatement/Program.cs):

```
using System;
namespace Wrox
{
  class Program
  {
    static void Main()
    {
      Console.WriteLine("Type in a string");
      string input;
      input = Console.ReadLine();
      if (input == "")
      {
        Console.WriteLine("You typed in an empty string.");
      }
      else if (input.Length < 5)
      {
        Console.WriteLine("The string had less than 5 characters.");
      }
      else if (input.Length < 10)
      {
        Console.WriteLine(
          "The string had at least 5 but less than 10 Characters.");
      }
      Console.WriteLine("The string was " + input);
    }
  }
}
```

There is no limit to how many else ifs you can add to an if clause.

Note that the previous example declares a string variable called input, gets the user to enter text at the command line, feeds this into input, and then tests the length of this string variable. The code also shows how easy string manipulation can be in C#. To find the length of input, for example, use input.Length.

Another point to note about the if statement is that you don't need to use the braces when there's only one statement in the conditional branch:

```
if (i == 0)
  Console.WriteLine("i is Zero"); // This will only execute if i == 0
  Console.WriteLine("i can be anything"); // Will execute whatever the
// value of i
```

However, for consistency, many programmers prefer to use curly braces whenever they use an if statement.

> **TIP** *Not using curly braces with* if *statements can lead to errors in maintaining the code. It happens too often that a second statement is added to the* if *statement that runs no matter whether the* if *returns true or false. Using curly braces every time avoids this coding error.*
>
> *A good guideline in regard to the* if *statement is to allow programmers to not use curly braces only when the statement is written in the same line as the* if *statement. With this guideline, programmers are less likely to add a second statement without adding curly braces.*

The if statements presented also illustrate some of the C# operators that compare values. Note in particular that C# uses == to compare variables for equality. Do not use = for this purpose. A single = is used to assign values.

In C#, the expression in the if clause must evaluate to a Boolean. It is not possible to test an integer directly (returned from a function, for example). You have to convert the integer that is returned to a Boolean true or false, for example, by comparing the value with zero or null:

```
if (DoSomething() != 0)
{
    // Non-zero value returned
}
else
{
    // Returned zero
}
```

The switch Statement

The switch / case statement is good for selecting one branch of execution from a set of mutually exclusive ones. It takes the form of a switch argument followed by a series of case clauses. When the expression in the switch argument evaluates to one of the values beside a case clause, the code immediately following the case clause executes. This is one example for which you don't need to use curly braces to join statements into blocks; instead, you mark the end of the code for each case using the break statement. You can also include a default case in the switch statement, which executes if the expression doesn't evaluate to any of the other cases. The following switch statement tests the value of the integerA variable:

```
switch (integerA)
{
  case 1:
    Console.WriteLine("integerA = 1");
    break;
  case 2:
    Console.WriteLine("integerA = 2");
    break;
  case 3:
    Console.WriteLine("integerA = 3");
    break;
  default:
    Console.WriteLine("integerA is not 1, 2, or 3");
    break;
}
```

Note that the case values must be constant expressions; variables are not permitted.

Though the switch.case statement should be familiar to C and C++ programmers, C#'s switch .case is a bit safer than its C++ equivalent. Specifically, it prohibits fall-through conditions in almost all cases. This means that if a case clause is fired early on in the block, later clauses cannot be fired unless you use a `goto` statement to indicate that you want them fired, too. The compiler enforces this restriction by flagging every `case` clause that is not equipped with a `break` statement as an error:

```
Control cannot fall through from one case label ('case 2:') to another
```

Although it is true that fall-through behavior is desirable in a limited number of situations, in the vast majority of cases it is unintended and results in a logical error that's hard to spot. Isn't it better to code for the norm rather than for the exception?

By getting creative with `goto` statements, you can duplicate fall-through functionality in your `switch` `.cases`. However, if you find yourself really wanting to, you probably should reconsider your approach. The following code illustrates both how to use `goto` to simulate fall-through, and how messy the resultant code can be:

```
// assume country and language are of type string
switch(country)
{
  case "America":
    CallAmericanOnlyMethod();
    goto case "Britain";
  case "France":
    language = "French";
    break;
  case "Britain":
    language = "English";
    break;
}
```

There is one exception to the no-fall-through rule, however, in that you can fall through from one case to the next if that case is empty. This allows you to treat two or more cases in an identical way (without the need for `goto` statements):

```
switch(country)
{
  case "au":
  case "uk":
  case "us":
    language = "English";
    break;
  case "at":
  case "de":
    language = "German";
    break;
}
```

One intriguing point about the `switch` statement in C# is that the order of the cases doesn't matter—you can even put the `default` case first! As a result, no two cases can be the same. This includes different constants that have the same value, so you can't, for example, do this:

```
// assume country is of type string
const string england = "uk";
const string britain = "uk";
switch(country)
{
  case england:
  case britain: // This will cause a compilation error.
    language = "English";
    break;
}
```

The previous code also shows another way in which the `switch` statement is different in C# compared to C++: In C#, you are allowed to use a string as the variable being tested.

> **NOTE** *With C# 7, the* switch *statement has been enhanced with pattern matching. Using pattern matching, the ordering of the cases becomes important. Read Chapter 13, "Functional Programming with C#," for more information about the* switch *statement using pattern matching.*

Loops

C# provides four different loops (for, while, do...while, and foreach) that enable you to execute a block of code repeatedly until a certain condition is met.

The for Loop

C# for loops provide a mechanism for iterating through a loop whereby you test whether a particular condition holds true before you perform another iteration. The syntax is

where:

- ➤ The initializer is the expression evaluated before the first loop is executed (usually initializing a local variable as a loop counter).
- ➤ The condition is the expression checked before each new iteration of the loop (this must evaluate to true for another iteration to be performed).
- ➤ The iterator is an expression evaluated after each iteration (usually incrementing the loop counter).

The iterations end when the condition evaluates to false.

The for loop is a so-called pretest loop because the loop condition is evaluated before the loop statements are executed; therefore, the contents of the loop won't be executed at all if the loop condition is false.

The for loop is excellent for repeating a statement or a block of statements for a predetermined number of times. The following example demonstrates typical usage of a for loop. It writes out all the integers from 0 to 99:

```
for (int i = 0; i < 100; i = i + 1)
{
    Console.WriteLine(i);
}
```

Here, you declare an int called i and initialize it to zero. This is used as the loop counter. You then immediately test whether it is less than 100. Because this condition evaluates to true, you execute the code in the loop, displaying the value 0. You then increment the counter by one, and walk through the process again. Looping ends when i reaches 100.

Actually, the way the preceding loop is written isn't quite how you would normally write it. C# has a shorthand for adding 1 to a variable, so instead of i = i + 1, you can simply write i++:

```
for (int i = 0; i < 100; i++)
{
    // ...
}
```

You can also make use of type inference for the iteration variable i in the preceding example. Using type inference, the loop construct would be as follows:

```
for (var i = 0; i < 100; i++)
{
    // ...
}
```

It's not unusual to nest `for` loops so that an inner loop executes once completely for each iteration of an outer loop. This approach is typically employed to loop through every element in a rectangular multidimensional array. The outermost loop loops through every row, and the inner loop loops through every column in a particular row. The following code displays rows of numbers. It also uses another `Console` method, `Console.Write`, which does the same thing as `Console.WriteLine` but doesn't send a carriage return to the output (code file `ForLoop/Program.cs`):

```
using System;

namespace Wrox
{
  class Program
  {
    static void Main()
    {
      // This loop iterates through rows
      for (int i = 0; i < 100; i+=10)
      {
        // This loop iterates through columns
        for (int j = i; j < i + 10; j++)
        {
          Console.Write($" {j}");
        }
        Console.WriteLine();
      }
    }
  }
}
```

Although `j` is an integer, it is automatically converted to a string so that the concatenation can take place.

The preceding sample results in this output:

```
 0 1 2 3 4 5 6 7 8 9
10 11 12 13 14 15 16 17 18 19
20 21 22 23 24 25 26 27 28 29
30 31 32 33 34 35 36 37 38 39
40 41 42 43 44 45 46 47 48 49
50 51 52 53 54 55 56 57 58 59
60 61 62 63 64 65 66 67 68 69
70 71 72 73 74 75 76 77 78 79
80 81 82 83 84 85 86 87 88 89
90 91 92 93 94 95 96 97 98 99
```

It is technically possible to evaluate something other than a counter variable in a `for` loop's test condition, but it is certainly not typical. It is also possible to omit one (or even all) of the expressions in the `for` loop. In such situations, however, you should consider using the `while` loop.

The while Loop

Like the `for` loop, `while` is a pretest loop. The syntax is similar, but `while` loops take only one expression:

```
while(condition)
  statement(s);
```

Unlike the `for` loop, the `while` loop is most often used to repeat a statement or a block of statements for a number of times that is not known before the loop begins. Usually, a statement inside the `while` loop's body will set a Boolean flag to `false` on a certain iteration, triggering the end of the loop, as in the following example:

```
bool condition = false;
while (!condition)
```

```
{
    // This loop spins until the condition is true.
    DoSomeWork();
    condition = CheckCondition(); // assume CheckCondition() returns a bool
}
```

The do...while Loop

The do...while loop is the post-test version of the while loop. This means that the loop's test condition is evaluated after the body of the loop has been executed. Consequently, do...while loops are useful for situations in which a block of statements must be executed at least one time, as in this example:

```
bool condition;
do
{
    // This loop will at least execute once, even if Condition is false.
    MustBeCalledAtLeastOnce();
    condition = CheckCondition();
} while (condition);
```

The foreach Loop

The foreach loop enables you to iterate through each item in a collection. For now, don't worry about exactly what a collection is (it is explained fully in Chapter 10, "Collections"); just understand that it is an object that represents a list of objects. Technically, for an object to count as a collection, it must support an interface called IEnumerable. Examples of collections include C# arrays, the collection classes in the System.Collections namespaces, and user-defined collection classes. You can get an idea of the syntax of foreach from the following code, if you assume that arrayOfInts is (unsurprisingly) an array of ints:

```
foreach (int temp in arrayOfInts)
{
    Console.WriteLine(temp);
}
```

Here, foreach steps through the array one element at a time. With each element, it places the value of the element in the int variable called temp and then performs an iteration of the loop.

Here is another situation where you can use type inference. The foreach loop would become the following:

```
foreach (var temp in arrayOfInts)
{
    // ...
}
```

temp would be inferred to int because that is what the collection item type is.

An important point to note with foreach is that you can't change the value of the item in the collection (temp in the preceding code), so code such as the following will not compile:

```
foreach (int temp in arrayOfInts)
{
    temp++;
    Console.WriteLine(temp);
}
```

If you need to iterate through the items in a collection and change their values, you must use a for loop instead.

Jump Statements

C# provides a number of statements that enable you to jump immediately to another line in the program. The first of these is, of course, the notorious goto statement.

The goto Statement

The goto statement enables you to jump directly to another specified line in the program, indicated by a *label* (this is just an identifier followed by a colon):

```
goto Label1;
Console.WriteLine("This won't be executed");
Label1:
  Console.WriteLine("Continuing execution from here");
```

A couple of restrictions are involved with goto. You can't jump into a block of code such as a for loop, you can't jump out of a class, and you can't exit a finally block after try...catch blocks (Chapter 14, "Errors and Exceptions," looks at exception handling with try.catch.finally).

The reputation of the goto statement probably precedes it, and in most circumstances, its use is sternly frowned upon. In general, it certainly doesn't conform to good object-oriented programming practices.

The break Statement

You have already met the break statement briefly—when you used it to exit from a case in a switch statement. In fact, break can also be used to exit from for, foreach, while, or do...while loops. Control switches to the statement immediately after the end of the loop.

If the statement occurs in a nested loop, control switches to the end of the innermost loop. If the break occurs outside a switch statement or a loop, a compile-time error occurs.

The continue Statement

The continue statement is similar to break, and you must use it within a for, foreach, while, or do...while loop. However, it exits only from the current iteration of the loop, meaning that execution restarts at the beginning of the next iteration of the loop rather than restarting outside the loop altogether.

The return Statement

The return statement is used to exit a method of a class, returning control to the caller of the method. If the method has a return type, return must return a value of this type; otherwise, if the method returns void, you should use return without an expression.

GETTING ORGANIZED WITH NAMESPACES

As discussed earlier in this chapter, namespaces provide a way to organize related classes and other types. Unlike a file or a component, a namespace is a logical, rather than a physical, grouping. When you define a class in a C# file, you can include it within a namespace definition. Later, when you define another class that performs related work in another file, you can include it within the same namespace, creating a logical grouping that indicates to other developers using the classes how they are related and used:

```
using System;
namespace CustomerPhoneBookApp
{
  public struct Subscriber
  {
    // Code for struct here..
  }
}
```

Placing a type in a namespace effectively gives that type a long name, consisting of the type's namespace as a series of names separated with periods (.), terminating with the name of the class. In the preceding example, the full name of the Subscriber struct is CustomerPhoneBookApp.Subscriber. This enables distinct classes with the same short name to be used within the same program without ambiguity. This full name is often called the *fully qualified name*.

You can also nest namespaces within other namespaces, creating a hierarchical structure for your types:

```
namespace Wrox
{
  namespace ProCSharp
  {
    namespace Basics
    {
      class NamespaceExample
      {
        // Code for the class here..
      }
    }
  }
}
```

Each namespace name is composed of the names of the namespaces it resides within, separated with periods, starting with the outermost namespace and ending with its own short name. Therefore, the full name for the `ProCSharp` namespace is `Wrox.ProCSharp`, and the full name of the `NamespaceExample` class is `Wrox.ProCSharp.Basics.NamespaceExample`.

You can use this syntax to organize the namespaces in your namespace definitions too, so the previous code could also be written as follows:

```
namespace Wrox.ProCSharp.Basics
{
  class NamespaceExample
  {
    // Code for the class here..
  }
}
```

Note that you are not permitted to declare a multipart namespace nested within another namespace.

Namespaces are not related to assemblies. It is perfectly acceptable to have different namespaces in the same assembly or to define types in the same namespace in different assemblies.

You should define the namespace hierarchy prior to starting a project. Generally the accepted format is `CompanyName.ProjectName.SystemSection`. In the previous example, Wrox is the company name, ProCSharp is the project, and in the case of this chapter, Basics is the section.

The using Directive

Obviously, namespaces can grow rather long and tiresome to type, and the capability to indicate a particular class with such specificity may not always be necessary. Fortunately, as noted earlier in this chapter, C# allows you to abbreviate a class's full name. To do this, list the class's namespace at the top of the file, prefixed with the `using` keyword. Throughout the rest of the file, you can refer to the types in the namespace simply by their type names:

```
using System;
using Wrox.ProCSharp;
```

As mentioned earlier, many C# files have the statement `using System;` simply because so many useful classes supplied by Microsoft are contained in the `System` namespace.

If two namespaces referenced by `using` statements contain a type of the same name, you need to use the full (or at least a longer) form of the name to ensure that the compiler knows which type to access. For example, suppose classes called `NamespaceExample` exist in both the `Wrox.ProCSharp.Basics` and `Wrox.ProCSharp.OOP` namespaces. If you then create a class called `Test` in the `Wrox.ProCSharp` namespace, and instantiate one of the `NamespaceExample` classes in this class, you need to specify which of these two classes you're talking about:

```
using Wrox.ProCSharp.OOP;
using Wrox.ProCSharp.Basics;
namespace Wrox.ProCSharp
{
  class Test
  {
    static void Main()
    {
      Basics.NamespaceExample nSEx = new Basics.NamespaceExample();
      // do something with the nSEx variable.
    }
  }
}
```

Your organization will probably want to spend some time developing a namespace convention so that its developers can quickly locate functionality that they need and so that the names of the organization's home-grown classes won't conflict with those in off-the-shelf class libraries. Guidelines on establishing your own namespace convention, along with other naming recommendations, are discussed later in this chapter.

Namespace Aliases

Another use of the `using` keyword is to assign aliases to classes and namespaces. If you need to refer to a very long namespace name several times in your code but don't want to include it in a simple `using` statement (for example, to avoid type name conflicts), you can assign an alias to the namespace. The syntax for this is as follows:

```
using alias = NamespaceName;
```

The following example (a modified version of the previous example) assigns the alias `Introduction` to the `Wrox.ProCSharp.Basics` namespace and uses this to instantiate a `NamespaceExample` object, which is defined in this namespace. Notice the use of the namespace alias qualifier (`::`). This forces the search to start with the `Introduction` namespace alias. If a class called `Introduction` had been introduced in the same scope, a conflict would occur. The `::` operator enables the alias to be referenced even if the conflict exists. The `NamespaceExample` class has one method, `GetNamespace`, which uses the `GetType` method exposed by every class to access a `Type` object representing the class's type. You use this object to return a name of the class's namespace (code file `NamespaceSample/Program.cs`):

```
using System;
using Introduction = Wrox.ProCSharp.Basics;

class Program
{
  static void Main()
  {
    Introduction::NamespaceExample NSEx = new Introduction::NamespaceExample();
    Console.WriteLine(NSEx.GetNamespace());
  }
}

namespace Wrox.ProCSharp.Basics
{
  class NamespaceExample
  {
    public string GetNamespace()
    {
      return this.GetType().Namespace;
    }
  }
}
```

UNDERSTANDING THE MAIN METHOD

As described at the beginning of this chapter, C# programs start execution at a method named Main. Depending on the execution environment there are different requirements.

➤ Have a static modifier applied

➤ Be in a class with any name

➤ Return a type of int or void

Although it is common to specify the public modifier explicitly—because by definition the method must be called from outside the program—it doesn't actually matter what accessibility level you assign to the entry-point method; it will run even if you mark the method as private.

The examples so far have shown only the Main method without any parameters. However, when the program is invoked, you can get the CLR to pass any command-line arguments to the program by including a parameter. This parameter is a string array, traditionally called args (although C# accepts any name). The program can use this array to access any options passed through the command line when the program is started.

The following example loops through the string array passed in to the Main method and writes the value of each option to the console window (code file ArgumentsSample/Program.cs):

```
using System;
namespace Wrox
{
  class Program
  {
    static void Main(string[] args)
    {
      for (int i = 0; i < args.Length; i++)
      {
        Console.WriteLine(args[i]);
      }
    }
  }
}
```

For passing arguments to the program when running the application from Visual Studio 2017, you can define the arguments in the Debug section of the project properties as shown in Figure 2-1. Running the application reveals the result to show all argument values to the console.

When you run the application from the command line using the .NET Core CLI tools, you just need to supply the arguments following the dotnet run command:

```
dotnet run arg1 arg2 arg3
```

In case you want to supply arguments that are in conflict with the arguments of the dotnet run command, you can add two dashes (--) before supplying the arguments of the program:

```
dotnet run -- arg1 arg2 arg3
```

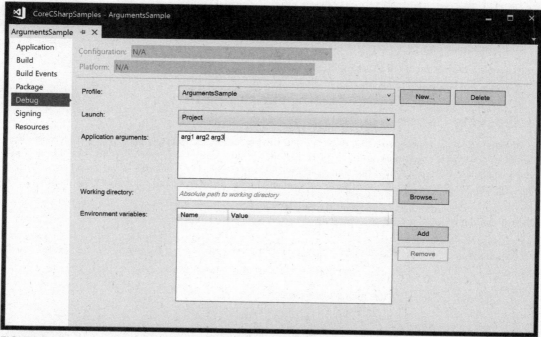

FIGURE 2-1

USING COMMENTS

The next topic—adding comments to your code—looks very simple on the surface, but it can be complex. Comments can be beneficial to other developers who may look at your code. Also, as you will see, you can use comments to generate documentation of your code for other developers to use.

Internal Comments Within the Source Files

As noted earlier in this chapter, C# uses the traditional C-type single-line (//..) and multiline (/* .. */) comments:

```
// This is a single-line comment
/* This comment
spans multiple lines. */
```

Everything in a single-line comment, from the // to the end of the line, is ignored by the compiler, and everything from an opening /* to the next */ in a multiline comment combination is ignored. Obviously, you can't include the combination */ in any multiline comments, because this will be treated as the end of the comment.

It is possible to put multiline comments within a line of code:

```
Console.WriteLine(/* Here's a comment! */ "This will compile.");
```

Use inline comments with care because they can make code hard to read. However, they can be useful when debugging if, for example, you temporarily want to try running the code with a different value somewhere:

```
DoSomething(Width, /*Height*/ 100);
```

Comment characters included in string literals are, of course, treated like normal characters:

```
string s = "/* This is just a normal string .*/";
```

XML Documentation

In addition to the C-type comments, illustrated in the preceding section, C# has a very neat feature: the capability to produce documentation in XML format automatically from special comments. These comments are single-line comments, but they begin with three slashes (///) instead of the usual two. Within these comments, you can place XML tags containing documentation of the types and type members in your code.

The tags in the following table are recognized by the compiler.

TAG	DESCRIPTION
`<c>`	Marks up text within a line as code—for example, `<c>int i = 10;</c>`.
`<code>`	Marks multiple lines as code.
`<example>`	Marks up a code example.
`<exception>`	Documents an exception class. (Syntax is verified by the compiler.)
`<include>`	Includes comments from another documentation file. (Syntax is verified by the compiler.)
`<list>`	Inserts a list into the documentation.
`<para>`	Gives structure to text.
`<param>`	Marks up a method parameter. (Syntax is verified by the compiler.)
`<paramref>`	Indicates that a word is a method parameter. (Syntax is verified by the compiler.)
`<permission>`	Documents access to a member. (Syntax is verified by the compiler.)
`<remarks>`	Adds a description for a member.
`<returns>`	Documents the return value for a method.
`<see>`	Provides a cross-reference to another parameter. (Syntax is verified by the compiler.)
`<seealso>`	Provides a "see also" section in a description. (Syntax is verified by the compiler.)
`<summary>`	Provides a short summary of a type or member.
`<typeparam>`	Describes a type parameter in the comment of a generic type.
`<typeparamref>`	Provides the name of the type parameter.
`<value>`	Describes a property.

Add some XML comments to the `Calculator.cs` file from the previous section. You add a `<summary>` element for the class and for its `Add` method, and a `<returns>` element and two `<param>` elements for the `Add` method:

```
// MathLib.cs
namespace Wrox.MathLib
{
  ///<summary>
  /// Wrox.MathLib.Calculator class.
  /// Provides a method to add two doublies.
  ///</summary>
  public class Calculator
  {
    ///<summary>
    /// The Add method allows us to add two doubles.
    ///</summary>
    ///<returns>Result of the addition (double)</returns>
    ///<param name="x">First number to add</param>
    ///<param name="y">Second number to add</param>
    public static double Add(double x, double y) => x + y;
  }
}
```

UNDERSTANDING C# PREPROCESSOR DIRECTIVES

Besides the usual keywords, most of which you have now encountered, C# also includes a number of commands that are known as *preprocessor directives*. These commands are never actually translated to any commands in your executable code, but they affect aspects of the compilation process. For example, you can use preprocessor directives to prevent the compiler from compiling certain portions of your code. You might do this if you are planning to release two versions of it—a basic version and an enterprise version that will have more features. You could use preprocessor directives to prevent the compiler from compiling code related to the additional features when you are compiling the basic version of the software. In another scenario, you might have written bits of code that are intended to provide you with debugging information. You probably don't want those portions of code compiled when you actually ship the software.

The preprocessor directives are all distinguished by beginning with the # symbol.

> **NOTE** C++ *developers will recognize the preprocessor directives as something that plays an important part in C and C++. However, there aren't as many preprocessor directives in C#, and they are not used as often. C# provides other mechanisms, such as custom attributes, that achieve some of the same effects as C++ directives. Also, note that C# doesn't actually have a separate preprocessor in the way that C++ does. The so-called preprocessor directives are actually handled by the compiler. Nevertheless, C# retains the name preprocessor directive because these commands give the impression of a preprocessor.*

The following sections briefly cover the purposes of the preprocessor directives.

#define and #undef

`#define` is used like this:

```
#define DEBUG
```

This tells the compiler that a symbol with the given name (in this case DEBUG) exists. It is a little bit like declaring a variable, except that this variable doesn't really have a value—it just exists. Also, this symbol isn't part of your actual code; it exists only for the benefit of the compiler, while the compiler is compiling the code, and has no meaning within the C# code itself.

#undef does the opposite, and removes the definition of a symbol:

```
#undef DEBUG
```

If the symbol doesn't exist in the first place, then #undef has no effect. Similarly, #define has no effect if a symbol already exists.

You need to place any #define and #undef directives at the beginning of the C# source file, before any code that declares any objects to be compiled.

#define isn't much use on its own, but when combined with other preprocessor directives, especially #if, it becomes very powerful.

> **NOTE** *Incidentally, you might notice some changes from the usual C# syntax. Preprocessor directives are not terminated by semicolons and they normally constitute the only command on a line. That's because for the preprocessor directives, C# abandons its usual practice of requiring commands to be separated by semicolons. If the compiler sees a preprocessor directive, it assumes that the next command is on the next line.*

#if, #elif, #else, and #endif

These directives inform the compiler whether to compile a block of code. Consider this method:

```
int DoSomeWork(double x)
{
    // do something
    #if DEBUG
    Console.WriteLine($"x is {x}");
    #endif
}
```

This code compiles as normal except for the Console.WriteLine method call contained inside the #if clause. This line is executed only if the symbol DEBUG has been defined by a previous #define directive. When the compiler finds the #if directive, it checks to see whether the symbol concerned exists, and compiles the code inside the #if clause only if the symbol does exist. Otherwise, the compiler simply ignores all the code until it reaches the matching #endif directive. Typical practice is to define the symbol DEBUG while you are debugging and have various bits of debugging-related code inside #if clauses. Then, when you are close to shipping, you simply comment out the #define directive, and all the debugging code miraculously disappears, the size of the executable file gets smaller, and your end users don't get confused by seeing debugging information. (Obviously, you would do more testing to ensure that your code still works without DEBUG defined.) This technique is very common in C and C++ programming and is known as *conditional compilation*.

The #elif (=else if) and #else directives can be used in #if blocks and have intuitively obvious meanings. It is also possible to nest #if blocks:

```
#define ENTERPRISE
#define W10
// further on in the file
#if ENTERPRISE
// do something
```

```
#if W10
// some code that is only relevant to enterprise
// edition running on W10
#endif
#elif PROFESSIONAL
// do something else
#else
// code for the leaner version
#endif
```

#if and #elif support a limited range of logical operators too, using the operators !, ==, !=, and ||. A symbol is considered to be true if it exists and false if it doesn't. For example:

```
#if W10 && (ENTERPRISE==false) // if W10 is defined but ENTERPRISE isn't
```

#warning and #error

Two other very useful preprocessor directives are #warning and #error. These will respectively cause a warning or an error to be raised when the compiler encounters them. If the compiler sees a #warning directive, it displays whatever text appears after the #warning to the user, after which compilation continues. If it encounters an #error directive, it displays the subsequent text to the user as if it is a compilation error message and then immediately abandons the compilation, so no IL code is generated.

You can use these directives as checks that you haven't done anything silly with your #define statements; you can also use the #warning statements to remind yourself to do something:

```
#if DEBUG && RELEASE
#error "You've defined DEBUG and RELEASE simultaneously!"
#endif
#warning "Don't forget to remove this line before the boss tests the code!"
Console.WriteLine("*I love this job.*");
```

#region and #endregion

The #region and #endregion directives are used to indicate that a certain block of code is to be treated as a single block with a given name, like this:

```
#region Member Field Declarations
int x;
double d;
Currency balance;
#endregion
```

This doesn't look that useful by itself; it doesn't affect the compilation process in any way. However, the real advantage is that these directives are recognized by some editors, including the Visual Studio editor. These editors can use the directives to lay out your code better on the screen. You find out how this works in Chapter 18, "Visual Studio 2017."

#line

The #line directive can be used to alter the filename and line number information that is output by the compiler in warnings and error messages. You probably won't want to use this directive very often. It's most useful when you are coding in conjunction with another package that alters the code you are typing before sending it to the compiler. In this situation, line numbers, or perhaps the filenames reported by the compiler, don't match up to the line numbers in the files or the filenames you are editing. The #line directive can be used to restore the match. You can also use the syntax #line default to restore the line to the default line numbering:

```
#line 164 "Core.cs" // We happen to know this is line 164 in the file
// Core.cs, before the intermediate
```

```
    // package mangles it.
    // later on
    #line default // restores default line numbering
```

#pragma

The #pragma directive can either suppress or restore specific compiler warnings. Unlike command-line options, the #pragma directive can be implemented on the class or method level, enabling fine-grained control over what warnings are suppressed and when. The following example disables the "field not used" warning and then restores it after the MyClass class compiles:

```
    #pragma warning disable 169
    public class MyClass
    {
        int neverUsedField;
    }
    #pragma warning restore 169
```

C# PROGRAMMING GUIDELINES

This final section of the chapter supplies the guidelines you need to bear in mind when writing C# programs. These are guidelines that most C# developers use. When you use these guidelines, other developers will feel comfortable working with your code.

Rules for Identifiers

This section examines the rules governing what names you can use for variables, classes, methods, and so on. Note that the rules presented in this section are not merely guidelines: they are enforced by the C# compiler.

Identifiers are the names you give to variables, to user-defined types such as classes and structs, and to members of these types. Identifiers are case sensitive, so, for example, variables named interestRate and InterestRate would be recognized as different variables. Following are a few rules determining what identifiers you can use in C#:

➤ They must begin with a letter or underscore, although they can contain numeric characters.

➤ You can't use C# keywords as identifiers.

The following table lists reserved C# keywords.

abstract	as	base	bool		
break	byte	case	catch		
char	checked	class	const		
continue	decimal	default	delegate		
do	double	else	enum		
event	explicit	extern	false		
finally	fixed	float	for		
foreach	goto	if	implicit		
in	int	interface	internal		
is	lock	long	namespace		

new	null	object	operator
out	override	params	private
protected	public	readonly	ref
return	sbyte	sealed	short
sizeof	stackalloc	static	string
struct	switch	this	throw
true	try	typeof	uint
ulong	unchecked	unsafe	ushort
using	virtual	void	volatile
while			

If you need to use one of these words as an identifier (for example, if you are accessing a class written in a different language), you can prefix the identifier with the @ symbol to indicate to the compiler that what follows should be treated as an identifier, not as a C# keyword (so abstract is not a valid identifier, but @ abstract is).

Finally, identifiers can also contain Unicode characters, specified using the syntax \uXXXX, where XXXX is the four-digit hex code for the Unicode character. The following are some examples of valid identifiers:

➤ Name
➤ Überfluß
➤ _Identifier
➤ \u005fIdentifier

The last two items in this list are identical and interchangeable (because 005f is the Unicode code for the underscore character), so obviously these identifiers couldn't both be declared in the same scope. Note that although syntactically you are allowed to use the underscore character in identifiers, this isn't recommended in most situations. That's because it doesn't follow the guidelines for naming variables that Microsoft has written to ensure that developers use the same conventions, making it easier to read one another's code.

> **NOTE** *You might wonder why some newer keywords added with the recent versions of C# are not in the list of reserved keywords. The reason is that if they had been added to the list of reserved keywords, it would have broken existing code that already made use of the new C# keywords. The solution was to enhance the syntax by defining these keywords as contextual keywords; they can be used only in some specific code places. For example, the async keyword can be used only with a method declaration, and it is okay to use it as a variable name. The compiler doesn't have a conflict with that.*

Usage Conventions

In any development language, certain traditional programming styles usually arise. The styles are not part of the language itself but rather are conventions—for example, how variables are named or how certain classes, methods, or functions are used. If most developers using that language follow the same conventions, it makes it easier for different developers to understand each other's code—which in turn generally helps program maintainability. Conventions do, however, depend on the language and the environment. For example, C++ developers programming on the Windows platform have traditionally used the prefixes `psz` or `lpsz` to indicate strings—`char *pszResult; char *lpszMessage;`—but on Unix machines it's more common not to use any such prefixes: `char *Result; char *Message;`.

Notice from the sample code in this book that the convention in C# is to name local variables without prefixes: `string result; string message;`.

> **NOTE** *The convention by which variable names are prefixed with letters that represent the data type is known as Hungarian notation. It means that other developers reading the code can immediately tell from the variable name what data type the variable represents. Hungarian notation is widely regarded as redundant in these days of smart editors and IntelliSense.*

Whereas many languages' usage conventions simply evolved as the language was used, for C# and the whole of the .NET Framework, Microsoft has written very comprehensive usage guidelines, which are detailed in the .NET/C# documentation. This means that, right from the start, .NET programs have a high degree of interoperability in terms of developers being able to understand code. The guidelines have also been developed with the benefit of some 20 years' hindsight in object-oriented programming. Judging by the relevant newsgroups, the guidelines have been carefully thought out and are well received in the developer community. Hence, the guidelines are well worth following.

Note, however, that the guidelines are not the same as language specifications. You should try to follow the guidelines when you can. Nevertheless, you won't run into problems if you have a good reason for not doing so—for example, you won't get a compilation error because you don't follow these guidelines. The general rule is that if you don't follow the usage guidelines, you must have a convincing reason. When you depart from the guidelines you should be making a conscious decision rather than simply not bothering. Also, if you compare the guidelines with the samples in the remainder of this book, you'll notice that in numerous examples I have chosen not to follow the conventions. That's usually because the conventions are designed for much larger programs than the samples; although the guidelines are great if you are writing a complete software package, they are not really suitable for small 20-line standalone programs. In many cases, following the conventions would have made the samples harder, rather than easier, to follow.

The full guidelines for good programming style are quite extensive. This section is confined to describing some of the more important guidelines, as well as those most likely to surprise you. To be absolutely certain that your code follows the usage guidelines completely, you need to refer to the Microsoft documentation.

Naming Conventions

One important aspect of making your programs understandable is how you choose to name your items—and that includes naming variables, methods, classes, enumerations, and namespaces.

It is intuitively obvious that your names should reflect the purpose of the item and should not clash with other names. The general philosophy in the .NET Framework is also that the name of a variable should reflect the purpose of that variable instance and not the data type. For example, `height` is a good name for a variable, whereas `integerValue` isn't. However, you are likely to find that principle is an ideal that is hard to achieve. Particularly when you are dealing with controls, in most cases you'll probably be happier sticking with variable names such as `confirmationDialog` and `chooseEmployeeListBox`, which do indicate the data type in the name.

The following sections look at some of the things you need to think about when choosing names.

Casing of Names

In many cases you should use *Pascal casing* for names. With Pascal casing, the first letter of each word in a name is capitalized: EmployeeSalary, ConfirmationDialog, PlainTextEncoding. Notice that nearly all the names of namespaces, classes, and members in the base classes follow Pascal casing. In particular, the convention of joining words using the underscore character is discouraged. Therefore, try not to use names such as employee_salary. It has also been common in other languages to use all capitals for names of constants. This is not advised in C# because such names are harder to read—the convention is to use Pascal casing throughout:

```
const int MaximumLength;
```

The only other casing convention that you are advised to use is *camel casing*. Camel casing is similar to Pascal casing, except that the first letter of the first word in the name is not capitalized: employeeSalary, confirmationDialog, plainTextEncoding. Following are three situations in which you are advised to use camel casing:

➤ For names of all private member fields in types:

Note, however, that often it is conventional to prefix names of member fields with an underscore:

➤ For names of all parameters passed to methods
➤ To distinguish items that would otherwise have the same name. A common example is when a property wraps around a field:

```
private string employeeName;
public string EmployeeName
{
  get
  {
    return employeeName;
  }
}
```

If you are wrapping a property around a field, you should always use camel casing for the private member and Pascal casing for the public or protected member, so that other classes that use your code see only names in Pascal case (except for parameter names).

You should also be wary about case sensitivity. C# is case sensitive, so it is syntactically correct for names in C# to differ only by the case, as in the previous examples. However, bear in mind that your assemblies might at some point be called from Visual Basic applications—and *Visual Basic is not case sensitive*. Hence, if you do use names that differ only by case, it is important to do so only in situations in which both names will never be seen outside your assembly. (The previous example qualifies as okay because camel case is used with the name that is attached to a private variable.) Otherwise, you may prevent other code written in Visual Basic from being able to use your assembly correctly.

Name Styles

Be consistent about your style of names. For example, if one of the methods in a class is called ShowConfirmationDialog, then you should not give another method a name such as ShowDialogWarning or WarningDialogShow. The other method should be called ShowWarningDialog.

Namespace Names

It is particularly important to choose Namespace names carefully to avoid the risk of ending up with the same name for one of your namespaces as someone else uses. Remember, namespace names are the *only* way that .NET distinguishes names of objects in shared assemblies. Therefore, if you use the same namespace name for your software package as another package, and both packages are used by the same program, problems will occur. Because of this, it's almost always a good idea to create a top-level namespace with the name of your company and then nest successive namespaces that narrow down the technology, group, or department you are working in or the name of the package for which your classes are intended. Microsoft recommends namespace names that begin with `<CompanyName>.<TechnologyName>`, as in these two examples:

```
WeaponsOfDestructionCorp.RayGunControllers
WeaponsOfDestructionCorp.Viruses
```

Names and Keywords

It is important that the names do not clash with any keywords. In fact, if you attempt to name an item in your code with a word that happens to be a C# keyword, you'll almost certainly get a syntax error because the compiler will assume that the name refers to a statement. However, because of the possibility that your classes will be accessed by code written in other languages, it is also important that you don't use names that are keywords in other .NET languages. Generally speaking, C++ keywords are similar to C# keywords, so confusion with C++ is unlikely, and those commonly encountered keywords that are unique to Visual C++ tend to start with two underscore characters. As with C#, C++ keywords are spelled in lowercase, so if you hold to the convention of naming your public classes and members with Pascal-style names, they will always have at least one uppercase letter in their names, and there will be no risk of clashes with C++ keywords. However, you are more likely to have problems with Visual Basic, which has many more keywords than C# does, and being non-case-sensitive means that you cannot rely on Pascal-style names for your classes and methods.

Check the Microsoft documentation at `https://docs.microsoft.com/dotnet/csharp/language-reference/keywords`. Here, you find a long list of C# keywords that you shouldn't use with classes and members.

Use of Properties and Methods

One area that can cause confusion regarding a class is whether a particular quantity should be represented by a property or a method. The rules are not hard and strict, but in general you should use a property if something should look and behave like a variable. (If you're not sure what a property is, see Chapter 3.) This means, among other things, that

- ➤ Client code should be able to read its value. Write-only properties are not recommended, so, for example, use a `SetPassword` method, not a write-only `Password` property.

- ➤ Reading the value should not take too long. The fact that something is a property usually suggests that reading it will be relatively quick.

- ➤ Reading the value should not have any observable and unexpected side effect. Furthermore, setting the value of a property should not have any side effect that is not directly related to the property. Setting the width of a dialog has the obvious effect of changing the appearance of the dialog on the screen. That's fine, because that's obviously related to the property in question.

- ➤ It should be possible to set properties in any order. In particular, it is not good practice when setting a property to throw an exception because another related property has not yet been set. For example, to use a class that accesses a database, you need to set `ConnectionString`, `UserName`, and `Password`, and then the author of the class should ensure that the class is implemented such that users can set them in any order.

- ➤ Successive reads of a property should give the same result. If the value of a property is likely to change unpredictably, you should code it as a method instead. `Speed`, in a class that monitors the motion of an automobile, is not a good candidate for a property. Use a `GetSpeed` method here; but `Weight` and `EngineSize` are good candidates for properties because they will not change for a given object.

If the item you are coding satisfies all the preceding criteria, it is probably a good candidate for a property. Otherwise, you should use a method.

Use of Fields

The guidelines are pretty simple here. Fields should almost always be private, although in some cases it may be acceptable for constant or read-only fields to be public. Making a field public may hinder your ability to extend or modify the class in the future.

The previous guidelines should give you a foundation of good practices, and you should use them in conjunction with a good object-oriented programming style.

A final helpful note to keep in mind is that Microsoft has been relatively careful about being consistent and has followed its own guidelines when writing the .NET base classes, so a very good way to get an intuitive feel for the conventions to follow when writing .NET code is to simply look at the base classes—see how classes, members, and namespaces are named, and how the class hierarchy works. Consistency between the base classes and your classes will facilitate readability and maintainability.

> **NOTE** *The new* `ValueTuple` *type contains public fields, whereas the old* `Tuple` *type instead used properties. Microsoft broke one of its own guidelines that's been defined for fields. Because variables of a tuple can be as simple as a variable of an* `int`, *and performance is paramount, it was decided to have public fields for value tuples. It just goes to show that there are no rules without exceptions. Read Chapter 13 for more information on tuples.*

SUMMARY

This chapter examined some of the basic syntax of C#, covering the areas needed to write simple C# programs. We covered a lot of ground, but much of it will be instantly recognizable to developers who are familiar with any C-style language (or even JavaScript).

You have seen that although C# syntax is similar to C++ and Java syntax, there are many minor differences. You have also seen that in many areas this syntax is combined with facilities to write code very quickly—for example, high-quality string handling facilities. C# also has a strongly defined type system, based on a distinction between value and reference types. Chapters 3 and 4 cover the C# object-oriented programming features.

3

Objects and Types

WROX.COM CODE DOWNLOADS FOR THIS CHAPTER

The wrox.com code downloads for this chapter are found at www.wrox.com on the Download Code tab. The source code is also available at https://github.com/ProfessionalCSharp/ProfessionalCSharp7 in the directory ObjectsAndTypes.

The code for this chapter is divided into the following major examples:

➤ MathSample

➤ MethodSample

➤ StaticConstructorSample

➤ StructsSample

➤ PassingByValueAndByReference

➤ OutKeywordSample

➤ EnumSample

➤ ExtensionMethods

CREATING AND USING CLASSES

So far, you've been introduced to some of the building blocks of the C# language, including variables, data types, and program flow statements, and you have seen a few very short complete programs containing little more than the Main method. What you haven't seen yet is how to put all these elements together to form a longer, complete program. The key to this lies in working with classes—the subject of this chapter. Chapter 4, "Object-Oriented Programming with C#," covers inheritance and features related to inheritance.

> **NOTE** *This chapter introduces the basic syntax associated with classes. However, we assume that you are already familiar with the underlying principles of using classes—for example, that you know what a constructor or a property is. This chapter is largely confined to applying those principles in C# code.*

CLASSES AND STRUCTS

Classes and structs are essentially templates from which you can create objects. Each object contains data and has methods to manipulate and access that data. The class defines what data and behavior each particular object (called an *instance*) of that class can contain. For example, if you have a class that represents a customer, it might define fields such as CustomerID, FirstName, LastName, and Address, which are used to hold information about a particular customer. It might also define functionality that acts upon the data stored in these fields. You can then instantiate an object of this class to represent one specific customer, set the field values for that instance, and use its functionality:

```
class PhoneCustomer
{
    public const string DayOfSendingBill = "Monday";
    public int CustomerID;
    public string FirstName;
    public string LastName;
}
```

Structs differ from classes because they do not need to be allocated on the heap (classes are reference types and are always allocated on the heap). Structs are value types and are usually stored on the stack. Also, structs cannot derive from a base struct.

You typically use structs for smaller data types for performance reasons. Storing value types on the stack avoids garbage collection. Another use case of structs are interop with native code; the layout of the struct can look the same as native data types.

In terms of syntax, however, structs look very similar to classes; the main difference is that you use the keyword struct instead of class to declare them. For example, if you wanted all PhoneCustomer instances to be allocated on the stack instead of the managed heap, you could write the following:

```
struct PhoneCustomerStruct
{
    public const string DayOfSendingBill = "Monday";
    public int CustomerID;
    public string FirstName;
    public string LastName;
}
```

For both classes and structs, you use the keyword new to declare an instance. This keyword creates the object and initializes it; in the following example, the default behavior is to zero out its fields:

```
var myCustomer = new PhoneCustomer(); // works for a class
var myCustomer2 = new PhoneCustomerStruct();// works for a struct
```

In most cases, you use classes much more often than structs. Therefore, this chapter covers classes first and then the differences between classes and structs and the specific reasons why you might choose to use a struct instead of a class. Unless otherwise stated, however, you can assume that code presented for a class works equally well for a struct.

> **NOTE** *An important difference between classes and structs is that objects of type of class are passed by reference, and objects of type of a struct are passed by value. This is explained later in this chapter in the section "Passing Parameters by Value and by Reference."*

CLASSES

A class contains members, which can be static or instance members. A static member belongs to the class; an instance member belongs to the object. With static fields, the value of the field is the same for every object. With instance fields, every object can have a different value. Static members have the static modifier attached.

The kind of members are explained in the following table.

MEMBER	DESCRIPTION
Fields	A field is a data member of a class. It is a variable of a type that is a member of a class.
Constants	Constants are associated with the class (although they do not have the static modifier). The compiler replaces constants everywhere they are used with the real value.
Methods	Methods are functions associated with a particular class.
Properties	Properties are sets of functions that can be accessed from the client in a similar way to the public fields of the class. C# provides a specific syntax for implementing read and write properties on your classes, so you don't have to use method names that are prefixed with the words Get or Set. Because there's a dedicated syntax for properties that is distinct from that for normal functions, the illusion of objects as actual things is strengthened for client code.
Constructors	Constructors are special functions that are called automatically when an object is instantiated. They must have the same name as the class to which they belong and cannot have a return type. Constructors are useful for initialization.
Indexers	Indexers allow your object to be accessed the same way as arrays. Indexers are explained in 6, "Operators and Casts."
Operators	Operators, at their simplest, are actions such as + or −. When you add two integers, you are, strictly speaking, using the + operator for integers. C# also allows you to specify how existing operators will work with your own classes (operator overloading). Chapter 6 looks at operators in detail.
Events	Events are class members that allow an object to notify a subscriber whenever something noteworthy happens, such as a field or property of the class changing, or some form of user interaction occurring. The client can have code, known as an event handler, that reacts to the event. Chapter 8, "Delegates, Lambdas, and Events," looks at events in detail.

continues

(continued)

MEMBER	DESCRIPTION
Destructors	The syntax of destructors or finalizers is similar to the syntax for constructors, but they are called when the CLR detects that an object is no longer needed. They have the same name as the class, preceded by a tilde (~). It is impossible to predict precisely when a finalizer will be called. Finalizers are discussed in Chapter 17, "Managed and Unmanaged Memory."
Types	Classes can contain inner classes. This is interesting if the inner type is only used in conjunction with the outer type.

Let's get into the details of class members.

Fields

Fields are any variables associated with the class. You have already seen fields in use in the PhoneCustomer class in the previous example.

After you have instantiated a PhoneCustomer object, you can then access these fields using the object.FieldName syntax, as shown in this example:

```
var customer1 = new PhoneCustomer();
customer1.FirstName = "Simon";
```

Constants can be associated with classes in the same way as variables. You declare a constant using the const keyword. If it is declared as public, then it is accessible from outside the class:

```
class PhoneCustomer
{
  public const string DayOfSendingBill = "Monday";
  public int CustomerID;
  public string FirstName;
  public string LastName;
}
```

Readonly Fields

To guarantee that fields of an object cannot be changed, you can declare fields with the readonly modifier. Fields with the readonly modifier can be assigned only values from constructors, which is different from the const modifier. With the const modifier, the compiler replaces the variable with its value everywhere it is used. The compiler already knows the value of the constant. Read-only fields are assigned during runtime from a constructor. Unlike const fields, read-only fields can be instance members. For using a read-only field as a class member, the static modifier needs to be assigned to the field.

Suppose that you have a program that edits documents, and for licensing reasons you want to restrict the number of documents that can be opened simultaneously. Assume also that you are selling different versions of the software, and it's possible for customers to upgrade their licenses to open more documents simultaneously. Clearly, this means you can't hard-code the maximum number in the source code. You would probably need a field to represent this maximum number. This field has to be read in—perhaps from some file storage—each time the program is launched. Therefore, your code might look something like this:

```
public class DocumentEditor
{
  private static readonly uint s_maxDocuments;
  static DocumentEditor()
  {
    s_maxDocuments = DoSomethingToFindOutMaxNumber();
  }
}
```

In this case, the field is static because the maximum number of documents needs to be stored only once per running instance of the program. This is why the field is initialized in the static constructor. If you had an instance readonly field, you would initialize it in the instance constructor(s). For example, presumably each document you edit has a creation date, which you wouldn't want to allow the user to change (because that would be rewriting the past!).

As noted earlier, the date is represented by the class System.DateTime. The following code initializes the _creationTime field in the constructor using the DateTime struct. After initialization of the Document class, the creation time cannot be changed anymore:

```
public class Document
{
  private readonly DateTime _creationTime;
  public Document()
  {
    _creationTime = DateTime.Now;
  }
}
```

_creationDate and s_maxDocuments in the previous code snippets are treated like any other fields, except that they are read-only, which means they can't be assigned outside the constructors:

```
void SomeMethod()
{
  s_maxDocuments = 10; // compilation error here. MaxDocuments is readonly
}
```

It's also worth noting that you don't have to assign a value to a readonly field in a constructor. If you don't assign a value, the field is left with the default value for its particular data type or whatever value you initialized it to at its declaration. That applies to both static and instance readonly fields.

It's a good idea *not* to declare fields public. If you change a public member of a class, every caller that's using this public member needs to be changed as well. For example, in case you want to introduce a check for the maximum string length with the next version, the public field needs to be changed to a property. Existing code that makes use of the public field must be recompiled for using this property (although the syntax from the caller side looks the same with properties). If you instead change the check within an existing property, the caller doesn't need to be recompiled for using the new version.

It's good practice to declare fields private and use properties to access the field, as described in the next section.

Properties

The idea of a *property* is that it is a method or a pair of methods dressed to look like a field. Let's change the field for the first name from the previous example to a private field with the variable name _firstName. The property named FirstName contains a get and set accessor to retrieve and set the value of the backing field:

```
class PhoneCustomer
{
  private string _firstName;
  public string FirstName
  {
    get
    {
      return _firstName;
    }
    set
    {
      _firstName = value;
    }
  }
  //...
}
```

The `get` accessor takes no parameters and must return the same type as the declared property. You should not specify any explicit parameters for the `set` accessor either, but the compiler assumes it takes one parameter, which is of the same type again, and which is referred to as `value`.

Let's get into another example with a different naming convention. The following code contains a property called `Age`, which sets a field called `age`. In this example, `age` is referred to as the backing variable for the property `Age`:

```
private int age;
public int Age
{
  get
  {
    return age;
  }
  set
  {
    age = value;
  }
}
```

Note the naming convention used here. You take advantage of C#'s case sensitivity by using the same name—Pascal-case for the public property, and camel-case for the equivalent private field if there is one. In earlier .NET versions, this naming convention was preferred by Microsoft's C# team. Recently they switched the naming convention to prefix field names by an underscore. This provides an extremely convenient way to identify fields in contrast to local variables.

> **NOTE** *Microsoft teams use either one or the other naming convention. For using private members of types, .NET doesn't have strict naming conventions. However, within a team the same convention should be used. The .NET Core team switched to using an underscore to prefix fields, which is the convention used in this book in most places (see* `https://github.com/dotnet/corefx/blob/master/Documentation/coding-guidelines/coding-style.md`*).*

Expression-Bodied Property Accessors

With C# 7, you can also write property accessors as expression-bodied members. For example, the previously shown property `FirstName` can be written using `=>`. This new feature reduces the need to write curly brackets, and the `return` keyword is omitted with the `get` accessor.

```
private string _firstName;
public string FirstName
{
  get => _firstName;
  set => _firstName = value;
}
```

When you use expression-bodied members, the implementation of the property accessor can be made up of only a single statement.

Auto-Implemented Properties

If there isn't going to be any logic in the properties `set` and `get`, then auto-implemented properties can be used. Auto-implemented properties implement the backing member variable automatically. The code for the earlier `Age` example would look like this:

```
public int Age { get; set; }
```

The declaration of a private field is not needed. The compiler creates this automatically. With auto-implemented properties, you cannot access the field directly as you don't know the name the compiler generates. If all you need to do with a property is read and write a field, the syntax for the property when you use auto-implemented properties is shorter than when you use expression-bodied property accessors.

By using auto-implemented properties, validation of the property cannot be done at the property set. Therefore, with the Age property you could not have checked to see if an invalid age is set.

Auto-implemented properties can be initialized using a *property initializer*:

```
public int Age { get; set; } = 42;
```

Access Modifiers for Properties

C# allows the set and get accessors to have differing access modifiers. This would allow a property to have a public get and a private or protected set. This can help control how or when a property can be set. In the following code example, notice that the set has a private access modifier but the get does not. In this case, the get takes the access level of the property. One of the accessors must follow the access level of the property. A compile error is generated if the get accessor has the protected access level associated with it because that would make both accessors have a different access level from the property.

```
public string Name
{
  get => _name;
  private set => _name = value;
}
```

Different access levels can also be set with auto-implemented properties:

```
public int Age { get; private set; }
```

> **NOTE** *Some developers may be concerned that the previous sections have presented a number of situations in which standard C# coding practices have led to very small functions—for example, accessing a field via a property instead of directly. Will this hurt performance because of the overhead of the extra function call? The answer is no. There's no need to worry about performance loss from these kinds of programming methodologies in C#. Recall that C# code is compiled to IL, then JIT compiled at runtime to native executable code. The JIT compiler is designed to generate highly optimized code and will ruthlessly inline code as appropriate (in other words, it replaces function calls with inline code). A method or property whose implementation simply calls another method or returns a field will almost certainly be inlined.*
>
> *Usually you do not need to change the inlining behavior, but you have some control to inform the compiler about inlining. Using the attribute* MethodImpl, *you can define that a method should not be inlined (*MethodImplOptions.NoInlining*), or inlining should be done aggressively by the compiler (*MethodImplOptions. AggressiveInlining*). With properties, you need to apply this attribute directly to the* get *and* set *accessors. Attributes are explained in detail in Chapter 16, "Reflection, Metadata, and Dynamic Programming."*

Read-Only Properties

It is possible to create a read-only property by simply omitting the set accessor from the property definition. Thus, to make Name a read-only property, you would do the following:

```
private readonly string _name;
public string Name
{
  get => _name;
}
```

Declaring the field with the readonly modifier only allows initializing the value of the property in the constructor.

> **WARNING** *Similar to creating read-only properties it is also possible to create a write-only property. Write-only properties can be created by omitting the* get *accessor. However, this is regarded as poor programming practice because it could be confusing to authors of client code. In general, it is recommended that if you are tempted to do this, you should use a method instead.*

Auto-Implemented Read-Only Properties

C# offers a simple syntax with auto-implemented properties to create read-only properties that access read-only fields. These properties can be initialized using property initializers.

```
public string Id { get; } = Guid.NewGuid().ToString();
```

Behind the scenes, the compiler creates a read-only field and also a property with a get accessor to this field. The code from the initializer moves to the implementation of the constructor and is invoked before the constructor body is called.

Read-only properties can also explicitly be initialized from the constructor as shown with this code snippet:

```
public class Person
{
  public Person(string name) => Name = name;

  public string Name { get; }
}
```

Expression-Bodied Properties

Since C# 6, properties with just a get accessor also can be implemented using expression-bodied properties. Similar to expression-bodied methods, expression-bodied properties don't need curly brackets and return statements. Expression-bodied properties are properties with the get accessor, but you don't need to write the get keyword. Instead of writing the get keyword, the code you previously implemented in the get accessor can now follow the lambda operator. With the Person class, the FullName property is implemented using an expression-bodied property and returns with this property the values of the FirstName and LastName properties combined (code file ClassesSample/Program.cs):

```
public class Person
{
  public Person(string firstName, string lastName)
  {
    FirstName = firstName;
    LastName = lastName;
  }
  public string FirstName { get; }
  public string LastName { get; }
  public string FullName => $"{FirstName} {LastName}";
}
```

Immutable Types

If a type contains members that can be changed, it is a *mutable* type. With the `readonly` modifier, the compiler complains if the state is changed. The state can be initialized only in the constructor. If an object doesn't have any members that can be changed—it has only `readonly` members—it is an *immutable* type. The content can be set only at initialization time. This is extremely useful with multithreading, as multiple threads can access the same object with the information and it can never change. Because the content can't change, synchronization is not necessary.

An example of an immutable type is the `String` class. This class does not define any member that is allowed to change its content. Methods such as `ToUpper` (which changes the string to uppercase) always return a new string, but the original string passed to the constructor remains unchanged.

> **NOTE** *.NET also offers immutable collections. These collection classes are covered in Chapter 11, "Special Collections."*

Anonymous Types

Chapter 2, "Core C#," discusses the `var` keyword in reference to implicitly typed variables. When you use `var` with the `new` keyword, you can create anonymous types. An anonymous type is simply a nameless class that inherits from `object`. The definition of the class is inferred from the initializer, just as with implicitly typed variables.

For example, if you need an object containing a person's first, middle, and last name, the declaration would look like this:

```
var captain = new
{
  FirstName = "James",
  MiddleName = "T",
  LastName = "Kirk"
};
```

This would produce an object with `FirstName`, `MiddleName`, and `LastName` properties. If you were to create another object that looked like this:

```
var doctor = new
{
  FirstName = "Leonard",
  MiddleName = string.Empty,
  LastName = "McCoy"
};
```

then the types of `captain` and `doctor` are the same. You could set `captain = doctor`, for example. This is only possible if all the properties match.

The names for the members of anonymous types can be inferred—if the values that are being set come from another object. This way, the initializer can be abbreviated. If you already have a class that contains the properties `FirstName`, `MiddleName`, and `LastName` and you have an instance of that class with the instance name `person`, then the `captain` object could be initialized like this:

```
var captain = new
{
  person.FirstName,
  person.MiddleName,
  person.LastName
};
```

The property names from the person object are inferred in the new object named captain, so the object named captain has FirstName, MiddleName, and LastName properties.

The actual type name of anonymous types is unknown; that's where the name comes from. The compiler "makes up" a name for the type, but only the compiler is ever able to make use of it. Therefore, you can't and shouldn't plan on using any type reflection on the new objects because you won't get consistent results.

Methods

Note that official C# terminology makes a distinction between functions and methods. In C# terminology, the term "function member" includes not only methods, but also other nondata members of a class or struct. This includes indexers, operators, constructors, destructors, and—perhaps somewhat surprisingly—properties. These are contrasted with data members: fields, constants, and events.

Declaring Methods

In C#, the definition of a method consists of any method modifiers (such as the method's accessibility), followed by the type of the return value, followed by the name of the method, followed by a list of input arguments enclosed in parentheses, followed by the body of the method enclosed in curly braces:

```
[modifiers] return_type MethodName([parameters])
{
   // Method body
}
```

Each parameter consists of the name of the type of the parameter, and the name by which it can be referenced in the body of the method. Also, if the method returns a value, a return statement must be used with the return value to indicate each exit point, as shown in this example:

```
public bool IsSquare(Rectangle rect)
{
   return (rect.Height == rect.Width);
}
```

If the method doesn't return anything, specify a return type of void because you can't omit the return type altogether; and if it takes no arguments, you still need to include an empty set of parentheses after the method name. In this case, including a return statement is optional—the method returns automatically when the closing curly brace is reached.

Expression-Bodied Methods

If the implementation of a method consists just of one statement, C# gives a simplified syntax to method definitions: *expression-bodied methods*. You don't need to write curly brackets and the return keyword with the new syntax. The operator => is used to distinguish the declaration of the left side of this operator to the implementation that is on the right side.

The following example is the same method as before, IsSquare, implemented using the expression-bodied method syntax. The right side of the lambda operator defines the implementation of the method. Curly brackets and a return statement are not needed. What's returned is the result of the statement, and the result needs to be of the same type as the method declared on the left side, which is a bool in this code snippet:

```
public bool IsSquare(Rectangle rect) => rect.Height == rect.Width;
```

Invoking Methods

The following example illustrates the syntax for definition and instantiation of classes, and definition and invocation of methods. The class Math defines instance and static members (code file MathSample/Math.cs):

```
public class Math
{
   public int Value { get; set; }
```

```
  public int GetSquare() => Value * Value;
  public static int GetSquareOf(int x) => x * x;
  public static double GetPi() => 3.14159;
}
```

The `Program` class makes use of the `Math` class, calls static methods, and instantiates an object to invoke instance members (code file `MathSample/Program.cs`):

```
using System;
namespace MathSample
{
  class Program
  {
    static void Main()
    {
      // Try calling some static functions.
      Console.WriteLine($"Pi is {Math.GetPi()}");
      int x = Math.GetSquareOf(5);
      Console.WriteLine($"Square of 5 is {x}");
      // Instantiate a Math object
      var math = new Math(); // instantiate a reference type
      // Call instance members
      math.Value = 30;
      Console.WriteLine($"Value field of math variable contains {math.Value}");
      Console.WriteLine($"Square of 30 is {math.GetSquare()}");
    }
  }
}
```

Running the `MathSample` example produces the following results:

```
Pi is 3.14159
Square of 5 is 25
Value field of math variable contains 30
Square of 30 is 900
```

As you can see from the code, the `Math` class contains a property that contains a number, as well as a method to find the square of this number. It also contains two static methods: one to return the value of pi and one to find the square of the number passed in as a parameter.

Some features of this class are not really good examples of C# program design. For example, `GetPi` would usually be implemented as a `const` field, but following good design would mean using some concepts that have not yet been introduced.

Method Overloading

C# supports method overloading—several versions of the method that have different signatures (that is, the same name but a different number of parameters and/or different parameter data types). To overload methods, simply declare the methods with the same name but different numbers of parameter types:

```
class ResultDisplayer
{
  public void DisplayResult(string result)
  {
    // implementation
  }

  public void DisplayResult(int result)
  {
    // implementation
  }
}
```

It's not just the parameter types that can differ; the number of parameters can differ too, as shown in the next example. One overloaded method can invoke another:

```
class MyClass
{
  public int DoSomething(int x)
  {
    return DoSomething(x, 10); // invoke DoSomething with two parameters
  }

  public int DoSomething(int x, int y)
  {
    // implementation
  }
}
```

> **NOTE** *With method overloading, it is not sufficient to only differ overloads by the return type. It's also not sufficient to differ by parameter names. The number of parameters and/or types needs to differ.*

Named Arguments

Invoking methods, the variable name need not be added to the invocation. However, if you have a method signature like the following to move a rectangle

```
public void MoveAndResize(int x, int y, int width, int height)
```

and you invoke it with the following code snippet, it's not clear from the invocation what numbers are used for what:

```
r.MoveAndResize(30, 40, 20, 40);
```

You can change the invocation to make it immediately clear what the numbers mean:

```
r.MoveAndResize(x: 30, y: 40, width: 20, height: 40);
```

Any method can be invoked using named arguments. You just need to write the name of the variable followed by a colon and the value passed. The compiler gets rid of the name and creates an invocation of the method just like the variable name would not be there—so there's no difference within the compiled code. C# 7.2 allows for non-trailing named arguments. When you use earlier C# versions, you need to supply names for all arguments after using the first named argument.

You can also change the order of variables this way, and the compiler rearranges it to the correct order. A big advantage you get with named arguments is shown in the next section with optional arguments.

Optional Arguments

Parameters can also be optional. You must supply a default value for optional parameters, which must be the last ones defined:

```
public void TestMethod(int notOptionalNumber, int optionalNumber = 42)
{
  Console.WriteLine(optionalNumber + notOptionalNumber);
}
```

This method can now be invoked using one or two parameters. Passing one parameter, the compiler changes the method call to pass 42 with the second parameter.

```
TestMethod(11);
TestMethod(11, 22);
```

You can define multiple optional parameters, as shown here:

```
public void TestMethod(int n, int opt1 = 11, int opt2 = 22, int opt3 = 33)
{
    Console.WriteLine(n + opt1 + opt2 + opt3);
}
```

This way, the method can be called using 1, 2, 3, or 4 parameters. The first line of the following code leaves the optional parameters with the values 11, 22, and 33. The second line passes the first three parameters, and the last one has a value of 33:

```
TestMethod(1);
TestMethod(1, 2, 3);
```

With multiple optional parameters, the feature of named arguments shines. Using named arguments, you can pass any of the optional parameters—for example, this example passes just the last one:

```
TestMethod(1, opt3: 4);
opt3: 4
```

Variable Number of Arguments

Using optional arguments, you can define a variable number of arguments. However, there's also a different syntax that allows passing a variable number of arguments—and this syntax doesn't have versioning issues.

Declaring the parameter of type array—the sample code uses an int array—and adding the params keyword, the method can be invoked using any number of int parameters.

```
public void AnyNumberOfArguments(params int[] data)
{
    foreach (var x in data)
    {
        Console.WriteLine(x);
    }
}
```

As the parameter of the method `AnyNumberOfArguments` is of type `int[]`, you can pass an `int` array, or because of the `params` keyword, you can pass one or any number of `int` values:

```
AnyNumberOfArguments(1);
AnyNumberOfArguments(1, 3, 5, 7, 11, 13);
```

If arguments of different types should be passed to methods, you can use an `object` array:

```
public void AnyNumberOfArguments(params object[] data)
{
    // ...
```

Now it is possible to use any type calling this method:

```
AnyNumberOfArguments("text", 42);
```

If the `params` keyword is used with multiple parameters that are defined with the method signature, `params` can be used only once, and it must be the last parameter:

```
Console.WriteLine(string format, params object[] arg);
```

Now that you've looked at the many aspects of methods, let's get into constructors, which are a special kind of methods.

Constructors

The syntax for declaring basic constructors is a method that has the same name as the containing class and that does not have any return type:

```
public class MyClass
{
    public MyClass()
    {
    }

    // rest of class definition
}
```

It's not necessary to provide a constructor for your class. We haven't supplied one for any of the examples so far in this book. In general, if you don't supply any constructor, the compiler generates a default one behind the scenes. It will be a very basic constructor that initializes all the member fields by zeroing them out (`null` reference for reference types, zero for numeric data types, and false for `bool`s). Often, that is adequate; if not, you need to write your own constructor.

Constructors follow the same rules for overloading as other methods—that is, you can provide as many overloads to the constructor as you want, provided they are clearly different in signature:

```
public MyClass() // zeroparameter constructor
{
    // construction code
}

public MyClass(int number) // another overload
{
    // construction code
}
```

However, if you supply any constructors that take parameters, the compiler does not automatically supply a default one. This is done only if you have not defined any constructors at all. In the following example, because a one-parameter constructor is defined, the compiler assumes that this is the only constructor you want to be available, so it does not implicitly supply any others:

```
public class MyNumber
{
```

```
    private int _number;
    public MyNumber(int number)
    {
      _number = number;
    }
}
```

If you now try instantiating a `MyNumber` object using a no-parameter constructor, you get a compilation error:

```
var numb = new MyNumber(); // causes compilation error
```

Note that it is possible to define constructors as private or protected, so that they are invisible to code in unrelated classes too:

```
public class MyNumber
{
  private int _number;
  private MyNumber(int number) // another overload
  {
    _number = number;
  }
}
```

This example hasn't actually defined any public, or even any protected, constructors for `MyNumber`. This would actually make it impossible for `MyNumber` to be instantiated by outside code using the `new` operator (though you might write a public static property or method in `MyNumber` that can instantiate the class). This is useful in two situations:

➤ If your class serves only as a container for some static members or properties, and therefore should never be instantiated. With this scenario, you can declare the class with the modifier `static`. With this modifier the class can contain only static members and cannot be instantiated.

➤ If you want the class to only ever be instantiated by calling a static member function (this is the so-called factory pattern approach to object instantiation). An implementation of the Singleton pattern is shown in the following code snippet.

```
public class Singleton
{
  private static Singleton s_instance;
  private int _state;
  private Singleton(int state)
  {
    _state = state;
  }
  public static Singleton Instance
  {
    get => s_instance ?? (s_instance = new Singleton(42);
  }
}
```

The `Singleton` class contains a private constructor, so you can instantiate it only within the class itself. To instantiate it, the static property `Instance` returns the field `s_instance`. If this field is not yet initialized (`null`), a new instance is created by calling the instance constructor. For the null check, the coalescing operator is used. If the left side of this operator is null, the right side of this operator is processed and the instance constructor invoked.

NOTE *The coalescing operator is explained in detail in Chapter 6.*

Expression Bodies with Constructors

If the implementation of a constructor consists of a single expression, the constructor can be implemented with an expression-bodied implementation:

```
public class Singleton
{
  private static Singleton s_instance;
  private int _state;
  private Singleton(int state) => _state = state;

  public static Singleton Instance =>
    s_instance ?? (s_instance = new Singleton(42);
}
```

Calling Constructors from Other Constructors

You might sometimes find yourself in the situation where you have several constructors in a class, perhaps to accommodate some optional parameters for which the constructors have some code in common. For example, consider the following:

```
class Car
{
  private string _description;
  private uint _nWheels;

  public Car(string description, uint nWheels)
  {
    _description = description;
    _nWheels = nWheels;
  }

  public Car(string description)
  {
    _description = description;
    _nWheels = 4;
  }
  // ...
}
```

Both constructors initialize the same fields. It would clearly be neater to place all the code in one location. C# has a special syntax known as a *constructor initializer* to enable this:

```
class Car
{
  private string _description;
  private uint _nWheels;
  public Car(string description, uint nWheels)
  {
    _description = description;
    _nWheels = nWheels;
  }
  public Car(string description): this(description, 4)
  {
  }
  // ...
```

In this context, the this keyword simply causes the constructor with the nearest matching parameters to be called. Note that any constructor initializer is executed before the body of the constructor. Suppose that the following code is run:

```
var myCar = new Car("Proton Persona");
```

In this example, the two-parameter constructor executes before any code in the body of the one-parameter constructor (though in this particular case, because there is no code in the body of the one-parameter constructor, it makes no difference).

A C# constructor initializer may contain either one call to another constructor in the same class (using the syntax just presented) or one call to a constructor in the immediate base class (using the same syntax, but using the keyword base instead of this). It is not possible to put more than one call in the initializer.

Static Constructors

One feature of C# is that it is also possible to write a static no-parameter constructor for a class. Such a constructor is executed only once, unlike the constructors written so far, which are instance constructors that are executed whenever an object of that class is created:

```
class MyClass
{
  static MyClass()
  {
    // initialization code
  }
  // rest of class definition
}
```

One reason for writing a static constructor is if your class has some static fields or properties that need to be initialized from an external source before the class is first used.

The .NET runtime makes no guarantees about when a static constructor will be executed, so you should not place any code in it that relies on it being executed at a particular time (for example, when an assembly is loaded). Nor is it possible to predict in what order static constructors of different classes will execute. However, what is guaranteed is that the static constructor will run at most once, and that it will be invoked before your code makes any reference to the class. In C#, the static constructor is usually executed immediately before the first call to any member of the class.

Note that the static constructor does not have any access modifiers. It's never called explicitly by any other C# code, but always by the .NET runtime when the class is loaded, so any access modifier such as public or private would be meaningless. For this same reason, the static constructor can never take any parameters, and there can be only one static constructor for a class. It should also be obvious that a static constructor can access only static members, not instance members, of the class.

It is possible to have a static constructor and a zero-parameter instance constructor defined in the same class. Although the parameter lists are identical, there is no conflict because the static constructor is executed when the class is loaded, but the instance constructor is executed whenever an instance is created. Therefore, there is no confusion about which constructor is executed or when.

If you have more than one class that has a static constructor, the static constructor that is executed first is undefined. Therefore, you should not put any code in a static constructor that depends on other static constructors having been or not having been executed. However, if any static fields have been given default values, these are allocated before the static constructor is called.

The next example illustrates the use of a static constructor. It is based on the idea of a program that has user preferences (which are presumably stored in some configuration file). To keep things simple, assume just one user preference—a quantity called BackColor that might represent the background color to be used in an application. Because we don't want to get into the details of writing code to read data from an external source here, assume also that the preference is to have a background color of red on weekdays and green on weekends. All the program does is display the preference in a console window, but that is enough to see a static constructor at work.

The class `UserPreferences` is declared with the `static` modifier; thus, it cannot be instantiated and can only contain static members. The static constructor initializes the `BackColor` property depending on the day of the week (code file `StaticConstructorSample/UserPreferences.cs`):

```
public static class UserPreferences
{
  public static Color BackColor { get; }
  static UserPreferences()
  {
    DateTime now = DateTime.Now;
    if (now.DayOfWeek == DayOfWeek.Saturday
        || now.DayOfWeek == DayOfWeek.Sunday)
    {
      BackColor = Color.Green;
    }
    else
    {
      BackColor = Color.Red;
    }
  }
}
```

This code makes use of the `System.DateTime` struct that is supplied with the .NET Framework. `DateTime` implements a static property `Now` that returns the current time. `DayOfWeek` is an instance property of `DateTime` that returns an enum value of type `DayOfWeek`.

`Color` is defined as an enum type and contains a few colors. The enum types are explained in detail later in the section Enums (code file `StaticConstructorSample/Color.cs`):

```
public enum Color
{
  White,
  Red,
  Green,
  Blue,
  Black
}
```

The `Main` method just invokes the `Console.WriteLine` method and writes the user preferences back color to the console (code file `StaticConstructorSample/Program.cs`):

```
class Program
{
  static void Main()
  {
    Console.WriteLine(
      $"User-preferences: BackColor is: {UserPreferences.BackColor}");
  }
}
```

Compiling and running the preceding code results in the following output:

```
User-preferences: BackColor is: Color Red
```

Of course, if the code is executed during the weekend, your color preference would be `Green`.

STRUCTS

So far, you have seen how classes offer a great way to encapsulate objects in your program. You have also seen how they are stored on the heap in a way that gives you much more flexibility in data lifetime but with a slight cost in performance. This performance cost is small thanks to the optimizations of managed heaps. However, in some situations all you really need is a small data structure. In those cases, a class provides more functionality than you need, and for best performance you probably want to use a struct. Consider the following example using a reference type:

```
public class Dimensions
{
  public Dimensions(double length, double width)
  {
    Length = length;
    Width = width;
  }
  public double Length { get; }
  public double Width { get; }
}
```

This code defines a class called `Dimensions`, which simply stores the length and width of an item. Suppose you're writing a furniture-arranging program that enables users to experiment with rearranging their furniture on the computer, and you want to store the dimensions of each item of furniture. All you have is two numbers, which you'll find convenient to treat as a pair rather than individually. There is no need for a lot of methods, or for you to be able to inherit from the class, and you certainly don't want to have the .NET runtime go to the trouble of bringing in the heap, with all the performance implications, just to store two doubles.

As mentioned earlier in this chapter, the only thing you need to change in the code to define a type as a struct instead of a class is to replace the keyword `class` with `struct`:

```
public struct Dimensions
{
  public Dimensions(double length, double width)
  {
    Length = length;
    Width = width;
  }

  public double Length { get; }
  public double Width { get; }
}
```

Defining functions for structs is also exactly the same as defining them for classes. You've already seen a constructor with the `Dimensions` struct. The following code demonstrates adding the property `Diagonal` to invoke the `Sqrt` method of the `Math` class (code file `StructsSample/Dimension.cs`):

```
public struct Dimensions
{
  public double Length { get; }
  public double Width { get; }
  public Dimensions(double length, double width)
  {
    Length = length;
    Width = width;
  }
  public double Diagonal => Math.Sqrt(Length * Length + Width * Width);
}
```

Structs are value types, not reference types. This means they are stored either in the stack or inline (if they are part of another object that is stored on the heap) and have the same lifetime restrictions as the simple data types:

➤ Structs do not support inheritance.

➤ There are some differences in the way constructors work for structs. If you do not supply a default constructor, the compiler automatically creates one and initializes the members to its default values.

➤ With a struct, you can specify how the fields are to be laid out in memory (this is examined in Chapter 16, which covers attributes).

Because structs are really intended to group data items together, you'll sometimes find that most or all of their fields are declared as public. Strictly speaking, this is contrary to the guidelines for writing .NET code—according to Microsoft, fields (other than const fields) should always be private and wrapped by public properties. However, for simple structs, many developers consider public fields to be acceptable programming practice.

> **NOTE** *Behind the scenes, the* int *type (*System.Int32*) is a struct with a public field. The new type* System.ValueType *is a struct that contains one or more public fields.* ValueTuple *is discussed in detail in Chapter 13, "Functional Programming with C#."*

The following sections look at some of these differences between structs and classes in more detail.

Structs Are Value Types

Although structs are value types, you can often treat them syntactically in the same way as classes. For example, with the definition of the Dimensions class in the previous section, you could write this:

```
var point = new Dimensions();
point.Length = 3;
point.Width = 6;
```

Note that because structs are value types, the new operator does not work in the same way as it does for classes and other reference types. Instead of allocating memory on the heap, the new operator simply calls the appropriate constructor, according to the parameters passed to it, initializing all fields. Indeed, for structs it is perfectly legal to write this:

```
Dimensions point;
point.Length = 3;
point.Width = 6;
```

If Dimensions were a class, this would produce a compilation error, because point would contain an uninitialized reference—an address that points nowhere, so you could not start setting values to its fields. For a struct, however, the variable declaration actually allocates space on the stack for the entire struct, so it's ready to assign values to. The following code, however, would cause a compilation error, with the compiler complaining that you are using an uninitialized variable:

```
Dimensions point;
double d = point.Length;
```

Structs follow the same rule as any other data type: Everything must be initialized before use. A struct is considered fully initialized either when the new operator has been called against it or when values have been individually assigned to all its fields. Also, of course, a struct defined as a member field of a class is initialized by being zeroed out automatically when the containing object is initialized.

The fact that structs are value types affects performance, though depending on how you use your struct, this can be good or bad. On the positive side, allocating memory for structs is very fast because this takes place inline or on the stack. The same is true when they go out of scope. Structs are cleaned up quickly and don't need to wait on garbage collection. On the negative side, whenever you pass a struct as a parameter or assign a struct to another struct (as in A = B, where A and B are structs), the full contents of the struct are copied, whereas for a class only the reference is copied. This results in a performance loss that varies according to the size of the struct, emphasizing the fact that structs are really intended for small data structures.

Note, however, that when passing a struct as a parameter to a method, you can avoid this performance loss by passing it as a ref parameter—in this case, only the address in memory of the struct will be passed in, which is just as fast as passing in a class. If you do this, though, be aware that it means the called method can, in principle, change the value of the struct. This is shown later in this chapter in the section "Passing Parameters by Value and by Reference."

Readonly structs

When you return a value type from a property, the caller receives a copy. Setting properties of this value type changes only the copy; the original value doesn't change. This can be confusing to the developer who's accessing the property. That's why a guideline for structs defines that *value types should be immutable*. Of course, this guideline is not valid for all value types because int, short, double... are not immutable, and the ValueTuple is also not immutable. However, most struct types are implemented as immutable.

When you use C# 7.2, the readonly modifier can be applied to a struct, and thus the compiler guarantees for immutability of the struct. The previously defined type Dimensions can be declared readonly when you use C# 7.2 because it contains only a constructor that changes its members. The properties only contain a get accessor, thus change is not possible (code file ReadOnlyStructSample/Dimensions.cs):

```
public readonly struct Dimensions
{
  public double Length { get; }
  public double Width { get; }

  public Dimensions(double length, double width)
  {
    Length = length;
    Width = width;
  }

  public double Diagonal => Math.Sqrt(Length * Length + Width * Width);
}
```

With the readonly modifier, the compiler complains in case the type contains changes to fields or properties that are applied after the object is created. With this modifier, the compiler can generate optimized code to not copy the contents of a struct when it is passed along; instead the compiler uses references because it can never change.

Structs and Inheritance

Structs are not designed for inheritance. This means it is not possible to inherit from a struct. The only exception to this is that structs, in common with every other type in C#, derive ultimately from the class System.Object. Hence, structs also have access to the methods of System.Object, and it is even possible to override them in structs; an obvious example would be overriding the ToString method. The actual inheritance chain for structs is that each struct derives from the class, System.ValueType, which in turn derives from System.Object. ValueType does not add any new members to Object but provides override implementations of some members of the base class that are more suitable for structs. Note that you cannot supply a different base class for a struct: Every struct is derived from ValueType.

> **NOTE** *Inheritance from* System.ValueType *only happens with structs when they are used as objects. Structs that cannot be used as objects are* ref structs. *These types have been available since C# 7.2. This feature is explained later in this chapter in the section "ref structs."*

> **NOTE** *To compare structural values, it's a good practice to implement the interface* IEquatable<T>. *This interface is discussed in Chapter 6.*

Constructors for Structs

You can define constructors for structs in a similar way as you do it for classes.

That said, the default constructor, which initializes all fields to zero values, is always present implicitly, even if you supply other constructors that take parameters. You can't create custom default constructors for structs.

```
public Dimensions(double length, double width)
{
  Length = length;
  Width = width;
}
```

Incidentally, you can supply a `Close` or `Dispose` method for a struct in the same way you do for a class. The `Dispose` method is discussed in detail in Chapter 17.

ref structs

Structs are not always put on the stack. They can also live on the heap. You can assign a struct to an object, which results in creating an object in the heap. Such a behavior can be a problem with some types. With .NET Core 2.1, the `Span` type allows access to memory on the stack. Copies of the `Span` type need to be atomic. This can only be guaranteed when the type stays on the stack. Also, the `Span` type can use managed pointers in its fields. Having such pointers on the heap can crash the application when the garbage collector runs. Thus, it needs to be guaranteed that the type stays on the stack.

With a new C# 7.2 language construct, reference types are stored on the heap and value types are typically stored on the stack but also can be stored on the heap. There's also a third type available—a value type that can only exist on the stack.

This type is created by applying the `ref` modifier to a struct as shown in the following code snippet. You can add properties, fields of value, reference types, and methods—just like other structs (code file `RefStructSample/ValueTypeOnly.cs`):

```
ref struct ValueTypeOnly
{
  //...
}
```

What can't be done with this type is to assign it to an object—for example, invoke methods of the `Object` base class such as `ToString`. This would incur boxing and create a reference type, which is not allowed with this type.

> **NOTE** *With most applications you'll not have a need to create a custom* `ref struct` *type. However, for high-performance applications where garbage collection needs to be reduced, there's need for this type. To get more information about* `ref struct` *and the reason for this type, along with* `ref return` *and* `ref locals`, *you should read Chapter 17 with details about the* `Span` *type and more information about* `ref`.

PASSING PARAMETERS BY VALUE AND BY REFERENCE

Let's assume you have a type named `A` with a property of type `int` named `X`. The method `ChangeA` receives a parameter of type `A` and changes the value of `X` to 2 (code file `PassingByValueAndReference/Program.cs`):

```
public static void ChangeA(A a)
{
  a.X = 2;
}
```

The `Main` method creates an instance of type `A`, initializes `X` to 1, and invokes the `ChangeA` method:

```
static void Main()
{
  A a1 = new A { X = 1 };
  ChangeA(a1);
  Console.WriteLine($"a1.X: {a1.X}");
}
```

What would you guess is the output? 1 or 2?

The answer is . . . it depends. You need to know if `A` is a class or a struct. Let's start with `A` as a struct:

```
public struct A
{
  public int X { get; set; }
}
```

Structs are passed by value; with that the variable `a` from the `ChangeA` method gets a copy from the variable `a1` that is put on the stack. Only the copy is changed and destroyed at the end of the method `ChangeA`. The content of `a1` never changes and stays 1.

This is completely different with `A` as a class:

```
public class A
{
  public int X { get; set; }
}
```

Classes are passed by reference. This way, `a` is a variable that references the same object on the heap as the variable `a1`. When `ChangeA` changes the value of the `X` property of `a`, the change makes it `a1.X` because it is the same object. Here, the result is 2.

> **NOTE** *To avoid this confusion on different behavior between classes and structs when members are changed, it's a good practice to make structs immutable. If a struct only has members that don't allow changing the state, you can't get into such a confusing situation. Of course, there's always an exception to the rule to make struct types immutable. The* `ValueTuple` *that is new with C# 7 is implemented as a mutable struct. However, with* `ValueTuple` *the public members are fields instead of properties (which is another violation of a guideline offering public fields). Because of the significance of tuples, and using them in similar ways as* int *and* float, *that's a good reason to violate some guidelines.*

ref Parameters

You can also pass structs by reference. Changing the declaration of the `ChangeA` method by adding the `ref` modifier, the variable is passed by reference—also if `A` is of type struct:

```
public static void ChangeA(ref A a)
{
  a.X = 2;
}
```

It's good to know this from the caller side as well, so with method parameters that have the `ref` modifier applied, this needs to be added on calling the method as well:

```
static void Main()
{
  A a1 = new A { X = 1 };
  ChangeA(ref a1);
  Console.WriteLine($"a1.X: {a1.X}");
}
```

Now the struct is passed by reference, likewise the class type, so the result is 2.

What about using the ref modifier with a class type? Let's change the implementation of the ChangeA method to this:

```
public static void ChangeA(A a)
{
  a.X = 2;
  a = new A { X = 3 };
}
```

Using A of type class, what result can be expected now? Of course, the result from the Main method will not be 1 because a pass by reference is done by class types. Setting a.X to 2, the original object a1 gets changed. However, the next line a = new A { X = 3 } now creates a new object on the heap, and a references the new object. The variable a1 used within the Main method still references the old object with the value 2. After the end of the ChangeA method, the new object on the heap is not referenced and can be garbage collected. So here the result is 2.

Using the ref modifier with A as a class type, a reference to a reference (or in C++ jargon, a pointer to a pointer) is passed, which allows allocating a new object, and the Main method shows the result 3:

```
public static void ChangeA(ref A a)
{
  a.X = 2;
  a = new A { X = 3 };
}
```

Finally, it is important to understand that C# continues to apply initialization requirements to parameters passed to methods. Any variable must be initialized before it is passed into a method, whether it is passed in by value or by reference.

> **NOTE** *With C# 7, you also can use the* ref *keyword with local variables and with the return type of a method. This new feature is discussed in Chapter 17.*

out Parameters

If a method returns one value, the method usually declares a return type and returns the result. What about returning multiple values from a method, maybe with different types? There are different options to do this. One option is to declare a class and struct and define all the information that should be returned as members of this type. Another option is to use a tuple type. Tuples are explained in Chapter 13, "Functional Programming with C#." The third option is to use the out keyword.

Let's get into an example by using the Parse method that is defined with the Int32 type. The ReadLine method gets a string from user input. Assuming the user enters a number, the int.Parse method converts the string and returns the number (code file OutKeywordSample/Program.cs):

```
string input1 = Console.ReadLine();
int result1 = int.Parse(input1);
Console.WriteLine($"result: {result1}");
```

However, users do not always enter the data you would like them to enter. In case the user does not enter a number, an exception is thrown. Of course, it is possible to catch the exception and work with the user accordingly, but this is not a good idea to do for a "normal" case. Maybe it can be assumed to be the "normal" case that the user enters wrong data. Dealing with exceptions is covered in Chapter 14, "Errors and Exceptions."

A better way to deal with the wrong type of data is to use a different method of the Int32 type: TryParse. TryParse is declared to return a bool type whether the parsing is successful or not. The result of the parsing (if it was successful) is returned with a parameter using the out modifier:

```
public static bool TryParse(string s, out int result);
```

Invoking this method, the result variable doesn't need to be initialized beforehand; the variable is initialized within the method. With C# 7, the variable can also be declared on method invocation. Similar to the ref keyword, the out keyword needs to be supplied on calling the method and not only with the method declaration:

```
string input2 = ReadLine();
if (int.TryParse(input2, out int result2))
{
  Console.WriteLine($"result: {result2}");
}
else
{
  Console.WriteLine("not a number");
}
```

> **NOTE** out var *is a new feature of C# 7. Before C# 7, an* out *variable needed to be declared before invoking the method. With C# 7, the declaration can happen calling the method. You can declare the variable using the* var *keyword (that's why the feature is known by* out var*), if the type is unambiguously defined by the method signature. You can also define the concrete type, as was shown in the previous code snippet. The scope of the variable is valid after the method invocation.*

in Parameters

C# 7.2 adds the in modifier to parameters. The out modifier allows returning values specified with the arguments. The in modifier guarantees the data that is sent into the method does not change (when passing a value type).

Let's define a simple mutable struct with the name AValueType and a public mutable field (code file InParameterSample/AValueType.cs):

```
struct AValueType
{
  public int Data;
}
```

Now when you define a method using the in modifier, the variable cannot be changed. Trying to change the mutable field Data, the compiler complains about not being able to assign a value to a member of the read-only variable because the variable is readonly. The in modifier makes the parameter a readonly variable (code file InParameterSample/Program.cs):

```
static void CantChange(in AValueType a)
{
  // a.Data = 43;  // does not compile - readonly variable
  Console.WriteLine(a.Data);
}
```

When invoking the method CantChange, you can invoke the method with or without passing the in modifier. This doesn't have an effect on the generated code.

Using value types with the in modifier not only helps to ensure that the memory cannot be changed but the compiler also can create better optimized code. Instead of copying the value type with the method invocation, the compiler can use references instead, and thus reduces the memory needed and increases performance.

> **NOTE** *The* in *modifier is mainly used with value types. However, you can use it with reference types as well. When using the* in *modifier with reference types, you can change the content of the variable, but not the variable itself.*

NULLABLE TYPES

Variables of reference types (classes) can be null while variables of value types (structs) cannot. This can be a problem with some scenarios, such as mapping C# types to database or XML types. A database or XML number can be null, whereas an int or double cannot be null.

One way to deal with this conflict is to use classes that map to database number types (which is done by Java). Using reference types that map to database numbers to allow the null value has an important disadvantage: It creates extra overhead. With reference types, the garbage collector is needed to clean up. Value types do not need to be cleaned up by the garbage collector; they are removed from memory when the variable goes out of scope.

C# has a solution for this: nullable types. A nullable type is a value type that can be null. You just have to put the ? after the type (which needs to be a struct). The only overhead a value type has compared to the underlying struct is a Boolean member that tells whether it is null.

With the following code snippet, x1 is a normal int, and x2 is a nullable int. Because x2 is a nullable int, null can be assigned to x2:

```
int x1 = 1;
int? x2 = null;
```

Because an int cannot have a value that cannot be assigned to int?, passing a variable of int to int? always succeeds and is accepted from the compiler:

```
int? x3 = x1;
```

The reverse is not true. int? cannot be directly assigned to int. This can fail, and thus a cast is required:

```
int x4 = (int)x3;
```

Of course, the cast generates an exception in a case where x3 is null. A better way to deal with that is to use the HasValue and Value properties of nullable types. HasValue returns true or false, depending on whether the nullable type has a value, and Value returns the underlying value. Using the conditional operator, x5 gets filled without possible exceptions. In a case where x3 is null, HasValue returns false, and here –1 is supplied to the variable x5:

```
int x5 = x3.HasValue ? x3.Value : -1;
```

Using the coalescing operator ??, there's a shorter syntax possible with nullable types. In a case where x3 is null, –1 is set with the variable x6; otherwise you take the value of x3:

```
int x6 = x3 ?? -1;
```

> **NOTE** With nullable types, you can use all operators that are available with the underlying types—for example, +, -, *, / and more with `int?`. *You can use nullable types with every struct type, not only with predefined C# types. You can read more about nullable types and what's behind the scenes in Chapter 5, "Generics."*

ENUM TYPES

An enumeration is a value type that contains a list of named constants, such as the `Color` type shown here. The enumeration type is defined by using the `enum` keyword (code file `EnumSample/Color.cs`):

```
public enum Color
{
  Red,
  Green,
  Blue
}
```

You can declare variables of `enum` types, such as the variable `c1`, and assign a value from the enumeration by setting one of the named constants prefixed with the name of the enum type (code file `EnumSample/Program.cs`):

```
private static void ColorSamples()
{
  Color c1 = Color.Red;
  Console.WriteLine(c1);
  //...
}
```

Running the program, the console output shows `Red`, which is the constant value of the enumeration.

By default, the type behind the enum type is an `int`. The underlying type can be changed to other integral types (byte, short, int, long with signed and unsigned variants). The values of the named constants are incremental values starting with 0, but they can be changed to other values:

```
public enum Color : short
{
  Red = 1,
  Green = 2,
  Blue = 3
}
```

You can change a number to an enumeration value and back using casts.

```
Color c2 = (Color)2;
short number = (short)c2;
```

You can also use an enum type to assign multiple options to a variable and not just one of the enum constants. To do this, the values assigned to the constants must be different bits, and the `Flags` attribute needs to be set with the enum.

The enum type `DaysOfWeek` defines different values for every day. Setting different bits can be done easily using hexadecimal values that are assigned using the `0x` prefix. The `Flags` attribute is information for the compiler for creating a different string representation of the values—for example, setting the value 3 to a variable of DaysOfWeek results in Monday, Tuesday when the Flags attribute is used (code file EnumSample/DaysOfWeek.cs):

```
[Flags]
public enum DaysOfWeek
{
  Monday = 0x1,
  Tuesday = 0x2,
  Wednesday = 0x4,
  Thursday = 0x8,
  Friday = 0x10,
  Saturday = 0x20,
  Sunday = 0x40
}
```

With such an enum declaration, you can assign a variable multiple values using the logical OR operator (code file EnumSample/Program.cs):

```
DaysOfWeek mondayAndWednesday = DaysOfWeek.Monday | DaysOfWeek.Wednesday;
Console.WriteLine(mondayAndWednesday);
```

Running the program, the output is a string representation of the days:

```
Monday, Tuesday
```

Setting different bits, it is also possible to combine single bits to cover multiple values, such as Weekend with a value of 0x60 that combines Saturday and Sunday with the logical OR operator, Workday to combine all the days from Monday to Friday, and AllWeek to combine Workday and Weekend with the logical OR operator (code file EnumSample/DaysOfWeek.cs):

```
[Flags]
public enum DaysOfWeek
{
  Monday = 0x1,
  Tuesday = 0x2,
  Wednesday = 0x4,
  Thursday = 0x8,
  Friday = 0x10,
  Saturday = 0x20,
  Sunday = 0x40,
  Weekend = Saturday | Sunday
  Workday = 0x1f,
  AllWeek = Workday | Weekend
}
```

With this in place, it's possible to assign DaysOfWeek.Weekend directly to a variable, but also assigning the separate values DaysOfWeek.Saturday and DaysOfWeek.Sunday combined with the logical OR operator results in the same. The output shown is the string representation of Weekend.

```
DaysOfWeek weekend = DaysOfWeek.Saturday | DaysOfWeek.Sunday;
Console.WriteLine(weekend);
```

Working with enumerations, the class Enum is sometimes a big help for dynamically getting some information about enum types. Enum offers methods to parse strings to get the corresponding enumeration constant, and to get all the names and values of an enum type.

The following code snippet uses a string to get the corresponding Color value using Enum.TryParse (code file EnumSample/Program.cs):

```
Color red;
if (Enum.TryParse<Color>("Red", out red))
{
  Console.WriteLine($"successfully parsed {red}");
}
```

> **NOTE** `Enum.TryParse<T>()` *is a generic method where* `T` *is a generic parameter type. This parameter type needs to be defined with the method invocation. Generic methods are explained in detail in Chapter 5.*

The `Enum.GetNames` method returns a string array of all the names of the enumeration:

```
foreach (var day in Enum.GetNames(typeof(Color)))
{
    Console.WriteLine(day);
}
```

When you run the application, this is the output:

```
Red
Green
Blue
```

To get all the values of the enumeration, you can use the method `Enum.GetValues`. `Enum.GetValues` returns an `Array` of the enum values. To get the integral value, it needs to be cast to the underlying type of the enumeration, which is done by the `foreach` statement:

```
foreach (short val in Enum.GetValues(typeof(Color)))
{
    Console.WriteLine(val);
}
```

PARTIAL CLASSES

The `partial` keyword allows the class, struct, method, or interface to span multiple files. Typically, a code generator of some type is generating part of a class, and so having the class in multiple files can be beneficial. Let's assume you want to make some additions to the class that is automatically generated from a tool. If the tool reruns then your changes are lost. The `partial` keyword is helpful for splitting the class in two files and making your changes to the file that is not defined by the code generator.

To use the `partial` keyword, simply place `partial` before `class`, `struct`, or `interface`. In the following example, the class `SampleClass` resides in two separate source files, `SampleClassAutogenerated.cs` and `SampleClass.cs`:

```
SampleClass.cs:
//SampleClassAutogenerated.cs
partial class SampleClass
{
    public void MethodOne() { }
}

//SampleClass.cs
partial class SampleClass
{
    public void MethodTwo() { }
}
```

When the project that these two source files are part of is compiled, a single type called `SampleClass` will be created with two methods: `MethodOne` and `MethodTwo`.

If any of the following keywords are used in describing the class, the same must apply to all partials of the same type:

➤ `public`

➤ `private`

- ➤ protected
- ➤ internal
- ➤ abstract
- ➤ sealed
- ➤ new
- ➤ generic constraints

Nested partials are allowed as long as the `partial` keyword precedes the `class` keyword in the nested type. Attributes, XML comments, interfaces, generic-type parameter attributes, and members are combined when the partial types are compiled into the type. Given these two source files:

```
// SampleClassAutogenerated.cs
[CustomAttribute]
partial class SampleClass: SampleBaseClass, ISampleClass
{
  public void MethodOne() { }
}

// SampleClass.cs
[AnotherAttribute]
partial class SampleClass: IOtherSampleClass
{
  public void MethodTwo() { }
}
```

the equivalent source file would be as follows after the compile:

```
[CustomAttribute]
[AnotherAttribute]
partial class SampleClass: SampleBaseClass, ISampleClass, IOtherSampleClass
{
  public void MethodOne() { }
  public void MethodTwo() { }
}
```

> **NOTE** *Although it may be tempting to create huge classes that span multiple files and possibly having different developers working on different files but the same class, the* partial *keyword was not designed for this use. With such a scenario, it would be better to split the big class into several smaller classes, having a class just for one purpose.*

Partial classes can contain *partial methods*. This is extremely useful if generated code should invoke methods that might not exist at all. The programmer extending the partial class can decide to create a custom implementation of the partial method, or do nothing. The following code snippet contains a partial class with the method `MethodOne` that invokes the method `APartialMethod`. The method `APartialMethod` is declared with the partial keyword; thus, it does not need any implementation. If there's not an implementation, the compiler removes the invocation of this method:

```
//SampleClassAutogenerated.cs
partial class SampleClass
{
  public void MethodOne()
  {
    APartialMethod();
  }
  public partial void APartialMethod();
}
```

An implementation of the partial method can be done within any other part of the partial class, as shown in the following code snippet. With this method in place, the compiler creates code within `MethodOne` to invoke this `APartialMethod` declared here:

```
// SampleClass.cs
partial class SampleClass: IOtherSampleClass
{
  public void APartialMethod()
  {
    // implementation of APartialMethod
  }
}
```

A partial method needs to be of type `void`. Otherwise the compiler cannot remove the invocation in case no implementation exists.

EXTENSION METHODS

There are many ways to extend a class. Inheritance, which is covered in Chapter 4, is a great way to add functionality to your objects. Extension methods are another option that can also be used to add functionality to classes. This option is also possible when inheritance cannot be used (for example, the class is sealed).

> **NOTE** *Extension methods can be used to extend interfaces. This way you can have common functionality for all the classes that implement this interface. Interfaces are explained in Chapter 4.*

Extension methods are static methods that can look like part of a class without actually being in the source code for the class.

Let's say you want the `string` type to be extended with a method to count the number of words within a string. The method `GetWordCount` makes use of the `String.Split` method to split up a string in a string array, and counts the number of elements within the array using the `Length` property (code file ExtensionMethods/Program.cs):

```
ExtensionMethods/Program.cs):
public static class StringExtension
{
  public static int GetWordCount(this string s) => s.Split().Length;
}
```

The `string` is extended by using the `this` keyword with the first parameter. This keyword defines the type that is extended.

Even though the extension method is static, you use standard method syntax. Notice that you call `GetWordCount` using the `fox` variable and not using the type name:

```
string fox = "the quick brown fox jumped over the lazy dogs down " +
"9876543210 times";
int wordCount = fox.GetWordCount();
Console.WriteLine($"{wordCount} words");
```

Behind the scenes, the compiler changes this to invoke the static method instead:

```
int wordCount = StringExtension.GetWordCount(fox);
```

Using the instance method syntax instead of calling a static method from your code directly results in a much nicer syntax. This syntax also has the advantage that the implementation of this method can be replaced by a different class without the need to change the code—just a new compiler run is needed.

How does the compiler find an extension method for a specific type? The this keyword is needed to match an extension method for a type, but also the namespace of the static class that defines the extension method needs to be opened. If you put the StringExtensions class within the namespace Wrox.Extensions, the compiler finds the GetWordCount method only if Wrox.Extensions is opened with the using directive. In case the type also defines an instance method with the same name, the extension method is never used. Any instance method already in the class takes precedence. When you have multiple extension methods with the same name to extend the same type, and when all the namespaces of these types are opened, the compiler results in an error that the call is ambiguous and it cannot decide between multiple implementations. If, however, the calling code is in one of these namespaces, this namespace takes precedence.

> **NOTE** *Language Integrated Query (LINQ) makes use of many extension methods. LINQ is discussed in Chapter 12, "Language Integrated Query."*

THE OBJECT CLASS

As indicated earlier, all .NET classes are ultimately derived from System.Object. In fact, if you don't specify a base class when you define a class, the compiler automatically assumes that it derives from Object. Because inheritance has not been used in this chapter, every class you have seen here is actually derived from System.Object. (As noted earlier, for structs this derivation is indirect—a struct is always derived from System.ValueType, which in turn derives from System.Object.)

The practical significance of this is that—besides the methods, properties, and so on that you define—you also have access to a number of public and protected member methods that have been defined for the Object class. These methods are available in all other classes that you define.

For the time being, the following list summarizes the purpose of each method:

> ToString—A fairly basic, quick-and-easy string representation. Use it when you want a quick idea of the contents of an object, perhaps for debugging purposes. It provides very little choice regarding how to format the data. For example, dates can, in principle, be expressed in a huge variety of formats, but DateTime.ToString does not offer you any choice in this regard. If you need a more sophisticated string representation—for example, one that takes into account your formatting preferences or the culture (the locale)—then you should implement the IFormattable interface (see Chapter 9, "Strings and Regular Expressions").

> GetHashCode—If objects are placed in a data structure known as a map (also known as a hash table or dictionary), it is used by classes that manipulate these structures to determine where to place an object in the structure. If you intend your class to be used as a key for a dictionary, you need to override GetHashCode. Some fairly strict requirements exist for how you implement your overload, which you learn about when you examine dictionaries in Chapter 10, "Collections."

> Equals (both versions) and ReferenceEquals—As you'll note by the existence of three different methods aimed at comparing the equality of objects, the .NET Framework has quite a sophisticated scheme for measuring equality. Subtle differences exist between how these three methods, along with the comparison operator, ==, are intended to be used. In addition, restrictions exist on how you should override the virtual, one-parameter version of Equals if you choose to do so, because certain base classes in the System.Collections namespace call the method and expect it to behave in certain ways. You explore the use of these methods in Chapter 6 when you examine operators.

> Finalize—Covered in Chapter 17, this method is intended as the nearest that C# has to C++-style destructors. It is called when a reference object is garbage collected to clean up resources. The Object implementation of Finalize doesn't actually do anything and is ignored by the garbage collector. You normally override Finalize if an object owns references to unmanaged resources that need to

be removed when the object is deleted. The garbage collector cannot do this directly because it only knows about managed resources, so it relies on any finalizers that you supply.

➤ GetType—This object returns an instance of a class derived from System.Type, so it can provide an extensive range of information about the class of which your object is a member, including base type, methods, properties, and so on. System.Type also provides the entry point into .NET's reflection technology. Chapter 16 examines this topic.

➤ MemberwiseClone—The only member of System.Object that isn't examined in detail anywhere in the book. That's because it is fairly simple in concept. It just makes a copy of the object and returns a reference (or in the case of a value type, a boxed reference) to the copy. Note that the copy made is a shallow copy, meaning it copies all the value types in the class. If the class contains any embedded references, then only the references are copied, not the objects referred to. This method is protected and cannot be called to copy external objects. Nor is it virtual, so you cannot override its implementation.

SUMMARY

This chapter examined C# syntax for declaring and manipulating objects. You have seen how to declare static and instance fields, properties, methods, and constructors. You have also seen new features that have been added with C# 7, such as expression-bodied members with constructors, property accessors, and out vars.

You have also seen how all types in C# derive ultimately from the type System.Object, which means that all types start with a basic set of useful methods, including ToString.

Inheritance comes up a few times throughout this chapter, and you examine implementation, interface inheritance, and the other aspects of object-orientation with C# in Chapter 4.

Object-Oriented Programming with C#

WHAT'S IN THIS CHAPTER?

➤ Types of inheritance
➤ Implementation inheritance
➤ Access modifiers
➤ Interfaces
➤ is and as Operators

WROX.COM CODE DOWNLOADS FOR THIS CHAPTER

The Wrox.com code downloads for this chapter are found at www.wrox.com on the Download Code tab. The source code is also available at https://github.com/ProfessionalCSharp/ProfessionalCSharp7 in the directory ObjectOrientation.

The code for this chapter is divided into the following major examples:

➤ VirtualMethods
➤ InheritanceWithConstructors
➤ UsingInterfaces

OBJECT ORIENTATION

C# is not a pure object-oriented programming language. C# offers multiple programming paradigms. However, object orientation is an important concept with C#, and it's a core principle of all the libraries offered by .NET.

The three most important concepts of object-orientation are *inheritance*, *encapsulation*, and *polymorphism*. Chapter 3, "Objects and Types," talks about creating individual classes to arrange properties, methods, and fields. When members of a type are declared private, they cannot be accessed from the outside. They are *encapsulated* within the type. This chapter's focus is on inheritance and polymorphism.

The previous chapter also explains that all classes ultimately derive from the class `System.Object`. This chapter covers how to create a hierarchy of classes and how polymorphism works with C#. It also describes all the C# keywords related to inheritance.

TYPES OF INHERITANCE

Let's start by reviewing some object-oriented (OO) terms and look at what C# does and does not support as far as inheritance is concerned.

> **Single inheritance**—With single inheritance, one class can derive from one base class. This is a possible scenario with C#.

> **Multiple inheritance**—Multiple inheritance allows deriving from multiple base classes. C# does not support multiple inheritance with classes, but it allows multiple inheritance with interfaces.

> **Multilevel inheritance**—Multilevel inheritance allows inheritance across a bigger hierarchy. Class B derives from class A, and class C derives from class B. Here, class B is also known as intermediate base class. This is supported and often used with C#.

> **Interface inheritance**—Interface inheritance defines inheritance with interfaces. Here, multiple inheritance is possible. Interfaces and interface inheritance is explained later in this chapter in the "Interfaces" section.

Let's discuss some specific issues with inheritance and C#.

Multiple Inheritance

Some languages such as C++ support what is known as *multiple inheritance*, in which a class derives from more than one other class. With implementation inheritance, multiple inheritance adds complexity and also overhead to the generated code even in cases where multiple inheritance is not used. Because of this, the designers of C# decided not to support multiple inheritance with classes because support for multiple inheritance increases complexity and adds overhead even in cases when multiple inheritance is not used.

C# does allow types to be derived from multiple interfaces. One type can *implement multiple interfaces*. This means that a C# class can be derived from one other class, and any number of interfaces. Indeed, we can be more precise: Thanks to the presence of `System.Object` as a common base type, every C# class (except for `Object`) has exactly one base class, and every C# class may additionally have any number of base interfaces.

Structs and Classes

Chapter 3 distinguishes between structs (value types) and classes (reference types). One restriction of using structs is that they do not support inheritance, beyond the fact that every struct is automatically derived from `System.ValueType`. Although it's true that you cannot code a type hierarchy of structs, it is possible for structs to implement interfaces. In other words, structs don't really support implementation inheritance, but they do support interface inheritance. The following summarizes the situation for any types that you define:

> *Structs* are always derived from `System.ValueType`. They can also implement any number of interfaces.

> *Classes* are always derived from either `System.Object` or a class that you choose. They can also implement any number of interfaces.

IMPLEMENTATION INHERITANCE

If you want to declare that a class derives from another class, use the following syntax:

```
class MyDerivedClass: MyBaseClass
```

```
{
  // members
}
```

If a class (or a struct) also derives from interfaces, the list of base class and interfaces is separated by commas:

```
public class MyDerivedClass: MyBaseClass, IInterface1, IInterface2
{
  // members
}
```

> **NOTE** *In case a class and interfaces are used to derive from, the class always must come first—before interfaces.*

For a struct, the syntax is as follows (it can only use interface inheritance):

```
public struct MyDerivedStruct: IInterface1, IInterface2
{
  // members
}
```

If you do not specify a base class in a class definition, the C# compiler assumes that `System.Object` is the base class. Hence, deriving from the `Object` class (or using the `object` keyword) is the same as not defining a base class.

```
class MyClass // implicitly derives from System.Object
{
  // members
}
```

Let's get into an example to define a base class `Shape`. Something that's common with shapes—no matter whether they are rectangles or ellipses—is that they have position and size. For position and size, corresponding classes are defined that are contained within the `Shape` class. The `Shape` class defines read-only properties `Position` and `Shape` that are initialized using auto property initializers (code file `VirtualMethods/Shape.cs`):

```
public class Position
{
  public int X { get; set; }
  public int Y { get; set; }
}

public class Size
{
  public int Width { get; set; }
  public int Height { get; set; }
}

public class Shape
{
  public Position Position { get; } = new Position();
  public Size Size { get; } = new Size();
}
```

Virtual Methods

By declaring a base class method as `virtual`, you allow the method to be overridden in any derived classes:

```
public class Shape
{
  public virtual void Draw() =>
    Console.WriteLine($"Shape with {Position} and {Size}");
}
```

In case the implementation is a one-liner, expression bodied methods (using the lambda operator) can also be used with the virtual keyword. This syntax can be used independent of the modifiers applied:

```
public class Shape
{
  public virtual void Draw() =>
    Console.WriteLine($"Shape with {Position} and {Size}");
}
```

It is also permitted to declare a property as virtual. For a virtual or overridden property, the syntax is the same as for a non-virtual property, with the exception of the keyword virtual, which is added to the definition. The syntax looks like this:

```
public virtual Size Size { get; set; }
```

Of course, it is also possible to use the full property syntax for virtual properties. The following code snippet makes use of C# 7 expression-bodied property accessors:

```
private Size _size;
public virtual Size Size
{
  get => _size;
  set => _size = value;
}
```

For simplicity, the following discussion focuses mainly on methods, but it applies equally well to properties.

The concepts behind virtual functions in C# are identical to standard OOP concepts. You can override a virtual function in a derived class; when the method is called, the appropriate method for the type of object is invoked. In C#, functions are not virtual by default but (aside from constructors) can be explicitly declared as virtual. This follows the C++ methodology: For performance reasons, functions are not virtual unless indicated. In Java, by contrast, all functions are virtual. C# differs from C++ syntax, though, because it requires you to declare when a derived class's function overrides another function, using the override keyword (code file VirtualMethods/ConcreteShapes.cs):

```
public class Rectangle : Shape
{
  public override void Draw() =>
    Console.WriteLine($"Rectangle with {Position} and {Size}");
}
```

This syntax for method overriding removes potential runtime bugs that can easily occur in C++, when a method signature in a derived class unintentionally differs slightly from the base version, resulting in the method failing to override the base version. In C#, this is picked up as a compile-time error because the compiler would see a function marked as override but would not see a base method for it to override.

The Size and Position types override the ToString method. This method is declared as virtual in the base class Object:

```
public class Position
{
  public int X { get; set; }
  public int Y { get; set; }
  public override string ToString() => $"X: {X}, Y: {Y}";
}

public class Size
{
  public int Width { get; set; }
  public int Height { get; set; }
  public override string ToString() => $"Width: {Width}, Height: {Height}";
}
```

> **NOTE** *The members of the base class* Object *are explained in Chapter 3.*

> **NOTE** *When overriding methods of the base class, the signature (all parameter types and the method name) and the return type must match exactly. If this is not the case then you can create a new member that does not override the base member.*

Within the Main method, a rectangle named r is instantiated, its properties initialized, and the method Draw invoked (code file VirtualMethods/Program.cs):

```
var r = new Rectangle();
r.Position.X = 33;
r.Position.Y = 22;
r.Size.Width = 200;
r.Size.Height = 100;
r.Draw();
```

Run the program to see the output of the Draw method:

```
Rectangle with X: 33, Y: 22 and Width: 200, Height: 100
```

Neither member fields nor static functions can be declared as virtual. The concept simply wouldn't make sense for any class member other than an instance function member.

Polymorphism

With polymorphism, the method that is invoked is defined dynamically and not during compile time. The compiler creates a virtual method table (vtable) that lists the methods that can be invoked during runtime, and it invokes the method based on the type at runtime.

Let's have a look at one example. The method DrawShape receives a Shape parameter and invokes the Draw method of the Shape class (code file VirtualMethods/Program.cs):

```
public static void DrawShape(Shape shape) => shape.Draw();
```

Use the rectangle created before to invoke the method. Although the method is declared to receive a Shape object, any type that derives from Shape (including the Rectangle) can be passed to this method:

Run the program to see the output of the Rectangle.Draw method instead of the Shape.Draw method. The output line starts with Rectangle. If the method of the base class wouldn't be virtual or the method from the derived class not overridden, the Draw method of the type of the declared object (the Shape) would be used, and thus the output would start with Shape:

```
Rectangle with X: 33, Y: 22 and Width: 200, Height: 100
```

Hiding Methods

If a method with the same signature is declared in both base and derived classes but the methods are not declared with the modifiers virtual and override, respectively, then the derived class version is said to *hide* the base class version.

In most cases, you would want to override methods rather than hide them. By hiding them you risk calling the wrong method for a given class instance. However, as shown in the following example, C# syntax is designed to ensure that the developer is warned at compile time about this potential problem, thus making it safer to hide methods if that is your intention. This also has versioning benefits for developers of class libraries.

Suppose that you have a class called Shape in a class library:

```
public class Shape
{
  // various members
}
```

At some point in the future, you write a derived class Ellipse that adds some functionality to the Shape base class. In particular, you add a method called MoveBy, which is not present in the base class:

```
public class Ellipse: Shape
{
  public void MoveBy(int x, int y)
  {
    Position.X += x;
    Position.Y += y;
  }
}
```

At some later time, the developer of the base class decides to extend the functionality of the base class and, by coincidence, adds a method that is also called MoveBy and that has the same name and signature as yours; however, it probably doesn't do the same thing. This new method might be declared virtual or not.

If you recompile the derived class you get a compiler warning because of a potential method clash. However, it can also happen easily that the new base class is used without compiling the derived class; it just replaces the base class assembly. The base class assembly could be installed in the global assembly cache (which is done by many Framework assemblies).

Now let's assume the MoveBy method of the base class is declared virtual and the base class itself invokes the MoveBy method. What method will be called? The method of the base class or the MoveBy method of the derived class that was defined earlier? Because the MoveBy method of the derived class is not defined with the override keyword (this was not possible because the base class MoveBy method didn't exist earlier), the compiler assumes the MoveBy method from the derived class is a completely different method that doesn't have any relation to the method of the base class; it just has the same name. This method is treated the same way as if it had a different name.

Compiling the Ellipse class generates a compilation warning that reminds you to use the new keyword to hide a method. In practice, not using the new keyword has the same compilation result, but you avoid the compiler warning:

```
public class Ellipse: Shape
{
  new public void Move(Position newPosition)
  {
    Position.X = newPosition.X;
    Position.Y = newPosition.Y;
  }
  //... other members
}
```

Instead of using the new keyword, you can also rename the method or override the method of the base class if it is declared virtual and serves the same purpose. However, in case other methods already invoke this method, a simple rename can lead to breaking other code.

> **NOTE** *The* new *method modifier shouldn't be used deliberately to hide members of the base class. The main purpose of this modifier is to deal with version conflicts and react to changes on base classes after the derived class was done.*

Calling Base Versions of Methods

C# has a special syntax for calling base versions of a method from a derived class: `base.<MethodName>`. For example, you have the `Move` method declared in the base class `Shape` and want to invoke it in the derived class `Rectangle` to use the implementation from the base class. To add functionality from the derived class, you can invoke it using base (code file `VirtualMethods/Shape.cs`):

```
public class Shape
{
  public virtual void Move(Position newPosition)
  {
    Position.X = newPosition.X;
    Position.Y = newPosition.Y;
    Console.WriteLine($"moves to {Position}");
  }
  //...other members
}
```

The `Move` method is overridden in the `Rectangle` class to add the term `Rectangle` to the console. After this text is written, the method of the base class is invoked using the base keyword (code file `VirtualMethods/ConcreteShapes.cs`):

```
public class Rectangle: Shape
{
  public override void Move(Position newPosition)
  {
    Console.Write("Rectangle ");
    base.Move(newPosition);
  }
  //...other members
}
```

Now move the rectangle to a new position (code file `VirtualMethods/Program.cs`):

```
r.Move(new Position { X = 120, Y = 40 });
```

Run the application to see output that is a result of the `Move` method in the `Rectangle` and the `Shape` classes:

```
Rectangle moves to X: 120, Y: 40
```

> **NOTE** *Using the* base *keyword, you can invoke any method of the base class—not just the method that is overridden.*

Abstract Classes and Methods

C# allows both classes and methods to be declared as abstract. An abstract class cannot be instantiated, whereas an abstract method does not have an implementation and must be overridden in any nonabstract derived class. Obviously, an abstract method is *automatically* virtual (although you don't need to supply the `virtual` keyword, and doing so results in a syntax error). If any class contains any abstract methods, that class is also abstract and must be declared as such.

Let's change the `Shape` class to be `abstract`. With this it is necessary to derive from this class. The new method `Resize` is declared abstract, and thus it can't have any implementation in the `Shape` class (code file `VirtualMethods/Shape.cs`):

```
public abstract class Shape
{
  public abstract void Resize(int width, int height); // abstract method
}
```

When deriving a type from the abstract base class, it is necessary to implement all abstract members. Otherwise, the compiler complains:

```
public class Ellipse : Shape
{
  public override void Resize(int width, int height)
  {
    Size.Width = width;
    Size.Height = height;
  }
}
```

Of course, the implementation could also look like the following example. Throwing an exception of type `NotImplementationException` is also an implementation, just not the implementation that was meant to be and usually just a temporary implementation during development:

```
public override void Resize(int width, int height)
{
  throw new NotImplementedException();
}
```

> **NOTE** *Exceptions are explained in detail in Chapter 14, "Errors and Exceptions."*

Using the abstract `Shape` class and the derived `Ellipse` class, you can declare a variable of a `Shape`. You cannot instantiate it, but you can instantiate an `Ellipse` and assign it to the `Shape` variable (code file `VirtualMethods/Program.cs`):

```
Shape s1 = new Ellipse();
DrawShape(s1);
```

Sealed Classes and Methods

In case it shouldn't be allowed to create a class that derives from your class, your class should be sealed. Adding the `sealed` modifier to a class doesn't allow you to create a subclass of it. Sealing a method means it's not possible to override this method.

```
sealed class FinalClass
{
  //...
}

class DerivedClass: FinalClass // wrong. Cannot derive from sealed class.
{
  //...
}
```

The most likely situation in which you'll mark a class or method as `sealed` is if the class or method is internal to the operation of the library, class, or other classes that you are writing, to ensure that any attempt to override some of its functionality might lead to instability in the code. For example, maybe you haven't tested inheritance and made the investment in design decisions for inheritance. If this is the case, it's better to mark your class `sealed`.

There's another reason to seal classes. With a sealed class, the compiler knows that derived classes are not possible, and thus the virtual table used for virtual methods can be reduced or eliminated, which can increase performance. The string class is sealed. As I haven't seen a single application not using strings, it's best to have this type as performant as possible. Making the class sealed is a good hint for the compiler.

Declaring a method as sealed serves a purpose similar to that for a class. The method can be an overridden method from a base class, but in the following example the compiler knows another class cannot extend the virtual table for this method; it ends here.

```
class MyClass: MyBaseClass
{
  public sealed override void FinalMethod()
  {
    // implementation
  }
}

class DerivedClass: MyClass
{
  public override void FinalMethod() // wrong. Will give compilation error
  {
  }
}
```

In order to use the sealed keyword on a method or property, it must have first been overridden from a base class. If you do not want a method or property in a base class overridden, then don't mark it as virtual.

Constructors of Derived Classes

Chapter 3 discusses how constructors can be applied to individual classes. An interesting question arises as to what happens when you start defining your own constructors for classes that are part of a hierarchy, inherited from other classes that may also have custom constructors.

Assume that you have not defined any explicit constructors for any of your classes. This means that the compiler supplies default zeroing-out constructors for all your classes. There is actually quite a lot going on under the hood when that happens, but the compiler is able to arrange it so that things work out nicely throughout the class hierarchy, and every field in every class is initialized to whatever its default value is. When you add a constructor of your own, however, you are effectively taking control of construction. This has implications right down through the hierarchy of derived classes, so you have to ensure that you don't inadvertently do anything to prevent construction through the hierarchy from taking place smoothly.

You might be wondering why there is any special problem with derived classes. The reason is that when you create an instance of a derived class, more than one constructor is at work. The constructor of the class you instantiate isn't by itself sufficient to initialize the class; the constructors of the base classes must also be called. That's why we've been talking about construction through the hierarchy.

With the earlier sample of the Shape type, properties have been initialized using the auto property initializer:

```
public class Shape
{
  public Position Position { get; } = new Position();
  public Size Size { get; } = new Size();
}
```

Behind the scenes, the compiler creates a default constructor for the class and moves the property initializer within this constructor:

```
public class Shape
{
  public Shape()
  {
    Position = new Position();
    Size = new Size();
  }

  public Position Position { get; };
  public Size Size { get; };
}
```

Of course, instantiating a `Rectangle` type that derives from the `Shape` class, the `Rectangle` needs `Position` and `Size`, and thus the constructor from the base class is invoked on constructing the derived object.

In case you don't initialize members within the default constructor, the compiler automatically initializes reference types to `null` and value types to `0`. Boolean types are initialized to `false`. The Boolean type is a value type, and `false` is the same as `0`, so it's the same rule that applies to the Boolean type.

With the `Ellipse` class, it's not necessary to create a default constructor if the base class defines a default constructor and you're okay with initializing all members to their defaults. Of course, you still can supply a constructor and call the base constructor using a *constructor initializer*:

```
public class Ellipse : Shape
{
  public Ellipse()
    : base()
  {
  }
}
```

The constructors are always called in the order of the hierarchy. The constructor of the class `System. Object` is first, and then progress continues down the hierarchy until the compiler reaches the class being instantiated. For instantiating the `Ellipse` type, the `Shape` constructor follows the `Object` constructor, and then the `Ellipse` constructor comes. Each of these constructors handles the initialization of the fields in its own class.

Now, make a change to the constructor of the `Shape` class. Instead of doing a default initialization with `Size` and `Position` properties, assign values within the constructor (code file `InheritanceWithConstructors/ Shape.cs`):

```
public abstract class Shape
{
  public Shape(int width, int height, int x, int y)
  {
    Size = new Size { Width = width, Height = height };
    Position = new Position { X = x, Y = y };
  }

  public Position Position { get; }
  public Size Size { get; }
}
```

When removing the default constructor and recompiling the program, the `Ellipse` and `Rectangle` classes can't compile because the compiler doesn't know what values should be passed to the only nondefault constructor of the base class. Here you need to create a constructor in the derived class and initialize the base class constructor with the *constructor initializer* (code file `InheritanceWithConstructors/ ConcreteShapes.cs`):

```
public Rectangle(int width, int height, int x, int y)
  : base(width, height, x, y)
{
}
```

Putting the initialization inside the constructor block is too late because the constructor of the base class is invoked before the constructor of the derived class is called. That's why there's a constructor initializer that is declared before the constructor block.

In case you want to allow creating `Rectangle` objects by using a default constructor, you can still do this. You can also do it if the constructor of the base class doesn't have a default constructor. You just need to assign the values for the base class constructor in the constructor initializer as shown. In the following snippet, named arguments are used because otherwise it would be hard to distinguish between `width`, `height`, `x`, and `y` values passed.

```
public Rectangle()
  : base(width: 0, height: 0, x: 0, y: 0)
{
}
```

> **NOTE** *Named arguments are discussed in Chapter 3.*

As you can see, this is a very neat and well-designed process. Each constructor handles initialization of the variables that are obviously its responsibility; and, in the process, your class is correctly instantiated and prepared for use. If you follow the same principles when you write your own constructors for your classes, even the most complex classes should be initialized smoothly and without any problems.

MODIFIERS

You have already encountered quite a number of so-called modifiers—keywords that can be applied to a type or a member. Modifiers can indicate the visibility of a method, such as `public` or `private`, or the nature of an item, such as whether a method is `virtual` or `abstract`. C# has a number of modifiers, and at this point it's worth taking a minute to provide the complete list.

Access Modifiers

Access modifiers indicate which other code items can view an item.

MODIFIER	APPLIES TO	DESCRIPTION
public	Any types or members	The item is visible to any other code.
protected	Any member of a type, and any nested type	The item is visible only to any derived type.
internal	Any types or members	The item is visible only within its containing assembly.
private	Any member of a type, and any nested type	The item is visible only inside the type to which it belongs.
protected internal	Any member of a type, and any nested type	The item is visible to any code within its containing assembly and to any code inside a derived type. Practically this means protected or internal, either `protected` (from any assembly) or `internal` (from within the assembly).
private protected	Any member of a type, and any nested type	Contrary to the access modifier `protected internal` which means either `protected` or `internal`, `private protected` combines `protected internal` with an *and*. Access is allowed only for derived types that are within the same assembly, but not from other assemblies. This access modifier is new with C# 7.2.

> **NOTE** `public`, `protected`, *and* `private` *are logical access modifiers.* `internal` *is a physical access modifier whose boundary is an assembly.*

Note that type definitions can be internal or public, depending on whether you want the type to be visible outside its containing assembly:

```
public class MyClass
{
  // ...
```

You cannot define types as protected, private, or protected internal because these visibility levels would be meaningless for a type contained in a namespace. Hence, these visibilities can be applied only to members. However, you can define nested types (that is, types contained within other types) with these visibilities because in this case the type also has the status of a member. Hence, the following code is correct:

```
public class OuterClass
{
  protected class InnerClass
  {
    // ...
  }
  // ...
}
```

If you have a nested type, the inner type is always able to see all members of the outer type. Therefore, with the preceding code, any code inside InnerClass always has access to all members of OuterClass, even where those members are private.

Other Modifiers

The modifiers in the following table can be applied to members of types and have various uses. A few of these modifiers also make sense when applied to types.

MODIFIER	APPLIES TO	DESCRIPTION
new	Function members	The member hides an inherited member with the same signature.
static	All members	The member does not operate on a specific instance of the class. This is also known as *class member* instead of instance member.
virtual	Function members only	The member can be overridden by a derived class.
abstract	Function members only	A virtual member that defines the signature of the member but doesn't provide an implementation.
override	Function members only	The member overrides an inherited virtual or abstract member.
sealed	Classes, methods, and properties	For classes, the class cannot be inherited from. For properties and methods, the member overrides an inherited virtual member but cannot be overridden by any members in any derived classes. Must be used in conjunction with override.
extern	Static [DllImport] methods only	The member is implemented externally, in a different language. The use of this keyword is explained in Chapter 17, "Managed and Unmanaged Memory."

INTERFACES

As mentioned earlier, by deriving from an interface, a class is declaring that it implements certain functions. Because not all object-oriented languages support interfaces, this section examines C#'s implementation of interfaces in detail. It illustrates interfaces by presenting the complete definition of one of the interfaces that has been predefined by Microsoft: `System.IDisposable`. `IDisposable` contains one method, `Dispose`, which is intended to be implemented by classes to clean up resources:

```
public interface IDisposable
{
  void Dispose();
}
```

This code shows that declaring an interface works syntactically in much the same way as declaring an abstract class. Be aware, however, that it is not permitted to supply implementations of any of the members of an interface. In general, an interface can contain only declarations of methods, properties, indexers, and events.

Compare interfaces to abstract classes: An abstract class can have implementations or abstract members without implementation. However, an interface can never have any implementation; it is purely abstract. Because the members of an interface are always abstract, the `abstract` keyword is not needed with interfaces.

Similarly to abstract classes, you can never instantiate an interface; it contains only the signatures of its members. In addition, you can declare variables of a type of an interface.

An interface has neither constructors (how can you construct something that you can't instantiate?) nor fields (because that would imply some internal implementation). An interface is also not allowed to contain operator overloads—although this possibility is always discussed with the language design and might change at some time in the future.

It's also not permitted to declare modifiers on the members in an interface definition. Interface members are always implicitly `public`, and they cannot be declared as `virtual`. That's up to implementing classes to decide. Therefore, it is fine for implementing classes to declare access modifiers, as demonstrated in the example in this section.

For example, consider `IDisposable`. If a class wants to declare publicly that it implements the `Dispose` method, it must implement `IDisposable`, which in C# terms means that the class derives from `IDisposable`:

```
class SomeClass: IDisposable
{
  // This class MUST contain an implementation of the
  // IDisposable.Dispose() method, otherwise
  // you get a compilation error.
  public void Dispose()
  {
    // implementation of Dispose() method
  }
  // rest of class
}
```

In this example, if `SomeClass` derives from `IDisposable` but doesn't contain a `Dispose` implementation with the exact same signature as defined in `IDisposable`, you get a compilation error because the class is breaking its agreed-on contract to implement `IDisposable`. Of course, it's no problem for the compiler if a class has a `Dispose` method but doesn't derive from `IDisposable`. The problem is that other code would have no way of recognizing that `SomeClass` has agreed to support the `IDisposable` features.

> **NOTE** IDisposable *is a relatively simple interface because it defines only one method. Most interfaces contain more members. The correct implementation of* IDisposable *is not really that simple; it's covered in Chapter 17.*

Defining and Implementing Interfaces

This section illustrates how to define and use interfaces by developing a short program that follows the interface inheritance paradigm. The example is based on bank accounts. Assume that you are writing code that will ultimately allow computerized transfers between bank accounts. Assume also for this example that there are many companies that implement bank accounts, but they have all mutually agreed that any classes representing bank accounts will implement an interface, IBankAccount, which exposes methods to deposit or withdraw money, and a property to return the balance. It is this interface that enables outside code to recognize the various bank account classes implemented by different bank accounts. Although the aim is to enable the bank accounts to communicate with each other to allow transfers of funds between accounts, that feature isn't introduced just yet.

To keep things simple, you keep all the code for the example in the same source file. Of course, if something like the example were used in real life, you could surmise that the different bank account classes would not only be compiled to different assemblies, but also be hosted on different machines owned by the different banks. That's all much too complicated for the purposes of this example. However, to maintain some realism, you define different namespaces for the different companies.

To begin, you need to define the IBankAccount interface (code file UsingInterfaces/IBankAccount.cs):

```
namespace Wrox.ProCSharp
{
  public interface IBankAccount
  {
    void PayIn(decimal amount);
    bool Withdraw(decimal amount);
    decimal Balance { get; }
  }
}
```

Notice the name of the interface, IBankAccount. It's a best-practice convention to begin an interface name with the letter I, to indicate it's an interface.

> **NOTE** *Chapter 2, "Core C#," points out that in most cases, .NET usage guidelines discourage the so-called Hungarian notation in which names are preceded by a letter that indicates the type of object being defined. Interfaces are one of the few exceptions for which Hungarian notation is recommended.*

The idea is that you can now write classes that represent bank accounts. These classes don't have to be related to each other in any way; they can be completely different classes. They will all, however, declare that they represent bank accounts by the mere fact that they implement the IBankAccount interface.

Let's start off with the first class, a saver account run by the Royal Bank of Venus (code file UsingInterfaces/VenusBank.cs):

```
namespace Wrox.ProCSharp.VenusBank
{
  public class SaverAccount: IBankAccount
  {
    private decimal _balance;
```

```
      public void PayIn(decimal amount) => _balance += amount;
      public bool Withdraw(decimal amount)
      {
        if (_balance >= amount)
        {
          _balance -= amount;
          return true;
        }
        Console.WriteLine("Withdrawal attempt failed.");
        return false;
      }
      public decimal Balance => _balance;
      public override string ToString() =>
        $"Venus Bank Saver: Balance = {_balance,6:C}";
    }
  }
```

It should be obvious what the implementation of this class does. You maintain a private field, balance, and adjust this amount when money is deposited or withdrawn. You display an error message if an attempt to withdraw money fails because of insufficient funds. Notice also that because we are keeping the code as simple as possible, we are not implementing extra properties, such as the account holder's name! In real life that would be essential information, of course, but for this example it's unnecessarily complicated.

The only really interesting line in this code is the class declaration:

```
public class SaverAccount: IBankAccount
```

You've declared that SaverAccount is derived from one interface, IBankAccount, and you have not explicitly indicated any other base classes (which means that SaverAccount is derived directly from System. Object). By the way, derivation from interfaces acts completely independently from derivation from classes.

Being derived from IBankAccount means that SaverAccount gets all the members of IBankAccount; but because an interface doesn't actually implement any of its methods, SaverAccount must provide its own implementations of all of them. If any implementations are missing, you can rest assured that the compiler will complain. Recall also that the interface just indicates the presence of its members. It's up to the class to determine whether it wants any of them to be virtual or abstract (though abstract functions are only allowed if the class itself is abstract). For this particular example, you don't have any reason to make any of the interface functions virtual.

To illustrate how different classes can implement the same interface, assume that the Planetary Bank of Jupiter also implements a class to represent one of its bank accounts—a Gold Account (code file UsingInterfaces/JupiterBank.cs):

```
namespace Wrox.ProCSharp.JupiterBank
{
  public class GoldAccount: IBankAccount
  {
    // ...
  }
}
```

The details of the GoldAccount class aren't presented here; in the sample code, it's basically identical to the implementation of SaverAccount. We stress that GoldAccount has no connection with SaverAccount, other than they both happen to implement the same interface.

Now that you have your classes, you can test them. You first need a few using declarations:

```
using Wrox.ProCSharp;
using Wrox.ProCSharp.VenusBank;
using Wrox.ProCSharp.JupiterBank;
```

Now you need a `Main` method (code file `UsingInterfaces/Program.cs`):

```
namespace Wrox.ProCSharp
{
  class Program
  {
    static void Main()
    {
      IBankAccount venusAccount = new SaverAccount();
      IBankAccount jupiterAccount = new GoldAccount();
      venusAccount.PayIn(200);
      venusAccount.Withdraw(100);
      Console.WriteLine(venusAccount.ToString());
      jupiterAccount.PayIn(500);
      jupiterAccount.Withdraw(600);
      jupiterAccount.Withdraw(100);
      Console.WriteLine(jupiterAccount.ToString());
    }
  }
}
```

This code produces the following output:

```
> BankAccounts
Venus Bank Saver: Balance = $100.00
Withdrawal attempt failed.
Jupiter Bank Saver: Balance = $400.00
```

The main point to notice about this code is the way that you have declared both your reference variables as `IBankAccount` references. This means that they can point to any instance of any class that implements this interface. However, it also means that you can call only methods that are part of this interface through these references—if you want to call any methods implemented by a class that are not part of the interface, you need to cast the reference to the appropriate type. In the example code, you were able to call `ToString` (not implemented by `IBankAccount`) without any explicit cast, purely because `ToString` is a `System.Object` method, so the C# compiler knows that it will be supported by any class (put differently, the cast from any interface to `System.Object` is implicit). Chapter 6, "Operators and Casts," covers the syntax for performing casts.

Interface references can in all respects be treated as class references—but the power of an interface reference is that it can refer to any class that implements that interface. For example, this allows you to form arrays of interfaces, whereby each element of the array is a different class:

```
IBankAccount[] accounts = new IBankAccount[2];
accounts[0] = new SaverAccount();
accounts[1] = new GoldAccount();
```

Note, however, that you would get a compiler error if you tried something like this:

```
accounts[1] = new SomeOtherClass(); // SomeOtherClass does NOT implement
// IBankAccount: WRONG!!
```

The preceding causes a compilation error similar to this:

```
Cannot implicitly convert type 'Wrox.ProCSharp. SomeOtherClass' to
'Wrox.ProCSharp.IBankAccount'
```

Interface Inheritance

It's possible for interfaces to inherit from each other in the same way that classes do. This concept is illustrated by defining a new interface, `ITransferBankAccount`, which has the same features as `IBankAccount` but also defines a method to transfer money directly to a different account (code file `UsingInterfaces/ITransferBankAccount`):

```
namespace Wrox.ProCSharp
{
    public interface ITransferBankAccount: IBankAccount
    {
        bool TransferTo(IBankAccount destination, decimal amount);
    }
}
```

Because `ITransferBankAccount` is derived from `IBankAccount`, it gets all the members of `IBankAccount` as well as its own. That means that any class that implements (derives from) `ITransferBankAccount` must implement all the methods of `IBankAccount`, as well as the new `TransferTo` method defined in `ITransferBankAccount`. Failure to implement all these methods results in a compilation error.

Note that the `TransferTo` method uses an `IBankAccount` interface reference for the destination account. This illustrates the usefulness of interfaces: When implementing and then invoking this method, you don't need to know anything about what type of object you are transferring money to—all you need to know is that this object implements `IBankAccount`.

To illustrate `ITransferBankAccount`, assume that the Planetary Bank of Jupiter also offers a current account. Most of the implementation of the `CurrentAccount` class is identical to implementations of `SaverAccount` and `GoldAccount` (again, this is just to keep this example simple—that won't normally be the case), so in the following code only the differences are highlighted (code file `UsingInterfaces/JupiterBank.cs`):

```
public class CurrentAccount: ITransferBankAccount
{
    private decimal _balance;
    public void PayIn(decimal amount) => _balance += amount;
    public bool Withdraw(decimal amount)
    {
        if (_balance >= amount)
        {
            _balance -= amount;
            return true;
        }
        Console.WriteLine("Withdrawal attempt failed.");
        return false;
    }

    public decimal Balance => _balance;
    public bool TransferTo(IBankAccount destination, decimal amount)
    {
        bool result = Withdraw(amount);
        if (result)
        {
            destination.PayIn(amount);
        }
        return result;
    }
    public override string ToString() =>
        $"Jupiter Bank Current Account: Balance = {_balance,6:C}";
}
```

The class can be demonstrated with this code:

```
static void Main()
{
    IBankAccount venusAccount = new SaverAccount();
    ITransferBankAccount jupiterAccount = new CurrentAccount();
    venusAccount.PayIn(200);
    jupiterAccount.PayIn(500);
    jupiterAccount.TransferTo(venusAccount, 100);
```

```
    Console.WriteLine(venusAccount.ToString());
    Console.WriteLine(jupiterAccount.ToString());
}
```

The preceding code produces the following output, which, as you can verify, shows that the correct amounts have been transferred:

```
> CurrentAccount
Venus Bank Saver: Balance = $300.00
Jupiter Bank Current Account: Balance = $400.00
```

IS AND AS OPERATORS

Before concluding inheritance with interfaces and classes, we need to have a look at two important operators related to inheritance: the `is` and `as` operators.

You've already seen that you can directly assign objects of a specific type to a base class or an interface—if the type has a direct relation in the hierarchy. For example, the `SaverAccount` created earlier can be directly assigned to an `IBankAccount` because the `SaverAccount` type implements the interface `IBankAccount`:

```
IBankAccount venusAccount = new SaverAccount();
```

What if you have a method accepting an object type, and you want to get access to the `IBankAccount` members? The object type doesn't have the members of the `IBankAccount` interface. You can do a cast. Cast the object (you can also use any parameter of type of any interface and cast it to the type you need) to an `IBankAccount` and work with that:

```
public void WorkWithManyDifferentObjects(object o)
{
    IBankAccount account = (IBankAccount)o;
    // work with the account
}
```

This works as long as you always supply an object of type `IBankAccount` to this method. Of course, if an object of type `object` is accepted, there will be the case when invalid objects are passed. This is when you get an `InvalidCastException`. It's never a good idea to accept exceptions in normal cases. You can read more about this in Chapter 14. This is where the `is` and `as` operators come into play.

Instead of doing the cast directly, it's a good idea to check whether the parameter implements the interface `IBankAccount`. The as operator works similar to the `cast` operator within the class hierarchy—it returns a reference to the object. However, it never throws an `InvalidCastException`. Instead, this operator returns null in case the object is not of the type asked for. Here, it is a good idea to verify for null before using the reference; otherwise a `NullReferenceException` will be thrown later using the following reference:

```
public void WorkWithManyDifferentObjects(object o)
{
    IBankAccount account = o as IBankAccount;
    if (account != null)
    {
        // work with the account
    }
}
```

Instead of using the as operator, you can use the `is` operator. The `is` operator returns `true` or `false`, depending on whether the condition is fulfilled and the object is of the specified type. If the condition is `true`, the resulting object is written to the variable declared of the matching type as shown in the following code snippet:

```
public void WorkWithManyDifferentObjects(object o)
{
    if (o is IBankAccount account)
```

```
    {
        // work with the account
    }
}
```

> **NOTE** *Adding the variable declaration to the* is *operator is a new feature of C# 7. This is part of the pattern matching functionality that is discussed in detail in Chapter 13, "Functional Programming with C#."*

Instead of having bad surprises by exceptions based on casts, conversions within the class hierarchy work well with the is and as operators.

SUMMARY

This chapter described how to code inheritance in C#. The chapter described how C# offers rich support for both multiple interface and single implementation inheritance and explained that C# provides a number of useful syntactical constructs designed to assist in making code more robust. These include the override keyword, which indicates when a function should override a base function; the new keyword, which indicates when a function hides a base function; and rigid rules for constructor initializers that are designed to ensure that constructors are designed to interoperate in a robust manner.

The next chapter continues with an important C# language construct: generics.

5

Generics

WROX.COM CODE DOWNLOADS FOR THIS CHAPTER

The Wrox.com code downloads for this chapter are found at www.wrox.com on the Download Code tab. The source code is also available at https://github.com/ProfessionalCSharp/ProfessionalCSharp7 in the directory Generics.

The code for this chapter is divided into the following major examples:

- ➤ Linked List Objects
- ➤ Linked List Sample
- ➤ Document Manager
- ➤ Variance
- ➤ Generic Methods
- ➤ Specialization

GENERICS OVERVIEW

Generics are an important concept of not only C# but also .NET. Generics are more than a part of the C# programming language; they are deeply integrated with the IL (Intermediate Language) code in the assemblies. With generics, you can create classes and methods that are independent of contained types. Instead of writing a number of methods or classes with the same functionality for different types, you can create just one method or class.

Another option to reduce the amount of code is using the `Object` class. However, passing using types derived from the `Object` class is not type safe. Generic classes make use of generic types that are replaced with specific types as needed. This allows for type safety: The compiler complains if a specific type is not supported with the generic class.

Generics are not limited to classes; in this chapter, you also see generics with interfaces and methods. You can find generics with delegates in Chapter 8, "Delegates, Lambdas, and Events."

Generics are not specific only to C#; similar concepts exist with other languages. For example, C++ templates have some similarity to generics. However, there's a big difference between C++ templates and .NET generics. With C++ templates, the source code of the template is required when a template is instantiated with a specific type. The C++ compiler generates separate binary code for each type that is an instance of a specific template. Unlike C++ templates, generics are not only a construct of the C# language but are defined with the Common Language Runtime (CLR). This makes it possible to instantiate generics with a specific type in Visual Basic even though the generic class was defined with C#.

The following sections explore the advantages and disadvantages of generics, particularly in regard to the following:

➤ Performance
➤ Type safety
➤ Binary code reuse
➤ Code bloat
➤ Naming guidelines

Performance

One of the big advantages of generics is performance. In Chapter 10, "Collections," you see non-generic and generic collection classes from the namespaces `System.Collections` and `System.Collections.Generic`. Using value types with non-generic collection classes results in boxing and unboxing when the value type is converted to a reference type, and vice versa.

> **NOTE** *Boxing and unboxing are discussed in Chapter 6, "Operators and Casts." Here is just a short refresher about these terms.*

Value types are stored on the stack, whereas reference types are stored on the heap. C# classes are reference types; structs are value types. .NET makes it easy to convert value types to reference types, so you can use a value type everywhere an object (which is a reference type) is needed. For example, an `int` can be assigned to an object. The conversion from a value type to a reference type is known as *boxing*. Boxing occurs automatically if a method requires an object as a parameter, and a value type is passed. In the other direction, a boxed value type can be converted to a value type by using unboxing. With unboxing, the cast operator is required.

The following example shows that the `ArrayList` class from the namespace `System.Collections` stores objects; the `Add` method is defined to require an object as a parameter, so an integer type is boxed. When the values from an `ArrayList` are read, unboxing occurs when the object is converted to an integer type. This may be obvious with the cast operator that is used to assign the first element of the `ArrayList` collection to the variable i1, but it also happens inside the `foreach` statement where the variable i2 of type `int` is accessed:

```
var list = new ArrayList();
list.Add(44); // boxing — convert a value type to a reference type
int i1 = (int)list[0]; // unboxing — convert a reference type to
// a value type
foreach (int i2 in list)
```

```
{
    Console.WriteLine(i2); // unboxing
}
```

Boxing and unboxing are easy to use but have a big performance impact, especially when iterating through many items.

Instead of using objects, the `List<T>` class from the namespace `System.Collections.Generic` enables you to define the type when it is used. In the example here, the generic type of the `List<T>` class is defined as `int`, so the `int` type is used inside the class that is generated dynamically from the Just-In-Time (JIT) compiler. Boxing and unboxing no longer happen:

```
var list = new List<int>();
list.Add(44); // no boxing — value types are stored in the List<int>
int i1 = list[0]; // no unboxing, no cast needed
foreach (int i2 in list)
{
    Console.WriteLine(i2);
}
```

Type Safety

Another feature of generics is type safety. As with the `ArrayList` class, if objects are used, any type can be added to this collection. The following example shows adding an integer, a string, and an object of type `MyClass` to the collection of type `ArrayList`:

```
var list = new ArrayList();
list.Add(44);
list.Add("mystring");
list.Add(new MyClass());
```

If this collection is iterated using the following `foreach` statement, which iterates using integer elements, the compiler accepts this code. However, because not all elements in the collection can be cast to an `int`, a runtime exception will occur:

```
foreach (int i in list)
{
    Console.WriteLine(i);
}
```

Errors should be detected as early as possible. With the generic class `List<T>`, the generic type `T` defines what types are allowed. With a definition of `List<int>`, only integer types can be added to the collection. The compiler doesn't compile this code because the `Add` method has invalid arguments:

```
var list = new List<int>();
list.Add(44);
list.Add("mystring"); // compile time error
list.Add(new MyClass()); // compile time error
```

Binary Code Reuse

Generics enable better binary code reuse. A generic class can be defined once and can be instantiated with many different types. Unlike C++ templates, it is not necessary to access the source code.

For example, here the `List<T>` class from the namespace `System.Collections.Generic` is instantiated with an `int`, a `string`, and a `MyClass` type:

```
var list = new List<int>();
list.Add(44);
var stringList = new List<string>();
stringList.Add("mystring");
var myClassList = new List<MyClass>();
myClassList.Add(new MyClass());
```

Generic types can be defined in one language and used from any other .NET language.

Code Bloat

You might be wondering how much code is created with generics when instantiating them with different specific types. Because a generic class definition goes into the assembly, instantiating generic classes with specific types doesn't duplicate these classes in the IL code. However, when the generic classes are compiled by the JIT compiler to native code, a new class for every specific value type is created. Reference types share all the same implementation of the same native class. This is because with reference types, only a 4-byte memory address (with 32-bit systems) is needed within the generic instantiated class to reference a reference type. Value types are contained within the memory of the generic instantiated class; and because every value type can have different memory requirements, a new class for every value type is instantiated.

Naming Guidelines

If generics are used in the program, it helps when generic types can be distinguished from non-generic types. Here are naming guidelines for generic types:

➤ Prefix generic type names with the letter T.

➤ If the generic type can be replaced by any class because there's no special requirement, and only one generic type is used, the character T is good as a generic type name:

```
public class List<T> { }
public class LinkedList<T> { }
```

➤ If there's a special requirement for a generic type (for example, it must implement an interface or derive from a base class), or if two or more generic types are used, use descriptive names for the type names:

```
public delegate void EventHandler<TEventArgs>(object sender,
  TEventArgs e);
public delegate TOutput Converter<TInput, TOutput>(TInput from);
public class SortedList<TKey, TValue> { }
```

CREATING GENERIC CLASSES

The example in this section starts with a normal, non-generic simplified linked list class that can contain objects of any kind, and then converts this class to a generic class.

With a linked list, one element references the next one. Therefore, you must create a class that wraps the object inside the linked list and references the next object. The class LinkedListNode contains a property named Value that is initialized with the constructor. In addition to that, the LinkedListNode class contains references to the next and previous elements in the list that can be accessed from properties (code file LinkedListObjects/LinkedListNode.cs):

```
public class LinkedListNode
{
  public LinkedListNode(object value) => Value = value;

  public object Value { get; }
  public LinkedListNode Next { get; internal set; }
  public LinkedListNode Prev { get; internal set; }
}
```

The LinkedList class includes First and Last properties of type LinkedListNode that mark the beginning and end of the list. The method AddLast adds a new element to the end of the list. First, an object of type LinkedListNode is created. If the list is empty, then the First and Last properties are set to the new element; otherwise, the new element is added as the last element to the list. By implementing the GetEnumerator method, it is possible to iterate through the list with the foreach statement. The GetEnumerator method makes use of the yield statement for creating an enumerator type:

```
public class LinkedList: IEnumerable
{
  public LinkedListNode First { get; private set; }
```

```
public LinkedListNode Last { get; private set; }
public LinkedListNode AddLast(object node)
{
  var newNode = new LinkedListNode(node);
  if (First == null)
  {
    First = newNode;
    Last = First;
  }
  else
  {
    LinkedListNode previous = Last;
    Last.Next = newNode;
    Last = newNode;
    Last.Prev = previous;
  }
  return newNode;
}

public IEnumerator GetEnumerator()
{
  LinkedListNode current = First;
  while (current != null)
  {
    yield return current.Value;
    current = current.Next;
  }
}
}
```

> **NOTE** *The* `yield` *statement creates a state machine for an enumerator. This statement is explained in Chapter 7, "Arrays."*

Now you can use the `LinkedList` class with any type. The following code segment instantiates a new `LinkedList` object and adds two integer types and one string type. As the integer types are converted to an object, boxing occurs as explained earlier in this chapter. With the `foreach` statement, unboxing happens. In the `foreach` statement, the elements from the list are cast to an integer, so a runtime exception occurs with the third element in the list because casting to an `int` fails (code file `LinkedListObjects/Program.cs`):

```
var list1 = new LinkedList();
list1.AddLast(2);
list1.AddLast(4);
list1.AddLast("6");
foreach (int i in list1)
{
  Console.WriteLine(i);
}
```

Now make a generic version of the linked list. A generic class is defined similarly to a normal class with the generic type declaration. You can then use the generic type within the class as a field member or with parameter types of methods. The class `LinkedListNode` is declared with a generic type `T`. The property `Value` is now type `T` instead of `object`; the constructor is changed as well to accept an object of type `T`. A generic type can also be returned and set, so the properties `Next` and `Prev` are now of type `LinkedListNode<T>` (code file `LinkedListSample/LinkedListNode.cs`):

```
public class LinkedListNode<T>
{
  public LinkedListNode(T value) => Value = value;
```

```
    public T Value { get; }
    public LinkedListNode<T> Next { get; internal set; }
    public LinkedListNode<T> Prev { get; internal set; }
}
```

In the following code, the class `LinkedList` is changed to a generic class as well. `LinkedList<T>` contains `LinkedListNode<T>` elements. The type `T` from the `LinkedList` defines the type `T` of the properties `First` and `Last`. The method `AddLast` now accepts a parameter of type `T` and instantiates an object of `LinkedListNode<T>`.

Besides the interface `IEnumerable`, a generic version is also available: `IEnumerable<T>`. `IEnumerable<T>` derives from `IEnumerable` and adds the `GetEnumerator` method, which returns `IEnumerator<T>`. `LinkedList<T>` implements the generic interface `IEnumerable<T>` (code file `LinkedListSample/LinkedList.cs`):

```
public class LinkedList<T>: IEnumerable<T>
{
    public LinkedListNode<T> First { get; private set; }
    public LinkedListNode<T> Last { get; private set; }
    public LinkedListNode<T> AddLast(T node)
    {
        var newNode = new LinkedListNode<T>(node);
        if (First == null)
        {
            First = newNode;
            Last = First;
        }
        else
        {
            LinkedListNode<T> previous = Last;
            Last.Next = newNode;
            Last = newNode;
            Last.Prev = previous;
        }
        return newNode;
    }

    public IEnumerator<T> GetEnumerator()
    {
        LinkedListNode<T> current = First;
        while (current != null)
        {
            yield return current.Value;
            current = current.Next;
        }
    }

    IEnumerator IEnumerable.GetEnumerator() => GetEnumerator();
}
```

> **NOTE** *Enumerators and the interfaces* `IEnumerable` *and* `IEnumerator` *are discussed in Chapter 7.*

Using the generic `LinkedList<T>`, you can instantiate it with an `int` type, and there's no boxing. Also, you get a compiler error if you don't pass an `int` with the method `AddLast`. Using the generic `IEnumerable<T>`, the `foreach` statement is also type safe, and you get a compiler error if that variable in the `foreach` statement is not an `int` (code file `LinkedListSample/Program.cs`):

```
var list2 = new LinkedList<int>();
list2.AddLast(1);
list2.AddLast(3);
```

```
    list2.AddLast(5);
    foreach (int i in list2)
    {
      Console.WriteLine(i);
    }
```

Similarly, you can use the generic `LinkedList<T>` with a `string` type and pass strings to the `AddLast` method:

```
    var list3 = new LinkedList<string>();
    list3.AddLast("2");
    list3.AddLast("four");
    list3.AddLast("foo");
    foreach (string s in list3)
    {
      Console.WriteLine(s);
    }
```

> **NOTE** *Every class that deals with the object type is a possible candidate for a generic implementation. Also, if classes make use of hierarchies, generics can be very helpful in making casting unnecessary.*

GENERICS FEATURES

When creating generic classes, you might need some additional C# keywords. For example, it is not possible to assign `null` to a generic type. In this case, the keyword `default` can be used, as demonstrated in the next section. If the generic type does not require the features of the `Object` class but you need to invoke some specific methods in the generic class, you can define constraints.

This section discusses the following topics:

➤ Default values

➤ Constraints

➤ Inheritance

➤ Static members

This example begins with a generic document manager, which is used to read and write documents from and to a queue. Start by creating a new Console project named `DocumentManager` and add the class `DocumentManager<T>`. The method `AddDocument` adds a document to the queue. The read-only property `IsDocumentAvailable` returns true if the queue is not empty (code file `DocumentManager/DocumentManager.cs`):

```
    using System;
    using System.Collections.Generic;
    namespace Wrox.ProCSharp.Generics
    {
      public class DocumentManager<T>
      {
        private readonly Queue<T> _documentQueue = new Queue<T>();
        private readonly object _lockQueue = new object();

        public void AddDocument(T doc)
        {
          lock (_lockQueue)
          {
            _documentQueue.Enqueue(doc);
          }
        }
```

```
      public bool IsDocumentAvailable => _documentQueue.Count > 0;
   }
}
```

Threading and the lock statement are discussed in Chapter 21, "Tasks and Parallel Programming."

Default Values

Now you add a `GetDocument` method to the `DocumentManager<T>` class. Inside this method the type `T` should be assigned to `null`. However, it is not possible to assign `null` to generic types. That's because a generic type can also be instantiated as a value type, and `null` is allowed only with reference types. To circumvent this problem, you can use the `default` keyword. With the `default` keyword, `null` is assigned to reference types and `0` is assigned to value types:

```
public T GetDocument()
{
  T doc = default;
  lock (_lockQueue)
  {
    doc = _documentQueue.Dequeue();
  }
  return doc;
}
```

> **NOTE** *The* `default` *keyword has multiple meanings depending on its context. The* `switch` *statement uses a* `default` *for defining the default case, and with generics* `default` *is used to initialize generic types either to* `null` *or to* `0`, *depending on whether it is a reference or value type.*

Constraints

If the generic class needs to invoke some methods from the generic type, you have to add constraints.

With `DocumentManager<T>`, all the document titles should be displayed in the `DisplayAllDocuments` method. The `Document` class implements the interface `IDocument` with the read-only properties `Title` and `Content` (code file `DocumentManager/Document.cs`):

```
public interface IDocument
{
  string Title { get; }
  string Content { get; }
}

public class Document: IDocument
{
  public Document(string title, string content)
  {
    Title = title;
    Content = content;
  }

  public string Title { get; }
  public string Content { get; }
}
```

To display the documents with the `DocumentManager<T>` class, you can cast the type `T` to the interface `IDocument` to display the title:

```
public void DisplayAllDocuments()
{
  foreach (T doc in documentQueue)
  {
    Console.WriteLine(((IDocument)doc).Title);
  }
}
```

The problem here is that doing a cast results in a runtime exception if type `T` does not implement the interface `IDocument`. Instead, it would be better to define a constraint with the `DocumentManager<TDocument>` class specifying that the type `TDocument` must implement the interface `IDocument`. To clarify the requirement in the name of the generic type, `T` is changed to `TDocument`. The `where` clause defines the requirement to implement the interface `IDocument` (code file `DocumentManager/DocumentManager.cs`):

```
public class DocumentManager<TDocument>
  where TDocument: IDocument
{
```

> **NOTE** *When adding a constraint to a generic type, it's a good idea to have some information with the generic parameter name. The sample code is now using* `TDocument` *instead of* `T` *for the generic parameter. For the compiler, the parameter name doesn't matter, but it is more readable.*

This way you can write the `foreach` statement in such a way that the type `TDocument` contains the property `Title`. You get support from Visual Studio IntelliSense and the compiler:

```
public void DisplayAllDocuments()
{
  foreach (TDocument doc in documentQueue)
  {
    Console.WriteLine(doc.Title);
  }
}
```

In the `Main` method, the `DocumentManager<TDocument>` class is instantiated with the type `Document` that implements the required interface `IDocument`. Then new documents are added and displayed, and one of the documents is retrieved (code file `DocumentManager/Program.cs`):

```
public static void Main()
{
  var dm = new DocumentManager<Document>();
  dm.AddDocument(new Document("Title A", "Sample A"));
  dm.AddDocument(new Document("Title B", "Sample B"));
  dm.DisplayAllDocuments();
  if (dm.IsDocumentAvailable)
  {
    Document d = dm.GetDocument();
    Console.WriteLine(d.Content);
  }
}
```

The `DocumentManager` now works with any class that implements the interface `IDocument`.

In the sample application, you've seen an interface constraint. Generics support several constraint types, indicated in the following table.

CONSTRAINT	DESCRIPTION
where T: struct	With a struct constraint, type T must be a value type.
where T: class	The class constraint indicates that type T must be a reference type.
where T: IFoo	Specifies that type T is required to implement interface IFoo.
where T: Foo	Specifies that type T is required to derive from base class Foo.
where T: new()	A constructor constraint; specifies that type T must have a default constructor.
where T1: T2	With constraints it is also possible to specify that type T1 derives from a generic type T2.

> **NOTE** *Constructor constraints can be defined only for the default constructor. It is not possible to define a constructor constraint for other constructors.*

With a generic type, you can also combine multiple constraints. The constraint where T: IFoo, new() with the MyClass<T> declaration specifies that type T implements the interface IFoo and has a default constructor:

```
public class MyClass<T>
  where T: IFoo, new()
{
  //...
```

> **NOTE** *One important restriction of the where clause with C# is that it's not possible to define operators that must be implemented by the generic type. Operators cannot be defined in interfaces. With the where clause, it is only possible to define base classes, interfaces, and the default constructor.*

Inheritance

The LinkedList<T> class created earlier implements the interface IEnumerable<T>:

```
public class LinkedList<T>: IEnumerable<T>
{
  //...
```

A generic type can implement a generic interface. The same is possible by deriving from a class. A generic class can be derived from a generic base class:

```
public class Base<T>
{
}

public class Derived<T>: Base<T>
{
}
```

The requirement is that the generic types of the interface must be repeated, or the type of the base class must be specified, as in this case:

```
public class Base<T>
{
}
```

```
public class Derived<T>: Base<string>
{
}
```

This way, the derived class can be a generic or non-generic class. For example, you can define an abstract generic base class that is implemented with a concrete type in the derived class. This enables you to write generic specialization for specific types:

```
public abstract class Calc<T>
{
  public abstract T Add(T x, T y);
  public abstract T Sub(T x, T y);
}

public class IntCalc: Calc<int>
{
  public override int Add(int x, int y) => x + y;
  public override int Sub(int x, int y) => x - y;
}
```

You can also create a partial specialization, such as deriving the StringQuery class from Query and defining only one of the generic parameters, for example, a string for TResult. For instantiating the StringQuery, you need only to supply the type for TRequest:

```
public class Query<TRequest, TResult>
{
}

public StringQuery<TRequest> : Query<TRequest, string>
{
}
```

Static Members

Static members of generic classes are shared with only one instantiation of the class, and they require special attention. Consider the following example, where the class StaticDemo<T> contains the static field x:

```
public class StaticDemo<T>
{
  public static int x;
}
```

Because the class StaticDemo<T> is used with both a string type and an int type, two sets of static fields exist:

```
StaticDemo<string>.x = 4;
StaticDemo<int>.x = 5;
Console.WriteLine(StaticDemo<string>.x); // writes 4
```

GENERIC INTERFACES

Using generics, you can define interfaces that define methods with generic parameters. In the linked list sample, you've already implemented the interface IEnumerable<out T>, which defines a GetEnumerator method to return IEnumerator<out T>. .NET offers a lot of generic interfaces for different scenarios; examples include IComparable<T>, ICollection<T>, and IExtensibleObject<T>. Often older, non-generic versions of the same interface exist; for example, .NET 1.0 had an IComparable interface that was based on objects. IComparable<in T> is based on a generic type:

```
public interface IComparable<in T>
{
  int CompareTo(T other);
}
```

> **NOTE** *Don't be confused by the* in *and* out *keywords used with the generic parameter. They are explained soon in the "Covariance and Contra-Variance" section.*

The older, non-generic `IComparable` interface requires an object with the `CompareTo` method. This requires a cast to specific types, such as to the `Person` class for using the `LastName` property:

```
public class Person: IComparable
{
  public int CompareTo(object obj)
  {
    Person other = obj as Person;
    return this.lastname.CompareTo(other.LastName);
  }
  //
```

When implementing the generic version, it is no longer necessary to cast the `object` to a `Person`:

```
public class Person: IComparable<Person>
{
  public int CompareTo(Person other) => LastName.CompareTo(other.LastName);

  //...
```

Covariance and Contra-Variance

Prior to .NET 4, generic interfaces were invariant. .NET 4 added important changes for generic interfaces and generic delegates: covariance and contra-variance. Covariance and contra-variance are used for the conversion of types with arguments and return types. For example, can you pass a `Rectangle` to a method that requests a `Shape`? Let's get into examples to see the advantages of these extensions.

With .NET, parameter types are covariant. Assume you have the classes `Shape` and `Rectangle`, and `Rectangle` derives from the `Shape` base class. The `Display` method is declared to accept an object of the `Shape` type as its parameter:

```
public void Display(Shape o) { }
```

Now you can pass any object that derives from the `Shape` base class. Because `Rectangle` derives from `Shape`, a `Rectangle` fulfills all the requirements of a `Shape` and the compiler accepts this method call:

```
var r = new Rectangle { Width= 5, Height=2.5 };
Display(r);
```

Return types of methods are contra-variant. When a method returns a `Shape` it is not possible to assign it to a `Rectangle` because a `Shape` is not necessarily always a `Rectangle`; but the opposite is possible. If a method returns a `Rectangle` as the `GetRectangle` method,

```
public Rectangle GetRectangle();
```

the result can be assigned to a `Shape`:

```
Shape s = GetRectangle();
```

Before version 4 of the .NET Framework, this behavior was not possible with generics. Since C# 4, the language is extended to support covariance and contra-variance with generic interfaces and generic delegates. Let's start by defining a `Shape` base class and a `Rectangle` class (code files `Variance/Shape.cs` and `Rectangle.cs`):

```
public class Shape
{
```

```
public double Width { get; set; }
public double Height { get; set; }
public override string ToString() => $"Width: {Width}, Height: {Height}";
}

public class Rectangle: Shape
{
}
```

Covariance with Generic Interfaces

A generic interface is covariant if the generic type is annotated with the out keyword. This also means that type T is allowed only with return types. The interface IIndex is covariant with type T and returns this type from a read-only indexer (code file Variance/IIndex.cs):

```
public interface IIndex<out T>
{
  T this[int index] { get; }
  int Count { get; }
}
```

The IIndex<T> interface is implemented with the RectangleCollection class. RectangleCollection defines Rectangle for generic type T:

> **NOTE** *If a read-write indexer is used with the IIndex interface, the generic type T is passed to the method and retrieved from the method. This is not possible with covariance; the generic type must be defined as invariant. Defining the type as invariant is done without out and in annotations (code file Variance/RectangleCollection.cs):*

```
public class RectangleCollection: IIndex<Rectangle>
{
  private Rectangle[] data = new Rectangle[3]
  {
    new Rectangle { Height=2, Width=5 },
    new Rectangle { Height=3, Width=7 },
    new Rectangle { Height=4.5, Width=2.9 }
  };

  private static RectangleCollection _coll;
  public static RectangleCollection GetRectangles() =>
    _coll ?? (_coll = new RectangleCollection());

  public Rectangle this[int index]
  {
    get
    {
      if (index < 0 || index > data.Length)
        throw new ArgumentOutOfRangeException(nameof(index));
      return data[index];
    }
  }

  public int Count => data.Length;
}
```

> **NOTE** *The* `RectangleCollection.GetRectangles` *method makes use of the coalescing operator. If the variable* `coll` *is* null, *the right side of the operator is invoked to create a new instance of* `RectangleCollection` *and assign it to the variable* `coll`, *which is returned from this method afterward. This operator is explained in detail in Chapter 6.*

The `RectangleCollection.GetRectangles` method returns a `RectangleCollection` that implements the `IIndex<Rectangle>` interface, so you can assign the return value to a variable `rectangle` of the `IIndex<Rectangle>` type. Because the interface is covariant, it is also possible to assign the returned value to a variable of `IIndex<Shape>`. Shape does not need anything more than a `Rectangle` has to offer. Using the `shapes` variable, the indexer from the interface and the `Count` property are used within the `for` loop (code file `Variance/Program.cs`):

```
public static void Main()
{
  IIndex<Rectangle> rectangles = RectangleCollection.GetRectangles();
  IIndex<Shape> shapes = rectangles;
  for (int i = 0; i < shapes.Count; i++)
  {
    Console.WriteLine(shapes[i]);
  }
}
```

Contra-Variance with Generic Interfaces

A generic interface is contra-variant if the generic type is annotated with the `in` keyword. This way, the interface is only allowed to use generic type `T` as input to its methods (code file `Variance/IDisplay.cs`):

```
public interface IDisplay<in T>
{
  void Show(T item);
}
```

The `ShapeDisplay` class implements `IDisplay<Shape>` and uses a `Shape` object as an input parameter (code file `Variance/ShapeDisplay.cs`):

```
public class ShapeDisplay: IDisplay<Shape>
{
  public void Show(Shape s) =>
    Console.WriteLine(
      $"{s.GetType().Name} Width: {s.Width}, Height: {s.Height}");
}
```

Creating a new instance of `ShapeDisplay` returns `IDisplay<Shape>`, which is assigned to the `shapeDisplay` variable. Because `IDisplay<T>` is contra-variant, it is possible to assign the result to `IDisplay<Rectangle>`, where `Rectangle` derives from `Shape`. This time the methods of the interface define only the generic type as input, and `Rectangle` fulfills all the requirements of a `Shape` (code file `Variance/Program.cs`):

```
public static void Main()
{
  //...
  IDisplay<Shape> shapeDisplay = new ShapeDisplay();
  IDisplay<Rectangle> rectangleDisplay = shapeDisplay;
  rectangleDisplay.Show(rectangles[0]);
}
```

GENERIC STRUCTS

Similar to classes, structs can be generic as well. They are very similar to generic classes with the exception of inheritance features. In this section you look at the generic struct Nullable<T>, which is defined by the .NET Framework.

An example of a generic struct in the .NET Framework is Nullable<T>. A number in a database and a number in a programming language have an important difference: A number in the database can be null, whereas a number in C# cannot be null. Int32 is a struct, and because structs are implemented as value types, they cannot be null. This difference often causes headaches and a lot of additional work to map the data. The problem exists not only with databases but also with mapping XML data to .NET types.

One solution is to map numbers from databases and XML files to reference types, because reference types can have a null value. However, this also means additional overhead during runtime.

With the structure Nullable<T>, this can be easily resolved. The following code segment shows a simplified version of how Nullable<T> is defined. The structure Nullable<T> defines a constraint specifying that the generic type T needs to be a struct. With classes as generic types, the advantage of low overhead is eliminated; and because objects of classes can be null anyway, there's no point in using a class with the Nullable<T> type. The only overhead in addition to the T type defined by Nullable<T> is the hasValue Boolean field that defines whether the value is set or null. Other than that, the generic struct defines the read-only properties HasValue and Value and some operator overloads. The operator overload to cast the Nullable<T> type to T is defined as explicit because it can throw an exception in case hasValue is false. The operator overload to cast to Nullable<T> is defined as implicit because it always succeeds:

```csharp
public struct Nullable<T>
  where T: struct
{
  public Nullable(T value)
  {
    _hasValue = true;
    _value = value;
  }

  private bool _hasValue;
  public bool HasValue => _hasValue;

  private T _value;
  public T Value
  {
    get
    {
      if (!_hasValue)
      {
        throw new InvalidOperationException("no value");
      }
      return _value;
    }
  }

  public static explicit operator T(Nullable<T> value) => _value.Value;

  public static implicit operator Nullable<T>(T value) =>
    new Nullable<T>(value);

  public override string ToString() => !HasValue ? string.Empty :
    _value.ToString();
}
```

In this example, Nullable<T> is instantiated with Nullable<int>. The variable x can now be used as an int, assigning values and using operators to do some calculation. This behavior is made possible by casting operators of the `Nullable<T>` type. However, x can also be `null`. The `Nullable<T>` properties `HasValue` and `Value` can check whether there is a value, and the value can be accessed:

```
Nullable<int> x;
x = 4;
x += 3;
if (x.HasValue)
{
    int y = x.Value;
}
x = null;
```

Because nullable types are used often, C# has a special syntax for defining variables of this type. Instead of using syntax with the generic structure, the ? operator can be used. In the following example, the variables x1 and x2 are both instances of a nullable int type:

```
Nullable<int> x1;
int? x2;
```

A nullable type can be compared with `null` and numbers, as shown. Here, the value of x is compared with `null`, and if it is not `null` it is compared with a value less than 0:

```
int? x = GetNullableType();
if (x == null)
{
    Console.WriteLine("x is null");
}
else if (x < 0)
{
    Console.WriteLine("x is smaller than 0");
}
```

Now that you know how `Nullable<T>` is defined, let's get into using nullable types. Nullable types can also be used with arithmetic operators. The variable x3 is the sum of the variables x1 and x2. If any of the nullable types have a `null` value, the result is `null`:

```
int? x1 = GetNullableType();
int? x2 = GetNullableType();
int? x3 = x1 + x2;
```

> **NOTE** *The* `GetNullableType` *method, which is called here, is just a placeholder for any method that returns a nullable* int. *For testing you can implement it to simply return* null *or to return any integer value.*

Non-nullable types can be converted to nullable types. With the conversion from a non-nullable type to a nullable type, an implicit conversion is possible where casting is not required. This type of conversion always succeeds:

```
int y1 = 4;
int? x1 = y1;
```

In the reverse situation, a conversion from a nullable type to a non-nullable type can fail. If the nullable type has a `null` value and the `null` value is assigned to a non-nullable type, then an exception of type `InvalidOperationException` is thrown. That's why the cast operator is required to do an explicit conversion:

```
int? x1 = GetNullableType();
int y1 = (int)x1;
```

Instead of doing an explicit cast, it is also possible to convert a nullable type to a non-nullable type with the coalescing operator. The coalescing operator uses the syntax `??` to define a default value for the conversion in case the nullable type has a value of null. Here, `y1` gets a 0 value if `x1` is null:

```
int? x1 = GetNullableType();
int y1 = x1 ?? 0;
```

GENERIC METHODS

In addition to defining generic classes, it is also possible to define generic methods. With a generic method, the generic type is defined with the method declaration. Generic methods can be defined within non-generic classes.

The method `Swap<T>` defines `T` as a generic type that is used for two arguments and a variable `temp`:

```
void Swap<T>(ref T x, ref T y)
{
  T temp;
  temp = x;
  x = y;
  y = temp;
}
```

A generic method can be invoked by assigning the generic type with the method call:

```
int i = 4;
int j = 5;
Swap<int>(ref i, ref j);
```

However, because the C# compiler can get the type of the parameters by calling the `Swap` method, it is not necessary to assign the generic type with the method call. The generic method can be invoked as simply as non-generic methods:

```
int i = 4;
int j = 5;
Swap(ref i, ref j);
```

Generic Methods Example

This example uses a generic method to accumulate all the elements of a collection. To show the features of generic methods, the following `Account` class, which contains `Name` and `Balance` properties, is used (code file `GenericMethods/Account.cs`):

```
public class Account
{
  public string Name { get; }
  public decimal Balance { get; }
  public Account(string name, Decimal balance)
  {
    Name = name;
    Balance = balance;
  }
}
```

All the accounts in which the balance should be accumulated are added to an accounts list of type `List<Account>` (code file `GenericMethods/Program.cs`):

```
var accounts = new List<Account>()
{
  new Account("Christian", 1500),
  new Account("Stephanie", 2200),
  new Account("Angela", 1800),
```

```
      new Account("Matthias", 2400),
      new Account("Katharina", 3800),
    };
```

A traditional way to accumulate all `Account` objects is by looping through them with a `foreach` statement, as shown here. Because the `foreach` statement uses the `IEnumerable` interface to iterate the elements of a collection, the argument of the `AccumulateSimple` method is of type `IEnumerable`. The `foreach` statement works with every object implementing `IEnumerable`. This way, the `AccumulateSimple` method can be used with all collection classes that implement the interface `IEnumerable<Account>`. In the implementation of this method, the property `Balance` of the `Account` object is directly accessed (code file `GenericMethods/Algorithms.cs`):

```
public static class Algorithms
{
  public static decimal AccumulateSimple(IEnumerable<Account> source)
  {
    decimal sum = 0;
    foreach (Account a in source)
    {
      sum += a.Balance;
    }
    return sum;
  }
}
```

The `AccumulateSimple` method is invoked like this:

```
decimal amount = Algorithms.AccumulateSimple(accounts);
```

Generic Methods with Constraints

The problem with the first implementation is that it works only with `Account` objects. This can be avoided by using a generic method.

The second version of the `Accumulate` method accepts any type that implements the interface `IAccount`. As you saw earlier with generic classes, you can restrict generic types with the `where` clause. You can use the same clause with generic methods that you use with generic classes. The parameter of the `Accumulate` method is changed to `IEnumerable<T>`, a generic interface that is implemented by generic collection classes (code file `GenericMethods/Algorithms.cs`):

```
public static decimal Accumulate<TAccount>(IEnumerable<TAccount> source)
  where TAccount: IAccount
{
  decimal sum = 0;
  foreach (TAccount a in source)
  {
    sum += a.Balance;
  }
  return sum;
}
```

The `Account` class is now refactored to implement the interface `IAccount` (code file `GenericMethods/Account.cs`):

```
public class Account: IAccount
{
  //...
```

The `IAccount` interface defines the read-only properties `Balance` and `Name` (code file `GenericMethods/IAccount.cs`):

```
public interface IAccount
{
```

```
    decimal Balance { get; }
    string Name { get; }
}
```

The new `Accumulate` method can be invoked by defining the `Account` type as a generic type parameter (code file GenericMethods/Program.cs):

```
decimal amount = Algorithm.Accumulate<Account>(accounts);
```

Because the generic type parameter can be automatically inferred by the compiler from the parameter type of the method, it is valid to invoke the `Accumulate` method this way:

```
decimal amount = Algorithm.Accumulate(accounts);
```

Generic Methods with Delegates

The requirement for the generic types to implement the interface `IAccount` may be too restrictive. The following example hints at how the `Accumulate` method can be changed by passing a generic delegate. Chapter 8 provides all the details about how to work with generic delegates, and how to use lambda expressions.

This `Accumulate` method uses two generic parameters: `T1` and `T2`. `T1` is used for the collection-implementing `IEnumerable<T1>` parameter, which is the first one of the methods. The second parameter uses the generic delegate `Func<T1, T2, TResult>`. Here, the second and third generic parameters are of the same `T2` type. A method needs to be passed that has two input parameters (`T1` and `T2`) and a return type of `T2` (code file GenericMethods/Algorithms.cs).

```
public static T2 Accumulate<T1, T2>(IEnumerable<T1> source,
  Func<T1, T2, T2> action)
{
  T2 sum = default(T2);
  foreach (T1 item in source)
  {
    sum = action(item, sum);
  }
  return sum;
}
```

In calling this method, it is necessary to specify the generic parameter types because the compiler cannot infer this automatically. With the first parameter of the method, the `accounts` collection that is assigned is of type `IEnumerable<Account>`. With the second parameter, a lambda expression is used that defines two parameters of type `Account` and `decimal`, and returns a decimal. This lambda expression is invoked for every item by the `Accumulate` method (code file GenericMethods/Program.cs):

```
decimal amount = Algorithm.Accumulate<Account, decimal>(
  accounts, (item, sum) => sum += item.Balance);
```

Don't scratch your head over this syntax yet. The sample should give you a glimpse of the possible ways to extend the `Accumulate` method. Chapter 8 covers lambda expressions in detail.

Generic Methods Specialization

You can overload generic methods to define specializations for specific types. This is true for methods with generic parameters as well. The `Foo` method is defined in four versions. The first accepts a generic parameter; the second one is a specialized version for the `int` parameter. The third `Foo` method accepts two generic parameters, and the fourth one is a specialized version of the third one with the first parameter of type `int`. During compile time, the best match is taken. If an `int` is passed, then the method with the `int` parameter is selected. With any other parameter type, the compiler chooses the generic version of the method (code file Specialization/Program.cs):

```
public class MethodOverloads
{
  public void Foo<T>(T obj) =>
    Console.WriteLine($"Foo<T>(T obj), obj type: {obj.GetType().Name}");
```

```
  public void Foo(int x) =>
    Console.WriteLine("Foo(int x)");

  public void Foo<T1, T2>(T1 obj1, T2 obj2) =>
    Console.WriteLine($"Foo<T1, T2>(T1 obj1, T2 obj2); " +
      $"{obj1.GetType().Name} {obj2.GetType().Name}");

  public void Foo<T>(int obj1, T obj2) =>
    Console.WriteLine($"Foo<T>(int obj1, T obj2); {obj2.GetType().Name}");

  public void Bar<T>(T obj) => Foo(obj);
}
```

The `Foo` method can now be invoked with any parameter type. The sample code passes `int` and `string` values to invoke all four `Foo` methods:

```
static void Main()
{
  var test = new MethodOverloads();
  test.Foo(33);
  test.Foo("abc");
  test.Foo("abc", 42);
  test.Foo(33, "abc");
}
```

Running the program, you can see by the output that the method with the best match is taken:

```
Foo(int x)
Foo<T>(T obj), obj type: String
Foo<T1, T2>(T1 obj1, T2 obj2); String Int32
Foo<T>(int obj1, T obj2); String
```

Be aware that the method invoked is defined during compile time and not runtime. This can be easily demonstrated by adding a generic `Bar` method that invokes the `Foo` method, passing the generic parameter value along:

```
public class MethodOverloads
{
  // ...
  public void Bar<T>(T obj) =>
    Foo(obj);
```

The `Main` method is now changed to invoke the `Bar` method passing an `int` value:

```
static void Main()
{
  var test = new MethodOverloads();
  test.Bar(44);
```

From the output on the console you can see that the generic `Foo` method was selected by the `Bar` method and not the overload with the `int` parameter. That's because the compiler selects the method that is invoked by the `Bar` method during compile time. Because the `Bar` method defines a generic parameter, and because there's a `Foo` method that matches this type, the generic `Foo` method is called. This is not changed during runtime when an `int` value is passed to the `Bar` method:

```
Foo<T>(T obj), obj type: Int32
```

SUMMARY

This chapter introduced a very important feature of the CLR: generics. With generic classes you can create type-independent classes, and generic methods allow type-independent methods. Interfaces, structs, and delegates can be created in a generic way as well. Generics make new programming styles possible. You've seen how algorithms, particularly actions and predicates, can be implemented to be used with different classes— and all are type safe. Generic delegates make it possible to decouple algorithms from collections.

You will see more features and uses of generics throughout this book. Chapter 8 introduces delegates that are often implemented as generics; Chapter 10 provides information about generic collection classes; and Chapter 12, "Language Integrated Query," discusses generic extension methods. The next chapter focuses on operators and casts.

Operators and Casts

WROX.COM CODE DOWNLOADS FOR THIS CHAPTER

The Wrox.com code downloads for this chapter are found at www.wrox.com on the Download Code tab. The source code is also available at https://github.com/ProfessionalCSharp/ProfessionalCSharp7 in the directory OperatorsAndCasts.

The code for this chapter is divided into the following major examples:

➤ OperatorsSample

➤ BinaryCalculations

➤ OperatorOverloadingSample

➤ OperatorOverloadingSample2

➤ OverloadingComparisonSample

➤ CustomIndexerSample

➤ CastingSample

OPERATORS AND CASTS

The preceding chapters have covered most of what you need to start writing useful programs using C#. This chapter continues the discussion with essential language elements and illustrates some powerful aspects of C# that enable you to extend its capabilities.

This chapter covers information about using operators, including operators that have been added with C# 6, such as the null-conditional operator and the `nameof` operator, as well as operator extensions of C# 7, such as pattern matching with the `is` operator. Later in this chapter, you see how operators are overloaded. The chapter also shows you how to implement custom functionality when using operators.

OPERATORS

C# operators are very similar to C++ and Java operators; however, there are differences.

C# supports the operators listed in the following table:

CATEGORY	OPERATOR	
Arithmetic	`+- * / %`	
Logical	`&	^ ˜ && ║ !`	
String concatenation	`+`	
Increment and decrement	`++- -`	
Bit shifting	`<< >>`	
Comparison	`== != < > <= >=`	
Assignment	`= += -= *= /= %= &= |= ^= <<= >>=`	
Member access (for objects and structs)	`.`	
Indexing (for arrays and indexers)	`[]`	
Cast	`()`	
Conditional (the ternary operator)	`?:`	
Delegate concatenation and removal (discussed in Chapter 8, "Delegates, Lambdas, and Events")	`+ -`	
Object creation	`new`	
Type information	`sizeof is typeof as`	
Overflow exception control	`checked unchecked`	
Indirection and address	`[]`	
Namespace alias qualifier (discussed in Chapter 2, "Core C#")	`::`	
Null coalescing operator	`??`	
Null-conditional operator	`?. ?[]`	
Name of an identifier	`nameof()`	

> **NOTE** *Note that four specific operators (`sizeof`, `*`, `->`, and `&`) are available only in unsafe code (code that bypasses C#'s type-safety checking), which is discussed in Chapter 17, "Managed and Unmanaged Memory."*

One of the biggest pitfalls to watch out for when using C# operators is that, as with other C-style languages, C# uses different operators for assignment (=) and comparison (==). For instance, the following statement means "let x equal three":

```
x = 3;
```

If you now want to compare x to a value, you need to use the double equals sign ==:

Fortunately, C#'s strict type-safety rules prevent the very common C error whereby assignment is performed instead of comparison in logical statements. This means that in C# the following statement will generate a compiler error:

```
if (x = 3) // compiler error
{
}
```

Visual Basic programmers who are accustomed to using the ampersand (&) character to concatenate strings will have to make an adjustment. In C#, the plus sign (+) is used instead for concatenation, whereas the & symbol denotes a logical AND between two different integer values. The pipe symbol, |, enables you to perform a logical OR between two integers. Visual Basic programmers also might not recognize the modulus (%) arithmetic operator. This returns the remainder after division, so, for example, x % 5 returns 2 if x is equal to 7.

You will use few pointers in C#, and therefore few indirection operators. More specifically, the only place you will use them is within blocks of unsafe code, because that is the only place in C# where pointers are allowed. Pointers and unsafe code are discussed in Chapter 17.

Operator Shortcuts

The following table shows the full list of shortcut assignment operators available in C#:

SHORTCUT OPERATOR	EQUIVALENT TO
x++, ++x	x = x + 1
x- -, - -x	x = x - 1
x += y	x = x + y
x -= y	x = x-y
x *= y	x = x * y
x /= y	x = x / y
x %= y	x = x % y
x >>= y	x = x >> y
x <<= y	x = x << y
x &= y	x = x & y
x |= y	x = x | y

You may be wondering why there are two examples each for the ++ increment and the – – decrement operators. Placing the operator *before* the expression is known as a prefix; placing the operator *after* the expression is known as a postfix. Note that there is a difference in the way they behave.

The increment and decrement operators can act both as entire expressions and within expressions. When used by themselves, the effect of both the prefix and postfix versions is identical and corresponds to the statement x = x + 1. When used within larger expressions, the prefix operator increments the value of x *before* the expression is evaluated; in other words, x is incremented and the new value is used in the expression. Conversely, the postfix operator increments the value of x *after* the expression is evaluated—the expression is evaluated using the original value of x. The following example uses the increment operator (++) as an example to demonstrate the difference between the prefix and postfix behavior (code file OperatorsSample/Program.cs):

```
int x = 5;
if (++x == 6) // true - x is incremented to 6 before the evaluation
{
  Console.WriteLine("This will execute");
}
if (x++ == 7) // false - x is incremented to 7 after the evaluation
{
  Console.WriteLine("This won't");
}
```

The first if condition evaluates to true because x is incremented from 5 to 6 *before* the expression is evaluated. The condition in the second if statement is false, however, because x is incremented to 7 only after the entire expression has been evaluated (while x == 6).

The prefix and postfix operators – –x and x– – behave in the same way, but decrement rather than increment the operand.

The other shortcut operators, such as += and -=, require two operands, and are used to modify the value of the first operand by performing an arithmetic or logical operation on it. For example, the next two lines are equivalent:

```
x += 5;
x = x + 5;
```

The following sections look at some of the primary and cast operators that you will frequently use within your C# code.

The Conditional-Expression Operator (?:)

The conditional-expression operator (?:), also known as the ternary operator, is a shorthand form of the if...else construction. It gets its name from the fact that it involves three operands. It allows you to evaluate a condition, returning one value if that condition is true, or another value if it is false. The syntax is as follows:

```
condition ? true_value: false_value
```

Here, condition is the Boolean expression to be evaluated, true_value is the value that is returned if condition is true, and false_value is the value that is returned otherwise.

When used sparingly, the conditional-expression operator can add a dash of terseness to your programs. It is especially handy for providing one of a couple of arguments to a function that is being invoked. You can use it to quickly convert a Boolean value to a string value of true or false. It is also handy for displaying the correct singular or plural form of a word (code file OperatorsSample/Program.cs):

```
int x = 1;
string s = x + " ";
```

```
s += (x == 1 ? "man": "men");
Console.WriteLine(s);
```

This code displays 1 man if x is equal to one but displays the correct plural form for any other number. Note, however, that if your output needs to be localized to different languages, you have to write more sophisticated routines to take into account the different grammatical rules of different languages.

The checked and unchecked Operators

Consider the following code:

```
byte b = byte.MaxValue;
b++;
Console.WriteLine(b);
```

The byte data type can hold values only in the range 0 to 255. Assigning byte.MaxValue to a byte results in 255. With 255, all bits of the 8 available bits in the bytes are set: 11111111. Incrementing this value by one causes an overflow and results in 0.

How the CLR handles this depends on a number of issues, including compiler options; so, whenever there's a risk of an unintentional overflow, you need some way to ensure that you get the result you want.

To do this, C# provides the checked and unchecked operators. If you mark a block of code as checked, the CLR enforces overflow checking, throwing an OverflowException if an overflow occurs. The following changes the preceding code to include the checked operator (code file OperatorsSample/Program.cs):

```
byte b = 255;
checked
{
  b++;
}
Console.WriteLine(b);
```

When you try to run this code, you get an error message like this:

```
System.OverflowException: Arithmetic operation resulted in an overflow.
```

You can enforce overflow checking for all unmarked code with the Visual Studio project settings Check for Arithmetic Overflow/Underflow in the Advance Build Settings. You can change this also directly in the csproj project file:

```
<PropertyGroup>
  <OutputType>Exe</OutputType>
  <TargetFramework>netcoreapp2.0</TargetFramework>
  <CheckForOverflowUnderflow>true</CheckForOverflowUnderflow>
</PropertyGroup>
```

If you want to suppress overflow checking, you can mark the code as unchecked:

```
byte b = 255;
unchecked
{
  b++;
}
Console.WriteLine(b);
```

In this case, no exception is raised, but you lose data because the byte type cannot hold a value of 256, the overflowing bits are discarded, and your b variable holds a value of zero (0).

Note that unchecked is the default behavior. The only time you are likely to need to explicitly use the unchecked keyword is when you need a few unchecked lines of code inside a larger block that you have explicitly marked as checked.

> **NOTE** *By default, overflow and underflow are not checked because enforcing checks has a performance impact. When you use checked as the default setting with your project, the result of every arithmetic operation needs to be verified whether the value is out of bounds. Arithmetic operations are also done with* `for` *loops using* `i++`. *For not having this performance impact, it's better to keep the default setting (Check for Arithmetic Overflow/Underflow) unchecked and use the* `checked` *operator where needed.*

The is Operator

The `is` operator allows you to check whether an object is compatible with a specific type. The phrase "is compatible" means that an object either is of that type or is derived from that type. For example, to check whether a variable is compatible with the `object` type, you could use the following bit of code (code file `OperatorsSample/Program.cs`):

```
int i = 10;
if (i is object)
{
    Console.WriteLine("i is an object");
}
```

`int`, like all C# data types, inherits from `object`; therefore, the expression `i is object` evaluates to `true` in this case, and the appropriate message will be displayed.

C# 7 extends the `is` operator with pattern matching. You can check for constants, types, and var. Examples of constant checks are shown in the following code snippet, which checks for the constant 42 and the constant null:

```
int i = 42;
if (i is 42)
{
    Console.WriteLine("i has the value 42");
}

object o = null;
if (o is null)
{
    Console.WriteLine("o is null");
}
```

Using the `is` operator with type matching, a variable can be declared right of the type. If the `is` operator returns `true`, the variable is filled with a reference to the object of the type. This variable can then be used within the scope of the `if` statement where the `is` operator is used:

```
public static void AMethodUsingPatternMatching(object o)
{
  if (o is Person p)
  {
    Console.WriteLine($"o is a Person with firstname {p.FirstName}");
  }
}
//...
AMethodUsingPatternMatching (new Person("Katharina", "Nagel"));
```

The as Operator

The `as` operator is used to perform explicit type conversions of reference types. If the type being converted is compatible with the specified type, conversion is performed successfully. However, if the types are incompatible, the as operator returns the value `null`. As shown in the following code, attempting to convert an `object` reference to a `string` returns `null` if the `object` reference does not actually refer to a `string` instance (code file `OperatorsSample/Program.cs`):

```
object o1 = "Some String";
object o2 = 5;
string s1 = o1 as string; // s1 = "Some String"
string s2 = o2 as string; // s2 = null
```

The as operator allows you to perform a safe type conversion in a single step without the need to first test the type using the is operator and then perform the conversion.

> **NOTE** *The* is *and* as *operators are shown with inheritance in Chapter 4, "Object Orientation with C#." Also check Chapter 13, "Functional Programming with C#" for more information on pattern matching and the* is *operator.*

The sizeof Operator

You can determine the size (in bytes) required on the stack by a value type using the `sizeof` operator (code file `OperatorsSample/Program.cs`):

```
Console.WriteLine(sizeof(int));
```

This displays the number 4 because an `int` is 4 bytes long.

You can also use the `sizeof` operator with structs if the struct contains only value types—for example, the `Point` class as shown here (code file `OperatorsSample/Point.cs`):

```
public struct Point
{
  public Point(int x, int y)
  {
    X = x;
    Y = y;
  }
  public int X { get; }
  public int Y { get; }
}
```

> **NOTE** *You cannot use* sizeof *with classes.*

Using `sizeof` with custom types, you need to write the code within an unsafe code block (code file `OperatorsSample/Program.cs`):

```
unsafe
{
  Console.WriteLine(sizeof(Point));
}
```

> **NOTE** *By default, unsafe code is not allowed. You need to specify the* AllowUnsafeBlocks *in the* csproj *project file. Chapter 17 looks at unsafe code in more detail.*

The typeof Operator

The `typeof` operator returns a `System.Type` object representing a specified type. For example, `typeof(string)` returns a `Type` object representing the `System.String` type. This is useful when you want to use reflection to find information about an object dynamically. For more information, see Chapter 16, "Reflection, Metadata, and Dynamic Programming."

The nameof Operator

The `nameof` operator is new since C# 6. This operator accepts a symbol, property, or method and returns the name.

How can this be used? One example is when the name of a variable is needed, as in checking a parameter for null:

```
public void Method(object o)
{
    if (o == null) throw new ArgumentNullException(nameof(o));
```

Of course, it would be similar to throw the exception by passing a string instead of using the `nameof` operator. However, passing a string doesn't give a compiler error if you misspell the name. Also, when you change the name of the parameter, you can easily miss changing the string passed to the `ArgumentNullException` constructor.

```
if (o == null) throw new ArgumentNullException("o");
```

Using the `nameof` operator for the name of a variable is just one use case. You can also use it to get the name of a property—for example, for firing a change event (using the interface `INotifyPropertyChanged`) in a property `set` accessor and passing the name of a property.

```
public string FirstName
{
  get => _firstName;
  set
  {
    _firstName = value;
    OnPropertyChanged(nameof(FirstName));
  }
}
```

The `nameof` operator can also be used to get the name of a method. This also works if the method is overloaded because all overloads result in the same value: the name of the method.

```
public void Method()
{
    Log($"{nameof(Method)} called");
```

The index Operator

You use the index operator (brackets) for accessing arrays in Chapter 7, "Arrays." In the following code snippet, the index operator is used to access the third element of the array named `arr1` by passing the number 2:

```
int[] arr1 = {1, 2, 3, 4};
int x = arr1[2]; // x == 3
```

Similar to accessing elements of an array, the index operator is implemented with collection classes (discussed in Chapter 10, "Collections").

The index operator doesn't require an integer within the brackets. Index operators can be defined with any type. The following code snippet creates a generic dictionary where the key is a `string`, and the value an `int`. With dictionaries, the key can be used with the indexer. In the following sample, the string `first` is passed to the index operator to set this element in the dictionary and then the same string is passed to the indexer to retrieve this element:

```
var dict = new Dictionary<string, int>();
dict["first"] = 1;
int x = dict["first"];
```

> **NOTE** *Later in this chapter in the "Implementing Custom Index Operators" section, you can read how to create index operators in your own classes.*

Nullable Types and Operators

An important difference between value types and reference types is that reference types can be `null`. A value type, such as `int`, cannot be `null`. This is a special issue on mapping C# types to database types. A database number can be `null`. In earlier C# versions, a solution was to use a reference type for mapping a nullable database number. However, this method affects performance because the garbage collector needs to deal with reference types. Now you can use a nullable `int` instead of a normal `int`. The overhead for this is just an additional Boolean that is used to check or set the `null` value. A nullable type still is a value type.

With the following code snippet, the variable `i1` is an `int` that gets 1 assigned to it. `i2` is a nullable `int` that has `i1` assigned. The nullability is defined by using the `?` with the type. `int?` can have an integer value assigned similar to the assignment of `i1`. The variable `i3` demonstrates that assigning `null` is also possible with nullable types (code file `NullableTypesSample/Program.cs`):

```
int i1 = 1;
int? i2 = 2;
int? i3 = null;
```

Every struct can be defined as a nullable type as shown with `long?` and `DateTime?`:

```
long? l1 = null;
DateTime? d1 = null;
```

If you use nullable types in your programs, you must always consider the effect a `null` value can have when used in conjunction with the various operators. Usually, when using a unary or binary operator with nullable types, the result will be `null` if one or both of the operands is `null`. For example:

```
int? a = null;
int? b = a + 4; // b = null
int? c = a * 5; // c = null
```

When comparing nullable types, if only one of the operands is `null`, the comparison always equates to `false`. This means that you cannot assume a condition is `true` just because its opposite is `false`, as often happens in programs using non-nullable types. For example, in the following example if a is null, the `else` clause is always invoked no matter whether b has a value of +5 or -5.

```
int? a = null;
int? b = -5;
if (a >= b) // if a or b is null, this condition is false
{
  Console.WriteLine("a >= b");
}
else
{
  Console.WriteLine("a < b");
}
```

> **NOTE** *The possibility of a* `null` *value means that you cannot freely combine nullable and non-nullable types in an expression. This is discussed in the section "Type Conversions" later in this chapter.*

> **NOTE** *When you use the C# keyword* `?` *with the type declaration—for example,* `int?`*—the compiler resolves this to use the generic type* `Nullable<int>`*. The C# compiler converts the shorthand notation to the generic type to reduce typing needs.*

The Null Coalescing Operator

The null coalescing operator (`??`) provides a shorthand mechanism to cater to the possibility of `null` values when working with nullable and reference types. The operator is placed between two operands—the first operand must be a nullable type or reference type, and the second operand must be of the same type as the first or of a type that is implicitly convertible to the type of the first operand. The null coalescing operator evaluates as follows:

- ➤ If the first operand is not `null`, then the overall expression has the value of the first operand.
- ➤ If the first operand is `null`, then the overall expression has the value of the second operand.

For example:

```
int? a = null;
int b;
b = a ?? 10; // b has the value 10
a = 3;
b = a ?? 10; // b has the value 3
```

If the second operand cannot be implicitly converted to the type of the first operand, a compile-time error is generated.

The null coalescing operator is not only important with nullable types but also with reference types. In the following code snippet, the property `Val` returns the value of the `_val` variable only if it is not null. In case it is null, a new instance of `MyClass` is created, assigned to the `_val` variable, and finally returned from the property. This second part of the expression within the `get` accessor only happens when the variable `_val` is null.

```
private MyClass _val;
public MyClass Val
{
  get => _val ?? (_val = new MyClass());
}
```

The Null-Conditional Operator

A feature of C# to reduce the number of code lines is the *null-conditional operator*. A great number of code lines in production code verifies null conditions. Before accessing members of a variable that is passed as a method parameter, it needs to be checked to determine whether the variable has a value of null. Otherwise a `NullReferenceException` would be thrown. A .NET design guideline specifies that code should never throw exceptions of these types and should always check for null conditions. However, such checks could be missed easily. This code snippet verifies whether the passed parameter `p` is not null. In case it is null, the method just returns without continuing:

```
public void ShowPerson(Person p)
{
  if (p == null) return;
```

```
    string firstName = p.FirstName;
    //...
}
```

Using the null-conditional operator to access the `FirstName` property (`p?.FirstName`), when `p` is `null`, only `null` is returned without continuing to the right side of the expression (code file `OperatorsSample/Program.cs`):

```
public void ShowPerson(Person p)
{
    string firstName = p?.FirstName;
    //...
}
```

When a property of an `int` type is accessed using the null-conditional operator, the result cannot be directly assigned to an `int` type because the result can be `null`. One option to resolve this is to assign the result to a nullable `int`:

```
int? age = p?.Age;
```

Of course, you can also solve this issue by using the null coalescing operator and defining another result (for example, `0`) in case the result of the left side is `null`:

```
int age1 = p?.Age ?? 0;
```

Multiple null-conditional operators can also be combined. Here the `Address` property of a `Person` object is accessed, and this property in turn defines a `City` property. Null checks need to be done for the `Person` object, and if it is not null, also for the result of the `Address` property:

```
Person p = GetPerson();
string city = null;
if (p != null && p.HomeAddress != null)
{
    city = p.HomeAddress.City;
}
```

When you use the null-conditional operator, the code becomes much simpler:

```
string city = p?.HomeAddress?.City;
```

You can also use the null-conditional operator with arrays. With the following code snippet, a `NullReferenceException` is thrown using the index operator to access an element of an array variable that is null:

```
int[] arr = null;
int x1 = arr[0];
```

Of course, traditional null checks could be done to avoid this exceptional condition. A simpler version uses `?[0]` to access the first element of the array. In case the result is `null`, the null coalescing operator returns the value for the `x1` variable:

```
int x1 = arr?[0] ?? 0;
```

Operator Precedence and Associativity

The following table shows the order of precedence of the C# operators. The operators at the top of the table are those with the highest precedence (that is, the ones evaluated first in an expression containing multiple operators).

GROUP	OPERATORS
Primary	`. ?. () [] ?[] x++ x-- new typeof sizeof checked unchecked`
Unary	`+ -! &DiacriticalTilde; ++x --x and casts`

GROUP	OPERATORS
Multiplication/division	`* / %`
Addition/subtraction	`+ -`
Shift operators	`<< >>`
Relational	`< ><= >= is as`
Comparison	`== !=`
Bitwise AND	`&`
Bitwise XOR	`^`
Bitwise OR	`|`
Logical AND	`&&`
Logical OR	`||`
Null coalescing	`??`
Conditional-expression operator	`?:`
Assignment and Lambda	`= += -= *= /= %= &= |= ^= <<= >>= >>>= =>`

Besides operator precedence, with binary operators you need to be aware of operator evaluations from left to right or right to left. With a few exceptions, all binary operators are left associative.

For example,

```
x + y + z
```

is evaluated as

```
(x + y) + z
```

You need to pay attention to the operator precedence before the associativity. With the following expression, first y and z are multiplied before the result of this multiplication is assigned to x, because multiplication has a higher precedency than addition:

```
x + y * z
```

The important exceptions with associativity are the assignment operators; these are right associative. The following expression is evaluated from right to left:

```
x = y = z
```

Because of the right associativity, all variables x, y, and z have the value 3 because it is evaluated from right to left. This wouldn't be the case if this operator would be evaluated from left to right:

```
int z = 3;
int y = 2;
int x = 1;
x = y = z;
```

An important right associative operator that might be misleading is the conditional-expression operator. The expression

```
a ? b: c ? d: e
```

is evaluated as

```
a = b: (c ? d: e)
```

because it is right-associative.

> **NOTE** *In complex expressions, avoid relying on operator precedence to produce the correct result. Using parentheses to specify the order in which you want operators applied clarifies your code and prevents potential confusion.*

USING BINARY OPERATORS

Working with binary values historically has been an important concept to understand when learning programming because the computer works with 0's and 1's. Many people probably missed learning this nowadays as they start to learn programming with Blocks, Scratch, and possibly JavaScript. If you are already fluent with 0 and 1, this section might still help you as a refresher.

With C# 7, working with binary values has become easier than it was in the past because of the use of digit separators and binary literals. Both of these features are discussed in Chapter 2, "Core C#." Binary operators have been available since the first version of C#, and they are covered in this section.

First, let's start with simple calculations using binary operators. The method `SimpleCalculations` first declares and initializes the variables `binary1` and `binary2` with binary values—using the binary literal and digit separators. Using the `&` operator, the two values are combined with the binary ADD operator and written to the variable `binaryAnd`. Following, the `|` operator is used to create the `binaryOr` variable, the `^` operator for the `binaryXOR` variable, and the `~` operator for the `reverse1` variable (code file BinaryCalculations/Program.cs):

```
static void SimpleCalculations()
{
  Console.WriteLine(nameof(SimpleCalculations));
  uint binary1 = 0b1111_0000_1100_0011_1110_0001_0001_1000;
  uint binary2 = 0b0000_1111_1100_0011_0101_1010_1110_0111;
  uint binaryAnd = binary1 & binary2;
  DisplayBits("AND", binaryAnd, binary1, binary2);
  uint binaryOR = binary1 | binary2;
  DisplayBits("OR", binaryOR, binary1, binary2);
  uint binaryXOR = binary1 ^ binary2;
  DisplayBits("XOR", binaryXOR, binary1, binary2);
  uint reverse1 = ~binary1;
  DisplayBits("NOT", reverse1, binary1);
  Console.WriteLine();
}
```

To display `uint` and `int` variables in a binary form, the extension method `ToBinaryString` is created. `Convert.ToString` offers an overload with two `int` parameters, where the second `int` value is the `toBase` parameter. Using this, you can format the output string binary by passing the value 2, octal (8), decimal (10), and hexadecimal (16). By default, if a binary value starts with 0 values, these values are ignored and not printed. The `PadLeft` method fills up these 0 values in the string. The number of string characters needed is calculated by the `sizeof` operator and a left shift of four bits. The `sizeof` operator returns the number of bytes for the specified type, as discussed earlier in this chapter. For displaying the bits, the number of bytes need to be multiplied by 8, which is the same as shifting three bits to the left. Another extension method is `AddSeparators`, which adds `_` separators after every four digits using LINQ methods (code file BinaryCalculations/BinaryExtensions.cs):

```
public static class BinaryExtensions
{
  public static string ToBinaryString(this uint number) =>
```

```
      Convert.ToString(number, toBase: 2).PadLeft(sizeof(uint) << 3, '0');
    public static string ToBinaryString(this int number) =>
      Convert.ToString(number, toBase: 2).PadLeft(sizeof(int) << 3, '0');

    public static string AddSeparators(this string number) =>
      string.Join('_',
        Enumerable.Range(0, number.Length / 4)
          .Select(i => number.Substring(i * 4, 4)).ToArray());
}
```

> **NOTE** *The* `AddSeparators` *method makes use of LINQ. LINQ is discussed in detail in Chapter 12, "Language Integrated Query."*

The method `DisplayBits`, which is invoked from the previously shown `SimpleCalculations` method, makes use of the `ToBinaryString` and `AddSeparators` extension methods. Here, the operands used for the operation are displayed, as well as the result (code file `BinaryCalculations/Program.cs`):

```
static void DisplayBits(string title, uint result, uint left,
  uint? right = null)
{
  Console.WriteLine(title);
  Console.WriteLine(left.ToBinaryString().AddSeparators());
  if (right.HasValue)
  {
    Console.WriteLine(right.Value.ToBinaryString().AddSeparators());
  }
  Console.WriteLine(result.ToBinaryString().AddSeparators());
  Console.WriteLine();
}
```

When you run the application, you can see the following output using the binary & operator. With this operator, the resulting bits are only 1 when both input values are also 1:

```
AND
1111_0000_1100_0011_1110_0001_0001_1000
0000_1111_1100_0011_0101_1010_1110_0111
0000_0000_1100_0011_0100_0000_0000_0000
```

Applying the binary | operator, the result bit is set (1) if one of the input bits is set:

```
OR
1111_0000_1100_0011_1110_0001_0001_1000
0000_1111_1100_0011_0101_1010_1110_0111
1111_1111_1100_0011_1111_1011_1111_1111
```

With the ^ operator, the result is set if just one of the original bits is set, but not both:

```
XOR
1111_0000_1100_0011_1110_0001_0001_1000
0000_1111_1100_0011_0101_1010_1110_0111
1111_1111_0000_0000_1011_1011_1111_1111
```

And finally, with the ~ operator, the result is the negation of the original:

```
NOT
1111_0000_1100_0011_1110_0001_0001_1000
0000_1111_0011_1100_0001_1110_1110_0111
```

Shifting Bits

As you've already seen in the previous sample, shifting three bits to the left is a multiplication by 8. A shift by one bit is a multiplication by 2. This is a lot faster than invoking the multiply operator— in case you need to multiply by 2, 4, 8, 16, 32, and so on.

The following code snippet sets one bit in the variable s1, and in the for loop the bit always shifts by one bit (code file BinaryCalculations/Program.cs):

```
static void ShiftingBits()
{
  Console.WriteLine(nameof(ShiftingBits));
  ushort s1 = 0b01;
  for (int i = 0; i < 16; i++)
  {
    Console.WriteLine($"{s1.ToBinarString()} {s1} hex: {s1:X}");
    s1 = (ushort)(s1 << 1);
  }
  Console.WriteLine();
}
```

With the program output you can see binary, decimal, and hexadecimal values with the loop:

```
0000000000000001 1 hex: 1
0000000000000010 2 hex: 2
0000000000000100 4 hex: 4
0000000000001000 8 hex: 8
0000000000010000 16 hex: 10
0000000000100000 32 hex: 20
0000000001000000 64 hex: 40
0000000010000000 128 hex: 80
0000000100000000 256 hex: 100
0000001000000000 512 hex: 200
0000010000000000 1024 hex: 400
0000100000000000 2048 hex: 800
0001000000000000 4096 hex: 1000
0010000000000000 8192 hex: 2000
0100000000000000 16384 hex: 4000
1000000000000000 32768 hex: 8000
```

Signed and Unsigned Numbers

One important thing to remember working with binaries is that using signed types such as int, long, short, the leftmost bit is used to represent the sign. When you use an int, the highest number available is 2147483647—the positive number of 31 bits or 0x7FFF FFFF. With an uint, the highest number available is 4294967295 or 0xFFFF FFFF. This represents the positive number of 32 bits. With the int, the other half of the number range is used for negative numbers.

To understand how negative numbers are represented, the following code snippet initializes the maxNumber variable to the highest positive number that fits into 31 bits using int.MaxValue. Then, in a for loop, the variable is incremented three times. From all the results, binary, decimal, and hexadecimal values are shown (code file BinaryCalculations/Program.cs):

```
private static void SignedNumbers()
{
  Console.WriteLine(nameof(SignedNumbers));

  void DisplayNumber(string title, int x) =>
    Console.WriteLine($"{title,-11} " +
```

```
          $"bin: {x.ToBinaryString().AddSeparators()}, " +
          $"dec: {x}, hex: {x:X}");

  int maxNumber = int.MaxValue;
  DisplayNumber("max int", maxNumber);
  for (int i = 0; i < 3; i++)
  {
    maxNumber++;
    DisplayNumber($"added {i + 1}", maxNumber);
  }
  Console.WriteLine();
  //...
}
```

With the output of the application, you can see all the bits—except for the sign bit—are set to achieve the maximum integer value. The output shows the same value in different formats—binary, decimal, and hexadecimal. Adding 1 to the first output results in an overflow of the int type setting the sign bit, and all other bits are 0. This is the highest negative value for the int type. After this result, two more increments are done:

```
max int    bin: 0111_1111_1111_1111_1111_1111_1111_1111, dec: 2147483647,
  hex: 7FFFFFFF
added 1    bin: 1000_0000_0000_0000_0000_0000_0000_0000, dec: -2147483648,
  hex: 80000000
added 2    bin: 1000_0000_0000_0000_0000_0000_0000_0001, dec: -2147483647,
  hex: 80000001
added 3    bin: 1000_0000_0000_0000_0000_0000_0000_0010, dec: -2147483646,
  hex: 80000002
```

With the next code snippet, the variable zero is initialized to 0. In the for loop, this variable is decremented three times:

```
int zero = 0;
DisplayNumber("zero", zero);
for (int i = 0; i < 3; i++)
{
  zero--;
  DisplayNumber($"subtracted {i + 1}", zero);
}
Console.WriteLine();
```

With the output, you can see 0 is represented with all the bits not set. Doing a decrement results in decimal -1, which is all the bits set—including the sign bit:

```
zero        bin: 0000_0000_0000_0000_0000_0000_0000_0000, dec: 0, hex: 0
subtracted 1 bin: 1111_1111_1111_1111_1111_1111_1111_1111, dec: -1, hex: FFFFFFFF
subtracted 2 bin: 1111_1111_1111_1111_1111_1111_1111_1110, dec: -2, hex: FFFFFFFE
subtracted 3 bin: 1111_1111_1111_1111_1111_1111_1111_1101, dec: -3, hex: FFFFFFFD
```

Next, start with the largest negative number for an int. The number is incremented three times:

```
int minNumber = int.MinValue;
DisplayNumber("min number", minNumber);
for (int i = 0; i < 3; i++)
{
  minNumber++;
  DisplayNumber($"added {i + 1}", minNumber);
}
Console.WriteLine();
```

The highest negative number was already shown earlier when overflowing the highest positive number. Earlier you saw this same number when int.MinValue was used. This number is then incremented three times:

```
min number  bin: 1000_0000_0000_0000_0000_0000_0000_0000, dec: -2147483648,
  hex: 80000000
```

```
added 1    bin: 1000_0000_0000_0000_0000_0000_0000_0001, dec: -2147483647,
  hex: 80000001
added 2    bin: 1000_0000_0000_0000_0000_0000_0000_0010, dec: -2147483646,
  hex: 80000002
added 3    bin: 1000_0000_0000_0000_0000_0000_0000_0011, dec: -2147483645,
  hex: 80000003
```

TYPE SAFETY

Chapter 1, ".NET Applications and Tools," noted that the Intermediate Language (IL) enforces strong type safety upon its code. Strong typing enables many of the services provided by .NET, including security and language interoperability. As you would expect from a language compiled into IL, C# is also strongly typed. Among other things, this means that data types are not always seamlessly interchangeable. This section looks at conversions between primitive types.

> **NOTE** *C# also supports conversions between different reference types and allows you to define how data types that you create behave when converted to and from other types. Both of these topics are discussed later in this chapter.*
>
> *Generics, however, enable you to avoid some of the most common situations in which you would need to perform type conversions. See Chapter 5, "Generics," and Chapter 10 for details.*

Type Conversions

Often, you need to convert data from one type to another. Consider the following code:

```
byte value1 = 10;
byte value2 = 23;
byte total;
total = value1 + value2;
Console.WriteLine(total);
```

When you attempt to compile these lines, you get the following error message:

```
Cannot implicitly convert type 'int' to 'byte'
```

The problem here is that when you add 2 bytes together, the result is returned as an `int`, not another `byte`. This is because a `byte` can contain only 8 bits of data, so adding 2 bytes together could very easily result in a value that cannot be stored in a single `byte`. If you want to store this result in a `byte` variable, you have to convert it back to a `byte`. The following sections discuss two conversion mechanisms supported by C#— *implicit* and *explicit*.

Implicit Conversions

Conversion between types can normally be achieved automatically (implicitly) only if you can guarantee that the value is not changed in any way. This is why the previous code failed; by attempting a conversion from an `int` to a `byte`, you were potentially losing 3 bytes of data. The compiler won't let you do that unless you explicitly specify that's what you want to do. If you store the result in a `long` instead of a `byte`, however, you will have no problems:

```
byte value1 = 10;
byte value2 = 23;
long total; // this will compile fine
total = value1 + value2;
Console.WriteLine(total);
```

Your program has compiled with no errors at this point because a `long` holds more bytes of data than a `byte`, so there is no risk of data being lost. In these circumstances, the compiler is happy to make the conversion for you, without your needing to ask for it explicitly.

The following table shows the implicit type conversions supported in C#:

FROM	TO
sbyte	short, int, long, float, double, decimal, BigInteger
byte	short, ushort, int, uint, long, ulong, float, double, decimal, BigInteger
short	int, long, float, double, decimal, BigInteger
ushort	int, uint, long, ulong, float, double, decimal, BigInteger
int	long, float, double, decimal, BigInteger
uint	long, ulong, float, double, decimal, BigInteger
long, ulong	float, double, decimal, BigInteger
float	double, BigInteger
char	ushort, int, uint, long, ulong, float, double, decimal, BigInteger

> **NOTE** `BigInteger` *is a struct that contains a number of any size. You can initialize it from smaller types, pass a number array to create one big number, or parse a string for a huge number. This type implements methods for mathematical calculations. The namespace for* `BigInteger` *is* `System.Numeric`*.*

As you would expect, you can perform implicit conversions only from a smaller integer type to a larger one, not from larger to smaller. You can also convert between integers and floating-point values; however, the rules are slightly different here. Though you can convert between types of the same size, such as `int`/`uint` to `float` and `long`/`ulong` to `double`, you can also convert from `long`/`ulong` back to `float`. You might lose 4 bytes of data doing this, but it only means that the value of the `float` you receive will be less precise than if you had used a `double`; the compiler regards this as an acceptable possible error because the magnitude of the value is not affected. You can also assign an unsigned variable to a signed variable as long as the value limits of the unsigned type fit between the limits of the signed variable.

Nullable types introduce additional considerations when implicitly converting value types:

➤ Nullable types implicitly convert to other nullable types following the conversion rules described for non-nullable types in the previous table; that is, `int?` implicitly converts to `long?`, `float?`, `double?`, and `decimal`.

➤ Non-nullable types implicitly convert to nullable types according to the conversion rules described in the preceding table; that is, `int` implicitly converts to `long?`, `float?`, `double?`, and `decimal?`.

➤ Nullable types do not implicitly convert to non-nullable types; you must perform an explicit conversion as described in the next section. That's because there is a chance that a nullable type will have the value `null`, which cannot be represented by a non-nullable type.

Explicit Conversions

Many conversions cannot be implicitly made between types, and the compiler returns an error if any are attempted. The following are some of the conversions that cannot be made implicitly:

- ➤ `int` to `short`—Data loss is possible.
- ➤ `int` to `uint`—Data loss is possible.
- ➤ `uint` to `int`—Data loss is possible.
- ➤ `float` to `int`—Everything is lost after the decimal point.
- ➤ Any numeric type to `char`—Data loss is possible.
- ➤ `decimal` to any numeric type—The decimal type is internally structured differently from both integers and floating-point numbers.
- ➤ `int?` to `int`—The nullable type may have the value `null`.

However, you can explicitly carry out such conversions using *casts*. When you cast one type to another, you deliberately force the compiler to make the conversion. A cast looks like this:

```
long val = 30000;
int i = (int)val; // A valid cast. The maximum int is 2147483647
```

You indicate the type to which you are casting by placing its name in parentheses before the value to be converted. If you are familiar with C, this is the typical syntax for casts. If you are familiar with the C++ special cast keywords such as `static_cast`, note that these do not exist in C#; you have to use the older C-type syntax.

Casting can be a dangerous operation to undertake. Even a simple cast from a `long` to an `int` can cause problems if the value of the original `long` is greater than the maximum value of an `int`:

```
long val = 3000000000;
int i = (int)val; // An invalid cast. The maximum int is 2147483647
```

In this case, you get neither an error nor the result you expect. If you run this code and output the value stored in `i`, this is what you get:

```
-1294967296
```

It is good practice to assume that an explicit cast does not return the results you expect. As shown earlier, C# provides a `checked` operator that you can use to test whether an operation causes an arithmetic overflow. You can use the `checked` operator to confirm that a cast is safe and to force the runtime to throw an overflow exception if it is not:

```
long val = 3000000000;
int i = checked((int)val);
```

Bearing in mind that all explicit casts are potentially unsafe, take care to include code in your application to deal with possible failures of the casts. Chapter 14, "Errors and Exceptions," introduces structured exception handling using the `try` and `catch` statements.

Using casts, you can convert most primitive data types from one type to another; for example, in the following code, the value `0.5` is added to `price`, and the total is cast to an `int`:

```
double price = 25.30;
int approximatePrice = (int)(price + 0.5);
```

This gives the price rounded to the nearest dollar. However, in this conversion, data is lost—namely, everything after the decimal point. Therefore, such a conversion should never be used if you want to continue to do more calculations using this modified price value. However, it is useful if you want to output the approximate value of a completed or partially completed calculation—if you don't want to bother the user with a lot of figures after the decimal point.

This example shows what happens if you convert an unsigned integer into a char:

```
ushort c = 43;
char symbol = (char)c;
Console.WriteLine(symbol);
```

The output is the character that has an ASCII number of 43: the + sign. You can try any kind of conversion you want between the numeric types (including char) and it will work, such as converting a decimal into a char, or vice versa.

Converting between value types is not restricted to isolated variables, as you have seen. You can convert an array element of type double to a struct member variable of type int:

```
struct ItemDetails
{
  public string Description;
  public int ApproxPrice;
}
//...
double[] Prices = { 25.30, 26.20, 27.40, 30.00 };
ItemDetails id;
id.Description = "Hello there.";
id.ApproxPrice = (int)(Prices[0] + 0.5);
```

To convert a nullable type to a non-nullable type or another nullable type where data loss may occur, you must use an explicit cast. This is true even when converting between elements with the same basic underlying type—for example, int? to int or float? to float. This is because the nullable type may have the value null, which cannot be represented by the non-nullable type. As long as an explicit cast between two equivalent non-nullable types is possible, so is the explicit cast between nullable types. However, when casting from a nullable type to a non-nullable type and the variable has the value null, an InvalidOperationException is thrown. For example:

```
int? a = null;
int b = (int)a; // Will throw exception
```

Using explicit casts and a bit of care and attention, you can convert any instance of a simple value type to almost any other. However, there are limitations on what you can do with explicit type conversions—as far as value types are concerned, you can only convert to and from the numeric and char types and enum types. You cannot directly cast Booleans to any other type or vice versa.

If you need to convert between numeric and string, you can use methods provided in the .NET class library. The Object class implements a ToString method, which has been overridden in all the .NET predefined types and which returns a string representation of the object:

```
int i = 10;
string s = i.ToString();
```

Similarly, if you need to parse a string to retrieve a numeric or Boolean value, you can use the Parse method supported by all the predefined value types:

```
string s = "100";
int i = int.Parse(s);
Console.WriteLine(i + 50); // Add 50 to prove it is really an int
```

Note that Parse registers an error by throwing an exception if it is unable to convert the string (for example, if you try to convert the string Hello to an integer). Again, exceptions are covered in Chapter 14.

Boxing and Unboxing

In Chapter 2 you learned that all types—both the simple predefined types, such as int and char, and the complex types, such as classes and structs—derive from the object type. This means you can treat even literal values as though they are objects:

```
string s = 10.ToString();
```

However, you also saw that C# data types are divided into value types, which are allocated on the stack, and reference types, which are allocated on the managed heap. How does this square with the capability to call methods on an int, if the int is nothing more than a 4-byte value on the stack?

C# achieves this through a bit of magic called *boxing*. Boxing and its counterpart, *unboxing*, enable you to convert value types to reference types and then back to value types. We include this in the section on casting because this is essentially what you are doing—you are casting your value to the object type. Boxing is the term used to describe the transformation of a value type to a reference type. Basically, the runtime creates a temporary reference-type box for the object on the heap.

This conversion can occur implicitly, as in the preceding example, but you can also perform it explicitly:

```
int myIntNumber = 20;
object myObject = myIntNumber;
```

Unboxing is the term used to describe the reverse process, whereby the value of a previously boxed value type is cast back to a value type. Here we use the term *cast* because this has to be done explicitly. The syntax is similar to explicit type conversions already described:

```
int myIntNumber = 20;
object myObject = myIntNumber; // Box the int
int mySecondNumber = (int)myObject; // Unbox it back into an int
```

A variable can be unboxed only if it has been boxed. If you execute the last line when myObject is not a boxed int, you get a runtime exception thrown at runtime.

One word of warning: When unboxing, you have to be careful that the receiving value variable has enough room to store all the bytes in the value being unboxed. C#'s ints, for example, are only 32 bits long, so unboxing a long value (64 bits) into an int, as shown here, results in an InvalidCastException:

```
long myLongNumber = 333333423;
object myObject = (object)myLongNumber;
int myIntNumber = (int)myObject;
```

COMPARING OBJECTS FOR EQUALITY

After discussing operators and briefly touching on the equality operator, it is worth considering for a moment what equality means when dealing with instances of classes and structs. Understanding the mechanics of object equality is essential for programming logical expressions and is important when implementing operator overloads and casts, the topic of the rest of this chapter.

The mechanisms of object equality vary depending on whether you are comparing reference types (instances of classes) or value types (the primitive data types, instances of structs, or enums). The following sections present the equality of reference types and value types independently.

Comparing Reference Types for Equality

You might be surprised to learn that System.Object defines three different methods for comparing objects for equality: ReferenceEquals and two versions of Equals: one method that is static and one virtual instance method that can be overridden. You can also implement the interface IEquality<T>, which defines an Equals method that has a generic type parameter instead of object. Add to this the comparison operator (==) and you actually have many ways to compare for equality. Some subtle differences exist between the different methods, which are examined next.

The ReferenceEquals Method

ReferenceEquals is a static method that tests whether two references refer to the same instance of a class, specifically whether the two references contain the same address in memory. As a static method, it cannot be overridden, so the System.Object implementation is what you always have. ReferenceEquals always returns true if supplied with two references that refer to the same object instance, and false otherwise. It does, however, consider null to be equal to null (code file EqualsSample/Program.cs):

```
static void ReferenceEqualsSample()
{
    SomeClass x = new SomeClass(), y = new SomeClass(), z = x;

    bool b1 = object.ReferenceEquals(null, null);// returns true
    bool b2 = object.ReferenceEquals(null, x);   // returns false
    bool b3 = object.ReferenceEquals(x, y);      // returns false because x and y
                                                 // references different objects
    bool b4 = object.ReferenceEquals(x, z);      // returns true because x and z
                                                 // references the same object

    //...
}
```

The Virtual Equals Method

The System.Object implementation of the virtual version of Equals also works by comparing references. However, because this method is virtual, you can override it in your own classes to compare objects by value. In particular, if you intend instances of your class to be used as keys in a dictionary, you need to override this method to compare values. Otherwise, depending on how you override Object.GetHashCode, the dictionary class that contains your objects either will not work at all or will work very inefficiently. Note that when overriding Equals, your override should never throw exceptions. Again, that's because doing so can cause problems for dictionary classes and possibly some other .NET base classes that internally call this method.

The Static Equals Method

The static version of Equals actually does the same thing as the virtual instance version. The difference is that the static version takes two parameters and compares them for equality. This method is able to cope when either of the objects is null; therefore, it provides an extra safeguard against throwing exceptions if there is a risk that an object might be null. The static overload first checks whether the references it has been passed are null. If they are both null, it returns true (because null is considered to be equal to null). If just one of them is null, it returns false. If both references actually refer to something, it calls the virtual instance version of Equals. This means that when you override the instance version of Equals, the effect is the same as if you were overriding the static version as well.

Comparison Operator (==)

It is best to think of the comparison operator as an intermediate option between strict value comparison and strict reference comparison. In most cases, writing the following means that you are comparing references:

```
bool b = (x == y); // x, y object references
```

However, it is accepted that there are some classes whose meanings are more intuitive if they are treated as values. In those cases, it is better to override the comparison operator to perform a value comparison.

Overriding operators is discussed next, but the obvious example of this is the System.String class for which Microsoft has overridden this operator to compare the contents of the strings rather than their references.

Comparing Value Types for Equality

When comparing value types for equality, the same principles hold as for reference types: ReferenceEquals is used to compare references, Equals is intended for value comparisons, and the comparison operator is viewed as an intermediate case. However, the big difference is that value types need to be boxed to be converted to references so that methods can be executed on them. In addition, Microsoft has already overloaded the instance Equals method in the System.ValueType class to test equality appropriate to value types. If you call sA.Equals(sB) where sA and sB are instances of some struct, the return value is true or false, according to whether sA and sB contain the same values in all their fields. On the other hand, no overload of == is available by default for your own structs. Writing (sA == sB) in any expression results in a compilation error unless you have provided an overload of == in your code for the struct in question.

Another point is that ReferenceEquals always returns false when applied to value types because, to call this method, the value types need to be boxed into objects. Even if you write the following, you still get the result of false:

```
bool b = ReferenceEquals(v,v);  // v is a variable of some value type
```

The reason is that v is boxed separately when converting each parameter, which means you get different references. Therefore, there really is no reason to call ReferenceEquals to compare value types because it doesn't make much sense.

Although the default override of Equals supplied by System.ValueType will almost certainly be adequate for the vast majority of structs that you define, you might want to override it again for your own structs to improve performance. Also, if a value type contains reference types as fields, you might want to override Equals to provide appropriate semantics for these fields because the default override of Equals will simply compare their addresses.

OPERATOR OVERLOADING

This section looks at another type of member that you can define for a class or a struct: the operator overload. Operator overloading is something that will be familiar to C++ developers. However, because the concept is new to both Java and Visual Basic developers, we explain it here. C++ developers will probably prefer to skip ahead to the main operator overloading example.

The point of operator overloading is that you do not always just want to call methods or properties on objects. Often, you need to do things like add quantities together, multiply them, or perform logical operations such as comparing objects. Suppose you defined a class that represents a mathematical matrix. In the world of math, matrices can be added together and multiplied, just like numbers. Therefore, it is quite plausible that you would want to write code like this:

```
Matrix a, b, c;
// assume a, b and c have been initialized
Matrix d = c * (a + b);
```

By overloading the operators, you can tell the compiler what + and * do when used in conjunction with a Matrix object, enabling you to write code like the preceding. If you were coding in a language that did not support operator overloading, you would have to define methods to perform those operations. The result would certainly be less intuitive and would probably look something like this:

```
Matrix d = c.Multiply(a.Add(b));
```

With what you have learned so far, operators such as + and * have been strictly for use with the predefined data types, and for good reason: The compiler knows what all the common operators mean for those data types. For example, it knows how to add two longs or how to divide one double by another double, and it can generate the appropriate intermediate language code. When you define your own classes or structs, however, you have to tell the compiler everything: what methods are available to call, what fields to store with each instance, and so on. Similarly, if you want to use operators with your own types, you have to tell the compiler what the relevant operators mean in the context of that class. You do that by defining overloads for the operators.

The other thing to stress is that overloading is not just concerned with arithmetic operators. You also need to consider the comparison operators, ==, <, >, !=, >=, and <=. Take the statement if (a==b). For classes, this statement, by default, compares the references a and b. It tests whether the references point to the same location in memory, rather than checking whether the instances actually contain the same data. For the string class, this behavior is overridden so that comparing strings really does compare the contents of each string. You might want to do the same for your own classes. For structs, the == operator does not do anything at all by default. Trying to compare two structs to determine whether they are equal produces a compilation error unless you explicitly overload == to tell the compiler how to perform the comparison.

In many situations, being able to overload operators enables you to generate more readable and intuitive code, including the following:

➤ Almost any mathematical object such as coordinates, vectors, matrices, tensors, functions, and so on. If you are writing a program that does some mathematical or physical modeling, you will almost certainly use classes representing these objects.

➤ Graphics programs that use mathematical or coordinate-related objects when calculating positions on-screen.

➤ A class that represents an amount of money (for example, in a financial program).

➤ A word processing or text analysis program that uses classes representing sentences, clauses, and so on. You might want to use operators to combine sentences (a more sophisticated version of concatenation for strings).

However, there are also many types for which operator overloading is not relevant. Using operator overloading inappropriately will make any code that uses your types far more difficult to understand. For example, multiplying two DateTime objects does not make any sense conceptually.

How Operators Work

To understand how to overload operators, it's quite useful to think about what happens when the compiler encounters an operator. Using the addition operator (+) as an example, suppose that the compiler processes the following lines of code:

```
int myInteger = 3;
uint myUnsignedInt = 2;
double myDouble = 4.0;
long myLong = myInteger + myUnsignedInt;
double myOtherDouble = myDouble + myInteger;
```

Now consider what happens when the compiler encounters this line:

```
long myLong = myInteger + myUnsignedInt;
```

The compiler identifies that it needs to add two integers and assign the result to a long. However, the expression myInteger + myUnsignedInt is really just an intuitive and convenient syntax for calling a method that adds two numbers. The method takes two parameters, myInteger and myUnsignedInt, and returns their sum. Therefore, the compiler does the same thing it does for any method call: It looks for the best matching overload of the addition operator based on the parameter types—in this case, one that takes two integers. As with normal overloaded methods, the desired return type does not influence the compiler's choice as to which version of a method it calls. As it happens, the overload called in the example takes two `int` parameters and returns an `int`; this return value is subsequently converted to a `long`.

The next line causes the compiler to use a different overload of the addition operator:

```
double myOtherDouble = myDouble + myInteger;
```

In this instance, the parameters are a `double` and an `int`, but there is no overload of the addition operator that takes this combination of parameters. Instead, the compiler identifies the best matching overload of the addition operator as being the version that takes two `double`s as its parameters, and it implicitly casts the `int` to a `double`. Adding two `double`s requires a different process from adding two integers. Floating-point numbers are stored as a mantissa and an exponent. Adding them involves bit-shifting the mantissa of one of the `double`s so that the two exponents have the same value, adding the mantissas, then shifting the mantissa of the result and adjusting its exponent to maintain the highest possible accuracy in the answer.

Now you are in a position to see what happens if the compiler finds something like this:

```
Vector vect1, vect2, vect3;
// initialize vect1 and vect2
vect3 = vect1 + vect2;
vect1 = vect1 * 2;
```

Here, `Vector` is the struct, which is defined in the following section. The compiler sees that it needs to add two `Vector` instances, `vect1` and `vect2`, together. It looks for an overload of the addition operator, which takes two `Vector` instances as its parameters.

If the compiler finds an appropriate overload, it calls up the implementation of that operator. If it cannot find one, it checks whether there is any other overload for + that it can use as a best match—perhaps something with two parameters of other data types that can be implicitly converted to `Vector` instances. If the compiler cannot find a suitable overload, it raises a compilation error, just as it would if it could not find an appropriate overload for any other method call.

Operator Overloading Example: The struct Vector

This section demonstrates operator overloading through developing a struct named `Vector` that represents a three-dimensional mathematical vector. Don't worry if mathematics is not your strong point—the vector example is very simple. As far as you are concerned here, a 3D vector is just a set of three numbers (`double`s) that tell you how far something is moving. The variables representing the numbers are called `_x`, `_y`, and `_z`: the `_x` tells you how far something moves east, `_y` tells you how far it moves north, and `_z` tells you how far it moves upward (in height). Combine the three numbers and you get the total movement. For example, if `_x=3.0`, `_y=3.0`, and `_z=1.0` (which you would normally write as (`3.0`, `3.0`, `1.0`)), you're moving 3 units east, 3 units north, and rising upward by 1 unit.

You can add or multiply vectors by other vectors or by numbers. Incidentally, in this context, we use the term *scalar*, which is math-speak for a simple number—in C# terms that is just a `double`. The significance of addition should be clear. If you move first by the vector (`3.0`, `3.0`, `1.0`) then move by the vector (`2.0`, `-4.0`, `-4.0`), the total amount you have moved can be determined by adding the two vectors. Adding vectors means adding each component individually, so you get (`5.0`, `-1.0`, `-3.0`). In this context, mathematicians write c=a+b, where a and b are the vectors and c is the resulting vector. You want to be able to use the `Vector` struct the same way.

> **NOTE** *The fact that this example is developed as a struct rather than a class is not significant with operator overloading. Operator overloading works in the same way for both structs and classes.*

Following is the definition for `Vector`—containing the read-only properties, constructors, and a `ToString` override so you can easily view the contents of a `Vector`, and, finally, that operator overload (code file `OperatorOverloadingSample/Vector.cs`):

```
struct Vector
{
  public Vector(double x, double y, double z)
  {
    X = x;
    Y = y;
    Z = z;
  }

  public Vector(Vector v)
  {
    X = v.X;
    Y = v.Y;
    Z = v.Z;
  }

  public double X { get; }
  public double Y { get; }
  public double Z { get; }
  public override string ToString() => $"( {X}, {Y}, {Z} )";
}
```

This example has two constructors that require specifying the initial value of the vector, either by passing in the values of each component or by supplying another `Vector` whose value can be copied. Constructors like the second one, that takes a single `Vector` argument, are often termed *copy constructors* because they effectively enable you to initialize a class or struct instance by copying another instance.

Here is the interesting part of the `Vector` struct—the operator overload that provides support for the addition operator:

```
public static Vector operator +(Vector left, Vector right) =>
new Vector(left.X + right.X, left.Y + right.Y, left.Z + right.Z);
```

The operator overload is declared in much the same way as a static method, except that the `operator` keyword tells the compiler it is actually an operator overload you are defining. The `operator` keyword is followed by the actual symbol for the relevant operator, in this case the addition operator (+). The return type is whatever type you get when you use this operator. Adding two vectors results in a vector; therefore, the return type is also a `Vector`. For this particular override of the addition operator, the return type is the same as the containing class, but that is not necessarily the case, as you see later in this example. The two parameters are the things you are operating on. For binary operators (those that take two parameters), such as the addition and subtraction operators, the first parameter is the value on the left of the operator, and the second parameter is the value on the right.

The implementation of this operator returns a new `Vector` that is initialized using `X`, `Y`, and `Z` properties from the `left` and `right` variables.

C# requires that all operator overloads be declared as `public` and `static`, which means they are associated with their class or struct, not with a particular instance. Because of this, the body of the operator overload has no access to non-static class members or the `this` identifier. This is fine because the parameters provide all the input data the operator needs to know to perform its task.

Now all you need to do is write some simple code to test the `Vector` struct (code file `OperatorOverloadingSample/Program.cs`):

```
static void Main()
{
  Vector vect1, vect2, vect3;
  vect1 = new Vector(3.0, 3.0, 1.0);
```

```
vect2 = new Vector(2.0, -4.0, -4.0);
vect3 = vect1 + vect2;
Console.WriteLine($"vect1 = {vect1}");
Console.WriteLine($"vect2 = {vect2}");
Console.WriteLine($"vect3 = {vect3}");
}
```

Compiling and running this code returns the following result:

```
vect1 = ( 3, 3, 1 )
vect2 = ( 2, -4, -4 )
vect3 = ( 5, -1, -3 )
```

In addition to adding vectors, you can multiply and subtract them and compare their values. In this section, you develop the Vector example further by adding a few more operator overloads. You won't develop the complete set that you'd probably need for a fully functional Vector type, but you develop enough to demonstrate some other aspects of operator overloading. First, you overload the multiplication operator to support multiplying vectors by a scalar and multiplying vectors by another vector.

Multiplying a vector by a scalar simply means multiplying each component individually by the scalar: for example, 2 * (1.0, 2.5, 2.0) returns (2.0, 5.0, 4.0). The relevant operator overload looks similar to this (code file OperatorOverloadingSample2/Vector.cs):

```
public static Vector operator *(double left, Vector right) =>
    new Vector(left * right.X, left * right.Y, left * right.Z);
```

This by itself, however, is not sufficient. If a and b are declared as type Vector, you can write code like this:

```
b = 2 * a;
```

The compiler implicitly converts the integer 2 to a double to match the operator overload signature. However, code like the following does not compile:

```
b = a * 2;
```

The point is that the compiler treats operator overloads exactly like method overloads. It examines all the available overloads of a given operator to find the best match. The preceding statement requires the first parameter to be a Vector and the second parameter to be an integer, or something to which an integer can be implicitly converted. You have not provided such an overload. The compiler cannot start swapping the order of parameters, so the fact that you've provided an overload that takes a double followed by a Vector is not sufficient. You need to explicitly define an overload that takes a Vector followed by a double as well. There are two possible ways of implementing this. The first way involves breaking down the vector multiplication operation in the same way that you have done for all operators so far:

```
public static Vector operator *(Vector left, double right) =>
    new Vector(right * left.X, right * left.Y, right * left.Z);
```

Given that you have already written code to implement essentially the same operation, however, you might prefer to reuse that code by writing the following:

```
public static Vector operator *(Vector left, double right) => right * left;
```

This code works by effectively telling the compiler that when it sees a multiplication of a Vector by a double, it can simply reverse the parameters and call the other operator overload. The sample code for this chapter uses the second version because it looks neater and illustrates the idea in action. This version also makes the code more maintainable because it saves duplicating the code to perform the multiplication in two separate overloads.

Next, you need to overload the multiplication operator to support vector multiplication. Mathematics provides a couple of ways to multiply vectors, but the one of interest here is known as the *dot product* or *inner product*, which actually returns a scalar as a result. That's the reason for this example—to demonstrate that arithmetic operators don't have to return the same type as the class in which they are defined.

In mathematical terms, if you have two vectors (x, y, z) and (X, Y, Z) then the inner product is defined to be the value of x*X + y*Y + z*Z. That might look like a strange way to multiply two things together, but it is actually very useful because it can be used to calculate various other quantities. If you ever write code that displays complex 3D graphics, such as using Direct3D or DirectDraw, you will almost certainly find that your code needs to work out inner products of vectors quite often as an intermediate step in calculating where to place objects on the screen. What's relevant here is that you want users of your Vector to be able to write double X = a*b to calculate the inner product of two Vector objects (a and b). The relevant overload looks like this:

```
public static double operator *(Vector left, Vector right) =>
    left.X * right.X + left.Y * right.Y + left.Z * right.Z;
```

Now that you understand the arithmetic operators, you can confirm that they work using a simple test method (code file OperatorOverloadingSample2/Program.cs):

```
static void Main()
{
  // stuff to demonstrate arithmetic operations
  Vector vect1, vect2, vect3;
  vect1 = new Vector(1.0, 1.5, 2.0);
  vect2 = new Vector(0.0, 0.0, -10.0);
  vect3 = vect1 + vect2;
  Console.WriteLine($"vect1 = {vect1}");
  Console.WriteLine($"vect2 = {vect2}");
  Console.WriteLine($"vect3 = vect1 + vect2 = {vect3}");
  Console.WriteLine($"2 * vect3 = {2 * vect3}");
  Console.WriteLine($"vect3 += vect2 gives {vect3 += vect2}");
  Console.WriteLine($"vect3 = vect1 * 2 gives {vect3 = vect1 * 2}");
  Console.WriteLine($"vect1 * vect3 = {vect1 * vect3}");
}
```

Running this code produces the following result:

```
vect1 = ( 1, 1.5, 2 )
vect2 = ( 0, 0, -10 )
vect3 = vect1 + vect2 = ( 1, 1.5, -8 )
2 * vect3 = ( 2, 3, -16 )
vect3 += vect2 gives ( 1, 1.5, -18 )
vect3 = vect1 * 2 gives ( 2, 3, 4 )
vect1 * vect3 = 14.5
```

This shows that the operator overloads have given the correct results; but if you look at the test code closely, you might be surprised to notice that it actually used an operator that wasn't overloaded—the addition assignment operator, +=:

```
Console.WriteLine($"vect3 += vect2 gives {vect3 += vect2}");
```

Although += normally counts as a single operator, it can be broken down into two steps: the addition and the assignment. Unlike the C++ language, C# does not allow you to overload the = operator; but if you overload +, the compiler automatically uses your overload of + to work out how to perform a += operation. The same principle works for all the assignment operators, such as -=, *=, /=, &=, and so on.

Overloading the Comparison Operators

As shown earlier in the section "Operators," C# has six comparison operators, and they are paired as follows:

➤   == and !=
➤   > and <
➤   >= and <=

> **NOTE** A .NET guideline defines that if the == operator returns true when comparing two objects, it should always return true. That's why you should only overload the == operator on immutable types.

The C# language requires that you overload these operators in pairs. That is, if you overload ==, you must overload != too; otherwise, you get a compiler error. In addition, the comparison operators must return a bool. This is the fundamental difference between these operators and the arithmetic operators. The result of adding or subtracting two quantities, for example, can theoretically be any type depending on the quantities. You have already seen that multiplying two Vector objects can be implemented to give a scalar. Another example involves the .NET base class System.DateTime. It's possible to subtract two DateTime instances, but the result is not a DateTime; instead it is a System.TimeSpan instance. By contrast, it doesn't really make much sense for a comparison to return anything other than a bool.

Apart from these differences, overloading the comparison operators follows the same principles as overloading the arithmetic operators. However, comparing quantities isn't always as simple as you might think. For example, if you simply compare two object references, you compare the memory address where the objects are stored. This is rarely the desired behavior of a comparison operator, so you must code the operator to compare the value of the objects and return the appropriate Boolean response. The following example overrides the == and != operators for the Vector struct. Here is the implementation of == (code file OverloadingComparisonSample/Vector.cs):

```
public static bool operator ==(Vector left, Vector right)
{
  if (object.ReferenceEquals(left, right)) return true;
  return left.X == right.X && left.Y == right.Y && left.Z == right.Z;
}
```

This approach simply compares two Vector objects for equality based on the values of their components. For most structs, that is probably what you will want to do, though in some cases you may need to think carefully about what you mean by equality. For example, if there are embedded classes, should you simply compare whether the references point to the same object (shallow comparison) or whether the values of the objects are the same (deep comparison)?

With a shallow comparison, the objects point to the same point in memory, whereas deep comparisons work with values and properties of the object to deem equality. You want to perform equality checks depending on the depth to help you decide what you want to verify.

> **NOTE** Don't be tempted to overload the comparison operator by only calling the instance version of the Equals method inherited from System.Object. If you do and then an attempt is made to evaluate (objA == objB), when objA happens to be null, you get an exception, as the .NET runtime tries to evaluate null.Equals(objB). Working the other way around (overriding Equals to call the comparison operator) should be safe.

You also need to override the != operator. Here is the simple way to do this:

```
public static bool operator !=(Vector left, Vector right) => !(left == right);
```

Now override the Equals and GetHashCode methods. These methods should always be overridden when the == operator is overridden. Otherwise the compiler complains with a warning.

```
public override bool Equals(object obj)
{
  if (obj == null) return false;
```

```
      return this == (Vector)obj;
   }

   public override int GetHashCode() =>
      X.GetHashCode() ^ (Y.GetHashCode() ^ Z.GetHashCode();
```

The `Equals` method can invoke in turn the `==` operator. The implementation of the hash code should be fast and always return the same value for the same object. This method is important when using dictionaries. Within dictionaries, it is used to build up the tree for objects, so it's best to distribute the returned values in the integer range. The `GetHashCode` method of the double type returns the integer representation of the double. For the `Vector` type, the hash values of the underlying types are just combined with XOR.

For value types, you should also implement the interface `IEquatable<T>`. This interface is a strongly typed version of the `Equals` method that is defined by the base class `Object`. Having all the other code already in place, you can easily do the implementation:

```
   public bool Equals(Vector other) => this == other;
```

As usual, you should quickly confirm that your override works with some test code. This time you'll define three `Vector` objects and compare them (code file `OverloadingComparisonSample/Program.cs`):

```
static void Main()
{
   var vect1 = new Vector(3.0, 3.0, -10.0);
   var vect2 = new Vector(3.0, 3.0, -10.0);
   var vect3 = new Vector(2.0, 3.0, 6.0);
   Console.WriteLine($"vect1 == vect2 returns {(vect1 == vect2)}");
   Console.WriteLine($"vect1 == vect3 returns {(vect1 == vect3)}");
   Console.WriteLine($"vect2 == vect3 returns {(vect2 == vect3)}");
   Console.WriteLine();
   Console.WriteLine($"vect1 != vect2 returns {(vect1 != vect2)}");
   Console.WriteLine($"vect1 != vect3 returns {(vect1 != vect3)}");
   Console.WriteLine($"vect2 != vect3 returns {(vect2 != vect3)}");
}
```

Running the example produces these results at the command line:

```
vect1 == vect2 returns True
vect1 == vect3 returns False
vect2 == vect3 returns False
vect1 != vect2 returns False
vect1 != vect3 returns True
vect2 != vect3 returns True
```

Which Operators Can You Overload?

It is not possible to overload all the available operators. The operators that you can overload are listed in the following table:

CATEGORY	OPERATORS	RESTRICTIONS	
Arithmetic binary	+, *, /, -, %	None	
Arithmetic unary	+, -, ++, --	None	
Bitwise binary	&, |, ^, <<, >>	None	
Bitwise unary	!, ~, true, false	The `true` and `false` operators must be overloaded as a pair.	

CATEGORY	OPERATORS	RESTRICTIONS
Comparison	==, !=,>=, <=>, <,	Comparison operators must be overloaded in pairs.
Assignment	+=, -=, *=, /=, >>=, <<=, %=, &=, |=, ^=	You cannot explicitly overload these operators; they are over-ridden implicitly when you override the individual operators such as +, -, %, and so on.
Index	[]	You cannot overload the index operator directly. The indexer member type, discussed in Chapter 2, allows you to support the index operator on your classes and structs.
Cast	()	You cannot overload the cast operator directly. User-defined casts (discussed in the last section of this chapter) allow you to define custom cast behavior.

> **NOTE** *You might wonder what is the reason for overloading the* `true` *and* `false` *operators. There's a good reason: what integer value is true or false is different based on the technology or framework you use. With many technologies, 0 is false and 1 is true; others define that any other value than 0 is true. You can also find technologies where –1 is false.*

IMPLEMENTING CUSTOM INDEX OPERATORS

Custom indexers cannot be implemented using the operator overloading syntax, but they can be implemented with a syntax that looks very similar to properties.

Start by looking at accessing array elements. Here, an array of `int` elements is created. The second code line uses the indexer to access the second element and pass 42 to it. The third line uses the indexer to access the third element and pass the element to the variable `x`.

```
int[] arr1 = {1, 2, 3};
arr1[1] = 42;
int x = arr1[2];
```

> **NOTE** *Arrays are explained in Chapter 7.*

The `CustomIndexerSample` makes use of these namespaces:

```
System

System.Collections.Generic

System.Linq
```

To create a custom indexer, first create a `Person` class with read-only properties `FirstName`, `LastName`, and `Birthday` (code file `CustomIndexerSample/Person.cs`):

```
public class Person
{
```

```csharp
    public DateTime Birthday { get; }
    public string FirstName { get; }
    public string LastName { get; }

    public Person(string firstName, string lastName, DateTime birthDay)
    {
      FirstName = firstName;
      LastName = lastName;
      Birthday = birthDay;
    }

    public override string ToString() => $"{FirstName} {LastName}";
}
```

The class `PersonCollection` defines a private array field that contains `Person` elements and a constructor where a number of `Person` objects can be passed (code file `CustomIndexerSample/PersonCollection.cs`):

```csharp
public class PersonCollection
{
  private Person[] _people;
  public PersonCollection(params Person[] people) =>
    _people = people.ToArray();
}
```

For allowing indexer-syntax to be used to access the `PersonCollection` and return `Person` objects, you can create an indexer. The indexer looks very similar to a property as it also contains `get` and `set` accessors. What's different is the name. Specifying an indexer makes use of the `this` keyword. The brackets that follow the `this` keyword specify the type that is used with the index. An array offers indexers with the `int` type, so `int` types are here used as well to pass the information directly to the contained array `_people`. The use of the `set` and `get` accessors is very similar to properties. The `get` accessor is invoked when a value is retrieved, the `set` accessor when a (`Person` object) is passed on the right side.

```csharp
public Person this[int index]
{
  get => _people[index];
  set => _people[index] = value;
}
```

With indexers, you cannot only define `int` types as the indexing type. Any type works, as is shown here with the `DateTime` struct as indexing type. This indexer is used to return every person with a specified birthday. Because multiple persons can have the same birthday, not a single `Person` object is returned but a list of persons with the interface `IEnumerable<Person>`. The `Where` method used makes the filtering based on a lambda expression. The `Where` method is defined in the namespace `System.Linq`:

```csharp
public IEnumerable<Person> this[DateTime birthDay]
{
  get => _people.Where(p => p.Birthday == birthDay);
}
```

The indexer using the `DateTime` type offers retrieving person objects, but doesn't allow you to set person objects as there's only a `get` accessor but no `set` accessor. A shorthand notation exists to create the same code with an expression-bodied member (the same syntax available with properties):

```csharp
public IEnumerable<Person> this[DateTime birthDay] =>
  _people.Where(p => p.Birthday == birthDay);
```

The `Main` method of the sample application creates a `PersonCollection` object and passes four `Person` objects to the constructor. With the first `WriteLine` method, the third element is accessed using the `get` accessor of the indexer with the `int` parameter. Within the `foreach` loop, the indexer with the `DateTime` parameter is used to pass a specified date (code file `CustomIndexerSample/Program.cs`):

```csharp
static void Main()
{
  var p1 = new Person("Ayrton", "Senna", new DateTime(1960, 3, 21));
```

```
        var p2 = new Person("Ronnie", "Peterson", new DateTime(1944, 2, 14));
        var p3 = new Person("Jochen", "Rindt", new DateTime(1942, 4, 18));
        var p4 = new Person("Francois", "Cevert", new DateTime(1944, 2, 25));
        var coll = new PersonCollection(p1, p2, p3, p4);
        Console.WriteLine(coll[2]);
        foreach (var r in coll[new DateTime(1960, 3, 21)])
        {
          Console.WriteLine(r);
        }
        Console.ReadLine();
    }
```

Running the program, the first `WriteLine` method writes `Jochen Rindt` to the console; the result of the `foreach` loop is `Ayrton Senna` as that person has the same birthday as is assigned within the second indexer.

USER-DEFINED CASTS

Earlier in this chapter (see the "Explicit Conversions" section), you learned that you can convert values between predefined data types through a process of casting. You also saw that C# allows two different types of casts: implicit and explicit. This section looks at these types of casts.

For an explicit cast, you explicitly mark the cast in your code by including the destination data type inside parentheses:

```
int i = 3;
long l = i; // implicit
short s = (short)i; // explicit
```

For the predefined data types, explicit casts are required where there is a risk that the cast might fail or some data might be lost. The following are some examples:

➤ When converting from an `int` to a `short`, the `short` might not be large enough to hold the value of the `int`.

➤ When converting from signed to unsigned data types, incorrect results are returned if the signed variable holds a negative value.

➤ When converting from floating-point to integer data types, the fractional part of the number will be lost.

➤ When converting from a nullable type to a non-nullable type, a value of `null` causes an exception.

By making the cast explicit in your code, C# forces you to affirm that you understand there is a risk of data loss, and therefore presumably you have written your code to take this into account.

Because C# allows you to define your own data types (structs and classes), it follows that you need the facility to support casts to and from those data types. The mechanism is to define a cast as a member operator of one of the relevant classes. Your cast operator must be marked as either `implicit` or `explicit` to indicate how you are intending it to be used. The expectation is that you follow the same guidelines as for the predefined casts: if you know that the cast is always safe regardless of the value held by the source variable, then you define it as `implicit`. Conversely, if you know there is a risk of something going wrong for certain values—perhaps some loss of data or an exception being thrown—then you should define the cast as `explicit`.

> **NOTE** *You should define any custom casts you write as explicit if there are any source data values for which the cast will fail or if there is any risk of an exception being thrown.*

The syntax for defining a cast is similar to that for overloading operators discussed earlier in this chapter. This is not a coincidence—a cast is regarded as an operator whose effect is to convert from the source type to the destination type. To illustrate the syntax, the following is taken from an example `struct` named `Currency`, which is introduced later in this section:

```
public static implicit operator float (Currency value)
{
  // processing
}
```

The return type of the operator defines the target type of the cast operation, and the single parameter is the source object for the conversion. The cast defined here allows you to implicitly convert the value of a `Currency` into a `float`. Note that if a conversion has been declared as `implicit`, the compiler permits its use either implicitly or explicitly. If it has been declared as `explicit`, the compiler only permits it to be used explicitly. In common with other operator overloads, casts must be declared as both `public` and `static`.

> **NOTE** *C++ developers will notice that this is different from C++, in which casts are instance members of classes.*

Implementing User-Defined Casts

This section illustrates the use of implicit and explicit user-defined casts in an example called `CastingSample`. In this example, you define a struct, `Currency`, which holds a positive USD ($) monetary value. C# provides the `decimal` type for this purpose, but it is possible you will still want to write your own struct or class to represent monetary values if you need to perform sophisticated financial processing and therefore want to implement specific methods on such a class.

> **NOTE** *The syntax for casting is the same for structs and classes. This example happens to be for a struct, but it would work just as well if you declared `Currency` as a class.*

Initially, the definition of the `Currency` struct is as follows (code file `CastingSample/Currency.cs`):

```
public struct Currency
{
  public uint Dollars { get; }
  public ushort Cents { get; }

  public Currency(uint dollars, ushort cents)
  {
    Dollars = dollars;
    Cents = cents;
  }

  public override string ToString() => $"${Dollars}.{Cents,-2:00}";
}
```

The use of unsigned data types for the `Dollar` and `Cents` properties ensures that a `Currency` instance can hold only positive values. It is restricted this way to illustrate some points about explicit casts later. You might want to use a class like this to hold, for example, salary information for company employees (people's salaries tend not to be negative!).

Start by assuming that you want to be able to convert `Currency` instances to `float` values, where the integer part of the `float` represents the dollars. In other words, you want to be able to write code like this:

```
var balance = new Currency(10, 50);
float f = balance; // We want f to be set to 10.5
```

To be able to do this, you need to define a cast. Hence, you add the following to your `Currency` definition:

```
public static implicit operator float (Currency value) =>
value.Dollars + (value.Cents/100.0f);
```

The preceding cast is implicit. It is a sensible choice in this case because, as it should be clear from the definition of `Currency`, any value that can be stored in the currency can also be stored in a `float`. There is no way that anything should ever go wrong in this cast.

> **NOTE** *There is a slight cheat here: In fact, when converting a* uint *to a* float*, there can be a loss in precision, but Microsoft has deemed this error sufficiently marginal to count the* uint-to-float *cast as implicit.*

However, if you have a `float` that you would like to be converted to a `Currency`, the conversion is not guaranteed to work. A `float` can store negative values, whereas `Currency` instances can't, and a `float` can store numbers of a far higher magnitude than can be stored in the (uint) `Dollar` field of `Currency`. Therefore, if a `float` contains an inappropriate value, converting it to a `Currency` could give unpredictable results. Because of this risk, the conversion from `float` to `Currency` should be defined as explicit. Here is the first attempt, which does not return quite the correct results, but it is instructive to examine why:

```
public static explicit operator Currency (float value)
{
  uint dollars = (uint)value;
  ushort cents = (ushort)((value-dollars)*100);
  return new Currency(dollars, cents);
}
```

The following code now successfully compiles:

```
float amount = 45.63f;
Currency amount2 = (Currency)amount;
```

However, the following code, if you tried it, would generate a compilation error because it attempts to use an explicit cast implicitly:

```
float amount = 45.63f;
Currency amount2 = amount; // wrong
```

By making the cast explicit, you warn the developer to be careful because data loss might occur. However, as you soon see, this is not how you want your `Currency` struct to behave. Try writing a test harness and running the sample. Here is the `Main` method, which instantiates a `Currency` struct and attempts a few conversions. At the start of this code, you write out the value of `balance` in two different ways—this is needed to illustrate something later in the example (code file `CastingSample/Program.cs`):

```
static void Main()
{
  try
  {
    var balance = new Currency(50,35);
    Console.WriteLine(balance);
    Console.WriteLine($"balance is {balance}"); // implicitly invokes ToString
```

```
      float balance2 = balance;
      Console.WriteLine($"After converting to float, = {balance2}");
      balance = (Currency) balance2;
      Console.WriteLine($"After converting back to Currency, = {balance}");
      Console.WriteLine("Now attempt to convert out of range value of " +
        "-$50.50 to a Currency:");

      checked
      {
        balance = (Currency) (-50.50);
        Console.WriteLine($"Result is {balance}");
      }
  }
  catch(Exception e)
  {
      Console.WriteLine($"Exception occurred: {e.Message}");
  }
}
```

Notice that the entire code is placed in a try block to catch any exceptions that occur during your casts. In addition, the lines that test converting an out-of-range value to Currency are placed in a checked block in an attempt to trap negative values. Running this code produces the following output:

```
50.35
Balance is $50.35
After converting to float, = 50.35
After converting back to Currency, = $50.34
Now attempt to convert out of range value of -$50.50 to a Currency:
Result is $4294967246.00
```

This output shows that the code did not quite work as expected. First, converting back from float to Currency gave a wrong result of $50.34 instead of $50.35. Second, no exception was generated when you tried to convert an obviously out-of-range value.

The first problem is caused by rounding errors. If a cast is used to convert from a float to a uint, the computer truncates the number rather than rounds it. The computer stores numbers in binary rather than decimal, and the fraction 0.35 cannot be exactly represented as a binary fraction (just as 1/3 cannot be represented exactly as a decimal fraction; it comes out as 0.3333 recurring). The computer ends up storing a value very slightly lower than 0.35 that can be represented exactly in binary format. Multiply by 100 and you get a number fractionally less than 35, which is truncated to 34 cents. Clearly, in this situation, such errors caused by truncation are serious, and the way to avoid them is to ensure that some intelligent rounding is performed in numerical conversions instead.

Luckily, Microsoft has written a class that does this: System.Convert. The System.Convert object contains a large number of static methods to perform various numerical conversions, and the one that we want is Convert.ToUInt16. Note that the extra care taken by the System.Convert methods comes at a performance cost. You should use them only when necessary.

Let's examine the second problem—why the expected overflow exception wasn't thrown. The issue here is this: The place where the overflow really occurs isn't actually in the Main routine at all—it is inside the code for the cast operator, which is called from the Main method. The code in this method was not marked as checked.

The solution is to ensure that the cast itself is computed in a checked context, too. With both this change and the fix for the first problem, the revised code for the conversion looks like the following:

```
public static explicit operator Currency (float value)
{
  checked
  {
    uint dollars = (uint)value;
```

```
    ushort cents = Convert.ToUInt16((value-dollars)*100);
    return new Currency(dollars, cents);
  }
}
```

Note that you use `Convert.ToUInt16` to calculate the cents, as described earlier, but you do not use it for calculating the dollar part of the amount. `System.Convert` is not needed when calculating the dollar amount because truncating the `float` value is what you want there.

> **NOTE** *The `System.Convert` methods also carry out their own overflow checking. Hence, for the particular case we are considering, there is no need to place the call to `Convert.ToUInt16` inside the checked context. The checked context is still required, however, for the explicit casting of `value` to dollars.*

You won't see a new set of results with this new `checked` cast just yet because you have some more modifications to make to the `CastingSample` example later in this section.

> **NOTE** *If you are defining a cast that will be used very often, and for which performance is at an absolute premium, you may prefer not to do any error checking. That is also a legitimate solution, provided that the behavior of your cast and the lack of error checking are very clearly documented.*

Casts Between Classes

The `Currency` example involves only classes that convert to or from `float`—one of the predefined data types. However, it is not necessary to involve any of the simple data types. It is perfectly legitimate to define casts to convert between instances of different structs or classes that you have defined. You need to be aware of a couple of restrictions, however:

➤ You cannot define a cast if one of the classes is derived from the other (these types of casts already exist, as you see later).

➤ The cast must be defined inside the definition of either the source or the destination data type.

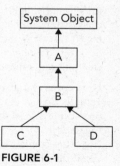

FIGURE 6-1

To illustrate these requirements, suppose that you have the class hierarchy shown in Figure 6-1.

In other words, classes C and D are indirectly derived from A. In this case, the only legitimate user-defined cast between A, B, C, or D would be to convert between classes C and D, because these classes are not derived from each other. The code to do so might look like the following (assuming you want the casts to be explicit, which is usually the case when defining casts between user-defined classes):

```
public static explicit operator D(C value)
{
  //...
}

public static explicit operator C(D value)
{
  //...
}
```

For each of these casts, you can choose where you place the definitions—inside the class definition of C or inside the class definition of D, but not anywhere else. C# requires you to put the definition of a cast inside either the source class (or struct) or the destination class (or struct). A side effect of this is that you cannot define a cast between two classes unless you have access to edit the source code for at least one of them. This is sensible because it prevents third parties from introducing casts into your classes.

After you have defined a cast inside one of the classes, you cannot also define the same cast inside the other class. Obviously, there should be only one cast for each conversion; otherwise, the compiler would not know which one to use.

Casts Between Base and Derived Classes

To see how these casts work, start by considering the case in which both the source and the destination are reference types, and consider two classes, MyBase and MyDerived, where MyDerived is derived directly or indirectly from MyBase.

First, from MyDerived to MyBase, it is always possible (assuming the constructors are available) to write this:

```
MyDerived derivedObject = new MyDerived();
MyBase baseCopy = derivedObject;
```

Here, you are casting implicitly from MyDerived to MyBase. This works because of the rule that any reference to a type MyBase is allowed to refer to objects of class MyBase or anything derived from MyBase. In OO programming, instances of a derived class are, in a real sense, instances of the base class, plus something extra. All the functions and fields defined on the base class are defined in the derived class, too.

Alternatively, you can write this:

```
MyBase derivedObject = new MyDerived();
MyBase baseObject = new MyBase();
MyDerived derivedCopy1 = (MyDerived) derivedObject; // OK
MyDerived derivedCopy2 = (MyDerived) baseObject; // Throws exception
```

This code is perfectly legal C# (in a syntactic sense, that is) and illustrates casting from a base class to a derived class. However, the final statement throws an exception when executed. When you perform the cast, the object being referred to is examined. Because a base class reference can, in principle, refer to a derived class instance, it is possible that this object is actually an instance of the derived class that you are attempting to cast to. If that is the case, the cast succeeds, and the derived reference is set to refer to the object. If, however, the object in question is not an instance of the derived class (or of any class derived from it), the cast fails and an exception is thrown.

Notice that the casts that the compiler has supplied, which convert between base and derived class, do not actually do any data conversion on the object in question. All they do is set the new reference to refer to the object if it is legal for that conversion to occur. To that extent, these casts are very different in nature from the ones that you normally define yourself. For example, in the CastingSample example earlier, you defined casts that convert between a Currency struct and a float. In the float-to-Currency cast, you actually instantiated a new Currency struct and initialized it with the required values. The predefined casts between base and derived classes do not do this. If you want to convert a MyBase instance into a real MyDerived object with values based on the contents of the MyBase instance, you cannot use the cast syntax to do this. The most sensible option is usually to define a derived class constructor that takes a base class instance as a parameter, and have this constructor perform the relevant initializations:

```
class DerivedClass: BaseClass
{
  public DerivedClass(BaseClass base)
  {
    // initialize object from the Base instance
  }
  // ...
```

Boxing and Unboxing Casts

The previous discussion focused on casting between base and derived classes where both participants were reference types. Similar principles apply when casting value types, although in this case it is not possible to simply copy references—some copying of data must occur.

It is not, of course, possible to derive from structs or primitive value types. Casting between base and derived structs invariably means casting between a primitive type or a struct and `System.Object`. (Theoretically, it is possible to cast between a struct and `System.ValueType`, though it is hard to see why you would want to do this.)

The cast from any struct (or primitive type) to `object` is always available as an implicit cast—because it is a cast from a derived type to a base type—and is just the familiar process of boxing. For example, using the `Currency` struct:

```
var balance = new Currency(40,0);
object baseCopy = balance;
```

When this implicit cast is executed, the contents of `balance` are copied onto the heap into a boxed object, and the `baseCopy` object reference is set to this object. What actually happens behind the scenes is this: When you originally defined the `Currency` struct, the .NET Framework implicitly supplied another (hidden) class, a boxed `Currency` class, which contains all the same fields as the `Currency` struct but is a reference type, stored on the heap. This happens whenever you define a value type, whether it is a `struct` or an `enum`, and similar boxed reference types exist corresponding to all the primitive value types of `int`, `double`, `uint`, and so on. It is not possible, or necessary, to gain direct programmatic access to any of these boxed classes in source code, but they are the objects that are working behind the scenes whenever a value type is cast to `object`. When you implicitly cast `Currency` to `object`, a boxed `Currency` instance is instantiated and initialized with all the data from the `Currency` struct. In the preceding code, it is this boxed `Currency` instance to which `baseCopy` refers. By these means, it is possible for casting from derived to base type to work syntactically in the same way for value types as for reference types.

Casting the other way is known as unboxing. Like casting between a base reference type and a derived reference type, it is an explicit cast because an exception is thrown if the object being cast is not of the correct type:

```
object derivedObject = new Currency(40,0);
object baseObject = new object();
Currency derivedCopy1 = (Currency)derivedObject; // OK
Currency derivedCopy2 = (Currency)baseObject; // Exception thrown
```

This code works in a way similar to the code presented earlier for reference types. Casting `derivedObject` to `Currency` works fine because `derivedObject` actually refers to a boxed `Currency` instance—the cast is performed by copying the fields out of the boxed `Currency` object into a new `Currency` struct. The second cast fails because `baseObject` does not refer to a boxed `Currency` object.

When using boxing and unboxing, it is important to understand that both processes actually copy the data into the new boxed or unboxed object. Hence, manipulations on the boxed object, for example, do not affect the contents of the original value type.

Multiple Casting

One thing you have to watch for when you are defining casts is that if the C# compiler is presented with a situation in which no direct cast is available to perform a requested conversion, it attempts to find a way of combining casts to do the conversion. For example, with the `Currency` struct, suppose the compiler encounters a few lines of code like this:

```
var balance = new Currency(10,50);
long amount = (long)balance;
double amountD = balance;
```

You first initialize a `Currency` instance, and then you attempt to convert it to a `long`. The trouble is that you haven't defined the cast to do that. However, this code still compiles successfully. Here's what happens: The compiler realizes that you have defined an implicit cast to get from `Currency` to `float`, and the compiler already knows how to explicitly cast a `float` to a `long`. Hence, it compiles that line of code into IL code that converts `balance` first to a `float`, and then converts that result to a `long`. The same thing happens in the final line of the code, when you convert `balance` to a `double`. However, because the cast from `Currency` to `float` and the predefined cast from `float` to `double` are both implicit, you can write this conversion in your code as an implicit cast. If you prefer, you could also specify the casting route explicitly:

```
var balance = new Currency(10,50);
long amount = (long)(float)balance;
double amountD = (double)(float)balance;
```

However, in most cases, this would be seen as needlessly complicating your code. The following code, by contrast, produces a compilation error:

```
var balance = new Currency(10,50);
long amount = balance;
```

The reason is that the best match for the conversion that the compiler can find is still to convert first to `float` and then to `long`. The conversion from `float` to `long` needs to be specified explicitly, though.

Not all of this by itself should give you too much trouble. The rules are, after all, fairly intuitive and designed to prevent any data loss from occurring without the developer knowing about it. However, the problem is that if you are not careful when you define your casts, it is possible for the compiler to select a path that leads to unexpected results. For example, suppose that it occurs to someone else in the group writing the `Currency` struct that it would be useful to be able to convert a `uint` containing the total number of cents in an amount into a `Currency` (cents, not dollars, because the idea is not to lose the fractions of a dollar). Therefore, this cast might be written to try to achieve this:

```
// Do not do this!
public static implicit operator Currency (uint value) =>
    new Currency(value/100u, (ushort)(value%100));
```

Note the `u` after the first 100 in this code to ensure that `value/100u` is interpreted as a `uint`. If you had written `value/100`, the compiler would have interpreted this as an `int`, not a `uint`.

The comment `Do not do this!` is clearly noted in this code, and here is why: The following code snippet merely converts a `jNuint` containing 350 into a `Currency` and back again; but what do you think `bal2` will contain after executing this?

```
uint bal = 350;
Currency balance = bal;
uint bal2 = (uint)balance;
```

The answer is not 350 but 3! Moreover, it all follows logically. You convert 350 implicitly to a `Currency`, giving the result `balance.Dollars = 3`, `balance.Cents = 50`. Then the compiler does its usual figuring out of the best path for the conversion back. `Balance` ends up being implicitly converted to a `float` (value 3.5), and this is converted explicitly to a `uint` with value 3.

Of course, other instances exist in which converting to another data type and back again causes data loss. For example, converting a `float` containing 5.8 to an `int` and back to a `float` again loses the fractional part, giving you a result of 5, but there is a slight difference in principle between losing the fractional part of a number and dividing an integer by more than 100. `Currency` has suddenly become a rather dangerous class that does strange things to integers!

The problem is that there is a conflict between how your casts interpret integers. The casts between `Currency` and `float` interpret an integer value of 1 as corresponding to one dollar, but the latest `uint`-to-`Currency` cast interprets this value as one cent. This is an example of very poor design. If you want your classes to be easy to use, you should ensure that all your casts behave in a way that is mutually compatible, in the sense that they intuitively give the same results. In this case, the solution is obviously to rewrite the uint-to-Currency cast so that it interprets an integer value of 1 as one dollar:

```
public static implicit operator Currency (uint value) =>
    new Currency(value, 0);
```

Incidentally, you might wonder whether this new cast is necessary at all. The answer is that it could be useful. Without this cast, the only way for the compiler to carry out a uint-to-Currency conversion would be via a float. Converting directly is a lot more efficient in this case, so having this extra cast provides performance benefits, though you need to ensure that it provides the same result as via a float, which you have now done. In other situations, you may also find that separately defining casts for different predefined data types enables more conversions to be implicit rather than explicit, though that is not the case here.

A good test of whether your casts are compatible is to ask whether a conversion will give the same results (other than perhaps a loss of accuracy as in float-to-int conversions) regardless of which path it takes. The Currency class provides a good example of this. Consider this code:

```
var balance = new Currency(50, 35);
ulong bal = (ulong) balance;
```

At present, there is only one way that the compiler can achieve this conversion: by converting the Currency to a float implicitly, then to a ulong explicitly. The float-to-ulong conversion requires an explicit conversion, but that is fine because you have specified one here.

Suppose, however, that you then added another cast, to convert implicitly from a Currency to a uint. You actually do this by modifying the Currency struct by adding the casts both to and from uint (code file CastingSample/Currency.cs):

```
public static implicit operator Currency (uint value) =>
    new Currency(value, 0);
public static implicit operator uint (Currency value) => value.Dollars;
```

Now the compiler has another possible route to convert from Currency to ulong: to convert from Currency to uint implicitly, then to ulong implicitly. Which of these two routes will it take? C# has some precise rules about the best route for the compiler when there are several possibilities. (The rules are not covered in this book, but if you are interested in the details, see the MSDN documentation.) The best answer is that you should design your casts so that all routes give the same answer (other than possible loss of precision), in which case it doesn't really matter which one the compiler picks. (As it happens in this case, the compiler picks the Currency-to-uint-to-ulong route in preference to Currency-to-float-to-ulong.)

To test casting the Currency to uint, add this test code to the Main method (code file CastingSample/Program.cs):

```
static void Main()
{
  try
  {
    var balance = new Currency(50,35);
    Console.WriteLine(balance);
    Console.WriteLine($"balance is {balance}");
    uint balance3 = (uint) balance;
    Console.WriteLine($"Converting to uint gives {balance3}");
  }
  catch (Exception ex)
  {
    Console.WriteLine($"Exception occurred: {e.Message}");
  }
}
```

Running the sample now gives you these results:

```
50
balance is $50.35
Converting to uint gives 50
```

The output shows that the conversion to `uint` has been successful, though, as expected, you have lost the cents part of the `Currency` in making this conversion. Casting a negative `float` to `Currency` has also produced the expected overflow exception now that the `float`-to-`Currency` cast itself defines a checked context.

However, the output also demonstrates one last potential problem that you need to be aware of when working with casts. The very first line of output does not display the balance correctly, displaying `50` instead of `50.35`.

So, what is going on? The problem here is that when you combine casts with method overloads, you get another source of unpredictability.

The `WriteLine` statement using the format string implicitly calls the `Currency.ToString` method, ensuring that the `Currency` is displayed as a string.

The very first code line with `WriteLine`, however, simply passes a raw `Currency` struct to the `WriteLine` method. Now, `WriteLine` has many overloads, but none of them takes a `Currency` struct. Therefore, the compiler starts fishing around to see what it can cast the `Currency` to in order to make it match up with one of the overloads of `WriteLine`. As it happens, one of the `WriteLine` overloads is designed to display `uint`s quickly and efficiently, and it takes a `uint` as a parameter—you have now supplied a cast that converts `Currency` implicitly to `uint`.

In fact, `WriteLine` has another overload that takes a `double` as a parameter and displays the value of that `double`. If you look closely at the output running the example previously where the cast to `uint` did not exist, you see that the first line of output displayed `Currency` as a `double`, using this overload. In that example, there wasn't a direct cast from `Currency` to `uint`, so the compiler picked `Currency`-to-`float`-to-`double` as its preferred way of matching up the available casts to the available `WriteLine` overloads. However, now that there is a direct cast to `uint` available in `SimpleCurrency2`, the compiler has opted for that route.

The upshot of this is that if you have a method call that takes several overloads and you attempt to pass it a parameter whose data type doesn't match any of the overloads exactly, then you are forcing the compiler to decide not only what casts to use to perform the data conversion, but also which overload, and hence which data conversion, to pick. The compiler always works logically and according to strict rules, but the results may not be what you expected. If there is any doubt, you are better off specifying which cast to use explicitly.

SUMMARY

This chapter looked at the standard operators provided by C#, described the mechanics of object equality, and examined how the compiler converts the standard data types from one to another. It also demonstrated how you can implement custom operator support on your data types using operator overloads. Finally, you looked at a special type of operator overload, the cast operator, which enables you to specify how instances of your types are converted to other data types.

The next chapter dives into arrays where the index operator has an important role.

7

Arrays

WHAT'S IN THIS CHAPTER?

- ➤ Simple arrays
- ➤ Multidimensional arrays
- ➤ Jagged arrays
- ➤ The Array class
- ➤ Arrays as parameters
- ➤ Enumerators
- ➤ Structural comparison
- ➤ Spans
- ➤ Array Pools

WROX.COM CODE DOWNLOADS FOR THIS CHAPTER

The Wrox.com code downloads for this chapter are found at www.wrox.com on the Download Code tab. The source code is also available at https://github.com/ProfessionalCSharp/ProfessionalCSharp7 in the directory Arrays.

The code for this chapter is divided into the following major examples:

- ➤ SimpleArrays
- ➤ SortingSample
- ➤ ArraySegment
- ➤ YieldSample
- ➤ StructuralComparison
- ➤ SpanSample
- ➤ ArrayPoolSample

MULTIPLE OBJECTS OF THE SAME TYPE

If you need to work with multiple objects of the same type, you can use collections (see Chapter 10, "Collections") and arrays. C# has a special notation to declare, initialize, and use arrays. Behind the scenes, the Array class comes into play, which offers several methods to sort and filter the elements inside the array. Using an enumerator, you can iterate through all the elements of the array.

> **NOTE** *For using multiple objects of different types, you can combine them using classes, structs, and tuples. Classes and structs are discussed in Chapter 3, "Objects and Types." Tuples are covered in Chapter 13, "Functional Programming with C#."*

SIMPLE ARRAYS

If you need to use multiple objects of the same type, you can use an array. An *array* is a data structure that contains a number of elements of the same type.

Array Declaration

An array is declared by defining the type of elements inside the array, followed by empty brackets and a variable name. For example, an array containing integer elements is declared like this:

```
int[] myArray;
```

Array Initialization

After declaring an array, memory must be allocated to hold all the elements of the array. An array is a reference type, so memory on the heap must be allocated. You do this by initializing the variable of the array using the new operator, with the type and the number of elements inside the array. Here, you specify the size of the array:

```
myArray = new int[4];
```

> **NOTE** *Value types and reference types are covered in Chapter 3.*

With this declaration and initialization, the variable myArray references four integer values that are allocated on the managed heap (see Figure 7-1).

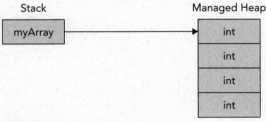

FIGURE 7-1

> **NOTE** *An array cannot be resized after its size is specified without copying all the elements. If you don't know how many elements should be in the array in advance, you can use a collection (see Chapter 10).*

Instead of using a separate line to declare and initialize an array, you can use a single line:

```
int[] myArray = new int[4];
```

You can also assign values to every array element using an array initializer. You can use array initializers only while declaring an array variable, not after the array is declared:

```
int[] myArray = new int[4] {4, 7, 11, 2};
```

If you initialize the array using curly brackets, you can also omit the size of the array because the compiler can count the number of elements:

```
int[] myArray = new int[] {4, 7, 11, 2};
```

There's even a shorter form using the C# compiler. Using curly brackets you can write the array declaration and initialization. The code generated from the compiler is the same as the previous result:

```
int[] myArray = {4, 7, 11, 2};
```

Accessing Array Elements

After an array is declared and initialized, you can access the array elements using an indexer. Arrays support only indexers that have integer parameters.

With the indexer, you pass the element number to access the array. The indexer always starts with a value of 0 for the first element. Therefore, the highest number you can pass to the indexer is the number of elements minus one, because the index starts at zero. In the following example, the array myArray is declared and initialized with four integer values. The elements can be accessed with indexer values 0, 1, 2, and 3.

```
int[] myArray = new int[] {4, 7, 11, 2};
int v1 = myArray[0]; // read first element
int v2 = myArray[1]; // read second element
myArray[3] = 44; // change fourth element
```

> **NOTE** *If you use a wrong indexer value that is bigger than the length of the array, an exception of type* IndexOutOfRangeException *is thrown.*

If you don't know the number of elements in the array, you can use the Length property, as shown in this for statement:

```
for (int i = 0; i < myArray.Length; i++)
{
   Console.WriteLine(myArray[i]);
}
```

Instead of using a for statement to iterate through all the elements of the array, you can also use the foreach statement:

```
foreach (var val in myArray)
{
   Console.WriteLine(val);
}
```

> **NOTE** *The* `foreach` *statement makes use of the* `IEnumerable` *and* `IEnumerator` *interfaces and traverses through the array from the first index to the last. This is discussed in detail later in this chapter.*

Using Reference Types

In addition to being able to declare arrays of predefined types, you can also declare arrays of custom types. Let's start with the following `Person` class, the properties `FirstName` and `LastName` using auto-implemented readonly properties, and an override of the `ToString` method from the `Object` class (code file `SimpleArrays/Person.cs`):

```
public class Person
{
  public Person(string firstName, string lastName)
  {
    FirstName = firstName;
    LastName = lastName;
  }

  public string FirstName { get; }
  public string LastName { get; }
  public override string ToString() => $"{FirstName} {LastName}";
}
```

Declaring an array of two `Person` elements is similar to declaring an array of `int`:

```
Person[] myPersons = new Person[2];
```

However, be aware that if the elements in the array are reference types, memory must be allocated for every array element. If you use an item in the array for which no memory was allocated, a `NullReferenceException` is thrown.

> **NOTE** *For information about errors and exceptions, see Chapter 14, "Errors and Exceptions."*

You can allocate every element of the array by using an indexer starting from 0 (code file `SimpleArrays/Program.cs`):

```
myPersons[0] = new Person("Ayrton", "Senna");
myPersons[1] = new Person("Michael", "Schumacher");
```

Figure 7-2 shows the objects in the managed heap with the `Person` array. `myPersons` is a variable that is stored on the stack. This variable references an array of `Person` elements that is stored on the managed heap. This array has enough space for two references. Every item in the array references a `Person` object that is also stored in the managed heap.

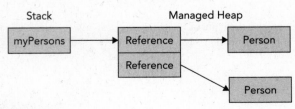

FIGURE 7-2

Similar to the `int` type, you can also use an array initializer with custom types:

```
Person[] myPersons2 =
{
  new Person("Ayrton", "Senna"),
  new Person("Michael", "Schumacher")
};
```

MULTIDIMENSIONAL ARRAYS

Ordinary arrays (also known as one-dimensional arrays) are indexed by a single integer. A multidimensional array is indexed by two or more integers.

$$a = \begin{bmatrix} 1, 2, 3 \\ 4, 5, 6 \\ 7, 8, 9 \end{bmatrix}$$

FIGURE 7-3

Figure 7-3 shows the mathematical notation for a two-dimensional array that has three rows and three columns. The first row has the values 1, 2, and 3, and the third row has the values 7, 8, and 9.

To declare this two-dimensional array with C#, you put a comma inside the brackets. The array is initialized by specifying the size of every dimension (also known as rank). Then the array elements can be accessed by using two integers with the indexer (code file `SimpleArrays/Program.cs`):

```
int[,] twodim = new int[3, 3];
twodim[0, 0] = 1;
twodim[0, 1] = 2;
twodim[0, 2] = 3;
twodim[1, 0] = 4;
twodim[1, 1] = 5;
twodim[1, 2] = 6;
twodim[2, 0] = 7;
twodim[2, 1] = 8;
twodim[2, 2] = 9;
```

> **NOTE** *After declaring an array, you cannot change the rank.*

You can also initialize the two-dimensional array by using an array indexer if you know the values for the elements in advance. To initialize the array, one outer curly bracket is used, and every row is initialized by using curly brackets inside the outer curly brackets:

```
int[,] twodim = {
  {1, 2, 3},
  {4, 5, 6},
  {7, 8, 9}
};
```

> **NOTE** *When using an array initializer, you must initialize every element of the array. It is not possible to defer the initialization of some values until later.*

By using two commas inside the brackets, you can declare a three-dimensional array:

```
int[,,] threedim = {
  { { 1, 2 }, { 3, 4 } },
  { { 5, 6 }, { 7, 8 } },
  { { 9, 10 }, { 11, 12 } }
};

Console.WriteLine(threedim[0, 1, 1]);
```

JAGGED ARRAYS

A two-dimensional array has a rectangular size (for example, 3 × 3 elements). A jagged array provides more flexibility in sizing the array. With a jagged array every row can have a different size.

Figure 7-4 contrasts a two-dimensional array that has 3 × 3 elements with a jagged array. The jagged array shown contains three rows, with the first row containing two elements, the second row containing six elements, and the third row containing three elements.

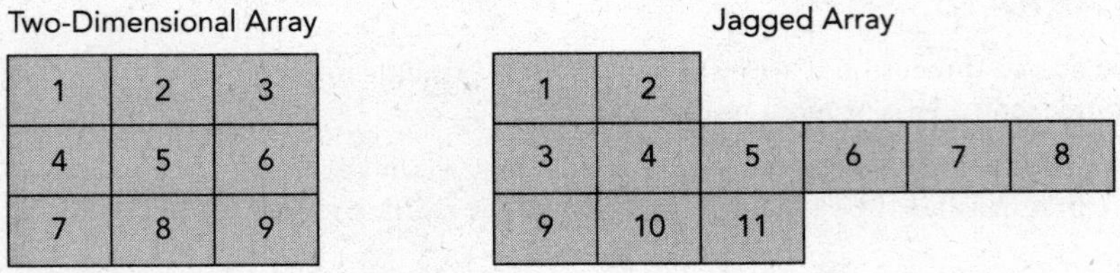

Two-Dimensional Array   Jagged Array

FIGURE 7-4

A jagged array is declared by placing one pair of opening and closing brackets after another. To initialize the jagged array, only the size that defines the number of rows in the first pair of brackets is set. The second brackets that define the number of elements inside the row are kept empty because every row has a different number of elements. Next, the element number of the rows can be set for every row (code file `SimpleArrays/Program.cs`):

```
int[][] jagged = new int[3][];
jagged[0] = new int[2] { 1, 2 };
jagged[1] = new int[6] { 3, 4, 5, 6, 7, 8 };
jagged[2] = new int[3] { 9, 10, 11 };
```

You can iterate through all the elements of a jagged array with nested `for` loops. In the outer `for` loop every row is iterated, and the inner `for` loop iterates through every element inside a row:

```
for (int row = 0; row < jagged.Length; row++)
{
  for (int element = 0; element < jagged[row].Length; element++)
  {
    Console.WriteLine($"row: {row}, element: {element}, " +
      $"value: {jagged[row][element]}");
  }
}
```

The output of the iteration displays the rows and every element within the rows:

```
row: 0, element: 0, value: 1
row: 0, element: 1, value: 2
row: 1, element: 0, value: 3
row: 1, element: 1, value: 4
row: 1, element: 2, value: 5
row: 1, element: 3, value: 6
row: 1, element: 4, value: 7
row: 1, element: 5, value: 8
row: 2, element: 0, value: 9
row: 2, element: 1, value: 10
row: 2, element: 2, value: 11
```

ARRAY CLASS

Declaring an array with brackets is a C# notation using the `Array` class. Using the C# syntax behind the scenes creates a new class that derives from the abstract base class `Array`. This makes it possible to use methods and properties that are defined with the `Array` class with every C# array. For example, you've already used the Length property or iterated through the array by using the foreach statement. By doing this, you are using the GetEnumerator method of the Array class.

Other properties implemented by the Array class are LongLength, for arrays in which the number of items doesn't fit within an integer, and Rank, to get the number of dimensions.

Let's have a look at other members of the Array class by getting into various features.

Creating Arrays

The Array class is abstract, so you cannot create an array by using a constructor. However, instead of using the C# syntax to create array instances, it is also possible to create arrays by using the static CreateInstance method. This is extremely useful if you don't know the type of elements in advance, because the type can be passed to the CreateInstance method as a Type object.

The following example shows how to create an array of type int with a size of 5. The first argument of the CreateInstance method requires the type of the elements, and the second argument defines the size. You can set values with the SetValue method, and read values with the GetValue method (code file SimpleArrays/Program.cs):

```
Array intArray1 = Array.CreateInstance(typeof(int), 5);
for (int i = 0; i < 5; i++)
{
    intArray1.SetValue(33, i);
}

for (int i = 0; i < 5; i++)
{
    Console.WriteLine(intArray1.GetValue(i));
}
```

You can also cast the created array to an array declared as int []:

```
int[] intArray2 = (int[])intArray1;
```

The CreateInstance method has many overloads to create multidimensional arrays and to create arrays that are not 0 based. The following example creates a two-dimensional array with 2 × 3 elements. The first dimension is 1 based; the second dimension is 10 based:

```
int[] lengths = { 2, 3 };
int[] lowerBounds = { 1, 10 };
Array racers = Array.CreateInstance(typeof(Person), lengths, lowerBounds);
```

Setting the elements of the array, the SetValue method accepts indices for every dimension:

```
racers.SetValue(new Person("Alain", "Prost"), 1, 10);
racers.SetValue(new Person("Emerson", "Fittipaldi"), 1, 11);
racers.SetValue(new Person("Ayrton", "Senna"), 1, 12);
racers.SetValue(new Person("Michael", "Schumacher"), 2, 10);
racers.SetValue(new Person("Fernando", "Alonso"), 2, 11);
racers.SetValue(new Person("Jenson", "Button"), 2, 12);
```

Although the array is not 0 based, you can assign it to a variable with the normal C# notation. You just have to take care not to cross the boundaries:

```
Person[,] racers2 = (Person[,])racers;
Person first = racers2[1, 10];
Person last = racers2[2, 12];
```

Copying Arrays

Because arrays are reference types, assigning an array variable to another one just gives you two variables referencing the same array. For copying arrays, the array implements the interface ICloneable. The Clone method that is defined with this interface creates a shallow copy of the array.

If the elements of the array are value types, as in the following code segment, all values are copied (see Figure 7-5):

```
int[] intArray1 = {1, 2};
int[] intArray2 = (int[])intArray1.Clone();
```

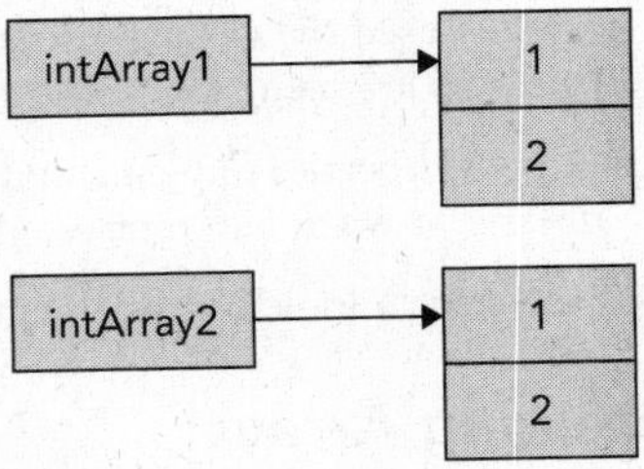

If the array contains reference types, only the references are copied, not the elements. Figure 7-6 shows the variables `beatles` and `beatlesClone`, where `beatlesClone` is created by calling the `Clone` method from `beatles`. The `Person` objects that are referenced are the same for `beatles` and `beatlesClone`. If you change a property of an element of `beatlesClone`, you change the same object of `beatles` (code file `SimpleArray/Program.cs`):

FIGURE 7-5

```
Person[] beatles = {
new Person { FirstName="John", LastName="Lennon" },
new Person { FirstName="Paul", LastName="McCartney" }
};
Person[] beatlesClone = (Person[])beatles.Clone();
```

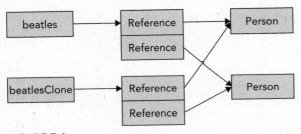

FIGURE 7-6

Instead of using the `Clone` method, you can use the `Array.Copy` method, which also creates a shallow copy. However, there's one important difference with `Clone` and `Copy`: `Clone` creates a new array; with `Copy` you have to pass an existing array with the same rank and enough elements.

> **NOTE** *If you need a deep copy of an array containing reference types, you have to iterate the array and create new objects.*

Sorting

The `Array` class uses the Quicksort algorithm to sort the elements in the array. The `Sort` method requires the interface `IComparable` to be implemented by the elements in the array. Simple types such as `System.String` and `System.Int32` implement `IComparable`, so you can sort elements containing these types.

With the sample program, the array name contains elements of type `string`, and this array can be sorted (code file `SortingSample/Program.cs`):

```
string[] names = {
    "Christina Aguilera",
    "Shakira",
    "Beyonce",
    "Lady Gaga"
};
Array.Sort(names);
```

```
    foreach (var name in names)
    {
       Console.WriteLine(name);
    }
```

The output of the application shows the sorted result of the array:

```
Beyonce
Christina Aguilera
Lady Gaga
Shakira
```

If you are using custom classes with the array, you must implement the interface IComparable. This interface defines just one method, CompareTo, which must return 0 if the objects to compare are equal; a value smaller than 0 if the instance should go before the object from the parameter; and a value larger than 0 if the instance should go after the object from the parameter.

Change the Person class to implement the interface IComparable<Person>. The comparison is first done on the value of the LastName by using the Compare method of the String class. If the LastName has the same value, the FirstName is compared (code file SortingSample/Person.cs):

```
public class Person: IComparable<Person>
{
   public int CompareTo(Person other)
   {
      if (other == null) return 1;
      int result = string.Compare(this.LastName, other.LastName);
      if (result == 0)
      {
         result = string.Compare(this.FirstName, other.FirstName);
      }
      return result;
   }
}
//...
```

Now it is possible to sort an array of Person objects by the last name (code file SortingSample/Program.cs):

```
Person[] persons = {
   new Person("Damon", "Hill"),
   new Person("Niki", "Lauda"),
   new Person("Ayrton", "Senna"),
   new Person("Graham", "Hill")
};
Array.Sort(persons);
foreach (var p in persons)
{
   Console.WriteLine(p);
}
```

Using the sort of the Person class, the output returns the names sorted by last name:

```
Damon Hill
Graham Hill
Niki Lauda
Ayrton Senna
```

If the Person object should be sorted differently, or if you don't have the option to change the class that is used as an element in the array, you can implement the interface IComparer or IComparer<T>. These interfaces define the method Compare. One of these interfaces must be implemented by the class that should be compared. The IComparer interface is independent of the class to compare. That's why the Compare method defines two arguments that should be compared. The return value is similar to the CompareTo method of the IComparable interface.

The class `PersonComparer` implements the `IComparer<Person>` interface to sort `Person` objects either by `firstName` or by `lastName`. The enumeration `PersonCompareType` defines the different sorting options that are available with `PersonComparer`: `FirstName` and `LastName`. How the compare should be done is defined with the constructor of the class `PersonComparer`, where a `PersonCompareType` value is set. The `Compare` method is implemented with a `switch` statement to compare either by `LastName` or by `FirstName` (code file SortingSample/PersonComparer.cs):

```
public enum PersonCompareType
{
  FirstName,
  LastName
}

public class PersonComparer: IComparer<Person>
{
  private PersonCompareType _compareType;
  public PersonComparer(PersonCompareType compareType) =>
    _compareType = compareType;

  public int Compare(Person x, Person y)
  {
    if (x is null && y is null) return 0;
    if (x is null) return 1;
    if (y is null) return -1;
    switch (_compareType)
    {
      case PersonCompareType.FirstName:
        return string.Compare(x.FirstName, y.FirstName);
      case PersonCompareType.LastName:
        return string.Compare(x.LastName, y.LastName);
      default:
        throw new ArgumentException("unexpected compare type");
    }
  }
}
```

Now you can pass a `PersonComparer` object to the second argument of the `Array.Sort` method. Here, the people are sorted by first name (code file SortingSample/Program.cs):

```
Array.Sort(persons, new PersonComparer(PersonCompareType.FirstName));
foreach (var p in persons)
{
  Console.WriteLine(p);
}
```

The persons array is now sorted by first name:

```
Ayrton Senna
Damon Hill
Graham Hill
Niki Lauda
```

> **NOTE** *The* Array *class also offers* Sort *methods that require a delegate as an argument. With this argument you can pass a method to do the comparison of two objects rather than relying on the* IComparable *or* IComparer *interfaces. Chapter 8, "Delegates, Lambdas, and Events," discusses how to use delegates.*

ARRAYS AS PARAMETERS

Arrays can be passed as parameters to methods, and returned from methods. Returning an array, you just have to declare the array as the return type, as shown with the following method `GetPersons`:

```
static Person[] GetPersons() =>
  new Person[] {
    new Person("Damon", "Hill"),
    new Person("Niki", "Lauda"),
    new Person("Ayrton", "Senna"),
    new Person("Graham", "Hill")
  };
```

Passing arrays to a method, the array is declared with the parameter, as shown with the method `DisplayPersons`:

```
static void DisplayPersons(Person[] persons)
{
  //...
}
```

ARRAY COVARIANCE

With arrays, covariance is supported. This means that an array can be declared as a base type and elements of derived types can be assigned to the elements.

For example, you can declare a parameter of type `object[]` as shown and pass a `Person[]` to it:

```
static void DisplayArray(object[] data)
{
  //...
}
```

> **NOTE** *Array covariance is only possible with reference types, not with value types. In addition, array covariance has an issue that can only be resolved with runtime exceptions. If you assign a Person array to an object array, the object array can then be used with anything that derives from the object. The compiler accepts, for example, passing a string to array elements. However, because a* `Person` *array is referenced by the object array, a runtime exception,* `ArrayTypeMismatchException`, *occurs.*

ENUMERATORS

By using the `foreach` statement you can iterate elements of a collection (see Chapter 10) without needing to know the number of elements inside the collection. The `foreach` statement uses an enumerator. Figure 7-7 shows the relationship between the client invoking the `foreach` method and the collection. The array or collection implements the `IEnumerable` interface with the `GetEnumerator` method. The `GetEnumerator` method returns an enumerator implementing the `IEnumerator` interface. The interface `IEnumerator` is then used by the `foreach` statement to iterate through the collection.

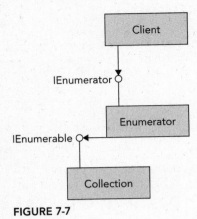

FIGURE 7-7

> **NOTE** *The* `GetEnumerator` *method is defined with the interface* `IEnumerable`. *The* `foreach` *statement doesn't really need this interface implemented in the collection class. It's enough to have a method with the name* `GetEnumerator` *that returns an object implementing the* `IEnumerator` *interface.*

IEnumerator Interface

The `foreach` statement uses the methods and properties of the `IEnumerator` interface to iterate all elements in a collection. For this, `IEnumerator` defines the property `Current` to return the element where the cursor is positioned, and the method `MoveNext` to move to the next element of the collection. `MoveNext` returns `true` if there's an element, and `false` if no more elements are available.

The generic version of this interface `IEnumerator<T>` derives from the interface IDisposable and thus defines a `Dispose` method to clean up resources allocated by the enumerator.

> **NOTE** *The* `IEnumerator` *interface also defines the* `Reset` *method for COM interoperability. Many .NET enumerators implement this by throwing an exception of type* `NotSupportedException`.

foreach Statement

The C# `foreach` statement is not resolved to a `foreach` statement in the IL code. Instead, the C# compiler converts the `foreach` statement to methods and properties of the `IEnumerator` interface. Here's a simple `foreach` statement to iterate all elements in the `persons` array and display them person by person:

```
foreach (var p in persons)
{
    Console.WriteLine(p);
}
```

The `foreach` statement is resolved to the following code segment. First, the `GetEnumerator` method is invoked to get an enumerator for the array. Inside a `while` loop, as long as `MoveNext` returns `true`, the elements of the array are accessed using the `Current` property:

```
IEnumerator<Person> enumerator = persons.GetEnumerator();
while (enumerator.MoveNext())
```

```
    {
      Person p = enumerator.Current;
      Console.WriteLine(p);
    }
```

yield Statement

Since the first release of C#, it has been easy to iterate through collections by using the `foreach` statement. With C# 1.0, it was still a lot of work to create an enumerator. C# 2.0 added the `yield` statement for creating enumerators easily. The `yield return` statement returns one element of a collection and moves the position to the next element, and `yield break` stops the iteration.

The next example shows the implementation of a simple collection using the `yield return` statement. The class `HelloCollection` contains the method `GetEnumerator`. The implementation of the `GetEnumerator` method contains two `yield return` statements where the strings `Hello` and `World` are returned (code file `YieldSample/Program.cs`):

```
using System;
using System.Collections;
namespace Wrox.ProCSharp.Arrays
{
  public class HelloCollection
  {
    public IEnumerator<string> GetEnumerator()
    {
      yield return "Hello";
      yield return "World";
    }
  }
}
```

> **NOTE** *A method or property that contains yield statements is also known as an iterator block. An iterator block must be declared to return an* IEnumerator *or* IEnumerable *interface, or the generic versions of these interfaces. This block may contain multiple* yield return *or* yield break *statements; a* return *statement is not allowed.*

Now it is possible to iterate through the collection using a `foreach` statement:

```
public void HelloWorld()
{
  var helloCollection = new HelloCollection();
  foreach (var s in helloCollection)
  {
    Console.WriteLine(s);
  }
}
```

With an iterator block, the compiler generates a yield type, including a state machine, as shown in the following code segment. The yield type implements the properties and methods of the interfaces `IEnumerator` and `IDisposable`. In the example, you can see the yield type as the inner class `Enumerator`. The `GetEnumerator` method of the outer class instantiates and returns a new yield type. Within the yield type, the variable `state` defines the current position of the iteration and is changed every time the method `MoveNext` is invoked. `MoveNext` encapsulates the code of the iterator block and sets the value of the `current` variable so that the `Current` property returns an object depending on the position:

```
public class HelloCollection
{
  public IEnumerator GetEnumerator() => new Enumerator(0);
```

```csharp
public class Enumerator: IEnumerator<string>, IEnumerator, IDisposable
{
  private int _state;
  private string _current;
  public Enumerator(int state) => _state = state;
  bool System.Collections.IEnumerator.MoveNext()
  {
    switch (state)
    {
      case 0:
        _current = "Hello";
        _state = 1;
        return true;
      case 1:
        _current = "World";
        _state = 2;
        return true;
      case 2:
        break;
    }
    return false;
  }

  void System.Collections.IEnumerator.Reset() =>
    throw new NotSupportedException();

  string System.Collections.Generic.IEnumerator<string>.Current => current;
  object System.Collections.IEnumerator.Current => current;
  void IDisposable.Dispose() { }
  }
}
```

> **NOTE** *Remember that the* `yield` *statement produces an enumerator, and not just a list filled with items. This enumerator is invoked by the* `foreach` *statement. As each item is accessed from the* `foreach`, *the enumerator is accessed. This makes it possible to iterate through huge amounts of data without reading all the data into memory in one turn.*

Different Ways to Iterate Through Collections

In a slightly larger and more realistic way than the Hello World example, you can use the `yield return` statement to iterate through a collection in different ways. The class `MusicTitles` enables iterating the titles in a default way with the `GetEnumerator` method, in reverse order with the `Reverse` method, and through a subset with the `Subset` method (code file `YieldSample/MusicTitles.cs`):

```csharp
public class MusicTitles
{
  string[] names = {"Tubular Bells", "Hergest Ridge", "Ommadawn", "Platinum"};

  public IEnumerator<string> GetEnumerator()
  {
    for (int i = 0; i < 4; i++)
    {
      yield return names[i];
    }
  }
}
```

```
public IEnumerable<string> Reverse()
{
  for (int i = 3; i >= 0; i-)
  {
    yield return names[i];
  }
}

public IEnumerable<string> Subset(int index, int length)
{
  for (int i = index; i < index + length; i++)
  {
    yield return names[i];
  }
}
}
```

> **NOTE** *The default iteration supported by a class is the* GetEnumerator *method, which is defined to return* IEnumerator. *Named iterations return* IEnumerable.

The client code to iterate through the string array first uses the GetEnumerator method, which you don't have to write in your code because it is used by default with the implementation of the foreach statement. Then the titles are iterated in reverse, and finally a subset is iterated by passing the index and number of items to iterate to the Subset method (code file YieldSample/Program.cs):

```
var titles = new MusicTitles();
foreach (var title in titles)
{
  Console.WriteLine(title);
}
Console.WriteLine();

Console.WriteLine("reverse");
foreach (var title in titles.Reverse())
{
  Console.WriteLine(title);
}
Console.WriteLine();

Console.WriteLine("subset");
foreach (var title in titles.Subset(2, 2))
{
  Console.WriteLine(title);
}
```

Returning Enumerators with Yield Return

With the yield statement you can also do more complex things, such as return an enumerator from yield return. Using the following Tic-Tac-Toe game as an example, players alternate putting a cross or a circle in one of nine fields. These moves are simulated by the GameMoves class. The methods Cross and Circle are the iterator blocks for creating iterator types. The variables cross and circle are set to Cross and Circle inside the constructor of the GameMoves class. By setting these fields, the methods are not invoked, but they are set to the iterator types that are defined with the iterator blocks. Within the Cross iterator block, information about the move is written to the console and the move number is incremented. If the move number is higher than 8, the iteration ends with `yield break`; otherwise, the enumerator object of the circle yield type is returned with each iteration. The `Circle` iterator block is very similar to the `Cross` iterator block; it just returns the cross iterator type with each iteration (code file `YieldSample/GameMoves.cs`):

```
public class GameMoves
{
  private IEnumerator _cross;
  private IEnumerator _circle;
  public GameMoves()
  {
    _cross = Cross();
    _circle = Circle();
  }
  private int _move = 0;
  const int MaxMoves = 9;

  public IEnumerator Cross()
  {
    while (true)
    {
      Console.WriteLine($"Cross, move {_move}");
      if (++_move >= MaxMoves)
      {
        yield break;
      }
      yield return _circle;
    }
  }

  public IEnumerator Circle()
  {
    while (true)
    {
      Console.WriteLine($"Circle, move {move}");
      if (++_move >= MaxMoves)
      {
        yield break;
      }
      yield return _cross;
    }
  }
}
```

From the client program, you can use the class `GameMoves` as follows. The first move is set by setting enumerator to the enumerator type returned by `game.Cross`. In a `while` loop, `enumerator.MoveNext` is called. The first time this is invoked, the `Cross` method is called, which returns the other enumerator with a `yield` statement. The returned value can be accessed with the `Current` property and is set to the `enumerator` variable for the next loop:

```
var game = new GameMoves();
IEnumerator enumerator = game.Cross();
while (enumerator.MoveNext())
{
  enumerator = enumerator.Current as IEnumerator;
}
```

The output of this program shows alternating moves until the last move:

```
Cross, move 0
Circle, move 1
Cross, move 2
Circle, move 3
Cross, move 4
```

```
Circle, move 5
Cross, move 6
Circle, move 7
Cross, move 8
```

STRUCTURAL COMPARISON

Arrays as well as tuples implement the interfaces `IStructuralEquatable` and `IStructuralComparable`. These interfaces compare not only references but also the content. This interface is implemented explicitly, so it is necessary to cast the arrays and tuples to this interface on use. `IStructuralEquatable` is used to compare whether two tuples or arrays have the same content; `IStructuralComparable` is used to sort tuples or arrays.

> **NOTE** *Tuples are discussed in Chapter 13.*

With the sample demonstrating `IStructuralEquatable`, the `Person` class implementing the interface `IEquatable` is used. `IEquatable` defines a strongly typed `Equals` method where the values of the `FirstName` and `LastName` properties are compared (code file `StructuralComparison/Person.cs`):

```csharp
public class Person: IEquatable<Person>
{
  public int Id { get; }
  public string FirstName { get; }
  public string LastName { get; }

  public Person(int id, string firstName, string lastName)
  {
    Id = id;
    FirstName = firstName;
    LastName = lastName;
  }

  public override string ToString() => $"{Id}, {FirstName} {LastName}";

  public override bool Equals(object obj)
  {
    if (obj == null)
    {
      return base.Equals(obj);
    }
    return Equals(obj as Person);
  }

  public override int GetHashCode() => Id.GetHashCode();

  public bool Equals(Person other)
  {
    if (other == null)
    return base.Equals(other);
    return Id == other.Id && FirstName == other.FirstName &&
    LastName == other.LastName;
  }
}
```

Now two arrays containing `Person` items are created. Both arrays contain the same `Person` object with the variable name `janet`, and two different `Person` objects that have the same content. The comparison operator `!=` returns `true` because there are indeed two different arrays referenced from two variable names, persons1 and persons2. Because the Equals method with one parameter is not overridden by the Array class, the same happens as with the == operator to compare the references, and they are not the same (code file StructuralComparison/Program.cs):

```
var janet = new Person("Janet", "Jackson");
Person[] people1 = {
  new Person("Michael", "Jackson"),
  janet
};
Person[] people2 = {
  new Person("Michael", "Jackson")
  janet
};

if (people1 != people2)
{
  Console.WriteLine("not the same reference");
}
```

Invoking the Equals method defined by the IStructuralEquatable interface—that is, the method with the first parameter of type object and the second parameter of type IEqualityComparer—you can define how the comparison should be done by passing an object that implements IEqualityComparer<T>. A default implementation of the IEqualityComparer is done by the EqualityComparer<T> class. This implementation checks whether the type implements the interface IEquatable, and invokes the IEquatable. Equals method. If the type does not implement IEquatable, the Equals method from the base class Object is invoked to do the comparison.

Person implements IEquatable<Person>, where the content of the objects is compared, and the arrays indeed contain the same content:

```
if ((people1 as IStructuralEquatable).Equals(people2,
  EqualityComparer<Person>.Default))
{
  Console.WriteLine("the same content");
}
```

SPANS

For a fast way to access managed or unmanaged continuous memory, you can use the Span<T> struct. One example where Span<T> can be used is an array; the Span<T> struct holds continuous memory behind the scenes. Another example is a long string. Using Span<T> with strings is covered in Chapter 9, "Strings and Regular Expressions."

Using Span<T>, you can directly access array elements. The elements of the array are not copied, but they can be used directly, which is faster than a copy.

In the following code snippet, first a simple int array is created and initialized. A Span<int> object is created, invoking the constructor and passing the array to the Span<int>. The Span<T> type offers an indexer, and thus the elements of the Span<T> can be accessed using this indexer. Here, the second element is changed to the value 11. Because the array arr1 is referenced from the span, the second element of the array is changed by changing the Span<T> element (code file SpanSample/Program.cs):

```
private static Span<int> IntroSpans()
{
  int[] arr1 = { 1, 4, 5, 11, 13, 18 };
  var span1 = new Span<int>(arr1);
  span1[1] = 11;
  Console.WriteLine($"arr1[1] is changed via span1[1]: {arr1[1]}");
  return span1;
}
```

Creating Slices

A powerful feature of Span<T> is that you can use it to access parts, or *slices,* of an array. Using the slices, the array elements are not copied; they're directly accessed from the span.

The following code snippet shows two ways to create slices. With the first one, a constructor overload is used to pass the start and length of the array that should be used. With the variable span3 that references this newly created Span<int>, it's only possible to access three elements of the array arr2, starting with the fourth element. Another overload of the constructor exists where you can pass just the start of the slice. With this overload, the remains of the array are taken until the end. You can also create a slice from a Span<T> object, invoking the Slice method. Similar overloads exist here. With the variable span4, the previously created span1 is used to create a slice with four elements starting with the third element of span1 (code file SpanSample/Program.cs):

```
private static Span<int> CreateSlices(Span<int> span1)
{
  Console.WriteLine(nameof(CreateSlices));
  int[] arr2 = { 3, 5, 7, 9, 11, 13, 15 };
  var span2 = new Span<int>(arr2);
  var span3 = new Span<int>(arr2, start: 3, length: 3);
  var span4 = span1.Slice(start: 2, length: 4);

  DisplaySpan("content of span3", span3);
  DisplaySpan("content of span4", span4);
  Console.WriteLine();
  return span2;
}
```

The DisplaySpan method is used to display the contents of a span. The method of the following code snippet makes use of the ReadOnlySpan. This span type can be used if you don't need to change the content that the span references, which is the case in the DisplaySpan method. ReadOnlySpan<T> is discussed later in this chapter in more detail:

```
private static void DisplaySpan(string title, ReadOnlySpan<int> span)
{
  Console.WriteLine(title);
  for (int i = 0; i < span.Length; i++)
  {
    Console.Write($"{span[i]}.");
  }
  Console.WriteLine();
}
```

When you run the application, the content of span3 and span4 is shown—a subset of the arr2 and arr1:

```
content of span3
9.11.13.
content of span4
6.8.10.12.
```

> **NOTE** Span<T> *is safe from crossing the boundaries. In cases when you're creating spans that exceed the contained array length, an exception of type* ArgumentOutOfRangeException *is thrown. Read Chapter 14 for more information on exception handling.*

Changing Values Using Spans

You've seen how to directly change elements of the array that are referenced by the span using the indexer of the Span<T> type. There are more options as shown in the following code snippet.

You can invoke the Clear method, which fills a span containing int types with 0; you can invoke the Fill method to fill the span with the value passed to the Fill method; and you can copy a Span<T> to another Span<T>. With the CopyTo method, if the destination span is not large enough, an exception of type ArgumentException is thrown. You can avoid this outcome by using the TryCopyTo method. This method doesn't throw an exception if the destination span is not large enough; instead it returns false as being not successful with the copy (code file SpanSample/Program.cs):

```
private static void ChangeValues(Span<int> span1, Span<int> span2)
{
  Console.WriteLine(nameof(ChangeValues));
  Span<int> span4 = span1.Slice(start: 4);
  span4.Clear();
  DisplaySpan("content of span1", span1);
  Span<int> span5 = span2.Slice(start: 3, length: 3);
  span5.Fill(42);
  DisplaySpan("content of span2", span2);
  span5.CopyTo(span1);
  DisplaySpan("content of span1", span1);

  if (!span1.TryCopyTo(span4))
  {
    Console.WriteLine("Couldn't copy span1 to span4 because span4 is " +
      "too small");
    Console.WriteLine($"length of span4: {span4.Length}, length of " +
      $"span1: {span1.Length}");
  }
  Console.WriteLine();
}
```

When you run the application, you can see the content of span1 where the last two numbers have been cleared using span4, the content of span2 where span5 was used to fill the value 42 with three elements, and again the content of span1 where the first three numbers have been copied over from span5. Copying span1 to span4 was not successful because span4 has just a length of 4, whereas span1 has a length of 6:

```
content of span1
2.11.6.8.0.0.
content of span2
3.5.7.42.42.42.15.
content of span1
42.42.42.8.0.0.
Couldn't copy span1 to span4 because span4 is too small
length of span4: 2, length of span1: 6
```

ReadOnly Spans

If you need only read-access to an array segment, you can use ReadOnlySpan<T> as was already shown in the DisplaySpan method. With ReadOnlySpan<T>, the indexer is read-only, and this type doesn't offer Clear and Fill methods. You can however, invoke the CopyTo method to copy the content of the ReadOnlySpan<T> to a Span<T>.

The following code snippet creates readOnlySpan1 from an array with the constructor of ReadOnlySpan<T>. readOnlySpan2 and readOnlySpan3 are created by direct assignments from Span<int> and int[]. Implicit cast operators are available with ReadOnlySpan<T> (code file SpanSample/Program.cs):

```
private static void ReadonlySpan(Span<int> span1)
{
    Console.WriteLine(nameof(ReadonlySpan));
```

```
        int[] arr = span1.ToArray();
        ReadOnlySpan<int> readOnlySpan1 = new ReadOnlySpan<int>(arr);
        DisplaySpan("readOnlySpan1", readOnlySpan1);

        ReadOnlySpan<int> readOnlySpan2 = span1;
        DisplaySpan("readOnlySpan2", readOnlySpan2);
        ReadOnlySpan<int> readOnlySpan3 = arr;
        DisplaySpan("readOnlySpan3", readOnlySpan3);
        Console.WriteLine();
    }
```

> **NOTE** *How to implement implicit cast operators is discussed in Chapter 6, "Operators and Casts."*

> **NOTE** *Previous editions of this book demonstrated the use of* ArraySegment<T>. *Although* ArraySegment<T> *is still available, it has some shortcomings, and you can use the more flexible* Span<T> *as a replacement. In case you're already using* ArraySegment<T>, *you can keep the code and interact with spans. The constructor of* Span<T> *also allows passing an* ArraySegment<T> *to create a* Span<T> *instance.*

ARRAY POOLS

If you have an application where a lot of arrays are created and destroyed, the garbage collector has some work to do. To reduce the work of the garbage collector, you can use array pools with the `ArrayPool` class. `ArrayPool` manages a pool of arrays. Arrays can be rented from and returned to the pool. Memory is managed from the `ArrayPool` itself.

Creating the Array Pool

You can create an `ArrayPool<T>` by invoking the static `Create` method. For efficiency, the array pool manages memory in multiple buckets for arrays of similar sizes. With the `Create` method, you can define the maximum array length and the number of arrays within a bucket before another bucket is required:

```
ArrayPool<int> customPool = ArrayPool<int>.Create(
    maxArrayLength: 40000, maxArraysPerBucket: 10);
```

The default for the `maxArrayLength` is 1024 * 1024 bytes, and the default for `maxArraysPerBucket` is 50. The array pool uses multiple buckets for faster access to arrays when many arrays are used. Arrays of similar sizes are kept in the same bucket as long as possible, and the maximum number of arrays is not reached.

You can also use a predefined shared pool by accessing the `Shared` property of the `ArrayPool<T>` class:

```
ArrayPool<int> sharedPool = ArrayPool<int>.Shared;
```

Renting Memory from the Pool

Requesting memory from the pool happens by invoking the `Rent` method. The `Rent` method accepts the minimum array length that should be requested. If memory is already available in the pool, it is returned. If it is not available, memory is allocated for the pool and returned afterward. In the following code snippet, an array of 1024, 2048, 3096, and so on elements is requested in a `for` loop (code file `ArrayPoolSample/Program.cs`):

```
private static void UseSharedPool()
{
```

```
        for (int i = 0; i < 10; i++)
        {
          int arrayLength = (i + 1) << 10;
          int[] arr = ArrayPool<int>.Shared.Rent(arrayLength);
          Console.WriteLine($"requested an array of {arrayLength} " +
            $"and received {arr.Length}");
          //...
        }
      }
```

The Rent method returns an array with at least the requested number of elements. The array returned could have more memory available. The shared pool keeps arrays with at least 16 elements. The element count of the arrays managed always duplicates—for example, 16, 32, 64, 128, 256, 512, 1024, 2048, 4096, 8192 elements and so on.

When you run the application, you can see that larger arrays are returned if the requested array size doesn't fit the arrays managed by the pool:

```
requested an array of 1024 and received 1024
requested an array of 2048 and received 2048
requested an array of 3072 and received 4096
requested an array of 4096 and received 4096
requested an array of 5120 and received 8192
requested an array of 6144 and received 8192
requested an array of 7168 and received 8192
requested an array of 8192 and received 8192
requested an array of 9216 and received 16384
requested an array of 10240 and received 16384
```

Returning Memory to the Pool

After you no longer need the array, you can return it to the pool. After the array is returned, you can later reuse it by another rent.

You return the array to the pool by invoking the Return method of the array pool and passing the array to the Return method. With an optional parameter, you can specify if the array should be cleared before it is returned to the pool. Without clearing it, the next one renting an array from the pool could read the data. Clearing the data, you avoid this, but you need more CPU time (code file: ArrayPoolSample/Program.cs):

```
ArrayPool<int>.Shared.Return(arr, clearArray: true);
```

> **NOTE** *Information about the garbage collector and how to get information about memory addresses is in Chapter 17, "Managed and Unmanaged Memory."*

SUMMARY

In this chapter, you've seen the C# notation to create and use simple, multidimensional, and jagged arrays. The Array class is used behind the scenes of C# arrays, enabling you to invoke properties and methods of this class with array variables.

You've seen how to sort elements in the array by using the IComparable and IComparer interfaces; and you've learned how to create and use enumerators, the interfaces IEnumerable and IEnumerator, and the yield statement.

The last sections of this chapter show you how to efficiently use arrays with Span<T> and ArrayPool.

The next chapter gets into details of more important features of C#: delegates, lambdas, and events.

8

Delegates, Lambdas, and Events

WHAT'S IN THIS CHAPTER?

➤ Delegates

➤ Lambda expressions

➤ Closures

➤ Events

WROX.COM CODE DOWNLOADS FOR THIS CHAPTER

The Wrox.com code downloads for this chapter are found at www.wrox.com on the Download Code tab. The source code is also available at https://github.com/ProfessionalCSharp/ProfessionalCSharp7 in the directory Delegates.

The code for this chapter is divided into the following major examples:

➤ Simple Delegates

➤ Bubble Sorter

➤ Lambda Expressions

➤ Events Sample

REFERENCING METHODS

Delegates are the .NET variant of addresses to methods. Compare this to C++, where a function pointer is nothing more than a pointer to a memory location that is not type-safe. You have no idea what a pointer is really pointing to, and items such as parameters and return types are not known. This is completely different with .NET; delegates are type-safe classes that define the return types and types of parameters. The delegate class not only contains a reference to a method, but can hold references to multiple methods.

Lambda expressions are directly related to delegates. When the parameter is a delegate type, you can use a lambda expression to implement a method that's referenced from the delegate.

This chapter explains the basics of delegates and lambda expressions, and shows you how to implement methods called by delegates with lambda expressions. It also demonstrates how .NET uses delegates as the means of implementing events.

DELEGATES

Delegates exist for situations in which you want to pass methods around to other methods. To see what that means, consider this line of code:

```
int i = int.Parse("99");
```

You are so used to passing data to methods as parameters, as in this example, that you don't consciously think about it, so the idea of passing methods around instead of data might sound a little strange. However, sometimes you have a method that does something, and rather than operate on data, the method might need to do something that involves invoking another method. To complicate things further, you do not know at compile time what this second method is. That information is available only at runtime and hence needs to be passed in as a parameter to the first method. That might sound confusing, but it should become clearer with a couple of examples:

➤ **Threads and tasks**—It is possible in C# to tell the computer to start a new sequence of execution in parallel with what it is currently doing. Such a sequence is known as a *thread*, and you start one using the `Start` method on an instance of one of the base classes, `System.Threading.Thread`. If you tell the computer to start a new sequence of execution, you must tell it where to start that sequence; that is, you must supply the details of a method in which execution can start. In other words, the constructor of the `Thread` class takes a parameter that defines the method to be invoked by the thread.

➤ **Generic library classes**—Many libraries contain code to perform various standard tasks. It is usually possible for these libraries to be self-contained, in the sense that you know when you write to the library exactly how the task must be performed. However, sometimes the task contains a subtask, which only the individual client code that uses the library knows how to perform. For example, say that you want to write a class that takes an array of objects and sorts them in ascending order. Part of the sorting process involves repeatedly taking two of the objects in the array and comparing them to see which one should come first. If you want to make the class capable of sorting arrays of any object, there is no way that it can tell in advance how to do this comparison. The client code that hands your class the array of objects must also tell your class how to do this comparison for the particular objects it wants sorted. The client code has to pass your class details of an appropriate method that can be called to do the comparison.

➤ **Events**—The general idea here is that often you have code that needs to be informed when some event takes place. GUI programming is full of situations like this. When the event is raised, the runtime needs to know what method should be executed. This is done by passing the method that handles the event as a parameter to a delegate. This is discussed later in this chapter.

In C and C++, you can just take the address of a function and pass it as a parameter. There's no type safety with C. You can pass any function to a method where a function pointer is required. Unfortunately, this direct approach not only causes some problems with type safety but also neglects the fact that when you are doing object-oriented programming, methods rarely exist in isolation; they usually need to be associated with a class instance before they can be called. Because of these problems, the .NET Framework does not syntactically permit this direct approach. Instead, if you want to pass methods around, you wrap the details of the method in a new kind of object: a delegate. Delegates, quite simply, are a special type of object—special in the sense that, whereas all the objects defined up to now contain data, a delegate contains the address of a method, or the address of multiple methods.

Declaring Delegates

When you want to use a class in C#, you do so in two stages. First, you need to define the class—that is, you need to tell the compiler what fields and methods make up the class. Then (unless you are using only static methods), you instantiate an object of that class. With delegates it is the same process. You start by declaring the delegates you want to use. Declaring delegates means telling the compiler what kind of method a delegate of that type will represent. Then you create one or more instances of that delegate. Behind the scenes, the compiler creates a class that represents the delegate.

The syntax for declaring delegates looks like this:

```
delegate void IntMethodInvoker(int x);
```

This declares a delegate called `IntMethodInvoker`, and indicates that each instance of this delegate can hold a reference to a method that takes one `int` parameter and returns `void`. The crucial point to understand about delegates is that they are type-safe. When you define the delegate, you provide full details about the signature and the return type of the method that it represents.

> **NOTE** *One good way to understand delegates is to think of a delegate as something that gives a name to a method signature and the return type.*

Suppose that you want to define a delegate called `TwoLongsOp` that represents a method that takes two `long`s as its parameters and returns a `double`. You could do so like this:

```
delegate double TwoLongsOp(long first, long second);
```

Or, to define a delegate that represents a method that takes no parameters and returns a `string`, you might write this:

```
delegate string GetAString();
```

The syntax is similar to that for a method definition, except there is no method body and the definition is prefixed with the keyword `delegate`. Because what you are doing here is basically defining a new class, you can define a delegate in any of the same places that you would define a class—that is to say, either inside another class, outside of any class, or in a namespace as a top-level object. Depending on how visible you want your definition to be, and the scope of the delegate, you can apply any of the normal access modifiers to delegate definitions—`public`, `private`, `protected`, and so on:

```
public delegate string GetAString();
```

> **NOTE** *We really mean what we say when we describe defining a delegate as defining a new class. Delegates are implemented as classes derived from the class* System. MulticastDelegate, *which is derived from the base class* System.Delegate. *The C# compiler is aware of this class and uses its delegate syntax to hide the details of the operation of this class. This is another good example of how C# works in conjunction with the base classes to make programming as easy as possible.*

After you have defined a delegate, you can create an instance of it so that you can use it to store details about a particular method.

> **NOTE** *There is an unfortunate problem with terminology here. When you are talking about classes, there are two distinct terms:* class, *which indicates the broader definition, and* object, *which means an instance of the class. Unfortunately, with delegates there is only the one term;* delegate *can refer to both the class and the object. When you create an instance of a delegate, what you have created is also referred to as a delegate. You need to be aware of the context to know which meaning is being used when we talk about delegates.*

Using Delegates

The following code snippet demonstrates the use of a delegate. It is a rather long-winded way of calling the `ToString` method on an `int` (code file `GetAStringDemo/Program.cs`):

```
private delegate string GetAString();
public static void Main()
{
  int x = 40;
  GetAString firstStringMethod = new GetAString(x.ToString);
  Console.WriteLine($"String is {firstStringMethod()}");
  // With firstStringMethod initialized to x.ToString(),
  // the above statement is equivalent to saying
  // Console.WriteLine($"String is {x.ToString()}");
}
```

This code instantiates a delegate of type `GetAString` and initializes it so it refers to the `ToString` method of the integer variable x. Delegates in C# always syntactically take a one-parameter constructor, the parameter being the method to which the delegate refers. This method must match the signature with which you originally defined the delegate. In this case, you would get a compilation error if you tried to initialize the variable `firstStringMethod` with any method that did not take any parameters and return a string. Notice that because `int.ToString` is an instance method (as opposed to a static one), you need to specify the instance (x) as well as the name of the method to initialize the delegate properly.

The next line uses the delegate to display the string. In any code, supplying the name of a delegate instance, followed by parentheses containing any parameters, has the same effect as calling the method wrapped by the delegate. Hence, in the preceding code snippet, the `Console.WriteLine` statement is completely equivalent to the commented-out line.

In fact, supplying parentheses to the delegate instance is the same as invoking the `Invoke` method of the delegate class. Because `firstStringMethod` is a variable of a delegate type, the C# compiler replaces `firstStringMethod` with `firstStringMethod.Invoke`:

```
firstStringMethod();
firstStringMethod.Invoke();
```

For less typing, at every place where a delegate instance is needed, you can just pass the name of the address. This is known by the term *delegate inference*. This C# feature works as long as the compiler can resolve the delegate instance to a specific type. The example initialized the variable `firstStringMethod` of type `GetAString` with a new instance of the delegate `GetAString`:

```
GetAString firstStringMethod = new GetAString(x.ToString);
```

You can write the same just by passing the method name with the variable x to the variable `firstStringMethod`:

```
GetAString firstStringMethod = x.ToString;
```

The code that is created by the C# compiler is the same. The compiler detects that a delegate type is required with `firstStringMethod`, so it creates an instance of the delegate type `GetAString` and passes the address of the method with the object x to the constructor.

> **NOTE** *Be aware that you can't type the brackets to the method name as* `x.ToString()` *and pass it to the delegate variable. This would be an invocation of the method. The invocation of the* `ToString` *method returns a string object that can't be assigned to the delegate variable. You can only assign the address of a method to the delegate variable.*

Delegate inference can be used anywhere a delegate instance is required. Delegate inference can also be used with events because events are based on delegates (as you see later in this chapter).

One feature of delegates is that they are type-safe to the extent that they ensure that the signature of the method being called is correct. However, interestingly, they don't care what type of object the method is being called against or even whether the method is a static method or an instance method.

> **NOTE** *An instance of a given delegate can refer to any instance or static method on any object of any type, provided that the signature of the method matches the signature of the delegate.*

To demonstrate this, the following example expands the previous code snippet so that it uses the `firstStringMethod` delegate to call a couple of other methods on another object—an instance method and a static method. For this, you use the `Currency` struct. The `Currency` struct has its own overload of `ToString` and a static method with the same signature to `GetCurrencyUnit`. This way, the same delegate variable can be used to invoke these methods (code file `GetAStringDemo/Currency.cs`):

```
struct Currency
{
  public uint Dollars;
  public ushort Cents;
  public Currency(uint dollars, ushort cents)
  {
    Dollars = dollars;
    Cents = cents;
  }

  public override string ToString() => $"${Dollars}.{Cents,2:00}";

  public static string GetCurrencyUnit() => "Dollar";

  public static explicit operator Currency (float value)
  {
    checked
    {
      uint dollars = (uint)value;
      ushort cents = (ushort)((value—dollars) * 100);
      return new Currency(dollars, cents);
    }
  }

  public static implicit operator float (Currency value) =>
    value.Dollars + (value.Cents / 100.0f);
```

```
    public static implicit operator Currency (uint value) =>
      new Currency(value, 0);

    public static implicit operator uint (Currency value) =>
      value.Dollars;
}
```

Now you can use the GetAString instance as follows (code file GetAStringDemo/Program.cs):

```
private delegate string GetAString();
public static void Main()
{
  int x = 40;
  GetAString firstStringMethod = x.ToString;
  Console.WriteLine($"String is {firstStringMethod()}");
  var balance = new Currency(34, 50);

  // firstStringMethod references an instance method
  firstStringMethod = balance.ToString;
  Console.WriteLine($"String is {firstStringMethod()}");

  // firstStringMethod references a static method
  firstStringMethod = new GetAString(Currency.GetCurrencyUnit);
  Console.WriteLine($"String is {firstStringMethod()}");
}
```

This code shows how you can call a method via a delegate and subsequently reassign the delegate to refer to different methods on different instances of classes, even static methods or methods against instances of different types of class, provided that the signature of each method matches the delegate definition.

When you run the application, you get the output from the different methods that are referenced by the delegate:

```
String is 40
String is $34.50
String is Dollar
```

However, you still haven't seen the process of passing a delegate to another method, and nothing particularly useful has been achieved yet. It is possible to call the ToString method of int and Currency objects in a much more straightforward way than using delegates. Unfortunately, the nature of delegates requires a fairly complex example before you can really appreciate their usefulness. The next section presents two delegate examples. The first one simply uses delegates to call a couple of different operations. It illustrates how to pass delegates to methods and how you can use arrays of delegates—although arguably it still doesn't do much that you couldn't do a lot more simply without delegates. The second, much more complex, example presents a BubbleSorter class, which implements a method to sort arrays of objects into ascending order. This class would be difficult to write without using delegates.

Simple Delegate Example

This example defines a MathOperations class that uses a couple of static methods to perform two operations on doubles. Then you use delegates to invoke these methods. The MathOperations class looks like this (code file SimpleDelegates/MathOperations):

```
class MathOperations
{
  public static double MultiplyByTwo(double value) => value * 2;
  public static double Square(double value) => value * value;
}
```

You invoke these methods as follows (code file SimpleDelegates/Program.cs):

```
using System;
```

```
namespace Wrox.ProCSharp.Delegates
{
  delegate double DoubleOp(double x);

  class Program
  {
    static void Main()
    {
      DoubleOp[] operations =
      {
        MathOperations.MultiplyByTwo,
        MathOperations.Square
      };

      for (int i=0; i < operations.Length; i++)
      {
        Console.WriteLine($"Using operations[{i}]:);
        ProcessAndDisplayNumber(operations[i], 2.0);
        ProcessAndDisplayNumber(operations[i], 7.94);
        ProcessAndDisplayNumber(operations[i], 1.414);
        Console.WriteLine();
      }
    }

    static void ProcessAndDisplayNumber(DoubleOp action, double value)
    {
      double result = action(value);
      Console.WriteLine($"Value is {value}, result of operation is {result}");
    }
  }
}
```

In this code, you instantiate an array of DoubleOp delegates (remember that after you have defined a delegate class, you can basically instantiate instances just as you can with normal classes, so putting some into an array is no problem). Each element of the array is initialized to refer to a different operation implemented by the MathOperations class. Then, you loop through the array, applying each operation to three different values. This illustrates one way of using delegates—to group methods together into an array so that you can call several methods in a loop.

The key lines in this code are the ones in which you pass each delegate to the ProcessAndDisplayNumber method, such as here:

```
ProcessAndDisplayNumber(operations[i], 2.0);
```

The preceding passes in the name of a delegate but without any parameters. Given that operations[i] is a delegate, syntactically:

➤ operations[i] means the delegate (that is, the method represented by the delegate)
➤ operations[i](2.0) means call this method, passing in the value in parentheses

The ProcessAndDisplayNumber method is defined to take a delegate as its first parameter:

```
static void ProcessAndDisplayNumber(DoubleOp action, double value)
```

Then, when in this method, you call:

```
double result = action(value);
```

This causes the method that is wrapped up by the action delegate instance to be called, and its return result stored in Result. Running this example gives you the following:

```
SimpleDelegate
Using operations[0]:
```

```
Value is 2, result of operation is 4
Value is 7.94, result of operation is 15.88
Value is 1.414, result of operation is 2.828
Using operations[1]:
Value is 2, result of operation is 4
Value is 7.94, result of operation is 63.0436
Value is 1.414, result of operation is 1.999396
```

Action<T> and Func<T> Delegates

Instead of defining a new delegate type with every parameter and return type, you can use the Action<T> and Func<T> delegates. The generic Action<T> delegate is meant to reference a method with void return. This delegate class exists in different variants so that you can pass up to 16 different parameter types. The Action class without the generic parameter is for calling methods without parameters. Action<in T> is for calling a method with one parameter; Action<in T1, in T2> for a method with two parameters; and Action<in T1, in T2, in T3, in T4, in T5, in T6, in T7, in T8> for a method with eight parameters.

The Func<T> delegates can be used in a similar manner. Func<T> allows you to invoke methods with a return type. Like Action<T>, Func<T> is defined in different variants to pass up to 16 parameter types and a return type. Func<out TResult> is the delegate type to invoke a method with a return type and without parameters. Func<in T, out TResult> is for a method with one parameter, and Func<in T1, in T2, in T3, in T4, out TResult> is for a method with four parameters.

The example in the preceding section declared a delegate with a double parameter and a double return type:

```
delegate double DoubleOp(double x);
```

Instead of declaring the custom delegate DoubleOp you can use the Func<in T, out TResult> delegate. You can declare a variable of the delegate type or, as shown here, an array of the delegate type:

```
Func<double, double>[] operations =
{
  MathOperations.MultiplyByTwo,
  MathOperations.Square
};
```

and use it with the ProcessAndDisplayNumber method as a parameter:

```
static void ProcessAndDisplayNumber(Func<double, double> action,
double value)
{
  double result = action(value);
  Console.WriteLine($"Value is {value}, result of operation is {result}");
}
```

BubbleSorter Example

You are now ready for an example that shows the real usefulness of delegates. You are going to write a class called BubbleSorter. This class implements a static method, Sort, which takes as its first parameter an array of objects, and rearranges this array into ascending order. For example, if you were to pass in this array of ints, {0, 5, 6, 2, 1}, it would rearrange this array into {0, 1, 2, 5, 6}.

The bubble-sorting algorithm is a well-known and very simple way to sort numbers. It is best suited to small sets of numbers, because for larger sets of numbers (more than about 10), far more efficient algorithms are available. It works by repeatedly looping through the array, comparing each pair of numbers and, if necessary, swapping them, so that the largest numbers progressively move to the end of the array. For sorting ints, a method to do a bubble sort might look like this:

```
bool swapped = true;
do
{
```

```
        swapped = false;
        for (int i = 0; i < sortArray.Length-1; i++)
        {
          if (sortArray[i] > sortArray[i+1])) // problem with this test
          {
            int temp = sortArray[i];
            sortArray[i] = sortArray[i + 1];
            sortArray[i + 1] = temp;
            swapped = true;
          }
        }
      } while (swapped);
```

This is all very well for ints, but you want your Sort method to be able to sort any object. In other words, if some client code hands you an array of Currency structs or any other class or struct that it may have defined, you need to be able to sort the array. This presents a problem with the line if (sortArray[i] < sortArray[i+1]) in the preceding code, because that requires you to compare two objects on the array to determine which one is greater. You can do that for ints, but how do you do it for a new class that doesn't implement the < operator? The answer is that the client code that knows about the class must pass in a delegate wrapping a method that does the comparison. Also, instead of using an int type for the *temp* variable, a generic Sort method can be implemented using a generic type.

With a generic Sort<T> method accepting type T, a comparison method is needed that has two parameters of type T and a return type of bool for the if comparison. This method can be referenced from a Func<T1, T2, TResult> delegate, where T1 and T2 are the same type: Func<T, T, bool>.

This way, you give your Sort<T> method the following signature:

```
    static public void Sort<T>(IList<T> sortArray, Func<T, T, bool> comparison)
```

The documentation for this method states that comparison must refer to a method that takes two arguments, and returns true if the value of the first argument is *smaller than* the second one.

Now you are all set. Here's the definition for the BubbleSorter class (code file BubbleSorter/ BubbleSorter.cs):

```
    class BubbleSorter
    {
      static public void Sort<T>(IList<T> sortArray, Func<T, T, bool> comparison)
      {
        bool swapped = true;
        do
        {
          swapped = false;
          for (int i = 0; i < sortArray.Count-1; i++)
          {
            if (comparison(sortArray[i+1], sortArray[i]))
            {
              T temp = sortArray[i];
              sortArray[i] = sortArray[i + 1];
              sortArray[i + 1] = temp;
              swapped = true;
            }
          }
        } while (swapped);
      }
    }
```

To use this class, you need to define another class, which you can use to set up an array that needs sorting. For this example, assume that the Mortimer Phones mobile phone company has a list of employees and wants them sorted according to salary. Each employee is represented by an instance of a class, `Employee`, which looks like this (code file `BubbleSorter/Employee.cs`):

```
class Employee
{
  public Employee(string name, decimal salary)
  {
    Name = name;
    Salary = salary;
  }

  public string Name { get; }
  public decimal Salary { get; }

  public override string ToString() => $"{Name}, {Salary:C}";
  public static bool CompareSalary(Employee e1, Employee e2) =>
    e1.Salary < e2.Salary;
}
```

Note that to match the signature of the `Func<T, T, bool>` delegate, you must define `CompareSalary` in this class as taking two `Employee` references and returning a Boolean. In the implementation, the comparison based on salary is performed.

Now you are ready to write some client code to request a sort (code file `BubbleSorter/Program.cs`):

```
using System;

namespace Wrox.ProCSharp.Delegates
{
  class Program
  {
    static void Main()
    {
      Employee[] employees =
      {
        new Employee("Bugs Bunny", 20000),
        new Employee("Elmer Fudd", 10000),
        new Employee("Daffy Duck", 25000),
        new Employee("Wile Coyote", 1000000.38m),
        new Employee("Foghorn Leghorn", 23000),
        new Employee("RoadRunner", 50000)
      };

      BubbleSorter.Sort(employees, Employee.CompareSalary);
      foreach (var employee in employees)
      {
        Console.WriteLine(employee);
      }
    }
  }
}
```

Running this code shows that the `Employees` are correctly sorted according to salary:

```
Elmer Fudd, $10,000.00
Bugs Bunny, $20,000.00
Foghorn Leghorn, $23,000.00
Daffy Duck, $25,000.00
RoadRunner, $50,000.00
Wile Coyote, $1,000,000.38
```

Multicast Delegates

So far, each of the delegates you have used wraps just one method call. Calling the delegate amounts to calling that method. If you want to call more than one method, you need to make an explicit call through a delegate more than once. However, it is possible for a delegate to wrap more than one method. Such a delegate is known as a *multicast delegate*. When a multicast delegate is called, it successively calls each method in order. For this to work, the delegate signature should return a void; otherwise, you would only get the result of the last method invoked by the delegate.

With a void return type, you can use the `Action<double>` delegate (code file `MulticastDelegates/Program.cs`):

```
class Program
{
  static void Main()
  {
    Action<double> operations = MathOperations.MultiplyByTwo;
    operations += MathOperations.Square;
```

In the earlier example, you wanted to store references to two methods, so you instantiated an array of delegates. Here, you simply add both operations into the same multicast delegate. Multicast delegates recognize the operators + and +=. Alternatively, you can expand the last two lines of the preceding code, as in this snippet:

```
Action<double> operation1 = MathOperations.MultiplyByTwo;
Action<double> operation2 = MathOperations.Square;
Action<double> operations = operation1 + operation2;
```

Multicast delegates also recognize the operators – and -= to remove method calls from the delegate.

> **NOTE** *In terms of what's going on under the hood, a multicast delegate is a class derived from* System.MulticastDelegate, *which in turn is derived from* System .Delegate. System.MulticastDelegate *has additional members to allow the chaining of method calls into a list.*

To illustrate the use of multicast delegates, the following code recasts the `SimpleDelegate` example into a new example: `MulticastDelegate`. Because you now need the delegate to refer to methods that return void, you rewrite the methods in the `MathOperations` class so they display their results instead of returning them (code file `MulticastDelegates/MathOperations.cs`):

```
class MathOperations
{
  public static void MultiplyByTwo(double value)
  {
    double result = value * 2;
    Console.WriteLine($"Multiplying by 2: {value} gives {result}");
  }

  public static void Square(double value)
  {
    double result = value * value;
    Console.WriteLine($"Squaring: {value} gives {result}");
  }
}
```

To accommodate this change, you also have to rewrite `ProcessAndDisplayNumber` (code file `MulticastDelegates/Program.cs`):

```
static void ProcessAndDisplayNumber(Action<double> action, double value)
{
  Console.WriteLine();
  Console.WriteLine($"ProcessAndDisplayNumber called with value = {value}");
  action(value);
}
```

Now you can try out your multicast delegate:

```
static void Main()
{
  Action<double> operations = MathOperations.MultiplyByTwo;
  operations += MathOperations.Square;
  ProcessAndDisplayNumber(operations, 2.0);
  ProcessAndDisplayNumber(operations, 7.94);
  ProcessAndDisplayNumber(operations, 1.414);
  Console.WriteLine();
}
```

Each time `ProcessAndDisplayNumber` is called, it displays a message saying that it has been called. Then the following statement causes each of the method calls in the `action` delegate instance to be called in succession:

```
action(value);
```

Running the preceding code produces this result:

```
ProcessAndDisplayNumber called with value = 2
Multiplying by 2: 2 gives 4
Squaring: 2 gives 4

ProcessAndDisplayNumber called with value = 7.94
Multiplying by 2: 7.94 gives 15.88
Squaring: 7.94 gives 63.0436

ProcessAndDisplayNumber called with value = 1.414
Multiplying by 2: 1.414 gives 2.828
Squaring: 1.414 gives 1.999396
```

If you are using multicast delegates, be aware that the order in which methods chained to the same delegate will be called is formally undefined. Therefore, avoid writing code that relies on such methods being called in any particular order.

Invoking multiple methods by one delegate might cause an even bigger problem. The multicast delegate contains a collection of delegates to invoke one after the other. If one of the methods invoked by a delegate throws an exception, the complete iteration stops. Consider the following `MulticastIteration` example. Here, the simple delegate `Action` that returns `void` without arguments is used. This delegate is meant to invoke the methods `One` and `Two`, which fulfill the parameter and return type requirements of the delegate. Be aware that method `One` throws an exception (code file `MulticastDelegatesUsingInvocationList/Program.cs`):

```
using System;

namespace Wrox.ProCSharp.Delegates
{
  class Program
  {
    static void One()
    {
```

```
        Console.WriteLine("One");
        throw new Exception("Error in one");
    }

    static void Two()
    {
        Console.WriteLine("Two");
    }
```

In the `Main` method, delegate `d1` is created to reference method `One`; next, the address of method `Two` is added to the same delegate. `d1` is invoked to call both methods. The exception is caught in a `try/catch` block:

```
static void Main()
{
    Action d1 = One;
    d1 += Two;
    try
    {
        d1();
    }
    catch (Exception)
    {
        Console.WriteLine("Exception caught");
    }
}
```

Only the first method is invoked by the delegate. Because the first method throws an exception, iterating the delegates stops here and method `Two` is never invoked. The result might differ because the order of calling the methods is not defined:

```
One
Exception Caught
```

> **NOTE** *Errors and exceptions are explained in detail in Chapter 14, "Errors and Exceptions."*

In such a scenario, you can avoid the problem by iterating the list on your own. The `Delegate` class defines the method `GetInvocationList` that returns an array of `Delegate` objects. You can now use this delegate to invoke the methods associated with them directly, catch exceptions, and continue with the next iteration (code file `MulticastDelegatesUsingInvocationList/Program.cs`):

```
static void Main()
{
    Action d1 = One;
    d1 += Two;
    Delegate[] delegates = d1.GetInvocationList();
    foreach (Action d in delegates)
    {
        try
        {
            d();
        }
        catch (Exception)
        {
            Console.WriteLine("Exception caught");
        }
    }
}
```

When you run the application with the code changes, you can see that the iteration continues with the next method after the exception is caught:

```
One
Exception caught
Two
```

Anonymous Methods

Up to this point, a method must already exist for the delegate to work (that is, the delegate is defined with the same signature as the method(s) it will be used with). However, there is another way to use delegates—with *anonymous methods*. An anonymous method is a block of code that is used as the parameter for the delegate.

The syntax for defining a delegate with an anonymous method doesn't change. It's when the delegate is instantiated that things change. The following simple console application shows how using an anonymous method can work (code file `AnonymousMethods/Program.cs`):

```
class Program
{
  static void Main()
  {
    string mid = ", middle part,";
    Func<string, string> anonDel = delegate(string param)
    {
      param += mid;
      param += " and this was added to the string.";
      return param;
    };
    Console.WriteLine(anonDel("Start of string"));
  }
}
```

The delegate `Func<string, string>` takes a single string parameter and returns a string. `anonDel` is a variable of this delegate type. Instead of assigning the name of a method to this variable, a simple block of code is used, prefixed by the delegate keyword, followed by a string parameter.

As you can see, the block of code uses a method-level string variable, `mid`, which is defined outside of the anonymous method and adds it to the parameter that was passed in. The code then returns the string value. When the delegate is called, a string is passed in as the parameter and the returned string is output to the console.

The benefit of using anonymous methods is that it reduces the amount of code you have to write. You don't need to define a method just to use it with a delegate. This becomes evident when you define the delegate for an event (events are discussed later in this chapter), and it helps reduce the complexity of code, especially where several events are defined. With anonymous methods, the code does not perform faster. The compiler still defines a method; the method just has an automatically assigned name that you don't need to know.

You must follow a couple of rules when using anonymous methods. You can't have a jump statement (`break`, `goto`, or `continue`) in an anonymous method that has a target outside of the anonymous method. The reverse is also true: A jump statement outside the anonymous method cannot have a target inside the anonymous method.

Unsafe code cannot be accessed inside an anonymous method, and the `ref` and `out` parameters that are used outside of the anonymous method cannot be accessed. Other variables defined outside of the anonymous method can be used.

If you have to write the same functionality more than once, don't use anonymous methods. In this case, instead of duplicating the code, write a named method. You have to write it only once and reference it by its name.

> **NOTE** *The syntax for anonymous methods was introduced with C# 2. With new programs you really don't need this syntax anymore because lambda expressions (explained in the next section) offer the same—and more—functionality. However, you'll find the syntax for anonymous methods in many places in existing source code, which is why it's good to know it.*
>
> *Lambda expressions have been available since C# 3.*

LAMBDA EXPRESSIONS

One way where lambda expressions are used is to assign a lambda expression to a delegate type: implement code inline. Lambda expressions can be used whenever you have a delegate parameter type. The previous example using anonymous methods is modified here to use a lambda expression.

```
class Program
{
  static void Main()
  {
    string mid = ", middle part,";
    Func<string, string> lambda = param =>
    {
      param += mid;
      param += " and this was added to the string.";
      return param;
    };
    Console.WriteLine(lambda("Start of string"));
  }
}
```

The left side of the lambda operator, =>, lists the parameters needed. The right side following the lambda operator defines the implementation of the method assigned to the variable `lambda`.

Parameters

With lambda expressions there are several ways to define parameters. If there's only one parameter, just the name of the parameter is enough. The following lambda expression uses the parameter named s. Because the delegate type defines a `string` parameter, s is of type `string`. The implementation invokes the `String.Format` method to return a string that is finally written to the console when the delegate is invoked: `change uppercase TEST` (code file `LambdaExpressions/Program.cs`):

```
Func<string, string> oneParam = s => $"change uppercase {s.ToUpper()}";
Console.WriteLine(oneParam("test"));
```

If a delegate uses more than one parameter, you can combine the parameter names inside brackets. Here, the parameters x and y are of type `double` as defined by the `Func<double, double, double>` delegate:

```
Func<double, double, double> twoParams = (x, y) => x * y;
Console.WriteLine(twoParams(3, 2));
```

For convenience, you can add the parameter types to the variable names inside the brackets. If the compiler can't match an overloaded version, using parameter types can help resolve the matching delegate:

```
Func<double, double, double> twoParamsWithTypes =
  (double x, double y) => x * y;
Console.WriteLine(twoParamsWithTypes(4, 2));
```

Multiple Code Lines

If the lambda expression consists of a single statement, a method block with curly brackets and a `return` statement are not needed. There's an implicit `return` added by the compiler:

```
Func<double, double> square = x => x * x;
```

It's completely legal to add curly brackets, a `return` statement, and semicolons. Usually it's just easier to read without them:

```
Func<double, double> square = x =>
{
  return x * x;
}
```

However, if you need multiple statements in the implementation of the lambda expression, curly brackets and the `return` statement are required:

```
Func<string, string> lambda = param =>
{
  param += mid;
  param += " and this was added to the string.";
  return param;
};
```

Closures

With lambda expressions you can access variables outside the block of the lambda expression. This is known by the term *closure*. Closures are a great feature, but they can also be very dangerous if not used correctly.

In the following example, a lambda expression of type `Func<int, int>` requires one int parameter and returns an int. The parameter for the lambda expression is defined with the variable x. The implementation also accesses the variable `someVal`, which is outside the lambda expression. As long as you do not assume that the lambda expression creates a new method that is used later when f is invoked, this might not look confusing at all. Looking at this code block, the returned value calling f should be the value from x plus 5, but this might not be the case (code file `LambdaExpressions/Program.cs`):

```
int someVal = 5;
Func<int, int> f = x => x + someVal;
```

Assuming the variable `someVal` is later changed, and then the lambda expression is invoked, the new value of `someVal` is used. The result here of invoking `f(3)` is 10:

```
someVal = 7;
WriteLine(f(3));
```

Similarly, when you're changing the value of a closure variable within the lambda expression, you can access the changed value outside of the lambda expression.

Now, you might wonder how it is possible at all to access variables outside of the lambda expression from within the lambda expression. To understand this, consider what the compiler does when you define a lambda expression. With the lambda expression `x => x + someVal`, the compiler creates an anonymous class that has a constructor to pass the outer variable. The constructor depends on how many variables you access from the outside. With this simple example, the constructor accepts an int. The anonymous class contains an anonymous method that has the implementation as defined by the lambda expression, with the parameters and return type:

```
public class AnonymousClass
{
  private int someVal;
```

```
    public AnonymousClass(int someVal)
    {
      this.someVal = someVal;
    }
    public int AnonymousMethod(int x) => x + someVal;
  }
```

Using the lambda expression and invoking the method creates an instance of the anonymous class and passes the value of the variable from the time when the call is made.

> **NOTE** *In case you are using closures with multiple threads, you can get into concurrency conflicts. It's best to only use immutable types for closures. This way it's guaranteed the value can't change, and synchronization is not needed.*

> **NOTE** *You can use lambda expressions anywhere the type is a delegate. Another use of lambda expressions is when the type is* Expression *or* Expression<T>, *in which case the compiler creates an expression tree. This feature is discussed in Chapter 12, "Language Integrated Query."*

EVENTS

Events are based on delegates and offer a publish/subscribe mechanism to delegates. You can find events everywhere across the framework. In Windows applications, the Button class offers the Click event. This type of event is a delegate. A handler method that is invoked when the Click event is fired needs to be defined, with the parameters as defined by the delegate type.

In the code example shown in this section, events are used to connect the CarDealer and Consumer classes. The CarDealer class offers an event when a new car arrives. The Consumer class subscribes to the event to be informed when a new car arrives.

Event Publisher

You start with a CarDealer class that offers a subscription based on events. CarDealer defines the event named NewCarInfo of type EventHandler<CarInfoEventArgs> with the event keyword. Inside the method NewCar, the event NewCarInfo is fired by invoking the method RaiseNewCarInfo. The implementation of this method verifies whether the delegate is not null and raises the event (code file EventsSample/CarDealer.cs):

```
using System;
namespace Wrox.ProCSharp.Delegates
{
  public class CarInfoEventArgs: EventArgs
  {
    public CarInfoEventArgs(string car) => Car = car;

    public string Car { get; }
  }

  public class CarDealer
  {
    public event EventHandler<CarInfoEventArgs> NewCarInfo;
```

```
    public void NewCar(string car)
    {
      Console.WriteLine($"CarDealer, new car {car}");
      NewCarInfo?.Invoke(this, new CarInfoEventArgs(car));
    }
  }
}
```

> **NOTE** *The null propagation operator.? used in the previous example is new since C# 6. This operator is discussed in Chapter 6, "Operators and Casts."*

The class `CarDealer` offers the event `NewCarInfo` of type `EventHandler<CarInfoEventArgs>`. As a convention, events typically use methods with two parameters; the first parameter is an object and contains the sender of the event, and the second parameter provides information about the event. The second parameter is different for various event types. .NET 1.0 defined several hundred delegates for events for all different data types. That's no longer necessary with the generic delegate `EventHandler<T>`. `EventHandler<TEventArgs>` defines a handler that returns `void` and accepts two parameters. With `EventHandler<TEventArgs>`, the first parameter needs to be of type object, and the second parameter is of type `T`. `EventHandler<TEventArgs>` also defines a constraint on `T`; it must derive from the base class `EventArgs`, which is the case with `CarInfoEventArgs`:

```
public event EventHandler<CarInfoEventArgs> NewCarInfo;
```

The delegate `EventHandler<TEventArgs>` is defined as follows:

```
public delegate void EventHandler<TEventArgs>(object sender, TEventArgs e)
where TEventArgs: EventArgs
```

Defining the event in one line is a C# shorthand notation. The compiler creates a variable of the delegate type `EventHandler<CarInfoEventArgs>` and adds methods to subscribe and unsubscribe from the delegate. The long form of the shorthand notation is shown next. This is very similar to auto-properties and full properties. With events, the `add` and `remove` keywords are used to add and remove a handler to the delegate:

```
private EventHandler<CarInfoEventArgs> _newCarInfo;
public event EventHandler<CarInfoEventArgs> NewCarInfo
{
  add => _newCarInfo += value;
  remove => _newCarInfo -= value;
}
```

> **NOTE** *The long notation to define events is useful if more needs to be done than just adding and removing the event handler, such as adding synchronization for multiple thread access. The UWP and WPF controls make use of the long notation to add bubbling and tunneling functionality with the events.*

The class `CarDealer` fires the event by calling the `Invoke` method of the delegate. This invokes all the handlers that are subscribed to the event. Remember, as previously shown with multicast delegates, the order of the methods invoked is not guaranteed. To have more control over calling the handler methods you can use the `Delegate` class method `GetInvocationList` to access every item in the delegate list and invoke each on its own, as shown earlier.

```
NewCarInfo?.Invoke(this, new CarInfoEventArgs(car));
```

Firing the event is just a one-liner. However, this is only with C# 6. Before C# 6, firing the event was more complex. Here is the same functionality implemented before C# 6. Before firing the event, you need to check whether the event is null. Because between a null check and firing the event the event could be set to null by another thread, a local variable is used, as shown in the following example:

```
EventHandler<CarInfoEventArgs> newCarInfo = NewCarInfo;
if (newCarInfo != null)
{
  newCarInfo(this, new CarInfoEventArgs(car));
}
```

Since C# 6, all this could be replaced by using null propagation, with a single code line as you've seen earlier.

Before firing the event, it is necessary to check whether the delegate NewCarInfo is not null. If no one subscribed, the delegate is null:

```
protected virtual void RaiseNewCarInfo(string car)
{
  NewCarInfo?.Invoke(this, new CarInfoEventArgs(car));
}
```

Event Listener

The class Consumer is used as the event listener. This class subscribes to the event of the CarDealer and defines the method NewCarIsHere that in turn fulfills the requirements of the EventHandler<CarInfoEventArgs> delegate with parameters of type object and CarInfoEventArgs (code file EventsSample/Consumer.cs):

```
public class Consumer
{
  private string _name;
  public Consumer(string name) => _name = name;

  public void NewCarIsHere(object sender, CarInfoEventArgs e)
  {
    Console.WriteLine($"{_name}: car {e.Car} is new");
  }
}
```

Now the event publisher and subscriber need to connect. This is done by using the NewCarInfo event of the CarDealer to create a subscription with +=. The consumer Valtteri subscribes to the event, then the consumer Max, and next Valtteri unsubscribes with -= (code file EventsSample/Program.cs):

```
class Program
{
  static void Main()
  {
    var dealer = new CarDealer();
    var valtteri = new Consumer("Valtteri");
    dealer.NewCarInfo += valtteri.NewCarIsHere;
    dealer.NewCar("Williams");

    var max = new Consumer("Max");
    dealer.NewCarInfo += max.NewCarIsHere;
    dealer.NewCar("Mercedes");
    dealer.NewCarInfo -= valtteri.NewCarIsHere;
    dealer.NewCar("Ferrari");
  }
}
```

Running the application, a Williams arrived and Valtteri was informed. After that, Max registers for the subscription as well, both Valtteri and Max are informed about the new Mercedes. Then Valtteri unsubscribes and only Max is informed about the Ferrari:

```
CarDealer, new car Williams
Valtteri: car Williams is new
CarDealer, new car Mercedes
Valtteri: car Mercedes is new
Max: car Mercedes is new
CarDealer, new car Ferrari
Max: car Ferrari is new
```

SUMMARY

This chapter provided the basics of delegates, lambda expressions, and events. You learned how to declare a delegate and add methods to the delegate list; you learned how to implement methods called by delegates with lambda expressions; and you learned the process of declaring event handlers to respond to an event, as well as how to create a custom event and use the patterns for raising the event.

Using delegates and events in the design of a large application can reduce dependencies and the coupling of layers. This enables you to develop components that have a higher reusability factor.

Lambda expressions are C# language features based on delegates. With these, you can reduce the amount of code you need to write. Lambda expressions are not only used with delegates, but also with the Language Integrated Query (LINQ) as you see in Chapter 12.

The next chapter covers the use of strings and regular expressions.

Strings and Regular Expressions

WROX.COM CODE DOWNLOADS FOR THIS CHAPTER

The Wrox.com code downloads for this chapter are found at www.wrox.com on the Download Code tab. The source code is also available at https://github.com/ProfessionalCSharp/ProfessionalCSharp7 in the directory StringsAndRegularExpressions.

The code for this chapter is divided into the following major examples:

Strings have been used consistently since the beginning of this book, as every program needs strings. However, you might not have realized that the stated mapping that the string keyword in C# refers to is the System.String .NET base class. String is a very powerful and versatile class, but it is by no means the only string-related class in the .NET armory. This chapter begins by reviewing the features of String and then looks at some nifty things you can do with strings using some of the other .NET classes—in particular those in the System.Text and System.Text.RegularExpressions namespaces. This chapter covers the following areas:

➤ **Building strings**—If you're performing repeated modifications on a string—for example, to build a lengthy string prior to displaying it or passing it to some other method or application—the String class can be very inefficient. When you find yourself in this kind of situation, another class, System.Text.StringBuilder, is more suitable because it has been designed exactly for this scenario.

➤ **Formatting expressions**—This chapter takes a closer look at the formatting expressions that have been used in the `Console.WriteLine` method throughout the past few chapters. These formatting expressions are processed using two useful interfaces: `IFormatProvider` and `IFormattable`. By implementing these interfaces on your own classes, you can define your own formatting sequences so that `Console.WriteLine` and similar classes display the values of your classes in whatever way you specify.

➤ **Regular expressions**—.NET also offers some very sophisticated classes that deal with cases in which you need to identify or extract substrings that satisfy certain fairly sophisticated criteria; for example, finding all occurrences within a string where a character or set of characters is repeated: finding all words that begin with "s" and contain at least one "n": or strings that adhere to an employee ID or a Social Security number construction. Although you can write methods to perform this kind of processing using the `String` class, writing such methods is cumbersome. Instead, some classes, specifically those from `System.Text.RegularExpressions`, are designed to perform this kind of processing.

➤ **Spans**—.NET Core offers the generic `Span` struct, which allows fast access to memory. `Span<T>` allows accessing slices of strings without copying the string.

EXAMINING SYSTEM.STRING

Before digging into the other string classes, this section briefly reviews some of the available methods in the `String` class itself.

`System.String` is a class specifically designed to store a string and allow a large number of operations on the string. In addition, due to the importance of this data type, C# has its own keyword and associated syntax to make it particularly easy to manipulate strings using this class.

You can concatenate strings using operator overloads:

```
string message1 = "Hello"; // returns "Hello"
message1 += ", There"; // returns "Hello, There"
string message2 = message1 + "!"; // returns "Hello, There!"
```

C# also allows extraction of a particular character using an indexer-like syntax:

```
string message = "Hello";
char char4 = message[4]; // returns 'o'. Note the string is zero-indexed
```

This enables you to perform such common tasks as replacing characters, removing whitespace, and changing case. The following table introduces the key methods.

METHOD	DESCRIPTION
Compare	Compares the contents of strings, taking into account the culture (locale) in assessing equivalence between certain characters.
CompareOrdinal	Same as Compare but doesn't take culture into account.
Concat	Combines separate string instances into a single instance.
CopyTo	Copies a specific number of characters from the selected index to an entirely new instance of an array.
Format	Formats a string containing various values and specifies how each value should be formatted.
IndexOf	Locates the first occurrence of a given substring or character in the string.

METHOD	DESCRIPTION
IndexOfAny	Locates the first occurrence of any one of a set of characters in a string.
Insert	Inserts a string instance into another string instance at a specified index.
Join	Builds a new string by combining an array of strings.
LastIndexOf	Same as IndexOf but finds the last occurrence.
LastIndexOfAny	Same as IndexOfAny but finds the last occurrence.
PadLeft	Pads out the string by adding a specified repeated character to the left side of the string.
PadRight	Pads out the string by adding a specified repeated character to the right side of the string.
Replace	Replaces occurrences of a given character or substring in the string with another character or substring.
Split	Splits the string into an array of substrings; the breaks occur wherever a given character occurs.
Substring	Retrieves the substring starting at a specified position in a string.
ToLower	Converts the string to lowercase.
ToUpper	Converts the string to uppercase.
Trim	Removes leading and trailing whitespace.

> **NOTE** *Please note that this table is not comprehensive; it is intended to give you an idea of the features offered by strings.*

Building Strings

As you have seen, String is an extremely powerful class that implements a large number of very useful methods. However, the String class has a shortcoming that makes it very inefficient for making repeated modifications to a given string—it is an *immutable* data type, which means that after you initialize a string object, that string object can never change. The methods and operators that appear to modify the contents of a string actually create new strings, copying across the contents of the old string if necessary. For example, consider the following code (code file StringSample/Program.cs):

```
string greetingText = "Hello from all the people at Wrox Press. ";
greetingText += "We do hope you enjoy this book as much as we enjoyed writing it.";
```

When this code executes, first an object of type System.String is created and initialized to hold the text Hello from all the people at Wrox Press. (Note that there's a space after the period.) When this happens, the .NET runtime allocates just enough memory in the string to hold this text (41 chars), and the variable greetingText is set to refer to this string instance.

In the next line, syntactically it looks like more text is being added onto the string, but it is not. Instead, a new string instance is created with just enough memory allocated to store the combined text—that's 104 characters in total. The original text, Hello from all the people at Wrox Press. , is copied into this new string instance along with the extra text: We do hope you enjoy this book as much as we enjoyed writing it. Then, the address stored in the variable greetingText is updated, so the variable correctly points to the new `String` object. The old `String` object is now unreferenced—there are no variables that refer to it—so it will be removed the next time the garbage collector comes along to clean out any unused objects in your application.

By itself, that doesn't look too bad, but suppose you wanted to create a very simple encryption scheme by adding 1 to the ASCII value of each character in the string. This would change the string to `Ifmmp gspn bmm uif qfpqmf bu Xspy Qsftt. Xf ep ipqf zpv fokpz uijt cppl bt nvdi bt xf fokpzfe xsjujoh ju`. Several ways of doing this exist, but the simplest and (if you are restricting yourself to using the `String` class) almost certainly the most efficient way is to use the `String.Replace` method, which replaces all occurrences of a given substring in a string with another substring. Using `Replace`, the code to encode the text looks like this (code file `StringSample/Program.cs`):

```csharp
string greetingText = "Hello from all the people at Wrox Press. ";
greetingText += "We do hope you enjoy this book as much as we " +
"enjoyed writing it.";
Console.WriteLine($"Not encoded:\n {greetingText}");
for(int i = 'z'; i>= 'a'; i--)
{
  char old1 = (char)i;
  char new1 = (char)(i+1);
  greetingText = greetingText.Replace(old1, new1);
}

for(int i = 'Z'; i>='A'; i--)
{
  char old1 = (char)i;
  char new1 = (char)(i+1);
  greetingText = greetingText.Replace(old1, new1);
}
Console.WriteLine($"Encoded:\n {greetingText}");
```

> **NOTE** *Simply, this code does not change Z to A or z to a. These letters are encoded to [and {, respectively.*

In this example, the `Replace` method works in a fairly intelligent way, to the extent that it won't create a new string unless it actually makes changes to the old string. The original string contained 23 different lowercase characters and three different uppercase ones. The `Replace` method will therefore have allocated a new string 26 times in total, with each new string storing 103 characters. That means because of the encryption process, there will be string objects capable of storing a combined total of 2,678 characters now sitting on the heap waiting to be garbage collected! Clearly, if you use strings to do text processing extensively, your applications will run into severe performance problems.

To address this kind of issue, Microsoft supplies the `System.Text.StringBuilder` class. `StringBuilder` is not as powerful as `String` in terms of the number of methods it supports. The processing you can do on a `StringBuilder` is limited to substitutions and appending or removing text from strings. However, it works in a much more efficient way.

When you construct a string using the `String` class, just enough memory is allocated to hold the string object. The `StringBuilder`, however, normally allocates more memory than is needed. You, as a developer, have the option to indicate how much memory the `StringBuilder` should allocate; but if you do not, the amount defaults to a value that varies according to the size of the string with which the `StringBuilder` instance is initialized. The `StringBuilder` class has two main properties:

➤ `Length`—Indicates the length of the string that it contains

➤ `Capacity`—Indicates the maximum length of the string in the memory allocation

Any modifications to the string take place within the block of memory assigned to the StringBuilder instance, which makes appending substrings and replacing individual characters within strings very efficient. Removing or inserting substrings is inevitably still inefficient because it means that the following part of the string must be moved. Only if you perform an operation that exceeds the capacity of the string is it necessary to allocate new memory and possibly move the entire contained string. In adding extra capacity, based on our experiments the StringBuilder appears to double its capacity if it detects that the capacity has been exceeded and no new value for capacity has been set.

For example, if you use a StringBuilder object to construct the original greeting string, you might write this code:

```
var greetingBuilder =
  new StringBuilder("Hello from all the people at Wrox Press. ", 150);
greetingBuilder.Append("We do hope you enjoy this book as much " +
  "as we enjoyed writing it");
```

> **NOTE** *To use the* StringBuilder *class, you need a* System.Text *reference in your code.*

This code sets an initial capacity of 150 for the StringBuilder. It is always a good idea to set a capacity that covers the likely maximum length of a string, to ensure that the StringBuilder does not need to relocate because its capacity was exceeded. By default, the capacity is set to 16. Theoretically, you can set a number as large as the number you pass in an int, although the system will probably complain that it does not have enough memory if you try to allocate the maximum of two billion characters (the theoretical maximum that a StringBuilder instance is allowed to contain).

Then, on calling the AppendFormat method, the remaining text is placed in the empty space, without the need to allocate more memory. However, the real efficiency gain from using a StringBuilder is realized when you make repeated text substitutions. For example, if you try to encrypt the text in the same way as before, you can perform the entire encryption without allocating any more memory whatsoever:

```
var greetingBuilder =
  new StringBuilder("Hello from all the people at Wrox Press. ", 150);
greetingBuilder.AppendFormat("We do hope you enjoy this book as much " +
  "as we enjoyed writing it");
Console.WriteLine("Not Encoded:\n" + greetingBuilder);
for(int i = 'z'; i>='a'; i--)
{
  char old1 = (char)i;
  char new1 = (char)(i+1);
  greetingBuilder = greetingBuilder.Replace(old1, new1);
}

for(int i = 'Z'; i>='A'; i--)
{
  char old1 = (char)i;
  char new1 = (char)(i+1);
  greetingBuilder = greetingBuilder.Replace(old1, new1);
}
Console.WriteLine($"Encoded:\n {greetingBuilder}");
```

This code uses the StringBuilder.Replace method, which does the same thing as String.Replace but without copying the string in the process. The total memory allocated to hold strings in the preceding code is 150 characters for the StringBuilder instance, as well as the memory allocated during the string operations performed internally in the final WriteLine statement.

Normally, you want to use StringBuilder to perform any manipulation of strings, and String to store or display the final result.

StringBuilder Members

You have seen a demonstration of one constructor of `StringBuilder`, which takes an initial string and capacity as its parameters. There are others. For example, you can supply only a string:

```
var sb = new StringBuilder("Hello");
```

Or you can create an empty `StringBuilder` with a given capacity:

```
var sb = new StringBuilder(20);
```

Apart from the `Length` and `Capacity` properties, there is a read-only `MaxCapacity` property that indicates the limit to which a given `StringBuilder` instance is allowed to grow. By default, this is specified by `int`. `MaxValue` (roughly two billion, as noted earlier), but you can set this value to something lower when you construct the `StringBuilder` object:

```
// This will set the initial capacity to 100, but the max will be 500.
// Hence, this StringBuilder can never grow to more than 500 characters,
// otherwise it will raise an exception if you try to do that.
var sb = new StringBuilder(100, 500);
```

You can also explicitly set the capacity at any time, though an exception is raised if you set the capacity to a value less than the current length of the string or a value that exceeds the maximum capacity:

```
var sb = new StringBuilder("Hello");
sb.Capacity = 100;
```

The following table lists the main `StringBuilder` methods.

METHOD	DESCRIPTION	
Append	Appends a string to the current string.	
AppendFormat	Appends a string that has been formatted from a format specifier.	
Insert	Inserts a substring into the current string.	
Remove	Removes characters from the current string.	
Replace	Replaces all occurrences of a character with another character or a substring with another substring in the current string.	
ToString	Returns the current string cast to a `System.String` object (overridden from `System.Object`).	

Several overloads of many of these methods exist.

> **NOTE** `AppendFormat` *is the method that is ultimately called when you call* `Console.` `WriteLine`, *which is responsible for determining what all the format expressions like* `{0:D}` *should be replaced with. This method is examined in the next section.*

There is no cast (either implicit or explicit) from `StringBuilder` to `String`. If you want to output the contents of a `StringBuilder` as a `String`, you must use the `ToString` method.

Now that you have been introduced to the `StringBuilder` class and have learned some of the ways in which you can use it to increase performance, be aware that this class does not always deliver the increased performance you are seeking. Basically, you should use the `StringBuilder` class when you are manipulating multiple strings. However, if you are just doing something as simple as concatenating two strings, you will find that System.String performs better.

STRING FORMATS

In previous chapters you've seen passing variables to strings with the $ prefix. This chapter examines what's behind this C# feature and covers all the other functionality offered by format strings.

String Interpolation

C# 6 introduced string interpolation by using the $ prefix for strings. The following example creates the string s2 using the $ prefix. This prefix allows having placeholders in curly brackets to reference results from code. {s1} is a placeholder in the string, where the compiler puts into the value of variable s1 into the string s2 (code file StringFormats/Program.cs):

```
string s1 = "World";
string s2 = $"Hello, {s1}";
```

In reality, this is just syntax sugar. From strings with the $ prefix, the compiler creates invocations to the String.Format method. So, the previous code snippet gets translated to this:

```
string s1 = "World";
string s2 = String.Format("Hello, {0}", s1);
```

The first parameter of the String.Format method that is used accepts a format string with placeholders that are numbered starting from 0, followed by the parameters that are put into the string holes.

The new string format is just a lot handier and doesn't require that much code to write.

It's not just variables you can use to fill in the holes of the string. Any method that returns a value can be used:

```
string s2 = $"Hello, {s1.ToUpper()}";
```

This translates to a similar statement:

```
string s2 = String.Format("Hello, {0}", s1.ToUpper());
```

It's also possible to have multiple holes in the string, like so:

```
int x = 3, y = 4;
string s3 = $"The result of {x} + {y} is {x + y}";
```

which translates to

```
string s3 = String.Format("The result of {0} and {1} is {2}", x, y, x + y);
```

FormattableString

What the interpolated string gets translated to can easily be seen by assigning the string to a FormattableString. The interpolated string can be directly assigned because the FormattableString is a better match than the normal string. This type defines a Format property that returns the resulting format string, an ArgumentCount property, and the method GetArgument to return the values:

```
int x = 3, y = 4;
FormattableString s = $"The result of {x} + {y} is {x + y}";
Console.WriteLine($"format: {s.Format}");
for (int i = 0; i < s.ArgumentCount; i++)
{
   Console.WriteLine($"argument {i}: {s.GetArgument(i)}");
}
```

Running this code snippet results in this output:

```
format: The result of {0} + {1} is {2}
argument 0: 3
argument 1: 4
argument 2: 7
```

> **NOTE** *The class* FormattableString *is defined in the* System *namespace but requires .NET 4.6. In case you would like to use the* FormattableString *with older .NET versions, you can create this type on your own, or use the StringInterpolationBridge NuGet package.*

Using Other Cultures with String Interpolation

Interpolated strings by default make use of the current culture. This can be changed easily. The helper method Invariant changes the interpolated string to use the invariant culture instead of the current one. As interpolated strings can be assigned to a FormattableString type, they can be passed to this method. FormattableString defines a ToString method that allows passing an IFormatProvider. The interface IFormatProvider is implemented by the CultureInfoclass. Passing CultureInfo.InvariantCulture to the IFormatProvider parameter changes the string to use the invariant culture:

```
private string Invariant(FormattableString s) =>
  s.ToString(CultureInfo.InvariantCulture);
```

> **NOTE** *Chapter 27, "Localization," discusses language-specific issues for format strings as well as cultures and invariant cultures.*

In the following code snippet, the Invariant method is used to pass a string to the second WriteLine method. The first invocation of WriteLine uses the current culture while the second one uses the invariant culture:

```
var day = new DateTime(2025, 2, 14);
Console.WriteLine($"{day:d}");
Console.WriteLine(Invariant($"{day:d}"));
```

If you have the English-US culture setting, the result is shown here. If you have a different culture configured with your system, the first result differs. In any case, you see a difference with the invariant culture:

```
2/14/2025
02/14/2015
```

For using the invariant culture, you don't need to implement your own method; instead you can use the static Invariant method of the FormattableString class directly:

```
Console.WriteLine(FormattableString.Invariant($"{day:d}"));
```

Escaping Curly Brackets

In case you want the curly brackets in an interpolated string, you can escape those using double curly brackets:

```
string s = "Hello";
Console.WriteLine($"{{s}} displays the value of s: {s}");
```

The WriteLine method is translated to this implementation:

```
Console.WriteLine(String.Format("{s} displays the value of {0}", s));
```

Thus, the output is this:

```
{s} displays the value of s : Hello
```

You can also escape curly brackets to build a new format string from a format string. Let's have a look at this code snippet:

```
string formatString = $"{s}, {{0}}";
string s2 = "World";
Console.WriteLine(formatString, s2);
```

With the string variable `formatString`, the compiler creates a call to `String.Format` just by putting a placeholder 0 to insert the variable `s`:

```
string formatString = String.Format("{0}, {{0}}", s);
```

This in turn results in this format string where the variable `s` is replaced with the value `Hello`, and the outermost curly brackets of the second format are removed:

```
string formatString = "Hello, {0}";
```

With the `WriteLine` method in the last line, now the string `World` gets inserted into the new placeholder 0 using the value of the variable `s2`:

```
Console.WriteLine("Hello, World");
```

DateTime and Number Formats

Other than just using string formats for placeholders, specific formats depending on a data type are available. Let's start with a date. A format string follows the expressions within the placeholder separated by a colon. Examples shown here are the D and d format for the `DateTime` type:

```
var day = new DateTime(2025, 2, 14);
Console.WriteLine($"{day:D}");
Console.WriteLine($"{day:d}");
```

The result shows a long date format string with the uppercase D and a short date string with the lowercase d:

```
Friday, February 14, 2025
2/14/2025
```

The `DateTime` type results in different outputs depending on uppercase or lowercase strings used. Depending on the language setting of your system, the output might look different. The date and time is language specific.

The `DateTime` type supports a lot of different standard format strings to have all date and time representations—for example, t for a short time format and T for a long time format, g and G to display date and time. All the other options are not discussed here, as you can find them in the MSDN documentation for the `ToString` method of the `DateTime` type.

> **NOTE** *One thing that should be mentioned is building a custom format string for* `DateTime`. *A custom date and time format string can combine format specifiers, such as dd-MMM-yyyy:*
>
> ```
> Console.WriteLine($"{day:dd-MMM-yyyy}");
> ```
>
> The result is shown here:
>
> ```
> 14-Feb-2025
> ```
>
> *This custom format string makes use of dd to display two digits for the day (this is important if the day is before the 10th; here you can see a difference between d and dd), MMM for an abbreviated name of the month (pay attention to uppercase; mm specifies minutes) and yyyy for the year with a four-digit number. Again, you can find all the other format specifiers for custom date and time format strings in the MSDN documentation.*

Format strings for numbers don't differentiate between uppercase and lowercase. Let's have a look at the n, e, x, and c standard numeric format strings:

```
int i = 2477;
Console.WriteLine($"{i:n} {i:e} {i:x} {i:c}");
```

The n format string defines a number format to show integral and decimal digits with group separators, e using exponential notation, x for a conversion to hexadecimal, and c to display a currency:

```
2,477.00 2.477000e+003 9ad $2,477.00
```

For numeric representations you can also use custom format strings. The # format specifier is a digit place-holder and displays a digit if available; otherwise no digit appears. The 0 format specifier is a zero place-holder and displays the corresponding digit or zero if a digit is not present.

```
double d = 3.1415;
Console.WriteLine($"{d:###.###}");
Console.WriteLine($"{d:000.000}");
```

With the double value from the sample code, the first result rounds the value after the comma to three digits; with the second result three digits before the comma are shown as well:

```
3.142
003.142
```

The Microsoft documentation gives information on all the standard numeric format strings for percent, round-trip and fixed-point displays, and custom format strings for different looks for exponential value displays, decimal points, group separators, and more.

Custom String Formats

Format strings are not restricted to built-in types; you can create your own format strings for your own types. You just need to implement the interface IFormattable.

Start with a simple Person class that contains FirstName and LastName properties (code file StringFormats/Person.cs):

```
public class Person
{
  public string FirstName { get; set; }
  public string LastName { get; set; }
}
```

For a simple string presentation of this class, the ToString method of the base class is overridden. This method returns a string consisting of FirstName and LastName:

```
public override string ToString() => FirstName + " " + LastName;
```

Other than a simple string representation, the Person class should also support the format strings F to just return the first name, L for the last name, and A, which stands for "all" and should give the same string representation as the ToString method. To implement custom strings, the interface IFormattable defines the method ToString with two parameters: a string parameter for the format and an IFormatProvider parameter. The IFormatProvider parameter is not used in the sample code. You can use this parameter for different representations based on the culture, as the CultureInfo class implements this interface.

Other classes that implement this interface are NumberFormatInfo and DateTimeFormatInfo. You can use these classes to configure string representations for numbers and DateTime passing instances to the second parameter of the ToString method. The implementation of the ToString method just uses the switch statement to return different strings based on the format string. To allow calling the ToString method directly just with the format string without a format provider, the ToString method is overloaded. This method in turn invokes the ToString method with two parameters:

```
public class Person : IFormattable
{
```

```
   public string FirstName { get; set; }
   public string LastName { get; set; }
   public override string ToString() => FirstName + " " + LastName;
   public virtual string ToString(string format) => ToString(format, null);

   public string ToString(string format, IFormatProvider formatProvider)
   {
     switch (format)
     {
       case null:
       case "A":
         return ToString();
       case "F":
         return FirstName;
       case "L":
         return LastName;
       default:
         throw new FormatException($"invalid format string {format}");
     }
   }
 }
```

With this in place, you can invoke the `ToString` method explicitly by passing a format string or implicitly by using string interpolation. The implicit call makes use of the two-parameter `ToString` passing `null` with the `IFormatProvider` parameter (code file `StringFormats/Program.cs`):

```
var p1 = new Person { FirstName = "Stephanie", LastName = "Nagel" };
Console.WriteLine(p1.ToString("F"));
Console.WriteLine($"{p1:F}");
```

REGULAR EXPRESSIONS

Regular expressions are one of those small technology aids that are incredibly useful in a wide range of programs. You can think of regular expressions as a mini-programming language with one specific purpose: to locate substrings within a large string expression. It is not a new technology; it originated in the UNIX environment and is commonly used with the Perl programming language, as well as with JavaScript. Regular expressions are supported by a number of .NET classes in the namespace `System. Text.RegularExpressions`. You can also find the use of regular expressions in various parts of the .NET Framework. For instance, they are used within the ASP.NET validation server controls.

If you are not familiar with the regular expressions language, this section introduces both regular expressions and their related .NET classes. If you are familiar with regular expressions, you may want to just skim through this section to pick out the references to the .NET base classes. You might like to know that the .NET regular expression engine is designed to be mostly compatible with Perl 5 regular expressions, although it has a few extra features.

Introduction to Regular Expressions

The regular expressions language is designed specifically for string processing. It contains two features:

➤ A set of escape codes for identifying specific types of characters. You are probably familiar with the use of the * character to represent any substring in command-line expressions. (For example, the command `Dir Re*` lists the files with names beginning with `Re`.) Regular expressions use many sequences like this to represent items such as *any one character, a word break, one optional character,* and so on.

➤ A system for grouping parts of substrings and intermediate results during a search operation.

With regular expressions, you can perform very sophisticated and high-level operations on strings. For example, you can do all the following:

➤ Identify (and perhaps either flag or remove) all repeated words in a string (for example, "The computer books books" to "The computer books").

➤ Convert all words to title case (for example, "this is a Title" to "This Is A Title").

➤ Convert all words longer than three characters to title case (for example, "this is a Title" to "This is a Title").

➤ Ensure that sentences are properly capitalized.

➤ Separate the various elements of a URI (for example, given `http://www.wrox.com`, extract the protocol, computer name, filename, and so on).

Of course, all these tasks can be performed in C# using the various methods on `System.String` and `System.Text.StringBuilder`. However, in some cases, this would require writing a fair amount of C# code. Using regular expressions, this code can normally be compressed to just a couple of lines. Essentially, you instantiate a `System.Text.RegularExpressions.RegEx` object (or, even simpler, invoke a static `RegEx` method), pass it the string to be processed, and pass in a regular expression (a string containing the instructions in the regular expressions language), and you're done.

A regular expression string looks at first sight rather like a regular string, but interspersed with escape sequences and other characters that have a special meaning. For example, the sequence `\b` indicates the beginning or end of a word (a word boundary), so if you wanted to indicate you were looking for the characters `th` at the beginning of a word, you would search for the regular expression, `\bth` (that is, the sequence word boundary-t-h). If you wanted to search for all occurrences of `th` at the end of a word, you would write `th\b` (the sequence t-h-word boundary). However, regular expressions are much more sophisticated than that and include, for example, facilities to store portions of text that are found in a search operation. This section only scratches the surface of the power of regular expressions.

> **NOTE** *For more on regular expressions, please see Andrew Watt's* Beginning Regular Expressions *(John Wiley & Sons, 2005).*

Suppose your application needed to convert U.S. phone numbers to an international format. In the United States, the phone numbers have the format 314-123-1234, which is often written as (314) 123-1234. When converting this national format to an international format, you have to include +1 (the country code of the United States) and add parentheses around the area code: +1 (314) 123-1234. As find-and-replace operations go, that is not too complicated. It would still require some coding effort if you were going to use the `String` class for this purpose (meaning you would have to write your code using the methods available from `System.String`). The regular expressions language enables you to construct a short string that achieves the same result.

This section is intended only as a very simple example, so it concentrates on searching strings to identify certain substrings, not on modifying them.

The RegularExpressionsPlayground Example

The regular expression samples in this chapter make use of the following namespaces:

```
System

System.Text.RegularExpressions
```

The rest of this section develops a short example called RegularExpressionsPlayground that illustrates some of the features of regular expressions, and how to use the .NET regular expressions engine in C# by performing and displaying the results of some searches. The text you are going to use as your sample document is part of the introduction to the previous edition of this book (code file RegularExpressionsPlayground/Program.cs):

```
const string text =
  @"Professional C# 6 and .NET Core 1.0 provides complete coverage " +
  "of the latest updates, features, and capabilities, giving you " +
  "everything you need for C#. Get expert instruction on the latest " +
  "changes to Visual Studio 2015, Windows Runtime, ADO.NET, ASP.NET, " +
  "Windows Store Apps, Windows Workflow Foundation, and more, with " +
  "clear explanations, no-nonsense pacing, and valuable expert insight. " +
  "This incredibly useful guide serves as both tutorial and desk " +
  "reference, providing a professional-level review of C# architecture " +
  "and its application in a number of areas. You'll gain a solid " +
  "background in managed code and .NET constructs within the context of " +
  "the 2015 release, so you can get acclimated quickly and get back to work.";
```

> **NOTE** *This code nicely illustrates the utility of verbatim strings that are prefixed by the @ symbol. This prefix is extremely helpful with regular expressions.*

This text is referred to as the *input string*. To get your bearings and get used to the regular expressions of .NET classes, you start with a basic plain-text search that does not feature any escape sequences or regular expression commands. Suppose that you want to find all occurrences of the string ion. This search string is referred to as the *pattern*. Using regular expressions and the input variable declared previously, you could write the following (code file RegularExpressionPlayground/Program.cs):

```
public static void Find1(text)
{
  const string pattern = "ion";
  MatchCollection matches = Regex.Matches(text, pattern,
    RegexOptions.IgnoreCase | RegexOptions.ExplicitCapture);
  WriteMatches(text, matches);
}
```

This code uses the static method Matches of the Regex class in the System.Text.RegularExpressions namespace. This method takes as parameters some input text, a pattern, and a set of optional flags taken from the RegexOptions enumeration. In this case, you have specified that all searching should be case-insensitive. The other flag, ExplicitCapture, modifies how the match is collected in a way that, for your purposes, makes the search a bit more efficient—you see why this is later in this chapter (although it does have other uses that we don't explore here). Matches returns a reference to a MatchCollection object. A *match* is the technical term for the results of finding an instance of the pattern in the expression. It is represented by the class System.Text.RegularExpressions.Match. Therefore, you return a MatchCollection that contains all the matches, each represented by a Match object. In the preceding code, you simply iterate over the collection and use the Index property of the Match class, which returns the index in the input text where the match was found.

The result of the Find1 method lists six matches with this output:

```
No. of matches: 6
Index: 7,       String: ion,    ofessional C#
Index: 172,     String: ion,    truction on t
Index: 300,     String: ion,    undation, and
Index: 334,     String: ion,    lanations, no
Index: 481,     String: ion,    ofessional-le
Index: 535,     String: ion,    lication in a
```

The following table details some of the `RegexOptions` enumerations.

MEMBER NAME	DESCRIPTION
CultureInvariant	Specifies that the culture of the string is ignored.
ExplicitCapture	Modifies the way the match is collected by making sure that valid captures are the ones that are explicitly named.
IgnoreCase	Ignores the case of the string that is input.
IgnorePatternWhitespace	Removes unescaped whitespace from the string and enables comments that are specified with the pound or hash sign.
Multiline	Changes the characters ^ and $ so that they are applied to the beginning and end of each line and not just to the beginning and end of the entire string.
RightToLeft	Causes the inputted string to be read from right to left instead of the default left to right (ideal for some Asian and other languages that are read in this direction).
Singleline	Specifies a single-line mode where the meaning of the dot (.) is changed to match every character.

So far, nothing is new from the preceding example apart from some .NET base classes. However, the power of regular expressions comes from that pattern string. The reason is that the pattern string is not limited to only plain text. As hinted earlier, it can also contain what are known as *meta-characters*, which are special characters that provide commands, as well as escape sequences, which work in much the same way as C# escape sequences. They are characters preceded by a backslash (\) and have special meanings.

For example, suppose you wanted to find words beginning with n. You could use the escape sequence \b, which indicates a word boundary (a word boundary is just a point where an alphanumeric character precedes or follows a whitespace character or punctuation symbol):

```
const string pattern = @"\bn";
MatchCollection myMatches = Regex.Matches(input, pattern,
RegexOptions.IgnoreCase |
RegexOptions.ExplicitCapture);
```

Notice the @ character in front of the string. You want the \b to be passed to the .NET regular expressions engine at runtime—you don't want the backslash intercepted by a well-meaning C# compiler that thinks it's an escape sequence in your source code.

If you want to find words ending with the sequence ure, you write this:

```
const string pattern = @"ure\b";
```

If you want to find all words beginning with the letter a and ending with the sequence ure (which has as its only match the words *architecture* in the example), you have to put a bit more thought into your code. You clearly need a pattern that begins with \ba and ends with ure\b, but what goes in the middle? You need to somehow tell the applications that between the a and the ure there can be any number of characters as long as none of them are whitespace. In fact, the correct pattern looks like this:

```
const string pattern = @"\ba\S*ure\b";
```

Eventually you will get used to seeing weird sequences of characters like this when working with regular expressions. It works quite logically. The escape sequence \S indicates any character that is not a whitespace character. The * is called a *quantifier*. It means that the preceding character can be repeated any number of times, including zero times. The sequence \S* means *any number of characters as long as they are not whitespace characters*. The preceding pattern, therefore, matches any single word that begins with a and ends with ure.

The following table lists some of the main special characters or escape sequences that you can use. It is not comprehensive; a fuller list is available in the Microsoft documentation.

SYMBOL	DESCRIPTION	EXAMPLE	MATCHES
^	Beginning of input text	^B	B, but only if first character in text
$	End of input text	X$	X, but only if last character in text
.	Any single character except the newline character (\)	i.ation	isation, ization
*	Preceding character may be repeated zero or more times	ra*t	rt, rat, raat, raaat, and so on
+	Preceding character may be repeated one or more times	ra+t	rat, raat, raaat and so on, but not rt
?	Preceding character may be repeated zero or one time	ra?t	rt and rat only
\s	Any whitespace character	\sa	[space]a, \ta, \na (\t and \n have the same meanings as in C#)
\S	Any character that isn't whitespace	\SF	aF, rF, cF, but not \tf
\b	Word boundary	ion\b	Any word ending in ion
\B	Any position that isn't a word boundary	\BX\B	Any X in the middle of a word

If you want to search for one of the meta-characters, you can do so by escaping the corresponding character with a backslash. For example, . (a single period) means any single character other than the newline character, whereas \. means a dot.

You can request a match that contains alternative characters by enclosing them in square brackets. For example, [1c] means one character that can be either 1 or c. If you wanted to search for any occurrence of the words map or man, you would use the sequence ma[np]. Within the square brackets, you can also indicate a range, for example [a-z], to indicate any single lowercase letter, [A-E] to indicate any uppercase letter between A and E (including the letters A and E themselves), or [0-9] to represent a single digit. A shorthand notation for [0-9] is \d. If you wanted to search for an integer (that is, a sequence that contains only the characters 0 through 9), you could write [0-9]+ or [\d]+.

The ^ has a different meaning used within square brackets. Used outside square brackets, it marks the beginning of input text. Within square brackets, it means any character except the following.

> **NOTE** *The use of the + character specifies there must be at least one such digit, but there may be more than one—so this would match 9, 83, 854, and so on.*

Displaying Results

In this section, you code the `RegularExpressionsPlayground` example to get a feel for how regular expressions work.

The core of the example is a method called `WriteMatches`, which writes out all the matches from a `MatchCollection` in a more detailed format. For each match, it displays the index of where the match was found in the input string, the string of the match, and a slightly longer string, which consists of the match plus up to 10 surrounding characters from the input text—up to five characters before the match and up to five afterward. (It is fewer than five characters if the match occurred within five characters of the beginning or end of the input text.) In other words, a match on the word `applications` that occurs near the end of the input text quoted earlier when starting with the `RegularExpressionPlayground` example would display `web applications imme` (five characters before and after the match), but a match on the final word `imme-diately` would display `ions immediately.` (only one character after the match), because after that you get to the end of the string. This longer string enables you to see more clearly where the regular expression locates the match (code file `RegularExpressionPlayground/Program.cs`):

```
public static void WriteMatches(string text, MatchCollection matches)
{
  Console.WriteLine($"Original text was: \n\n{text}\n");
  Console.WriteLine($"No. of matches: {matches.Count}");
  foreach (Match nextMatch in matches)
  {
    int index = nextMatch.Index;
    string result = nextMatch.ToString();
    int charsBefore = (index < 5) ? index : 5;
    int fromEnd = text.Length - index - result.Length;
    int charsAfter = (fromEnd < 5) ? fromEnd : 5;
    int charsToDisplay = charsBefore + charsAfter + result.Length;
    Console.WriteLine($"Index: {index}, \tString: {result}, \t" +
      "{text.Substring(index - charsBefore, charsToDisplay)}");
  }
}
```

The bulk of the processing in this method is devoted to the logic of figuring out how many characters in the longer substring it can display without overrunning the beginning or end of the input text. Note that you use another property on the `Match` object, `Value`, which contains the string identified for the match. Other than that, `RegularExpressionsPlayground` simply contains a number of methods with names such as `Find1`, `Find2`, and so on, which perform some of the searches based on the examples in this section. For example, `Find2` looks for any string that contains a at the beginning of a word and `ure` at the end:

```
public static void Find2(string text)
{
  string pattern = @"\ba\S*ure\b";
  MatchCollection matches = Regex.Matches(text, pattern,
  RegexOptions.IgnoreCase);
  Console.WriteMatches(text, matches);
}
```

Along with this is a simple `Main` method that you can edit to select one of the `Find<n>` methods:

```
public static void Main()
{
  Find2();
  Console.ReadLine();
}
```

The code also needs to make use of the `RegularExpressions` namespace:

```
using System;
using System.Text.RegularExpressions;
```

Running the example with the `Find2` method shown previously gives this result:

```
No. of matches: 1
Index: 506,      String: architecture,   f C# architecture and
```

Matches, Groups, and Captures

One nice feature of regular expressions is that you can group characters. It works the same way as compound statements in C#. In C#, you can group any number of statements by putting them in braces, and the result is treated as one compound statement. In regular expression patterns, you can group any characters (including meta-characters and escape sequences), and the result is treated as a single character. The only difference is that you use parentheses instead of braces. The resultant sequence is known as a group.

For example, the pattern `(an)+` locates any occurrences of the sequence an. The + quantifier applies only to the previous character, but because you have grouped the characters together, it now applies to repeats of an treated as a unit. This means that if you apply `(an)+` to the input text, bananas came to Europe late in the annals of history, the anan from bananas is identified; however, if you write an+, the program selects the ann from annals, as well as two separate sequences of an from bananas. The expression `(an)+` identifies occurrences of an, anan, ananan, and so on, whereas the expression an+ identifies occurrences of an, ann, annn, and so on.

> **NOTE** *You might be wondering why with the preceding example* `(an)+` *selects* anan *from the word "banana" but doesn't identify either of the two occurrences of* an *from the same word. The rule is that matches must not overlap. If a couple of possibilities would overlap, then by default the longest possible sequence is matched.*

Groups are even more powerful than that. By default, when you form part of the pattern into a group, you are also asking the regular expression engine to remember any matches against just that group, as well as any matches against the entire pattern. In other words, you are treating that group as a pattern to be matched and returned in its own right. This can be extremely useful if you want to break up strings into component parts.

For example, URIs have the format `<protocol>://<address>:<port>`, where the port is optional. An example of this is `http://www.wrox.com:80`. Suppose you want to extract the protocol, the address, and the port from a URI in which there may or may not be whitespace (but no punctuation) immediately following the URI. You could do so using this expression:

```
\b(https?)(://)([.\w]+)([\s:]([\d]{2,5})?)\b
```

Here is how this expression works: First, the leading and trailing `\b` sequences ensure that you consider only portions of text that are entire words. Within that, the first group, `(https?)` identifies either the http or https protocol. `?` after the s character specifies that this character might come 0 or 1 times, thus http and https are allowed. The parentheses cause the protocol to be stored as a group.

The second group is a simple one with `(://)`. This just specifies the characters `://` in that order.

The third group `([.\w]+)` is more interesting. This group contains a parenthetical expression of either the `.` character (dot) or any alphanumeric character specified by `\w`. These characters can be repeated any time, and thus matches www.wrox.com.

The fourth group `([\s:]([\d]{2,5})?)` is a longer expression that contains an inner group. The first parenthetical expression within this group allows either whitespace characters specified by `\s` or the colon. The inner group specifies a digit with `[\d]`. The expression `{2,5}` specifies that the preceding character (the digit) is allowed at least two times and not more than five times. The complete expression with the digits is allowed 0 or 1 time specified by `?` that follows the inner group. Having this group optional is very important because the port number is not always specified in a URI; in fact, it is usually absent.

Let's define a string to run this expression on (code file `RegularExpressionsPlayground/Program.cs`):

```
string line = "Hey, I've just found this amazing URI at " +
"http:// what was it -oh yes https://www.wrox.com or " +
"http://www.wrox.com:80";
```

The code to match with this expression uses the `Matches` method similar to what was used before. The difference is that you iterate all `Group` objects within the `Match.Groups` property and write the resulting index and value of every group to the console:

```
string pattern = @"\b(https?)(://)([.\w]+)([\s:]([\d]{2,4})?)?\b";
var r = new Regex(pattern);
MatchCollection mc = r.Matches(line);
foreach (Match m in mc)
{
  Console.WriteLine($"Match: {m}");
  foreach (Group g in m.Groups)
  {
    if (g.Success)
    {
      Console.WriteLine($"group index: {g.Index}, value: {g.Value}");
    }
  }
  Console.WriteLine();
}
```

Running the program, these groups and values are found:

```
Match https://www.wrox.com
group index 70, value: https://www.wrox.com
group index 70, value: https
group index 75, value: ://
group index 78, value: www.wrox.com
group index 90, value:
Match http://www.wrox.com:80
group index 94, value http://www.wrox.com:80
group index 94, value: http
group index 98, value: ://
group index 101, value: www.wrox.com
group index 113, value: :80
group index 114, value: 80
```

With this, the URI from the text is matched, and the different parts of the URI are nicely grouped. However, grouping offers more features. Some groups, such as the separation between the protocol and the address, can be ignored, and groups can also be named.

Change the regular expression to name every group and to ignore some. Specifying `?<name>` at the beginning of a group names a group. For example, the regular expression groups for protocol, address, and port are named accordingly. You ignore groups using `?:` at the group's beginning. Don't be confused by `?::/` within the group. You are searching for `://`, and the group is ignored by placing `?:` in front of this:

```
string pattern = @"\b(?<protocol>https?)(?::://)" +
@"(?<address>[.\w]+)([\s:](?<port>[\d]{2,4})?)?\b";
```

To get the groups from a regular expression, the `Regex` class defines the method `GetGroupNames`. In the code snippet, all the group names are used with every match to write group name and values using the `Groups` property and indexer:

```
Regex r = new Regex(pattern, RegexOptions.ExplicitCapture);
MatchCollection mc = r.Matches(line);
foreach (Match m in mc)
```

```
{
    Console.WriteLine($"match: {m} at {m.Index}");
    foreach (var groupName in r.GetGroupNames())
    {
        Console.WriteLine($"match for {groupName}: {m.Groups[groupName].Value}");
    }
}
```

When you run the program, you can see the name of the groups with their values:

```
match: https://www.wrox.com at 70
match for 0: https://www.wrox.com
match for protocol: https
match for address: www.wrox.com
match for port:
match: http://www.wrox.com:80 at 94
match for 0: http://www.wrox.com:80
match for protocol: http
match for address: www.wrox.com
match for port: 80
```

STRINGS AND SPANS

Today's programming code often deals with long strings that need to be manipulated. For example, the Web API returns a long string in JSON or XML format. Splitting up such large strings into many smaller strings means that many objects are created, and the garbage collector has a lot to do afterward to free the memory from these strings when they are no longer needed.

.NET Core has a new way around this: the `Span<T>` type. This type is covered in Chapter 7, "Arrays." This type references a slice of an array without the need to copy its contents. Likewise, `Span<T>` can be used to reference a slice of a string without the need to copy the original content.

The following code snippet creates a span from a very long string referenced by the variable text. It's the same string as used previously with regular expressions. A `ReadOnlySpan<char>` is returned from the `AsSpan` extension method. `AsSpan` extends the string type and returns a `ReadOnlySpan<char>`, as a string consists of char elements. Internally, `Span<T>` makes use of the `ref` keyword to keep references. With the `Slice` method, a slice from the complete string is taken. The start is selected with the first parameter, the index where the text `Visual` is first found in the string. From there, 13 characters are used as defined by the second parameter. The result again is a `ReadOnlySpan`. Only with the `ToArray` method of the span is memory allocated. The `ToArray` method allocates memory needed by the slide. The char array then is passed to the constructor of the string type to create a new string (code file `SpanWithStrings/Program.cs`):

```
int ix = text.IndexOf("Visual");
ReadOnlySpan<char> spanToText = text.AsSpan();
ReadOnlySpan<char> slice = spanToText.Slice(ix, 13);

string newString = new string(slice.ToArray());
Console.WriteLine(newString);
```

The newly allocated string from the slice contains Visual Studio.

> **NOTE** *Spans with arrays are covered in Chapter 7. Read more about spans mapping to native memory and the* ref *keyword in Chapter 17, "Managed and Unmanaged Memory." The Web API returning JSON or XML is covered in Chapter 32, "Web API." You can read details about JSON and XML in Bonus Chapter 2, "XML and JSON," which you can find online.*

SUMMARY

You have quite several available data types at your disposal when working with the .NET Framework. One of the most frequently used types in your applications (especially applications that focus on submitting and retrieving data) is the `string` data type. The importance of `string` is the reason why this book has an entire chapter that focuses on how to use the `string` data type and manipulate it in your applications.

When working with strings in the past, it was quite common to just slice and dice the strings as needed using concatenation. With the .NET Framework, you can use the `StringBuilder` class to accomplish a lot of this task with better performance than before.

Another feature of strings is the string interpolation. In most applications this feature can make string handling a lot easier.

Advanced string manipulation using regular expressions is an excellent tool to search through and validate your strings.

Last, you've seen how the `Span` struct can be used efficiently to work with large strings without the need to allocate and release memory blocks.

The next chapter is the first of two parts covering different collection classes.

10

Collections

WROX.COM CODE DOWNLOADS FOR THIS CHAPTER

The Wrox.com code downloads for this chapter are found at http://www.wrox.com on the Download Code tab. The source code is also available at https://github.com/ProfessionalCSharp/ProfessionalCSharp7 in the directory Collections.

The code for this chapter is divided into the following major examples:

➤ List Samples
➤ Queue Sample
➤ Linked List Sample
➤ Sorted List Sample
➤ Dictionary Sample
➤ Set Sample

OVERVIEW

Chapter 7, "Arrays," covers arrays and the interfaces implemented by the Array class. The size of arrays is fixed. If the number of elements is dynamic, you should use a collection class instead of an array.

List<T> is a collection class that can be compared to arrays; but there are also other kinds of collections: queues, stacks, linked lists, dictionaries, and sets. The other collection classes have partly different APIs to access the elements in the collection and often a different internal structure for how the items are stored in memory. This chapter covers these collection classes and their differences, including performance differences.

COLLECTION INTERFACES AND TYPES

Most collection classes are in the `System.Collections` and `System.Collections.Generic` namespaces. Generic collection classes are located in the `System.Collections.Generic` namespace. Collection classes that are specialized for a specific type are located in the `System.Collections.Specialized` namespace. Thread-safe collection classes are in the `System.Collections.Concurrent` namespace. Immutable collection classes are in the `System.Collections.Immutable` namespace.

Of course, there are also other ways to group collection classes. Collections can be grouped into lists, collections, and dictionaries based on the interfaces that are implemented by the collection class.

> **NOTE** *You can read detailed information about the interfaces* `IEnumerable` *and* `IEnumerator` *in Chapter 7.*

The following table describes the most important interfaces implemented by collections and lists.

INTERFACE	DESCRIPTION
`IEnumerable<T>`	The interface `IEnumerable` is required by the `foreach` statement. This interface defines the method `GetEnumerator`, which returns an enumerator that implements the `IEnumerator` interface.
`ICollection<T>`	`ICollection<T>` is implemented by generic collection classes. With this you can get the number of items in the collection `Count` property), and copy the collection to an array (`CopyTo` method). You can also add and remove items from the collection (`Add`, `Remove`, `Clear`).
`IList<T>`	The `IList<T>` interface is for lists where elements can be accessed from their position. This interface defines an indexer, as well as ways to insert or remove items from specific positions (`Insert`, `RemoveAt` methods). `IList<T>` derives from `ICollection<T>`.
`ISet<T>`	This interface is implemented by sets. Sets allow combining different sets into a union, getting the intersection of two sets, and checking whether two sets overlap. `ISet<T>` derives from `ICollection<T>`.
`IDictionary<TKey, TValue>`	The interface `IDictionary<TKey, TValue>` is implemented by generic collection classes that have a key and a value. With this interface all the keys and values can be accessed, items can be accessed with an indexer of type key, and items can be added or removed.
`ILookup<TKey, TValue>`	Like the `IDictionary<TKey, TValue>` interface, lookups have keys and values. However, with lookups the collection can contain multiple values with one key.
`IComparer<T>`	The interface `IComparer<T>` is implemented by a comparer and used to sort elements inside a collection with the `Compare` method.
`IEqualityComparer<T>`	`IEqualityComparer<T>` is implemented by a comparer that can be used for keys in a dictionary. With this interface the objects can be compared for equality.

LISTS

For resizable lists, .NET offers the generic class List<T>. This class implements the IList, ICollection, IEnumerable, IList<T>, ICollection<T>, and IEnumerable<T> interfaces.

The following examples use the members of the class Racer as elements to be added to the collection to represent a Formula-1 racer. This class has five properties: Id, FirstName, LastName, Country, and the number of Wins. With the constructors of the class, the name of the racer and the number of wins can be passed to set the members. The method ToString is overridden to return the name of the racer. The class Racer also implements the generic interface IComparable<T> for sorting racer elements and IFormattable (code file ListSamples/Racer.cs):

```
public class Racer: IComparable<Racer>, IFormattable
{
  public int Id { get; }
  public string FirstName { get; }
  public string LastName { get; }
  public string Country { get; }
  public int Wins { get; }

  public Racer(int id, string firstName, string lastName, string country)
    :this(id, firstName, lastName, country, wins: 0)
  { }

  public Racer(int id, string firstName, string lastName, string country,int wins)
  {
    Id = id;
    FirstName = firstName;
    LastName = lastName;
    Country = country;
    Wins = wins;
  }

  public override string ToString() => $"{FirstName} {LastName}";

  public string ToString(string format, IFormatProvider formatProvider)
  {
    if (format == null) format = "N";
    switch (format.ToUpper())
    {
      case "N": // name
        return ToString();
      case "F": // first name
        return FirstName;
      case "L": // last name
        return LastName;
      case "W": // Wins
        return $"{ToString()}, Wins: {Wins}";
      case "C": // Country
        return $"{ToString()}, Country: {Country}";
      case "A": // All
        return $"{ToString()}, Country: {Country} Wins: {Wins}";
      default:
        throw new FormatException(String.Format(formatProvider,
          $"Format {format} is not supported"));
    }
  }

  public string ToString(string format) => ToString(format, null);
```

```
        public int CompareTo(Racer other)
        {
          int compare = LastName?.CompareTo(other?.LastName) ?? -1;
          if (compare == 0)
          {
            return FirstName?.CompareTo(other?.FirstName) ?? -1;
          }
          return compare;
        }
      }
```

Creating Lists

You can create list objects by invoking the default constructor. With the generic class `List<T>`, you must specify the type for the values of the list with the declaration. The following code shows how to declare a `List<T>` with int and a list with `Racer` elements. `ArrayList` is a non-generic list that accepts any `Object` type for its elements.

Using the default constructor creates an empty list. As soon as elements are added to the list, the capacity of the list is extended to allow 4 elements. If the fifth element is added, the list is resized to allow 8 elements. If 8 elements are not enough, the list is resized again to contain 16 elements. With every resize the capacity of the list is doubled.

```
var intList = new List<int>();
var racers = new List<Racer>();
```

When the capacity of the list changes, the complete collection is reallocated to a new memory block. With the implementation of `List<T>`, an array of type `T` is used. With reallocation, a new array is created, and `Array.Copy` copies the elements from the old array to the new array. To save time, if you know the number of elements in advance, that should be in the list; you can define the capacity with the constructor. The following example creates a collection with a capacity of 10 elements. If the capacity is not large enough for the elements added, the capacity is resized to 20 and then to 40 elements—doubled again:

```
List<int> intList = new List<int>(10);
```

You can get and set the capacity of a collection by using the `Capacity` property:

```
intList.Capacity = 20;
```

The capacity is not the same as the number of elements in the collection. The number of elements in the collection can be read with the `Count` property. Of course, the capacity is always larger or equal to the number of items. As long as no element was added to the list, the count is 0:

```
Console.WriteLine(intList.Count);
```

If you are finished adding elements to the list and don't want to add any more, you can get rid of the unneeded capacity by invoking the `TrimExcess` method; however, because the relocation takes time, `TrimExcess` has no effect if the item count is more than 90 percent of capacity:

```
intList.TrimExcess();
```

Collection Initializers

You can also assign values to collections using collection initializers. The syntax of collection initializers is similar to array initializers, which are explained in Chapter 7. With a collection initializer, values are assigned to the collection within curly brackets at the time the collection is initialized:

```
var intList = new List<int>() {1, 2};
var stringList = new List<string>() { "one", "two" };
```

> **NOTE** *Collection initializers are not reflected within the IL code of the compiled assembly. The compiler converts the collection initializer to invoke the Add method for every item from the initializer list.*

Adding Elements

You can add elements to the list with the Add method, shown in the following example. The generic instantiated type defines the parameter type of the Add method:

```
var intList = new List<int>();
intList.Add(1);
intList.Add(2);
var stringList = new List<string>();
stringList.Add("one");
stringList.Add("two");
```

The variable racers is defined as type List<Racer>. With the new operator, a new object of the same type is created. Because the class List<T> was instantiated with the concrete class Racer, now only Racer objects can be added with the Add method. In the following sample code, five Formula-1 racers are created and added to the collection. The first three are added using the collection initializer, and the last two are added by explicitly invoking the Add method (code file ListSamples/Program.cs):

```
var graham = new Racer(7, "Graham", "Hill", "UK", 14);
var emerson = new Racer(13, "Emerson", "Fittipaldi", "Brazil", 14);
var mario = new Racer(16, "Mario", "Andretti", "USA", 12);
var racers = new List<Racer>(20) {graham, emerson, mario};
racers.Add(new Racer(24, "Michael", "Schumacher", "Germany", 91));
racers.Add(new Racer(27, "Mika", "Hakkinen", "Finland", 20));
```

With the AddRange method of the List<T> class, you can add multiple elements to the collection at once. The method AddRange accepts an object of type IEnumerable<T>, so you can also pass an array as shown here (code file ListSamples/Program.cs):

```
racers.AddRange(new Racer[] {
  new Racer(14, "Niki", "Lauda", "Austria", 25),
  new Racer(21, "Alain", "Prost", "France", 51)});
```

> **NOTE** *The collection initializer can be used only during declaration of the collection. The AddRange method can be invoked after the collection is initialized. In case you get the data dynamically after creating the collection, you need to invoke AddRange.*

If you know some elements of the collection when instantiating the list, you can also pass any object that implements IEnumerable<T> to the constructor of the class. This is very similar to the AddRange method (code file ListSamples/Program.cs):

```
var racers = new List<Racer>(
  new Racer[] {
    new Racer(12, "Jochen", "Rindt", "Austria", 6),
    new Racer(22, "Ayrton", "Senna", "Brazil", 41) });
```

Inserting Elements

You can insert elements at a specified position with the `Insert` method (code file `ListSamples/Program.cs`):

```
racers.Insert(3, new Racer(6, "Phil", "Hill", "USA", 3));
```

The method `InsertRange` offers the capability to insert a number of elements, similar to the `AddRange` method shown earlier.

If the index set is larger than the number of elements in the collection, an exception of type `ArgumentOutOfRangeException` is thrown.

Accessing Elements

All classes that implement the `IList` and `IList<T>` interface offer an indexer, so you can access the elements by using an indexer and passing the item number. The first item can be accessed with an index value 0. By specifying `racers[3]`, for example, you access the fourth element of the list:

```
Racer r1 = racers[3];
```

When you use the `Count` property to get the number of elements, you can do a `for` loop to iterate through every item in the collection, and you can use the indexer to access every item (code file `ListSamples/Program.cs`):

```
for (int i = 0; i < racers.Count; i++)
{
   Console.WriteLine(racers[i]);
}
```

> **NOTE** *Indexed access to collection classes is available with* `ArrayList`, `StringCollection`, *and* `List<T>`.

Because `List<T>` implements the interface `IEnumerable`, you can iterate through the items in the collection using the `foreach` statement as well (code file `ListSamples/Program.cs`):

```
foreach (var r in racers)
{
   Console.WriteLine(r);
}
```

> **NOTE** *Chapter 7 explains how the* `foreach` *statement is resolved by the compiler to make use of the* `IEnumerable` *and* `IEnumerator` *interfaces.*

Removing Elements

You can remove elements by index or pass the item that should be removed. Here, the fourth element is removed from the collection:

```
racers.RemoveAt(3);
```

You can also directly pass a `Racer` object to the `Remove` method to remove this element. Removing by index is faster, because here the collection must be searched for the item to remove. The `Remove` method first searches in the collection to get the index of the item with the `IndexOf` method and then uses the index to remove the item. `IndexOf` first checks whether the item type implements the interface `IEquatable<T>`. If it does, the Equals method of this interface is invoked to find the item in the collection that is the same as the one passed to the method. If this interface is not implemented, the Equals method of the Object class is used to compare the items. The default implementation of the Equals method in the Object class does a bitwise compare with value types, but compares only references with reference types.

> **NOTE** *Chapter 6, "Operators and Casts," explains how you can override the* Equals *method.*

In the following example, the racer referenced by the variable graham is removed from the collection. The variable graham was created earlier when the collection was filled. Because the interface IEquatable<T> and the Object.Equals method are not overridden with the Racer class, you cannot create a new object with the same content as the item that should be removed and pass it to the Remove method (code file ListSamples/Program.cs):

```
if (!racers.Remove(graham))
{
  Console.WriteLine("object not found in collection");
}
```

The method RemoveRange removes a number of items from the collection. The first parameter specifies the index where the removal of items should begin; the second parameter specifies the number of items to be removed:

```
int index = 3;
int count = 5;
racers.RemoveRange(index, count);
```

To remove all items with some specific characteristics from the collection, you can use the RemoveAll method. This method uses the Predicate<T> parameter when searching for elements, which is discussed next. To remove all elements from the collection, use the Clear method defined with the ICollection<T> interface.

Searching

There are different ways to search for elements in the collection. You can get the index to the found item, or the item itself. You can use methods such as IndexOf, LastIndexOf, FindIndex, FindLastIndex, Find, and FindLast. To just check whether an item exists, the List<T> class offers the Exists method.

The method IndexOf requires an object as parameter and returns the index of the item if it is found inside the collection. If the item is not found, –1 is returned. Remember that IndexOf is using the IEquatable<T> interface to compare the elements (code file ListSamples/Program.cs):

```
int index1 = racers.IndexOf(mario);
```

With the IndexOf method, you can also specify that the complete collection should not be searched, instead specifying an index where the search should start and the number of elements that should be iterated for the comparison.

Instead of searching a specific item with the IndexOf method, you can search for an item that has some specific characteristics that you can define with the FindIndex method. FindIndex requires a parameter of type Predicate:

```
public int FindIndex(Predicate<T> match);
```

The Predicate<T> type is a delegate that returns a Boolean value and requires type T as parameter. If the predicate returns true, there's a match, and the element is found. If it returns false, the element is not found, and the search continues.

```
public delegate bool Predicate<T>(T obj);
```

With the `List<T>` class that is using `Racer` objects for type `T`, you can pass the address of a method that returns a `bool` and defines a parameter of type `Racer` to the `FindIndex` method. Finding the first racer of a specific country, you can create the `FindCountry` class as shown next. The `FindCountryPredicate` method has the signature and return type defined by the `Predicate<T>` delegate. The `Find` method uses the variable `country` to search for a country that you can pass with the constructor of the class (code file `ListSamples/FindCountry.cs`):

```
public class FindCountry
{
  public FindCountry(string country) => _country = country;

  private string _country;

  public bool FindCountryPredicate(Racer racer) =>
    racer?.Country == _country;
}
```

With the `FindIndex` method, you can create a new instance of the `FindCountry` class, pass a country string to the constructor, and pass the address of the `Find` method. In the following example, after `FindIndex` completes successfully, `index2` contains the index of the first item where the `Country` property of the racer is set to `Finland` (code file `ListSamples/Program.cs`):

```
int index2 = racers.FindIndex(new FindCountry("Finland").FindCountryPredicate);
```

Instead of creating a class with a handler method, you can use a lambda expression here as well. The result is the same as before. Now the lambda expression defines the implementation to search for an item where the `Country` property is set to `Finland`:

```
int index3 = racers.FindIndex(r => r.Country == "Finland");
```

Like the `IndexOf` method, with the `FindIndex` method you can also specify the index where the search should start and the count of items that should be iterated through. To do a search for an index beginning from the last element in the collection, you can use the `FindLastIndex` method.

The method `FindIndex` returns the index of the found item. Instead of getting the index, you can also go directly to the item in the collection. The `Find` method requires a parameter of type `Predicate<T>`, much as the `FindIndex` method. The `Find` method in the following example searches for the first racer in the list that has the `FirstName` property set to `Niki`. Of course, you can also do a `FindLast` search to find the last item that fulfills the predicate.

```
Racer racer = racers.Find(r => r.FirstName == "Niki");
```

To get not only one but all the items that fulfill the requirements of a predicate, you can use the `FindAll` method. The `FindAll` method uses the same `Predicate<T>` delegate as the `Find` and `FindIndex` methods. The `FindAll` method does not stop when the first item is found; instead the `FindAll` method iterates through every item in the collection and returns all items for which the predicate returns `true`.

With the `FindAll` method invoked in the next example, all racer items are returned where the property `Wins` is set to more than 20. All racers who won more than 20 races are referenced from the `bigWinners` list:

```
List<Racer> bigWinners = racers.FindAll(r => r.Wins > 20);
```

Iterating through the variable `bigWinners` with a `foreach` statement gives the following result:

```
foreach (Racer r in bigWinners)
{
  Console.WriteLine($"{r:A}");
}
Michael Schumacher, Germany Wins: 91
Niki Lauda, Austria Wins: 25
Alain Prost, France Wins: 51
```

The result is not sorted, but you'll see that done next.

> **NOTE** *Format specifiers and the* `IFormattable` *interface is discussed in detail in Chapter 9, "Strings and Regular Expressions."*

Sorting

The `List<T>` class enables sorting its elements by using the `Sort` method. `Sort` uses the quick sort algorithm whereby all elements are compared until the complete list is sorted.

You can use several overloads of the `Sort` method. The arguments that can be passed are a generic delegate `Comparison<T>`, the generic interface `IComparer<T>`, and a range together with the generic interface `IComparer<T>`:

```
public void List<T>.Sort();
public void List<T>.Sort(Comparison<T>);
public void List<T>.Sort(IComparer<T>);
public void List<T>.Sort(Int32, Int32, IComparer<T>);
```

Using the `Sort` method without arguments is possible only if the elements in the collection implement the interface `IComparable`.

Here, the class `Racer` implements the interface `IComparable<T>` to sort racers by the last name:

```
racers.Sort();
```

If you need to do a sort other than the default supported by the item types, you need to use other techniques, such as passing an object that implements the `IComparer<T>` interface.

The class `RacerComparer` implements the interface `IComparer<T>` for `Racer` types. This class enables you to sort by the first name, last name, country, or number of wins. The kind of sort that should be done is defined with the inner enumeration type `CompareType`. The `CompareType` is set with the constructor of the class `RacerComparer`. The interface `IComparer<Racer>` defines the method `Compare`, which is required for sorting. In the implementation of this method, the `Compare` and `CompareTo` methods of the `string` and `int` types are used (code file `ListSamples/RacerComparer.cs`):

```
public class RacerComparer : IComparer<Racer>
{
  public enum CompareType
  {
    FirstName,
    LastName,
    Country,
    Wins
  }
  private CompareType _compareType;
  public RacerComparer(CompareType compareType)
  {
    _compareType = compareType;
  }

  public int Compare(Racer x, Racer y)
  {
    if (x == null && y == null) return 0;
    if (x == null) return -1;
    if (y == null) return 1;
    int result;
    switch (_compareType)
    {
      case CompareType.FirstName:
        return string.Compare(x.FirstName, y.FirstName);
```

```
        case CompareType.LastName:
          return string.Compare(x.LastName, y.LastName);
        case CompareType.Country:
          result = string.Compare(x.Country, y.Country);
          if (result == 0)
            return string.Compare(x.LastName, y.LastName);
          else
            return result;
        case CompareType.Wins:
          return x.Wins.CompareTo(y.Wins);
        default:
          throw new ArgumentException("Invalid Compare Type");
      }
    }
  }
}
```

> **NOTE** *The* Compare *method returns 0 if the two elements passed to it are equal with the order. If a value less than 0 is returned, the first argument is less than the second. With a value larger than 0, the first argument is greater than the second. Passing null with an argument, the method shouldn't throw a* NullReferenceException*. Instead, null should take its place before any other element; thus –1 is returned if the first argument is null, and +1 if the second argument is null.*

You can now use an instance of the RacerComparer class with the Sort method. Passing the enumeration RacerComparer.CompareType.Country sorts the collection by the property Country:

```
racers.Sort(new RacerComparer(RacerComparer.CompareType.Country));
```

Another way to do the sort is by using the overloaded Sort method, which requires a Comparison<T> delegate:

```
public void List<T>.Sort(Comparison<T>);
```

Comparison<T> is a delegate to a method that has two parameters of type T and a return type int. If the parameter values are equal, the method must return 0. If the first parameter is less than the second, a value less than zero must be returned; otherwise, a value greater than zero is returned:

```
public delegate int Comparison<T>(T x, T y);
```

Now you can pass a lambda expression to the Sort method to do a sort by the number of wins. The two parameters are of type Racer, and in the implementation the Wins properties are compared by using the int method CompareTo. Also in the implementation, r2 and r1 are used in reverse order, so the number of wins is sorted in descending order. After the method has been invoked, the complete racer list is sorted based on the racer's number of wins:

```
racers.Sort((r1, r2) => r2.Wins.CompareTo(r1.Wins));
```

You can also reverse the order of a complete collection by invoking the Reverse method.

Read-Only Collections

After collections are created they are read/write, of course; otherwise, you couldn't fill them with any values. However, after the collection is filled, you can create a read-only collection. The List<T> collection has the method AsReadOnly that returns an object of type ReadOnlyCollection<T>. The class ReadOnlyCollection<T> implements the same interfaces as List<T>, but all methods and properties that change the collection throw a NotSupportedException. Beside the interfaces of List<T>, ReadOnlyCollection<T> also implements the interfaces IReadOnlyCollection<T> and IReadOnlyList<T>. With the members of these interfaces, the collection cannot be changed.

QUEUES

A queue is a collection whose elements are processed first in, first out (FIFO), meaning the item that is put first in the queue is read first. Examples of queues are standing in line at the airport, a human resources queue to process employee applicants, print jobs waiting to be processed in a print queue, and a thread waiting for the CPU in a round-robin fashion. Sometimes the elements of a queue differ in their priority. For example, in the queue at the airport, business passengers are processed before economy passengers. In this case, multiple queues can be used, one queue for each priority. At the airport this is easily handled with separate check-in queues for business and economy passengers. The same is true for print queues and threads. You can have an array or a list of queues whereby one item in the array stands for a priority. Within every array item there's a queue, where processing happens using the FIFO principle.

> **NOTE** *Later in this chapter, a different implementation with a linked list is used to define a list of priorities.*

A queue is implemented with the `Queue<T>` class in the namespace `System.Collections.Generic`. Internally, the `Queue<T>` class uses an array of type T, similar to the `List<T>` type. It implements the interfaces `IEnumerable<T>` and `ICollection`, but it doesn't implement `ICollection<T>` because this interface defines `Add` and `Remove` methods that shouldn't be available for queues.

The `Queue<T>` class does not implement the interface `IList<T>`, so you cannot access the queue using an indexer. The queue just allows you to add an item to it, which is put at the end of the queue (with the `Enqueue` method), and to get items from the head of the queue (with the `Dequeue` method).

Figure 10-1 shows the items of a queue. The `Enqueue` method adds items to one end of the queue; the items are read and removed at the other end of the queue with the `Dequeue` method. Invoking the `Dequeue` method once more removes the next item from the queue.

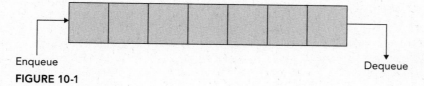

Enqueue   Dequeue

FIGURE 10-1

Methods of the `Queue<T>` class are described in the following table.

SELECTED QUEUE <T> MEMBERS	DESCRIPTION
Count	Returns the number of items in the queue.
Enqueue	Adds an item to the end of the queue.
Dequeue	Reads and removes an item from the head of the queue. If there are no more items in the queue when the Dequeue method is invoked, an exception of type InvalidOperationException is thrown.
Peek	Reads an item from the head of the queue but does not remove the item.
TrimExcess	Resizes the capacity of the queue. The Dequeue method removes items from the queue, but it doesn't resize the capacity of the queue. To get rid of the empty items at the beginning of the queue, use the TrimExcess method.

When creating queues, you can use constructors similar to those used with the List<T> type. The default constructor creates an empty queue, but you can also use a constructor to specify the capacity. As items are added to the queue, the capacity is increased to hold 4, 8, 16, and 32 items if the capacity is not defined. Like the List<T> class, the capacity is always doubled as required. The default constructor of the non-generic Queue class is different because it creates an initial array of 32 empty items. With an overload of the constructor, you can also pass any other collection that implements the IEnumerable<T> interface that is copied to the queue.

The following example demonstrating the use of the Queue<T> class is a document management application. One thread is used to add documents to the queue, and another thread reads documents from the queue and processes them.

The items stored in the queue are of type Document. The Document class defines a title and content (code file QueueSample/Document.cs):

```
public class Document
{
  public string Title { get; }
  public string Content { get; }
  public Document(string title, string content)
  {
    Title = title;
    Content = content;
  }
}
```

The DocumentManager class is a thin layer around the Queue<T> class. It defines how to handle documents: adding documents to the queue with the AddDocument method and getting documents from the queue with the GetDocument method.

Inside the AddDocument method, the document is added to the end of the queue using the Enqueue method. The first document from the queue is read with the Dequeue method inside GetDocument. Because multiple threads can access the DocumentManager concurrently, access to the queue is locked with the lock statement.

> **NOTE** *Threading and the* lock *statement are discussed in Chapter 21, "Tasks and Parallel Programming."*

IsDocumentAvailable is a read-only Boolean property that returns true if there are documents in the queue and false if not (code file QueueSample/DocumentManager.cs):

```
public class DocumentManager
{
  private readonly object _syncQueue = new object();
  private readonly Queue<Document> _documentQueue = new Queue<Document>();

  public void AddDocument(Document doc)
  {
    lock (_syncQueue)
    {
      _documentQueue.Enqueue(doc);
    }
  }

  public Document GetDocument()
  {
    Document doc = null;
    lock (_syncQueue)
    {
      doc = _documentQueue.Dequeue();
    }
```

```
        return doc;
    }


    public bool IsDocumentAvailable => _documentQueue.Count > 0;
}
```

The class `ProcessDocuments` processes documents from the queue in a separate task. The only method that can be accessed from the outside is `Start`. In the `Start` method, a new task is instantiated. A `ProcessDocuments` object is created to start the task, and the `Run` method is defined as the start method of the task. The `StartNew` method of the `TaskFactory` (which is accessed from the static `Factory` property of the `Task` class) requires a delegate `Action` parameter where the address of the `Run` method can be passed to. The `StartNew` method of the `TaskFactory` immediately starts the task.

With the `Run` method of the `ProcessDocuments` class, an endless loop is defined. Within this loop, the property `IsDocumentAvailable` is used to determine whether there is a document in the queue. If so, the document is taken from the `DocumentManager` and processed. Processing in this example is writing information only to the console. In a real application, the document could be written to a file, written to the database, or sent across the network (code file QueueSample/ProcessDocuments.cs):

```csharp
public class ProcessDocuments
{
    public static Task Start(DocumentManager dm) =>
        Task.Run(new ProcessDocuments(dm).Run);

    protected ProcessDocuments(DocumentManager dm) =>
        _documentManager = dm ?? throw new ArgumentNullExcption(nameof(dm));

    private DocumentManager _documentManager;

    protected async Task Run()
    {
        while (true)
        {
            if (_documentManager.IsDocumentAvailable)
            {
                Document doc = _documentManager.GetDocument();
                Console.WriteLine("Processing document {0}", doc.Title);
            }
            await Task.Delay(new Random().Next(20));
        }
    }
}
```

In the `Main` method of the application, a `DocumentManager` object is instantiated, and the document processing task is started. Then 1,000 documents are created and added to the `DocumentManager` (code file QueueSample/Program.cs):

```csharp
public class Program
{
    public static async Task Main()
    {
        var dm = new DocumentManager();

        Task processDocuments = ProcessDocuments.Start(dm);

        // Create documents and add them to the DocumentManager
        for (int i = 0; i < 1000; i++)
        {
            var doc = new Document($"Doc {i.ToString()}", "content");
            dm.AddDocument(doc);
            Console.WriteLine($"Added document {doc.Title}");
            await Task.Delay(new Random().Next(20));
        }
```

```
      await processDocuments;
      Console.ReadLine();
   }
}
```

> **NOTE** *With the* `QueueSample`, *the* `Main` *method is declared to return a* `Task`. *This feature requires at least C# 7.1. You can read more about asynchronous* `Main` *methods in Chapter 15, "Asynchronous Programming."*

When you start the application, the documents are added to and removed from the queue, and you get output like the following:

```
Added document Doc 279
Processing document Doc 236
Added document Doc 280
Processing document Doc 237
Added document Doc 281
Processing document Doc 238
Processing document Doc 239
Processing document Doc 240
Processing document Doc 241
Added document Doc 282
Processing document Doc 242
Added document Doc 283
Processing document Doc 243
```

A real-life scenario using the task described with the sample application might be an application that processes documents received with a Web API service.

STACKS

A stack is another container that is very similar to the queue. You just use different methods to access the stack. The item that is added last to the stack is read first, so the stack is a *last in, first out* (LIFO) container.

Figure 10-2 shows the representation of a stack where the `Push` method adds an item to the stack, and the `Pop` method gets the item that was added last.

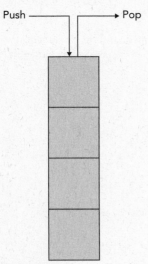

FIGURE 10-2

Like the `Queue<T>` class, the `Stack<T>` class implements the interfaces `IEnumerable<T>` and `ICollection`.

Members of the `Stack<T>` class are listed in the following table.

SELECTED STACK<T> MEMBERS	DESCRIPTION
Count	Returns the number of items in the stack.
Push	Adds an item on top of the stack.
Pop	Removes and returns an item from the top of the stack. If the stack is empty, an exception of type `InvalidOperationException` is thrown.
Peek	Returns an item from the top of the stack but does not remove the item.
Contains	Checks whether an item is in the stack and returns `true` if it is.

In this example, three items are added to the stack with the `Push` method. With the `foreach` method, all items are iterated using the `IEnumerable` interface. The enumerator of the stack does not remove the items; it just returns them item by item (code file `StackSample/Program.cs`):

```
var alphabet = new Stack<char>();
alphabet.Push('A');
alphabet.Push('B');
alphabet.Push('C');
foreach (char item in alphabet)
{
  Console.Write(item);
}
Console.WriteLine();
```

Because the items are read in order from the last item added to the first, the following result is produced:

```
CBA
```

Reading the items with the enumerator does not change the state of the items. With the `Pop` method, every item that is read is also removed from the stack. This way, you can iterate the collection using a `while` loop and verify the `Count` property if items still exist:

```
var alphabet = new Stack<char>();
alphabet.Push('A');
alphabet.Push('B');
alphabet.Push('C');
Console.Write("First iteration: ");
foreach (char item in alphabet)
{
  Console.Write(item);
}
Console.WriteLine();
Console.Write("Second iteration: ");
while (alphabet.Count > 0)
{
  Console.Write(alphabet.Pop());
}
Console.WriteLine();
```

The result gives CBA twice—once for each iteration. After the second iteration, the stack is empty because the second iteration used the `Pop` method:

```
First iteration: CBA
Second iteration: CBA
```

LINKED LISTS

`LinkedList<T>` is a doubly linked list, whereby one element references the next and the previous one, as shown in Figure 10-3. This way you can easily walk forward through the complete list by moving to the next element, or backward by moving to the previous element.

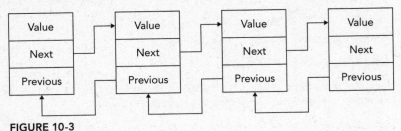

FIGURE 10-3

The advantage of a linked list is that if items are inserted anywhere in the list, the linked list is very fast. When an item is inserted, only the `Next` reference of the previous item and the `Previous` reference of the next item must be changed to reference the inserted item. With the `List<T>` class, when an element is inserted all subsequent elements must be moved.

Of course, there's also a disadvantage with linked lists. Items of linked lists can be accessed only one after the other. It takes a long time to find an item that's somewhere in the middle or at the end of the list.

A linked list cannot just store the items inside the list; together with every item, the linked list must have information about the next and previous items. That's why the `LinkedList<T>` contains items of type `LinkedListNode<T>`. With the class `LinkedListNode<T>`, you can get to the next and previous items in the list. The `LinkedListNode<T>` class defines the properties `List`, `Next`, `Previous`, and `Value`. The `List` property returns the `LinkedList<T>` object that is associated with the node. `Next` and `Previous` are for iterating through the list and accessing the next or previous item. `Value` returns the item that is associated with the node. `Value` is of type `T`.

The `LinkedList<T>` class itself defines members to access the first (`First`) and last (`Last`) item of the list, to insert items at specific positions (`AddAfter`, `AddBefore`, `AddFirst`, `AddLast`), to remove items from specific positions (`Remove`, `RemoveFirst`, `RemoveLast`), and to find elements where the search starts from either the beginning (`Find`) or the end (`FindLast`) of the list.

The sample application to demonstrate linked lists uses a linked list together with a list. The linked list contains documents as in the queue example, but the documents have an additional priority associated with them. The documents will be sorted inside the linked list depending on the priority. If multiple documents have the same priority, the elements are sorted according to the time when the document was inserted.

Figure 10-4 describes the collections of the sample application. `LinkedList<Document>` is the linked list containing all the `Document` objects. The figure shows the title and priority of the documents. The title indicates when the document was added to the list: The first document added has the title `"One"`, the second document has the title `"Two"`, and so on. You can see that the documents `One` and `Four` have the same priority, 8, but because `One` was added before `Four`, it is earlier in the list.

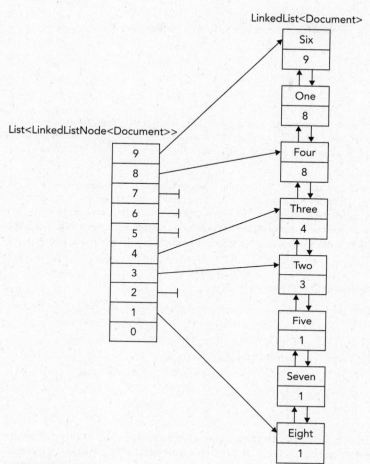

LinkedList<Document>

List<LinkedListNode<Document>>

FIGURE 10-4

When new documents are added to the linked list, they should be added after the last document that has the same priority. The LinkedList<Document> collection contains elements of type LinkedListNode<Document>. The class LinkedListNode<T> adds Next and Previous properties to walk from one node to the next. For referencing such elements, the List<T> is defined as List<LinkedListNode<Document>>. For fast access to the last document of every priority, the collection List<LinkedListNode> contains up to 10 elements, each referencing the last document of every priority. In the upcoming discussion, the reference to the last document of every priority is called the priority node.

Using the previous example, the Document class is extended to contain the priority, which is set with the constructor of the class (code file LinkedListSample/Document.cs):

```
public class Document
{
  public string Title { get; }
  public string Content { get; }
```

```
      public byte Priority { get; }
      public Document(string title, string content, byte priority)
      {
        Title = title;
        Content = content;
        Priority = priority;
      }
    }
```

The heart of the solution is the `PriorityDocumentManager` class. This class is very easy to use. With the public interface of this class, new `Document` elements can be added to the linked list, the first document can be retrieved, and for testing purposes it also has a method to display all elements of the collection as they are linked in the list.

The class `PriorityDocumentManager` contains two collections. The collection of type `LinkedList <Document>` contains all documents. The collection of type `List<LinkedListNode<Document>>` contains references of up to 10 elements that are entry points for adding new documents with a specific priority. Both collection variables are initialized with the constructor of the class `PriorityDocumentManager`. The list collection is also initialized with `null` (code file `LinkedListSample/PriorityDocumentManager.cs`):

```
    public class PriorityDocumentManager
    {
      private readonly LinkedList<Document> _documentList;
      // priorities 0.9
      private readonly List<LinkedListNode<Document>> _priorityNodes;
      public PriorityDocumentManager()
      {
        _documentList = new LinkedList<Document>();
        _priorityNodes = new List<LinkedListNode<Document>>(10);
        for (int i = 0; i < 10; i++)
        {
          _priorityNodes.Add(new LinkedListNode<Document>(null));
        }
      }
    }
```

Part of the public interface of the class is the method `AddDocument`. `AddDocument` does nothing more than call the private method `AddDocumentToPriorityNode`. The reason for having the implementation inside a different method is that `AddDocumentToPriorityNode` may be called recursively, as you will see soon:

```
    public void AddDocument(Document d)
    {
      if (d == null) throw new ArgumentNullException(nameof(d));
      AddDocumentToPriorityNode(d, d.Priority);
    }
```

The first action that is done in the implementation of `AddDocumentToPriorityNode` is a check to see if the priority fits in the allowed priority range. Here, the allowed range is between 0 and 9. If a wrong value is passed, an exception of type `ArgumentException` is thrown.

Next, you check whether there's already a priority node with the same priority as the priority that was passed. If there's no such priority node in the list collection, `AddDocumentToPriorityNode` is invoked recursively with the priority value decremented to check for a priority node with the next lower priority.

If there's no priority node with the same priority or any priority with a lower value, the document can be safely added to the end of the linked list by calling the method `AddLast`. In addition, the linked list node is referenced by the priority node that's responsible for the priority of the document.

If there's an existing priority node, you can get the position inside the linked list where the document should be inserted. In the following example, you must determine whether a priority node already exists with the correct priority, or if there's just a priority node that references a document with a lower priority. In the first case, you can insert the new document after the position referenced by the priority node. Because the priority node always must reference the last document with a specific priority, the reference of the priority node must be set. It gets more complex if only a priority node referencing a document with a lower priority exists. Here, the document must be inserted before all documents with the same priority as the priority node. To get the first document of the same priority, a `while` loop iterates through all linked list nodes, using the `Previous` property, until a linked list node is reached that has a different priority. This way, you know the position where the document must be inserted, and the priority node can be set:

```
private void AddDocumentToPriorityNode(Document doc, int priority)
{
  if (priority > 9 || priority < 0)
    throw new ArgumentException("Priority must be between 0 and 9");
  if (_priorityNodes[priority].Value == null)
  {
    --priority;
    if (priority <= 0)
    {
      // check for the next lower priority
      AddDocumentToPriorityNode(doc, priority);
    }
    else // now no priority node exists with the same priority or lower
      // add the new document to the end
    {
      _documentList.AddLast(doc);
      _priorityNodes[doc.Priority] = _documentList.Last;
    }
    return;
  }
  else // a priority node exists
  {
    LinkedListNode<Document> prioNode = _priorityNodes[priority];
    if (priority == doc.Priority)
    // priority node with the same priority exists
    {
      _documentList.AddAfter(prioNode, doc);
      // set the priority node to the last document with the same priority
      _priorityNodes[doc.Priority] = prioNode.Next;
    }
    else // only priority node with a lower priority exists
    {
      // get the first node of the lower priority
      LinkedListNode<Document> firstPrioNode = prioNode;
      while (firstPrioNode.Previous != null &&
        firstPrioNode.Previous.Value.Priority == prioNode.Value.Priority)
      {
        firstPrioNode = prioNode.Previous;
        prioNode = firstPrioNode;
      }
      _documentList.AddBefore(firstPrioNode, doc);
      // set the priority node to the new value
      _priorityNodes[doc.Priority] = firstPrioNode.Previous;
    }
  }
}
```

Now only simple methods are left for discussion. `DisplayAllNodes` does a `foreach` loop to display the priority and the title of every document to the console.

The method `GetDocument` returns the first document (the document with the highest priority) from the linked list and removes it from the list:

```
public void DisplayAllNodes()
{
  foreach (Document doc in documentList)
```

```
    {
      Console.WriteLine($"priority: {doc.Priority}, title {doc.Title}");
    }
  }

  // returns the document with the highest priority
  // (that's first in the linked list)
  public Document GetDocument()
  {
    Document doc = _documentList.First.Value;
    _documentList.RemoveFirst();
    return doc;
  }
```

In the `Main` method, the `PriorityDocumentManager` is used to demonstrate its functionality. Eight new documents with different priorities are added to the linked list, and then the complete list is displayed (code file `LinkedListSample/Program.cs`):

```
public static void Main()
{
  var pdm = new PriorityDocumentManager();
  pdm.AddDocument(new Document("one", "Sample", 8));
  pdm.AddDocument(new Document("two", "Sample", 3));
  pdm.AddDocument(new Document("three", "Sample", 4));
  pdm.AddDocument(new Document("four", "Sample", 8));
  pdm.AddDocument(new Document("five", "Sample", 1));
  pdm.AddDocument(new Document("six", "Sample", 9));
  pdm.AddDocument(new Document("seven", "Sample", 1));
  pdm.AddDocument(new Document("eight", "Sample", 1));
  pdm.DisplayAllNodes();
}
```

With the processed result, you can see that the documents are sorted first by priority and second by when the document was added:

```
priority: 9, title six
priority: 8, title one
priority: 8, title four
priority: 4, title three
priority: 3, title two
priority: 1, title five
priority: 1, title seven
priority: 1, title eight
```

SORTED LIST

If the collection you need should be sorted based on a key, you can use `SortedList<TKey, TValue>`. This class sorts the elements based on a key. You can use any type for the value and also for the key.

The following example creates a sorted list for which both the key and the value are of type `string`. The default constructor creates an empty list, and then two books are added with the `Add` method. With overloaded constructors, you can define the capacity of the list and pass an object that implements the interface `IComparer<TKey>`, which is used to sort the elements in the list.

The first parameter of the `Add` method is the key (the book title); the second parameter is the value (the ISBN). Instead of using the `Add` method, you can use the indexer to add elements to the list. The indexer requires the key as index parameter. If a key already exists, the `Add` method throws an exception of type `ArgumentException`. If the same key is used with the indexer, the new value replaces the old value (code file `SortedListSample/Program.cs`):

```
var books = new SortedList<string, string>();
books.Add("Professional WPF Programming", "978-0-470-04180-2");
```

```
books.Add("Professional ASP.NET MVC 5", "978-1-118-79475-3");

books["Beginning C# 6 Programming"] = "978-1-119-09668-9";
books["Professional C# 6 and .NET Core 1.0"] = "978-1-119-09660-3";
```

> **NOTE** `SortedList<TKey, TValue>` *allows only one value per key. If you need multiple values per key you can use* `Lookup<TKey, TElement>`.

You can iterate through the list using a `foreach` statement. Elements returned by the enumerator are of type `KeyValuePair<TKey, TValue>`, which contains both the key and the value. The key can be accessed with the `Key` property, and the value can be accessed with the `Value` property:

```
foreach (KeyValuePair<string, string> book in books)
{
  Console.WriteLine($"{book.Key}, {book.Value}");
}
```

The iteration displays book titles and ISBN numbers ordered by the key:

```
Beginning C# 6 Programming, 978-1-119-09668-9
Professional ASP.NET MVC 5, 978-1-118-79475-3
Professional C# 6 and .NET Core 1.0, 978-1-119-09660-3
Professional WPF Programming, 978-0-470-04180-2
```

You can also access the values and keys by using the `Values` and `Keys` properties. The `Values` property returns `IList<TValue>` and the `Keys` property returns `IList<TKey>`, so you can use these properties with a `foreach`:

```
foreach (string isbn in books.Values)
{
  Console.WriteLine(isbn);
}
foreach (string title in books.Keys)
{
  Console.WriteLine(title);
}
```

The first loop displays the values, and next the keys:

```
978-1-119-09668-9
978-1-118-79475-3
978-1-119-09660-3
978-0-470-04180-2
Beginning C# 6 Programming
Professional ASP.NET MVC 5
Professional C# 6 and .NET Core 1.0
Professional WPF Programming
```

If you try to access an element with an indexer and passing a key that does not exist, an exception of type `KeyNotFoundException` is thrown. To avoid that exception, you can use the method `ContainsKey`, which returns `true` if the key passed exists in the collection, or you can invoke the method `TryGetValue`, which tries to get the value but doesn't throw an exception if it isn't found:

```
string title = "Professional C# 8";
if (!books.TryGetValue(title, out string isbn))
{
  Console.WriteLine($"{title} not found");
}
```

DICTIONARIES

A dictionary represents a sophisticated data structure that enables you to access an element based on a key. Dictionaries are also known as hash tables or maps. The main feature of dictionaries is fast lookup based on keys. You can also add and remove items freely, a bit like a `List<T>`, but without the performance overhead of having to shift subsequent items in memory.

Figure 10-5 shows a simplified representation of a dictionary. Here employee-ids such as B4711 are the keys added to the dictionary. The key is transformed into a hash. With the hash a number is created to associate an index with the values. The index then contains a link to the value. The figure is simplified because it is possible for a single index entry to be associated with multiple values, and the index can be stored as a tree.

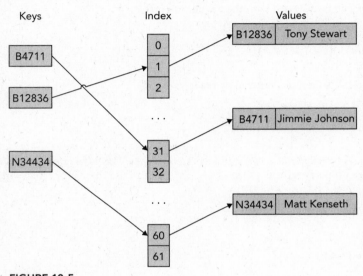

FIGURE 10-5

.NET offers several dictionary classes. The main class you use is `Dictionary<TKey, TValue>`.

Dictionary Initializers

C# offers a syntax to initialize dictionaries at declaration. A dictionary with a key of `int` and a value of `string` can be initialized as follows:

```
var dict = new Dictionary<int, string>()
{
    [3] = "three",
    [7] = "seven"
};
```

Here, two elements are added to the dictionary. The first element has a key of 3 and a string value three; the second element has a key of 7 and a string value seven. This initializer syntax is easily readable and uses the same syntax as accessing the elements in the dictionary.

Key Type

A type that is used as a key in the dictionary must override the method `GetHashCode` of the `Object` class. Whenever a dictionary class needs to determine where an item should be located, it calls the `GetHashCode` method. The `int` that is returned by `GetHashCode` is used by the dictionary to calculate an index of where to place the element. We won't go into this part of the algorithm; what you should know is that it involves prime numbers, so the capacity of a dictionary is a prime number.

The implementation of `GetHashCode` must satisfy the following requirements:

➤ The same object should always return the same value.

➤ Different objects can return the same value.

➤ It must not throw exceptions.

➤ It should use at least one instance field.

➤ The hash code should not change during the lifetime of the object.

Besides requirements that must be satisfied by the `GetHashCode` implementation, it's also good practice to satisfy these requirements:

➤ It should execute as quickly as possible; it must be inexpensive to compute.

➤ The hash code value should be evenly distributed across the entire range of numbers that an `int` can store.

> **NOTE** *Good performance of the dictionary is based on a good implementation of the method* `GetHashCode`.

What's the reason for having hash code values evenly distributed across the range of integers? If two keys return hashes that have the same index, the dictionary class needs to start looking for the nearest available free location to store the second item—and it will have to do some searching to retrieve this item later. This is obviously going to hurt performance. In addition, if a lot of your keys are tending to provide the same storage indexes for where they should be stored, this kind of clash becomes more likely. However, because of the way that Microsoft's part of the algorithm works, this risk is minimized when the calculated hash values are evenly distributed between `int.MinValue` and `int.MaxValue`.

Besides having an implementation of `GetHashCode`, the key type also must implement the `IEquatable<T>`. `Equals` method or override the `Equals` method from the `Object` class. Because different key objects may return the same hash code, the method `Equals` is used by the dictionary comparing keys. The dictionary examines whether two keys, such as A and B, are equal; it invokes `A.Equals(B)`. This means that you must ensure that the following is always true: If `A.Equals(B)` is true, then `A.GetHashCode` and `B.GetHashCode` must always return the same hash code.

This may seem a subtle point, but it is crucial. If you contrived some way of overriding these methods so that the preceding statement were not always true, a dictionary that uses instances of this class as its keys would not work properly. Instead, you'd find funny things happening. For example, you might place an object in the dictionary and then discover that you could never retrieve it, or you might try to retrieve an entry and have the wrong entry returned.

> **NOTE** *For this reason, the C# compiler displays a compilation warning if you supply an override for* `Equals` *but don't supply an override for* `GetHashCode`.

For `System.Object` this condition is true because `Equals` simply compares references, and `GetHashCode` returns a hash that is based solely on the address of the object. This means that hash tables based on a key that doesn't override these methods will work correctly. However, the problem with this approach is that keys are regarded as equal only if they are the same object. That means when you place an object in the dictionary, you must hang on to the reference to the key; you can't simply instantiate another key object later with the same value. If you don't override `Equals` and `GetHashCode`, the type is not very convenient to use in a dictionary.

Incidentally, `System.String` implements the interface `IEquatable` and overloads `GetHashCode` appropriately. `Equals` provides value comparison, and `GetHashCode` returns a hash based on the value of the string. Strings can be used conveniently as keys in dictionaries.

Number types such as `Int32` also implement the interface `IEquatable` and overload `GetHashCode`. However, the hash code returned by these types simply maps to the value. If the number you would like to use as a key is not itself distributed around the possible values of an integer, using integers as keys doesn't fulfill the rule of evenly distributing key values to get the best performance. `Int32` is not meant to be used in a dictionary.

If you need to use a key type that does not implement `IEquatable` and does not override `GetHashCode` according to the key values you store in the dictionary, you can create a comparer implementing the interface `IEqualityComparer<T>`. `IEqualityComparer<T>` defines the methods `GetHashCode` and `Equals` with an argument of the object passed, so you can offer an implementation different from the object type itself. An overload of the `Dictionary<TKey, TValue>` constructor allows passing an object implementing `IEqualityComparer<T>`. If such an object is assigned to the dictionary, this class is used to generate the hash codes and compare the keys.

Dictionary Example

The dictionary example in this section is a program that sets up a dictionary of employees. The dictionary is indexed by `EmployeeId` objects, and each item stored in the dictionary is an `Employee` object that stores details of an employee.

The struct `EmployeeId` is implemented to define a key to be used in a dictionary. The members of the class are a prefix character and a number for the employee. Both these variables are read-only and can be initialized only in the constructor to ensure that keys within the dictionary shouldn't change. When you have read-only variables it is guaranteed that they can't be changed. The fields are filled within the constructor. The `ToString` method is overloaded to get a string representation of the employee ID. As required for a key type, `EmployeeId` implements the interface `IEquatable` and overloads the method `GetHashCode` (code file `DictionarySample/EmployeeId.cs`):

```
public class EmployeeIdException : Exception
{
  public EmployeeIdException(string message) : base(message) { }
}

public struct EmployeeId : IEquatable<EmployeeId>
{
  private readonly char _prefix;
  private readonly int _number;
  public EmployeeId(string id)
  {
    if (id == null) throw new ArgumentNullException(nameof(id));
    _prefix = (id.ToUpper())[0];
    int numLength = id.Length - 1;
    try
    {
      _number = int.Parse(id.Substring(1, numLength > 6 ? 6 : numLength));
    }
    catch (FormatException)
    {
      throw new EmployeeIdException("Invalid EmployeeId format");
    }
  }
```

```
    public override string ToString() => _prefix.ToString() +
      $"{number,6:000000}";

    public override int GetHashCode() => (number ^ number << 16) * 0x15051505;

    public bool Equals(EmployeeId other) =>
      (prefix == other?.prefix && number == other?.number);

    public override bool Equals(object obj) => Equals((EmployeeId)obj);

    public static bool operator ==(EmployeeId left, EmployeeId right) =>
      left.Equals(right);

    public static bool operator !=(EmployeeId left, EmployeeId right) =>
      !(left == right);
}
```

The `Equals` method that is defined by the `IEquatable<T>` interface compares the values of two `EmployeeId` objects and returns `true` if both values are the same. Instead of implementing the `Equals` method from the `IEquatable<T>` interface, you can also override the `Equals` method from the `Object` class:

```
    public bool Equals(EmployeeId other) =>
      prefix == other.prefix && number == other.number;
```

With the number variable, a value from 1 to around 190,000 is expected for the employees. This doesn't fill the range of an integer. The algorithm used by `GetHashCode` shifts the number 16 bits to the left, then does an XOR (exclusive OR) with the original number, and finally multiplies the result by the hex value 15051505. The hash code is evenly distributed across the range of an integer:

```
    public override int GetHashCode() => (number ^ number << 16) * 0x1505_1505;
```

> **NOTE** *On the Internet, you can find a lot more complex algorithms that have a better distribution across the integer range. You can also use the* `GetHashCode` *method of a string to return a hash.*

The `Employee` class is a simple entity class containing the name, salary, and ID of the employee. The constructor initializes all values, and the method `ToString` returns a string representation of an instance. The implementation of `ToString` uses a format string to create the string representation for performance reasons (code file `DictionarySample/Employee.cs`):

```
    public class Employee
    {
      private string _name;
      private decimal _salary;
      private readonly EmployeeId _id;
      public Employee(EmployeeId id, string name, decimal salary)
      {
        _id = id;
        _name = name;
        _salary = salary;
      }

      public override string ToString() =>
        $"{id.ToString()}: {name, -20} {salary:C}";
    }
```

In the `Main` method of the sample application, a new `Dictionary<TKey, TValue>` instance is created, where the key is of type `EmployeeId` and the value is of type `Employee`. The constructor allocates a capacity of 31 elements. Remember that capacity is based on prime numbers. However, when you assign a value that is not a prime number, you don't need to worry. The `Dictionary<TKey, TValue>` class itself takes the next prime number that follows the integer passed to the constructor to allocate the capacity. After creating the employee objects and IDs, they are added to the newly created dictionary using the new dictionary initializer syntax. Of course, you can also invoke the `Add` method of the dictionary to add objects instead (code file `DictionarySample/Program.cs`):

```
static void Main()
{
  var idJimmie = new EmployeeId("C48");
  var jimmie = new Employee(idJimmie, "Jimmie Johnson", 150926.00m);

  var idJoey = new EmployeeId("F22");
  var joey = new Employee(idJoey, "Joey Logano", 45125.00m);

  var idKyle = new EmployeeId("T18");
  var kyle = new Employee(idKyle, "Kyle Bush", 78728.00m);

  var idCarl = new EmployeeId("T19");
  var carl = new Employee(idCarl, "Carl Edwards", 80473.00m);

  var idMatt = new EmployeeId("T20");
  var matt = new Employee(idMatt, "Matt Kenseth", 113970.00m);

  var employees = new Dictionary<EmployeeId, Employee>(31)
  {
    [idJimmie] = jimmie,
    [idJoey] = joey,
    [idKyle] = kyle,
    [idCarl] = carl,
    [idMatt] = matt
  };

  foreach (var employee in employees.Values)
  {
    Console.WriteLine(employee);
  }
  //...
```

After the entries are added to the dictionary, inside a `while` loop employees are read from the dictionary. The user is asked to enter an employee number to store in the variable `userInput`, and the user can exit the application by entering **X**. If the key is in the dictionary, it is examined with the `TryGetValue` method of the `Dictionary<TKey, TValue>` class. `TryGetValue` returns `true` if the key is found and `false` otherwise. If the value is found, the value associated with the key is stored in the employee variable. This value is written to the console.

> **NOTE** *You can also use an indexer of the* `Dictionary<TKey, TValue>` *class instead of* `TryGetValue` *to access a value stored in the dictionary. However, if the key is not found, the indexer throws an exception of type* `KeyNotFoundException`.

```
while (true)
{
  Console.Write("Enter employee id (X to exit)> ");
  var userInput =ReadLine();
  userInput = userInput.ToUpper();
  if (userInput == "X") break;
  EmployeeId id;
  try
```

```
    {
        id = new EmployeeId(userInput);
        if (!employees.TryGetValue(id, out Employee employee))
        {
            Console.WriteLine($"Employee with id {id} does not exist");
        }
        else
        {
            Console.WriteLine(employee);
        }
    }
    catch (EmployeeIdException ex)
    {
        Console.WriteLine(ex.Message);
    }
}
```

Running the application produces the following output:

```
C000048: Jimmie Johnson      $150,926.00
F000022: Joey Logano         $45,125.00
T000018: Kyle Bush           $78,728.00
T000019: Carl Edwards        $80,473.00
T000020: Matt Kenseth        $113,970.00
Enter employee id (X to exit)> T18
T000018: Kyle Bush           $78,728.00
Enter employee id (X to exit)> C48
C000048: Jimmie Johnson      $150,926.00
Enter employee id (X to exit)> X
Press any key to continue . . .
```

Lookups

Dictionary<TKey, TValue> supports only one value per key. The class Lookup<TKey, TElement> resembles a Dictionary<TKey, TValue> but maps keys to a collection of values. This class is implemented in the assembly System.Core and defined with the namespace System.Linq.

Lookup<TKey, TElement> cannot be created as a normal dictionary. Instead, you must invoke the method ToLookup, which returns a Lookup<TKey, TElement> object. The method ToLookup is an extension method that is available with every class implementing IEnumerable<T>. In the following example, a list of Racer objects is filled. Because List<T> implements IEnumerable<T>, the ToLookup method can be invoked on the racers list. This method requires a delegate of type Func<TSource, TKey> that defines the selector of the key. Here, the racers are selected based on their country by using the lambda expression r => r.Country. The foreach loop accesses only the racers from Australia by using the indexer (code file LookupSample/Program.cs):

```
var racers = new List<Racer>();
racers.Add(new Racer("Jacques", "Villeneuve", "Canada", 11));
racers.Add(new Racer("Alan", "Jones", "Australia", 12));
racers.Add(new Racer("Jackie", "Stewart", "United Kingdom", 27));
racers.Add(new Racer("James", "Hunt", "United Kingdom", 10));
racers.Add(new Racer("Jack", "Brabham", "Australia", 14));

var lookupRacers = racers.ToLookup(r => r.Country);

foreach (Racer r in lookupRacers["Australia"])
{
    Console.WriteLine(r);
}
```

> **NOTE** *You can read more about extension methods in Chapter 12, "Language Integrated Query." Lambda expressions are explained in Chapter 8, "Delegates, Lambdas, and Events."*

The output shows the racers from Australia:

```
Alan Jones
Jack Brabham
```

Sorted Dictionaries

SortedDictionary<TKey, TValue> is a binary search tree in which the items are sorted based on the key. The key type must implement the interface IComparable<TKey>. If the key type is not sortable, you can also create a comparer implementing IComparer<TKey> and assign the comparer as a constructor argument of the sorted dictionary.

Earlier in this chapter you read about SortedList<TKey, TValue>. SortedDictionary<TKey, TValue> and SortedList<TKey, TValue> have similar functionality, but because SortedList<TKey, TValue> is implemented as a list that is based on an array, and SortedDictionary<TKey, TValue> is implemented as a dictionary, the classes have different characteristics:

➤ SortedList<TKey, TValue> uses less memory than SortedDictionary<TKey, TValue>.

➤ SortedDictionary<TKey, TValue> has faster insertion and removal of elements.

➤ When populating the collection with already sorted data, SortedList<TKey, TValue> is faster if capacity changes are not needed.

> **NOTE** SortedList *consumes less memory than* SortedDictionary. SortedDictionary *is faster with inserts and the removal of unsorted data.*

SETS

A collection that contains only distinct items is known by the term *set*. .NET Core includes two sets, HashSet<T> and SortedSet<T>, that both implement the interface ISet<T>. HashSet<T> contains an unordered list of distinct items; with SortedSet<T> the list is ordered.

The ISet<T> interface offers methods to create a union of multiple sets, to create an intersection of sets, or to provide information if one set is a superset or subset of another.

In the following sample code, three new sets of type string are created and filled with Formula-1 cars. The HashSet<T> class implements the ICollection<T> interface. However, the Add method is implemented explicitly and a different Add method is offered by the class, as you can see here. The Add method differs by the return type; a Boolean value is returned to provide the information if the element was added. If the element was already in the set, it is not added, and false is returned (code file SetSample/Program.cs):

```
var companyTeams = new HashSet<string>()
{ "Ferrari", "McLaren", "Mercedes" };

var traditionalTeams = new HashSet<string>() { "Ferrari", "McLaren" };

var privateTeams = new HashSet<string>()
{ "Red Bull", "Toro Rosso", "Force India", "Sauber" };
```

```
if (privateTeams.Add("Williams"))
{
  Console.WriteLine("Williams added");
}

if (!companyTeams.Add("McLaren"))
{
  Console.WriteLine("McLaren was already in this set");
}
```

The result of these two `Add` methods is written to the console:

```
Williams added
McLaren was already in this set
```

The methods `IsSubsetOf` and `IsSupersetOf` compare a set with a collection that implements the `IEnumerable<T>` interface and returns a Boolean result. Here, `IsSubsetOf` verifies whether every element in `traditionalTeams` is contained in `companyTeams`, which is the case; `IsSupersetOf` verifies whether `traditionalTeams` has any additional elements compared to `companyTeams`:

```
if (traditionalTeams.IsSubsetOf(companyTeams))
{
  Console.WriteLine("traditionalTeams is subset of companyTeams");
}
if (companyTeams.IsSupersetOf(traditionalTeams))
{
  Console.WriteLine("companyTeams is a superset of traditionalTeams");
}
```

The output of this verification is shown here:

```
traditionalTeams is a subset of companyTeams
companyTeams is a superset of traditionalTeams
```

Williams is a traditional team as well, which is why this team is added to the `traditionalTeams` collection:

```
traditionalTeams.Add("Williams");
if (privateTeams.Overlaps(traditionalTeams))
{
  Console.WriteLine("At least one team is the same with traditional " +
    "and private teams");
}
```

Because there's an overlap, this is the result:

```
At least one team is the same with traditional and private teams.
```

The variable `allTeams` that references a new `SortedSet<string>` is filled with a union of `companyTeams`, `privateTeams`, and `traditionalTeams` by calling the `UnionWith` method:

```
var allTeams = new SortedSet<string>(companyTeams);
allTeams.UnionWith(privateTeams);
allTeams.UnionWith(traditionalTeams);
Console.WriteLine();
Console.WriteLine("all teams");
foreach (var team in allTeams)
{
  Console.WriteLine(team);
}
```

Here, all teams are returned but every team is listed just once because the set contains only unique values; and because the container is a `SortedSet<string>`, the result is ordered:

```
Ferrari
Force India
Lotus
```

```
McLaren
Mercedes
Red Bull
Sauber
Toro Rosso
Williams
```

The method `ExceptWith` removes all private teams from the `allTeams` set:

```
allTeams.ExceptWith(privateTeams);
WriteLine();
WriteLine("no private team left");
foreach (var team in allTeams)
{
   Console.WriteLine(team);
}
```

The remaining elements in the collection do not contain any private teams:

```
Ferrari
McLaren
Mercedes
```

PERFORMANCE

Many collection classes offer the same functionality as others; for example, `SortedList` offers nearly the same features as `SortedDictionary`. However, often there's a big difference in performance. Whereas one collection consumes less memory, the other collection class is faster with retrieval of elements. The MSDN documentation often provides performance hints about methods of the collection, giving you information about the time the operation requires in *big-O* notation:

➤ O(1)

➤ O(log n)

➤ O(n)

O(1) means that the time this operation needs is constant no matter how many items are in the collection. For example, the `ArrayList` has an `Add` method with O(1) behavior. No matter how many elements are in the list, it always takes the same amount of time when adding a new element to the end of the list. The `Count` property provides the number of items, so it is easy to find the end of the list.

O(n) means it takes the worst-case time of N to perform an operation on the collection. The `Add` method of `ArrayList` can be an O(n) operation if a reallocation of the collection is required. Changing the capacity causes the list to be copied, and the time for the copy increases linearly with every element.

O(log n) means that the time needed for the operation increases with every element in the collection, but the increase of time for each element is not linear but logarithmic. `SortedDictionary<TKey, TValue>` has O(log n) behavior for inserting operations inside the collection; `SortedList<TKey, TValue>` has O(n) behavior for the same functionality. Here, `SortedDictionary<TKey, TValue>` is a lot faster because it is more efficient to insert elements into a tree structure than into a list.

The following table lists collection classes and their performance for different actions such as adding, inserting, and removing items. Using this table, you can select the best collection class for the purpose of your use. The left column lists the collection class. The Add column gives timing information about adding items to the collection. The `List<T>` and the `HashSet<T>` classes define `Add` methods to add items to the collection. With other collection classes, use a different method to add elements to the collection; for example, the `Stack<T>` class defines a `Push` method, and the `Queue<T>` class defines an `Enqueue` method. You can find this information in the table as well.

If there are multiple big-O values in a cell, the reason is that if a collection needs to be resized, resizing takes a while. For example, with the `List<T>` class, adding items needs O(1). If the capacity of the collection is not large enough and the collection needs to be resized, the resize requires O(n) time. The larger the collection, the longer the resize operation takes. It's best to avoid resizes by setting the capacity of the collection to a value that can hold all the elements.

If the table cell contains *n/a*, the operation is *not applicable* with this collection type.

COLLECTION	ADD	INSERT	REMOVE	ITEM	SORT	FIND
List<T>	O(1) or O(n) if the collection must be resized	O(n)	O(n)	O(1)	O (n log n), worst case O(n ^ 2)	O(n)
Stack<T>	Push, O(1), or O(n) if the stack must be resized	n/a	Pop, O(1)	n/a	n/a	n/a
Queue<T>	Enqueue, O(1), or O(n) if the queue must be resized	n/a	Dequeue, O(1)	n/a	n/a	n/a
HashSet<T>	O(1) or O(n) if the set must be resized	Add O(1) or O(n)	O(1)	n/a	n/a	n/a
SortedSet<T>	O(1) or O(n) if the set must be resized	Add O(1) or O(n)	O(1)	n/a	n/a	n/a
LinkedList<T>	AddLast O(1)	Add After O(1)	O(1)	n/a	n/a	O(n)
Dictionary <TKey, TValue>	O(1) or O(n)	n/a	O(1)	O(1)	n/a	n/a
SortedDictionary-<TKey, TValue>	O(log n)	n/a	O(log n)	O(log n)	n/a	n/a
SortedList <TKey, TValue>	O(n) for unsorted data, O(log n) for end of list, O(n) if resize is needed	n/a	O(n)	O(log n) to read/write, O(log n) if the key is in the list, O(n) if the key is not in the list	n/a	n/a

SUMMARY

This chapter looked at working with different kinds of generic collections. Arrays are fixed in size, but you can use lists for dynamically growing collections. For accessing elements on a first-in, first-out basis, there's a queue; and you can use a stack for last-in, first-out operations. Linked lists allow for fast insertion and removal of elements but are slow for searching. With keys and values, you can use dictionaries, which are fast for searching and inserting elements. Sets are useful for unique items and can be ordered (`SortedSet<T>`) or not ordered (`HashSet<T>`).

Chapter 11, "Special Collections," gives you details about some special collection classes.

11

Special Collections

WROX.COM CODE DOWNLOADS FOR THIS CHAPTER

The Wrox.com code downloads for this chapter are found at http://www.wrox.com on the Download Code tab. The source code is also available at https://github.com/ProfessionalCSharp/ProfessionalCSharp7 in the directory SpecialCollections.

The code for this chapter is divided into the following major examples:

➤ BitArray Sample

➤ BitVector Sample

➤ Observable Collection Sample

➤ Immutable Collections Sample

➤ Pipeline Sample

OVERVIEW

Chapter 10, "Collections," covers lists, queues, stacks, dictionaries, and linked lists. This chapter continues with special collections, such as collections for dealing with bits, collections that can be observed when changed, collections that cannot be changed, and collections that can be accessed from multiple threads simultaneously.

WORKING WITH BITS

If you need to deal with a number of bits, C# 7 has extensions like the binary literal and the number separator that are covered in Chapter 2, "Core C#," and Chapter 6, "Operators and Casts." When you work with binary data, you can also use the class BitArray and the struct BitVector32.

BitArray is located in the namespace System.Collections, and BitVector32 is in the namespace System.Collections.Specialized. The most important difference between these two types is that BitArray is resizable—which is useful if you don't have advance knowledge of the number of bits needed—and it can contain a large number of bits. BitVector32 is stack-based and therefore faster. BitVector32 contains only 32 bits, which are stored in an integer.

BitArray

The class BitArray is a reference type that contains an array of ints, where for every 32 bits a new integer is used. Members of this class are described in the following table.

BITARRAY MEMBERS	DESCRIPTION
Count Length	The get accessor of both Count and Length return the number of bits in the array. With the Length property, you can also define a new size and resize the collection.
Item Get Set	You can use an indexer to read and write bits in the array. The indexer is of type bool. Instead of using the indexer, you can also use the Get and Set methods to access the bits in the array.
SetAll	The method SetAll sets the values of all bits according to the parameter passed to the method.
Not	The method Not generates the inverse of all bits of the array.
And Or Xor	With the methods And, Or, and Xor, you can combine two BitArray objects. The And method does a binary AND, where the result bits are set only if the bits from both input arrays are set. The Or method does a binary OR, where the result bits are set if one or both input arrays are set. The Xor method is an exclusive OR, where the result is set if only one of the input bits is set.

> **NOTE** *In Chapter 6 covers bitwise operators that can be used with number types such as* byte, short, int, *and* long. *The* BitArray *class has similar functionality but can be used with a different number of bits than the C# types.*

The BitArraySample makes use of the following namespaces:

```
System

System.Collections

System.Text
```

The extension method GetBitsFormat iterates through a BitArray and writes 1 or 0 to the console, depending on whether the bit is set. For better readability, a separator character is added every four bits (code file BitArraySample/BitArrayExtensions.cs):

```
public static class BitArrayExtensions
{
  public static string GetBitsFormat(this BitArray bits)
  {
    var sb = new StringBuilder();
    for (int i = bits.Length - 1; i >= 0; i--)
```

```
        {
          sb.Append(bits[i] ? 1 : 0);
          if (i != 0 && i % 4 == 0)
          {
            sb.Append("_");
          }
        }
        return sb.ToString();
      }
    }
```

The example to demonstrate the `BitArray` class creates a bit array with nine bits, indexed from 0 to 8. The `SetAll` method sets all nine bits to `true`. Then the `Set` method changes bit 1 to `false`. Instead of the `Set` method, you can also use an indexer, as shown with index 5 and 7: (code file `BitArraySample/ Program.cs`):

```
var bits1 = new BitArray(9);
bits1.SetAll(true);
bits1.Set(1, false);
bits1[5] = false;
bits1[7] = false;
Console.Write("initialized: ");
Console.WriteLine(bits1.GetBitsFormat());
```

This is the displayed result of the initialized bits:

```
initialized: 1_0101_1101
```

The `Not` method generates the inverse of the bits of the `BitArray`:

```
Console.Write("not ");
Console.Write(bits1.GetBitsFormat());
bits1.Not();
Console.Write(" = ");
Console.WriteLine(bits1.GetBitsFormat());
```

The result of `Not` is all bits inversed. If the bit were `true`, it is `false`; and if it were `false`, it is `true`:

```
not 1_0101_1101 = 0_1010_0010
```

In the following example, a new `BitArray` is created. With the constructor, the variable `bits1` is used to initialize the array, so the new array has the same values. Then the values for bits 0, 1, and 4 are set to different values. Before the `Or` method is used, the bit arrays `bits1` and `bits2` are displayed. The `Or` method changes the values of `bits1`:

```
var bits2 = new BitArray(bits1);
bits2[0] = true;
bits2[1] = false;
bits2[4] = true;
Console.Write($"{bits1.GetBitsFormat()} OR {bits2.GetBitsFormat()}");
Console.Write(" = ");
bits1.Or(bits2);
Console.WriteLine(bits1.GetBitsFormat());
```

With the `Or` method, the set bits are taken from both input arrays. In the result, the bit is set if it was set with either the first or the second array:

```
0_1010_0010 OR 0_1011_0001 = 0_1011_0011
```

Next, the `And` method is used to operate on `bits2` and `bits1`:

```
Console.Write($"{bits2.GetBitsFormat()} AND {bits1.GetBitsFormat()}");
Console.Write(" = ");
bits2.And(bits1);
Console.WriteLine(bits2.GetBitsFormat());
```

The result of the `And` method only sets the bits where the bit was set in both input arrays:

```
0_1011_0001 AND 0_1011_0011 = 0_1011_0001
```

Finally, the `Xor` method is used for an exclusive `OR`:

```
Console.Write($"{bits1.GetBitsFormat()} XOR {bits2.GetBitsFormat()}");
bits1.Xor(bits2);
Console.Write(" = ");
Console.WriteLine(bits1.GetBitsFormat());
```

With the `Xor` method, the resultant bits are set only if the bit was set either in the first or the second input, but not both:

```
0_1011_0011 XOR 0_1011_0001 = 0_0000_0010
```

BitVector32

If you know in advance how many bits you need, you can use the `BitVector32` structure instead of `BitArray`. `BitVector32` is more efficient because it is a value type and stores the bits on the stack inside an integer. With a single integer you have a place for 32 bits. If you need more bits, you can use multiple `BitVector32` values or the `BitArray`. The `BitArray` can grow as needed; this is not an option with `BitVector32`.

The following table shows the members of `BitVector` that are very different from `BitArray`:

BITVECTOR MEMBERS	DESCRIPTION
Data	The property `Data` returns the data behind the `BitVector32` as an integer.
Item	The values for the `BitVector32` can be set using an indexer. The indexer is overloaded; you can get and set the values using a mask or a section of type `BitVector32.Section`.
CreateMask	`CreateMask` is a static method that you can use to create a mask for accessing specific bits in the `BitVector32`.
CreateSection	`CreateSection` is a static method that you can use to create several sections within the 32 bits.

The `BitVectorSample` makes use of the following namespaces:

```
System

System.Collections.Specialized

System.Linq
```

The following example creates a `BitVector32` with the default constructor, whereby all 32 bits are initialized to `false`. Then masks are created to access the bits inside the bit vector. The first call to `CreateMask` creates a mask to access the first bit. After `CreateMask` is invoked, `bit1` has a value of 1. Invoking `CreateMask` once more and passing the first mask as a parameter to `CreateMask` returns a mask to access the second bit, which is 2. `bit3` then has a value of 4 to access bit number 3, and `bit4` has a value of 8 to access bit number 4.

Then the masks are used with the indexer to access the bits inside the bit vector and to set the fields accordingly (code file `BitVectorSample/Program.cs`):

```
var bits1 = new BitVector32();
int bit1 = BitVector32.CreateMask();
```

```
int bit2 = BitVector32.CreateMask(bit1);
int bit3 = BitVector32.CreateMask(bit2);
int bit4 = BitVector32.CreateMask(bit3);
int bit5 = BitVector32.CreateMask(bit4);
bits1[bit1] = true;
bits1[bit2] = false;
bits1[bit3] = true;
bits1[bit4] = true;
bits1[bit5] = true;
Console.WriteLine(bits1);
```

The `BitVector32` has an overridden `ToString` method that not only displays the name of the class but also 1 or 0 if the bits are set or not, respectively:

```
BitVector32{00000000000000000000000000011101}
```

Instead of creating a mask with the `CreateMask` method, you can define the mask yourself; you can also set multiple bits at once. The hexadecimal value `abcdef` is the same as the binary value `1010 1011 1100 1101 1110 1111`. All the bits defined with this value are set:

```
bits1[0xabcdef] = true;
Console.WriteLine(bits1);
```

With the output shown you can verify the bits that are set:

```
BitVector32{00000000101010111100110111101111}
```

Separating the 32 bits to different sections can be extremely useful. For example, an IPv4 address is defined as a four-byte number that is stored inside an integer. You can split the integer by defining four sections. With a multicast IP message, several 32-bit values are used. One of these 32-bit values is separated in these sections: 16 bits for the number of sources, 8 bits for a querier's query interval code, 3 bits for a querier's robustness variable, a 1-bit suppress flag, and 4 bits that are reserved. You can also define your own bit meanings to save memory.

The following example simulates receiving the value `0x79abcdef` and passes this value to the constructor of `BitVector32`, so that the bits are set accordingly:

```
int received = 0x79abcdef;
BitVector32 bits2 = new BitVector32(received);
Console.WriteLine(bits2);
```

The bits are shown on the console as initialized:

```
BitVector32{01111001101010111100110111101111}
```

Then six sections are created. The first section requires 12 bits, as defined by the hexadecimal value `0xfff` (12 bits are set); section B requires 8 bits; section C, 4 bits; sections D and E, 3 bits; and section F, 2 bits. The first call to `CreateSection` just receives `0xfff` to allocate the first 12 bits. With the second call to `CreateSection`, the first section is passed as an argument, so the next section continues where the first section ended. `CreateSection` returns a value of type `BitVector32` `.Section` that contains the offset and the mask for the section:

```
// sections: FF EEE DDD CCCC BBBBBBBB
// AAAAAAAAAAAA
BitVector32.Section sectionA = BitVector32.CreateSection(0xfff);
BitVector32.Section sectionB = BitVector32.CreateSection(0xff, sectionA);
BitVector32.Section sectionC = BitVector32.CreateSection(0xf, sectionB);
BitVector32.Section sectionD = BitVector32.CreateSection(0x7, sectionC);
BitVector32.Section sectionE = BitVector32.CreateSection(0x7, sectionD);
BitVector32.Section sectionF = BitVector32.CreateSection(0x3, sectionE);
```

Passing a `BitVector32.Section` to the indexer of the `BitVector32` returns an int just mapped to the section of the bit vector. As shown next, the extension method, `ToBinaryString`, returns a string representation of the int number:

```
Console.WriteLine($"Section A: {bits2[sectionA].ToBinaryString()}");
Console.WriteLine($"Section B: {bits2[sectionB].ToBinaryString()}");
Console.WriteLine($"Section C: {bits2[sectionC].ToBinaryString()}");
Console.WriteLine($"Section D: {bits2[sectionD].ToBinaryString()}");
Console.WriteLine($"Section E: {bits2[sectionE].ToBinaryString()}");
Console.WriteLine($"Section F: {bits2[sectionF].ToBinaryString()}");
```

The method `ToBinaryString` receives the bits in an integer and returns a string representation containing 0 and 1. With the implementation, the `Convert.ToString` method is used to create a binary representation using the `toBase` parameter value 2. With the `AddSeparators` extension method, after every four bits a separator character is inserted with the help of the `string.Join` method to combine an array to a string, and LINQ methods. LINQ is covered in the next chapter in detail (code file `BitVectorSample/BinaryExtensions.cs`):

```
public static class BinaryExtensions
{
  public static string AddSeparators(this string number) =>
    number.Length <= 4 ? number :
      string.Join("_",
        Enumerable.Range(0, number.Length / 4)
          .Select(i => number.Substring(i * 4, 4)).ToArray());

  public static string ToBinaryString(this int number) =>
    Convert.ToString(number, toBase: 2).AddSeparators();
}
```

The result displays the bit representation of sections A to F, which you can now verify with the value that was passed into the bit vector:

```
Section A: 1101_1110_1111
Section B: 1011_1100
Section C: 1010
Section D: 1
Section E: 111
Section F: 1
```

OBSERVABLE COLLECTIONS

In case you need information when items in the collection are removed or added, you can use the `ObservableCollection<T>` class. This class originally was defined for WPF so that the UI is informed about collection changes. It's now used with Universal Windows Apps the same way. The namespace of this class is `System.Collections.ObjectModel`.

`ObservableCollection<T>` derives from the base class `Collection<T>` that can be used to create custom collections and it uses `List<T>` internally. From the base class, the virtual methods `SetItem` and `RemoveItem` are overridden to fire the `CollectionChanged` event. Clients of this class can register to this event by using the interface `INotifyCollectionChanged`.

The `ObservableCollectionSample` makes use of the following namespaces:

```
System

System.Collections.ObjectModel

System.Collections.Specialized
```

This example demonstrates using an `ObservableCollection<string>` where the method `Data_CollectionChanged` is registered to the `CollectionChanged` event. Two items are added to the end—one item is inserted, and one item is removed (code file `ObservableCollectionSample/Program.cs`):

```
var data = new ObservableCollection<string>();
data.CollectionChanged += Data_CollectionChanged;
data.Add("One");
data.Add("Two");
data.Insert(1, "Three");
data.Remove("One");
```

The method `Data_CollectionChanged` receives `NotifyCollectionChangedEventArgs` containing information about changes to the collection. The `Action` property provides information if an item was added or removed. With removed items, the `OldItems` property is set and lists the removed items. With added items, the `NewItems` property is set and lists the new items:

```
public static void Data_CollectionChanged(object sender,
  NotifyCollectionChangedEventArgs e)
{
  Console.WriteLine($"action: {e.Action.ToString()}");
  if (e.OldItems != null)
  {
    Console.WriteLine($"starting index for old item(s): {e.OldStartingIndex}");
    Console.WriteLine("old item(s):");
    foreach (var item in e.OldItems)
    {
      Console.WriteLine(item);
    }
  }
  if (e.NewItems != null)
  {
    Console.WriteLine($"starting index for new item(s): {e.NewStartingIndex}");
    Console.WriteLine("new item(s): ");
    foreach (var item in e.NewItems)
    {
      Console.WriteLine(item);
    }
  }
  Console.WriteLine();
}
```

Running the application results in the following output. First the items `One` and `Two` are added to the collection, and thus the `Add` action is shown with the index `0` and `1`. The third item, `Three`, is inserted on position 1 so it shows the action `Add` with index `1`. Finally, the item `One` is removed as shown with the action `Remove` and index `0`:

```
action: Add
starting index for new item(s): 0
new item(s):
One
action: Add
starting index for new item(s): 1
new item(s):
Two
action: Add
starting index for new item(s): 1
new item(s):
Three
action: Remove
starting index for old item(s): 0
old item(s):
One
```

IMMUTABLE COLLECTIONS

If an object can change its state, it is hard to use it from multiple simultaneously running tasks. Synchronization is necessary with these collections. If an object cannot change state, it's a lot easier to use it from multiple threads. An object that can't change is an immutable object. Collections that cannot be changed are immutable collections.

> **NOTE** *The topics of using multiple tasks and threads and programming with asynchronous methods are explained in detail in Chapter 15, "Asynchronous Programming," and Chapter 21, "Tasks and Parallel Programming."*

Comparing read-only collections that have been discussed in the previous chapter with immutable collections, there's a big difference: read-only collections make use of an interface to mutable collections. Using this interface, the collection cannot be changed. However, if someone still has a reference to the mutable collection, it still can be changed. With immutable collections, nobody can change this collection.

The `ImmutableCollectionSample` makes use of the following namespaces:

```
System

System.Collections.Generic

System.Collections.Immutable
```

Let's start with a simple immutable string array. You can create the array with the static `Create` method as shown. The `Create` method is overloaded where other variants of this method allow passing any number of elements. Pay attention that two different types are used here: the non-generic `ImmutableArray` class with the static `Create` method and the generic `ImmutableArray` struct that is returned from the `Create` method. In the following code snippet an empty array is created (code file `ImmutableCollectionSample/Program.cs`):

```
ImmutableArray<string> a1 = ImmutableArray.Create<string>();
```

An empty array is not very useful. The `ImmutableArray<T>` type offers an `Add` method to add elements. However, contrary to other collection classes, the `Add` method does not change the immutable collection itself. Instead, a new immutable collection is returned. So, after the call of the `Add` method, a1 is still an empty collection, and a2 is an immutable collection with one element. The `Add` method returns the new immutable collection:

```
ImmutableArray<string> a2 = a1.Add("Williams");
```

With this, it is possible to use this API in a fluent way and invoke one `Add` method after the other. The variable a3 now references an immutable collection containing four elements:

```
ImmutableArray<string> a3 =
    a2.Add("Ferrari").Add("Mercedes").Add("Red Bull Racing");
```

With each of these stages using the immutable array, the complete collections are not copied with every step. Instead, the immutable types make use of shared state and only copy the collection when it's necessary.

However, it's even more efficient to first fill the collection and then make it an immutable array. When some manipulation needs to take place, you can again use a mutable collection. A builder class offered by the immutable types helps with that.

To see this in action, first an `Account` class is created that is put into the collection. This type itself is immutable and cannot be changed by using read-only auto properties (code file `ImmutableCollectionSample/Account.cs`):

```
public class Account
{
  public Account(string name, decimal amount)
  {
    Name = name;
    Amount = amount;
  }

  public string Name { get; }
  public decimal Amount { get; }
}
```

Next a `List<Account>` collection is created and filled with sample accounts (code file `ImmutableCollectionSample/Program.cs`):

```
var accounts = new List<Account>()
{
  new Account("Scrooge McDuck", 667377678765m),
  new Account("Donald Duck", -200m),
  new Account("Ludwig von Drake", 20000m)
};
```

From the accounts collection, an immutable collection can be created with the extension method `ToImmutableList`. This extension method is available as soon as the namespace `System.Collections.Immutable` is opened.

```
ImmutableList<Account> immutableAccounts = accounts.ToImmutableList();
```

The variable `immutableAccounts` can be enumerated like other collections. It just cannot be changed:

```
foreach (var account in immutableAccounts)
{
  Console.WriteLine($"{account.Name} {account.Amount}");
}
```

Instead of using the `foreach` statement to iterate immutable lists, you can use the `ForEach` method that is defined with `ImmutableList<T>`. This method requires an `Action<T>` delegate as parameter and thus a lambda expression can be assigned:

```
immutableAccounts.ForEach(a => Console.WriteLine($"{a.Name} {a.Amount}"));
```

Working with these collections, methods like `Contains`, `FindAll`, `FindLast`, `IndexOf`, and others are available. Because these methods are like the methods from other collection classes discussed in Chapter 10, they are not explicitly shown here.

In case you need to change the content for immutable collections, the collections offer methods like `Add`, `AddRange`, `Remove`, `RemoveAt`, `RemoveRange`, `Replace`, and `Sort`. These methods are very different from normal collection classes as the immutable collection that is used to invoke the methods is never changed, but these methods return a new immutable collection.

Using Builders with Immutable Collections

Creating new immutable collections from existing ones can be done easily with the mentioned `Add`, `Remove`, and `Replace` methods. However, this is not very efficient if you need to do multiple changes such as adding and removing elements for the new collection. For creating new immutable collections by doing more changes, you can create a builder.

Let's continue with the sample code and make multiple changes to the account objects in the collection. For doing this, you can create a builder by invoking the `ToBuilder` method. This method returns a collection that you can change. In the sample code, all accounts with an amount larger than 0 are removed. The original immutable collection is not changed. After the change with the builder is completed, a new immutable collection is created by invoking the `ToImmutable` method of the `Builder`. This collection is used next to output all overdrawn accounts:

```
ImmutableList<Account>.Builder builder = immutableAccounts.ToBuilder();
for (int i = 0; i > builder.Count; i++)
{
  Account a = builder[i];
  if (a.Amount < 0)
  {
    builder.Remove(a);
  }
}
ImmutableList<Account> overdrawnAccounts = builder.ToImmutable();
overdrawnAccounts.ForEach(a =< WriteLine($"{a.Name} {a.Amount}"));
```

Other than removing elements with the `Remove` method, the `Builder` type offers the methods `Add`, `AddRange`, `Insert`, `RemoveAt`, `RemoveAll`, `Reverse`, and `Sort` to change the mutable collection. After finishing the mutable operations, invoke `ToImmutable` to get the immutable collection again.

Immutable Collection Types and Interfaces

Other than `ImmutableArray` and `ImmutableList`, the NuGet package `System.Collections.Immutable` offers some more immutable collection types as shown in the following table:

IMMUTABLE TYPE	DESCRIPTION
`ImmutableArray<T>`	`ImmutableArray<T>` is a struct that uses an array type internally but doesn't allow changes to the underlying type. This struct implements the interface `IImmutableList<T>`.
`ImmutableList<T>`	`ImmutableList<T>` uses a binary tree internally to map the objects and implements the interface `IImmutableList<T>`.
`ImmutableQueue<T>`	`ImmutableQueue<T>` implements the interface `IImmutableQueue<T>` that allows access to elements first-in-first-out with `Enqueue`, `Dequeue`, and `Peek`.
`ImmutableStack<T>`	`ImmutableStack<T>` implements the interface `IImmutableStack<T>` that allows access to elements first-in-last-out with `Push`, `Pop`, and `Peek`.
`ImmutableDictionary<TKey, TValue>`	`ImmutableDictionary<TKey, TValue>` is an immutable collection with unordered key/value pair elements implementing the interface `IImmutableDictionary<TKey, TValue>`.
`ImmutableSortedDictionary<TKey, TValue>`	`ImmutableSortedDictionary<TKey, TValue>` is an immutable collection with ordered key/value pair elements implementing the interface `IImmutableDictionary<TKey, TValue>`.

IMMUTABLE TYPE	DESCRIPTION
ImmutableHashSet<T>	ImmutableHashSet<T> is an immutable unordered hash set implementing the interface IImmutableSet<T>. This interface offers set functionality explained in Chapter 10.
ImmutableSortedSet<T>	ImmutableSortedSet<T> is an immutable ordered set implementing the interface IImmutableSet<T>.

Like the normal collection classes, immutable collections implement interfaces as well—such as IImmutableList<T>, IImmutableQueue<T>, and IImmutableStack<T>. The big difference with these immutable interfaces is that all the methods that make a change in the collection return a new collection.

Using LINQ with Immutable Arrays

For using LINQ with immutable arrays, the class ImmutableArrayExtensions defines optimized versions for LINQ methods such as Where, Aggregate, All, First, Last, Select, and SelectMany. All that you need to use the optimized versions is to directly use the ImmutableArray type and open the System.Linq namespace.

The Where method defined with the ImmutableArrayExtensions type looks like this to extend the ImmutableArray<T> type:

```
public static IEnumerable<T> Where<T>(
this ImmutableArray<T> immutableArray, Func<T, bool> predicate);
```

The normal LINQ extension method extends IEnumerable<T>. Because ImmutableArray<T> is a better match, the optimized version is used calling LINQ methods.

> **NOTE** *LINQ is explained in detail in Chapter 12, "Language Integrated Query."*

CONCURRENT COLLECTIONS

Immutable collections can easily be used from multiple threads because they cannot be changed. In case you want to use collections that should be changed from multiple threads, .NET offers thread-safe collection classes within the namespace System.Collections.Concurrent. Thread-safe collections are guarded against multiple threads accessing them in conflicting ways.

For thread-safe access of collections, the interface IProducerConsumerCollection<T> is defined. The most important methods of this interface are TryAdd and TryTake. TryAdd tries to add an item to the collection, but this might fail if the collection is locked from adding items. To provide this information, the method returns a Boolean value indicating success or failure. TryTake works the same way to inform the caller about success or failure, and returns on success an item from the collection. The following list describes the collection classes from the System.Collections.Concurrent namespace and its functionality:

➤ ConcurrentQueue<T>—This class is implemented with a lock-free algorithm and uses 32 item arrays that are combined in a linked list internally. Methods to access the elements of the queue are Enqueue, TryDequeue, and TryPeek. The naming of these methods is very similar to the methods of Queue<T> that you know already, with the difference of the Try prefix to indicate that the method call might fail.

Because this class implements the interface IProducerConsumerCollection<T>, the methods TryAdd and TryTake just invoke Enqueue and TryDequeue.

➤ `ConcurrentStack<T>`—Very similar to `ConcurrentQueue<T>` but with other item access methods, this class defines the methods `Push`, `PushRange`, `TryPeek`, `TryPop`, and `TryPopRange`. Internally this class uses a linked list of its items.

➤ `ConcurrentBag<T>`—This class doesn't define any order in which to add or take items. It uses a concept that maps threads to arrays used internally and thus tries to reduce locks. The methods to access elements are `Add`, `TryPeek`, and `TryTake`.

➤ `ConcurrentDictionary<TKey, TValue>`—This is a thread-safe collection of keys and values. `TryAdd`, `TryGetValue`, `TryRemove`, and `TryUpdate` are methods to access the members in a nonblocking fashion. Because the items are based on keys and values, `ConcurrentDictionary<TKey, TValue>` does not implement `IProducerConsumerCollection<T>`.

➤ `BlockingCollection<T>`—A collection that blocks and waits until it is possible to do the task by adding or taking the item, `BlockingCollection<T>` offers an interface to add and remove items with the `Add` and `Take` methods. These methods block the thread and wait until the task becomes possible. The `Add` method has an overload whereby you also can pass a `CancellationToken`. This token enables canceling a blocking call. If you don't want the thread to wait for an endless time, and you don't want to cancel the call from the outside, the methods `TryAdd` and `TryTake` are offered as well, whereby you can also specify a timeout value for the maximum amount of time you would like to block the thread and wait before the call should fail.

The `ConcurrentXXX` collection classes are thread-safe, returning false if an action is not possible with the current state of threads. You always have to check whether adding or taking the item was successful before moving on. You can't trust the collection to always fulfill the task.

`BlockingCollection<T>` is a decorator to any class implementing the `IProducerConsumerCollection<T>` interface and by default uses `ConcurrentQueue<T>`. With the constructor you can also pass any other class that implements `IProducerConsumerCollection<T>`—such as `ConcurrentBag<T>` and `ConcurrentStack<T>`.

Creating Pipelines

A great use for these concurrent collection classes is with pipelines. One task writes some content to a collection class while another task can read from the collection at the same time.

The following sample application demonstrates the use of the `BlockingCollection<T>` class with multiple tasks that form a pipeline. The first pipeline is shown in Figure 11-1. The task for the first stage reads filenames and adds them to a queue. While this task is running, the task for stage 2 can already start to read the filenames from the queue and load their content. The result is written to another queue. Stage 3 can be started at the same time to read the content from the second queue and process it. Here, the result is written to a dictionary.

In this scenario, the next stage can only start when stage 3 is completed and the content is finally processed with a full result in the dictionary. The next steps are shown in Figure 11-2. Stage 4 reads from the dictionary, converts the data, and writes it to a queue. Stage 5 adds color information to the items and puts them in another queue. The last stage displays the information. Stages 4 to 6 can run concurrently as well.

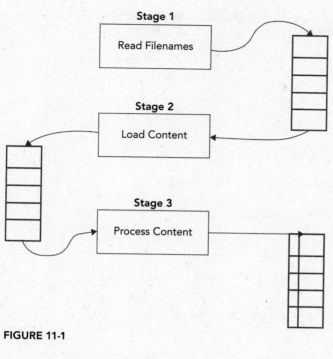

FIGURE 11-1

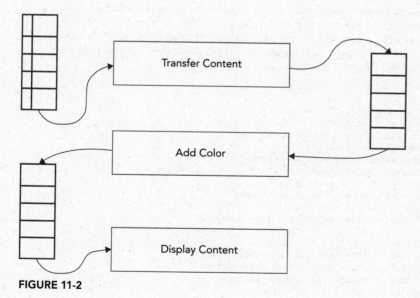

FIGURE 11-2

The `Info` class represents items that are maintained by the pipeline (code file `PipelineSample/Info.cs`):

```csharp
public class Info
{
  public Info(string word, int count)
  {
    Word = word;
    Count = count;
  }

  public string Word { get; }
  public int Count { get; }
  public string Color { get; set; }

  public override string ToString() => $"{Count} times: {Word}";
}
```

The `PipelineSample` makes use of the following namespaces:

> System
>
> System.Collections.Generic
>
> System.Collections.Concurrent
>
> System.IO
>
> System.Linq
>
> System.Threading.Tasks

Looking at the code of this sample application, the complete pipeline is managed within the method `StartPipeline`. Here, the collections are instantiated and passed to the various stages of the pipeline. The first stage is processed with `ReadFilenamesAsync`, and the second and third stages, `LoadContentAsync` and `ProcessContentAsync`, are running simultaneously. The fourth stage, however, can only start when the first three stages are completed (code file `PipelineSample/Program.cs`):

```csharp
public static async Task StartPipelineAsync()
{
  var fileNames = new BlockingCollection<string>();
  var lines = new BlockingCollection<string>();
  var words = new ConcurrentDictionary<string, int>();
  var items = new BlockingCollection<Info>();
  var coloredItems = new BlockingCollection<Info>();
  Task t1 = PipelineStages.ReadFilenamesAsync(@"../../..", fileNames);
  ColoredConsole.WriteLine("started stage 1");
  Task t2 = PipelineStages.LoadContentAsync(fileNames, lines);
  ConsoleHelper.WriteLine("started stage 2");
  Task t3 = PipelineStages.ProcessContentAsync(lines, words);
  await Task.WhenAll(t1, t2, t3);
  ConsoleHelper.WriteLine("stages 1, 2, 3 completed");
  Task t4 = PipelineStages.TransferContentAsync(words, items);
  Task t5 = PipelineStages.AddColorAsync(items, coloredItems);
  Task t6 = PipelineStages.ShowContentAsync(coloredItems);
  ColoredConsole.WriteLine("stages 4, 5, 6 started");
  await Task.WhenAll(t4, t5, t6);
  ColoredConsole.WriteLine("all stages finished");
}
```

> **NOTE** *This example application makes use of tasks and the* async *and* await
> *keywords, which are explained in detail in Chapter 15. You can read more about
> threads, tasks, and synchronization in Chapter 21. File I/O is discussed in Chapter 22,
> "Files and Streams."*

The example writes information to the console using the `ColoredConsole` class. This class provides an easy way to change the color for console output and uses synchronization to avoid returning output with the wrong colors (code file `PipelineSample/ColoredConsole.cs`):

```
public static class ColoredConsole
{
  private static object syncOutput = new object();
  public static void WriteLine(string message)
  {
    lock (syncOutput)
    {
      Console.WriteLine(message);
    }
  }

  public static void WriteLine(string message, string color)
  {
    lock (syncOutput)
    {
      Console.ForegroundColor = (ConsoleColor)Enum.Parse(
        typeof(ConsoleColor), color);
      Console.WriteLine(message);
      Console.ResetColor();
    }
  }
}
```

Using a BlockingCollection

Let's get into the first stage of the pipeline. `ReadFilenamesAsync` receives a `BlockingCollection<T>` where it can write its output. The implementation of this method uses an enumerator to iterate C# files within the specified directory and its subdirectories. The filenames are added to the `BlockingCollection<T>` with the `Add` method. After adding filenames is completed, the `CompleteAdding` method is invoked to inform all readers that they should not wait for any additional items in the collection (code file `PipelineSample/PipelineStages.cs`):

```
public static class PipelineStages
{
  public static Task ReadFilenamesAsync(string path,
    BlockingCollection<string> output)
  {
    return Task.Factory.StartNew(() =>
    {
      foreach (string filename in Directory.EnumerateFiles(path, "*.cs",
        SearchOption.AllDirectories))
      {
        output.Add(filename);
        ColoredConsole.WriteLine($"stage 1: added {filename}");
      }
      output.CompleteAdding();
    }, TaskCreationOptions.LongRunning);
  }
  //. . .
```

> **NOTE** *If you have a reader that reads from a* `BlockingCollection<T>` *at the same time a writer adds items, it is important to invoke the* `CompleteAdding` *method. Otherwise, the reader would wait for more items to arrive within the* `foreach` *loop.*

The next stage is to read the file and add its content to another collection, which is done from the `LoadContentAsync` method. This method uses the filenames passed with the input collection, opens the file, and adds all lines of the file to the output collection. With the `foreach` loop, the method `GetConsumingEnumerable` is invoked with the input blocking collection to iterate the items. It's possible to use the `input` variable directly without invoking `GetConsumingEnumerable`, but this would only iterate the current state of the collection, and not the items that are added afterward.

```
public static async Task LoadContentAsync(BlockingCollection<string> input,
  BlockingCollection<string> output)
{
  foreach (var filename in input.GetConsumingEnumerable())
  {
    using (FileStream stream = File.OpenRead(filename))
    {
      var reader = new StreamReader(stream);
      string line = null;
      while ((line = await reader.ReadLineAsync()) != null)
      {
        output.Add(line);
        ColoredConsole.WriteLine($"stage 2: added {line}");
      }
    }
  }
  output.CompleteAdding();
}
```

> **NOTE** *If a reader is reading a collection at the same time while it is filled, you need to get the enumerator of the blocking collection with the method* `GetConsumingEnumerable` *instead of iterating the collection directly.*

Using a ConcurrentDictionary

Stage 3 is implemented in the `ProcessContentAsync` method. This method gets the lines from the input collection, and then splits and filters words to an output dictionary. The method `AddOrUpdate` is a method from the `ConcurrentDictionary` type. If the key is not yet added to the dictionary, the second parameter defines the value that should be set. If the key is already available in the dictionary, the `updateValueFactory` parameter defines how the value should be changed. In this case, the existing value is just incremented by one:

```
public static Task ProcessContentAsync(BlockingCollection<string> input,
  ConcurrentDictionary<string, int> output)
{
  return Task.Factory.StartNew(() =>
  {
    foreach (var line in input.GetConsumingEnumerable())
    {
      string[] words = line.Split(' ', ';', '\t', '{', '}', '(', ')', ':',
        ',', '"');
      foreach (var word in words.Where(w => !string.IsNullOrEmpty(w)))
      {
        output.AddOrUpdate(key: word, addValue: 1,
```

```
            updateValueFactory: (s, i) => ++i);
          ColoredConsole.WriteLine($"stage 3: added {word}");
        }
      }
    }, TaskCreationOptions.LongRunning);
  }
```

Running the application with the first three stages, you'll see output like the following, where the stages operate interleaved:

```
stage 3: added DisplayBits
stage 3: added bits2
stage 3: added Write
stage 3: added =
stage 3: added bits1.Or
stage 2: added DisplayBits(bits2);
stage 2: added Write(" and ");
stage 2: added DisplayBits(bits1);
stage 2: added WriteLine();
stage 2: added DisplayBits(bits2);
```

Completing the Pipeline

After the first three stages are completed, the next three stages can run in parallel again.
`TransferContentAsync` gets the data from the dictionary, converts it to the type `Info`, and puts it into the output `BlockingCollection<T>` (code file `PipelineSample/PipelineStages.cs`):

```
public static Task TransferContentAsync(
  ConcurrentDictionary<string, int> input,
  BlockingCollection<Info> output)
{
  return Task.Factory.StartNew(() =>
  {
    foreach (var word in input.Keys)
    {
      if (input.TryGetValue(word, out int value))
      {
        var info = new Info { Word = word, Count = value };
        output.Add(info);
        ColoredConsole.WriteLine($"stage 4: added {info}");
      }
    }
    output.CompleteAdding();
  }, TaskCreationOptions.LongRunning);
}
```

The pipeline stage `AddColorAsync` sets the `Color` property of the `Info` type depending on the value of the `Count` property:

```
public static Task AddColorAsync(BlockingCollection<Info> input,
  BlockingCollection<Info> output)
{
  return Task.Factory.StartNew(() =>
  {
    foreach (var item in input.GetConsumingEnumerable())
    {
      if (item.Count > 40)
      {
        item.Color = "Red";
      }
      else if (item.Count > 20)
      {
        item.Color = "Yellow";
      }
```

```
      else
      {
        item.Color = "Green";
      }
      output.Add(item);
      ColoredConsole.WriteLine($"stage 5: added color {item.Color} to {item}");
    }
    output.CompleteAdding();
  }, TaskCreationOptions.LongRunning);
}
```

The last stage writes the resulting items to the console in the specified color:

```
public static Task ShowContentAsync(BlockingCollection<Info> input)
{
  return Task.Factory.StartNew(() =>
  {
    foreach (var item in input.GetConsumingEnumerable())
    {
      ColoredConsole.WriteLine($"stage 6: {item}", item.Color);
    }
  }, TaskCreationOptions.LongRunning);
}
```

Running the application results in the following output, and you'll see that it is colored:

```
stage 6: 20 times: static
stage 6: 3 times: Count
stage 6: 2 times: t2
stage 6: 1 times: bits2[sectionD]
stage 6: 3 times: set
stage 6: 2 times: Console.ReadLine
stage 6: 3 times: started
stage 6: 1 times: builder.Remove
stage 6: 1 times: reader
stage 6: 2 times: bit4
stage 6: 1 times: ForegroundColor
stage 6: 1 times: all
all stages finished
```

SUMMARY

This chapter looked at working with special collections. The chapter introduced you to `BitArray` and `BitVector32`, which are optimized for working with a collection of bits.

Not only bits are stored in the `ObservableCollection<T>` class. This class raises events when items change in the list. Chapters 33 through 37 use this class with Windows and Xamarin apps.

This chapter also explained that immutable collections are a guarantee that the collection never changes, and thus can be easily used in multithreaded applications.

The last part of this chapter looked at concurrent collections where one thread can be used to fill the collection while another thread simultaneously retrieves items from the same collection.

Chapter 12 gives you details about Language Integrated Query (LINQ).

12

Language Integrated Query

WROX.COM CODE DOWNLOADS FOR THIS CHAPTER

The Wrox.com code downloads for this chapter are found at www.wrox.com on the Download Code tab. The source code is also available at https://github.com/ProfessionalCSharp/ProfessionalCSharp7 in the directory LINQ.

The code for this chapter is divided into the following major examples:

➤ LINQ Intro

➤ Enumerable Sample

➤ Parallel LINQ

➤ Expression Trees

LINQ OVERVIEW

LINQ (Language Integrated Query) integrates query syntax inside the C# programming language, making it possible to access different data sources with the same syntax. LINQ accomplishes this by offering an abstraction layer.

This chapter describes the core principles of LINQ and the language extensions for C# that make the C# LINQ Query possible.

> **NOTE** *For details about using LINQ across the database, you should read Chapter 26, "Entity Framework Core." For information about querying XML data, read Bonus Chapter 2, "XML and JSON," (which you can find online) after reading this chapter.*

This chapter starts with a simple LINQ query before diving into the full potential of LINQ. The C# language offers integrated query language that is converted to method calls. This section shows you how the conversion looks so you can use all the possibilities of LINQ.

Lists and Entities

The LINQ queries in this chapter are performed on a collection containing Formula-1 champions from 1950 to 2016. This data needs to be prepared with classes and lists within a .NET Standard library.

This library makes use of these namespaces:

System

System.Collections.Generic

For the entities, the type `Racer` is defined. `Racer` defines several properties and an overloaded `ToString` method to display a racer in a string format. This class implements the interface `IFormattable` to support different variants of format strings, and the interface `IComparable<Racer>`, which can be used to sort a list of racers based on the `LastName`. For more advanced queries, the class `Racer` contains not only single-value properties such as `FirstName`, `LastName`, `Wins Country`, and `Starts`, but also properties that contain a collection, such as `Cars` and `Years`. The `Years` property lists all the years of the championship title. Some racers have won more than one title. The `Cars` property is used to list all the cars used by the driver during the title years (code file `DataLib/Racer.cs`):

```csharp
public class Racer: IComparable<Racer>, IFormattable
{
  public Racer(string firstName, string lastName, string country,
    int starts, int wins)
    : this(firstName, lastName, country, starts, wins, null, null) { }

  public Racer(string firstName, string lastName, string country,
    int starts, int wins, IEnumerable<int> years, IEnumerable<string> cars)
  {
    FirstName = firstName;
    LastName = lastName;
    Country = country;
    Starts = starts;
    Wins = wins;
    Years = years != null ? new List<int>(years) : new List<int>();
    Cars = cars != null ? new List<string>(cars) : new List<string>();
  }

  public string FirstName { get; }
  public string LastName { get; }
  public int Wins { get; }
  public string Country { get; }
  public int Starts { get; }
  public IEnumerable<string> Cars { get; }
  public IEnumerable<int> Years { get; }

  public override string ToString() => $"{FirstName} {LastName}";

  public int CompareTo(Racer other) => LastName.Compare(other?.LastName);

  public string ToString(string format) => ToString(format, null);

  public string ToString(string format, IFormatProvider formatProvider)
  {
    switch (format)
    {
      case null:
```

```
        case "N":
          return ToString();
        case "F":
          return FirstName;
        case "L":
          return LastName;
        case "C":
          return Country;
        case "S":
          return Starts.ToString();
        case "W":
          return Wins.ToString();
        case "A":
          return $"{FirstName} {LastName}, {Country}; starts: {Starts}, wins: {Wins}";
        default:
          throw new FormatException($"Format {format} not supported");
      }
    }
  }
```

A second entity class is `Team`. This class just contains the name and an array of years for constructor championships. Like a driver championship, there's a constructor championship for the best team of a year (code file `DataLib/Team.cs`):

```
public class Team
{
  public Team(string name, params int[] years)
  {
    Name = name;
    Years = years != null ? new List<int>(years) : new List<int>();
  }
  public string Name { get; }
  public IEnumerable<int> Years { get; }
}
```

The class `Formula1` returns a list of racers in the method `GetChampions`. The list is filled with all Formula-1 champions from the years 1950 to 2016 (code file `DataLib/Formula1.cs`):

```
public static class Formula1
{
  private static List<Racer> s_racers;
  public static IList<Racer> GetChampions() => s_racers ??
    (s_racers = InitalizeRacers());

  private static List<Racer> InitializeRacers =>
    new List<Racer>
    {
      new Racer("Nino", "Farina", "Italy", 33, 5, new int[] { 1950 },
        new string[] { "Alfa Romeo" }),
      new Racer("Alberto", "Ascari", "Italy", 32, 10, new int[] { 1952, 1953 },
        new string[] { "Ferrari" }),
      new Racer("Juan Manuel", "Fangio", "Argentina", 51, 24,
        new int[] { 1951, 1954, 1955, 1956, 1957 },
        new string[] { "Alfa Romeo", "Maserati", "Mercedes", "Ferrari" }),
      new Racer("Mike", "Hawthorn", "UK", 45, 3, new int[] { 1958 },
        new string[] { "Ferrari" }),
      new Racer("Phil", "Hill", "USA", 48, 3, new int[] { 1961 },
        new string[] { "Ferrari" }),
      new Racer("John", "Surtees", "UK", 111, 6, new int[] { 1964 },
        new string[] { "Ferrari" }),
      new Racer("Jim", "Clark", "UK", 72, 25, new int[] { 1963, 1965 },
        new string[] { "Lotus" }),
      new Racer("Jack", "Brabham", "Australia", 125, 14,
```

```
            new int[] { 1959, 1960, 1966 }, new string[] { "Cooper", "Brabham" }),
         new Racer("Denny", "Hulme", "New Zealand", 112, 8, new int[] { 1967 },
            new string[] { "Brabham" }),
         new Racer("Graham", "Hill", "UK", 176, 14, new int[] { 1962, 1968 },
            new string[] { "BRM", "Lotus" }),
         new Racer("Jochen", "Rindt", "Austria", 60, 6, new int[] { 1970 },
            new string[] { "Lotus" }),
         new Racer("Jackie", "Stewart", "UK", 99, 27,
            new int[] { 1969, 1971, 1973 }, new string[] { "Matra", "Tyrrell" }),
         //...
      }
      //...
   }
```

Where queries are done across multiple lists, the `GetConstructorChampions` method that follows returns the list of all constructor championships (these championships have been around since 1958):

```
   private static List<Team> s_teams;
   public static IList<Team> GetContructorChampions()
   {
     if (s_teams == null)
     {
       s_teams = new List<Team>()
       {
         new Team("Vanwall", 1958),
         new Team("Cooper", 1959, 1960),
         new Team("Ferrari", 1961, 1964, 1975, 1976, 1977, 1979, 1982, 1983, 1999,
            2000, 2001, 2002, 2003, 2004, 2007, 2008),
         new Team("BRM", 1962),
         new Team("Lotus", 1963, 1965, 1968, 1970, 1972, 1973, 1978),
         new Team("Brabham", 1966, 1967),
         new Team("Matra", 1969),
         new Team("Tyrrell", 1971),
         new Team("McLaren", 1974, 1984, 1985, 1988, 1989, 1990, 1991, 1998),
         new Team("Williams", 1980, 1981, 1986, 1987, 1992, 1993, 1994, 1996,
            1997),
         new Team("Benetton", 1995),
         new Team("Renault", 2005, 2006),
         new Team("Brawn GP", 2009),
         new Team("Red Bull Racing", 2010, 2011, 2012, 1013),
         new Team("Mercedes", 2014, 2015, 2016, 2017)
       };
     }
     return s_teams;
   }
```

LINQ Query

The sample application demonstrating LINQ is a console application using these namespaces:

`System`

`System.Collections.Generic`

`System.Linq`

Using these prepared lists and objects from the previously created library, you can do a LINQ query—for example, a query to get all world champions from Brazil sorted by the highest number of wins. To accomplish this, you could use methods of the `List<T>` class—for example, the `FindAll` and `Sort` methods. However, using LINQ there's a simpler syntax (code file `LINQIntro/Program.cs`):

```
   static void LINQQuery()
   {
```

```
var query = from r in Formula1.GetChampions()
            where r.Country == "Brazil"
            orderby r.Wins descending
            select r;

foreach (Racer r in query)
{
    Console.WriteLine($"{r:A}");
}
}
```

The result of this query shows world champions from Brazil ordered by number of wins:

```
Ayrton Senna, Brazil; starts: 161, wins: 41
Nelson Piquet, Brazil; starts: 204, wins: 23
Emerson Fittipaldi, Brazil; starts: 143, wins: 14
```

The expression

```
from r in Formula1.GetChampions()
where r.Country == "Brazil"
orderby r.Wins descending
select r;
```

is a LINQ query. The clauses `from`, `where`, `orderby`, `descending`, and `select` are predefined keywords in this query.

The query expression must begin with a `from` clause and end with a `select` or `group` clause. In between you can optionally use `where`, `orderby`, `join`, `let`, and additional `from` clauses.

> **NOTE** *The variable* `query` *just has the LINQ query assigned to it. The query is not performed by this assignment, but rather as soon as the query is accessed using the* `foreach` *loop. This is discussed in more detail later in the section "Deferred Query Execution."*

Extension Methods

The compiler converts the LINQ query to invoke method calls instead of the LINQ query. LINQ offers various extension methods for the `IEnumerable<T>` interface, so you can use the LINQ query across any collection that implements this interface. An extension method is defined as a static method whose first parameter defines the type it extends, and it is declared in a static class.

Extension methods make it possible to write a method to a class that doesn't already offer the method at first. You can also add a method to any class that implements a specific interface, so multiple classes can make use of the same implementation.

For example, wouldn't you like to have a `Foo` method with the `String` class? The `String` class is sealed, so it is not possible to inherit from this class; but you can create an extension method, as shown in the following code:

```
public static class StringExtension
{
    public static void Foo(this string s)
    {
        Console.WriteLine($"Foo invoked for {s}");
    }
}
```

The `Foo` method extends the `string` class, as is defined with the first parameter. For differentiating extension methods from normal static methods, the extension method also requires the `this` keyword with the first parameter.

Indeed, it is now possible to use the `Foo` method with the `string` type:

```
string s = "Hello";
s.Foo();
```

The result shows `Foo` invoked for `Hello` in the console, because `Hello` is the string passed to the `Foo` method.

This might appear to be breaking object-oriented rules because a new method is defined for a type without changing the type or deriving from it. However, this is not the case. The extension method cannot access private members of the type it extends. Calling an extension method is just a new syntax for invoking a static method. With the string you can get the same result by calling the method `Foo` this way:

```
string s = "Hello";
StringExtension.Foo(s);
```

To invoke the static method, write the class name followed by the method name. Extension methods are a different way to invoke static methods. You don't have to supply the name of the class where the static method is defined. Instead, because of the parameter type the static method is selected by the compiler. You just import the namespace that contains the class to get the `Foo` extension method in the scope of the `String` class.

One of the classes that define LINQ extension methods is `Enumerable` in the namespace `System.Linq`. You just import the namespace to open the scope of the extension methods of this class. A sample implementation of the `Where` extension method is shown in the following code. The first parameter of the `Where` method that includes the `this` keyword is of type `IEnumerable<T>`. This enables the `Where` method to be used with every type that implements `IEnumerable<T>`. A few examples of types that implement this interface are arrays and `List<T>`. The second parameter is a `Func<T, bool>` delegate that references a method that returns a Boolean value and requires a parameter of type `T`. This predicate is invoked within the implementation to examine whether the item from the `IEnumerable<T>` source should be added into the destination collection. If the method is referenced by the delegate, the `yield return` statement returns the item from the source to the destination:

```
public static IEnumerable<TSource> Where<TSource>(
  this IEnumerable<TSource> source,
  Func<TSource, bool> predicate)
{
  foreach (TSource item in source)
  {
    if (predicate(item))
      yield return item;
  }
}
```

Because `Where` is implemented as a generic method, it works with any type that is contained in a collection. Any collection implementing `IEnumerable<T>` is supported.

> **NOTE** *The extension methods here are defined in the namespace* `System.Linq` *in the assembly* `System.Core`.

Now it's possible to use the extension methods `Where`, `OrderByDescending`, and `Select` from the class `Enumerable`. Because each of these methods returns `IEnumerable<TSource>`, it is possible to invoke one method after the other by using the previous result. With the arguments of the extension methods, anonymous methods that define the implementation for the delegate parameters are used (code file `LINQIntro/Program.cs`):

```
static void ExtensionMethods()
{
  var champions = new List<Racer>(Formula1.GetChampions());
  IEnumerable<Racer> brazilChampions =
    champions.Where(r =< r.Country == "Brazil")
      .OrderByDescending(r =< r.Wins)
      .Select(r =< r);

  foreach (Racer r in brazilChampions)
  {
    Console.WriteLine($"{r:A}");
  }
}
```

Deferred Query Execution

During runtime, the query expression does not run immediately as it is defined. The query runs only when the items are iterated.

Let's have a look once more at the extension method `Where`. This extension method makes use of the `yield return` statement to return the elements where the predicate is true. Because the `yield return` statement is used, the compiler creates an enumerator and returns the items as soon as they are accessed from the enumeration:

```
public static IEnumerable<T> Where<T>(this IEnumerable<T> source,
  Func<T, bool> predicate)
  {
    foreach (T item in source)
    {
      if (predicate(item))
      {
        yield return item;
      }
    }
  }
}
```

This has a very interesting and important effect. In the following example a collection of `string` elements is created and filled with first names. Next, a query is defined to get all names from the collection whose first letter is J. The collection should also be sorted. The iteration does not happen when the query is defined. Instead, the iteration happens with the `foreach` statement, where all items are iterated. Only one element of the collection fulfills the requirements of the `where` expression by starting with the letter J: Juan. After the iteration is done and `Juan` is written to the console, four new names are added to the collection. Then the iteration is done again (code file `LINQIntro/Program.cs`):

```
static void DeferredQuery()
{
  var names = new List<string> { "Nino", "Alberto", "Juan", "Mike", "Phil" };
  var namesWithJ = from n in names
                   where n.StartsWith("J")
                   orderby n
                   select n;

  Console.WriteLine("First iteration");
  foreach (string name in namesWithJ)
  {
    Console.WriteLine(name);
  }
  Console.WriteLine();
```

```
    names.Add("John");
    names.Add("Jim");
    names.Add("Jack");
    names.Add("Denny");
    Console.WriteLine("Second iteration");

    foreach (string name in namesWithJ)
    {
        Console.WriteLine(name);
    }
```

Because the iteration does not happen when the query is defined, but does happen with every foreach, changes can be seen, as the output from the application demonstrates:

```
First iteration
Juan
Second iteration
Jack
Jim
John
Juan
```

Of course, you also must be aware that the extension methods are invoked every time the query is used within an iteration. Most of the time this is very practical, because you can detect changes in the source data. However, sometimes this is impractical. You can change this behavior by invoking the extension methods ToArray, ToList, and the like. In the following example, you can see that ToList iterates through the collection immediately and returns a collection implementing IList<string>. The returned list is then iterated through twice; in between iterations, the data source gets new names:

```
var names = new List<string> { "Nino", "Alberto", "Juan", "Mike", "Phil" };
var namesWithJ = (from n in names
                  where n.StartsWith("J")
                  orderby n
                  select n).ToList();

Console.WriteLine("First iteration");
foreach (string name in namesWithJ)
{
    Console.WriteLine(name);
}
Console.WriteLine();

names.Add("John");
names.Add("Jim");
names.Add("Jack");
names.Add("Denny");
Console.WriteLine("Second iteration");
foreach (string name in namesWithJ)
{
    Console.WriteLine(name);
}
```

The result indicates that in between the iterations the output stays the same although the collection values have changed:

```
First iteration
Juan
Second iteration
Juan
```

STANDARD QUERY OPERATORS

Where, OrderByDescending, and Select are only a few of the query operators defined by LINQ. The LINQ query defines a declarative syntax for the most common operators. There are many more query operators available with the Enumerable class.

The following table lists the standard query operators defined by the Enumerable class.

STANDARD QUERY OPERATORS	DESCRIPTION
Where OfType<TResult>	*Filtering operators* define a restriction to the elements returned. With the Where query operator you can use a predicate; for example, a Lambda expression that returns a bool. OfType<TResult> filters the elements based on the type and returns only the elements of the type TResult.
Select SelectMany	*Projection operators* are used to transform an object into a new object of a different type. Select and SelectMany define a projection to select values of the result based on a selector function.
OrderBy ThenBy OrderByDescending ThenByDescending Reverse	*Sorting operators* change the order of elements returned. OrderBy sorts values in ascending order; OrderByDescending sorts values in descending order. ThenBy and ThenByDescending operators are used for a secondary sort if the first sort gives similar results. Reverse reverses the elements in the collection.
Join GroupJoin	*Join operators* are used to combine collections that might not be directly related to each other. With the Join operator a join of two collections based on key selector functions can be done. This is like the JOIN you know from SQL. The GroupJoin operator joins two collections and groups the results.
GroupBy ToLookup	*Grouping operators* put the data into groups. The GroupBy operator groups elements with a common key. ToLookup groups the elements by creating a one-to-many dictionary.
Any All Contains	*Quantifier operators* return a Boolean value if elements of the sequence satisfy a specific condition. Any, All, and Contains are quantifier operators. Any determines whether any element in the collection satisfies a predicate function; All determines whether all elements in the collection satisfy a predicate. Contains checks whether a specific element is in the collection.
Take Skip TakeWhile SkipWhile	*Partitioning operators* return a subset of the collection. Take, Skip, TakeWhile, and SkipWhile are partitioning operators. With these, you get a partial result. With Take, you have to specify the number of elements to take from the collection; Skip ignores the specified number of elements and takes the rest. TakeWhile takes the elements as long as a condition is true. SkipWhile skips the elements if the condition is true.
Distinct Union Intersect Except Zip	*Set operators* return a collection set. Distinct removes duplicates from a collection. With the exception of Distinct, the other set operators require two collections. Union returns unique elements that appear in either of the two collections. Intersect returns elements that appear in both collections. Except returns elements that appear in just one collection. Zip combines two collections into one.

continues

(continued)

STANDARD QUERY OPERATORS	DESCRIPTION
First FirstOrDefault Last LastOrDefault ElementAt ElementAtOrDefault Single SingleOrDefault	*Element operators* return just one element. First returns the first element that satisfies a condition. FirstOrDefault is like First, but it returns a default value of the type if the element is not found. Last returns the last element that satisfies a condition. With ElementAt, you specify the position of the element to return. Single returns only the one element that satisfies a condition. If more than one element satisfies the condition, an exception is thrown. All the XXOrDefault methods are like the methods that start with the same prefix, but they return the default value of the type if the element is not found.
Count Sum Min Max Average Aggregate	*Aggregate operators* compute a single value from a collection. With aggregate operators, you can get the sum of all values, the number of all elements, the element with the lowest or highest value, an average number, and so on.
ToArray AsEnumerable ToList ToDictionary Cast\<TResult\>	*Conversion operators* convert the collection to an array: IEnumerable, IList, IDictionary, and so on. The Cast method casts every item of the collection to the generic argument type.
Empty Range Repeat	*Generation* operators return a new sequence. The collection is empty using the Empty operator; Range returns a sequence of numbers, and Repeat returns a collection with one repeated value.

The following sections provide examples demonstrating how to use these operators.

Filtering

This section looks at some examples for a query. The sample application is a console application making use of these namespaces:

```
System
System.Collections.Generic
System.Linq
```

This sample application available with the code download offers passing command-line arguments for every different feature shown. In the Debug section in the Properties page, you can configure the command-line arguments as needed to run the different sections of the application. Using the command line, you can invoke the commands using the .NET Core command-line utility in this way:

```
dotnet run -- -f
```

which passes the argument -f to the application.

With the where clause, you can combine multiple expressions—for example, get only the racers from Brazil and Austria who won more than 15 races. The result type of the expression passed to the where clause just needs to be of type bool (code file EnumerableSample/FilteringSamples.cs):

```csharp
static void Filtering()
{
  var racers = from r in Formula1.GetChampions()
               where r.Wins > 15 &&
               (r.Country == "Brazil" || r.Country == "Austria")
               select r;

  foreach (var r in racers)
  {
    Console.WriteLine($"{r:A}");
  }
}
```

Starting the program with this LINQ query returns Niki Lauda, Nelson Piquet, and Ayrton Senna, as shown here:

```
Niki Lauda, Austria, Starts: 173, Wins: 25
Nelson Piquet, Brazil, Starts: 204, Wins: 23
Ayrton Senna, Brazil, Starts: 161, Wins: 41
```

Not all queries can be done with the LINQ query syntax, and not all extension methods are mapped to LINQ query clauses. Advanced queries require using extension methods. To better understand complex queries with extension methods, it's good to see how simple queries are mapped. Using the extension methods Where and Select produces a query very similar to the LINQ query done before (code file EnumerableSample/FilteringSamples.cs):

```csharp
static void FilteringWithMethods()
{
  var racers = Formula1.GetChampions()
    .Where(r => r.Wins > 15 &&
      (r.Country == "Brazil" || r.Country == "Austria"))
      .Select(r => r);
  //...
}
```

Filtering with Index

One scenario in which you can't use the LINQ query is an overload of the Where method. With an overload of the 3Where method, you can pass a second parameter that is the index. The index is a counter for every result returned from the filter. You can use the index within the expression to do some calculation based on the index. In the following example, the index is used within the code that is called by the Where extension method to return only racers whose last name starts with A if the index is even (code file EnumerableSample/FilteringSamples.cs):

```csharp
static void FilteringWithIndex()
{
  var racers = Formula1.GetChampions()
    .Where((r, index) => r.LastName.StartsWith("A") && index % 2 != 0);

  foreach (var r in racers)
  {
    Console.WriteLine($"{r:A}");
  }
}
```

The racers with last names beginning with the letter A are Alberto Ascari, Mario Andretti, and Fernando Alonso. Because Mario Andretti is positioned within an index that is odd, he is not in the result:

```
Alberto Ascari, Italy; starts: 32, wins: 10
Fernando Alonso, Spain; starts: 279, wins: 33
```

Type Filtering

For filtering based on a type you can use the `OfType` extension method. Here the array data contains both `string` and `int` objects. Using the extension method `OfType`, passing the string class to the generic parameter returns only the strings from the collection (code file EnumerableSample/FilteringSamples.cs):

```
static void TypeFiltering()
{
  object[] data = { "one", 2, 3, "four", "five", 6 };
  var query = data.OfType<string>();

  foreach (var s in query)
  {
    Console.WriteLine(s);
  }
}
```

Running this code, the strings one, four, and five are displayed:

```
one
four
five
```

Compound from

If you need to do a filter based on a member of the object that itself is a sequence, you can use a compound `from`. The `Racer` class defines a property `Cars`, where `Cars` is a string array. For a filter of all racers who were champions with a Ferrari, you can use the LINQ query shown next. The first `from` clause accesses the `Racer` objects returned from `Formula1.GetChampions`. The second `from` clause accesses the `Cars` property of the `Racer` class to return all cars of type `string`. Next the cars are used with the where clause to filter only the racers who were champions with a Ferrari (code file EnumerableSample/CompoundFromSamples.cs):

```
static void CompoundFrom()
{
  var ferrariDrivers = from r in Formula1.GetChampions()
                       from c in r.Cars
                       where c == "Ferrari"
                       orderby r.LastName
                       select r.FirstName + " " + r.LastName;
  //...
}
```

If you are curious about the result of this query, following are all Formula-1 champions driving a Ferrari:

```
Alberto Ascari
Juan Manuel Fangio
Mike Hawthorn
Phil Hill
Niki Lauda
Kimi Räikkönen
Jody Scheckter
Michael Schumacher
John Surtees
```

The C# compiler converts a compound `from` clause with a LINQ query to the `SelectMany` extension method. `SelectMany` can be used to iterate a sequence of a sequence. The overload of the `SelectMany` method that is used with the example is shown here:

```
public static IEnumerable<TResult> SelectMany<TSource, TCollection, TResult> (
    this IEnumerable<TSource> source,
    Func<TSource,
    IEnumerable<TCollection>> collectionSelector,
    Func<TSource, TCollection, TResult> resultSelector);
```

The first parameter is the implicit parameter that receives the sequence of `Racer` objects from the `GetChampions` method. The second parameter is the `collectionSelector` delegate where the inner sequence is defined. With the lambda expression `r => r.Cars`, the collection of cars should be returned. The third parameter is a delegate that is now invoked for every car and receives the `Racer` and `Car` objects. The lambda expression creates an anonymous type with a `Racer` and a `Car` property. Because of this `SelectMany` method, the hierarchy of racers and cars is flattened and a collection of new objects of an anonymous type for every car is returned.

This new collection is passed to the `Where` method so that only the racers driving a Ferrari are filtered. Finally, the `OrderBy` and `Select` methods are invoked (code file `EnumerableSample/ CompoundFromSamples.cs`):

```
static void CompoundFromWithMethods()
{
    var ferrariDrivers = Formula1.GetChampions()
        .SelectMany(r => r.Cars, (r, c) => new { Racer = r, Car = c })
        .Where(r => r.Car == "Ferrari")
        .OrderBy(r => r.Racer.LastName)
        .Select(r => r.Racer.FirstName + " " + r.Racer.LastName);
    //...
}
```

Resolving the generic `SelectMany` method to the types that are used here, the types are resolved as follows. In this case the source is of type `Racer`, the filtered collection is a `string` array, and of course the name of the anonymous type that is returned is not known and is shown here as `TResult`:

```
public static IEnumerable<TResult> SelectMany<Racer, string, TResult> (
    this IEnumerable<Racer> source,
    Func<Racer, IEnumerable<string>> collectionSelector,
    Func<Racer, string, TResult> resultSelector);
```

Because the query was just converted from a LINQ query to extension methods, the result is the same as before.

Sorting

To sort a sequence, the `orderby` clause was used already. This section reviews the earlier example, now with the `orderby descending` clause. Here the racers are sorted based on the number of wins as specified by the key selector in descending order (code file `EnumerableSample/SortingSamples.cs`):

```
static void SortDescending()
{
    var racers = from r in Formula1.GetChampions()
                 where r.Country == "Brazil"
                 orderby r.Wins descending
                 select r;
    //...
}
```

The orderby clause is resolved to the OrderBy method, and the orderby descending clause is resolved to the OrderByDescending method (code file EnumerableSample/SortingSamples.cs):

```
static void SortDescendingWithMethods()
{
  var racers = Formula1.GetChampions()
    .Where(r => r.Country == "Brazil")
    .OrderByDescending(r => r.Wins)
    .Select(r => r);
  //...
}
```

The OrderBy and OrderByDescending methods return IOrderedEnumerable<TSource>. This interface derives from the interface IEnumerable<TSource> but contains an additional method, CreateOrdered-Enumerable<TSource>. This method is used for further ordering of the sequence. If two items are the same based on the key selector, ordering can continue with the ThenBy and ThenByDescending methods. These methods require an IOrderedEnumerable<TSource> to work on but return this interface as well. Therefore, you can add any number of ThenBy and ThenByDescending methods to sort the collection.

Using the LINQ query, you just add all the different keys (with commas) for sorting to the orderby clause. In the next example, the sort of all racers is done first based on country, next on last name, and finally on first name. The Take extension method that is added to the result of the LINQ query is used to return the first 10 results (code file EnumerableSample/SortingSamples.cs):

```
static void SortMultiple()
{
  var racers = (from r in Formula1.GetChampions()
                orderby r.Country, r.LastName, r.FirstName
                select r).Take(10);
  //...
}
```

The sorted result is shown here:

```
Argentina: Fangio, Juan Manuel
Australia: Brabham, Jack
Australia: Jones, Alan
Austria: Lauda, Niki
Austria: Rindt, Jochen
Brazil: Fittipaldi, Emerson
Brazil: Piquet, Nelson
Brazil: Senna, Ayrton
Canada: Villeneuve, Jacques
Finland: Hakkinen, Mika
```

Doing the same with extension methods makes use of the OrderBy and ThenBy methods (code file EnumerableSample/SortingSamples.cs):

```
static void SortMultipleWithMethods()
{
  var racers = Formula1.GetChampions()
    .OrderBy(r => r.Country)
    .ThenBy(r => r.LastName)
    .ThenBy(r => r.FirstName)
    .Take(10);
  //...
}
```

Grouping

To group query results based on a key value, the `group` clause can be used. Now the Formula-1 champions should be grouped by country, and the number of champions within a country should be listed. The clause `group r by r.Country into g` groups all the racers based on the `Country` property and defines a new identifier `g` that can be used later to access the group result information. The result from the `group` clause is ordered based on the extension method `Count` that is applied on the group result; and if the count is the same, the ordering is done based on the key. This is the country because this was the key used for grouping. The `where` clause filters the results based on groups that have at least two items, and the `select` clause creates an anonymous type with the `Country` and `Count` properties (code file `EnumerableSample/GroupingSamples.cs`):

```
static void Grouping()
{
  var countries = from r in Formula1.GetChampions()
                  group r by r.Country into g
                  orderby g.Count() descending, g.Key
                  where g.Count() >= 2
                  select new
                  {
                    Country = g.Key,
                    Count = g.Count()
                  };

  foreach (var item in countries)
  {
    Console.WriteLine($"{item.Country, -10} {item.Count}");
  }
}
```

The result displays the collection of objects with the `Country` and `Count` properties:

```
UK          10
Brazil      3
Finland     3
Germany     3
Australia   2
Austria     2
Italy       2
USA         2
```

Doing the same with extension methods, the `groupby` clause is resolved to the `GroupBy` method. What's interesting with the declaration of the `GroupBy` method is that it returns an enumeration of objects implementing the `IGrouping` interface. The `IGrouping` interface defines the `Key` property, so you can access the key of the group after defining the call to this method:

```
public static IEnumerable<IGrouping<TKey, TSource>> GroupBy<TSource, TKey>(
    this IEnumerable<TSource> source, Func<TSource, TKey> keySelector);
```

The `group r by r.Country into g` clause is resolved to `GroupBy(r => r.Country)` and returns the group sequence. The group sequence is first ordered by the `OrderByDescending` method, then by the `ThenBy` method. Next, the `Where` and `Select` methods that you already know are invoked (code file `EnumerableSample/GroupingSamples.cs`):

```
static void GroupingWithMethods()
{
  var countries = Formula1.GetChampions()
    .GroupBy(r => r.Country)
    .OrderByDescending(g => g.Count())
```

```
      .ThenBy(g => g.Key)
      .Where(g => g.Count() >= 2)
      .Select(g => new
      {
        Country = g.Key,
        Count = g.Count()
      });
```

Variables Within the LINQ Query

With the LINQ query as it is written for grouping, the Count method is called multiple times. You can change this by using the let clause. let allows defining variables within the LINQ query (code file EnumerableSample/GroupingSamples.cs):

```
static void GroupingWithVariables()
{
  var countries = from r in Formula1.GetChampions()
                  group r by r.Country into g
                  let count = g.Count()
                  orderby count descending, g.Key
                  where count >= 2
                  select new
                  {
                    Country = g.Key,
                    Count = count
                  };
  //...
}
```

Using the method syntax, the Count method was invoked multiple times as well. To define extra data to pass to the next method (what is really done by the let clause), you can use the Select method to create anonymous types. Here an anonymous type with Group and Count properties is created. A collection of items with these properties is passed to the OrderByDescending method where the sort is based on the Count property of this anonymous type:

```
static void GroupingWithAnonymousTypes()
{
  var countries = Formula1.GetChampions()
    .GroupBy(r => r.Country)
    .Select(g => new { Group = g, Count = g.Count() })
    .OrderByDescending(g => g.Count)
    .ThenBy(g => g.Group.Key)
    .Where(g => g.Count >= 2)
    .Select(g => new
    {
      Country = g.Group.Key,
      Count = g.Count
    });
  //...
}
```

Take care with the number of interim objects created based on the let clause or Select method. When you query through large lists, the number of objects created that need to be garbage collected later can have a huge impact on performance.

Grouping with Nested Objects

If the grouped objects should contain nested sequences, you can do that by changing the anonymous type created by the select clause. With this example, the returned countries should contain not only the properties for the name of the country and the number of racers, but also a sequence of the names of the racers.

This sequence is assigned by using an inner `from`/`in` clause assigned to the `Racers` property. The inner `from` clause is using the `g` group to get all racers from the group, order them by last name, and create a new string based on the first and last name (code file `EnumerableSample/GroupingSamples.cs`):

```
static void GroupingAndNestedObjects()
{
  var countries = from r in Formula1.GetChampions()
                  group r by r.Country into g
                  let count = g.Count()
                  orderby count descending, g.Key
                  where count >= 2
                  select new
                  {
                    Country = g.Key,
                    Count = count,
                    Racers = from r1 in g
                             orderby r1.LastName
                             select r1.FirstName + " " + r1.LastName
                  };

  foreach (var item in countries)
  {
    Console.WriteLine($"{item.Country, -10} {item.Count}");
    foreach (var name in item.Racers)
    {
      Console.Write($"{name}; ");
    }
    Console.WriteLine();
  }
}
```

Using extension methods, the inner `Racer` objects are created using the group variable `g` of type `IGrouping` where the `Key` property is the key for the grouping—the country in this case—and the items of a group can be accessed using the `Group` property:

```
static void GroupingAndNestedObjectsWithMethods()
{
  var countries = Formula1.GetChampions()
    .GroupBy(r => r.Country)
    .Select(g => new
    {
      Group = g,
      Key = g.Key,
      Count = g.Count()
    })
    .OrderByDescending(g => g.Count)
    .ThenBy(g => g.Key)
    .Where(g => g.Count >= 2)
    .Select(g => new
    {
      Country = g.Key,
      Count = g.Count,
      Racers = g.Group.OrderBy(r => r.LastName)
        .Select(r => r.FirstName + " " + r.LastName)
    });
  //...
}
```

The output now lists all champions from the specified countries:

```
UK         10
Jenson Button; Jim Clark; Lewis Hamilton; Mike Hawthorn; Graham Hill;
Damon Hill; James Hunt; Nigel Mansell; Jackie Stewart; John Surtees;
```

```
Brazil       3
Emerson Fittipaldi; Nelson Piquet; Ayrton Senna;
Finland      3
Mika Hakkinen; Kimi Raikkonen; Keke Rosberg;
Germany      3
Nico Rosberg; Michael Schumacher; Sebastian Vettel;
Australia    2
Jack Brabham; Alan Jones;
Austria      2
Niki Lauda; Jochen Rindt;
Italy        2
Alberto Ascari; Nino Farina;
USA          2
Mario Andretti; Phil Hill;
```

Inner Join

You can use the `join` clause to combine two sources based on specific criteria. First, however, let's get two lists that should be joined. With Formula-1, there are drivers and a constructor champions. The drivers are returned from the method `GetChampions`, and the constructors are returned from the method `GetConstructorChampions`. It would be interesting to get a list by year in which every year lists the driver and the constructor champions.

To do this, the first two queries for the racers and the teams are defined (code file `EnumerableSample/JoinSamples.cs`):

```
static void InnerJoin()
{
   var racers = from r in Formula1.GetChampions()
                from y in r.Years
                select new
                {
                  Year = y,
                  Name = r.FirstName + " " + r.LastName
                };

   var teams = from t in Formula1.GetContructorChampions()
               from y in t.Years
               select new
               {
                 Year = y,
                 Name = t.Name
               };
   //...
}
```

Using these two queries, a join is done based on the year of the driver champion and the year of the team champion with the `join` clause. The `select` clause defines a new anonymous type containing `Year`, `Racer`, and `Team` properties:

```
var racersAndTeams = (from r in racers
                      join t in teams on r.Year equals t.Year
                      select new
                      {
                        r.Year,
                        Champion = r.Name,
                        Constructor = t.Name
                      }).Take(10);
Console.WriteLine("Year World Champion\t Constructor Title");
```

```
foreach (var item in racersAndTeams)
{
  Console.WriteLine($"{item.Year}: {item.Champion,-20} {item.Constructor}");
}
```

Of course, you can also combine this into just one LINQ query, but that's a matter of taste:

```
var racersAndTeams =
  (from r in
   from r1 in Formula1.GetChampions()
   from yr in r1.Years
   select new
   {
     Year = yr,
     Name = r1.FirstName + " " + r1.LastName
   }
   join t in
     from t1 in Formula1.GetContructorChampions()
     from yt in t1.Years
     select new
     {
       Year = yt,
       Name = t1.Name
     }
   on r.Year equals t.Year
   orderby t.Year
   select new
   {
     Year = r.Year,
     Racer = r.Name,
     Team = t.Name
   }).Take(10);
```

Using extension methods, the racers and teams can be joined by invoking the Join method, passing the teams with the first argument to join them with the racers, specifying the key selectors for the outer and the inner collection, and defining the result selector with the last argument (code file EnumerableSample/JoinSamples.cs):

```
static void InnerJoinWithMethods()
{
  var racers = Formula1.GetChampions()
    .SelectMany(r => r.Years, (r1, year) =>
    new
    {
      Year = year,
      Name = $"{r1.FirstName} {r1.LastName}"
    });

  var teams = Formula1.GetConstructorChampions()
    .SelectMany(t => t.Years, (t, year) =>
    new
    {
      Year = year,
      Name = t.Name
    });

  var racersAndTeams = racers.Join(
    teams,
    r => r.Year,
    t => t.Year,
    (r, t) =>
      new
```

```
        {
          Year = r.Year,
          Champion = r.Name,
          Constructor = t.Name
        }).OrderBy(item => item.Year).Take(10);
    //...
    }
```

The output displays data from the anonymous type for the first 10 years in which both a drivers' and constructor championship took place:

```
Year World Champion Constructor Title
1958: Mike Hawthorn Vanwall
1959: Jack Brabham Cooper
1960: Jack Brabham Cooper
1961: Phil Hill Ferrari
1962: Graham Hill BRM
1963: Jim Clark Lotus
1964: John Surtees Ferrari
1965: Jim Clark Lotus
1966: Jack Brabham Brabham
1967: Denny Hulme Brabham
```

Figure 12-1 shows a graphical presentation of two collections combined with an inner join. Using an inner join, the results are matches with both collections.

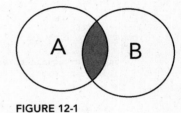

FIGURE 12-1

Left Outer Join

The output from the previous join sample started with the year 1958—
the first year when both the drivers' and constructor championship started. The drivers' championship started earlier, in the year 1950. With an inner join, results are returned only when matching records are found. To get a result with all the years included, you can use a *left outer join*. A left outer join returns all the elements in the left sequence even when no match is found in the right sequence.

The earlier LINQ query is changed to a left outer join. A left outer join is defined with the join clause together with the DefaultIfEmpty method. If the left side of the query (the racers) does not have a matching constructor champion, the default value for the right side is defined by the DefaultIfEmpty method (code file EnumerableSample/JoinSamples.cs):

```
static void LeftOuterJoin()
{
  //...
  var racersAndTeams =
    (from r in racers
     join t in teams on r.Year equals t.Year into rt
     from t in rt.DefaultIfEmpty()
     orderby r.Year
     select new
     {
       Year = r.Year,
       Champion = r.Name,
       Constructor = t == null ? "no constructor championship" : t.Name
     }).Take(10);
  //...
  }
```

Doing the same query with the extension methods, the GroupJoin method is used. The first three parameters are similar with Join and GroupJoin. The result of GroupJoin is different. Instead of a flat list that is returned from the Join method, GroupJoin returns a list where every matching item of the first list contains a list of matches from the second list. Using the following `SelectMany` method, the list is flattened again. In case no teams are available for a match, the `Constructors` property is assigned to the default value of the type, which is null with classes. When you create the anonymous type, the `Constructor` property gets the string "no constructor championship" assigned if the team is `null` (code file `EnumerableSample/JoinSamples.cs`):

```
static void LeftOuterJoinWithMethods()
{
  //...
  var racersAndTeams =
    racers.GroupJoin(
      teams,
      r => r.Year,
      t => t.Year,
      (r, ts) => new
      {
        Year = r.Year,
        Champion = r.Name,
        Constructors = ts
      })
      .SelectMany(
        rt => rt.Constructors.DefaultIfEmpty(),
        (r, t) => new
        {
          Year = r.Year,
          Champion = r.Champion,
          Constructor = t?.Name ?? "no constructor championship"
        });
  //...
}
```

> **NOTE** *Other usages of the* `GroupJoin` *method are shown in the next section.*

Running the application with this query, the output starts with the year 1950 as shown here:

```
Year Champion Constructor Title
1950: Nino Farina no constructor championship
1951: Juan Manuel Fangio no constructor championship
1952: Alberto Ascari no constructor championship
1953: Alberto Ascari no constructor championship
1954: Juan Manuel Fangio no constructor championship
1955: Juan Manuel Fangio no constructor championship
1956: Juan Manuel Fangio no constructor championship
1957: Juan Manuel Fangio no constructor championship
1958: Mike Hawthorn Vanwall
1959: Jack Brabham Cooper
```

Figure 12-2 shows a graphical presentation of two collections combined with a left outer join. Using a left outer join, the results are not just matches with both collections A and B but also include the right collection B.

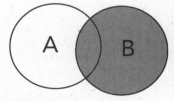

FIGURE 12-2

Group Join

A left outer join makes use of a group join together with the `into` clause. It uses partly the same syntax as the group join. The group join just doesn't need the `DefaultIfEmpty` method.

With a group join, two independent sequences can be joined, whereby one sequence contains a list of items for one element of the other sequence.

The following example uses two independent sequences. One is the list of champions that you already know from previous examples. The second sequence is a collection of `Championship` types. The `Championship` type is shown in the next code snippet. This class contains the year of the championship and the racers with the first, second, and third positions of the year with the properties `Year`, `First`, `Second`, and `Third` (code file `DataLib/Championship.cs`):

```csharp
public class Championship
{
  public Championship(int year, string first, string second, string third)
  {
    Year = year;
    First = first;
    Second = second:
    Third = third;
  }

  public int Year { get; }
  public string First { get; }
  public string Second { get; }
  public string Third { get; }
}
```

The collection of championships is returned from the method `GetChampionships` as shown in the following code snippet (code file `DataLib/Formula1.cs`):

```csharp
private static List<Championship> s_championships;
public static IEnumerable<Championship> GetChampionships()
{
  if (s_championships == null)
  {
    s_championships = new List<Championship>
    {
      new Championship(1950, "Nino Farina", "Juan Manuel Fangio",
        "Luigi Fagioli"),
      new Championship(1951, "Juan Manuel Fangio", "Alberto Ascari",
        "Froilan Gonzalez"),
      //...
    }
  }
  return s_championships;
}
```

The list of champions should be combined with the list of racers that are found within the first three positions in every year of championships, and for every world champion the results for every year should be displayed.

Because in the list of championships every item contains three racers, this list needs to be flattened first. One way to do this is by using a compound from. As there's no collection available with a property of a single item, but instead the three properties `First`, `Second`, and `Third` need to be combined and flattened, a new `List<T>` is created that is filled with information from these properties. For a newly created object, custom classes and anonymous types can be used as you've already seen several times. This time, we use a new feature of C# 7 and create a tuple. Tuples contain members of different types and can be created using tuple literals with parentheses as shown in the following code snippet. Here, a flat list of tuples contains the year, position in the championship, first name, and last name information from racers (code file `EnumerableSample/JoinSamples.cs`):

```csharp
static void GroupJoin()
{
```

```
var racers = from cs in Formula1.GetChampionships()
             from r in new List<
                (int Year, int Position, string FirstName, string LastName)>()
             {
                (cs.Year, Position: 1, FirstName: cs.First.FirstName(),
                 LastName: cs.First.LastName()),
                (cs.Year, Position: 2, FirstName: cs.Second.FirstName(),
                 LastName: cs.Second.LastName()),
                (cs.Year, Position: 3, FirstName: cs.Third.FirstName(),
                 LastName: cs.Third.LastName())
             }
             select r;
//...
}
```

> **NOTE** *Chapter 13, "Functional Programming with C#," gives detailed information about tuples. The sample code here makes use of a tuple enhancement available with C# 7.1, thus the compiler setting must be configured to use at least version 7.1.*

The extension methods `FirstName` and `LastName` use the last blank character to split up the string (code file `EnumerableSample/StringExtensions.cs`):

```csharp
public static class StringExtensions
{
  public static string FirstName(this string name) =>
    name.Substring(0, name.LastIndexOf(' '));

  public static string LastName(this string name) =>
    name.Substring(name.LastIndexOf(' ') + 1);
}
```

With a join clause the racers from both lists can be combined. `Formula1.GetChampions` returns a list of Racers, and the `racers` variable returns the list of tuples that contains the year, the result, and the names of racers. It's not enough to compare the items from these two collections by using the last name. Sometimes a racer and his father can be found in the list (for example, Damon Hill and Graham Hill), so it's necessary to compare the items by both `FirstName` and `LastName`. You do this by creating a new tuple type for both lists. Using the `into` clause, the result from the second collection is put into the variable `yearResults`. `yearResults` is created for every racer in the first collection and contains the results of the matching first name and last name from the second collection. Finally, with the LINQ query a new tuple type is created that contains the needed information (code file `EnumerableSample/JoinSamples.cs`):

```csharp
static void GroupJoin()
{
  //...
  var q = (from r in Formula1.GetChampions()
           join r2 in racers on
           (
             r.FirstName,
             r.LastName
           )
           equals
           (
             r2.FirstName,
             r2.LastName
           )
           into yearResults
           select
```

```
                       (
                          r.FirstName,
                          r.LastName,
                          r.Wins,
                          r.Starts,
                          Results: yearResults
                       ));

    foreach (var r in q)
    {
       Console.WriteLine($"{r.FirstName} {r.LastName}");
       foreach (var results in r.Results)
       {
          Console.WriteLine($"\t{results.Year} {results.Position}");
       }
    }
}
```

The last results from the `foreach` loop are shown next. Jenson Button has been among the top three for three years—2004 as third, 2009 as first, and 2011 as second; Sebastian Vettel was world champion four times and had the second position in 2009 and the third in 2015; and Nico Rosberg was world champion in 2016, and was in the second position two times in 2014 and 2015:

```
Jenson Button
         2004 3
         2009 1
         2011 2
Sebastian Vettel
         2009 2
         2010 1
         2011 1
         2012 1
         2013 1
         2015 3
Nico Rosberg
         2014 2
         2015 2
         2016 1
```

Using `GroupJoin` with extension methods, the syntax probably looks easier to catch. First, the compound from is done with the `SelectMany` method. This part is not very different, and tuples are used again. The `GroupJoin` method is invoked by passing the racers with the first parameter to join the champions with the flattened racers, and the match for both collections with the second and third parameters. The fourth parameter receives the racer from the first collection and a collection of the second. This is the results containing the position and the year, which are written to the `Results` tuple member (code file `EnumerableSample/JoinSamples.cs`):

```
static void GroupJoinWithMethods()
{
  var racers = Formula1.GetChampionships()
    .SelectMany(cs => new List<(int Year, int Position, string FirstName,
       string LastName)>
    {
      (cs.Year, Position: 1, FirstName: cs.First.FirstName(),
        LastName: cs.First.LastName()),
      (cs.Year, Position: 2, FirstName: cs.Second.FirstName(),
        LastName: cs.Second.LastName()),
      (cs.Year, Position: 3, FirstName: cs.Third.FirstName(),
        LastName: cs.Third.LastName())
    });
```

```
      var q = Formula1.GetChampions()
        .GroupJoin(racers,
          r1 => (r1.FirstName, r1.LastName),
          r2 => (r2.FirstName, r2.LastName),
          (r1, r2s) => (r1.FirstName, r1.LastName, r1.Wins, r1.Starts,
            Results: r2s));
      //...
    }
```

Set Operations

The extension methods `Distinct`, `Union`, `Intersect`, and `Except` are *set* operations. The following example creates a sequence of Formula-1 champions driving a Ferrari and another sequence of Formula-1 champions driving a McLaren, and then determines whether any driver has been a champion driving both cars. Of course, that's where the `Intersect` extension method can help.

First, you need to get all champions driving a Ferrari. This uses a simple LINQ query with a compound `from` to access the property `Cars` that's returning a sequence of string objects:

```
      var ferrariDrivers = from r in Formula1.GetChampions()
                           from c in r.Cars
                           where c == "Ferrari"
                           orderby r.LastName
                           select r;
```

Now the same query with a different parameter of the `where` clause is needed to get all McLaren racers. It's not a good idea to write the same query again. Another option is to create a method in which you can pass the parameter `car`. In case the method wouldn't be needed in other places, you can create a *local function*. `racersByCar` is the name of a local function that is implemented as a lambda expression containing a LINQ query. The local function `racersByCar` is defined within the scope of the method `SetOperations`, and thus it can be invoked only within this method. The LINQ `Intersect` extension method is used to get all racers who won the championship with a Ferrari and a McLaren (code file `EnumerableSample/LinqSamples.cs`):

```
    static void SetOperations()
    {
      IEnumerable<Racer> racersByCar(string car) =>
        from r in Formula1.GetChampions()
        from c in r.Cars
        where c == car
        orderby r.LastName
        select r;

      Console.WriteLine("World champion with Ferrari and McLaren");
      foreach (var racer in
        racersByCar("Ferrari").Intersect(racersByCar("McLaren")))
      {
        Console.WriteLine(racer);
      }
    }
```

> **NOTE** *Local functions are a new feature of C# 7 and are discussed in detail in Chapter 13.*

The result is just one racer, Niki Lauda:

```
    World champion with Ferrari and McLaren
    Niki Lauda
```

> **NOTE** *The set operations compare the objects by invoking the* GetHashCode *and* Equals *methods of the entity class. For custom comparisons, you can also pass an object that implements the interface* IEqualityComparer<T>*. In the preceding example, the* GetChampions *method always returns the same objects, so the default comparison works. If that's not the case, the set methods offer overloads in which a comparison can be defined.*

Zip

The Zip method enables you to merge two related sequences into one with a predicate function.

First, two related sequences are created, both with the same filtering (country Italy) and ordering. For merging this is important, as item 1 from the first collection is merged with item 1 from the second collection, item 2 with item 2, and so on. In case the count of the two sequences is different, Zip stops when the end of the smaller collection is reached.

The items in the first collection have a Name property, and the items in the second collection have LastName and Starts properties.

Using the Zip method on the collection racerNames requires the second collection racerNamesAndStarts as the first parameter. The second parameter is of type Func<TFirst, TSecond, TResult>. This parameter is implemented as a lambda expression and receives the elements of the first collection with the parameter first, and the elements of the second collection with the parameter second. The implementation creates and returns a string containing the Name property of the first element and the Starts property of the second element (code file EnumerableSample/LinqSamples.cs):

```csharp
static void ZipOperation()
{
  var racerNames = from r in Formula1.GetChampions()
                   where r.Country == "Italy"
                   orderby r.Wins descending
                   select new
                   {
                     Name = r.FirstName + " " + r.LastName
                   };

  var racerNamesAndStarts = from r in Formula1.GetChampions()
                            where r.Country == "Italy"
                            orderby r.Wins descending
                            select new
                            {
                              r.LastName,
                              r.Starts
                            };

  var racers = racerNames.Zip(racerNamesAndStarts,
               (first, second) => first.Name + ", starts: second.Starts);

  foreach (var r in racers)
  {
    Console.WriteLine(r);
  }
}
```

The result of this merge is shown here:

```
Alberto Ascari, starts: 32
Nino Farina, starts: 33
```

Partitioning

Partitioning operations such as the extension methods `Take` and `Skip` can be used for easy paging—for example, to display just five racers on the first page, and continue with the next five on the following pages.

With the LINQ query shown here, the extension methods `Skip` and `Take` are added to the end of the query. The `Skip` method first ignores a number of items calculated based on the page size and the actual page number; the `Take` method then takes a number of items based on the page size (code file `EnumerableSample/LinqSamples.cs`):

```
static void Partitioning()
{
  int pageSize = 5;
  int numberPages = (int)Math.Ceiling(Formula1.GetChampions().Count() /
    (double)pageSize);

  for (int page = 0; page < numberPages; page++)
  {
    Console.WriteLine($"Page {page}");

    var racers = (from r in Formula1.GetChampions()
                  orderby r.LastName, r.FirstName
                  select r.FirstName + " " + r.LastName).
                 Skip(page * pageSize).Take(pageSize);

    foreach (var name in racers)
    {
      Console.WriteLine(name);
    }
    Console.WriteLine();
  }
}
```

Here is the output of the first three pages:

```
Page 0
Fernando Alonso
Mario Andretti
Alberto Ascari
Jack Brabham
Jenson Button

Page 1
Jim Clark
Juan Manuel Fangio
Nino Farina
Emerson Fittipaldi
Mika Hakkinen

Page 2
Lewis Hamilton
Mike Hawthorn
Damon Hill
Graham Hill
Phil Hill
```

Paging can be extremely useful with Windows or web applications, showing the user only a part of the data.

> **NOTE** *Note an important behavior of this paging mechanism: Because the query is done with every page, changing the underlying data affects the results. New objects are shown as paging continues. Depending on your scenario, this can be advantageous to your application. If this behavior is not what you need, you can do the paging not over the original data source but by using a cache that maps to the original data.*

With the `TakeWhile` and `SkipWhile` extension methods you can also pass a predicate to retrieve or skip items based on the result of the predicate.

Aggregate Operators

The aggregate operators such as `Count`, `Sum`, `Min`, `Max`, `Average`, and `Aggregate` do not return a sequence; instead they return a single value.

The `Count` extension method returns the number of items in the collection. In the following example, the `Count` method is applied to the `Years` property of a `Racer` to filter the racers and return only those who won more than three championships. Because the same count is needed more than once in the same query, a variable `numberYears` is defined by using the `let` clause (code file `EnumerableSample/LinqSamples.cs`):

```
static void AggregateCount()
{
  var query = from r in Formula1.GetChampions()
              let numberYears = r.Years.Count()
              where numberYears >= 3
              orderby numberYears descending, r.LastName
              select new
              {
                Name = r.FirstName + " " + r.LastName,
                TimesChampion = numberYears
              };

  foreach (var r in query)
  {
    Console.WriteLine($"{r.Name} {r.TimesChampion}");
  }
}
```

The result is shown here:

```
Michael Schumacher 7
Juan Manuel Fangio 5
Lewis Hamilton 4
Alain Prost 4
Sebastian Vettel 4
Jack Brabham 3
Niki Lauda 3
Nelson Piquet 3
Ayrton Senna 3
Jackie Stewart 3
```

The `Sum` method summarizes all numbers of a sequence and returns the result. In the next example, `Sum` is used to calculate the sum of all race wins for a country. First the racers are grouped based on country; then, with the new anonymous type created, the `Wins` property is assigned to the sum of all wins from a single country (code file `EnumerableSample/LinqSamples.cs`):

```
static void AggregateSum()
{
  var countries = (from c in
                   from r in Formula1.GetChampions()
```

```
                    group r by r.Country into c
                    select new
                    {
                       Country = c.Key,
                       Wins = (from r1 in c
                              select r1.Wins).Sum()
                    }
                    orderby c.Wins descending, c.Country
                    select c).Take(5);

        foreach (var country in countries)
        {
          Console.WriteLine("{country.Country} {country.Wins}");
        }
    }
```

The most successful countries based on the Formula-1 race champions are as follows:

```
UK 216
Germany 162
Brazil 78
France 51
Finland 45
```

The methods `Min`, `Max`, `Average`, and `Aggregate` are used in the same way as `Count` and `Sum`. `Min` returns the minimum number of the values in the collection, and `Max` returns the maximum number. `Average` calculates the average number. With the `Aggregate` method you can pass a lambda expression that performs an aggregation of all the values.

Conversion Operators

In this chapter you've already seen that query execution is deferred until the items are accessed. Using the query within an iteration, the query is executed. With a conversion operator, the query is executed immediately, and the result is returned in an array, a list, or a dictionary.

In the next example, the `ToList` extension method is invoked to immediately execute the query and put the result into a `List<T>` (code file `EnumerableSample/LinqSamples.cs`):

```
static void ToList()
{
    List<Racer> racers = (from r in Formula1.GetChampions()
                          where r.Starts > 200
                          orderby r.Starts descending
                          select r).ToList();

    foreach (var racer in racers)
    {
        Console.WriteLine($"{racer} {racer:S}");
    }
}
```

The result of this query shows Jenson Button first:

```
Jenson Button 306
Fernando Alonso 291
Michael Schumacher 287
Kimi Räikkönen 271
Nico Rosberg 207
Nelson Piquet 204
```

It's not always that simple to get the returned objects into the list. For example, for fast access from a car to a racer within a collection class, you can use the new class `Lookup<TKey, TElement>`.

> **NOTE** *The* `Dictionary<TKey, TValue>` *class supports only a single value for a key. With the class* `Lookup<TKey, TElement>` *from the namespace* `System.Linq`, *you can have multiple values for a single key. These classes are covered in detail in Chapter 10, "Collections."*

Using the compound `from` query, the sequence of racers and cars is flattened, and an anonymous type with the properties `Car` and `Racer` is created. With the lookup that is returned, the key should be of type `string` referencing the car, and the value should be of type `Racer`. To make this selection, you can pass a key and an element selector to one overload of the `ToLookup` method. The key selector references the `Car` property, and the element selector references the `Racer` property (code file `EnumerableSample/LinqSamples.cs`):

```
static void ToLookup()
{
  var racers = (from r in Formula1.GetChampions()
                from c in r.Cars
                select new
                {
                  Car = c,
                  Racer = r
                }).ToLookup(cr => cr.Car, cr => cr.Racer);

  if (racers.Contains("Williams"))
  {
    foreach (var williamsRacer in racers["Williams"])
    {
      Console.WriteLine(williamsRacer);
    }
  }
}
```

The result of all "Williams" champions accessed using the indexer of the `Lookup` class is shown here:

```
Alan Jones
Keke Rosberg
Nigel Mansell
Alain Prost
Damon Hill
Jacques Villeneuve
```

In case you need to use a LINQ query over an untyped collection, such as the `ArrayList`, you can use the `Cast` method. In the following example, an `ArrayList` collection that is based on the `Object` type is filled with `Racer` objects. To make it possible to define a strongly typed query, you can use the `Cast` method (code file `EnumerableSample/LinqSamples.cs`):

```
static void ConvertWithCast
{
  var list = new System.Collections.ArrayList(Formula1.GetChampions()
    as System.Collections.ICollection);

  var query = from r in list.Cast<Racer>()
              where r.Country == "USA"
              orderby r.Wins descending
              select r;

  foreach (var racer in query)
  {
    Console.WriteLine("{racer:A}", racer);
  }
}
```

The results include the only Formula 1 champions from the U.S.:

```
Mario Andretti, country: USA, starts: 128, wins: 12
Phil Hill, country: USA, starts: 48, wins: 3
```

Generation Operators

The generation operators `Range`, `Empty`, and `Repeat` are not extension methods, but normal static methods that return sequences. With LINQ to Objects, these methods are available with the `Enumerable` class.

Have you ever needed a range of numbers filled? Nothing is easier than using the `Range` method. This method receives the start value with the first parameter and the number of items with the second parameter (code file `EnumerableSample/LinqSamples.cs`):

```
static void GenerateRange()
{
  var values = Enumerable.Range(1, 20);
  foreach (var item in values)
  {
    Console.Write($"{item} ", item);
  }
  Console.WriteLine();
}
```

> **NOTE** *The* `Range` *method does not return a collection filled with the values as defined. This method does a deferred query execution like the other methods. It returns a* `RangeEnumerator` *that simply does a* `yield` *return with the values incremented.*

Of course, the result now looks like this:

```
1 2 3 4 5 6 7 8 9 10 11 12 13 14 15 16 17 18 19 20
```

You can combine the result with other extension methods to get a different result—for example, using the `Select` extension method:

```
var values = Enumerable.Range(1, 20).Select(n => n * 3);
```

The `Empty` method returns an iterator that does not return values. This can be used for parameters that require a collection for which you can pass an empty collection.

The `Repeat` method returns an iterator that returns the same value a specific number of times.

PARALLEL LINQ

The class `ParallelEnumerable` in the `System.Linq` namespace splits the work of queries across multiple threads that run simultaneously. Although the `Enumerable` class defines extension methods to the `IEnumerable<T>` interface, most extension methods of the `ParallelEnumerable` class are extensions for the class `ParallelQuery<TSource>`. One important exception is the `AsParallel` method, which extends `IEnumerable<TSource>` and returns `ParallelQuery<TSource>`, so a normal collection class can be queried in a parallel manner.

Parallel Queries

To demonstrate Parallel LINQ (PLINQ), a large collection is needed. With small collections you don't see any effect when the collection fits inside the CPU's cache. In the following code, a large `int` collection is filled with random values (code file `ParallelLinqSample/Program.cs`):

```
static IEnumerable<int> SampleData()
```

```
    {
        const int arraySize = 50000000;
        var r = new Random();
        return Enumerable.Range(0, arraySize).Select(x => r.Next(140)).ToList();
    }
```

Now you can use a LINQ query to filter the data, do some calculations, and get an average of the filtered data. The query defines a filter with the where clause to summarize only the items with values < 20, and then the aggregation function sum is invoked. The only difference to the LINQ queries you've seen so far is the call to the AsParallel method:

```
    static void LinqQuery(IEnumerable<int> data)
    {
        var res = (from x in data.AsParallel()
                   where Math.Log(x) < 4
                   select x).Average();
        //...
    }
```

Like the LINQ queries shown already, the compiler changes the syntax to invoke the methods AsParallel, Where, Select, and Average. AsParallel is defined with the ParallelEnumerable class to extend the IEnumerable<T> interface, so it can be called with a simple array. AsParallel returns ParallelQuery<TSource>. Because of the returned type, the Where method chosen by the compiler is ParallelEnumerable.Where instead of Enumerable.Where. In the following code, the Select and Average methods are from ParallelEnumerable as well. In contrast to the implementation of the Enumerable class, with the ParallelEnumerable class the query is *partitioned* so that multiple threads can work on the query. The collection can be split into multiple parts whereby different threads work on each part to filter the remaining items. After the partitioned work is completed, *merging* must occur to get the summary result of all parts:

```
    static void ExtensionMethods(IEnumerable<int> data)
    {
        var res = data.AsParallel()
          .Where(x => Math.Log(x) < 4)
          .Select(x => x).Average();
        //...
    }
```

When you run this code, you can also start the task manager, so you can confirm that all CPUs of your system are busy. If you remove the AsParallel method, multiple CPUs might not be used. Of course, if you don't have multiple CPUs on your system, then don't expect to see an improvement with the parallel version.

Partitioners

The AsParallel method is an extension not only to the IEnumerable<T> interface, but also to the Partitioner class. With this you can influence the partitions to be created.

The Partitioner class is defined within the namespace System.Collections.Concurrent and has different variants. The Create method accepts arrays or objects implementing IList<T>. Depending on that, as well as on the parameter loadBalance , which is of type Boolean and available with some overloads of the method, a different partitioner type is returned. For arrays, the classes DynamicPartitionerForArray<TSource> and StaticPartitionerForArray<TSource>, are used. Both of which derive from the abstract base class OrderablePartitioner<TSource>.

In the following example, the code from the "Parallel Queries" section is changed to manually create a partitioner instead of relying on the default one (code file ParallelLinqSample/Program.cs):

```
    static void UseAPartitioner(IList<int> data)
    {
```

```
        var result = (from x in Partitioner.Create(data, true).AsParallel()
                        where Math.Log(x) < 4
                        select x).Average();
    //...
    }
```

You can also influence the parallelism by invoking the methods `WithExecutionMode` and `WithDegreeOfParallelism`. With `WithExecutionMode` you can pass a value of `ParallelExecutionMode`, which can be `Default` or `ForceParallelism`. By default, Parallel LINQ avoids parallelism with high over-head. With the method `WithDegreeOfParallelism` you can pass an integer value to specify the maximum number of tasks that should run in parallel. This is useful if not all CPU cores should be used by the query.

> **NOTE** *You can read more about tasks and threads in Chapter 21, "Tasks and Parallel Programming."*

Cancellation

.NET offers a standard way to cancel long-running tasks, and this is also true for Parallel LINQ.

To cancel a long-running query, you can add the method `WithCancellation` to the query and pass a `CancellationToken` to the parameter. The `CancellationToken` is created from the `CancellationTokenSource`. The query is run in a separate thread where the exception of type `OperationCanceledException` is caught. This exception is fired if the query is cancelled. From the main thread the task can be cancelled by invoking the `Cancel` method of the `CancellationTokenSource` (code file `ParallelLinqSample/Program.cs`):

```
static void UseCancellation(IEnumerable<int> data)
{
  var cts = new CancellationTokenSource();

  Task.Run(() =>
  {
    try
    {
      var res = (from x in data.AsParallel().WithCancellation(cts.Token)
                    where Math.Log(x) < 4
                    select x).Average();

      Console.WriteLine($"query finished, sum: {res}");
    }
    catch (OperationCanceledException ex)
    {
      Console.WriteLine(ex.Message);
    }
  });
  Console.WriteLine("query started");
  Console.Write("cancel? ");
  string input = ReadLine();
  if (input.ToLower().Equals("y"))
  {
    // cancel!
    cts.Cancel();
  }
}
```

> **NOTE** *You can read more about cancellation and the* `CancellationToken` *in Chapter 21.*

EXPRESSION TREES

With LINQ to Objects, the extension methods require a delegate type as parameter; this way, a lambda expression can be assigned to the parameter. Lambda expressions can also be assigned to parameters of type `Expression<T>`. The C# compiler defines different behavior for lambda expressions depending on the type. If the type is `Expression<T>`, the compiler creates an expression tree from the lambda expression and stores it in the assembly. The expression tree can be analyzed during runtime and optimized for querying against the data source.

Let's turn to a query expression that was used previously:

```
var brazilRacers = from r in racers
                   where r.Country == "Brazil"
                   orderby r.Wins
                   select r;
```

The preceding query expression uses the extension methods `Where`, `OrderBy`, and `Select`. The `Enumerable` class defines the `Where` extension method with the delegate type `Func<T, bool>` as parameter predicate:

```
public static IEnumerable<TSource> Where<TSource>(
    this IEnumerable<TSource> source, Func<TSource, bool> predicate);
```

This way, the lambda expression is assigned to the predicate. Here, the lambda expression is like an anonymous method, as explained earlier:

```
Func<Racer, bool> predicate = r => r.Country == "Brazil";
```

The `Enumerable` class is not the only class for defining the `Where` extension method. The `Where` extension method is also defined by the class `Queryable<T>`. This class has a different definition of the `Where` extension method:

```
public static IQueryable<TSource> Where<TSource>(
    this IQueryable<TSource> source,
    Expression<Func<TSource, bool>> predicate);
```

Here, the lambda expression is assigned to the type `Expression<T>`, which behaves differently:

```
Expression<Func<Racer, bool>> predicate = r => r.Country == "Brazil";
```

Instead of using delegates, the compiler emits an expression tree to the assembly. The expression tree can be read during runtime. Expression trees are built from classes derived from the abstract base class `Expression`. The `Expression` class is not the same as `Expression<T>`. Some of the expression classes that inherit from `Expression` include `BinaryExpression`, `ConstantExpression`, `InvocationExpression`, `LambdaExpression`, `NewExpression`, `NewArrayExpression`, `TernaryExpression`, `UnaryExpression`, and more. The compiler creates an expression tree resulting from the lambda expression.

For example, the lambda expression `r.Country == "Brazil"` makes use of `ParameterExpression`, `MemberExpression`, `ConstantExpression`, and `MethodCallExpression` to create a tree and store the tree in the assembly. This tree is then used during runtime to create an optimized query to the underlying data source.

With the sample application, the method `DisplayTree` is implemented to display an expression tree graphically on the console. In the following example, an `Expression` object can be passed, and depending on the expression type some information about the expression is written to the console. Depending on the type of the expression, DisplayTree is called recursively (code file ExpressionTreeSample/Program.cs):

```
static void DisplayTree(int indent, string message,
  Expression expression)
{
  string output = $"{string.Empty.PadLeft(indent, '>')} {message} " +
    $"! NodeType: {expression.NodeType}; Expr: {expression}";

  indent++;

  switch (expression.NodeType)
  {
    case ExpressionType.Lambda:
      Console.WriteLine(output);
      LambdaExpression lambdaExpr = (LambdaExpression)expression;
      foreach (var parameter in lambdaExpr.Parameters)
      {
        DisplayTree(indent, "Parameter", parameter);
      }
      DisplayTree(indent, "Body", lambdaExpr.Body);
      break;
    case ExpressionType.Constant:
      ConstantExpression constExpr = (ConstantExpression)expression;
      Console.WriteLine($"{output} Const Value: {constExpr.Value}");
      break;
    case ExpressionType.Parameter:
      ParameterExpression paramExpr = (ParameterExpression)expression;
      Console.WriteLine($"{output} Param Type: {paramExpr.Type.Name}");
      break;
    case ExpressionType.Equal:
    case ExpressionType.AndAlso:
    case ExpressionType.GreaterThan:
      BinaryExpression binExpr = (BinaryExpression)expression;
      if (binExpr.Method != null)
      {
        Console.WriteLine($"{output} Method: {binExpr.Method.Name}");
      }
      else
      {
        Console.WriteLine(output);
      }
      DisplayTree(indent, "Left", binExpr.Left);
      DisplayTree(indent, "Right", binExpr.Right);
      break;
    case ExpressionType.MemberAccess:
      MemberExpression memberExpr = (MemberExpression)expression;
      Console.WriteLine($"{output} Member Name: {memberExpr.Member.Name}, " +
        " Type: {memberExpr.Expression}");
      DisplayTree(indent, "Member Expr", memberExpr.Expression);
      break;
    default:
      Console.WriteLine();
      Console.WriteLine($"{expression.NodeType} {expression.Type.Name}");
      break;
  }
}
```

> **NOTE** *The method* DisplayTree *does not deal with all expression types—only the types that are used with the following example expression.*

The expression that is used for showing the tree is already well known. It's a lambda expression with a Racer parameter, and the body of the expression takes racers from Brazil only if they have won more than six races:

```
Expression<Func<Racer, bool>> expression =
  r => r.Country == "Brazil" && r.Wins > 6;
```

Looking at the tree result, you can see from the output that the lambda expression consists of a Parameter and an AndAlso node type. The AndAlso node type has an Equal node type to the left and a GreaterThan node type to the right. The Equal node type to the left of the AndAlso node type has a MemberAccess node type to the left and a Constant node type to the right, and so on:

```
Lambda! NodeType: Lambda; Expr: r => ((r.Country == "Brazil") AndAlso (r.Wins > 6))
> Parameter! NodeType: Parameter; Expr: r Param Type: Racer
> Body! NodeType: AndAlso; Expr: ((r.Country == "Brazil") AndAlso (r.Wins > 6))
>> Left! NodeType: Equal; Expr: (r.Country == "Brazil") Method: op_Equality
>>> Left! NodeType: MemberAccess; Expr: r.Country Member Name: Country, Type: String
>>>> Member Expr! NodeType: Parameter; Expr: r Param Type: Racer
>>> Right! NodeType: Constant; Expr: "Brazil" Const Value: Brazil
>> Right! NodeType: GreaterThan; Expr: (r.Wins > 6)
>>> Left! NodeType: MemberAccess; Expr: r.Wins Member Name: Wins, Type: Int32
>>>> Member Expr! NodeType: Parameter; Expr: r Param Type: Racer
>>> Right! NodeType: Constant; Expr: 6 Const Value: 6
```

Examples where the Expression<T> type is used are with the Entity Framework Core and the client provider for WCF Data Services. These technologies define methods with Expression<T> parameters. This way the LINQ provider accessing the database can create a runtime-optimized query by reading the expressions to get the data from the database.

LINQ PROVIDERS

.NET includes several LINQ providers. A LINQ provider implements the standard query operators for a specific data source. LINQ providers might implement more extension methods than are defined by LINQ, but the standard operators must at least be implemented. LINQ to XML implements additional methods that are particularly useful with XML, such as the methods Elements, Descendants, and Ancestors defined by the class Extensions in the System.Xml.Linq namespace.

Implementation of the LINQ provider is selected based on the namespace and the type of the first parameter. The namespace of the class that implements the extension methods must be opened; otherwise, the extension class is not in scope. The parameter of the Where method defined by LINQ to Objects and the Where method defined by LINQ to Entities is different.

The Where method of LINQ to Objects is defined with the Enumerable class:

```
public static IEnumerable<TSource> Where<TSource>(
    this IEnumerable<TSource> source, Func<TSource, bool> predicate);
```

Inside the System.Linq namespace is another class that implements the operator Where. This implementation is used by LINQ to Entities. You can find the implementation in the class Queryable:

```
public static IQueryable<TSource> Where<TSource>(
    this IQueryable<TSource> source,
    Expression<Func<TSource, bool>> predicate);
```

Both classes are implemented in the System.Core assembly in the System.Linq namespace. How does the compiler select what method to use, and what's the magic with the Expression type? The lambda expression is the same regardless of whether it is passed with a Func<TSource, bool> parameter or an Expression<Func<TSource, bool>> parameter—only the compiler behaves differently. The selection is done based on the source parameter. The method that matches best based on its parameters is chosen by the compiler. Properties of Entity Framework Core contexts are of type `DbSet<TEntity>`. `DbSet<TEntity>` implements `IQueryable<TEntity>`, and thus Entity Framework Core uses the `Where` method of the `Queryable` class.

SUMMARY

This chapter described and demonstrated the LINQ query and the language constructs on which the query is based, such as extension methods and lambda expressions. You've looked at the various LINQ query operators—not only for filtering and ordering of data sources, but also for partitioning, grouping, doing conversions, joins, and so on.

With Parallel LINQ, you've seen how longer queries can easily be parallelized.

Another important concept of this chapter is the expression tree. Expression trees enable building the query to the data source at runtime because the tree is stored in the assembly. You can read about its great advantages in Chapter 26. LINQ is a very in-depth topic, and you can see Bonus Chapter 2 for information on using LINQ with XML data. Other third-party providers are also available for download, such as LINQ to MySQL, LINQ to Amazon, LINQ to Flickr, LINQ to LDAP, and LINQ to SharePoint. No matter what data source you have, with LINQ you can use the same query syntax.

The next chapter covers functional programming. Many of the newer C# features are based on this programming paradigm.

13

Functional Programming with C#

WHAT'S IN THIS CHAPTER?

➤ Functional programming overview
➤ Expression-bodied members
➤ Extension methods
➤ The `using static` declaration
➤ Local functions
➤ Tuples
➤ Pattern matching

WROX.COM CODE DOWNLOADS FOR THIS CHAPTER

You can find the wrox.com code downloads for this chapter at www.wrox.com. The source code is also available at https://github.com/ProfessionalCSharp/ProfessionalCSharp7 in the directory FunctionalProgramming.

The code for this chapter is divided into the following major examples:

➤ ExpressionBodiedMembers
➤ LocalFunctions
➤ Tuples
➤ PatternMatching

WHAT IS FUNCTIONAL PROGRAMMING?

C# never has been a pure *object-oriented* programming language. From the beginning, C# has been a *component-oriented* programming language. What does component-oriented mean? C# offers inheritance and polymorphism that's also used by object-oriented programming languages; in addition, it offers native support for properties, events, and annotations via attributes. Later versions with LINQ and expressions have also included *declarative programming*. Using declarative LINQ expressions, the compiler saves an expression tree that is used later by a provider to dynamically generate SQL statements.

> **NOTE** *Object-oriented features of C# are discussed in Chapter 4, "Object-Oriented Programming with C#," events are covered in Chapter 8, "Delegates, Lambdas, and Events," and LINQ is covered in Chapter 12, "Language Integrated Query."*

C# is not purely bound to a single programming language paradigm. Instead, features that are practical with today's applications created with C# are added to the syntax of C#. In the last years more and more features associated with *functional programming* have been added as well.

What are the foundations of functional programming? The most important concepts of functional programming are based on two approaches: avoiding state mutation and having functions as a first-class concept. The next two sections get more into details on these two things.

> **NOTE** *This chapter does not claim to give you all the information to write applications with the pure functional programming paradigm. Complete books are needed for this. (If you want to write programs with this paradigm, you should consider switching to the F# programming language instead of using C#.) This chapter goes a pragmatic way—like C# does. Some features used with functional programming are useful with all application types; that's why these features are offered in C#. Over time, more and more functional programming features will be added to C# in a way that fits the C# programming style.*

Avoiding State Mutation

With the programming language F#, which is a functional-first language, creating a custom type, an object of this type is by default immutable. An object can be initialized in a constructor, but it can't be changed later. If mutability is needed, the type needs to be explicitly declared to be mutable. This is different with C#.

With C#, some of the predefined types are immutable such as the string type. Methods that are used to change the string always return a new string. What about collections? The methods used by LINQ don't change a collection. Instead, methods such as Where and OrderBy return a new collection that is filtered and a new collection that is ordered.

On the other hand, the List<T> collection offers methods for sorting that are implemented in a mutable way; the original collection is sorted. For more immutability, .NET offers complete immutable collections in the namespace System.Collections.Immutable. These collections don't offer methods that change the collection. Instead, new collections are always returned.

What's the advantage of using immutable types? Because it's guaranteed no one can change an instance, multiple threads can be used to access it concurrently without the need for synchronization. With immutable types, it's also easier to create unit tests.

For creating custom types, some features were added with C# 6 to create immutable types. Since C# 6, you have been able to create an auto implemented read-only property with just a get accessor:

```
public string FirstName { get; }
```

Out of this, the compiler creates a read-only field that can be initialized only in the constructor and a property with a get accessor returning this field.

> **NOTE** *Strings are covered in Chapter 9, "Strings and Regular Expressions."*
> *Immutable collections are covered in Chapter 11, "Special Collections."*

Because of some library requirements, where you can use immutable types is somewhat limited. Over the last years, the limitations have been removed in more and more places. For example, the NuGet package `Newtonsoft.Json` allows using immutable types for JSON serialization and deserialization. This library makes use of a constructor that matches arguments needed to create an instance. Entity Framework was such a limitation in the last years. However, since Entity Framework Core 1.1, table columns can be mapped to fields instead of to read/write properties.

> **NOTE** *JSON serialization is covered in Bonus Chapter 2, "XML and JSON," which you can find online. Entity Framework Core is covered in Chapter 26, "Entity Framework Core." Threads and synchronization are covered in Chapter 21, "Tasks and Parallel Programming."*

> **NOTE** *This chapter does not cover the C# features to create immutable types because this is already covered in Chapter 3, "Objects and Types." C# allows creating auto-implemented properties just with a* get *accessor where the compiler creates a* readonly *field and a* get *accessor returning the value of this field. Future versions of C# are planned to have more features to create immutable types, such as records.*

Functions as First Class

With functional programming, functions are first class. This means that functions can be used as arguments of functions, functions can be returned from functions, and functions can be assigned to variables.

This always has been possible with C#: Delegates can hold addresses of functions, delegates can be used as arguments of methods, and delegates can be returned from methods. However, you need to be aware that comparing the invocation of a normal function to the invocation of a delegate, the delegate has some overhead associated. With a delegate, an instance of a delegate class is created, and this instance holds a collection of method references. When you invoke a delegate, the collection is iterated to invoke every method assigned to the delegate.

> **NOTE** *Delegates are covered in Chapter 8.*

Higher-Order Functions

Functional programming defines the term *higher-order function* as a function that takes another function as parameter or that returns a function. Some do both. With a C# implementation, delegates are used as parameters and return types of a method.

Examples of higher-order functions are methods defined for LINQ as you've seen in the previous chapter. For example, the `Where` method receives a `Func<TSource, bool>` predicate:

```
public static IEnumerable<TSource> Where(this IEnumerable<TSource> source,
  Func<TSource, bool> predicate);
```

How a higher-order function can both receive a function as a parameter as well as return a function is shown later in this chapter.

Pure Functions

Functional programming defines the term *pure function*. Pure functions should be preferred if possible. Pure functions fulfill two requirements:

➤ Pure functions always return the same result for the same arguments that are passed.

➤ Pure functions don't result in a side effect, such as changing state, or depend on external sources.

Of course, not all methods can be implemented as a pure function. Pure functions just have the advantage that testing becomes easy; there's no external dependency.

When creating a method to access external sources, you might think about splitting the method into two parts: a part that is pure with probably complex logic and a part that cannot be pure.

Now that you've had an overview of the important concepts of functional programming, it's time to get into C# syntax details on how C# helps these concepts.

EXPRESSION-BODIED MEMBERS

C# 6 allowed expression-bodied members with methods and properties that only defined a get accessor. Now, with C# 7, expression-bodied members can be used everywhere as long as only one statement is used with the implementation. With functional programming, many methods are only one-liners, and thus this feature can be used often; the number of code lines is reduced because as curly brackets are not needed.

> **NOTE** *This feature is already introduced in other chapters of this book, such as expression-bodied properties and expression-bodied methods in Chapter 3 and expression-bodied event accessors in Chapter 8, so not every aspect of them is covered in this chapter.*

Let's look at the following code snippet in which expression-bodied members are used with property accessors—the get and set accessors—with the implementation of the ToString method, and the implementation of the constructor. The constructor is defined to accept the name as a string parameter and requires this to split the string into first name and last name. This is done with one statement where first the string is split up into a string array, and next this string array is used to extract two strings, named _firstName and _lastName, using out parameters (code file ExpressionBodiedMembers/Person.cs):

```
public class Person
{
  public Person(string name) =>
    name.Split(' ').ToStrings(out _firstName, out _lastName);

  private string _firstName;
  public string FirstName
  {
    get => _firstName;
    set => _firstName = value;
  }

  private string _lastName;
  public string LastName
```

```
  {
    get => _lastName;
    set => _lastName = value;
  }

  public override string ToString() => $"{FirstName} {LastName}";
}
```

The custom `out` parameters are filled with the extension method `ToStrings` from the following code snippet. This is an extension method for the string array, and it moves the elements of the array to the output parameters (code file `ExpressionBodiedMembers/StringArrayExtensions.cs`):

```
public static class StringArrayExtensions
{
  public static void ToStrings(this string[] values, out string value1,
    out string value2)
  {
    if (values == null) throw new ArgumentNullException(nameof(values));
    if (values.Length != 2) throw new IndexOutOfRangeException(
      "only arrays with 2 values allowed");

    value1 = values[0];
    value2 = values[1];
  }
}
```

With all this in place, a `Person` can be created with the name consisting of one string, and the `FirstName` and `LastName` properties accessed to read the name (code file `ExpressionBodiedMembers/Program.cs`):

```
Person p = new Person("Katharina Nagel");
Console.WriteLine($"{p.FirstName} {p.LastName}");
```

EXTENSION METHODS

Extension methods already have been covered in Chapter 12, and the previous section of this chapter implements a custom extension method. However, as extension methods help a lot with functional programming concepts, so I'm showing another example here.

With functional programming, many methods are very short and consist of a single statement, whereas expression-bodied members like those shown earlier help reduce the number of code lines. For example, the `using` statement can be changed to a method instead. The following extension method named `Use` is an extension method for all classes implementing the `IDisposable` interface. The `using` statement is used within the implementation to release the item after its use. For the user of the item, an `Action<T>` delegate can be passed to the `Use` method (code file `UsingStatic/FunctionalExtensions.cs`:

```
public static class FunctionalExtensions
{
  public static void Use<T>(this T item, Action<T> action)
    where T : IDisposable
  {
    using (item)
    {
      action(item);
    }
  }
}
```

A sample class that implements the interface `IDisposable` is defined with the `Resource` class. This class offers the `Foo` method in addition to the `IDisposable` functionality (code file `UsingStatic/Resource.cs`):

```
class Resource : IDisposable
{
```

```
public void Foo() => Console.WriteLine("Foo");

private bool disposedValue = false;

protected virtual void Dispose(bool disposing)
{
  if (!disposedValue)
  {
    if (disposing)
    {
      Console.WriteLine("release resource");
    }
    disposedValue = true;
  }
}

public void Dispose() => Dispose(true);
}
```

Now think about how a typical using statement block for accessing this Resource object would look:

```
using (var r = new Resource())
{
  r.Foo();
}
```

With the Use method, accessing and disposing of the resource can be done in a single statement (code file UsingStatic/Program.cs):

```
new Resource().Use(r => r.Foo());
```

USING STATIC

Many practical extensions can be implemented with extension methods, such as you've seen with the Use extension method or the many extension methods for LINQ that are covered in Chapter 12. You'll also see many extension methods offered by .NET in many of the following chapters of the book.

Not all practical extensions have a type that can be extended. For some scenarios simple static methods can be advantageous. For easier invocation of these methods, the using static declaration can be used to get rid of the class name.

For example, instead of writing

```
Console.WriteLine("Hello World!");
```

you can write

```
WriteLine("Hello World!");
```

if System.Console is opened:

```
using static System.Console;
```

After using this declaration, you can use all static members of the class Console—such as WriteLine, Write, ReadLine, Read, Beep, and others—without writing the Console class. You just need to make sure to not get into conflicts when opening static members of other classes, or using methods of a base class when static methods were meant.

Let's get into a practical example. High-order functions take functions as parameters, return a function, or do both. When working with functions, it can be useful to combine two functions to one.

You do this with the Compose method, as shown in the following code snippet (code file UsingStatic/FunctionalExtensions.cs):

```
public static class FunctionalExtensions
{
  //...
  public static Func<T1, TResult> Compose<T1, T2, TResult>(
    Func<T1, T2> f1, Func<T2, TResult> f2) =>
      a => f2(f1(a));
}
```

This generic method defines three type parameters and two parameters of the delegate type Func. Just remember, the delegate Func<T, TResult> references a method with one argument and a return type that can be of a different type. The Compose method accepts two Func parameters to pass two methods that are combined to one. The first method (f1) passed to Compose can have two different types—one for input (T1) and one for output (T2)—whereas the second method (f2) passed needs the same input type (T2) as the output type (T2) of the first method and can have a different output type (TResult). The Compose method itself returns a Func delegate with the same input type (T1) as the first method, and the same output type as the second method (TResult). The implementation might look a little scary because two lambda operators follow one after the other. This construct will become clear as you understand what the method returns: a method. The method that is returned is of type Func<T1, TResult>. After the first lambda operator, a => f2(f1(a)); defines this method. The variable a is of type T1, and the return of the method is of type TResult, which is the same result type as returned from f2. f2 receives f1 with the input as parameter.

To use the Compose method, first two delegates f1 and f2 are created that add 1 or 2 to the input. These delegates are combined with the Compose method. The Compose method can be invoked without a class name because the using static declaration opens the static members of the class FunctionalExtensions. After creating f3 with the Compose method, the f3 method is invoked (code file UsingStatic/Program.cs):

```
using System;
using static System.Console;
using static UsingStatic.FunctionalExtensions;

namespace UsingStatic
{
  class Program
  {
    static void Main()
    {
      //...

      Func<int, int> f1 = x => x + 1;
      Func<int, int> f2 = x => x + 2;
      Func<int, int> f3 = Compose(f1, f2);
      var x1 = f3(39);
      WriteLine(x1);
      //...
    }
  }
}
```

The result written to the console is, of course, 42.

As the Compose method is declared, the parameter types can be different between the input and the output. In the following code snippet, the first method passed to the Compose method receives a string and returns a Person object; the second method receives a Person and returns a string. If the compiler can't identify the parameter type from the variable and the return type, the concrete delegate type must be specified as shown with the method that receives a string and returns a Person. The variable name alone doesn't help the compiler to know its type. With the second method passed to the `Compose` method it's already clear that the input is of the same type as the return from the first method, so a type specification is not necessary. After the invocation of the `Compose` method, the variable `greetPerson` is a combination of the two input methods:

```
var greetPerson = Compose(
  new Func<string, Person>(name => new Person(name)),
  person => $"Hello, {person.FirstName}");

WriteLine(greetPerson("Mario Andretti"));
```

Invoking the `greetPerson` method with the string `Mario Andretti` in the `WriteLine` method, writes the string `Hello, Mario` to the console.

LOCAL FUNCTIONS

A new feature of C# 7 is *local functions*: Methods can be declared within methods. A local function is declared within the scope of a method, a property accessor, a constructor, or lambda expressions. A local function can only be invoked within the scope of the containing member. Instead of using a private method that is needed in just one place, you can use a local function.

Let's get into an example and start without a local function—a lambda expression that will be replaced by a local function in the next turn. The following code snippet declares a lambda expression that's assigned to the delegate variable `add`. The variable `add` is in the scope of the method `IntroWithLambdaExpression`, and thus it can be invoked only within this method (code file `LocalFunctions/Program.cs`):

```
private static void IntroWithLambdaExpression()
{
  Func<int, int, int> add = (x, y) =>
  {
    return x + y;
  };
  int result = add(37, 5);
  Console.WriteLine(result);
}
```

Instead of declaring a lambda expression, you can define a local function. A local function is declared in a similar way to a normal method, with a return type, the name, and parameters. The local function is invoked in the same way as the lambda expression shown earlier:

```
private static void IntroWithLocalFunctions()
{
  int add(int x, int y)
  {
    return x + y;
  }
  int result = add(37, 5);
  Console.WriteLine(result);
}
```

Compared to the lambda expression, the syntax is simpler with the local function, and the local function also performs better. Whereas a delegate needs an instance of a class and a collection of references to methods, with a local function only the reference to the function is needed, and this function can be invoked directly. The overhead is like other methods.

Of course, if the local function can be implemented with a single statement, the implementation can be done using an expression-bodied member:

```
private static void IntroWithLocalFunctionsWithExpressionBodies()
{
  int add(int x, int y) => x + y;
```

```
        int result = add(37, 5);
        Console.WriteLine(result);
    }
```

Within the method body, the local function can be implemented in any location. There's no need to implement them in the top of the body; it can also be implemented elsewhere, and the local function can be invoked before that. This behavior is like normal methods. However, unlike normal methods, local functions cannot be virtual, abstract, private, or use other modifiers. The only modifiers allowed are async and unsafe.

Like lambda expressions, local functions can access variables from the outer scope (also known as closures) as shown in the following code snippet where the local function accesses variable z, which is defined outside of the local function:

```
    private static void IntroWithLocalFunctionsWithClosures()
    {
        int z = 3;
        int result = add(37, 5);
        Console.WriteLine(result);

        int add(int x, int y) => x + y + z;
    }
```

> **NOTE** *The only modifiers allowed with local functions are* async *and* unsafe. *The* async *modifier is explained in Chapter 15, "Asynchronous Programming," and the* unsafe *modifier is explained in Chapter 17, "Managed and Unmanaged Memory."*

A reason to use local functions is if you need the functionality only within the scope of a method (or property, constructor, and so on). There still would be other options to local functions. Performance is a good reason to use local functions instead of lambda expressions. In comparing local functions to normal private methods, local functions don't have a performance advantage. Of course, local functions can use closures, whereas private methods can't. Is this enough reason to use local functions? To understand the real benefits of local functions, you need to see some useful examples, which are shown in the next sections.

Local Functions with the yield Statement

The previous chapter, "Language Integrated Query," includes a simple implementation of the Where method with the yield statement. What isn't covered there is the checking of parameters. Let's add this to the implementation of the Where1 method, checking the source and predicate parameters for null (code file LocalFunctions/EnumerableExtensions.cs):

```
    public static IEnumerable<T> Where1<T>(this IEnumerable<T> source,
      Func<T, bool> predicate)
    {
        if (source == null) throw new ArgumentNullException(nameof(source));
        if (predicate == null) throw new ArgumentNullException(nameof(predicate));

        foreach (T item in source)
        {
            if (predicate(item))
            {
                yield return item;
            }
        }
    }
```

Writing code to test for the `ArgumentNullException`, the preprocessor statement `#line` is defined to start with the source code line 1000. The exception does not happen in the line 1004 where the null is passed to the `Where1` method; instead it happens in line 1006 with the `foreach` statement. The reason for finding this error late is because of the deferred execution of the `yield` statement in the implementation of the `Where1` method (code file `LocalFunctions/Program.cs`):

```
private static void YieldSampleSimple()
{
#line 1000
    Console.WriteLine(nameof(YieldSampleSimple));
    try
    {
        string[] names = { "James", "Niki", "John", "Gerhard", "Jack" };
        var q = names.Where1(null);

        foreach (var n in q)  // callstack position for exception
        {
            Console.WriteLine(n);
        }
    }
    catch (ArgumentNullException ex)
    {
        Console.WriteLine(ex);
    }
    Console.WriteLine();
}
```

To fix this issue, and to give earlier error information to the caller, the `Where1` method is implemented in two parts with the `Where2` method. Here, the `Where2` method just checks for incorrect parameters and does not include yield statements. The implementation with yield return is done in a separate private method, the `WhereImpl`. This method is invoked from the `Where2` method after the input parameters have been checked (code file `LocalFunctions/EnumerationExtensions.cs`):

```
public static IEnumerable<T> Where2<T>(this IEnumerable<T> source,
    Func<T, bool> predicate)
{
    if (source == null) throw new ArgumentNullException(nameof(source));
    if (predicate == null) throw new ArgumentNullException(nameof(predicate));

    return Where2Impl(source, predicate);
}

private static IEnumerable<T> Where2Impl<T>(IEnumerable<T> source,
    Func<T, bool> predicate)
{
    foreach (T item in source)
    {
        if (predicate(item))
        {
            yield return item;
        }
    }
}
```

Calling the method now, the stack trace shows the error happened in line 1004, where the `Where2` method was invoked (code file `LocalFunctions/Program.cs`):

```
private static void YieldSampleWithPrivateMethod()
{
#line 1000
    Console.WriteLine(nameof(YieldSampleWithPrivateMethod));
    try
```

```
        {
            string[] names = { "James", "Niki", "John", "Gerhard", "Jack" };
            var q = names.Where2(null);   // callstack position for exception

            foreach (var n in q)
            {
                Console.WriteLine(n);
            }
        }
        catch (ArgumentNullException ex)
        {
            Console.WriteLine(ex);
        }
        Console.WriteLine();
    }
```

The issue was fixed with the Where2 method. However, now you have a private method that is needed in only one place. The body of the Where2 method includes parameter checks and the invocation of the method Where2Impl. This is a great scenario for a private method. The implementation of the Where3 method includes the checks for the input parameters as before, as well as a private function instead of the previous private method Where2Impl. The local function can have a simpler signature, as it's possible to access the variable's source and predicate from the outer scope (code file LocalFunctions/EnumerableExtensions.cs):

```
public static IEnumerable<T> Where3<T>(this IEnumerable<T> source,
    Func<T, bool> predicate)
{
    if (source == null) throw new ArgumentNullException(nameof(source));
    if (predicate == null) throw new ArgumentNullException(nameof(predicate));

    return Iterator();

    IEnumerable<T> Iterator()
    {
        foreach (T item in source)
        {
            if (predicate(item))
            {
                yield return item;
            }
        }
    }
}
```

Invoking the method Where3 results in the same behavior as invoking the method Where2. The stack trace shows the issue with the invocation of the Where3 method.

Recursive Local Functions

Another scenario that uses local function is recursive invocation, which is shown in the next example with the QuickSort method. Here, the local function Sort is invoked recursively until the collection is sorted (code file LocalFunctions/Algorithms.cs):

```
public static void QuickSort<T>(T[] elements) where T : IComparable<T>
{
    void Sort(int start, int end)
    {
        int i = start, j = end;
        var pivot = elements[(start + end) / 2];

        while (i <= j)
        {
```

```
      while (elements[i].CompareTo(pivot) < 0) i++;
      while (elements[j].CompareTo(pivot) > 0) j--;
      if (i <= j)
      {
        T tmp = elements[i];
        elements[i] = elements[j];
        elements[j] = tmp;
        i++;
        j--;
      }
    }
    if (start < j) Sort(start, j);
    if (i < end) Sort(i, end);
  }

  Sort(0, elements.Length - 1);
}
```

> **NOTE** *When using C#, you need to be careful with recursive calls. A recursive loop such as the following ends after about 24,000 iterations because of a stack overflow. The C# compiler does not implement* tail call optimization *as the F# compiler does. With tail call optimization, recursive calls are converted to iterations to not consume this stack space.*

```
public static void WhenDoesItEnd()
{
  Console.WriteLine(nameof(WhenDoesItEnd));
  void InnerLoop(int ix)
  {
    Console.WriteLine(ix++);
    InnerLoop(ix);
  }
  InnerLoop(1);
}
```

TUPLES

Tuples enable you to combine objects of different types. With arrays, you can combine objects of the same type, whereas tuples allow using different combinations of types. Tuples help reduce the need for the following two things:

➤ Defining custom classes or structs for returning multiple values

➤ Defining parameters to return multiple values from methods.

Tuples have been in the .NET Framework since version 4.0 in the form of generic `Tuple` classes. However, they have not been used much as the different objects of a tuple can be accessed using `Item1`, `Item2`, `Item3`, and so on properties, and this is neither very attractive nor does it give any information about its meaning.

This changes with C# 7, which offers tuple functionality integrated in the programming language, and this gives great improvements as shown in the next example, which uses a simple immutable `Person` class (code file `TuplesSample/Person.cs`):

```
public class Person
{
  public Person(string firstName, string lastName)
  {
    FirstName = firstName;
```

```
        LastName = lastName;
    }
    public string FirstName { get; }
    public string LastName { get; }

    public override string ToString() => $"{FirstName} {LastName}";
    //...
}
```

Declaring and Initializing Tuples

A tuple can be declared using parentheses and initialized using a tuple literal that is created with parentheses as well. In the following code snippet, on the left side a tuple variable t is declared containing a string, an int, and a Person. On the right side, a tuple literal is used to create a tuple with the string magic, the number 42, and a Person object initialized using a constructor of the Person class. The tuple can be accessed using the variable t with the members declared in the parentheses (s, i, and p in this example; code file Tuples/Program.cs):

```
private static void IntroTuples()
{
    (string s, int i, Person p) t = ("magic", 42, new Person(
        "Stephanie", "Nagel"));
    Console.WriteLine($"s: {t.s}, i: {t.i}, p: {t.p}");
    //...
}
```

When you run the application, the output shows the values of the tuple:

```
s: magic, i: 42, p: Stephanie Nagel
```

The tuple literal also can be assigned to a tuple variable without declaring its members. This way the members of the tuple are accessed using the member names of the ValueTuple struct: Item1, Item2, and Item3:

```
private static void IntroTuples()
{
    //...
    var t2 = ("magic", 42, new Person("Matthias", "Nagel"));
    Console.WriteLine($"string: {t2.Item1}, int: {t2.Item2},
        person: {t2.Item3}");
    //...
}
```

You can assign names to the tuple in the tuple literal by defining the name followed by a colon, which is the same syntax as with object literals:

```
private static void IntroTuples()
{
    //...
    var t3 = (s: "magic", i: 42, p: new Person("Matthias", "Nagel"));
    Console.WriteLine($"s: {t3.s}, i: {t3.i}, p: {t3.p}");
    //...
}
```

With all this, names are just a convenience. You can assign one tuple to another one when the types match; the names do not matter:

```
private static void IntroTuples()
{
    //...
    (string astring, int anumber, Person aperson) t4 = t3;
    Console.WriteLine($"s: {t4.astring}, i: {t4.anumber}, p: {t4.aperson}");
}
```

Tuple Deconstruction

You also can deconstruct tuples into variables. To do this you just need to remove the tuple variable from the previous code sample and just define variable names in parentheses. The variables can then be directly accessed that contain the values of the tuple parts (code file `Tuples/Program.cs`):

```
private static void TupleDeconstruction()
{
  (string s, int i, Person p) = ("magic", 42, new Person("Stephanie",
    "Nagel"));
  Console.WriteLine($"s: {s}, i: {i}, p: {p}");
  //...
}
```

You can also declare the variables for deconstruction using the `var` keyword; the types are defined by the tuple literal. You can also declare the variables before initialization and deconstruct the tuple to existing variables:

```
private static void TupleDeconstruction()
{
  //...
  (var s1, var i1, var p1) = ("magic", 42, new Person("Stephanie", "Nagel"));
  Console.WriteLine($"s: {s1}, i: {i1}, p: {p1}");

  string s2;
  int i2;
  Person p2;
  (s2, i2, p2) = ("magic", 42, new Person("Katharina", "Nagel"));
  Console.WriteLine($"s: {s2}, i: {i2}, p: {p2}");
  //...
}
```

In case you don't need all the parts of the tuple, you can use _ to ignore this part as shown here:

```
private static void TupleDeconstruction()
{
  //...
  (string s3, _, _) = ("magic", 42, new Person("Katharina", "Nagel"));
  Console.WriteLine(s3);
}
```

> **NOTE** *Probably you already used _ when you invoked methods with* out *parameter modifiers for cases where the result was not needed. In this scenario, using _ is only a naming convention. Using _ with tuples is different. You don't need to declare a type, and you can use _ multiple times; it's a compiler feature to ignore this part with deconstruction.*

Returning Tuples

Let's get into a more useful example: a method returning a tuple. The method `Divide` from the following code snippet receives two parameters and returns a tuple consisting of two `int` values. The result is returned with a tuple literal (code file `Tuples/Program.cs`):

```
static (int result, int remainder) Divide(int dividend, int divisor)
{
  int result = dividend / divisor;
```

```
    int remainder = dividend % divisor;
    return (result, remainder);
}
```

The result is deconstructed into the `result` and `remainder` variables:

```
private static void ReturningTuples()
{
    (int result, int remainder) = Divide(7, 2);
    Console.WriteLine($"7 / 2 - result: {result}, remainder: {remainder}");
}
```

> **NOTE** *Using tuples, you can avoid declaring method signatures with* out *parameters.*
> out *parameters cannot be used with* async *methods; this restriction does not apply*
> *with tuples.*

Behind the Scenes

Using the new tuple syntax, the C# compiler creates `ValueTuple` structures behind the scenes. .NET defines multiple `ValueTuple` structures for one to seven generic parameters, and another one where the eighth parameter can be another tuple. Using a tuple literal results in an invocation of `Tuple.Create`. The Tuple structure defines fields named `Item1`, `Item2`, `Item3`, and so on to access all the items (code file `Tuples/Program.cs`):

```
private static void BehindTheScenes()
{
    (string s, int i) t1 = ("magic", 42); // tuple literal
    Console.WriteLine($"{t1.s} {t1.i}");
    ValueTuple<string, int> t2 = ValueTuple.Create("magic", 42);
    Console.WriteLine($"{t2.Item1}, {t2.Item2}");
}
```

How does the naming of the fields come from returning tuples from methods? A method signature, as shown here with the `Divide` method,

```
public static (int result, int remainder) Divide(int dividend, int divisor)
```

is translated to the return of a `ValueTuple` with the `TupleElementNames` attribute for the return type:

```
[return: TupleElementNames(new string[] {"result", "remainder" })]
public static ValueTuple<int, int> Divide(int dividend, int divisor)
```

When using this manner of invoking the method, the compiler reads the information from the attribute to match the names to the `ItemX` fields. With the invocation, the `ItemX` fields are used instead of the nicer names.

With the automatic usage of the `TupleElementNames` attribute, a method returning a tuple can be declared inside a library (code file `TuplesLib/SimpleMath.cs`):

```
public class SimpleMath
{
    public static (int result, int remainder) Divide(int dividend, int divisor)
    {
        int result = dividend / divisor;
        int remainder = dividend % divisor;
        return (result, remainder);
    }
}
```

The library is used from the console application where the `result` and `remainder` names are directly available:

```
private static void UseALibrary()
{
  var t = SimpleMath.Divide(5, 3);
  Console.WriteLine($"result: {t.result}, remainder: {t.remainder}");
}
```

Whereas the `older` Tuple type is a class, the new tuple `ValueTuple` is a struct. This reduces the work needed by the garbage collector as value types are stored on the stack. The old `Tuple` type is implemented as an immutable class with read-only properties. With the new `ValueTuple`, the members are public fields. Public fields make this type mutable (code file `Tuples/Program.cs`):

```
static void Mutability()
{
  // old tuple is a immutable reference type
  Tuple<string, int> t1 = Tuple.Create("old tuple", 42);
  // t1.Item1 = "new string"; // not possible with Tuple

  // new tuple is a mutable value type
  (string s, int i) t2 = ("new tuple", 42);
  t2.s = "new string";
  t2.i = 43;
  t2.i++;

  Console.WriteLine($"new string: {t2.s} int: {t2.i}");
}
```

> **NOTE** *It looks like Microsoft broke some rules with* `ValueType`: *Structs should be immutable, and fields should not be declared public. However, the new tuples can be compared to simple value types such as* `int` *and* `long`; *breaking the rules with tuples is completely excusable to also get best performance optimizations.*

Compatibility of ValueTuple with Tuple

The older tuple types haven't been used much because of the unkind naming. However, for programs using the `Tuple` type, there's an easy conversion to a `ValueTuple`.

The `Tuple` type can be converted to a `ValueTuple` by invoking the `ToValueTuple` extension method. As the old `Tuple` type doesn't offer the nicer names, you need to define the names with parentheses (code file `Tuples/Program.cs`):

```
static void TupleCompatibility()
{
  // convert Tuple to ValueTuple
  Tuple<string, int, bool, Person> t1 = Tuple.Create("a string", 42, true,
    new Person("Katharina", "Nagel"));
  Console.WriteLine($"old tuple - string: {t1.Item1}, number: {t1.Item2},
    bool: {t1.Item3}, Person: {t1.Item4}");
  (string s, int i, bool b, Person p) t2 = t1.ToValueTuple();
  Console.WriteLine($"new tuple - string: {t2.s}, number: {t2.i}, bool: {t2.b},
    Person: {t2.p}");
  //...
}
```

Old tuples can also be deconstructed to specific fields. The following example shows deconstructing the tuple t1 to the fields s, i, and b:

```
static void TupleCompatibility()
{
    //...
    (string s, int i, bool b, Person p) = t1; // Deconstruct
    Console.WriteLine($"new tuple - string: {s}, number: {i}, bool: {b},
        Person {p}");
    //...
}
```

It's also possible to do this the other way around. New value tuples can be converted to tuples with the ToTuple method. Of course, then you need to specify the members using Item1, Item2, Item3, and so on.

```
static void TupleCompatibility()
{
    //...
    // convert ValueTuple to Tuple
    Tuple<string, int, bool, Person> t3 = t2.ToTuple();
    Console.WriteLine($"old tuple - string: {t1.Item1}, number: {t1.Item2}, " +
        $"bool: {t1.Item3}, Person: {t1.Item4}");
}
```

Infer Tuple Names

A new feature of C# 7.1 is the inference of tuple names. The Divide method declared earlier returns a tuple with the names result and remainder. The returned tuple is written to the variable t1 where these names are used to access the tuple fields. When you invoke the Divide method the second time, the tuple result is written to a tuple with the names res and rem. From the returned tuple, the result is written to res, and remainder is written to rem. t3 is created using a tuple literal where the res and rem fields are defined, and the values from tuple t1 are assigned accordingly. The fourth tuple in this example makes use of name inference. t4 is created using a tuple literal where the names are the same as the names from tuple t1. Accessing the result and remainder fields without giving a name to the tuple members takes the same names as coming from t1. t4 also has members named result and remainder (code file Tuples/Program.cs):

```
private static void TupleNames()
{
    var t1 = Divide(9, 4);
    Console.WriteLine($"{t1.result}, {t1.remainder}");

    (int res, int rem) t2 = Divide(11, 3);
    Console.WriteLine($"{t2.res}, {t2.rem}");

    var t3 = (res: t1.result, rem: t1.remainder);

    // use inferred names
    var t4 = (t1.result, t1.remainder);
    Console.WriteLine($"{t4.result}, {t4.remainder}");
}
```

> **NOTE** *Inference of tuple names requires at least C# 7.1. You need to specify this version using* LangVersion *in the* csproj *project file or by using the Project Settings in Visual Studio.*

Tuples with Linked Lists

A practical use of tuples is with linked lists. With a linked list, an item (which is a `LinkedListNode`) contains the value and a reference to the next item. In the following code snippet, you create a `LinkedList` that contains 10 elements. Then the `do/while` statement is used to walk through this list. Within the loop, a tuple literal is used to access the `Value` and `Next` properties of the `LinkedListNode`. With deconstruction, the value is written to the variable `value`, and the next item in the linked list is written to the variable `node`, which itself is the `LinkedListNode` again (code file `Tuples/Program.cs`):

```
static void TuplesWithLinkedList()
{
  Console.WriteLine(nameof(TuplesWithLinkedList));
  var list = new LinkedList<int>(Enumerable.Range(0, 10));

  int value;
  LinkedListNode<int> node = list.First;
  do
  {
    (value, node) = (node.Value, node.Next);
    Console.WriteLine(value);
  } while (node != null);
  Console.WriteLine();
}
```

> **NOTE** *Linked lists are discussed in Chapter 10, "Collections."*

Tuples with LINQ

The previous chapter demonstrates anonymous types and tuples with a LINQ statement. Let's change one LINQ query from anonymous types to tuples. The following LINQ query creates an anonymous type with `LastName` and `Starts` property in the parameter of the `Select` method (code file `Tuples/Program.cs`):

```
static void UsingAnonymousTypes()
{
  var racerNamesAndStarts = Formula1.GetChampions()
    .Where(r => r.Country == "Italy")
    .OrderByDescending(r => r.Wins)
    .Select(r => new
    {
      r.LastName,
      r.Starts
    });

  foreach (var r in racerNamesAndStarts)
  {
    Console.WriteLine($"{r.LastName}, starts: {r.Starts}");
  }
}
```

Changing the curly brackets to parentheses creates a tuple with the fields `LastName` and `Starts`:

```
static void UsingTuples()
{
  var racerNamesAndStarts = Formula1.GetChampions()
    .Where(r => r.Country == "Italy")
    .OrderByDescending(r => r.Wins)
    .Select(r =>
      (
```

```
      r.LastName,
      r.Starts
    ));

  foreach (var r in racerNamesAndStarts)
  {
    Console.WriteLine($"{r.LastName}, starts: {r.Starts}");
  }
}
```

> **NOTE** *With anonymous types, a class is created, and thus instances of this class are allocated on the heap and need to be collected from the garbage collector. By comparison, tuples are value types and stored on the stack. Tuples can have a performance advantage.*

Deconstruction

You've already seen deconstruction with tuples—writing tuples into simple variables. Deconstruction can also be done with any type: deconstructing a class or struct into its parts.

For example, the previously shown `Person` class can be deconstructed into first name and last name (code file `Tuples/Program.cs`):

```
private static void Deconstruct()
{
  var p1 = new Person("Katharina", "Nagel");

  (var first, var last) = p1;
  Console.WriteLine($"{first} {last}");
}
```

All that needs to be done is to create a `Deconstruct` method that fills the separate parts into `out` parameters (code file `Tuples/Person.cs`):

```
public class Person
{
  public Person(string firstName, string lastName)
  {
    FirstName = firstName;
    LastName = lastName;
  }
  public string FirstName { get; }
  public string LastName { get; }

  public override string ToString() => $"{FirstName} {LastName}";

  public void Deconstruct(out string firstName, out string lastName)
  {
    firstName = FirstName;
    lastName = LastName;
  }
}
```

Deconstruction is implemented with the method name `Deconstruct`. This method is always of type `void` and returns the part with `out` parameters. You might wonder why a method creating a tuple can't be implemented by returning a tuple. The reason is that overloads are allowed. You can implement multiple `Deconstruct` methods using different parameter types. This wouldn't be possible when returning a tuple. With C#, an overloaded method cannot be selected just by its return type.

Deconstruction with Extension Methods

Deconstruction can also be implemented without adding a `Deconstruct` method to the class that should be deconstructed: by using extension methods. The following code example defines an extension method for the `Racer` type to deconstruct a `Racer` to firstName, lastName, starts, and wins (code file Tuples/RacerExtensions.cs):

```
public static class RacerExtensions
{
  public static void Deconstruct(this Racer r, out string firstName,
    out string lastName, out int starts, out int wins)
  {
    firstName = r.FirstName;
    lastName = r.LastName;
    starts = r.Starts;
    wins = r.Wins;
  }
}
```

The following code snippet deconstructs a `Racer` to the variables `first` and `last`. Starts and wins are ignored (code file Tuples/Program.cs):

```
static void DeconstructWithExtensionsMethods()
{
  var racer = Formula1.GetChampions().Where(
    r => r.LastName == "Lauda").First();
  (string first, string last, _, _) = racer;
  Console.WriteLine($"{first} {last}");
}
```

Tuples are one of the most important improvements (if not the most important one) of C# 7. Next, let's get into pattern matching, which is another great feature of C# 7.

PATTERN MATCHING

From an object-oriented view, it would be best to always use concrete types and interfaces to solve a problem. However, often this is not easy to do. From a database, a query might give you different object types that are not related to any hierarchy. When you access API services, a list or a single object can be returned—or perhaps nothing at all is returned. Thus, a method often should work with diverse types. This is where pattern matching can help.

For the example, an array of different objects is created. The array named `data` contains null with the first element, the integer with the value 42, a string, an object of type `Person`, and an array containing `Person` objects (code file PatternMatching/Program.cs):

```
static void Main()
{
  var p1 = new Person("Katharina", "Nagel");
  var p2 = new Person("Matthias", "Nagel");
  var p3 = new Person("Stephanie", "Nagel");
  object[] data = { null, 42, "astring", p1, new Person[] { p2, p3 } };

  foreach (var item in data)
  {
    IsOperator(item);
  }

  foreach (var item in data)
  {
    SwitchStatement(item);
  }
}
```

With pattern matching in C# 7, the is operator and the switch statement have been enhanced with three kinds of patterns: the *const pattern*, the *type pattern*, and the *var pattern*. Let's get into details starting with the is operator.

Pattern Matching with the is Operator

A simple match with the is operator is the *const pattern*. With this pattern, you can compare an object to constant values such as null or 42 (code file PatternMatching/Program.cs):

```
static void IsOperator(object item)
{
  // const pattern
  if (item is null)
  {
    Console.WriteLine("item is null");
  }

  if (item is 42)
  {
    Console.WriteLine("item is 42");
  }
  //...
}
```

When you run the application with the previously declared array, the first two items of the array match with the two if statements as shown in this program output:

```
item is null
item is 42
```

> **NOTE** *Parameters of methods usually have been checked for null comparing to null using the equal operator. For example,*
>
> ```
>         if (item == null) throw ArgumentNullException("null");
> ```
>
> *This can now be replaced using pattern matching:*
>
> ```
>         if (item is null) throw ArgumentNullException("null");
> ```
>
> *Behind the scenes, the C# compiler generates the same Intermediate Language (IL) code.*

The most interesting pattern match is the *type pattern*. With this pattern you can match for a specific type, such as int or string. This pattern also enables you to declare a variable, such as if (item is int i). The variable i is assigned to the item if the pattern applies:

```
static void IsOperator(object item)
{
  //...
  // type pattern
  if (item is int)
  {
    Console.WriteLine($"Item is of type int");
  }

  if (item is int i)
  {
    Console.WriteLine($"Item is of type int with the value {i}");
  }
```

```
if (item is string s)
{
    Console.WriteLine($"Item is a string: {s}");
}
//...
}
```

With the previous type patterns, these matches apply with the value 42 and the string astring:

```
Item is of type int
Item is of type int with a value 42
Item is a string: astring
```

Declaring a variable of the type allows strongly typed access. You can access all the members of the type without the need for a cast. This also allows using logical operators in the if statement to check for other constraints than just the type, such as if the FirstName starts with the string Ka:

```
static void IsOperator(object item)
{
    //...
    if (item is Person p && p.FirstName.StartsWith("Ka"))
    {
        Console.WriteLine($"Item is a person: {p.FirstName} {p.LastName}");
    }

    if (item is IEnumerable<Person> people)
    {
        string names = string.Join(", ",
            people.Select(p1 => p1.FirstName).ToArray());
        Console.WriteLine($"it's a Person collection containing {names}");
    }
    //...
}
```

With the previous two type patterns and the object array applied, these matches apply:

```
Item is a person: Katharina Nagel
it's a Person collection containing Matthias, Stephanie
```

One more pattern type needs to be discussed: the *var pattern*. Everything can be applied to a var; you just get the concrete type. With the sample code, the GetType method is invoked to get the name of the type and to write the concrete type to the console. When the value is null, the var pattern applies as well. That's why the null-conditional operator is used with the every variable. every is null if the item is null, which writes the string null to the console:

```
static void IsOperator(object item)
{
    //...
    // var pattern
    if (item is var every)
    {
        Console.WriteLine($"it's var of type {every?.GetType().Name ?? "null"} " +
            $"with the value {every ?? "nothing"}");
    }
}
```

The output of the application for the var pattern shows that all items of the array match with this pattern:

```
it's var of type null with the value nothing
it's var of type Int32 with the value 42
it's var of type String with the value astring
it's var of type Person with the value Katharina Nagel
it's var of type Person[] with the value PatternMatching.Person[]
```

Pattern Matching with the switch Statement

With the switch statement, the three pattern types can be used as well. The following code snippet shows the const pattern with cases for null and 42; the type pattern for int, string, and Person; and the var pattern. Like the extension of the is operator, with the switch statement a variable can be specified with the type pattern to write the matching result to this variable. You also can apply an additional filter with the when clause. The first type match for the Person class applies only when the FirstName property of the Person has the value Katharina. With the switch statement, the ordering of the cases is important. As soon as one case applies, the other cases are not checked further. If the first match to the Person type with the when clause applies, the second case for Person does not apply. That's why when filtering must be done before general cases for a type. The var pattern that is defined with the last case matches with every object passed to the switch. However, this case is checked only if none of the other cases that are defined earlier apply. The default clause can be on every position of the switch statement, and it applies only if none of the cases match. It's just a good practice to put this clause last (code file PatternMatching/Program.cs):

```
static void SwitchStatement(object item)
{
  switch (item)
  {
    case null:
    case 42:
      Console.WriteLine("it's a const pattern");
      break;
    case int i:
      Console.WriteLine($"it's a type pattern with int: {i}");
      break;
    case string s:
      Console.WriteLine($"it's a type pattern with string: {s}");
      break;
    case Person p when p.FirstName == "Katharina":
      Console.WriteLine($"type pattern match with Person and " +
        $"when clause: {p}");
      break;
    case Person p:
      Console.WriteLine($"type pattern match with Person: {p}");
      break;
    case var every:
      Console.WriteLine($"var pattern match: {every?.GetType().Name}");
      break;
    default:
  }
}
```

When you run the application, the const pattern of the switch statement applies with null and 42, the string pattern applies with the string astring, with the Person object the first Person case applies, and finally, the Person array matches the var pattern—because no other pattern applied earlier. A match to the type pattern with the int type did not apply because the const pattern was an earlier match:

```
it's a const pattern
it's a const pattern
it's a type pattern with string: astring
type pattern match with Person and when clause: Katharina Nagel
var pattern match: Person[]
```

Pattern Matching with Generics

If you need pattern matching with generics, you need the compiler be configured to at least C# 7.1. C# 7.1 adds pattern matching for generics. With C# 7, you can define a generic method as shown and use the is operator to check a variable of a generic type for a specific type to apply (code file `PatternMatching/HttpManager.cs`):

```
public void Send<T>(T package)
{
  if (package is HealthPackage hp)
  {
    hp.CheckHealth();
  }
  //...
}
```

You can do pattern matching with generics similarly to the manner you use with generic classes. You can also use generics with pattern matching and the `switch` statement as well.

> **NOTE** *Generic methods and generic classes are discussed in Chapter 5, "Generics."*

SUMMARY

In this chapter, you've seen new features of C# 7 such as local functions, tuples, and pattern matching. All these features are coming from the functional programming paradigm, but all are very useful for creating normal .NET applications. Local functions are useful in a few scenarios, such as for allowing better error handling with delayed methods using the `yield` statement. Tuples offer an efficient way to combine different data types. It's not necessary to always create custom classes for such combinations.

You've also seen how tuples can replace anonymous types in LINQ queries. Pattern matching allows dealing with different types using enhancements of the `is` operator and the `switch` statement.

The next chapter goes into the details of errors and exceptions.

14

Errors and Exceptions

WHAT'S IN THIS CHAPTER?

➤ Looking at the exception classes

➤ Using `try...catch...finally` to capture exceptions

➤ Filtering exceptions

➤ Creating user-defined exceptions

➤ Retrieving caller information

WROX.COM CODE DOWNLOADS FOR THIS CHAPTER

The Wrox.com code downloads for this chapter are found at www.wrox.com on the Download Code tab. The source code is also available at https://github.com/ProfessionalCSharp/ProfessionalCSharp7 in the directory ErrorsAndExceptions.

The code for this chapter is divided into the following major examples:

➤ Simple Exceptions

➤ ExceptionFilters

➤ RethrowExceptions

➤ Solicit Cold Call

➤ Caller Information

INTRODUCTION

Errors happen, and they are not always caused by the person who coded the application. Sometimes your application generates an error because of an action that was initiated by the end user of the application, or it might be simply due to the environmental context in which your code is running. In any case, you should anticipate errors occurring in your applications and code accordingly.

.NET has enhanced the ways in which you deal with errors. C#'s mechanism for handling error conditions enables you to provide custom handling for each type of error condition, as well as to separate the code that identifies errors from the code that handles them.

No matter how good your coding is, your programs should be capable of handling any possible errors that might occur. For example, in the middle of some complex processing of your code, you might discover that it doesn't have permission to read a file; or, while it is sending network requests, the network might go down. In such exceptional situations, it is not enough for a method to simply return an appropriate error code—there might be 15 or 20 nested method calls, so what you really want the program to do is jump back up through all those calls to exit the task completely and take the appropriate counteractions. The C# language has very good facilities for handling this kind of situation, through the mechanism known as *exception handling*.

This chapter covers catching and throwing exceptions in many different scenarios. You see exception types from different namespaces and their hierarchy, and you find out how to create custom exception types. You discover different ways to catch exceptions—for example, how to catch exceptions with the exact exception type or a base class. You also see how to deal with nested `try` blocks, and how you could catch exceptions that way. For code that should be invoked no matter whether an exception occurs or the code continues with any error, you are introduced to creating `try`/`finally` code blocks.

By the end of this chapter, you will have a good grasp of advanced exception handling in your C# applications.

EXCEPTION CLASSES

In C#, an exception is an object created (or *thrown*) when a particular exceptional error condition occurs. This object contains information that should help identify the problem. Although you can create your own exception classes (and you do so later), .NET includes many predefined exception classes—too many to provide a comprehensive list here. The class hierarchy diagram in Figure 14-1 shows a few of these classes to give you a sense of the general pattern. This section provides a quick survey of some of the exceptions available in the .NET base class library.

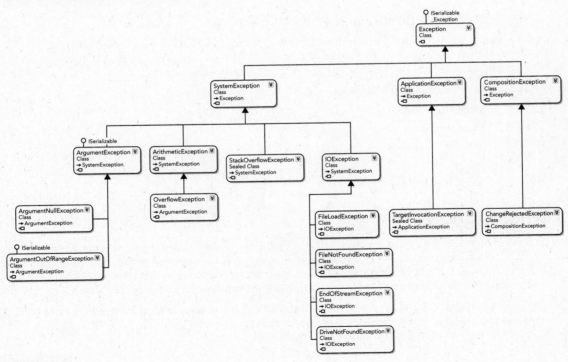

FIGURE 14-1

All the classes in Figure 14-1 are part of the System namespace, except for IOException and CompositionException and the classes derived from these two classes. IOException and its derived classes are part of the namespace System.IO. The System.IO namespace deals with reading from and writing to files. CompositionException and its derived classes are part of the namespace System.ComponentModel .Composition. This namespace deals with dynamically loading parts and components. In general, there is no specific namespace for exceptions. Exception classes should be placed in whatever namespace is appropriate to the classes that can generate them—hence, I/O-related exceptions are in the System.IO namespace. You find exception classes in quite a few of the base class namespaces.

The generic exception class, System.Exception, is derived from System.Object, as you would expect for a .NET class. In general, you should not throw generic System.Exception objects in your code, because they provide no specifics about the error condition.

Two important classes in the hierarchy are derived from System.Exception:

➤ SystemException—This class is for exceptions that are usually thrown by the .NET runtime or that are considered to be of a generic nature and might be thrown by almost any application. For example, StackOverflowException is thrown by the .NET runtime if it detects that the stack is full. However, you might choose to throw ArgumentException or its subclasses in your own code if you detect that a method has been called with inappropriate arguments. Subclasses of SystemException include classes that represent both fatal and nonfatal errors.

➤ ApplicationException—With the initial design of NET, this class was meant to be the base class for custom application exception classes. However, some exception classes that are thrown by the CLR derive from this base class (for example, TargetInvocationException), and exceptions thrown from applications derive from SystemException (for example, ArgumentException). Therefore, it's no longer a good practice to derive custom exception types from ApplicationException, as this doesn't offer any benefits. Instead, custom exception classes can derive directly from the Exception base class. Many pre-defined exception classes directly derive from Exception.

Other exception classes that might come in handy include the following:

➤ StackOverflowException—This exception is thrown when the area of memory allocated to the stack is full. A stack overflow can occur if a method continuously calls itself recursively. This is generally a fatal error, because it prevents your application from doing anything apart from terminating (in which case it is unlikely that even the finally block will execute). Trying to handle errors like this yourself is usually pointless; instead, you should have the application gracefully exit.

➤ EndOfStreamException—The usual cause of an EndOfStreamException is an attempt to read past the end of a file. A *stream* represents a flow of data between data sources. Streams are covered in detail in Chapter 23, "Networking."

➤ OverflowException—An example when this occurs is if you attempt to cast an int containing a value of -40 to a uint in a checked context.

The other exception classes shown in Figure 14-1 are not discussed here. They are just shown to illustrate the hierarchy of exception classes.

The class hierarchy for exceptions is somewhat unusual in that most of these classes do not add any functionality to their respective base classes. However, in the case of exception handling, the common reason for adding inherited classes is to indicate more specific error conditions. Often, it isn't necessary to override methods or add any new ones (although it is not uncommon to add extra properties that carry extra information about the error condition). For example, you might have a base ArgumentException class intended for method calls whereby inappropriate values are passed in, and an ArgumentNullException class derived from it, which is intended to handle a null argument if passed.

CATCHING EXCEPTIONS

Given that .NET includes a selection of predefined base class exception objects, this section describes how you use them in your code to trap error conditions. In dealing with possible error conditions in C# code, you typically divide the relevant part of your program into blocks of three different types:

➤ try blocks encapsulate the code that forms part of the normal operation of your program and that might encounter some serious error conditions.

➤ catch blocks encapsulate the code dealing with the various error conditions that your code might have encountered by working through any of the code in the accompanying try block. This block could also be used for logging errors.

➤ finally blocks encapsulate the code that cleans up any resources or takes any other action that you normally want handled at the end of a try or catch block. It is important to understand that the finally block is executed whether an exception is thrown. Because the purpose of the finally block is to contain cleanup code that should always be executed, the compiler flags an error if you place a return statement inside a finally block. An example of using the finally block is closing any connections that were opened in the try block. Understand that the finally block is completely optional. If your application does not require any cleanup code (such as disposing of or closing any open objects), then there is no need for this block.

The following steps outline how these blocks work together to trap error conditions:

1. The execution flow first enters the try block.

2. If no errors occur in the try block, execution proceeds normally through the block, and when the end of the try block is reached, the flow of execution jumps to the finally block if one is present (Step 5). However, if an error does occur within the try block, execution jumps to a catch block (Step 3).

3. The error condition is handled in the catch block.

4. At the end of the catch block, execution automatically transfers to the finally block if one is present.

5. The finally block is executed (if present).

The C# syntax used to bring all this about looks roughly like this:

```
try
{
   // code for normal execution
}
catch
{
   // error handling
}
finally
{
   // clean up
}
```

A few variations on this theme exist:

➤ You can omit the finally block because it is optional.

➤ You can also supply as many catch blocks as you want to handle specific types of errors. However, you don't want to get too carried away and have a huge number of catch blocks.

➤ You can define filters with catch blocks to catch the exception with the specific block only if the filter matches.

➤ You can omit the catch blocks altogether, in which case the syntax serves not to identify exceptions but to guarantee that code in the finally block will be executed when execution leaves the try block. This is useful if the try block contains several exit points.

So far so good, but the question that has yet to be answered is this: If the code is running in the `try` block, how does it know when to switch to the `catch` block if an error occurs? If an error is detected, the code does something known as *throwing an exception*. In other words, it instantiates an exception object class and throws it:

```
throw new OverflowException();
```

Here, you have instantiated an exception object of the `OverflowException` class. As soon as the application encounters a `throw` statement inside a `try` block, it immediately looks for the `catch` block associated with that `try` block. If more than one `catch` block is associated with the `try` block, it identifies the correct `catch` block by checking which exception class the `catch` block is associated with. For example, when the `OverflowException` object is thrown, execution jumps to the following `catch` block:

```
catch (OverflowException ex)
{
   // exception handling here
}
```

In other words, the application looks for the `catch` block that indicates a matching exception class instance of the same class (or of a base class).

With this extra information, you can expand the `try` block just demonstrated. Assume, for the sake of argument, that two possible serious errors can occur in the `try` block: an overflow and an array out of bounds. Assume also that your code contains two Boolean variables, `Overflow` and `OutOfBounds`, which indicate whether these conditions exist. You have already seen that a predefined exception class exists to indicate overflow (`OverflowException`); similarly, an `IndexOutOfRangeException` class exists to handle an array that is out of bounds.

Now your `try` block looks like this:

```
try
{
   // code for normal execution
   if (Overflow == true)
   {
      throw new OverflowException();
   }
   // more processing
   if (OutOfBounds == true)
   {
      throw new IndexOutOfRangeException();
   }
   // otherwise continue normal execution
}
catch (OverflowException ex)
{
   // error handling for the overflow error condition
}
catch (IndexOutOfRangeException ex)
{
   // error handling for the index out of range error condition
}
finally
{
   // clean up
}
```

This is because you can have `throw` statements that are nested in several method calls inside the `try` block, but the same `try` block continues to apply even as execution flow enters these other methods. If the application encounters a `throw` statement, it immediately goes back up through all the method calls on the stack, looking for the end of the containing `try` block and the start of the appropriate `catch` block. During this process, all the local variables in the intermediate method calls will correctly go out of scope. This makes the `try...catch` architecture well suited to the situation described at the beginning of this section, whereby the error occurs inside a method call that is nested inside 15 or 20 method calls, and processing must stop immediately.

As you can probably gather from this discussion, `try` blocks can play a very significant role in controlling the flow of your code's execution. However, it is important to understand that exceptions are intended for exceptional conditions, hence their name. You wouldn't want to use them as a way of controlling when to exit a `do...while` loop.

Exceptions and Performance

Exception handling has a performance implication. In cases that are common, you shouldn't use exceptions to deal with errors. For example, when converting a string to a number, you can use the `Parse` method of the `int` type. This method throws a `FormatException` in case the `string` passed to this method can't be converted to a number, and it throws an `OverflowException` if a number can be converted but it doesn't fit into an `int`:

```
static void NumberDemo1(string n)
{
    if (n is null) throw new ArgumentNullException(nameof(n));
    try
    {
        int i = int.Parse(n);
        Console.WriteLine($"converted: {i}");
    }
    catch (FormatException ex)
    {
        Console.WriteLine(ex.Message);
    }
    catch (OverflowException ex)
    {
        Console.WriteLine(ex.Message);
    }
}
```

If the method `NumberDemo1` usually is used only in a way to pass numbers in a string and receiving not a number is exceptional, it's okay to program it this way. However, in cases when it's normal from the program flow to expect strings that cannot be converted, you can use the `TryParse` method. This method doesn't throw an exception if the string cannot be converted to a number. Instead, `TryParse` returns `true` if parsing succeeds, and it returns `false` if parsing fails:

```
static void NumberDemo2(string n)
{
    if (n is null) throw new ArgumentNullException(nameof(n));
    if (int.TryParse(n, out int result))
    {
        Console.WriteLine($"converted {result}");
    }
    else
    {
        Console.WriteLine("not a number");
    }
}
```

Implementing Multiple Catch Blocks

The easiest way to see how `try...catch...finally` blocks work in practice is with a couple of examples. The first example is called `SimpleExceptions`. It repeatedly asks the user to type in a number and then displays it. However, for the sake of this example, imagine that the number must be between 0 and 5; otherwise, the program isn't able to process the number properly. Therefore, you throw an exception if the user types anything outside this range. The program then continues to ask for more numbers for processing until the user simply presses the Enter key without entering anything.

> **NOTE** *You should note that this code does not provide a good example of when to use exception handling, but it shows good practice on how to use exception handling. As their name suggests, exceptions are provided for other than normal circumstances. Users often type silly things, so this situation doesn't really count. Normally, your program handles incorrect user input by performing an instant check and asking the user to retype the input if it isn't valid. However, generating exceptional situations is difficult in a small example that you can read through in a few minutes, so I will tolerate this less-than-ideal one to demonstrate how exceptions work. The examples that follow present more realistic situations.*

The code for `SimpleExceptions` looks like this (code file `SimpleExceptions/Program.cs`):

```csharp
public class Program
{
  public static void Main()
  {
    while (true)
    {
      try
      {
        string userInput;
        Console.Write("Input a number between 0 and 5 " +
          "(or just hit return to exit)> ");
        userInput = Console.ReadLine();

        if (string.IsNullOrEmpty(userInput))
        {
          break;
        }
        int index = Convert.ToInt32(userInput);
        if (index < 0 || index > 5)
        {
          throw new IndexOutOfRangeException($"You typed in {userInput}");
        }
        Console.WriteLine($"Your number was {index}");
      }
      catch (IndexOutOfRangeException ex)
      {
        Console.WriteLine("Exception: " +
          $"Number should be between 0 and 5. {ex.Message}");
      }
      catch (Exception ex)
      {
        Console.WriteLine($"An exception was thrown. Message was: " +
          $"{ex.Message}");
      }
      finally
      {
        Console.WriteLine("Thank you\n");
      }
    }
  }
}
```

The core of this code is a `while` loop, which continually uses `ReadLine` to ask for user input. `ReadLine` returns a string, so your first task is to convert it to an `int` using the `System.Convert.ToInt32` method. The `System.Convert` class contains various useful methods to perform data conversions, and it provides an alternative to the `int.Parse` method. In general, `System.Convert` contains methods to perform various type conversions. Recall that the C# compiler resolves `int` to instances of the `System.Int32` base class.

> **NOTE** *It is also worth pointing out that the parameter passed to the `catch` block is scoped to that `catch` block—which is why you can use the same parameter name, ex, in successive `catch` blocks in the preceding code.*

In the preceding example, you also check for an empty string because it is your condition for exiting the `while` loop. Notice how the `break` statement breaks right out of the enclosing `try` block as well as the `while` loop because this is valid behavior. Of course, when execution breaks out of the `try` block, the `Console.WriteLine` statement in the `finally` block is executed. Although you just display a greeting here, more commonly you will be doing tasks like closing file handles and calling the `Dispose` method of various objects to perform any cleanup. After the application leaves the `finally` block, it simply carries on executing into the next statement that it would have executed had the `finally` block not been present. In the case of this example, though, you iterate back to the start of the `while` loop and enter the `try` block again (unless the `finally` block was entered as a result of executing the `break` statement in the `while` loop, in which case you simply exit the `while` loop).

Next, you check for your exception condition:

```
if (index < 0 || index > 5)
{
    throw new IndexOutOfRangeException($"You typed in {userInput}");
}
```

When throwing an exception, you need to specify what type of exception to throw. Although the class `System.Exception` is available, it is intended only as a base class. It is considered bad programming practice to throw an instance of this class as an exception, because it conveys no information about the nature of the error condition. Instead, .NET contains many other exception classes that are derived from `Exception`. Each of these matches a particular type of exception condition, and you are free to define your own as well. The goal is to provide as much information as possible about the particular exception condition by throwing an instance of a class that matches the particular error condition. In the preceding example, `System.IndexOutOfRangeException` is the best choice for the circumstances. `IndexOutOfRangeException` has several constructor overloads. The one chosen in the example takes a string describing the error. Alternatively, you might choose to derive your own custom `Exception` object that describes the error condition in the context of your application.

Suppose that the user next types a number that is not between 0 and 5. The number is picked up by the `if` statement and an `IndexOutOfRangeException` object is instantiated and thrown. At this point, the application immediately exits the `try` block and hunts for a `catch` block that handles `IndexOutOfRangeException`. The first `catch` block it encounters is this:

```
catch (IndexOutOfRangeException ex)
{
    Console.WriteLine($"Exception: Number should be between 0 and 5." +
        $"{ex.Message}");
}
```

Because this `catch` block takes a parameter of the appropriate class, the `catch` block receives the exception instance and is executed. In this case, you display an error message and the `Exception.Message` property (which corresponds to the string passed to the `IndexOutOfRangeException`'s constructor). After executing this `catch` block, control then switches to the `finally` block, just as if no exception had occurred.

Notice that in the example you have also provided another `catch` block:

```
catch (Exception ex)
{
   Console.WriteLine($"An exception was thrown. Message was: {ex.Message}");
}
```

This `catch` block would also be capable of handling an `IndexOutOfRangeException` if it weren't for the fact that such exceptions will already have been caught by the previous `catch` block. A reference to a base class can also refer to any instances of classes derived from it, and all exceptions are derived from `Exception`. This `catch` block isn't executed because the application executes only the first suitable `catch` block it finds from the list of available `catch` blocks. This catch block isn't executed when an exception of type `IndexOutOfRangeException` is thrown. The application only executes the first suitable catch block it finds from the list of available catch blocks. This second catch block catches other exceptions derived from the Exception base class. Be aware that the three separate calls to methods within the try block (`Console.ReadLine`, `Console.Write`, and `Convert.ToInt32`) might throw other exceptions.

If the user types something that is not a number—say a or `hello`—the `Convert.ToInt32` method throws an exception of the class `System.FormatException` to indicate that the string passed into `ToInt32` is not in a format that can be converted to an int. When this happens, the application traces back through the method calls, looking for a handler that can handle this exception. Your first `catch` block (the one that takes an `IndexOutOfRangeException`) will not do. The application then looks at the second `catch` block. This one will do because `FormatException` is derived from `Exception`, so a `FormatException` instance can be passed in as a parameter here.

The structure of the example is fairly typical of a situation with multiple `catch` blocks. You start with `catch` blocks that are designed to trap specific error conditions. Then, you finish with more general blocks that cover any errors for which you have not written specific error handlers. Indeed, the order of the `catch` blocks is important. Had you written the previous two blocks in the opposite order, the code would not have compiled, because the second `catch` block is unreachable (the `Exception` catch block would catch all exceptions). Therefore, the uppermost `catch` blocks should be the most granular options available, ending with the most general options.

Now that you have analyzed the code for the example, you can run it. The following output illustrates what happens with different inputs and demonstrates both the `IndexOutOfRangeException` and the `FormatException` being thrown:

```
SimpleExceptions
Input a number between 0 and 5 (or just hit return to exit)> 4
Your number was 4
Thank you
Input a number between 0 and 5 (or just hit return to exit)> 0
Your number was 0
Thank you
Input a number between 0 and 5 (or just hit return to exit)> 10
Exception: Number should be between 0 and 5. You typed in 10
Thank you
Input a number between 0 and 5 (or just hit return to exit)> hello
An exception was thrown. Message was: Input string was not in a correct format.
Thank you
Input a number between 0 and 5 (or just hit return to exit)>
Thank you
```

Catching Exceptions from Other Code

The previous example demonstrates the handling of two exceptions. One of them, `IndexOutOfRangeException`, was thrown by your own code. The other, `FormatException`, was thrown from inside one of the base classes. It is very common for code in a library to throw an exception if it detects that a problem has occurred, or if one of the methods has been called inappropriately by being passed the wrong parameters. However, library code rarely attempts to catch exceptions; this is regarded as the responsibility of the client code.

Often, exceptions are thrown from the base class libraries while you are debugging. The process of debugging to some extent involves determining why exceptions have been thrown and removing the causes. Your aim should be to ensure that by the time the code is actually shipped, exceptions occur only in very exceptional circumstances and, if possible, are handled appropriately in your code.

System.Exception Properties

The example illustrated the use of only the Message property of the exception object. However, a number of other properties are available in System.Exception, as shown in the following table.

PROPERTY	DESCRIPTION
Data	Enables you to add key/value statements to the exception that can be used to supply extra information about it.
HelpLink	A link to a help file that provides more information about the exception.
InnerException	If this exception was thrown inside a catch block, then InnerException contains the exception object that sent the code into that catch block.
Message	Text that describes the error condition.
Source	The name of the application or object that caused the exception.
StackTrace	Provides details about the method calls on the stack (to help track down the method that threw the exception).
HResult	A numerical value that is assigned to the exception.
TargetSite	A .NET reflection object that describes the method that threw the exception.

The property value for StackTrace is supplied automatically by the .NET runtime if a stack trace is available. Source will always be filled in by the .NET runtime as the name of the assembly in which the exception was raised (though you might want to modify the property in your code to give more specific information), whereas Data, Message, HelpLink, and InnerException must be filled in by the code that threw the exception, by setting these properties immediately before throwing the exception. For example, the code to throw an exception might look something like this:

```
if (ErrorCondition == true)
{
  var myException = new ClassMyException("Help!!!!");
  myException.Source = "My Application Name";
  myException.HelpLink = "MyHelpFile.txt";
  myException.Data["ErrorDate"] = DateTime.Now;
  myException.Data.Add("AdditionalInfo", "Contact Bill from the Blue  Team");
  throw myException;
}
```

Here, ClassMyException is the name of the particular exception class you are throwing. Note that it is common practice for the names of all exception classes to end with Exception. In addition, note that the Data property is assigned in two possible ways.

Exception Filters

Since version 6, C# has allowed exception filters. A catch block runs only if the filter returns `true`. You can have different catch blocks that act differently when catching different exception types. In some scenarios, it's useful to have the catch blocks act differently based on the content of an exception. For example, when using the Windows Runtime, you often get COM exceptions for all different kinds of exceptions, or when doing network calls you get a network exception for many different scenarios—for example, if the server is not available, or the data supplied do not match the expectations. It's good to react to these errors differently. Some exceptions can be recovered in different ways, while with others the user might need some information.

The following code sample throws the exception of type `MyCustomException` and sets the `ErrorCode` property of this exception (code file `ExceptionFilters/Program.cs`):

```
public static void ThrowWithErrorCode(int code)
{
    throw new MyCustomException("Error in Foo") { ErrorCode = code };
}
```

In the `Main` method, the `try` block safeguards the method invocation with two catch blocks. The first catch block uses the `when` keyword to filter only exceptions if the `ErrorCode` property equals `405`. The expression for the `when` clause needs to return a Boolean value. If the result is `true`, this catch block handles the exception. If it is `false`, other catches are looked for. Passing `405` to the method `ThrowWithErrorCode`, the filter returns `true`, and the first `catch` handles the exception. Passing another value, the filter returns `false` and the second `catch` handles the exception. With filters, you can have multiple handlers to handle the same exception type.

Of course, you can also remove the second `catch` block and not handle the exception in that circumstance.

```
try
{
    ThrowWithErrorCode(405);
}
catch (MyCustomException ex) when (ex.ErrorCode == 405)
{
    Console.WriteLine($"Exception caught with filter {ex.Message} " +
        $"and {ex.ErrorCode}");
}
catch (MyCustomException ex)
{
    Console.WriteLine($"Exception caught {ex.Message} and {ex.ErrorCode}");
}
```

Re-throwing Exceptions

When you catch exceptions it's also very common to re-throw exceptions. You can change the exception type while throwing the exception again. With this you can give the caller more information about what happened. The original exception might not have enough information about the context of what was going on. You can also log exception information and give the caller different information. For example, for a user running the application, exception information does not really help. A system administrator reading log files can react accordingly.

An issue with re-throwing exceptions is that the caller often needs to find out the reason for what happened with the earlier exception, and where this did happen. Depending on how exceptions are thrown, stack trace information might be lost. For you to see the different options on re-throwing exceptions, the sample program `RethrowExceptions` shows the different options.

For this sample, two custom exception types are created. The first one, `MyCustomException`, defines the property `ErrorCode` in addition to the members of the base class `Exception`; the second one, `AnotherCustomException`, supports passing an inner exception (code file `RethrowExceptions/MyCustomException.cs`):

```
public class MyCustomException : Exception
{
  public MyCustomException(string message)
    : base(message) { }

  public int ErrorCode { get; set; }
}

public class AnotherCustomException : Exception
{
  public AnotherCustomException(string message, Exception innerException)
    : base(message, innerException) { }
}
```

The method `HandleAll` invokes the methods `HandleAndThrowAgain`, `HandleAndThrowWithInner-Exception`, `HandleAndRethrow`, and `HandleWithFilter`. The exception that is thrown is caught to write the exception message as well as the stack trace to the console. To better find what line numbers are referenced from the stack trace, the `#line` preprocessor directive is used that restarts the line numbering. With this, the invocation of the methods using the delegate m is in line 114 (code file `RethrowExceptions/Program.cs`):

```
#line 100
public static void HandleAll()
{
  var methods = new Action[]
  {
    HandleAndThrowAgain,
    HandleAndThrowWithInnerException,
    HandleAndRethrow,
    HandleWithFilter
  };

  foreach (var m in methods)
  {
    try
    {
      m(); // line 114
    }
    catch (Exception ex)
    {
      Console.WriteLine(ex.Message);
      Console.WriteLine(ex.StackTrace);
      if (ex.InnerException != null)
      {
        Console.WriteLine($"\tInner Exception{ex.Message}");
        Console.WriteLine(ex.InnerException.StackTrace);
      }
      Console.WriteLine();
    }
  }
}
```

The method `ThrowAnException` is the one to throw the first exception. This exception is thrown in line 8002. During development, it helps to know where this exception is thrown:

```
#line 8000
public static void ThrowAnException(string message)
```

```
{
    throw new MyCustomException(message); // line 8002
}
```

Naïve Use to Rethrow the Exception

The method `HandleAndThrowAgain` does nothing more than log the exception to the console and throw it again using `throw ex`:

```
#line 4000
public static void HandleAndThrowAgain()
{
    try
    {
        ThrowAnException("test 1");
    }
    catch (Exception ex)
    {
        Console.WriteLine($"Log exception {ex.Message} and throw again");
        throw ex; // you shouldn't do that - line 4009
    }
}
```

Running the application, a simplified output showing the stack-trace (without the namespace and the full path to the code files) is shown here:

```
Log exception test 1 and throw again
test 1
at Program.HandleAndThrowAgain() in Program.cs:line 4009
at Program.HandleAll() in Program.cs:line 114
```

The stack trace shows the call to the m method within the `HandleAll` method, which in turn invokes the `HandleAndThrowAgain` method. The information where the exception is thrown at first is completely lost in the call stack of the final catch. This makes it hard to find the original reason of an error. Usually it's not a good idea to just throw the same exception with `throw` passing the exception object.

Changing the Exception

One useful scenario is to change the type of the exception and add information to the error. This is done in the method `HandleAndThrowWithInnerException`. After logging the error, a new exception of type `AnotherException` is thrown passing ex as the inner exception:

```
#line 3000
public static void HandleAndThrowWithInnerException()
{
    try
    {
        ThrowAnException("test 2"); // line 3004
    }
    catch (Exception ex)
    {
        Console.WriteLine($"Log exception {ex.Message} and throw again");
        throw new AnotherCustomException("throw with inner exception", ex); // 3009
    }
}
```

Checking the stack trace of the outer exception, you see line numbers 3009 and 114 similar to before. However, the inner exception gives the original reason of the error. It gives the line of the method that invoked the erroneous method (3004) and the line where the original (the inner) exception was thrown (8002):

```
Log exception test 2 and throw again
throw with inner exception
```

```
at Program.HandleAndThrowWithInnerException() in Program.cs:line 3009
at Program.HandleAll() in Program.cs:line 114
Inner Exception throw with inner exception
at Program.ThrowAnException(String message) in Program.cs:line 8002
at Program.HandleAndThrowWithInnerException() in Program.cs:line 3004
```

No information is lost this way.

> **NOTE** *When trying to find reasons for an error, have a look at whether an inner exception exists. This often gives helpful information.*

> **NOTE** *When catching exceptions, it's good practice to change the exception when rethrowing. For example, catching an* SqlException *can result in throwing a business-related exception such as* InvalidIsbnException.

Rethrowing the Exception

In case the exception type should not be changed, the same exception can be rethrown just with the throw statement. Using throw without passing an exception object throws the current exception of the catch block and keeps the exception information:

```
#line 2000
public static void HandleAndRethrow()
{
  try
  {
    ThrowAnException("test 3");
  }
  catch (Exception ex)
  {
    Console.WriteLine($"Log exception {ex.Message} and rethrow");
    throw; // line 2009
  }
}
```

With this in place, the stack information is not lost. The exception was originally thrown in line 8002, and rethrown in line 2009. Line 114 contains the delegate m that invoked HandleAndRethrow:

```
Log exception test 3 and rethrow
test 3
at Program.ThrowAnException(String message) in Program.cs:line 8002
at Program.HandleAndRethrow() in Program.cs:line 2009
at Program.HandleAll() in Program.cs:line 114
```

Using Filters to Add Functionality

When rethrowing exceptions using the throw statement, the call stack contains the address of the throw. When you use exception filters, it is possible to not change the call stack at all. Now add a when keyword that passes a filter method. This filter method named Filter logs the message and always returns false. That's why the catch block is never invoked:

```
#line 1000
public void HandleWithFilter()
{
```

```
    try
    {
      ThrowAnException("test 4"); // line 1004
    }
    catch (Exception ex) when(Filter(ex))
    {
      Console.WriteLine("block never invoked");
    }
}
#line 1500
public bool Filter(Exception ex)
{
  Console.WriteLine($"just log {ex.Message}");
  return false;
}
```

Now when you look at the stack trace, the exception originates in the `HandleAll` method in line 114 that in turn invokes `HandleWithFilter`, line 1004 contains the invocation to `ThrowAnException`, and line 8002 contains the line where the exception was thrown:

```
just log test 4
test 4
at Program.ThrowAnException(String message) in Program.cs:line 8002
at Program.HandleWithFilter() in Program.cs:line 1004
at RethrowExceptions.Program.HandleAll() in Program.cs:line 114
```

> **NOTE** *The primary use of exception filters is to filter exceptions based on a value of the exception. Exception filters can also be used for other effects, such as writing log information without changing the call stack. However, exception filters should be fast running, so you should only do simple checks and avoid side effects. Logging is one of the excusable exceptions.*

What Happens If an Exception Isn't Handled?

Sometimes an exception might be thrown but there is no `catch` block in your code that is able to handle that kind of exception. The `SimpleExceptions` example can serve to illustrate this. Suppose, for example, that you omitted the `FormatException` and catch-all `catch` blocks, and supplied only the block that traps an `IndexOutOfRangeException`. In that circumstance, what would happen if a `FormatException` were thrown?

The answer is that the .NET runtime would catch it. Later in this section, you learn how you can nest `try` blocks; and, in fact, there is already a nested `try` block behind the scenes in the example. The .NET runtime has effectively placed the entire program inside another huge `try` block—it does this for every .NET program. This `try` block has a `catch` handler that can catch any type of exception. If an exception occurs that your code does not handle, the execution flow simply passes right out of your program and is trapped by this `catch` block in the .NET runtime. However, the results of this probably will not be what you want, as the execution of your code is terminated promptly. The user sees a dialog that complains that your code has not handled the exception and provides any details about the exception the .NET runtime was able to retrieve. At least the exception has been caught!

In general, if you are writing an executable, try to catch as many exceptions as you reasonably can and handle them in a sensible way. If you are writing a library, it is normally best to catch exceptions that you can handle in a useful way, or where you can add additional information to the context and throw other exception types as shown in the previous section. Assume that the calling code handles any errors it encounters.

USER-DEFINED EXCEPTION CLASSES

In the previous section, you already created a user-defined exception. You are now ready to look at a larger example that illustrates exceptions. This example, called `SolicitColdCall`, contains two nested `try` blocks and illustrates the practice of defining your own custom exception classes and throwing another exception from inside a `try` block.

This example assumes that a sales company wants to increase its customer base. The company's sales team is going to phone a list of people to invite them to become customers, a practice known in sales jargon as *cold-calling*. To this end, you have a text file available that contains the names of the people to be cold-called. The file should be in a well-defined format in which the first line contains the number of people in the file and each subsequent line contains the name of the next person. In other words, a correctly formatted file of names might look like this:

```
4
George Washington
Benedict Arnold
John Adams
Thomas Jefferson
```

This version of cold-calling is designed to display the name of the person on the screen (perhaps for the salesperson to read). That is why only the names, and not the phone numbers, of the individuals are contained in the file.

For this example, your program asks the user for the name of the file and then simply reads it in and displays the names of people. That sounds like a simple task, but even so a couple of things can go wrong and require you to abandon the entire procedure:

➤ The user might type the name of a file that does not exist. This is caught as a `FileNotFound` exception.

➤ The file might not be in the correct format. There are two possible problems here. One, the first line of the file might not be an integer. Two, there might not be as many names in the file as the first line of the file indicates. In both cases, you want to trap this oddity as a custom exception that has been written especially for this purpose, `ColdCallFileFormatException`.

There is something else that can go wrong that doesn't cause you to abandon the entire process but does mean you need to abandon a person's name and move on to the next name in the file (and therefore trap it by an inner `try` block). Some people are spies working for rival sales companies, so you obviously do not want to let these people know what you are up to by accidentally phoning one of them. For simplicity, assume that you can identify who the spies are because their names begin with B. Such people should have been screened out when the data file was first prepared, but in case any have slipped through, you need to check each name in the file and throw a `SalesSpyFoundException` if you detect a sales spy. This, of course, is another custom exception object.

Finally, you implement this example by coding a class, `ColdCallFileReader`, which maintains the connection to the cold-call file and retrieves data from it. You code this class in a safe way, which means that its methods all throw exceptions if they are called inappropriately—for example, if a method that reads a file is called before the file has even been opened. For this purpose, you write another exception class: `UnexpectedException`.

Catching the User-Defined Exceptions

The code sample for user-defined exceptions makes use of the following namespaces:

```
System

System.IO
```

Start with the Main method of the SolicitColdCall sample, which catches your user-defined exceptions. Note that you need to call up file-handling classes in the System.IO namespace as well as the System namespace (code file SolicitColdCall/Program.cs):

```
public class Program
{
  public static void Main()
  {
    Console.Write("Please type in the name of the file " +
      "containing the names of the people to be cold called > ");
    string fileName = ReadLine();
    ColdCallFileReaderLoop1(fileName);
    Console.WriteLine();
    Console.ReadLine();
  }

  public static ColdCallfFileReaderLoop1(string filename)
  {
    var peopleToRing = new ColdCallFileReader();
    try
    {
      peopleToRing.Open(fileName);
      for (int i = 0; i < peopleToRing.NPeopleToRing; i++)
      {
        peopleToRing.ProcessNextPerson();
      }
      Console.WriteLine("All callers processed correctly");
    }
    catch(FileNotFoundException)
    {
      Console.WriteLine($"The file {fileName} does not exist");
    }
    catch(ColdCallFileFormatException ex)
    {
      Console.WriteLine($"The file {fileName} appears to have been corrupted");
      Console.WriteLine($"Details of problem are: {ex.Message}");
      if (ex.InnerException != null)
      {
        Console.WriteLine($"Inner exception was: {ex.InnerException.Message}");
      }
    }
    catch(Exception ex)
    {
      Console.WriteLine($"Exception occurred:\n{ex.Message}");
    }
    finally
    {
      peopleToRing.Dispose();
    }
  }
}
```

This code is a little more than just a loop to process people from the file. You start by asking the user for the name of the file. Then you instantiate an object of a class called ColdCallFileReader, which is defined shortly. The ColdCallFileReader class is the class that handles the file reading. Notice that you do this outside the initial try block—that's because the variables that you instantiate here need to be available in the subsequent catch and finally blocks, and if you declare them inside the try block they would go out of scope at the closing curly brace of the try block, where the compiler would complain about it.

In the try block, you open the file (using the ColdCallFileReader.Open method) and loop over all the people in it. The ColdCallFileReader.ProcessNextPerson method reads in and displays the name of the next person in the file, and the `ColdCallFileReader.NPeopleToRing` property indicates how many people should be in the file (obtained by reading the file's first line). There are three `catch` blocks: one for `FileNotFoundException`, one for `ColdCallFileFormatException`, and one to trap any other .NET exceptions.

In the case of a `FileNotFoundException`, you display a message to that effect. Notice that in this `catch` block, the exception instance is not actually used at all. This `catch` block is used to illustrate the user-friendliness of the application. Exception objects generally contain technical information that is useful for developers, but not the sort of stuff you want to show to end users. Therefore, in this case you create a simpler message of your own.

For the `ColdCallFileFormatException` handler, you have done the opposite, specifying how to obtain fuller technical information, including details about the inner exception, if one is present.

Finally, if you catch any other generic exceptions, you display a user-friendly message, instead of letting any such exceptions fall through to the .NET runtime. Note that here you are not handling any other exceptions that aren't derived from `System.Exception` because you are not calling directly into non-.NET code.

The `finally` block is there to clean up resources. In this case, that means closing any open file—performed by the `ColdCallFileReader.Dispose` method.

> **NOTE** C# *offers the* `using` *statement where the compiler itself creates a* `try/finally` *block calling the* `Dispose` *method in the finally block. The using statement is available on objects implementing a* `Dispose` *method. You can read the details of the using statement in Chapter 17, "Managed and Unmanaged Memory."*

Throwing the User-Defined Exceptions

Now take a look at the definition of the class that handles the file reading and (potentially) throws your user-defined exceptions: `ColdCallFileReader`. Because this class maintains an external file connection, you need to ensure that it is disposed of correctly in accordance with the principles outlined for the disposing of objects in Chapter 4, "Object-Oriented Programming with C#." Therefore, you derive this class from `IDisposable`.

First, you declare some private fields (code file `SolicitColdCall/ColdCallFileReader.cs`):

```
public class ColdCallFileReader: IDisposable
{
    private FileStream _fs;
    private StreamReader _sr;
    private uint _nPeopleToRing;
    private bool _isDisposed = false;
    private bool _isOpen = false;
```

`FileStream` and `StreamReader`, both in the `System.IO` namespace, are the base classes that you use to read the file. `FileStream` enables you to connect to the file in the first place, whereas `StreamReader` is designed to read text files and implements a method, `ReadLine`, which reads a line of text from a file. You look at `StreamReader` more closely in Chapter 22, "Files and Streams," which discusses file handling in depth.

The `_isDisposed` field indicates whether the `Dispose` method has been called. `ColdCallFileReader` is implemented so that after `Dispose` has been called, it is not permitted to reopen connections and reuse the object. `_isOpen` is also used for error checking—in this case, checking whether the `StreamReader` actually connects to an open file.

The process of opening the file and reading in that first line—the one that tells you how many people are in the file—is handled by the Open method:

```
public void Open(string fileName)
{
  if (_isDisposed)
  {
    throw new ObjectDisposedException("peopleToRing");
  }
  _fs = new FileStream(fileName, FileMode.Open);
  _sr = new StreamReader(_fs);
  try
  {
    string firstLine = _sr.ReadLine();
    _nPeopleToRing = uint.Parse(firstLine);
    _isOpen = true;
  }
  catch (FormatException ex)
  {
    throw new ColdCallFileFormatException(
      $"First line isn\'t an integer {ex}");
  }
}
```

The first thing you do in this method (as with all other ColdCallFileReader methods) is check whether the client code has inappropriately called it after the object has been disposed of, and if so, throw a predefined ObjectDisposedException object. The Open method checks the _isDisposed field to determine whether Dispose has already been called. Because calling Dispose implies that the caller has now finished with this object, you regard it as an error to attempt to open a new file connection if Dispose has been called.

Next, the method contains the first of two inner try blocks. The purpose of this one is to catch any errors resulting from the first line of the file not containing an integer. If that problem arises, the .NET runtime throws a FormatException, which you trap and convert to a more meaningful exception that indicates a problem with the format of the cold-call file. Note that System.FormatException is there to indicate format problems with basic data types, not with files, so it's not a particularly useful exception to pass back to the calling routine in this case. The new exception thrown will be trapped by the outermost try block. Because no cleanup is needed here, there is no need for a finally block.

If everything is fine, you set the isOpen field to true to indicate that there is now a valid file connection from which data can be read.

The ProcessNextPerson method also contains an inner try block:

```
public void ProcessNextPerson()
{
  if (_isDisposed)
  {
    throw new ObjectDisposedException("peopleToRing");
  }
  if (!_isOpen)
  {
    throw new UnexpectedException(
      "Attempted to access coldcall file that is not open");
  }
  try
  {
    string name = _sr.ReadLine();
    if (name == null)
    {
```

```
               throw new ColdCallFileFormatException("Not enough names");
            }
            if (name[0] == 'B')
            {
               throw new SalesSpyFoundException(name);
            }
            Console.WriteLine(name);
         }
         catch(SalesSpyFoundException ex)
         {
            Console.WriteLine(ex.Message);
         }
         finally
         {
         }
      }
```

Two possible problems exist with the file here (assuming there actually is an open file connection; the `ProcessNextPerson` method checks this first). One, you might read in the next name and discover that it is a sales spy. If that condition occurs, then the exception is trapped by the first `catch` block in this method. Because that exception has been caught here, inside the loop, it means that execution can subsequently continue in the `Main` method of the program, and the subsequent names in the file continue to be processed.

A problem might also occur if you try to read the next name and discover that you have already reached the end of the file. The `StreamReader` object's `ReadLine` method works like this: If it has gone past the end of the file, it doesn't throw an exception but simply returns `null`. Therefore, if you find a null string, you know that the format of the file was incorrect because the number in the first line of the file indicated a larger number of names than were actually present in the file. If that happens, you throw a `ColdCallFileFormatException`, which will be caught by the outer exception handler (which causes the execution to terminate).

Again, you don't need a `finally` block here because there is no cleanup to do; however, this time an empty `finally` block is included just to show that you can do so, if you want.

The example is nearly finished. You have just two more members of `ColdCallFileReader` to look at: the `NPeopleToRing` property, which returns the number of people that are supposed to be in the file, and the `Dispose` method, which closes an open file. Notice that the `Dispose` method returns immediately if it has already been called—this is the recommended way of implementing it. It also confirms that there actually is a file stream to close before closing it. This example is shown here to illustrate defensive coding techniques:

```csharp
public uint NPeopleToRing
{
   get
   {
      if (_isDisposed)
      {
         throw new ObjectDisposedException("peopleToRing");
      }
      if (!_isOpen)
      {
         throw new UnexpectedException(
            "Attempted to access cold-call file that is not open");
      }
      return _nPeopleToRing;
   }
}
```

```
public void Dispose()
{
  if (_isDisposed)
  {
    return;
  }
  _isDisposed = true;
  _isOpen = false;
  _fs?.Dispose();
  _fs = null;
}
```

Defining the User-Defined Exception Classes

Finally, you need to define three of your own exception classes. Defining your own exception is quite easy because there are rarely any extra methods to add. It is just a case of implementing a constructor to ensure that the base class constructor is called correctly. Here is the full implementation of SalesSpyFoundException (code file SolicitColdCall/SalesSpyFoundException.cs):

```
public class SalesSpyFoundException: Exception
{
  public SalesSpyFoundException(string spyName)
    : base($"Sales spy found, with name {spyName}")
  {
  }

  public SalesSpyFoundException(string spyName, Exception innerException)
    : base($"Sales spy found with name {spyName}", innerException)
  {
  }
}
```

Notice that it is derived from Exception, as you would expect for a custom exception. In fact, in practice, you would probably have added an intermediate class, something like ColdCallFileException, derived from Exception, and then derived both of your exception classes from this class. This ensures that the handling code has that extra-fine degree of control over which exception handler handles each exception. However, to keep the example simple, you will not do that.

You have done one bit of processing in SalesSpyFoundException. You have assumed that the message passed into its constructor is just the name of the spy found, so you turn this string into a more meaningful error message. You have also provided two constructors: one that simply takes a message, and one that also takes an inner exception as a parameter. When defining your own exception classes, it is best to include, at a minimum, at least these two constructors (although you will not actually be using the second SalesSpyFoundException constructor in this example).

Now for the ColdCallFileFormatException. This follows the same principles as the previous exception, but you don't do any processing on the message (code file SolicitColdCall/ColdCallFileFormatException.cs):

```
public class ColdCallFileFormatException: Exception
{
  public ColdCallFileFormatException(string message)
    : base(message)
  {
  }

  public ColdCallFileFormatException(string message, Exception innerException)
    : base(message, innerException)
  {
  }
}
```

Finally, you have `UnexpectedException`, which looks much the same as `ColdCallFileFormatException` (code file `SolicitColdCall/UnexpectedException.cs`):

```
public class UnexpectedException: Exception
{
  public UnexpectedException(string message)
    : base(message)
  {
  }

  public UnexpectedException(string message, Exception innerException)
    : base(message, innerException)
  {
  }
}
```

Now you are ready to test the program. First, try the `people.txt` file. The contents are defined here:

```
4
George Washington
Benedict Arnold
John Adams
Thomas Jefferson
```

This has four names (which match the number given in the first line of the file), including one spy. Then try the following `people2.txt` file, which has an obvious formatting error:

```
49
George Washington
Benedict Arnold
John Adams
Thomas Jefferson
```

Finally, try the example but specify the name of a file that does not exist, such as `people3.txt`. Running the program three times for the three filenames returns these results:

```
SolicitColdCall
Please type in the name of the file containing the names of the people to be cold
called > people.txt
George Washington
Sales spy found, with name Benedict Arnold
John Adams
Thomas Jefferson
All callers processed correctly
SolicitColdCall
Please type in the name of the file containing the names of the people to be cold
called > people2.txt
George Washington
Sales spy found, with name Benedict Arnold
John Adams
Thomas Jefferson
The file people2.txt appears to have been corrupted.
Details of the problem are: Not enough names
SolicitColdCall
Please type in the name of the file containing the names of the people to be cold
called > people3.txt
The file people3.txt does not exist.
```

This application has demonstrated a number of different ways in which you can handle the errors and exceptions that you might find in your own applications.

CALLER INFORMATION

When dealing with errors, it is often helpful to get information about the error where it occurred. Earlier in this chapter, the #line preprocessor directive is used to change the line numbering of the code to get better information with the call stack. Getting the line numbers, filenames, and member names from within code, you can use attributes and optional parameters that are directly supported by the C# compiler. The attributes CallerLineNumber, CallerFilePath, and CallerMemberName, defined within the namespace System.Runtime.CompilerServices, can be applied to parameters. Normally with optional parameters, the compiler assigns the default values on method invocation in case these parameters are not supplied with the call information. With caller information attributes, the compiler doesn't fill in the default values; it instead fills in the line number, file path, and member name.

The code sample CallerInformation makes use of the following namespaces:

```
System

System.Runtime.CompilerServices
```

The Log method from the following code snippet demonstrates how to use these attributes. With the implementation, the information is written to the console (code file CallerInformation/Program.cs):

```csharp
public void Log([CallerLineNumber] int line = -1,
[CallerFilePath] string path = null,
[CallerMemberName] string name = null)
{
  Console.WriteLine((line < 0) ? "No line" : "Line " + line);
  Console.WriteLine((path == null) ? "No file path" : path);
  Console.WriteLine((name == null) ? "No member name" : name);
  Console.WriteLine();
}
```

Let's invoke this method with some different scenarios. In the following Main method, the Log method is called by using an instance of the Program class, within the set accessor of the property, and within a lambda expression. Argument values are not assigned to the method, enabling the compiler to fill it in:

```csharp
public static void Main()
{
  var p = new Program();
  p.Log();
  p.SomeProperty = 33;
  Action a1 = () => p.Log();
  a1();
}

private int _someProperty;
public int SomeProperty
{
  get => _someProperty;
  set
  {
    Log();
    _someProperty = value;
  }
}
```

The result of the running program is shown next. Where the Log method was invoked, you can see the line numbers, the filename, and the caller member name. With the Log inside the Main method, the member name is Main. The invocation of the Log method inside the set accessor of the property SomeProperty shows SomeProperty. The Log method inside the lambda expression doesn't show the name of the generated method, but instead the name of the method where the lambda expression was invoked (Main), which is more useful, of course.

```
Line 12
c:\ProCSharp\ErrorsAndExceptions\CallerInformation\Program.cs
Main
Line 26
c:\ProCSharp\ErrorsAndExceptions\CallerInformation\Program.cs
SomeProperty
Line 14
c:\ProCSharp\ErrorsAndExceptions\CallerInformation\Program.cs
Main
```

Using the `Log` method within a constructor, the caller member name shows `ctor`. With a destructor, the caller member name is `Finalize`, as this is the method name generated.

> **NOTE** *The destructor and finalizer are covered in Chapter 17.*

> **NOTE** *A great use of the* `CallerMemberName` *attribute is with the implementation of the interface* `INotifyPropertyChanged`. *This interface requires the name of the property to be passed with the method implementation. You can see the implementation of this interface in several chapters in this book—for example, Chapter 34, "Patterns with XAML Apps."*

SUMMARY

This chapter examined the rich mechanism C# provides for dealing with error conditions through exceptions. You are not limited to the generic error codes that could be output from your code; instead, you have the capability to go in and uniquely handle the most granular of error conditions. Sometimes these error conditions are provided to you through .NET itself; at other times, though, you might want to code your own error conditions as illustrated in this chapter. In either case, you have many ways to protect the workflow of your applications from unnecessary and dangerous faults.

The next chapter goes into important keywords for asynchronous programming: `async` and `await`.

15

Asynchronous Programming

WHAT'S IN THIS CHAPTER?

➤ The importance of asynchronous programming
➤ Asynchronous patterns
➤ Foundations of asynchronous programming
➤ Error handling with asynchronous methods
➤ Asynchronous programming with Windows Apps

WROX.COM CODE DOWNLOADS FOR THIS CHAPTER

The Wrox.com code downloads for this chapter are found at www.wrox.com on the Download Code tab. The source code is also available at https://github.com/ProfessionalCSharp/ProfessionalCSharp7 in the directory Async.

The code for this chapter is divided into the following major examples:

➤ AsyncHistory
➤ Foundations
➤ Error Handling
➤ AsyncWindowsApp

WHY ASYNCHRONOUS PROGRAMMING IS IMPORTANT

The .NET Framework 4.5 added the Task Parallel Library (TPL) to .NET to make parallel programming easier. C# 5.0 added two keywords to make asynchronous programming easier: async and await. These two keywords are the main focus of this chapter.

With *asynchronous programming* a method is called that runs in the background (typically with the help of a thread or task), and the calling thread is not blocked.

In this chapter, you can read about different patterns on asynchronous programming such as the *asynchronous pattern*, the *event-based asynchronous pattern*, and the *task-based asynchronous pattern* (TAP). TAP makes use of the async and await keywords. When you compare these patterns, you can see the real advantage of this style of asynchronous programming.

After discussing the different patterns, you see the foundation of asynchronous programming by creating tasks and invoking asynchronous methods. You find out what's behind the scenes with continuation tasks and the synchronization context.

Error handling needs some special emphasis; as with asynchronous tasks, some scenarios require some different handling with errors.

The last part of this chapter discusses specific scenarios with Universal Windows apps, what you need to be aware of with asynchronous programming.

> **NOTE** *Chapter 21, "Tasks and Parallel Programming," covers other information about parallel programming.*

Users find it annoying when an application does not immediately react to requests. With the mouse, we have become accustomed to experiencing a delay, as we've learned that behavior over several decades. With a touch UI, an application needs to immediately react to requests. Otherwise, the user tries to redo the action.

Because asynchronous programming was hard to achieve with older versions of the .NET Framework, it was not always done when it should have been. One of the applications that blocked the UI thread fairly often is an older version of Visual Studio. With that version, opening a solution containing hundreds of projects meant you could take a long coffee break. Visual Studio 2017 offers the *Lightweight Solution Load* feature, which loads projects only as needed and with the selected project loaded first. Since Visual Studio 2015, the NuGet package manager is no longer implemented as a modal dialog. The new NuGet package manager can load information about packages asynchronously while you do other things at the same time. These are just a few examples of important changes built into Visual Studio related to asynchronous programming.

Many APIs with .NET offer both a synchronous and an asynchronous version. Because the synchronous version of the API was a lot easier to use, it was often used where it wasn't appropriate. With the new Windows Runtime (WinRT), if an API call is expected to take longer than 40 milliseconds, only an asynchronous version is available. Since C# 5.0, programming asynchronously is as easy as programming in a synchronous manner, so there shouldn't be any barrier to using the asynchronous APIs, but of course there can be traps, which are covered in this chapter.

.NET HISTORY OF ASYNCHRONOUS PROGRAMMING

Before stepping into the new `async` and `await` keywords, it is best to understand asynchronous patterns from the .NET Framework. Asynchronous features have been available since .NET Framework 1.0, and many classes in the .NET Framework implement one or more such patterns.

Here, we start doing a synchronous networking call followed by the different asynchronous patterns:

➤ Asynchronous pattern

➤ Event-based asynchronous pattern

➤ Task-based asynchronous pattern

The *asynchronous pattern*, which was the first way of handling asynchronous features, is not only available with several APIs but also with a base functionality such as the delegate type.

Because doing updates on the UI—both with Windows Forms and WPF—with the asynchronous pattern is quite complex, .NET Framework 2.0 introduced the *event-based asynchronous pattern*. With this pattern, an event handler is invoked from the thread that owns the synchronization context, so updating UI code is easily handled with this pattern. Previously, this pattern was also known with the name *asynchronous component pattern*.

With the .NET Framework 4.5, another way to achieve asynchronous programming was introduced: the *task-based asynchronous pattern* (TAP). This pattern is based on the `Task` type and makes use of a compiler feature with the keywords `async` and `await`.

The sample code for the `HistorySample` uses at least C# 7.1 and these namespaces:

```
System

System.IO

System.Net

System.Threading.Tasks
```

A sample app doing an HTTP request is a good use case as several of the System.Net APIs offer synchronous as well as asynchronous APIs.

Synchronous Call

Let's start with the synchronized version using the `WebClient` class. This class offers several synchronous APIs, such as `DownloadString`, `DownloadFile`, and `DownloadData`. In the following code snippet, `DownloadString` makes an HTTP request and writes the response in the string content. A substring of this string is written to the console (code file `AsyncHistory/Program.cs`):

```
private const string url = "http://www.cninnovation.com";

private static void SynchronizedAPI()
{
  Console.WriteLine(nameof(SynchronizedAPI));
  using (var client = new WebClient())
  {
    string content = client.DownloadString(url);
    Console.WriteLine(content.Substring(0, 100));
  }
  Console.WriteLine();
}
```

The method `DownloadString` blocks the calling thread until the result is returned. It's not a good idea to invoke this method from the user interface thread of the client application because it blocks the user interface. The wait is unpleasant to the user because the application is unresponsive during this network call.

Asynchronous Pattern

One way to make the call asynchronously is by using the asynchronous pattern. Many APIs of .NET offer the asynchronous pattern. With the .NET Framework, also the delegate type supports this pattern. Just be aware that when you invoke these methods of the delegate with .NET Core, an exception with the information that the platform is not supported is thrown.

The asynchronous pattern defines a `BeginXXX` method and an `EndXXX` method. For example, if a synchronous method `DownloadString` is offered, the asynchronous variants would be `BeginDownloadString` and `EndDownloadString`. The `BeginXXX` method takes all input arguments of the synchronous method, and `EndXXX` takes the output arguments and return type to return the result. With the asynchronous pattern, the `BeginXXX` method also defines a parameter of `AsyncCallback`, which accepts a delegate that is invoked as soon as the asynchronous method is completed. The `BeginXXX` method returns `IAsyncResult`, which can be used for polling to verify whether the call is completed, and to wait for the end of the method.

The `WebClient` class doesn't offer an implementation of the asynchronous pattern. Instead, the `WebRequest` class can be used. The `WebRequest` class itself is used by the `WebClient`. `WebRequest` offers this pattern with the methods `BeginGetResponse` and `EndGetResponse` (`GetResponse` is the synchronous version of this API).

In the following code snippet, a `WebRequest` is created using the `Create` method of the `WebRequest` class. Using this request object, the `BeginGetResponse` method starts the asynchronous HTTP GET request to the server. The calling thread is not blocked. The first parameter of the method is an `AsyncCallback`. This is a delegate referencing a `void` method with an `IAsyncResult` argument. The implementation is done with the local function `ReadResponse`. This method is invoked as soon as the network request is completed. Within the implementation, the request object is used again to retrieve the result using `GetResponseStream`. In the code sample, `Stream` and `StreamReader` are used to access the returned string content (code file `AsyncHistory/Program.cs`):

```
private static void AsynchronousPattern()
{
  Console.WriteLine(nameof(AsynchronousPattern));
  WebRequest request = WebRequest.Create(url);
  IAsyncResult result = request.BeginGetResponse(ReadResponse, null);

  void ReadResponse(IAsyncResult ar)
  {
    using (WebResponse response = request.EndGetResponse(ar))
    {
      Stream stream = response.GetResponseStream();
      var reader = new StreamReader(stream);
      string content = reader.ReadToEnd();
      Console.WriteLine(content.Substring(0, 100));
      Console.WriteLine();
    }
  }
}
```

Because a local function is used with the implementation, the request variable from the outer scope can be directly accessed with the closure functionality of the local function. Similar behavior is available with lambda expressions. In case a separate method would be used, the request object must be passed to this method. This is possible by passing the request object as the second argument of the `BeginGetResponse` method. This parameter can be retrieved in the called method using the `AsyncState` property of the `IAsyncResult`.

> **NOTE** *Local functions are explained in Chapter 13, "Functional Programming with C#."*

There's a problem with using the asynchronous pattern with UI applications: The method invoked from the `AsyncCallback` is not running in the UI thread, thus you cannot access members of UI elements without switching to the UI thread. An exception with the information `The calling thread cannot access this object because a different thread owns it.` would be the thrown. To make this easier, the .NET Framework 2.0 introduced the event-based asynchronous pattern, which makes it easier to deal with UI updates. This pattern is discussed next.

Event-Based Asynchronous Pattern

The method `EventBasedAsyncPattern` makes use of the event-based asynchronous pattern. This pattern defines a method with the suffix `Async`. Again, the example code uses the `WebClient` class. With the synchronous method `DownloadString`, the `WebClient` class offers the asynchronous variant `DownloadStringAsync`. When the request is completed, the `DownloadStringCompleted` event is fired. With the event handler of this event, the result can be retrieved. The `DownloadStringCompleted` event is of type `DownloadStringCompletedEventHandler`. The second argument is of type `DownloadStringCompletedEventArgs`. This argument returns the result string with the `Result` property (code file `AsyncHistory/Program.cs`):

```csharp
private static void EventBasedAsyncPattern()
{
  Console.WriteLine(nameof(EventBasedAsyncPattern));
  using (var client = new WebClient())
  {
    client.DownloadStringCompleted += (sender, e) =>
    {
      Console.WriteLine(e.Result.Substring(0, 100));
    };
    client.DownloadStringAsync(new Uri(url));
    Console.WriteLine();
  }
}
```

With the `DownloadStringCompleted` event, the event handler is invoked with the thread that holds the synchronization context. Using Windows Forms, WPF, and the Universal Windows Platform, this is the UI thread. Thus, you can directly access UI elements from the event handler. This is the big advantage of this pattern compared to the asynchronous pattern.

The difference between this event-based asynchronous pattern and synchronous programming is the order of method calls; they're reversed for the asynchronous pattern. Before invoking the asynchronous method, you need to define what happens when the method call is completed. The following section plunges into the new world of asynchronous programming with the `async` and `await` keywords.

Task-Based Asynchronous Pattern

The `WebClient` class was updated with the .NET Framework 4.5 to offer the task-based asynchronous pattern (TAP) as well. This pattern defines a suffix `Async` method that returns a `Task` type. Because the `WebClient` class already offers a method with the `Async` suffix to implement the task-based asynchronous pattern, the new method has the name `DownloadStringTaskAsync`.

The method `DownloadStringTaskAsync` is declared to return `Task<string>`. You do not need to declare a variable of `Task<string>` to assign the result from `DownloadStringTaskAsync`; instead, you can declare a variable of type `string`, and you can use the `await` keyword. The `await` keyword unblocks the thread to do other tasks. As soon as the method `DownloadStringTaskAsync` completes its background processing, the UI thread can continue and get the result from the background task to the string variable `resp`. Also, the code following this line continues (code file `AsyncHistory/Program.cs`):

```csharp
private static async Task TaskBasedAsyncPatternAsync()
{
  Console.WriteLine(nameof(TaskBasedAsyncPatternAsync));
  using (var client = new WebClient())
  {
    string content = await client.DownloadStringTaskAsync(url);
    Console.WriteLine(content.Substring(0, 100));
    Console.WriteLine();
  }
}
```

> **NOTE** *The* `async` *keyword creates a state machine similar to the* `yield` *return statement, which is discussed in Chapter 7, "Arrays."*

The code is much simpler now. There is no blocking, and no manually switching back to the UI thread, as this is done automatically. Also, the code follows the same order as you're used to with synchronous programming.

> **NOTE** *A more modern HTTP client is implemented with the class* `HttpClient`*. This class offers only asynchronous methods supporting the task-based asynchronous pattern. How this class can be used is explained in Chapter 23, "Networking."*

Async Main Method

The entry point of the console application, the `Main` method, has the `async` modifier applied to allow the `await` keyword in the implementation. Using this declaration of the `Main` method to return a task requires C# 7.1 (code file `AsyncHistory/Program.cs`):

```
static async Task Main()
{
    SynchronizedAPI();
    AsynchronousPattern();
    EventBasedAsyncPattern();
    await TaskBasedAsyncPatternAsync();
    Console.ReadLine();
}
```

> **NOTE** *To specify version 7.1 of the C# compiler you need to add the* `LangVersion` *element to the* `csproj` *project file, or you can make a change to Visual Studio in the Advanced Build Project Settings.*

Now that you've seen the advantages of the `async` and `await` keywords, the next section examines the programming foundation behind these keywords.

FOUNDATION OF ASYNCHRONOUS PROGRAMMING

The `async` and `await` keywords are just a compiler feature. The compiler creates code by using the `Task` class. Instead of using the new keywords, you could get the same functionality with C# 4 and methods of the `Task` class; it's just not as convenient.

This section gives information about what the compiler does with the async and await keywords. It shows you an effortless way to create an asynchronous method and demonstrates how to invoke multiple asynchronous methods in parallel. You also see how you can change a class to offer the asynchronous pattern with the new keywords.

The sample code for all the `Foundations` sample makes use of these namespaces:

```
System

System.Collections.Generic

System.IO

System.Linq

System.Net

System.Runtime.CompilerServices

System.Threading

System.Threading.Tasks
```

To better understand what's going on, the `TraceThreadAndTask` method is created to write thread and task information to the console. `Task.CurrentId` returns the identifier of the task. `Thread.CurrentThread.ManagedThreadId` returns the identifier of the current thread (code file `Foundations/Program.cs`):

```
public static void TraceThreadAndTask(string info)
{
    string taskInfo = Task.CurrentId == null ? "no task" : "task " +
        Task.CurrentId;

    Console.WriteLine($"{info} in thread {Thread.CurrentThread.ManagedThreadId}" +
        $"and {taskInfo}");
}
```

Creating Tasks

Let's start with the synchronous method `Greeting`, which takes a while before returning a string (code file `Foundations/Program.cs`):

```
static string Greeting(string name)
{
    TraceThreadAndTask($"running {nameof(Greeting)}");
    Task.Delay(3000).Wait();
    return $"Hello, {name}";
}
```

To make such a method asynchronously, you define the method `GreetingAsync`. The task-based asynchronous pattern specifies that an asynchronous method is named with the `Async` suffix and returns a task. `GreetingAsync` is defined to have the same input parameters as the `Greeting` method but returns `Task<string>`. `Task<string>` defines a task that returns a string in the future. A simple way to return a task is by using the `Task.Run` method. The generic version `Task.Run<string>()` creates a task that returns a string. As the compiler already knows the return type from the implementation (`Greeting` returns a string), you can also simplify the implementation by just using `Task.Run()`:

```
static Task<string> GreetingAsync(string name) =>
    Task.Run<string>(() =>
    {
        TraceThreadAndTask($"running {nameof(GreetingAsync)}");
        return Greeting(name);
    });
```

Calling an Asynchronous Method

You can call this asynchronous method `GreetingAsync` by using the `await` keyword on the task that is returned. The `await` keyword requires the method to be declared with the `async` modifier. The code within this method does not continue before the `GreetingAsync` method is completed. However, you can reuse the thread that started the `CallerWithAsync` method. This thread is not blocked (code file `Foundations/Program.cs`):

```
private async static void CallerWithAsync()
{
```

```
    TraceThreadAndTask($"started {nameof(CallerWithAsync)}");
    string result = await GreetingAsync("Stephanie");
    Console.WriteLine(result);
    TraceThreadAndTask($"ended {nameof(CallerWithAsync)}");
}
```

When you run the application, you can see from the first output that there's no task. The GreetingAsync method is running in a task, and this task is using a different thread from the caller. The synchronous Greeting method then runs in this task. As the Greeting method returns, the GreetingAsync method returns, and the scope is back in the CallerWithAsync method after the await. Now, the CallerWithAsync method runs in a different thread than before. There's not a task anymore, but although the method started with thread 2, after the await thread 3 was used. The await made sure that the continuation happens after the task was completed, but it now uses a different thread. This behavior is different between Console applications and applications that have a synchronization context as you see later in this chapter in the "Async with Windows Apps" section:

```
started CallerWithAsync in thread 2 and no task
running GreetingAsync in thread 3 and task 1
running Greeting in thread 3 and task 1
Hello, Stephanie
ended CallerWithAsync in thread 3 and no task
```

Instead of passing the result from the asynchronous method to a variable, you can also use the await keyword directly by passing an argument. Here, the result from the GreetingAsync method is awaited as it was in the previous code snippet, but this time the result is directly passed to the Console.WriteLine method:

```
private async static void CallerWithAsync2()
{
    TraceThreadAndTask($"started {nameof(CallerWithAsync2)}");
    Console.WriteLine(await GreetingAsync("Stephanie"));
    TraceThreadAndTask($"ended {nameof(CallerWithAsync2)}");
}
```

> **NOTE** With C# 7, the async modifier can be used with methods that return void or return an object that offers the GetAwaiter method. .NET offers the Task and ValueTask types. With the Windows Runtime you also can use IAsyncOperation. You should avoid using the async modifier with void methods; read more about this in the "Error Handling" section later in this chapter.

The next section explains what's driving the await keyword. Behind the scenes, continuation tasks are used.

Using the Awaiter

You can use the async keyword with any object that offers the GetAwaiter method and returns an awaiter. An awaiter implements the interface INotifyCompletion with the method OnCompleted. This method is invoked when the task is completed. With the following code snippet, instead of using await on the Task, the GetAwaiter method of the task is used. GetAwaiter from the Task class returns a TaskAwaiter. Using the OnCompleted method, a local function is assigned that is invoked when the task is completed (code file Foundations/Program.cs):

```
private static void CallerWithAwaiter()
{
    TraceThreadAndTask($"starting {nameof(CallerWithAwaiter)}");
    TaskAwaiter<string> awaiter = GreetingAsync("Matthias").GetAwaiter();
    awaiter.OnCompleted(OnCompleteAwaiter);
```

```
    void OnCompleteAwaiter()
    {
      Console.WriteLine(awaiter.GetResult());
      TraceThreadAndTask($"ended {nameof(CallerWithAwaiter)}");
    }
}
```

When you run the application, you can see a result similar to the scenario in which you used the `await` keyword:

```
starting CallerWithAwaiter in thread 2 and no task
running GreetingAsync in thread 3 and task 1
running Greeting in thread 3 and task 1
Hello, Matthias
ended CallerWithAwaiter in thread 3 and no task
```

The compiler converts the `await` keyword by putting all the code that follows within the block of a `OnCompleted` method.

Continuation with Tasks

You can also handle continuation by using features of the `Task` object. `GreetingAsync` returns a `Task<string>` object. The `Task` object contains information about the task created, and allows waiting for its completion. The `ContinueWith` method of the `Task` class defines the code that should be invoked as soon as the task is finished. The delegate assigned to the `ContinueWith` method receives the completed task with its argument, which allows accessing the result from the task using the `Result` property (code file `Foundations/Program.cs`):

```
private static void CallerWithContinuationTask()
{
  TraceThreadAndTask("started CallerWithContinuationTask");

  var t1 = GreetingAsync("Stephanie");

  t1.ContinueWith(t =>
  {
    string result = t.Result;
    Console.WriteLine(result);

    TraceThreadAndTask("ended CallerWithContinuationTask");
  });
}
```

Synchronization Context

If you verify the thread that is used within the methods you will find that in all three methods—`CallerWithAsync CallerWithAwaiter`, and `CallerWithContinuationTask`—different threads are used during the lifetime of the methods. One thread is used to invoke the method `GreetingAsync`, and another thread takes action after the `await` keyword or within the code block in the `ContinueWith` method.

With a console application usually this is not an issue. However, you have to ensure that at least one foreground thread is still running before all background tasks that should be completed are finished. The sample application invokes `Console.ReadLine` to keep the main thread running until the return key is pressed.

With applications that are bound to a specific thread for some actions (for example, with WPF applications or Windows apps, UI elements can only be accessed from the UI thread), this is an issue.

Using the `async` and `await` keywords you don't have to do any special actions to access the UI thread after an `await` completion. By default, the generated code switches the thread to the thread that has the synchronization context. A WPF application sets a `DispatcherSynchronizationContext`, and a Windows Forms application sets a `WindowsFormsSynchronizationContext`. Windows apps use the

WinRTSynchronizationContext. If the calling thread of the asynchronous method is assigned to the synchronization context, then with the continuous execution after the await, by default the same synchronization context is used. If the same synchronization context shouldn't be used, you must invoke the Task method ConfigureAwait(continueOnCapturedContext: false). An example that illustrates this usefulness is a Windows app in which the code that follows the await is not using any UI elements. In this case, it is faster to avoid the switch to the synchronization context.

Using Multiple Asynchronous Methods

Within an asynchronous method you can call multiple asynchronous methods. How you code this depends on whether the results from one asynchronous method are needed by another.

Calling Asynchronous Methods Sequentially

You can use the await keyword to call every asynchronous method. In cases where one method is dependent on the result of another method, this is very useful. Here, the second call to GreetingAsync is completely independent of the result of the first call to GreetingAsync. Thus, the complete method MultipleAsyncMethods could return the result faster if await is not used with every single method, as shown in the following example (code file Foundations/Program.cs):

```
private async static void MultipleAsyncMethods()
{
    string s1 = await GreetingAsync("Stephanie");
    string s2 = await GreetingAsync("Matthias");
    Console.WriteLine($"Finished both methods.{Environment.NewLine} " +
        $"Result 1: {s1}{Environment.NewLine} Result 2: {s2}");
}
```

Using Combinators

If the asynchronous methods are not dependent on each other, it is a lot faster not to await on each separately; instead assign the return of the asynchronous method to a Task variable. The GreetingAsync method returns Task<string>. Both these methods can now run in parallel. Combinators can help with this. A combinator accepts multiple parameters of the same type and returns a value of the same type. The passed parameters are "combined" to one. Task combinators accept multiple Task objects as parameter and return a Task.

The sample code invokes the Task.WhenAll combinator method that you can await to have both tasks finished (code file Foundations/Program.cs):

```
private async static void MultipleAsyncMethodsWithCombinators1()
{
    Task<string> t1 = GreetingAsync("Stephanie");
    Task<string> t2 = GreetingAsync("Matthias");
    await Task.WhenAll(t1, t2);
    Console.WriteLine($"Finished both methods.{Environment.NewLine} " +
        $"Result 1: {t1.Result}{Environment.NewLine} Result 2: {t2.Result}");
}
```

The Task class defines the WhenAll and WhenAny combinators. The Task returned from the WhenAll method is completed as soon as all tasks passed to the method are completed; the Task returned from the WhenAny method is completed as soon as one of the tasks passed to the method is completed.

The WhenAll method of the Task type defines several overloads. If all the tasks return the same type, you can use an array of this type for the result of the await. The GreetingAsync method returns a Task<string>, and awaiting for this method results in a string. Therefore, you can use Task.WhenAll to return a string array:

```
private async static void MultipleAsyncMethodsWithCombinators2()
{
```

```
        Task<string> t1 = GreetingAsync("Stephanie");
        Task<string> t2 = GreetingAsync("Matthias");
        string[] result = await Task.WhenAll(t1, t2);
        Console.WriteLine($"Finished both methods.{Environment.NewLine} " +
          $"Result 1: {result[0]}{Enviornment.NewLine} Result 2: {result[1]}");
      }
```

The WhenAll method is of practical use when the waiting task can continue only when all tasks it's waiting for are finished. The WhenAny method can be used when the calling task can do some work when any task it's waiting for is completed. It can use a result from the task to go on.

Using ValueTasks

C# 7 is more flexible with the await keyword; it can now await any object offering the GetAwaiter method. A new type that can be used with await is ValueTask. Contrary to the Task which is a class, ValueTask is a struct. This has a performance advantage as the ValueTask doesn't have an object on the heap.

What is the real overhead of a Task object compared to the asynchronous method call? A method that needs to be invoked asynchronously typically has a lot more overhead than an object on the heap. Most times, the overhead of a Task object on the heap can be ignored—but not always. For example, a method can have one path where data is retrieved from a service with an asynchronous API. With this data retrieval, the data is written to a local cache. When you invoke the method the second time, the data can be retrieved in a fast manner without needing to create a Task object.

The sample method GreetingValueTaskAsync does exactly this. In case the name is already found in the dictionary, the result is returned as a ValueTask. If the name isn't in the dictionary, the GreetingAsync method is invoked, which returns a Task. Awaiting on this task to retrieve the result, a ValueTask is returned again (code file Foundations/Program.cs):

```
    private readonly static Dictionary<string, string> names = new Dictionary<string, string>();

    static async ValueTask<string> GreetingValueTaskAsync(string name)
    {
      if (names.TryGetValue(name, out string result))
      {
        return result;
      }
      else
      {
        result = await GreetingAsync(name);
        names.Add(name, result);
        return result;
      }
    }
```

The UseValueTask method invokes the method GreetingValueTaskAsync two times with the same name. The first time, the data is retrieved using the GreetingAsync method; the second time, data is found in the dictionary and returned from there:

```
    private static async void UseValueTask()
    {
      string result = await GreetingValueTaskAsync("Katharina");
      Console.WriteLine(result);
      string result2 = await GreetingValueTaskAsync("Katharina");
      Console.WriteLine(result2);
    }
```

In case a method doesn't use the async modifier and a ValueTask needs to be returned, ValueTask objects can be created using the constructor passing the result, or passing a Task object:

```
    static ValueTask<string> GreetingValueTask2Async(string name)
    {
```

```
if (names.TryGetValue(name, out string result))
{
  return new ValueTask<string>(result);
}
else
{
  Task<string> t1 = GreetingAsync(name);

  TaskAwaiter<string> awaiter = t1.GetAwaiter();
  awaiter.OnCompleted(OnCompletion);
  return new ValueTask<string>(t1);

  void OnCompletion()
  {
    names.Add(name, awaiter.GetResult());
  }
}
}
```

Converting the Asynchronous Pattern

Not all classes from the .NET Framework introduced the new asynchronous method style. There are still many classes that offer the asynchronous pattern with the BeginXXX and EndXXX methods and not with task-based asynchronous methods; you will see this when you work with different classes from the framework. However, you can convert the asynchronous pattern to the new task-based asynchronous pattern.

This example uses the HttpWebRequest class with the BeginGetResponse method to convert this method to the task-based async pattern. Task.Factory.FromAsync is a generic method that offers a few overloads to convert the asynchronous pattern to the task-based asynchronous pattern. With the sample application, when the BeginGetResponse method of the HttpWebRequest is invoked, the asynchronous network request is started. This method returns an IAsyncResult, which is the first argument to the FromAsync method. The second argument is a reference to the method EndGetResponse, and it requires a delegate with the IAsyncResult argument—which the EndGetResponse method is. The second argument also requires a return of WebResponse as defined by the generic parameter for the FromAsync method. The EndGetResponse method is invoked by the task helper functionality when the IAsyncResult signals completion (code file Foundations/Program.cs):

```
private static async void ConvertingAsyncPattern()
{
  HttpWebRequest request = WebRequest.Create("http://www.microsoft.com")
    as HttpWebRequest;

  using (WebResponse response = await Task.Factory.FromAsync<WebResponse>(
    request.BeginGetResponse(null, null), request.EndGetResponse))
  {
    Stream stream = response.GetResponseStream();
    using (var reader = new StreamReader(stream))
    {
      string content = reader.ReadToEnd();
      Console.WriteLine(content.Substring(0, 100));
    }
  }
}
```

> **WARNING** *With legacy applications, often the* BeginInvoke *method of the delegate is used when using the asynchronous pattern. The compiler does not complain when you use this method from a .NET Core application. However, during runtime you get a platform not supported exception.*

ERROR HANDLING

Chapter 14, "Errors and Exceptions," provides detailed coverage of errors and exception handling. However, in the context of asynchronous methods, you should be aware of some special handling of errors.

The code for the `ErrorHandling` example makes use of these namespaces:

```
System

System.Threading.Tasks
```

Let's start with a simple method that throws an exception after a delay (code file `ErrorHandling/Program.cs`):

```
static async Task ThrowAfter(int ms, string message)
{
  await Task.Delay(ms);
  throw new Exception(message);
}
```

If you call the asynchronous method without awaiting it, you can put the asynchronous method within a try/catch block—and the exception will not be caught. That's because the method `DontHandle` has already completed before the exception from `ThrowAfter` is thrown. You need to await the `ThrowAfter` method, as shown in the example that follows in the next section. Pay attention that the exception is not caught in this code snippet:

```
private static void DontHandle()
{
  try
  {
    ThrowAfter(200, "first");
    // exception is not caught because this method is finished
    // before the exception is thrown
  }
  catch (Exception ex)
  {
    Console.WriteLine(ex.Message);
  }
}
```

> **WARNING** *Asynchronous methods that return* void *cannot be awaited. The issue with this is that exceptions that are thrown from* async void *methods cannot be caught. That's why it is best to return a* Task *type from an asynchronous method. Handler methods or overridden base methods are exempted from this rule.*

Handling Exceptions with Asynchronous Methods

A good way to deal with exceptions from asynchronous methods is to use `await` and put a try/catch statement around it, as shown in the following code snippet. The `HandleOneError` method releases the thread after calling the `ThrowAfter` method asynchronously, but it keeps the `Task` referenced to continue as soon as the task is completed. When that happens (which, in this case, is when the exception is thrown after two seconds), the `catch` matches and the code within the `catch` block is invoked (code file `ErrorHandling/Program.cs`):

```
private static async void HandleOneError()
{
  try
  {
```

```
      await ThrowAfter(2000, "first");
    }
    catch (Exception ex)
    {
      Console.WriteLine($"handled {ex.Message}");
    }
}
```

Handling Exceptions with Multiple Asynchronous Methods

What if two asynchronous methods are invoked and both throw exceptions? In the following example, first the `ThrowAfter` method is invoked, which throws an exception with the message `first` after two seconds. After this method is completed, the `ThrowAfter` method is invoked, throwing an exception after one second. Because the first call to `ThrowAfter` already throws an exception, the code within the `try` block does not continue to invoke the second method, instead landing within the `catch` block to deal with the first exception (code file `ErrorHandling/Program.cs`):

```
private static async void StartTwoTasks()
{
  try
  {
    await ThrowAfter(2000, "first");
    await ThrowAfter(1000, "second"); // the second call is not invoked
    // because the first method throws
    // an exception
  }
  catch (Exception ex)
  {
    Console.WriteLine($"handled {ex.Message}");
  }
}
```

Now start the two calls to `ThrowAfter` in parallel. The first method throws an exception after two seconds and the second one after one second. With `Task.WhenAll` you wait until both tasks are completed, whether an exception is thrown or not. Therefore, after a wait of about two seconds, `Task.WhenAll` is completed, and the exception is caught with the `catch` statement. However, you only see the exception information from the first task that is passed to the `WhenAll` method. It's not the task that threw the exception first (which is the second task), but the first task in the list:

```
private async static void StartTwoTasksParallel()
{
  try
  {
    Task t1 = ThrowAfter(2000, "first");
    Task t2 = ThrowAfter(1000, "second");
    await Task.WhenAll(t1, t2);
  }
  catch (Exception ex)
  {
    // just display the exception information of the first task
    // that is awaited within WhenAll
    Console.WriteLine($"handled {ex.Message}");
  }
}
```

One way to get the exception information from all tasks is to declare the task variables `t1` and `t2` outside of the `try` block, so they can be accessed from within the `catch` block. Here you can check the status of the task to determine whether they are in a faulted state with the `IsFaulted` property. In case of an exception, the `IsFaulted` property returns true. The exception information itself can be accessed by using `Exception`

.InnerException of the Task class. Another, and usually better, way to retrieve exception information from all tasks is demonstrated next.

Using AggregateException Information

To get the exception information from all failing tasks, you can write the result from Task.WhenAll to a Task variable. This task is then awaited until all tasks are completed. Otherwise the exception would still be missed. As described in the last section, with the catch statement only the exception of the first task can be retrieved. However, now you have access to the Exception property of the outer task. The Exception property is of type AggregateException. This exception type defines the property InnerExceptions (not only InnerException), which contains a list of all the exceptions that have been awaited for. Now you can easily iterate through all the exceptions (code file ErrorHandling/Program.cs):

```
private static async void ShowAggregatedException()
{
  Task taskResult = null;
  try
  {
    Task t1 = ThrowAfter(2000, "first");
    Task t2 = ThrowAfter(1000, "second");
    await (taskResult = Task.WhenAll(t1, t2));
  }
  catch (Exception ex)
  {
    Console.WriteLine($"handled {ex.Message}");
    foreach (var ex1 in taskResult.Exception.InnerExceptions)
    {
      Console.WriteLine($"inner exception {ex1.Message}");
    }
  }
}
```

ASYNC WITH WINDOWS APPS

Using the async keyword with Universal Windows Platform (UWP) apps works the same as what you've already seen in this chapter. However, you need to be aware that after calling await from the UI thread, when the asynchronous method returns, you're by default back in the UI thread. This makes it easy to update UI elements after the asynchronous method is completed.

> **NOTE** *To build and create Universal Windows Platform (UWP) app, you need Windows 10, and your Windows system must be configured in "developer mode." Enable the developer mode by opening the Windows settings, chose the Update & Security tile, select the "For developers" category, and click the radio button "Developer mode." This allows your system to run sideloaded apps (apps without installing them from the Windows Store), and adds a Windows package for the developer mode.*

To understand the functionality—and the issues—a Universal Windows App is created. This app contains five buttons and a TextBlock element to demonstrate different scenarios (code file AsyncWindowsApps/MainPage.xaml):

```
<StackPanel>
  <Button Content="Start Async" Click="OnStartAsync" Margin="4" />
```

```
    <Button Content="Start Async with Config" Click="OnStartAsyncConfigureAwait"
      Margin="4" />
    <Button Content="Start Async with Thread Switch"
      Click="OnStartAsyncWithThreadSwitch" Margin="4" />
    <Button Content="Use IAsyncOperation" Click="OnIAsyncOperation" Margin="4" />
    <Button Content="Deadlock" Click="OnStartDeadlock" Margin="4" />
    <TextBlock x:Name="text1" Margin="4" />
</StackPanel>
```

> **NOTE** *Programming UWP apps is covered in detail in Chapters 33 to 36.*

In the `OnStartAsync` method, the thread ID of the UI thread is written to the `TextBlock` element. Next the asynchronous method `Task.Delay`, which does not block the UI thread, is invoked, and after this method completed the thread ID is written to the `TextBlock` again (code file `AsyncWindowsApps/MainPage.xaml.cs`):

```
private async void OnStartAsync(object sender, RoutedEventArgs e)
{
    text1.Text = $"UI thread: {GetThread()}";
    await Task.Delay(1000);
    text1.Text += $"\n after await: {GetThread()}";
}
```

For accessing the thread ID, you use the `Environment` class. With UWP apps, the `Thread` class is not available—at least not until build 15063:

```
private string GetThread() => $"thread: {Environment.CurrentManagedThreadId}";
```

When you run the application, you can see similar output in the text element. Contrary to console applications, with UWP apps defining a synchronization context, after the await you can see the same thread as before. This allows direct access to UI elements:

```
UI thread: thread 3
after await: thread 3
```

Configure Await

In case you don't need access to UI elements, you can configure `await` to not use the synchronization context. The following code snippet demonstrates the configuration and also shows why you shouldn't access UI elements from a background thread.

With the method `OnStartAsyncConfigureAwait`, after writing the ID of the UI thread to the text information, the local function `AsyncFunction` is invoked. In this local function, the starting thread is written before the asynchronous method `Task.Delay` is invoked. Using the task returned from this method, the `ConfigureAwait` is invoked. With this method, the task is configured by passing the `continueOn-CapturedContext` argument set to `false`. With this context configuration, you see that the thread after the await is not the UI thread anymore. Using a different thread to write the result to the `result` variable is okay. What you should never do is shown in the `try` block: accessing UI elements from a non-UI thread. The exception you get contains the `HRESULT` value as shown in the `when` clause. Just this exception is caught in the `catch`: the result is returned to the caller. With the caller, `ConfigureAwait` is invoked as well, but this time the `continueOnCapturedContext` is set to true. Here, both before and after the await, the method is running in the UI thread (code file `AsyncWindowsApp/MainWindow.xaml.cs`):

```
private async void OnStartAsyncConfigureAwait(object sender, RoutedEventArgs e)
{
    text1.Text = $"UI thread: {GetThread()}";
```

```
string s = await AsyncFunction().ConfigureAwait(
  continueOnCapturedContext: true);

// after await, with continueOnCapturedContext true we are back in the UI thread
text1.Text += $"\n{s}\nafter await: {GetThread()}";

async Task<string> AsyncFunction()
{
  string result = $"\nasync function: {GetThread()}\n";
  await Task.Delay(1000).ConfigureAwait(continueOnCapturedContext: false);
  result += $"\nasync function after await : {GetThread()}";

  try
  {
    text1.Text = "this is a call from the wrong thread";
    return "not reached";
  }
  catch (Exception ex) when (ex.HResult == -2147417842)
  {
    return result;
    // we know it's the wrong thread
    // don't access UI elements from the previous try block
  }
}
}
```

> **NOTE** *Exception handling and filtering is explained in Chapter 14.*

When you run the application, you can see output similar to the following. In the async local function after the await, a different thread is used. The text "not reached" is never written, because the exception is thrown:

```
UI thread: thread 3
async function: thread 3
async function after await: thread 6
after await: thread 3
```

> **WARNING** *In later UWP chapters in this book, data binding is used instead of directly accessing properties of UI elements. However, with UWP you also can't write properties that are bound to UI elements from a non UI-thread.*

Switch to the UI Thread

In some scenarios, there's no effortless way around using a background thread and accessing UI elements. Here, you can switch to the UI thread with the CoreDispatcher object that is returned from the Dispatcher property. The Dispatcher property is defined in the DependencyObject class. DependencyObject is a base class of UI elements. Invoking the RunAsync method of the CoreDispatcher object runs the passed lambda expression again in a UI thread (code file AsyncWindowsApp/MainWindow.xaml.cs):

```
private async void OnStartAsyncWithThreadSwitch(object sender, RoutedEventArgs e)
{
  text1.Text = $"UI thread: {GetThread()}";

  string s = await AsyncFunction();
```

```
text1.Text += $"\nafter await: {GetThread()}";

async Task<string> AsyncFunction()
{
  string result = $"\nasync function: {GetThread()}\n";
  await Task.Delay(1000).ConfigureAwait(continueOnCapturedContext: false);
  result += $"\nasync function after await : {GetThread()}";

  await Dispatcher.RunAsync(CoreDispatcherPriority.Normal, () =>
  {
    text1.Text +=
      $"\nasync function switch back to the UI thread: {GetThread()}";
  });
  return result;
}
}
```

When you run the application, you can see always the UI thread used when using `RunAsync`:

```
UI Thread: thread 3
async function switch back to the UI thread: thread 3
async function: thread 3
async function after await: thread 5
after await: thread 3
```

Using IAsyncOperation

Asynchronous methods are defined by the Windows Runtime to not return a `Task` or a `ValueTask`. `Task` and `ValueTask` are not part of the Windows Runtime. Instead, these methods return an object that implements the interface `IAsyncOperation`. `IAsyncOperation` does not define the method `GetAwaiter` as needed by the `await` keyword. However, an `IAsyncOperation` is automatically converted to a `Task` when you use the `await` keyword. You can also use the `AsTask` extension method to convert an `IAsyncOperation` object to a task.

With the example application, in the method `OnIAsyncOperation`, the `ShowAsync` method of the `MessageDialog` is invoked. This method returns an `IAsyncOperaition`, and you can simply use the `await` keyword to get the result (code file `AsyncWindowsApp/MainWindow.xaml.cs`):

```
private async void OnIAsyncOperation(object sender, RoutedEventArgs e)
{
  var dlg = new MessageDialog("Select One, Two, Or Three", "Sample");

  dlg.Commands.Add(new UICommand("One", null, 1));
  dlg.Commands.Add(new UICommand("Two", null, 2));
  dlg.Commands.Add(new UICommand("Three", null, 3));

  IUICommand command = await dlg.ShowAsync();

  text1.Text = $"Command {command.Id} with the label {command.Label} invoked";
}
```

Avoid Blocking Scenarios

It's dangerous using `Wait` on a `Task` and the `async` keyword together. With applications using the synchronization context, this can easily result in a deadlock.

In the method `OnStartDeadlock`, the local function `DelayAsync` is invoked. `DelayAsync` waits on the completion of `Task.Delay` before continuing in the foreground thread. However, the caller invokes the `Wait` method on the task returned from `DelayAsync`. The `Wait` method blocks the calling thread until the task is completed. In this case, the `Wait` is invoked from the foreground thread, so the `Wait` blocks the foreground thread. The `await` on `Task.Delay` can never complete, because the foreground thread is not available. This is a classical deadlock scenario (code file `AsyncWindowsApps/MainWindow.xaml.cs`):

```
private void OnStartDeadlock(object sender, RoutedEventArgs e)
{
  DelayAsync().Wait();
}

private async Task DelayAsync()
{
  await Task.Delay(1000);
}
```

> **WARNING** *Avoid using* `Wait` *and* `await` *together in applications using the synchronization context.*

SUMMARY

This chapter introduced the `async` and `await` keywords. Having looked at several examples, you've seen the advantages of the task-based asynchronous pattern compared to the asynchronous pattern and the event-based asynchronous pattern available with earlier editions of .NET.

You've also seen how easy it is to create asynchronous methods with the help of the `Task` class, and learned how to use the `async` and `await` keywords to wait for these methods without blocking threads. Finally, you looked at the error-handling aspect of asynchronous methods.

For more information on parallel programming, and details about threads and tasks, see Chapter 21.

The next chapter continues with core features of C# and .NET and gives detailed information on reflection, metadata, and dynamic programming.

16

Reflection, Metadata, and Dynamic Programming

WHAT'S IN THIS CHAPTER?

➤ Using custom attributes
➤ Inspecting the metadata at runtime using reflection
➤ Building access points from classes that enable reflection
➤ Working with the dynamic type
➤ Creating dynamic objects with DynamicObject and ExpandoObject

WROX.COM CODE DOWNLOADS FOR THIS CHAPTER

The Wrox.com code downloads for this chapter are found at www.wrox.com on the Download Code tab. The source code is also available at https://github.com/ProfessionalCSharp/ProfessionalCSharp7 in the directory ReflectionAndDynamic.

The code for this chapter is divided into the following major examples:

➤ LookupWhatsNew
➤ TypeView
➤ VectorClass
➤ WhatsNewAttributes
➤ Dynamic
➤ DynamicFileReader

INSPECTING CODE AT RUNTIME AND DYNAMIC PROGRAMMING

This chapter focuses on custom attributes, reflection, and dynamic programming. Custom attributes are mechanisms that enable you to associate custom metadata with program elements. This metadata is created at compile time and embedded in an assembly. *Reflection* is a generic term that describes the capability to inspect and manipulate program elements at runtime. For example, reflection allows you to do the following:

- ➤ Enumerate the members of a type.
- ➤ Instantiate a new object.
- ➤ Execute the members of an object.
- ➤ Find out information about a type.
- ➤ Find out information about an assembly.
- ➤ Inspect the custom attributes applied to a type.
- ➤ Create and compile a new assembly.

This list represents a great deal of functionality and encompasses some of the most powerful and complex capabilities provided by the .NET class library. Because one chapter does not have the space to cover all the capabilities of reflection, I focus on those elements that you are likely to use most frequently.

To demonstrate custom attributes and reflection, in this chapter you first develop an example based on a company that regularly ships upgrades of its software and wants to have details about these upgrades documented automatically. In the example, you define custom attributes that indicate the date when program elements were last modified, and what changes were made. You then use reflection to develop an application that looks for these attributes in an assembly and can automatically display all the details about what upgrades have been made to the software since a given date.

Another example in this chapter considers an application that reads from or writes to a database and uses custom attributes as a way to mark which classes and properties correspond to which database tables and columns. By reading these attributes from the assembly at runtime, the program can automatically retrieve or write data to the appropriate location in the database, without requiring specific logic for each table or column.

The second big aspect of this chapter is dynamic programming, which has been a part of the C# language since version 4 when the `dynamic` type was added. The growth of languages such as Ruby and Python, and the increased use of JavaScript, have intensified interest in dynamic programming. Although C# is still a statically typed language, the additions for dynamic programming give the C# language capabilities that some developers are looking for. Using dynamic language features allows for calling script functions from within C#.

In this chapter, you look at the `dynamic` type and the rules for using it. You also see what an implementation of `DynamicObject` looks like and how you can use it. `ExpandoObject`, which is the frameworks implementation of `DynamicObject`, is also covered.

CUSTOM ATTRIBUTES

You have already seen in this book how you can define attributes on various items within your program. These attributes have been defined by Microsoft as part of .NET, and many of them receive special support from the C# compiler. This means that for those particular attributes, the compiler can customize the compilation process in specific ways—for example, laying out a struct in memory according to the details in the `StructLayout` attributes.

.NET also enables you to define your own attributes. Obviously, these attributes don't have any effect on the compilation process because the compiler has no intrinsic awareness of them. However, these attributes are emitted as metadata in the compiled assembly when they are applied to program elements.

By itself, this metadata might be useful for documentation purposes, but what makes attributes really powerful is that by using reflection, your code can read this metadata and use it to make decisions at runtime. This means that the custom attributes that you define can directly affect how your code runs. For example, custom attributes can be used to enable declarative code access security checks for custom permission classes, to associate information with program elements that can then be used by testing tools, or when developing extensible frameworks that allow the loading of plug-ins or modules.

Writing Custom Attributes

To understand how to write your own custom attributes, it is useful to know what the compiler does when it encounters an element in your code that has a custom attribute applied to it. To take the database example, suppose that you have a C# property declaration that looks like this:

```
[FieldName("SocialSecurityNumber")]
public string SocialSecurityNumber
{
  get {
   //...
```

When the C# compiler recognizes that this property has an attribute applied to it (`FieldName`), it first appends the string `Attribute` to this name, forming the combined name `FieldNameAttribute`. The compiler then searches all the namespaces in its search path (those namespaces that have been mentioned in a `using` statement) for a class with the specified name. Note that if you mark an item with an attribute whose name already ends in the string `Attribute`, the compiler does not add the string to the name a second time; it leaves the attribute name unchanged. Therefore, the preceding code is equivalent to this:

```
[FieldNameAttribute("SocialSecurityNumber")]
public string SocialSecurityNumber
{
  get {
   //...
```

The compiler expects to find a class with this name, and it expects this class to be derived directly or indirectly from `System.Attribute`. The compiler also expects that this class contains information governing the use of the attribute. In particular, the attribute class needs to specify the following:

➤ The types of program elements to which the attribute can be applied (classes, structs, properties, methods, and so on)

➤ Whether it is legal for the attribute to be applied more than once to the same program element

➤ Whether the attribute, when applied to a class or interface, is inherited by derived classes and interfaces

➤ The mandatory and optional parameters the attribute takes

If the compiler cannot find a corresponding attribute class, or if it finds one but the way that you have used that attribute does not match the information in the attribute class, the compiler raises a compilation error. For example, if the attribute class indicates that the attribute can be applied only to classes, but you have applied it to a struct definition, a compilation error occurs.

Continuing with the example, assume that you have defined the `FieldName` attribute like this:

```
[AttributeUsage(AttributeTargets.Property,
  AllowMultiple=false, Inherited=false)]
public class FieldNameAttribute: Attribute
{
  private string _name;
  public FieldNameAttribute(string name)
  {
    _name = name;
  }
}
```

The following sections discuss each element of this definition.

Specifying the AttributeUsage Attribute

The first thing to note is that the attribute class itself is marked with an attribute—the System .AttributeUsage attribute. This is an attribute defined by Microsoft for which the C# compiler provides special support. (You could argue that AttributeUsage isn't an attribute at all; it is more like a meta-attribute, because it applies only to other attributes, not simply to any class.) The primary purpose of AttributeUsage is to identify the types of program elements to which your custom attribute can be applied. This information is provided by the first parameter of the AttributeUsage attribute. This parameter is mandatory, and it is of an enumerated type, AttributeTargets. In the previous example, you have indicated that the FieldName attribute can be applied only to properties, which is fine, because that is exactly what you have applied it to in the earlier code fragment. The members of the AttributeTargets enumeration are as follows:

- ➤ All
- ➤ Assembly
- ➤ Class
- ➤ Constructor
- ➤ Delegate
- ➤ Enum
- ➤ Event
- ➤ Field
- ➤ GenericParameter
- ➤ Interface
- ➤ Method
- ➤ Module
- ➤ Parameter
- ➤ Property
- ➤ ReturnValue
- ➤ Struct

This list identifies all the program elements to which you can apply attributes. Note that when applying the attribute to a program element, you place the attribute in square brackets immediately before the element. However, two values in the preceding list do not correspond to any program element: Assembly and Module. An attribute can be applied to an assembly or a module as a whole, rather than to an element in your code; in this case the attribute can be placed anywhere in your source code, but it must be prefixed with the Assembly or Module keyword:

```
[assembly:SomeAssemblyAttribute(Parameters)]
[module:SomeAssemblyAttribute(Parameters)]
```

When indicating the valid target elements of a custom attribute, you can combine these values using the bitwise OR operator. For example, if you want to indicate that your FieldName attribute can be applied to both properties and fields, you use the following:

```
[AttributeUsage(AttributeTargets.Property | AttributeTargets.Field,
    AllowMultiple=false, Inherited=false)]
public class FieldNameAttribute: Attribute
```

You can also use AttributeTargets.All to indicate that your attribute can be applied to all types of program elements. The AttributeUsage attribute also contains two other parameters: AllowMultiple and Inherited. These are specified using the syntax of <ParameterName>=<ParameterValue>, instead of simply specifying the values for these parameters. These parameters are optional—you can omit them.

The `AllowMultiple` parameter indicates whether an attribute can be applied more than once to the same item. The fact that it is set to `false` indicates that the compiler should raise an error if it sees something like this:

```
[FieldName("SocialSecurityNumber")]
[FieldName("NationalInsuranceNumber")]
public string SocialSecurityNumber
{
    //...
```

If the `Inherited` parameter is set to `true`, an attribute applied to a class or interface is also automatically applied to all derived classes or interfaces. If the attribute is applied to a method or property, it automatically applies to any overrides of that method or property, and so on.

Specifying Attribute Parameters

This section demonstrates how you can specify the parameters that your custom attribute takes. When the compiler encounters a statement such as the following, it examines the parameters passed into the attribute—which is a string—and looks for a constructor for the attribute that takes exactly those parameters:

```
[FieldName("SocialSecurityNumber")]
public string SocialSecurityNumber
{
    //...
```

If the compiler finds an appropriate constructor, it emits the specified metadata to the assembly. If the compiler does not find an appropriate constructor, a compilation error occurs. As discussed later in this chapter, reflection involves reading metadata (attributes) from assemblies and instantiating the attribute classes they represent. Because of this, the compiler must ensure that an appropriate constructor exists that allows the runtime instantiation of the specified attribute.

In the example, you have supplied just one constructor for `FieldNameAttribute`, and this constructor takes one string parameter. Therefore, when applying the `FieldName` attribute to a property, you must supply one string as a parameter, as shown in the preceding code.

To allow a choice of what types of parameters should be supplied with an attribute, you can provide different constructor overloads, although normal practice is to supply just one constructor and use properties to define any other optional parameters, as explained next.

Specifying Optional Attribute Parameters

As demonstrated with the `AttributeUsage` attribute, an alternative syntax enables optional parameters to be added to an attribute. This syntax involves specifying the names and values of the optional parameters. It works through `public` properties or fields in the attribute class. For example, suppose that you modify the definition of the `SocialSecurityNumber` property as follows:

```
[FieldName("SocialSecurityNumber", Comment="This is the primary key field")]
public string SocialSecurityNumber { get; set; }
{
    //...
```

In this case, the compiler recognizes the `<ParameterName>=<ParameterValue>` syntax of the second parameter and does not attempt to match this parameter to a `FieldNameAttribute` constructor. Instead, it looks for a `public` property or field (although public fields are not considered good programming practice, so normally you will work with properties) of that name that it can use to set the value of this parameter. If you want the previous code to work, you have to add some code to `FieldNameAttribute`:

```
[AttributeUsage(AttributeTargets.Property,
    AllowMultiple=false, Inherited=false)]
public class FieldNameAttribute : Attribute
{
```

```
    public string Comment { get; set; }
    private string _fieldName;
    public FieldNameAttribute(string fieldName)
    {
      _fieldName = fieldname;
    }
    //...
}
```

Custom Attribute Example: WhatsNewAttributes

In this section you start developing the example mentioned at the beginning of the chapter.
WhatsNewAttributes provides for an attribute that indicates when a program element was last modified. This is a more ambitious code example than many of the others in that it consists of three separate assemblies:

➤ WhatsNewAttributes—Contains the definitions of the attributes

➤ VectorClass—Contains the code to which the attributes have been applied

➤ LookUpWhatsNew—Contains the project that displays details about items that have changed

Of these, only the LookUpWhatsNew assembly is a console application of the type that you have used up until now. The remaining two assemblies are libraries—they each contain class definitions but no program entry point.

The WhatsNewAttributes Library

This section starts with the core WhatsNewAttributes .NET Standard library. The source code is contained in the file WhatsNewAttributes.cs, which is located in the WhatsNewAttributes project of the WhatsNewAttributes solution in the example code for this chapter.

The WhatsNewAttributes.cs file defines two attribute classes, LastModifiedAttribute and SupportsWhatsNewAttribute. You use the attribute LastModifiedAttribute to mark when an item was last modified. It takes two mandatory parameters (parameters that are passed to the constructor): the date of the modification and a string containing a description of the changes. One optional parameter named issues (for which a public property exists) can be used to describe any outstanding issues for the item.

In practice, you would probably want this attribute to apply to anything. To keep the code simple, its usage is limited here to classes, methods, and constructors. You allow it to be applied more than once to the same item (AllowMultiple=true) because an item might be modified more than once, and each modification has to be marked with a separate attribute instance.

SupportsWhatsNew is a smaller class representing an attribute that doesn't take any parameters. The purpose of this assembly attribute is to mark an assembly for which you are maintaining documentation via the LastModifiedAttribute. This way, the program that examines this assembly later knows that the assembly it is reading is one on which you are actually using your automated documentation process. Here is the complete source code for this part of the example (code file WhatsNewAttributes/WhatsNewAttributes.cs):

```
[AttributeUsage(AttributeTargets.Class | AttributeTargets.Method |
  AttributeTargets.Constructor, AllowMultiple=true, Inherited=false)]
public class LastModifiedAttribute: Attribute
{
  private readonly DateTime _dateModified;
  private readonly string _changes;
  public LastModifiedAttribute(string dateModified, string changes)
  {
    _dateModified = DateTime.Parse(dateModified);
    _changes = changes;
  }
```

```
   public DateTime DateModified => _dateModified;

   public string Changes => _changes;

   public string Issues { get; set; }
}

[AttributeUsage(AttributeTargets.Assembly)]
public class SupportsWhatsNewAttribute: Attribute
{
}
```

Based on what has been discussed, this code should be fairly clear. Notice, however, that the properties DateModified and Changes are read-only. Using the expression syntax, the compiler creates get accessors. There is no need for set accessors because you are requiring these parameters to be set in the constructor as mandatory parameters. You need the get accessors so that you can read the values of these attributes.

The VectorClass Library

The VectorClass .NET Standard library references the WhatsNewAttributes library. After adding the using declarations, the global assembly attribute marks the assembly to support the WhatsNew attributes (code file VectorClass/Vector.cs):

```
[assembly: SupportsWhatsNew]
```

The sample code for VectorClass makes use of the following namespaces:

```
System

System.Collections

System.Collections.Generic

WhatsNewAttributes
```

Now for the code for the Vector class. Some LastModified attributes are added to the class to mark changes:

```
[LastModified("19 Jul 2017", "updated for C# 7 and .NET Core 2")]
[LastModified("6 Jun 2015", "updated for C# 6 and .NET Core")]
[LastModified("14 Deb 2010", "IEnumerable interface implemented: " +
  "Vector can be treated as a collection")]
[LastModified("10 Feb 2010", "IFormattable interface implemented " +
  "Vector accepts N and VE format specifiers")]
public class Vector : IFormattable, IEnumerable<double>
{
  public Vector(double x, double y, double z)
  {
    X = x;
    Y = y;
    Z = z;
  }

  [LastModified("19 Jul 2017", "Reduced the number of code lines")]
  public Vector(Vector vector)
    : this (vector.X, vector.Y, vector.Z { }

  public double X { get; }
  public double Y { get; }
  public double Z { get; }

  public string ToString(string format, IFormatProvider formatProvider)
  {
    //...
```

You also mark the contained `VectorEnumerator` class:

```
[LastModified("6 Jun 2015",
  "Changed to implement the generic interface IEnumerator<T>")]
[LastModified("14 Feb 2010",
  "Class created as part of collection support for Vector")]
private class VectorEnumerator : IEnumerator<double>
{
```

The version number for the library is defined in the `csproj` project file (project file `VectorClass/VectorClass.csproj`):

```
<PropertyGroup>
  <TargetFramework>netstandard2.0</TargetFramework>
  <Version>2.1.0</Version>
</PropertyGroup>
```

That's as far as you can get with this example for now. You are unable to run anything yet because all you have are two libraries. After taking a look at reflection in the next section, you will develop the final part of the example, in which you look up and display these attributes.

USING REFLECTION

In this section, you take a closer look at the `System.Type` class, which enables you to access information concerning the definition of any data type. You also look at the `System.Reflection.Assembly` class, which you can use to access information about an assembly or to load that assembly into your program. Finally, you combine the code in this section with the code in the previous section to complete the `WhatsNewAttributes` example.

The System.Type Class

So far you have used the `Type` class only to hold the reference to a type as follows:

```
Type t = typeof(double);
```

Although previously referred to as a class, `Type` is an abstract base class. Whenever you instantiate a `Type` object, you are actually instantiating a class derived from `Type`. `Type` has one derived class corresponding to each actual data type, though in general the derived classes simply provide different overloads of the various `Type` methods and properties that return the correct data for the corresponding data type. They do not typically add new methods or properties. In general, there are three common ways to obtain a `Type` reference that refers to any given type.

➤ You can use the C# `typeof` operator as shown in the preceding code. This operator takes the name of the type (not in quotation marks, however) as a parameter.

➤ You can use the `GetType` method, which all classes inherit from `System.Object`:

```
double d = 10;
Type t = d.GetType();
```

`GetType` is called against a variable, rather than taking the name of a type. Note, however, that the `Type` object returned is still associated with only that data type. It does not contain any information that relates to that instance of the type. The `GetType` method can be useful if you have a reference to an object but you are not sure what class that object is actually an instance of.

➤ You can call the static method of the `Type` class, `GetType`:

```
Type t = Type.GetType("System.Double");
```

`Type` is really the gateway to much of the reflection functionality. It implements a huge number of methods and properties—far too many to provide a comprehensive list here. However, the following subsections should give you a good idea of the kinds of things you can do with the `Type` class. Note that the available properties are all read-only; you use Type to find out about the data type—you cannot use it to make any modifications to the type!

Type Properties

You can divide the properties implemented by Type into three categories. First, a number of properties retrieve the strings containing various names associated with the class, as shown in the following table:

PROPERTY	RETURNS
Name	The name of the data type
FullName	The fully qualified name of the data type (including the namespace name)
Namespace	The name of the namespace in which the data type is defined

Second, it is possible to retrieve references to further type objects that represent related classes, as shown in the following table.

PROPERTY	RETURNS TYPE REFERENCE CORRESPONDING TO
BaseType	The immediate base type of this type
UnderlyingSystemType	The type to which this type maps in the .NET runtime (recall that certain .NET base types actually map to specific predefined types recognized by IL). This member is only available in the full Framework.

A number of Boolean properties indicate whether this type is, for example, a class, an enum, and so on. These properties include IsAbstract, IsArray, IsClass, IsEnum, IsInterface, IsPointer, IsPrimitive (one of the predefined primitive data types), IsPublic, IsSealed, and IsValueType. The following example uses a primitive data type:

```
Type intType = typeof(int);
Console.WriteLine(intType.IsAbstract); // writes false
Console.WriteLine(intType.IsClass); // writes false
Console.WriteLine(intType.IsEnum); // writes false
Console.WriteLine(intType.IsPrimitive); // writes true
Console.WriteLine(intType.IsValueType); // writes true
```

This example uses the Vector class:

```
Type vecType = typeof(Vector);
Console.WriteLine(vecType.IsAbstract); // writes false
Console.WriteLine(vecType.IsClass); // writes true
Console.WriteLine(vecType.IsEnum); // writes false
Console.WriteLine(vecType.IsPrimitive); // writes false
Console.WriteLine(vecType.IsValueType); // writes false
```

Finally, you can also retrieve a reference to the assembly in which the type is defined. This is returned as a reference to an instance of the System.Reflection.Assembly class, which is examined shortly:

```
Type t = typeof (Vector);
Assembly containingAssembly = new Assembly(t);
```

Methods

Most of the methods of System.Type are used to obtain details about the members of the corresponding data type—the constructors, properties, methods, events, and so on. Quite a large number of methods exist, but they all follow the same pattern. For example, two methods retrieve details about the methods of the data type: GetMethod and GetMethods. GetMethod returns a reference to a System.Reflection.

`MethodInfo` object, which contains details about a method. `GetMethods` returns an array of such references. As the names suggest, the difference is that `GetMethods` returns details about all the methods, whereas `GetMethod` returns details about just one method with a specified parameter list. Both methods have overloads that take an extra parameter, a `BindingFlags` enumerated value that indicates which members should be returned—for example, whether to return public members, instance members, static members, and so on.

For example, the simplest overload of `GetMethods` takes no parameters and returns details about all the public methods of the data type:

```
Type t = typeof(double);
foreach (MethodInfo nextMethod in t.GetMethods())
{
  //...
}
```

The member methods of `Type` that follow the same pattern are shown in the following table. Note that plural names return an array.

TYPE OF OBJECT RETURNED	METHOD(S)	
ConstructorInfo	GetConstructor, GetConstructors	
EventInfo	GetEvent, GetEvents	
FieldInfo	GetField, GetFields	
MemberInfo	GetMember, GetMembers, GetDefaultMembers	
MethodInfo	GetMethod, GetMethods	
PropertyInfo	GetProperty, GetProperties	

The `GetMember` and `GetMembers` methods return details about any or all members of the data type, regardless of whether these members are constructors, properties, methods, and so on.

The TypeView Example

This section demonstrates some of the features of the `Type` class with a short example, `TypeView`, which you can use to list the members of a data type. The example demonstrates how to use `TypeView` for a `double`; however, you can swap this type with any other data type just by changing one line of the code in the example.

The result of running the application is this output to the console:

```
Analysis of type Double
Type Name: Double
Full Name: System.Double
Namespace: System
Base Type: ValueType
public members:
System.Double Method IsInfinity
System.Double Method IsPositiveInfinity
System.Double Method IsNegativeInfinity
System.Double Method IsNaN
System.Double Method CompareTo
System.Double Method CompareTo
System.Double Method Equals
System.Double Method op_Equality
System.Double Method op_Inequality
System.Double Method op_LessThan
```

```
System.Double Method op_GreaterThan
System.Double Method op_LessThanOrEqual
System.Double Method op_GreaterThanOrEqual
System.Double Method Equals
System.Double Method GetHashCode
System.Double Method ToString
System.Double Method ToString
System.Double Method ToString
System.Double Method ToString
System.Double Method Parse
System.Double Method Parse
System.Double Method Parse
System.Double Method Parse
System.Double Method TryParse
System.Double Method TryParse
System.Double Method GetTypeCode
System.Object Method GetType
System.Double Field MinValue
System.Double Field MaxValue
System.Double Field Epsilon
System.Double Field NegativeInfinity
System.Double Field PositiveInfinity
System.Double Field NaN
```

The console displays the name, full name, and namespace of the data type as well as the name of the base type. Next, it simply iterates through all the public instance members of the data type, displaying for each member the declaring type, the type of member (method, field, and so on), and the name of the member. The *declaring type* is the name of the class that actually declares the type member (for example, System.Double if it is defined or overridden in System.Double, or the name of the relevant base type if the member is simply inherited from a base class).

TypeView does not display signatures of methods because you are retrieving details about all public instance members through MemberInfo objects, and information about parameters is not available through a MemberInfo object. To retrieve that information, you would need references to MethodInfo and other more specific objects, which means that you would need to obtain details about each type of member separately.

The sample code for TypeView makes use of the following namespaces:

```
System

System.Reflection

System.Text
```

TypeView does display details about all public instance members for doubles, the only details defined are fields and methods. The entire code is in one class, Program, which has a couple of static methods and one static field, a StringBuilder instance called OutputText, which is used to build the text to be displayed in the message box. The Main method and class declaration look like this (code file TypeView/Program.cs):

```
class Program
{
  private static StringBuilder OutputText = new StringBuilder();

  static void Main()
  {
    // modify this line to retrieve details of any other data type
    Type t = typeof(double);
    AnalyzeType(t);
    Console.WriteLine($"Analysis of type {t.Name}");
    Console.WriteLine(OutputText.ToString());
    Console.ReadLine();
  }
  //...
}
```

The `Main` method implementation starts by declaring a `Type` object to represent your chosen data type. You then call a method, `AnalyzeType`, which extracts the information from the `Type` object and uses it to build the output text. Finally, you write the output to the console. `AnalyzeType` is where the bulk of the work is done:

```
static void AnalyzeType(Type t)
{
  TypeInfo typeInfo = t.GetTypeInfo();
  AddToOutput($"Type Name: {t.Name}");
  AddToOutput($"Full Name: {t.FullName}");
  AddToOutput($"Namespace: {t.Namespace}");

  Type tBase = t.BaseType;
  if (tBase != null)
  {
    AddToOutput($"Base Type: {tBase.Name}");
  }

  AddToOutput("\npublic members:");
  foreach (MemberInfo NextMember in t.GetMembers())
  {
    AddToOutput($"{member.DeclaringType} {member.MemberType} {member.Name}");
  }
}
```

You implement the `AnalyzeType` method by calling various properties of the `Type` object to get the information you need concerning the type names and then calling the `GetMembers` method to get an array of `MemberInfo` objects that you can use to display the details for each member. Note that you use a helper method, `AddToOutput`, to build the text to be displayed:

```
static void AddToOutput(string Text) =>
  OutputText.Append("\n" + Text);
```

The Assembly Class

The `Assembly` class is defined in the `System.Reflection` namespace and provides access to the metadata for a given assembly. It also contains methods that enable you to load and even execute an assembly—assuming that the assembly is an executable. As with the `Type` class, `Assembly` contains too many methods and properties to cover here, so this section is confined to covering those methods and properties that you need to get started and that you use to complete the `WhatsNewAttributes` example.

Before you can do anything with an `Assembly` instance, you need to load the corresponding assembly into the running process. You can do this with either the static members `Assembly.Load` or `Assembly.LoadFrom`. The difference between these methods is that `Load` takes the name of the assembly, and the runtime searches in a variety of locations in an attempt to locate the assembly. These locations include the local directory and the global assembly cache. `LoadFrom` takes the full path name of an assembly and does not attempt to find the assembly in any other location:

```
Assembly assembly1 = Assembly.Load("SomeAssembly");
Assembly assembly2 = Assembly.LoadFrom
  (@"C:\My Projects\Software\SomeOtherAssembly");
```

A number of other overloads of both methods exist, which supply additional security information. After you have loaded an assembly, you can use various properties on it to find out, for example, its full name:

```
string name = assembly1.FullName;
```

Getting Details About Types Defined in an Assembly

One nice feature of the `Assembly` class is that it enables you to obtain details about all the types that are defined in the corresponding assembly. You simply call the `Assembly.GetTypes` method, which returns an array of `System.Type` references containing details about all the types. You can then manipulate these `Type` references as explained in the previous section:

```
Type[] types = theAssembly.GetTypes();
foreach(Type definedType in types)
{
    DoSomethingWith(definedType);
}
```

Getting Details About Custom Attributes

The methods you use to find out which custom attributes are defined on an assembly or type depend on the type of object to which the attribute is attached. If you want to find out what custom attributes are attached to an assembly as a whole, you need to call a `static` method of the `Attribute` class, `GetCustomAttributes`, passing in a reference to the assembly:

> **NOTE** *This is actually quite significant. You might have wondered why, when you defined custom attributes, you had to go to all the trouble of actually writing classes for them, and why Microsoft didn't come up with some simpler syntax. Well, the answer is here. The custom attributes genuinely exist as objects, and when an assembly is loaded you can read in these attribute objects, examine their properties, and call their methods.*

```
Attribute[] definedAttributes =
    Attribute.GetCustomAttributes(assembly1);
// assembly1 is an Assembly object
```

`GetCustomAttributes`, which is used to get assembly attributes, has a few overloads. If you call it without specifying any parameters other than an assembly reference, it simply returns all the custom attributes defined for that assembly. You can also call `GetCustomAttributes` by specifying a second parameter, which is a `Type` object that indicates the attribute class in which you are interested. In this case, `GetCustomAttributes` returns an array consisting of all the attributes present that are of the specified type.

Note that all attributes are retrieved as plain `Attribute` references. If you want to call any of the methods or properties you defined for your custom attributes, you need to cast these references explicitly to the relevant custom attribute classes. You can obtain details about custom attributes that are attached to a given data type by calling another overload of `Assembly.GetCustomAttributes`, this time passing a `Type` reference that describes the type for which you want to retrieve any attached attributes. To obtain attributes that are attached to methods, constructors, fields, and so on, however, you need to call a `GetCustomAttributes` method that is a member of one of the classes `MethodInfo`, `ConstructorInfo`, `FieldInfo`, and so on.

If you expect only a single attribute of a given type, you can call the `GetCustomAttribute` method instead, which returns a single `Attribute` object. You will use `GetCustomAttribute` in the `WhatsNewAttributes` example to find out whether the `SupportsWhatsNew` attribute is present in the assembly. To do this, you call `GetCustomAttribute`, passing in a reference to the `WhatsNewAttributes` assembly, and the type of the `SupportsWhatsNewAttribute` attribute. If this attribute is present, you get an `Attribute` instance. If no instances of it are defined in the assembly, you get `null`. If two or more instances are found, `GetCustomAttribute` throws a `System.Reflection.AmbiguousMatchException`. This is what that call would look like:

```
Attribute supportsAttribute =
    Attribute.GetCustomAttributes(assembly1, typeof(SupportsWhatsNewAttribute));
```

Completing the WhatsNewAttributes Example

You now have enough information to complete the WhatsNewAttributes example by writing the source code for the final assembly in the sample, the LookUpWhatsNew assembly. This part of the application is a console application. However, it needs to reference the other assemblies of WhatsNewAttributes and VectorClass.

The sample code for the LookupWhatsNew project references the libraries WhatsNewAttributes and VectorClass and makes uses the following namespaces:

```
System

System.Collections.Generic

System.Linq

System.Reflection

System.Text

WhatsNewAttributes
```

The Program class contains the main program entry point as well as the other methods. All the methods you define are in this class, which also has two static fields—outputText, which contains the text as you build it in preparation for writing it to the message box, and backDateTo, which stores the date you have selected. All modifications made since this date will be displayed. Normally, you would display a dialog inviting the user to pick this date, but we don't want to get sidetracked into that kind of code. For this reason, backDateTo is hard-coded to a value of 1 Feb 2017. You can easily change this date when you download the code (code file LookupWhatsNew/Program.cs):

```csharp
class Program
{
  private static readonly StringBuilder outputText = new StringBuilder(1000);
  private static DateTime backDateTo = new DateTime(2017, 2, 1);

  static void Main()
  {
    Assembly theAssembly = Assembly.Load(new AssemblyName("VectorClass"));
    Attribute supportsAttribute = theAssembly.GetCustomAttribute(
      typeof(SupportsWhatsNewAttribute));

    AddToOutput($"Assembly: {theAssembly.FullName}");
    if (supportsAttribute == null)
    {
      AddToOutput("This assembly does not support WhatsNew attributes");
      return;
    }
    else
    {
      AddToOutput("Defined Types:");
    }

    IEnumerable<Type> types = theAssembly.ExportedTypes;
    foreach(Type definedType in types)
    {
      DisplayTypeInfo(definedType);
    }

    Console.WriteLine($"What\`s New since {backDateTo:D}");
    Console.WriteLine(outputText.ToString());
    Console.ReadLine();
  }
  //...
}
```

The `Main` method first loads the `VectorClass` assembly, and then verifies that it is marked with the `SupportsWhatsNew` attribute. You know `VectorClass` has the `SupportsWhatsNew` attribute applied to it because you have only recently compiled it, but this is a check that would be worth making if users were given a choice of which assembly they want to check.

Assuming that all is well, you use the `Assembly.ExportedTypes` property to get a collection of all the types defined in this assembly, and then loop through them. For each one, you call a method, `DisplayTypeInfo`, which adds the relevant text, including details regarding any instances of `LastModifiedAttribute`, to the `outputText` field. Finally, you show the complete text to the console. The `DisplayTypeInfo` method looks like this (code file `LookupWhatsNew/Program.cs`):

```
private static void DisplayTypeInfo(Type type)
{
  // make sure we only pick out classes
  if (!type.GetTypeInfo().IsClass)
  {
    return;
  }

  AddToOutput($"{Environment.NewLine}class {type.Name}");

  IEnumerable<LastModifiedAttribute> lastModifiedAttributes =
    type.GetTypeInfo().GetCustomAttributes()
    .OfType<LastModifiedAttribute>()
    .Where(a => a.DateModified >= backDateTo).ToArray();

  if (attributes.Count() == 0)
  {
    AddToOutput($"\tNo changes to the class {type.Name}" +
      $"{Environment.NewLine}");
  }
  else
  {
    foreach (LastFieldModifiedAttribute attribute in lastModifiedattributes)
    {
      WriteAttributeInfo(attribute);
    }
  }

  AddToOutput("changes to methods of this class:");

  foreach (MethodInfo method in
    type.GetTypeInfo().DeclaredMembers.OfType<MethodInfo>())
  {
    IEnumerable<LastModifiedAttribute> attributesToMethods =
      method.GetCustomAttributes().OfType<LastModifiedAttribute>()
        .Where(a => a.DateModified >= backDateTo).ToArray();

    if (attributesToMethods.Count() > 0)
    {
      AddToOutput($"{method.ReturnType} {method.Name}()");
      foreach (Attribute attribute in attributesToMethods)
      {
        WriteAttributeInfo(attribute);
      }
    }
  }
}
```

Notice that the first thing you do in this method is check whether the `Type` reference you have been passed actually represents a class. Because, to keep things simple, you have specified that the `LastModified` attribute can be applied only to classes or member methods, you would be wasting time by doing any processing if the item is not a class (it could be a class, delegate, or enum).

Next, you use the `type.GetTypeInfo().GetCustomAttributes()` method to determine whether this class has any `LastModifiedAttribute` instances attached to it. If so, you add their details to the output text, using a helper method, `WriteAttributeInfo`.

Finally, you use the `DeclaredMembers` property of the `TypeInfo` type to iterate through all the member methods of this data type, and then do the same with each method as you did for the class—check whether it has any `LastModifiedAttribute` instances attached to it; if so, you display them using `WriteAttributeInfo`.

The next bit of code shows the `WriteAttributeInfo` method, which is responsible for determining what text to display for a given `LastModifiedAttribute` instance. Note that this method is passed an `Attribute` reference, so it needs to cast this to a `LastModifiedAttribute` reference first. After it has done that, it uses the properties that you originally defined for this attribute to retrieve its parameters. It confirms that the date of the attribute is sufficiently recent before actually adding it to the text for display (code file `LookupWhatsNew/Program.cs`):

```
private static void WriteAttributeInfo(Attribute attribute)
{
  if (attribute is LastModifiedAttribute lastModifiedAttribute)
  {
    AddToOutput($"\tmodified: {lastModifiedAttribute.DateModified:D}: " +
      $"{lastModifiedAttribute.Changes}");

    if (lastModifiedAttribute.Issues != null)
    {
      AddToOutput($"\tOutstanding issues: {lastModifiedAttribute.Issues}");
    }
  }
}
```

Finally, here is the helper `AddToOutput` method:

```
static void AddToOutput(string text) =>
  outputText.Append($"{Environment.NewLine}{text}");
```

Running this code produces the results shown here:

```
What`s New since Wednesday, February 1, 2017
Assembly: VectorClass, Version=2.1.0.0, Culture=neutral, PublicKeyToken=null
Defined Types:

class Vector
      modified: Wednesday, July 19, 2017: updated for C# 7 and .NET Core 2
changes to methods of this class:
System.String ToString()
      modified: Wednesday, July 19, 2017: changed ijk format from StringBuilder to format string
```

Note that when you list the types defined in the `VectorClass` assembly, you actually pick up two classes: `Vector` and the embedded `VectorEnumerator` class. In addition, note that because the `backDateTo` date of 1 Feb is hard-coded in this example, you actually pick up the attributes that are dated July 19 but not those dated earlier.

USING DYNAMIC LANGUAGE EXTENSIONS FOR REFLECTION

Until now you've used reflection for reading metadata. You can also use reflection to create instances dynamically from types that aren't known at compile time. The next sample shows creating an instance of the `Calculator` class without the compiler knowing of this type at compile time. The assembly `CalculatorLib` is loaded dynamically without adding a reference. During runtime, the `Calculator` object is instantiated, and a method is called. After you know how to use the Reflection API, you'll do the same using the C# `dynamic` keyword. This keyword has been part of the C# language since version 4.

Creating the Calculator Library

The library that is loaded is a simple Class Library (.NET Standard) containing the type `Calculator` with implementations of the `Add` and `Subtract` methods. As the methods are really simple, they are implemented using the expression syntax (code file `CalculatorLib/Calculator.cs`):

```
public class Calculator
{
  public double Add(double x, double y) => x + y;
  public double Subtract(double x, double y) => x - y;
}
```

After you compile the library, copy the generated DLL to the folder `c:/addins`.

Instantiating a Type Dynamically

For using reflection to create the `Calculator` instance dynamically, you create a Console App (.NET Core) with the name `ClientApp`.

The constant `CalculatorTypeName` defines the name of the `Calculator` type, including the namespace. The `Main` method requires a command-line argument with the path to the library and then invokes the methods `UsingReflection` and `UsingReflectionWithDynamic`, two variants doing reflection (code file `DynamicSamples/ClientApp/Program.cs`):

```
class Program
{
  private const string CalculatorTypeName = "CalculatorLib.Calculator";

  static void Main(string[] args)
  {
    if (args.Length != 1)
    {
      ShowUsage();
      return;
    }
    UsingReflection(args[0]);
    UsingReflectionWithDynamic(args[0]);
  }

  private static void ShowUsage()
  {
    Console.WriteLine($"Usage: {nameof(ClientApp)} path");
    Console.WriteLine();
    Console.WriteLine("Copy CalculatorLib.dll to an addin directory");
    Console.WriteLine("and pass the absolute path of this directory " +
      "when starting the application to load the library");
  }
```

Before using reflection to invoke a method, you need to instantiate the `Calculator` type. The method `GetCalculator` loads the assembly dynamically using the method `LoadFile` of the `Assembly` class and creates an instance of the `Calculator` type with the `CreateInstance` method:

```
private static object GetCalculator()
{
  Assembly assembly = Assembly.LoadFile(CalculatorLibPath);
  return assembly.CreateInstance(CalculatorTypeName);
}
```

The sample code for the `ClientApp` makes use of the following dependency and .NET namespaces:

Dependency

```
System.Runtime.Loader
```

.NET Namespaces

```
Microsoft.CSharp.RuntimeBinder
System
System.Reflection
```

Invoking a Member with the Reflection API

Next, the Reflection API is used to invoke the method Add of the Calculator instance. First, the calculator instance is retrieved with the helper method GetCalculator. If you would like to add a reference to the CalculatorLib, you could use new Calculator to create an instance. But here it's not that easy.

Invoking the method using reflection has the advantage that the type does not need to be available at compile time. You could add it at a later time just by copying the library in the specified directory. To invoke the member using reflection, the Type object of the instance is retrieved using GetType—a method of the base class Object. With the help of the extension method GetMethod, a MethodInfo object for the method Add is accessed. The MethodInfo defines the Invoke method to call the method using any number of parameters. The first parameter of the Invoke method needs the instance of the type where the member is invoked. The second parameter is of type object[] to pass all the parameters needed by the invocation. You're passing the values of the x and y variables here (code file DynamicSamples/ClientApp/Program.cs):

```
private static void UsingReflection()
{
  double x = 3;
  double y = 4;
  object calc = GetCalculator();

  object result = calc.GetType().GetMethod("Add")
    .Invoke(calc, new object[] { x, y });
  Console.WriteLine($"the result of {x} and {y} is {result}");
}
```

When you run the program, the calculator is invoked, and this result is written to the console:

```
The result of 3 and 4 is 7
```

This is quite some work to do for calling a member dynamically. The next section looks at how easy it is to use the dynamic keyword.

Invoking a Member with the Dynamic Type

Using reflection with the dynamic keyword, the object that is returned from the GetCalculator method is assigned to a variable of a dynamic type. The GetCalculator method itself is not changed; it still returns an object. The result is returned to a variable that is of type dynamic. With this, the Add method is invoked, and two double values are passed to it (code file DynamicSamples/ClientApp/Program.cs):

```
private static void ReflectionNew()
{
  double x = 3;
  double y = 4;
  dynamic calc = GetCalculator();
  double result = calc.Add(x, y);
  Console.WriteLine($"the result of {x} and {y} is {result}");
}
```

The syntax is really simple; it looks like calling a method with strongly typed access. However, there's no IntelliSense within Visual Studio because you can immediately see coding this from the Visual Studio editor, so it's easy to make typos.

There's also no compile-time check. The compiler runs fine when you invoke the `Multiply` method. Just remember you only defined `Add` and `Subtract` methods with the calculator.

```
try
{
  result = calc.Multiply(x, y);
}
catch (RuntimeBinderException ex)
{
  Console.WriteLine(ex);
}
```

When you run the application and invoke the `Multiply` method, you get a `RuntimeBinderException`:

```
Microsoft.CSharp.RuntimeBinder.RuntimeBinderException: 'CalculatorLib.Calculator'
  does not contain a definition for 'Multiply'
  at CallSite.Target(Closure , CallSite , Object , Double , Double )
  at System.Dynamic.UpdateDelegates.UpdateAndExecute3[T0,T1,T2,TRet](CallSite
  site, T0 arg0, T1 arg1, T2 arg2)
  at ClientApp.Program.UsingReflectionWithDynamic(String addinPath) in...
```

Using the `dynamic` type also has more overhead compared to accessing objects in a strongly typed manner. Therefore, the keyword is useful only in some specific scenarios such as reflection. You don't have a compiler check invoking the `InvokeMember` method of the `Type`; instead, a string is passed for the name of the member. Using the `dynamic` type, which has a simpler syntax, has a big advantage compared to using the Reflection API in such scenarios.

The `dynamic` type can also be used with COM integration and scripting environments as shown after discussing the dynamic keyword more in detail.

THE DYNAMIC TYPE

The `dynamic` type enables you to write code that bypasses compile-time type checking. The compiler assumes that the operation defined for an object of type `dynamic` is valid. If that operation isn't valid, the error isn't detected until runtime. This is shown in the following example:

```
class Program
{
  static void Main()
  {
    var staticPerson = new Person();
    dynamic dynamicPerson = new Person();
    staticPerson.GetFullName("John", "Smith");
    dynamicPerson.GetFullName("John", "Smith");
  }
}

class Person
{
  public string FirstName { get; set; }
  public string LastName { get; set; }
  public string GetFullName() => $"{FirstName} {LastName}";
}
```

This example does not compile because of the call to `staticPerson.GetFullName()`. There isn't a method on the `Person` object that takes two parameters, so the compiler raises the error. If that line of code were commented out, the example would compile. If executed, a runtime error would occur. The exception that is raised is `RuntimeBinderException`. The `RuntimeBinder` is the object in the runtime that evaluates the call to determine whether `Person` really does support the method that was called. Binding is discussed later in the chapter.

Unlike the var keyword, an object that is defined as *dynamic* can change type during runtime. Remember that when the var keyword is used, the determination of the object's type is delayed. After the type is defined, it can't be changed. Not only can you change the type of a dynamic object, you can change it many times. This differs from casting an object from one type to another. When you cast an object, you are creating a new object with a different but compatible type. For example, you cannot cast an int to a Person object. In the following example, you can see that if the object is a dynamic object, you can change it from int to Person:

```
dynamic dyn;
dyn = 100;
Console.WriteLine(dyn.GetType());
Console.WriteLine(dyn);
dyn = "This is a string";
Console.WriteLine(dyn.GetType());
Console.WriteLine(dyn);
dyn = new Person() { FirstName = "Bugs", LastName = "Bunny" };
Console.WriteLine(dyn.GetType());
Console.WriteLine($"{dyn.FirstName} {dyn.LastName}");
```

The result of executing this code would be that the dyn object actually changes type from System.Int32 to System.String to Person. If dyn had been declared as an int or string, the code would not have compiled.

> **NOTE** *There are a couple of limitations to the dynamic type. A dynamic object does not support extension methods. Nor can anonymous functions (lambda expressions) be used as parameters to a dynamic method call, so LINQ does not work well with dynamic objects. Most LINQ calls are extension methods, and lambda expressions are used as arguments to those extension methods.*

Dynamic Behind the Scenes

So what's going on behind the scenes to make the dynamic functionality available with C#? C# is a statically typed language. That hasn't changed. Take a look at the IL (Intermediate Language) that's generated when the dynamic type is used.

First, this is the example C# code that you're looking at (code file DynamicSamples/DecompileSample/Program.cs):

```
class Program
{
  static void Main()
  {
    StaticClass staticObject = new StaticClass();
    DynamicClass dynamicObject = new DynamicClass();
    Console.WriteLine(staticObject.IntValue);
    Console.WriteLine(dynamicObject.DynValue);
    Console.ReadLine();
  }
}

class StaticClass
{
  public int IntValue = 100;
}
```

```
class DynamicClass
{
  public dynamic DynValue = 100;
}
```

Besides the `Program` class, you have two classes: `StaticClass` and `DynamicClass`. `StaticClass` has a single field that returns an `int`. `DynamicClass` has a single field that returns a `dynamic` object. The `Main` method creates these objects and prints out the value that the methods return. Simple enough.

Now comment out the references to the `DynamicClass` in `Main` like this:

```
static void Main()
{
  StaticClass staticObject = new StaticClass();
  //DynamicClass dynamicObject = new DynamicClass();
  Console.WriteLine(staticObject.IntValue);
  //Console.WriteLine(dynamicObject.DynValue);
  Console.ReadLine();
}
```

Using the `ildasm` tool, you can look at the IL that is generated for the `Main` method:

```
.method private hidebysig static void  Main() cil managed
{
  .entrypoint
  // Code size       22 (0x16)
  .maxstack  8
  IL_0000:  newobj     instance void DecompileSample.StaticClass::.ctor()
  IL_0005:  ldfld      int32 DecompileSample.StaticClass::IntValue
  IL_000a:  call       void [System.Console]System.Console::WriteLine(int32)
  IL_000f:  call       string [System.Console]System.Console::ReadLine()
  IL_0014:  pop
  IL_0015:  ret
} // end of method Program::Main
```

Without getting into the details of IL, you can still pretty much tell what's going on just by looking at this section of code. Line 0000, the `StaticClass` constructor, is called. Line 0005 calls the `IntValue` field of `StaticClass`. The next line writes out the value.

Now comment out the `StaticClass` references and uncomment the `DynamicClass` references:

```
static void Main()
{
  //StaticClass staticObject = new StaticClass();
  DynamicClass dynamicObject = new DynamicClass();
  //Console.WriteLine(staticObject.IntValue);
  Console.WriteLine(dynamicObject.DynValue);
  Console.ReadLine();
}
```

Compile the application again, and the following is generated:

```
.method private hidebysig static void  Main() cil managed
{
  .entrypoint
  // Code size       119 (0x77)
  .maxstack  9
  .locals init (class DecompileSample.DynamicClass V_0)
  IL_0000:  newobj     instance void DecompileSample.DynamicClass::.ctor()
  IL_0005:  stloc.0
  IL_0006:  ldsfld     class [System.Linq.Expressions]System.Runtime.CompilerServices.
CallSite`1<class [System.Runtime]System.Action`3<class [System.Linq.Expressions]System.
Runtime.CompilerServices.CallSite,class [System.Runtime]System.Type,object>> DecompileSample.
Program/'<>o__0'::'<>p__0'
```

```
IL_000b:  brtrue.s    IL_004c
IL_000d:  ldc.i4      0x100
IL_0012:  ldstr       „WriteLine"
IL_0017:  ldnull
IL_0018:  ldtoken     DecompileSample.Program
IL_001d:  call        class [System.Runtime]System.Type [System.Runtime]System.Type::GetTypeFr
omHandle(valuetype [System.Runtime]System.RuntimeTypeHandle)
IL_0022:  ldc.i4.2
IL_0023:  newarr      [Microsoft.CSharp]Microsoft.CSharp.RuntimeBinder.CSharpArgumentInfo
IL_0028:  dup
IL_0029:  ldc.i4.0
IL_002a:  ldc.i4.s    33
IL_002c:  ldnull
IL_002d:  call        class [Microsoft.CSharp]Microsoft.CSharp.RuntimeBinder.
CSharpArgumentInfo [Microsoft.CSharp]Microsoft.CSharp.RuntimeBinder.CSharpArgumentInfo::Create(
valuetype [Microsoft.CSharp]Microsoft.CSharp.RuntimeBinder.CSharpArgumentInfoFlags,
string)
IL_0032:  stelem.ref
IL_0033:  dup
IL_0034:  ldc.i4.1
IL_0035:  ldc.i4.0
IL_0036:  ldnull
IL_0037:  call        class [Microsoft.CSharp]Microsoft.CSharp.RuntimeBinder.
CSharpArgumentInfo [Microsoft.CSharp]Microsoft.CSharp.RuntimeBinder.CSharpArgumentInfo::Create(
valuetype [Microsoft.CSharp]Microsoft.CSharp.RuntimeBinder.CSharpArgumentInfoFlags,
string)
IL_003c:  stelem.ref
IL_003d:  call        class [System.Linq.Expressions]System.Runtime.CompilerServices.
CallSiteBinder [Microsoft.CSharp]Microsoft.CSharp.RuntimeBinder.Binder::InvokeMember(valuetype
[Microsoft.CSharp]Microsoft.CSharp.RuntimeBinder.CSharpBinderFlags,
string,
class [System.Runtime]System.Collections.Generic.IEnumerable`1<class [System.Runtime]System.
Type>,
class [System.Runtime]System.Type,
class [System.Runtime]System.Collections.Generic.IEnumerable`1<class [Microsoft.CSharp]
Microsoft.CSharp.RuntimeBinder.CSharpArgumentInfo>)
IL_0042:  call        class [System.Linq.Expressions]System.Runtime.CompilerServices.
CallSite`1<!0> class [System.Linq.Expressions]System.Runtime.CompilerServices.CallSite`1<class
[System.Runtime]System.Action`3<class [System.Linq.Expressions]System.Runtime.CompilerServices.
CallSite,class [System.Runtime]System.Type,object>>::Create(class [System.Linq.Expressions]
System.Runtime.CompilerServices.CallSiteBinder)
IL_0047:  stsfld      class [System.Linq.Expressions]System.Runtime.CompilerServices.
CallSite`1<class [System.Runtime]System.Action`3<class [System.Linq.Expressions]System.
Runtime.CompilerServices.CallSite,class [System.Runtime]System.Type,object>> DecompileSample.
Program/'<>o__0'::'<>p__0'
IL_004c:  ldsfld      class [System.Linq.Expressions]System.Runtime.CompilerServices.
CallSite`1<class [System.Runtime]System.Action`3<class [System.Linq.Expressions]System.
Runtime.CompilerServices.CallSite,class [System.Runtime]System.Type,object>> DecompileSample.
Program/'<>o__0'::'<>p__0'
IL_0051:  ldfld       !0 class [System.Linq.Expressions]System.Runtime.CompilerServices.
CallSite`1<class [System.Runtime]System.Action`3<class [System.Linq.Expressions]System.Runtime.
CompilerServices.CallSite,class [System.Runtime]System.Type,object>>::Target
IL_0056:  ldsfld      class [System.Linq.Expressions]System.Runtime.CompilerServices.
CallSite`1<class [System.Runtime]System.Action`3<class [System.Linq.Expressions]System.
Runtime.CompilerServices.CallSite,class [System.Runtime]System.Type,object>> DecompileSample.
Program/'<>o__0'::'<>p__0'
```

```
    IL_005b:  ldtoken      [System.Console]System.Console
    IL_0060:  call         class [System.Runtime]System.Type
[System.Runtime]System.Type::GetTypeFromHandle(valuetype [System.Runtime]System.
RuntimeTypeHandle)
    IL_0065:  ldloc.0
    IL_0066:  ldfld        object DecompileSample.DynamicClass::DynValue
    IL_006b:  callvirt     instance void class [System.Runtime]System.Action`3<class [System.
Linq.Expressions]System.Runtime.CompilerServices.CallSite,class [System.Runtime]System.
Type,object>::Invoke(!0,
!1,
!2)
    IL_0070:  call         string [System.Console]System.Console::ReadLine()
    IL_0075:  pop
    IL_0076:  ret
} // end of method Program::Main
```

It's safe to say that the C# compiler is doing a little extra work to support the dynamic type. Looking at the generated code, you can see references to System.Runtime.CompilerServices.CallSite and System.Runtime.CompilerServices.CallSiteBinder.

The CallSite is a type that handles the lookup at runtime. When a call is made on a dynamic object at runtime, something has to check that object to determine whether the member really exists. The call site caches this information, so the lookup doesn't have to be performed repeatedly. Without this process, performance in looping structures would be questionable.

After the CallSite does the member lookup, the CallSiteBinder is invoked. It takes the information from the call site and generates an expression tree representing the operation to which the binder is bound.

There is obviously a lot going on here. Great care has been taken to optimize what would appear to be a very complex operation. Clearly, using the dynamic type can be useful, but it does come with a price.

DYNAMICOBJECT AND EXPANDOOBJECT

What if you want to create your own dynamic object? You have a couple of options for doing that: by deriving from DynamicObject or by using ExpandoObject. Using DynamicObject is a little more work than using ExpandoObject because with DynamicObject you have to override a couple of methods. ExpandoObject is a sealed class that is ready to use.

DynamicObject

Consider an object that represents a person. Normally, you would define properties for the first name, middle name, and last name. Now imagine the capability to build that object during runtime, with the system having no prior knowledge of what properties the object might have or what methods the object might support. That's what having a DynamicObject-based object can provide. There might be very few times when you need this sort of functionality, but until now the C# language had no way of accommodating such a requirement (code file DynamicSamples/DynamicSample/WroxDynamicObject.cs):

```
public class WroxDynamicObject : DynamicObject
{
  private Dictionary<string, object> _dynamicData =
    new Dictionary<string, object>();

  public override bool TryGetMember(GetMemberBinder binder, out object result)
  {
    bool success = false;
    result = null;
    if (_dynamicData.ContainsKey(binder.Name))
    {
```

```
        result = _dynamicData[binder.Name];
        success = true;
      }
      else
      {
        result = "Property Not Found!";
      }
      return success;
    }

    public override bool TrySetMember(SetMemberBinder binder, object value)
    {
      _dynamicData[binder.Name] = value;
      return true;
    }

    public override bool TryInvokeMember(InvokeMemberBinder binder,
      object[] args, out object result)
    {
      dynamic method = _dynamicData[binder.Name];
      result = method((DateTime)args[0]);
      return result != null;
    }
  }
}
```

First look at what the `DynamicObject` looks like (code file `DynamicSamples/DynamicSample/ WroxDyamicObject.cs`):

In this example, you're overriding three methods: `TrySetMember`, `TryGetMember`, and `TryInvokeMember`.

`TrySetMember` adds the new method, property, or field to the object. In this case, you store the member information in a `Dictionary` object. The `SetMemberBinder` object that is passed into the `TrySetMember` method contains the `Name` property, which is used to identify the element in the `Dictionary`.

The `TryGetMember` retrieves the object stored in the `Dictionary` based on the `GetMemberBinder Name` property.

Here is the code that makes use of the new dynamic object just created (code file `DynamicSamples/ DynamicSample/Program.cs`):

```
dynamic wroxDyn = new WroxDynamicObject();
wroxDyn.FirstName = "Bugs";
wroxDyn.LastName = "Bunny";
Console.WriteLine(wroxDyn.GetType());
Console.WriteLine($"{wroxDyn.FirstName} {wroxDyn.LastName}");
```

It looks simple enough, but where is the call to the methods you overrode? That's where .NET helps. `DynamicObject` handles the binding for you; all you have to do is reference the properties `FirstName` and `LastName` as if they were there all the time.

You can also easily add a method. You can use the same `WroxDynamicObject` and add a `GetTomorrowDate` method to it. It takes a `DateTime` object and returns a date string representing the next day. Here's the code:

```
dynamic wroxDyn = new WroxDynamicObject();
Func<DateTime, string> GetTomorrow = today => today.AddDays(1).ToShortDateString();
wroxDyn.GetTomorrowDate = GetTomorrow;
Console.WriteLine($"Tomorrow is {wroxDyn.GetTomorrowDate(DateTime.Now)}");
```

You create the delegate `GetTomorrow` using `Func<T, TResult>`. The method the delegate represents is the call to `AddDays`. One day is added to the `Date` that is passed in, and a string of that date is returned. The delegate is then set to `GetTomorrowDate` on the `wroxDyn` object. The last line calls the new method, passing in the current day's date. Hence the dynamic magic and you have an object with a valid method.

ExpandoObject

ExpandoObject works similarly to the WroxDynamicObject created in the previous section. The difference is that you don't have to override any methods, as shown in the following code example (code file DynamicSamples/DynamicSample/WroxDynamicObject.cs):

```
static void DoExpando()
{
  dynamic expObj = new ExpandoObject();
  expObj.FirstName = "Daffy";
  expObj.LastName = "Duck";
  Console.WriteLine($"{expObj.FirstName} {expObj.LastName}");
  Func<DateTime, string> GetTomorrow = today =>
    today.AddDays(1).ToShortDateString();

  expObj.GetTomorrowDate = GetTomorrow;
  Console.WriteLine($"Tomorrow is {expObj.GetTomorrowDate(DateTime.Now)}");
  expObj.Friends = new List<Person>();
  expObj.Friends.Add(new Person() { FirstName = "Bob", LastName = "Jones" });
  expObj.Friends.Add(new Person() { FirstName = "Robert",
    LastName = "Jones" });
  expObj.Friends.Add(new Person() { FirstName = "Bobby", LastName = "Jones" });
  foreach (Person friend in expObj.Friends)
  {
    Console.WriteLine($"{friend.FirstName} {friend.LastName}");
  }
}
```

Notice that this code is almost identical to what you did earlier. You add a FirstName and LastName property, add a GetTomorrow function, and then do one additional thing: add a collection of Person objects as a property of the object.

At first glance it might seem that this is no different from using the dynamic type, but there are a couple of subtle differences that are important. First, you can't just create an empty dynamic typed object. The dynamic type must have something assigned to it. For example, the following code won't work:

```
dynamic dynObj;
dynObj.FirstName = "Joe";
```

As shown in the previous example, this is possible with ExpandoObject.

Second, because the dynamic type has to have something assigned to it, it reports back the type assigned to it if you do a GetType call. For example, if you assign an int, it reports back that it is an int. This doesn't happen with ExpandoObject or an object derived from DynamicObject.

If you have to control the addition and access of properties in your dynamic object, then deriving from DynamicObject is your best option. With DynamicObject, you can use several methods to override and control exactly how the object interacts with the runtime. For other cases, using the dynamic type or the ExpandoObject might be appropriate.

Following is another example of using dynamic and ExpandoObject. Assume that the requirement is to develop a general-purpose comma-separated values (CSV) file parsing tool. You won't know from one execution to another what data will be in the file, only that the values will be comma-separated and that the first line will contain the field names.

First, open the file and read in the stream. You can use a simple helper method to do this (code file DynamicSamples/DynamicFileReader/DynamicFileHelper.cs):

```
public class DynamicFileHelper
{
  //...
  private StreamReader OpenFile(string fileName)
```

```
        {
          if(File.Exists(fileName))
          {
            return new StreamReader(fileName);
          }
          return null;
        }
        //...
      }
```

This just opens the file and creates a new `StreamReader` to read the file contents.

Now you want to get the field names, which you can do easily by reading in the first line from the file and using the `Split` function to create a string array of field names:

```
string[] headerLine = fileStream.ReadLine().Split(',').Trim().ToArray();
```

Next is the interesting part. You read in the next line from the file, create a string array just like you did with the field names, and start creating your dynamic objects. Here's what the code looks like (code file `DynamicSamples/DynamicFileReader/DynamicFileHelper.cs`):

```
public class DynamicFileHelper
{
  //...
  public IEnumerable<dynamic> ParseFile(string fileName)
  {
    var retList = new List<dynamic>();
    while (fileStream.Peek() > 0)
    {
      string[] dataLine = fileStream.ReadLine().Split(',').Trim().ToArray();
      dynamic dynamicEntity = new ExpandoObject();
      for(int i=0;i<headerLine.Length;i++)
      {
        ((IDictionary<string,object>)dynamicEntity).Add(headerLine[i],
          dataLine[i]);
      }
      retList.Add(dynamicEntity);
    }
    return retList;
  }
  //...
}
```

After you have the string array of field names and data elements, you create a new `ExpandoObject` and add the data to it. Notice that you cast the `ExpandoObject` to a `Dictionary` object. You use the field name as the key and the data as the value. Then you can add the new object to the `retList` object you created and return it to the code that called the method.

What makes this nice is you have a section of code that can handle any data you give it. The only requirements in this case are ensuring that the field names are the first line and that everything is comma-separated. This concept could be expanded to other file types or even to a `DataReader`.

Using this CSV file content that is available with the sample code download

```
FirstName, LastName, City, State
Niki, Lauda, Vienna, Austria
Carlos, Reutemann, Santa Fe, Argentine
Sebastian, Vettel, Thurgovia, Switzerland
```

and this `Main` method to read the sample file `EmployeeList.txt` (code file `DynamicSamples/DynamicFileReader/Program.cs`):

```
static void Main()
{
  var helper = new DynamicFileHelper();
```

```
    var employeeList = helper.ParseFile("EmployeeList.txt");
    foreach (var employee in employeeList)
    {
      Console.WriteLine($"{employee.FirstName} {employee.LastName} lives in " +
        $"{employee.City}, {employee.State}.");
    }
    Console.ReadLine();
  }
```

results in this output to the console:

```
Niki Lauda lives in Vienna, Austria.
Carlos Reutemann lives in Santa Fe, Argentine.
Sebastian Vettel lives in Thurgovia, Switzerland.
```

SUMMARY

This chapter illustrated using the `Type` and `Assembly` classes, which are the primary entry points through which you can access the extensive capabilities provided by reflection.

In addition, this chapter demonstrated a specific aspect of reflection that you are likely to use more often than any other—the inspection of custom attributes. You learned how to define and apply your own custom attributes, and how to retrieve information about custom attributes at runtime.

The second focus of this chapter was working with the dynamic type. Using `ExpandoObject` in place of multiple objects can reduce the number of lines of code significantly. Also using the DLR and adding scripting languages like Python or Ruby can help you build a more polymorphic application that can be changed easily without recompiling.

The next chapter gives details on freeing resources with the `IDisposable` interface, releasing native resources, and working with `unsafe` C# code.

17

Managed and Unmanaged Memory

WHAT'S IN THIS CHAPTER?

➤ Allocating space on the stack and heap at runtime

➤ Garbage collection

➤ Releasing unmanaged resources using destructors and the `System.IDisposable` interface

➤ The syntax for using pointers in C#

➤ Reference semantics

➤ Using the `Span` type

➤ Platform Invoke to access native APIs

WROX.COM CODE DOWNLOADS FOR THIS CHAPTER

The Wrox.com code downloads for this chapter are found at www.wrox.com on the Download Code tab. The source code is also available at https://github.com/ProfessionalCSharp/ProfessionalCSharp7 in the directory Memory.

The code for this chapter is divided into the following major examples:

➤ PointerPlayground

➤ PointerPlayground2

➤ QuickArray

➤ ReferenceSemantics

➤ SpanSample

➤ PlatformInvokeSample

MEMORY

Variables are stored on the stack. The data it references can be on the stack (structs) or on the heap (classes). Structs also can be boxed, so objects on the heap are created. The garbage collector needs to free up unmanaged objects that are no longer needed from the managed heap. Using native APIs, memory can be allocated on the native heap. The garbage collector is not responsible for memory allocated on the native heap. You have to free this memory on your own. There's a lot to consider with regard to memory.

When you use a managed environment, you can easily be misled to not pay attention to memory management because the *garbage collector* (GC) deals with that anyway. A lot of work is done by the GC; it's very practical to know how it works, what the small and the large object heap are, and what data types are stored within the stack. Also, while the garbage collector deals with managed resources, what about unmanaged ones? You have to free them on your own. Probably your programs are fully managed programs, but what about the types of the Framework? For example, file types (discussed in Chapter 22, "Files and Streams"), wrap a native file handle. This file handle needs to be released. To release this handle early, it's good to know the IDisposable interface and the using statement that's explained in this chapter.

Other aspects are important as well. Although several language constructs make it easier to create immutable types, mutable objects have an advantage as well. The string class is an immutable type that's been available since .NET Framework 1.0. Nowadays we often have to deal with large strings. When manipulating the string, the GC needs to clean up a lot of objects. Directly accessing the memory of the string and making changes makes a mutable and in different scenarios a more performant program. The Span type that makes this possible has been discussed in Chapter 9, "Strings and Regular Expressions," and in Chapter 7, "Arrays." With arrays you've also seen the ArrayPool class that also offers reducing the work of the GC.

This chapter starts with various aspects of memory management and memory access. A good understanding of memory management and knowledge of the pointer capabilities provided by C# will better enable you to integrate C# code with legacy code and perform efficient memory manipulation in performance-critical systems. This chapter covers new ways to use the ref keyword in C# 7 for return types and local variables. This feature reduces the need for unsafe code and using pointers with C#. This chapter also discusses more details about using the Span type to access a different kind of memory, such as the managed heap, the native heap, and the stack.

MEMORY MANAGEMENT UNDER THE HOOD

One of the advantages of C# programming is that the programmer does not need to worry about detailed memory management; the garbage collector deals with the problem of memory cleanup on your behalf. As a result, you get something that approximates the efficiency of languages such as C++ without the complexity of having to handle memory management yourself as you do in C++. However, although you do not have to manage memory manually, it still pays to understand what is going on behind the scenes. Understanding how your program manages memory under the covers will help you increase the speed and performance of your applications. This section looks at what happens in the computer's memory when you allocate variables.

> **NOTE** *The precise details of many of the topics of this section are not presented here. This section serves as an abbreviated guide to the general processes rather than as a statement of exact implementation.*

Value Data Types

Windows uses a system known as *virtual addressing*, in which the mapping from the memory address seen by your program to the actual location in hardware memory is entirely managed by Windows. As a result, each process of a 32-bit application sees 4GB of available memory, regardless of how much hardware memory you actually have in your computer (with 64-bit applications on 64-bit processors this number is greater). This memory contains everything that is part of the program, including the executable code, any DLLs loaded by the code, and the contents of all variables used when the program runs. This 4GB of memory is known as the *virtual address* space or *virtual memory*. For convenience, this chapter uses the shorthand *memory*.

> **NOTE** *With .NET Core applications by default applications are built as portable applications. A portable application runs on both 32- and 64-bit environments on Windows and on Linux as long as the .NET Core runtime is installed on the system. Not all APIs are available on all platforms, especially if you use native APIs. For this, you can specify specific platforms with your .NET Core application as explained in Chapter 1, ".NET Applications and Tools."*

Each memory location in the available 4GB is numbered starting from zero. To access a value stored at a particular location in memory, you need to supply the number that represents that memory location. In any compiled high-level language, the compiler converts human-readable variable names into memory addresses that the processor understands.

Somewhere inside a processor's virtual memory is an area known as the *stack*. The *stack* stores value data types that are not members of objects. In addition, when you call a method, the stack is used to hold a copy of any parameters passed to the method. To understand how the stack works, you need to understand the importance of variable *scope* in C#. If variable a goes into scope before variable b, then b will always go out of scope first. Consider the following code:

```
{
  int a;
  // do something
  {
    int b;
    // do something else
  }
}
```

First, the variable a is declared. Then, inside the inner code block, b is declared. Then the inner code block terminates and b goes out of scope, then a goes out of scope. Therefore, the lifetime of b is entirely contained within the lifetime of a. The idea that you always de-allocate variables in the reverse order of how you allocate them is crucial to the way the stack works.

Note that b is in a different block from code (defined by a different nesting of curly braces). For this reason, it is contained within a different scope. This is termed as *block scope* or *structure scope*.

You do not know exactly where in the address space the stack is—you don't need to know for C# development. A *stack pointer* (a variable maintained by the operating system) identifies the next free location on the stack. When your program first starts running, the stack pointer will point to just past the end of the block of memory that is reserved for the stack. The stack fills downward, from high memory addresses to low addresses. As data is put on the stack, the stack pointer is adjusted accordingly, so it always points to just past the next free location. This is illustrated in Figure 17-1, which shows a stack pointer with a value of 800000 (0xC3500 (in hex); the next free location is the address 799999.

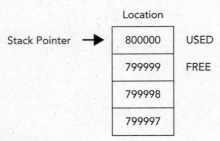

FIGURE 17-1

The following code tells the compiler that you need space in memory to store an integer and a double, and these memory locations are referred to as nRacingCars and engineSize. The line that declares each variable indicates the point at which you start requiring access to this variable. The closing curly brace of the block in which the variables are declared identifies the point at which both variables go out of scope:

```
{
  int nRacingCars = 10;
  double engineSize = 3000.0;
  // do calculations;
}
```

Assuming that you use the stack shown in Figure 17-1, when the variable nRacingCars comes into scope and is assigned the value 10, the value 10 is placed in locations 799996 through 799999, the 4 bytes just below the location pointed to by the stack pointer (4 bytes because that's how much memory is needed to store an int). To accommodate this, 4 is subtracted from the value of the stack pointer, so it now points to the location 799996, just after the new first free location (799995).

The next line of code declares the variable engineSize (a double) and initializes it to the value 3000.0. A double occupies eight bytes, so the value 3000.0 is placed in locations 799988 through 799995 on the stack, and the stack pointer is decremented by eight, so that it again points to the location just after the next free location on the stack.

When engineSize goes out of scope, the runtime knows that it is no longer needed. Because of the way variable lifetimes are always nested, you can guarantee that whatever happened while engineSize was in scope, the stack pointer is now pointing to the location where engineSize is stored. To remove engineSize from the stack, the stack pointer is incremented by eight and it now points to the location immediately after the end of engineSize. At this point in the code, you are at the closing curly brace, so nRacingCars also goes out of scope. The stack pointer is incremented by 4. When another variable comes into scope after engineSize and nRacingCars have been removed from the stack, it overwrites the memory descending from location 799999, where nRacingCars was stored.

If the compiler hits a line such as int i, j, then the order of variables coming into scope looks indeterminate. Both variables are declared at the same time and go out of scope at the same time. In this situation, it does not matter in what order the two variables are removed from memory. The compiler internally always ensures that the one that was put in memory first is removed last, thus preserving the rule that prohibits crossover of variable lifetimes.

Reference Data Types

Although the stack provides very high performance, it is not flexible enough to be used for all variables. The requirement that the lifetime of a variable must be nested is too restrictive for many purposes. Often, you need to use a method to allocate memory for storing data and keeping that data available long after that method has exited. This possibility exists whenever storage space is requested with the new operator—as is the case for all reference types. That is where the *managed heap* comes in.

If you have done any C++ coding that required low-level memory management, you are familiar with the heap. The managed heap is not quite the same as the native heap C++ uses, however; the managed heap works under the control of the garbage collector and provides significant benefits compared to traditional heaps.

The managed heap (or heap for short) is just another area of memory from the processor's available memory. The following code demonstrates how the heap works and how memory is allocated for reference data types:

```
void DoWork()
{
  Customer arabel;
  arabel = new Customer();
  Customer otherCustomer2 = new EnhancedCustomer();
}
```

This code assumes the existence of two classes, `Customer` and `EnhancedCustomer`. The `EnhancedCustomer` class extends the `Customer` class.

First, you declare a `Customer` reference called `arabel`. The space for this is allocated on the stack, but remember that this is only a reference, not an actual `Customer` object. The `arabel` reference occupies 4 bytes, enough space to hold the address at which a `Customer` object will be stored. (You need 4 bytes to represent a memory address as an integer value between 0 and 4GB.)

The next line,

```
arabel = new Customer();
```

does several things. First, it allocates memory on the heap to store a `Customer` object (a real object, not just an address). Then it sets the value of the variable `arabel` to the address of the memory it has allocated to the new `Customer` object. (It also calls the appropriate `Customer` constructor to initialize the fields in the class instance, but you don't need to worry about that here.)

The `Customer` instance is not placed on the stack—it is placed on the heap. In this example, you don't know precisely how many bytes a `Customer` object occupies, but assume for the sake of argument that it is 32. These 32 bytes contain the instance fields of `Customer` as well as some information that .NET uses to identify and manage its class instances.

To find a storage location on the heap for the new `Customer` object, the .NET runtime looks through the heap and grabs the first adjacent, unused block of 32 bytes. Again, for the sake of argument, assume that this happens to be at address `200000`, and that the `arabel` reference occupied locations `799996` through `799999` on the stack. This means that before instantiating the `arabel` object, the memory content looks like Figure 17-2.

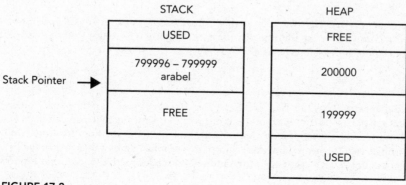

FIGURE 17-2

After allocating the new `Customer` object, the content of memory looks like Figure 17-3. Note that unlike the stack, memory in the heap is allocated upward, so the free space is above the used space.

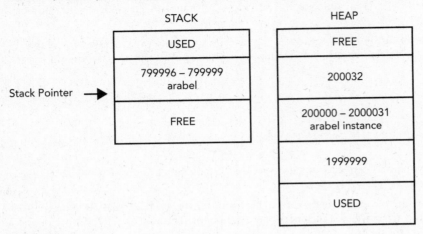

FIGURE 17-3

The next line of code both declares a `Customer` reference and instantiates a `Customer` object. In this instance, space on the stack for the `otherCustomer2` reference is allocated and space for the `mrJones` object is allocated on the heap in a single line of code:

```
Customer otherCustomer2 = new EnhancedCustomer();
```

This line allocates 4 bytes on the stack to hold the `otherCustomer2` reference, stored at locations `799992` through `799995`. The `otherCustomer2` object is allocated space on the heap starting at location `200032`.

It is clear from the example that the process of setting up a reference variable is more complex than that for setting up a value variable, and there is performance overhead. In fact, the process is somewhat oversimplified here, because the .NET runtime needs to maintain information about the state of the heap, and this information needs to be updated whenever new data is added to the heap. Despite this overhead, you now have a mechanism for allocating variables that is not constrained by the limitations of the stack. By assigning the value of one reference variable to another of the same type, you have two variables that reference the same object in memory. When a reference variable goes out of scope, it is removed from the stack as described in the previous section, but the data for a referenced object is still sitting on the heap. The data remains on the heap until either the program terminates or the garbage collector removes it, which happens only when it is no longer referenced by any variables.

That is the power of reference data types, and you will see this feature used extensively in C# code. It means that you have a high degree of control over the lifetime of your data, because it is guaranteed to exist in the heap as long as you are maintaining some reference to it.

Garbage Collection

The previous discussion and diagrams show the managed heap working very much like the stack, to the extent that successive objects are placed next to each other in memory. This means that you can determine where to place the next object by using a heap pointer that indicates the next free memory location, which is adjusted as you add more objects to the heap. However, things are complicated by the fact that the lives of the heap-based objects are not coupled with the scope of the individual stack-based variables that reference them.

When the garbage collector runs, it removes all those objects from the heap that are no longer referenced. The GC finds all referenced objects from a root table of references and continues to the tree of referenced objects. Immediately after, the heap has objects scattered on it, which are mixed up with memory that has just been freed (see Figure 17-4).

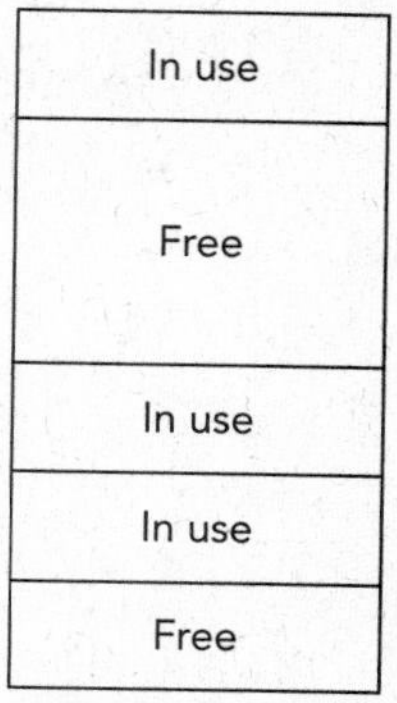

If the managed heap stayed like this, allocating space for new objects would be an awkward process, with the runtime having to search through the heap for a block of memory big enough to store each new object. However, the garbage collector does not leave the heap in this state. As soon as the garbage collector has freed all the objects it can, it compacts the heap by moving all the remaining objects to form one continuous block of memory. This means that the heap can continue working just like the stack, as far as locating where to store new objects. Of course, when the objects are moved about, all the references to those objects need to be updated with the correct new addresses, but the garbage collector handles that, too.

In use
Free
In use
In use
Free

FIGURE 17-4

This action of compacting by the garbage collector is where the managed heap works very differently from unmanaged heaps. With the managed heap, it is just a question of reading the value of the heap pointer, rather than iterating through a linked list of addresses to find somewhere to put the new data.

> **NOTE** *Generally, the garbage collector runs when the .NET runtime determines that garbage collection is required. You can force the garbage collector to run at a certain point in your code by calling* `System.GC.Collect`. `System.GC` *is a .NET class that represents the garbage collector, and the* `Collect` *method initiates a garbage collection. The* `GC` *class is intended for rare situations in which you know that it's a good time to call the garbage collector; for example, if you have just de-referenced a large number of objects in your code. However, the logic of the garbage collector does not guarantee that all unreferenced objects will be removed from the heap in a single garbage collection pass.*

> **NOTE** *It is useful to run* `GC.Collect` *during testing. With this you can see memory leaks where objects that should have been garbage collected are still alive. Because the garbage collector does a good job, it's not a good idea to collect memory programmatically in your production code. If you invoke* `Collect` *programmatically, objects move faster to the next generation, as shown next. This causes more time for the GC to run.*

When objects are created, they are placed within the managed heap. The first section of the heap is called the generation 0 section, or gen 0. As your new objects are created, they are moved into this section of the heap. Therefore, this is where the youngest objects reside.

Your objects remain there until the first collection of objects occurs through the garbage collection process. The objects that remain alive after this cleansing are compacted and then moved to the next section or generational part of the heap—the generation 1, or gen 1, section.

At this point, the generation 0 section is empty, and all new objects are again placed in this section. Older objects that survived the GC (garbage collection) process are further down in the generation 1 section. This movement of aged items actually occurs one more time. The next collection process that occurs is then repeated. This means that the items that survived the GC process from the generation 1 section are moved to the generation 2 section, and the gen 0 items go to gen 1, again leaving gen 0 open for new objects.

> **NOTE** *A garbage collection occurs when you allocate an item that exceeds the capacity of the generation 0 section or when a* `GC.Collect` *is called.*

This process greatly improves the performance of your application. Typically, your youngest objects are the ones that can be collected, and a large number of younger-related objects might be reclaimed as well. If these objects reside next to each other in the heap, then the garbage collection is faster. In addition, because related objects are residing next to each other, program execution is faster all around.

Another performance-related aspect of garbage collection in .NET is how the framework deals with larger objects that are added to the heap. Under the covers of .NET, larger objects have their own managed heap, referred to as the large object heap. When objects greater than 85,000 bytes are utilized, they go to this special heap rather than the main heap. Your .NET application doesn't know the difference, as this is all managed for you. Because compressing large items in the heap is expensive, it isn't done for the objects residing in the large object heap.

To improve GC even more, collections on the generation 2 section and from the large object heap are now done on a background thread. This means that application threads are only blocked for generation 0 and generation 1 collections, which reduces the overall pause time, especially for large-scale server apps. This feature is on by default for both servers and workstations.

Another optimization to help in application performance is GC balancing. This is specific to server GC. Typically, a server will have a pool of threads doing roughly the same thing. The memory allocation will be similar across all the threads. For servers there is one GC heap per logical server. So, when one of the heaps runs out of memory and triggers a GC, all of the other heaps most likely will benefit from the GC as well. If a thread happens to use a lot more memory than other threads and it causes a GC, the other threads may not be close to requiring the GC so it's not efficient. The GC will balance the heaps—both the small object heap and also the large object heap. By doing this balancing process, you can reduce unnecessary collection.

To take advantage of hardware with lots of memory, the GC has added the `GCSettings.LatencyMode` property. Setting the property to one of the values in the `GCLatencyMode` enumeration gives a little control to how the GC performs collections. The following table shows the possible values for the `GCLatencyMode` that can be used.

MEMBER	DESCRIPTION
`Batch`	Disables the concurrency settings and sets the GC for maximum throughput with the expense of responsiveness. This overrides the configuration setting.
`Interactive`	The default behavior on a workstation. This uses garbage collection concurrency and balances throughput and responsiveness.
`LowLatency`	Conservative GC. Full collections only occur when there is memory pressure on the system. This setting should only be used for short periods of time to perform specific operations.
`SustainedLowLatency`	Does full blocking collections only when there is system memory pressure.
`NoGCRegion`	New with .NET 4.6. With `GCSettings`, this is a read-only property. You can set it within a code block calling `GC.TryStartNoGCRegion` and `EndNoGCRegion`. Invoking `TryStartNoGCRegion` you define the size of the memory that needs to be available, which the GC tries to reach. After a successful call to `TryStartNoGCRegion` you define that the garbage collector should not run—until calling `EndNoGCRegion`.

The amount of time that the `LowLatency` or `NoGCRegion` settings are used should be kept to a minimum. The amount of memory being allocated should be as small as possible. An out-of-memory error could occur if you're not careful.

STRONG AND WEAK REFERENCES

The garbage collector cannot reclaim memory of an object that still has a reference—that is a strong reference. It can reclaim managed memory that is not referenced from the root table directly or indirectly. However, sometimes it can be missed to release references.

> **NOTE** *In case you have objects that reference each other but are not referenced from the root table—for example Object A references B, B references C, and C references A—the GC can destroy all these objects.*

When the class or struct is instantiated in the application code, it has a strong reference as long as there is any other code that references it. For example, if you have a class called `MyClass` and you create a reference to objects based on that class and call the variable `myClassVariable` as follows, as long as `myClassVariable` is in scope there is a strong reference to the `MyClass` object:

```
var myClassVariable = new MyClass();
```

This means that the garbage collector cannot clean up the memory used by the `MyClass` object. Generally, this is a good thing because you might need to access the `MyClass` object. You might create a cache object that has references to several other objects, like this:

```
var myCache = new MyCache();
myCache.Add(myClassVariable);
```

Now you're finished using the `myClassVariable`. It can go out of scope, or you assign `null`:

```
myClassVariable = null;
```

In case the garbage collector runs now, it can't release the memory that was referenced by the `myClassVariable`, because the object is still referenced from the cache object. Such references can easily be missed, and you can avoid this using the `WeakReference`.

A weak reference allows the object to be created and used, but if the garbage collector happens to run, it collects the object and frees up the memory. This is not something you would typically want to do because of potential bugs and performance issues, but there are certainly situations in which it makes sense. Weak references also don't make sense with small objects, as weak references have an overhead on their own, and that might be bigger than the small object.

Weak references are created using the `WeakReference` class. With the constructor, you can pass a strong reference. The sample code creates a `DataObject` and passes the reference returned from the constructor. On using `WeakReference`, you can check the `IsAlive` property. For using the object again, the `Target` property of `WeakReference` returns a strong reference. In case the value of the property returned is not null, you can use the strong reference. Because the object could be collected at any time, it's important that the existence of the object is valid before trying to reference it. After retrieving the strong reference successfully, you can use it in a normal way, and now it can't be garbage collected because you have a strong reference again:

```
// Instantiate a weak reference to MathTest object
var myWeakReference = new WeakReference(new DataObject());
if (myWeakReference.IsAlive)
{
  DataObject strongReference = myWeakReference.Target as DataObject;
  if (strongReference != null)
```

```
      {
        // use the strongReference
      }
    }
    else
    {
      // reference not available
    }
```

WORKING WITH UNMANAGED RESOURCES

The presence of the garbage collector means that you usually do not need to worry about objects you no longer need; you simply allow all references to those objects to go out of scope and let the garbage collector free memory as required. However, the garbage collector does not know how to free unmanaged resources (such as file handles, network connections, and database connections). When managed classes encapsulate direct or indirect references to unmanaged resources, you need to make special provisions to ensure that the unmanaged resources are released when an instance of the class is garbage collected.

When defining a class, you can use two mechanisms to automate the freeing of unmanaged resources. These mechanisms are often implemented together because each provides a slightly different approach:

➤ Declare a *destructor* (or finalizer) as a member of your class.

➤ Implement the System.IDisposable interface in your class.

The following sections discuss each of these mechanisms in turn and then look at how to implement the mechanisms together for best results.

Destructors or Finalizers

You have seen that constructors enable you to specify actions that must take place whenever an instance of a class is created. Conversely, destructors are called before an object is destroyed by the garbage collector. Given this behavior, a destructor would initially seem like a great place to put code to free unmanaged resources and perform a general cleanup. Unfortunately, things are not so straightforward.

> **NOTE** *Although we talk about destructors in C#, in the underlying .NET architecture these are known as finalizers. When you define a destructor in C#, what is emitted into the assembly by the compiler is actually a* Finalize *method. It doesn't affect any of your source code, but you need to be aware of it when examining generated Intermediate Language (IL) code.*

The syntax for a destructor will be familiar to C++ developers. It looks like a method, with the same name as the containing class, but prefixed with a tilde (~). It has no return type, and takes no parameters or access modifiers. Here is an example:

```
class MyClass
{
  ~MyClass()
  {
    // Finalizer implementation
  }
}
```

When the C# compiler compiles a destructor, it implicitly translates the destructor code to the equivalent of an override of the Finalize method, which ensures that the Finalize method of the parent class is executed. The following example shows the C# code equivalent to the Intermediate Language (IL) that the compiler would generate for the ~MyClass destructor:

```
protected override void Finalize()
{
  try
  {
    // Finalizer implementation
  }
  finally
  {
    base.Finalize();
  }
}
```

As shown, the code implemented in the ~MyClass destructor is wrapped in a `try` block contained in the `Finalize` method. A call to the parent's `Finalize` method is ensured by placing the call in a `finally` block. You can read about `try` and `finally` blocks in Chapter 14, "Errors and Exceptions."

Experienced C++ developers make extensive use of destructors, sometimes not only to clean up resources but also to provide debugging information or perform other tasks. C# destructors are used far less than their C++ equivalents. The problem with C# destructors as compared to their C++ counterparts is that they are nondeterministic. When a C++ object is destroyed, its destructor runs immediately. However, because of the way the garbage collector works when using C#, there is no way to know when an object's destructor will actually execute. Hence, you cannot place any code in the destructor that relies on being run at a certain time, and you should not rely on the destructor being called for different class instances in any particular order. When your object is holding scarce and critical resources that need to be freed as soon as possible, you do not want to wait for garbage collection.

Another problem with C# destructors is that the implementation of a destructor delays the final removal of an object from memory. Objects that do not have a destructor are removed from memory in one pass of the garbage collector, but objects that have destructors require two passes to be destroyed: The first pass calls the destructor without removing the object, and the second pass actually deletes the object. In addition, the runtime uses a single thread to execute the `Finalize` methods of all objects. If you use destructors frequently, and use them to execute lengthy cleanup tasks, the impact on performance can be noticeable.

The IDisposable Interface

In C#, the recommended alternative to using a destructor is using the `System.IDisposable` interface. The `IDisposable` interface defines a pattern (with language-level support) that provides a deterministic mechanism for freeing unmanaged resources and avoids the garbage collector–related problems inherent with destructors. The `IDisposable` interface declares a single method named `Dispose`, which takes no parameters and returns `void`. Here is an implementation for `MyClass`:

```
class MyClass: IDisposable
{
  public void Dispose()
  {
    // implementation
  }
}
```

The implementation of `Dispose` should explicitly free all unmanaged resources used directly by an object and call `Dispose` on any encapsulated objects that also implement the `IDisposable` interface. In this way, the `Dispose` method provides precise control over when unmanaged resources are freed.

Suppose that you have a class named `ResourceGobbler`, which relies on the use of some external resource and implements `IDisposable`. If you want to instantiate an instance of this class, use it, and then dispose of it, you could do so like this:

```
var theInstance = new ResourceGobbler();
// do your processing
theInstance.Dispose();
```

Unfortunately, this code fails to free the resources consumed by `theInstance` if an exception occurs during processing, so you should write the code as follows using a `try` block (as covered in detail in Chapter 14):

```
ResourceGobbler theInstance = null;
try
{
  theInstance = new ResourceGobbler();
  // do your processing
}
finally
{
  theInstance?.Dispose();
}
```

The using Statement

Using `try/finally` ensures that `Dispose` is always called on `theInstance` and that any resources consumed by it are always freed, even if an exception occurs during processing. However, if you always had to repeat such a construct, it would result in confusing code. C# offers a syntax that you can use to guarantee that `Dispose` is automatically called against an object that implements `IDisposable` when its reference goes out of scope. The syntax to do this involves the `using` keyword—though now in a very different context, which has nothing to do with namespaces. The following code generates IL code equivalent to the `try` block just shown:

```
using (var theInstance = new ResourceGobbler())
{
  // do your processing
}
```

The `using` statement, followed in brackets by a reference variable declaration and instantiation, causes that variable to be scoped to the accompanying statement block. In addition, when that variable goes out of scope, its `Dispose` method is called automatically, even if an exception occurs.

> **NOTE** *The* using *keyword has multiple uses with C#. The* using *declaration is used to import namespaces. The* using *statement works with objects implementing* IDisposable *and invokes the* Dispose *method with the end of the using scope.*

> **NOTE** *With several classes both a* Close *and a* Dispose *method exists. If it is common to close a resource (such as a file and a database), both* Close *and* Dispose *have been implemented. Here, the* Close *method simply calls* Dispose. *This approach provides clarity in the use of these classes and supports the* using *statement. Newer classes only implement the* Dispose *method as we're already used to it.*

Implementing IDisposable and a Destructor

The previous sections discussed two alternatives for freeing unmanaged resources used by the classes you create:

➤ The execution of a destructor is enforced by the runtime but is nondeterministic and places an unacceptable overhead on the runtime because of the way garbage collection works.

➤ The IDisposable interface provides a mechanism that enables users of a class to control when resources are freed but requires discipline to ensure that Dispose is called.

If you are creating a finalizer, you should also implement the IDisposable interface. You implement IDisposable on the assumption that most programmers will call Dispose correctly, but implement a destructor as a safety mechanism in case Dispose is not called. Here is an example of a dual implementation:

```
public class ResourceHolder: IDisposable
{
  private bool _isDisposed = false;
  public void Dispose()
  {
    Dispose(true);
    GC.SuppressFinalize(this);
  }

  protected virtual void Dispose(bool disposing)
  {
    if (!_isDisposed)
    {
      if (disposing)
      {
        // Cleanup managed objects by calling their
        // Dispose() methods.
      }
      // Cleanup unmanaged objects
    }
    _isDisposed = true;
  }

  ~ResourceHolder()
  {
    Dispose(false);
  }

  public void SomeMethod()
  {
    // Ensure object not already disposed before execution of any method
    if(_isDisposed)
    {
      throw new ObjectDisposedException("ResourceHolder");
    }
    // method implementation...
  }
}
```

You can see from this code that there is a second protected overload of Dispose that takes one bool parameter—and this is the method that does all the cleaning up. Dispose(bool) is called by both the destructor and by IDisposable.Dispose. The point of this approach is to ensure that all cleanup code is in one place.

The parameter passed to `Dispose(bool)` indicates whether `Dispose(bool)` has been invoked by the destructor or by `IDisposable.Dispose`—`Dispose(bool)` should not be invoked from anywhere else in your code. The idea is this:

➤ If a consumer calls `IDisposable.Dispose`, that consumer is indicating that all managed and unmanaged resources associated with that object should be cleaned up.

➤ If a destructor has been invoked, all resources still need to be cleaned up. However, in this case, you know that the destructor must have been called by the garbage collector and you should not attempt to access other managed objects because you can no longer be certain of their state. In this situation, the best you can do is clean up the known unmanaged resources and hope that any referenced managed objects also have destructors that will perform their own cleaning up.

The `_isDisposed` member variable indicates whether the object has already been disposed of and ensures that you do not try to dispose of member variables more than once. It also enables you to test whether an object has been disposed of before executing any instance methods, as shown in `SomeMethod`. This simplistic approach is not thread-safe and depends on the caller ensuring that only one thread is calling the method concurrently. Requiring a consumer to enforce synchronization is a reasonable assumption and one that is used repeatedly throughout the .NET class libraries (in the `Collection` classes, for example). Threading and synchronization are discussed in Chapter 21, "Tasks and Parallel Programming." Finally, `IDisposable.Dispose` contains a call to the method `System.GC.SuppressFinalize`. `GC` is the class that represents the garbage collector, and the `SuppressFinalize` method tells the garbage collector that a class no longer needs to have its destructor called. Because your implementation of `Dispose` has already done all the cleanup required, there's nothing left for the destructor to do. Calling `SuppressFinalize` means that the garbage collector will treat that object as if it doesn't have a destructor at all.

IDisposable and Finalizer Rules

Learning about finalizers and the `IDisposable` interface you already learned the Dispose pattern and some rules on using these constructs. Because releasing resources is such an important aspect with managed code, the rules are summarized in this list:

➤ If your class defines a member that implements `IDisposable`, the class should also implement `IDisposable`.

➤ Implementing `IDisposable` does not mean that you should also implement a finalizer. Finalizers create additional overhead with both creating an object and releasing the memory of the object as an additional pass from the GC is needed. You should implement a finalizer only if needed—for example, to release native resources. To release native resources, a finalizer is really needed.

➤ If a finalizer is implemented, you should also implement the interface `IDisposable`. This way the native resource can be released earlier, not only when the GC is finding out about the occupied resource.

➤ Within the finalization code implementation, don't access objects that might have been finalized already. The order of finalizers is not guaranteed.

➤ If an object you use implements the `IDisposable` interface, call the `Dispose` method when the object is no longer needed. In case you're using this object within a method, the using statement comes handy. In case the object is a member of the class, make the class implement `IDisposable` as well.

UNSAFE CODE

As you have just seen, C# is very good at hiding much of the basic memory management from the developer, thanks to the garbage collector and the use of references. However, sometimes you will want direct access to memory. For example, you might want to access a function in an external (non-.NET) DLL that requires a pointer to be passed as a parameter (as many Windows API functions do), or possibly for performance reasons. This section examines the C# facilities that provide direct access to the content of memory.

Accessing Memory Directly with Pointers

Although I am introducing *pointers* as if they are a new topic, in reality pointers are not new at all. You have been using references freely in your code, and a reference is simply a type-safe pointer. You have already seen how variables that represent objects and arrays actually store the memory address of where the corresponding data (the *referent*) is stored. A pointer is simply a variable that stores the address of something else in the same way as a reference. The *difference* is that C# does not allow you direct access to the address contained in a reference variable. With a reference, the variable is treated syntactically as if it stores the actual content of the referent.

C# references are designed to make the language simpler to use and to prevent you from inadvertently doing something that corrupts the contents of memory. With a pointer, however, the actual memory address is available to you. This gives you a lot of power to perform new kinds of operations. For example, you can add 4 bytes to the address in order to examine or even modify whatever data happens to be stored 4 bytes further in memory.

There are two main reasons for using pointers:

➤ **Backward compatibility**—Despite all the facilities provided by the .NET runtime, it is still possible to call native Windows API functions, and for some operations this may be the only way to accomplish your task. These API functions are generally written in C++ or C# and often require pointers as parameters. However, in many cases it is possible to write the `DllImport` declaration in a way that avoids use of pointers—for example, by using the `System.IntPtr` class.

➤ **Performance**—On those occasions when speed is of the utmost importance, pointers can provide a route to optimized performance. If you know what you are doing, you can ensure that data is accessed or manipulated in the most efficient way. However, be aware that more often than not, there are other areas of your code where you can likely make the necessary performance improvements without resorting to using pointers. Try using a code profiler to look for the bottlenecks in your code; Visual Studio includes a code profiler.

Low-level memory access has a price. The syntax for using pointers is more complex than that for reference types, and pointers are unquestionably more difficult to use correctly. You need good programming skills and an excellent ability to think carefully and logically about what your code is doing to use pointers successfully. Otherwise, it is very easy to introduce subtle, difficult-to-find bugs into your program when using pointers. For example, it is easy to overwrite other variables, cause stack overflows, access areas of memory that don't store any variables, or even overwrite information about your code that is needed by the .NET runtime, thereby crashing your program.

Despite these issues, pointers remain a very powerful and flexible tool in the writing of efficient code.

> **WARNING** *I strongly advise against using pointers unnecessarily because your code will not only be harder to write and debug, but it will also fail the memory type safety checks imposed by the CLR.*

Writing Unsafe Code with the unsafe Keyword

As a result of the risks associated with pointers, C# allows the use of pointers only in blocks of code that you have specifically marked for this purpose. The keyword to do this is `unsafe`. You can mark an individual method as being `unsafe` like this:

```
unsafe int GetSomeNumber()
{
    // code that can use pointers
}
```

Any method can be marked as unsafe, regardless of what other modifiers have been applied to it (for example, static methods or virtual methods). In the case of methods, the unsafe modifier applies to the method's parameters, allowing you to use pointers as parameters. You can also mark an entire class or struct as unsafe, which means that all its members are assumed unsafe:

```
unsafe class MyClass
{
  // any method in this class can now use pointers
}
```

Similarly, you can mark a member as unsafe:

```
class MyClass
{
  unsafe int* pX; // declaration of a pointer field in a class
}
```

Or you can mark a block of code within a method as unsafe:

```
void MyMethod()
{
  // code that doesn't use pointers
  unsafe
  {
    // unsafe code that uses pointers here
  }

  // more 'safe' code that doesn't use pointers
}
```

Note, however, that you cannot mark a local variable by itself as unsafe:

```
int MyMethod()
{
  unsafe int *pX; // WRONG
}
```

If you want to use an unsafe local variable, you need to declare and use it inside a method or block that is unsafe. There is one more step before you can use pointers. The C# compiler rejects unsafe code unless you tell it that your code includes unsafe blocks. You can configure unsafe code by setting the AllowUnsafeBlocks in the csproj project file as shown, or you can select the Allow Unsafe Code check box in the Visual Studio Build Project Properties settings:

```
<PropertyGroup>
  <AllowUnsafeBlocks>True</AllowUnsafeBlocks>
</PropertyGroup>
```

Pointer Syntax

After you have marked a block of code as unsafe, you can declare a pointer using the following syntax:

```
int* pWidth, pHeight;
double* pResult;
byte*[] pFlags;
```

This code declares four variables: pWidth and pHeight are pointers to integers, pResult is a pointer to a double, and pFlags is an array of pointers to bytes. It is common practice to use the prefix p in front of names of pointer variables to indicate that they are pointers. When used in a variable declaration, the symbol * indicates that you are declaring a pointer (that is, something that stores the address of a variable of the specified type).

When you have declared variables of pointer types, you can use them in the same way as normal variables, but first you need to learn two more operators:

➤ & means take the address of, and converts a value data type to a pointer—for example, int to *int. This operator is known as the address operator.

➤ * means get the content of this address, and converts a pointer to a value data type—for example, *float to float. This operator is known as the indirection operator (or the de-reference operator).

You can see from these definitions that & and * have opposite effects.

> **NOTE** *You might be wondering how it is possible to use the symbols & and * in this manner because these symbols also refer to the operators of bitwise AND (&) and multiplication (*). Actually, it is always possible for both you and the compiler to know what is meant in each case because with the pointer meanings, these symbols always appear as unary operators—they act on only one variable and appear in front of that variable in your code. By contrast, bitwise AND and multiplication are binary operators—they require two operands.*

The following code shows examples of how to use these operators:

```
int x = 10;
int* pX, pY;
pX = &x;
pY = pX;
*pY = 20;
```

You start by declaring an integer, x, with the value 10 followed by two pointers to integers, pX and pY. You then set pX to point to x (that is, you set the content of pX to the address of x). Then you assign the value of pX to pY, so that pY also points to x. Finally, in the statement *pY = 20, you assign the value 20 as the contents of the location pointed to by pY—in effect changing x to 20 because pY happens to point to x. Note that there is no particular connection between the variables pY and x. It is just that at the present time, pY happens to point to the memory location at which x is held.

To get a better understanding of what is going on, consider that the integer x is stored at memory locations 0x12F8C4 through 0x12F8C7 (1243332 to 1243335 in decimal) on the stack (there are four locations because an int occupies 4 bytes). Because the stack allocates memory downward, this means that the variables pX will be stored at locations 0x12F8C0 to 0x12F8C3, and pY will end up at locations 0x12F8BC to 0x12F8BF. Note that pX and pY also occupy 4 bytes each. That is not because an int occupies 4 bytes, but because on a 32-bit application you need 4 bytes to store an address. With these addresses, after executing the previous code, the stack will look like Figure 17-5.

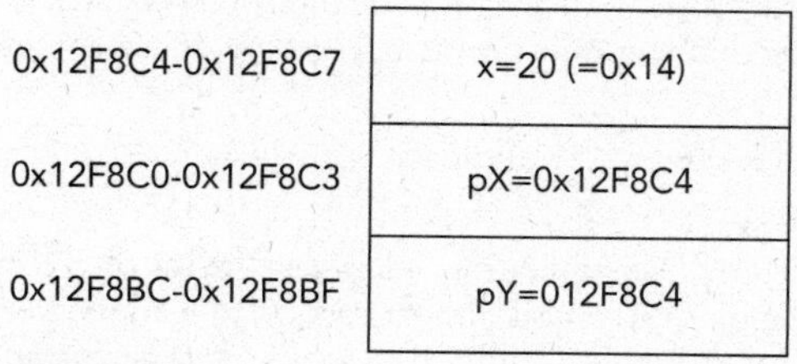

0x12F8C4-0x12F8C7	x=20 (=0x14)
0x12F8C0-0x12F8C3	pX=0x12F8C4
0x12F8BC-0x12F8BF	pY=012F8C4

FIGURE 17-5

> **NOTE** *Although this process is illustrated with integers, which are stored consecutively on the stack on a 32-bit processor, this does not happen for all data types. The reason is that 32-bit processors work best when retrieving data from memory in 4-byte chunks. Memory on such machines tends to be divided into 4-byte blocks, and each block is sometimes known under Windows as a DWORD because this was the name of a 32-bit unsigned* int *in pre-.NET days. It is most efficient to grab DWORDs from memory—storing data across DWORD boundaries normally results in a hardware performance hit. For this reason, the .NET runtime normally pads out data types so that the memory they occupy is a multiple of 4. For example, a short occupies 2 bytes, but if a short is placed on the stack, the stack pointer will still be decremented by 4, not 2, so the next variable to go on the stack will still start at a DWORD boundary.*

You can declare a pointer to any value type (that is, any of the predefined types uint, int, byte, and so on, or to a struct). However, it is not possible to declare a pointer to a class or an array; this is because doing so could cause problems for the garbage collector. To work properly, the garbage collector needs to know exactly what class instances have been created on the heap, and where they are; but if your code started manipulating classes using pointers, you could very easily corrupt the information on the heap concerning classes that the .NET runtime maintains for the garbage collector. In this context, any data type that the garbage collector can access is known as a *managed type*. Pointers can only be declared as *unmanaged* types because the garbage collector cannot deal with them.

Casting Pointers to Integer Types

Because a pointer really stores an integer that represents an address, you won't be surprised to know that the address in any pointer can be converted to or from any integer type. Pointer-to-integer-type conversions must be explicit. Implicit conversions are not available for such conversions. For example, it is perfectly legitimate to write the following:

```
int x = 10;
int* pX, pY;
pX = &x;
pY = pX;
*pY = 20;
ulong y = (ulong)pX;
int* pD = (int*)y;
```

The address held in the pointer pX is cast to a `ulong` and stored in the variable y. You have then cast y back to an `int*` and stored it in the new variable pD. Hence, now pD also points to the value of x.

The primary reason for casting a pointer value to an integer type is to display it. The interpolation string (and similarly `Console.Write`) does not have any overloads that can take pointers, but they do accept and display pointer values that have been cast to integer types:

```
WriteLine($"Address is {pX}"); // wrong -- will give a compilation error
WriteLine($"Address is {(ulong)pX}"); // OK
```

You can cast a pointer to any of the integer types. However, because an address occupies 4 bytes on 32-bit systems, casting a pointer to anything other than a uint, long, or ulong is almost certain to lead to overflow errors. (An int causes problems because its range is from roughly –2 billion to 2 billion, whereas an address runs from zero to about 4 billion.) If you are creating a 64-bit application, you need to cast the pointer to ulong.

It is also important to be aware that the checked keyword does not apply to conversions involving pointers. For such conversions, exceptions are not raised when overflows occur, even in a checked context. The .NET runtime assumes that if you are using pointers, you know what you are doing and are not worried about possible overflows.

Casting Between Pointer Types

You can also explicitly convert between pointers pointing to different types. For example, the following is perfectly legal code:

```
byte aByte = 8;
byte* pByte= &aByte;
double* pDouble = (double*)pByte;
```

However, if you try something like this, be careful. In this example, if you look at the `double` value pointed to by `pDouble`, you are actually looking up some memory that contains a `byte` (aByte), combined with some other memory, and treating it as if this area of memory contained a `double`, which does not give you a meaningful value. However, you might want to convert between types to implement the equivalent of a C `union`, or you might want to cast pointers from other types into pointers to `sbyte` to examine individual bytes of memory.

void Pointers

If you want to maintain a pointer but not specify to what type of data it points, you can declare it as a pointer to a `void`:

```
int* pointerToInt;
void* pointerToVoid;
pointerToVoid = (void*)pointerToInt;
```

The main use of this is if you need to call an API function that requires `void*` parameters. Within the C# language, there isn't a great deal that you can do using `void` pointers. In particular, the compiler flags an error if you attempt to de-reference a `void` pointer using the `*` operator.

Pointer Arithmetic

It is possible to add or subtract integers to and from pointers. However, the compiler is quite clever about how it arranges this. For example, suppose that you have a pointer to an `int` and you try to add 1 to its value. The compiler assumes that you actually mean you want to look at the memory location following the `int`, and hence it increases the value by 4 bytes—the size of an `int`. If it is a pointer to a `double`, adding 1 actually increases the value of the pointer by 8 bytes, the size of a `double`. Only if the pointer points to a `byte` or `sbyte` (1 byte each) does adding 1 to the value of the pointer actually change its value by 1.

You can use the operators +, -, +=, -=, ++, and -- with pointers, with the variable on the right side of these operators being a `long` or `ulong`.

> **NOTE** *It is not permitted to carry out arithmetic operations on void pointers.*

For example, assume the following definitions:

```
uint u = 3;
byte b = 8;
double d = 10.0;
uint* pUint= &u; // size of a uint is 4
byte* pByte = &b; // size of a byte is 1
double* pDouble = &d; // size of a double is 8
```

Next, assume the addresses to which these pointers point are as follows:

➤   pUint: 1243332

➤   pByte: 1243328

➤   pDouble: 1243320

Then execute this code:

```
++pUint; // adds (1*4) = 4 bytes to pUint
pByte -= 3; // subtracts (3*1) = 3 bytes from pByte
double* pDouble2 = pDouble + 4; // pDouble2 = pDouble + 32 bytes (4*8 bytes)
```

The pointers now contain this:

➤   pUint: 1243336

➤   pByte: 1243325

➤   pDouble2: 1243352

> **NOTE** *The general rule is that adding a number* X *to a pointer to type* T *with value* P *gives the result* P + X*(sizeof(T)). If successive values of a given type are stored in successive memory locations, pointer addition works very well, allowing you to move pointers between memory locations. If you are dealing with types such as* byte *or* char, *though, with sizes not in multiples of 4, successive values will not, by default, be stored in successive memory locations.*

You can also subtract one pointer from another pointer, if both pointers point to the same data type. In this case, the result is a long whose value is given by the difference between the pointer values divided by the size of the type that they represent:

```
double* pD1 = (double*)1243324; // note that it is perfectly valid to
// initialize a pointer like this.
double* pD2 = (double*)1243300;
long L = pD1-pD2; // gives the result 3 (=24/sizeof(double))
```

The sizeof Operator

This section has been referring to the size of various data types. If you need to use the size of a type in your code, you can use the sizeof operator, which takes the name of a data type as a parameter and returns the number of bytes occupied by that type, as shown in this example:

```
int x = sizeof(double);
```

This sets x to the value 8.

The advantage of using sizeof is that you don't have to hard-code data type sizes in your code, making your code more portable. For the predefined data types, sizeof returns the following values:

```
sizeof(sbyte) = 1; sizeof(byte) = 1;
sizeof(short) = 2; sizeof(ushort) = 2;
sizeof(int) = 4; sizeof(uint) = 4;
sizeof(long) = 8; sizeof(ulong) = 8;
sizeof(char) = 2; sizeof(float) = 4;
sizeof(double) = 8; sizeof(bool) = 1;
```

You can also use sizeof for structs that you define yourself, although, in that case, the result depends on what fields are in the struct. You cannot use sizeof for classes.

Pointers to Structs: The Pointer Member Access Operator

Pointers to structs work in exactly the same way as pointers to the predefined value types. There is, however, one condition: The struct must not contain any reference types. This is due to the restriction mentioned earlier that pointers cannot point to any reference types. To avoid this, the compiler flags an error if you create a pointer to any struct that contains any reference types.

Suppose that you had a struct defined like this:

```
struct MyStruct
{
   public long X;
   public float F;
}
```

You could define a pointer to it as follows:

```
MyStruct* pStruct;
```

Then you could initialize it like this:

```
var myStruct = new MyStruct();
pStruct = &myStruct;
```

It is also possible to access member values of a struct through the pointer:

```
(*pStruct).X = 4;
(*pStruct).F = 3.4f;
```

However, this syntax is a bit complex. For this reason, C# defines another operator that enables you to access members of structs through pointers using a simpler syntax. It is known as the *pointer member access operator*, and the symbol is a dash followed by a greater-than sign, so it looks like an arrow: ->.

> **NOTE** C++ *developers will recognize the pointer member access operator because* C++ *uses the same symbol for the same purpose.*

Using the pointer member access operator, the previous code can be rewritten like this:

```
pStruct->X = 4;
pStruct->F = 3.4f;
```

You can also directly set up pointers of the appropriate type to point to fields within a struct,

```
long* pL = &(Struct.X);
float* pF = &(Struct.F);
```

or,

```
long* pL = &(pStruct->X);
float* pF = &(pStruct->F);
```

Pointers to Class Members

As indicated earlier, it is not possible to create pointers to classes. That is because the garbage collector does not maintain any information about pointers—only about references—so creating pointers to classes could cause garbage collection to not work properly.

However, most classes do contain value type members, and you might want to create pointers to them. This is possible, but it requires a special syntax. For example, suppose that you rewrite the struct from the previous example as a class:

```
class MyClass
{
```

```
    public long X;
    public float F;
}
```

Then you might want to create pointers to its fields, X and F, in the same way as you did earlier. Unfortunately, doing so produces a compilation error:

```
var myObject = new MyClass();
long* pL = &(myObject.X); // wrong -- compilation error
float* pF = &(myObject.F); // wrong -- compilation error
```

Although X and F are unmanaged types, they are embedded in an object, which sits on the heap. During garbage collection, the garbage collector might move MyObject to a new location, which would leave pL and pF pointing to the wrong memory addresses. Because of this, the compiler does not let you assign addresses of members of managed types to pointers in this manner.

The solution is to use the fixed keyword, which tells the garbage collector that there may be pointers referencing members of certain objects, so those objects must not be moved. The syntax for using fixed looks like this when you want to declare only one pointer:

```
var myObject = new MyClass();
fixed (long* pObject = &(myObject.X))
{
  // do something
}
```

You define and initialize the pointer variable in the brackets following the keyword fixed. This pointer variable (pObject in the example) is scoped to the fixed block identified by the curly braces. As a result, the garbage collector knows not to move the myObject object while the code inside the fixed block is executing.

If you want to declare more than one pointer, you can place multiple fixed statements before the same code block:

```
var myObject = new MyClass();
fixed (long* pX = &(myObject.X))
fixed (float* pF = &(myObject.F))
{
  // do something
}
```

You can nest entire fixed blocks if you want to fix several pointers for different periods:

```
var myObject = new MyClass();
fixed (long* pX = &(myObject.X))
{
  // do something with pX
  fixed (float* pF = &(myObject.F))
  {
    // do something else with pF
  }
}
```

You can also initialize several variables within the same fixed block, if they are of the same type:

```
var myObject = new MyClass();
var myObject2 = new MyClass();
fixed (long* pX = &(myObject.X), pX2 = &(myObject2.X))
{
  // etc.
}
```

In all these cases, it is immaterial whether the various pointers you are declaring point to fields in the same or different objects or to static fields not associated with any class instance.

Pointer Example: PointerPlayground

For understanding pointers, it's best to write a program using pointers and to use the debugger. The following code snippet is from an example named `PointerPlayground`. It does some simple pointer manipulation and displays the results, enabling you to see what is happening in memory and where variables are stored (code file `PointerPlayground/Program.cs`):

```csharp
class Program
{
  unsafe static void Main()
  {
    int x=10;
    short y = -1;
    byte y2 = 4;
    double z = 1.5;
    int* pX = &x;
    short* pY = &y;
    double* pZ = &z;

    Console.WriteLine($"Address of x is 0x{(ulong)&x:X}, " +
      $"size is {sizeof(int)}, value is {x}");
    Console.WriteLine($"Address of y is 0x{(ulong)&y2:X}, " +
      $"size is {sizeof(short)}, value is {y}");
    Console.WriteLine($"Address of y2 is 0x{(ulong)&y2:X}, " +
      $"size is {sizeof(byte)}, value is {y2}");
    Console.WriteLine($"Address of z is 0x{(ulong)&z:X}, " +
      $"size is {sizeof(double)}, value is {z}");
    Console.WriteLine($"Address of pX=&x is 0x{(ulong)&pX:X}, " +
      $"size is {sizeof(int*)}, value is 0x{(ulong)pX:X}");
    Console.WriteLine($"Address of pY=&y is 0x{(ulong)&pY:X}, " +
      $"size is {sizeof(short*)}, value is 0x{(ulong)pY:X}");
    Console.WriteLine($"Address of pZ=&z is 0x{(ulong)&pZ:X}, " +
      $"size is {sizeof(double*)}, value is 0x{(ulong)pZ:X}");
    *pX = 20;
    Console.WriteLine($"After setting *pX, x = {x}");
    Console.WriteLine($"*pX = {*pX}");
    pZ = (double*)pX;
    Console.WriteLine($"x treated as a double = {*pZ}");
    Console.ReadLine();
  }
}
```

This code declares four value variables:

➤   An int `x`

➤   A short `y`

➤   A byte `y2`

➤   A double `z`

It also declares pointers to three of these values: `pX`, `pY`, and `pZ`.

Next, you display the value of these variables as well as their size and address. Note that in taking the address of `pX`, `pY`, and `pZ`, you are effectively looking at a pointer *to* a pointer—an address of an address of a value. Also, in accordance with the usual practice when displaying addresses, you have used the `{0:X}` format specifier in the `WriteLine` commands to ensure that memory addresses are displayed in hexadecimal format.

Finally, you use the pointer `pX` to change the value of `x` to 20 and do some pointer casting to see what happens if you try to treat the content of `x` as if it were a `double`.

Compiling and running this code results in the following output:

```
Address of x is 0x376943D5A8, size is 4, value is 10
Address of y is 0x376943D5A0, size is 2, value is -1
Address of y2 is 0x376943D598, size is 1, value is 4
Address of z is 0x376943D590, size is 8, value is 1.5
Address of pX=&x is 0x376943D588, size is 8, value is 0x376943D5A8
Address of pY=&y is 0x376943D580, size is 8, value is 0x376943D5A0
Address of pZ=&z is 0x376943D578, size is 8, value is 0x376943D590
After setting *pX, x = 20
*pX = 20
x treated as a double = 9.88131291682493E-323
```

> **NOTE** *When you run the application with the CoreCLR, different addresses are shown every time you run the application.*

Checking through these results confirms the description of how the stack operates presented in the "Memory Management Under the Hood" section earlier in this chapter. It allocates successive variables moving downward in memory. Notice how it also confirms that blocks of memory on the stack are always allocated in multiples of 4 bytes. For example, y is a short (of size 2) and has the (hex) address 0xD4E710, indicating that the memory locations reserved for it are locations 0xD4E710 through 0xD4E713. If the .NET runtime had been strictly packing up variables next to each other, Y would have occupied just two locations, 0xD4E712 and 0xD4713.

The next example illustrates pointer arithmetic, as well as pointers to structs and class members. This example is named PointerPlayground2. To start, you define a struct named CurrencyStruct, which represents a currency value as dollars and cents. You also define an equivalent class named CurrencyClass (code file PointerPlayground2/Currency.cs):

```
internal struct CurrencyStruct
{
  public long Dollars;
  public byte Cents;
  public override string ToString() => $"$ {Dollars}.{Cents}";
}

internal class CurrencyClass
{
  public long Dollars = 0;
  public byte Cents = 0;
  public override string ToString() => $"$ {Dollars}.{Cents}";
}
```

Now that you have your struct and class defined, you can apply some pointers to them. Following is the code for the new example. Because the code is fairly long, I'm going through it in detail. You start by displaying the size of CurrencyStruct, creating a couple of CurrencyStruct instances and creating some CurrencyStruct pointers. You use the pAmount pointer to initialize the members of the amount1 CurrencyStruct and then display the addresses of your variables (code file PointerPlayground2/Program.cs):

```
unsafe static void Main()
{
  Console.WriteLine($"Size of CurrencyStruct struct is " +
    $"{sizeof(CurrencyStruct)}");
  CurrencyStruct amount1, amount2;
  CurrencyStruct* pAmount = &amount1;
  long* pDollars = &(pAmount->Dollars);
```

```
        byte* pCents = &(pAmount->Cents);
        Console.WriteLine("Address of amount1 is 0x{(ulong)&amount1:X}");
        Console.WriteLine("Address of amount2 is 0x{(ulong)&amount2:X}");
        Console.WriteLine("Address of pAmount is 0x{(ulong)&pAmount:X}");
        Console.WriteLine("Address of pDollars is 0x{(ulong)&pDollars:X}");
        Console.WriteLine("Address of pCents is 0x{(ulong)&pCents:X}");

        pAmount->Dollars = 20;
        *pCents = 50;
        Console.WriteLine($"amount1 contains {amount1}");
        //...
    }
```

Now you do some pointer manipulation that relies on your knowledge of how the stack works. Due to the order in which the variables were declared, you know that amount2 will be stored at an address immediately below amount1. The sizeof(CurrencyStruct) operator returns 16 (as demonstrated in the screen output coming up), so CurrencyStruct occupies a multiple of 4 bytes. Therefore, after you decrement your currency pointer, it points to amount2:

```
    --pAmount; // this should get it to point to amount2
    Console.WriteLine($"amount2 has address 0x{(ulong)pAmount:X} " +
        $"and contains {*pAmount}");
```

Notice that when you call Console.WriteLine, you display the contents of amount2, but you haven't yet initialized it. What is displayed is random garbage—whatever happened to be stored at that location in memory before execution of the example. There is an important point here: Normally, the C# compiler would prevent you from using an uninitialized variable, but when you start using pointers, it is very easy to circumvent many of the usual compilation checks. In this case, you have done so because the compiler has no way of knowing that you are actually displaying the contents of amount2. Only you know that, because your knowledge of the stack means that you can tell what the effect of decrementing pAmount will be. After you start doing pointer arithmetic, you will find that you can access all sorts of variables and memory locations that the compiler would usually stop you from accessing, hence the description of pointer arithmetic as unsafe.

Next, you do some pointer arithmetic on your pCents pointer. pCents currently points to amount1.Cents, but the aim here is to get it to point to amount2.Cents, again using pointer operations instead of directly telling the compiler that's what you want to do. To do this, you need to decrement the address pCents contains by sizeof(Currency):

```
    // do some clever casting to get pCents to point to cents
    // inside amount2
    CurrencyStruct* pTempCurrency = (CurrencyStruct*)pCents;
    pCents = (byte*) ( --pTempCurrency );
    Console.WriteLine("Address of pCents is now 0x{0:X}", (ulong)&pCents);
```

Finally, you use the fixed keyword to create some pointers that point to the fields in a class instance and use these pointers to set the value of this instance. Notice that this is also the first time that you have been able to look at the address of an item stored on the heap, rather than the stack:

```
    Console.WriteLine("\nNow with classes");
    // now try it out with classes
    var amount3 = new CurrencyClass();
    fixed(long* pDollars2 = &(amount3.Dollars))
    fixed(byte* pCents2 = &(amount3.Cents))
    {
      Console.WriteLine($"amount3.Dollars has address 0x{(ulong)pDollars2:X}");
      Console.WriteLine($"amount3.Cents has address 0x{(ulong)pCents2:X}");
      *pDollars2 = -100;
      Console.WriteLine($"amount3 contains {amount3}");
    }
```

Compiling and running this code gives output similar to this:

```
Size of CurrencyStruct struct is 16
Address of amount1 is 0xD290DCD7C0
Address of amount2 is 0xD290DCD7B0
Address of pAmount is 0xD290DCD7A8
Address of pDollars is 0xD290DCD7A0
Address of pCents is 0xD290DCD798
amount1 contains $ 20.50
amount2 has address 0xD290DCD7B0 and contains $ 0.0
Address of pCents is now 0xD290DCD798
Now with classes
amount3.Dollars has address 0xD292C91A70
amount3.Cents has address 0xD292C91A78
amount3 contains $ -100.0
```

Notice in this output the uninitialized value of `amount2` that is displayed, and notice that the size of the `CurrencyStruct` struct is 16—somewhat larger than you would expect given the size of its fields (a `long` and a `byte` should total 9 bytes).

Using Pointers to Optimize Performance

Until now, all the examples have been designed to demonstrate the various things that you can do with pointers. You have played around with memory in a way that is probably interesting only to people who like to know what's happening under the hood, but that doesn't really help you write better code. Now you're going to apply your understanding of pointers and see an example of how judicious use of pointers has a significant performance benefit.

Creating Stack-Based Arrays

This section explores one of the main areas in which pointers can be useful: creating high-performance, low-overhead arrays on the stack. As discussed in Chapter 2, "Core C#," C# includes rich support for handling arrays. Chapter 7, "Arrays," give more details on arrays. Although C# makes it very easy to use both one-dimensional and rectangular or jagged multidimensional arrays, it suffers from the disadvantage that these arrays are actually objects; they are instances of `System.Array`. This means that the arrays are stored on the heap, with all the overhead that this involves. There may be occasions when you need to create a short-lived, high-performance array and don't want the overhead of reference objects. You can do this by using pointers, although this is easy only for one-dimensional arrays.

To create a high-performance array, you need to use a keyword: `stackalloc`. The `stackalloc` command instructs the .NET runtime to allocate an amount of memory on the stack. When you call `stackalloc`, you need to supply it with two pieces of information:

➤ The type of data you want to store
➤ The number of these data items you need to store

For example, to allocate enough memory to store 10 `decimal` data items, you can write the following:

```
decimal* pDecimals = stackalloc decimal[10];
```

This command simply allocates the stack memory; it does not attempt to initialize the memory to any default value. This is fine for the purpose of this example because you are creating a high-performance array, and initializing values unnecessarily would hurt performance.

Similarly, to store 20 `double` data items, you write this:

```
double* pDoubles = stackalloc double[20];
```

Although this line of code specifies the number of variables to store as a constant, this can equally be a quantity evaluated at runtime. Therefore, you can write the previous example like this:

```
int size;
size = 20; // or some other value calculated at runtime
double* pDoubles = stackalloc double[size];
```

You can see from these code snippets that the syntax of stackalloc is slightly unusual. It is followed immediately by the name of the data type you want to store (which must be a value type) and then by the number of items you need space for, in square brackets. The number of bytes allocated is this number multiplied by sizeof(data type). The use of square brackets in the preceding code sample suggests an array, which is not too surprising. If you have allocated space for 20 doubles, then what you have is an array of 20 doubles. The simplest type of array that you can have is a block of memory that stores one element after another (see Figure 17-6).

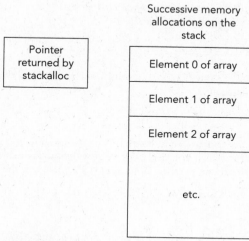

FIGURE 17-6

This diagram also shows the pointer returned by stackalloc, which is always a pointer to the allocated data type that points to the top of the newly allocated memory block. To use the memory block, you simply de-reference the returned pointer. For example, to allocate space for 20 doubles and then set the first element (element 0 of the array) to the value 3.0, write this:

```
double* pDoubles = stackalloc double[20];
*pDoubles = 3.0;
```

To access the next element of the array, you use pointer arithmetic. As described earlier, if you add 1 to a pointer, its value will be increased by the size of whatever data type it points to. In this case, that's just enough to take you to the next free memory location in the block that you have allocated. Therefore, you can set the second element of the array (element number 1) to the value 8.4:

```
double* pDoubles = stackalloc double[20];
*pDoubles = 3.0;
*(pDoubles + 1) = 8.4;
```

By the same reasoning, you can access the element with index X of the array with the expression *(pDoubles+ X).

Effectively, you have a means by which you can access elements of your array, but for general-purpose use, this syntax is too complex. Fortunately, C# defines an alternative syntax using square brackets. C# gives a very precise meaning to square brackets when they are applied to pointers; if the variable p is any pointer type and X is an integer, then the expression p[X] is always interpreted by the compiler as meaning *(p+X). This is true for all pointers, not only those initialized using stackalloc. With this shorthand notation, you now have a very convenient syntax for accessing your array. In fact, it means that you have exactly the same syntax for accessing one-dimensional, stack-based arrays as you do for accessing heap-based arrays that are represented by the System.Array class:

```
double* pDoubles = stackalloc double [20];
```

```
pDoubles[0] = 3.0; // pDoubles[0] is the same as *pDoubles
pDoubles[1] = 8.4; // pDoubles[1] is the same as *(pDoubles+1)
```

> **NOTE** *This idea of applying array syntax to pointers is not new. It has been a fundamental part of both the C and the C++ languages ever since those languages were invented. Indeed, C++ developers will recognize the stack-based arrays they can obtain using* stackalloc *as being essentially identical to classic stack-based C and C++ arrays. This syntax and the way it links pointers and arrays is one reason why the C language became popular in the 1970s, and the main reason why the use of pointers became such a popular programming technique in C and C++.*

Although your high-performance array can be accessed in the same way as a normal C# array, a word of caution is in order. The following code in C# raises an exception:

```
double[] myDoubleArray = new double [20];
myDoubleArray[50] = 3.0;
```

The exception occurs because you are trying to access an array using an index that is out of bounds; the index is 50, whereas the maximum allowed value is 19. However, if you declare the equivalent array using stackalloc, there is no object wrapped around the array that can perform bounds checking. Hence, the following code does *not* raise an exception:

```
double* pDoubles = stackalloc double [20];
pDoubles[50] = 3.0;
```

In this code, you allocate enough memory to hold 20 doubles. Then you set sizeof(double) memory locations, starting at the location given by the start of this memory + 50*sizeof(double) to hold the double value 3.0. Unfortunately, that memory location is way outside the area of memory that you have allocated for the doubles. There is no knowing what data might be stored at that address. At best, you might have used some currently unused memory, but it is equally possible that you might have just overwritten some locations in the stack that were being used to store other variables or even the return address from the method currently being executed. Again, you see that the high performance to be gained from pointers comes at a cost; you need to be certain you know what you are doing, or you will get some very strange run-time bugs.

QuickArray Example

The discussion of pointers ends with a stackalloc example called QuickArray. In this example, the program simply asks users how many elements they want to be allocated for an array. The code then uses stackalloc to allocate an array of longs that size. The elements of this array are populated with the squares of the integers starting with 0, and the results are displayed on the console (code file QuickArray/ Program.cs):

```
class Program
{
  unsafe static void Main()
  {
    Console.Write("How big an array do you want? \n> ");
    string userInput = ReadLine();
    uint size = uint.Parse(userInput);
    long* pArray = stackalloc long[(int) size];
    for (int i = 0; i < size; i++)
    {
      pArray[i] = i*i;
    }
```

```
        for (int i = 0; i < size; i++)
        {
           Console.WriteLine($"Element {i} = {*(pArray + i)}");
        }
        Console.ReadLine();
     }
  }
```

Here is the output from the `QuickArray` example:

```
How big an array do you want?
> 15
Element 0 = 0
Element 1 = 1
Element 2 = 4
Element 3 = 9
Element 4 = 16
Element 5 = 25
Element 6 = 36
Element 7 = 49
Element 8 = 64
Element 9 = 81
Element 10 = 100
Element 11 = 121
Element 12 = 144
Element 13 = 169
Element 14 = 196
```

REFERENCE SEMANTICS

Chapter 3, "Objects and Types," shows the `ref` keyword in action when passing arguments to methods. When passing a struct by value, the contents of the struct is copied. Passing a struct by reference (using the `ref` keyword), the new variable references the same data.

Using C# 7.0, you also can use the `ref` keyword as a modifier of the return type, and as modifier with local variables. With C# 7.2, the `readonly` modifier can be added to the `ref` keyword to not allow changes. C# 7.2 also adds the `in` keyword for passing value types by reference without allowing them to change. These new features are discussed in this section.

On one hand, it's preferable to have immutable types, as these types allow access from multiple threads without the need for synchronization, as no thread can change a value. However, immutable types also mean that a lot of data needs to be copied. With value types, data need to be copied, which, of course, also costs performance. Using reference types, different variables are needed to reference the same data on the heap, and probably this data also needs a copy. For example, the `string` type is immutable. Methods of the `string` type such as `ToUpper` and `ToLower` never change the string, but instead return a new string. Such objects need to be garbage collected when they are no longer referenced. You've seen the functionality of the garbage collector earlier in this chapter in the "Garbage Collection" section. To avoid excessive use of the garbage collector and to copy data without needing to use `IntPtr` and `unsafe` code, the enhanced functionality of the `ref` keyword is of immense help.

The `ReferenceSemantics` example makes use of these namespaces:

`System`

`System.Linq`

Have a look at the following `Data` class. This class contains the value type `int` with the variable name `_anumber` that is initialized in the constructor. The method `Show` writes the current value of the of the number to the console. The most interesting part is the `GetNumber` method. Within the implementation, the variable _anumber is returned using the ref keyword to return a reference to it. This is made possible by the declaration of the return type of GetNumber; it is declared of type ref int to return a reference to an int. The method GetReadonlyNumber is a method that returns a ref readonly int. ref readonly is new with C# 7.2 to return a value type by reference, but not to allow it to change by the caller (code file ReferenceSemantics/Data.cs):

```
public class Data
{
  public Data(int anumber) => _anumber = anumber;
  private int _anumber;

  public ref int GetNumber() => ref _anumber;

  public ref readonly int GetReadonlyNumber() => ref _anumber;

  public void Show() => Console.WriteLine($"Data: {_anumber}");
}
```

Let's use the Data class and invoke the GetNumber method. The method is declared to return ref int. However, in the following code snippet, the result is written to an int. n is a local variable that keeps an int, and the result from GetNumber is copied to this variable. When you change the value of the local variable, the data from within the Data class is not changed (code file ReferenceSemantics/Program.cs):

```
static void UseMember()
{
  Console.WriteLine(nameof(UseMember));
  var d = new Data(11);
  int n = d.GetNumber();
  n = 42;
  d.Show();
  Console.WriteLine();
}
```

When you run the application, the output shows that the Data class still contains the initialized data after the change of the local variable:

```
UseMember
Data: 11
```

Making a small change to the implementation in the method UseRefMember, the GetNumber method is invoked to return a ref specifying the ref keyword before the method, and the variable n to be a ref local, and thus it directly references _anumber within the Data class. A local variable can also be declared with the ref readonly modifier. The result of the method GetNumber returning a ref int can be assigned to a ref readonly int. This guarantees that the variable n2 cannot be changed. The compiler complains if n2 would be changed (code file ReferenceSemantics/Program.cs):

```
static void UseRefMember()
{
  Console.WriteLine(nameof(UseRefMember));
  var d = new Data(11);
  ref int n = ref d.GetNumber();
  n = 42;
  d.Show();

  ref readonly int n2 = d.GetNumber();
  // n2 = 42; // not allowed - it's readonly!
  Console.WriteLine();
}
```

When you run the application with this change, the data within the Data class is changed. Fast direct access is possible without needing to use IntPtr and unsafe code:

```
UseRefMember
Data: 42
```

Next, let's invoke the method GetReadonlyNumber. This method returns ref readonly int. You can assign the result to an int. Assigning a ref to an int makes a copy. The copy can be changed, but doesn't change the original. Assigning the result to a ref readonly int passes the result by reference, but the result cannot be changed (code file ReferenceSemantics/Program.cs):

```
static void UseReadonlyRefMember()
{
  Console.WriteLine(nameof(UseReadonlyRefMember));
  var d = new Data(11);
  int n = d.GetReadonlyNumber();  // create a copy
  n = 42;
  d.Show();

  // ref int n = d.GetReadonlyNumber(); // not allowed
  ref readonly int n2 = ref d.GetReadonlyNumber();
  // n2 = 42; // not allowed
  Console.WriteLine();
}
```

The result of this method is an unchanged Data member:

```
UseRefMember
Data: 11
```

Passing ref and returning ref

Let's get into another example: passing a ref int and returning a ref int. The Max method receives x and y parameters by ref, and returns the higher of these two values by ref (code file ReferenceSemantics/Program.cs):

```
static ref int Max(ref int x, ref int y)
{
  if (x > y) return ref x;
  else return ref y;
}
```

Without needing to make copies of the variables x and y, passing them to the method Max gives a fast way to return the higher value. This can be really useful if this method is invoked often:

```
static void UseMax()
{
  Console.WriteLine(nameof(UseMax));
  int x = 4, y = 5;
  ref int z = ref Max(ref x, ref y);
  Console.WriteLine($"{z} is the max of {x} and {y}");
  //...
}
```

This is the message returned:

```
5 is the max of 4 and 5
```

Returning a reference is fast because behind the scenes you use only pointers. However, this also means that the original item where the reference points to can be changed. For example, changing the variable z that references the data from x or y, depending what's larger, also changes the value of the original variable:

```
static void UseMax()
{
  //...
  z = x + y;
  Console.WriteLine($"y after changing z: {y}");

  Console.WriteLine();
}
```

When you run the program, you can see that y now has the value that was assigned to z:

```
y after changing z: 9
```

Ref and Arrays

Another example to show the features of ref return and ref local shows this keyword with arrays. The class Container defines a member of type int [] that is initialized in the constructor. The GetItem method returns an item of the array by reference. This allows of a fast path directly within the array of the container (code file ReferenceSemantics/Container.cs):

```
public class Container
{
    public Container(int[] data) => _data = data;
    private int[] _data;

    //...

    public ref int GetItem(int index) => ref _data[index];

    public void ShowAll()
    {
      Console.WriteLine(string.Join(", ", _data));
      Console.WriteLine();
    }
}
```

When using this Container, a sample array containing a list of 10 items is passed to the constructor. The fourth item is retrieved from the GetItem method, this item is changed to 33, and finally all the items are written to the console using the ShowAll method (code file ReferenceSemantics/Program.cs):

```
private static void UseItemOfContainer()
{
  Console.WriteLine(nameof(UseItemOfContainer));
  var c = new Container(Enumerable.Range(0, 10).Select(x => x).ToArray());
  ref int item = ref c.GetItem(3);
  item = 33;
  c.ShowAll();
  Console.WriteLine();
}
```

When you run the application, you can see the fourth item changed from the outside:

```
UseItemOfContainer
0, 1, 2, 33, 4, 5, 6, 7, 8, 9
```

Let's see what can be done not only with items of arrays but with complete arrays by adding the GetData method. This method returns a reference to the array itself (code file ReferenceSemantics/ Container.cs):

```
public class Container
{
```

```
//...

    public ref int[] GetData() => ref _data;

    //...
}
```

Using the `GetData` method of the `Container` class, a reference from the array is returned and written to the `ref` local variable `d1`. A new array with three elements is assigned to this variable (code file `ReferenceSemantics/Program.cs`):

```
private static void UseArrayOfContainer()
{
  Console.WriteLine(nameof(UseArrayOfContainer));
  var c = new Container(Enumerable.Range(0, 10).Select(x => x).ToArray());
  ref int[] d1 = ref c.GetData();
  d1 = new int[] { 4, 5, 6 };
  c.ShowAll();
  Console.WriteLine();
}
```

Because a reference to the array is returned, the complete array can be replaced. The container now contains the newly created array with the elements 4, 5, and 6:

```
UseArrayOfContainer
4, 5, 6
```

> **NOTE** *The* `ref` *keyword for* `ref` *returns and* `ref` *locals requires references that stay alive when returning the reference. For example, you can return references to value types as long as they are contained in a reference type, and thus are on the managed heap. Using structs, you cannot define methods to return references of members of the struct. You can return references to structs that are received as references, as you've seen with the* `Max` *method. These value types are guaranteed alive with the return of the method, because they are passed by the caller that waits for the return of the method.*

> **NOTE** *Chapter 3, "Objects and Types," covers defining parameters with the* `ref`*,* `out`*, and* `in` *modifiers. These modifiers are important in regard to reference semantics as well. Using the* `in` *parameter that's new with C# 7.2 with value types defines that the value type is passed by reference (similar to using the* `ref` *keyword with the parameter), but doesn't allow changing it.* `in` *is like* `ref` `readonly` *for the parameters.*

SPAN<T>

Chapter 3 includes creating reference types (classes) and value types (structs). Instances of classes are stored on the managed heap. The value of structs can be stored on the stack, or, when boxing is used, on the managed heap. Now we have another kind: a type that can have its value only on the stack but never on the heap, sometimes called *ref-like types*. Boxing is not possible with these types. Such a type is declared with the `ref struct` keyword. Using `ref struct` gives some additional behaviors and restrictions. The restrictions are the following:

➤ They can't be added as array items.
➤ They can't be used as generic type argument.

➤ They can't be boxed.

➤ They can't be static fields.

➤ They can only be instance fields of ref-like types.

`Span<T>` and `ReadOnlySpan<T>` are ref-like types covered in this section. These types are already covered in Chapter 7 with extension methods for arrays and in Chapter 9 with extension methods for strings. Here, additional features are covered to reference data on the managed heap, the stack, and the native heap.

Spans Referencing the Managed Heap

A `Span` can reference memory on the managed heap, as you've shown in Chapters 7 and 9. In the following code snippet, an array is created, and with the extension method `AsSpan`, a new `Span` is created referencing the memory of the array on the managed heap. After creating the `Span` referenced from the variable span1, a slice of the `Span` is created that is filled with the value 42. The next `Console.WriteLine` writes the values of the span span1 to the console (code file `SpanSample/Program.cs`):

```
private static void SpanOnTheHeap()
{
  Console.WriteLine(nameof(SpanOnTheHeap));
  Span<int> span1 = (new int[] { 1, 5, 11, 71, 22, 19, 21, 33 }).AsSpan();

  span1.Slice(start: 4, length: 3).Fill(42);

  Console.WriteLine(string.Join(", ", span1.ToArray()));

  Console.WriteLine();
}
```

When you run the application, you can see the output of span1 with the 42 filled within the slice of the span:

```
SpanOnTheHeap
1, 5, 11, 71, 42, 42, 42, 33
```

Spans Referencing the Stack

`Span` can be used to reference memory on the stack. Referencing a single variable on the stack is not as interesting as referencing a block of memory; that's why the following code snippet makes use of the `stackalloc` keyword. `stackalloc` returns a `long*` which requires the method `SpanOnTheStack` to be declared unsafe. A constructor of the `Span` type allows passing a pointer with the additional parameter for the size. Next, the variable span1 is used with the indexer to fill every item (code file `SpanSample/Program.cs`):

```
private static unsafe void SpanOnTheStack()
{
  Console.WriteLine(nameof(SpanOnTheStack));

  long* lp = stackalloc long[20];
  var span1 = new Span<long>(lp, 20);

  for (int i = 0; i < 20; i++)
  {
    span1[i] = i;
  }

  Console.WriteLine(string.Join(", ", span1.ToArray()));
  Console.WriteLine();
}
```

When you run the program, the following output shows the span with the initialized data on the stack:

```
SpanOnTheStack
0, 1, 2, 3, 4, 5, 6, 7, 8, 9, 10, 11, 12, 13, 14, 15, 16, 17, 18, 19
```

Spans Referencing the Native Heap

A great feature of spans is they can also reference memory on the native heap. Memory on the native heap usually is allocated from native APIs. In the following code snippet, the `AllocHGlobal` method of the `Marshal` class is used to allocate 100 bytes on the native heap. The `Marshal` class returns a pointer with the `IntPtr` type. To directly access the `int*`, the `ToPointer` method of `IntPtr` is invoked. This is the pointer required by the constructor of the `Span` class. Writing `int` values to this memory, you need to pay attention how many bytes are needed. As an `int` contains 32 bits, the number of bytes is divided by 4 with a bit shift of two bits. After this, the native memory is filled by invoking the `Fill` method of the `Span`. With a for loop, every item referenced from the `Span` is written to the console (code file `SpanSample/Program.cs`):

```csharp
private static unsafe void SpanOnNativeMemory()
{
  Console.WriteLine(nameof(SpanOnNativeMemory));
  const int nbytes = 100;
  IntPtr p = Marshal.AllocHGlobal(nbytes);
  try
  {
    int* p2 = (int*)p.ToPointer();
    Span<int> span = new Span<int>(p2, nbytes >> 2);
    span.Fill(42);

    int max = nbytes >> 2;
    for (int i = 0; i < max; i++)
    {
      Console.Write($"{span[i]} ");
    }
    Console.WriteLine();
  }
  finally
  {
    Marshal.FreeHGlobal(p);
  }
  Console.WriteLine();
}
```

When you run the application, the values stored in the native heap are written to the console:

```
SpanOnNativeMemory
42 42 42 42 42 42 42 42 42 42 42 42 42 42 42 42 42 42 42 42 42 42 42 42 42
```

> **NOTE** *Using* Span *to access native memory and the stack, unsafe code was needed because of the memory allocation and creation of the* Span *by passing a pointer. After the initialization, unsafe code is no longer required using the* Span.

Span Extension Methods

For the `Span` type, extension methods are defined to make it easier to work with this type. The following code snippet demonstrates the use of the `Overlaps`, the `Reverse`, and the `IndexOf` methods. With the `Overlaps` method, it is checked if the span that is used to invoke this extension method overlaps the span passed with the argument. The `Reverse` method reverses the content of the span. The `IndexOf` method returns the index of the span passed with the argument (code file `SpanSample/Program.cs`):

```
private static void SpanExtensions()
{
  Console.WriteLine(nameof(SpanExtensions));
  Span<int> span1 = (new int[] { 1, 5, 11, 71, 22, 19, 21, 33 }).AsSpan();
  Span<int> span2 = span1.Slice(3, 4);
  bool overlaps = span1.Overlaps(span2);
  Console.WriteLine($"span1 overlaps span2: {overlaps}");
  span1.Reverse();
  Console.WriteLine($"span1 reversed: {string.Join(", ", span1.ToArray())}");
  Console.WriteLine($"span2 (a slice) after reversing span1: " +
    $"{string.Join(", ", span2.ToArray())}");
  int index = span1.IndexOf(span2);
  Console.WriteLine($"index of span2 in span1: {index}");
  Console.WriteLine();
}
```

Running the program produces this output:

```
SpanExtensions
span1 overlaps span2: True
span1 reversed: 33, 21, 19, 22, 71, 11, 5, 1
span2 (a slice) after reversing span1: 22, 71, 11, 5
index of span2 in span1: 3
```

Other extension methods defined for the `Span` type are `StartWith` to check if a span starts with the sequence of another span, `SequenceEqual` to compare the sequence of two spans, `SequenceCompareTo` for ordering of sequences, and `LastIndexOf` which returns the first matching index starting from the end of the span.

PLATFORM INVOKE

Not all the features of Windows API calls are available from .NET. This is true not only for old Windows API calls but also for very new features. Maybe you've written some DLLs that export unmanaged methods and you would like to use them from C# as well.

To reuse an unmanaged library that doesn't contain COM objects—it contains only exported functions— you can use Platform Invoke (P/Invoke). With P/Invoke, the CLR loads the DLL that includes the function that should be called and marshals the parameters.

To use the unmanaged function, first you have to determine the name of the function as it is exported. You can do this by using the `dumpbin` tool with the `/exports` option.

For example, the command

```
dumpbin /exports c:\windows\system32\kernel32.dll | more
```

lists all exported functions from the DLL `kernel32.dll`. In the example, you use the `CreateHardLink` Windows API function to create a hard link to an existing file. With this API call, you can have several filenames that reference the same file as long as the filenames are on one hard disk only. This API call is not available from .NET Core, so you must use platform invoke.

To call a native function, you have to define a C# external method with the same number of arguments, and the argument types that are defined with the unmanaged method must have mapped types with managed code.

The Windows API call `CreateHardLink` has this definition in C++:

```
BOOL CreateHardLink(
LPCTSTR lpFileName,
```

```
        LPCTSTR lpExistingFileName,
        LPSECURITY_ATTRIBUTES lpSecurityAttributes);
```

This definition must be mapped to .NET data types. The return type is a BOOL with unmanaged code; this simply maps to the bool data type. LPCTSTR defines a long pointer to a const string. The Windows API uses the Hungarian naming convention for the data type. LP is a long pointer, C is a const, and STR is a null-terminated string. The T marks the type as a generic type, and the type is resolved to either LPCSTR (an ANSI string) or LPWSTR (a wide Unicode string), depending on the compiler's settings to 32 or 64 bit. C strings map to the .NET type String. LPSECURITY_ATTRIBUTES, which is a long pointer to a struct of type SECURITY_ATTRIBUTES. Because you can pass NULL to this argument, mapping this type to IntPtr is okay. The C# declaration of this method must be marked with the extern modifier because there's no implementation of this method within the C# code. Instead, the method implementation is in the DLL kernel32.dll, which is referenced with the attribute [DllImport]. The return type of the .NET declaration CreateHardLink is of type bool, and the native method CreateHardLink returns a BOOL, so some additional clarification is useful. Because there are different Boolean data types with C++ (for example, the native bool and the Windows-defined BOOL, which have different values), the attribute [MarshalAs] specifies to what native type the .NET type bool should map:

```
[DllImport("kernel32.dll", SetLastError="true",
   EntryPoint="CreateHardLink", CharSet=CharSet.Unicode)]
[return: MarshalAs(UnmanagedType.Bool)]
public static extern bool CreateHardLink(string newFileName,
   string existingFilename, IntPtr securityAttributes);
```

> **NOTE** *The website* http://www.pinvoke.net *is very helpful with the conversion from native to managed code.*

The settings that you can specify with the attribute [DllImport] are listed in the following table.

DLLIMPORT PROPERTY OR FIELD	DESCRIPTION
EntryPoint	You can give the C# declaration of the function a different name than the one it has with the unmanaged library. The name of the method in the unmanaged library is defined in the field EntryPoint.
CallingConvention	Depending on the compiler or compiler settings that were used to compile the unmanaged function, you can use different calling conventions. The calling convention defines how the parameters are handled and where to put them on the stack. You can define the calling convention by setting an enumerable value. The Windows API usually uses the StdCall calling convention on the Windows operating system, and it uses the Cdecl calling convention on Windows CE. Setting the value to CallingConvention.Winapi works for the Windows API in both the Windows and the Windows CE environments.
CharSet	String parameters can be either ANSI or Unicode. With the CharSet setting, you can define how strings are managed. Possible values that are defined with the CharSet enumeration are Ansi, Unicode, and Auto. CharSet.Auto uses Unicode on the Windows NT platform, and ANSI on Microsoft's older operating systems.
SetLastError	If the unmanaged function sets an error by using the Windows API SetLastError, you can set the SetLastError field to true. This way, you can read the error number afterward by using Marshal.GetLastWin32Error.

To make the `CreateHardLink` method easier to use from a .NET environment, you should follow these guidelines:

➤ Create an internal class named `NativeMethods` that wraps the platform invoke method calls.

➤ Create a public class to offer the native method functionality to .NET applications.

➤ Use security attributes to mark the required security.

In the following example, the public method `CreateHardLink` in the class `FileUtility` is the method that can be used by .NET applications. This method has the filename arguments reversed compared to the native Windows API method `CreateHardLink`. The first argument is the name of the existing file, and the second argument is the new file. This is similar to other classes in the framework, such as `File.Copy`. Because the third argument used to pass the security attributes for the new filename is not used with this implementation, the public method has just two parameters. The return type is changed as well. Instead of returning an error by returning the value `false`, an exception is thrown. In case of an error, the unmanaged method `CreateHardLink` sets the error number with the unmanaged API `SetLastError`. To read this value from .NET, the `[DllImport]` field `SetLastError` is set to `true`. Within the managed method `CreateHardLink`, the error number is read by calling `Marshal.GetLastWin32Error`. To create an error message from this number, the `Win32Exception` class from the namespace `System.ComponentModel` is used. This class accepts an error number with the constructor, and returns a localized error message. In case of an error, an exception of type `IOException` is thrown, which has an inner exception of type `Win32Exception`. The public method `CreateHardLink` has the `FileIOPermission` attribute applied to check whether the caller has the necessary permission (code file `PInvokeSampleLib/NativeMethods.cs`).

```
[SecurityCritical]
internal static class NativeMethods
{
  [DllImport("kernel32.dll", SetLastError = true,
    EntryPoint = "CreateHardLinkW", CharSet = CharSet.Unicode)]
  [return: MarshalAs(UnmanagedType.Bool)]
  private static extern bool CreateHardLink(
  [In, MarshalAs(UnmanagedType.LPWStr)] string newFileName,
  [In, MarshalAs(UnmanagedType.LPWStr)] string existingFileName,
  IntPtr securityAttributes);
  internal static void CreateHardLink(string oldFileName,
    string newFileName)
  {
    if (!CreateHardLink(newFileName, oldFileName, IntPtr.Zero))
    {
      var ex = new Win32Exception(Marshal.GetLastWin32Error());
      throw new IOException(ex.Message, ex);
    }
  }
}


public static class FileUtility
{
  [FileIOPermission(SecurityAction.LinkDemand, Unrestricted = true)]
  public static void CreateHardLink(string oldFileName,
    string newFileName)
  {
    NativeMethods.CreateHardLink(oldFileName, newFileName);
  }
}
```

This library uses the following dependency and namespaces:

Dependency:

```
System.Security.Permissions
```

Namespaces:

System

System.IO

System.Runtime.InteropServices

System.Security

System.Security.Permissions

> **WARNING** *The PlatformInvoke sample compiles successfully on Linux but doesn't run because the library* `kernel32.dll` *cannot be found on the Linux operating system.*

You can now use this class to easily create hard links. If the file passed with the first argument of the program does not exist, you get an exception with the message: `The system cannot find the file specified`. If the file exists, you get a new filename referencing the original file. You can easily verify this by changing text in one file; it shows up in the other file as well (code file `PInvokeSample/Program.cs`):

```
class Program
{
  static void Main(string[] args)
  {
    if (args.Length != 2)
    {
      Console.WriteLine("usage: PInvokeSample " +
        "existingfilename newfilename");
      return;
    }
    try
    {
      FileUtility.CreateHardLink(args[0], args[1]);
    }
    catch (IOException ex)
    {
      Console.WriteLine(ex.Message);
    }
  }
}
```

With native method calls on Windows, often you have to use Windows handles. A Window handle is a 32- or 64-bit value for which, depending on the handle types, some values are not allowed. With .NET 1.0 for handles, usually the `IntPtr` structure was used because you can set every possible 32-bit value with this structure. However, with some handle types, this led to security problems and possible threading race conditions and leaked handles with the finalization phase. That's why .NET 2.0 introduced the `SafeHandle` class. The class `SafeHandle` is an abstract base class for every Windows handle. Derived classes inside the `Microsoft.Win32.SafeHandles` namespace are `SafeHandleZeroOrMinusOneIsInvalid` and `SafeHandleMinusOneIsInvalid`. As the name indicates, these classes do not accept invalid 0 or −1 values. Further derived handle types are `SafeFileHandle`, `SafeWaitHandle`, `SafeNCryptHandle`, and `SafePipeHandle`, which can be used by the specific Windows API calls.

For example, to map the Windows API `CreateFile`, you can use the following declaration to return a `SafeFileHandle`. Of course, usually you could use the .NET classes `File` and `FileInfo` instead.

```
[DllImport("Kernel32.dll", SetLastError = true,
  CharSet = CharSet.Unicode)]
internal static extern SafeFileHandle CreateFile(
```

```
string fileName,
[MarshalAs(UnmanagedType.U4)] FileAccess fileAccess,
[MarshalAs(UnmanagedType.U4)] FileShare fileShare,
IntPtr securityAttributes,
[MarshalAs(UnmanagedType.U4)] FileMode creationDisposition,
int flags,
SafeFileHandle template);
```

SUMMARY

Remember that in order to become a truly proficient C# programmer, you must have a solid understanding of how memory allocation and garbage collection work. This chapter described how the CLR manages and allocates memory on the heap and the stack. It also illustrated how to write classes that free unmanaged resources correctly, and how to use pointers in C#. These are both advanced topics that are poorly understood and often implemented incorrectly by novice programmers. At a minimum, this chapter should have helped you understand how to release resources using the IDisposable interface and the using statement.

You've also seen C# 7.0 and 7.2 enhancements passing values by reference and returning values by reference, particularly ref return and ref locals, as well as using the ref readonly modifier.

The next chapter covers a roundtrip through all features of Visual Studio 2017.

18

Visual Studio 2017

WHAT'S IN THIS CHAPTER?

➤ Using Visual Studio 2017

➤ Creating and working with projects

➤ Debugging

➤ Refactoring with Visual Studio

➤ Working with various technologies: UWP, ASP.NET Core, and more

➤ Analyzing applications

➤ Creating and using containers with Docker

WORKING WITH VISUAL STUDIO 2017

At this point, you should be familiar with the C# language and almost ready to move on to the applied sections of the book, which cover how to use C# to program a variety of applications. Before doing that, however, it's important to understand how you can use Visual Studio and some of the features provided by the .NET environment to get the best from your programs.

This chapter explains what programming in the .NET environment means in practice. It covers Visual Studio, the main development environment in which you will write, compile, debug, and optimize your C# programs, and provides guidelines for writing good applications. Visual Studio is the main IDE used for numerous purposes, including writing ASP.NET and ASP.NET Core web applications, Windows Presentation Foundation (WPF) applications, and apps for the Universal Windows Platform (UWP), and for accessing services created by the ASP.NET Web.

This chapter also explores what it takes to build applications that are targeted at .NET Core.

Visual Studio 2017 is a fully integrated development environment. It is designed to make the process of writing your code, debugging it, and compiling it to an assembly to be shipped as easy as possible. This means that Visual Studio gives you a very sophisticated multiple-document–interface application in which you can do just about everything related to developing your code. It offers the following features:

➤ **Text editor**—Using this editor, you can write your C# (as well as Visual Basic, C++, F#, JavaScript, XAML, JSON, and SQL) code. This text editor is quite sophisticated. For example, as you type, it automatically lays out your code by indenting lines, matching start and end brackets of code blocks, and color-coding keywords. It also performs some syntax checks as you type, and underlines code that causes compilation errors, also known as design-time debugging. In addition, it features IntelliSense, which automatically displays the names of classes, fields, or methods as you begin to type them. As you start typing parameters to methods, it also shows you the parameter lists for the available overloads. Figure 18-1 shows the IntelliSense feature in action with a UWP app. This dialog has a new feature with Visual Studio 2017: You can use the buttons at the bottom to select to see only properties, events, or methods. This helps a lot with the large member lists.

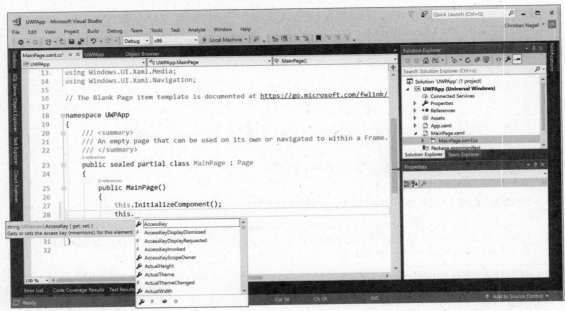

FIGURE 18-1

➤ **Design view editor**—This editor enables you to place user-interface and data-access controls in your project; Visual Studio automatically adds the necessary C# code to your source files to instantiate these controls in your project. (This is possible because all .NET controls are instances of base classes.)

➤ **Supporting windows**—These windows enable you to view and modify aspects of your project, such as the classes in your source code, as well as the available properties (and their startup values) for Windows Forms and Web Forms classes. You can also use these windows to specify compilation options, such as which assemblies your code needs to reference.

➤ **Integrated debugger**—It is in the nature of programming that your code will not run correctly the first time you try it. Or the second time. Or the third time. Visual Studio seamlessly links to a debugger for you, enabling you to set breakpoints and watches on variables from within the environment.

➤ **Integrated Microsoft help**—Visual Studio enables you to access the Microsoft documentation from within the IDE. For example, if you are not sure of the meaning of a keyword while using the text editor, simply select the keyword and press the F1 key, and Visual Studio accesses `https://docs .microsoft.com` to show you related topics. Similarly, if you are not sure what a certain compilation error means, you can bring up the documentation for that error by selecting the error message and pressing F1.

➤ **Access to other programs**—Visual Studio can also access some other utilities that enable you to examine and modify aspects of your computer or network, without your having to leave the developer environment. With the tools available, you can check running services and database connections, look directly into your SQL Server tables, browse your Microsoft Azure Cloud services, and even browse the Web using a web browser window.

➤ **Visual Studio extensions**—Some extensions of Visual Studio are already installed with a normal installation of Visual Studio, and many more extensions from both Microsoft and third parties are available. These extensions enable you to analyze code, offer project or item templates, access other services, and more. With the .NET Compiler Platform, integration of tools with Visual Studio has become easier.

> **NOTE** *By pressing Ctrl+Space, you can bring back the IntelliSense list box if you need it or if for any reason it is not visible. In case you want to see some code below the IntelliSense box, just keep pressing the Ctrl button.*

The recent releases of Visual Studio had some interesting progress. One big part was with the user interface, the other big part with the background functionality and the .NET Compiler Platform.

With the user interface, Visual Studio 2010 redesigned the shell to be based on WPF instead of native Windows controls. Visual Studio 2012 had some user interface (UI) changes based on this. In particular, the UI was enhanced to have more focus on the main work area—the editor—and to allow doing more tasks directly from the code editor instead of needing to use many other tools. Of course, you need some tools outside the code editor, but more functionality has been built into a few of these tools, so the number of tools typically needed can be reduced. With Visual Studio 2017, some more UI features have been enhanced. You can immediately see the first UI enhancement in the Visual Studio Installer, which has taken some inspiration from the design of the Windows 8 tiles to make it easier to select Workloads (see Figure 18-2).

With the .NET Compiler Platform (code name Roslyn), the .NET compiler has been completely rewritten; it now integrates functionality throughout the compiler pipeline, such as syntax analysis, semantics analysis, binding, and code emitting. Based on this, Microsoft had to rewrite many Visual Studio integration tools. The code editor, IntelliSense, and refactoring are all based on the .NET Compiler Platform.

For XAML code editing, Visual Studio and Blend for Visual Studio share the same engines. Not only the code engines are the same: while Visual Studio 2013 got the XAML engine from Blend, since Blend for Visual Studio 2015, Blend got the shell from Visual Studio. As you start Blend for Visual Studio you see that it looks like Visual Studio, and you can immediately start working with it.

Another special feature of Visual Studio is search. Visual Studio has so many commands and features that it is often hard to find the menu or toolbar button you are looking for. Just enter a part of the command you're looking for into the Quick Launch, and you'll see available options. Quick Launch is located at the top-right corner of the window (see Figure 18-3). Search functionality is also available from the toolbox, Solution Explorer, the code editor (which you can invoke by pressing Ctrl+F), the assemblies on the Reference Manager, and more.

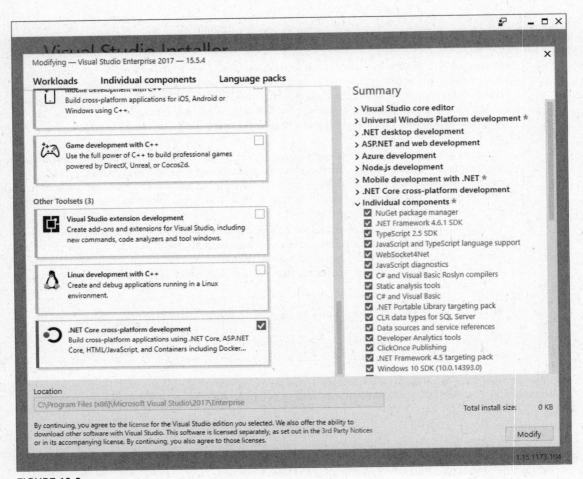

FIGURE 18-2

Visual Studio Editions

Visual Studio 2017 is available in a few editions. The least expensive is Visual Studio 2017 Community Edition, which is free in some cases. It's free for individual developers, open-source projects, academic research, education, and small professional teams.

You can purchase the Professional and Enterprise editions. Only the Enterprise edition includes all the features. Exclusive to the Enterprise edition is IntelliTrace, load testing, and some architecture tools. The Microsoft Fakes framework (unit test isolation) is only available with Visual Studio Enterprise. This chapter's tour of Visual Studio 2017 includes a few features that are available only with specific editions. For detailed information about the features of each edition of Visual Studio 2017, see https://www.visualstudio.com/vs/compare/.

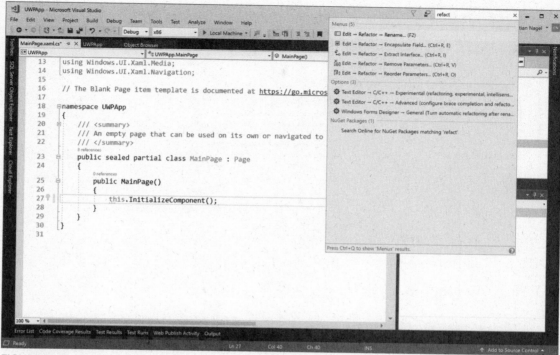

FIGURE 18-3

Visual Studio Settings

When you start Visual Studio the first time, you are asked to select a settings collection that matches your environment, for example, General Development, Visual Basic, Visual C#, Visual C++, or Web Development. These different settings reflect the different tools historically used for these languages. When writing applications on the Microsoft platform, different tools were used to create Visual Basic, C++, and web applications. Similarly, Visual Basic, Visual C++, and Visual InterDev had completely different programming environments, with completely different settings and tool options. Now, you can create apps for all these technologies with Visual Studio, but Visual Studio still offers the keyboard shortcuts that you can choose based on Visual Basic, Visual C++, and Visual InterDev. Of course, you also can select specific C# settings as well.

After choosing the main category of settings to define keyboard shortcuts, menus, and the position of tool windows, you can change every setting with Tools ⇨ Customize (toolbars and commands) and Tools ⇨ Options (here you find the settings for all the tools). You can also reset the settings collection with Tools ⇨ Import and Export Settings, which invokes a wizard that enables you to select a default collection of settings (see Figure 18-4).

FIGURE 18-4

The following sections walk through the process of creating, coding, and debugging a project, demonstrating what Visual Studio can do to help you at each stage.

CREATING A PROJECT

After installing Visual Studio 2017, you will want to start your first project. With Visual Studio, you rarely start with a blank file and then add C# code, in the way that you have been doing in the previous chapters in this book. (Of course, the option of asking for an empty application project is there if you really do want to start writing your code from scratch or if you are going to create a solution that will contain a few projects.)

Instead, the idea is that you tell Visual Studio roughly what type of project you want to create, and it generates the files and C# code that provide a framework for that type of project. You then proceed to add your code to this outline. For example, if you want to build a Windows desktop application (a WPF application), Visual Studio starts you off with an XAML file and a file containing C# source code that creates a basic form. This form can communicate with Windows and receiving events. It can be maximized, minimized, or resized; all you need to do is add the controls and functionality you want. If your application is intended to be a command-line utility (a console application), Visual Studio gives you a basic namespace, a class, and a `Main` method to get you started.

Last, but hardly least, when you create your project, Visual Studio also sets up the compilation options that you are likely to supply to the C# compiler—whether it is to compile to a command-line application, a library, or a WPF application. It also tells the compiler which base class libraries and NuGet packages you need to reference (a WPF GUI application needs to reference many of the WPF-related libraries; a console application probably does not). Of course, you can modify all these settings as you are editing if necessary.

The first time you start Visual Studio, you are presented with an IDE containing menus, a toolbar, and a page with getting-started information, how-to videos, and latest news (see Figure 18-5). The Start Page contains various links to useful websites and links to some actual articles, and it enables you to open existing projects or start a new project altogether.

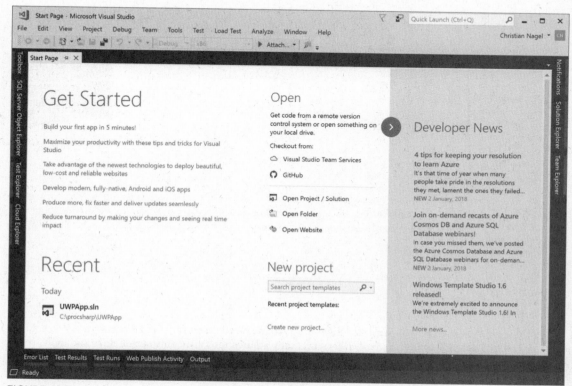

FIGURE 18-5

In the case of Figure 18-5, the Start Page reflects what is shown after you have already used Visual Studio 2017, as it includes a list of the most recently edited projects. You can just click one of these projects to open it again.

Multi-Targeting .NET

Visual Studio enables you to target the version of the .NET version that you want to work with. When you open the New Project dialog, shown in Figure 18-6, a drop-down list in the top area of the dialog displays the available options.

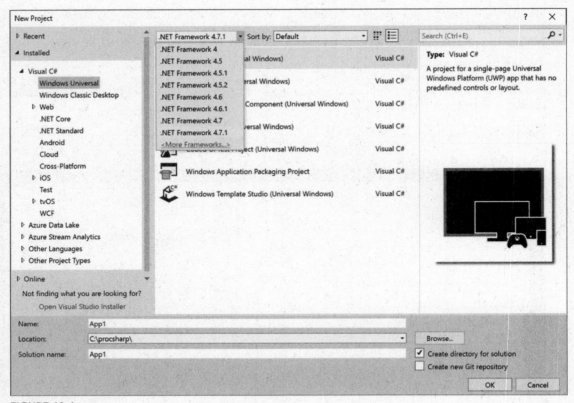

FIGURE 18-6

In this case, you can see that the drop-down list enables you to target the .NET Frameworks 44, 4.5, 4.5.1, 4.5.2, 4.6, 4.6.1, 4.7, and 4.7.1. However, with many application types, this option does not apply. If you create .NET Core apps, or Windows Universal apps, it doesn't matter what you select. However, you can change the .NET Core version or Windows Runtime version target later.

If you want to change the target framework with a .NET Core application, you can right-click the project in the Solution Explorer, select the Project Properties, choose the Application tab, and select the .NET Core version from the Target Framework list (see Figure 18-7).

This is not that different with Windows apps. Here, right-click the project in the Solution Explorer, select the Project Properties, choose the Application tab, and now you can select the target and the minimum build versions, as shown in Figure 18-8.

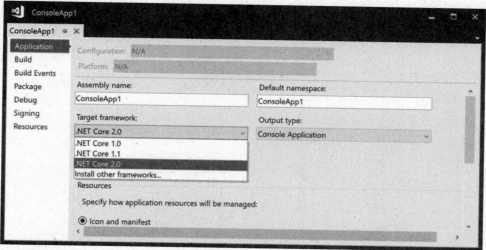

FIGURE 18-7

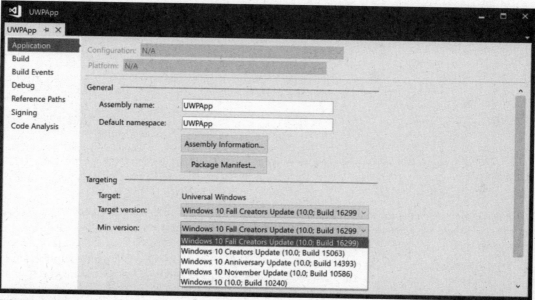

FIGURE 18-8

Selecting a Project Type

To create a new project, select File ➪ New Project from the Visual Studio menu. The New Project dialog displays (see Figure 18-9), giving you your first inkling of the variety of projects you can create.

FIGURE 18-9

Using this dialog, you effectively select the initial framework files and code you want Visual Studio to generate for you, the programming language you want to create your project with, and different categories of application types.

The following tables describe the most important options that are available to you under the Visual C# projects as related to this book. Legacy project templates you might still need are not covered here; for these, you should consult older editions of this book.

Using Windows Universal Project Templates

The first table covers templates for the Universal Windows Platform. These templates are available on both Windows 10 and Windows 8.1, but you need a Windows 10 system to test the application. The templates are used to create applications running on Windows 10 using any device family—the PC, X-Box, IoT devices, and more.

IF YOU CHOOSE. . .	YOU GET THE C# CODE AND COMPILATION OPTIONS TO GENERATE. . .
Blank App (Universal Windows)	A basic empty Universal Windows app with XAML, without styles and other base classes.
Class Library (Universal Windows)	A .NET class library that can be called up by other Windows Store apps programmed with .NET. You can use the API of the Windows Runtime within this library.
Windows Runtime Component (Universal Windows)	A Windows Runtime class library that can be called up by other Windows Store apps developed with different programming languages (C#, C++, JavaScript).
Unit Test App (Universal Windows)	A library that contains unit tests for Universal Windows Platform apps.
Coded UI Test Project (Universal Windows)	A project to define coded UI tests for Windows apps.
Windows Application Packaging Project	A WPF or Windows Forms project. You can build a Windows 10 installation package and mix the app with modern Windows 10 code.

> **NOTE** *For Windows 10, the number of default templates for Universal apps have been reduced. Creating Windows Store apps for Windows 8, Visual Studio offers more project templates to predefine Grid-based, Split-based, or Hub-based apps. For Windows 10 only an empty template is available. You can either start with the empty template or consider using the Windows Template Studio as a starter. The Windows Template Studio project template is available as soon as you install the Windows Template Studio Visual Studio extension from Microsoft, which is available via Tools ⇨ Extensions and Updates.*

Using .NET Core Project Templates

Interesting enhancements with Visual Studio 2017 are available with the .NET Core project templates. Initially, there are five selections, which are described in the following table.

IF YOU CHOOSE. . .	YOU GET THE C# CODE AND COMPILATION OPTIONS TO GENERATE. . .
Console App (.NET Core)	A console app with .NET Core. This is the template you primarily used when creating the code for the previous chapters.
Class Library (.NET Core)	A class library that can be used with .NET Core applications. Don't use this template if you want to share the library between .NET Core, Universal Apps, and Xamarin. Look for the Standard Library instead. You need to use this library for creating some specific .NET Core features that are not available with .NET Standard.
Unit Test Project (.NET Core)	A unit test project to test .NET Core and .NET Standard projects and libraries with MSTest.
xUnit Test Project (.NET Core)	A unit test project to test.NET Core and .NET Standard projects and libraries with xUnit.
ASP.NET Core Web Application	An ASP.NET Core web application, no matter whether it's a website returning HTML code to the client or a service returning JSON. The selections that are available after you have selected this project template are described in the next table.

After selecting the ASP.NET Core Web Application Template, you get the choice of selecting some precon-figured templates as shown in Figure 18-10. Use the combo box at the top to choose between .NET Core and .NET Framework. ASP.NET Core runs on .NET Framework as well, not only on .NET Core. Then you can select the ASP.NET Core version number, which depends on the SDKs you've installed. A selection of .NET Framework is only useful if you need to use legacy libraries that only run with the .NET Framework. Otherwise keep the selection with .NET Core. If you select .NET Core and ASP.NET Core 2.0, you see a similar screen to Figure 18-10. These templates are described in the following table.

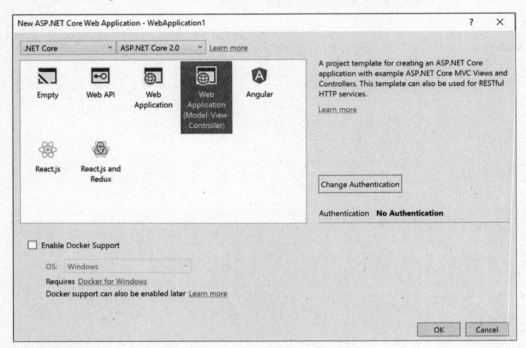

FIGURE 18-10

IF YOU CHOOSE. . .	YOU GET THE C# CODE AND COMPILATION OPTIONS TO GENERATE. . .
Empty	An ASP.NET Core web application. When choosing this template, you do not get a complete empty project, but a good starter to create a basic web app with .NET Core. This template is the template to start with in the Chapter 30, "ASP.NET Core," and Chapter 31, "ASP.NET Core MVC." You'll learn what needs to be added.
Web API	A service offering a Web API using ASP.NET Core. The Web API template makes it possible to easily create RESTful services. This project is covered in Chapter 32, "Web API."
Web Application	A web application with Razor Pages. This is a new option with ASP.NET Core 2.0 and is covered in Chapter 31.
MVC	A web application using ASP.NET Core MVC. This template makes use of the full-blown Model-View-Controller pattern. You can use this to create a rich web application. This template is covered in Chapter 31 as well.

IF YOU CHOOSE...	YOU GET THE C# CODE AND COMPILATION OPTIONS TO GENERATE...
Angular	A web application using the Angular script library to create a Single Page Application (SPA) together with ASP.NET Core for the backend services.
React.js	A web application using React.js and ASP.NET Core for the backend services. React.js is another SPA technology.
React.js and Redux	A web application using React.js and Redux for the client, and ASP.NET Core for the backend services. This time, the Redux library is used in addition to React.js.

Using .NET Standard Templates

This category includes just a single template, but it is so important to get coverage here. You can create a Class Library (.NET Standard). From now on this is the preferred class library to create. This library can be shared between .NET Framework, .NET Core, Universal Apps, Xamarin, and more technologies. You just need to pay attention to the version of the .NET Standard you select after creating this library.

.NET Standard libraries are covered in detail in Chapter 19, "Libraries, Assemblies, Packages, and NuGet."

> **NOTE** *The .NET Standard Library replaces the Portable Library. Portable Libraries are now listed as legacy in Visual Studio.*

By far this is not a full list of the Visual Studio 2017 project templates, but it reflects some of the most commonly used templates.

EXPLORING AND CODING A PROJECT

This section looks at the features that Visual Studio provides to help you add and explore code with your project. You find out about using the Solution Explorer to explore files and code, use features from the editor—such as IntelliSense and code snippets—and explore other windows, such as the Properties window and the Document Outline.

Solution Explorer

After creating a project—for example, a Console App (.NET Core) that was used mostly in earlier chapters—the most important tool you will use, other than the code editor, is the *Solution Explorer*. With this tool you can navigate through all files and items of your project, and see all the classes and members of classes.

> **NOTE** *When running a console app from within Visual Studio, there's a common misconception that it's necessary to have a* `Console.ReadLine` *method at the last line of the* `Main` *method to keep the console window open. That's not the case. You can start the application with Debug ⇨ Start without Debugging (or press Ctrl+F5) instead of Debug ⇨ Start Debugging (or F5). This keeps the window open until you press a key. Using F5 to start the application makes sense if breakpoints are set, and then Visual Studio halts at the breakpoints anyway.*

Working with Projects and Solutions

The Solution Explorer displays your projects and solutions. It's important to understand the distinction between these:

➤ A *project* is a set of all the source-code files and resources that will compile into a single assembly (or in some cases, a single module). For example, a project might be a class library or a Windows GUI application.

➤ A *solution* is the set of all the projects that make up a particular software package (application).

To understand this distinction, consider what happens when you ship a project, which consists of more than one assembly. For example, you might have a user interface, custom controls, and other components that ship as libraries of parts of the application. You might even have a different user interface for administrators, and a service that is called across the network. Each of these parts of the application might be contained in a separate assembly, and hence they are regarded by Visual Studio as separate projects. However, it is quite likely that you will be coding these projects in parallel and in conjunction with one another. Thus, it is quite useful to be able to edit them all as one single unit in Visual Studio. Visual Studio enables this by regarding all the projects as forming one solution, and treating the solution as the unit that it reads in and allows you to work on.

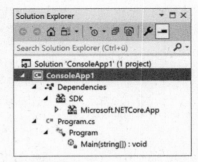

Up until now, this chapter has been loosely talking about creating a console project. In fact, in the example you are working on, Visual Studio has created a solution for you—although this particular solution contains just one project. You can see this scenario reflected in the Solution Explorer (see Figure 18-11), which contains a tree structure that defines your solution.

In this case, the project contains your source file, `Program.cs`, as well as a project configuration file, `ConsoleApp1.csproj`, which enables you to define project descriptions, versions, and dependencies.

FIGURE 18-11

The project file is not clearly seen in Solution Explorer. You just need to select the project (ConsoleApp1 in Figure 18-11) and then select Edit ConsoleApp1.csproj from the context menu (either click the Menu button on your keyboard or right-click). With .NET Core projects, you can do this without unloading the solution. When you work with other project types (for example, Universal Windows Apps), you first need to unload the solution before you edit the project file directly from within Visual Studio.

The Solution Explorer also indicates the NuGet packages and projects that your project references. You can see this by expanding the `Dependencies` folder in the Solution Explorer.

> **NOTE** *With older project types you see a* `References` *folder instead of* `Dependencies`.

If you have not changed any of the default settings in Visual Studio, you will probably find the Solution Explorer in the top-right corner of your screen. If you cannot see it, just go to the View menu and select Solution Explorer.

The solution is described by a file with the extension `.sln`; in this example, it is `ConsoleApp1.sln`. The solution file is a text file that contains information about all the projects contained within the solution, as well as global items that can be used with all contained projects.

REVEALING HIDDEN FILES

By default, Solution Explorer hides some files. By clicking the button Show All Files on the Solution Explorer toolbar, you can display all hidden files. For example, the `bin` and `obj` directories store compiled and intermediate files. Subfolders of `obj` hold various temporary or intermediate files; subfolders of `bin` hold the compiled assemblies.

Adding Projects to a Solution

As you work through the following sections, you see how Visual Studio works with Windows apps and console apps. To that end, you create a Windows project called `SimpleApp` that you add to your current solution, `ConsoleApp1`.

> **NOTE** *Creating the* `SimpleApp` *project means that you end up with a solution containing a UWP app and a console app. That is not a very common scenario—you are more likely to have one application and several libraries—but it enables you to see more code! You might, however, create a solution like this if, for example, you are writing a utility that you want to run either as a UWP app or as a command-line utility, or you need some extra command-line features with your app.*

You can create the new project in several ways. One way is to select New ⇨ Project from the File menu (as you have done already), or you can select Add ⇨ New Project from the File menu. Selecting Add ⇨ New Project from the File menu brings up the familiar Add New Project dialog; as shown in Figure 18-12, however, Visual Studio wants to create the new project in the preexisting `ConsoleApp1` location of the solution.

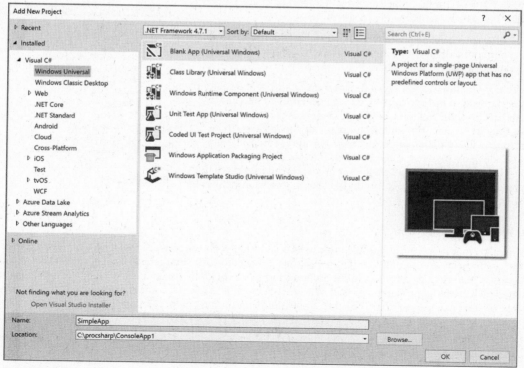

FIGURE 18-12

If you select this option, a new project is added, so the `ConsoleApp1` solution now contains a console application and a Blank App (Universal Windows).

> **NOTE** *In accordance with Visual Studio's language independence, the new project does not need to be a C# project. It is perfectly acceptable to put a C# project, a Visual Basic project, and a C++ project in the same solution. We will stick with C# here because this is a C# book!*

With the platform versions, select Target and Minimum versions that are installed on your system. You can select the latest version for both the Target and the Minimum version (see Figure 18-13).

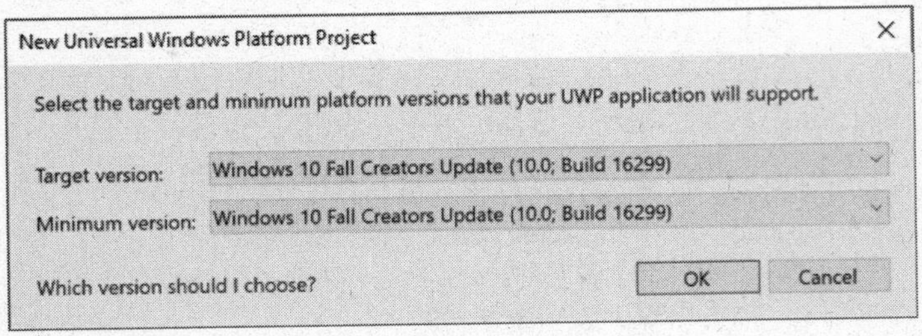

New Universal Windows Platform Project   ×

Select the target and minimum platform versions that your UWP application will support.

Target version: Windows 10 Fall Creators Update (10.0; Build 16299)   ˅

Minimum version: Windows 10 Fall Creators Update (10.0; Build 16299)   ˅

Which version should I choose?   OK   Cancel

FIGURE 18-13

Of course, this means that `ConsoleApp1` is not really an appropriate name for the solution anymore. To change the name, you can right-click the name of the solution and select Rename from the context menu. Call the new solution `DemoSolution`. The Solution Explorer window should now look like Figure 18-14.

As you can see, Visual Studio has made your newly added UWP project automatically reference some of the extra base classes that are important for UWP functionality.

Note that if you look in Windows Explorer, the name of the solution file has changed to `DemoSolution.sln`. In general, if you want to rename any files, the Solution Explorer window is the best place to do so, because Visual Studio then automatically updates any references to that file in the other project files. If you rename files using only Windows Explorer, you might break the solution because Visual Studio is not able to locate all the files it needs to read into the IDE. As a result, you need to manually edit the project and solution files to update the file references.

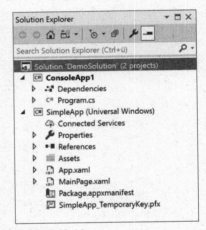

FIGURE 18-14

Setting the Startup Project

Bear in mind that if you have multiple projects in a solution, you need to configure which one should run as the startup project. You can also configure multiple projects to start simultaneously. There are a lot of ways to do this. After selecting a project in the Solution Explorer, the context menu offers a Set as Startup Project option, which enables one startup project at a time. You can also use the context menu Debug ⇨ Start new instance to start one project after the other. To simultaneously start more than one project, click the solution in the Solution Explorer and select the context menu Set Startup Projects. This opens the dialog shown in Figure 18-15. After you check Multiple Startup Projects, you can define what projects should be started.

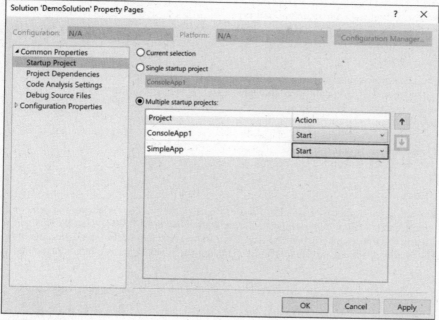

FIGURE 18-15

Discovering Types and Members

A UWP application contains a lot more initial code than a console application when Visual Studio first creates it. That is because creating a window is an intrinsically more complex process. Chapter 34, "Patterns with XAML Apps," discusses the code for a UWP application in detail. For now, have a look at the XAML code in `MainPage.xaml` and in the C# source code `MainPage.xaml.cs`. There's also some hidden generated C# code. Iterating through the tree in the Solution Explorer, below `MainPage.xaml.cs` you find the class `MainPage`. With all the code files, the Solution Explorer shows the types within that file. Within the type `MainPage` you can see the members of the class. `_contentLoaded` is a field of type `bool`. Clicking this field opens the file `MainPage.g.i.cs`. This file—a part of the `MainPage` class—is generated by the designer and contains initialization code.

Previewing Items

A feature offered by the Solution Explorer is the button to Preview Selected Items. When this button is enabled, and you click an item in the Solution Explorer, the editor for this item opens, as usual. However, if the item was not opened previously, the tab flow of the editor shows the new opened item in the rightmost position. Now, when you click another item, the previously opened one is closed. This helps significantly with reducing the number of open items.

In the editor tab of the previewed item is the Keep Open button, which promotes the item to stay open even when another item is clicked; the tab for the item that you're keeping open moves to the left.

Using Scopes

Setting scopes allows you to focus on a specific part of the solution. The list of items shown by the Solution Explorer can grow huge. For example, opening the context menu of a type enables you to select the base type from the menu Base Types. Here you can see the complete inheritance hierarchy of the type, as shown in Figure 18-16.

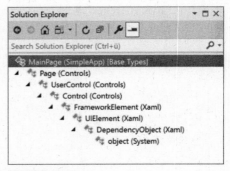

Because Solution Explorer contains more information than you can easily view with one screen, you can open multiple Solution Explorer windows at once with the menu option New Solution Explorer View, and you can set the scope to a specific element—for example, to a project or a class—by selecting Scope to This from the context menu. To return to the previous scope, click the Back button.

FIGURE 18-16

Adding Items to a Project

Directly from within Solution Explorer you can add different items to the project. Selecting the project and selecting the context menu Add ⇨ New Item opens the dialog shown in Figure 18-17. Another way to get to the same dialog is by using the main menu Project ⇨ Add New Item. Here you find many different categories, such as code items to add classes or interfaces, items for using the ASP.NET Core or other technologies, and a lot more.

Managing References and Dependencies

Adding references with Visual Studio needs some special considerations because of differences with project types. Depending on the project type, you see Dependencies or References in the Solution Explorer. Opening the context menu while clicking on this item, you can see the Add References menu item to open the Reference Manager.

The Reference Manager, shown in Figure 18-18, enables you to add references to other projects in the same solution, add references to shared projects in the same solution, and browse for assemblies.

> **NOTE** *Shared projects enable you to share code between different technologies without creating a library. This feature is covered in Chapter 19.*

Depending on the project types you're adding references to, the Reference Manager gives different options. With .NET Framework projects, you can also reference shared assemblies and COM objects.

When you're creating Universal Windows Platform apps, you can reference Universal Windows Extensions, for example API extensions available with Windows IoT or Windows Mobile, as shown in Figure 18-19.

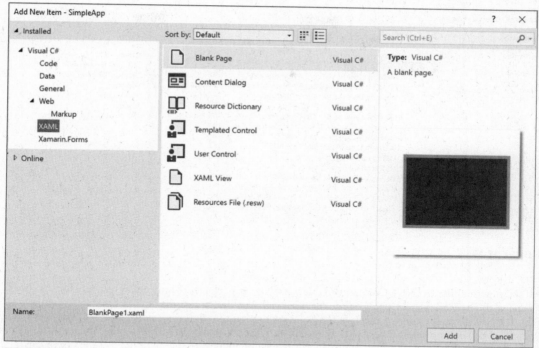

FIGURE 18-17

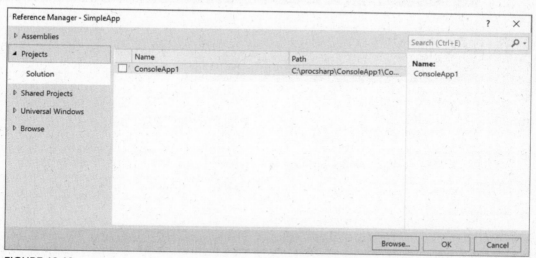

FIGURE 18-18

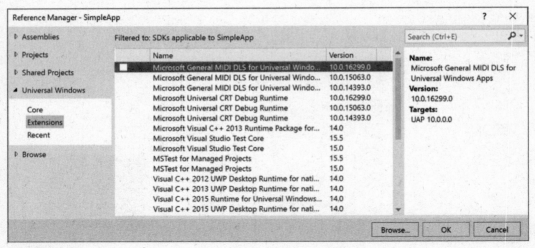

FIGURE 18-19

All the functionality of .NET Core is available with NuGet packages. Many enhancements for the .NET Framework are available with NuGet packages as well. You can access the NuGet Package Manager (see Figure 18-20) from the context menu in the Solution Explorer, or you can select Project ⇨ Manage NuGet Packages. You can browse for new packages to install, see the packages installed, and update installed packages. Figure 18-20 shows an indication that a package update is available with the installed packages.

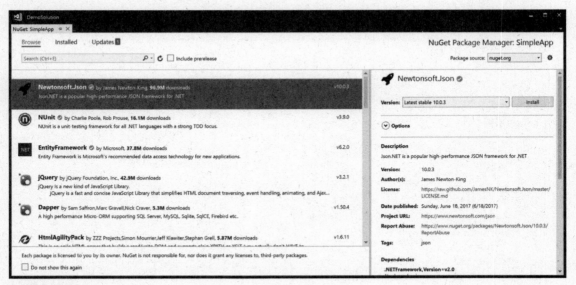

FIGURE 18-20

You can configure the sources of NuGet packages by opening the Options dialog by selecting Tools ⇨ Options. In the Options dialog select the NuGet Package Manager ⇨ Package Sources in the tree view (see Figure 18-21). By default, Microsoft's NuGet server is configured, but you can also configure other NuGet servers or your own. With .NET Core and ASP.NET Core 1.0, Microsoft offers feeds with NuGet packages that are updated on a daily basis.

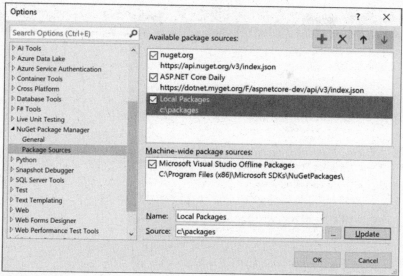

FIGURE 18-21

Using the NuGet Package Manager, you can not only select the package source, but you can also select a filter to see all packages that are installed, or where an upgrade is available, and search for packages on the server.

> **NOTE** *With ASP.NET Core, JavaScript libraries are no longer used from NuGet server. Instead, JavaScript package managers, such as NPM and Bower, are directly supported from within Visual Studio 2017. This is discussed in Chapter 30.*

Another option you have with dependencies or references is the menu Add Connected Service. This opens the dialog as shown in Figure 18-22, which allows easily adding specific features to your applications. Selecting one of these packages adds NuGet packages, makes some configuration changes in the app, and usually opens a web page to help what needs to be done next. You can access more Connected Services via the Find More Services... link in this dialog.

Working with the Code Editor

The Visual Studio code editor is where most of your development work takes place. This editor increased in size in Visual Studio after the removal of some toolbars from the default configuration, and the removal of borders from the menus, toolbars, and tab headers. The following sections look at some of the most useful features of this editor.

The Folding Editor

One notable feature of Visual Studio is its use of a folding editor as its default code editor. Figure 18-23 shows the code for the console application that you generated earlier. Notice the little minus signs on the left-hand side of the window. These signs mark the points where the editor assumes that a new block of code (or documentation comment) begins. You can click these icons to close the view of the corresponding block of code just as you would close a node in a tree control (see Figure 18-24).

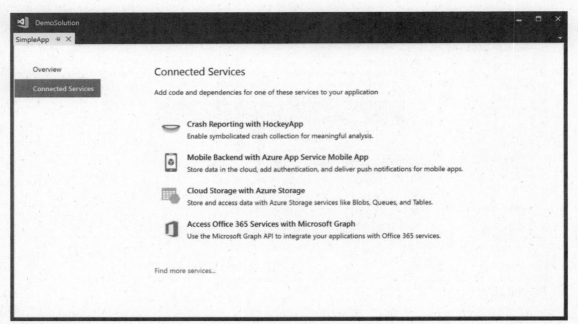

FIGURE 18-22

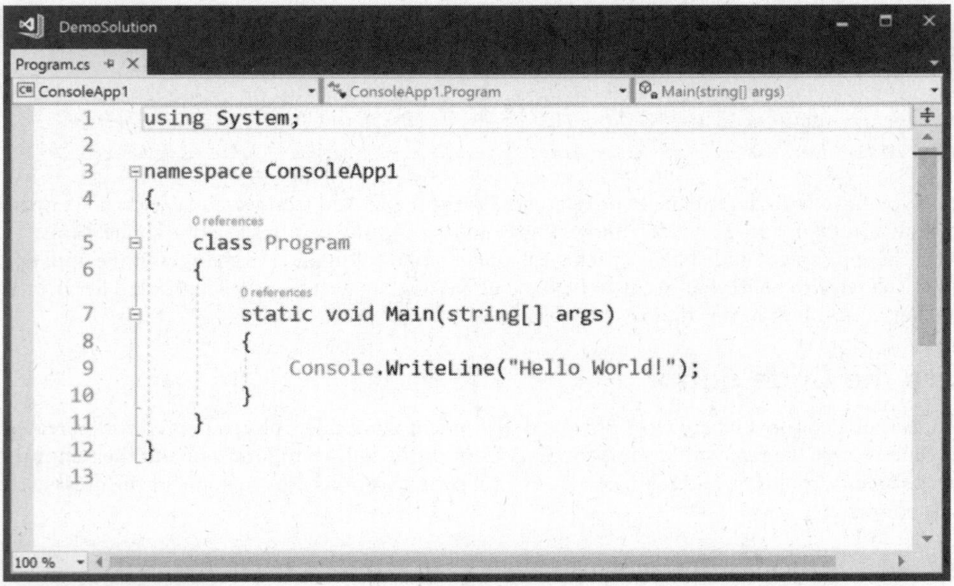

```csharp
using System;

namespace ConsoleApp1
{
    class Program
    {
        static void Main(string[] args)
        {
            Console.WriteLine("Hello World!");
        }
    }
}
```

FIGURE 18-23

DemoSolution
Program.cs
ConsoleApp1
ConsoleApp1.Program
Main(string[] args)
using System;
namespace ConsoleApp1
{
0 references
class Program...
}
100 %

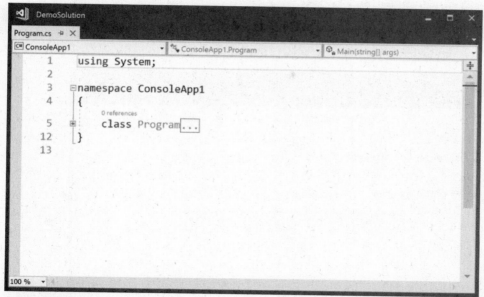

FIGURE 18-24

This means that while you are editing you can focus on just the areas of code you want to look at, hiding the bits of code you are not interested in working with at that moment. If you do not like the way the editor has chosen to block off your code, you can indicate your own blocks of collapsible code with the C# preprocessor directives, `#region` and `#endregion`. For example, to collapse the code inside the `Main` method, you would add the code shown in Figure 18-25.

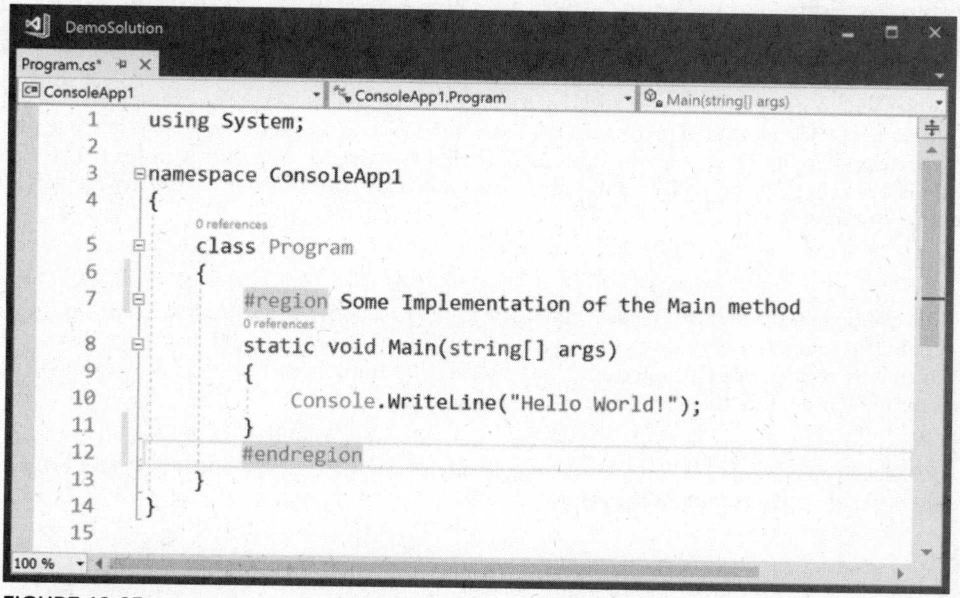

DemoSolution
Program.cs*
ConsoleApp1
ConsoleApp1.Program
Main(string[] args)
using System;
namespace ConsoleApp1
{
0 references
class Program
{
#region Some Implementation of the Main method
0 references
static void Main(string[] args)
{
Console.WriteLine("Hello World!");
}
#endregion
}
}
100 %

FIGURE 18-25

The code editor automatically detects the #region block and places a new minus sign by the #region directive, enabling you to close the region. Enclosing this code in a region enables the editor to close it (see Figure 18-26), marking the area with the comment you specified in the #region directive. The compiler, however, ignores the directives and compiles the Main method as normal.

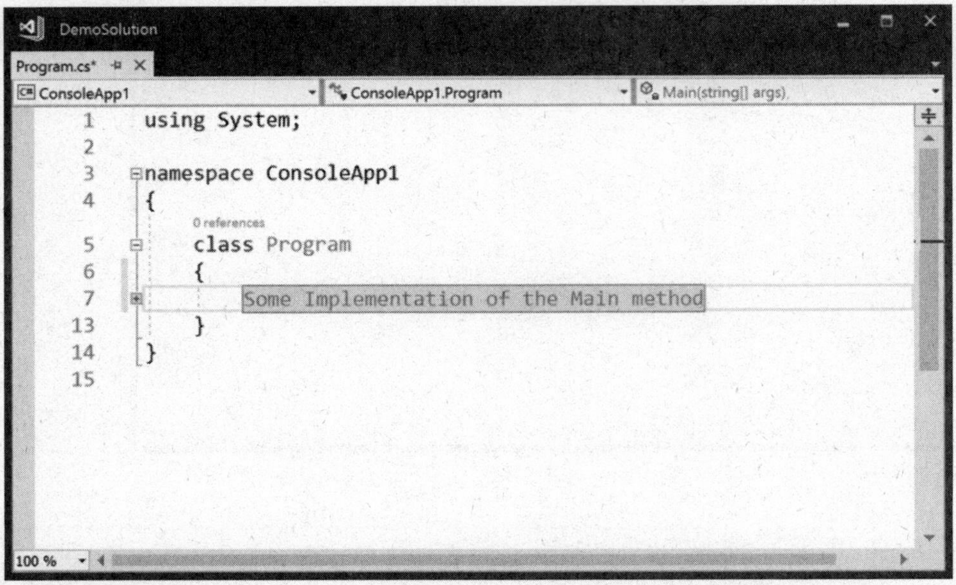

FIGURE 18-26

Navigating Within the Editor

On the top line of the editor are three combo boxes. The right combo box enables you to navigate between members of the type you're in. The middle combo box enables you to navigate between types. The left combo box enables you to navigate between different applications or frameworks. For example, if you are working on the source code of a shared project, in the left combo box of the editor you can select one of the projects where the shared project is used to see the code that is active for the selected project. The code that is not compiled for the selected project is dimmed. You can create code segments for different platforms using C# preprocessor commands.

IntelliSense

In addition to the folding editor feature, Visual Studio's code editor also incorporates Microsoft's popular *IntelliSense* capability, which not only saves you typing but also ensures that you use the correct parameters. IntelliSense remembers your preferred choices and starts with these initially instead of at the beginning of the sometimes rather lengthy lists that IntelliSense can now provide.

The code editor also performs some syntax checking on your code, underlining these errors with a short wavy line, even before you compile the code. Hovering the mouse pointer over the underlined text brings up a small box that contains a description of the error.

CodeLens

Did you ever change a method and wonder, "Did I miss a method calling this?" With the CodeLens it's easy to find callers. The number of references is directly shown in the editor (see Figure 18-27). When you click the references link, the CodeLens opens so you can see the code of the callers and navigate to them.

FIGURE 18-27

If the source code is checked into a source control system like Visual Studio Online using Git or TFS, you can also see the authors and changes made. If you're using unit tests (covered in Chapter 28), you can see the number of successful and failing test runs, and you can immediately switch to detailed information.

> **NOTE** *The CodeLens is not available in the Visual Studio Community edition.*

Using Code Snippets

Great productivity features from the code editor are *code snippets*. Just by writing cw<tab><tab> in the editor, the editor creates a Console.WriteLine();. Visual Studio comes with many code snippets, including the following:

➤ do, for, forr, foreach, and while for creating loops

➤ equals for an implementation of the Equals method

➤ attribute and exception for creating Attribute- and Exception-derived types

You can see all the code snippets available with the Code Snippets Manager (see Figure 18-28) by selecting Tools ⇨ Code Snippets Manager. You can also create custom snippets.

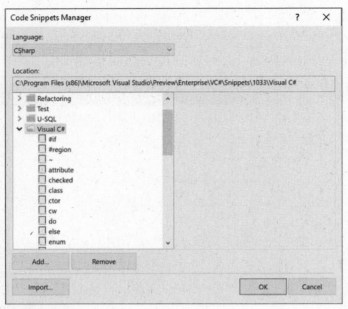

FIGURE 18-28

EditorConfig

Visual Studio supports different coding styles. With earlier editions of Visual Studio, you could configure your environment for a coding style. However, when you work with different projects, you might need different coding styles. EditorConfig supports different coding styles if you configure the Follow Project Coding Conventions option in Tools ⇨ Options ⇨ Text Editor ⇨ General.

To use EditorConfig you can add `.editorconfig` files to the project directory or a subdirectory. The configuration applies for all the source code files in this directory and subdirectories. In subdirectories, you can add more `.editorconfig` files that overrule the configuration from a parent directory.

The `.editorconfig` file used by the ASP.NET Core MVC team is shown in the following code snippet. With this file you can define the indent size based on different file extensions, and you can also define coding guidelines—for example, if var should be preferred or disallowed, if the this qualifier should or should not be used, if C# defined types should be preferred to .NET types, if throw expressions should be allowed, and so on. With these settings, you can define whether the editor should generate a suggestion, a warning, or an error:

```
# EditorConfig is awesome:http://EditorConfig.org

# top-most EditorConfig file
root = true

# Don't use tabs for indentation.
[*]
indent_style = space
# (Please don't specify an indent_size here; that has too many unintended
# consequences.)

# Code files
[*.{cs,csx,vb,vbx}]
indent_size = 4
```

```
# Xml project files
[*.{csproj,vbproj,vcxproj,vcxproj.filters,proj,projitems,shproj}]
indent_size = 2

# Xml config files
[*.{props,targets,ruleset,config,nuspec,resx,vsixmanifest,vsct}]
indent_size = 2

# JSON files
[*.json]
indent_size = 2

# Dotnet code style settings:
[*.cs]
# Sort using and Import directives with System.* appearing first
dotnet_sort_system_directives_first = true

# Don't use this. qualifier
dotnet_style_qualification_for_field = false:suggestion
dotnet_style_qualification_for_property = false:suggestion

# use int x = .. over Int32
dotnet_style_predefined_type_for_locals_parameters_members = true:suggestion

# use int.MaxValue over Int32.MaxValue
dotnet_style_predefined_type_for_member_access = true:suggestion

# Require var all the time.
csharp_style_var_for_built_in_types = true:suggestion
csharp_style_var_when_type_is_apparent = true:suggestion
csharp_style_var_elsewhere = true:suggestion

# Disallow throw expressions.
csharp_style_throw_expression = false:suggestion

# Newline settings
csharp_new_line_before_open_brace = all
csharp_new_line_before_else = true
csharp_new_line_before_catch = true
csharp_new_line_before_finally = true
csharp_new_line_before_members_in_object_initializers = true
csharp_new_line_before_members_in_anonymous_types = true
```

Using this `.editorconfig` file, you can see a suggestion by typing `int x = 42` as shown in Figure 18-29. Pay attention because you might need to re-open your source code after changing `.editorconfig` to have the new configuration activated.

> **NOTE** *You can get details about the file format, plugins for various editors, the editorconfig project page, and more on* http://editorconfig.org.

Learning and Understanding Other Windows

In addition to the code editor and Solution Explorer, Visual Studio provides other windows that enable you to view and/or manage your projects from different points of view.

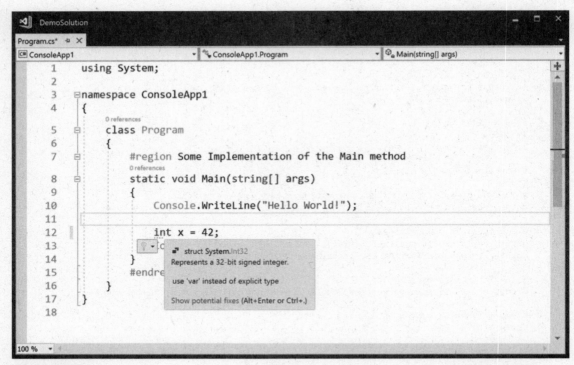

FIGURE 18-29

> **NOTE** *The rest of this section describes several other windows. If any of these windows are not visible on your monitor, you can select them from the View menu. To show the design view and code editor, right-click the filename in Solution Explorer and select View Designer or View Code from the context menu, or select the item from the toolbar at the top of Solution Explorer. The design view and code editor share the same tabbed window.*

Using the Design View Window

If you are designing a user interface application, such as a Windows app, or a Class Library (Universal Windows), you can use the Design View window. This window presents a visual overview of what your form will look like. You normally use the Design View window in conjunction with a window known as the *toolbox*. The toolbox contains many .NET components that you can drag onto your program. Toolbox components vary according to project type. Figure 18-30 shows the items displayed within a Windows app.

FIGURE 18-30

To add your own custom categories to the toolbox, execute the following steps:

1. Right-click any category.
2. Select Add Tab from the context menu.

You can move your code snippets to the items in the toolbox, so you can easily access them. You can also place other tools in the toolbox by selecting Choose Items from the same context menu; this is particularly useful for adding your own custom components or Universal Windows Components that are not present in the toolbox by default, as shown in Figure 18-31.

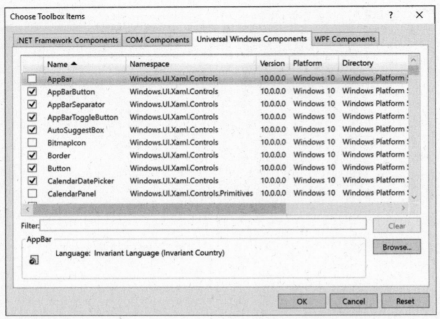

FIGURE 18-31

Using the Properties Window

As mentioned in the first part of the book, .NET classes can implement properties. The Properties window is available with projects and files and when you're selecting items using the Design view. Figure 18-32 shows the Properties view with a control of a Windows app.

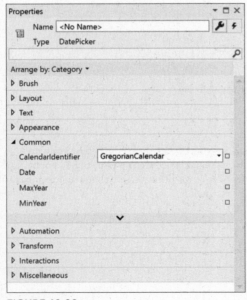

FIGURE 18-32

With this window you can see all the properties of an item and configure it accordingly. You can change some properties by entering text in a text box; others have predefined selections, and some have a custom editor. You can also add event handlers to events with the Properties window.

Using the Class View Window

Although the Solution Explorer can show classes and members of classes, that's normally the job of the Class View (see Figure 18-33). To invoke the class view, select View ⇨ Class View. The Class View shows the hierarchy of the namespaces and classes in your code. It provides a tree view that you can expand to see which namespaces contain what classes, and what classes contain what members.

FIGURE 18-33

A nice feature of the Class View is that if you right-click the name of any item for which you have access to the source code, then the context menu displays the Go To Definition option, which takes you to the definition of the item in the code editor. Alternatively, you can do this by double-clicking the item in Class View (or, indeed, by right-clicking the item you want in the source code editor and choosing the same option from the resulting context menu). The context menu also enables you to add a field, method, property, or indexer to a class. In other words, you specify the details for the relevant member in a dialog, and the code is added for you. This feature can be particularly useful for adding properties and indexers, as it can save you quite a bit of typing.

Using the Object Browser Window

An important aspect of programming in the .NET environment is being able to find out what methods and other code items are available in the base classes and any other libraries that you are referencing from your assembly. This feature is available through a window called the Object Browser (see Figure 18-34). You can access this window by selecting Object Browser from the View menu in Visual Studio 2017. With this tool you can browse for and select existing component sets—such as .NET Framework versions from 4 to 4.7.1, what's available with the Windows Runtime, and .NET for UWP—and view the classes and members of the classes that are available with this subset. You can select the Windows Runtime by selecting Universal Windows in the Browse drop-down to find all namespaces, types, and methods of this native new API for UWP apps.

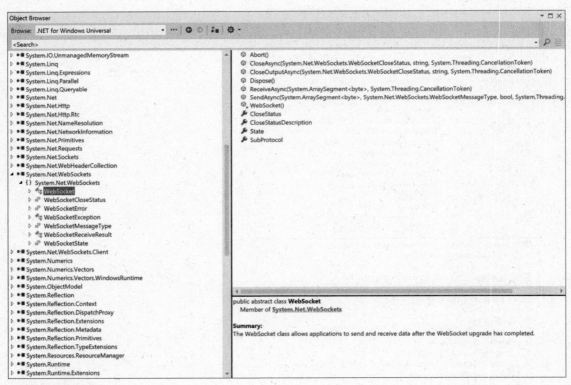

FIGURE 18-34

> **NOTE** *Don't be annoyed with the Object Browser that many selections offered from the drop-down list don't show any results. This is by design.*

Using the Server Explorer Window

You can use the Server Explorer window, shown in Figure 18-35, to find out about aspects of the computers in your network while coding. With the Servers section, you can find information about services running (which is extremely useful in developing Windows Services), create new performance counts, and access the event logs. The Data Connections section enables not only connecting to existing databases and querying data, but also creating a new database. Visual Studio 2017 also has a lot of Microsoft Azure information built in to Server Explorer, including options for App Services, Virtual Machines, Notifications, Storage, and more.

Using the Cloud Explorer

The Cloud Explorer (see Figure 18-36) is an explorer that is available with Visual Studio 2017 if you install the Azure SDK. With the Cloud Explorer you can get access to your Microsoft Azure subscription and have access to your resources, view log files, attach debuggers, start and stop services, go directly to the Azure portal, and start debug sessions.

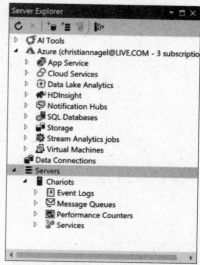

FIGURE 18-35

Using the Document Outline

A window available with WPF and UWP apps is the Document Outline. Figure 18-37 shows this window opened with an application from Bonus Chapter 1, "Composition," which you can find online. Here, you can view the logical structure and hierarchy of the XAML elements, lock elements to prevent changing them unintentionally, easily move elements within the hierarchy, group elements within a new container element, and change layout types.

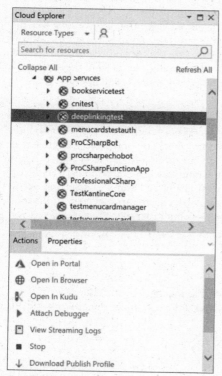

FIGURE 18-36

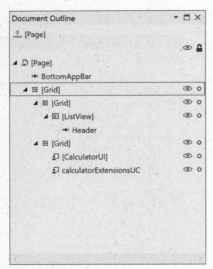

FIGURE 18-37

With this tool you can also create XAML templates and graphically edit data binding.

Arranging Windows

While exploring Visual Studio, you might have noticed that many of the windows have some interesting functionality that's more reminiscent of toolbars. In particular, they can all either float (also on a second display), or they can be docked. When they are docked, they display an extra icon that looks like a pin next to the minimize button in the top-right corner of each window. This icon really does act like a pin—you can use it to pin the window open. A pinned window (the pin is displayed vertically) behaves just like the regular windows you are used to. When windows are unpinned (the pin is displayed horizontally), however, they remain open only as long as they have the focus. As soon as they lose the focus (because you clicked or moved your mouse somewhere else), they smoothly retreat into the main border around the entire Visual Studio application. Pinning and unpinning windows provides another way to make the best use of the limited space on your screen.

A feature with Visual Studio 2017 is that you can store different layouts. It's likely that you're running in different environments. For example, in your office you might have connected your laptop to two big screens, but this is not the case when you're programming in a plane, where you only have a single screen. In the past, you probably always arranged the windows according to your needs and had to change this several times a day. Another scenario in which you might need different layouts is when you're doing web development and creating UWP and Xamarin apps. Now you can save your layout and easily switch from one to the other. From the Window menu, select Save Window Layout to save your current arrangement of the tools. Use Window ➪ Apply Window Layout to select one of your saved layouts to arrange the windows as you have saved them.

BUILDING A PROJECT

Visual Studio is not only about coding your projects. It is an IDE that manages the full life cycle of your project, including the building or compiling of your solutions. This section examines the options that Visual Studio provides for building your project.

Building, Compiling, and Making Code

Before examining the various build options, it is important to clarify some terminology. You will often see three different terms used in connection with the process of getting from your source code to some sort of executable code: *compiling*, *building*, and *making*. The origin of these three terms reflects the fact that until recently, the process of getting from source code to executable code involved more than one step (this is still the case in C++). This was due in large part to the number of source files in a program.

In C++, for example, each source file needs to be compiled individually. This results in what are known as *object files*, each containing something like executable code, but where each object file relates to only one source file. To generate an executable, these object files need to be linked together, a process that is officially known as *linking*. The combined process was usually referred to—at least on the Windows platform—as building your code. However, in C# terms the compiler is more sophisticated, able to read in and treat all your source files as one block. Hence, there is not really a separate linking stage, so in the context of C#, the terms *compile* and *build* are used interchangeably.

The term *make* basically means the same thing as *build*, although it is not really used in the context of C#. The term *make* originated on old mainframe systems on which, when a project was composed of many source files, a separate file would be written containing instructions to the compiler on how to build a project—which files to include and what libraries to link to, and so on. This file was generally known as a *makefile* and it is still quite standard on UNIX systems. The MSBuild project file something like the old makefile; it's just a new advanced XML variant. With MSBuild projects, you can use the `MSBuild` command with the project file as input, and all the sources will be compiled. Using build files is very helpful on a separate build server on which all developers check their code in, and overnight the build process is done. Chapter 1 mentions the .NET Core command line (CLI) tools, the command line to build with the .NET Core environment, which now uses MSBuild behind the scenes.

Debugging and Release Builds

The idea of having separate builds is very familiar to C++ developers, and to a lesser degree to those with a Visual Basic background. The point here is that when you are debugging, you typically want your executable to behave differently from when you are ready to ship the software. When you are ready to ship your software, you want the executable to be as small and fast as possible. Unfortunately, these two requirements are not compatible with your needs when you are debugging code, as explained in the following sections.

Optimization

High performance is achieved partly by the compiler's many optimizations of the code. This means that the compiler actively looks at your source code as it is compiling to identify places where it can modify the precise details of what you are doing in a way that does not change the overall effect but makes things more efficient. For example, suppose the compiler encountered the following source code:

```
double InchesToCm(double ins) => ins * 2.54;
// later on in the code
Y = InchesToCm(X);
```

It might replace it with this:

```
Y = X * 2.54;
```

Similarly, it might replace

```
{
    string message = "Hi";
    Console.WriteLine(message);
}
```

with this:

```
Console.WriteLine("Hi");
```

By doing so, the compiler bypasses having to declare any unnecessary object reference in the process.

It is not possible to exactly pin down what optimizations the C# compiler does—nor whether the two previous examples would occur with any particular situation—because those kinds of details are not documented. (Chances are good that for managed languages such as C#, the previous optimizations would occur at JIT compilation time, not when the C# compiler compiles source code to assembly.) Obviously, for proprietary reasons, companies that write compilers are usually quite reluctant to provide many details about the tricks that their compilers use. Note that optimizations do not affect your source code—they affect only the contents of the executable code. However, the previous examples should give you a good idea of what to expect from optimizations.

The problem is that although optimizations like the examples just shown help a great deal in making your code run faster, they are detrimental for debugging. In the first example, suppose that you want to set a breakpoint inside the InchesToCm method to see what is going on in there. How can you possibly do that if the executable code does not actually have an InchesToCm method because the compiler has removed it? Moreover, how can you set a watch on the Message variable when that does not exist in the compiled code either?

Debugger Symbols

During debugging, you often have to look at the values of variables, and you specify them by their source code names. The trouble is that executable code generally does not contain those names—the compiler replaces the names with memory addresses. .NET has modified this situation somewhat to the extent that certain items in assemblies are stored with their names, but this is true of only a small minority of items—such as public classes and methods—and those names will still be removed when the assembly is JIT-compiled. Asking the debugger to tell you the value in the variable called HeightInInches is not going to get you very far if, when the debugger examines the executable code, it sees only addresses and no reference to the name HeightInInches anywhere.

Therefore, to debug properly, you need to make extra debugging information available in the executable. This information includes, among other things, names of variables and line information that enables the debugger to match up which executable machine assembly language instructions correspond to your original source code instructions. You will not, however, want that information in a release build, both for proprietary reasons (debugging information makes it a lot easier for other people to disassemble your code) and because it increases the size of the executable.

Extra Source Code Debugging Commands

A related issue is that quite often while you are debugging there will be extra lines in your code to display crucial debugging-related information. Obviously, you want the relevant commands removed entirely from the executable before you ship the software. You could do this manually, but wouldn't it be so much easier if you could simply mark those statements in some way so that the compiler ignores them when it is compiling your code to be shipped? You've already seen in the first part of the book how this can be done in C# by defining a suitable processor symbol, and possibly using this in conjunction with the Conditional attribute, giving you what is known as *conditional compilation*.

What all these factors add up to is that you need to compile almost all commercial software in a slightly different way when debugging than in the final product that is shipped. Visual Studio can handle this because, as you have already seen, it stores details about all the options it is supposed to pass to the compiler when it has your code compiled. All that Visual Studio must do to support different types of builds is store more than one set of such details. These different sets of build information are referred to as *configurations*. When you create a project, Visual Studio automatically gives you two configurations—Debug and Release:

> ➤ **Debug**—This configuration commonly specifies that no optimizations are to take place, extra debugging information is to be present in the executable, and the compiler is to assume that the debug preprocessor symbol Debug is present unless it is explicitly #undefined in the source code.

> **Release**—This configuration specifies that the compiler should optimize the compilation, that there should be no extra debugging information in the executable, and that the compiler should not assume that any particular preprocessor symbol is present.

You can define your own configurations as well. You might want to do this, for example, to set up professional-level builds and enterprise-level builds so that you can ship two versions of the software. In the past, because of issues related to Unicode character encodings being supported on Windows NT but not on Windows 95, it was common for C++ projects to feature a Unicode configuration and an MBCS (multi-byte character set) configuration.

Selecting a Configuration

At this point you might be wondering how Visual Studio, given that it stores details about more than one configuration, determines which one to use when arranging for a project to be built. The answer is that there is always an active configuration, which is the configuration that is used when you ask Visual Studio to build a project. (Note that configurations are set for each project, rather than each solution.)

By default, when you create a project, the Debug configuration is the active configuration. You can change which configuration is the active one by clicking the Build menu option and selecting the Configuration Manager item. It is also available through a drop-down menu in the main Visual Studio toolbar.

Editing Configurations

In addition to choosing the active configuration, you can also examine and edit the configurations. To do this, select the relevant project in Solution Explorer and then select Properties from the Project menu. This brings up a sophisticated dialog. (Alternatively, you can access the same dialog by right-clicking the name of the project in Solution Explorer and then selecting Properties from the context menu.)

This dialog contains a tabbed view that enables you to select many different general areas to examine or edit. Space does not permit showing these areas, but this section outlines a couple of the most important ones.

Depending on the project type, the options available are very different. First, look at the properties of the Universal Windows application in Figure 18-38, which shows a tabbed view of the available properties. This screenshot shows the general Application settings.

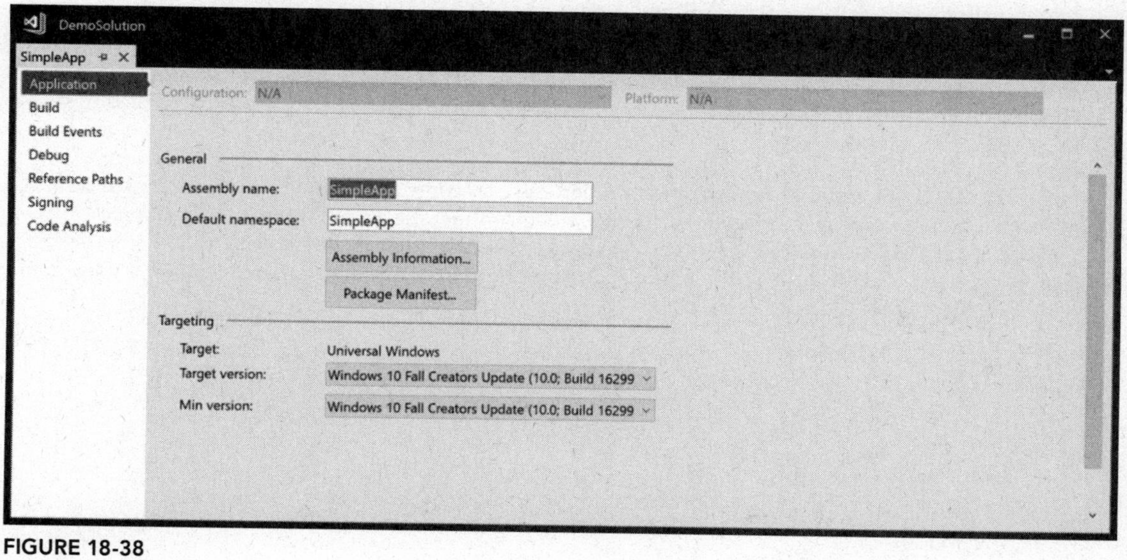

FIGURE 18-38

Among the points to note are that you can select the name of the assembly as well as the default namespace generated with the new items. By clicking the Assembly Information button, you can enter version numbers, title, description, company, and other information. Clicking the Package Manifest button switches to the Package Manifest editor covered in Chapter 33.

Figure 18-39 shows the same configuration for a .NET Core Console application. You also can see Application settings, but this screen looks different. Assembly name and default namespace are also configurable, but here you can select the version of the target framework, the output type of the app, and a startup object in case you have multiple Main methods.

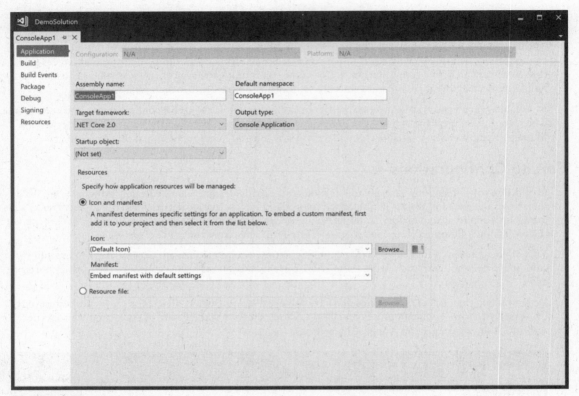

FIGURE 18-39

Figure 18-40 shows the build configuration properties of the Universal Windows app. Note that a list box near the top of the dialog enables you to specify which configuration you want to look at. You can see—in the case of the Debug configuration—that the compiler assumes that the DEBUG and TRACE preprocessor symbols have been defined. In addition, the code is not optimized, extra debug information is generated, and the .NET Native tool chain is not used.

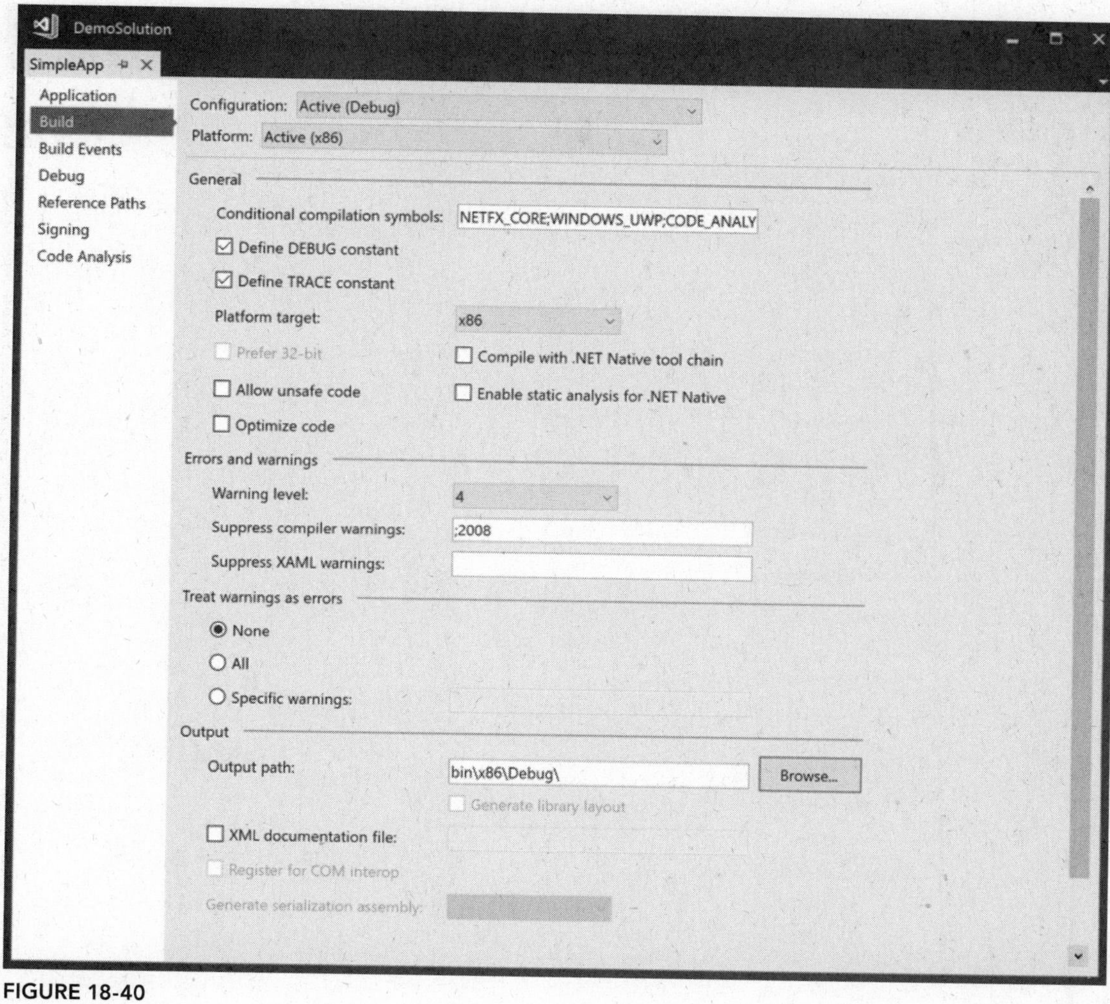

FIGURE 18-40

Figure 18-41 shows the build configuration properties of a .NET Core project. Again, in the debug configuration, code is not optimized, and DEBUG and TRACE preprocessor symbols have been defined.

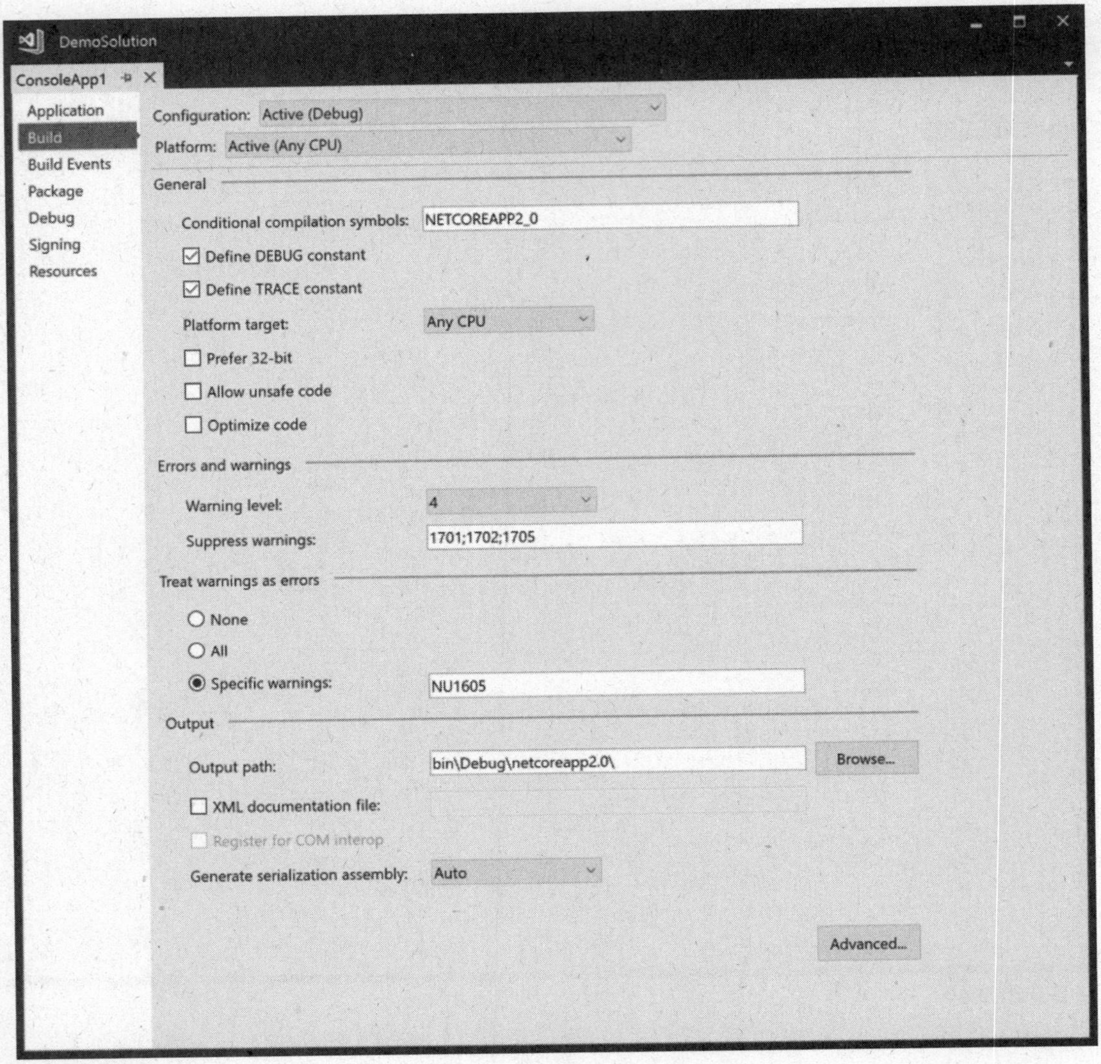

FIGURE 18-41

DEBUGGING YOUR CODE

At this point, you are ready to run and debug the application. In C#, the main technique involved in debugging is simply setting breakpoints and using them to examine what is going on in your code at a certain point in its execution.

Setting Breakpoints

You can set breakpoints from Visual Studio on any line of your code that is executed. The simplest way is to click the line in the code editor, within the shaded area near the far left of the document window (or press the F9 key when the appropriate line is selected). This sets up a breakpoint on that line, which pauses execution and transfers control to the debugger as soon as that line is reached in the execution process. A breakpoint is indicated by a red circle to the left of the line in the code editor. Visual Studio also highlights the line by displaying the text and background in a different color. Clicking the circle again removes the breakpoint.

If breaking every time at a particular line is not adequate for your problem, you can also set conditional breakpoints. To do this, select Debug ⇨ Windows ⇨ Breakpoints. This brings up a dialog that requests details about the breakpoint you want to set. When you click the Settings of a breakpoint (see Figure 18-42), you can do the following:

➤ Specify conditions—for example, you can specify to hit the breakpoint only if a conditional expression returns true. You can also specify a hit count to break a loop that has been passed a certain number of times.

➤ Set actions to log a message to the Output Window and continue execution.

With this dialog you also have the option to export and import breakpoint settings, which is useful for working with different breakpoint arrangements depending on what scenario you want to debug into, and to store the debug settings.

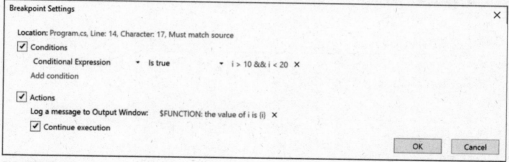

FIGURE 18-42

Using Data Tips and Debugger Visualizers

After a breakpoint has been hit, you will usually want to investigate the values of variables. The simplest way to do this is to hover the mouse cursor over the name of the variable in the code editor. This causes a little *data tip* box (shown in Figure 18-43) that shows the value of that variable to pop up, which can also be expanded for greater detail.

Some of the values shown in the data tip offer a magnifying glass. Clicking this magnifying class provides one or more options to use a *debugger visualizer*—depending on the type. Figure 18-44 shows the JSON Visualizer, which displays JSON content. Several other visualizers are available as well, such as HTML, XML, and Text visualizers.

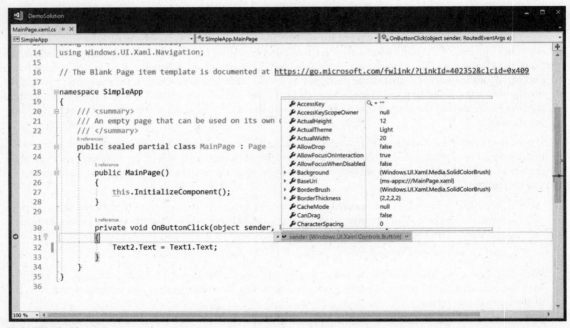

FIGURE 18-43

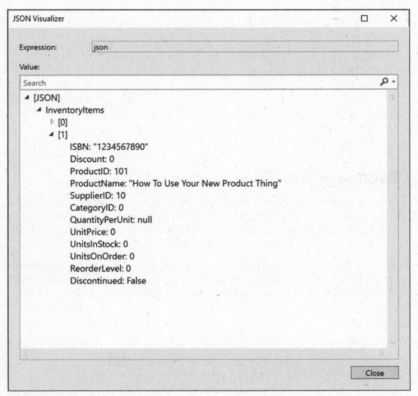

FIGURE 18-44

Live Visual Tree

A feature of Visual Studio 2017 offered for XAML-based applications is the Live Visual Tree. While debugging a UWP and WPF application, you can open the Live Visual Tree (see Figure 18-45) via Debug ⇨ Windows ⇨ Live Visual Tree to see the live tree of the XAML elements including its properties in the Live Property Explorer. Using this window, you can click the Selection button to select an element in the UI to see its element in the live tree. In the Live Property Explorer, you can directly change properties, and see the results on the running application.

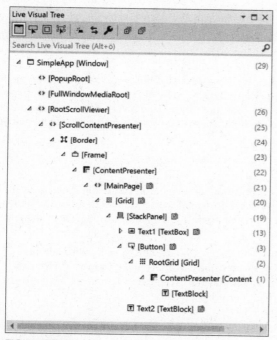

FIGURE 18-45

Monitoring and Changing Variables

Sometimes you might prefer a more continuous look at values. For that you can use the *Autos*, *Locals*, and *Watch* windows to examine the contents of variables. Each of these windows is designed to monitor different variables:

➤ **Autos**—Monitors the last few variables that have been accessed as the program was executing.

➤ **Locals**—Monitors variables that are accessible in the method currently being executed.

➤ **Watch**—Monitors any variables that you have explicitly specified by typing their names into the Watch window. You can drag and drop variables to the Watch window.

These windows are only visible when the program is running under the debugger. If you do not see them, select Debug ⇨ Windows, and then select the desired menu. The Watch window offers four different windows in case there's so much to watch and you want to group that. With all these windows you can both watch and change the values, enabling you to try different paths in the program without leaving the debugger. The Locals window is shown in Figure 18-46.

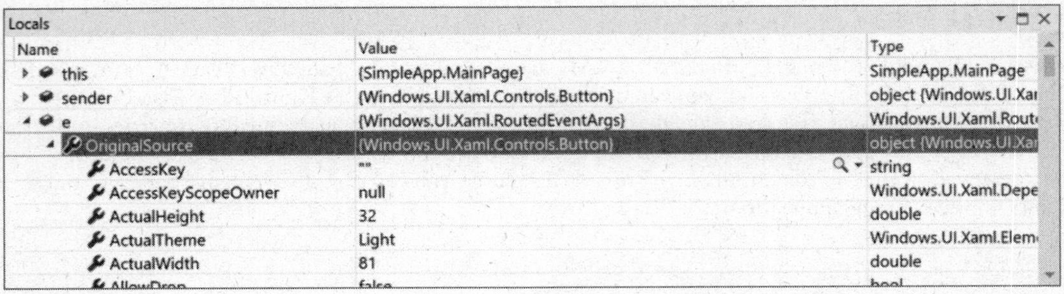

FIGURE 18-46

Another window that doesn't directly relate to the other windows discussed but is still an important one for monitoring and changing variables is the *Immediate window*. This window also makes it possible for you to look at variable values. You can use this window to enter code and run it. This is very helpful when you're doing some tests during a debug session; it enables you to home in on details, try a method out, and change a debug run dynamically.

Exceptions

Exceptions are great when you are ready to ship your application, ensuring that error conditions are handled appropriately. Used well, they can ensure that users are never presented with technical or annoying dialogs. Unfortunately, exceptions are not so great when you are trying to debug your application. The problem is twofold:

➤ If an exception occurs when you are debugging, you often do not want it to be handled automatically—especially if automatically handling it means retiring gracefully and terminating execution! Rather, you want the debugger to help you determine why the exception has occurred. Of course, if you have written good, robust, defensive code, your program automatically handles almost anything—including the bugs that you want to detect!

➤ If an exception for which you have not written a handler occurs, the .NET runtime still searches for one. Unfortunately, by the time it discovers there isn't one, it will have terminated your program. There will not be a call stack left, and you will not be able to look at the values of any of your variables because they will all have gone out of scope.

Of course, you can set breakpoints in your catch blocks, but that often does not help very much because when the catch block is reached, flow of execution will, by definition, have exited the corresponding try block. That means the variables you probably wanted to examine the values of, to figure out what has gone wrong, will have gone out of scope. You will not even be able to look at the stack trace to find what method was being executed when the throw statement occurred because control will have left that method. Setting the breakpoints at the throw statement obviously solves this; but if you are coding defensively, there will be many throw statements in your code. How can you tell which one threw the exception?

Visual Studio provides a very neat answer to all of this. You can configure the exception types where the debugger should break. This is configured in the menu Debug ➪ Windows ➪ Exception Settings. With this window (see Figure 18-47) you can specify what happens when an exception is thrown. You can choose to continue execution or to stop and start debugging—in which case execution stops and the debugger steps in at the throw statement.

What makes this a powerful tool is that you can customize the behavior according to which class of exception is thrown. You can configure to break into the debugger whenever it encounters any exception thrown by a .NET base class, but not to break into the debugger for specific exception types.

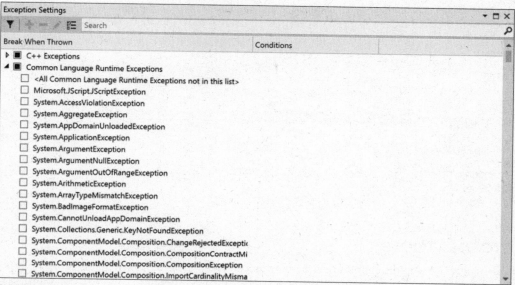

FIGURE 18-47

Visual Studio is aware of all the exception classes available in the .NET base classes, and of quite a few exceptions that can be thrown outside the .NET environment. Visual Studio is not automatically aware of any custom exception classes that you write, but you can manually add your exception classes to the list, and specify which of your exceptions should cause execution to stop immediately. To do this, just click the Add button (which is enabled when you have selected a top-level node from the tree) and type in the name of your exception class.

Multithreading

Visual Studio also offers great support for debugging multithreaded programs. When debugging multi-threaded programs, you must understand that the program behaves differently depending on whether it is running in the debugger or not. If you reach a breakpoint, Visual Studio stops all threads of the program, so you have the chance to access the current state of all the threads. To switch between different threads, you can enable the Debug Location toolbar. This toolbar contains a combo box for all processes and another combo box for all threads of the running application. When you select a different thread, you find the code line where the thread currently halts and the variables currently accessible from different threads. The Tasks window (shown in Figure 18-48) shows all running tasks, including their statuses, locations, task names, the current threads that are used by the tasks, the application domains, and the process identifiers. This window also indicates when different threads block each other, causing a deadlock.

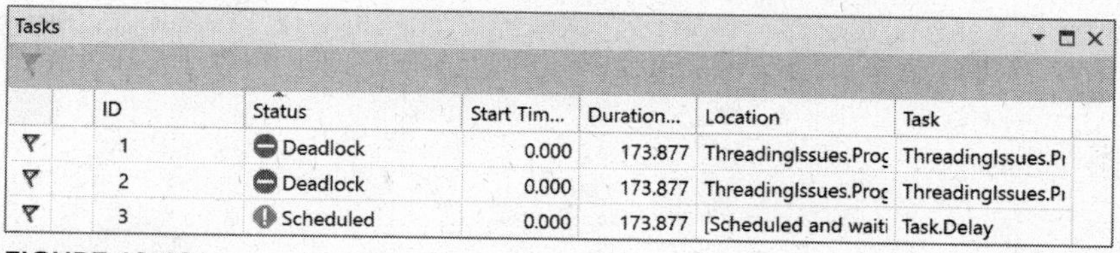

	ID	Status	Start Tim...	Duration...	Location	Task
▼	1	⛔ Deadlock	0.000	173.877	ThreadingIssues.Proç	ThreadingIssues.Pr
▼	2	⛔ Deadlock	0.000	173.877	ThreadingIssues.Proç	ThreadingIssues.Pr
▼	3	ⓘ Scheduled	0.000	173.877	[Scheduled and waiti	Task.Delay

FIGURE 18-48

Figure 18-49 shows the Parallel Stacks window, where you can see different threads or tasks (depending on the selection) in a hierarchical view. You can jump to the source code directly by clicking the task or thread.

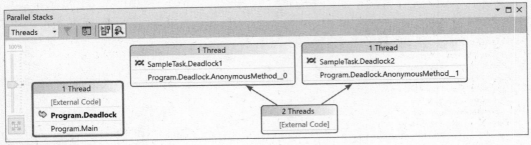

FIGURE 18-49

REFACTORING TOOLS

Many developers develop their applications first for functionality. After the functionality is in place, they *rework* their applications to make them more manageable and more readable. This process is called *refactoring*. Refactoring involves reworking code for readability and performance, providing type safety, and ensuring that applications adhere to standard OO (object-oriented) programming practices. Reworking also happens when updates are made to applications.

The C# environment of Visual Studio 2017 includes a set of refactoring tools, which you can find under the Refactoring option in the Visual Studio menu. To see this in action, create a new class called Car in Visual Studio:

```
public class Car
{
  public string _color;
  public string _doors;

  public int Go()
  {
    int speedMph = 100;
    return speedMph;
  }
}
```

Now suppose that for the purpose of refactoring, you want to change the code a bit so that the color and door variables are encapsulated in public .NET properties. The refactoring capabilities of Visual Studio 2017 enable you to simply right-click either of these properties in the document window and select Quick Actions. You see different options for refactoring, such as generating a constructor to fill the fields or to generate the methods Equals and GetHashCode or to encapsulate the fields as shown in Figure 18-50.

From this dialog you can provide the name of the property and click the Preview link, or you can directly accept the changes. When you select the button to encapsulate the fields, the code is reworked into the following:

```
public class Car
{
  private string _color;
  private string _doors;

  public string Color { get => _color; set => _color = value; }
  public string Doors { get => _doors; set => _doors = value; }
```

```
    public int Go()
    {
      int speedMph = 100;
      return speedMph;
    }
}
```

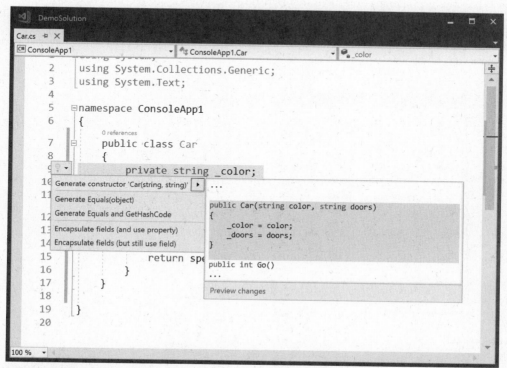

FIGURE 18-50

As you can see, these code fixes make it quite simple to refactor your code—not only on one page but throughout an entire application. Also included are capabilities to do the following:

➤ Rename method names, local variables, fields, and more.

➤ Extract methods from a selection of code.

➤ Extract interfaces based on a set of existing type members.

➤ Promote local variables to parameters.

➤ Rename or reorder parameters.

You will find that the refactoring capabilities provided by Visual Studio 2017 offer a great way to get cleaner, more readable, and better-structured code.

DIAGNOSTIC TOOLS

Visual Studio 2017 offers many useful tools that can help you analyze and proactively troubleshoot your application. This section looks at some of these Visual Studio analysis tools.

Like the architecture tools, the analyzer tools are available with Visual Studio 2017 Enterprise.

To analyze a complete run of the application, you can use the diagnostics tools. These tools enable you to find what methods are called, how often methods are called, how much time is spent in what methods, how much memory is used, and much more. With Visual Studio 2017, the diagnostics tools are started automatically when you start the debugger. With the diagnostics tools, you can also see IntelliTrace (historical debugging) events (see Figure 18-51). When you hit a breakpoint, you can have a look at previous information in time such as previous breakpoints, exceptions that were thrown, database access, ASP.NET Core events, tracing, or user input gestures, such as a user clicking a button. By clicking the information of previous events, you can have a look at local variables, the call stack, and method calls that were done. This makes it easy to find problems without restarting a debug session and setting breakpoints to methods that have been invoked before you see the issue.

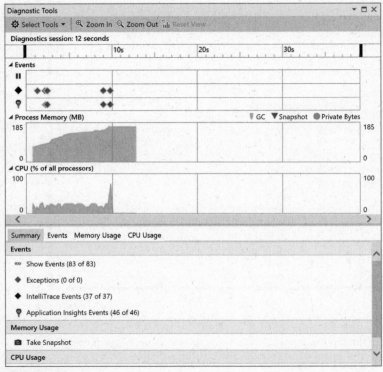

FIGURE 18-51

> **NOTE** *IntelliTrace is only available in the Visual Studio 2017 Enterprise edition.*

Another way to start diagnostics tools is to start them via the profiler: Debug ⇨ Performance Profiler or Analyze ⇨ Performance Profiler. Here you have more control over the features to start (see Figure 18-52). Depending on the project type used, more or fewer features are available. With UWP projects you can see the application timeline, memory usage, CPU usage, and memory. Other tools are HTML UI Responsiveness, JavaScript Memory, UI Analysis, and a Performance Wizard.

The first option, Application Timeline (see Figure 18-53), gives information about the UI thread and the time it is spending in parsing, layout, rendering, I/O, and application code. Depending on where the most time is spent, you know where optimization can be useful.

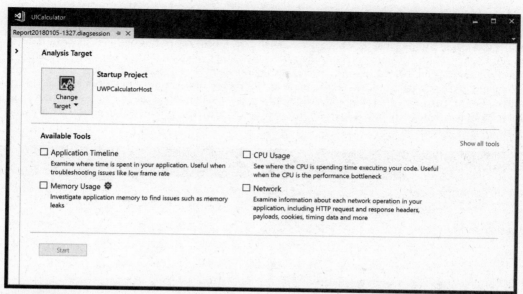

FIGURE 18-52

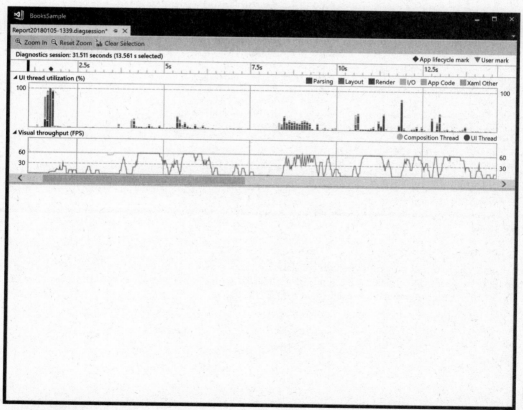

FIGURE 18-53

If you select the CPU Usage option (Figure 18-54), the overhead of monitoring is low. With this option, performance information is sampled after specific time intervals. You don't see all method calls invoked, especially if they are running just for a short time. Again, the advantage of this option is low overhead. When running a profiling session, you must always be aware that you're monitoring not only the performance of the application, but the performance of getting the data as well. You shouldn't profile all data at once, as sampling all the data influences the outcome. Collecting information about .NET memory allocation helps you identify memory leaks and provides information about what type of objects need how much memory. Resource contention data helps with the analysis of threads, enabling you to easily identify whether different threads block each other.

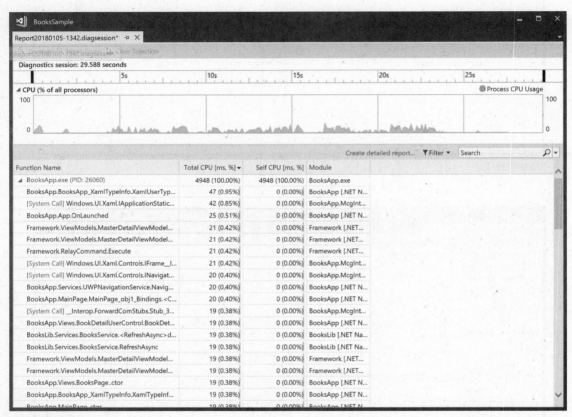

FIGURE 18-54

After an analysis run is completed, you can get detailed report information as shown in Figure 18-55. You can see CPU usage by the application, a hot path indicating which functions are taking the most time, and a sorted list of the functions that have used the most CPU time.

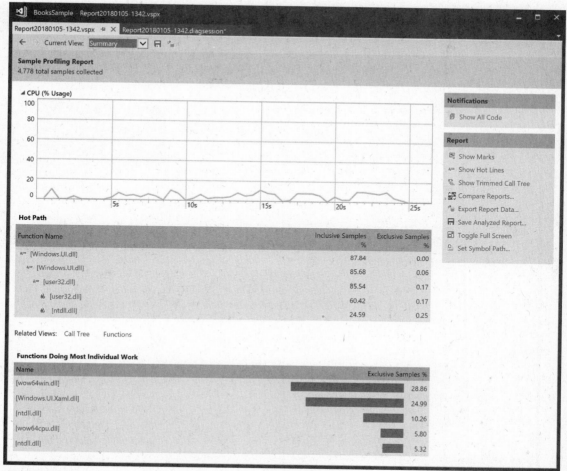

FIGURE 18-55

The profiler has many more screens—too many to show here. One view is a function view that you can sort based on the number of calls made to the function, or the elapsed inclusive and exclusive times used by the function. This information can help you identify methods deserving of another look in terms of performance, whereas others might not be worthwhile because they are not called often, or they do not take an inordinate amount of time.

Clicking within a function, you can invoke details about it, as shown in Figure 18-56. This enables you to see which functions are called and immediately step into the source code. The Caller/Callee view also provides information about what functions have been called by what function.

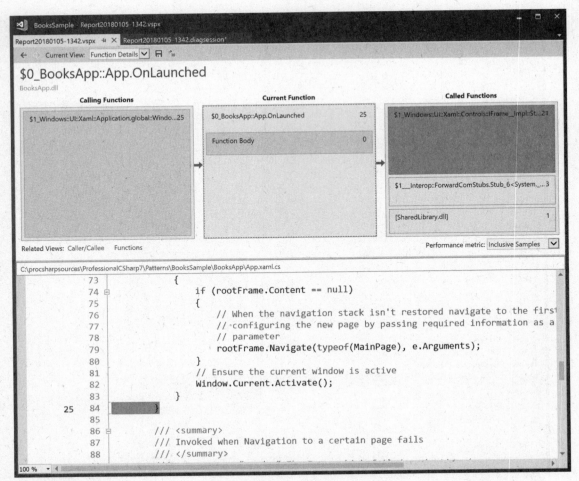

FIGURE 18-56

CREATING AND USING CONTAINERS WITH DOCKER

A great new feature of Visual Studio is its Docker integration. Because Docker is relatively new in the .NET world, it deserves an introduction.

What is Docker good for? Docker offers virtualization; it's a container technology that enables you to package and deploy applications and services isolated with all its dependencies. Compared to a virtual machine, it's lightweight because the images can be a lot smaller as one image is based on another one. One Docker container also doesn't need to reserve one CPU core and memory because they can be shared. Development can create a Docker image that's used by production. It's no longer, "It runs on my machine."

Here are the key terms to understand about Docker:

- ➤ **Image**—A deployment unit. An image is a package that includes all dependencies (frameworks) and configuration needed to run the application. An image can derive from other images. After an image is created, it is immutable.

- ➤ **Registry**—A store where you can find Docker images. Docker's official registry, where you can find thousands of images, is at `https://hub.docker.com`. At `https://hub.docker.com/r/microsoft/dotnet/` you can pull official Microsoft .NET Core images for Linux and Windows Server.

- ➤ **Container**—A running image. The container is a runtime environment for one application or service. You can scale it by creating multiple instances of a container from the same image. A container runs in a host. You can download Docker Community Edition for Windows from `https://store.docker.com/editions/community/docker-ce-desktop-windows` to host Docker on Windows 10. Microsoft Azure has several offerings to run your Docker images in the cloud.

- ➤ **Dockerfile**—A text file with instructions to build a Docker image. You can use the Docker command line to process the `dockerfile`.

To understand Docker, it's best to try it out.

Hello Docker!

After installing Docker Community Edition, you can use the Docker commands to pull and run Docker containers. The first command to start with is the Docker version of "Hello World!" From the command line, you just need to invoke `docker run hello-world`. When you start this the first time, you can see a result like the following output shows. Because the Docker image hello-world is not yet locally installed, the Docker image is pulled from the Docker registry and started. After a successful download, you'll see `Hello from Docker!` displayed:

```
> docker run hello-world
Unable to find image 'hello-world:latest' locally
latest: Pulling from library/hello-world
ca4f61b1923c: Pull complete
Digest: sha256:ca0eeb6fb05351dfc8759c20733c91def84cb8007aa89a5bf606bc8b315b9fc7
Status: Downloaded newer image for hello-world:latest

Hello from Docker!
```

When you invoke the command a second time, because the Docker image is already downloaded locally, you get immediate results:

```
> docker run hello-world
Hello from Docker!
```

Running ASP.NET Core in a Docker Container

Next, let's pull a Docker container from Microsoft and create and run an ASP.NET Core application.

To pull and run the container, you start the command `docker run` with these options:

```
> docker run -p 8000:80 -e "ASPNETCORE_URLS=http://+:80" -it --rm microsoft/dotnet
```

The option `-p` maps the port 80 from the container to the port 8000 outside the container. On your local system, port 80 is probably already occupied by a web server. The option `-e` sets an environmental variable within the container. By setting the environmental variable `ASPNETCORE_URLS`, you can specify the port number that is the listening port used by the Kestrel server hosting ASP.NET Core. The option -it starts the container interactive with a terminal; thus, when the command completes, you type in the command prompt of the container. The option --rm removes the container if it already exists before the container is downloaded again. The last part of the command specifies the image to be pulled from the hub and started. The image microsoft/dotnet contains the .NET Core SDK with the command-line tools.

> **NOTE** microsoft/dotnet *pulls the latest* microsoft/dotnet *Docker image with the released SDK. By adding tags to the name, you can pull specific versions and also pull a version with just the runtime that can be used for production.* microsoft/dotnet:<version>-sdk *retrieves the .NET Core SDK,* microsoft/dotnet:<version>-runtime *an image with the runtime, and* microsoft/dotnet:<version>-runtime-deps *a smaller image that doesn't include the runtime but does include the native binaries needed for hosting self-contained apps. Self-contained apps are explained in Chapter 1, ".NET Applications and Tools." Details on the images are available at* https://hub.docker.com/r/microsoft/dotnet/.

When you start the command, the image is pulled from the Docker hub, started, and you can enter in the Docker container. Let's create an ASP.NET Core MVC application and start it with the following commands:

```
# mkdir websample
# cd websample
# dotnet new mvc
# dotnet restore
# dotnet build
# dotnet run
```

Now you can access http://localhost:8000 from a browser outside of the container and access the ASP .NET Core website in the container. From outside the Docker container, you can use the command

```
> docker images
```

to see all the downloaded images and

```
> docker container list
```

to see the active containers running. This is a shorthand notation:

```
> docker ps
```

Creating a Dockerfile

With the commands used so far, you've seen how to pull and run a Docker container. Next let's create a custom Docker image that runs an ASP.NET Core application. This time, you create a release build and build a publish package.

First, you use the ASP.NET Core CLI to create an ASP.NET Core MVC web application. Passing -c Release to the dotnet build command builds release code. The option -o ./Publish for the dotnet publish command writes the output for publishing in the Publish subdirectory.

```
> mkdir DockerSample
> cd DockerSample
> dotnet new mvc
> dotnet restore
> dotnet build -c Release
> dotnet publish -c Release -o ./Publish
```

Next, create a `dockerfile` in the same directory as the web application, in the current directory of the command prompt (code file `DockerSample/dockerfile`):

```
FROM microsoft/aspnetcore
WORKDIR /app
COPY ./publish .
RUN dir .
ENTRYPOINT [ "dotnet", "/app/DockerSample.dll" ]
RUN echo 'completed building image'
```

> **WARNING** *When running Docker on Linux, pay attention to the case sensitivity of the filenames. With Linux, the file* `dockersample.dll` *is different from* `DockerSample.dll`.

Let's get through every command. A `dockerfile` starts with a `FROM`. The newly built image is based on the image `microsoft/aspnetcore`. This image contains only the runtime. For a build-image, you can use `microsoft/aspnetcore-build`. `microsoft/aspnetcore` itself is based on `microsoft/dotnet`. The `microsoft/aspnetcore` image contains a set of native images for the ASP.NET Core libraries, so no time is spent on the first run to compile the libraries.

```
FROM microsoft/aspnetcore
```

The next command sets the working directory inside the image to be created to the `/app` folder.

```
WORKDIR /app
```

The `COPY` command copies the content from the local `./Publish` directory to the current directory inside the image—the previously defined working directory:

```
COPY ./publish .
```

The next command just displays the file in the current directory to see if the copy succeeded:

```
RUN dir .
```

The `ENTRYPOINT` defines the command that should be started when running the container with its arguments. At runtime, the ASP.NET Core app is started with `dotnet` and the name of the DLL:

```
ENTRYPOINT [ "dotnet", "/app/dockersample.dll" ]
```

With the `dockerfile` in place, you can build a docker image with the command `docker build`. The option `-t` gives a name to the image. The last `.` in the command defines the directory that should be searched for the `dockerfile`:

```
> docker build -t mysampleapp .
```

> **NOTE** *With the* `-t` *option of the* `docker build` *command, you can tag the image— for example, with a version number such as* `docker build -t mysampleapp:1.4 .`

After a successful build, you can run the Docker image and map port 80 from the container to port 8002 outside of the container:

```
> docker run -p 8002:80 mysampleapp
```

When you use the production code and the precompiled ASP.NET Core image, you experience a fast response as you use the browser to access the ASP.NET Core web application.

Using Visual Studio

Now let's get into Visual Studio 2017. How is the experience of Docker integrated? A web application using the project template Web Application (Model-View-Controller) is created. The project is named `WebAppWithVS`. You'll see this name in the generated `dockerfile`. With the first dialog, you can already enable Docker support by selecting a check box and choosing between a Linux or Windows container (Figure 18-57). Leave this option deselected. It's easy to add Docker support later.

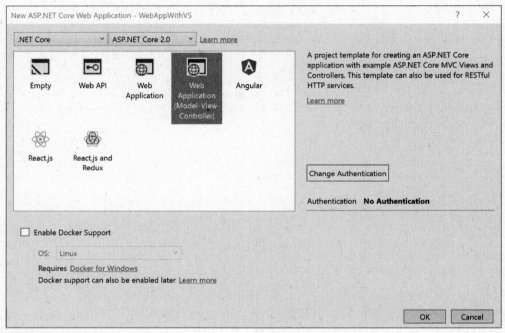

FIGURE 18-57

When you use the project template, the same files are created as when you use the command line. You can add Docker support to an existing project by selecting Project ⇨ Docker Support. In the dialog shown in Figure 18-58 you select the target OS. Let's host it on Linux.

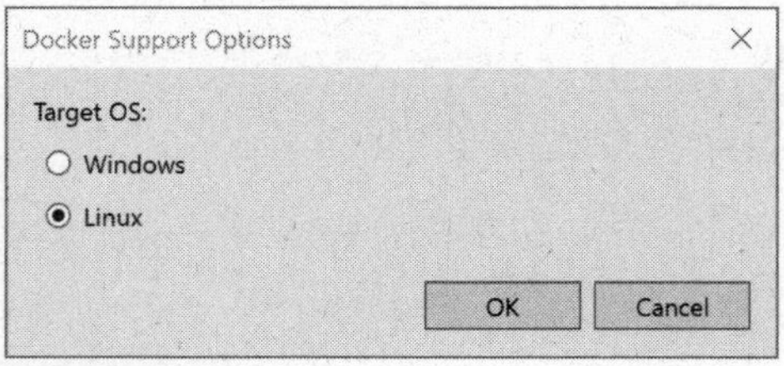

FIGURE 18-58

Now you get a `dockerfile` with the project. This `dockerfile` includes more than one `FROM` for *multi-stage docker builds*. Here, multiple images are created depending on whether a debug or release build is done. Let's get through this file with multiple steps. The first `FROM` is based on the image `microsoft/aspnet-core:2.0`, which is defined `AS base` to reference it with the name `base` later. With the first image definition, the working directory is set to `/app`, and the port number `80` is exposed (code file `WebAppWithVS/Dockerfile`):

```
FROM microsoft/aspnetcore:2.0 AS base
WORKDIR /app
EXPOSE 80
```

The second `FROM` is completely independent of the first one. This `FROM` defines the image base `aspnetcore-build:2.0`. The image with the `build` tag is the ASP.NET Core image, including the SDK. The working directory is now `/src`. Next, two `COPY` commands are used to copy the solution and the project file to the `src` directory. Running `dotnet restore` restores all NuGet packages, and the next `COPY` command copies the complete folder with its subdirectories to the `src` directory. The new working directory is set to the folder of the web application—before running `dotnet build`:

```
FROM microsoft/aspnetcore-build:2.0 AS build
WORKDIR /src
COPY *.sln ./
COPY WebAppWithVS/WebAppWithVS.csproj WebAppWithVS/
RUN dotnet restore
COPY . .
WORKDIR /src/WebAppWithVS
RUN dotnet build -c Release -o /app
```

The next image definition makes use of the previously configured build image: `FROM build AS publish`. The new name is `publish`, where the .NET command `dotnet publish` is invoked to create the files for publication in the `/app` subdirectory:

```
FROM build AS publish
RUN dotnet publish -c Release -o /app
```

The last `FROM` defines an image named `final` that's based on the first image defined: the `base` image. The working directory is now `/app`. The `COPY` command copies the `/app` directory from the previously defined `publish` image (the publish was done to the `/app` directory) to the working directory. Finally, the entry point of the container is set to the `dotnet` command:

```
FROM base AS final
WORKDIR /app
COPY --from=publish /app .
ENTRYPOINT ["dotnet", "WebAppWithVS.dll"]
```

With the `Dockerfile` in place, you just need to invoke the Docker commands as shown previously to create the images needed. However, instead of using the Docker commands you can use *Docker Compose*, which is a tool to run multiple Docker applications. For this tool you need a YAML file that defines services that make up the application. From the services, dockerfiles are referenced to build the images.

As you add Docker support with Visual Studio to a project, you can find another project in the solution: `docker-compose`. The `docker-compose` project contains files using the YAML syntax with the `yml` file extension.

> **NOTE** *YAML (YAML Ain't Markup Language) is a syntax created that is not as verbose as XML. YAML uses whitespaces with the syntax.*

The file `docker-compose.yml` is automatically created. After the version number for Docker Compose, `services:` lists the services that are built. The service name `webappwithvs` needs to match the value in the `<DockerServiceName>` element defined in the CSPROJ configuration file. The CSPROJ file also lists the `Microsoft.Docker.Sdk` that's used to trigger this project. The name of the image that's created is specified by `image`. You can change this image name. The image name is tagged with `dev` (for the Debug build) and latest (for the Release build) (configuration file `WebAppWithVS/docker-compose/docker-compose.yml`):

```
version: '3'

services:
  webappwithvs:
    image: webappwithvs
    build:
      context: .
      dockerfile: WebApWithVS/Dockerfile
```

Building and running the project with debug and release builds now creates and runs images with the names `webappwithvs:dev` and `webappwithvs:latest`. While this is already a great feature of Visual Studio to automatically build the images, the best is that you can set breakpoints, start the debugger, and debug from Visual Studio running on a Windows machine into Docker images running on Linux—all on the same system!

SUMMARY

This chapter explored one of the most important programming tools in the .NET environment: Visual Studio 2017. The bulk of the chapter examined how this tool facilitates writing code in C#.

You've learned about various project templates, the Solution Explorer, and various features of the editor. You've also debugged your code. You've seen refactoring in action and been introduced to the new integration of Docker.

The first part of the book concludes with this chapter. The next chapter starts to dive into .NET Standard libraries by covering libraries, assemblies, and NuGet packages.

PART II
.NET Core and the Windows Runtime

19

Libraries, Assemblies, Packages, and NuGet

WHAT'S IN THIS CHAPTER?

➤ Differences between libraries, assemblies, packages
➤ Creating libraries
➤ Using .NET Standard
➤ Using shared projects
➤ Creating NuGet packages

WROX.COM CODE DOWNLOADS FOR THIS CHAPTER

The wrox.com code downloads for this chapter are found at www.wrox.com on the Download Code tab. The source code is also available at https://github.com/ProfessionalCSharp/ProfessionalCSharp7 in the directory Libraries.

The code for this chapter is divided into the following major examples:

➤ UsingLibs
➤ UsingLegacyLibs
➤ UsingASharedProject
➤ CreateNuGet

THE HELL OF LIBRARIES

Libraries make it possible for you to reuse code in multiple applications. With Windows, libraries have a long history, and architecture guidelines have taken different directions with newer technologies. Before .NET, dynamic link libraries (DLLs) could be shared between different applications. These DLLs have been installed in a shared directory. It wasn't possible to have multiple versions of these libraries on the same system, but they should have been upward compatible. Of course, this wasn't always the case. In addition, there were problems with application installations that did not pay attention to the guidelines and replaced a shared library with an older one. This was the DLL Hell.

.NET tried to solve this with *assemblies*. Assemblies are libraries that could be shared. In addition to normal DLLs, assemblies contain extensible metadata with information about the library and a version number, and it's possible to install multiple versions side by side in the *global assembly cache*. Microsoft tried to fix versioning issues, but this added another layer of complexity.

Let's assume you're using library A and B from your application X (see Figure 19-1). Application X references version 1.1 from library A and version 1.0 from library B. The issue is that library B references library A as well, but it references a different version—version 1.0. One process can only have one version of a library loaded. What version of the library A is loaded into the process? In case library B is used before library A, version 1.0 wins. This is a big issue as soon as application X needs to use library A itself.

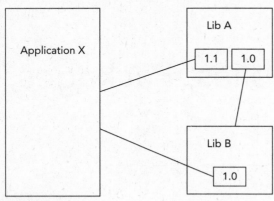

FIGURE 19-1

To avoid this issue, you could configure assembly redirects. You can define an assembly redirect for application X to load version 1.1 from library A. Library B then needs to use version 1.1 from library A as well. In case library A is upward-compatible, this shouldn't be an issue.

Of course, compatibility doesn't always exist, and issues can be more complex. Publishers of components can create a publisher policy to define redirects with the library itself. This redirect can be overridden by the application. There's a lot of complexity with this, which resulted in Assembly Hell.

> **NOTE** *With .NET Core there's no global sharing of assemblies as it was with the .NET Framework. Only the .NET runtime can be shared between different applications.*

NuGet packages add another abstraction layer to libraries. A NuGet package can contain multiple versions of one or more assemblies, along with other stuff, such as automatic configuration of assembly redirects.

Instead of waiting for new .NET Framework releases, you could add functionality via NuGet packages, which allowed for faster updates of the packages. NuGet packages are a great delivery vehicle. Some libraries like Entity Framework switched to NuGet to allow for faster updates than the .NET Framework offered.

However, there are some issues with NuGet. Often adding NuGet packages to projects fail. NuGet packages might not be compatible with the project. When adding packages was successful, it can happen that the package made some incorrect configuration with the project, e.g. wrong binding redirects. This results in the feeling of the NuGet Package Hell. The problems from DLLs moved to different abstraction layers and are indeed different. With newer NuGet versions and advancements in NuGet, Microsoft has tried to solve the issues with NuGet.

Directions in the architecture of .NET Core also changed. With .NET Core, packages have been made more granular. For example, with the .NET Framework, the Console class is inside the mscorlib assembly, which is an assembly needed by every .NET Framework application. Of course, not every .NET application needs the Console class. With .NET Core 1.0, a separate package System.Console exists that contains the Console class and a few related classes. The goal was to make it easier to update and select what packages are really needed. With some Beta versions of .NET Core 1.0, the project files contained a large list of packages, which didn't make development easier. Just before the release of .NET Core 1.0, Microsoft introduced meta-packages (or reference-packages). A meta-package doesn't include code but instead a list of other packages.

With .NET Core 2.0 includes another simplification. When you created a "Hello, World!" Console application with .NET Core 1.1, the generated project.asset.json file has a size of 313 KB. This file (in the obj directory) shows the tree of dependencies. With .NET Core 2.0, the file size was reduced to 33 KB because of larger packages with fewer references.

This chapter goes into the detail of assemblies and NuGet packages, explains how to share code using .NET Standard libraries, and also explains differences with Windows Runtime components.

ASSEMBLIES

An assembly is a library or executable that includes additional metadata. Using .NET Core, the application containing the Main method is created as a library with the file extension .dll. This DLL needs a hosting process to load this library, which you do using dotnet run, or just dotnet from a runtime environment. When you create standalone applications with .NET Core, different executables are created for every platform to load the library.

Let's have a look at a simple "Hello, World!" console application created in the directory ConsoleApp, using the command

```
> dotnet new console
```

After building the application, the DLL can be found in the bin/debug/netcoreapp2.0 directory. The netcoreapp2.0 directory depends on the target framework listed in the csproj project file.

Assembly information can be read using the ildasm.exe (IL Disassembler) command-line utility. Ildasm.exe shows the types of the assembly with its members, with the additional metadata as shown in Figure 19-2.

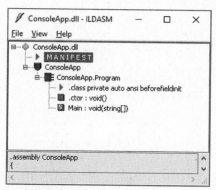

FIGURE 19-2

Clicking MANIFEST (refer to Figure 19-2), opens metadata information for the assembly as shown in Figure 19-3. The assembly which has the name ConsoleApp, references the assemblies System.Runtime and System.Console. You also can see several configured assembly attributes such as `AssemblyCompanyNameAttribute`, `AssemblyConfigurationAttribute`, `AssemblyDescriptionAttribute`, `AssemblyFileVersionAttribute`, and others.

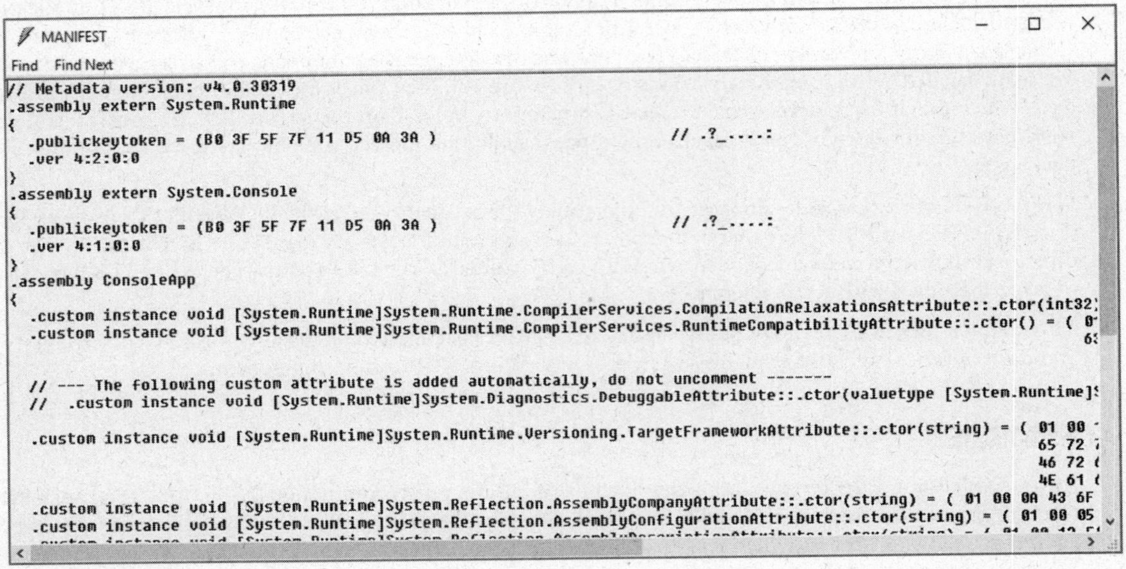

FIGURE 19-3

Assembly metadata that describes the application can be configured using Visual Studio; select Package in the Project Properties (see Figure 19-4).

Of course, you can also directly edit the project file (code file `ConsoleApp/ConsoleApp.csproj`):

```xml
<Project Sdk="Microsoft.NET.Sdk">

  <PropertyGroup>
    <OutputType>Exe</OutputType>
    <TargetFramework>netcoreapp2.0</TargetFramework>
    <Authors>Christian Nagel</Authors>
    <Company>CN innovation</Company>
    <Product>Sample App</Product>
    <Description>Sample App for Professional C#</Description>
    <Copyright>Copyright (c) CN innovation</Copyright>
    <PackageProjectUrl>https://github.com/ProfessionalCSharp
    </PackageProjectUrl>
    <RepositoryUrl>https://github.com/ProfessionalCSharp/ProfessionalCSharp7
    </RepositoryUrl>
    <RepositoryType>git</RepositoryType>
    <PackageTags>Wrox Press, Sample, Libraries</PackageTags>
  </PropertyGroup>

</Project>
```

> **NOTE** *With previous projects, such metadata information was typically added to the file* `AssemblyInfo.cs` *by adding this information with global C# attributes. You can still do it this way, but then you need to configure the* `csproj` *file to not automatically generate the attributes.*

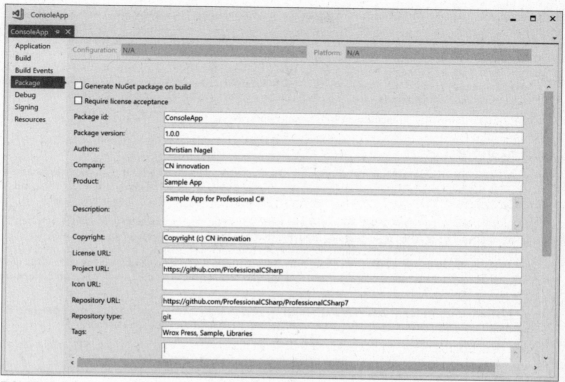

FIGURE 19-4

CREATING LIBRARIES

You can use shared code by creating libraries. With Visual Studio 2017, you've many options to create libraries, as shown here:

- ➤ Class Library (.NET Core)
- ➤ Class Library (.NET Standard)
- ➤ Class Library (.NET Framework)
- ➤ WPF Custom Control Library (.NET Framework)
- ➤ WPF User Control Library (.NET Framework)
- ➤ Windows Forms Control Library (.NET Framework)
- ➤ Class Library (Universal Windows)
- ➤ Class Library (Legacy Portable)
- ➤ Shared Project

The Shared Project listed is not really a class library, but you can use it for sharing code from multiple projects. See the section "Using Shared Projects" later in this chapter for more information.

The class libraries identified with .NET Framework in the preceding list are meant to be used with .NET Framework applications, and they can have specific restrictions. The WPF User Control Library and WPF Custom Control Library can be used only from WPF applications. Similarly, the Windows Forms Control Library can be used only from Windows Forms applications.

Class Library (Legacy Portable) already has *legacy* in its name. This project template, which was originally known as Portable Class Library (PCL) shouldn't be used with new applications. This library enables you to share code between different technologies, such as sharing code between Silverlight, WPF, Xamarin, .NET Core, and so on. Depending on the platform and version selection, different APIs are available. The more platforms and the older the version chosen, the fewer APIs are available. As more and more platforms have been added, this increased the complexity of the definitions and also increased complexity on using portable libraries from portable libraries.

.NET Standard provides a replacement for portable libraries.

.NET Standard

The .NET Standard makes a linear definition of APIs available, which is different than the matrix definition with APIs that was available for portable libraries. Every version of the .NET Standard adds APIs, and APIs are never removed.

The higher the version of the .NET Standard, the more APIs you can use. However, the .NET Standard doesn't implement the APIs; it just defines the APIs that need to be implemented by a .NET platform. This can be compared to interfaces and concrete classes. An interface just defines a contract for members that need to be implemented by a class. With the .NET Standard, the .NET Standard specifies what APIs need to be available, and a .NET platform—supporting a specific version of the standard—needs to implement these APIs.

You can find which APIs are available with which standard version, as well as the differences between the standards, at `https://github.com/dotnet/standard/tree/master/docs/versions`.

Every version of the .NET Standard adds APIs to the standard:

➤   .NET Standard 1.1 added 2,414 APIs to .NET Standard 1.0.

➤   Version 1.2 added just 46 APIs.

➤   With 1.3, 3,314 APIs were added.

➤   Version 1.4 added only 18 Cryptography APIs .

➤   Version 1.5 mainly enhanced reflection support and added 242 APIs.

➤   Version 1.6 added more Cryptography APIs and enhanced regular expressions, with a total of 146 additional APIs.

With .NET Standard 2.0, Microsoft made a big investment to make it easier to move legacy applications to .NET Core. With this new standard, 19,507 APIs have been added. Not all of these APIs were new. Some were already implemented with .NET Framework 4.6.1. For example, old APIs like `DataSet`, `DataTable`, and others are now available with the .NET Standard. This was a move to make it easier to bring legacy applications to the .NET Standard. A huge investment was needed for .NET Core, because .NET Core 2.0 implements the .NET Standard 2.0.

What APIs are not in the standard and never will be? Platform-specific APIs are not expected to be part of the .NET Standard. For example, *Windows Presentation Foundation (WPF)* and *Windows Forms* define Windows-specific APIs that will not make it into the standard. You can, however, create WPF and Windows Forms applications and use .NET Standard libraries from there. You cannot create .NET Standard libraries that contain WPF or Windows Forms controls.

New APIs that are tested are coming first to .NET Core. As soon as the APIs stabilize, there's a good chance they will be available with a future version of the .NET Standard.

Let's get into more details on the platform support of .NET Standard. If you need to support Windows Phone Silverlight 8.1, you need to restrict your library to the APIs that are available with .NET Standard 1.0. Of course, nowadays there's typically no need to support any Silverlight version. Let's get into more important .NET platforms.

For using libraries from the Universal Windows Platform, you need to pay attention to what build number you want to support. If you're supporting only the *Fall Creators Update of Windows 10*, you can already use .NET Standard 2.0. For supporting the Creators Update and older Windows 10 builds, you just can go up to .NET Standard 1.4. Newer versions are not possible in such cases. If you create a library containing ASP.NET Core 1.1 controllers, the library needs to be version 1.6 of the standard.

> **NOTE** *To support the most platforms possible, you need to select a lower .NET Standard version. To have more APIs available, select a higher .NET Standard version.*

Creating a .NET Standard Library

To create a .NET Standard library, you can use the .NET Core CLI tools with the command

```
dotnet new classlib
```

Using the .NET Core 2.0 CLI tools, this creates a library with this `csproj` definition (code file `UsingLibs/SimpleLib/SimpleLib.csproj`):

```
<Project Sdk="Microsoft.NET.Sdk">
  <PropertyGroup>
    <TargetFramework>netstandard2.0</TargetFramework>
  </PropertyGroup>
</Project>
```

You can change the version of the .NET Standard library by changing the `TargetFramework` element. From Visual Studio, you can use the Application Settings of the Project Properties to change the .NET Standard version (see Figure 19-5).

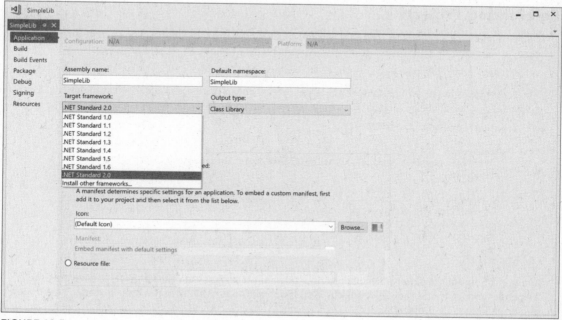

FIGURE 19-5

Solution Files

When you work with multiple projects (for example, a console application and a library), it's helpful to work with solution files. With the newer versions of the .NET Core CLI tools, you can use solutions from the command line as well as using them from Visual Studio. For example,

```
> dotnet new sln
```

creates a solution file in the current directory.

Using the `dotnet sln add` command, you can add projects to the solution file:

```
dotnet sln add SimpleLib/SimpleLib.csproj
```

The project files are added to the solution file as shown in the following snippet (solution file `UsingLibs\UsingLibs.sln`):

```
Microsoft Visual Studio Solution File, Format Version 12.00
# Visual Studio 15
VisualStudioVersion = 15.0.26124.0
MinimumVisualStudioVersion = 15.0.26124.0
Project("{FAE04EC0-301F-11D3-BF4B-00C04F79EFBC}") = "SimpleLib",
    "SimpleLib\SimpleLib.csproj", "{C58F9225-7407-45A0-932A-81AC3906F228}"
EndProject
Project("{FAE04EC0-301F-11D3-BF4B-00C04F79EFBC}") = "ConsoleApp",
    "ConsoleApp\ConsoleApp.csproj", "{31E6F88A-C0BC-4277-A9E9-19DAFDEB1A7A}"
EndProject
Global
# ...
```

When you're using Visual Studio, you can select the solution in the Solution Explorer to add new projects. From the context menu, select Add and then select Existing Project to add existing projects.

Referencing Projects

You can reference a library by using the `dotnet add reference` command. The current directory just needs to be positioned in the directory of the project where the library should be added:

```
dotnet add reference ..\SimpleLib\SimpleLib.csproj
```

The reference is added using a `ProjectReference` element in the `csproj` file (project file `UsingLibs/ConsoleApp/ConsoleApp.csproj`):

```
<Project Sdk="Microsoft.NET.Sdk">

  <ItemGroup>
    <ProjectReference Include="..\SimpleLib\SimpleLib.csproj" />
  </ItemGroup>

  <PropertyGroup>
    <OutputType>Exe</OutputType>
    <TargetFramework>netcoreapp2.0</TargetFramework>
  </PropertyGroup>

</Project>
```

Using the Solution Explorer in Visual Studio, you can add projects to other projects by selecting the Dependencies node and then selecting the Add Reference command from the Project menu. This dialog box shown in Figure 19-6 opens.

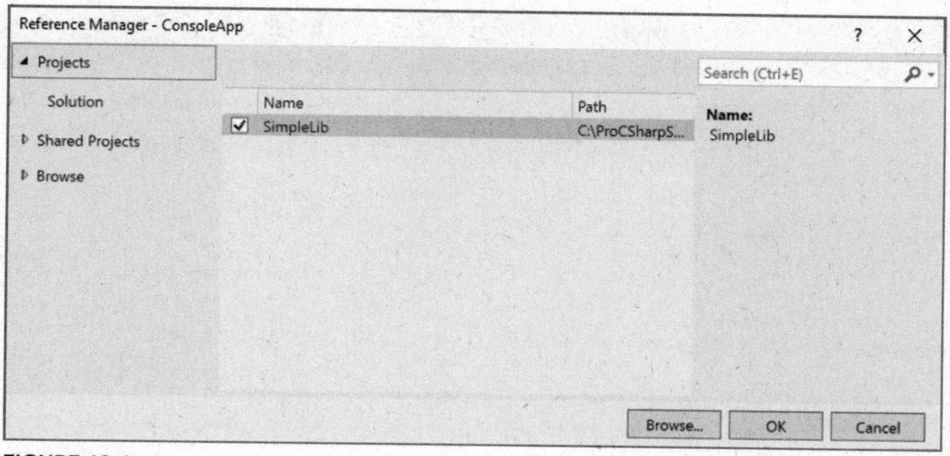

FIGURE 19-6

Referencing NuGet Packages

If the library is already packaged within a NuGet package, the NuGet package can be directly referenced with the command `dotnet add package`:

```
dotnet add package Microsoft.Composition
```

Instead of adding a `ProjectReference` as before, this adds a `PackageReference`:

```xml
<Project Sdk="Microsoft.NET.Sdk">
  <ItemGroup>
    <ProjectReference Include="..\SimpleLib\SimpleLib.csproj" />
  </ItemGroup>
  <ItemGroup>
    <PackageReference Include="Microsoft.Composition" Version="1.0.31" />
  </ItemGroup>
  <PropertyGroup>
    <OutputType>Exe</OutputType>
    <TargetFramework>netcoreapp2.0</TargetFramework>
  </PropertyGroup>
</Project>
```

To request a specific version of the package, you can specify the `--version` option with the .NET Core CLI command. With Visual Studio, you can use the NuGet Package Manager (see Figure 19-7) to find packages and select a specific version of the package. With this tool, you also can get details on the package with links to the project and licensing information.

> **NOTE** *Not all the packages you find on www.nuget.org are useful with your application. You should check licensing information to make sure the license fits with your project needs. Also, you should check the package author. If it's an open-source package, how active is the community behind it?*

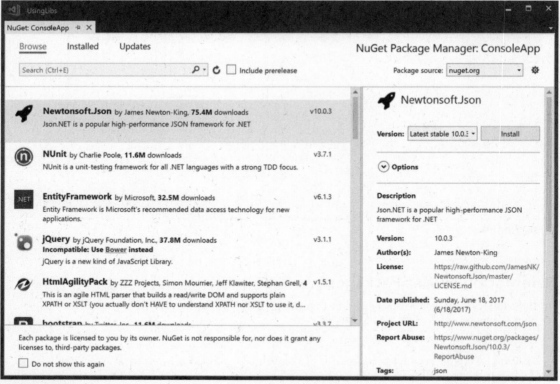

FIGURE 19-7

NuGet Sources

Where are the packages coming from? www.nuget.org is a server where Microsoft and third parties upload .NET packages. After the packages have been downloaded from the NuGet server for the first time, the packages are stored in the user profile. Thus, it becomes a lot faster to create another project with the same packages.

On Windows, the directory for the packages in the user profile is %userprofile%\.nuget\packages. Other temporary directories are used as well. To get all the information about these directories, it's best to install the NuGet command-line utility, which you can download from https://dist.nuget.org/.

To see the folders for the global packages, the HTTP cache, and the temp packages, you can use nuget locals:

```
> nuget locals all -list
```

In some companies, it's permissible to use only packages that have been approved and are stored in a local NuGet server. The default configuration for the NuGet server is in the file NuGet.Config in the directory %appdata%/nuget.

A default configuration looks similar to the following NuGet.Config file. Packages are loaded from https://api.nuget.org and the local NuGetFallbackFolder:

```
<?xml version="1.0" encoding="utf-8"?>
<configuration>
  <packageSources>
```

```
            <add key="nuget.org" value="https://api.nuget.org/v3/index.json"
                protocolVersion="3" />
            <add key="CliFallbackFolder"
                value="C:\Users\chris\.dotnet\NuGetFallbackFolder" />
        </packageSources>
    </configuration>
```

You can change the defaults by adding and removing package sources.

Microsoft doesn't store packages from the daily build on the main NuGet server. To use daily builds of .NET Core NuGet packages, you need to configure other NuGet servers. You can also configure local directories where you put your custom NuGet packages. The following `NuGet.Config` file adds a local directory and the nightly feed of .NET Core packages to the package sources.

```
<configuration>
  <packageSources>
    <add key="local packages" value="C:\git\mypackages" />
    <add key="dotnet-core"
      value="https://dotnet.myget.org/F/dotnet-core/api/v3/index.json" />
  </packageSources>
</configuration>
```

Instead of changing the default configuration file, you can place a configuration file into the project directory. This way, the configured package sources are valid only for the project.

Using .NET Framework Libraries

As already mentioned earlier in the chapter, a big advantage of the .NET Standard 2.0 is the additional APIs coming from the .NET Framework. This makes it easier to move legacy .NET applications to the new .NET.

.NET Standard libraries can be used from many different .NET technologies. Of course, you can reference .NET Standard libraries from .NET Core, but also from Mono and .NET Framework projects. A WPF application can make use of a .NET Standard library. Such a scenario was already possible with libraries created with .NET Core 1.0. But now, with .NET Standard 2.0, the interop scenario is extended. You can also reference an old .NET Framework library from a .NET Standard library as long as the .NET Framework library uses only APIs available with the .NET Standard.

How is this possible? Trying such interop scenarios with earlier .NET Core versions often resulted in compilation errors—for example, the object type is defined two times. The reason for such issues can be easily explained. With older .NET technologies, such as the .NET Framework, core types such as the `object` class are defined in `mscorlib`. With newer technologies such as .NET Core, the object type is defined in `System.Runtime`. Using both, you often ended up with duplicates of objects and other core types.

.NET Standard 2.0 changed the behavior. The .NET Standard defines an API set, but not an implementation. The complete implementation of the API needs to be done from the .NET platform, such as .NET Framework and .NET Core. The standard is implemented using type forwarding, which is forwarding types of the standard to a concrete implementation. The new library that lists the types from the .NET Standard is `NetStandard.dll`. This library is different for every platform. `NetStandard.dll` lists the types but doesn't contain any implementation. Instead, this library contains type forwarders to the specific implementation. For example, when you add a .NET Standard library to a .NET framework project, the `NetStandard.dll` is referenced automatically and contains a type forwarder for the `System.Console` class to the `mscorlib` assembly:

```
.class extern forwarder System.Console
{
   .assembly extern mscorlib
}
```

Accordingly, with a .NET Core project, the `NetStandard.dll` contains a redirect of `System.Console` to the library `System.Console`:

```
.class extern forwarder System.Console
{
  .assembly extern System.Console
}
```

Let's see this in action by creating a legacy .NET Framework library with the class `Legacy`. The methods `ConsoleMessage` and `WindowsMessage` just write output. `ConsoleMessage` writes output to the console. `WindowsMessage`, makes use of the .NET Framework library `System.Windows.Forms`, and opens a `MessageBox`. Additionally, the method `ShowConsoleType` gives information where the `Console` class is coming from (code file `UsingLegacyLibs/DotnetFrameworkLib/Legacy.cs`):

```
public class Legacy
{
  public static void ConsoleMessage(string message)
  {
    Console.WriteLine($"From the .NET Framework Lib: {message}");
  }

  public static void ShowConsoleType()
  {
    Console.WriteLine($"The type {nameof(Console)} is from " +
      $"{Assembly.GetAssembly(typeof(Console)).FullName}");
  }

  public static void WindowsMessage(string message)
  {
    MessageBox.Show($"Windows Forms: {message}");
  }
}
```

What you need to be pay attention to in this scenario is that the `Console` class is part of .NET Standard, but the `MessageBox` class is not. Windows Forms is specific to Windows and will not be a part of the .NET Standard.

Next, a .NET Standard Library references this .NET Framework library. You can handle this in a simple way by adding a reference to the project. The project file contains a `ProjectReference` to the .NET Framework library (project file `UsingLegacyLibs/DotnetStandardLib/DotnetStandardLib.csproj`):

```
<Project Sdk="Microsoft.NET.Sdk">
  <PropertyGroup>
    <TargetFramework>netstandard2.0</TargetFramework>
  </PropertyGroup>
  <ItemGroup>
    <ProjectReference Include="..\DotnetFrameworkLib\DotnetFrameworkLib.csproj" />
  </ItemGroup>
</Project>
```

The `Wrapper` class defined in the .NET Standard library just forwards the method calls to the .NET Framework library. There's no compilation error on building the .NET Standard library when referencing the .NET Framework library (code file `UsingLegacyLibs/DotnetStandardLib/Wrapper.cs`):

```
public class Wrapper
{
  public static void ConsoleMessage(string message) =>
    Legacy.ConsoleMessage(message);

  public static void WindowsMessage(string message) =>
    Legacy.WindowsMessage(message);

  public static void ShowConsoleType() => Legacy.ShowConsoleType();
}
```

Next, a .NET Core console application makes use of the `Wrapper` class. The `Program` class invokes the three methods. However, check the handling of the `FileNotFoundException` exception when calling the `WindowsMessage` method (code file `UsingLegacyLibs/UsingLegacyLibs/Program.cs`):

```
static void Main()
{
  Wrapper.ConsoleMessage("Hello from .NET Core");
  Wrapper.ShowConsoleType();
  try
  {
    Wrapper.WindowsMessage("Hello from .NET Core");
  }
  catch (FileNotFoundException ex)
  {
    Console.WriteLine(ex.Message);
  }
}
```

The application runs as shown in the following output. The `Console` class is from the `System.Console` assembly. Invoking `WindowsMessage` results in a `FileNotFoundException` because the `System.Windows.Forms` assembly cannot be found:

```
From the .NET Framework Lib: Hello from .NET Core
The type Console is from System.Console, Version=4.1.0.0, Culture=neutral,
PublicKeyToken=b03f5f7f11d50a3a
Could not load file or assembly 'System.Windows.Forms, Version=4.0.0.0,
Culture=neutral, PublicKeyToken=b77a5c561934e089'.
The system cannot find the file specified.
```

When you create a .NET Framework Console application, there's no need to wrap the invocation of the `WindowsMessage` call into a try/catch handler because `System.Windows.Forms` is available (code file `UsingLegacyLibs/DotnetFrameworkApp/Program.cs`):

```
static void Main()
{
  Wrapper.ConsoleMessage("Hello from the .NET Framework");
  Wrapper.ShowConsoleType();
  Wrapper.WindowsMessage("Hello from the .NET Framework");
}
```

Running this application shows that the `Console` class is coming from the `mscorlib` assembly, and a window pops up for the `MessageBox`:

```
From the .NET Framework Lib: Hello from the .NET Framework
The type Console is from mscorlib, Version=4.0.0.0, Culture=neutral,
PublicKeyToken=b77a5c561934e089
```

> **WARNING** *It's easy to reference .NET Framework assemblies from .NET Core applications and build the application. However, this does not mean that every functionality of the .NET Framework assembly is available—only the types that are defined in the .NET Standard. Using just these types enables you to use .NET Framework libraries on Linux.*
>
> *Usually it's better to go for compilation errors if types are not available. Rebuilding .NET Framework libraries as .NET Standard libraries gives you this feature. Just in case you don't have the source code available, such as from vendors that don't offer .NET Standard libraries yet, you can still use the library from .NET Core. To check binaries and find out what types are not compatible with which version of the .NET Standard, you can use the .NET Portability Analyzer that is available as a command-line tool and a Visual Studio extension (see* `https://github.com/Microsoft/dotnet-apiport`*).*

Running the .NET Portability analyzer on the sample .NET Framework library shows you information on what platform versions support particular types and members (see table).

TARGET TYPE	TARGET MEMBER	.NET CORE	.NET FRAMEWORK	.NET STANDARD
DialogResult	DialogResult	Not supported	Supported: 1.1+	Not supported
MessageBox	MessageBox	Not supported	Supported: 1.1+	Not supported
MessagBox	Show	Not supported	Supported: 1.1+	Not supported
Assembly	GetAssembly	Supported: 2.0+	Supported: 1.1+	Supported: 2.0+

USING SHARED PROJECTS

Shared projects are not really libraries, but they are still helpful in sharing code. Shared projects give an alternative to a library to share the code but include the code with the project that references the shared project. This way, platform-specific code can be added to the shared project. However, this feature is useful only if not too much code is different. When there are a lot of code differences, it might be a better idea to create platform-specific libraries.

With the following code example, a .NET Core application and a Universal Windows App are created, and both reference a shared project. The shared project contains code that can be used with both platforms, but each also contains code that is platform specific.

The difference starts with namespaces that are not available everywhere. You can use preprocessor directives to check for conditional compilation symbols. The preprocessor directive `Windows_UWP` is defined with Universal Windows apps (code file `UsingASharedProject/SharedProject/Message.cs`):

```
using System;
using System.Threading.Tasks;
#if WINDOWS_UWP
using Windows.UI.Popups;
#endif
```

The `Message` class defines `Show`, `ShowAsync`, and `Add` methods. The `Add` method is available for every platform. The `Show` method is available only when the `NETCOREAPP2_0` directive is defined, and the `ShowAsync` method is available only for UWP apps. The class can be defined with the `internal` access modifier because it's not used outside of the assembly boundaries:

```
internal class Message
{
#if NETCOREAPP2_0
  public static void Show(string message)
  {
    Console.WriteLine(message);
  }
#elif WINDOWS_UWP
  public static async Task ShowAsync(string message)
  {
    await new MessageDialog(message).ShowAsync();
  }
#endif
  public static int Add(int x, int y) => x + y;
}
```

Using Visual Studio, a shared project can be added from the Reference Manager with the Shared Project selection as shown in Figure 19-8. Source code is included, and the Import element is used with the project file (project file UsingASharedProject/UsingASharedProject/UsingASharedProject.csproj):

```
<Project Sdk="Microsoft.NET.Sdk">
  <PropertyGroup>
    <OutputType>Exe</OutputType>
    <TargetFramework>netcoreapp2.0</TargetFramework>
  </PropertyGroup>
  <Import Project="..\SharedProject\SharedProject.projitems" Label="Shared" />
</Project>
```

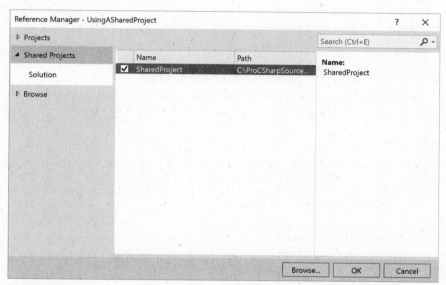

FIGURE 19-8

The Message class can now be used similarly to the way it would be used as a class of the same project (code file UsingASharedProject/UsingASharedProject/Program.cs):

```
using SharedProject;

namespace UsingASharedProject
{
  class Program
  {
    static void Main()
    {
      Message.Show(".NET Core");
    }
  }
}
```

From the UWP application, the Message class can be used in the same way. Here, the ShowAsync method is invoked in the Click handler of a Button (code file UsingASharedProject/UniversalApp/MainPage .xaml.cs):

```
private async void OnButtonClick(object sender, RoutedEventArgs e)
{
  await Message.ShowAsync("Hello from UWP");
}
```

> **NOTE** *When you work with the Visual Studio editor on the source code of the shared project, you can select the drop-down view on top of the editor to select the current project you would like to work with. This grays out the code that is currently not available based on the defined preprocessor definitions.*

CREATING NUGET PACKAGES

We've taken an excursion to shared projects, but now let's continue with libraries—and creating NuGet packages from libraries. NuGet packages can be created easily by using the .NET Core CLI tools and with Visual Studio 2017.

NuGet Packages with the Command Line

Metadata information about the NuGet package can be added to the project file csproj as shown earlier in the "Assemblies" section. To create a NuGet package from the command line, you can use the dotnet pack command:

```
> dotnet pack --configuration Release
```

Remember to set the configuration. By default, the Debug configuration is built. After a successful packaging, you can find the NuGet package in the directory bin/Release or related directories, depending on the selected configuration with the file extension .nupkg. A .nupkg file is a zip file that contains the binary with additional metadata. You can rename this file to a zip file to see its contents.

You can copy the generated NuGet package to a folder on your system or to a network share to make it available to your team. The sample is copied to the folder c:/MyPackages. To use this folder, the NuGet .config file can be changed to include this package source as shown in the section NuGet Sources. You also can reference the folder directly using the dotnet add package command:

```
> dotnet add package SampleLib --source c:/MyPackages
```

Supporting Multiple Platforms

The .NET Standard 2.0 has been enhanced to support a lot more APIs that are available on every new .NET platform. However, this is still not enough for some applications. You might either need legacy libraries that use more APIs than are available from the .NET Standard, or you might need features that are different between APIs such as WPF, UWP, and Xamarin. .NET Core also offers more features than are available from the .NET Standard.

Previously you've seen how Shared Projects can be used to support different platforms. Another option is to create different binaries from the same source code as shown in the next example.

The sample library SampleLib supports both .NET Standard 2.0 as well as .NET Framework 4.7 with different binaries. To build multiple binaries, the TargetFramework element can be changed to TargetFrameworks, and all the *target framework monikers* for the target frameworks where binaries should be created are listed within. The example adds the target framework monikers netstandard2.0 and net47. For code differences based on the target frameworks, different conditional compilation symbols are defined (project file CreateNuGet/SampleLib/SampleLib.csproj):

```
<Project Sdk="Microsoft.NET.Sdk">
  <PropertyGroup>
    <TargetFrameworks>netstandard2.0;net47</TargetFrameworks>
    <!-- Metadata information -->
  </PropertyGroup>

  <PropertyGroup Condition="'$(TargetFramework)'=='netstandard2.0'">
    <DefineConstants>NETSTANDARD2_0</DefineConstants>
  </PropertyGroup>

  <PropertyGroup Condition="'$(TargetFramework)'=='net47'">
    <DefineConstants>DOTNET47</DefineConstants>
  </PropertyGroup>
</Project>
```

> **NOTE** *The list of target framework monikers is shown at* https://docs.microsoft
> .com/nuget/schema/target-frameworks.

With the code, so you can easily see different functionality, different strings are initialized with different values, and this value is returned from the Show method (code file CreateNuGet/SampleLib/Demo.cs):

```
public class Demo
{
#if NETSTANDARD2_0
  private static string s_info = ".NET Standard 2.0";
#elif DOTNET47
  private static string s_info = ".NET 4.7";
#else
  private static string s_info = "Unknown";
#endif

  public static string Show() => s_info;
}
```

With this setup, you build the application with multiple target frameworks, and a DLL for every target framework is created. When you create a NuGet, one package is created that contains all the libraries.

When you create a .NET Core Console application, you can build the application for multiple target frameworks as well. Like the library before, with the console application multiple target frameworks are configured. The console application will be built for .NET Core 2.0 and the .NET Framework 4.7 (project file CreateNuGet/DotnetCaller/DotnetCaller.csproj):

```
<TargetFrameworks>netcoreapp2.0;net47</TargetFrameworks>
```

It's also possible to add packages only for specific target frameworks. You can do this with the dotnet add package command by adding the --framework option:

```
> dotnet add package SampleLib --framework net47 --source c:/MyPackages
```

This shows up with a condition based on the target framework in the project file as shown:

```
<ItemGroup Condition="'$(TargetFramework)' == 'net47'">
  <PackageReference Include="SampleLib" Version="1.2.0" />
</ItemGroup>
```

With the sample application, the same package is needed, but different assemblies from the package need to be selected. This is done automatically based on the project, and the package just needs to be added to the project. The complete project file for the console application is shown here (project file `CreateNuGet/DotnetCaller/DotnetCaller.csproj`):

```
<Project Sdk="Microsoft.NET.Sdk">
  <PropertyGroup>
    <OutputType>Exe</OutputType>
    <TargetFrameworks>netcoreapp2.0;net47</TargetFrameworks>
  </PropertyGroup>
  <ItemGroup>
    <PackageReference Include="SampleLib" Version="1.2.0" />
  </ItemGroup>
</Project>
```

Building the console application creates multiple binaries that contain references to different libraries.

```
> dotnet run --framework net47
```

results in the output

```
.NET 4.7
```

Using the .NET Core variant

```
> dotnet run --framework netcoreapp2.0
```

results in this output

```
.NET Standard 2.0
```

Be aware that selecting a different .NET Framework version, such as .NET 4.6.1, also results in .NET Standard 2.0. This is because the library built with .NET Framework 4.7 is not compatible with .NET 4.6.1 (only newer versions of .NET Framework are), but .NET 4.6.1 is compatible with .NET Standard 2.0, so this library matches.

NuGet Packages with Visual Studio

Visual Studio 2017 allows you to create packages. In the Solution Explorer, when you select the project, you can open the context menu and select Pack to create a NuGet package. In the Project properties of the Package settings, you can also select to create a NuGet package on every build. This is probably overkill if you don't plan to distribute packages on every build. However, with this setting you should configure the package metadata as well as the assembly and package version (see Figure 19-9).

You can use packages within Visual Studio by selecting Dependencies in the Solution Explorer, opening the context menu, and selecting Manage NuGet Packages. This opens the NuGet Package Manager (see Figure 19-10) where you can select the package sources (including the packages from the local folder if you configured this via clicking on the Settings icon). You can browse the available packages, see the packages installed with the project, and check whether updates of packages are available.

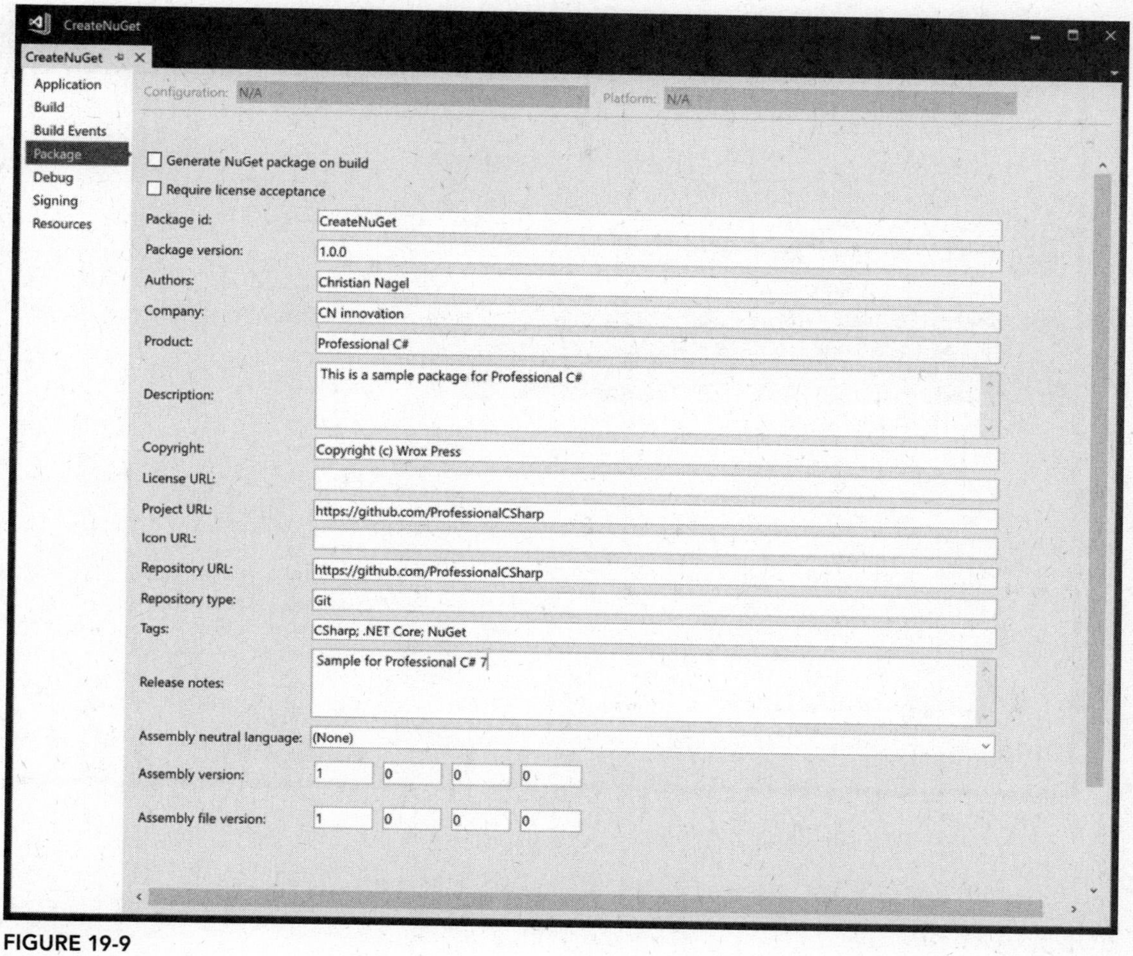

FIGURE 19-9

> **NOTE** *In case you want to create NuGet packages not only for internal use but also for publishing on the NuGet server, only adding the library to the NuGet file is not enough. You can add a readme file, add libraries from related projects, define dependencies, and create build scripts. For this, you need the NuGet utility from* www.nuget.org. *Visit* https://docs.microsoft.com/nuget *to get more information about how to do this.*

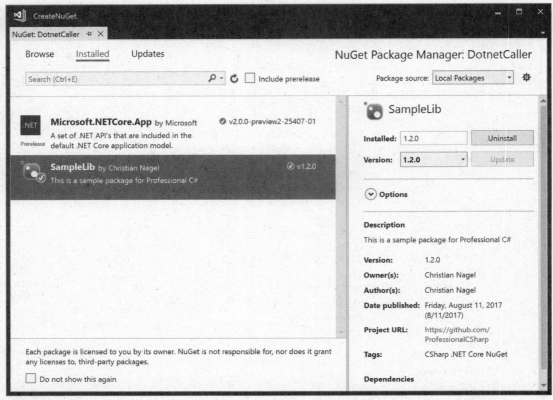

FIGURE 19-10

SUMMARY

This chapter explained the differences between DLLs, assemblies, and NuGet packages. You've seen how to create and distribute libraries with NuGet packages.

The .NET Standard defines an API set that is implemented from different .NET platforms. You've seen how a .NET Standard library can be used from .NET Core and the .NET Framework, and how types come from different libraries, such as mscorlib and System.Runtime.

The next chapter gets into the details of an important pattern: dependency injection. In this chapter you learn about another way of sharing code with different platforms by injecting platform-specific features.

20

Dependency Injection

WHAT'S IN THIS CHAPTER?

➤ Defining dependency injection

➤ Using dependency injection with Microsoft.Extensions .DependencyInjection

➤ Working with lifetime of services

➤ Using options and configuration to initialize services

➤ Using DI to create platform independence for WPF, UWP, and Xamarin

➤ Using other dependency injection containers

WROX.COM CODE DOWNLOADS FOR THIS CHAPTER

The wrox.com code downloads for this chapter are found at www.wrox.com on the Download Code tab. The source code is also available at https://github.com/ProfessionalCSharp/ProfessionalCSharp7 in the directory DependencyInjection. The code for this chapter is divided into the following major examples:

➤ NoDI

➤ WithDI

➤ WithDIContainer

➤ ServicesLifetime

➤ DIWithOptions

➤ DIWithConfigurations

➤ PlatformIndependenceSample

➤ DIWithAutofac

WHAT IS DEPENDENCY INJECTION?

Faster development cycles demand unit tests and better updatability. Making some code changes should not result in errors in unexpected places. Creating more modular applications where dependencies are reduced helps with that.

Dependency injection (DI) allows injection dependencies from the outside of a class, thus the class where the dependency is injected only needs to know about a contract (usually a C# interface). The class can be independent of the creation of its objects.

Dependency injection allows for easier unit tests. With the unit test, only a specific class needs testing, and the dependencies needed can be replaced by a special mock class that contains test data.

You can also use different implementations to differentiate between production mode and development mode. For example, in production you might need to access an SAP server, or you might need to authenticate with a specific active directory that is not accessible for all developers. During development, during every debug session you don't want to wait to have a successful authentication, and you don't need the SAP server to develop the user interface. Here you can have—for the same contract—different implementations where authentication is simulated, and you can work with test data instead of accessing the SAP server.

You can also use different implementations with different platforms. You can, for example, create a .NET Standard library where all the common functionality is implemented for UWP, WPF, and Xamarin applications, and you can redirect to platform-specific code as needed.

Dependency injection also enables you to replace standard functionality with custom features. ASP.NET Core and Entity Framework Core is heavily based on dependency injection. These technologies use hundreds of contracts—for example, to find a controller, to map a HTTP request to a controller, to convert data received to a parameter, to map a database table to an entity type, and so on. You easily can replace the custom functionality by using a different implementation.

DI is the core pattern of agile software development and continuous software delivery practices.

A *dependency injection container* is not required with dependency injection, but it helps for managing the dependencies. As soon as you have a growing list of services managed by the dependency injection container, you can see its advantages. ASP.NET Core and Entity Framework Core use `Microsoft.Extensions .DependencyInjection` as a container to manage all the dependencies to manage hundreds of services.

Although dependency injection and dependency injection containers increase the complexity in very small applications, as soon as your application grows larger and needs multiple services, dependency injection reduces the complexity and fosters implementations that are not tightly bound.

This chapter starts with a small application that doesn't use dependency injection; in subsequent examples it turns into an application that does use dependency injection and uses a dependency injection container. This chapter also covers lifetime management and configuration of services. In the last sections of this chapter you see how you can use dependency injection to cover platform-specific services with WPF, UWP, and Xamarin. Finally, the chapter discusses integrating third-party containers with `Microsoft.Extensions .DependencyInjection`.

Using a Service Without Dependency Injection

Let's start an example without using dependency injection; later we'll change it to use dependency injection. The service implementation that is used is defined in the class `GreetingService`. This class defines the method `Greet` that returns a string (code file `NoDI/GreetingService.cs`):

```
public class GreetingService
{
  public string Greet(string name) => $"Hello, {name}";
}
```

The class `HomeController` makes use of this service. In the `Hello` method, the `GreetingService` is instantiated, and the `Greet` method is invoked (code file `NoDI/HomeController.cs`):

```
public class HomeController
{
  public string Hello(string name)
```

```
    {
        var service = new GreetingService();
        return service.Greet(name);
    }
}
```

Let's have a look at the `Main` method of the `Program` class. Here, the `HomeController` is instantiated, the `Hello` method invoked, and the result is written to the console (code file `NoDI/Program.cs`):

```
static void Main()
{
    var controller = new HomeController();
    string result = controller.Hello("Stephanie");
    Console.WriteLine(result);
}
```

The program is working, and `Hello, Stephanie` is written to the console. What are the issues with that?

The `HomeController` and `GreetingService` are tightly coupled. It's not easy to replace the `GreetingService` in the `HomeController` for a different implementation. This `GreetingService` is a simple one that returns a `string`. In normal applications, you typically have a more complex scenario—for example, the `GreetingService` might access an API service using HTTP requests, or it might access the database using Entity Framework. You might want to change the service used in one place instead of finding all the places where the service is used.

Also, when you create a unit test for the `HomeController`, the `GreetingService` is tested as well. With a unit test, you want to test just the functionality of the methods of a single class without using other dependencies. In the `HomeController`, the `GreetingService` cannot be easily replaced for unit tests. Technically it's possible to make replacements of the internal implementation of the `GreetingService` method for unit tests. With the Microsoft Fakes framework, it is possible to change the implementation of the method by replacing specific methods and properties of the `GreetingService` class. This change is defined with the unit test and happens only when the unit test runs: "faking" the original method by a different one. There are better ways to do this: by using dependency injection.

In the next section, you see how to change this implementation to use dependency injection.

> **NOTE** *Entity Framework Core is covered in detail in Chapter 26, "Entity Framework Core." Check Chapter 28, "Testing," for more information on unit testing. API services are explained in Chapter 32, "ASP.NET Web API."*

Using Dependency Injection

Let's make the `HomeController` independent of the implementation of the `GreetingService`. You can do this by creating the interface `IGreetingService` that defines the functionality needed by the `HomeController` (code file `WithDI/IGreetingService.cs`):

```
public interface IGreetingService
{
    string Greet(string name);
}
```

`GreetingService` now implements the interface `IGreetingService` (code file `WithDI/GreetingService.cs`):

```
public class GreetingService : IGreetingService
{
    public string Greet(string name) => $"Hello, {name}";
}
```

All the `HomeController` now needs is a reference to an object that implements the interface `IGreetingService`. This is injected with the constructor of the `HomeController`, assigned to the private field, and used with the method `Hello` (code file `WithDI/HomeController.cs`):

```
public class HomeController
{
  private readonly IGreetingService _greetingService;
  public HomeController(IGreetingService greetingService)
  {
    _greetingService = greetingService ??
      throw new ArgumentNullException(nameof(greetingService));
  }

  public string Hello(string name) => _greetingService.Greet(name);
}
```

With this implementation, the `HomeController` makes use of the *inversion of control* design principle. The `HomeController` doesn't instantiate the `GreetingService` like it did before. Instead, the control to define the concrete class that is used by the `HomeController` is given to the outside; in other words, the control is inversed.

> **NOTE** Inversion of control *is also known as the* Hollywood principle: *Don't call us; we call you.*
>
> *Inversion of control also reduces the dependencies on different technologies and creates more common code. For example, you can use the same view-models and service contracts from WPF, UWP, and Xamarin applications in a common .NET Standard library. Some services need to be implemented differently with WPF, UWP, and Xamarin. The implementation for such services can come from the hosting application, whereas the contract is defined and used in a .NET Standard library. Read Chapter 34, "Patterns with XAML Apps," for more information on view-models.*

The class `HomeController` doesn't have a dependency on the implementation of a concrete implementation of the `IGreetingService` interface. The `HomeController` can use any class that implements the interface `IGreetingService`. The class just needs to implement all members of this interface. Now, the dependency needs to be injected from the outside, passing a concrete implementation to the constructor of the `HelloController` class. With the sample code, the inversion of control design principle is implemented using the dependency injection pattern with *constructor injection*. It's called constructor injection because the interface is injected in the constructor. The dependency needs to be injected to create a `HomeController` instance.

Let's change the `Main` method to pass a concrete implementation of the `IGreetingService` to the `HomeController`. Here, the dependency is injected (code file `WithDI/Program.cs`):

```
static void Main()
{
  var controller = new HomeController(new GreetingService());
  string result = controller.Hello("Matthias");
  Console.WriteLine(result);
}
```

Creating a unit test for the `Hello` method of the `HomeController`, a different implementation can be injected—for example, a `MockGreetingService` implementing `IGreetingService`.

The sample application is currently very small. The only thing that needs to be injected is a single concrete class that implements a contract. This class is instantiated at the same time you instantiate the HomeController. In real applications, you need to deal with many interfaces and implementations, and you also need to share instances. A simple way for doing this is to use a dependency injection container that manages all the dependencies. In the next section, the application is changed to use the Microsoft .Extensions.DependencyInjection container.

USING THE .NET CORE DI CONTAINER

With a dependency injection container, you can have one place in your application where you define what contracts map to which specific implementation, and you also can specify if a service should be used as a singleton, or a new instance should be created every time it's used.

In the next sample, let's use the previously created GreetingService to implement IGreetingService as well as the HomeController class, but this time we use a dependency injection container.

The sample WithDIContainer makes use of these NuGet packages and namespaces:

Packages

Microsoft.Extensions.DependencyInjection

Namespaces

System

Microsoft.Extensions.DependencyInjection

Within the Program class, now the RegisterServices method is defined. Here, a new ServiceCollection object is instantiated. ServiceCollection is defined in the namespace Microsoft .Extensions.DependencyInjection after you add the NuGet package Microsoft.Extensions .DependencyInjection. When you use AddSingleton and AddTransient, extension methods to the ServiceCollection are used to register the types that need to be known by the DI container. With the sample application, both the GreetingService and the HomeController are registered in the container, which allows retrieving the HomeController from the container.

The class GreetingService is instantiated when the IGreetingService interface is requested. The HomeController itself does not implement an interface. With this DI container configuration, the HomeController is instantiated when the HomeController is requested. The DI container configuration also defines the lifetime of the services. With GreetingService, the same instance always is returned when IGreetingService is requested. This is different with the HomeController. With the HomeController with every request to retrieve a HomeController, a new instance is created. The lifetime information for the services is specified by using the AddSingleton and the AddTransient methods. Later in this chapter, you can read more about the lifetime of these services.

Invoking the method BuildServiceProvider returns a ServiceProvider object that can then be used to access the services registered (code file WithDIContainer/Program.cs):

```
static ServiceProvider RegisterServices()
{
  var services = new ServiceCollection();
  services.AddSingleton<IGreetingService, GreetingService>();
  services.AddTransient<HomeController>();
  return services.BuildServiceProvider();
}
```

> **NOTE** *With .NET Core 1.1, the* `BuildServiceProvider` *returned the interface* `IServiceProvider` *instead of returning the concrete class* `ServiceProvider`. *With .NET Core 1.1,* `ServiceProvider` *was declared internal and thus could be used from the outside only via its public interface* `IServiceProvider`. *The implementation changed with .NET Core 2.0 to make the* `ServiceProvider` *class public, and to change the method declaration of* `BuildServiceProvider` *to return* `ServiceProvider`. *This allows directly accessing the* `Dispose` *method of the* `ServiceProvider` *without the need to cast the returned object to* `IDisposable` *to invoke* `Dispose`.

> **NOTE** *In case you add the same interface contract multiple times to the services collection, the last one added wins on getting the interface from the container. This makes it easy to replace contracts with different implementations if you need some other functionality, such as with services implemented by ASP.NET Core or Entity Framework Core.*
>
> *On the other hand, with the* `ServiceCollection` *class you also have access to remove services and to retrieve a list of all services for a specific contract.*

Next, let's change the `Main` method to invoke the `RegisterServices` method for making the registration within the DI container and then to invoke the `GetRequiredService` method of the `ServiceProvider` to get a reference to a `HomeController` instance (code file `WithDIContainer/Program.cs`):

```
static void Main()
{
  using (ServiceProvider container = RegisterServices())
  {
    var controller = container.GetRequiredService<HomeController>();
    string result = controller.Hello("Katharina");
    Console.WriteLine(result);
  }
}
```

> **NOTE** *With the* `ServiceProvider` *class, different overloads of* `GetService` *and* `GetRequiredService` *exists. The method that is directly implemented in the* `ServiceProvider` *class is* `GetService` *with a* `Type` *parameter. The generic method* `GetService<T>` *is an extension method that takes the generic type parameter and passes it to the* `GetService` *method.*
>
> *If the service is not available in the container,* `GetService` *returns* null. *The extension method* `GetRequiredService` *checks for a* null *result and throws an* `InvalidOperationException` *in case the service is not found. In case the service provider implements the interface* `ISupportsRequiredService`, *the extension method* `GetRequiredService` *invokes the* `GetRequiredService` *of the provider. The container of .NET Core 2.0 does not implement this interface, but some third-party containers do.*

When you start the application, on the request of the `GetRequiredService` method, the DI container creates an instance of the `HomeController` class. The `HomeController` constructor requires an object implementing `IGreetingService`. This interface is also registered with the container; for `IGreetingService` a `GreetingService` object needs to be returned. The `GreetingService` class has a default constructor, so the container can create an instance and pass this instance to the constructor of the `HomeController`. This instance is used with the controller variable, and it's used as before to invoke the `Hello` method.

What happens if not every dependency is registered with the DI container? To see this in action, you can remove the configuration of the `IGreetingService` with the DI container. In that case, the container throws the `InvalidOperationException`. This error message is shown: `Unable to resolve service for type 'WithDIContainer.IGreetingService' while attempting to activate 'WithDIContainer.HomeController'`.

LIFETIME OF SERVICES

The lifetime of services defines how long a service instance exists. Does it exist for the lifetime of the application? Is a new instance created on every request? There's also something in-between, as you will see here.

Registering a service as a singleton always returns the same instance, and registering a service as transient returns a new object every time the service is injected. There are more options available, and more issues to think about. Let's start with another example showing the lifetime features and issues. The example also implements the `IDisposable` interface with the services, so you can see how this is dealt with.

The sample `ServicesLifetime` makes use of the following NuGet package and namespaces:

Package

`Microsoft.Extensions.DependencyInjection`

Namespaces

`System`

`Microsoft.Extensions.DependencyInjection`

To easily differentiate between different instances, every service instantiated will be given a different number. The number is created from a shared service. This shared service defines a simple interface `INumberService` to return a number (code file `ServicesLifetime/INumberService.cs`):

```
public interface INumberService
{
    int GetNumber();
}
```

The implementation of `INumberService` always returns a new number in the `GetNumber` method. This service will be registered as a singleton to have the number shared between the other services (code file `ServicesLifetime/NumberService.cs`):

```
public class NumberService : INumberService
{
    private int _number = 0;
    public int GetNumber() => Interlocked.Increment(ref _number);
}
```

The other services that will be looked at are defined by the interface contracts `IServiceA`, `IServiceB`, and `IServiceC` with the corresponding methods `A`, `B`, and `C`. The following code snippet shows the contract for `IServiceA` (code file `ServicesLifetime/IServiceA.cs`):

```
public interface IServiceA
{
    void A();
}
```

With the implementation of `ServiceA`, the constructor needs injection of the `INumberService`. With this service, the number is retrieved to assign it to the private field _n. With the implementation of the constructor, the method `A`, and the `Dispose` method that implements the `IDisposable` interface, console output is written, so you can see lifetime information (code file `ServicesLifetime/ServiceA.cs`):

```csharp
public class ServiceA : IServiceA, IDisposable
{
  private int _n;
  public ServiceA(INumberService numberService)
  {
    _n = numberService.GetNumber();
    Console.WriteLine($"ctor {nameof(ServiceA)}, {_n}");
  }

  public void A() => Console.WriteLine($"{nameof(A)}, {_n}");

  public void Dispose() =>
    Console.WriteLine($"disposing {nameof(ServiceA)}, {_n}");
}
```

> **NOTE** *The* `IDiposable` *interface is explained in detail in Chapter 17, "Managed and Unmanaged Memory."*

In addition to the services, the controller `ControllerX` is implemented. `ControllerX` requires constructor injection of three services: `IServiceA`, `IServiceB`, and `INumberService`. With the method `M`, two of the injected services are invoked. Also, constructor and `Dispose` information is written to the console (code file `ServicesLifetime/ControllerX.cs`):

```csharp
public class ControllerX : IDisposable
{
  private readonly IServiceA _serviceA;
  private readonly IServiceB _serviceB;
  private readonly int _n;
  private int _countm = 0;
  public ControllerX(IServiceA serviceA, IServiceB serviceB,
    INumberService numberService)
  {
    _n = numberService.GetNumber();

    Console.WriteLine($"ctor {nameof(ControllerX)}, {_n}");
    _serviceA = serviceA;
    _serviceB = serviceB;
  }

  public void M()
  {
    Console.WriteLine($"invoked {nameof(M)} for the {++_countm}. time");
    _serviceA.A();
    _serviceB.B();
  }

  public void Dispose() => Console.WriteLine(
      $"disposing {nameof(ControllerX)}, {_n}");
}
```

Using Singleton and Transient Services

Let's start registering singleton and transient services. RegisterServices is implemented as a local function within the method SingletonAndTransient. Here, the services ServiceA, ServiceB, and NumberService and the controller class ControllerX are registered. The NumberService needs to be registered as a singleton to have shared state. ServiceA is registered as a singleton as well. ServiceB and ControllerX are registered transient (code file ServicesLifetime/Program.cs):

```
private static void SingletonAndTransient()
{
  Console.WriteLine(nameof(SingletonAndTransient));

  ServiceProvider RegisterServices()
  {
    IServiceCollection services = new ServiceCollection();
    services.AddSingleton<IServiceA, ServiceA>();
    services.AddTransient<IServiceB, ServiceB>();
    services.AddTransient<ControllerX>();
    services.AddSingleton<INumberService, NumberService>();
    return services.BuildServiceProvider();
  }
  //...
}
```

AddSingleton and AddTransient are extension methods that make it easier to register services with the Microsoft.Extensions.DependencyInjection framework. Instead of using these helpful methods, you can also register services with the Add method (which is itself invoked by the convenient methods). The Add method requires a ServiceDescriptor that contains the service type, the implementation type, and the kind of the service. The kind of the service is specified using the ServiceLifetime enum type. ServiceLifetime defines the values Singleton, Transient, and Scoped:

```
services.Add(new ServiceDescriptor(typeof(ControllerX),
    typeof(ControllerX), ServiceLifetime.Transient));
```

> **NOTE** The Add method of the ServiceCollection class is explicitly implemented for the interface IServiceCollection. With this, you can see the method only when you use the interface IServiceCollection and not when you have a variable of the ServiceCollection type. Explicit interface implementation is covered in Chapter 4, "Object-Oriented Programming with C#."

The local function RegisterServices method is invoked to retrieve the ServiceProvider, get the ControllerX two times, and invoke the method M before the ServiceProvider gets disposed (code file ServicesLifetime/Program.cs):

```
private static void SingletonAndTransient()
{
  //...
  using (ServiceProvider container = RegisterServices())
  {
    ControllerX x = container.GetRequiredService<ControllerX>();
    x.M();
    x.M();
```

```
        Console.WriteLine($"requesting {nameof(ControllerX)}");
        ControllerX x2 = container.GetRequiredService<ControllerX>();
        x2.M();

        Console.WriteLine();
    }
}
```

> **NOTE** *Local functions are explained in Chapter 13, "Functional Programming with C#."*

When you run the application, you can see when the `ControllerX` is requested, `ServiceA` and `ServiceB` are instantiated, and the `NumberService` returns a new number every time the `GetNumber` method is invoked. When the `ControllerX` is requested the second time, not only is the `ControllerX` newly created but also `ServiceB` is created and is registered transient. With `ServiceB`, the same instance is used as before, and no new instance is created:

```
SingletonAndTransient
requesting ControllerX
ctor ServiceA, 1
ctor ServiceB, 2
ctor ControllerX, 3
invoked M for the 1. time
A, 1
B, 2
invoked M for the 2. time
A, 1
B, 2
requesting ControllerX
ctor ServiceB, 4
ctor ControllerX, 5
invoked M for the 1. time
A, 1
B, 4

disposing ControllerX, 5
disposing ServiceB, 4
disposing ControllerX, 3
disposing ServiceB, 2
disposing ServiceA, 1
```

Using Scoped Services

Services can also be registered within a scope. This is something in-between transient and singleton. With singleton, only a single instance is created. Transient creates a new instance every time the service is requested from the container. With scoped, always the same instance is returned from the same scope, but from a different scope a different instance is returned. Scopes are by default defined with ASP.NET Core web applications. Here, the scope is a HTTP Web request. With the scoped service, the same instance is returned if the request to the container is coming from the same HTTP request. With different HTTP requests, other instances are returned. This allows for easily sharing state inside an HTTP request.

With non-ASP.NET Core web applications you need to create the scope for yourself to get advantages of scoped services.

Let's start registering services with the local function `RegisterServices`. `ServiceA` is registered as a scoped service, `ServiceB` as singleton, and `ServiceC` as transient (code file `ServicesLifetime/Program.cs`):

```
private static void UsingScoped()
{
```

```
    Console.WriteLine(nameof(UsingScoped));

    ServiceProvider RegisterServices()
    {
      var services = new ServiceCollection();
      services.AddSingleton<INumberService, NumberService>();
      services.AddScoped<IServiceA, ServiceA>();
      services.AddSingleton<IServiceB, ServiceB>();
      services.AddTransient<IServiceC, ServiceC>();
      return services.BuildServiceProvider();
    }
    //...
  }
```

You can create a scope invoking the `CreateScope` method of the `ServiceProvider`. This returns a scope object that implements the interface `IServiceScope`. From there you can access the `ServiceProvider` belonging to this scope where you can request the services from the container. With the following code snippet, `ServiceA` and `ServiceC` are requested two times, whereas `ServiceB` is requested just once. Then the methods A, B, and C are invoked:

```
    private static void UsingScoped()
    {
      //...
      using (ServiceProvider container = RegisterServices())
      {
        using (IServiceScope scope1 = container.CreateScope())
        {
          IServiceA a1 = scope1.ServiceProvider.GetService<IServiceA>();
          a1.A();
          IServiceA a2 = scope1.ServiceProvider.GetService<IServiceA>();
          a2.A();
          IServiceB b1 = scope1.ServiceProvider.GetService<IServiceB>();
          b1.B();
          IServiceC c1 = scope1.ServiceProvider.GetService<IServiceC>();
          c1.C();
          IServiceC c2 = scope1.ServiceProvider.GetService<IServiceC>();
          c2.C();
        }

        Console.WriteLine("end of scope1");
      //...
    }
```

After the first scope is disposed, another scope is created. With the second scope, again the services `ServiceA`, `ServiceB`, and `ServiceC` are requested and methods invoked:

```
    private static void UsingScoped()
    {
      //...
      Console.WriteLine("end of scope1");

      using (IServiceScope scope2 = container.CreateScope())
      {
        IServiceA a3 = scope2.ServiceProvider.GetService<IServiceA>();
        a3.A();
        IServiceB b2 = scope2.ServiceProvider.GetService<IServiceB>();
        b2.B();
        IServiceC c3 = scope2.ServiceProvider.GetService<IServiceC>();
        c3.C();
      }
      Console.WriteLine("end of scope2");
      Console.WriteLine();
    }
```

When you run the application, you can see the services for the instances are created, methods are invoked, and they're automatically disposed. As `ServiceA` is registered as scoped, within the same scope the same instance is used. `ServiceC` is registered as transient, so here an instance is created with every request to the container. At the end of the scope, the transient and scoped services are automatically disposed, but not `ServiceB`. `ServiceB` is registered as singleton and thus needs to survive the end of the scope:

```
UsingScoped
ctor ServiceA, 1
A, 1
A, 1
ctor ServiceB, 2
B, 2
ctor ServiceC, 3
C, 3
ctor ServiceC, 4
C, 4
disposing ServiceC, 4
disposing ServiceC, 3
disposing ServiceA, 1
end of scope1
```

Starting the second scope, `ServiceA` and `ServiceB` are instantiated again. When you request `ServiceB`, the same object previously created is returned. At the end of the scope, `ServiceA` and `ServiceC` are disposed again. `ServiceB` is disposed after disposing the root provider:

```
ctor ServiceA, 5
A, 5
B, 2
ctor ServiceC, 6
C, 6
disposing ServiceC, 6
disposing ServiceA, 5
end of scope2

disposing ServiceB, 2
```

> **NOTE** *You don't need to invoke the* `Dispose` *method on services to release them. With services implementing the* `IDisposable` *interface, the container invokes the* `Dispose` *method. Transient and scoped services are disposed when the scope is disposed. Singleton services are disposed when the root provider is disposed.*
>
> *With .NET Core 2.0, the service instances are disposed in the reverse order they have been created. This is important when one service needs another one injected. For example,* `ServiceA` *requires* `ServiceB` *to be injected. Thus,* `ServiceB` *is created first, followed by* `ServiceA`*. With disposing,* `ServiceA` *is disposed first and can still access methods from* `ServiceB` *while it's being disposed. This behavior is different from .NET Core 1.0 where disposing of service instances happened in the order the service instances were created.*

Using Custom Factories

Other than defining to use transient, scoped, and singleton, you can also create a custom factory or pass an existing instance to the container. The following code snippet shows how you can do this.

You can pass a previously created instance to the container by using an overload of the `AddSingleton` method. Here, in the `RegisterServices` method, a `NumberService` object is created first, and then it's passed to the `AddSingleton` method. Using the `GetService` method, or injecting it in the constructor, is not different from the code you've seen before. You just need to be aware that the container is not responsible for invoking the Dispose method in this case. With objects creating and passing to the container, it's your responsibility to dispose these objects (if the objects need disposing at all). You also can use a factory method that is used to create the instance instead of letting the service be created from the container. In case the service needs a custom initialization or defines constructors that aren't supported by the DI container, this is a useful option. You can pass a delegate with an IServiceProvider parameter and return the service instance to the AddSingleton, AddScoped, and AddTransient methods. With the sample code, the local function named CreateServiceBFactory returns a ServiceB object. In case the constructor of the service implementation needs other services, these can be retrieved using the passed IServiceProvider instance (code file ServicesLifetime/Program.cs):

```csharp
private static void CustomFactories()
{
  Console.WriteLine(nameof(CustomFactories));

  IServiceB CreateServiceBFactory(IServiceProvider provider) =>
    new ServiceB(provider.GetService<INumberService>());

  ServiceProvider RegisterServices()
  {
    var numberService = new NumberService();

    var services = new ServiceCollection();
    services.AddSingleton<INumberService>(numberService);  // add existing

    services.AddTransient<IServiceB>(CreateServiceBFactory);  // use a factory
    services.AddSingleton<IServiceA, ServiceA>();
    return services.BuildServiceProvider();
  }

  using (ServiceProvider container = RegisterServices())
  {
    IServiceA a1 = container.GetService<IServiceA>();
    IServiceA a2 = container.GetService<IServiceA>();
    IServiceB b1 = container.GetService<IServiceB>();
    IServiceB b2 = container.GetService<IServiceB>();
  }
  Console.WriteLine();
}
```

INITIALIZATION OF SERVICES USING OPTIONS

You've already seen that a service can be injected in another service. This can also be used to initialize a service with options. You cannot define non-service contracts with the constructor of a service for initialization because the container does not know how to initialize this. Services are needed. However, to pass options for a service, you can also use a service that is already available with .NET Core.

The sample DIWithOptions makes use of these NuGet packages and namespaces:

Packages

Microsoft.Extensions.DependencyInjection

Microsoft.Extensions.Options

Namespaces

System

Microsoft.Extensions.DependencyInjection

Microsoft.Extensions.Options

The sample code makes use of the previously used `GreetingService` with modifications to pass options. The configuration values needed by the service are defined with the class `GreetingServiceOptions`. The sample code requires a `string` parameter with the `From` property (code file `DIWithOptions/GreetingServiceOptions.cs`):

```
public class GreetingServiceOptions
{
  public string From { get; set; }
}
```

The options for the service can be passed by specifying a constructor with an `IOptions<T>` parameter. The previously defined class `GreetingServiceOptions` is the generic type used with `IOptions`. The value passed to the constructor is used to initialize the field `_from` (code file `DIWithOptions/GreetingService.cs`):

```
public class GreetingService : IGreetingService
{
  public GreetingService(IOptions<GreetingServiceOptions> options) =>
    _from = options.Value.From;

  private readonly string _from;

  public string Greet(string name) => $"Hello, {name}! Greetings from {_from}";
}
```

> **NOTE** *The* `IOptions` *interface and the service used with options is implemented in the NuGet package* `Microsoft.Extensions.Options`*.*

For making it easy to register the service with the DI container, the extension method `AddGreetingService` is defined. This method extends the `IServiceCollection` interface and allows passing the `GreetingServiceOptions` with a delegate. In the implementation, the `Configure` method is used to specify the configuration with the `IOptions` interface. The `Configure` method is an extension method for `IServiceCollection` in the `Microsoft.Extensions.Options` NuGet package (code file `DIWithOptions/GreetingServiceExtensions.cs`):

```
public static class GreetingServiceExtensions
{
  public static IServiceCollection AddGreetingService(
    this IServiceCollection collection,
    Action<GreetingServiceOptions> setupAction)
  {
    if (collection == null)
      throw new ArgumentNullException(nameof(collection));
    if (setupAction == null)
      throw new ArgumentNullException(nameof(setupAction));

    collection.Configure(setupAction);
    return collection.AddTransient<IGreetingService, GreetingService>();
  }
}
```

The `HomeController` that makes use of the `GreetingService` with constructor injection doesn't need any change (code file `DIWithOptions/HomeController.cs`):

```
public class HomeController
{
  private readonly IGreetingService _greetingService;
  public HomeController(IGreetingService greetingService)
```

```
    {
      _greetingService = greetingService;
    }

    public string Hello(string name) => _greetingService.Greet(name);
  }
```

You can now register the services with the helper method `AddGreetingService`. The configuration for the `GreetingService` is done here by passing the required options. What's also needed is a service that implements the `IOptions` interface. Here, an extension method can be used as well: `AddOptions`. This method adds several interfaces and maps it to implementations that are used with options (code file `DIWithOptions/Program.cs`):

```
static ServiceProvider RegisterServices()
{
  var services = new ServiceCollection();
  services.AddOptions();
  services.AddGreetingService(options =>
  {
    options.From = "Christian";
  });
  services.AddTransient<HomeController>();
  return services.BuildServiceProvider();
}
```

The service can now be used like before. The `HomeController` is retrieved from the container, and constructor injection is used in the `HomeController` where the `IGreetingService` is used:

```
static void Main()
{
  using (var container = RegisterServices())
  {
    var controller = container.GetService<HomeController>();
    string result = controller.Hello("Katharina");
    Console.WriteLine(result);
  }
}
```

When you run the application, now the options are used:

```
Hello, Katharina! Greetings from Christian
```

USING CONFIGURATION FILES

Options as shown in the previous section also can be used when a service needs to be configured from a configuration file. However, there's a more direct way to do this: You can use the .NET configuration features in conjunction with an extension to the options. Options can be extended with configuration using the NuGet package `Microsoft.Extensions.Options.ConfigurationExtensions`.

The sample `DIWithConfiguration` makes use of these NuGet packages and namespaces:

Packages

`Microsoft.Extensions.Configuration`

`Microsoft.Extensions.Configuration.Json`

`Microsoft.ExtensionsDependencyInjection`

`Microsoft.Extensions.Options`

`Microsoft.Extensions.Options.ConfigurationExtensions`

Namespaces

```
System

Microsoft.Extensions.Configuration

Microsoft.Extensions.DependencyInjection

Microsoft.Extensions.Options
```

The sample code is based on the sample from the previous section, but now options are extended with configuration. No change needs to be done with the GreetingService class; it's still initialized using the IOptions interface. What's changed is the AddGreetingService extension method, which makes it easier to use the service. The second parameter of this method is now of type IConfiguration to receive configuration values. The config parameter is used for passing it to the Configure extension method. The Configure extension method is different one from the one used previously; this one is defined in the NuGet package Microsoft.Extensions.Options.ConfigurationExtensions (code file DIWithConfiguration/GreetingServiceExtensions.cs):

```
public static class GreetingServiceExtensions
{
  public static IServiceCollection AddGreetingService(
    this IServiceCollection collection, IConfiguration config)
  {
    if (collection == null)
      throw new ArgumentNullException(nameof(collection));
    if (config == null) throw new ArgumentNullException(nameof(config));

    collection.Configure<GreetingServiceOptions>(config);
    return collection.AddTransient<IGreetingService, GreetingService>();
  }
}
```

Configuration can be read from environmental variables, program arguments, and from files with different formats such as XML, INI, and JSON files. Here, the provider to read JSON configuration is used for adding the NuGet packages Microsoft.Extensions.Configuration and Microsoft.Extensions .Json. In the method DefineConfiguration, first a ConfigurationBuilder is created, and then fluent API is used to configure the base path for the directory where the JSON file can be read and to configure the JSON file itself. The file appsettings.json is used to read the configuration. After the setup of the ConfigurationBuilder, invoking the Build method returns an object that implements IConfiguration where the configuration values can be accessed (code file DIWithConfiguration/Program.cs):

```
static void DefineConfiguration()
{
  IConfigurationBuilder configBuilder = new ConfigurationBuilder()
    .SetBasePath(Directory.GetCurrentDirectory())
    .AddJsonFile("appsettings.json");
  Configuration = configBuilder.Build();
}

public static IConfiguration Configuration { get; set; }
```

The configuration file specifies the From settings for the GreetingService configuration (configuration file DIWithConfiguration/appsettings.json:

```
{
  "GreetingService": {
```

```
        "From": "Matthias"
    }
}
```

The `ServiceCollection` is configured like it was before. The `IOptions` interface needs to be specified as well. What's different is that the new version of the `AddGreetingService` extension method that passes the `IConfiguration` value. This can be done by accessing the `Configuration` property that's defined previously to read the section `GreetingService`, which passes the values that contain this section (code file `DIWithConfiguration/Program.cs`):

```
static ServiceProvider RegisterServices()
{
  var services = new ServiceCollection();
  services.AddOptions();
  services.AddSingleton<IGreetingService, GreetingService>();
  services.AddGreetingService(
    Configuration.GetSection("GreetingService"));
  services.AddTransient<HomeController>();
  return services.BuildServiceProvider();
}
```

Before registering the services, the configuration needs to be specified. You do this in the `Main` method as shown. When you run the application, it behaves like it did before, but the configuration comes from a file:

```
static void Main()
{
  DefineConfiguration();
  var container = RegisterServices();
  var controller = container.GetService<HomeController>();
  string result = controller.Hello("Katharina");
  Console.WriteLine(result);
}
```

CREATING PLATFORM INDEPENDENCE

Dependency injection also can be used to use platform-specific features from platform-independent libraries. For example, you can create a .NET Standard Library that is used from WPF, UWP, and Xamarin applications, and it makes calls into platform-specific APIs. Calling a Web API can be implemented so it's completely platform independent. Doing such simple things like opening a message dialog is platform specific.

The next sample solution, `PlatformIndependenceSample`, consists of the projects in the following table.

`DISampleLib`	This is a .NET Standard library consisting of services, service contracts, and a view-model. Because the message service is platform specific, for this service only a contract is defined within the library (`IMessageService`).
`WPFClient`	The WPF client application references the `DISampleLib` and contains a reference to the NuGet package `Microsoft.Extensions.DependencyInjection`. This application defines a user interface with XAML and makes use of the view-model and services from the .NET Standard library. For the interface `IMessageService`, the service `WPFMessageService` is implemented in the WPF project.
`UWPClient`	The UWP client application is like the WPF application. It just needs a different implementation of the `IMessageService`: `UWPMessageService`.
`XamarinClient`	With Xamarin, a Xamarin.Forms application was created. This results in a project for Android, a project for iOS, and a project for UWP. Common code (you can share the user interface) is in a shared project. With every single Xamarin.Forms project the .NET Standard library and the NuGet package `Microsoft.Extensions.DependencyInjection` need to be referenced. The code for the user interface, the setup of the DI container, and the implementation of the `IMessageService` interface—`XamarinMessageService`—is common between UWP, Android, and iPhone in the shared project.

> **NOTE** *To have the Xamarin project templates available with Visual Studio, you need to install the workload Mobile development with .NET using the Visual Studio Installer. You can also use Visual Studio for Mac. To successfully compile for iOS, you also need a Mac.*

.NET Standard Library

Let's start with the .NET Standard library implementing services and contracts. The interface `IMessageService` is a contract. This contract defines the method `ShowMessageAsync`, where a pop-up window should be shown on calling this method. As mentioned previously, creating these dialogs is not possible from .NET Standard (code file `PlatformIndependenceSample/DISampleLib/IMessageService.cs`):

```
public interface IMessageService
{
   Task ShowMessageAsync(string message);
}
```

The interface `IMessageService` is used in the class `ShowMessageViewModel`. The object implementing this interface will be injected with the constructor of `ShowMessageViewModel`. This view-model class defines the command `ShowMessageCommand` that is fired from the user interfaces of the specific platforms. On firing of this command, the `ShowMessageAsync` method of the `IMessageService` is invoked (code file `PlatformIndependenceSample/DISampleLib/ShowMessageViewModel.cs`):

```
public class ShowMessageViewModel
{
   private readonly IMessageService _messageService;
   public ShowMessageViewModel(IMessageService messageService)
   {
     _messageService = messageService ??
       throw new ArgumentNullException(nameof(messageService));
```

```
        ShowMessageCommand = new RelayCommand(ShowMessage);
    }

    public ICommand ShowMessageCommand { get; }

    public void ShowMessage()
    {
        _messageService.ShowMessageAsync("A message from the view-model");
    }
}
```

WPF Application

The first client application using this library is the WPF application. The `WPFMessageService` class implements the `IMessageService` interface. With WPF, dialogs can be opened using `MessageBox.Show`. This class does not offer asynchronous functionality; thus, a completed task is returned to fulfill the contract from the `ShowMessageAsync` method (code file `PlatformIndependenceSample/WPFClient/WPFMessageService.cs`):

```
public class WPFMessageService : IMessageService
{
    public Task ShowMessageAsync(string message)
    {
        MessageBox.Show(message);
        return Task.CompletedTask;
    }
}
```

In the `App` class, the DI container is created, and the services are registered. The `WPFMessageService` class is mapped to the `IMessageService` interface (code file `PlatformIndependenceSample/WPFClient/App.xaml.cs`):

```
protected override void OnStartup(StartupEventArgs e)
{
    base.OnStartup(e);
    RegisterServices();
}

public void RegisterServices()
{
    var services = new ServiceCollection();
    services.AddSingleton<IMessageService, WPFMessageService>();
    services.AddTransient<ShowMessageViewModel>();
    Container = services.BuildServiceProvider();
}

public IServiceProvider Container { get; private set; }
```

In the code-behind file of the user interface, the `ViewModel` property is set by requesting `ShowMessageViewModel` from the container (code file `PlatformIndependenceSample/WPFClient/MainWindow.xaml.cs`):

```
public MainWindow()
{
    InitializeComponent();
    ViewModel = (Application.Current as App)
        .Container.GetService<ShowMessageViewModel>();
    this.DataContext = this;
}

public ShowMessageViewModel ViewModel { get; }
```

With the XAML code, the `Button` element defines a `Command` property that binds to the `ShowMessageCommand` of the view-model (XAML file `PlatformIndependenceSample/WPFClient/MainWindow.xaml`):

```
<Button Content="Click Me!"
   Command="{Binding ViewModel.ShowMessageCommand, Mode=OneTime}" />
```

When you run the application, clicking the button invokes the command in the view-model that is requested from the container, and the command handler invokes a service that in turn is implemented with the WPF application to show the `MessageBox` shown in Figure 20-1.

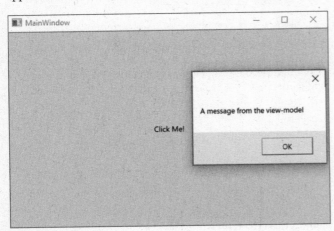

FIGURE 20-1

UWP Application

The UWP application is very similar to the WPF application, but there are some important differences. The first one shows up with the `UWPMessageService` class; to show a dialog, the `MessageDialog` class is used. This class offers the async method `ShowAsync` (code file `PlatformIndependenceSample/UWPClient/UWPMessageService.cs`):

```
public class UWPMessageService : IMessageService
{
  public async Task ShowMessageAsync(string message) =>
    await new MessageDialog(message).ShowAsync();
}
```

The DI container is filled in the same way except that the `UWPMessageSerivce` is now used to fulfill the contract for the `IMessageService` interface (code file `PlatformIndependenceSample/UWPClient/App.xaml.cs`):

```
public void RegisterServices()
{
  var services = new ServiceCollection();
  services.AddSingleton<IMessageService, UWPMessageService>();
  services.AddTransient<ShowMessageViewModel>();
  Container = services.BuildServiceProvider();
}

public IServiceProvider Container { get; private set; }
```

Requesting the view-model from the container is done in the same way as with WPF (code file `PlatformIndependenceSample/UWPClient/MainPage.xaml.cs`):

```
public MainPage()
{
  this.InitializeComponent();
  ViewModel = (Application.Current as App)
    .Container.GetService<ShowMessageViewModel>();
}

public ShowMessageViewModel ViewModel { get; }
```

Another difference with UWP is the use of compiled binding, but this is not really related to dependency injection (XAML file `PlatformIndependenceSample/UWPClient/MainPage.xaml`):

```
<Button Content="Click Me!"
  Command="{x:Bind ViewModel.ShowMessageCommand, Mode=OneTime}" />
```

When you run the application, you can see the same behavior, but with UWP user interfaces (Figure 20-2).

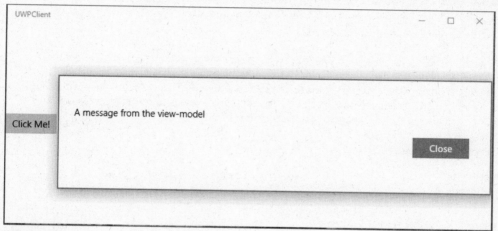

FIGURE 20-2

Xamarin Application

When you implement the same features with a Xamarin.Forms application, there's another interesting approach with dependency injection. With Xamarin.Forms, the method to show a message dialog requires a `Page` object, so the `XamarinMessageService` that's implementing `IMessageService` needs to be configured for receiving a `Page` object. It's not possible to change the `IMessageService`, as the `Page` type is not available with a .NET Standard library. It's also not possible to use an extra configuration property with the `XamarinMessageService` class, as this class is instantiated from the view-model type that is also implemented in the .NET Standard library. A good approach is to add another service with a service contract that is only used within Xamarin.Forms application. The `XamarinMessageService` constructor demands an object implementing the `IPageService` interface. This service is then used to retrieve the Page, and with this the `DisplayAlert` method can be invoked (code file `PlatformIndependenceSample/XamarinClient/XamarinMessageService.cs`):

```
public class XamarinMessageService : IMessageService
{
  private readonly IPageService _pageService;
```

```
public XamarinMessageService(IPageService pageService)
{
  _pageService = pageService;
}

public Task ShowMessageAsync(string message)
{
  return _pageService.Page.DisplayAlert("Message", message, "Close");
}
}
```

The contract IPageService just defines a Page property as needed for the dialog (code file PlatformIndependenceSample/XamarinClient/IPageService.cs):

```
public interface IPageService
{
  Page Page { get; set; }
}
```

The implementation of the IPageService is just a simple auto-property (code file PlatformIndependenceSample/XamarinClient/PageService.cs):

```
public class PageService : IPageService
{
  public Page Page { get; set; }
}
```

The container is created in the App class. This time, the XamarinMessageSerivce is mapped as implementation for the IMessageService contract, and IPageService needs to be listed, too (code file PlatformIndependenceSample/XamarinClient/App.xaml.cs):

```
public App()
{
  InitializeComponent();
  RegisterServices();

  MainPage = new XamarinClient.MainPage();
}

public void RegisterServices()
{
  var services = new ServiceCollection();
  services.AddSingleton<IPageService, PageService>();
  services.AddSingleton<IMessageService, XamarinMessageService>();
  services.AddTransient<ShowMessageViewModel>();
  Container = services.BuildServiceProvider();
}

public IServiceProvider Container { get; private set; }
```

In the code-behind file, the Page property needs to be associated with the PageService (code file PlatformIndependenceSample/XamarinClient/MainPage.xaml.cs):

```
public MainPage()
{
  InitializeComponent();
  IServiceProvider container = (Application.Current as App).Container;
  ViewModel = container.GetService<ShowMessageViewModel>();
  this.BindingContext = this;
  container.GetService<IPageService>().Page = this;
}

public ShowMessageViewModel ViewModel { get; }
```

The XAML code looks like the previous samples (XAML file `PlatformIndependenceSample/XamarinClient/MainPage.xaml`):

```
<Button Text="Click Me!"
    Command="{Binding ViewModel.ShowMessageCommand, Mode=OneWay}" />
```

When you run the application, the alert message pops up, as shown in Figure 20-3.

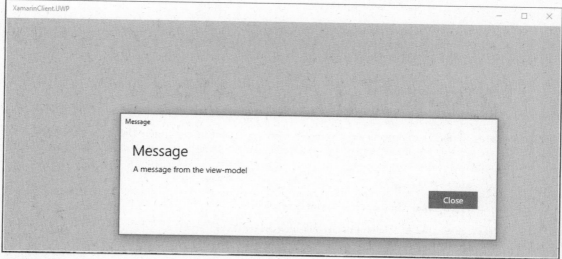

FIGURE 20-3

USING OTHER DI CONTAINERS

`Microsoft.Extensions.DependencyInjection` is a simple DI container; many third-party containers offer additional functionality. For example, Autofac allows configuration of the services in a configuration file.

While ASP.NET Core uses `Microsoft.Extensions.DependencyInjection`, you can also configure this—using an adapter—to use other third-party dependency injection containers, such as Autofac, Rezolver, Scan, Neleus, CuteAnt, fm, Dryloc, CuteAnt, Stashbox, and others. You just need to add an adapter in the form of a NuGet package and make the initialization according to the container's needs.

The sample project `DIWithAutofac` uses the same `GreetingService` and `HomeController` as implemented previously, but it uses the Autofac dependency injection container adapter. For this, these NuGet packages and namespaces are needed:

Packages

`Autofac.Extensions.DependencyInjection`

`Microsoft.ExtensionsDependencyInjection`

Namespaces

`Autofac`

`Autofac.Extensions.DependencyInjection`

`Microsoft.Extensions.DependencyInjection`

`System`

For using the Autofac container adapter, the services are registered in a `ServiceCollection` like before. Instead of creating an `IServiceProvider`, now you use a `ContainerBuilder` from Autofac. This builder can be populated with the `ServiceCollection` that invokes the `Populate` method. This is a way of adding the hundreds of ASP.NET Core services to this container. The container also supports several `Register` methods to add managed services. The `Build` method now creates a container and returns it with the `IContainer` interface (code file `DIWithAutoFac/Program.cs`):

```
static IContainer RegisterServices()
{
  var services = new ServiceCollection();
  services.AddSingleton<IGreetingService, GreetingService>();
  services.AddTransient<HomeController>();

  var builder = new ContainerBuilder();
  builder.Populate(services);
  return builder.Build();
}
```

The `Resolve` method can now be used to resolve services from this container. Other than this, no changes are needed. The `HomeController` receives `GreetingService` via dependency injection (code file `DIWithAutoFac/Program.cs`):

```
static void Main()
{
  using (IContainer container = RegisterServices())
  {
    var controller = container.Resolve<HomeController>();
    string result = controller.Hello("Katharina");
    Console.WriteLine(result);
  }
}
```

SUMMARY

This chapter served as an introduction to dependency injection and continued using Microsoft's container `Microsoft.Extensions.DependencyInjection` with various scenarios including configuration via options and .NET Core configuration. You've also seen how to use dependency injection with different platforms by using platform-specific features with WPF, UWP, and Xamarin.

This book contains several chapters in which dependency injection has an important role. Chapter 26 shows how dependency injection is used with Entity Framework Core, and how you can replace built-in functionality. You can read in Chapter 28 about using dependency injection with unit tests and mocking functionality that should not be tested by a unit test. Chapter 30 and the chapters that follow it cover how dependency injection is used with ASP.NET Core. You will see hundreds of services registered in a container. Chapter 34 shows the MVVM pattern and other patterns that are used with XAML-based applications. Dependency injection is an important foundation in those applications.

Chapter 21 goes into the detail of parallel programming with the `Task` and `Parallel` classes that help you use multiple cores from the operating system. Issues that come up when you use multiple tasks are covered as well.

21

Tasks and Parallel Programming

WHAT'S IN THIS CHAPTER?

➤ An overview of multi-threading
➤ Working with the Parallel class
➤ Working with Tasks
➤ Using the Cancellation framework
➤ Using the Data Flow Library
➤ Working with timers
➤ Understanding threading issues
➤ Using the lock keyword
➤ Synchronizing with Monitor
➤ Synchronizing with mutexes
➤ Working with Semaphore and SemaphoreSlim
➤ Using ManualResetEvent, AutoResetEvent, and CountdownEvent
➤ Working with Barrier
➤ Managing readers and writers with ReaderWriterLockSlim

WROX.COM CODE DOWNLOADS FOR THIS CHAPTER

The Wrox.com code downloads for this chapter are found at www.wrox.com on the Download Code tab. The source code is also available at https://github.com/ProfessionalCSharp/ProfessionalCSharp7 in the directory Tasks.

The code for this chapter is divided into the following major examples:

➤ Parallel
➤ Task
➤ Cancellation
➤ DataFlow
➤ Timer

➤ WinAppTimer

➤ ThreadingIssues

➤ SynchronizationSamples

➤ BarrierSample

➤ ReaderWriterLockSample

OVERVIEW

There are several reasons for using multiple threads. Suppose that you are making a network call from an application that might take some time. You don't want to stall the user interface and force the user to wait idly until the response is returned from the server. The user could perform some other actions in the meantime or even cancel the request that was sent to the server. Using threads can help.

For all activities that require a wait—for example, because of file, database, or network access—you can start a new thread to fulfill other activities at the same time. Even if you have only processing-intensive tasks to do, threading can help. Multiple threads of a single process can run on different CPUs, or, nowadays, on different cores of a multiple-core CPU, at the same time.

You must be aware of some issues when running multiple threads, however. Because they can run during the same time, you can easily get into problems if the threads access the same data. To avoid that, you must implement synchronization mechanisms.

.NET offers an abstraction mechanism to threads: tasks. Tasks allow building relations between tasks—for example, one task should continue when the first one is completed. You can also build a hierarchy consisting of multiple tasks.

Instead of using tasks, you can implement parallel activities using the `Parallel` class. You need to differentiate *data parallelism* where working with some data is processed simultaneously between different tasks, or *task parallelism* where different functions are executed simultaneously.

When creating parallel programs, you have a lot of different options. You should use the simplest option that fits your scenario. This chapter starts with the `Parallel` class that offers very easy parallelism. If this is all you need, just use this class. In case you need more control, such as when you need to manage a relation between tasks or to define a method that returns a task, the `Task` class is the way to go.

This chapter also covers the data flow library, which might be the easiest one to use if you need an actor-based programming to flow data through pipelines.

In case you even need more control over parallelism, such as setting priorities, the `Thread` class might be the one to use.

> **NOTE** *The use of asynchronous methods with the* `async` *and* `await` *keywords is covered in Chapter 15, "Asynchronous Programming."*
>
> *One variant of task parallelism is offered by Parallel LINQ, which is covered in Chapter 12, "Language Integrated Query."*

Creating a program that runs multiple tasks in parallel can lead to race conditions and deadlocks. You need to be aware of synchronization techniques.

It is best when you can avoid synchronization by not sharing data between threads. Of course, this is not always possible. If data sharing is necessary, you must use synchronization so that only one task at a time accesses and changes the shared state. In case you don't pay attention to synchronization, race conditions and deadlocks can apply. A big issue with race conditions and deadlocks is that errors can occur from time to time. With a higher number of CPU cores, error numbers can increase. Such errors usually are hard to find. So, it's best to pay attention to synchronization from the beginning.

Using multiple tasks is easy if the tasks don't access the same variables. You can avoid this situation to a certain degree, but at some point, you will find some data needs to be shared. When sharing data, you need to apply synchronization techniques. When threads access the same data and you don't apply synchronization, you are lucky when the problem pops up immediately. However, this is rarely the case. This chapter shows race conditions and deadlocks, and how you can avoid them by applying synchronization mechanisms.

.NET offers several options for synchronization. You can use synchronization objects within a process or across processes. You can use them to synchronize one task or multiple tasks to access one or more resources. Synchronization objects can also be used to inform tasks that something completed. All these synchronization objects are covered in this chapter.

> **NOTE** *The need for synchronization can be partly avoided by using immutable data structures as much as possible. With immutable data structures, the data can only be initialized, but cannot be changed afterward. That's why synchronization is not needed with these types.*

After this long introduction, let's start with the `Parallel` class—an uncomplicated way to add parallelism to your application.

PARALLEL CLASS

One great abstraction of threads is the `Parallel` class. With this class, both data and task parallelism are offered. This class is in the namespace `System.Threading.Tasks`.

The `Parallel` class defines static methods for a parallel `for` and `foreach`. With the C# statements `for` and `foreach`, the loop is run from one thread. The `Parallel` class uses multiple tasks and, thus, multiple threads for this job.

Whereas the `Parallel.For` and `Parallel.ForEach` methods invoke the same code during each iteration, `Parallel.Invoke` enables you to invoke different methods concurrently. `Parallel.Invoke` is for task parallelism, and `Parallel.ForEach` is for data parallelism.

Looping with the Parallel.For Method

The `Parallel.For` method is like the C# `for` loop statement for performing a task a number of times. With `Parallel.For`, the iterations run in parallel. The order of iteration is not defined.

The sample code for `ParallelSamples` makes use of the following namespaces:

Namespaces

```
System

System.Linq

System.Threading

System.Threading.Tasks
```

> **NOTE** *This sample makes use of command-line arguments. To work through the different features, pass different arguments as shown on startup of the sample application, or by checking the* `Main` *method. From Visual Studio, you can pass command-line arguments in the Debug options of the project properties. Using the dotnet command line, to pass the command-line argument* `-p`, *you can start the command* `dotnet run -- -p`.

For having information about the thread and the task, the following `Log` method writes thread and task identifiers to the console (code file `ParallelSamples/Program.cs`):

```
public static void Log(string prefix) =>
  Console.WriteLine($"{prefix}, task: {Task.CurrentId}, " +
    $"thread: {Thread.CurrentThread.ManagedThreadId}");
```

Let's get into the `Parallel.For` method. With this method, the first two parameters define the start and end of the loop. The following example has the iterations from 0 to 9. The third parameter is an `Action<int>` delegate. The integer parameter is the iteration of the loop that is passed to the method referenced by the delegate. The return type of `Parallel.For` is the struct `ParallelLoopResult`, which provides information if the loop is completed:

```
public static void ParallelFor()
{
  ParallelLoopResult result =
    Parallel.For(0, 10, i =>
    {
      Log($"S {i}");
      Task.Delay(10).Wait();
      Log($"E {i}");
    });
  Console.WriteLine($"Is completed: {result.IsCompleted}");
}
```

In the body of `Parallel.For`, the index, task identifier, and thread identifier are written to the console. As shown in the following output, the order is not guaranteed. You will see different results if you run this program once more. This run of the program had the order 2-4-0-6-8 and so on with nine tasks and six threads. A task does not necessarily map to one thread: a thread can be reused by different tasks.

```
S 2 task: 1, thread: 3
S 4 task: 2, thread: 4
S 0 task: 4, thread: 2
S 6 task: 5, thread: 5
S 8 task: 3, thread: 6
E 6 task: 5, thread: 5
E 0 task: 4, thread: 2
S 1 task: 4, thread: 2
E 4 task: 2, thread: 4
S 5 task: 8, thread: 4
E 2 task: 1, thread: 3
S 9 task: 9, thread: 3
E 8 task: 3, thread: 6
S 3 task: 7, thread: 8
S 7 task: 6, thread: 5
E 5 task: 8, thread: 4
E 1 task: 4, thread: 2
E 3 task: 7, thread: 8
E 7 task: 6, thread: 5
E 9 task: 9, thread: 3
Is completed: True
```

The delay within the parallel body waits for 10 milliseconds to have a better chance to create new threads. If you remove this line, you see fewer threads and tasks to be used.

What you can also see with the result is that every end-log of a loop uses the same thread and task as the start-log. Using `Task.Delay` with the `Wait` method blocks the current thread until the delay ends.

Change the previous example to now use the `await` keyword with the `Task.Delay` method (code file `ParallelSamples/Program.cs`):

```
public static void ParallelForWithAsync()
{
  ParallelLoopResult result =
    Parallel.For(0, 10, async i =>
    {
      Log($"S {i}");
      await Task.Delay(10);
      Log($"E {i}");
    });
  Console.WriteLine($"is completed: {result.IsCompleted}");
}
```

The result is in the following code snippet. With the output after the `Thread.Delay` method you can see the thread change. For example, loop iteration 8, which had thread ID 7 before the delay, has thread ID 5 after the delay. You can also see that tasks no longer exist—there are only threads—and here previous threads are reused. Another important aspect is that the `For` method of the `Parallel` class is completed without waiting for the delay. The `Parallel` class waits for the tasks it created, but it doesn't wait for other background activity. It is also possible that you won't see the output from the methods after the delay at all—if the main thread (which is a foreground thread) is finished, all the background threads are stopped. Foreground and background threads are discussed in the next chapter.

```
S 0, task: 5, thread: 1
S 8, task: 8, thread: 7
S 6, task: 7, thread: 8
S 4, task: 9, thread: 6
S 2, task: 6, thread: 5
S 7, task: 7, thread: 8
S 1, task: 5, thread: 1
S 5, task: 9, thread: 6
S 9, task: 8, thread: 7
S 3, task: 6, thread: 5
Is completed: True
E 2, task: , thread: 8
E 0, task: , thread: 8
E 8, task: , thread: 5
E 6, task: , thread: 7
E 4, task: , thread: 6
E 5, task: , thread: 7
E 7, task: , thread: 7
E 1, task: , thread: 6
E 3, task: , thread: 5
E 9, task: , thread: 8
```

> **WARNING** *As demonstrated here, although using async features with .NET and C# is very easy, it's still important to know what's happening behind the scenes, and you have to pay attention to some issues.*

Stopping Parallel.For Early

You can also break `Parallel.For` early without looping through all the iterations. A method overload of the `For` method accepts a third parameter of type `Action<int, ParallelLoopState>`. By defining a method with these parameters, you can influence the outcome of the loop by invoking the `Break` or `Stop` methods of the `ParallelLoopState`.

Remember, the order of iterations is not defined (code file `ParallelSamples/Program.cs`):

```
public static void StopParallelForEarly()
{
  ParallelLoopResult result =
    Parallel.For(10, 40, (int i, ParallelLoopState pls) =>
    {
      Log($"S {i}");
      if (i > 12)
      {
        pls.Break();
        Log($"break now... {i}");
      }
      Task.Delay(10).Wait();
      Log($"E {i}");
    });
  Console.WriteLine($"Is completed: {result.IsCompleted}");
  Console.WriteLine($"lowest break iteration: {result.LowestBreakIteration}");
}
```

This run of the application demonstrates that the iteration breaks up with a value higher than 12, but other tasks can simultaneously run, and tasks with other values can run. All the tasks that have been started before the break can continue to the end. You can use the `LowestBreakIteration` property to ignore results from tasks that you do not need:

```
S 31, task: 6, thread: 8
S 17, task: 7, thread: 5
S 10, task: 5, thread: 1
S 24, task: 8, thread: 6
break now 24, task: 8, thread: 6
S 38, task: 9, thread: 7
break now 38, task: 9, thread: 7
break now 31, task: 6, thread: 8
break now 17, task: 7, thread: 5
E 17, task: 7, thread: 5
E 10, task: 5, thread: 1
S 11, task: 5, thread: 1
E 38, task: 9, thread: 7
E 24, task: 8, thread: 6
E 31, task: 6, thread: 8
E 11, task: 5, thread: 1
S 12, task: 5, thread: 1
E 12, task: 5, thread: 1
S 13, task: 5, thread: 1
break now 13, task: 5, thread: 1
E 13, task: 5, thread: 1
Is completed: False
lowest break iteration: 13
```

Parallel For Initialization

`Parallel.For` might use several threads to do the loops. If you need an initialization that should be done with every thread, you can use the `Parallel.For<TLocal>` method. The generic version of the `For` method accepts—in addition to the `from` and `to` values—three delegate parameters. The first parameter is of type

Func<TLocal>. Because the example here uses a string for TLocal, the method needs to be defined as Func<string>, a method returning a string. This method is invoked only once for each thread that is used to do the iterations.

The second delegate parameter defines the delegate for the body. In the example, the parameter is of type Func<int, ParallelLoopState, string, string>. The first parameter is the loop iteration; the second parameter, ParallelLoopState, enables stopping the loop, as shown earlier. With the third parameter, the body method receives the value that is returned from the init method. The body method also needs to return a value of the type that was defined with the generic For parameter.

The last parameter of the For method specifies a delegate, Action<TLocal>; in the example, a string is received. This method, a thread exit method, is called only once for each thread (code file ParallelSamples/Program.cs):

```csharp
public static void ParallelForWithInit()
{
  Parallel.For<string>(0, 10, () =>
  {
    // invoked once for each thread
    Log($"init thread");
    return $"t{Thread.CurrentThread.ManagedThreadId}";
  },
  (i, pls, str1) =>
  {
    // invoked for each member
    Log($"body i {i} str1 {str1}");
    Task.Delay(10).Wait();
    return $"i {i}";
  },
  (str1) =>
  {
    // final action on each thread
    Log($"finally {str1}");
  });
}
```

The result of running this program once is shown here:

```
init thread task: 7, thread: 6
init thread task: 6, thread: 5
body i: 4 str1: t6 task: 7, thread: 6
body i: 2 str1: t5 task: 6, thread: 5
init thread task: 5, thread: 1
body i: 0 str1: t1 task: 5, thread: 1
init thread task: 9, thread: 8
body i: 8 str1: t8 task: 9, thread: 8
init thread task: 8, thread: 7
body i: 6 str1: t7 task: 8, thread: 7
body i: 1 str1: i 0 task: 5, thread: 1
finally i 2 task: 6, thread: 5
init thread task: 16, thread: 5
finally i 8 task: 9, thread: 8
init thread task: 17, thread: 8
body i: 9 str1: t8 task: 17, thread: 8
finally i 6 task: 8, thread: 7
init thread task: 18, thread: 7
body i: 7 str1: t7 task: 18, thread: 7
finally i 4 task: 7, thread: 6
init thread task: 15, thread: 10
body i: 3 str1: t10 task: 15, thread: 10
body i: 5 str1: t5 task: 16, thread: 5
finally i 1 task: 5, thread: 1
```

```
finally i 5 task: 16, thread: 5
finally i 3 task: 15, thread: 10
finally i 7 task: 18, thread: 7
finally i 9 task: 17, thread: 8
```

The output shows that the init method is called only once for each thread; the body of the loop receives the first string from the initialization and passes this string to the next iteration of the body with the same thread. Lastly, the final action is invoked once for each thread and receives the last result from every body.

With this functionality, this method fits perfectly to accumulate a result of a huge data collection.

Looping with the Parallel.ForEach Method

Parallel.ForEach iterates through a collection implementing IEnumerable in a way like the foreach statement, but in an asynchronous manner. Again, the order is not guaranteed (code file ParallelSamples/ Program.cs):

```
public static void ParallelForEach()
{
    string[] data = {"zero", "one", "two", "three", "four", "five",
    "six", "seven", "eight", "nine", "ten", "eleven", "twelve"};
    ParallelLoopResult result =
        Parallel.ForEach<string>(data, s =>
        {
            Console.WriteLine(s);
        });
}
```

If you need to break up the loop, you can use an overload of the ForEach method with a ParallelLoopState parameter. You can do this in the same way you did earlier with the For method. An overload of the ForEach method can also be used to access an indexer to get the iteration number, as shown here:

```
Parallel.ForEach<string>(data, (s, pls, l) =>
{
    Console.WriteLine($"{s} {l}");
});
```

Invoking Multiple Methods with the Parallel.Invoke Method

If multiple tasks should run in parallel, you can use the Parallel.Invoke method, which offers the task parallelism pattern. Parallel.Invoke allows the passing of an array of Action delegates, whereby you can assign methods that should run. The example code passes the Foo and Bar methods to be invoked in parallel (code file ParallelSamples/Program.cs):

```
public static void ParallelInvoke()
{
    Parallel.Invoke(Foo, Bar);
}

public static void Foo() =>
    Console.WriteLine("foo");

public static void Bar() =>
    Console.WriteLine("bar");
```

The Parallel class is very easy to use—for both task and data parallelism. If more control is needed, and you don't want to wait until the action started with the Parallel class is completed, the Task class comes in handy. Of course, it's also possible to combine the Task and Parallel classes.

TASKS

For more control over the parallel actions, you can use the `Task` class from the namespace `System .Threading.Tasks`. A *task* represents some unit of work that should be done. This unit of work can run in a separate thread, and it is also possible to start a task in a synchronized manner, which results in a wait for the calling thread. With tasks, you have an abstraction layer but also a lot of control over the underlying threads.

Tasks provide much more flexibility in organizing the work you need to do. For example, you can define continuation work—what should be done after a task is complete. This can be differentiated based on whether the task was successful. You can also organize tasks in a hierarchy. For example, a parent task can create new children tasks. Optionally, this can create a dependency, so canceling a parent task also cancels its child tasks.

Starting Tasks

To start a task, you can use either the `TaskFactory` or the constructor of the `Task` and the `Start` method. The `Task` constructor gives you more flexibility in creating the task.

The sample code for `TaskSamples` makes use of the following namespaces:

Namespaces

```
System

System.Linq

System.Threading

System.Threading.Tasks
```

When starting a task, an instance of the `Task` class can be created, and the code that should run can be assigned with an `Action` or `Action<object>` delegate, with either no parameters or one object parameter. In the following example, a method is defined with one parameter: `TaskMethod`. The implementation invokes the `Log` method where the ID of the task and the ID of the thread are written to the console, as well as information if the thread is coming from a thread pool, and if the thread is a background thread. Writing multiple messages to the console is synchronized by using the `lock` keyword with the `s_logLock` synchronization object. This way, parallel calls to `Log` can be done, and multiple writes to the console are not interleaving each other. Otherwise the `title` could be written by one task, and the thread information follows by another task (code file `TaskSamples/Program.cs`):

```csharp
public static void TaskMethod(object o)
{
  Log(o?.ToString());
}

private static object s_logLock = new object();
public static void Log(string title)
{
  lock (s_logLock)
  {
    Console.WriteLine(title);
    Console.WriteLine($"Task id: {Task.CurrentId?.ToString() ?? "no task"}, " +
      $"thread: {Thread.CurrentThread.ManagedThreadId}");
    Console.WriteLine($"is pooled thread: " +
      $"{Thread.CurrentThread.IsThreadPoolThread}");
    Console.WriteLine($"is background thread: " +
      $"{Thread.CurrentThread.IsBackground}");
    Console.WriteLine();
  }
}
```

The following sections describe different ways to start a new task.

Tasks Using the Thread Pool

In this section, diverse ways are shown to start a task that uses a thread from the thread pool. The thread pool offers a pool of background threads. The thread pool manages threads on its own, increasing or decreasing the number of threads within the pool as needed. Threads from the pool are used to fulfill some actions and returned to the pool afterward.

The first way to create a task is with an instantiated TaskFactory, where the method TaskMethod is passed to the StartNew method, and the task is immediately started. The second approach uses the static Factory property of the Task class to get access to the TaskFactory, and to invoke the StartNew method. This is very similar to the first version in that it uses a factory, but there's less control over factory creation. The third approach uses the constructor of the Task class. When the Task object is instantiated, the task does not run immediately. Instead, it is given the status Created. The task is then started by calling the Start method of the Task class. The fourth approach calls the Run method of the Task that immediately starts the task. The Run method doesn't have an overloaded variant to pass an Action<object> delegate, but it's easy to simulate this by assigning a lambda expression of type Action, and using the parameter within its implementation (code file TaskSamples/Program.cs):

```
public void TasksUsingThreadPool()
{
  var tf = new TaskFactory();
  Task t1 = tf.StartNew(TaskMethod, "using a task factory");
  Task t2 = Task.Factory.StartNew(TaskMethod, "factory via a task");
  var t3 = new Task(TaskMethod, "using a task constructor and Start");
  t3.Start();
  Task t4 = Task.Run(() => TaskMethod("using the Run method"));
}
```

The output returned with these variants is as follows. All these versions create a new task, and a thread from the thread pool is used:

```
using a task factory
Task id: 1, thread: 4
is pooled thread: True
is background thread: True

factory via a task
Task id: 2, thread: 3
is pooled thread: True
is background thread: True

using a task constructor and Start
Task id: 3, thread: 5
is pooled thread: True
is background thread: True

using the Run method
Task id: 4, thread: 6
is pooled thread: True
is background thread: True
```

With both the Task constructor and the StartNew method of the TaskFactory, you can pass values from the enumeration TaskCreationOptions. Using this creation option, you can change how the task should behave differently, as is shown in the next sections.

Synchronous Tasks

A task does not necessarily mean to use a thread from a thread pool—it can use other threads as well. Tasks can also run synchronously, with the same thread as the calling thread. The following code snippet uses the method RunSynchronously of the Task class (code file TaskSamples/Program.cs):

```
private static void RunSynchronousTask()
{
```

```
    TaskMethod("just the main thread");
    var t1 = new Task(TaskMethod, "run sync");
    t1.RunSynchronously();
}
```

Here, the `TaskMethod` is first called directly from the main thread before it is invoked from the newly created `Task`. As you can see from the following console output, the main thread doesn't have a task ID. It is not a pooled thread. Calling the method `RunSynchronously` uses the same thread as the calling thread, but creates a task if one wasn't created previously:

```
just the main thread
Task id: no task, thread: 2
is pooled thread: False
is background thread: False

run sync
Task id: 1, thread: 2
is pooled thread: False
is background thread: False
```

Tasks Using a Separate Thread

If the code of a task should run for a longer time, you should use `TaskCreationOptions.LongRunning` to instruct the task scheduler to create a new thread, rather than use a thread from the thread pool. This way, the thread doesn't need to be managed by the thread pool. When a thread is taken from the thread pool, the task scheduler can decide to wait for an already running task to be completed and use this thread instead of creating a new thread with the pool. With a long-running thread, the task scheduler knows immediately that it doesn't make sense to wait for this one. The following code snippet creates a long-running task (code file `TaskSamples/Program.cs`):

```
private static void LongRunningTask()
{
  var t1 = new Task(TaskMethod, "long running",
    TaskCreationOptions.LongRunning);
  t1.Start();
}
```

Indeed, using the option `TaskCreationOptions.LongRunning`, a thread from the thread pool is not used. Instead, a new thread is created:

```
long running
Task id: 5, thread: 7
is pooled thread: False
is background thread: True
```

Futures—Results from Tasks

When a task is finished, it can write some stateful information to a shared object. Such a shared object must be thread-safe. Another option is to use a task that returns a result. Such a task is also known as *future* as it returns a result in the future. With early versions of the Task Parallel Library (TPL), the class had the name `Future` as well. Now it is a generic version of the `Task` class. With this class it is possible to define the type of the result that is returned with a task.

A method that is invoked by a task to return a result can be declared with any return type. The following example method `TaskWithResult` returns two `int` values with the help of a tuple. The input of the method can be void or of type `object`, as shown here (code file `TaskSamples/Program.cs`):

```
public static (int Result, int Remainder) TaskWithResult(object division)
{
  (int x, int y) = ((int x, int y))division;
  int result = x / y;
```

```
        int remainder = x % y;
        Console.WriteLine("task creates a result...");
        return (result, remainder);
    }
```

> **NOTE** *Tuples allow you to combine multiple values into one. Tuples are explained in Chapter 13, "Functional Programming with C#."*

When you define a task to invoke the method `TaskWithResult`, you use the generic class `Task<TResult>`. The generic parameter defines the return type. With the constructor, the method is passed to the `Func` delegate, and the second parameter defines the input value. Because this task needs two input values in the `object` parameter, a tuple is created as well. Next, the task is started. The `Result` property of the `Task` instance `t1` blocks and waits until the task is completed. Upon task completion, the `Result` property contains the result from the task:

```
public static void TaskWithResultDemo()
{
    var t1 = new Task<(int Result, int Remainder)>(TaskWithResult, (8, 3));
    t1.Start();
    Console.WriteLine(t1.Result);
    t1.Wait();
    Console.WriteLine($"result from task: {t1.Result.Result} " +
        $"{t1.Result.Remainder}");
}
```

Continuation Tasks

With tasks, you can specify that after a task is finished another specific task should start to run—for example, a new task that uses a result from the previous one or should do some cleanup if the previous task failed.

Whereas the task handler has either no parameter or one object parameter, the continuation handler has a parameter of type `Task`. Here, you can access information about the originating task (code file `TaskSamples/Program.cs`):

```
private static void DoOnFirst()
{
    Console.WriteLine($"doing some task {Task.CurrentId}");
    Task.Delay(3000).Wait();
}

private static void DoOnSecond(Task t)
{
    Console.WriteLine($"task {t.Id} finished");
    Console.WriteLine($"this task id {Task.CurrentId}");
    Console.WriteLine("do some cleanup");
    Task.Delay(3000).Wait();
}
```

A continuation task is defined by invoking the `ContinueWith` method on a task. You could also use the `TaskFactory` for this. `t1.OnContinueWith(DoOnSecond)` means that a new task invoking the method `DoOnSecond` should be started as soon as the task `t1` is finished. You can start multiple tasks when one task is finished, and a continuation task can have another continuation task, as this next example demonstrates (code file `TaskSamples/Program.cs`):

```
public static void ContinuationTasks()
{
    Task t1 = new Task(DoOnFirst);
    Task t2 = t1.ContinueWith(DoOnSecond);
```

```
        Task t3 = t1.ContinueWith(DoOnSecond);
        Task t4 = t2.ContinueWith(DoOnSecond);
        t1.Start();
    }
```

So far, the continuation tasks have been started when the previous task was finished, regardless of the result. With values from `TaskContinuationOptions`, you can define that a continuation task should only start if the originating task was successful (or faulted). Some of the possible values are `OnlyOnFaulted`, `NotOnFaulted`, `OnlyOnCanceled`, `NotOnCanceled`, and `OnlyOnRanToCompletion`:

```
Task t5 = t1.ContinueWith(DoOnError, TaskContinuationOptions.OnlyOnFaulted);
```

> **NOTE** *The compiler-generated code from the* `await` *keyword discussed in Chapter 15 makes use of continuation tasks.*

Task Hierarchies

With task continuations, one task is started after another. Tasks can also form a hierarchy. When a task starts a new task, a parent/child hierarchy is started.

In the code snippet that follows, within the task of the parent, a new task object is created, and the task is started. The code to create a child task is the same as that to create a parent task. The only difference is that the task is created from within another task (code file `TaskSamples/Program.cs`):

```
public static void ParentAndChild()
{
    var parent = new Task(ParentTask);
    parent.Start();
    Task.Delay(2000).Wait();
    Console.WriteLine(parent.Status);
    Task.Delay(4000).Wait();
    Console.WriteLine(parent.Status);
}

private static void ParentTask()
{
    Console.WriteLine($"task id {Task.CurrentId}");
    var child = new Task(ChildTask);
    child.Start();
    Task.Delay(1000).Wait();
    Console.WriteLine("parent started child");
}

private static void ChildTask()
{
    Console.WriteLine("child");
    Task.Delay(5000).Wait();
    Console.WriteLine("child finished");
}
```

If the parent task is finished before the child task, the status of the parent task is shown as `WaitingForChildrenToComplete`. The parent task is completed with the status `RanToCompletion` as soon as all children tasks are completed as well. Of course, this is not the case if the parent creates a task with the `TaskCreationOption` `DetachedFromParent`.

Canceling a parent task also cancels the children. The cancellation framework is discussed next.

Returning Tasks from Methods

A method that returns a task with results is declared to return `Task<T>`—for example, a method that returns a task with a collection of strings:

```
public Task<IEnumerable<string>> TaskMethodAsync()
{
}
```

Creating methods that access the network or data access are often asynchronous, with such a result so you can use task features to deal with the results (for example, by using the `async` keyword as explained in Chapter 15). In case you have a synchronous path or need to implement an interface that is defined that way with synchronous code, there's no need to create a task for the sake of the result value. The `Task` class offers creating a result with a completed task that is finished with the status `RanToCompletion` using the method `FromResult`:

```
return Task.FromResult<IEnumerable<string>>(
  new List<string>() { "one", "two" });
```

Waiting for Tasks

Probably you've already seen the `WhenAll` and `WaitAll` methods of the `Task` class and wondered what the difference might be. Both methods wait for all tasks that are passed to these methods to complete. The `WaitAll` method blocks the calling task until all tasks that are waited for are completed. The `WhenAll` method returns a task which in turn allows you to use the `async` keyword to wait for the result, and it does not block the waiting task.

Although the `WhenAll` and `WaitAll` methods are finished when all the tasks you are waiting for are completed, you can wait for just one task of a list to be completed with `WhenAny` and `WaitAny`. Like the `WhenAll` and `WaitAll` methods, the `WaitAny` method blocks the calling task, whereas `WhenAny` returns a task that can be awaited.

A method that already has been used several times with several samples is the `Task.Delay` method. You can specify a number of milliseconds to wait before the task that is returned from this method is completed.

In case all that should be done is to give up the CPU and thus allow other tasks to run, you can invoke the `Task.Yield` method. This method gives up the CPU and lets other tasks run. In case no other task is waiting to run, the task calling `Task.Yield` continues immediately. Otherwise it needs to wait until the CPU is scheduled again for the calling task.

Value Tasks

In case a method sometimes runs asynchronously, but not always, the `Task` class might be some overhead that's not needed. .NET now offers `ValueTask` that is a struct compared to the `Task` that is a class, thus the `ValueTask` doesn't have the overhead of an object in the heap. Usually invoking asynchronous methods, such as making calls to an API server or a database, the overhead of the `Task` type can be ignored compared to the time needed for the work to be done. However, there are some cases where the overhead cannot be ignored, such as when a method is called thousands of times, and it rarely really needs a call across the network. This is a scenario where the `ValueTask` becomes handy.

Let's get into an example. The method `GetTheRealData` simulates a method that usually takes a long time, accessing data from the network or a database. Here, sample data is generated with the `Enumerable` class. Together with the time, the data is retrieved, a result in the form of a tuple is returned. This method returns a `Task` as we are used to (code file `ValueTaskSample/Program.cs`):

```
public static Task<(IEnumerable<string> data, DateTime retrievedTime)>
  GetTheRealData() =>
```

```
Task.FromResult(
  (Enumerable.Range(0, 10)
    .Select(x => $"item {x}").AsEnumerable(), DateTime.Now));
```

The interesting part now follows in the method `GetSomeData`. This method is declared to return a `ValueTask`. With the implementation, first a check is done if cached data is not older than 5 seconds. If the cached data is not older, the cached data is directly returned and passed to the `ValueTask` constructor. This doesn't really need a background thread; the data can be directly returned. In case the cache is older, the `GetTheRealData` method is invoked. This method needs a real task and could occur with some delay (code file `ValueTaskSample/Program.cs`):

```
private static DateTime _retrieved;
private static IEnumerable<string> _cachedData;
public static async ValueTask<IEnumerable<string>> GetSomeDataAsync()
{
  if (_retrieved >= DateTime.Now.AddSeconds(-5))
  {
    Console.WriteLine("data from the cache");
    return await new ValueTask<IEnumerable<string>>(_cachedData);
  }

  Console.WriteLine("data from the service");
  (_cachedData, _retrieved) = await GetTheRealData();
  return _cachedData;
}
```

> **NOTE** *The constructor of the* `ValueTask` *accepts type* `TResult` *for the data to be returned, or* `Task<TResult>` *to supply a Task returned from methods that do run asynchronously.*

The `Main` method includes a loop to invoke the `GetSomeDataAsync` method several times with a delay after every iteration (code file `ValueTaskSample/Program.cs`):

```
static async Task Main(string[] args)
{
  for (int i = 0; i < 20; i++)
  {
    IEnumerable<string> data = await GetSomeDataAsync();
    await Task.Delay(1000);
  }
  Console.ReadLine();
}
```

When you run the application, you can see that the data is returned from the cache, and after the cache is invalidated, the service is accessed first before the cache is used again.

```
data from the service
data from the cache
data from the cache
data from the cache
data from the cache
data from the service
data from the cache
data from the cache
data from the cache
data from the cache
data from the service
data from the cache
...
```

> **NOTE** *Probably you don't have scenarios yet where you can't ignore the overhead from tasks compared to value tasks. However, having this core feature in the framework allows for upcoming features such as async streams or async operators in a future C# version.*

CANCELLATION FRAMEWORK

.NET includes a cancellation framework to enable the canceling of long-running tasks in a standard manner. Every blocking call should support this mechanism. Of course, not every blocking call currently implements this new technology, but more and more are doing so. Among the technologies that offer this mechanism already are tasks, concurrent collection classes, and Parallel LINQ, as well as several synchronization mechanisms.

The cancellation framework is based on cooperative behavior; it is not forceful. A long-running task checks whether it is canceled and returns control accordingly.

A method that supports cancellation accepts a CancellationToken parameter. This class defines the property IsCancellationRequested, whereby a long operation can check to see whether it should abort. Other ways for a long operation to check for cancellation include using a WaitHandle property that is signaled when the token is canceled or using the Register method. The Register method accepts parameters of type Action and ICancelableOperation. The method that is referenced by the Action delegate is invoked when the token is canceled. This is like the ICancelableOperation, whereby the Cancel method of an object implementing this interface is invoked when the cancellation is done.

The sample code for cancellation samples makes use of the following namespaces:

Namespaces

```
System

System.Threading

System.Threading.Tasks
```

Cancellation of Parallel.For

This section starts with a simple example using the Parallel.For method. The Parallel class provides overloads for the For method, whereby you can pass a parameter of type ParallelOptions. With ParallelOptions, you can pass a CancellationToken. The CancellationToken is generated by creating a CancellationTokenSource. CancellationTokenSource implements the interface ICancelableOperation and can therefore be registered with the CancellationToken and allows cancellation with the Cancel method. The example doesn't call the Cancel method directly but uses the CancelAfter method to cancel the token after 500 milliseconds.

Within the implementation of the For loop, the Parallel class verifies the outcome of the CancellationToken and cancels the operation. Upon cancellation, the For method throws an exception of type OperationCanceledException, which is caught in the example. With the CancellationToken, it is possible to register for information when the cancellation is done. This is accomplished by calling the Register method and passing a delegate that is invoked on cancellation (code file CancellationSamples/Program.cs):

```
public static void CancelParallelFor()
{
  var cts = new CancellationTokenSource();
  cts.Token.Register(() => Console.WriteLine("*** token cancelled"));
```

```
    // send a cancel after 500 ms
    cts.CancelAfter(500);
    try
    {
      ParallelLoopResult result =
        Parallel.For(0, 100, new ParallelOptions
        {
          CancellationToken = cts.Token,
        },
        x =>
        {
          Console.WriteLine($"loop {x} started");
          int sum = 0;
          for (int i = 0; i < 100; i++)
          {
            Task.Delay(2).Wait();
            sum += i;
          }
          Console.WriteLine($"loop {x} finished");
        });
    }
    catch (OperationCanceledException ex)
    {
      Console.WriteLine(ex.Message);
    }
}
```

When you run the application, you get output like the following. Iteration 0, 50, 25, 75, and 1 were all started. This is on a system with a quad-core CPU. With the cancellation, all other iterations were canceled before starting. The iterations that were started are allowed to finish because cancellation is always done in a cooperative way to avoid the risk of resource leaks when iterations are canceled somewhere in between:

```
loop 0 started
loop 50 started
loop 25 started
loop 75 started
loop 1 started
*** token cancelled
loop 75 finished
loop 50 finished
loop 1 finished
loop 0 finished
loop 25 finished
The operation was canceled.
```

Cancellation of Tasks

The same cancellation pattern is used with tasks. First, a new `CancellationTokenSource` is created. If you need just one cancellation token, you can use a default token by accessing `Task.Factory .CancellationToken`. Then, like the previous code, the task is canceled after 500 milliseconds. The task doing the major work within a loop receives the cancellation token via the `TaskFactory` object. The cancellation token is assigned to the `TaskFactory` by setting it in the constructor. This cancellation token is used by the task to check whether cancellation is requested by checking the `IsCancellationRequested` property of the `CancellationToken` (code file `CancellationSamples/Program.cs`):

```
public void CancelTask()
{
  var cts = new CancellationTokenSource();
  cts.Token.Register(() => Console.WriteLine("*** task cancelled"));
  // send a cancel after 500 ms
  cts.CancelAfter(500);
```

```
Task t1 = Task.Run(() =>
{
  Console.WriteLine("in task");
  for (int i = 0; i < 20; i++)
  {
    Task.Delay(100).Wait();
    CancellationToken token = cts.Token;
    if (token.IsCancellationRequested)
    {
      Console.WriteLine("cancelling was requested, " +
        "cancelling from within the task");
      token.ThrowIfCancellationRequested();
      break;
    }
    Console.WriteLine("in loop");
  }
  Console.WriteLine("task finished without cancellation");
}, cts.Token);

try
{
  t1.Wait();
}
catch (AggregateException ex)
{
  Console.WriteLine($"exception: {ex.GetType().Name}, {ex.Message}");
  foreach (var innerException in ex.InnerExceptions)
  {
    Console.WriteLine($"inner exception: {ex.InnerException.GetType()}," +
      $"{ex.InnerException.Message}");
  }
}
}
```

When you run the application, you can see that the task starts, runs for a few loops, and gets the cancellation request. The task is canceled and throws a `TaskCanceledException`, which is initiated from the method call `ThrowIfCancellationRequested`. With the caller waiting for the task, you can see that the exception `AggregateException` is caught and contains the inner exception `TaskCanceledException`. This is used for a hierarchy of cancellations—for example, if you run a `Parallel.For` within a task that is canceled as well. The final status of the task is `Canceled`:

```
in task
in loop
in loop
in loop
in loop
*** task cancelled
cancelling was requested, cancelling from within the task
exception: AggregateException, One or more errors occurred.
inner exception: TaskCanceledException, A task was canceled.
```

DATA FLOW

The `Parallel` and `Task` classes, and Parallel LINQ, help a lot with data parallelism. However, these classes do not directly support dealing with data flow or transforming data in parallel. For this, you can use *Task Parallel Library Data Flow*, or *TPL Data Flow*.

The sample code for the data flow samples makes use of the following namespaces:

Namespaces

```
System
```

```
System.IO

System.Threading

System.Threading.Tasks

System.Threading.Tasks.DataFlow
```

Using an Action Block

The heart of TPL Data Flow is data blocks. These blocks can act as a source to offer some data or a target to receive data, or both. Let's start with a simple example, a data block that receives some data and writes it to the console. The following code snippet defines an ActionBlock that receives a string and writes information to the console. The Main method reads user input within a while loop, and posts every string read to the ActionBlock by calling the Post method. The Post method posts an item to the ActionBlock, which deals with the message asynchronously, writing the information to the console (code file SimpleDataFlowSample/Program.cs):

```
static void Main()
{
  var processInput = new ActionBlock<string>(s =>
  {
    Console.WriteLine($"user input: {s}");
  });
  bool exit = false;
  while (!exit)
  {
    string input = ReadLine();
    if (string.Compare(input, "exit", ignoreCase: true) == 0)
    {
      exit = true;
    }
    else
    {
      processInput.Post(input);
    }
  }
}
```

Source and Target Blocks

When the method assigned to the ActionBlock from the previous example executes, the ActionBlock uses a task to do the execution in parallel. You could verify this by checking the task and thread identifiers and writing these to the console. Every block implements the interface IDataflowBlock, which contains the property Completion, which returns a Task, and the methods Complete and Fault. Invoking the Complete method, the block no longer accepts any input or produces any more output. Invoking the Fault method puts the block into a faulting state.

As mentioned earlier, a block can be either a source or a target, or both. In this case, the ActionBlock is a target block and thus implements the interface ITargetBlock. ITargetBlock derives from IDataflowBlock and defines the OfferMessage method, in addition to the members of the IDataBlock interface. OfferMessage sends a message that can be consumed by the block. An API that is easier to use than OfferMessage is the Post method, which is implemented as an extension method for the ITargetBlock interface. The Post method was also used by the sample application.

The ISourceBlock interface is implemented by blocks that can act as a data source. ISourceBlock offers methods in addition to the members of the IDataBlock interface to link to a target block and to consume messages.

The BufferBlock acts as both a source and a target, implementing both ISourceBlock and ITargetBlock. In the next example, this BufferBlock is used to both post messages and receive messages (code file SimpleDataFlowSample/Program.cs):

The Producer method reads strings from the console and writes them to the BufferBlock by invoking the Post method:

```
public static void Producer()
{
  bool exit = false;
  while (!exit)
  {
  string input = ReadLine();
  if (string.Compare(input, "exit", ignoreCase: true) == 0)
  {
    exit = true;
  }
  else
  {
    s_buffer.Post(input);
  }
  }
}
```

The Consumer method contains a loop to receive data from the BufferBlock by invoking the ReceiveAsync method. ReceiveAsync is an extension method for the ISourceBlock interface:

```
public static async Task ConsumerAsync()
{
  while (true)
  {
    string data = await s_buffer.ReceiveAsync();
    Console.WriteLine($"user input: {data}");
  }
}
```

Now, you just need to start the producer and consumer. You do this with two independent tasks in the Main method:

```
static void Main()
{
  Task t1 = Task.Run(() => Producer());
  Task t2 = Task.Run(async () => await ConsumerAsync());
  Task.WaitAll(t1, t2);
}
```

When you run the application, the producer task reads data from the console, and the consumer receives the data to write it to the console.

Connecting Blocks

This section creates a pipeline by connecting multiple blocks. First, three methods are created that will be used by the blocks. The GetFileNames method receives a directory path and yields the filenames that end with the .cs extension (code file DataFlowSample/Program.cs):

```
public static IEnumerable<string> GetFileNames(string path)
{
  foreach (var fileName in Directory.EnumerateFiles(path, "*.cs"))
  {
    yield return fileName;
  }
}
```

The `LoadLines` method receives a list of filenames and yields every line of the files:

```
public static IEnumerable<string> LoadLines(IEnumerable<string> fileNames)
{
  foreach (var fileName in fileNames)
  {
    using (FileStream stream = File.OpenRead(fileName))
    {
      var reader = new StreamReader(stream);
      string line = null;
      while ((line = reader.ReadLine()) != null)
      {
        //WriteLine($"LoadLines {line}");
        yield return line;
      }
    }
  }
}
```

The third method, `GetWords`, receives the `lines` collection and splits it up line by line to `yield return` a list of words:

```
public static IEnumerable<string> GetWords(IEnumerable<string> lines)
{
  foreach (var line in lines)
  {
    string[] words = line.Split(' ', ';', '(', ')', '{', '}', '.', ',');
    foreach (var word in words)
    {
      if (!string.IsNullOrEmpty(word))
        yield return word;
    }
  }
}
```

To create the pipeline, the `SetupPipeline` method creates three `TransformBlock` objects. The `TransformBlock` is a source and target block that transforms the source by using a delegate. The first `TransformBlock` is declared to transform a `string` to `IEnumerable<string>`. The transformation is done by the `GetFileNames` method that is invoked within the lambda expression passed to the constructor of the first block. Similarly, the next two `TransformBlock` objects are used to invoke the `LoadLines` and `GetWords` methods:

```
public static ITargetBlock<string> SetupPipeline()
{
  var fileNamesForPath = new TransformBlock<string, IEnumerable<string>>(
    path => GetFileNames(path));

  var lines = new TransformBlock<IEnumerable<string>, IEnumerable<string>>(
    fileNames => LoadLines(fileNames));

  var words = new TransformBlock<IEnumerable<string>, IEnumerable<string>>(
    lines2 => GetWords(lines2));
```

The last block defined is an `ActionBlock`. This block has been used before and is just a target block to receive data:

```
  var display = new ActionBlock<IEnumerable<string>>(
    coll =>
    {
      foreach (var s in coll)
      {
        Console.WriteLine(s);
      }
    });
```

Finally, the blocks are connected to each other. fileNamesForPath is linked to the lines block. The result from fileNamesForPath is passed to the lines block. The lines block links to the words block, and the words block links to the display block. Last, the block to start the pipeline is returned:

```
fileNamesForPath.LinkTo(lines);
lines.LinkTo(words);
words.LinkTo(display);
return fileNamesForPath;
}
```

The Main method now needs to kick off the pipeline. Invoking the Post method to pass a directory, the pipeline starts and finally writes words from the C# source code to the console. Here, it would be possible to start multiple requests for the pipeline, passing more than one directory, and doing these tasks in parallel:

```
static void Main()
{
  var target = SetupPipeline();
  target.Post(".");
  Console.ReadLine();
}
```

With this brief introduction to the TPL Data Flow library, you've seen the principal way to work with this technology. This library offers a lot more functionality, such as different blocks that deal with data differently. The BroadcastBlock allows passing the input source to multiple targets (for example, writing data to a file and displaying it), the JoinBlock joins multiple sources to one target, and the BatchBlock batches input into arrays. Using DataflowBlockOptions options allows configuration of a block, such as the maximum number of items that are processed within a single task and passing a cancellation token that allows canceling a pipeline. With links, you can also filter messages and only pass messages that fulfill a specified predicate.

TIMERS

With a timer, you can do a repeat invocation of a method. Two timers will be covered in this section: the Timer class from the System.Threading namespace and the DispatcherTimer for XAML-based apps.

Using the System.Threading.Timer class, you can pass the method to be invoked as the first parameter in the constructor. This method must fulfill the requirements of the TimerCallback delegate, which defines a void return type and an object parameter. With the second parameter of the constructor, you can pass any object, which is then received with the object argument in the callback method. For example, you can pass an Event object to signal the caller. The third parameter specifies the time span during which the callback should be invoked the first time. With the last parameter, you specify the repeating interval for the callback. If the timer should fire only once, set the fourth parameter to the value -1.

If the time interval should be changed after creating the Timer object, you can pass new values with the Change method (code file TimerSample/Program.cs):

```
private static void ThreadingTimer()
{
  void TimeAction(object o) =>
    Console.WriteLine($"System.Threading.Timer {DateTime.Now:T}");

  using (var t1 = new Timer(TimeAction, null,
    TimeSpan.FromSeconds(2), TimeSpan.FromSeconds(3)))
  {
    Task.Delay(15000).Wait();
  }
}
```

The `DispatcherTimer` from the namespace `Windows.UI.Xaml` (for UWP apps) is a timer for XAML-based apps where the event handler is called within the UI thread, thus it is possible to directly access user interface elements.

The sample application to demonstrate the `DispatcherTimer` is a Windows app that shows the hand of a clock that switches every second. The following XAML code defines the commands that enable you to start and stop the clock (code file `WinAppTimer/MainPage.xaml`):

```
<Page.TopAppBar>
  <CommandBar IsOpen="True">
    <AppBarButton Icon="Play" Click="{x:Bind OnTimer}" />
    <AppBarButton Icon="Stop" Click="{x:Bind OnStopTimer}" />
  </CommandBar>
</Page.TopAppBar>
```

The hand of the clock is defined using the shape `Line`. To rotate the line, you use a `RotateTransform` element:

```
<Canvas Width="300" Height="300">
  <Ellipse Width="10" Height="10" Fill="Red" Canvas.Left="145"
    Canvas.Top="145" />
  <Line Canvas.Left="150" Canvas.Top="150" Fill="Green" StrokeThickness="3"
    Stroke="Blue" X1="0" Y1="0" X2="120" Y2="0" >
    <Line.RenderTransform>
      <RotateTransform CenterX="0" CenterY="0" Angle="270" x:Name="rotate" />
    </Line.RenderTransform>
  </Line>
</Canvas>
```

> **NOTE** *XAML shapes are explained in Chapter 35, "Styling XAML Apps."*

The `DispatcherTimer` object is created in the `MainPage` class. In the constructor, the handler method is assigned to the `Tick` event, and the `Interval` is specified to be one second. The timer is started in the `OnTimer` method—the method that gets called when the user clicks the `Play` button in the `CommandBar` (code file `WinAppTimer/MainPage.xaml.cs`):

```
private DispatcherTimer _timer = new DispatcherTimer();
public MainPage()
{
  this.InitializeComponent();
  _timer.Tick += OnTick;
  _timer.Interval = TimeSpan.FromSeconds(1);
}

private void OnTimer()
{
  _timer.Start();
}

private void OnTick(object sender, object e)
{
  double newAngle = rotate.Angle + 6;
  if (newAngle >= 360) newAngle = 0;
  rotate.Angle = newAngle;
}
```

```
private void OnStopTimer()
{
    _timer.Stop();
}
```

When you run the application, the clock hand is shown (see Figure 21-1).

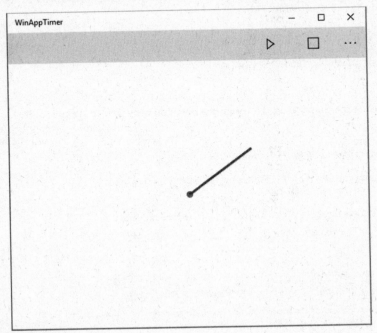

FIGURE 21-1

THREADING ISSUES

Programming with multiple threads is challenging. When starting multiple threads that access the same data, you can get intermittent problems that are hard to find. The problems are the same whether you use tasks, Parallel LINQ, or the `Parallel` class. To avoid getting into trouble, you must pay attention to synchronization issues and the problems that can occur with multiple threads. This section covers two in particular: race conditions and deadlocks.

> **NOTE** *Before synchronizing custom collection classes with the synchronization types shown here, you should also read Chapter 11, "Special Collections," to learn about collections that are already thread-safe: concurrent collections.*

The sample code for the `ThreadingIssues` sample makes use of these namespaces:

```
System.Diagnostics

System.Threading

System.Threading.Tasks

static System.Console
```

You can start the sample application `ThreadingIssues` with command-line arguments to simulate either race conditions or deadlocks.

Race Conditions

A race condition can occur if two or more threads access the same objects and access to the shared state is not synchronized. To demonstrate a race condition, the following example defines the class `StateObject`, with an `int` field and the method `ChangeState`. In the implementation of `ChangeState`, the state variable is verified to determine whether it contains 5; if it does, the value is incremented. `Trace.Assert` is the next statement, which immediately verifies that state now contains the value 6.

After incrementing by 1 a variable that contains the value 5, you might assume that the variable now has the value 6; but this is not necessarily the case. For example, if one thread has just completed the `if (_state == 5)` statement, it might be preempted, with the scheduler running another thread. The second thread now goes into the `if` body and, because the state still has the value 5, the state is incremented by 1 to 6. The first thread is then scheduled again, and in the next statement the state is incremented to 7. This is when the race condition occurs, and the assert message is shown (code file `ThreadingIssues/SampleTask.cs`):

```
public class StateObject
{
  private int _state = 5;
  public void ChangeState(int loop)
  {
    if (_state == 5)
    {
      _state++;
      if (_state != 6)
      {
        Console.WriteLine($"Race condition occurred after {loop} loops");
        Trace.Fail("race condition");
      }
    }
    _state = 5;
  }
}
```

You can verify this by defining a method for a task. The method `RaceCondition` of the class `SampleTask` gets a `StateObject` as a parameter. Inside an endless `while` loop, the `ChangeState` method is invoked. The variable `i` is used just to show the loop number in the assert message:

```
public class SampleTask
{
  public void RaceCondition(object o)
  {
    Trace.Assert(o is StateObject, "o must be of type StateObject");
    StateObject state = o as StateObject;
    int i = 0;
    while (true)
    {
      state.ChangeState(i++);
    }
  }
}
```

In the `Main` method of the program, a new `StateObject` is created that is shared among all the tasks. `Task` objects are created by invoking the `RaceCondition` method with the lambda expression that is passed to the `Run` method of the `Task`. The main thread then waits for user input. However, there's a good chance that the program will halt before reading user input because a race condition will happen:

```
public void RaceConditions()
{
  var state = new StateObject();
```

```
for (int i = 0; i < 2; i++)
{
    Task.Run(() => new SampleTask().RaceCondition(state));
}
}
```

When you start the program, you get race conditions. How long it takes until the first race condition happens depends on your system and whether you build the program as a release build or a debug build. With a release build, the problem happens more often because the code is optimized. If you have multiple CPUs in your system or dual-/quad-core CPUs, where multiple threads can run concurrently, the problem also occurs more often than with a single-core CPU. The problem occurs with a single-core CPU because thread scheduling is preemptive, but the problem doesn't occur that often.

In one run of the program on my system, I saw an error after 85,232 loops; in another run, the error manifested after 70,037 loops. If you start the application multiple times, you always get different results.

You can avoid the problem by locking the shared object. You do this inside the thread by locking the variable state, which is shared among the threads, with the `lock` statement, as shown in the following example. Only one thread can exist inside the lock block for the state object. Because this object is shared among all threads, a thread must wait at the lock if another thread has the lock for state. As soon as the lock is accepted, the thread owns the lock and gives it up at the end of the lock block. If every thread changing the object referenced with the state variable is using a lock, the race condition no longer occurs:

```
public class SampleTask
{
    public void RaceCondition(object o)
    {
        Trace.Assert(o is StateObject, "o must be of type StateObject");
        StateObject state = o as StateObject;
        int i = 0;
        while (true)
        {
            lock (state) // no race condition with this lock
            {
                state.ChangeState(i++);
            }
        }
    }
}
```

> **NOTE** *With the downloaded sample code, you need to uncomment the lock statements for solving the issues with race conditions.*

Instead of performing the lock when using the shared object, you can make the shared object thread-safe. In the following code, the `ChangeState` method contains a `lock` statement. Because you cannot lock the state variable itself (only reference types can be used for a lock), the variable `sync` of type `object` is defined and used with the `lock` statement. If a lock is done using the same synchronization object every time the value state is changed, race conditions no longer happen:

```
public class StateObject
{
    private int _state = 5;
    private _object sync = new object();
    public void ChangeState(int loop)
    {
        lock (_sync)
        {
            if (_state == 5)
```

```
    {
      _state++;
      if (_state != 6)
      {
        Console.WriteLine($"Race condition occured after {loop} loops");
        Trace.Fail($"race condition at {loop}");
      }
    }
    _state = 5;
  }
}
```

Deadlocks

Too much locking can get you in trouble as well. In a deadlock, at least two threads halt and wait for each other to release a lock. As both threads wait for each other, a deadlock occurs, and the threads wait endlessly.

To demonstrate deadlocks, the following code instantiates two objects of type StateObject and passes them with the constructor of the SampleTask class. Two tasks are created: one task running the method Deadlock1 and the other task running the method Deadlock2 (code file ThreadingIssues/Program.cs):

```
var state1 = new StateObject();
var state2 = new StateObject();
new Task(new SampleTask(state1, state2).Deadlock1).Start();
new Task(new SampleTask(state1, state2).Deadlock2).Start();
```

The methods Deadlock1 and Deadlock2 now change the state of two objects: s1 and s2. That's why two locks are generated. Deadlock1 first does a lock for s1 and next for s2. Deadlock2 first does a lock for s2 and then for s1. Now, occasionally the lock for s1 in Deadlock1 is resolved. Next, a thread switch occurs, and Deadlock2 starts to run and gets the lock for s2. The second thread now waits for the lock of s1. Because it needs to wait, the thread scheduler schedules the first thread again, which now waits for s2. Both threads now wait and don't release the lock as long as the lock block is not ended. This is a typical deadlock (code file ThreadingIssues/SampleTask.cs):

```
public class SampleTask
{
  public SampleTask(StateObject s1, StateObject s2)
  {
    _s1 = s1;
    _s2 = s2;
  }
  private StateObject _s1;
  private StateObject _s2;

  public void Deadlock1()
  {
    int i = 0;
    while (true)
    {
      lock (_s1)
      {
        lock (_s2)
        {
          _s1.ChangeState(i);
          _s2.ChangeState(i++);
          Console.WriteLine($"still running, {i}");
        }
      }
    }
  }
```

```
public void Deadlock2()
{
  int i = 0;
  while (true)
  {
    lock (_s2)
    {
      lock (_s1)
      {
        _s1.ChangeState(i);
        _s2.ChangeState(i++);
        Console.WriteLine($"still running, {i}");
      }
    }
  }
}
```

As a result, the program runs some loops and soon becomes unresponsive. The message "still running" is written a few times to the console. Again, how soon the problem occurs depends on your system configuration, and the result will vary.

A deadlock problem is not always as obvious as it is here. One thread locks _s1 and then _s2; the other thread locks _s2 and then _s1. In this case, you just need to change the order so that both threads perform the locks in the same order. In a bigger application, the locks might be hidden deeply inside a method. You can prevent this problem by designing a good lock order in the initial architecture of the application, and by defining timeouts for the locks, as demonstrated in the next section.

THE LOCK STATEMENT AND THREAD SAFETY

C# has its own keyword for the synchronization of multiple threads: the lock statement. The lock statement provides an easy way to hold and release a lock. Before adding lock statements, however, let's look at another race condition. The class SharedState demonstrates using shared state between threads and shares an integer value (code file SynchronizationSamples/SharedState.cs):

```
public class SharedState
{
  public int State { get; set; }
}
```

The sample code for all the following synchronization samples uses the following namespaces:

```
System

System.Collections.Generic

System.Linq

System.Text

System.Threading

System.Threading.Tasks
```

The class Job contains the method DoTheJob, which is the entry point for a new task. With the implementation, the State of the SharedState object is incremented 50,000 times. The variable sharedState is initialized in the constructor of this class (code file SynchronizationSamples/Job.cs):

```
public class Job
{
  private SharedState _sharedState;
  public Job(SharedState sharedState)
```

```
  {
    _sharedState = sharedState;
  }

  public void DoTheJob()
  {
    for (int i = 0; i < 50000; i++)
    {
      _sharedState.State += 1;
    }
  }
}
```

In the `Main` method, a `SharedState` object is created and passed to the constructor of 20 `Task` objects. All tasks are started. After starting the tasks, the `Main` method waits until every one of the 20 tasks is completed. After the tasks are completed, the summarized value of the shared state is written to the console. With 50,000 loops and 20 tasks, a value of 1,000,000 could be expected. Often, however, this is not the case (code file `SynchronizationSamples/Program.cs`):

```
class Program
{
  static void Main()
  {
    int numTasks = 20;
    var state = new SharedState();
    var tasks = new Task[numTasks];
    for (int i = 0; i < numTasks; i++)
    {
      tasks[i] = Task.Run(() => new Job(state).DoTheJob());
    }
    Task.WaitAll(tasks);
    Console.WriteLine($"summarized {state.State}");
  }
}
```

The results of multiple runs of the application are as follows:

```
summarized 424687
summarized 465708
summarized 581754
summarized 395571
summarized 633601
```

The behavior is different every time, but none of the results are correct. As noted earlier, you will see big differences between debug and release builds, and the type of CPU that you are using also affects results. If you change the loop count to smaller values, you often will get correct values—but not every time. In this case the application is small enough to see the problem easily; in a large application, the reason for such a problem can be hard to find.

You must add synchronization to this program. To do so, use the `lock` keyword. Defining the object with the `lock` statement means that you wait to get the lock for the specified object. You can pass only a reference type. Locking a value type would just lock a copy, which wouldn't make any sense. In any case, the C# compiler issues an error if value types are used with the `lock` statement. As soon as the lock is granted—only one thread gets the lock—the block of the `lock` statement can run. At the end of the `lock` statement block, the lock for the object is released, and another thread waiting for the lock can be granted access to it:

```
lock (obj)
{
  // synchronized region
}
```

To lock static members, you can place the lock on the type object or a static member:

```
lock (typeof(StaticClass))
{
}
```

You can make the instance members of a class thread-safe by using the `lock` keyword. This way, only one thread at a time can access the methods `DoThis` and `DoThat` for the same instance:

```
public class Demo
{
  public void DoThis()
  {
    lock (this)
    {
      // only one thread at a time can access the DoThis and DoThat methods
    }
  }

  public void DoThat()
  {
    lock (this)
    {
    }
  }
}
```

However, because the object of the instance can also be used for synchronized access from the outside, and you can't control this from the class itself, you can apply the SyncRoot pattern. With the SyncRoot pattern, a private object named `_syncRoot` is created, and this object is used with the `lock` statements:

```
public class Demo
{
  private object _syncRoot = new object();
  public void DoThis()
  {
    lock (_syncRoot)
    {
      // only one thread at a time can access the DoThis and DoThat methods
    }
  }

  public void DoThat()
  {
    lock (_syncRoot)
    {
    }
  }
}
```

Using locks costs time and is not always necessary. You can create two versions of a class: synchronized and unsynchronized. This is demonstrated in the next example code by changing the class `Demo`. The class `Demo` is not synchronized, as shown in the implementation of the `DoThis` and `DoThat` methods. The class also defines the `IsSynchronized` property, whereby the client can get information about the synchronization option of the class. To make a synchronized variant of the `Demo` class, you use the static method `Synchronized` to pass an unsynchronized object, and this method returns an object of type `SynchronizedDemo`. `SynchronizedDemo` is implemented as an inner class that is derived from the base class `Demo` and overrides the virtual members of the base class. The overridden members make use of the SyncRoot pattern:

```
public class Demo
{
  private class SynchronizedDemo: Demo
```

```
    {
      private object _syncRoot = new object();
      private Demo _d;
      public SynchronizedDemo(Demo d)
      {
        _d = d;
      }

      public override bool IsSynchronized => true;

      public override void DoThis()
      {
        lock (_syncRoot)
        {
          _d.DoThis();
        }
      }

      public override void DoThat()
      {
        lock (_syncRoot)
        {
          _d.DoThat();
        }
      }
    }

    public virtual bool IsSynchronized => false;

    public static Demo Synchronized(Demo d)
    {
      if (!d.IsSynchronized)
      {
        return new SynchronizedDemo(d);
      }
      return d;
    }

    public virtual void DoThis()
    {
    }

    public virtual void DoThat()
    {
    }
  }
```

Bear in mind that when you use the SynchronizedDemo class, only methods are synchronized. There is no synchronization for invoking other members of this class.

Now, change the SharedState class that was not synchronized at first to use the SyncRoot pattern. If you try to make the SharedState class thread-safe by locking access to the properties with the SyncRoot pattern, you still get the race condition shown earlier in the "Race Conditions" section:

```
public class SharedState
{
  private int _state = 0;
  private object _syncRoot = new object();
  public int State // there's still a race condition,
  // don't do this!
  {
```

```
        get { lock (_syncRoot) { return _state; }}
        set { lock (_syncRoot) { _state = value; }}
    }
}
```

The thread that invokes the `DoTheJob` method is accessing the `get` accessor of the `SharedState` class to get the current value of the state, and then the `set` accessor sets the new value for the state. In between calling the `get` and `set` accessors, the object is not locked, and another thread can read the interim value (code file `SynchronizationSamples/Job.cs`):

```
public void DoTheJob()
{
  for (int i = 0; i < 50000; i++)
  {
    _sharedState.State += 1;
  }
}
```

Therefore, it is better to leave the `SharedState` class as it was earlier, without thread safety (code file `SynchronizationSamples/SharedState.cs`):

```
public class SharedState
{
  public int State { get; set; }
}
```

In addition, add the `lock` statement where it belongs, inside the method `DoTheJob` (code file `SynchronizationSamples/Job.cs`):

```
public void DoTheJob()
{
  for (int i = 0; i < 50000; i++)
  {
    lock (_sharedState)
    {
      _sharedState.State += 1;
    }
  }
}
```

This way, the results of the application are always as expected.

> **NOTE** *Using the* `lock` *statement in one place does not mean that all other threads accessing the object are waiting. You have to explicitly use synchronization with every thread accessing the shared state.*

Of course, you can also change the design of the `SharedState` class and offer incrementing as an atomic operation. This is a design question—what should be an atomic functionality of the class? The next code snippet just keeps the increment locked:

```
public class SharedState
{
  private int _state = 0;
  private object _syncRoot = new object();
  public int State => _state;
  public int IncrementState()
  {
    lock (_syncRoot)
    {
      return ++_state;
    }
  }
}
```

There is, however, a faster way to lock the increment of the state, as shown in the next section.

INTERLOCKED

The `Interlocked` class is used to make simple statements for variables atomic. `i++` is not thread-safe. It consists of getting a value from the memory, incrementing the value by 1, and storing the value back in memory. These operations can be interrupted by the thread scheduler. The `Interlocked` class provides methods for incrementing, decrementing, exchanging, and reading values in a thread-safe manner.

Using the `Interlocked` class is much faster than other synchronization techniques. However, you can use it only for simple synchronization issues.

For example, instead of using the `lock` statement to lock access to the variable `someState` when setting it to a new value, in case it is null, you can use the `Interlocked` class, which is faster:

```
lock (this)
{
  if (_someState == null)
  {
    _someState = newState;
  }
}
```

The faster version with the same functionality uses the `Interlocked.CompareExchange` method.

Instead of performing incrementing inside a `lock` statement as shown here:

```
public int State
{
  get
  {
    lock (this)
    {
      return ++_state;
    }
  }
}
```

you can use `Interlocked.Increment`, which is faster:

```
public int State
{
  get => Interlocked.Increment(ref _state);
}
```

MONITOR

The C# compiler resolves the `lock` statement to use the `Monitor` class. The following `lock` statement

```
lock (obj)
{
  // synchronized region for obj
}
```

is resolved to invoke the `Enter` method, which waits until the thread gets the lock of the object. Only one thread at a time may be the owner of the object lock. As soon as the lock is resolved, the thread can enter the synchronized section. The `Exit` method of the `Monitor` class releases the lock. The compiler puts the `Exit` method into a `finally` handler of a `try` block so that the lock is also released if an exception is thrown:

```
Monitor.Enter(obj);
try
{
  // synchronized region for obj
```

```
}
finally
{
  Monitor.Exit(obj);
}
```

> **NOTE** *Chapter 14, "Errors and Exceptions," covers the* try/finally *block.*

The `Monitor` class has a big advantage over the `lock` statement of C#: You can add a timeout value for waiting to get the lock. Therefore, instead of endlessly waiting to get the lock, you can use the `TryEnter` method shown in the following example, passing a timeout value that defines the maximum amount of time to wait for the lock. If the lock for `obj` is acquired, `TryEnter` sets the Boolean `ref` parameter to `true` and performs synchronized access to the state guarded by the object `obj`. If `obj` is locked for more than 500 milliseconds by another thread, `TryEnter` sets the variable `lockTaken` to `false`, and the thread does not wait any longer but is used to do something else. Maybe later, the thread can try to acquire the lock again.

```
bool _lockTaken = false;
Monitor.TryEnter(_obj, 500, ref _lockTaken);
if (_lockTaken)
  {
  try
  {
    // acquired the lock
    // synchronized region for obj
  }
  finally
  {
    Monitor.Exit(obj);
  }
}
else
{
  // didn't get the lock, do something else
}
```

SPINLOCK

If the overhead on object-based lock objects (`Monitor`) would be too high because of garbage collection, you can use the `SpinLock` struct. `SpinLock` is useful if you have many locks (for example, for every node in a list) and hold times are always extremely short. You should avoid holding more than one `SpinLock`, and don't call anything that might block.

Other than the architectural differences, `SpinLock` is very similar in usage to the `Monitor` class. You acquire the lock with `Enter` or `TryEnter` and release the lock with `Exit`. `SpinLock` also offers two properties to provide information about whether it is currently locked: `IsHeld` and `IsHeldByCurrentThread`.

> **NOTE** *Be careful when passing* SpinLock *instances around. Because* SpinLock *is defined as a* struct, *assigning one variable to another creates a copy. Always pass* SpinLock *instances by reference.*

WAITHANDLE

WaitHandle is an abstract base class that you can use to wait for a signal to be set. You can wait for different things, because WaitHandle is a base class and some classes are derived from it.

With WaitHandle, you can wait for one signal to occur (WaitOne), multiple objects that all must be signaled (WaitAll), or one of multiple objects (WaitAny). WaitAll and WaitAny are static members of the WaitHandle class and accept an array of WaitHandle parameters.

WaitHandle has a SafeWaitHandle property with which you can assign a native handle to an operating system resource and wait for that handle. For example, you can assign a SafeFileHandle to wait for a file I/O operation to complete.

The classes Mutex, EventWaitHandle, and Semaphore are derived from the base class WaitHandle, so you can use any of these with waits.

MUTEX

Mutex (mutual exclusion) is one of the classes of the .NET Framework that offers synchronization across multiple processes. It is very similar to the Monitor class in that there is just one owner. That is, only one thread can get a lock on the mutex and access the synchronized code regions that are secured by the mutex.

With the constructor of the Mutex class, you can define whether the mutex should initially be owned by the calling thread, define a name for the mutex, and determine whether the mutex already exists. In the following example, the third parameter is defined as an out parameter to receive a Boolean value if the mutex was newly created. If the value returned is false, the mutex was already defined. The mutex might be defined in a different process, because a mutex with a name is known to the operating system and is shared among different processes. If no name is assigned to the mutex, the mutex is unnamed and not shared among different processes.

```
bool createdNew;
var mutex = new Mutex(false, "ProCSharpMutex", out createdNew);
```

To open an existing mutex, you can also use the method Mutex.OpenExisting, which doesn't require the same .NET privileges as creating the mutex with the constructor.

Because the Mutex class derives from the base class WaitHandle, you can do a WaitOne to acquire the mutex lock and be the owner of the mutex during that time. The mutex is released by invoking the ReleaseMutex method:

```
if (mutex.WaitOne())
{
  try
  {
  // synchronized region
  }
  finally
  {
    mutex.ReleaseMutex();
  }
}
else
{
  // some problem happened while waiting
}
```

Because a named mutex is known system-wide, you can use it to keep an application from being started twice. In the following console application, the constructor of the `Mutex` object is invoked. Then it is verified whether the mutex with the name `SingletonAppMutex` exists already. If it does, the application exits (code file `SingletonUsingMutex/Program.cs`):

```
static void Main()
{
  bool mutexCreated;
  var mutex = new Mutex(false, "SingletonAppMutex", out mutexCreated);
  if (!mutexCreated)
  {
    Console.WriteLine("You can only start one instance of the application.");
    Console.WriteLine("Exiting.");
    return;
  }
  Console.WriteLine("Application running");
  Console.WriteLine("Press return to exit");
  Console.ReadLine();
}
```

SEMAPHORE

A semaphore is very similar to a mutex, but unlike the mutex, the semaphore can be used by multiple threads at once. A semaphore is a counting mutex, meaning that with a semaphore you can define the number of threads that are allowed to access the resource guarded by the semaphore simultaneously. This is useful if you need to limit the number of threads that can access the available resources. For example, if a system has three physical I/O ports available, three threads can access them simultaneously, but a fourth thread needs to wait until the resource is released by one of the other threads.

.NET Core provides two classes with semaphore functionality: `Semaphore` and `SemaphoreSlim`. `Semaphore` can be named, can use system-wide resources, and allows synchronization between different processes. `SemaphoreSlim` is a lightweight version that is optimized for shorter wait times.

In the following example application, in the `Main` method six tasks are created along with one semaphore with a count of 3. In the constructor of the `Semaphore` class, you can define the count for the number of locks that can be acquired with the semaphore (the second parameter) and the number of locks that are free initially (the first parameter). If the first parameter has a lower value than the second parameter, the difference between the values defines the already allocated semaphore count. As with the mutex, you can also assign a name to the semaphore to share it among different processes. Here a `SemaphoreSlim` object is created that can only be used within the process. After the `SemaphoreSlim` object is created, six tasks are started, and they all wait for the same semaphore (code file `SemaphoreSample/Program.cs`):

```
class Program
{
  static void Main()
  {
    int taskCount = 6;
    int semaphoreCount = 3;
    var semaphore = new SemaphoreSlim(semaphoreCount, semaphoreCount);
    var tasks = new Task[taskCount];
    for (int i = 0; i < taskCount; i++)
    {
      tasks[i] = Task.Run(() => TaskMain(semaphore));
    }
    Task.WaitAll(tasks);
    Console.WriteLine("All tasks finished");
  }
  //...
```

In the task's main method, `TaskMain`, the task does a `Wait` to lock the semaphore. Remember that the semaphore has a count of 3, so three tasks can acquire the lock. Task 4 must wait, and here the timeout of 600 milliseconds is defined as the maximum wait time. If the lock cannot be acquired after the wait time has elapsed, the task writes a message to the console and repeats the wait in a loop. As soon as the lock is acquired, the thread writes a message to the console, sleeps for some time, and releases the lock. Again, with the release of the lock it is important that the resource be released in all cases. That's why the `Release` method of the `SemaphoreSlim` class is invoked in a `finally` handler (code file `SemaphoreSample/Program.cs`):

```
// ...
public static void TaskMain(SemaphoreSlim semaphore)
{
  bool isCompleted = false;
  while (!isCompleted)
  {
    if (semaphore.Wait(600))
    {
      try
      {
        Console.WriteLine($"Task {Task.CurrentId} locks the semaphore");
        Task.Delay(2000).Wait();
      }
      finally
      {
        Console.WriteLine($"Task {Task.CurrentId} releases the semaphore");
        semaphore.Release();
        isCompleted = true;
      }
    }
    else
    {
      Console.WriteLine($"Timeout for task {Task.CurrentId}; wait again");
    }
  }
}
```

When you run the application, you can indeed see that with four threads, the lock is made immediately. The tasks with IDs 7, 8, and 9 must wait. The wait continues in the loop until one of the other threads releases the semaphore:

```
Task 4 locks the semaphore
Task 5 locks the semaphore
Task 6 locks the semaphore
Timeout for task 7; wait again
Timeout for task 7; wait again
Timeout for task 8; wait again
Timeout for task 7; wait again
Timeout for task 8; wait again
Timeout for task 7; wait again
Timeout for task 9; wait again
Timeout for task 8; wait again
Task 5 releases the semaphore
Task 7 locks the semaphore
Task 6 releases the semaphore
Task 4 releases the semaphore
Task 8 locks the semaphore
Task 9 locks the semaphore
Task 8 releases the semaphore
Task 7 releases the semaphore
Task 9 releases the semaphore
All tasks finished
```

EVENTS

Like mutex and semaphore objects, events are also system-wide synchronization resources. For using system events from managed code, the .NET Framework offers the classes `ManualResetEvent`, `AutoResetEvent`, `ManualResetEventSlim`, and `CountdownEvent` in the namespace `System.Threading`.

> **NOTE** *The event keyword from C# that is covered in Chapter 8, "Delegates, Lambdas, and Events," has nothing to do with the event classes from the namespace* `System.Threading`; *the event keyword is based on delegates. However, both event classes are .NET wrappers to the system-wide native event resource for synchronization.*

You can use events to inform other tasks that some data is present, that something is completed, and so on. An event can be signaled or not signaled. A task can wait for the event to be in a signaled state with the help of the `WaitHandle` class, discussed earlier.

A `ManualResetEventSlim` is signaled by invoking the `Set` method, and it's returned to a nonsignaled state with the `Reset` method. If multiple threads are waiting for an event to be signaled and the `Set` method is invoked, then all threads waiting are released. In addition, if a thread invokes the `WaitOne` method but the event is already signaled, the waiting thread can continue immediately.

An `AutoResetEvent` is also signaled by invoking the `Set` method, and you can set it back to a nonsignaled state with the `Reset` method. However, if a thread is waiting for an auto-reset event to be signaled, the event is automatically changed into a nonsignaled state when the wait state of the first thread is finished. This way, if multiple threads are waiting for the event to be set, only one thread is released from its wait state. It is not the thread that has been waiting the longest for the event to be signaled, but the thread waiting with the highest priority.

To demonstrate events with the `ManualResetEventSlim` class, the following class `Calculator` defines the method `Calculation`, which is the entry point for a task. With this method, the task receives input data for calculation and writes the result to the variable result that can be accessed from the `Result` property. As soon as the result is completed (after a random amount of time), the event is signaled by invoking the `Set` method of the `ManualResetEventSlim` (code file `EventSample/Calculator.cs`):

```
public class Calculator
{
  private ManualResetEventSlim _mEvent;
  public int Result { get; private set; }

  public Calculator(ManualResetEventSlim ev)
  {
    _mEvent = ev;
  }

  public void Calculation(int x, int y)
  {
    Console.WriteLine($"Task {Task.CurrentId} starts calculation");
    Task.Delay(new Random().Next(3000)).Wait();
    Result = x + y;
    // signal the event-completed!
    Console.WriteLine($"Task {Task.CurrentId} is ready");
    _mEvent.Set();
  }
}
```

The `Main` method of the program defines arrays of four `ManualResetEventSlim` objects and four `Calculator` objects. Every `Calculator` is initialized in the constructor with a `ManualResetEventSlim` object, so every task gets its own event object to signal when it is completed. Now, the `Task` class is used to enable different tasks to run the calculation (code file `EventSample/Program.cs`):

```
class Program
{
  static void Main()
  {
    const int taskCount = 4;
    var mEvents = new ManualResetEventSlim[taskCount];
    var waitHandles = new WaitHandle[taskCount];
    var calcs = new Calculator[taskCount];
    for (int i = 0; i < taskCount; i++)
    {
      int i1 = i;
      mEvents[i] = new ManualResetEventSlim(false);
      waitHandles[i] = mEvents[i].WaitHandle;
      calcs[i] = new Calculator(mEvents[i]);
      Task.Run(() => calcs[i1].Calculation(i1 + 1, i1 + 3));
    }
  //...
```

The `WaitHandle` class is now used to wait for any one of the events in the array. `WaitAny` waits until any one of the events is signaled. In contrast to `ManualResetEvent`, `ManualResetEventSlim` does not derive from `WaitHandle`. That's why a separate collection of `WaitHandle` objects is kept, which is filled from the `WaitHandle` property of the `ManualResetEventSlim` class. `WaitAny` returns an index value that provides information about the event that was signaled. The returned value matches the index of the `WaitHandle` array that is passed to `WaitAny`. Using this index, information from the signaled event can be read:

```
for (int i = 0; i < taskCount; i++)
{
  int index = WaitHandle.WaitAny(waitHandles);
  if (index == WaitHandle.WaitTimeout)
  {
    Console.WriteLine("Timeout!!");
  }
  else
  {
    mEvents[index].Reset();
    Console.WriteLine($"finished task for {index}, result:
    {calcs[index].Result}");
  }
}
```

When starting the application, you can see the tasks doing the calculation and setting the event to inform the main thread that it can read the result. At random times, depending on whether the build is a debug or release build and on your hardware, you might see different orders and a different number of tasks performing calls:

```
Task 4 starts calculation
Task 5 starts calculation
Task 6 starts calculation
Task 7 starts calculation
Task 7 is ready
finished task for 3, result: 10
Task 4 is ready
finished task for 0, result: 4
Task 6 is ready
finished task for 1, result: 6
Task 5 is ready
finished task for 2, result: 8
```

In a scenario like this, to fork some work into multiple tasks and later join the result, the new `CountdownEvent` class can be very useful. Instead of creating a separate event object for every task, you need to create only one. `CountdownEvent` defines an initial number for all the tasks that set the event, and after the count is reached, the `CountdownEvent` is signaled.

The `Calculator` class is modified to use the `CountdownEvent` instead of the `ManualResetEvent`. Rather than set the signal with the `Set` method, `CountdownEvent` defines the `Signal` method (code file `EventSampleWithCountdownEvent/Calculator.cs`):

```
public class Calculator
{
  private CountdownEvent _cEvent;
  public int Result { get; private set; }

  public Calculator(CountdownEvent ev)
  {
    _cEvent = ev;
  }

  public void Calculation(int x, int y)
  {
    Console.WriteLine($"Task {Task.CurrentId} starts calculation");
    Task.Delay(new Random().Next(3000)).Wait();
    Result = x + y;
    // signal the event-completed!
    Console.WriteLine($"Task {Task.CurrentId} is ready");
    _cEvent.Signal();
  }
}
```

You can now simplify the `Main` method so that it's only necessary to wait for the single event. If you don't deal with the results separately as it was done before, this new edition might be all that's needed:

```
const int taskCount = 4;
var cEvent = new CountdownEvent(taskCount);
var calcs = new Calculator[taskCount];
for (int i = 0; i < taskCount; i++)
{
  calcs[i] = new Calculator(cEvent);
  int i1 = i;
  Task.Run(() => calcs[i1].Calculation, Tuple.Create(i1 + 1, i1 + 3));
}
cEvent.Wait();

Console.WriteLine("all finished");
for (int i = 0; i < taskCount; i++)
{
  Console.WriteLine($"task for {i}, result: {calcs[i].Result}");
}
```

BARRIER

For synchronization, the `Barrier` class is great for scenarios in which work is forked into multiple tasks and the work must be joined afterward. `Barrier` is used for participants that need to be synchronized. While the job is active, you can dynamically add participants—for example, child tasks that are created from a parent task. Participants can wait until the work is done by all the other participants before continuing.

The `BarrierSample` is somewhat complex, but it's worthwhile to demonstrate the features of the Barrier type. The sample creates multiple collections of two million random strings. Multiple tasks are used to iterate through the collection and count the number of strings, starting with a, b, c, and so on. The work is not only distributed between different tasks, but also within a task. After all tasks are iterated through the first collection of strings, the result is summarized, and the tasks continue later with the next collection.

The method `FillData` creates a collection and fills it with random strings (code file `BarrierSample/Program.cs`):

```
public static IEnumerable<string> FillData(int size)
{
  var r = new Random();
  return Enumerable.Range(0, size).Select(x => GetString(r));
}

private static string GetString(Random r)
{
  var sb = new StringBuilder(6);
  for (int i = 0; i < 6; i++)
  {
    sb.Append((char)(r.Next(26) + 97));
  }
  return sb.ToString();
}
```

A helper method to show information about a `Barrier` is defined with the method `LogBarrierInformation`:

```
private static void LogBarrierInformation(string info, Barrier barrier)
{
  Console.WriteLine($"Task {Task.CurrentId}: {info}. " +
    $"{barrier.ParticipantCount} current and " +
    $"{barrier.ParticipantsRemaining} remaining participants, " +
    $"phase {barrier.CurrentPhaseNumber}");
}
```

The `CalculationInTask` method defines the job performed by a task. With the parameters, the third parameter references the `Barrier` instance. The data that is used for the calculation is an array of `IList<string>`. The last parameter, a jagged `int` array, will be used to write the results as the task progresses.

The task makes the processing in a loop. With every loop, an array element of `IList<string>[]` is processed. After every loop is completed, the `Task` signals that it's ready by invoking the `SignalAndWait` method, and it waits until all the other tasks are ready with this processing as well. This loop continues until the task is fully finished. Then the task removes itself from the barrier by invoking the method `RemoveParticipant` (code file `BarrierSample/Program.cs`):

```
private static void CalculationInTask(int jobNumber, int partitionSize,
  Barrier barrier, IList<string>[] coll, int loops, int[][] results)
{
  LogBarrierInformation("CalculationInTask started", barrier);
  for (int i = 0; i < loops; i++)
  {
    var data = new List<string>(coll[i]);
    int start = jobNumber * partitionSize;
    int end = start + partitionSize;
    Console.WriteLine($"Task {Task.CurrentId} in loop {i}: partition " +
      $"from {start} to {end}");
    for (int j = start; j < end; j++)
    {
      char c = data[j][0];
      results[i][c - 97]++;
    }
    Console.WriteLine($"Calculation completed from task {Task.CurrentId} " +
      $"in loop {i}. {results[i][0]} times a, {results[i][25]} times z");
```

624 | CHAPTER 21 TASKS AND PARALLEL PROGRAMMING

```
        LogBarrierInformation("sending signal and wait for all", barrier);
        barrier.SignalAndWait();
        LogBarrierInformation("waiting completed", barrier);
    }
    barrier.RemoveParticipant();
    LogBarrierInformation("finished task, removed participant", barrier);
}
```

With the `Main` method, a `Barrier` instance is created. In the constructor, you can specify the number of participants. In the example, this number is 3 (`numberTasks + 1`) because there are two created tasks, and the `Main` method is a participant as well. Using `Task.Run`, two tasks are created to fork the iteration through the collection into two parts. After starting the tasks, using `SignalAndWait`, the main method signals its completion and waits until all remaining participants either signal their completion or remove themselves as participants from the barrier. As soon as all participants are ready with one iteration, the results from the tasks are zipped together with the `Zip` extension method. Then the next iteration is done to wait for the next results from the tasks (code file `BarrierSample/Program.cs`):

```
static void Main()
{
    const int numberTasks = 2;
    const int partitionSize = 1000000;
    const int loops = 5;
    var taskResults = new Dictionary<int, int[][]>();
    var data = new List<string>[loops];
    for (int i = 0; i < loops; i++)
    {
        data[i] = new List<string>(FillData(partitionSize * numberTasks);
    }

    var barrier = new Barrier(numberTasks + 1);
    LogBarrierInformation("initial participants in barrier", barrier);
    for (int i = 0; i < numberTasks; i++)
    {
        barrier.AddParticipant();
        int jobNumber = i;
        taskResults.Add(i, new int[loops][]);
        for (int loop = 0; loop < loops; loop++)
        {
            taskResult[i, loop] = new int[26];
        }
        Console.WriteLine("Main - starting task job {jobNumber}");
        Task.Run(() => CalculationInTask(jobNumber, partitionSize,
            barrier, data, loops, taskResults[jobNumber]));
    }

    for (int loop = 0; loop < 5; loop++)
    {
        LogBarrierInformation("main task, start signaling and wait", barrier);
        barrier.SignalAndWait();
        LogBarrierInformation("main task waiting completed", barrier);
        int[][] resultCollection1 = taskResults[0];
        int[][] resultCollection2 = taskResults[1];
        var resultCollection = resultCollection1[loop].Zip(
            resultCollection2[loop], (c1, c2) => c1 + c2);
        char ch = 'a';
        int sum = 0;
        foreach (var x in resultCollection)
        {
            Console.WriteLine($"{ch++}, count: {x}");
```

```
        sum += x;
    }
    LogBarrierInformation($"main task finished loop {loop}, sum: {sum}",
      barrier);
}

Console.WriteLine("finished all iterations");
Console.ReadLine();
}
```

> **NOTE** *Jagged arrays are explained in Chapter 7, "Arrays." The* Zip *extension method is explained in Chapter 12, "Language Integrated Query."*

When you run the application, you can see output like the following. In the output you can see that every call to AddParticipant increases the participant count as well as the remaining participant count. As soon as one participant invokes SignalAndWait, the remaining participant count is decremented. When the remaining participant count reaches 0, the wait of all participants ends, and the next phase begins:

```
Task : initial participants in barrier. 1 current and 1 remaining participants,
phase 0.
Main - starting task job 0
Main - starting task job 1
Task : main task, starting signaling and wait. 3 current and
3 remaining participants, phase 0.
Task 4: CalculationInTask started. 3 current and 2 remaining participants, phase 0.
Task 5: CalculationInTask started. 3 current and 2 remaining participants, phase 0.
Task 4 in loop 0: partition from 0 to 1000000
Task 5 in loop 0: partition from 1000000 to 2000000
Calculation completed from task 4 in loop 0. 38272 times a, 38637 times z
Task 4: sending signal and wait for all. 3 current and
2 remaining participants, phase 0.
Calculation completed from task 5 in loop 0. 38486 times a, 38781 times z
Task 5: sending signal and wait for all. 3 current and
1 remaining participants, phase 0.
Task 5: waiting completed. 3 current and 3 remaining participants, phase 1
Task 4: waiting completed. 3 current and 3 remaining participants, phase 1
Task : main waiting completed. 3 current and 3 remaining participants, phase 1
```

READERWRITERLOCKSLIM

For a locking mechanism to allow multiple readers but only one writer for a resource, you can use the class ReaderWriterLockSlim. This class offers a locking functionality in which multiple readers can access the resource if no writer locked it, and only a single writer can lock the resource.

The ReaderWriterLockSlim class has blocking and nonblocking methods to acquire a read lock, such as EnterReadLock (blocking) and TryEnterReadLock (nonblocking), and to acquire a write lock with EnterWriteLock (blocking) and TryEnterWriteLock (nonblocking). If a task reads first and writes afterward, it can acquire an upgradable read lock with EnterUpgradableReadLock or TryEnterUpgradableReadLock. With this lock, the write lock can be acquired without releasing the read lock.

Several properties of this class offer information about the held locks, such as CurrentReadCount, WaitingReadCount, WaitingUpgradableReadCount, and WaitingWriteCount.

The following example creates a collection containing six items and a ReaderWriterLockSlim object. The method ReaderMethod acquires a read lock to read all items of the list and write them to the console.

The method `WriterMethod` tries to acquire a write lock to change all values of the collection. In the `Main` method, six tasks are started that invoke either the method `ReaderMethod` or the method `WriterMethod` (code file ReaderWriterLockSample/Program.cs):

```csharp
class Program
{
  private static List<int> _items = new List<int>() { 0, 1, 2, 3, 4, 5};
  private static ReaderWriterLockSlim _rwl =
    new ReaderWriterLockSlim(LockRecursionPolicy.SupportsRecursion);

  public static void ReaderMethod(object reader)
  {
    try
    {
      _rwl.EnterReadLock();
      for (int i = 0; i < _items.Count; i++)
      {
        Console.WriteLine($"reader {reader}, loop: {i}, item: {_items[i]}");
        Task.Delay(40).Wait();
      }
    }
    finally
    {
      _rwl.ExitReadLock();
    }
  }

  public static void WriterMethod(object writer)
  {
    try
    {
      while (!_rwl.TryEnterWriteLock(50))
      {
        Console.WriteLine($"Writer {writer} waiting for the write lock");
        Console.WriteLine($"current reader count: {_rwl.CurrentReadCount}");
      }
      Console.WriteLine($"Writer {writer} acquired the lock");
      for (int i = 0; i < _items.Count; i++)
      {
        _items[i]++;
        Task.Delay(50).Wait();
      }
      Console.WriteLine($"Writer {writer} finished");
    }
    finally
    {
      _rwl.ExitWriteLock();
    }
  }

  static void Main()
  {
    var taskFactory = new TaskFactory(TaskCreationOptions.LongRunning,
      TaskContinuationOptions.None);
    var tasks = new Task[6];
    tasks[0] = taskFactory.StartNew(WriterMethod, 1);
    tasks[1] = taskFactory.StartNew(ReaderMethod, 1);
    tasks[2] = taskFactory.StartNew(ReaderMethod, 2);
    tasks[3] = taskFactory.StartNew(WriterMethod, 2);
    tasks[4] = taskFactory.StartNew(ReaderMethod, 3);
    tasks[5] = taskFactory.StartNew(ReaderMethod, 4);
    Task.WaitAll(tasks);
  }
}
```

When you run the application, the following shows that the first writer gets the lock first. The second writer and all readers need to wait. Next, the readers can work concurrently, while the second writer still waits for the resource:

```
Writer 1 acquired the lock
Writer 2 waiting for the write lock
current reader count: 0
Writer 2 waiting for the write lock
current reader count: 0
Writer 2 waiting for the write lock
current reader count: 0
Writer 2 waiting for the write lock
current reader count: 0
Writer 1 finished
reader 4, loop: 0, item: 1
reader 1, loop: 0, item: 1
Writer 2 waiting for the write lock
current reader count: 4
reader 2, loop: 0, item: 1
reader 3, loop: 0, item: 1
reader 4, loop: 1, item: 2
reader 1, loop: 1, item: 2
reader 3, loop: 1, item: 2
reader 2, loop: 1, item: 2
Writer 2 waiting for the write lock
current reader count: 4
reader 4, loop: 2, item: 3
reader 1, loop: 2, item: 3
reader 2, loop: 2, item: 3
reader 3, loop: 2, item: 3
Writer 2 waiting for the write lock
current reader count: 4
reader 4, loop: 3, item: 4
reader 1, loop: 3, item: 4
reader 2, loop: 3, item: 4
reader 3, loop: 3, item: 4
reader 4, loop: 4, item: 5
reader 1, loop: 4, item: 5
Writer 2 waiting for the write lock
current reader count: 4
reader 2, loop: 4, item: 5
reader 3, loop: 4, item: 5
reader 4, loop: 5, item: 6
reader 1, loop: 5, item: 6
reader 2, loop: 5, item: 6
reader 3, loop: 5, item: 6
Writer 2 waiting for the write lock
current reader count: 4
Writer 2 acquired the lock
Writer 2 finished
```

LOCKS WITH AWAIT

In case you try to use the lock keyword while having the async keyword in the lock block, you get this compilation error: cannot await in the body of a lock statement. The reason is that after the async completes, the method might run in a different thread than before the async keyword. The lock keyword needs to release the lock in the same thread as the lock is acquired.

Such a code block results in compilation errors:

```
static async Task IncorrectLockAsync()
{
    lock (s_syncLock)
```

```
  {
    Console.WriteLine($"{nameof(IncorrectLockAsync)} started");
    await Task.Delay(500);  // compiler error: cannot await in the body
      // of a lock statement
    Console.WriteLine($"{nameof(IncorrectLockAsync)} ending");
  }
}
```

How can this be solved? You cannot use a Monitor for this, as the Monitor needs to release the lock from the same thread where it entered the lock. The lock keyword is based on Monitor.

While the Mutex object can be used for synchronization across different processes, it has the same issues: it grants a lock for a thread. Releasing the lock from a different thread is not possible. Instead, you can use the Semaphore—or the SemaphoreSlim class. Semaphores can release the semaphore from a different thread.

The following code snippet waits to acquire a semaphore using WaitAsync on a SemaphoreSlim object. The SemaphoreSlim object is initialized with a count of 1, thus the wait on the semaphore is only granted once. In the finally code block, the semaphore is released by invoking the Release method (code file LockAcrossAwait/Program.cs):

```
private static SemaphoreSlim s_asyncLock = new SemaphoreSlim(1);
static async Task LockWithSemaphore(string title)
{
  Console.WriteLine($"{title} waiting for lock");
  await s_asyncLock.WaitAsync();
  try
  {
    Console.WriteLine($"{title} {nameof(LockWithSemaphore)} started");
    await Task.Delay(500);
    Console.WriteLine($"{title} {nameof(LockWithSemaphore)} ending");
  }
  finally
  {
    s_asyncLock.Release();
  }
}
```

Let's try to invoke this method from multiple tasks concurrently. The method RunUseSemaphoreAsync starts six tasks to invoke the LockWithSemaphore method concurrently:

```
static async Task RunUseSemaphoreAsync()
{
  Console.WriteLine(nameof(RunUseSemaphoreAsync));
  string[] messages = { "one", "two", "three", "four", "five", "six" };
  Task[] tasks = new Task[messages.Length];

  for (int i = 0; i < messages.Length; i++)
  {
    string message = messages[i];

    tasks[i] = Task.Run(async () =>
    {
      await LockWithSemaphore(message);
    });
  }

  await Task.WhenAll(tasks);
  Console.WriteLine();
}
```

Running the program, you can see that multiple tasks are started concurrently, but after the semaphore is locked, all other tasks need to wait until the semaphore is released again:

```
RunLockWithAwaitAsync
two waiting for lock
two LockWithSemaphore started
three waiting for lock
five waiting for lock
four waiting for lock
six waiting for lock
one waiting for lock
two LockWithSemaphore ending
three LockWithSemaphore started
three LockWithSemaphore ending
five LockWithSemaphore started
five LockWithSemaphore ending
four LockWithSemaphore started
four LockWithSemaphore ending
six LockWithSemaphore started
six LockWithSemaphore ending
one LockWithSemaphore started
one LockWithSemaphore ending
```

To make the use of the lock easier, you can create a class that implements the IDisposable interface to manage the resource. With this class, you can use the using statement in the same way as the lock statement is used to lock and release the semaphore.

The following code snippet implements the AsyncSemaphore class that allocates a SemaphoreSlim in the constructor, and on invoking the WaitAsync method on the AsyncSemaphore, the inner class SemaphoreReleaser is returned that implements the interface IDisposable. On calling the Dispose method, the semaphore is released (code file LockAcrossAwait/AsyncSemaphore.cs):

```csharp
public sealed class AsyncSemaphore
{
  private class SemaphoreReleaser : IDisposable
  {
    private SemaphoreSlim _semaphore;

    public SemaphoreReleaser(SemaphoreSlim semaphore) =>
      _semaphore = semaphore;

    public void Dispose() => _semaphore.Release();
  }

  private SemaphoreSlim _semaphore;
  public AsyncSemaphore() =>
    _semaphore = new SemaphoreSlim(1);

  public async Task<IDisposable> WaitAsync()
  {
    await _semaphore.WaitAsync();
    return new SemaphoreReleaser(_semaphore) as IDisposable;
  }
}
```

Changing the implementation from the LockWithSemaphore method shown previously, now a using statement can be used where the semaphore is locked. Remember, the using statement creates a catch/finally block, and in the finally block the Dispose method gets invoked (code file LockAcrossAwait/Program.cs):

```csharp
private static AsyncSemaphore s_asyncSemaphore = new AsyncSemaphore();
static async Task UseAsyncSemaphore(string title)
{
  using (await s_asyncSemaphore.WaitAsync())
```

```
    {
      Console.WriteLine($"{title} {nameof(LockWithSemaphore)} started");
      await Task.Delay(500);
      Console.WriteLine($"{title} {nameof(LockWithSemaphore)} ending");
    }
  }
```

Using the `UseAsyncSemaphore` method similar to the `LockWithSemaphore` method results in the same behavior. However, with a class written once, locking across await becomes simpler.

SUMMARY

This chapter explored how to code applications that use multiple tasks by using the `System.Threading .Tasks` namespace. Using multithreading in your applications takes careful planning. Too many threads can cause resource issues, and not enough threads can cause your application to be sluggish and perform poorly. With tasks, you get an abstraction to threads. This abstraction helps you avoid creating too many threads because threads are reused from a pool.

You've seen various ways to create multiple tasks, such as the `Parallel` class, which offers both task and data parallelism with `Parallel.Invoke`, `Parallel.ForEach`, and `Parallel.For`. With the `Task` class, you've seen how to gain more control over parallel programming. Tasks can run synchronously in the calling thread, using a thread from a thread pool, and a separate new thread can be created. Tasks also offer a hierarchical model that enables the creation of child tasks, also providing a way to cancel a complete hierarchy.

The cancellation framework offers a standard mechanism that can be used in the same manner with different classes to cancel a task early.

You've seen several synchronization objects that are available with .NET, and with which scenario what synchronization object has its advantage. An easy synchronization can be done using the `lock` keyword. Behind the scenes, it's the `Monitor` type that allows setting timeouts, which is not possible with the `lock` keyword. For synchronization between processes, the `Mutex` object offers similar functionality. With the `Semaphore` object you've seen a synchronization object with a count—some tasks are allowed to run concurrently. To inform others of information that is ready, various kinds of event objects have been discussed, such as the `AutoResetEvent`, `ManualResetEvent`, and `CountdownEvent`. A straightforward way to have multiple readers and one writer is offered by the `ReaderWriterLock`. The `Barrier` type allows for more complex scenarios where multiple tasks can run concurrently until a synchronization point is reached. As soon as all tasks reach this point, all can continue concurrently to meet at the next synchronization point.

Here are some final guidelines regarding threading:

➤ Try to keep synchronization requirements to a minimum. Synchronization is complex and blocks threads. You can avoid it if you try to avoid sharing state. Of course, this is not always possible.

➤ Static members of a class should be thread-safe. Usually, this is the case with classes in the .NET Framework.

➤ Instance state does not need to be thread-safe. For best performance, synchronization is best used outside the class where it is needed, and not with every member of the class. Instance members of .NET Framework classes usually are not thread-safe. In the Microsoft API documentation, you can find this information documented for every class of the .NET Framework in the "Thread Safety" section.

The next chapter gives information on another core .NET topic: files and streams.

22

Files and Streams

WHAT'S IN THIS CHAPTER?

➤ Exploring the directory structure

➤ Moving, copying, and deleting files and folders

➤ Reading and writing text in files

➤ Using streams to read and write files

➤ Using readers and writers to read and write files

➤ Compressing files

➤ Monitoring file changes

➤ Communicating using pipes

➤ Using Windows Runtime streams

WROX.COM CODE DOWNLOADS FOR THIS CHAPTER

The Wrox.com code downloads for this chapter are found at www.wrox.com on the Download Code tab. The source code is also available at https://github.com/ProfessionalCSharp/ProfessionalCSharp7 in the directory FilesAndStreams.

The code for this chapter is divided into the following major examples:

➤ DriveInformation

➤ WorkingWithFilesAndFolders

➤ StreamSamples

➤ ReaderWriterSamples

➤ CompressFileSample

➤ FileMonitor

➤ MemoryMappedFiles

➤ NamedPipes

➤ AnonymousPipes

➤ WindowsAppEditor

INTRODUCTION

When you're reading and writing to files and directories you can use simple APIs, or you can use advanced ones that offer more features. You also have to differentiate between .NET classes and functionality offered from the Windows Runtime. From Universal Windows Platform (UWP) Windows apps, you don't have access to the file system in any directory; you have access only to specific directories. Alternatively, you can let the user pick files. This chapter covers all these options. You'll read and write files by using a simple API and get into more features by using streams. You'll use both .NET types and types from the Windows Runtime, and you'll mix both of these technologies to take advantage of .NET features with the Windows Runtime.

As you use streams, you also learn about compressing data and sharing data between different tasks using memory mapped files and pipes.

MANAGING THE FILE SYSTEM

The classes used to browse around the file system and perform operations such as moving, copying, and deleting files are shown in Figure 22-1.

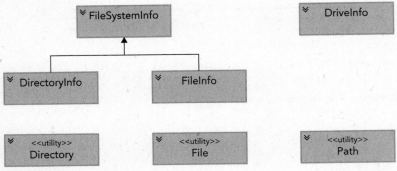

FIGURE 22-1

The following list explains the function of these classes:

➤ `FileSystemInfo`—The base class represents any file system object.

➤ `FileInfo` and `File`—These classes represent a file on the file system.

➤ `DirectoryInfo` and `Directory`—These classes represent a folder on the file system.

➤ `Path`—This class contains static members that you can use to manipulate pathnames.

➤ `DriveInfo`—This class provides properties and methods that provide information about a selected drive.

> **NOTE** *Directories or folders? These terms are often used interchangeably. Directory is a classical term for a file system object. A directory contains files and other directories. A folder has its origin with Apple's Lisa and is a GUI object. Often it is associated with an icon to map to a directory.*

Notice in the previous list that two classes are used to work with folders and two classes are for working with files. Which one of these classes you use depends largely on how many operations you need to access that folder or file:

➤ `Directory` and `File` contain only static methods and are never instantiated. You use these classes by supplying the path to the appropriate file system object whenever you call a member method. If you want to do only one operation on a folder or file, using these classes is more efficient because it saves the overhead of creating a .NET object.

➤ `DirectoryInfo` and `FileInfo` implement roughly the same public methods as `Directory` and `File`, as well as some public properties and constructors, but they are stateful and the members of these classes are not static. You need to instantiate these classes before each instance is associated with a particular folder or file. This means that these classes are more efficient if you are performing multiple operations using the same object. That's because they read in the authentication and other information for the appropriate file system object on construction, and then they do not need to read that information again, no matter how many methods and so on you call against each object (class instance). In comparison, the corresponding stateless classes need to check the details of the file or folder again with every method you call.

Checking Drive Information

Before working with files and folders, let's check the drives of the system. You use the `DriveInfo` class, which can perform a scan of a system to provide a list of available drives and then dig in deeper to provide a large amount of detail about any of the drives.

To demonstrate using the `DriveInfo` class, the following example creates a simple Console application that lists information of all the available drives on a computer.

The sample code for `DriveInformation` makes use of the following namespaces:

```
System

System.IO
```

The following code snippet invokes the static method `DriveInfo.GetDrives`. This method returns an array of `DriveInfo` objects. With this array, every drive that is ready is accessed to write information about the drive name, type, and format, and it also shows size information (code file `DriveInformation/Program.cs`):

```
DriveInfo[] drives = DriveInfo.GetDrives();
foreach (DriveInfo drive in drives)
{
  if (drive.IsReady)
  {
    Console.WriteLine($"Drive name: {drive.Name}");
    Console.WriteLine($"Format: {drive.DriveFormat}");
    Console.WriteLine($"Type: {drive.DriveType}");
    Console.WriteLine($"Root directory: {drive.RootDirectory}");
    Console.WriteLine($"Volume label: {drive.VolumeLabel}");
    Console.WriteLine($"Free space: {drive.TotalFreeSpace}");
    Console.WriteLine($"Available space: {drive.AvailableFreeSpace}");
    Console.WriteLine($"Total size: {drive.TotalSize}");
    Console.WriteLine();
  }
}
```

When I run this program on my Windows system, which doesn't have a DVD drive but has a solid-state disk (SSD) and a memory card, I see this information:

```
Drive name: C:\
Format: NTFS
Type: Fixed
Root directory: C:\
Volume label: Windows
Free space: 289063882752
Available space: 289063882752
Total size: 509571969024

Drive name: D:\
Format: exFAT
Type: Removable
Root directory: D:\
Volume label:
Free space: 196831477760
Available space: 196831477760
Total size: 196832395264
```

On my Mac, drive letters are not available, but you can also see Ram and Network types as they are accessible using File APIs on Unix-based systems:

```
Drive name: /
Format: hfs
Type: Fixed
Root directory: /
Volume label: /
Free space: 170332930048
Available space: 170070786048
Total size: 249769230336

Drive name: /dev
Format: devs
Type: Ram
Root directory: /dev
Volume label: /dev
Free space: 0
Available space: 0
Total size: 184832

Drive name: /net
Format: autofs
Type: Network
Root directory: /net
Volume label: /net
Free space: 0
Available space: 0
Total size: 0
```

Working with the Path Class

For accessing files and directories, the names of the files and directories need to be defined—including parent folders. When you combine multiple folders and files using string concatenation operators, you can easily miss a separator character or use one too many characters. The `Path` class can help with this because this class adds missing separator characters, and it also deals with different platform requirements on Windows- and Unix-based systems.

The `Path` class exposes some static methods that make operations on pathnames easier. For example, suppose that you want to display the full pathname for a file, `ReadMe.txt`, in the folder `D:\Projects`. You could find the path to the file using the following code:

```
Console.WriteLine(Path.Combine(@"D:\Projects", "ReadMe.txt"));
```

`Path.Combine` is the method of this class that you are likely to use most often, but `Path` also implements other methods that supply information about the path or the required format for it.

With the public fields `VolumeSeparatorChar`, `DirectorySeparatorChar`, `AltDirectorySeparatorChar`, and `PathSeparator` you can get the platform-specific character that is used to separate drives, folders, and files, and the separator of multiple paths. With Windows, these characters are `:`, `\`, `/`, and `;`.

The `Path` class also helps with accessing the user-specific temp folder (`GetTempPath`) and creating temporary (`GetTempFileName`) and random filenames (`GetRandomFileName`). Pay attention that the method `GetTempFileName` includes the folder, whereas `GetRandomFileName` just returns the filename without any folder.

The sample code for `WorkingWithFilesAndDirectories` makes use of the following namespaces:

```
System

System.Collections.Generic

System.IO
```

This sample application offers several command line arguments to start the different functionality of the program. Just start the program without command lines or check the source code to see all the different options.

The `Environment` class defines a list of special folders. The following code snippet returns the documents folder by passing the enumeration value `SpecialFolder.MyDocuments` to the `GetFolderPath` method (code file `WorkingWithFilesAndDirectories/Program.cs`):

```
private static string GetDocumentsFolder() =>
    Environment.GetFolderPath(Environment.SpecialFolder.MyDocuments);
```

`Environment.SpecialFolder` is a huge enumeration that gives values for music, pictures, program files, app data, and many other folders.

Creating Files and Folders

Now let's get into using the `File`, `FileInfo`, `Directory`, and `DirectoryInfo` classes. First, the method `CreateAFile` creates the file `Sample1.txt` and adds the string `Hello, World!` to the file. An easy way to create a text file is to invoke the method `WriteAllText` of the `File` class. This method takes a filename and the string that should be written to the file. Everything is done with a single call (code file `WorkingWithFilesAndDirectories/Program.cs`):

```
const string Sample1FileName = "Sample1.md";
// ...

public static void CreateAFile()
{
  string fileName = Path.Combine(GetDocumentsFolder(), Sample1FileName);
  File.WriteAllText(fileName, "Hello, World!");
}
```

To copy a file, you can use either the `Copy` method of the `File` class or the `CopyTo` method of the `FileInfo` class:

```
var file = new FileInfo(fileName1);
file.CopyTo(fileName2);
File.Copy(fileName1", fileName2);
```

The first code snippet using `FileInfo` takes slightly longer to execute because of the need to instantiate an object named file, but it leaves file ready for you to perform further actions on the same file. When you use the second example, there is no need to instantiate an object to copy the file.

You can instantiate a `FileInfo` or `DirectoryInfo` class by passing to the constructor a string containing the path to the corresponding file system object. You have just seen the process for a file. For a folder, the code looks similar:

```
var myFolder = new DirectoryInfo(directory1);
```

If the path represents an object that does not exist, an exception is not thrown at construction; instead it's thrown the first time you call a method that actually requires the corresponding file system object to be there. You can find out whether the object exists and is of the appropriate type by checking the `Exists` property, which is implemented by both of these classes:

```
var test = new FileInfo(@"C:\Windows");
Console.WriteLine(test.Exists);
```

Note that for this property to return true, the corresponding file system object must be of the appropriate type. In other words, if you instantiate a `FileInfo` object by supplying the path of a folder, or you instantiate a `DirectoryInfo` object by giving it the path of a file, `Exists` has the value `false`. Most of the properties and methods of these objects return a value if possible—they won't necessarily throw an exception just because the wrong type of object has been called, unless they are asked to do something that is impossible. For example, the preceding code snippet might first display `false` (because `C:\Windows` is a directory), but it still displays the time the folder was created because a directory has that information. However, if you tried to open the directory as if it were a file, using the `FileInfo.Open` method, you'd get an exception.

You move and delete files or directories using the `MoveTo` and `Delete` methods of the `FileInfo` and `DirectoryInfo` classes. The equivalent methods on the `File` and `Directory` classes are `Move` and `Delete`. The `FileInfo` and `File` classes also implement the methods `CopyTo` and `Copy`, respectively. However, no methods exist to copy complete folders—you need to do that by copying each file in the folder.

Using all of these methods is quite intuitive. You can find detailed descriptions in the Microsoft documentation.

Accessing and Modifying File Properties

Let's get some information about files. You can use both the `File` and `FileInfo` classes to access file information. The `File` class defines static method, whereas the `FileInfo` class offers instance methods. The following code snippet shows how to use `FileInfo` to retrieve multiple information. If you instead used the `File` class, the access would be slower because every access would mean a check to determine whether the user is allowed to get this information. With the `FileInfo` class, the check happens only when calling the constructor.

The sample code creates a new `FileInfo` object and writes the result of the properties `Name`, `DirectoryName`, `IsReadOnly`, `Extension`, `Length`, `CreationTime`, `LastAccessTime`, and `Attributes` to the console (code file `WorkingWithFilesAndDirectories/Program.cs`):

```
private static void FileInformation(string fileName)
{
    var file = new FileInfo(fileName);
    Console.WriteLine($"Name: {file.Name}");
```

```
Console.WriteLine($"Directory: {file.DirectoryName}");
Console.WriteLine($"Read only: {file.IsReadOnly}");
Console.WriteLine($"Extension: {file.Extension}");
Console.WriteLine($"Length: {file.Length}");
Console.WriteLine($"Creation time: {file.CreationTime:F}");
Console.WriteLine($"Access time: {file.LastAccessTime:F}");
Console.WriteLine($"File attributes: {file.Attributes}");
}
```

Passing the `Program.cs` filename of the current directory to this method,

```
FileInformation("./Program.cs");
```

results in this output (on my machine):

```
Name: Program.cs
Directory: C:\ProCSharpSources\files\ProfessionalCSharp7\FilesAndStreams\F
ilesAndStreamsSamples\WorkingWithFilesAndDirectories
Read only: False
Extension: .cs
Length: 7637
Creation time: Friday, September 1, 2017 12:48:51 PM
Access time: Friday, September 1, 2017 4:07:12 PM
File attributes: Archive
```

A few of the properties of the `FileInfo` class cannot be set; they only define get accessors. It's not possible to retrieve the filename, the file extension, and the length of the file. The creation time and last access time can be set. The method `ChangeFileProperties` writes the creation time of a file to the console and later changes the creation time to a date in the year 2025.

```
private static void ChangeFileProperties()
{
  string fileName = Path.Combine(GetDocumentsFolder(), Sample1FileName);
  var file = new FileInfo(fileName);
  if (!file.Exists)
  {
    Console.WriteLine($"Create the file {Sample1FileName} before calling this method");
    Console.WriteLine("You can do this by invoking this program with the -c argument");
    return;
  }
  Console.WriteLine($"creation time: {file.CreationTime:F}");
  file.CreationTime = new DateTime(2025, 12, 24, 15, 0, 0);
  Console.WriteLine($"creation time: {file.CreationTime:F}");
}
```

Running the program shows the initial creation time of the file as well as the creation time after it has been changed. Creating files in the future (at least specifying the creation time) is possible with this technique.

```
creation time: Sunday, December 20, 2015 9:41:49 AM
creation time: Wednesday, December 24, 2025 3:00:00 PM
```

> **NOTE** *Being able to manually modify these properties might seem strange at first, but it can be quite useful. For example, if you have a program that effectively modifies a file by simply reading it in, deleting it, and creating a new file with the new contents, you would probably want to modify the creation date to match the original creation date of the old file.*

Using File to Read and Write

With `File.ReadAllText` and `File.WriteAllText` you can read and write a file using a single string. Instead of using one string, you can also use file operations that use a string for every line in a file as shown here.

Instead of reading all lines to a single string, a string array is returned from the method `File` `.ReadAllLines`. With this method you can do a different handling based on every line, but still the complete file needs to be read into memory (code file `WorkingWithFilesAndFolders/Program.cs`):

```
public static void ReadingAFileLineByLine(string fileName)
{
  string[] lines = File.ReadAllLines(fileName);
  int i = 1;
  foreach (var line in lines)
  {
    Console.WriteLine($"{i++}. {line}");
  }
  //...
}
```

To read line by line without needing to wait until all lines have been read, you can use the method `File` `.ReadLines`. This method returns `IEnumerable<string>`, where you can already start looping through the file before the complete file has been read:

```
public static void ReadingAFileLineByLine(string fileName)
{
  //...
  IEnumerable<string> lines = File.ReadLines(fileName);
  i = 1;
  foreach (var line in lines)
  {
    Console.WriteLine($"{i++}. {line}");
  }
}
```

For writing a string collection, you can use the method `File.WriteAllLines`. This method accepts a filename and an `IEnumerable<string>` type as parameter:

```
public static void WriteAFile()
{
  string fileName = Path.Combine(GetDocumentsFolder(), "movies.txt");
  string[] movies =
  {
    "Snow White And The Seven Dwarfs",
    "Gone With The Wind",
    "Casablanca",
    "The Bridge On The River Kwai",
    "Some Like It Hot"
  };
  File.WriteAllLines(fileName, movies);
}
```

To append strings to an existing file, you use `File.AppendAllLines`:

```
string[] moreMovies =
{
  "Psycho",
  "Easy Rider",
  "Star Wars",
  "The Matrix"
};
File.AppendAllLines(fileName, moreMovies);
```

ENUMERATING FILES

For working with multiple files, you can use the `Directory` class. `Directory` defines the method `GetFiles` that returns a string array of all files in the directory. The method `GetDirectories` returns a string array of all directories.

All of these methods define overloads that allow passing a search pattern and a value of the SearchOption enumeration. SearchOption enables you to walk through all subdirectories or to stay in the top-level directory by using the value `AllDirectories` or `TopDirectoriesOnly`. The search pattern doesn't allow passing regular expressions as are discussed in Chapter 9, "Strings and Regular Expressions"; it passes only simple expressions using * for any characters and ? for single characters.

When you walk through a huge directory (or subdirectories), the methods `GetFiles` and `GetDirectories` need to have the complete result before the result is returned. An alternative is to use the methods `EnumerateDirectories` and `EnumerateFiles`. These methods offer the same parameters for the search pattern and options, but they immediately start returning a result with `IEnumerable<string>`.

Let's get into an example: Within a directory and all its subdirectories, all files that end with Copy are deleted in case another file exists with the same name and size. You can simulate this easily by selecting all files in a folder by pressing Ctrl+A on the keyboard, entering Ctrl+C on the keyboard for copy, and entering Ctrl+V on the keyboard while the mouse is still in the same folder to paste. The new files have the Copy postfix applied.

The method `DeleteDuplicateFiles` iterates all files in the directory that is passed with the first argument, walking through all subdirectories using the option `SearchOption.AllDirectories`. Within the foreach statement, the current file in the iteration is compared to the file in the previous iteration. In cases where the filename is the same and only the `Copy` postfix is different, and if the size of the files is the same as well, the copied file is deleted by invoking `FileInfo.Delete` (code file `WorkingWithFilesAndFolders/Program.cs`):

```csharp
private void DeleteDuplicateFiles(string directory, bool checkOnly)
{
  IEnumerable<string> fileNames = Directory.EnumerateFiles(directory,
    "*", SearchOption.AllDirectories);
  string previousFileName = string.Empty;
  foreach (string fileName in fileNames)
  {
    string previousName = Path.GetFileNameWithoutExtension(previousFileName);
    if (!string.IsNullOrEmpty(previousFileName) &&
      previousName.EndsWith("Copy") &&
      fileName.StartsWith(previousFileName.Substring(
        0, previousFileName.LastIndexOf(" - Copy"))))
    {
      var copiedFile = new FileInfo(previousFileName);
      var originalFile = new FileInfo(fileName);
      if (copiedFile.Length == originalFile.Length)
      {
        Console.WriteLine($"delete {copiedFile.FullName}");
        if (!checkOnly)
        {
          copiedFile.Delete();
        }
      }
    }
    previousFileName = fileName;
  }
}
```

WORKING WITH STREAMS

Now let's get into more powerful options that are available when you work with files: streams. The idea of a stream has been around for a very long time. A stream is an object used to transfer data. The data can be transferred in one of two directions:

➤ If the data is being transferred from some outside source into your program, it is called reading from the stream.

➤ If the data is being transferred from your program to some outside source, it is called *writing* to the stream.

Very often, the outside source will be a file, but that is not always the case. Other possibilities include the following:

➤ Reading or writing data on the network using some network protocol, where the intention is for this data to be picked up by or sent from another computer

➤ Reading from or writing to a named pipe

➤ Reading from or writing to an area of memory

Some streams allow only writing, some streams allow only reading, and some streams allow random access. Random access enables you to position a cursor randomly within a stream—for example, to start reading from the start of the stream to later move to the end of the stream, and continue with a position in the middle of the stream.

Of these examples, Microsoft has supplied a .NET class for writing to or reading from memory: the System.IO.MemoryStream object. The System.Net.Sockets.NetworkStream object handles network data. The Stream class does not make any assumptions of the nature of the data source. It can be file streams, memory streams, network streams, or any data source you can think of.

Some streams can also be chained. For example, the DeflateStream can be used to compress data. This stream in turn can write to the FileStream, MemoryStream, or NetworkStream. The CryptoStream enables you to encrypt data. It's also possible to chain the DeflateStream to the CryptoStream to write in turn to the FileStream.

> **NOTE** *Chapter 24, "Security," explains how you can use the* CryptoStream.

Using streams, the outside source might even be a variable within your own code. This might sound paradoxical, but the technique of using streams to transmit data between variables can be a useful trick for converting data between data types. The C language used something similar—the sprintf function—to convert between integer data types and strings or to format strings.

The advantage of having a separate object for the transfer of data, rather than using the FileInfo or DirectoryInfo classes to do this, is that separating the concept of transferring data from the particular data source makes it easier to swap data sources. Stream objects themselves contain a lot of generic code that concerns the movement of data between outside sources and variables in your code. By keeping this code separate from any concept of a particular data source, you make it easier for this code to be reused in different circumstances.

Although it's not that easy to directly read and write to streams, you can use readers and writers. This is another separation of concerns. Readers and writers can read and write to streams. For example, the StringReader and StringWriter classes are part of the same inheritance tree as two classes that you use later to read and write text files. The classes will almost certainly share a substantial amount of code behind the scenes. Figure 22-2 illustrates the hierarchy of stream-related classes in the System.IO namespace.

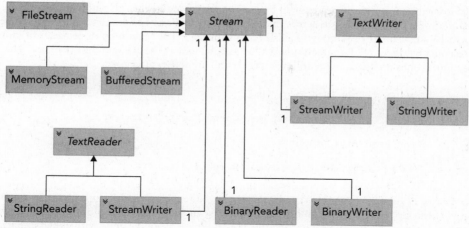

FIGURE 22-2

As far as reading and writing files goes, the classes that concern us most are the following:

➤ `FileStream`—This class is intended for reading and writing binary data in a file.

➤ `StreamReader` and `StreamWriter`—These classes are designed specifically for reading from and writing to streams offering APIs for text formats.

➤ `BinaryReader` and `BinaryWriter`—These classes are designed for reading and writing to streams offering APIs for binary data.

The difference between using these classes and directly using the underlying stream objects is that a basic stream works in bytes. For example, suppose that as part of the process of saving some document you want to write the contents of a variable of type `long` to a binary file. Each `long` occupies 8 bytes, and if you use an ordinary binary stream you would have to explicitly write each of those 8 bytes of memory.

In C# code, you would have to perform some bitwise operations to extract each of those 8 bytes from the `long` value. Using a `BinaryWriter` instance, you can encapsulate the entire operation in an overload of the `BinaryWriter.Write` method, which takes a `long` as a parameter, and which places those 8 bytes into the stream (and if the stream is directed to a file, into the file). A corresponding `BinaryReader.Read` method extracts 8 bytes from the stream and recovers the value of the `long`.

Working with File Streams

Let's get into programming streams reading and writing files. A `FileStream` instance is used to read or write data to or from a file. To construct a `FileStream`, you need four pieces of information:

➤ The *file* you want to access.

➤ The *mode*, which indicates how you want to open the file. For example, are you intending to create a new file or open an existing file? If you are opening an existing file, should any write operations be interpreted as overwriting the contents of the file or appending to the file?

➤ The *access*, which indicates how you want to access the file. For example, do you want to read from or write to the file or do both?

➤ The *share* access, which specifies whether you want exclusive access to the file. Alternatively, are you willing to have other streams access the file simultaneously? If so, should other streams have access to read the file, to write to it, or to do both?

The first piece of information is usually represented by a string that contains the full pathname of the file, and this chapter considers only those constructors that require a string here. Besides those, however, some additional constructors take a native Windows handle to a file instead. The remaining three pieces of information are represented by three .NET enumerations called `FileMode`, `FileAccess`, and `FileShare`. The values of these enumerations are listed in the following table and are self-explanatory:

ENUMERATION	VALUES	
`FileMode`	`Append`, `Create`, `CreateNew`, `Open`, `OpenOrCreate`, or `Truncate`	
`FileAccess`	`Read`, `ReadWrite`, or `Write`	
`FileShare`	`Delete`, `Inheritable`, `None`, `Read`, `ReadWrite`, or `Write`	

Note that in the case of `FileMode`, exceptions can be thrown if you request a mode that is inconsistent with the existing status of the file. `Append`, `Open`, and `Truncate` throw an exception if the file does not already exist, and `CreateNew` throws an exception if it does. `Create` and `OpenOrCreate` cope with either scenario, but `Create` deletes any existing file to replace it with a new, initially empty, one. The `FileAccess` and `FileShare` enumerations are bitwise flags, so values can be combined with the C# bitwise OR operator, |.

Creating a FileStream

The sample code for StreamSamples makes use of the following namespaces:

```
System

System.Collections.Generic

System.Globalization

System.IO

System.Linq

System.Text

System.Threading.Tasks
```

There are a large number of constructors for the `FileStream`. The following sample uses one with four parameters (code file `StreamSamples/Program.cs`):

➤ The filename

➤ The `FileMode` enumeration with the `Open` value to open an existing file

➤ The `FileAccess` enumeration with the `Read` value to read the file

➤ The `FileShare` enumeration with a `Read` value to allow other programs to read but not change the file at the same time

```
private void ReadFileUsingFileStream(string fileName)
{
  const int bufferSize = 4096;
  using (var stream = new FileStream(fileName, FileMode.Open,
    FileAccess.Read, FileShare.Read))
  {
    ShowStreamInformation(stream);
    Encoding encoding = GetEncoding(stream);
    //...
```

Instead of using the constructor of the `FileStream` class to create a `FileStream` object, you can create a `FileStream` directly using the `File` class with the `OpenRead` method. The `OpenRead` method opens a file (similar to `FileMode.Open`), returns a stream that can be read (`FileAccess.Read`), and also allows other processes read access (`FileShare.Read`):

```
using (FileStream stream = File.OpenRead(filename))
{
  //...
```

Getting Stream Information

The `Stream` class defines the properties `CanRead`, `CanWrite`, `CanSeek`, and `CanTimeout` that you can read to get information about what can be done with a stream. For reading and writing streams, the timeout values `ReadTimeout` and `WriteTimeout` specify timeouts in milliseconds. Setting these values can be important in networking scenarios to make sure the user does not have to wait too long when reading or writing the stream fails. The `Position` property returns the current position of the cursor in the stream. Every time some data is read from the stream, the position moves to the next byte that will be read. The sample code writes information about the stream to the console (code file `StreamSamples/Program.cs`):

```
private void ShowStreamInformation(Stream stream)
{
  Console.WriteLine($"stream can read: {stream.CanRead}, " +
    $"can write: {stream.CanWrite}, can seek: {stream.CanSeek}, " +
    $"can timeout: {stream.CanTimeout}");
  Console.WriteLine($"length: {stream.Length}, position: {stream.Position}");
  if (stream.CanTimeout)
  {
    Console.WriteLine($"read timeout: {stream.ReadTimeout} " +
      $"write timeout: {stream.WriteTimeout} ");
  }
}
```

When you run the program with the file stream that has been opened, you get the following output. The position is currently 0 as read has not yet happened:

```
stream can read: True, can write: False, can seek: True, can timeout: False
length: 1113, position: 0
```

Analyzing Text File Encodings

With text files, the next step is to read the first bytes of the stream—the preamble. The *preamble* gives information about how the file is encoded (the text format used). This is also known as *byte order mark* (BOM).

You can read a stream by using `ReadByte` that reads just a byte from the stream, or the `Read` method that fills a byte array. With the `GetEncoding` sample method, an array of 5 bytes is created, and the byte array is filled from the `Read` method. The second and third parameters specify the offset within the byte array and the count of the number of bytes that are available to fill. The `Read` method returns the number of bytes read; the stream might be smaller than the buffer. In case no more characters are available to read, the `Read` method returns 0.

The sample code analyzes the first characters of the stream to return the detected encoding and positions the stream after the encoding characters (code file `StreamSamples/Program.cs`):

```
private Encoding GetEncoding(Stream stream)
{
  if (!stream.CanSeek) throw new ArgumentException(
    "require a stream that can seek");

  Encoding encoding = Encoding.ASCII;
  byte[] bom = new byte[5];
  int nRead = stream.Read(bom, offset: 0, count: 5);
  if (bom[0] == 0xff && bom[1] == 0xfe && bom[2] == 0 && bom[3] == 0)
  {
```

```
            Console.WriteLine("UTF-32");
            stream.Seek(4, SeekOrigin.Begin);
            return Encoding.UTF32;
        }
        else if (bom[0] == 0xff && bom[1] == 0xfe)
        {
            Console.WriteLine("UTF-16, little endian");
            stream.Seek(2, SeekOrigin.Begin);
            return Encoding.Unicode;
        }
        else if (bom[0] == 0xfe && bom[1] == 0xff)
        {
            Console.WriteLine("UTF-16, big endian");
            stream.Seek(2, SeekOrigin.Begin);
            return Encoding.BigEndianUnicode;
        }
        else if (bom[0] == 0xef && bom[1] == 0xbb && bom[2] == 0xbf)
        {
            Console.WriteLine("UTF-8");
            stream.Seek(3, SeekOrigin.Begin);
            return Encoding.UTF8;
        }
        stream.Seek(0, SeekOrigin.Begin);
        return encoding;
    }
```

The start of a file can begin with the characters FF and FE. The order of these bytes gives information about how the document is stored. Two-byte Unicode can be stored in little or big endian. With FF followed by FE, it's little endian, and when FE is followed by FF, it's big endian. This endianness goes back to mainframes by IBM that used big endian for byte ordering, and PDP11 systems from Digital Equipment that used little endian. Communicating across the network with computers that have different endianness requires changing the order of bytes on one side. Nowadays, the Intel CPU architecture uses little endian, and the ARM architecture allows switching between little and big endian.

What's the other difference between these encodings? With ASCII, 7 bits are enough for every character. Originally based on the English alphabet, ASCII offers lowercase, uppercase, and control characters. Extended ASCII makes use of the 8th bit to allow switching to language-specific characters. Switching is not easy as it requires paying attention to the code map and also does not provide enough characters for some Asian languages. UTF-16 (Unicode Text Format) solves this by having 16 bits for every character. Because UTF-16 is still not enough for historical glyphs, UTF-32 uses 32 bits for every character. Although Windows NT 3.1 switched to UTF-16 for the default text encoding (from a Microsoft extension of ASCII before), nowadays the most-used text format is UTF-8. With the web, UTF-8 turned out to be the most-used text format since 2007 (this superseded ASCII, which had been the most common character encoding before). UTF-8 uses a variable length for character definitions. One character is defined by using between 1 and 6 bytes. UTF-8 is detected by this character sequence at the beginning of a file: 0xEF, 0xBB, 0xBF.

Reading Streams

After opening the file and creating the stream, the file is read using the Read method. This is repeated until the method returns 0. A string is created using the Encoder created from the GetEncoding method defined earlier. Do not forget to close the stream using the Dispose method. If possible, use the using statement—as is done with this code sample—to dispose the stream automatically (code file StreamSamples/Program.cs):

```
    public static void ReadFileUsingFileStream(string fileName)
    {
        const int BUFFERSIZE = 256;
        using (var stream = new FileStream(fileName, FileMode.Open,
```

```
                    FileAccess.Read, FileShare.Read))
                {
                    ShowStreamInformation(stream);
                    Encoding encoding = GetEncoding(stream);
                    byte[] buffer = new byte[bufferSize];
                    bool completed = false;
                    do
                    {
                        int nread = stream.Read(buffer, 0, BUFFERSIZE);
                        if (nread == 0) completed = true;
                        if (nread < BUFFERSIZE)
                        {
                            Array.Clear(buffer, nread, BUFFERSIZE - nread);
                        }
                        string s = encoding.GetString(buffer, 0, nread);
                        Console.WriteLine($"read {nread} bytes");
                        Console.WriteLine(s);
                    } while (!completed);
                }
            }
```

Writing Streams

How streams can be written is demonstrated by writing a simple string to a text file. To create a stream that can be written to, the `File.OpenWrite` method can be used. This time a temporary filename is created with the help of `Path.GetTempFileName`. The default file extension defined by the `GetTempFileName` is changed to txt with `Path.ChangeExtension` (code file StreamSamples/Program.cs):

```
public static void WriteTextFile()
{
    string tempTextFileName = Path.ChangeExtension(Path.GetTempFileName(),
        "txt");
    using (FileStream stream = File.OpenWrite(tempTextFileName))
    {
        //...
```

When you're writing a UTF-8 file, the preamble needs to be written to the file. This can be done by sending the 3 bytes of the UTF-8 preamble to the stream with the `WriteByte` method:

```
stream.WriteByte(0xef);
stream.WriteByte(0xbb);
stream.WriteByte(0xbf);
```

There's an alternative for doing this. You don't need to remember the bytes to specify the encoding. The Encoding class already has this information. The `GetPreamble` method returns a byte array with the preamble for the file. This byte array is written using the `Write` method of the `Stream` class:

```
byte[] preamble = Encoding.UTF8.GetPreamble();
stream.Write(preamble, 0, preamble.Length);
```

Now the content of the file can be written. As the `Write` method requires byte arrays to write, strings need to be converted. For converting a string to a byte array with UTF-8, `Encoding.UTF8.GetBytes` does the job before the byte array is written:

```
string hello = "Hello, World!";
byte[] buffer = Encoding.UTF8.GetBytes(hello);
stream.Write(buffer, 0, buffer.Length);
Console.WriteLine($"file {stream.Name} written");
```

You can open the temporary file using an editor such as Notepad, and it will use the correct encoding.

Copying Streams

Now let's combine reading and writing from streams by copying the file content. With the next code snippet, the readable stream is opened with `File.OpenRead`, and the writeable stream is opened with `File.OpenWrite`. A buffer is read using the `Stream.Read` method and written with `Stream.Write` (code file `StreamSamples/Program.cs`):

```
public static void CopyUsingStreams(string inputFile, string outputFile)
{
  const int BUFFERSIZE = 4096;
  using (var inputStream = File.OpenRead(inputFile))
  using (var outputStream = File.OpenWrite(outputFile))
  {
    byte[] buffer = new byte[BUFFERSIZE];
    bool completed = false;
    do
    {
      int nRead = inputStream.Read(buffer, 0, BUFFERSIZE);
      if (nRead == 0) completed = true;
      outputStream.Write(buffer, 0, nRead);
    } while (!completed);
  }
}
```

To copy a stream, it's not necessary to write the code to read and write a stream. Instead, you can use the `CopyTo` method of the `Stream` class, as shown here (code file `StreamSamples/Program.cs`):

```
public static void CopyUsingStreams2(string inputFile, string outputFile)
{
  using (var inputStream = File.OpenRead(inputFile))
  using (var outputStream = File.OpenWrite(outputFile))
  {
    inputStream.CopyTo(outputStream);
  }
}
```

Using Random Access to Streams

Random access to streams provides an advantage in that—even with large files—you can access a specific position within the file in a fast way.

To see random access in action, the following code snippet creates a large file. This code snippet creates the file `sampledata.data` with records that are all the same length and contain a number, a text, and a random date. The number of records that is passed to the method is created with the help of the `Enumerable.Range` method. The `Select` method creates an anonymous type that contains `Number`, `Text`, and `Date` properties. Out of these records, a string with # pre- and postfix is created, with a fixed length for every value and a ; separator between each value. The `WriteAsync` method writes the record to the stream (code file `StreamSamples/Program.cs`):

```
const string SampleFilePath = "./samplefile.data";
public static async Task CreateSampleFile(int nRecords)
{
  FileStream stream = File.Create(SampleFilePath);
  using (var writer = new StreamWriter(stream))
  {
    var r = new Random();
    var records = Enumerable.Range(0, nRecords).Select(x => new
    {
      Number = x,
```

```
    Text = $"Sample text {r.Next(200)}",
    Date = new DateTime(Math.Abs((long)((r.NextDouble() * 2 - 1) *
      DateTime.MaxValue.Ticks)))
  });

  foreach (var rec in records)
  {
    string date = rec.Date.ToString("d", CultureInfo.InvariantCulture);
    string s =
      $"#{rec.Number,8};{rec.Text,-20};{date}#{Environment.NewLine}";
    await writer.WriteAsync(s);
  }
  }
}
```

> **NOTE** *Chapter 17, "Managed and Unmanaged Memory," explains that every object implementing* `IDisposable` *should be disposed. In the previous code snippet, it looks like* `FileStream` *is not disposed. However, that's not the case. The* `StreamWriter` *takes control over the used resource and disposes the stream when the* `StreamWriter` *is disposed. To keep the stream opened for a longer period than the* `StreamWriter`, *you can configure this with the constructor of the* `StreamWriter`. *In that case, you need to dispose the stream explicitly.*

Now let's position a cursor randomly within the stream to read different records. The user is asked to enter a record number that should be accessed. The byte in the stream that should be accessed is based on the record number and the record size. The Seek method of the Stream class now enables you to position the cursor within the stream. The second argument specifies whether the position is based on the beginning of the stream, the end of the stream, or the current position (code file StreamSamples/Program.cs):

```
public static void RandomAccessSample()
{
  try
  {
    using (FileStream stream = File.OpenRead(SampleFilePath))
    {
      byte[] buffer = new byte[RECORDSIZE];
      do
      {
        try
        {
          Console.Write("record number (or 'bye' to end): ");
          string line = Console.ReadLine();
          if (line.ToUpper().CompareTo("BYE") == 0) break;
          if (int.TryParse(line, out int record))
          {
            stream.Seek((record - 1) * RECORDSIZE, SeekOrigin.Begin);
            stream.Read(buffer, 0, RECORDSIZE);
            string s = Encoding.UTF8.GetString(buffer);
            Console.WriteLine($"record: {s}");
          }
        }
        catch (Exception ex)
        {
          Console.WriteLine(ex.Message);
        }
```

```
        } while (true);
        Console.WriteLine("finished");
    }
}
catch (FileNotFoundException)
{
    Console.WriteLine("Create the sample file using the option -sample first");
}
}
```

With this you can experiment with creating a file with 1.5 million records or more. A file this size is slow when you open it using Notepad, but it is extremely fast when you use random access. Depending on your system and the CPU and disk type, you might use higher or lower values for the tests.

> **NOTE** *In case the records that should be accessed are not fixed size, it still can be useful to use random access for large files. One way to deal with this is to write the position of the records to the beginning of the file. Another option is to read a larger block where the record could be and find the record identifier and the record limiters within the memory block.*

Using Buffered Streams

For performance reasons, when you read or write to or from a file, the output is buffered. This means that if your program asks for the next 2 bytes of a file stream, and the stream passes the request on to Windows, then Windows will not connect to the file system and then locate and read the file off the disk just to get 2 bytes. Instead, Windows retrieves a large block of the file at one time and stores this block in an area of memory known as a *buffer*. Subsequent requests for data from the stream are satisfied from the buffer until the buffer runs out, at which point Windows grabs another block of data from the file.

Writing to files works in the same way. For files, this is done automatically by the operating system, but you might have to write a stream class to read from some other device that is not buffered. If so, you can create a BufferedStream, which implements a buffer itself, and pass the stream that should be buffered to the constructor. Note, however, that BufferedStream is not designed for the situation in which an application frequently alternates between reading and writing data.

USING READERS AND WRITERS

Reading and writing text files using the FileStream class requires working with byte arrays and dealing with the encoding as described in the previous section. There's an easier way to do this: using readers and writers. You can use the StreamReader and StreamWriter classes to read and write to the FileStream, and you have an easier job not dealing with byte arrays and encodings.

That's because these classes work at a slightly higher level and are specifically geared to reading and writing text. The methods that they implement can automatically detect convenient points to stop reading text, based on the contents of the stream. In particular:

➤ These classes implement methods to read or write one line of text at a time: StreamReader .ReadLine and StreamWriter.WriteLine. In the case of reading, this means that the stream automatically determines where the next carriage return is and stops reading at that point. In the case of writing, it means that the stream automatically appends the carriage return–line feed combination to the text that it writes out.

➤ By using the StreamReader and StreamWriter classes, you don't need to worry about the encoding used in the file.

The sample code for `ReaderWriterSamples` makes use of the following namespaces:

```
System

System.Collections.Generic

System.Globalization

System.IO

System.Linq

System.Text

System.Threading.Tasks
```

The StreamReader Class

Let's start with the `StreamReader` by converting the previous example to read a file to use the `StreamReader`. It looks a lot easier now. The constructor of the `StreamReader` receives the `FileStream`. You can check for the end of the file by using the `EndOfStream` property, and you read lines using the `ReadLine` method (code file `ReaderWriterSamples/Program.cs`):

```
public static void ReadFileUsingReader(string fileName)
{
  var stream = new FileStream(fileName, FileMode.Open, FileAccess.Read,
    FileShare.Read);
  using (var reader = new StreamReader(stream))
  {
    while (!reader.EndOfStream)
    {
      string line = reader.ReadLine();
      Console.WriteLine(line);
    }
  }
}
```

It's no longer necessary to deal with byte arrays and the encoding. However, pay attention; the `StreamReader` by default uses the UTF-8 encoding. You can let the `StreamReader` use the encoding as it is defined by the preamble in the file by specifying a different constructor:

```
var reader = new StreamReader(stream, detectEncodingFromByteOrderMarks: true);
```

You can also explicitly specify the encoding:

```
var reader = new StreamReader(stream, Encoding.Unicode);
```

Other constructors enable you to set the buffer to be used; the default is 1024 bytes. Also, you can specify that the underlying stream should not be closed on closing the reader. By default, when the reader is closed (using the `Dispose` method), the underlying stream is closed as well.

Instead of explicitly instantiating a new `StreamReader`, you can create a `StreamReader` by using the `OpenText` method of the `File` class:

```
var reader = File.OpenText(fileName);
```

With the code snippet to read the file, the file was read line by line using the `ReadLine` method. The `StreamReader` also allows reading the complete file from the position of the cursor in the stream using `ReadToEnd`:

```
string content = reader.ReadToEnd();
```

The `StreamReader` also allows the content to read to a char array. This is similar to the `Read` method of the `Stream` class; it doesn't read to a byte array but instead to a char array. Remember, the char type uses two bytes. This is perfect for 16-bit Unicode, but is not as useful with UTF-8 where a single character can be between one and six bytes long:

```
int nChars = 100;
char[] charArray = new char[nChars];
int nCharsRead = reader.Read(charArray, 0, nChars);
```

The StreamWriter Class

The `StreamWriter` works in the same way as the `StreamReader`, except that you use `StreamWriter` only to write to a file (or to another stream). The following code snippet shows creating a `StreamWriter` passing a `FileStream`. Then a passed string array is written to the stream (code file `ReaderWriterSamples/Program.cs`):

```
public static void WriteFileUsingWriter(string fileName, string[] lines)
{
  var outputStream = File.OpenWrite(fileName);
  using (var writer = new StreamWriter(outputStream))
  {
    byte[] preamble = Encoding.UTF8.GetPreamble();
    outputStream.Write(preamble, 0, preamble.Length);
    writer.Write(lines);
  }
}
```

Remember that the `StreamWriter` is using the UTF-8 format by default to write the text content. You can define alternative contents by setting an `Encoding` object in the constructor. Also, similarly to the constructor of the `StreamReader`, the `StreamWriter` allows specifying the buffer size and whether the underlying stream should not be closed on closing of the writer.

The `Write` method of the `StreamWriter` defines 17 overloads that allow passing strings and several .NET data types. Using the methods passing the .NET data types, remember that all these are changed to strings with the specified encoding. To write the data types in binary format, you can use the `BinaryWriter` that's shown next.

Reading and Writing Binary Files

To read and write binary files, one option is to directly use the stream types; in this case, it's good to use byte arrays for reading and writing. Another option is to use readers and writers defined for this scenario: `BinaryReader` and `BinaryWriter`. You use them similarly to the way you use `StreamReader` and `StreamWriter` except `BinaryReader` and `BinaryWriter` don't use any encoding. Files are written in binary format rather than text format.

Unlike the `Stream` type, `BinaryWriter` defines 18 overloads for the `Write` method. The overloads accept different types, as shown in the following code snippet that writes a `double`, an `int`, a `long`, and a `string` (code file `ReaderWriterSamples/Program.cs`):

```
public static void WriteFileUsingBinaryWriter(string binFile)
{
  var outputStream = File.Create(binFile);
  using (var writer = new BinaryWriter(outputStream))
  {
    double d = 47.47;
    int i = 42;
    long l = 987654321;
    string s = "sample";
    writer.Write(d);
    writer.Write(i);
    writer.Write(l);
    writer.Write(s);
  }
}
```

To read the file again, you can use a `BinaryReader`. This class defines methods to read all the different types, such as `ReadDouble`, `ReadInt32`, `ReadInt64`, and `ReadString`, which are shown here:

```
public static void ReadFileUsingBinaryReader(string binFile)
{
  var inputStream = File.Open(binFile, FileMode.Open);
  using (var reader = new BinaryReader(inputStream))
  {
    double d = reader.ReadDouble();
    int i = reader.ReadInt32();
    long l = reader.ReadInt64();
    string s = reader.ReadString();
    Console.WriteLine($"d: {d}, i: {i}, l: {l}, s: {s}");
  }
}
```

The order for reading the file must match exactly the order in which it has been written. Creating your own binary format, you need to know what and how it is stored and read accordingly. The older Microsoft Word document was using a binary file format, whereas the newer `docx` file extension is a zip file. How zip files can be read and written is explained in the next section.

COMPRESSING FILES

.NET includes types to compress and decompress streams using different algorithms. You can use `DeflateStream`, `GZipStream`, and `BrotliStream` to compress and decompress streams; the `ZipArchive` class enables you to create and read ZIP files.

Both `DeflateStream` and `GZipStream` use the same algorithm for compression (in fact, `GZipStream` uses `DeflateStream` behind the scenes), but `GZipStream` adds a cyclic redundancy check to detect data corruption. Brotli is a relatively new open-source compression algorithm from Google. The speed of Brotli is similar to deflate, but it offers a better compression. Contrary to most other compression algorithms, it uses a dictionary for often-used words for better compression. Nowadays this algorithm is supported by most modern browsers.

Using a zip file has the advantage that you can compress files to an archive (with ZipArchive), and you can open this archive directly with Windows Explorer; it's been built in to Windows since 1998. You can't open a gzip archive with Windows Explorer; you need third-party tools for gzip.

> **NOTE** *The algorithm used by* `DeflateStream` *and* `GZipStream` *is the* deflate *algorithm. This algorithm is defined by RFC 1951 (*`https://tools.ietf.org/html/rfc1951`*). This algorithm is widely thought to be not covered by patents, which is why it is in widespread use.*
>
> *Brotli is available on GitHub at* `https://github.com/google/brotli` *and defined by RFC 7932 (*`https://tools.ietf.org/html/rfc7932`*).*

The sample code for CompressFileSample makes use of the following dependency and namespaces:

Dependency

```
System.IO.Compression.Brotli
```

Namespaces

```
System
```

```
System.Collections.Generic
```

```
System.IO

System.IO.Compression

System.Text
```

Using the Deflate Stream

As explained earlier, a feature from streams is that you can chain them. To compress a stream, all that's needed is to create `DeflateStream` and pass another stream (in this example, the `outputStream` to write a file) to the constructor, with the argument `CompressionMode.Compress` for compression. Writing to this stream either using the `Write` method or by using other features, such as the `CopyTo` method as shown in this code snippet, is all that's needed for file compression (code file `CompressFileSample/Program.cs`):

```
public static void CompressFile(string fileName, string compressedFileName)
{
  using (FileStream inputStream = File.OpenRead(fileName))
  {
    FileStream outputStream = File.OpenWrite(compressedFileName);
    using (var compressStream =
      new DeflateStream(outputStream, CompressionMode.Compress))
    {
      inputStream.CopyTo(compressStream);
    }
  }
}
```

To decompress the deflate-compressed file again, the following code snippet opens the file using a `FileStream` and creates the `DeflateStream` object with `CompressionMode.Decompress` passing the file stream for decompression. The `Stream.CopyTo` method copies the decompressed stream to a `MemoryStream`. This code snippet then makes use of a `StreamReader` to read the data from the `MemoryStream` and write the output to the console. The `StreamReader` is configured to leave the assigned `MemoryStream` open (using the `leaveOpen` argument), so the `MemoryStream` could also be used after closing the reader:

```
public static void DecompressFile(string fileName)
{
  FileStream inputStream = File.OpenRead(fileName);
  using (MemoryStream outputStream = new MemoryStream())
  using (var compressStream = new DeflateStream(inputStream,
    CompressionMode.Decompress))
  {
    compressStream.CopyTo(outputStream);
    outputStream.Seek(0, SeekOrigin.Begin);
    using (var reader = new StreamReader(outputStream, Encoding.UTF8,
      detectEncodingFromByteOrderMarks: true, bufferSize: 4096,
      leaveOpen: true))
    {
      string result = reader.ReadToEnd();
      Console.WriteLine(result);
    }
    // you could use the outputStream after the StreamReader is closed
  }
}
```

Using Brotli

Using `BrotliStream`, compression with Brotli is like using deflate. You just need to add the NuGet package `System.IO.Compression.Brotli` and instantiate the `BrotliStream` class (code file `CompressFileSample/Program.cs`):

```
public static void CompressFileWithBrotli(string fileName,
  string compressedFileName)
{
  using (FileStream inputStream = File.OpenRead(fileName))
  {
    FileStream outputStream = File.OpenWrite(compressedFileName);
    using (var compressStream =
      new BrotliStream(outputStream, CompressionMode.Compress))
    {
      inputStream.CopyTo(compressStream);
    }
  }
}
```

Decompression works accordingly using `BrotliStream`:

```
public static void DecompressFileWithBrotli(string fileName)
{
  FileStream inputStream = File.OpenRead(fileName);
  using (MemoryStream outputStream = new MemoryStream())
  using (var compressStream = new BrotliStream(inputStream,
    CompressionMode.Decompress))
  {
    compressStream.CopyTo(outputStream);
    outputStream.Seek(0, SeekOrigin.Begin);
    using (var reader = new StreamReader(outputStream, Encoding.UTF8,
      detectEncodingFromByteOrderMarks: true, bufferSize: 4096,
      leaveOpen: true))
    {
      string result = reader.ReadToEnd();
      Console.WriteLine(result);
    }
  }
}
```

Zipping Files

Today, the ZIP file format is the standard for many different file types. Word documents (`docx`) as well as NuGet packages are all stored as a ZIP file. With .NET, it's easy to create a ZIP archive.

For creating a ZIP archive, you can create an object of `ZipArchive`. A `ZipArchive` contains multiple `ZipArchiveEntry` objects. The `ZipArchive` class is not a stream, but it uses a stream to read or write to (this is similar to the reader and writer classes discussed earlier). The following code snippet creates a `ZipArchive` that writes the compressed content to the file stream opened with `File.OpenWrite`. What's added to the ZIP archive is defined by the directory passed. `Directory.EnumerateFiles` enumerates all the files in the directory and creates a `ZipArchiveEntry` object for every file. Invoking the `Open` method creates a `Stream` object. With the `CopyTo` method of the `Stream` that is read, the file is compressed and written to the `ZipArchiveEntry` (code file `CompressFileSample/Program.cs`):

```
public static void CreateZipFile(string directory, string zipFile)
{
  FileStream zipStream = File.OpenWrite(zipFile);
```

```
using (var archive = new ZipArchive(zipStream, ZipArchiveMode.Create))
{
  IEnumerable<string> files = Directory.EnumerateFiles(
    directory, "*", SearchOption.TopDirectoryOnly);
  foreach (var file in files)
  {
    ZipArchiveEntry entry = archive.CreateEntry(Path.GetFileName(file));
    using (FileStream inputStream = File.OpenRead(file))
    using (Stream outputStream = entry.Open())
    {
      inputStream.CopyTo(outputStream);
    }
  }
}
```

WATCHING FILE CHANGES

With `FileSystemWatcher`, you can monitor file changes. Events are fired on creating, renaming, deleting, and changing files. This can be used in scenarios where you need to react on file changes—for example, with a server when a file is uploaded, or in a case where a file is cached in memory and the cache needs to be invalidated when the file changes.

As `FileSystemWatcher` is easy to use, let's directly get into a sample. The sample code for `FileMonitor` makes use of the following namespaces:

```
System

System.IO
```

The sample code starts watching files in the method `WatchFiles`. Using the constructor of the `FileSystemWatcher`, you can supply the directory that should be watched. You can also provide a filter to filter only specific files that match with the filter expression. When you set the property `IncludeSubdirectories`, you can define whether only the files in the specified directory should be watched or whether files in subdirectories should also be watched. With the `Created`, `Changed`, `Deleted`, and `Renamed` events, event handlers are supplied. All of these events are of type `FileSystemEventHandler` with the exception of the `Renamed` event that is of type `RenamedEventHandler`. `RenamedEventHandler` derives from `FileSystemEventHandler` and offers additional information about the event (code file `FileMonitor/Program.cs`):

```
private static FileSystemWatcher s_watcher;

public static void WatchFiles(string path, string filter)
{
  s_watcher = new FileSystemWatcher(path, filter)
  {
    IncludeSubdirectories = true
  };
  s_watcher.Created += OnFileChanged;
  s_watcher.Changed += OnFileChanged;
  s_watcher.Deleted += OnFileChanged;
  s_watcher.Renamed += OnFileRenamed;
  s_watcher.EnableRaisingEvents = true;
  Console.WriteLine("watching file changes...");
}
```

The information that is received with a file change is of type `FileSystemEventArgs`. It contains the name of the file that changed as well as the kind of change that is an enumeration of type `WatcherChangeTypes`:

```
private static void OnFileChanged(object sender, FileSystemEventArgs e)
{
  Console.WriteLine($"file {e.Name} {e.ChangeType}");
}
```

On renaming the file, additional information is received with the `RenamedEventArgs` parameter. This type derives from `FileSystemEventArgs` and defines additional information about the original name of the file:

```
private static void OnFileRenamed(object sender, RenamedEventArgs e)
{
  Console.WriteLine($"file {e.OldName} {e.ChangeType} to {e.Name}");
}
```

When you start the application by specifying a folder to watch and `*.txt` as the filter, the following is the output after creating the file `sample1.txt`, adding content, renaming it to `sample2.txt`, and finally deleting it:

```
watching file changes...
file New Text Document.txt Created
file New Text Document.txt Renamed to sample1.txt
file sample1.txt Changed
file sample1.txt Changed
file sample1.txt Renamed to sample2.txt
file sample2.txt Deleted
```

WORKING WITH MEMORY MAPPED FILES

Memory mapped files enable you to access files or shared memory from different processes. There are several scenarios and features with this technology:

➤ Fast random access to huge files using maps of the file

➤ Sharing of files between different processes or tasks

➤ Sharing of memory between different processes or tasks

➤ Using accessors to directly read and write from memory positions

➤ Using streams to read and write

The memory mapped files API allows you to use either a physical file or shared memory—where the system's page file is used as a backing store. The shared memory can be bigger than the available physical memory, so a backing store is needed. You can create a memory mapped file to a specific file or shared memory. With either of these options, you can assign a name for the memory map. Using a name allows different processes to have access to the same shared memory.

After you've created the memory map, you can create a view. A view is used to map a part of the complete memory mapped file to access it for reading or writing.

The `MemoryMappedFilesSample` makes use of the following namespaces:

```
System

System.IO

System.IO.MemoryMappedFiles

System.Threading

System.Threading.Tasks
```

The sample application demonstrates working with a memory mapped file using both view accessors and streams using multiple tasks. One task creates the memory mapped file and writes data to it; the other task reads data.

> **NOTE** *The sample code makes use of tasks and events. Read Chapter 21, "Tasks and Parallel Programming," for more information about tasks, and synchronization between tasks.*

Some infrastructure is needed for creating the tasks and signaling when the map is ready, and the data is written. The name of the map and ManualResetEventSlim objects are defined as a member of the Program class (code file MemoryMappedFilesSample/Program.cs):

```
private ManualResetEventSlim _mapCreated =
  new ManualResetEventSlim(initialState: false);

private ManualResetEventSlim _dataWrittenEvent =
  new ManualResetEventSlim(initialState: false);

private const string MAPNAME = "SampleMap";
```

Tasks are started within the Main method with the Task.Run method:

```
public void Run()
{
  Task.Run(() => WriterAsync());
  Task.Run(() => Reader());
  Console.WriteLine("tasks started");
  Console.ReadLine();
}
```

Now let's create readers and writers using accessors.

Using Accessors to Create Memory Mapped Files

To create a memory-based memory mapped file, the writer invokes the MemoryMappedFile.CreateOrOpen method. This method either opens the object with the name specified with the first parameter, or it creates a new one if it doesn't exist. To open existing files, you can use the method OpenExisting. For accessing physical files, you can use the method CreateFromFile.

Other parameters used in the sample code are the size of the memory mapped file and the access needed. After the memory mapped file is created, the event _mapCreated is signaled to give other tasks the information that the memory mapped file is created and can be opened. Invoking the method CreateViewAccessor returns a MemoryMappedViewAccessor to access the shared memory. With the view accessor, you can define an offset and size that is used by this task. Of course, the maximum size that you can use is the size of the memory mapped file itself. This view is used for writing; thus, the file access is set to MemoryMappedFileAccess.Write.

Next, you can write primitive data types to the shared memory using overloaded Write methods of the MemoryMappedViewAccessor. The Write method always needs position information designating where the data should be written to. After all the data is written, an event is signaled to inform the reader that it is now possible to start reading (code file MemoryMappedFilesSample/Program.cs):

```
private async Task WriterAsync()
{
  try
  {
    using (MemoryMappedFile mappedFile = MemoryMappedFile.CreateOrOpen(
      MAPNAME, 10000, MemoryMappedFileAccess.ReadWrite))
    {
      _mapCreated.Set(); // signal shared memory segment created
      Console.WriteLine("shared memory segment created");
      using (MemoryMappedViewAccessor accessor = mappedFile.CreateViewAccessor(
        0, 10000, MemoryMappedFileAccess.Write))
      {
        for (int i = 0, pos = 0; i < 100; i++, pos += 4)
        {
          accessor.Write(pos, i);
          Console.WriteLine($"written {i} at position {pos}");
          await Task.Delay(10);
        }
```

```
            _dataWrittenEvent.Set(); // signal all data written
            Console.WriteLine("data written");
          }
        }
      }
      catch (Exception ex)
      {
        Console.WriteLine($"writer {ex.Message}");
      }
    }
```

The reader first waits for the map to be created before opening the memory mapped file using `MemoryMappedFile.OpenExisting`. The reader just needs read access to the map. After that, similar to the writer before, a view accessor is created. Before reading data, you wait for the `_dataWrittenEvent` to be set. Reading is similar to writing in that you supply a position where the data should be accessed, but different `Read` methods, such as `ReadInt32`, are defined for reading the different data types:

```
    private void Reader()
    {
      try
      {
        Console.WriteLine("reader");
        _mapCreated.Wait();
        Console.WriteLine("reader starting");
        using (MemoryMappedFile mappedFile = MemoryMappedFile.OpenExisting(
          MAPNAME, MemoryMappedFileRights.Read))
        {
          using (MemoryMappedViewAccessor accessor = mappedFile.CreateViewAccessor(
            0, 10000, MemoryMappedFileAccess.Read))
          {
            _dataWrittenEvent.Wait();
            Console.WriteLine("reading can start now");
            for (int i = 0; i < 400; i += 4)
            {
              int result = accessor.ReadInt32(i);
              Console.WriteLine($"reading {result} from position {i}");
            }
          }
        }
      }
      catch (Exception ex)
      {
        Console.WriteLine($"reader {ex.Message}");
      }
    }
```

When you run the application, you might see output such as this:

```
reader
reader starting
tasks started
shared memory segment created
written 0 at position 0
written 1 at position 4
written 2 at position 8
...
written 99 at 396
data written
reading can start now
reading 0 from position 0
reading 1 from position 4
...
```

Using Streams to Create Memory Mapped Files

Instead of writing primitive data types with memory mapped files, you can instead use streams. Streams enable you to use readers and writers, as described earlier in this chapter. Now create a writer to use a `StreamWriter`. The method `CreateViewStream` from the `MemoryMappedFile` returns a `MemoryMappedViewStream`. This method is very similar to the `CreateViewAccessor` method used earlier in defining a view inside the map; with the offset and size, it is convenient to use all the features of streams. The `WriteLineAsync` method is then used to write a string to the stream. As the `StreamWriter` caches writes, the stream position is not updated with every write; it's updated only when the writer writes blocks. For flushing the cache with every write, you set the `AutoFlush` property of the `StreamWriter` to true (code file MemoryMappedFilesSample/Program.cs):

```
private async Task WriterUsingStreams()
{
  try
  {
    using (MemoryMappedFile mappedFile = MemoryMappedFile.CreateOrOpen(
      MAPNAME, 10000, MemoryMappedFileAccess.ReadWrite))
    {
      _mapCreated.Set(); // signal shared memory segment created
      Console.WriteLine("shared memory segment created");
      MemoryMappedViewStream stream = mappedFile.CreateViewStream(
        0, 10000, MemoryMappedFileAccess.Write);
      using (var writer = new StreamWriter(stream))
      {
        writer.AutoFlush = true;
        for (int i = 0; i < 100; i++)
        {
          string s = $"some data {i}";
          Console.WriteLine($"writing {s} at {stream.Position}");
          await writer.WriteLineAsync(s);
        }
      }
      _dataWrittenEvent.Set(); // signal all data written
      Console.WriteLine("data written");
    }
  }
  catch (Exception ex)
  {
    Console.WriteLine($"writer {ex.Message}");
  }
}
```

The reader similarly creates a mapped view stream with `CreateViewStream`, but this time for read access. Now it's possible to use `StreamReader` methods to read content from the shared memory:

```
private async Task ReaderUsingStreams()
{
  try
  {
    Console.WriteLine("reader");
    _mapCreated.Wait();
    Console.WriteLine("reader starting");
    using (MemoryMappedFile mappedFile = MemoryMappedFile.OpenExisting(
      MAPNAME, MemoryMappedFileRights.Read))
    {
      MemoryMappedViewStream stream = mappedFile.CreateViewStream(
        0, 10000, MemoryMappedFileAccess.Read);
      using (var reader = new StreamReader(stream))
      {
        _dataWrittenEvent.Wait();
```

```
      Console.WriteLine("reading can start now");
      for (int i = 0; i < 100; i++)
      {
        long pos = stream.Position;
        string s = await reader.ReadLineAsync();
        Console.WriteLine($"read {s} from {pos}");
      }
    }
  }
}
catch (Exception ex)
{
  Console.WriteLine($"reader {ex.Message}");
}
}
```

When you run the application, you can see the data written and read. When the data is being written, the position within the stream is always updated because the AutoFlush property is set. When data is being read, always 1024 byte blocks are read.

```
tasks started
reader
reader starting
shared memory segment created
writing some data 0 at 0
writing some data 1 at 13
writing some data 2 at 26
writing some data 3 at 39
writing some data 4 at 52
...
data written
reading can start now
read some data 0 from 0
read some data 1 from 1024
read some data 2 from 1024
read some data 3 from 1024
...
```

When communicating via memory mapped files, you have to synchronize the reader and the writer, so the reader knows when data is available. Pipes, which are discussed in the next section, give other options in such a scenario.

COMMUNICATING WITH PIPES

For communication between threads and processes, and also fast communication between different systems, you can use pipes. With .NET, pipes are implemented as streams and thus you have an option to not only send bytes into a pipe, but you can use all the stream features, such as readers and writers.

Pipes are implemented as different kinds—as *named pipes*, where the name can be used to connect to each end, and *anonymous pipes*. Anonymous pipes cannot be used to communicate between different systems; they can be used only for communication between a child and parent process or for communication between different tasks.

The code for all the pipe samples makes use of the following namespaces:

```
System

System.IO

System.IO.Pipes

System.Threading

System.Threading.Tasks
```

Let's start with named pipes for communication between different processes. With the first sample application, two console applications are used. One acts as server and reads data from a pipe; the other one writes messages to the pipe.

Creating a Named Pipe Server

You create the server by creating a new instance of NamedPipeServerStream. NamedPipeServerStream derives from the base class PipeStream that in turn derives from the Stream base class and thus can use all the features of streams—for example, you can create a CryptoStream or a GZipStream to write encrypted or compressed data into the named pipe. The constructor requires a name for the pipe that can be used by multiple processes communicating via the pipe.

The second argument that is used in the following code snippet defines the direction of the pipe. The server stream is used for reading, and thus the direction is set to PipeDirection.In. Named pipes can also be bidirectional for reading and writing; you use PipeDirection.InOut. Anonymous pipes can be only unidirectional. Next, the named pipe waits until the writing party connects by calling the WaitForConnection method. Next, within a loop (until the message "bye" is received), the pipe server reads messages to a buffer array and writes the message to the console (code file PipesReader/Program.cs):

```
private static void PipesReader(string pipeName)
{
  try
  {
    using (var pipeReader =
      new NamedPipeServerStream(pipeName, PipeDirection.In))
    {
      pipeReader.WaitForConnection();
      Console.WriteLine("reader connected");
      const int BUFFERSIZE = 256;
      bool completed = false;
      while (!completed)
      {
        byte[] buffer = new byte[BUFFERSIZE];
        int nRead = pipeReader.Read(buffer, 0, BUFFERSIZE);
        string line = Encoding.UTF8.GetString(buffer, 0, nRead);
        Console.WriteLine(line);
        if (line == "bye") completed = true;
      }
    }
    Console.WriteLine("completed reading");
    Console.ReadLine();
  }
  catch (Exception ex)
  {
    Console.WriteLine(ex.Message);
  }
}
```

The following are some other options that you can configure with named pipes:

➤ You can set the enumeration PipeTransmissionMode to Byte or Message. With bytes, a continuous stream is sent; with messages every message can be retrieved.

➤ With the pipe options, you can specify WriteThrough to immediately write to the pipe and not to the cache.

➤ You can configure buffer sizes for input and output.

➤ You configure pipe security to designate who is allowed to read and write to the pipe. Security is discussed in Chapter 24.

➤ You can configure inheritability of the pipe handle, which is important for communicating with child processes.

Because the `NamedPipeServerStream` is a `Stream`, you can use `StreamReader` instead of reading from the byte array; this method simplifies the code:

```
var pipeReader = new NamedPipeServerStream(pipeName, PipeDirection.In);
using (var reader = new StreamReader(pipeReader))
{
  pipeReader.WaitForConnection();
  Console.WriteLine("reader connected");
  bool completed = false;
  while (!completed)
  {
    string line = reader.ReadLine();
    Console.WriteLine(line);
    if (line == "bye") completed = true;
  }
}
```

Creating a Named Pipe Client

Now you need a client. As the server reads messages, the client writes them.

You create the client by instantiating a `NamedPipeClientStream` object. Because named pipes can communicate across the network, you need a server name in addition to the pipe name and the direction of the pipe. The client connects by invoking the `Connect` method. After the connection succeeds, messages are sent to the server by invoking `WriteLine` on the `StreamWriter`. By default, messages are not sent immediately; they are cached. The message is pushed to the server by invoking the `Flush` method. You can also immediately pass all the messages without invoking the `Flush` method. For this, you have to configure the option to write through the cache on creating the pipe (code file `PipesWriter/Program.cs`):

```
public static void PipesWriter(string serverName, string pipeName)
{
  var pipeWriter = new NamedPipeClientStream(serverName,
    pipeName, PipeDirection.Out);
  using (var writer = new StreamWriter(pipeWriter))
  {
    pipeWriter.Connect();
    Console.WriteLine("writer connected");
    bool completed = false;
    while (!completed)
    {
      string input = ReadLine();
      if (input == "bye") completed = true;
      writer.WriteLine(input);
      writer.Flush();
    }
  }
  Console.WriteLine("completed writing");
}
```

For starting two projects from within Visual Studio, you can configure multiple startup projects with Project ⇨ Set Startup Projects. When you run the application, input from one console is echoed in the other one.

Creating Anonymous Pipes

Let's do something similar with anonymous pipes. With anonymous pipes two tasks are created that communicate with each other. For signaling the pipe creation, you use a `ManualResetEventSlim` object as you did with the memory mapped files. In the `Run` method of the `Program` class, two tasks are created that invoke the `Reader` and `Writer` methods (code file `AnonymousPipes/Program.cs`):

```
private string _pipeHandle;
private ManualResetEventSlim _pipeHandleSet;
```

```
static void Main()
{
  var p = new Program();
  p.Run();
  Console.ReadLine();
}

public void Run()
{
  _pipeHandleSet = new ManualResetEventSlim(initialState: false);
  Task.Run(() => Reader());
  Task.Run(() => Writer());
  Console.ReadLine();
}
```

The server side acts as a reader by creating an `AnonymousPipeServerStream` and defining the `PipeDirection.In`. The other side of the communication needs to know about the client handle of the pipe. This handle is converted to a string from the method `GetClientHandleAsString` and assigned to the `_pipeHandle` variable. This variable will be used later by the client that acts as a writer. After the initial process, the pipe server can be acted on as a stream because it is a stream:

```
private void Reader()
{
  try
  {
    var pipeReader = new AnonymousPipeServerStream(PipeDirection.In,
      HandleInheritability.None);
    using (var reader = new StreamReader(pipeReader))
    {
      _pipeHandle = pipeReader.GetClientHandleAsString();
      Console.WriteLine($"pipe handle: {_pipeHandle}");
      _pipeHandleSet.Set();
      bool end = false;
      while (!end)
      {
        string line = reader.ReadLine();
        Console.WriteLine(line);
        if (line == "end") end = true;
      }
      Console.WriteLine("finished reading");
    }
  }
  catch (Exception ex)
  {
    Console.WriteLine(ex.Message);
  }
}
```

The client code waits until the variable `_pipeHandleSet` is signaled, and thus can open the pipe handle referenced by the `_pipeHandle` variable. Later processing continues with a `StreamWriter`:

```
private void Writer()
{
  Console.WriteLine("anonymous pipe writer");
  _pipeHandleSet.Wait();
  var pipeWriter = new AnonymousPipeClientStream(
    PipeDirection.Out, _pipeHandle);
  using (var writer = new StreamWriter(pipeWriter))
  {
    writer.AutoFlush = true;
    Console.WriteLine("starting writer");
    for (int i = 0; i < 5; i++)
```

```
          {
            writer.WriteLine($"Message {i}");
            Task.Delay(500).Wait();
          }
          writer.WriteLine("end");
        }
    }
```

When you run the application, the two tasks communicate and send data between the tasks.

USING FILES AND STREAMS WITH THE WINDOWS RUNTIME

With the Windows Runtime, you implement streams with native types. Although they are implemented with native code, they look like .NET types. However, there's a difference you need to be aware of: For streams, the Windows Runtime implements its own types in the namespace `Windows.Storage.Streams`. Here you can find classes such as `FileInputStream`, `FileOutputStream`, and `RandomAccessStreams`. All these classes are based on interfaces, for example, `IInputStream`, `IOutputStream`, and `IRandomAccessStream`. You'll also find the concept of readers and writers. Windows Runtime readers and writers are the types `DataReader` and `DataWriter`.

Let's look at what's different from the .NET streams you've seen so far and how .NET streams and types can map to these native types.

Windows App Editor

Let's create an editor starting with the Blank App (Universal Windows) Visual Studio template.

To add commands for opening and saving a file, a `CommandBar` with `AppBarButton` elements is added to the main page (code file `WindowsAppEditor/MainPage.xaml`):

```xml
<Page.BottomAppBar>
  <CommandBar IsOpen="True">
    <AppBarButton Icon="OpenFile" Label="Open" Click="{x:Bind OnOpen}" />
    <AppBarButton Icon="Save" Label="Save" Click="{x:Bind OnSave}" />
  </CommandBar>
</Page.BottomAppBar>
```

The `TextBox` added to the `Grid` fill receive the contents of the file:

```xml
<Grid Background="{ThemeResource ApplicationPageBackgroundThemeBrush}">
  <TextBox x:Name="text1" HorizontalTextAlignment="Left"
    AcceptsReturn="True" />
</Grid>
```

The `OnOpen` handle first starts the dialog where the user can select a file. Remember, you used the `OpenFileDialog` earlier. With Windows apps, you can use pickers. To open files, the `FileOpenPicker` is the preferred type. You can configure this picker to define the proposed start location for the user. You set the `SuggestedStartLocation` to `PickerLocationId.DocumentsLibrary` to open the user's documents folder. The `PickerLocationId` is an enumeration that defines various special folders.

Next, the `FileTypeFilter` collection specifies the file types that should be listed for the user. Finally, the method `PickSingleFileAsync` returns the file selected from the user. To allow users to select multiple files, you can use the method `PickMultipleFilesAsync` instead. This method returns a `StorageFile`. `StorageFile` is defined in the namespace `Windows.Storage`. This class is the equivalent of the `FileInfo` class for opening, creating, copying, moving, and deleting files (code file `WindowsAppEditor/MainPage.xaml.cs`):

```csharp
public async void OnOpen()
{
  try
```

```
    {
      var picker = new FileOpenPicker()
      {
        ViewMode = PickerViewMode.Thumbnail,
        SuggestedStartLocation = PickerLocationId.DocumentsLibrary
      };
      picker.FileTypeFilter.Add(".txt");
      picker.FileTypeFilter.Add(".md");

      StorageFile file = await picker.PickSingleFileAsync();
      //...
```

Now, open the file using `OpenReadAsync`. This method returns a stream that implements the interface `IRandomAccessStreamWithContentType`, which derives from the interfaces `IRandomAccessStream`, `IInputStream`, `IOuputStream`, `IContentProvider`, and `IDisposable`. `IRandomAccessStream` allows random access to a stream with the `Seek` method, and it gives information about the size of a stream. `IInputStream` defines the method `ReadAsync` to read from a stream. `IOutputStream` is the opposite; it defines the methods `WriteAsync` and `FlushAsync`. `IContentTypeProvider` defines the property `ContentType` that gives information about the content of the file. Remember the encodings of the text files? Now it would be possible to read the content of the stream invoking the method `ReadAsync`. However, the Windows Runtime also knows the reader's and writer's concepts that have already been discussed. A `DataReader` accepts an `IInputStream` with the constructor. The `DataReader` type defines methods to read primitive data types such as `ReadInt16`, `ReadInt32`, and `ReadDateTime`. You can read a byte array with `ReadBytes`, and a string with `ReadString`. The `ReadString` method requires the number of characters to read. The string is assigned to the `Text` property of the `TextBox` control to display the content:

```
    //...
    if (file != null)
    {
      IRandomAccessStreamWithContentType stream = await file.OpenReadAsync();
      using (var reader = new DataReader(stream))
      {
        await reader.LoadAsync((uint)stream.Size);
        text1.Text = reader.ReadString((uint)stream.Size);
      }
    }
  }
  catch (Exception ex)
  {
    var dlg = new MessageDialog(ex.Message, "Error");
    await dlg.ShowAsync();
  }
```

> **NOTE** *Like the readers and the writers of the .NET Framework, the `DataReader` and `DataWriter` manages the stream that is passed with the constructor. On disposing the reader or writer, the stream gets disposed as well. With .NET classes, to keep the underlying stream open for a longer time you can set the `leaveOpen` argument in the constructor. With the Windows Runtime types, you can detach the stream from the readers and writers by invoking the method `DetachStream`.*

On saving the document, the `OnSave` method is invoked. First, the `FileSavePicker` is used to allow the user to select the document—similar to the `FileOpenPicker`. Next, the file is opened using `OpenTransactedWriteAsync`. The NTFS file system supports transactions; these are not covered from the .NET Framework but are available with the Windows Runtime. `OpenTransactedWriteAsync` returns a `StorageStreamTransaction` object that implements the interface `IStorageStreamTransaction`. This object itself is not a stream (although the name might lead you to believe this), but it contains a stream that you can reference with the `Stream` property. This property returns an `IRandomAccessStream` stream. As you can create a `DataReader`, you can create a `DataWriter` to write primitive data types, including strings as in this example. The `StoreAsync` method finally writes the content from the buffer to the stream. The transaction needs to be committed by invoking the `CommitAsync` method before disposing the writer:

```
public async void OnSave()
{
  try
  {
    var picker = new FileSavePicker()
    {
      SuggestedStartLocation = PickerLocationId.DocumentsLibrary,
      SuggestedFileName = "New Document"
    };
    picker.FileTypeChoices.Add("Plain Text", new List<string>() { ".txt" });
    StorageFile file = await picker.PickSaveFileAsync();
    if (file != null)
    {
      using (StorageStreamTransaction tx =
        await file.OpenTransactedWriteAsync())
      {
        IRandomAccessStream stream = tx.Stream;
        stream.Seek(0);
        using (var writer = new DataWriter(stream))
        {
          writer.WriteString(text1.Text);
          tx.Stream.Size = await writer.StoreAsync();
          await tx.CommitAsync();
        }
      }
    }
  }
  catch (Exception ex)
  {
    var dlg = new MessageDialog(ex.Message, "Error");
    await dlg.ShowAsync();
  }
}
```

The `DataWriter` doesn't add the preamble defining the kind of Unicode file to the stream. You need to do that explicitly, as explained earlier in this chapter. The `DataWriter` just deals with the encoding of the file by setting the `UnicodeEncoding` and `ByteOrder` properties. The default setting is `UnicodeEncoding.Utf8` and `ByteOrder.BigEndian`. Instead of working with the `DataWriter`, you can also take advantage of the features of the `StreamReader` and `StreamWriter` as well as the .NET `Stream` class, as shown in the next section.

Mapping Windows Runtime Types to .NET Types

Let's start with reading the file. To convert a Windows Runtime stream to a .NET stream for reading, you can use the extension method `AsStreamForRead`. This method is defined in the namespace `System.IO` (that must be opened) in the assembly `System.Runtime.WindowsRuntime`. This method creates a new `Stream` object that manages the `IInputStream`. Now, you can use it as a normal .NET stream, as shown previously—for example, passing it to a `StreamReader` and using this reader to access the file:

```
public async void OnOpenDotnet()
{
  try
  {
    var picker = new FileOpenPicker()
    {
```

```
        ViewMode = PickerViewMode.Thumbnail,
        SuggestedStartLocation = PickerLocationId.DocumentsLibrary
      };
      picker.FileTypeFilter.Add(".txt");
      picker.FileTypeFilter.Add(".md");

      StorageFile file = await picker.PickSingleFileAsync();
      if (file != null)
      {
        IRandomAccessStreamWithContentType wrtStream =
          await file.OpenReadAsync();
        Stream stream = wrtStream.AsStreamForRead();
        using (var reader = new StreamReader(stream))
        {
          text1.Text = await reader.ReadToEndAsync();
        }
      }
    }
    catch (Exception ex)
    {
      var dlg = new MessageDialog(ex.Message, "Error");
      await dlg.ShowAsync();
    }
  }
```

All the Windows Runtime stream types can easily be converted to .NET streams and the other way around. The following table lists the methods needed:

CONVERT FROM	CONVERT TO	METHOD	
IRandomAccessStream	Stream	AsStream	
IInputStream	Stream	AsStreamForRead	
IOutputStream	Stream	AsStreamForWrite	
Stream	IInputStream	AsInputStream	
Stream	IOutputStream	AsOutputStream	
Stream	IRandomAccessStream	AsRandomAccessStream	

Now save the change to the file as well. The stream for writing is converted with the extension method `AsStreamForWrite`. Now, this stream can be written using the `StreamWriter` class. The code snippet also writes the preamble for the UTF-8 encoding to the file:

```
  public async void OnSaveDotnet()
  {
    try
    {
      var picker = new FileSavePicker()
      {
        SuggestedStartLocation = PickerLocationId.DocumentsLibrary,
        SuggestedFileName = "New Document"
      };
      picker.FileTypeChoices.Add("Plain Text", new List<string>() { ".txt" });
      StorageFile file = await picker.PickSaveFileAsync();
      if (file != null)
      {
        StorageStreamTransaction tx = await file.OpenTransactedWriteAsync();
        using (var writer = new StreamWriter(tx.Stream.AsStreamForWrite()))
        {
```

```
        byte[] preamble = Encoding.UTF8.GetPreamble();
        await stream.WriteAsync(preamble, 0, preamble.Length);
        await writer.WriteAsync(text1.Text);
        await writer.FlushAsync();
        tx.Stream.Size = (ulong)stream.Length;
        await tx.CommitAsync();
      }
    }
  }
  catch (Exception ex)
  {
    var dlg = new MessageDialog(ex.Message, "Error");
    await dlg.ShowAsync();
  }
}
```

SUMMARY

In this chapter, you examined how to use the .NET classes to access the file system from your C# code. You have seen that in both cases the base classes expose simple but powerful object models that make it very easy to perform almost any kind of action in these areas. For the file system, these actions are copying files; moving, creating, and deleting files and folders; and reading and writing both binary and text files.

You've seen how to compress files using both the deflate algorithm and ZIP files. The FileSystemWatcher was used to get information when files change. You've also seen how to communicate with the help of shared memory as well as named and anonymous pipes. Finally, you've seen how to map .NET streams to Windows Runtime streams to take advantage of .NET features within Windows apps.

In some other chapters of the book you can see streams in action. For example, Chapter 23, "Networking," uses streams to send data across the network. Reading and writing XML files and streaming large XML files are shown in Bonus Chapter 2/JSON," which you can find online.

The next chapter covers the foundation of networking and sending streams across the network.

23

Networking

WHAT'S IN THIS CHAPTER?

➤ Using HttpClient

➤ Manipulating IP addresses and performing DNS lookups

➤ Creating a server with WebListener

➤ Socket programming with TCP, UDP, and socket classes

WROX.COM CODE DOWNLOADS FOR THIS CHAPTER

The Wrox.com code downloads for this chapter are found at `http://www.wrox.com` on the Download Code tab. The source code is also available at `https://github.com/ProfessionalCSharp/ProfessionalCSharp7` in the directory `Networking`.

The code for this chapter is divided into the following major examples:

➤ HttpClientSample

➤ WinAppHttpClient

➤ HttpServer

➤ Utilities

➤ DnsLookup

➤ HttpClientUsingTcp

➤ TcpServer

➤ WinAppTcpClient

➤ UdpReceiver

➤ UdpSender

➤ SocketServer

➤ SocketClient

NETWORKING

This chapter takes a practical approach to networking, mixing examples with a discussion of relevant theory and networking concepts as appropriate. This chapter is not a guide to computer networking but an introduction to using the .NET for network communication.

This chapter shows you how to create both clients and servers using network protocols. It starts with the simplest case: sending an HTTP request to a server and storing the information that's sent back in the response.

Then you see how to create an HTTP server, using utility classes to split up and create URIs and resolve hostnames to IP addresses. You are also introduced to sending and receiving data via TCP and UDP and find out how to make use of the Socket class.

The two namespaces of most interest for networking are System.Net and System.Net.Sockets. The System.Net namespace is generally concerned with higher-level operations, such as downloading and uploading files, and making web requests using HTTP and other protocols, whereas System.Net.Sockets contains classes to perform lower-level operations. You will find these classes useful when you want to work directly with sockets or protocols, such as TCP/IP. The methods in these classes closely mimic the Windows socket (Winsock) API functions derived from the Berkeley sockets interface. You will also find that some of the objects that this chapter works with are found in the System.IO namespace.

THE HTTPCLIENT CLASS

The HttpClient class is used to send an HTTP request and receive the response from the request. It is in the System.Net.Http namespace. The classes in the System.Net.Http namespace help make it easy to consume web services for both clients and server.

The HttpClient class derives from the HttpMessageInvoker class. This base class implements the SendAsync method. The SendAsync method is the workhorse of the HttpClient class. As you see later in this section, there are several derivatives of this method to use. As the name implies, the SendAsync method call is asynchronous. This enables you to write a fully asynchronous system for calling web services.

> **WARNING** *The* HttpClient *class implements the* IDisposable *interface. As a general guideline, objects implementing* IDisposable *should be disposed after its use. This is also true for the* HttpClient *class. However, the* Dispose *method of the* HttpClient *does not immediately release the associated socket; it is released after a timeout. This timeout can take 20 seconds. With this timeout, using many* HttpClient *object instances can lead to the program running out of sockets. The solution: The* HttpClient *class is built for reuse. You can use this class with many requests and not create a new instance every time.*

Making an Asynchronous Get Request

In the download code examples for this chapter is HttpClientSample. It calls a web service asynchronously in different ways. To call using the different ways demonstrated by the sample, you use command-line arguments.

The sample code makes use of the following namespaces:

```
System

System.Linq

System.Net

System.Net.Http

System.Net.Http.Headers

System.Threading

System.Threading.Tasks
```

The first code snippet instantiates an HttpClient object and assigns it to the private field _httpClient for reuse. The HttpClient object is thread-safe, so a single HttpClient object can be used to handle multiple requests. Each instance of HttpClient maintains its own thread pool, so requests between HttpClient instances are isolated.

Invoking the GetAsync makes an HTTP GET request to the server. You pass in the address of the method you're going to call. The GetAsync call is overloaded to take either a string or a URI object. The example calls into Microsoft's OData sample site http://services.odata.org, but you could alter that address to call any number of REST web services.

The call to GetAsync returns an HttpResponseMessage object. The HttpResponseMessage class represents a response including headers, status, and content. Checking the IsSuccessfulStatusCode property of the response tell you whether the request was successful. With a successful call, the content returned is retrieved as a string using the ReadAsStringAsync method (code file HttpClientSample/HttpClientSamples.cs):

```
private const string NorthwindUrl =
  "http://services.data.org/Northwind/Northwind.svc/Regions";
private const string IncorrectUrl =
  "http://services.data.org/Northwind1/Northwind.svc/Regions";

private HttpClient _httpClient;
public HttpClient HttpClient =>
  _httpClient ?? (_httpClient = new HttpClient());

private async Task GetDataSimpleAsync()
{
  HttpResponseMessage response = await HttpClient.GetAsync(NorthwindUrl);
  if(response.IsSuccessStatusCode)
    {
      Console.WriteLine($"Response Status Code: {(int)response.StatusCode} " +
        $"{response.ReasonPhrase}");
      string responseBodyAsText = await response.Content.ReadAsStringAsync();
      Console.WriteLine($"Received payload of {responseBodyAsText.Length} characters");
      Console.WriteLine();
      Console.WriteLine(responseBodyAsText);
    }
  }
}
```

Executing this code with the command-line argument -s should produce the following output:

```
Response Status Code: 200 OK
Received payload of 3379 characters
<?xml version="1.0" encoding="utf-8"?>
<!- ... ->
```

> **NOTE** *Because the* HttpClient *class used the* GetAsync *method call with the* await *keyword, the calling thread returned and could do some other work. When the result is available from the* GetAsync *method a thread continues with the method, and the response is written to the* response *variable. The* await *keyword is explained in Chapter 15, "Asynchronous Programming." Creating and using tasks is explained in Chapter 21, "Tasks and Parallel Programming."*

Throwing Exceptions

Invoking the GetAsync method of the HttpClient class by default doesn't generate an exception if the method fails. This could be easily changed by invoking the EnsureSuccessStatusCode method with the HttpResponseMessage. This method checks whether IsSuccessStatusCode is false and throws an exception otherwise (code file HttpClientSample/HttpClientSamples.cs):

```
private async Task GetDataWithExceptionsAsync()
{
  try
  {
    HttpResponseMessage response = await HttpClient.GetAsync(IncorrectUrl);
    response.EnsureSuccessStatusCode();
    ConsoleWriteLine($"Response Status Code: {(int)response.StatusCode} " +
      $"{response.ReasonPhrase}");
    string responseBodyAsText = await response.Content.ReadAsStringAsync();
    Console.WriteLine($"Received payload of {responseBodyAsText.Length} characters");
    Console.WriteLine();
    Console.WriteLine(responseBodyAsText);
  }
  catch (Exception ex)
  {
    Console.WriteLine($"{ex.Message}");
  }
}
```

Passing Headers

You didn't set or change any of the headers when you made the request, but the DefaultRequestHeaders property on HttpClient enables you to do just that. You can add headers to the collection using the Add method. After you set a header value, the header and header value are sent with every request that this instance of HttpClient sends.

By default, the response content will be in XML format. You can change this by adding an Accept header to the request to use JSON. Add the following line just before the call to GetAsync and the content is returned in JSON format:

```
client.DefaultRequestHeaders.Add("Accept", "application/json;odata=verbose");
```

Adding and removing the header and running the example will result in the content in both XML and JSON formats.

The `HttpRequestHeaders` object returned from the `DefaultHeaders` property has several helper properties to many of the standard headers. You can read the values of the headers from these properties, but they are read only. To set a value, you need to use the `Add` method. In the code snippet, the HTTP Accept header is added. Depending on the Accept header received by the server, the server can return different data formats based on the client's needs. When you send the Accept header `application/json`, the client informs the server that it accepts data in JSON format. Header information is shown with the `ShowHeaders` method that is also invoked when receiving the response from the server (code file `HttpClientSample/HttpClientSamples.cs`):

```
public Task GetDataWithHeadersAsync()
{
  try
  {
    HttpClient.DefaultRequestHeaders.Add("Accept",
      "application/json;odata=verbose");
    ShowHeaders("Request Headers:", HttpClient.DefaultRequestHeaders);

    HttpResponseMessage response = await client.GetAsync(NorthwindUrl);
    HttpClient.EnsureSuccessStatusCode();
    ShowHeaders("Response Headers:", response.Headers);
    //...
  }
}
```

Contrary to the previous sample, the `ShowHeaders` method was added, taking an `HttpHeaders` object as a parameter. `HttpHeaders` is the base class for `HttpRequestHeaders` and `HttpResponseHeaders`. The specialized classes both add helper properties to access headers directly. The `HttpHeader` object is defined as a `KeyValuePair<string, IEnumerable<string>>`. This means that each header can have more than one value in the collection. Because of this, it's important that if you want to change a value in a header, you need to remove the original value and add the new value.

The `ShowHeaders` function is pretty simple. It iterates all headers in `HttpHeaders`. The enumerator returns `KeyValuePair<string, IEnumerable<string>>` elements and shows a stringified version of the values for every key:

```
public void ShowHeaders(string title, HttpHeaders headers)
{
  Console.WriteLine(title);
  foreach (var header in headers)
  {
    string value = string.Join(" ", header.Value);
    Console.WriteLine($"Header: {header.Key} Value: {value}");
  }
  Console.WriteLine();
}
```

Running this code will now display any headers for the request:

```
Request Headers:
Header: Accept Value: application/json; odata=verbose
Response Headers:
Header: Cache-Control Value: private
Header: Date Value: Thu, 31 Aug 2017 09:58:09 GMT
Header: Server Value: Microsoft-IIS/8.0
Header: Set-Cookie Value:
ARRAffinity=a5ee7717b148daedb0164e6e19088a5a78c47693a6
0e57422887d7e011fb1e5e;Path=/;Domain=services.odata.org
Header: Vary Value: *
Header: X-Content-Type-Options Value: nosniff
```

```
Header: DataServiceVersion Value: 2.0;
Header: X-AspNet-Version Value: 4.0.30319
Header: X-Powered-By Value: ASP.NET
Header: Access-Control-Allow-Origin Value: *
Header: Access-Control-Allow-Methods Value: GET
Header: Access-Control-Allow-Headers Value: Accept, Origin, Content-Type,
MaxDataServiceVersion
Header: Access-Control-Expose-Headers Value: DataServiceVersion
```

Because the client now requests JSON data, the server returns JSON, and you can also see this information:

```
Response Status Code: 200 OK
Received payload of 1551 characters
{"d":{"results":[{"__metadata":{"id":"http://services.odata.org/Northwind/
Northwind.svc/Regions(1) ", "uri":
```

Accessing the Content

The previous code snippets have shown you how to access the Content property to retrieve a string. The Content property in the response returns an HttpContent object. In order to get the data from the HttpContent object you need to use one of the methods supplied. In the example, the ReadAsStringAsync method was used. It returns a string representation of the content. As the name implies, this is an async call. Instead of using the async keyword, the Result property could be used as well. Calling the Result property blocks the call until it's finished and then continues with execution.

Other methods to get the data from the HttpContent object are ReadAsByteArrayAsync, which returns a byte array of the data, and ReadAsStreamAsync, which returns a stream. You can also load the content into a memory buffer using LoadIntoBufferAsync.

The Headers property returns the HttpContentHeaders object. This works exactly the same way the request and response headers do in the previous example.

> **NOTE** *Instead of using the* GetAsync *and* ReadAsStringAsync *methods of the* HttpClient *and* HttpContent *classes, the* HttpClient *class also offers the method* GetStringAsync *that returns a string without the need to invoke two methods. However, when using this method, you don't have that much control over the error status and other information.*

> **NOTE** *Note Streams are explained in Chapter 22, "Files and Streams."*

Customizing Requests with HttpMessageHandler

The HttpClient class can take an HttpMessageHandler as a parameter to its constructor. This makes it possible for you to customize the request. You can pass an instance of the HttpClientHandler. There are numerous properties that can be set for things such as ClientCertificates, Pipelining, CachePolicy, ImpersonationLevel, and so on.

With the next code snippet, a SampleMessageHandler is instantiated and passed to the HttpClient constructor: (code file HttpClientSample/HttpClientSamples.cs):

```
private HttpClient _httpClientWithMessageHandler;
public HttpClient HttpClientWithMessageHandler =>
```

```
_httpClientWithMessageHandler ?? (_httpClientWithMessageHandler =
    new HttpClient(new SampleMessageHandler("error")));
```

The purpose of this handler type, `SampleMessageHandler`, is to take a string as a parameter and either display it in the console, or, if the message is "error," set the response's status code to `Bad Request`. If you create a class that derives from `HttpClientHandler`, you can override a few properties and the method `SendAsync`. `SendAsync` is typically overridden because the request to the server can be influenced. If the `_displayMessage` is set to "error", an `HttpResponseMessage` with a bad request is returned. The method needs a `Task` returned. For the error case, asynchronous methods do not need to be called; that's why the error is simply returned with `Task.FromResult` (code file `HttpClientSample/SampleMessageHandler.cs`):

```
public class SampleMessageHandler : HttpClientHandler
{
  private string _message;
  public SampleMessageHandler(string message) =>
    _message = message;

  protected override Task<HttpResponseMessage> SendAsync(
    HttpRequestMessage request, CancellationToken cancellationToken)
  {
    Console.WriteLine($"In SampleMessageHandler {_message}");
    if (_message == "error")
    {
      var response = new HttpResponseMessage(HttpStatusCode.BadRequest);
      return Task.FromResult<HttpResponseMessage>(response);
    }
    return base.SendAsync(request, cancellationToken);
  }
}
```

There are many reasons to add a custom handler. The handler pipeline is set so that multiple handlers can be added. Besides the default, there is the `DelegatingHandler`, which executes some code and then "delegates" the call back to the inner or next handler. The `HttpClientHandler` is the last handler in line and sends the request to the addressee. Figure 23-1 shows the pipeline. Each `DelegatingHandler` added would call the next or inner handler finally ending at the `HttpClientHandler`-based handler.

Creating an HttpRequestMessage Using SendAsync

Behind the scenes, the `GetAsync` method of the `HttpClient` class invokes the `SendAsync` method. Instead of using the `GetAsync` method, you can also use the `SendAsync` method to send an HTTP request. With `SendAsync` you have even more control over defining the request. The constructor of the `HttpRequestMessage` class is overloaded to pass a value of the `HttpMethod`. The `GetAsync` method creates an HTTP request with `HttpMethod.Get`. Using `HttpMethod`, you can not only send GET, POST, PUT, and DELETE requests but you can also send also HEAD, OPTIONS, and TRACE. With the `HttpRequestMessage` object in place, you can invoke the `SendAsync` method with the `HttpClient` (code file `HttpClientSample/HttpClientSamples.cs`):

```
private async Task GetDataAdvancedAsync()
{
  var request = new HttpRequestMessage(HttpMethod.Get, NorthwindUrl);
  HttpResponseMessage response = await client.SendAsync(request);
  //...
}
```

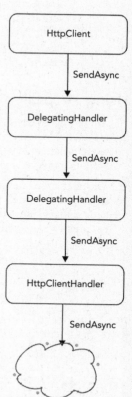

FIGURE 23-1

> **NOTE** *This chapter only makes HTTP GET requests with the* `HttpClient` *class. The* `HttpClient` *class also allows sending HTTP POST, PUT, and DELETE requests using the* `PostAsync`, `PutAsync`, *and* `DeleteAsync` *methods. These methods are used in Chapter 32, "ASP.NET Web API," where these requests are done to invoke corresponding action methods in the web service.*

After the `HttpRequestMessage` object is created, the header and content can be supplied by using the `Headers` and `Content` properties. With the `Version` property, the HTTP version can be specified.

> **NOTE** *HTTP/1.0 was specified in the year 1996 followed by 1.1 just a few years later. With 1.0, the connection was always closed after the server returned the data; with 1.1, a keep-alive header was added where the client was able to put his or her wish to keep the connection alive as the client might make more requests to receive not only the HTML code, but also CSS and JavaScript files and images. After HTTP/1.1 was defined in 1999, it took 16 years until HTTP/2 was done in the year 2015. What are the advantages of version 2? HTTP/2 allows multiple concurrent requests on the same connection, header information is compressed, the client can define which of the resources is more important, and the server can send resources to the client via server push. HTTP/2 supporting server push means WebSockets will practically be obsolete as soon as HTTP/2 is supported everywhere. All the newer versions of browsers, as well as IIS running on Windows 10 and Windows Server 2016, support HTTP/2. With .NET Core, HTTP/2 is planned (at the time of this writing) with a future milestone; see* `https://github.com/dotnet/corefx/issues/23134`.

Using HttpClient with Windows Runtime

At the time of writing this book, the `HttpClient` class used with console applications doesn't support HTTP/2. However, the `HttpClient` class used with the Universal Windows Platform has a different implementation that is based on features of the Windows 10 API. With this, `HttpClient` supports HTTP/2, and even uses this version by default.

The next code sample shows a Universal Windows app that makes an HTTP request to a link that is entered in a `TextBox` and shows the result, as well as giving information about the HTTP version. The following code snippet shows the major elements of the XAML code, and Figure 23-2 shows the user interface of the running app (code file `WinAppHttpClient/MainPage.xaml`):

```
<StackPanel Orientation="Horizontal">
  <TextBox Header="Url" Text="{x:Bind Url, Mode=TwoWay}" MinWidth="200"
    Margin="5" />
  <Button Content="Send" Click="{x:Bind OnSendRequest}" Margin="10,5,5,5"
    VerticalAlignment="Bottom" />
</StackPanel>
<TextBox Header="Version" Text="{x:Bind Version, Mode=OneWay}" Grid.Row="1"
  Margin="5" IsReadOnly="True" />
<TextBox AcceptsReturn="True" IsReadOnly="True"
  Text="{x:Bind Result, Mode=OneWay}" Grid.Row="2"
  ScrollViewer.HorizontalScrollBarVisibility="Auto"
  ScrollViewer.VerticalScrollBarVisibility="Auto" />
```

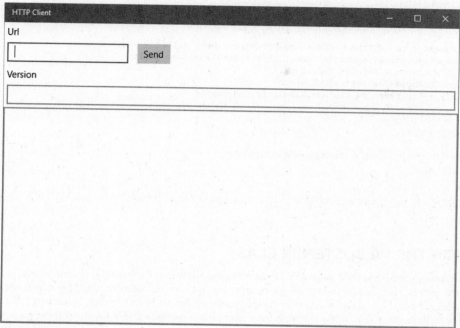

FIGURE 23-2

> **NOTE** *XAML code and dependency properties are explained in Chapter 33, "Windows Apps," and compiled binding is covered in Chapter 34, "Patterns with XAML Apps."*

The properties `Url`, `Version`, and `Result` are implemented as dependency properties for making automatic updates to the UI. The following code snippet shows the `Url` property (code file `WinAppHttpClient/MainPage.xaml.cs`):

```
public string Url
{
  get => (string)GetValue(UrlProperty);
  set => SetValue(UrlProperty, value);
}

public static readonly DependencyProperty UrlProperty =
  DependencyProperty.Register("Url", typeof(string), typeof(MainPage),
    new PropertyMetadata(string.Empty));
```

The `HttpClient` class is used in the `OnSendRequest` method. This method is invoked when clicking the `Send` button in the UI. As in the previous sample, the `SendAsync` method is used to make the HTTP request. To see that the request is indeed making a request using the HTTP/2 version, you can check the `request.Version` property from the debugger. The version answered from the server coming from `response.Version` is written to the `Version` property that is bound in the UI. Nowadays, most servers just support the HTTP 1.1 version. As mentioned previously, HTTP/2 is supported by Windows Server 2016:

```
private async void OnSendRequest()
{
  try
```

```
    {
      using (var client = new HttpClient())
      {
        var request = new HttpRequestMessage(HttpMethod.Get, Url);
        HttpResponseMessage response = await client.SendAsync(request);
        Version = response.Version.ToString();
        response.EnsureSuccessStatusCode();
        Result = await response.Content.ReadAsStringAsync();
      }
    }
    catch (Exception ex)
    {
      await new MessageDialog(ex.Message).ShowAsync();
    }
  }
```

Running the application, you make a request to `https://http2.akamai.com/demo` to see HTTP/2 returned.

WORKING WITH THE WEBLISTENER CLASS

Using Internet Information Server (IIS) as an HTTP server is usually a great approach because you have access to a lot of features, such as scalability, health monitoring, a graphical user interface for administration, and a lot more. However, you can also easily create your own simple HTTP server. Since the .NET Framework 2.0, you have been able to use the `HttpListener`, but now since .NET Core 1.0 there's a new one: the `WebListener` class.

The sample code of the `HttpServer` makes use of the following dependency and namespaces:

Dependency

`Microsoft.Net.Http.Server`

Namespaces

`Microsoft.Net.Http.Server`

`System`

`System.Collections.Generic`

`System.Linq`

`System.Net`

`System.Reflection`

`System.Text`

`System.Threading.Tasks`

The sample code for the HTTP server is a Console Application (Package) that allows passing a list of URL prefixes that defines where the server listens. An example of such a prefix is `http://localhost:8082/samples` where the server listens only to requests on port 8082 on the localhost if the path starts with samples. No matter what path follows, the server handles the request. To not only support requests from localhost, you can use the + character, such as `http://+:8082/samples`. This way the server is also accessible from all its hostnames. In case you are not starting Visual Studio from elevated mode, the user running the listener needs allowance. You can do this by running a command prompt in elevated mode and adding the URL using this `netsh` command:

```
>netsh http add urlacl url=http://+:8082/samples user=Everyone
```

The sample code checks the arguments if at least one prefix is passed and invokes the `StartServer` method afterward (code file `HttpServer/Program.cs`):

```csharp
static async Task Main(string[] args)
{
  if (args.Length < 1)
  {
    ShowUsage();
    return;
  }
  await StartServerAsync(args);
  Console.ReadLine();
}

private static void ShowUsage()
{
  Console.WriteLine("Usage: HttpServer Prefix [Prefix2] [Prefix3] [Prefix4]");
}
```

The heart of the program is the `StartServer` method. Here, the `WebListener` class is instantiated, and the prefixes as defined from the command argument list are added. Calling the `Start` method of the `WebListener` class registers the port on the system. Next, after calling the `GetContextAsync` method, the listener waits for a client to connect and send data. As soon as a client sends an HTTP request, the request can be read from the `HttpContext` object that is returned from `GetContextAsync`. For both the request that is coming from the client and the answer that is sent, the `HttpContext` object is used. The `Request` property returns a `Request` object. The `Request` object contains the HTTP header information. With an HTTP POST request, the `Request` also contains the body. The `Response` property returns a `Response` object, which allows you to return header information (using the `Headers` property), status code (`StatusCode` property), and the response body (the `Body` property):

```csharp
public static async Task StartServerAsync(params string[] prefixes)
{
  try
  {
    Console.WriteLine($"server starting at");
    var listener = new WebListener();
    foreach (var prefix in prefixes)
    {
      listener.UrlPrefixes.Add(prefix);
      Console.WriteLine($"\t{prefix}");
    }
    listener.Start();
    do
    {
      using (RequestContext context = await listener.GetContextAsync())
      {
        context.Response.Headers.Add("content-type",
        new string[] { "text/html" });
        context.Response.StatusCode = (int)HttpStatusCode.OK;
        byte[] buffer = GetHtmlContent(context.Request);
        await context.Response.Body.WriteAsync(buffer, 0, buffer.Length);
      }
    } while (true);
  }
  catch (Exception ex)
  {
    Console.WriteLine(ex.Message);
  }
}
```

The sample code returns an HTML file that is retrieved using the `GetHtmlContent` method. This method makes use of the `htmlFormat` format string with two placeholders in the heading and the body. The `GetHtmlContent` method fills in the placeholders using the `string.Format` method. To fill the HTML body, two helper methods are used that retrieve the header information from the request and all the property values of the `Request` object—GetHeaderInfo and GetRequestInfo:

```
private static string htmlFormat =
  "<!DOCTYPE html><html><head><title>{0}</title></head>" +
  "<body>{1}</body></html>";

private static byte[] GetHtmlContent(Request request)
{
  string title = "Sample WebListener";
  var sb = new StringBuilder("<h1>Hello from the server</h1>");
  sb.Append("<h2>Header Info</h2>");
  sb.Append(string.Join(" ", GetHeaderInfo(request.Headers)));
  sb.Append("<h2>Request Object Information</h2>");
  sb.Append(string.Join(" ", GetRequestInfo(request)));
  string html = string.Format(htmlFormat, title, sb.ToString());
  return Encoding.UTF8.GetBytes(html);
}
```

The `GetHeaderInfo` method retrieves the keys and values from the `HeaderCollection` to return a `div` element that contains every key and value:

```
private static IEnumerable<string> GetHeaderInfo(HeaderCollection headers) =>
  headers.Keys.Select(key =>
    $"<div>{key}: {string.Join(",", headers.GetValues(key))}</div>");
```

The `GetRequestInfo` method makes use of reflection to get all the properties of the Request type, and returns the property names as well as its values:

```
private static IEnumerable<string> GetRequestInfo(Request request) =>
  request.GetType().GetProperties().Select(
    p => $"<div>{p.Name}: {p.GetValue(request)}</div>");
```

> **NOTE** *The* GetHeaderInfo *and* GetRequestInfo *methods make use of expression-bodied member functions, LINQ, and reflection. Expression-bodied member functions are explained in Chapter 3, "Objects and Types." Chapter 12, "Language Integrated Query," explains LINQ. Chapter 16, "Reflection, Metadata, and Dynamic Programming," includes reflection as an important topic.*

Running the server and using a browser such as Google Chrome to access the server using a URL such as `http://[hostname]:8082/samples/Hello?sample=text` results in output as shown in Figure 23-3.

> **NOTE** *To access localhost from the Edge browser, you need to enable localhost loopback, which you can do via* about :flags. *On some Windows 10 builds there are issues accessing localhost from the Edge browser event if localhost loopback is enabled. In such cases use other browsers, such as Internet Explorer.*

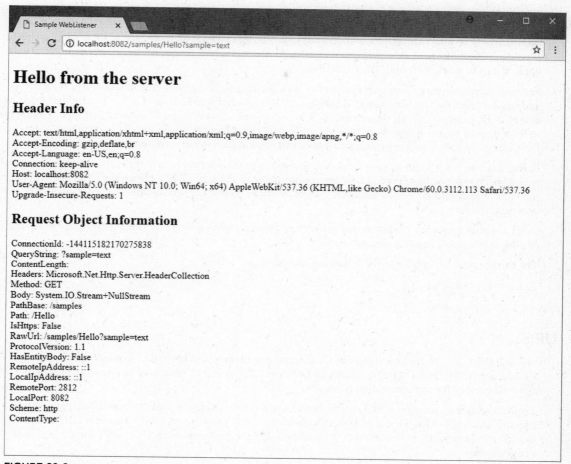

FIGURE 23-3

WORKING WITH UTILITY CLASSES

After dealing with HTTP requests and responses using classes that abstract the HTTP protocol like `HttpClient` and `WebListener`, let's have a look at some utility classes that make web programming easier when dealing with URIs and IP addresses.

On the Internet, you identify servers as well as clients by IP address or host name (also referred to as a Domain Name System (DNS) name). Generally speaking, the host name is the human-friendly name that you type in a web browser window, such as www.wrox.com or www.cninnovation.com. An IP address is the identifier that computers use to recognize each other. IP addresses are the identifiers used to ensure that web requests and responses reach the appropriate machines. It is even possible for a computer to have more than one IP address.

| CHAPTER 23 NETWORKING

An IP address can be a 32-bit or 128-bit value, depending on whether Internet Protocol version 4 (IPv4) or Internet Protocol version 6 (IPv6) is used. An example of a 32-bit IP address is `192.168.1.100`. Because there are now so many computers and other devices vying for a spot on the Internet, IPv6 was developed. IPv6 can potentially provide a maximum number of about 3×10^{38} unique addresses. .NET enables your applications to work with both IPv4 and IPv6.

For host names to work, you must first send a network request to translate the host name into an IP address—a task that's carried out by one or more DNS servers. A *DNS server* stores a table that maps host names to IP addresses for all the computers it knows about, as well as the IP addresses of other DNS servers to look up host names it does not know about. Your local computer should always know about at least one DNS server. Network administrators configure this information when a computer is set up.

Before sending out a request, your computer first asks the DNS server to give it the IP address corresponding to the host name you have typed in. When it is armed with the correct IP address, the computer can address the request and send it over the network. All this work normally happens behind the scenes while the user is browsing the web.

.NET supplies a number of classes that are able to assist with the process of looking up IP addresses and finding information about host computers.

The sample code makes use of the following namespaces:

```
System

System.Net
```

URIs

`Uri` and `UriBuilder` are two classes in the `System` namespace, and both are intended to represent a URI. `Uri` enables you to parse, combine, and compare URIs, and `UriBuilder` enables you to build a URI given the strings for the component parts.

The following code snippet demonstrates features of the `Uri` class. The constructor allows passing relative and absolute URLs. This class defines several read-only properties to access parts of a URL such as the scheme, hostname, port number, query strings, and the segments of an URL (code file `Utilities/Program.cs`):

```csharp
public static void UriSample(string url)
{
  var page = new Uri(url);
  Console.WriteLine($"scheme: {page.Scheme}");
  Console.WriteLine($"host: {page.Host}, type: {page.HostNameType}, " +
    $"idn host: {page.IdnHost}");
  Console.WriteLine($"port: {page.Port}");
  Console.WriteLine($"path: {page.AbsolutePath}");
  Console.WriteLine($"query: {page.Query}");

  foreach (var segment in page.Segments)
  {
    Console.WriteLine($"segment: {segment}");
  }
  //...
}
```

When you run the application and pass this URL and this string that contains a path and a query string `http://www.amazon.com/Professional-C-6-0-Christian-Nagel/dp/111909660X/ref=sr_1_4?ie=UTF8&amqid=1438459506&sr=8-4&keywords=professional+c%23+6`, you get the following output:

```
scheme: http
host: www.amazon.com, type: Dns, idn host: www.amazon.com
port: 80
```

```
path: /Professional-C-6-0-Christian-Nagel/dp/111909660X/ref=sr_1_4
query: ?ie=UTF8&qid=1438459506&sr=8-4&keywords=professional+c%23+6
segment: /
segment: Professional-C-6-0-Christian-Nagel/
segment: dp/
segment: 111909660X/
segment: ref=sr_1_4
```

Unlike the `Uri` class, the `UriBuilder` defines read-write properties, as shown in the following code snippet. You can create an `UriBuilder` instance, assign these properties, and get a URL returned from the `Uri` property:

```
public static void UriSample(string url)
{
    // ...
    var builder = new UriBuilder();
    builder.Host = "www.cninnovation.com";
    builder.Port = 80;
    builder.Path = "training/MVC";
    Uri uri = builder.Uri;
    Console.WriteLine(uri);
}
```

Instead of using properties with the `UriBuilder`, this class also offers several overloads of the constructor where the parts of an URL can be passed as well.

IPAddress

`IPAddress` represents an IP address. The address itself is available as a byte array using the `GetAddressBytes` property and may be converted to a dotted decimal format with the `ToString` method. `IPAddress` also implements static `Parse` and `TryParse` methods that effectively perform the reverse conversion of `ToString`—converting from a dotted decimal string to an `IPAddress`. The code sample also accesses the `AddressFamily` property and converts an IPv4 address to IPv6, and vice versa (code file `Utilities/Program.cs`):

```
public static void IPAddressSample(string ipAddressString)
{
    IPAddress address;
    if (!IPAddress.TryParse(ipAddressString, out address))
    {
        Console.WriteLine($"cannot parse {ipAddressString}");
        return;
    }
    byte[] bytes = address.GetAddressBytes();
    for (int i = 0; i < bytes.Length; i++)
    {
        Console.WriteLine($"byte {i}: {bytes[i]:X}");
    }
    Console.WriteLine($"family: {address.AddressFamily}, " +
        $"map to ipv6: {address.MapToIPv6()}, map to ipv4: {address.MapToIPv4()}");
    // ...
```

Passing the address 65.52.128.33 to the method results in this output:

```
byte 0: 41
byte 1: 34
byte 2: 80
byte 3: 21
family: InterNetwork, map to ipv6: ::ffff:65.52.128.33, map to ipv4: 65.52.128.3
3
```

The `IPAddress` class also defines static properties to create special addresses such as loopback, broadcast, and anycast:

```
public static void IPAddressSample(string ipAddressString)
{
  //...
  Console.WriteLine($"IPv4 loopback address: {IPAddress.Loopback}");
  Console.WriteLine($"IPv6 loopback address: {IPAddress.IPv6Loopback}");
  Console.WriteLine($"IPv4 broadcast address: {IPAddress.Broadcast}");
  Console.WriteLine($"IPv4 any address: {IPAddress.Any}");
  Console.WriteLine($"IPv6 any address: {IPAddress.IPv6Any}");
}
```

With a *loopback* address, the network hardware is bypassed. This is the IP address that represents the host-name localhost.

The *broadcast* address is an address that addresses every node in a local network. Such an address is not available with IPv6, as this concept is not used with the newer version of the Internet Protocol. After the initial definition of IPv4, multicasting was added for IPv6. With multicasting, a group of nodes is addressed instead of all nodes. With IPv6, multicasting completely replaces broadcasting. Both broadcast and multi-cast are shown in code samples later in this chapter when using UDP.

With an *anycast* one-to-many routing is used as well, but the data stream is only transmitted to the node closest in the network. This is useful for load balancing. With IPv4, the Border Gateway Protocol (BGP) routing protocol is used to find the shortest path in the network; with IPv6 this feature is inherent.

When you run the application, you can see the following addresses for IPv4 and IPv6:

```
IPv4 loopback address: 127.0.0.1
IPv6 loopback address: ::1
IPv4 broadcast address: 255.255.255.255
IPv4 any address: 0.0.0.0
IPv6 any address: ::
```

IPHostEntry

The `IPHostEntry` class encapsulates information related to a particular host computer. This class makes the host name available via the `HostName` property (which returns a string), and the `AddressList` property returns an array of `IPAddress` objects. You are going to use the `IPHostEntry` class in the next example.

Dns

The `Dns` class can communicate with your default DNS server to retrieve IP addresses.

The `DnsLookup` sample code makes use of the following namespaces:

    System

    System.Net

    System.Threading.Tasks

The sample application is implemented as a Console Application (package) that loops to ask the user for hostnames (you can also add an IP address instead) to get an `IPHostEntry` via `Dns.GetHostEntryAsync`. From the `IPHostEntry`, the address list is accessed using the `AddressList` property. All the addresses of the host, as well as the `AddressFamily`, are written to the console (code file `DnsLookup/Program.cs`):

```
static void Main()
{
  do
  {
    Console.Write("Hostname:\t");
    string hostname = ReadLine();
```

```
      if (hostname.CompareTo("exit") == 0)
      {
        Console.WriteLine("bye!");
        return;
      }

      OnLookupAsync(hostname).Wait();
      Console.WriteLine();
    } while (true);
  }

  public static async Task OnLookupAsync(string hostname)
  {
    try
    {
      IPHostEntry ipHost = await Dns.GetHostEntryAsync(hostname);
      Console.WriteLine($"Hostname: {ipHost.HostName}");
      foreach (IPAddress address in ipHost.AddressList)
      {
        Console.WriteLine($"Address Family: {address.AddressFamily}");
        Console.WriteLine($"Address: {address}");
      }
    }
    catch (Exception ex)
    {
      Console.WriteLine(ex.Message);
    }
  }
}
```

Run the application and enter a few hostnames to see output such as the following. With the hostname www .orf.at, you can see that this hostname defines multiple IP addresses.

```
Hostname: www.cninnovation.com
Hostname: www.cninnovation.com
Address Family: InterNetwork
Address: 65.52.128.33
Hostname: www.orf.at
Hostname: www.orf.at
Address Family: InterNetwork
Address: 194.232.104.150
Address Family: InterNetwork
Address: 194.232.104.139
Address Family: InterNetwork
Address: 194.232.104.140
Address Family: InterNetwork
Address: 194.232.104.142
Address Family: InterNetwork
Address: 194.232.104.141
Address Family: InterNetwork
Address: 194.232.104.149
Hostname: exit
bye!
```

> **NOTE** The Dns class is somewhat limited—for example, you can't define to use a server that's different than the default DNS server. Also, the Aliases property of the IPHostEntry is not populated from the method GetHostEntryAsync. It's only populated from obsolete methods of the Dns class, and these don't populate this property fully. For a full use of DNS lookups, it's better to use a third-party library.

Now it's time to move to some lower-level protocols such as TCP and UDP.

USING TCP

The HTTP protocol is based on the Transmission Control Protocol (TCP). With TCP, the client first needs to open a connection to the server before sending commands. With HTTP, textual commands are sent. The `HttpClient` and `WebListener` classes hide the details of the HTTP protocol. When you are using TCP classes and you send HTTP requests, you need to know more about the HTTP protocol. The TCP classes don't offer functionality for the HTTP protocol; you have to do this on your own. On the other side, the TCP classes give more flexibility because you can use these classes also with other protocols based on TCP.

The TCP classes offer simple methods for connecting and sending data between two endpoints. An endpoint is the combination of an IP address and a port number. Existing protocols have well-defined port numbers—for example, HTTP uses port 80, whereas SMTP uses port 25. The Internet Assigned Numbers Authority, IANA (www.iana.org), assigns port numbers to these well-known services. Unless you are implementing a well-known service, you should select a port number higher than 1,024.

TCP traffic makes up the majority of traffic on the Internet today. It is often the protocol of choice because it offers guaranteed delivery, error correction, and buffering. The `TcpClient` class encapsulates a TCP connection and provides a number of properties to regulate the connection, including buffering, buffer size, and timeouts. Reading and writing is accomplished by requesting a `NetworkStream` object via the `GetStream` method.

The `TcpListener` class listens for incoming TCP connections with the `Start` method. When a connection request arrives, you can use the `AcceptSocket` method to return a socket for communication with the remote machine, or you can use the `AcceptTcpClient` method to use a higher-level `TcpClient` object for communication. The easiest way to see how the `TcpListener` and `TcpClient` classes work together is to go through some examples.

Creating an HTTP Client Using TCP

First, create a Console Application (Package) that will send an HTTP request to a web server. You've previously done this with the `HttpClient` class, but with the `TcpClient` class you need to take a deeper look into the HTTP protocol.

The `HttpClientUsingTcp` sample code makes use of the following namespaces:

```
System

System.IO

System.Net.Sockets

System.Text

System.Threading.Tasks
```

The application accepts one command-line argument to pass the name of the server. With this, the method `RequestHtmlAsync` is invoked to make an HTTP request to the server. It returns a string with the `Result` property of the `Task` (code file `HttpClientUsingTcp/Program.cs`):

```
static void Main(string[] args)
{
  if (args.Length != 1)
  {
    ShowUsage();
  }
  Task<string> t1 = RequestHtmlAsync(args[0]);
  Console.WriteLine(t1.Result);
  Console.ReadLine();
}
```

```
private static void ShowUsage()
{
  Console.WriteLine("Usage: HttpClientUsingTcp hostname");
}
```

Now let's look at the most important parts of the `RequestHtmlAsync` method. First, a `TcpClient` object is instantiated. Second, with the method `ConnectAsync`, a TCP connection to the host is made at port 80, the default port for HTTP. Third, a stream to read and write using this connection is retrieved via the `GetStream` method:

```
private const int ReadBufferSize = 1024;
public static async Task<string> RequestHtmlAsync(string hostname)
{
  try
  {
    using (var client = new TcpClient())
    {
      await client.ConnectAsync(hostname, 80);
      NetworkStream stream = client.GetStream();
      //...
    }
  }
}
```

The stream can now be used to write a request to the server and read the response. HTTP is a text-based protocol; that's why it's easy to define the request in a string. To make a simple request to the server, the header defines the HTTP method `GET` followed by the path of the URL / and the HTTP version `HTTP/1.1`. The second line defines the `Host` header with the hostname and port number, and the third line defines the `Connection` header. Typically, with the `Connection` header the client requests `keep-alive` to ask the server to keep the connection open as the client expects to make more requests. Here we're just making a single request to the server, so the server should close the connection, thus `close` is set to the `Connection` header. To end the header information, you need to add an empty line to the request by using `\r\n`. The header information is sent with UTF-8 encoding by calling the `WriteAsync` method of the `NetworkStream`. To immediately send the buffer to the server, the `FlushAsync` method is invoked. Otherwise the data might be kept in the local cache:

```
//...
string header = "GET / HTTP/1.1\r\n" +
$"Host: {hostname}:80\r\n" +
"Connection: close\r\n" +
"\r\n";
byte[] buffer = Encoding.UTF8.GetBytes(header);
await stream.WriteAsync(buffer, 0, buffer.Length);
await stream.FlushAsync();
```

Now you can continue the process by reading the answer from the server. As you don't know how big the answer will be, you create a `MemoryStream` that grows dynamically. The answer from the server is temporarily written to a byte array using the `ReadAsync` method, and the content of this byte array is added to the `MemoryStream`. After all the data is read from the server, a `StreamReader` takes control to read the data from the stream into a string and return it to the caller:

```
var ms = new MemoryStream();
buffer = new byte[ReadBufferSize];
int read = 0;
do
{
  read = await stream.ReadAsync(buffer, 0, ReadBufferSize);
  ms.Write(buffer, 0, read);
  Array.Clear(buffer, 0, buffer.Length);
```

```
        } while (read > 0);
        ms.Seek(0, SeekOrigin.Begin);
        var reader = new StreamReader(ms);
        return reader.ReadToEnd();
    }
    //...
```

When you pass a website to the program, you see a successful request with HTML content shown in the console.

Now it's time to create a TCP listener with a custom protocol.

Creating a TCP Listener

Creating your own protocol based on TCP needs requires some advance thought about the architecture. You can define your own binary protocol where every bit is saved on the data transfer, but it's more complex to read; alternatively, you can use a text-based format such as HTTP or FTP. Should a session stay open or be closed with every request? Does the server need to keep state for a client, or is all the data sent with every request?

The custom server will support some simple functionality, such as echo and reverse a message that is sent. Another feature of the custom server is that the client can send state information and retrieve it again using another call. The state is stored temporarily in a session state. Although it's a simple scenario, you get the idea of what's needed to set this up.

The `TcpServer` sample code is implemented as a Console App (.NET Core) and makes use of the following namespaces:

```
System

System.Collections

System.Collections.Concurrent

System.Linq

System.Net.Sockets

System.Text

System.Threading

System.Threading.Tasks

static TcpServer.CustomProtocol
```

The custom TCP listener supports a few requests, as shown in the following table.

REQUEST	DESCRIPTION
`HELO::v1.0`	This command needs to be sent after initiating the connection. Other commands will not be accepted.
`ECHO::message`	The `ECHO` command returns the message to the caller.
`REV::message`	The `REV` command reserves the message and returns it to the caller.
`BYE`	The `BYE` command closes the connection.
`SET::key=value`	The `SET` command sets the server-side state that can be retrieved with the `GET` command.
`GET::key`	

The first line of the request is a session-identifier prefixed by ID. This needs to be sent with every request except the HELO request. This is used as a state identifier.

All the constants of the protocol are defined in the static class CustomProtocol (code file TcpServer/CustomProtocol.cs):

```
public static class CustomProtocol
{
  public const string SESSIONID = "ID";
  public const string COMMANDHELO = "HELO";
  public const string COMMANDECHO = "ECO";
  public const string COMMANDREV = "REV";
  public const string COMMANDBYE = "BYE";
  public const string COMMANDSET = "SET";
  public const string COMMANDGET = "GET";
  public const string STATUSOK = "OK";
  public const string STATUSCLOSED = "CLOSED";
  public const string STATUSINVALID = "INV";
  public const string STATUSUNKNOWN = "UNK";
  public const string STATUSNOTFOUND = "NOTFOUND";
  public const string STATUSTIMEOUT = "TIMOUT";
  public const string SEPARATOR = "::";
  public static readonly TimeSpan SessionTimeout = TimeSpan.FromMinutes(2);
}
```

The Run method (which is invoked from the Main method) starts a timer that cleans up all the session state every minute. The major functionality of the Run method is the start of the server by invoking the method RunServerAsync (code file TcpServer/Program.cs):

```
static void Main()
{
  var p = new Program();
  p.Run();
}

public void Run()
{
  using (var timer = new Timer(TimerSessionCleanup, null,
    TimeSpan.FromMinutes(1), TimeSpan.FromMinutes(1)))
  {
    RunServerAsync().Wait();
  }
}
```

The most important part of the server regarding the TcpListener class is in the method RunServerAsync. The TcpListener is instantiated using the constructor the IP address and port number where the listener can be accessed. Calling the Start method, the listener starts listening for client connections. The AcceptTcpClientAsync waits until a client connects. As soon as a client is connected, a TcpClient instance is returned that allows communication with the client. This instance is passed to the RunClientRequest method, where the request is dealt with.

```
private async Task RunServerAsync()
{
  try
  {
    var listener = new TcpListener(IPAddress.Any, portNumber);
    Console.WriteLine($"listener started at port {portNumber}");
    listener.Start();
    while (true)
    {
      Console.WriteLine("waiting for client...");
      TcpClient client = await listener.AcceptTcpClientAsync();
```

```
      Task t = RunClientRequest(client);
    }
  }
  catch (Exception ex)
  {
    Console.WriteLine($"Exception of type {ex.GetType().Name}, Message: {ex.Message}");
  }
}
```

To read and write from and to the client, the GetStream method of the TcpClient returns a
NetworkStream. First you need to read the request from the client. You do this by using the ReadAsync
method. The ReadAsync method fills a byte array. This byte array is converted to a string using the
Encoding class. The information received is written to the console and passed to the ParseRequest helper
method. Depending on the result of the ParseRequest method, an answer for the client is created and
returned to the client using the WriteAsync method.

```
private Task RunClientRequestAsync(TcpClient client)
{
  return Task.Run(async () =>
  {
    try
    {
      using (client)
      {
        Console.WriteLine("client connected");
        using (NetworkStream stream = client.GetStream())
        {
          bool completed = false;
          do
          {
            byte[] readBuffer = new byte[1024];
            int read = await stream.ReadAsync(readBuffer, 0, readBuffer.Length);
            string request = Encoding.ASCII.GetString(readBuffer, 0, read);
            Console.WriteLine($"received {request}");

            byte[] writeBuffer = null;
            string response = string.Empty;
            ParseResponse resp = ParseRequest(request, out string sessionId,
              out string result);
            switch (resp)
            {
              case ParseResponse.OK:
                string content = $"{STATUSOK}::{SESSIONID}::{sessionId}";
                if (!string.IsNullOrEmpty(result))
                {
                  content += $"{SEPARATOR}{result}";
                }
                response = $"{STATUSOK}{SEPARATOR}{SESSIONID}{SEPARATOR}" +
                  $"{sessionId}{SEPARATOR}{content}";
                break;
              case ParseResponse.CLOSE:
                response = $"{STATUSCLOSED}";
                completed = true;
                break;
              case ParseResponse.TIMEOUT:
                response = $"{STATUSTIMEOUT}";
                break;
              case ParseResponse.ERROR:
                response = $"{STATUSINVALID}";
                break;
```

```
                default:
                    break;
            }
            writeBuffer = Encoding.ASCII.GetBytes(response);
            await stream.WriteAsync(writeBuffer, 0, writeBuffer.Length);
            await stream.FlushAsync();
            Console.WriteLine($"returned {Encoding.ASCII.GetString(
                writeBuffer, 0, writeBuffer.Length)}");
        } while (!completed);
    }
}
catch (Exception ex)
{
    Console.WriteLine($"Exception in client request handling " +
        "of type {ex.GetType().Name}, Message: {ex.Message}");
}
Console.WriteLine("client disconnected");
});
}
```

The `ParseRequest` method parses the request and filters out the session identifier. The first call to the server (HELO) is the only call where a session identifier is not passed from the client; here it is created using the `SessionManager`. With the second and later requests, `requestColl[0]` must contain ID, and `request-Coll[1]` must contain the session identifier. Using this identifier, the `TouchSession` method updates the current time of the session identifier if the session is still valid. If it is not valid, a timeout is returned. For the functionality of the service, the `ProcessRequest` method is invoked:

```
private ParseResponse ParseRequest(string request, out string sessionId,
    out string response)
{
    sessionId = string.Empty;
    response = string.Empty;
    string[] requestColl = request.Split(
    new string[] { SEPARATOR }, StringSplitOptions.RemoveEmptyEntries);
    if (requestColl[0] == COMMANDHELO) // first request
    {
        sessionId = _sessionManager.CreateSession();
    }
    else if (requestColl[0] == SESSIONID) // any other valid request
    {
        sessionId = requestColl[1];
        if (!_sessionManager.TouchSession(sessionId))
        {
            return ParseResponse.TIMEOUT;
        }
        if (requestColl[2] == COMMANDBYE)
        {
            return ParseResponse.CLOSE;
        }
        if (requestColl.Length >= 4)
        {
            response = ProcessRequest(requestColl);
        }
    }
    else
    {
        return ParseResponse.ERROR;
    }
    return ParseResponse.OK;
}
```

The `ProcessRequest` method contains a switch statement to handle the different requests. This method in turn makes use of the `CommandActions` class to echo or reverse the message received. To store and retrieve the session state, the `SessionManager` is used:

```
private string ProcessRequest(string[] requestColl)
{
  if (requestColl.Length < 4)
    throw new ArgumentException("invalid length requestColl");

  string sessionId = requestColl[1];
  string response = string.Empty;
  string requestCommand = requestColl[2];
  string requestAction = requestColl[3];
  switch (requestCommand)
  {
    case COMMANDECHO:
      response = _commandActions.Echo(requestAction);
      break;
    case COMMANDREV:
      response = _commandActions.Reverse(requestAction);
      break;
    case COMMANDSET:
      response = _sessionManager.ParseSessionData(sessionId, requestAction);
      break;
    case COMMANDGET:
      response = $"{_sessionManager.GetSessionData(sessionId, requestAction)}";
      break;
    default:
      response = STATUSUNKNOWN;
      break;
  }
  return response;
}
```

The `CommandActions` class defines simple methods `Echo` and `Reverse` that return the action string or return the string reversed (code file `TcpServer/CommandActions.cs`):

```
public class CommandActions
{
  public string Reverse(string action) => string.Join("", action.Reverse());
  public string Echo(string action) => action;
}
```

After checking the main functionality of the server with the `Echo` and `Reverse` methods, it's time to get into the session management. What's needed on the server is an identifier and the time the session was last accessed for the purpose of removing the oldest sessions (code file `TcpServer/SessionManager.cs`):

```
public struct Session
{
  public string SessionId { get; set; }
  public DateTime LastAccessTime { get; set; }
}
```

The `SessionManager` contains thread-safe dictionaries that store all sessions and session data. When you're using multiple clients, the dictionaries can be accessed from multiple threads simultaneously. That's why thread-safe dictionaries from the namespace `System.Collections.Concurrent` are used. The `CreateSession` method creates a new session and adds it to the _sessions dictionary:

```
public class SessionManager
{
  private readonly ConcurrentDictionary<string, Session> _sessions =
    new ConcurrentDictionary<string, Session>();
  private readonly ConcurrentDictionary<string, Dictionary<string, string>>
```

```
      _sessionData =
        new ConcurrentDictionary<string, Dictionary<string, string>>();

    public string CreateSession()
    {
      string sessionId = Guid.NewGuid().ToString();
      if (_sessions.TryAdd(sessionId,
        new Session
        {
          SessionId = sessionId,
          LastAccessTime = DateTime.UtcNow
        }))
      {
        return sessionId;
      }
      else
      {
        return string.Empty;
      }
    }
    //...
  }
```

The `CleanupAllSessions` method is called every minute from a timer thread to remove all sessions that haven't been used recently. This method in turn invokes `CleanupSession`, which removes a single session. `CleanupSession` is also invoked when the client sends the BYE message:

```
public void CleanupAllSessions()
{
  foreach (var session in _sessions)
  {
    if (session.Value.LastAccessTime + SessionTimeout >= DateTime.UtcNow)
    {
      CleanupSession(session.Key);
    }
  }
}

public void CleanupSession(string sessionId)
{
  if (_sessionData.TryRemove(sessionId, out Dictionary<string, string> removed))
  {
    Console.WriteLine($"removed {sessionId} from session data");
  }
  if (_sessions.TryRemove(sessionId, out Session header))
  {
    Console.WriteLine($"removed {sessionId} from sessions");
  }
}
```

The `TouchSession` method updates the `LastAccessTime` of the session, and returns `false` if the session is no longer valid:

```
public bool TouchSession(string sessionId)
{
  if (!_sessions.TryGetValue(sessionId, out Session oldHeader))
  {
    return false;
  }
  Session updatedHeader = oldHeader;
  updatedHeader.LastAccessTime = DateTime.UtcNow;
  _sessions.TryUpdate(sessionId, updatedHeader, oldHeader);
  return true;
}
```

For setting session data, the request needs to be parsed. The action that is received for session data contains key and value separated by the equal sign, such as x=42. This is parsed from the ParseSessionData method, which in turn calls the SetSessionData method:

```csharp
public string ParseSessionData(string sessionId, string requestAction)
{
  string[] sessionData = requestAction.Split('=');
  if (sessionData.Length != 2) return STATUSUNKNOWN;
  string key = sessionData[0];
  string value = sessionData[1];
  SetSessionData(sessionId, key, value);
  return $"{key}={value}";
}
```

SetSessionData either adds or updates the session state in the dictionary. The GetSessionData retrieves the value, or returns NOTFOUND:

```csharp
public string GetSessionData(string sessionId, string key)
{
  if (!_sessionData.TryGetValue(sessionId, out Dictionary<string, string> data))
  {
    data = new Dictionary<string, string>();
    data.Add(key, value);
    _sessionData.TryAdd(sessionId, data);
  }
  else
  {
    if (data.TryGetValue(key, out string val))
    {
      data.Remove(key);
    }
    data.Add(key, value);
  }
}

public string GetSessionData(string sessionId, string key)
{
  if (_sessionData.TryGetValue(sessionId, out Dictionary<string, string> data))
  {
    if (data.TryGetValue(key, out string value))
    {
      return value;
    }
  }
  return STATUSNOTFOUND;
}
```

After compiling the listener, you can start the program. Now you need a client to connect to the server.

Creating a TCP Client

The client for the example is a UWP app with the name WinAppTCPClient. This application allows connecting to the TCP server as well as sending all the different commands that are supported by the custom protocol.

> **NOTE** *For using UWP with the* TcpClient *class, you need a version that supports .NET Standard 2.0, which starts with the Fall Creators Update of Windows 10. The downloadable code samples also include a WPF sample project.*

The user interface of the application is shown in Figure 23-4. The left-upper part allows connecting to the server. In the top-left part, a ComboBox lists all commands, and the Send button sends the command to the server. In the middle section, the session identifier and the status of the request sent will be shown. The controls in the lower part show the information received from the server and allow you to clear this information.

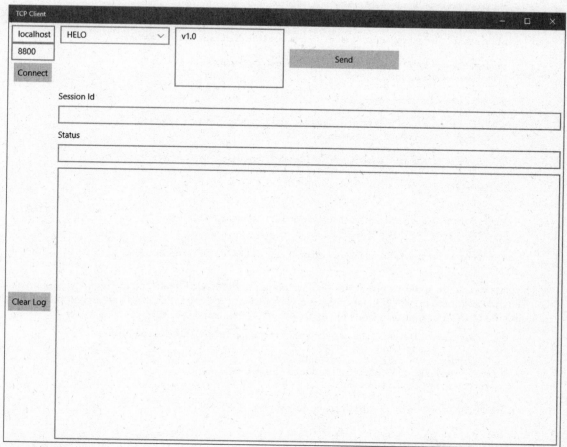

FIGURE 23-4

The classes CustomProtocolCommand and CustomProtocolCommands are used for data binding in the user interface. With CustomProtocolCommand, the Name property shows the name of the command while the Action property is the data that is entered by the user to send with the command. The class CustomProtocolCommands contains a list of the commands that are bound to the ComboBox (code file WinAppTcpClient/CustomProtocolCommands.cs):

```
public class CustomProtocolCommand
{
  public CustomProtocolCommand(string name)
    : this(name, null) { }

  public CustomProtocolCommand(string name, string action)
  {
    Name = name;
```

```
      Action = action;
    }

    public string Name { get; }
    public string Action { get; set; }

    public override string ToString() => Name;
}

public class CustomProtocolCommands : IEnumerable<CustomProtocolCommand>
{
  private readonly List<CustomProtocolCommand> _commands =
    new List<CustomProtocolCommand>();

  public CustomProtocolCommands()
  {
    string[] commands = { "HELO", "BYE", "SET", "GET", "ECO", "REV" };
    foreach (var command in commands)
    {
      _commands.Add(new CustomProtocolCommand(command));
    }
    _commands.Single(c => c.Name == "HELO").Action = "v1.0";
  }

  public IEnumerator<CustomProtocolCommand> GetEnumerator() =>
    _commands.GetEnumerator();

  IEnumerator IEnumerable.GetEnumerator() => _commands.GetEnumerator();
}
```

The class `MainPage` contains properties that are bound to the XAML code and methods that are invoked based on user interactions. This class creates an instance of the `TcpClient` class and several properties that are bound to the user interface (code file `WinAppTcpClient/MainPage.xaml.cs`):

```
public partial class MainPage : Page, INotifyPropertyChanged, IDisposable
{
  private TcpClient _client = new TcpClient();
  private readonly CustomProtocolCommands _commands =
    new CustomProtocolCommands();

  public MainWindow() => InitializeComponent();

  private string _remoteHost = "localhost";
  public string RemoteHost
  {
    get => _remoteHost;
    set => SetProperty(ref _remoteHost, value);
  }

  private int _serverPort = 8800;
  public int ServerPort
  {
    get => _serverPort;
    set => SetProperty(ref _serverPort, value);
  }

  private string _sessionId;
  public string SessionId
  {
    get => return _sessionId;
    set => SetProperty(ref _sessionId, value);
  }
```

```
    private CustomProtocolCommand _activeCommand;
    public CustomProtocolCommand ActiveCommand
    {
      get => _activeCommand;
      set => SetProperty(ref _activeCommand, value);
    }

    private string _log;
    public string Log
    {
      get => _log;
      set => SetProperty(ref _log, value);
    }

    private string _status;
    public string Status
    {
      get => return _status;
      set => SetProperty(ref _status, value);
    }
    //...
}
```

The method OnConnect is called when the user clicks the Connect button. The connection to the TCP server is made, invoking the ConnectAsync method of the TcpClient class. In case the connection is in a stale mode, and the OnConnect method is invoked once more, a SocketException is thrown where the ErrorCode is set to 0x2748. A C# exception filter is used here to handle this case of the SocketException and create a new TcpClient, so invoking OnConnect once more likely succeeds (code file WinAppTcpClient/MainPage.xaml.cs):

```
    private async void OnConnect(object sender, RoutedEventArgs e)
    {
      try
      {
        await _client.ConnectAsync(RemoteHost, ServerPort);
      }
      catch (SocketException ex) when (ex.ErrorCode == 0x2748)
      {
        _client.Dispose();
        _client = new TcpClient();
        await new MessageDialog("please retry connect").ShowAsync();
      }
      catch (Exception ex)
      {
        await new MessageDialog(ex.Message).ShowAsync();
      }
    }
```

Sending requests to the TCP server is handled by the method OnSendCommand. The code here is very similar to the sending and receiving code on the server. The GetStream method returns a NetworkStream, and this is used to write (WriteAsync) data to the server and read (ReadAsync) data from the server (code file WinAppTcpClient/MainPage.xaml.cs):

```
    private async void OnSendCommand(object sender, RoutedEventArgs e)
    {
      try
      {
        if (!VerifyIsConnected()) return;
        NetworkStream stream = _client.GetStream();
        byte[] writeBuffer = Encoding.ASCII.GetBytes(GetCommand());
        await stream.WriteAsync(writeBuffer, 0, writeBuffer.Length);
        await stream.FlushAsync();
```

```
        byte[] readBuffer = new byte[1024];
        int read = await stream.ReadAsync(readBuffer, 0, readBuffer.Length);
        string messageRead = Encoding.ASCII.GetString(readBuffer, 0, read);
        Log += messageRead + Environment.NewLine;
        ParseMessage(messageRead);
    }
    catch (Exception ex)
    {
        await new MessageDialog(ex.Message).ShowAsync();
    }
}
```

To build up the data that can be sent to the server, the `GetCommand` method is invoked from within `OnSendCommand`. `GetCommand` in turn invokes the method `GetSessionHeader` to build up the session identifier, and then takes the `ActiveCommand` property (of type `CustomProtocolCommand`) that contains the selected command name and the entered data:

```
private string GetCommand() =>
  $"{GetSessionHeader()}{ActiveCommand?.Name}::{ActiveCommand?.Action}";

private string GetSessionHeader()
{
  if (string.IsNullOrEmpty(SessionId)) return string.Empty;
  return $"ID::{SessionId}::";
}
```

The `ParseMessage` method is used after the data is received from the server. This method splits up the message to set the `Status` and `SessionId` properties:

```
private void ParseMessage(string message)
{
  if (string.IsNullOrEmpty(message)) return;
  string[] messageColl = message.Split(
    new string[] { "::" }, StringSplitOptions.RemoveEmptyEntries);
  Status = messageColl[0];
  SessionId = GetSessionId(messageColl);
}
```

When you run the application, you can connect to the server, select commands, set values for echo and reverse returns, and see all the messages coming from the server, as shown in Figure 23-5.

TCP Versus UDP

The next protocol covered is UDP (User Datagram Protocol). UDP is a simple protocol with little overhead. Before sending and receiving data with TCP, a connection needs to be made. This is not necessary with UDP. With UDP, just start sending or receiving. Of course, that means that UDP has less overhead than TCP, but it is also more unreliable. When you send data with UDP, you don't get information when this data is received. UDP is often used for situations in which the speed and performance requirements outweigh the reliability requirements—for example, video streaming. UDP also offers broadcasting messages to a group of nodes. On the other hand, TCP offers a number of features to confirm the delivery of data. TCP provides error correction and retransmission in the case of lost or corrupted packets. Last, but hardly least, TCP buffers incoming and outgoing data and guarantees that a sequence of packets scrambled in transmission is reassembled before delivery to the application. Even with the extra overhead, TCP is the most widely used protocol across the Internet because of its high reliability.

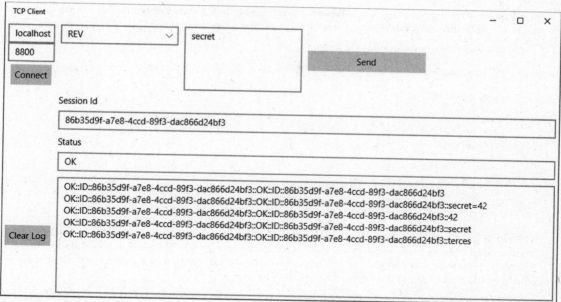

FIGURE 23-5

USING UDP

To demonstrate UDP, you create two Console Application (Package) projects that show various features of UDP: directly sending data to a host, broadcasting data to all hosts on the local network, and multicasting data to a group of nodes that belong to the same group.

The `UdpSender` and `UdpReceiver` projects use the following namespaces:

```
System

System.Linq

System.Net

System.Net.Sockets

System.Text

System.Threading.Tasks
```

Building a UDP Receiver

Start with the receiving application. This application makes use of command-line arguments where you can control the different features of the application. A command-line argument that is required is `-p`, which specifies the port number where the receiver is available to receive data. An optional argument is `-g` with a group address for multicasting. The `ParseCommandLine` method parses the command-line arguments and puts the results into the variables `port` and `groupAddress` (code file `UdpReceiver/Program.cs`):

```
static async Task Main(string[] args)
{
  if (!ParseCommandLine(args, out int port, out string groupAddress))
  {
    ShowUsage();
    return;
  }
  await ReaderAsync(port, groupAddress);
  Console.ReadLine();
}

private static void ShowUsage()
{
  Console.WriteLine("Usage: UdpReceiver -p port [-g groupaddress]");
}
```

The `Reader` method creates a `UdpClient` object with the port number that's passed in the program arguments. The `ReceiveAsync` method waits until some data arrives. This data can be found with the `UdpReceiveResult` with the `Buffer` property. After the data is encoded to a string, it's written to the console to continue the loop and wait for the next data to receive:

```
private static async Task ReaderAsync(int port, string groupAddress)
{
  using (var client = new UdpClient(port))
  {
    if (groupAddress != null)
    {
      client.JoinMulticastGroup(IPAddress.Parse(groupAddress));
      Console.WriteLine(
        $"joining the multicast group {IPAddress.Parse(groupAddress)}");
    }

    bool completed = false;
    do
    {
      Console.WriteLine("starting the receiver");
      UdpReceiveResult result = await client.ReceiveAsync();
      byte[] datagram = result.Buffer;
      string received = Encoding.UTF8.GetString(datagram);
      Console.WriteLine($"received {received}");
      if (received == "bye")
      {
        completed = true;
      }
    } while (!completed);
    Console.WriteLine("receiver closing");
    if (groupAddress != null)
    {
      client.DropMulticastGroup(IPAddress.Parse(groupAddress));
    }
  }
}
```

When you start the application, it waits for a sender to send data. For the time being, ignore the multicast group and just use the argument with the port number because multicasting is discussed after you create the sender.

Creating a UDP Sender

The UDP sender application also enables you to configure it by passing command-line options. It has more options than the receiving application. Besides the command-line argument -p to specify the port number, the sender allows -b for a broadcast to all nodes in the local network, -h to identify a specific host, -g to specify a group, and -ipv6 to indicate that IPv6 should be used instead of IPv4 (code file UdpSender/Program.cs):

```
static async Task Main(string[] args)
{
  if (!ParseCommandLine(args, out int port, out string hostname, out bool broadcast,
    out string groupAddress, out bool ipv6))
  {
    ShowUsage();
    Console.ReadLine();
    return;
  }

  IPEndpoint endpoint = await GetIPEndPointAsync(port, hostname, broadcast,
    groupAddress, ipv6);
  await SenderAsync(endpoint, broadcast, groupAddress);
  Console.WriteLine("Press return to exit...");
  Console.ReadLine();
}

private static void ShowUsage()
{
  Console.WriteLine("Usage: UdpSender -p port [-g groupaddress | -b | -h hostname] " +
    "[-ipv6]");
  Console.WriteLine("\t-p port number\tEnter a port number for the sender");
  Console.WriteLine("\t-g group address\tGroup address in the range 224.0.0.0 " +
    "to 239.255.255.255");
  Console.WriteLine("\t-b\tFor a broadcast");
  Console.WriteLine("\t-h hostname\tUse the hostname option if the message should " +
    "be sent to a single host");
}
```

To send data, you need an IPEndPoint. Depending on the program arguments, you create this in different ways. With a broadcast, IPv4 defines the address 255.255.255.255 that is returned from IPAddress .Broadcast. There's no IPv6 address for broadcast because IPv6 doesn't support broadcasts. IPv6's replacement for broadcasts are multicasts. Multicasts have been added to IPv4 as well. When you're passing a hostname, the hostname is resolved using DNS lookup using the Dns class. The method GetHostEntryAsync returns an IPHostEntry where the IPAddress can be retrieved from the AddressList property. Depending on whether IPv4 or IPv6 is used, a different IPAddress is taken from this list. Depending on your network environment, only one of these address types might work. If a group address is passed to the method, the address is parsed using IPAddress.Parse:

```
public static async Task<IPEndPoint> GetIPEndPoint(int port, string hostName,
bool broadcast, string groupAddress, bool ipv6)
{
  IPEndPoint endpoint = null;
  try
  {
    if (broadcast)
    {
      endpoint = new IPEndPoint(IPAddress.Broadcast, port);
    }
    else if (hostName != null)
```

```
    {
      IPHostEntry hostEntry = await Dns.GetHostEntryAsync(hostName);
      IPAddress address = null;
      if (ipv6)
      {
        address = hostEntry.AddressList.Where(
            a => a.AddressFamily == AddressFamily.InterNetworkV6)
          .FirstOrDefault();
      }
      else
      {
        address = hostEntry.AddressList.Where(
            a => a.AddressFamily == AddressFamily.InterNetwork)
          .FirstOrDefault();
      }
      if (address == null)
      {
        Func<string> ipversion = () => ipv6 ? "IPv6" : "IPv4";
        Console.WriteLine($"no {ipversion()} address for {hostName}");
        return null;
      }
      endpoint = new IPEndPoint(address, port);
    }
    else if (groupAddress != null)
    {
      endpoint = new IPEndPoint(IPAddress.Parse(groupAddress), port);
    }
    else
    {
      throw new InvalidOperationException($"{nameof(hostName)}, "
        + "{nameof(broadcast)}, or {nameof(groupAddress)} must be set");
    }
  }
  catch (SocketException ex)
  {
    Console.WriteLine(ex.Message);
  }
  return endpoint;
}
```

Now, regarding the UDP protocol, the most important part of the sender follows. After creating a `UdpClient` instance and converting a string to a byte array, data is sent using the `SendAsync` method. Note that neither the receiver needs to listen, nor the sender needs to connect. UDP is really simple. However, in a case in which the sender sends the data to nowhere—nobody receives the data—you also don't get any error messages:

```
private async Task Sender(IPEndpoint endpoint, bool broadcast,
  string groupAddress)
{
  try
  {
    string localhost = Dns.GetHostName();
    using (var client = new UdpClient())
    {
      client.EnableBroadcast = broadcast;
      if (groupAddress != null)
      {
        client.JoinMulticastGroup(IPAddress.Parse(groupAddress));
      }
      bool completed = false;
      do
```

```
        {
          Console.WriteLine("Enter a message or bye to exit");
          string input = Console.ReadLine();
          Console.WriteLine();
          completed = input == "bye";
          byte[] datagram = Encoding.UTF8.GetBytes($"{input} from {localhost}");
          int sent = await client.SendAsync(datagram, datagram.Length, endpoint);
        } while (!completed);

        if (groupAddress != null)
        {
          client.DropMulticastGroup(IPAddress.Parse(groupAddress));
        }
      }
    }
    catch (SocketException ex)
    {
      Console.WriteLine(ex.Message);
    }
  }
```

Now you can start the receiver with this option:

```
-p 9400
```

and the sender with this option:

```
-p 9400 -h localhost
```

You can enter data in the sender that will arrive in the receiver. If you stop the receiver, you can go on sending without detecting any error. You can also try to use a hostname instead of localhost and run the receiver on a different system.

With the sender, you can add the -b option and remove the hostname to send a broadcast to all nodes listening to port 9400 on the same network:

```
-p 9400 -b
```

Be aware that broadcasts don't cross most routers, and of course you can't use broadcasts on the Internet. This situation is different with multicasts, discussed next.

Using Multicasts

Broadcasts don't cross routers, but multicasts can. Multicasts have been invented to send messages to a group of systems—all nodes that belong to the same group. With IPv4, specific IP addresses are reserved for multicast use. The addresses start with 224.0.0.0 to 239.255.255.253. Many of these addresses are reserved for specific protocols—for example, for routers—but 239.0.0.0/8 can be used privately within an organization. This is very similar to IPv6, which has well-known IPv6 multicast addresses for different routing protocols. Addresses f::/16 are local within an organization; addresses ffxe::/16 have global scope and can be routed over public Internet.

For a sender or receiver to use multicasts, it must join a multicast group by invoking the JoinMulticastGroup method of the UdpClient:

```
client.JoinMulticastGroup(IPAddress.Parse(groupAddress));
```

To leave the group again, you can invoke the method DropMulticastGroup:

```
client.DropMulticastGroup(IPAddress.Parse(groupAddress));
```

When you start both the receiver and sender with these options,

```
-p 9400 -g 230.0.0.1
```

they both belong to the same group, and multicasting is in action. As with broadcasting, you can start multiple receivers and multiple senders. The receivers will receive nearly all messages from each receiver.

USING SOCKETS

The HTTP protocol is based on TCP, and thus the `HttpXX` classes offered an abstraction layer over the `TcpXX` classes. The `TcpXX` classes, however, give you more control. You can even get more control than offered by the `TcpXX` or `UdpXX` classes with sockets. With sockets, you can use different protocols, not only protocols based on TCP or UDP, and also create your own protocol. What might be even more important is that you can have more control over TCP- or UDP-based protocols.

The `SocketServerSender` and `SocketClient` projects are implemented as Console Application (Package) and use these namespaces:

```
System

System.Linq

System.IO

System.Net

System.Net.Sockets

System.Text

System.Threading

System.Threading.Tasks
```

Creating a Listener Using Sockets

Let's start with a server that listens to incoming requests. The server requires a port number that is expected with the program arguments. With this, it invokes the `Listener` method (code file `SocketServer/Program.cs`):

```csharp
static void Main(string[] args)
{
  if (args.Length != 1)
  {
    ShowUsage();
    return;
  }

  if (!int.TryParse(args[0], out int port))
  {
    ShowUsage();
    return;
  }

  Listener(port);
  Console.ReadLine();
}

private void ShowUsage()
{
  Console.WriteLine("SocketServer port");
}
```

The most important code with regard to sockets is in the following code snippet. The listener creates a new `Socket` object. With the constructor, the `AddressFamily`, `SocketType`, and `ProtocolType` are supplied.

The `AddressFamily` is a large enumeration that offers many different networks. Examples are *DECnet*, which was released 1975 by Digital Equipment and used as main network communication between PDP-11 systems; Banyan VINES, which was used to connect client machines; and, of course, `InetnetWork` for IPv4 and `InternetWorkV6` for IPv6. As mentioned previously, you can use sockets for a large number of networking protocols. The second parameter `SocketType` specifies the kind of socket. Examples are `Stream` for TCP, `Dgram` for UDP, or `Raw` for raw sockets. The third parameter is an enumeration for the `ProtocolType`. Examples are `IP`, `Ucmp`, `Udp`, `IPv6`, and `Raw`. The settings you choose need to match. For example, using TCP with IPv4, the address family must be `InterNetwork`, the socket type `Stream`, and the protocol type `Tcp`. To create a UDP communication with IPv4, the address family needs to be set to `InterNetwork`, the socket type `Dgram`, and the protocol type `Udp`.

```
public static void Listener(int port)
{
    var listener = new Socket(AddressFamily.InterNetwork, SocketType.Stream,
    ProtocolType.Tcp);
    listener.ReceiveTimeout = 5000; // receive timout 5 seconds
    listener.SendTimeout = 5000; // send timeout 5 seconds
    //...
```

The listener socket returned from the constructor is bound to an IP address and port numbers. With the sample code, the listener is bound to all local IPv4 addresses and the port number is specified with the argument. Calling the `Listen` method starts the listening mode of the socket. The socket can now accept incoming connection requests. Specifying the parameter with the `Listen` method defines the size of the backlog queue—how many clients can connect concurrently before their connection is dealt with:

```
public static void Listener(int port)
{
    //...
    listener.Bind(new IPEndPoint(IPAddress.Any, port));
    listener.Listen(backlog: 15);
    Console.WriteLine($"listener started on port {port}");
    //...
```

Waiting for the client to connect happens in the `Accept` method of the `Socket` class. This method blocks the thread until a client connects. After a client connects, this method needs to be invoked again to fulfill requests of other clients; this is why this method is called within a `while` loop. For the listening, a separate task, which can be canceled from the calling thread, is started. The task to read and write using the socket happens within the method `CommunicateWithClientUsingSocketAsync`. This method receives the `Socket` instance that is bound to the client to read and write:

```
public static void Listener(int port)
{
    //...
    var cts = new CancellationTokenSource();
    var tf = new TaskFactory(TaskCreationOptions.LongRunning,
    TaskContinuationOptions.None);
    tf.StartNew(() => // listener task
    {
        Console.WriteLine("listener task started");
        while (true)
        {
            if (cts.Token.IsCancellationRequested)
            {
                cts.Token.ThrowIfCancellationRequested();
                break;
            }
            Console.WriteLine("waiting for accept");

            Socket client = listener.Accept();
            if (!client.Connected)
            {
```

```
            Console.WriteLine("not connected");
            continue;
        }
        Console.WriteLine($"client connected local address " +
            $"{((IPEndPoint)client.LocalEndPoint).Address} and port " +
            $"{((IPEndPoint)client.LocalEndPoint).Port}, remote address " +
            $"{((IPEndPoint)client.RemoteEndPoint).Address} and port " +
            $"{((IPEndPoint)client.RemoteEndPoint).Port}");
        Task t = CommunicateWithClientUsingSocketAsync(client);
    }
    listener.Dispose();
    Console.WriteLine("Listener task closing");
}, cts.Token);
Console.WriteLine("Press return to exit");
Console.ReadLine();
cts.Cancel();
}
```

For the communication with the client, a new task is created. This frees the listener task to immediately make the next iteration to wait for the next client connection. The `Receive` method of the `Socket` class accepts a buffer where data can be read to as well as flags for the socket. This byte array is converted to a string and sent back to the client with a small change using the `Send` method:

```
private static Task CommunicateWithClientUsingSocketAsync(Socket socket)
{
    return Task.Run(() =>
    {
        try
        {
            using (socket)
            {
                bool completed = false;
                do
                {
                    byte[] readBuffer = new byte[1024];
                    int read = socket.Receive(readBuffer, 0, 1024, SocketFlags.None);
                    string fromClient = Encoding.UTF8.GetString(readBuffer, 0, read);
                    Console.WriteLine($"read {read} bytes: {fromClient}");
                    if (string.Compare(fromClient, "shutdown", ignoreCase: true) == 0)
                    {
                        completed = true;
                    }
                    byte[] writeBuffer = Encoding.UTF8.GetBytes($"echo {fromClient}");
                    int send = socket.Send(writeBuffer);
                    Console.WriteLine($"sent {send} bytes");
                } while (!completed);
            }
            Console.WriteLine("closed stream and client socket");
        }
        catch (Exception ex)
        {
            Console.WriteLine(ex.Message);
        }
    });
}
```

The server is ready as it is. However, let's look at different ways to make the read and write communication by extending the abstraction level.

Using NetworkStream with Sockets

You've already used the `NetworkStream` class with the `TcpClient` and `TcpListener` classes. The `NetworkStream` constructor allows passing a `Socket`, so you can use the `Stream` methods `Read` and `Write` instead of socket's `Send` and `Receive` methods. With the constructor of the `NetworkStream` you can define whether the stream should own the socket. If—as in this code snippet—the stream owns the socket, the socket will be closed when the stream is closed (code file `SocketServer/Program.cs`):

```
private static async Task CommunicateWithClientUsingNetworkStreamAsync(
  Socket socket)
{
  try
  {
    using (var stream = new NetworkStream(socket, ownsSocket: true))
    {
      bool completed = false;
      do
      {
        byte[] readBuffer = new byte[1024];
        int read = await stream.ReadAsync(readBuffer, 0, 1024);
        string fromClient = Encoding.UTF8.GetString(readBuffer, 0, read);
        Console.WriteLine($"read {read} bytes: {fromClient}");
        if (string.Compare(fromClient, "shutdown", ignoreCase: true) == 0)
        {
          completed = true;
        }
        byte[] writeBuffer = Encoding.UTF8.GetBytes($"echo {fromClient}");
        await stream.WriteAsync(writeBuffer, 0, writeBuffer.Length);
      } while (!completed);
    }
    Console.WriteLine("closed stream and client socket");
  }
  catch (Exception ex)
  {
    Console.WriteLine(ex.Message);
  }
}
```

To use this method in the code sample, you need to change the `Listener` method to invoke the method `CommunicateWithClientUsingNetworkStreamAsync` instead of the method `CommunicateWithClientUsingSocketAsync`.

Using Readers and Writers with Sockets

Let's add one more abstraction layer. Because the `NetworkStream` derives from the `Stream` class, you can also use readers and writers to access the socket. What you need to pay attention to is the lifetime of the readers and writers. Calling the `Dispose` method of a reader or writer also disposes the underlying stream. That's why a constructor of the `StreamReader` and `StreamWriter` was selected where the `leaveOption` argument can be set to true. With this in place, the underlying stream is not disposed on disposing the readers and writers. The `NetworkStream` is disposed on the end of the outer `using` statement, and this in turn closes the socket because here the socket is owned. There's another aspect that you need to be aware of when using writers with sockets: By default, the writer doesn't flush the data, so they are kept in the cache until the cache is full. Using network streams, you might need to get an answer faster. Here you can set the `AutoFlush` property to true (an alternative would be to invoke the `FlushAsync` method):

```
public static async Task CommunicateWithClientUsingReadersAndWritersAsync(
  Socket socket)
{
  try
  {
```

```
      using (var stream = new NetworkStream(socket, ownsSocket: true))
      using (var reader = new StreamReader(stream, Encoding.UTF8, false,
        8192, leaveOpen: true))
      using (var writer = new StreamWriter(stream, Encoding.UTF8,
        8192, leaveOpen: true))
      {
        writer.AutoFlush = true;
        bool completed = false;
        do
        {
          string fromClient = await reader.ReadLineAsync();
          Console.WriteLine($"read {fromClient}");
          if (string.Compare(fromClient, "shutdown", ignoreCase: true) == 0)
          {
            completed = true;
          }
          await writer.WriteLineAsync($"echo {fromClient}");
        } while (!completed);
      }
      Console.WriteLine("closed stream and client socket");
    }
    catch (Exception ex)
    {
      Console.WriteLine(ex.Message);
    }
  }
}
```

To use this method in the code sample, you need to change the `Listener` method to invoke
the method `CommunicateWithClientUsingReadersAndWritersAsync` instead of the method
`CommunicateWithClientUsingSocketAsync`.

> **NOTE** *Streams, readers, and writers are explained in detail in Chapter 22.*

Implementing a Receiver Using Sockets

The receiver application `SocketClient` is implemented as a Console Application (Package) as well. With
the command-line arguments, the hostname and the port number of the server need to be passed. With a
successful command-line parsing, the method `SendAndReceive` is invoked to communicate with the server
(code file `SocketClient/Program.cs`):

```
static async Task Main(string[] args)
{
  if (args.Length != 2)
  {
    ShowUsage();
    return;
  }

  string hostName = args[0];
  if (!int.TryParse(args[1], out int port))
  {
    ShowUsage();
    return;
  }
  Console.WriteLine("press return when the server is started");
  Console.ReadLine();
  await SendAndReceiveAsync(hostName, port);
```

```
      Console.ReadLine();
    }

    private static void ShowUsage()
    {
      Console.WriteLine("Usage: SocketClient server port");
    }
```

The `SendAndReceive` method uses DNS name resolution to get the `IPHostEntry` from the hostname. This `IPHostEntry` is used to get an IPv4 address of the host. After the `Socket` instance is created (in the same way it was created for the server code), the address is used with the `Connect` method to make a connection to the server. After the connection was done, the methods `Sender` and `Receiver` are invoked that create different tasks, which enables you to run these methods concurrently. The receiver client can simultaneously read and write from and to the server:

```
public static async Task SendAndReceiveAsync(string hostName, int port)
{
  try
  {
    IPHostEntry ipHost = await Dns.GetHostEntryAsync(hostName);
    IPAddress ipAddress = ipHost.AddressList.Where(
      address => address.AddressFamily == AddressFamily.InterNetwork).First();
    if (ipAddress == null)
    {
      Console.WriteLine("no IPv4 address");
      return;
    }

    using (var client = new Socket(AddressFamily.InterNetwork,
      SocketType.Stream, ProtocolType.Tcp))
    {
      client.Connect(ipAddress, port);
      Console.WriteLine("client successfully connected");
      var stream = new NetworkStream(client);
      var cts = new CancellationTokenSource();
      Task tSender = SenderAsync(stream, cts);
      Task tReceiver = ReceiverAsync(stream, cts.Token);
      await Task.WhenAll(tSender, tReceiver);
    }
  }
  catch (SocketException ex)
  {
    Console.WriteLine(ex.Message);
  }
}
```

> **NOTE** *If you change the filtering of the address list to get an IPv6 address instead of an IPv4 address, you also need to change the* `Socket` *invocation to create a socket for the IPv6 address family.*

The `Sender` method asks the user for input and sends this data to the network stream with the `WriteAsync` method. The `Receiver` method receives data from the stream with the `ReadAsync` method. After the user enters the termination string, cancellation is sent from the `Sender` task via a `CancellationToken`:

```
public static async Task SenderAsync(NetworkStream stream,
  CancellationTokenSource cts)
{
  Console.WriteLine("Sender task");
```

```
    while (true)
    {
      Console.WriteLine("enter a string to send, shutdown to exit");
      string line = Console.ReadLine();
      byte[] buffer = Encoding.UTF8.GetBytes($"{line}\r\n");
      await stream.WriteAsync(buffer, 0, buffer.Length);
      await stream.FlushAsync();
      if (string.Compare(line, "shutdown", ignoreCase: true) == 0)
      {
        cts.Cancel();
        Console.WriteLine("sender task closes");
        break;
      }
    }
  }

  private const int ReadBufferSize = 1024;

  public static async Task ReceiverAsync(NetworkStream stream,
    CancellationToken token)
  {
    try
    {
      stream.ReadTimeout = 5000;
      Console.WriteLine("Receiver task");
      byte[] readBuffer = new byte[ReadBufferSize];
      while (true)
      {
        Array.Clear(readBuffer, 0, ReadBufferSize);
        int read = await stream.ReadAsync(readBuffer, 0, ReadBufferSize, token);
        string receivedLine = Encoding.UTF8.GetString(readBuffer, 0, read);
        Console.WriteLine($"received {receivedLine}");
      }
    }
    catch (OperationCanceledException ex)
    {
      Console.WriteLine(ex.Message);
    }
  }
```

When you run both the client and server, you can see communication across TCP.

> **NOTE** *The sample code implements a TCP client and server. TCP requires a connection before sending and receiving data; this is done by calling the* Connect *method. For UDP, the* Connect *method could be invoked as well, but it doesn't do a connection. With UDP, instead of calling the* Connect *method, you can use the* SendTo *and* ReceiveFrom *methods instead. These methods require an* EndPoint *parameter where the endpoint is defined just when sending and receiving.*

> **NOTE** *Cancellation tokens are explained in Chapter 21.*

SUMMARY

This chapter described the .NET classes available in the `System.Net` namespace for communication across networks. You have seen some of the .NET base classes that deal with opening client connections on the network and Internet, and how to send requests to and receive responses from servers.

As a rule of thumb, when programming with classes in the `System.Net` namespace, you should always try to use the most generic class possible. For instance, using the `TcpClient` class instead of the `Socket` class isolates your code from many of the lower-level socket details. Moving one step higher, the `HttpClient` class is an easy way to make use of the HTTP protocol.

This book covers much more networking than the core networking features you've seen in this chapter. Chapter 32 covers ASP.NET Web API to offer services using the HTTP protocol. In Bonus Chapter 3, which you can find online, you read about WebHooks and SignalR—two technologies that offers event-driven communication.

In the next chapter, you read about security. You can see the `CryptoStream` in action for encrypting streams, no matter whether they are used with files or networking.

24

Security

WROX.COM CODE DOWNLOADS FOR THIS CHAPTER

The Wrox.com code downloads for this chapter are found at www.wrox.com on the Download Code tab. The source code is also available in the GitHub repository https://github.com/ ProfessionalCSharp/ProfessionalCSharp7 in the folder Security. The code for this chapter is divided into the following major examples:

➤ WindowsPrincipal
➤ SigningDemo
➤ SecureTransfer
➤ RSASample
➤ DataProtection
➤ UserSecretsSample
➤ FileAccessControl
➤ WebApplicationSecurity

INTRODUCTION

Security has several key elements that you need to consider to make your applications secure. The primary one, of course, is the user of the application. Is the user the person authorized to access the application, or someone posing as the user? How can this user be trusted? As you see in this chapter, ensuring the security of an application in regard of the user is a two-part process: First, users need to be authenticated, and then they need to be authorized to verify that they are allowed to use the requested resources.

What about data that is stored or sent across the network? Is it possible for someone to access this data, for example, by using a network sniffer? Encryption of data is important in this regard. Some technologies, such as Windows Communication Foundation (WCF), provide encryption capabilities by simple configuration, so you can see what's done behind the scenes.

Yet another aspect is the application itself. If the application is hosted by a web provider, how is the application restricted from doing harm to the server?

This chapter explores the features available in .NET to help you manage security, demonstrating how .NET protects you from malicious code, how to administer security policies, and how to access the security subsystem programmatically.

You can also read about the issues you need to be aware of when making web applications secure.

VERIFYING USER INFORMATION

Two fundamental pillars of security are authentication and authorization. *Authentication* is the process of identifying the user, and *authorization* occurs afterward to verify that the identified user is allowed to access a specific resource. This section shows how to get information about users with identities and principals.

Working with Windows Identities

You can identify the user running the application by using an *identity*. The WindowsIdentity class represents a Windows user. If you don't identify the user with a Windows account, you can use other classes that implement the interface IIdentity. With this interface you have access to the name of the user, information about whether the user is authenticated, and the authentication type.

A *principal* is an object that contains the identity of the user and the roles to which the user belongs. The interface IPrincipal defines the property Identity, which returns an IIdentity object, and the method IsInRole with which you can verify that the user is a member of a specific role. A *role* is a collection of users who have the same security permissions, and it is the unit of administration for users. Roles can be Windows groups or just a collection of strings that you define.

The principal classes available with .NET are WindowsPrincipal, GenericPrincipal, and RolePrincipal. Since .NET 4.5, these principal types derive from the base class ClaimsPrincipal. You can also create a custom principal class that implements the interface IPrincipal or derives from ClaimsPrincipal.

The sample code runs only on Windows and makes use of the following dependency and namespaces:

Dependency

System.Security.Principal.Windows

Namespaces

System

System.Collections.Generic

System.Security.Claims

System.Security.Principal

The following example creates a Console App (.NET Core) that provides access to the principal in an application that, in turn, enables you to access the underlying Windows account. You need to import the System.Security.Principal and System.Security.Claims namespaces. The Main method invokes the method `ShowIdentityInformation` to write information about the `WindowsIdentity` to the console, `ShowPrincipal` to write additional information that is available with principals, and `ShowClaims` to write information about claims (code file `WindowsPrincipal/Program.cs`):

```
static void Main()
{
  WindowsIdentity identity = ShowIdentityInformation();
  WindowsPrincipal principal = ShowPrincipal(identity);
  ShowClaims(principal.Claims);
}
```

The method `ShowIdentityInformation` creates a `WindowsIdentity` object by invoking the static `GetCurrent` method of the `WindowsIdentity` and accesses its properties to show the identity type, name of the identity, authentication type, and other values (code file `WindowsPrincipal/Program.cs`):

```
public static WindowsIdentity ShowIdentityInformation()
{
  WindowsIdentity identity = WindowsIdentity.GetCurrent();
  if (identity == null)
  {
    Console.WriteLine("not a Windows Identity");
    return null;
  }
  Console.WriteLine($"IdentityType: {identity}");
  Console.WriteLine($"Name: {identity.Name}");
  Console.WriteLine($"Authenticated: {identity.IsAuthenticated}");
  Console.WriteLine($"Authentication Type: {identity.AuthenticationType}");
  Console.WriteLine($"Anonymous? {identity.IsAnonymous}");
  Console.WriteLine($"Access Token: " +
    $"{identity.AccessToken.DangerousGetHandle()}");
  Console.WriteLine();
  return identity;
}
```

All identity classes, such as `WindowsIdentity`, implement the `IIdentity` interface, which contains three properties—`AuthenticationType`, `IsAuthenticated`, and `Name`—for all derived identity classes to implement. The other properties you've seen with the `WindowsIdentity` are specific to this kind of identity.

When you run the application, you see information like what's shown in the following snippet. The authentication type shows CloudAP because I'm logged into the system using a Microsoft Live account. Active Directory shows up in the authentication type if you're using Active Directory:

```
IdentityType: System.Security.Principal.WindowsIdentity
Name: THEROCKS\Christian
Authenticated: True
Authentication Type: CloudAP
Anonymous? False
Access Token: 564
```

Windows Principals

A principal contains an identity and offers additional information, such as roles the user belongs to. Principals implement the interface `IPrincipal`, which offers the method `IsInRole` in addition to an `Identity` property. With Windows, all the Windows groups the user is member of are mapped to roles. The method `IsInRole` is overloaded to accept a security identifier, a role string, or an enumeration value of the `WindowsBuiltInRole` enumeration. The sample code verifies whether the user belongs to the built-in roles User and Administrator (code file `WindowsPrincipal/Program.cs`):

```
public static WindowsPrincipal ShowPrincipal(WindowsIdentity identity)
{
  Console.WriteLine("Show principal information");
  WindowsPrincipal principal = new WindowsPrincipal(identity);
```

```
    if (principal == null)
    {
      Console.WriteLine("not a Windows Principal");
      return null;
    }
    Console.WriteLine($"Users? {principal.IsInRole(WindowsBuiltInRole.User)}");
    Console.WriteLine(
      $"Administrators? {principal.IsInRole(WindowsBuiltInRole.Administrator)}");
    Console.WriteLine();
    return principal;
  }
```

When I run the application, my account belongs to the role Users but not Administrator, and I get the following result:

```
Show principal information
Users? True
Administrators? False
```

It is enormously beneficial to be able to easily access details about the current users and their roles. With this information, you can make decisions about what actions should be permitted or denied. The ability to make use of roles and Windows user groups provides the added benefit that administration can be handled using standard user administration tools, and you can usually avoid altering the code when user roles change.

All the principal classes derive from the base class ClaimsPrincipal. This way, it's possible to access claims from users with the Claims property of a principal object. The following section looks at claims.

Using Claims

Claims offer a lot more flexibility compared to roles. A *claim* is a statement made about an identity from an authority. An authority such as the Active Directory or the Microsoft Live account authentication service makes claims about users—for example, the claim of the name of the user, claims about groups the user belongs to, or a claim about the age. Is the user already of age 21 or older and eligible for accessing specific resources?

The method ShowClaims accesses a collection of claims to write subject, issuer, claim type, and more options to the console (code file WindowsPrincipal/Program.cs):

```
public static void ShowClaims(IEnumerable<Claim> claims)
{
  Console.WriteLine("Claims");
  foreach (var claim in claims)
  {
    Console.WriteLine($"Subject: {claim.Subject}");
    Console.WriteLine($"Issuer: {claim.Issuer}");
    Console.WriteLine($"Type: {claim.Type}");
    Console.WriteLine($"Value type: {claim.ValueType}");
    Console.WriteLine($"Value: {claim.Value}");
    foreach (var prop in claim.Properties)
    {
      Console.WriteLine($"\tProperty: {prop.Key} {prop.Value}");
    }
    Console.WriteLine();
  }
}
```

Here is an extract of the claims from the Microsoft Live account, which provides information about the name, the primary ID, and the group identifiers:

```
Claims
Subject: System.Security.Principal.WindowsIdentity
Issuer: AD AUTHORITY
```

```
Type: http://schemas.xmlsoap.org/ws/2005/05/identity/claims/name
Value type: http://www.w3.org/2001/XMLSchema#string
Value: THEROCKS\Christian

Subject: System.Security.Principal.WindowsIdentity
Issuer: AD AUTHORITY
Type: http://schemas.microsoft.com/ws/2008/06/identity/claims/primarysid
Value type: http://www.w3.org/2001/XMLSchema#string
Value: S-1-5-21-1413171511-313453878-1364686672-1001
    Property: http://schemas.microsoft.com/ws/2008/06/identity/claims/
    windowssubauthority NTAuthority

Subject: System.Security.Principal.WindowsIdentity
Issuer: AD AUTHORITY
Type: http://schemas.microsoft.com/ws/2008/06/identity/claims/groupsid
Value type: http://www.w3.org/2001/XMLSchema#string
Value: S-1-1-0
    Property: http://schemas.microsoft.com/ws/2008/06/identity/claims/
    windowssubauthority WorldAuthority

Subject: System.Security.Principal.WindowsIdentity
Issuer: AD AUTHORITY
Type: http://schemas.microsoft.com/ws/2005/05/identity/claims/denyonlysid
Value type: http://www.w3.org/2001/XMLSchema#string
Value: S-1-5-114
    Property: http://schemas.microsoft.com/ws/2008/06/identity/claims/
    windowssubauthority NTAuthority
...
```

You can add claims to a Windows identity from a claim provider. You can also add a claim from a simple client program, such as the age claim here:

```
identity.AddClaim(new Claim("Age", "25"));
```

Using claims from a program, it's just a matter to trust this claim. Is this claim true—the age 25? Claims can also be lies. Adding this claim from the client application, you can see that the issuer of this claim is the LOCAL AUTHORITY. Information from the AD AUTHORITY (the Active Directory) is more trustworthy, but here you need to trust the Active Directory system administrators.

The `WindowsIdentity` deriving from the base class `ClaimsIdentity` offers several methods checking for claims or retrieving specific claims. To test whether a claim is available, you can use the `HasClaim` method:

```
bool hasName = identity.HasClaim(c => c.Type == ClaimTypes.Name);
```

To retrieve specific claims, the method `FindAll` needs a predicate to define a match:

```
var groupClaims = identity.FindAll(c => c.Type == ClaimTypes.GroupSid);
```

> **NOTE** *A claim type can be a simple string like the* `"Age"` *type used earlier. The* `ClaimType` *defines a list of known types such as* `Country`, `Email`, `Name`, `MobilePhone`, `UserData`, `Surname`, `PostalCode`, *and several more.*

ENCRYPTING DATA

Confidential data should be secured so that it cannot be read by unprivileged users. This is valid for both data that is sent across the network and stored data. You can encrypt such data with symmetric or asymmetric encryption keys.

With a symmetric key, you can use the same key for encryption and decryption. With asymmetric encryption, different keys are used for encryption and decryption: a public key and a private key. Something encrypted using a public key can be decrypted with the corresponding private key. This also works the other way around: Something encrypted using a private key can be decrypted by using the corresponding public key, but not the private key. It's practically impossible to calculate the private or public key from the other one.

Public and private keys are always created as a pair. The public key can be made available to everybody, and even put on a website, but the private key must be safely locked away. Following are some examples that demonstrate how public and private keys are used for encryption.

If Alice sends a message to Bob (see Figure 24-1), and she wants to ensure that no one other than Bob can read the message, she uses Bob's public key. The message is encrypted using Bob's public key. Bob opens the message and can decrypt it using his secretly stored private key. This key exchange guarantees that only Bob can read Alice's message.

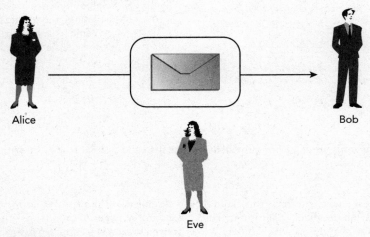

Alice

Bob

Eve

FIGURE 24-1

There is one problem, however: Bob can't be sure that the mail comes from Alice. Eve can use Bob's public key to encrypt messages sent to Bob and pretend to be Alice. We can extend this principle using public/private keys. Let's start again with Alice sending a message to Bob. Before Alice encrypts the message using Bob's public key, she adds her signature and encrypts the signature using her own private key. Then she encrypts the mail using Bob's public key. Therefore, it is guaranteed that no one other than Bob can read the message. When Bob decrypts it, he detects an encrypted signature. The signature can be decrypted using Alice's public key. For Bob, it is not a problem to access Alice's public key because the key is public. After decrypting the signature, Bob can be sure that it was Alice who sent the message.

The encryption and decryption algorithms using symmetric keys are a lot faster than those using asymmetric keys. The problem with symmetric keys is that the keys must be exchanged in a safe manner. With network communication, one way to do this is by using asymmetric keys first for the key exchange and then symmetric keys for encryption of the data that is sent across the wire.

.NET contains classes for encryption in the namespace System.Security.Cryptography. Several symmetric and asymmetric algorithms are implemented. You can find algorithm classes for many different purposes. Some of the classes have a Cng prefix or suffix. CNG is short for *Cryptography Next Generation*, which is a newer version of the native Windows Crypto API. This API makes it possible to write a program independently of the algorithm by using a provider-based model.

The following table lists encryption classes and their purposes from the namespace `System.Security.Cryptography`. The classes without a `Cng`, `Managed`, or `CryptoServiceProvider` suffix are abstract base classes, such as `MD5`. The `Managed` suffix means that this algorithm is implemented with managed code; other classes might wrap native Windows API calls. The suffix `CryptoServiceProvider` is used with classes that implement the abstract base class. The `Cng` suffix is used with classes that make use of the new Cryptography CNG API.

CATEGORY	CLASSES	DESCRIPTION
Hash	`MD5 SHA1 SHA1Managed  SHA256 SHA256Managed SHA256Cng  SHA384 SHA384Managed SHA512 SHA512Managed`	The purpose of hash algorithms is to create a fixed-length hash value from binary strings of arbitrary length. These algorithms are used with digital signatures and for data integrity. If the same binary string is hashed again, the same hash result is returned. MD5 (Message Digest Algorithm 5), developed at RSA Laboratories, is faster than SHA1. SHA1 is stronger against brute force attacks. The SHA algorithms were designed by the National Security Agency (NSA). MD5 uses a 128-bit hash size; SHA1 uses 160 bits. The other SHA algorithms contain the hash size in the name. SHA512 is the strongest of these algorithms, with a hash size of 512 bits; it is also the slowest.
Symmetric	`DES DESCryptoServiceProvider TripleDESTripleDESCryptoServiceProvider Aes AesCryptoServiceProvider AesManaged RC2 RC2CryptoServiceProvider Rijndael RijndaelManaged`	Symmetric key algorithms use the same key for encryption and decryption of data. Data Encryption Standard (DES) is now considered insecure because it uses only 56 bits for the key size and can be broken in less than 24 hours. Triple-DES is the successor to DES and has a key length of 168 bits, but the effective security it provides is only 112-bit. Advanced Encryption Standard (AES) has a key size of 128, 192, or 256 bits. Rijndael is very similar to AES but offers more key size options. AES is an encryption standard adopted by the U.S. government.

continues

(continued)

CATEGORY	CLASSES	DESCRIPTION

Asymmetric	`DSA DSACryptoServiceProvider`
	`ECDsa ECDsaCng ECDiffieHellman`
	`ECDiffieHellmanCng RSA`
	`RSACryptoServiceProvider RSACng`
		Asymmetric algorithms use different keys for encryption and decryption. The Rivest, Shamir, Adleman (RSA) algorithm was the first one used for signing as well as encryption. This algorithm is widely used in e-commerce protocols. RSACng is a class new with .NET 4.6 and .NET Core that is based on a Cryptography Next Generation (CNG) implementation. Digital Signature Algorithm (DSA) is a United States Federal Government standard for digital signatures. Elliptic Curve DSA (ECDSA) and EC Diffie-Hellman use algorithms based on elliptic curve groups. These algorithms are more secure, with shorter key sizes. For example, having a key size of 1024 bits for DSA is similar in security to 160 bits for ECDSA. As a result, ECDSA is much faster. EC Diffie-Hellman is an algorithm used to exchange private keys in a secure way over a public channel.

The following section includes some examples demonstrating how these algorithms can be used programmatically.

> **WARNING** *Be aware that all classes with the* `Cng` *pre- or postfix (belonging to Windows Cryptography Next Generation, CNG), are supported only on Windows. They do not run on Linux or Mac. These APIs throw a* `PlatformNotSupportedException` *on Linux.*

Creating and Verifying a Signature

The first example demonstrates a signature using the ECDSA algorithm, described in the preceding table, for signing. Alice creates a signature that is encrypted with her private key and can be accessed using her public key. This way, it is guaranteed that the signature is from Alice.

The sample application `SigningDemo` makes use of the following dependency and namespaces:

Dependency

```
System.Security.Cryptography.Cng
```

Namespaces

```
System

System.Security.Cryptography

System.Text
```

First, look at the major steps in the `Main` method: Alice's keys are created, and the string `"Alice"` is signed and then verified to be the signature from Alice by using the public key. The message that is signed is converted to a byte array by using the `Encoding` class. To write the encrypted signature to the console, the byte array that contains the signature is converted to a string with the method `Convert .ToBase64String` (code file `SigningDemo/Program.cs`):

```
private CngKey _aliceKeySignature;
private byte[] _alicePubKeyBlob;

static void Main()
{
  var p = new Program();
  p.Run();
}

public void Run()
{
  InitAliceKeys();
  byte[] aliceData = Encoding.UTF8.GetBytes("Alice");
  byte[] aliceSignature = CreateSignature(aliceData, aliceKeySignature);
  Console.WriteLine($"Alice created signature: " +
    $"{Convert.ToBase64String(aliceSignature)}");
  if (VerifySignature(aliceData, aliceSignature, alicePubKeyBlob))
  {
    Console.WriteLine("Alice signature verified successfully");
  }
}
```

> **WARNING** *Never convert encrypted data to a string using the* `Encoding` *class. The* `Encoding` *class verifies and converts invalid values that are not allowed with Unicode; therefore, converting the string back to a byte array can yield a different result.*

`InitAliceKeys` is the method that creates a new key pair for Alice. This key pair is stored in a static field, so it can be accessed from the other methods. The `Create` method of `CngKey` gets the algorithm as an argument to define a key pair for the algorithm. With the `Export` method, the public key of the key pair is exported. This public key can be given to Bob for verification of the signature. Alice keeps the private key. Instead of creating a key pair with the `CngKey` class, you can open existing keys that are stored in the key store. Usually Alice would have a certificate containing a key pair in her private store, and the store could be accessed with `CngKey.Open`:

```
private void InitAliceKeys()
{
  _aliceKeySignature = CngKey.Create(CngAlgorithm.ECDsaP521);
  _alicePubKeyBlob =
    aliceKeySignature.Export(CngKeyBlobFormat.GenericPublicBlob);
}
```

With the key pair, Alice can create the signature using the `ECDsaCng` class. The constructor of this class receives the `CngKey`—which contains both the public and private keys—from Alice. The private key is used to sign the data with the `SignData` method:

```
public byte[] CreateSignature(byte[] data, CngKey key)
{
  byte[] signature;
  using (var signingAlg = new ECDsaCng(key))
  {
    signature = signingAlg.SignData(data, HashAlgorithmName.SHA512);
    signingAlg.Clear();
  }
  return signature;
}
```

To verify that the signature was really from Alice, Bob checks the signature by using the public key from Alice. The byte array containing the public key blob can be imported to a `CngKey` object with the static `Import` method. The `ECDsaCng` class is then used to verify the signature by invoking `VerifyData`:

```
public bool VerifySignature(byte[] data, byte[] signature, byte[] pubKey)
{
  bool retValue = false;
  using (CngKey key = CngKey.Import(pubKey, CngKeyBlobFormat.GenericPublicBlob))
  using (var signingAlg = new ECDsaCng(key))
  {
    retValue = signingAlg.VerifyData(data, signature, HashAlgorithmName.SHA512);
    signingAlg.Clear();
  }
  return retValue;
}
```

Implementing Secure Data Exchange

The next example helps explain public/private key principles, exchanging a secret between two parties, and communication with symmetric keys. A secret can be exchanged between two parties using the EC Diffie-Hellman algorithm. This algorithm allows exchanging a secret just by using public and private keys and exchanging the public key between two parties. At the time of this writing, an implementation of this algorithm is not available with .NET Core; it's available only with the .NET Framework running on Windows. In your applications you typically don't need to implement this functionality because it's already offered by infrastructure services.

> **NOTE** At the time of this writing, .NET Core just includes the `ECDiffieHellman` abstract base class that can be used by implementers to create concrete classes. A concrete class is not yet here, that's why this sample uses only .NET 4.7.1.

The sample application `SecureTransfer` has the target framework set to `net471` and makes use of the following dependencies and namespaces:

Dependencies

`System.Security.Cryptography.Algorithms`

`System.Security.Cryptography.Cng`

`System.Security.Cryptography.Csp`

`System.Security.Cryptography.Primitives`

Namespaces

```
System

System.IO

System.Security.Cryptography

System.Text

System.Threading.Tasks
```

The `Main` method contains the primary functionality. Alice creates an encrypted message and sends it to Bob. Before the message is created and sent, key pairs are created for Alice and Bob. Bob has access only to Alice's public key, and Alice has access only to Bob's public key (code file `SecureTransfer/Program.cs`):

```
private CngKey _aliceKey;
private CngKey _bobKey;
private byte[] _alicePubKeyBlob;
private byte[] _bobPubKeyBlob;

static async Task Main()
{
  var p = new Program();
  await p.RunAsync();
  Console.ReadLine();
}

public async Task RunAsync()
{
  try
  {
    CreateKeys();
    byte[] encrytpedData =
      await AliceSendsDataAsync("This is a secret message for Bob");
    await BobReceivesDataAsync(encrytpedData);
  }
  catch (Exception ex)
  {
    Console.WriteLine(ex.Message);
  }
}
```

In the implementation of the `CreateKeys` method, keys are created to be used with the EC Diffie-Hellman 521 algorithm:

```
public void CreateKeys()
{
  aliceKey = CngKey.Create(CngAlgorithm.ECDiffieHellmanP521);
  bobKey = CngKey.Create(CngAlgorithm.ECDiffieHellmanP521);
  alicePubKeyBlob = aliceKey.Export(CngKeyBlobFormat.EccPublicBlob);
  bobPubKeyBlob = bobKey.Export(CngKeyBlobFormat.EccPublicBlob);
}
```

In the method `AliceSendsDataAsync`, the string that contains text characters is converted to a byte array by using the `Encoding` class. An `ECDiffieHellmanCng` object is created and initialized with the key pair from Alice. Alice creates a symmetric key by using her key pair and the public key from Bob, calling the method `DeriveKeyMaterial`. The returned symmetric key is used with the symmetric algorithm AES to encrypt the data. `AesCryptoServiceProvider` requires the key and an initialization vector (IV). The IV is generated dynamically from the method `GenerateIV`. The symmetric key is exchanged with the help of the EC Diffie-Hellman algorithm, but the IV must also be exchanged. From a security standpoint, it is OK to transfer the IV unencrypted across the network—only the key exchange must be secured. The IV is stored first as content in the memory stream, followed by the encrypted data where the `CryptoStream` class uses the `encryptor` created by the `AesCryptoServiceProvider` class. Before the encrypted data is accessed from the memory stream, the crypto stream must be closed. Otherwise, end bits would be missing from the encrypted data:

```
public async Task<byte[]> AliceSendsDataAsync(string message)
{
  Console.WriteLine($"Alice sends message: {message}");
  byte[] rawData = Encoding.UTF8.GetBytes(message);
  byte[] encryptedData = null;
  using (var aliceAlgorithm = new ECDiffieHellmanCng(aliceKey))
  using (CngKey bobPubKey = CngKey.Import(bobPubKeyBlob,
    CngKeyBlobFormat.EccPublicBlob))
  {
    byte[] symmKey = aliceAlgorithm.DeriveKeyMaterial(bobPubKey);
    Console.WriteLine("Alice creates this symmetric key with " +
      $"Bobs public key information: {Convert.ToBase64String(symmKey)}");
    using (var aes = new AesCryptoServiceProvider())
    {
      aes.Key = symmKey;
      aes.GenerateIV();
      using (ICryptoTransform encryptor = aes.CreateEncryptor())
      using (var ms = new MemoryStream())
      {
        // create CryptoStream and encrypt data to send
        using (var cs = new CryptoStream(ms, encryptor,
        CryptoStreamMode.Write))
        {
          // write initialization vector not encrypted
          await ms.WriteAsync(aes.IV, 0, aes.IV.Length);
          cs.Write(rawData, 0, rawData.Length);
        }
        encryptedData = ms.ToArray();
      }
      aes.Clear();
    }
  }
  Console.WriteLine("Alice: message is encrypted: "+
    $"{Convert.ToBase64String(encryptedData)}");
  Console.WriteLine();
  return encryptedData;
}
```

Bob receives the encrypted data in the argument of the method `BobReceivesDataAsync`. First, the unencrypted initialization vector must be read. The `BlockSize` property of the class `AesCryptoServiceProvider` returns the number of bits for a block. The number of bytes can be calculated by dividing by 8, and the fastest way to do this is by doing a bit shift of 3 bits (shifting by 1 bit is a division by 2, 2 bits by 4, and 3 bits by 8). With the `for` loop, the first bytes of the raw bytes that contain the IV unencrypted are written to the array `iv`. Next, an `ECDiffieHellmanCng` object is instantiated with the key pair from Bob. Using the public key from Alice, the symmetric key is returned from the method `DeriveKeyMaterial`.

Comparing the symmetric keys created from Alice and Bob shows that the same key value is created. Using this symmetric key and the initialization vector, the message from Alice can be decrypted with the `AesCryptoServiceProvider` class:

```
public async Task BobReceivesDataAsync(byte[] encryptedData)
{
  Console.WriteLine("Bob receives encrypted data");
  byte[] rawData = null;
  var aes = new AesCryptoServiceProvider();
```

```
    int nBytes = aes.BlockSize 3;
    byte[] iv = new byte[nBytes];
    for (int i = 0; i < iv.Length; i++)
    {
      iv[i] = encryptedData[i];
    }
    using (var bobAlgorithm = new ECDiffieHellmanCng(bobKey))
    using (CngKey alicePubKey = CngKey.Import(alicePubKeyBlob,
      CngKeyBlobFormat.EccPublicBlob))
    {
      byte[] symmKey = bobAlgorithm.DeriveKeyMaterial(alicePubKey);
      Console.WriteLine("Bob creates this symmetric key with " +
        $"Alices public key information: {Convert.ToBase64String(symmKey)}");
      aes.Key = symmKey;
      aes.IV = iv;
      using (ICryptoTransform decryptor = aes.CreateDecryptor())
      using (MemoryStream ms = new MemoryStream())
      {
        using (var cs = new CryptoStream(ms, decryptor, CryptoStreamMode.Write))
        {
          await cs.WriteAsync(encryptedData, nBytes,
            encryptedData.Length - nBytes);
        }
        rawData = ms.ToArray();
        Console.WriteLine("Bob decrypts message to: " +
          $"{Encoding.UTF8.GetString(rawData)}");
      }
      aes.Clear();
    }
  }
```

Running the application returns output like the following. The message from Alice is encrypted, and then decrypted by Bob with the securely exchanged symmetric key.

```
Alice sends message: this is a secret message for Bob
Alice creates this symmetric key with Bobs public key information:
q4D182m7lyev9Nlp6f0av2Jvc0+LmHF5zEjXwlOlI3Y=
Alice: message is encrypted: WpOxvUoWH5XY31wC8aXcDWeDUWa6zaSObfGcQCpKixzlTJ9exb
tkF5Hp2WPSZWL9V9n13toBg7hgjPbrVzN2A==
Bob receives encrypted data
Bob creates this symmetric key with Alices public key information:
q4D182m7lyev9Nlp6f0av2Jvc0+LmHF5zEjXwlOlI3Y=
Bob decrypts message to: this is a secret message for Bob
```

Signing and Hashing Using RSA

A new cryptography algorithm class is RSACng. RSA (the name comes from the algorithm designers Ron Rivest, Adi Shamir, and Leonard Adlerman) is an asymmetric algorithm that is widely used. Although the RSA algorithm was already available with .NET with the RSA and RSACryptoServiceProvider classes, RSACng is a class based on the CNG API and is similar in use to the ECDSACng class shown earlier.

With the sample application shown in this section, Alice creates a document, hashes it to make sure it doesn't get changed, and signs it with a signature to guarantee that the document is generated by Alice. Bob receives the document and checks the guarantees from Alice to make sure the document hasn't been tampered with.

The RSA sample code makes use of the following dependency and namespaces:

Dependency

```
System.Security.Cryptography.Cng
```

Namespaces

```
System

System.IO

System.Linq
```

The `Main` method of the application is structured to start with Alice's tasks to invoke the method `AliceTasks` to create a document, a hash code, and a signature. This information is then passed to Bob's tasks to invoke the method `BobTasks` (code file `RSASample/Program.cs`):

```
class Program
{
  private CngKey _aliceKey;
  private byte[] _alicePubKeyBlob;

  static void Main()
  {
    var p = new Program();
    p.Run();
  }

  public void Run()
  {
    AliceTasks(out byte[] document, out byte[] hash, out byte[] signature);
    BobTasks(document, hash, signature);
  }
  //...
}
```

The method `AliceTasks` first creates the keys needed by Alice, converts the message to a byte array, hashes the byte array, and adds a signature:

```
public void AliceTasks(out byte[] data, out byte[] hash, out byte[] signature)
{
  InitAliceKeys();
  data = Encoding.UTF8.GetBytes("Best greetings from Alice");
  hash = HashDocument(data);
  signature = AddSignatureToHash(hash, _aliceKey);
}
```

Like before, the keys needed by Alice are created using the `CngKey` class. As the RSA algorithm is being used now, the enumeration value `CngAlgorithm.Rsa` is passed to the `Create` method to create public and private keys. Only the public key is given to Bob, so the public key is extracted with the `Export` method:

```
private void InitAliceKeys()
{
  _aliceKey = CngKey.Create(CngAlgorithm.Rsa);
  _alicePubKeyBlob = _aliceKey.Export(CngKeyBlobFormat.GenericPublicBlob);
}
```

The `HashDocument` method is invoked from Alice's tasks to create a hash code for the document. The hash code is created using one of the hash algorithm classes: SHA384. No matter how long the document is, the hash code always has the same length. Creating the hash code for the same document again results in the same hash code. Bob needs to use the same algorithm on the document. If the same hash code is returned, the document hasn't been changed.

```
private byte[] HashDocument(byte[] data)
{
  using (var hashAlg = SHA384.Create())
  {
    return hashAlg.ComputeHash(data);
  }
}
```

Adding a signature guarantees that the document is from Alice. Here, the hash is signed using the RSACng class. Alice's CngKey, including the public and private keys, is passed to the constructor of the RSACng class; the signature is created by invoking the SignHash method. When the hash is signed, the SignHash method needs to know about the algorithm of the hash; HashAlgorithmName.SHA384 is the algorithm that was used to create the hash. Also, the RSA padding is needed. Possible options with the RSASignaturePadding enumeration are Pss and Pkcs1:

```
private byte[] AddSignatureToHash(byte[] hash, CngKey key)
{
  using (var signingAlg = new RSACng(key))
  {
    byte[] signed = signingAlg.SignHash(hash,
      HashAlgorithmName.SHA384, RSASignaturePadding.Pss);
    return signed;
  }
}
```

After hashing and signing from Alice, Bob's tasks can start in the method BobTasks. Bob receives the document data, the hash code, and the signature, and he uses Alice's public key. First, Alice's public key is imported using CngKey.Import and assigned to the aliceKey variable. Next, Bob uses the helper methods IsSignatureValid and IsDocumentUnchanged to verify whether the signature is valid and the document unchanged. Only if both conditions are true, the document is written to the console:

```
public void BobTasks(byte[] data, byte[] hash, byte[] signature)
{
  CngKey aliceKey = CngKey.Import(_alicePubKeyBlob,
  CngKeyBlobFormat.GenericPublicBlob);
  if (!IsSignatureValid(hash, signature, aliceKey))
  {
    Console.WriteLine("signature not valid");
    return;
  }
  if (!IsDocumentUnchanged(hash, data))
  {
    Console.WriteLine("document was changed");
    return;
  }
  Console.WriteLine("signature valid, document unchanged");
  Console.WriteLine($"document from Alice: {Encoding.UTF8.GetString(data)}");
}
```

To verify if the signature is valid, the public key from Alice is used to create an instance of the RSACng class. With this class, the VerifyHash method is used to pass the hash, signature, and algorithm information that was used earlier. Now Bob knows the information is from Alice:

```
private bool IsSignatureValid(byte[] hash, byte[] signature, CngKey key)
{
  using (var signingAlg = new RSACng(key))
  {
    return signingAlg.VerifyHash(hash, signature, HashAlgorithmName.SHA384,
      RSASignaturePadding.Pss);
  }
}
```

To verify that the document data is unchanged, Bob hashes the document again and uses the LINQ extension method SequenceEqual to verify whether the hash code is the same as was sent earlier. If the hashes are the same, it can be assumed that the document was not changed:

```
private bool IsDocumentUnchanged(byte[] hash, byte[] data)
{
  byte[] newHash = HashDocument(data);
  return newHash.SequenceEqual(hash);
}
```

When you run the application, you see output like what's shown here. When you debug the application, you can change the document data after it's hashed by Alice and see that Bob doesn't accept the changed document. To change the document data, you can easily change the value in the Watch window of the debugger.

```
signature valid, document unchanged
document from Alice: Best greetings from Alice
```

PROTECTING DATA

After encrypting, signing, and hashing data, let's move the abstraction layer higher. This section gets into protecting data—storing security-sensitive data. When data is used with web applications, the client used cannot be trusted. This is where the data protection API takes place.

Another kind of data that needs to be protected is configuration data. Configuration data—such as SQL connection strings (including username and password) or some access tokens to AWS or Microsoft Azure—shouldn't be put into a public source code repository. This information can easily be misused. Indeed, bots are used to crawl over public GitHub repositories to find secret keys and use them, for example to spin up virtual machines to farm Bitcoins. App Secrets offer a way for storing secrets in a user profile.

Both these technologies, data protection and user secrets, are covered in this section.

Implementing Data Protection

With the .NET Framework, the namespace `System.Security.DataProtection` contains a `DpApiDataProtector` class that wraps the native Windows Data Protection API (DPAPI). Because these classes are based on Windows, they do not offer the flexibility and features needed with .NET Core, that's why the ASP.NET team created classes with the `Microsoft.AspNetCore.DataProtection` namespace.

With this library, trusted information can be stored for later retrieval, and the storage media (such as using hosting environments from a third party) cannot be trusted itself, so the information needs to be stored encrypted on the host.

The sample application is a simple Console App (.NET Core) that enables you to read and write information using data protection. With this sample, you see the flexibility and features of the ASP.NET data protection.

The data protection sample code makes use of the following dependencies and namespaces:

Dependencies

`Microsoft.AspNetCore.DataProtection`

`Microsoft.Extensions.DependencyInjection`

Namespaces

`Microsoft.AspNetCore.DataProtection`

`Microsoft.Extensions.DependencyInjection`

`System`

`System.IO`

`System.Linq`

You can start the console application by using the `-r` and `-w` command-line arguments to either read or write from the storage. Also, you need to use the command line to set a filename to read and write. After checking the command-line arguments, the data protection is initialized calling the `SetupDataProtection` helper method. This method returns an object of type `MySafe` that embeds an `IDataProtector`. After that, depending on the command-line arguments, either the `Write` or `Read` method is invoked (code file `DataProtectionSample/Program.cs`):

```
class Program
{
  private const string readOption = "-r";
  private const string writeOption = "-w";
  private readonly string[] options = { readOption, writeOption };
  static void Main(string[] args)
  {
    if (args.Length != 2 || args.Intersect(options).Count() != 1)
    {
      ShowUsage();
      return;
    }

    string fileName = args[1];
    MySafe safe = SetupDataProtection();
    switch (args[0])
    {
      case writeOption:
        Write(safe, fileName);
        break;
      case readOption:
        Read(safe, fileName);
        break;
      default:
        ShowUsage();
        break;
    }
  }
  //...
}
```

The class `MySafe` holds a member of `IDataProtector`. This interface defines the members `Protect` and `Unprotect` to encrypt and decrypt data. This interface defines `Protect` and `Unprotect` methods with byte array arguments and returning byte arrays. However, the sample code directly sends and returns strings from the `Encrypt` and `Decrypt` methods using extension methods that are defined within the `Microsoft.AspNetCore.DataProtection.Abstractions` NuGet package. The `MySafe` class receives an `IDataProtectionProvider` interface via dependency injection. With this interface, a `IDataProtector` is returned passing a purpose string. The same string needs to be used when reading and writing from this safe (code file `DataProtectionSample/MySafe.cs`):

```
public class MySafe
{
  private IDataProtector _protector;
  public MySafe(IDataProtectionProvider provider) =>
    _protector = provider.CreateProtector("MySafe.MyProtection.v2");

  public string Encrypt(string input) => _protector.Protect(input);
  public string Decrypt(string encrypted) => _protector.Unprotect(encrypted);
}
```

With the `SetupDataProtection` method, the `AddDataProtection` extension method is invoked to add data protection via dependency injection, and to configure it. The `AddDataProtection` method registers default services and returns an `IDataProtectionBuilder` that can be used to configure data protection further using a fluent API. The sample code persists the key to the actual directory passing a `DirectoryInfo` instance to the method `PersistKeysToFileSystem`. Another option is to persist the key to the registry

(PersistKeysToRegistry), and you can create your own method to persist the key to a custom store. The lifetime of the created keys is defined by the method SetDefaultKeyLifetime. Next, the keys are protected by calling ProtectKeysWithDpapi. This method protects the keys using the DPAPI, which encrypts the stored keys with the current user. ProtectKeysWithCertificate allows using a certificate for key protection. The API also defines the method UseEphemeralDataProtectionProvider in which keys are stored just in memory. When the application is started again, new keys need to be generated. This is a great feature for unit testing (code file DataProtectionSample/Program.cs):

```
public static MySafe SetupDataProtection()
{
  var serviceCollection = new ServiceCollection();
  serviceCollection.AddDataProtection()
    .PersistKeysToFileSystem(new DirectoryInfo("."))
    .SetDefaultKeyLifetime(TimeSpan.FromDays(20))
    .ProtectKeysWithDpapi();

  IServiceProvider services = serviceCollection.BuildServiceProvider();

  return ActivatorUtilities.CreateInstance<MySafe>(services);
}
```

> **NOTE** *Dependency injection is explained in detail in Chapter 20, "Dependency Injection."*

Now the heart of the data protection application is implemented, and the Write and Read methods can take advantage of MySafe to encrypt and decrypt the user's content:

```
public static void Write(MySafe safe, string fileName)
{
  Console.WriteLine("enter content to write:");
  string content = Console.ReadLine();
  string encrypted = safe.Encrypt(content);
  File.WriteAllText(fileName, encrypted);
  Console.WriteLine($"content written to {fileName}");
}

public static void Read(MySafe safe, string fileName)
{
  string encrypted = File.ReadAllText(fileName);
  string decrypted = safe.Decrypt(encrypted);
  Console.WriteLine(decrypted);
}
```

User Secrets

Having the connection string in the configuration file is not a big problem as long as Windows authentication is used. When you store username and password with the connection string, it can be a big issue to add the connection string to a configuration file and store the configuration file along with the source code repository. Having a public repository and storing Amazon or Azure keys with the configuration can lead to losing thousands of dollars very quickly. Hackers' background jobs comb through public GitHub repositories to find Amazon keys to hijack accounts and create virtual machines for making Bitcoins. Visit https://www.humankode.com/security/how-a-bug-in-visual-studio-2015-exposed-my-source-code-on-github-and-cost-me-6500-in-a-few-hours to find out more about the situation.

.NET Core has some mitigations around this: user secrets. With user secrets, configuration is not stored in a configuration file of the project; it is stored in a configuration file associated with your account.

The user secrets sample code makes use of the following dependencies and namespaces:

Dependencies

```
Microsoft.Extensions.Configuration

Microsoft.Extensions.Configuration.CommandLine

Microsoft.Extensions.Configuration.EnvironmentVariables

Microsoft.Extensions.Configuration.Json

Microsoft.Extensions.Configuration.UserSecrets
```

Namespaces

```
Microsoft.Extensions.Configuration

System

System.IO
```

To have the user secrets command-line extension for the dotnet CLI tools, a reference to `Microsoft.Extensions.SecretManager.Tools` needs to be added to the `csproj` file (project file `UserSecretsSample/UserSecretsSample.csproj`):

```xml
<ItemGroup>
  <DotNetCliToolReference Include="Microsoft.Extensions.SecretManager.Tools"
    Version="2.0.0" />
</ItemGroup>
```

In addition, you need to define an initial ID by adding a value to the `UserSecretsId` element in the project file (project file `UserSecretsSample/UserSecretsSample.csproj`):

```xml
<PropertyGroup>
  <OutputType>Exe</OutputType>
  <TargetFramework>netcoreapp2.0</TargetFramework>
  <UserSecretsId>UserSecretsSample-Id</UserSecretsId>
</PropertyGroup>
```

This secret ID just needs to be unique on your local system to not mix up configuration values from different projects. Thus, it's a good idea to have the project name contained in the identifier.

The sample application defines using configuration from a JSON file, environmental variables, the command line, and user secrets. User secrets are configured to invoke the extension method `AddUserSecrets` with the `ConfigurationBuilder`. This provider is added only if the application is built with debug mode enabled. Remember, this provider is available only when you're running the application with the user profile that has user secrets enabled. The overloaded method of `AddUserSecrets` requires the user secrets ID as a parameter—the same identifier that has been used with the configuration (code file `UserSecretsSample/Program.cs`):

```csharp
static void Main(string[] args)
{
  var configBuilder = new ConfigurationBuilder();
  configBuilder.SetBasePath(Directory.GetCurrentDirectory())
    .AddJsonFile("appsettings.json")
    .AddEnvironmentVariables()
    .AddCommandLine(args);

#if DEBUG
  configBuilder.AddUserSecrets("UserSecretsSample-Id");
#endif
  IConfigurationRoot configuration = configBuilder.Build();
  //...
}
```

> **NOTE** *Read more about application configuration with* Microsoft.Extensions
> .Configuration *in Chapter 30, "ASP.NET Core."*

With the JSON configuration file appsettings.json, a value to the key NotASecret is written. This configuration file should not contain sensitive configuration information when the project is added to a public source code repository (configuration file UserSecretsSample/appsettings.json):

```
{
  "NotASecret": "this is not a secret"
}
```

Because the SecretManager tool has been configured with the project file, you can use the dotnet command-line tool to set, list, remove, and clear secrets. The following command sets the secret with the key Secret1:

```
> dotnet user-secrets set Secret1 "this is a secret"
```

Use dotnet user-secrets list to show all user secrets, and dotnet user-secrets clear to remove all user secrets.

On a Windows system, user secrets are stored in the folder %APPDATA%\microsoft\UserSecrets\ <userSecretsId>\secrets.json. On a Linux system, the secrets are stored in ~/.microsoft/ usersecrets/<userSecretsId>/secrets.json.

To read the configuration values, no matter where the configuration is stored, the variable of type IConfigurationRoot can be used. Using the indexer, the values stored with the corresponding keys can be read, no matter whether the configuration was stored in the JSON file or with user secrets (code file UserSecretsSample/Program.cs):

```
string notASecret1 = configuration["NotASecret"];
Console.WriteLine($"not a secret: {notASecret1}");

string secretValue1 = configuration["Secret1"];
Console.WriteLine($"secret: {secretValue1}");
```

On the production system, the private profile where the user secrets are stored are not available. Depending on the technology used, different providers can be used. For example, with Azure App Services, configuration can be configured with the Azure portal, and retrieved using environmental variables. You also can use the Azure Key Vault configuration provider to read configuration from Azure Key Vault secrets.

ACCESS CONTROL TO RESOURCES

Operating system resources such as files and registry keys, as well as handles of a named pipe, are secured by using an access control list (ACL). Figure 24-2 shows the structure mapping this. Associated with the resource is a security descriptor that contains information about the owner of the resource. It references two access control lists: a discretionary access control list (DACL) and a system access control list (SACL). The DACL defines who has access; the SACL defines audit rules for security event logging. An ACL contains a list of access control entries (ACEs), which contain a type, a security identifier, and rights. With the DACL, the ACE can be of type access allowed or access denied. Some of the rights that you can set and get with a file are create, read, write, delete, modify, change permissions, and take ownership.

The classes to read and modify access control are in the namespace System.Security.AccessControl. The following program demonstrates reading the access control list from a file.

The sample application FileAccessControl makes use of the following dependencies and namespaces:

Dependencies

```
System.IO.FileSystem
```

```
System.IO.FileSystem.AccessControl
```

Namespaces

```
System
```

```
System.IO
```

```
System.Security.AccessControl
```

```
System.Security.Principal
```

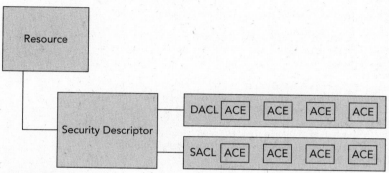

FIGURE 24-2

> **WARNING** *Access control APIs are available only on Windows, not on Linux or Mac.* System.IO.FileSystem.AccessControl *APIs are part of the resource management on Windows.*

The `FileStream` class defines the `GetAccessControl` method, which returns a `FileSecurity` object. `FileSecurity` is the .NET class that represents a security descriptor for files. `FileSecurity` derives from the base classes `ObjectSecurity`, `CommonObjectSecurity`, `NativeObjectSecurity`, and `FileSystemSecurity`. Other classes that represent a security descriptor are `CryptoKeySecurity`, `EventWaitHandleSecurity`, `MutexSecurity`, `RegistrySecurity`, `SemaphoreSecurity`, `PipeSecurity`, and `ActiveDirectorySecurity`. All these objects can be secured using an ACL. In general, the corresponding .NET class defines the method `GetAccessControl` to return the corresponding security class; for example, the `Mutex.GetAccessControl` method returns a `MutexSecurity`, and the `PipeStream`.`GetAccessControl` method returns a `PipeSecurity`.

The `FileSecurity` class defines methods to read and change the DACL and SACL. The method `GetAccessRules` returns the DACL in the form of the class `AuthorizationRuleCollection`. To access the SACL, you can use the method `GetAuditRules`.

With the method `GetAccessRules`, you can specify whether inherited access rules, and not only access rules directly defined with the object, should be used. The last parameter defines the type of the security identifier that should be returned. This type must derive from the base class `IdentityReference`. Possible types are `NTAccount` and `SecurityIdentifier`. Both these classes represent users or groups; the `NTAccount` class finds the security object by its name and the `SecurityIdentifier` class finds the security object by a unique security identifier.

The returned `AuthorizationRuleCollection` contains `AuthorizationRule` objects. The `AuthorizationRule` is the .NET representation of an ACE. In the following example, a file is accessed, so the `AuthorizationRule` can be cast to a `FileSystemAccessRule`. With ACEs of other resources, different .NET representations exist, such as `MutexAccessRule` and `PipeAccessRule`. With the `FileSystemAccessRule` class, the properties `AccessControlType`, `FileSystemRights`, and `IdentityReference` return information about the ACE (code file `FileAccessControl/Program.cs`).

```csharp
class Program
{
  static void Main(string[] args)
  {
    string filename = null;
    if (args.Length == 0) return;
    filename = args[0];
    using (FileStream stream = File.Open(filename, FileMode.Open))
    {
      FileSecurity securityDescriptor = stream.GetAccessControl();
      AuthorizationRuleCollection rules =
        securityDescriptor.GetAccessRules(true, true,
          typeof(NTAccount));
      foreach (AuthorizationRule rule in rules)
      {
        var fileRule = rule as FileSystemAccessRule;
        Console.WriteLine($"Access type: {fileRule.AccessControlType}");
        Console.WriteLine($"Rights: {fileRule.FileSystemRights}");
        Console.WriteLine($"Identity: {fileRule.IdentityReference.Value}");
        Console.WriteLine();
      }
    }
  }
}
```

By running the application and passing a filename, you can see the ACL for the file. The following output lists full control to Administrators and System, modification rights to authenticated users, and read and execute rights to all users belonging to the group Users:

```
Access type: Allow
Rights: FullControl
Identity: BUILTIN\Administrators
Access type: Allow
Rights: FullControl
Identity: NT AUTHORITY\SYSTEM
Access type: Allow
Rights: FullControl
Identity: BUILTIN\Administrators
Access type: Allow
Rights: FullControl
Identity: TheOtherSide\Christian
```

Setting access rights is very similar to reading access rights. To set access rights, several resource classes that can be secured offer the `SetAccessControl` and `ModifyAccessControl` methods. The following code modifies the ACL of a file by invoking the `SetAccessControl` method from the `File` class. To this method a `FileSecurity` object is passed. The `FileSecurity` object is filled with `FileSystemAccessRule` objects. The access rules listed here deny write access to the Sales group, give read access to the Everyone group, and give full control to the Developers group:

> **NOTE** *This program runs on your system only if the Windows groups Sales and Developers are defined. You can change the program to use groups that are available in your environment.*

```csharp
private void WriteAcl(string filename)
{
  var salesIdentity = new NTAccount("Sales");
  var developersIdentity = new NTAccount("Developers");
```

```
    var everyOneIdentity = new NTAccount("Everyone");
    var salesAce = new FileSystemAccessRule(salesIdentity,
    FileSystemRights.Write, AccessControlType.Deny);
    var everyoneAce = new FileSystemAccessRule(everyOneIdentity,
    FileSystemRights.Read, AccessControlType.Allow);
    var developersAce = new FileSystemAccessRule(developersIdentity,
    FileSystemRights.FullControl, AccessControlType.Allow);
    var securityDescriptor = new FileSecurity();
    securityDescriptor.SetAccessRule(everyoneAce);
    securityDescriptor.SetAccessRule(developersAce);
    securityDescriptor.SetAccessRule(salesAce);
    File.SetAccessControl(filename, securityDescriptor);
}
```

> **NOTE** *You can verify the access rules by opening the Properties window and selecting a file in Windows Explorer. Select the Security tab to see the ACL.*

WEB SECURITY

Web applications have some specific security issues you need to be aware of with applications that allow user input. User input cannot be trusted. Verifying input data on the client using JavaScript or built-in HTML5 features is only for the convenience of the user. Errors can be shown without making an extra network request to the server. However, the client cannot be trusted. HTTP requests can be intercepted, and the user (a hacker) can make different requests that bypass the HTML5 and JavaScript validation.

This section looks at common issues with web applications, and what you need to be aware of avoiding the issues.

> **NOTE** *This section makes use of ASP.NET Core and ASP.NET MVC. Read Chapter 30 and Chapter 31, "ASP.NET Core MVC" for more information on these technologies.*

Encoding

Never trust user input. Writing user information to a database and using this information to display on a website can be the cause of a typical hack. For example, a community website was showing the latest five new users on the home page. One of the new users managed to add a script to the username, and the script did a redirect to a malicious website. Because the user information was shown for every user coming to this site, every user was redirected.

Let's have a look at how easy it is to simulate and to avoid such a behavior with the next example. In the following code snippet, the /echo URL is mapped to an answer that returns the input from the user assigned to the x parameter that sends the response using context.Response.WriteAsync (code file ASPNETCoreMVCSecurity/Startup.cs):

```
app.Map("/echo", app1 =>
{
  app1.Run(async context =>
  {
    string data = context.Request.Query["x"];
    await context.Response.WriteAsync(data);
  });
});
```

Now passing the request

```
http://localhost:24897/echo?x=I'm a nice user
```

The string `I'm a nice user` is returned to the browser. This is not that bad, but users can't play differently. For example, users can input HTML code such as this:

```
http://localhost:24897/echo?x=<h1>Is this wanted?</h1>
```

The result shows the input string is formatted with the HTML `H1` tag. Users can do more bad things by entering JavaScript code:

```
localhost:24897/echo?x=<script>alert("this is bad");</script>
```

In most browsers, a pop-up window where the user entered text shows up. In case you try this with Google Chrome, there's a separate measure to avoid this issue. This browser shows an error page, `This page isn't working` with additional information `ERR_BLOCKED_BY_XSS_AUDITOR`.

If you try to avoid this issue by checking for `<script>` elements with the input and not return a thing in that case, you'll likely fail. Instead of using the `<script>` element, users can also use Unicode numbers for the angle brackets with the same result. Instead, let's encode the user input to not let it be interpreted by the browser.

You can use the `HTMLEncoder` class from the namespace `System.Text.Encodings.Web` to encode user input:

```
app.Map("/echoenc", app1 =>
{
  app1.Run(async context =>
  {
    string data = context.Request.Query["x"];
    await context.Response.WriteAsync(HtmlEncoder.Default.Encode(data));
  });
});
```

When you use `HtmlEncoder` class, the user can enter `<h1>` elements with the input `http://localhost:24897/echoenc?x=<h1>this gets converted</h1>`. As result, `<h1>this gets converted</h1>` is shown in the browser. The `<` character is encoded to `&lt;`, and thus displayed as text. The complete encoded string is:

```
&lt;h1&gt;this gets converted&lt;/h1&gt;
```

Similarly, the script element is converted and doesn't run as script in the browser.

> **NOTE** *You can use the* `HtmlEncoder` *class to allow specific inputs to go through—for example, you might allow the user to add* `<b>` *elements. You can create an encoder with accepted inputs using the* `HtmlEncoder.Create` *method. Nowadays a preferred method is to allow the user to make some formatting by using Markdown and converting Markdown to HTML. You can read my blog article about Markdown at* `https://csharp.christiannagel.com/2016/07/03/markdown/`.

The sample code has so far made use of ASP.NET Core functionality. When you directly return a string from an ASP.NET Core MVC controller or inside a view, encoding happens by default. You need to make extra investment to not encode the result here.

Just returning a string with an ASP.NET Core controller results in an encoded string (code file `ASPNETCoreMVCSecurity/Controllers/HomeController.cs`):

```
public string Echo(string x) => x;
```

To send an unencoded string, the `Content` method of the `Controller` base class can be used, and you specify that the content is returned as text/html:

```
public IActionResult EchoUnencoded(string x) => Content(x, "text/html");
```

Let's go a step further on using Razor code in a view. Here, the `EchoWithView` method passes the input data from the user using `ViewBag.SampleData` to a view (code file `ASPNETCoreMVCSecurity/Controllers/HomeController.cs`):

```
public IActionResult EchoWithView(string x)
{
  ViewBag.SampleData = x;
  return View();
}
```

In the view, encoding happens by default. Passing the input data using the Razor expression `@data`. `data` is a local variable where the passed `ViewBag` information is assigned. For not making use of encoding, the `Html` helper class with the method `Raw` can be used (code file `ASPNETCoreMVCSecurity/Views/Home/EchoWithView.cshtml`):

```
@{
   string data = ViewBag.SampleData;
}
<div>
  this is encoded
</div>
<div>@data</div>

<br />
<div>
  This is not encoded
</div>
<div>
  @Html.Raw(@data)
</div>
```

> **NOTE** *When explicitly sending unencoded data to the client, you need to make sure the input can be trusted—for example, HTML converted from Markdown instead of directly returning user input.*

> **NOTE** *You can use the* `UrlEncoder` *class when using user input for URL strings similarly to how you use the* `HtmlEncoder` *class when using user input as HTML content.*

SQL Injection

Another common problem with web applications is SQL injection. As with HTML encoding, the issue can easily be avoided by using built-in functionality.

The following code snippet creates a SQL string that directly assigns the input parameter in the `SqlSample` controller method. With this, the user can enter `;SELECT * FROM Table Users`, and all this information is shown to the user:

```
public IActionResult SqlSample(string id)
{
  string connectionString = GetConnectionString();
```

```
var sqlConnection = new SqlConnection(connectionString);
SqlCommand command = sqlConnection.CreateCommand();
// don't do this - string concatenation for SQL commands!
command.CommandText = "SELECT * FROM Customers WHERE City = " + id;
sqlConnection.Open();
using (SqlDataReader reader =
  command.ExecuteReader(System.Data.CommandBehavior.CloseConnection))
{
  var sb = new StringBuilder();
  while (reader.Read())
  {
    for (int i = 0; i < reader.FieldCount; i++)
    {
      sb.Append(reader[i]);
    }
    sb.AppendLine();
  }
  ViewBag.Data = sb.ToString();
}
return View(); }
```

You should never use string concatenation with SQL statements. Instead, you can easily avoid this problem by using parameters or implicitly using Entity Framework Core parameters.

> **NOTE** *Using SQL commands is covered in Chapter 25, "ADO.NET and Transactions." Entity Framework Core is covered in Chapter 26, "Entity Framework Core."*

Cross-Site Request Forgery

Cross-site request forgery (XSRF) is an attack in which a malicious website tries to replay a user and enter data without the user knowing.

Let's get into an example where the user enters book information in a form. Book is a simple model class containing Title and Publisher properties. Within the HomeController, the EditBook method returns a view (code file ASPNETCoreMVCSecurity/Controllers/HomeController.cs):

```
public IActionResult EditBook() => View();
```

The view defines simple input data where the user can enter title and publisher information, and pass this information to the server with a HTTP POST request (code file ASPNETCoreMVCSecurity/Views/EditBook.cshtml):

```
@{
    ViewData["Title"] = "EditBook";
}
<h2>Edit Book</h2>

<form asp-controller="Home" asp-action="EditBook" method="post">
  <label for="title">Title:</label>
  <input type="text" id="title" name="title" />
  <br />
  <label for="publisher">Publisher:</label>
  <input type="text" id="publisher" name="publisher" />
  <br />
  <input type="submit" value="Submit" />
</form>
```

With the HTTP POST request, the following `EditBook` method is invoked to display a view with the entered user data (code file `ASPNETCoreMVCSecurity/Controllers/HomeController.cs`):

```
[HttpPost]
public IActionResult EditBook(Book book) => View("EditBookResult", book);
```

When you run the application while opening the URL `http://localhost:24897/Home/EditBook`, book information can be entered, the submit button clicked, the information is received from the controller, and the book information is shown in the view result.

Meanwhile, a malicious website just needs to use the same link to post the data in its own form. Check the following code snippet with the form element referencing the same URL as before. This form is hosted from a different website, `http//localhost:9817/dothis.html`. Here it's only a different port, but it could be a different domain name as well. The user doesn't need to enter anything with the form (the input elements are hidden, thus not shown to the user). The user just needs to click the submit button without knowing something different happens behind the scenes (code file `HackingSite/wwwroot/dothis.html`):

```
<h1>Click this for a win!</h1>

<!-- form has a redirect to the website being hacked -->
<form action="http://localhost:24897/Home/EditBook" method="post">
  <input type="hidden" value="bad book title" name="title" />
  <input type="hidden" value="bad publisher" name="publisher" />
  <input type="submit" value="Click Now!" />
</form>
```

When you click this link, the malicious data is transmitted to the website on behalf of the user. If the user is authenticated with the Book website and didn't sign out, the data is submitted on behalf of the user, and probably some ordering happened with a different delivery address.

To avoid this behavior, ASP.NET Core offers anti forgery tokens. Such a token needs to be created from the form that should be used from the user to enter valid data and is validated on receiving the data.

The edit book form is now changed to include this token with the HTML helper method `AntiForgeryToken` (code file `ASPNETCoreMVCSecurity/Views/EditBook.cshtml`):

```
<form asp-controller="Home" asp-action="EditBook" method="post">
  @Html.AntiForgeryToken()

  <label for="title">Title:</label>
  <input type="text" id="title" name="title" />
  <br />
  <label for="publisher">Publisher:</label>
  <input type="text" id="publisher" name="publisher" />
  <br />
  <input type="submit" value="Submit" />
</form>
```

When you run the application, you can see a hidden form field with the automatically generated token. When the data is retrieved, the token is validated using the `ValidateAntiForgeryToken` attribute (code file `ASPNETCoreMVCSecurity/Controllers/HomeController.cs`):

```
[HttpPost]
[ValidateAntiForgeryToken]
public IActionResult EditBook(Book book) => View("EditBookResult", book);
```

When you run the malicious website now, a response is returned without accepting invalid data.

SUMMARY

This chapter covered several aspects of security with .NET applications. Users are represented by identities and principals, classes that implement the interface `IIdentity` and `IPrincipal`. You've also seen how to access claims from identities.

A brief overview of cryptography demonstrated how the signing and encrypting of data enable the exchange of keys in a secure way. .NET offers both symmetric and asymmetric cryptography algorithms as well as hashing and signing.

With access control lists you can read and modify access to operating system resources such as files. You program ACLs similarly to the way you program secure pipes, registry keys, Active Directory entries, and many other operating system resources.

In many cases you can work with security from higher abstraction levels. For example, using HTTPS to access a web server, keys for encryption are exchanged behind the scenes. The `File` class offers an `Encrypt` method (using the NTFS file system) to easily encrypt files. Still it's important to know what happens behind this functionality.

Regarding web applications, you've seen common issues on trusting user input that results in various attacks, including cross-site request forgery. You've seen how various issues can be avoided using encoding and anti-forgery request tokens to avoid XSRF.

The next two chapters make use of data in the database, starting with ADO.NET.

25

ADO.NET and Transactions

WROX.COM CODE DOWNLOADS FOR THIS CHAPTER

The Wrox.com code downloads for this chapter are found at www.wrox.com on the Download Code tab. The source code is also available in the GitHub repository https://github.com/ProfessionalCSharp/ProfessionalCSharp7 in the folder ADONET. The code for this chapter is divided into the following major examples:

➤ ConnectionSamples
➤ CommandSamples
➤ AsyncSamples
➤ TransactionSamples
➤ SystemTransactionSamples

ADO.NET OVERVIEW

This chapter discusses how to access a relational database like SQL Server from your C# programs using ADO.NET. It shows you how to connect to and disconnect from a database, how to use queries, and how to add and update records. You learn the various command object options and see how commands can be used for each of the options presented by the SQL Server provider classes; how to call stored procedures with command objects; and how to use transactions.

ADO.NET previously shipped different database providers: a provider for SQL Server and one for Oracle, using OLEDB and ODBC. The OLEDB technology is discontinued, so this provider shouldn't be used with new applications. Accessing the Oracle database, Microsoft's provider is discontinued as well because a provider from Oracle (http://www.oracle.com/technetwork/topics/dotnet/products) better fits the needs. For other data sources (also for Oracle), many third-party providers are available. Before using the ODBC provider, you should use a provider specific for the data source you access. The code samples in this chapter are based on SQL Server, but you can easily change it to use different connection and command objects, such as `OracleConnection` and `OracleCommand` when accessing the Oracle database instead of `SqlConnection` and `SqlCommand`.

> **NOTE** *This chapter does not cover the* `DataSet` *to have tables in memory, although they are supported by .NET Core 2.0. Datasets enable you to retrieve records from a database and store the content within in-memory data tables with relations. Datasets have been used a lot with earlier versions of .NET. Now, you can use Entity Framework Core (EF Core) instead. EF Core is covered in Chapter 26, "Entity Framework Core." This newer technology enables you to have object relations instead of table-based relations.*

Sample Database

The examples in this chapter use the *Books* database for SQL Server. A backup file of this database is part of the source code download in the directory `CreateDatabase`. Using the backup file, you can restore the database backup using SQL Server Management Studio as shown in Figure 25-1. As an alternative, you can also use the SQL script `CreateBooks.sql` to create the database. In case you don't have SQL Server Management Studio on your system, you can download a free version from `https://docs.microsoft.com/ sql/ssms/download-sql-server-management-studio-ssms`.

The SQL server used with this chapter is SQL Server LocalDb. This is a database server that is installed as part of Visual Studio. You can use any other SQL Server edition as well; you just need to change the connection string accordingly.

NuGet Packages and Namespaces

The sample code for all the ADO.NET samples makes use of the following dependencies and namespaces:

Dependencies

```
Microsoft.Extensions.Configuration
```

```
Microsoft.Extensions.Configuration.Json
```

```
System.Data.SqlClient
```

Namespaces

```
Microsoft.Extensions.Configuration
```

```
System
```

```
System.Collections
```

```
System.Data
```

```
System.Data.SqlClient
```

```
System.IO
```

```
System.Threading.Tasks
```

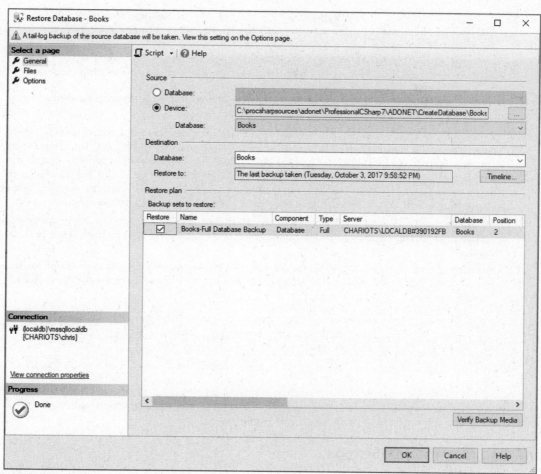

FIGURE 25-1

USING DATABASE CONNECTIONS

To access the database, you need to provide connection parameters, such as the machine on which the database is running and possibly your login credentials. You make a connection to SQL Server using the `SqlConnection` class.

The following code snippet illustrates how to create, open, and close a connection to the Books database (code file `ConnectionSamples/Program.cs`):

```
public static void OpenConnection()
{
  string connectionString = @"server=(localdb)\MSSQLLocalDB;" +
    "integrated security=SSPI;database=Books";

  var connection = new SqlConnection(connectionString);
  connection.Open();
  // Do something useful
  Console.WriteLine("Connection opened");
  connection.Close();
}
```

> **NOTE** *The* SqlConnection *class implements the* IDisposable *interface with the* Dispose *method in addition to the* Close *method. Both do the same, to release the connection. With this, you can use the* using *statement to close the connection.*

In the example connection string, the parameters used are as follows (the parameters are delimited by a semicolon in the connection string):

➤ server=(localdb)\MSSQLLocalDB—This denotes the database server to connect to. SQL Server permits several separate database server instances to be running on the same machine. Here, you are connecting to the localdb Server and the MSSQLLocalDB SQL Server instance that is created with the installation of SQL Server. If you are using the local installation of SQL Server, change this part to server=(local). Instead of using the keyword server, you can use Data Source instead. Connecting to SQL Azure, you can set Data Source=servername.database.windows.net.

➤ database=Books—This describes the database instance to connect to; each SQL Server process can expose several database instances. Instead of the keyword database, you can instead use Initial Catalog.

➤ integrated security=SSPI—This uses Windows Authentication to connect to the database. In case you are using SQL Azure, you need to set User Id and Password instead, or use the Azure Active Directory.

> **NOTE** *You can find great information about connection strings with many different databases at* http://www.connectionstrings.com.

The ConnectionSamples example opens a database connection using the defined connection string and then closes that connection. After you have opened the connection, you can issue commands against the data source; when you are finished, you can close the connection.

Managing Connection Strings

Instead of hard-coding the connection string with the C# code, it is better to read it from a configuration file. With .NET Core, configuration files can be JSON or XML formats, or read from environmental variables. With the following sample, the connection string is read from a JSON configuration file (code file ConnectionSamples/config.json):

```
{
  "Data": {
    "DefaultConnection": {
    "ConnectionString":
      "Server=(localdb)\\MSSQLLocalDB;Database=Books;
        Trusted_Connection=True;"
    }
  }
}
```

The JSON file can be read using the Configuration API defined in the NuGet package Microsoft .Extensions.Configuration. To use JSON configuration files, the NuGet package Microsoft .Extensions.Configuration.Json is added as well. For reading a configuration file, the ConfigurationBuilder is created. The AddJsonFile extension method adds the JSON file config .json to read configuration information from this file—if it is in the same path as the program. To configure a different path, you can invoke the method SetBasePath. Invoking the Build method of the ConfigurationBuilder builds up the configuration from all the added configuration files and returns an object implementing the IConfiguration interface. With this, the configuration values can be retrieved, such as the configuration value for Data:DefaultConnection:ConnectionString (code file ConnectionSamples/Program.cs):

```
public static void ConnectionUsingConfig()
{
  var configurationBuilder = new ConfigurationBuilder()
    .SetBasePath(Directory.GetCurrentDirectory())
    .AddJsonFile("config.json");
  IConfiguration config = configurationBuilder.Build();
  string connectionString = config["Data:DefaultConnection:ConnectionString"];
  Console.WriteLine(connectionString);
}
```

Connection Pools

When two-tier applications were done several years ago it was a good idea to open the connection on application start and close it only when the application was closed. Nowadays, this is not a good idea. The reason for this program architecture was that it takes some time to open a connection. Now, closing a connection doesn't close the connection with the server. Instead, the connection is added to a connection pool. When you open the connection again, it can be taken from the pool, thus it is very fast to open a connection; it only takes time to open the first connection.

Pooling can be configured with several options in the connection string. Setting the option Pooling to false disables the connection pool; by default, it's enabled—Pooling = true. Min Pool Size and Max Pool Size enable you to configure the number of connections in the pool. By default, Min Pool Size has a value of 0 and Max Pool Size has a value of 100. Connection Lifetime defines how long a connection should stay inactive in the pool before it is really released.

Connection Information

After creating a connection, you can register event handlers to get some information about the connection. The SqlConnection class defines the InfoMessage and StateChange events. The InfoMessage event is fired every time an information or warning message is returned from SQL Server. The StateChange event is fired when the state of the connection changes—for example, the connection is opened or closed (code file ConnectionSamples/Program.cs):

```
public static void ConnectionInformation()
{
  using (var connection = new SqlConnection(GetConnectionString()))
  {
    connection.InfoMessage += (sender, e) =>
    {
      Console.WriteLine($"warning or info {e.Message}");
    };

    connection.StateChange += (sender, e) =>
    {
      Console.WriteLine($"current state: {e.CurrentState}, before: " +
        $"{e.OriginalState}");
    };
    try
    {
      connection.StatisticsEnabled = true;
      connection.FireInfoMessageEventOnUserErrors = true;
      connection.Open();

      Console.WriteLine("connection opened");
      //... Read some records
```

```
    }
    catch (Exception ex)
    {
      Console.WriteLine(ex.Message);
    }
  }
}
```

When you run the application, you can see the `StateChange` event fired and the `Open` and `Closed` state:

```
current state: Open, before: Closed
connection opened
... output reading records
current state: Closed, before: Open
```

In case an exception happens, by default the `InfoMessage` event is not fired. You can change this behavior by setting the property `FireInfoMessageEventOnUserErrors`. Then with an error, e.g. using the `Titl` property instead of `Title`, you can see this information with the application:

```
current state: Open, before: Closed
connection opened
warning or info: Invalid column name 'Titl'.
... output reading records
current state: Closed, before: Open
```

The `SqlConnection` class also offers statistic information. You just need to set the `StatisticsEnabled` property, then you can retrieve the statistics from the `RetrieveStatistics` method. This method returns the statistic with an object implementing the `IDictionary` interface:

```
IDictionary statistics = connection.RetrieveStatistics();
ShowStatistics(statistics);
connection.ResetStatistics();
```

The method `ShowStatistics` iterates all keys of the received `IDictionary` interface and displays all values:

```
private static void ShowStatistics(IDictionary statistics)
{
  Console.WriteLine("Statistics");
  foreach (var key in statistics.Keys)
  {
    Console.WriteLine($"{key}, value: {statistics[key]}");
  }
  Console.WriteLine();
}
```

Retrieving all records from the Books table shows this statistical information from the connection:

```
BuffersReceived, value: 1
BuffersSent, value: 1
BytesReceived, value: 142
BytesSent, value: 124
CursorOpens, value: 0
IduCount, value: 0
IduRows, value: 0
PreparedExecs, value: 0
Prepares, value: 0
SelectCount, value: 0
SelectRows, value: 0
ServerRoundtrips, value: 1
SumResultSets, value: 0
Transactions, value: 0
UnpreparedExecs, value: 1
ConnectionTime, value: 140
ExecutionTime, value: 456
NetworkServerTime, value: 8
```

COMMANDS

The "Using Database Connections" section briefly touched on the idea of issuing commands against a database. A command is, in its simplest form, a string of text containing SQL statements to be issued to the database. A command could also be a stored procedure, shown later in this section.

A command can be constructed by passing the SQL statement as a parameter to the constructor of the Command class, as shown in this example (code file CommandSamples/Program.cs):

```
public static void CreateCommand()
{
  using (var connection = new SqlConnection(GetConnectionString()))
  {
    string sql = "SELECT [Title], [Publisher], [ReleaseDate] " +
      "FROM [ProCSharp].[Books]";
    var command = new SqlCommand(sql, connection);
    connection.Open();
    //...
  }
}
```

A command can also be created by invoking the CreateCommand method of the SqlConnection and assigning the SQL statement to the CommandText property:

```
SqlCommand command = connection.CreateCommand();
command.CommandText = sql;
```

Commands often need parameters. For example, the following SQL statement requires a Title parameter. Don't be incited to use string concatenation to build up parameters. Instead, always use the parameter features of ADO.NET:

```
string sql = "SELECT [Title], [Publisher], [ReleaseDate] " +
"FROM [ProCSharp].[Books] WHERE lower([Title]) LIKE @Title";
var command = new SqlCommand(sql, connection);
```

When you add the parameter to the SqlCommand object, there's a simple way to use the Parameters property that returns a SqlParameterCollection and the AddWithValue method:

```
command.Parameters.AddWithValue("Title", "Professional C#%");
```

A more efficient method that's more programming work is to use overloads of the Add method by passing the name and the SQL data type:

```
command.Parameters.Add("TitleStart", SqlDbType.NVarChar, 50);
command.Parameters["Title"].Value = "Professional C#%";
```

It's also possible to create a SqlParameter object and add this to the SqlParameterCollection.

> **NOTE** *Don't be inclined to use string concatenation with SQL parameters. This is often misused for SQL injection attacks. Using* SqlParameter *objects inhibits such attacks.*

After you have defined the command, you need to execute it. There are several ways to issue the statement, depending on what, if anything, you expect to be returned from that command. The SqlCommand class provides the following ExecuteXX methods:

➤   ExecuteNonQuery—Executes the command but does not return any output

➤   ExecuteReader—Executes the command and returns a typed IDataReader

➤   ExecuteScalar—Executes the command and returns the value from the first column of the first row of any result set

ExecuteNonQuery

The ExecuteNonQuery method is commonly used for UPDATE, INSERT, or DELETE statements, for which the only returned value is the number of records affected. This method can, however, return results if you call a stored procedure that has output parameters. The sample code creates a new record within the ProCSharp .Books table. Figure 25-2 shows the design view of this table with Visual Studio 2017.

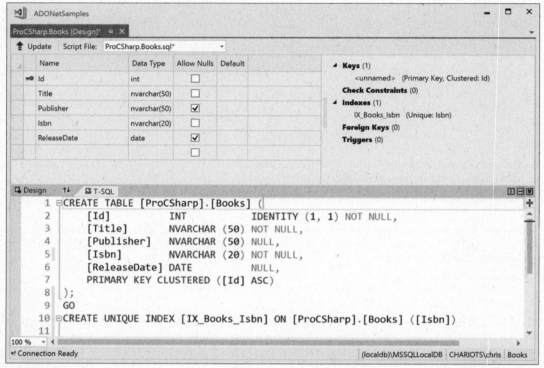

FIGURE 25-2

This table has an Id as primary key that is an identity column and thus does not need to be supplied creating the record. The Title and Isbn columns do not allow null (see Figure 25-2), but other columns do. In the sample code, all the columns are filled with values. The method ExecuteNonQuery defines the SQL INSERT statement, adds values for the parameters, and invokes the ExecuteNonQuery method of the SqlCommand class (code file CommandSamples/Program.cs):

```
public static void ExecuteNonQuery
{
  try
  {
    using (var connection = new SqlConnection(GetConnectionString()))
    {
      string sql = "INSERT INTO [ProCSharp].[Books] " +
        "([Title], [Publisher], [Isbn], [ReleaseDate]) " +
        "VALUES (@Title, @Publisher, @Isbn, @ReleaseDate)";
      var command = new SqlCommand(sql, connection);
      command.Parameters.AddWithValue("Title",
        "Professional C# 7 and .NET Core 2.0");
```

```
            command.Parameters.AddWithValue("Publisher", "Wrox Press");
            command.Parameters.AddWithValue("Isbn", "978-1119449270");
            command.Parameters.AddWithValue("ReleaseDate", new DateTime(2018, 4, 2));

            connection.Open();
            int records = command.ExecuteNonQuery();
            Console.WriteLine($"{records} record(s) inserted");
        }
    }
    catch (SqlException ex)
    {
        Console.WriteLine(ex.Message);
    }
}
```

ExecuteNonQuery returns the number of rows affected by the command as an int. When you run the method the first time, one record is inserted. When you run the same method a second time, you get an exception because of a unique index conflict. The Isbn has a unique index defined and thus is allowed only once. To run the method a second time, you need to delete the created record first.

ExecuteScalar

On many occasions it is necessary to return a single result from a SQL statement, such as the count of records in a given table or the current date/time on the server. You can use the ExecuteScalar method in such situations:

```
public static void ExecuteScalar()
{
    using (var connection = new SqlConnection(GetConnectionString()))
    {
        string sql = "SELECT COUNT(*) FROM [ProCSharp].[Books]";
        SqlCommand command = connection.CreateCommand();
        command.CommandText = sql;
        connection.Open();
        object count = command.ExecuteScalar();
        Console.WriteLine($"counted {count} book records");
    }
}
```

The method returns an object, which you can cast to the appropriate type if required. If the SQL you are calling returns only one column, it is preferable to use ExecuteScalar over any other method of retrieving that column. That also applies to stored procedures that return a single value.

ExecuteReader

The ExecuteReader method executes the command and returns a data reader object. The object returned can be used to iterate through the record(s) returned. The ExecuteReader sample makes use of an SQL query that is defined with the local function GetBookQuery in the method ExecuteReader (code file CommandSamples/Program.cs):

```
public static void ExecuteReader(string titleParameter)
{
    string GetBookQuery() =>
        "SELECT [Id], [Title], [Publisher], [ReleaseDate] "+
        "FROM [ProCSharp].[Books] WHERE lower([Title]) LIKE @Title " +
        "ORDER BY [ReleaseDate] DESC";
    //...
}
```

> **NOTE** *Local functions are explained in Chapter 13, "Functional Programming with C#."*

When you invoke the method ExecuteReader of the SqlCommand object, a SqlDataReader is returned. Note that the SqlDataReader needs to be disposed after it has been used. Also note that this time the SqlConnection object is not explicitly disposed at the end of the method. Passing the parameter CommandBehavior.CloseConnection to the ExecuteReader method automatically closes the connection on closing of the reader. If you don't supply this setting, you still need to close the connection.

For reading the records from the data reader, the Read method is invoked within a while loop. The first call to the Read method moves the cursor to the first record returned. When Read is invoked again, the cursor is positioned to the next record—if there's a record available. The Read method returns false if no record is available at the next position. When accessing the values of the columns, different GetXXX methods are invoked, such as GetInt32, GetString, and GetDateTime. These methods are strongly typed as they return the specific type needed, such as int, string, and DateTime. The index passed to these methods corresponds to the columns retrieved with the SQL SELECT statement, so the index stays the same even if the database structure changes. With the strongly typed GetXXX methods you need to pay attention to values where null is returned from the database; here the GetXXX method throws an exception with a value type returned. With the data retrieved, the ReleaseDate can be null. To avoid an exception in this case, the C# conditional statement ?: is used to check whether the value is null with the SqlDataReader.IsDbNull method. In that case, null is assigned to a nullable DateTime. Only if the value is not null, the DateTime is accessed with the GetDateTime method (code file CommandSamples/Program.cs):

```csharp
public static void ExecuteReader(string title)
{
  //...

  var connection = new SqlConnection(GetConnectionString());
  var command = new SqlCommand(GetBookQuery(), connection);
  var parameter = new SqlParameter("Title", SqlDbType.NVarChar, 50)
  {
    Value = $"{title}%"
  };
  command.Parameters.Add(parameter);

  connection.Open();
  using (SqlDataReader reader =
    command.ExecuteReader(CommandBehavior.CloseConnection))
  {
    while (reader.Read())
    {
      int id = reader.GetInt32(0);
      string bookTitle = reader.GetString(1);
      string publisher = reader.GetString(2);
      DateTime? releaseDate =
        reader.IsDbNull(3) ? (DateTime?)null : reader.GetDateTime(3);
      DateTime from = reader.GetDateTime(4);
      Console.WriteLine($"{id,5}. {bookTitle,-40} {publisher,-15} " +
        $"{releaseDate:d}");
    }
  }
}
```

When you run the application and pass the title Professional C# to the ExecuteReader method, you see this output:

```
1015. Professional C# 7 and .NET Core 2.0    Wrox Press    4/2/2018
   1. Professional C# 6 and .NET Core 1.0    Wrox Press    4/11/2016
```

```
   2. Professional C# 5.0 and .NET 4.5.1       Wrox Press      2/9/2014
  11. Professional C# 2012 and .NET 4.5        Wrox Press      10/18/2012
   9. Professional C# 4 and .NET 4             Wrox Press      3/8/2010
   8. Professional C# 2008                     Wrox Press      5/24/2008
  18. Professional C# 2005 with .NET 3.0       Wrox Press      6/12/2007
  12. Professional C# 2005                     Wrox Press      11/7/2005
   6. Professional C# 3rd Edition              Wrox Press      6/2/2004
  10. Professional C# 2nd Edition              Wrox Press      3/28/2002
1010. Professional C# Web Services             Wrox Press      12/1/2001
1012. Professional C# (Beta 2 Edition)         Wrox Press      6/1/2001
```

With the `SqlDataReader`, instead of using the typed methods `GetXXX`, you can use the untyped indexer that returns an object. With this, you need to cast to the corresponding type:

```
int id = (int)reader[0];
string bookTitle = (string)reader[1];
string publisher = (string)reader[2];
DateTime? releaseDate = (DateTime?)reader[3];
```

The indexer of the `SqlDataReader` also allows a `string` to be used instead of the `int`, passing the column name. This is the slowest method of these different options, but it might fulfill your needs. Compared to the time it costs to make a service call, the additional time needed to access the indexer can be ignored:

```
int id = (int)reader["Id"];
string bookTitle = (string)reader["Title"];
string publisher = (string)reader["Publisher"];
DateTime? releaseDate = (DateTime?)reader["ReleaseDate"];
```

Calling Stored Procedures

Calling a stored procedure with a command object is just a matter of defining the name of the stored procedure, adding a definition for each parameter of the procedure, and then executing the command with one of the methods presented in the previous section.

The following sample calls the stored procedure `GetBooksByPublisher` to get all the books from a publisher. This stored procedure receives one parameter to return records of the requested books:

```
CREATE PROCEDURE [ProCSharp].[GetBooksByPublisher]
  @publisher nvarchar(50)
AS
  SELECT [Id], [Title], [Publisher], [ReleaseDate] FROM [ProCSharp].[Books]
  WHERE [Publisher] = @publisher ORDER BY [ReleaseDate]
```

To invoke the stored procedure, the `CommandText` of the `SqlCommand` object is set to the name of the stored procedure, and the `CommandType` is set to `CommandType.StoredProcedure`. Other than that, the command is invoked similarly to the way you've seen before. The parameter is created using the `CreateParameter` method of the `SqlCommand` object, but you can use other methods to create the parameter used earlier as well. With the parameter, the `SqlDbType`, `ParameterName`, and `Value` properties are filled. Because the stored procedure returns records, it is invoked by calling the method `ExecuteReader` (code file `CommandSamples/Program.cs`):

```
private static void StoredProcedure(string publisher)
{
  using (var connection = new SqlConnection(GetConnectionString()))
  {
    SqlCommand command = connection.CreateCommand();
    command.CommandText = "[ProCSharp].[GetBooksByPublisher]";
    command.CommandType = CommandType.StoredProcedure;
    SqlParameter p1 = command.CreateParameter();
    p1.SqlDbType = SqlDbType.NvarChar;
    p1.ParameterName = "@Publisher";
    p1.Value = publisher;
```

```
      command.Parameters.Add(p1);
      connection.Open();
      using (SqlDataReader reader = command.ExecuteReader())
      {
        while (reader.Read())
        {
          int recursionLevel = (int)reader["Id"];
          string title = (string)reader["Title"];
          string pub = (string)reader["Publisher"];
          DateTime releaseDate = (DateTime)reader["ReleaseDate"];
          Console.WriteLine($"{title} - {pub}; {releaseDate:d}");
        }
      }
    }
  }
}
```

When you run the application and pass the publisher Wrox Press, you get the result as shown:

```
Professional C# (Beta 2 Edition) - Wrox Press; 6/1/2001
Beginning C# - Wrox Press; 9/15/2001
Professional C# Web Services - Wrox Press; 12/1/2001
Professional C# 2nd Edition - Wrox Press; 3/28/2002
Beginning Visual C# - Wrox Press; 8/20/2002
Professional .NET Network Programming - Wrox Press; 10/1/2002
ASP to ASP.NET Migration Handbook - Wrox Press; 2/1/2003
Professional C# 3rd Edition - Wrox Press; 6/2/2004
Professional C# 2005 - Wrox Press; 11/7/2005
Beginning Visual C# 2005 - Wrox Press; 11/7/2005
Professional C# 2005 with .NET 3.0 - Wrox Press; 6/12/2007
Beginning Visual C# 2008 - Wrox Press; 5/5/2008
Professional C# 2008 - Wrox Press; 5/24/2008
Professional C# 4 and .NET 4 - Wrox Press; 3/8/2010
Beginning Visual C# 2010 - Wrox Press; 4/5/2010
Real World .NET, C#, and Silverlight - Wrox Press; 11/22/2011
Professional C# 2012 and .NET 4.5 - Wrox Press; 10/18/2012
Beginning Visual C# 2012 Programming - Wrox Press; 12/4/2012
Professional C# 5.0 and .NET 4.5.1 - Wrox Press; 2/9/2014
Professional C# 6 and .NET Core 1.0 - Wrox Press; 4/11/2016
Professional C# 7 and .NET Core 2.0 - Wrox Press; 4/2/2018
```

Depending on the return of the stored procedure, you need to invoke the stored procedure with ExecuteReader, ExecuteScalar, or ExecuteNonQuery.

With a stored procedure that contains Output parameters, you need to specify the Direction property of the SqlParameter. By default, the direction is ParameterDirection.Input:

```
var pOut = new SqlParameter();
pOut.Direction = ParameterDirection.Output;
```

ASYNCHRONOUS DATA ACCESS

Accessing the database can take some time. Here you shouldn't block the user interface. The ADO.NET classes offer task-based asynchronous programming by offering asynchronous methods in addition to the synchronous ones. The following code snippet is like the previous one using the SqlDataReader, but it makes use of Async method calls. The connection is opened with SqlConnection.OpenAsync, the reader is returned from the method SqlCommand.ExecuteReaderAsync, and the records are retrieved using SqlDataReader.ReadAsync. With all these methods, the calling thread is not blocked but can do other work before getting the result (code file AsyncSamples/Program.cs):

```
public static async Task Main()
{
  await ReadAsync("Wrox Press");
```

```
    }

    public static async Task ReadAsync(int productId)
    {
        var connection = new SqlConnection(GetConnectionString());

        string sql = "SELECT [Title], [Publisher], [ReleaseDate] " +
          "FROM [ProCSharp].[Books] WHERE lower([Title]) " +
          "LIKE @Title ORDER BY [ReleaseDate]";

        var command = new SqlCommand(sql, connection);
        var titleParameter = new SqlParameter("Title", SqlDbType.NVarChar, 50);
        titleParameter.Value = title;
        command.Parameters.Add(titleParameter);

        await connection.OpenAsync();

        using (SqlDataReader reader =
          await command.ExecuteReaderAsync(CommandBehavior.CloseConnection))
        {
            while (await reader.ReadAsync())
            {
                int id = reader.GetInt32(0);
                string bookTitle = reader.GetString(1);
                string publisher = reader[2].ToString();
                DateTime? releaseDate =
                  reader.IsDBNull(3) ? (DateTime?)null : reader.GetDateTime(3);
                Console.WriteLine($"{id,5}. {bookTitle,-40} {publisher,-15} " +
                  $"{releaseDate:d}");
            }
        }
    }
}
```

> **NOTE** *The asynchronous* Main *method requires at least C# 7.1.*

Using the asynchronous method calls is not only advantageous with Windows applications but also useful on the server side for making multiple calls simultaneous. The asynchronous methods of the ADO.NET API have overloads to support the CancellationToken for an earlier stop of a long-running method.

> **NOTE** *For more information about asynchronous method calls and the* CancellationToken, *read Chapter 15, "Asynchronous Programming."*

TRANSACTIONS WITH ADO.NET

By default, a single command is running within a transaction. If you need to issue multiple commands, and either all of these or none happen, you can start and commit transactions explicitly.

Transactions are described by the term ACID. ACID is a four-letter acronym for *atomicity, consistency, isolation,* and *durability*:

➤ **Atomicity**—Represents one unit of work. With a transaction, either the complete unit of work succeeds, or nothing is changed.

➤ **Consistency**—The state before the transaction was started and after the transaction is completed must be valid. During the transaction, the state may have interim values.

➤ **Isolation**—Transactions that happen concurrently are isolated from the state, which is changed during a transaction. Transaction A cannot see the interim state of transaction B until the transaction is completed.

➤ **Durability**—After a transaction is completed, it must be stored in a durable way. This means that if the power goes down or the server crashes, the state must be recovered at reboot.

> **NOTE** *Transactions and valid state can easily be described as a wedding ceremony. A bridal couple is standing before a transaction coordinator. The transaction coordinator asks the first of the couple: "Do you want to marry this person on your side?" If the first one agrees, the second is asked: "Do you want to marry this person?" If the second one declines, the first receives a rollback. A valid state with this transaction is only that both are married, or none are. If both agree, the transaction is committed, and both are in the married state. If one denies, the transaction is aborted, and both stay in the unmarried state. An invalid state is that one is married, and the other is not. The transaction guarantees that the result is never in an invalid state.*

With ADO.NET, transactions can be started by invoking the `BeginTransaction` method of the `SqlConnection`. A transaction is always associated with one connection; you can't create ADO.NET transactions over multiple connections. The method `BeginTransaction` returns an `SqlTransaction` that in turn needs to be used with the commands running under the same transaction (code file `TransactionSamples/Program.cs`):

```
public static void TransactionSample()
{
  using (var connection = new SqlConnection(GetConnectionString()))
  {
    await connection.OpenAsync();
    SqlTransaction tx = connection.BeginTransaction();
    //...
  }
}
```

The code sample creates a record in the `ProCSharp.Books` table. Using the SQL clause `INSERT INTO`, a record is added. The `Books` table defines an auto-increment identifier that is returned with the second SQL statement `SELECT SCOPE_IDENTITY()` that returns the created identifier. After the `SqlCommand` object is instantiated, the connection is assigned by setting the `Connection` property, and the transaction is assigned by setting the `Transaction` property. With ADO.NET transactions, you cannot assign the transaction to a command that uses a different connection. However, you can also create commands with the same connection that are not related to a transaction:

```
public static void TransactionSample()
{
  //...
  try
  {
    string sql = "INSERT INTO [ProCSharp].[Books] " +
      "([Title], [Publisher], [Isbn], [ReleaseDate])" +
      "VALUES (@Title, @Publisher, @Isbn, @ReleaseDate); " +
      "SELECT SCOPE_IDENTITY()";

    var command = new SqlCommand
    {
      CommandText = sql,
      Connection = connection,
      Transaction = tx
    }
    //...
}
```

> **NOTE** *You might wonder why the* `OpenAsync` *and* `BeginTransaction` *methods are defined outside of the* `try` *block. These calls can fail, too. For example, if the* `OpenAsync` *method fails, the exception is not caught in the local* `catch` *block, but instead a matching* `catch` *is searched for outside of the* `TransactionSample` *method. It's a good way to deal with such exceptions separately. The* `tx` *variable needs to be declared outside of the* `try` *block—otherwise it wouldn't be possible to use it in the* `catch`.

After defining the parameters and filling the values, the command is executed by invoking the method `ExecuteScalarAsync`. This time the `ExecuteScalarAsync` method is used with the `INSERT INTO` clause because the complete SQL statement ends by returning a single result: The created identifier is returned from `SELECT SCOPE_IDENTITY()`. In case you set a breakpoint after the `WriteLine` method and check the result in the database, you will not see the new record in the database although the created identifier is already returned. The reason is that the transaction is not yet committed:

```
public static void TransactionSample()
{
  //...
  var p1 = new SqlParameter("Title", SqlDbType.NVarChar, 50);
  var p2 = new SqlParameter("Publisher", SqlDbType.NVarChar, 50);
  var p3 = new SqlParameter("Isbn", SqlDbType.NVarChar, 20);
  var p4 = new SqlParameter("ReleaseDate", SqlDbType.Date);
  command.Parameters.AddRange(new SqlParameter[] { p1, p2, p3, p4 });

  command.Parameters["Title"].Value = "Professional C# 8 and .NET Core 3.0";
  command.Parameters["Publisher"].Value = "Wrox Press";
  command.Parameters["Isbn"].Value = "42-08154711";
  command.Parameters["ReleaseDate"].Value = new DateTime(2020, 9, 2);

  object id = await command.ExecuteScalarAsync();
  Console.WriteLine($"record added with id: {id}");
  //...
}
```

Now another record can be created within the same transaction. With the sample code, the same command is used that has the connection and transaction still associated, just the values are changed before invoking `ExecuteScalarAsync` again. You could also create a new `SqlCommand` object that accesses a different table in the same database. The transaction is committed invoking the `Commit` method of the `SqlTransaction` object. After the commit, you can see the new records in the database:

```
public static void TransactionSample()
{
  //...
  command.Parameters["Title"].Value = "Professional C# 9 and .NET Core 4.0";
  command.Parameters["Publisher"].Value = "Wrox Press";
  command.Parameters["Isbn"].Value = "42-08154711";
  command.Parameters["ReleaseDate"].Value = new DateTime(2022, 11, 2);

  id = await command.ExecuteScalarAsync();
  Console.WriteLine($"record added with id: {id}");

  tx.Commit();
}
catch (Exception ex)
{
  Console.WriteLine($"error {ex.Message}, rolling back");
  tx.Rollback();
}
}
```

Did you check the `Isbn` number with both records? It's the same. Because the database table is specified with a unique index on the `Isbn` number, writing the second records fail with an exception of type `SqlException` and the exception information `Cannot insert duplicate key row in object 'ProCSharp.Books' with unique index 'IX_Books_Isbn'. The duplicate key value is (42-08154711)`. As a result, the `Rollback` method makes an undo of all the SQL commands in the same transaction. The state is reset as it was before the transaction was started. This way, the first record is not written to the database as well.

In case you run the program in debugging mode and have a breakpoint active for too long, the transaction will be aborted because the transaction timeout is reached. Transactions are not meant to have user input while the transaction is active. It's also not useful to increase the transaction timeout for user input, because having a transaction active causes locks within the database. Depending on the records you read and write, either row locks, page locks, or table locks can happen. You can influence the locks and thus performance of the database by setting an isolation level for creating the transaction. However, this also influences the ACID properties of the transaction—for example, not everything is isolated.

The default isolation level that is applied to the transaction is `ReadCommitted`. The following table shows the different options you can set.

ISOLATION LEVEL	DESCRIPTION
ReadUncommitted	Transactions are not isolated from each other. With this level, there is no wait for locked records from other transactions. This way, uncommitted data can be read from other transactions—dirty reads. This level is usually only used for reading records for which it does not matter if you read interim changes, such as reports.
ReadCommitted	Waits for records with a write-lock from other transactions. This way, a dirty read cannot happen. This level sets a read-lock for the current record read and a write-lock for the records being written until the transaction is completed. During the reading of a sequence of records, with every new record that is read, the prior record is unlocked. That's why nonrepeatable reads can happen.
RepeatableRead	Holds the lock for the records read until the transaction is completed. This way, the problem of nonrepeatable reads is avoided. Phantom reads can still occur.
Serializable	Holds a range lock. While the transaction is running, it is not possible to add a new record that belongs to the same range from which the data is being read.
Snapshot	With this level a snapshot is done from the actual data. This level reduces the locks as modified rows are copied. That way, other transactions can still read the old data without needing to wait for releasing of the lock.
Unspecified	Indicates that the provider is using an isolation level that is different from the values defined by the `IsolationLevel` enumeration.
Chaos	This level is like `ReadUncommitted`, but in addition to performing the actions of the `ReadUncommitted` value, `Chaos` does not lock updated records.

The following table summarizes the problems that can occur because of setting the most commonly used transaction isolation levels.

ISOLATION LEVEL	DIRTY READS	NONREPEATABLE READS	PHANTOM READS
ReadUncommitted	Y	Y	Y
ReadCommitted	N	Y	Y

ISOLATION LEVEL	DIRTY READS	NONREPEATABLE READS	PHANTOM READS
RepeatableRead	N	N	Y
Serializable	Y	Y	Y

TRANSACTIONS WITH SYSTEM.TRANSACTIONS

Another way to deal with transactions is by using System.Transactions. These classes have been available since .NET Framework 2.0 but have not been available with .NET Core 1.1. With .NET Core 2.1, these types are back, and can be used from ADO.NET (starting with version 4.5 of System.Data.SqlClient) as well as Entity Framework Core 2.1.

The System.Transactions namespace defines several classes for transactions. Probably the most important class is Transaction. This can be used to directly access ambient transactions, to give information about the transaction, and to start a rollback if something fails. The following table describes the properties and methods of the Transaction class:

TRANSACTION CLASS MEMBER	DESCRIPTION
Current	The property Current is a static property. Transaction.Current returns an ambient transaction if one exists. Ambient transactions are discussed later in this chapter.
IsolationLevel	The IsolationLevel property returns an object of type IsolationLevel. IsolationLevel is an enumeration that defines what access other transactions have to the interim result of the transaction. Check the section "Transactions with ADO.NET" earlier in this chapter for more information about isolation levels.
TransactionInformation	The TransactionInformation property returns a TransactionInformation object, which provides information about the current state of the transaction, the time when the transaction was created, and transaction identifiers.
Rollback	With the Rollback method, you can abort a transaction and undo everything that is part of the transaction, setting all results to the state before the transaction.
DependentClone	With the DependentClone method, you can create a transaction that depends on the current transaction.
TransactionCompleted	TransactionCompleted is an event that is fired when the transaction is completed—either successfully or unsuccessfully. With an event handler object of type TransactionCompletedEventHandler, you can access the Transaction object and read its state.

The sample application (a .NET Core Console App) showing the features of System.Transactions makes use of the following dependencies and namespaces:

Dependencies

```
Microsoft.Extensions.Configuration
```

```
Microsoft.Extensions.Configuration.Json

System.Data.SqlClient
```

Namespaces

```
Microsoft.Extensions.Configuration

System

System.Data.SqlClient

System.IO

System.Linq

System.Threading.Tasks

System.Transactions
```

The code sample defines a `Utilities` class with some helper methods that are used throughout the different samples. (code file `SystemTransactionSamples/Utilities.cs`):

```csharp
public class Utilities
{
  public static bool AbortTx()
  {
    Console.WriteLine("Abort the transaction (y/n)?");
    return Console.ReadLine().ToLower().Equals("y");
  }

  public static void DisplayTransactionInformation(string title,
    TransactionInformation info)
  {
    if (info == null) throw new ArgumentNullException(nameof(info));

    Console.WriteLine(title);
    Console.WriteLine($"Creation time: {info.CreationTime:T}");
    Console.WriteLine($"Status: {info.Status}");
    Console.WriteLine($"Local Id: {info.LocalIdentifier}");
    Console.WriteLine($"Distributed Id: {info.DistributedIdentifier}");
    Console.WriteLine();
  }
}
```

> **NOTE** *The sample code asks the user if the transaction should be aborted. This is good for demonstration purposes, but you should never have user interactions within a transaction in a real application. Records are locked while a transaction is active. You don't want to hinder other users to work because one user has locks opened because of these locks.*
>
> *You also need to pay attention to the transaction timeout. If the user input takes more time than the transaction timeout, the transaction is aborted.*

This sample makes use of the same database as the previous samples, but there's an important change. This time the `Book` type is defined to map information from the `Books` table (code file `SystemTransactionSamples/Book.cs`):

```csharp
public class Book
{
  public int Id { get; set; }
  public string Title { get; set; }
```

```
    public string Publisher { get; set; }
    public string Isbn { get; set; }
    public DateTime? ReleaseDate { get; set; }
}
```

The `BookData` class maps the `Book` type to the database and implements the `AddBookAsync` method to add a new record to the `Books` table. The implementation looks like the implementation you've seen it before when invoking the `ExecuteNonQuery` method to insert a new record, but there is an important difference. This time, the `System.Transactions.Transaction` is enlisted using the `SqlConnection` method `EnlistTransaction`. This way the `SqlConnection` participates with the outcome of this transaction (code file `SystemTransactionSamples/BookData.cs`):

```csharp
public class BookData
{
  public async Task AddBookAsync(Book book, Transaction tx)
  {
    using (SqlConnection connection = new SqlConnection(GetConnectionString()))
    {
      string sql = "INSERT INTO [ProCSharp].[Books] ([Title], [Publisher], " +
        "[Isbn], [ReleaseDate]) " +
        "VALUES (@Title, @Publisher, @Isbn, @ReleaseDate)";

      await connection.OpenAsync();
      if (tx != null)
      {
        connection.EnlistTransaction(tx);
      }
      var command = connection.CreateCommand();
      command.CommandText = sql;
      command.Parameters.AddWithValue("Title", book.Title);
      command.Parameters.AddWithValue("Publisher", book.Publisher);
      command.Parameters.AddWithValue("Isbn", book.Isbn);
      command.Parameters.AddWithValue("ReleaseDate", book.ReleaseDate);

      await command.ExecuteNonQueryAsync();
    }
  }
  //...
}
```

Committable Transactions

The `Transaction` class cannot be committed programmatically; it does not have a method to commit the transaction. The base class `Transaction` just supports aborting the transaction. The only transaction class that supports a commit is the class `CommittableTransaction`.

In the `CommittableTransactionAsync` method, first a transaction of type `CommittableTransaction` is created, and information is shown to the console. Then a `Book` object is created, which is written to the database from the `AddBookAsync` method. If you verify the record in the database from outside the transaction, you cannot see the book added until the transaction is completed. If the transaction fails, there is a rollback, and the book is not written to the database.

After the `AddBookAsync` method is invoked, the `AbortTx` method is called to ask the user whether the transaction should be aborted. If the user aborts, an exception of type `ApplicationException` is thrown and, in the `catch` block, a rollback is performed by calling the method `Rollback` of the `Transaction` class. The record is not written to the database. If the user does not abort, the `Commit` method commits the transaction, and the final state of the transaction is committed (code file `SystemTransactionSamples/Program.cs`):

```csharp
static async Task CommittableTransactionAsync()
{
  var tx = new CommittableTransaction();
```

```
DisplayTransactionInformation("TX created", tx.TransactionInformation);

try
{
  var b = new Book
  {
    Title = "A Dog in The House",
    Publisher = "Pet Show",
    Isbn = RandomIsbn(),
    ReleaseDate = new DateTime(2018, 11, 24)
  };
  var data = new BookData();
  await data.AddBookAsync(b, tx);

  if (AbortTx())
  {
    throw new ApplicationException("transaction abort by the user");
  }
  tx.Commit();
}
catch (Exception ex)
{
  Console.WriteLine(ex.Message);
  Console.WriteLine();
  tx.Rollback();
}

DisplayTransactionInformation("TX completed", tx.TransactionInformation);
}
```

As shown in the following output of the application, the transaction is active and has a local identifier. In addition, the user has chosen to abort the transaction. After the transaction is finished, you can see the aborted state:

```
TX created
Creation time: 7:29:36 PM
Status: Active
Local Id: c090c903-3f74-44b2-92a7-7607e33b787c:1
Distributed Id: 00000000-0000-0000-0000-000000000000

Abort the transaction (y/n)?
y
transaction abort by the user

TX completed
Creation time: 7:29:36 PM
Status: Aborted
Local Id: c090c903-3f74-44b2-92a7-7607e33b787c:1
Distributed Id: 00000000-0000-0000-0000-000000000000
```

With the second output of the application that follows, the transaction is not aborted by the user. The transaction has the status Committed, and the data is written to the database:

```
TX created
Creation time: 7:30:59 PM
Status: Active
Local Id: e60feb38-e3b2-4ede-992d-f93296a363a4:1
Distributed Id: 00000000-0000-0000-0000-000000000000

Abort the transaction (y/n)?
n
TX completed
```

```
Creation time: 7:30:59 PM
Status: Committed
Local Id: e60feb38-e3b2-4ede-992d-f93296a363a4:1
Distributed Id: 00000000-0000-0000-0000-000000000000
```

Dependent Transactions

With dependent transactions, you can influence one transaction among multiple tasks or threads. A dependent transaction depends on another transaction and influences the outcome of the transaction.

The sample method `DependentTransactions` first creates a root transaction using `CommittableTransaction`. This transaction object is used to create a dependent transaction with the method `DependentClone`. This `DependentTransaction` is passed to a separate task in the local function `UsingDependentTransactionAsync`. A dependent transaction can be marked as completed as is done invoking the `Complete` method.

The `DependentClone` method requires and argument of type `DependentCloneOption`, which is an enumeration with the values `BlockCompleteUntilComplete` and `RollbackIfNotComplete`. This option is important if the root transaction completes before the dependent transaction. Setting the option to `RollbackIfNotComplete`, the transaction aborts if the dependent transaction didn't invoke the `Complete` method before the `Commit` method of the root transaction. Setting the option to `BlockCommitUntilComplete`, the method `Commit` waits (blocks) until the outcome is defined by all dependent transactions.

Next, the `Commit` method of the `CommittableTransaction` class is invoked if the user does not abort the transaction (code file `SystemTransactions/Program.cs`):

```csharp
static void DependentTransactions()
{
  async Task UsingDependentTransactionAsync(DependentTransaction dtx)
  {
    dtx.TransactionCompleted += (sender, e) =>
      DisplayTransactionInformation("Depdendent TX completed",
        e.Transaction.TransactionInformation);

    DisplayTransactionInformation("Dependent Tx", dtx.TransactionInformation);

    await Task.Delay(2000);

    dtx.Complete();
    DisplayTransactionInformation("Dependent Tx send complete",
      dtx.TransactionInformation);
  }

  var tx = new CommittableTransaction();
  DisplayTransactionInformation("Root Tx created",
    tx.TransactionInformation);

  try
  {
    DependentTransaction depTx = tx.DependentClone(
      DependentCloneOption.BlockCommitUntilComplete);
    Task t1 = Task.Run(() => UsingDependentTransactionAsync(depTx));

    if (AbortTx())
    {
      throw new ApplicationException("transaction abort by the user");
    }
    tx.Commit();
  }
  catch (Exception ex)
```

```
    {
      Console.WriteLine(ex.Message);
      tx.Rollback();
    }

    DisplayTransactionInformation("TX completed", tx.TransactionInformation);
  }
```

The following output of the application shows the root transaction and its identifier. Because of the option `DependentCloneOption.BlockCommitUntilComplete`, the root transaction waits in the `Commit` method until the outcome of the dependent transaction is defined. As soon as the dependent transaction is finished, the transaction is committed:

```
Root Tx created
Creation time: 7:50:32 PM
Status: Active
Local Id: 87268b8c-076d-4823-af58-944b861bd4fe:1
Distributed Id: 00000000-0000-0000-0000-000000000000

Abort the transaction (y/n)?
Dependent Tx
Creation time: 7:50:32 PM
Status: Active
Local Id: 87268b8c-076d-4823-af58-944b861bd4fe:1
Distributed Id: 00000000-0000-0000-0000-000000000000

Dependent Tx send complete
Creation time: 7:50:32 PM
Status: Active
Local Id: 87268b8c-076d-4823-af58-944b861bd4fe:1
Distributed Id: 00000000-0000-0000-0000-000000000000

n
Depdendent TX completed
Creation time: 7:50:32 PM
Status: Committed
Local Id: 87268b8c-076d-4823-af58-944b861bd4fe:1
Distributed Id: 00000000-0000-0000-0000-000000000000

TX completed
Creation time: 7:50:32 PM
Status: Committed
Local Id: 87268b8c-076d-4823-af58-944b861bd4fe:1
Distributed Id: 00000000-0000-0000-0000-000000000000
```

Ambient Transactions

The biggest advantage of the classes in the `System.Transactions` namespace is the ambient transaction feature. With ambient transactions, there is no need to manually enlist a connection with a transaction; this is done automatically from the resources supporting ambient transactions.

An ambient transaction is associated with the current thread. You can get and set the ambient transaction with the static property `Transaction.Current`. APIs supporting ambient transactions check this property to get an ambient transaction and to enlist with the transaction. ADO.NET connections support ambient transactions.

You can create a `CommittableTransaction` object and assign it to the property `Transaction.Current` to initialize the ambient transaction. Another way (and typically the preferred way) is with the `TransactionScope` class. The constructor of `TransactionScope` creates an ambient transaction.

> **NOTE** *If an ADO.NET connection should not enlist with an ambient transaction, you can set the value* `Enlist=false` *with the connection string.*

For using the `TransactionScope`, another `AddBook` method is created that just adds a record to the `Books` table without explicitly enlisting to a transaction (code file `SystemTransactionSamples/BookData.cs`):

```
public void AddBook(Book book)
{
  using (SqlConnection connection = new SqlConnection(GetConnectionString()))
  {
    string sql = "INSERT INTO [ProCSharp].[Books] ([Title], [Publisher], " +
      "[Isbn], [ReleaseDate]) " +
      "VALUES (@Title, @Publisher, @Isbn, @ReleaseDate)";

    connection.Open();

    var command = connection.CreateCommand();
    command.CommandText = sql;
    command.Parameters.AddWithValue("Title", book.Title);
    command.Parameters.AddWithValue("Publisher", book.Publisher);
    command.Parameters.AddWithValue("Isbn", book.Isbn);
    command.Parameters.AddWithValue("ReleaseDate", book.ReleaseDate);

    command.ExecuteNonQuery();
  }
}
```

Important methods of the `TransactionScope` are `Complete` and `Dispose`. The `Complete` method sets the success bit for the scope, and the `Dispose` method finishes the scope and commits or rolls back the transaction if the scope is a root scope.

Because the `TransactionScope` class implements the `IDisposable` interface, you can define the scope with the `using` statement. The default constructor creates a new transaction. In the following code snippet, immediately after creating the `TransactionScope` instance, a lambda expression invoking `DisplayTransactionInformation` is assigned to the `TransactionCompleted` event to get information when the transaction is completed. Before this event fires, immediately after the creation of the transaction, the property `Transaction.Current` is accessed to display the current state of the transaction on the console. After that, a new `Book` object is created, and the previously created `AddBook` method is invoked. In case the user does not abort the transaction, the `Complete` method of the `TransactionScope` is invoked. The end of the using block invokes the `Dispose` method of the `TransactionScope`. If the `Complete` method was invoked, and if every other party participating in the transaction (for example, the SQL connection) has the success bit set, the transaction is committed. In case any party was not successful with the transaction that includes the `TransactionScope` when `Complete` was not invoked, the transaction is aborted (code file `SystemTransactionSamples/Program.cs`):

```
static void AmbientTransactions()
{
  using (var scope = new TransactionScope())
  {
    Transaction.Current.TransactionCompleted += (sender, e) =>
      DisplayTransactionInformation("TX completed",
        e.Transaction.TransactionInformation);

    DisplayTransactionInformation("Ambient TX created",
      Transaction.Current.TransactionInformation);

    var b = new Book
    {
```

```
        Title = "Cats in The House",
        Publisher = "Pet Show",
        Isbn = RandomIsbn(),
        ReleaseDate = new DateTime(2019, 11, 24)
    };
    var data = new BookData();
    data.AddBook(b);

    if (!AbortTx())
    {
        scope.Complete();
    }
    else
    {
        Console.WriteLine("transaction abort by the user");
    }

  } // scope.Dispose();
}
```

When you run the application, you can see an active ambient transaction after an instance of the `TransactionSope` class is created. The last output of the application is the output from the `TransactionCompleted` event handler to display the finished transaction state:

```
Ambient TX created
Creation time: 7:53:10 AM
Status: Active
Local Id: 0e28b708-9dd7-4b17-bf41-c09f963928cf:1
Distributed Id: 00000000-0000-0000-0000-000000000000

Abort the transaction (y/n)?
n
TX completed
Creation time: 7:53:10 AM
Status: Committed
Local Id: 0e28b708-9dd7-4b17-bf41-c09f963928cf:1
Distributed Id: 00000000-0000-0000-0000-000000000000
```

Nested Scopes with Ambient Transactions

With the `TransactionScope` class you can also nest scopes. The nested scope can be directly inside an outer scope or within a method that is invoked from the scope. A nested scope can use the same transaction as the outer scope, suppress the transaction, or create a new transaction that is independent from the outer scope. The requirement for the scope is defined with a `TransactionScopeOption` enumeration that is passed to the constructor of the `TransactionScope` class.

The following table describes the values and corresponding functionality available with the `TransactionScope` enumeration.

TRANSACTIONSCOPE MEMBER	DESCRIPTION
Required	Required defines that the scope requires a transaction. If the outer scope already contains an ambient transaction, the inner scope uses the existing transaction. If an ambient transaction does not exist, a new transaction is created. If both scopes share the same transaction, every scope influences the outcome of the transaction. Only if all scopes set the success bit, the transaction can commit. If one scope does not invoke the Complete method before the root scope is disposed, the transaction is aborted.

TRANSACTIONSCOPE MEMBER	DESCRIPTION
RequiresNew	RequiresNew always creates a new transaction. If the outer scope already defines a transaction, the transaction from the inner scope is completely independent. Both transactions can commit or abort independently.
Suppress	With Suppress, the scope does not contain an ambient transaction, whether the outer scope contains a transaction.

The next example defines two scopes. The inner scope is configured to require a new transaction with the option TransactionScopeOption.RequiresNew (code file SystemTransactionSamples/Program.cs):

```
static void NestedScopes()
{
  using (var scope = new TransactionScope())
  {
    Transaction.Current.TransactionCompleted += (sender, e) =>
      DisplayTransactionInformation("TX completed",
        e.Transaction.TransactionInformation);

    DisplayTransactionInformation("Ambient TX created",
      Transaction.Current.TransactionInformation);

    var b = new Book
    {
      Title = "Dogs in The House",
      Publisher = "Pet Show",
      Isbn = RandomIsbn(),
      ReleaseDate = new DateTime(2020, 11, 24)
    };
    var data = new BookData();
    data.AddBook(b);

    using (var scope2 = new
      TransactionScope(TransactionScopeOption.RequiresNew))
    {
      Transaction.Current.TransactionCompleted += (sender, e) =>
        DisplayTransactionInformation("Inner TX completed",
          e.Transaction.TransactionInformation);

      DisplayTransactionInformation("Inner TX scope",
        Transaction.Current.TransactionInformation);

      var b1 = new Book
      {
        Title = "Dogs and Cats in The House",
        Publisher = "Pet Show",
        Isbn = RandomIsbn(),
        ReleaseDate = new DateTime(2021, 11, 24)
      };
      var data1 = new BookData();
      data1.AddBook(b1);

      scope2.Complete();
    }

    scope.Complete();
  }
```

When you run the application, you can see different transaction identifiers of the outer scope and the inner scope where the inner scope appends :2 to the GUID, and the outer scope :1. These transactions are independent of each other:

```
Ambient TX created
Creation time: 8:20:09 AM
Status: Active
Local Id: d4e3a180-49d6-4c16-b4c9-89a9c6d4ace9:1
Distributed Id: 00000000-0000-0000-0000-000000000000

Inner TX scope
Creation time: 8:20:11 AM
Status: Active
Local Id: d4e3a180-49d6-4c16-b4c9-89a9c6d4ace9:2
Distributed Id: 00000000-0000-0000-0000-000000000000

Inner TX completed
Creation time: 8:20:11 AM
Status: Committed
Local Id: d4e3a180-49d6-4c16-b4c9-89a9c6d4ace9:2
Distributed Id: 00000000-0000-0000-0000-000000000000

TX completed
Creation time: 8:20:09 AM
Status: Committed
Local Id: d4e3a180-49d6-4c16-b4c9-89a9c6d4ace9:1
Distributed Id: 00000000-0000-0000-0000-000000000000
```

If you change the creation of the inner scope to use `TransactionScopeOption.Required`, you can see the same transaction is used with the outer and the inner scope:

```
Ambient TX created
Creation time: 8:23:52 AM
Status: Active
Local Id: 95181f71-0268-40f0-8f12-471a01a83638:1
Distributed Id: 00000000-0000-0000-0000-000000000000

Inner TX scope
Creation time: 8:23:52 AM
Status: Active
Local Id: 95181f71-0268-40f0-8f12-471a01a83638:1
Distributed Id: 00000000-0000-0000-0000-000000000000

TX completed
Creation time: 8:23:52 AM
Status: Committed
Local Id: 95181f71-0268-40f0-8f12-471a01a83638:1
Distributed Id: 00000000-0000-0000-0000-000000000000

Inner TX completed
Creation time: 8:23:52 AM
Status: Committed
Local Id: 95181f71-0268-40f0-8f12-471a01a83638:1
Distributed Id: 00000000-0000-0000-0000-000000000000
```

SUMMARY

In this chapter, you've seen the core foundation of ADO.NET. You first looked at the `SqlConnection` object to open a connection to SQL Server. You've seen how to retrieve the connection string from a configuration file.

This chapter explained how to use connections properly so that they can be closed as early as possible, which preserves valuable resources. All the connection classes implement the `IDisposable` interface, called when the object is placed within a `using` statement. If there is one thing you should take away from this chapter, it is the importance of closing database connections as early as possible.

With commands you've seen passing parameters, getting a single return value, and retrieving records using the `SqlDataReader`. You've also seen how stored procedures can be invoked using the `SqlCommand` object.

Like other parts of the framework where processing can take some time, ADO.NET implements the task-based async pattern that was shown as well. You've also seen how to create and use transactions with ADO .NET.

With `System.Transactions`, you've seen a different way to deal with transactions—transactions that can be independent of the SQL connection whereas the SQL connection automatically enlists to the transaction when ambient transactions are used.

The next chapter is about Entity Framework Core that offers an abstraction to data access by offering a mapping between relations in the database and object hierarchies and uses ADO.NET classes behind the scenes when you're accessing a relational database.

26

Entity Framework Core

WHAT'S IN THIS CHAPTER?

➤ Introducing Entity Framework Core

➤ Using dependency injection with Entity Framework

➤ Conventions, annotations, and the fluent API

➤ Using queries, compiled queries, global query filters

➤ Defining relationships with conventions, annotations, and the fluent API

➤ Using table per hierarchy, table splitting, and owned entities

➤ Object tracking

➤ Updating objects and object trees

➤ Conflict handling with updates

➤ Using transactions

➤ Using migrations with the .NET CLI tools

WROX.COM CODE DOWNLOADS FOR THIS CHAPTER

The Wrox.com code downloads for this chapter are found at www.wrox.com on the Download Code tab. The source code is also available at https://github.com/ProfessionalCSharp/ProfessionalCSharp7 in the directory EFCore. The code for this chapter is divided into the following major examples:

➤ Intro

➤ Books Sample

➤ UsingDependencyInjection

➤ Menus Sample

➤ Menus with Data Annotations

➤ Relations with Annotations/Conventions/FluentAPI

➤ Table per Hierarchy

➤ Conflict Handling Sample

➤ Transactions Sample

HISTORY OF ENTITY FRAMEWORK

Entity Framework and Entity Framework Core (EF Core) are frameworks offering mapping of entities to relationships. With these, you can create types that map to database tables, create database queries using LINQ, create and update objects, and write them to the database.

After many years of changes to Entity Framework, EF Core is a complete rewrite. Let's have a look at the history of Entity Framework to see the reasons for the rewrite.

➤ **Entity Framework 1**—The first version of Entity Framework was not ready with .NET 3.5, but it was soon available with .NET 3.5 SP1. Another product offering somewhat similar functionality that was already available with .NET 3.5 was LINQ to SQL. Both LINQ to SQL and Entity Framework offered similar features from a wide view. However, LINQ to SQL was simpler to use but was only available for accessing SQL Server. Entity Framework was provider-based and offered access to several different relational databases. It included more features, such as many-to-many mapping without the need for mapping objects, and n-to-n mapping was possible. One disadvantage of Entity Framework was that it required model types to derive from the `EntityObject` base class. Mapping the objects to relations was done using an EDMX file that contains XML. The XML contained is defined by three schemas: The Conceptual Schema Definition (CSD) defines the object types with their properties and associations; the Storage Schema Definition (SSD) defines the database tables, columns, and relations; and the Mapping Schema Language (MSL) defines how the CSD and SSD map to each other.

➤ **Entity Framework 4**—Entity Framework 4 was available with .NET 4 and received major improvements, many coming from LINQ to SQL ideas. Because of the big changes, versions 2 and 3 have been skipped. With this edition, *lazy loading* was added to fetch relations on accessing a property. Creating a database was possible after designing a model using *SQL Data Definition Language* (DDL). The two models using Entity Framework were now *Database First* or *Model First*. Possibly the most important feature added was the support for Plain Old CLR Objects (POCO), so it was no longer necessary to derive from the base class `EntityObject`.

With later updates (such as Entity Framework 4.1, 4.2), additional features have been added with NuGet packages. This allowed adding features faster. Entity Framework 4.1 offers the *Code First* model where the EDMX file to define the mappings is no longer used. Instead, all the mapping is defined using C# code— either using attributes or with a fluent API to define the mapping using code.

Entity Framework 4.3 added support for *Migrations*. With this, it is possible to define updates to the database schemas using C# code. The database update can be automatically applied from the application using the database.

➤ **Entity Framework 5**—The NuGet package for Entity Framework 5 supported both .NET Framework 4.5 and .NET Framework 4.0 applications. However, many of the features of Entity Framework 5 only have been available with .NET Framework 4.5. Entity Framework was still based on types that are installed on the system with .NET Framework 4.5. New with this release were performance improvements as well as supporting new SQL Server features, such as spatial data types, and many of these features have not been available when using it with .NET Framework 4.0 applications.

➤ **Entity Framework 6**—Entity Framework 6 solved some issues with Entity Framework 5, which was partly a part of the framework installed on the system and partly available via NuGet extensions. Now the complete code of Entity Framework has moved to NuGet packages. For not creating conflicts, a new namespace was used. When porting apps to the new version, the namespace had to be changed.

➤ **Entity Framework Core (EF Core)**—This version of Entity Framework got a new name and was a complete rewrite of Entity Framework. EF Core is available not only on Windows but also on Linux and Mac. It supports both relational databases and NoSQL data stores.

This book covers *Entity Framework Core 2.0*. This version no longer supports the XML file mapping with CSDL, SSDL, and MSL. Only Code First is supported now—the model that was added with Entity Framework 4.1. Code First doesn't mean that the database can't exist first. You can either create the database first or define the database purely from code; both options are possible.

> **NOTE** *The name* Code First *is somewhat misleading. With Code First, either the code or the database can be created first. Originally with the beta version of Code First, the name was* Code Only. *Because the other model options had* First *in their names, the name* Code Only *was changed as well.*

Entity Framework Core 1.0 did not support all the features that were offered by Entity Framework 6. Entity Framework Core 2.0 catches up but still doesn't support all the features of Entity Framework 6. However, it also has some new features Entity Framework 6 doesn't have.

You just need to pay attention to what version of Entity Framework you are using. There are many valid reasons to stay with Entity Framework 6, but using ASP.NET Core on non-Windows platforms, using Entity Framework with the Universal Windows Platform, using Xamarin, and using nonrelational data stores all require the use of EF Core.

This chapter introduces you to EF Core. It starts with a simple model reading and writing information from SQL Server. Later, relations are added, and you will be introduced to the change tracker and conflict handling when writing to the database. Creating and modifying database schemas using migrations is another important part of this chapter.

> **NOTE** *This chapter uses the Books database. This database is included with the download of the code samples at* www.wrox.com. *Other databases used with the samples are created from the code.*

INTRODUCING EF CORE

The first example uses a single `Book` type and maps this type to the `Books` table in a SQL Server database. You write records to the database and then read, update, and delete them.

With the first example, you can create the database first or let the database be created from the application. To create the database first, you can use the SQL Server Object Explorer that is part of Visual Studio 2017. Select the database instance `(localdb)\MSSQLLocalDB`. This database is installed with the installation of Visual Studio). Click the Databases node in the tree view and select Add New Database. The sample database `WroxBooks` has only a single table named `Books`.

You can create the table `Books` by selecting the Tables node within the `WroxBooks` database and then selecting Add New Table. Using the designer shown in Figure 26-1, or by entering the SQL DDL statement in the T-SQL editor, you can create the table `Books`. The following code snippet shows the T-SQL code for creating the table. When you click the Update button, you can submit the changes to the database.

```
CREATE TABLE [dbo].[Books]
(
    [BookId] INT IDENTITY(1, 1) NOT NULL,
    [Title] NVARCHAR(50) NOT NULL,
    [Publisher] NVARCHAR(25) NULL,
    CONSTRAINT [PK_Books] PRIMARY KEY CLUSTERED ([BookId] ASC)
)
```

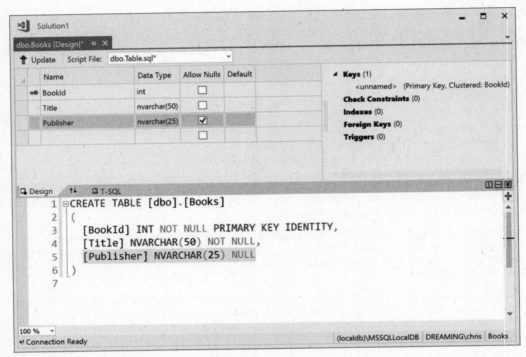

FIGURE 26-1

The sample applications used in this chapter are all .NET Core console applications and make use of the following NuGet dependencies and namespaces:

Dependencies

```
Microsoft.EntityFrameworkCore
```

```
Microsoft.EntityFrameworkCore.SqlServer
```

```
Microsoft.EntityFramework.Design
```

```
Microsoft.Extensions.DependencyInjection
```

```
Microsoft.Extensions.Logging.Console
```

Namespaces

```
Microsoft.EntityFrameworkCore
```

```
Microsoft.EntityFrameworkCore.ChangeTracking
```

```
Microsoft.EntityFrameworkCore.Diagnostics
```

```
Microsoft.EntityFrameworkCore.Infrastructure
```

```
Microsoft.EntityFrameworkCore.Metadata.Builders
```

```
Microsoft.Extensions.DependencyInjection
```

```
Microsoft.Extensions.Logging
```

```
System
```

```
System.Collections.Generic
```

```
System.ComponentModel.DataAnnotations

System.ComponentModel.DataAnnotations.Schema

System.Linq

System.Threading.Tasks
```

Creating a Model

The sample application `BookSample` for accessing the `Books` database is a .NET Core console app. With this application, the class `Book` is a simple entity type that defines three properties. The `BookId` property maps to the primary key of the table, the `Title` property to the `Title` column, and the `Publisher` property to the `Publisher` column. With the `Title` property, the `Required` attribute is applied because the mapping column has a `NOT NULL` definition in the database. Lengths for the `Title` and `Publisher` properties are applied using the `StringLength` attribute. This also maps with the columns in the database. To map the type to the `Books` table, the `Table` attribute is applied to the type (code file `Intro/Book.cs`):

```csharp
[Table("Books")]
public class Book
{
    public int BookId { get; set; }
    [Required]
    [StringLength(50)]
    public string Title { get; set; }
    [StringLength(30)]
    public string Publisher { get; set; }
}
```

Conventions, Annotations, and Fluent API

EF Core is using three concepts to define the model: conventions, annotations, and the fluent API. With conventions, some things happen automatically. For example, naming a property of type `int` or `Guid` with an Id postfix maps the property to a primary key.

Conventions can be overridden using annotations—specifying attributes. The previous example used the `Table` attribute to map the `Book` type to the `Books` table. There's also a convention for mapping to the table; this is using a property name of a context. Creating contexts is shown in the next section. Conventions do not exist for every annotation. `Required` and `StringLength` attributes have been used as well. Annotations are more powerful than conventions; you can do more.

Instead of using annotations, you can also use a fluent API, which means configuration is done via code rather than using attributes. With a fluent API, the return value of a method can be used to invoke the next method. The fluent API for EF Core is more powerful than the annotations are; you can do more. The fluent API is shown later in this chapter in the section "Creating a Model."

Creating a Context

The association of the `Book` table with the database is done creating the `BooksContext` class. This class derives from the base class `DbContext`. The `BooksContext` class defines the `Books` property that is of type `DbSet<Book>`. This type allows creating queries and adding `Book` instances for storing it in the database. To define the connection string, the `OnConfiguring` method of the `DbContext` can be overridden. Here, the `UseSqlServer` extension method maps the context to a SQL Server database (code file `BooksSample/BooksContext.cs`):

```csharp
public class BooksContext: DbContext
{
    private const string ConnectionString =
        @"server=(localdb)\MSSQLLocalDb;database=WroxBooks;" +
```

```
        @"trusted_connection=true";

    public DbSet<Book> Books { get; set; }

    protected override void OnConfiguring(DbContextOptionsBuilder optionsBuilder)
    {
      base.OnConfiguring(optionsBuilder);
      optionsBuilder.UseSqlServer(ConnectionString);
    }
}
```

> **NOTE** *Another way to define the connection string is by using dependency injection, which is shown later in this chapter in the section "Using Dependency Injection."*

Creating the Database

The model and the context classes are defined. Now it's also possible to create the database programmatically. First, the `BooksContext` object is instantiated. The `using` statement makes sure that the database connection is closed at the end of the using scope.

When you use the `Database` property of the `DbContext`, a `DatabaseFacade` is returned. You can use this to create and delete databases, and to directly send SQL statements. Invoking the method `EnsureCreatedAsync` makes sure that the database is created. If the database already exists, this method returns false. If the database does not exist, the database is created according to the definition of the context and the model, and true is returned (code file `Intro/Program.cs`):

```
private async Task CreateTheDatabaseAsync()
{
  using (var context = new BooksContext())
  {
    bool created = await context.Database.EnsureCreatedAsync();
    string creationInfo = created ? "created" : "exists";
    Console.WriteLine($"database {creationInfo}");
  }
}
```

When you run the program, if you already created the database earlier, the string `database exists` is written to the console. In case you didn't create the database earlier, the database is created, followed by the string `database created`.

> **NOTE** *Many of the code samples make use of the asynchronous methods of EF Core, such as `EnsureCreatedAsync` and `SaveChangesAsync`. If you don't need async functionality—for example, in your console applications or probably web applications—you can use the synchronous variant of these methods. Although async has some overhead, the synchronous versions of these APIs block the calling thread. `EnsureCreated` and `SaveChanges` are the synchronous APIs while `EnsureCreatedAsync` and `SaveChangesAsync` are the asynchronous APIs. Read more about the asynchronous methods in Chapter 15, "Asynchronous Programming," and Chapter 21, "Tasks and Parallel Programming."*

> **NOTE** *Using the* Async *variants of the context methods allows starting the operation in the background. However, you cannot start multiple operations on the same context parallel. You need to* await *for an operation to complete before starting the next operation.*

Deleting the Database

Deleting the database is programmatically very similar to its creation. You just need to invoke the method EnsureDeletedAsync of the DatabaseFacade:

```
private async Task DeleteDatabaseAsync()
{
  Console.Write("Delete the database? ");
  string input = Console.ReadLine();
  if (input.ToLower() == "y")
  {
    using (var context = new BooksContext())
    {
      bool deleted = await context.Database.EnsureDeletedAsync();
      string deletionInfo = deleted ? "deleted" : "not deleted";
      Console.WriteLine($"database {deletionInfo}");
    }
  }
}
```

Just make sure you don't delete a database that should not be deleted. Pay attention to the connection string you use.

Writing to the Database

After the database and the Books table are created, you can fill the table with data. The AddBookAsync method is created to add a Book object to the database. AddBookAsync just adds the Book object to the context, it doesn't write it to the database. The object is written on invoking the method SaveChangesAsync (code file Intro/Program.cs):

```
private async Task AddBookAsync(string title, string publisher)
{
  using (var context = new BooksContext())
  {
    var book = new Book
    {
      Title = title,
      Publisher = publisher
    };
    await context.Books.AddAsync(book);
    int records = await context.SaveChangesAsync();
    Console.WriteLine($"{records} record added");
  }
  Console.WriteLine();
}
```

For adding a list of books, you can use the AddRange method:

```
private async Task AddBooksAsync()
{
  using (var context = new BooksContext())
```

```
    {
      var b1 = new Book
      {
        Title = "Professional C# 6 and .NET Core 1.0",
        Publisher = "Wrox Press"
      };
      var b2 = new Book
      {
        Title = "Professional C# 5 and .NET 4.5.1",
        Publisher = "Wrox Press"
      };
      var b3 = new Book
      {
        Title = "JavaScript for Kids",
        Publisher = "Wrox Press"
      };
      var b4 = new Book
      {
        Title = "Web Design with HTML and CSS",
        Publisher = "For Dummies"
      };
      await context.AddRangeAsync(b1, b2, b3, b4);
      int records = await context.SaveChangesAsync();
      Console.WriteLine($"{records} records added");
    }
    Console.WriteLine();
  }
```

When you run the application and invoke these methods, you can see the data written to the database using the SQL Server Object Explorer.

Reading from the Database

To read the data from C# code, you just need to invoke the BooksContext and access the Books property. Accessing this property creates a SQL statement to retrieve all books from the database (code file Intro/ Program.cs):

```
private async Task ReadBooksAsync()
{
  using (var context = new BooksContext())
  {
    List<Book> books = await context.Books.ToListAsync();
    foreach (var b in books)
    {
      Console.WriteLine($"{b.Title} {b.Publisher}");
    }
  }
  Console.WriteLine();
}
```

When you open the IntelliTrace Events window during debugging, you can see the SQL statement that is sent to the database (this requires Visual Studio Enterprise edition):

```
SELECT [b].[BookId], [b].[Publisher], [b].[Title]
FROM [Books] AS [b]
```

Entity Framework offers a LINQ provider. With that, you can create LINQ queries to access the database. You can either use the method syntax as shown here:

```
private async Task QueryBooksAsync()
{
  using (var context = new BooksContext())
```

```
  {
    List<Book> wroxBooks = context.Books
      .Where(b => b.Publisher == "Wrox Press")
      .ToListAsync();

    foreach (var b in wroxBooks)
    {
      Console.WriteLine($"{b.Title} {b.Publisher}");
    }
  }
  Console.WriteLine();
}
```

or use the declarative LINQ query syntax:

```
var wroxBooks = await (from b in context.Books
                       where b.Publisher == "Wrox Press"
                       select b).ToListAsync();
```

With both syntax variants, this SQL statement is sent to the database:

```
SELECT [b].[BookId], [b].[Publisher], [b].[Title]
FROM [Books] AS [b]
WHERE [b].[Publisher] = 'Wrox Press'
```

> **NOTE** *LINQ is discussed in detail in Chapter 12, "Language Integrated Query."*

Updating Records

Updating records can be easily achieved just by changing objects that have been loaded with the context, and invoking SaveChangesAsync (code file Intro/Program.cs):

```
private async Task UpdateBookAsync()
{
  using (var context = new BooksContext())
  {
    int records = 0;
    Book book = await context.Books
      .Where(b => b.Title == "Professional C# 7")
      .FirstOrDefaultAsync();

    if (book != null)
    {
      book.Title = "Professional C# 7 and .NET Core 2.0";
      records = await context.SaveChangesAsync();
    }
    Console.WriteLine($"{records} record updated");
  }
  Console.WriteLine();
}
```

Deleting Records

Finally, let's clean up the database and delete all records. You do this by retrieving all records and invoking the Remove or RemoveRange method to set the state of the objects in the context to deleted. Invoking the SaveChangesAsync method now deletes the records from the database and invokes SQL Delete statements for every object (code file Intro/Program.cs):

```
private async Task DeleteBooksAsync()
{
  using (var context = new BooksContext())
```

```
    {
      var books = context.Books;
      context.Books.RemoveRange(books);
      int records = await context.SaveChangesAsync();
      Console.WriteLine($"{records} records deleted");
    }
    Console.WriteLine();
}
```

> **NOTE** *An object-relational mapping tool such as EF Core is not useful with all scenarios. Deleting all objects was not done efficiently with the sample code. Instead of sending a* DELETE *statement to the database for every record to delete, you can delete all records using a single SQL statement. How this can be done is explained in Chapter 25, "ADO.NET." EF Core is not that bad in such scenarios, as multiple statements can be combined into a batch statement, as shown later in the chapter in the section "Batching."*

Now that you've seen how to add, query, update, and delete records, this chapter steps into features behind the scenes and gets into advanced scenarios using Entity Framework.

Logging

To see the SQL statements sent to the database, you can open the profiler with SQL Server, open the Intellitrace Events in Visual Studio (Debug ➪ Windows ➪ Intellitrace Events), which requires the Enterprise edition of Visual Studio, or just enable logging. With logging, you can write trace information where you like to.

EF Core internally uses a dependency injection container (using `Microsoft.Extensions.DependencyInjection`) that has the interface `ILoggerFactory` registered. You can access this interface and register your own logger provider.

The following code snippet uses `BooksContext` to register a new logger. First, the `IServiceProvider` of the context is retrieved using the `GetInfrastructure` extension method. This extension method is defined in the namespace `Microsoft.EntityFrameworkCore.Infrastructure`. Using the `IServiceProvider`, services registered with the container can be retrieved, such as the interface `ILoggerFactory`. This interface is used from the EF Core infrastructure to write log information. With this interface, you can add log providers such as the Console log provider. This log provider is defined in the NuGet package `Microsoft.Extensions.Logging.Console`. The provider defines the `AddConsole` extension method to the `ILoggerFactory`, which makes it easy to add it as a log provider. Here, the log provider is configured to write informational logs (code file `Intro/Program.cs`):

```
private void AddLogging()
{
  using (var context = new BooksContext())
  {
    IServiceProvider provider = context.GetInfrastructure<IServiceProvider>();
    ILoggerFactory loggerFactory = provider.GetService<ILoggerFactory>();
    loggerFactory.AddConsole(LogLevel.Information);
  }
}
```

You need to make this configuration with only one context. The registration is done in the infrastructure of EF Core, thus as soon as this is configured for the application, logging is done with every context instantiated. For example, the `QueryBooksAsync` method implemented earlier now shows this logging information on the console:

```
info: Microsoft.EntityFrameworkCore.Database.Command[200101]
      Executed DbCommand (131ms) [Parameters=[], CommandType='Text',
```

```
    CommandTimeout='30']
SELECT [b].[BookId], [b].[Publisher], [b].[Title]
FROM [Books] AS [b]
WHERE [b].[Publisher] = N'Wrox Press'
```

> **NOTE** *Dependency injection and* `Microsoft.Extensions.DependencyInjection`
> *is covered in detail in Chapter 20, "Dependency Injection." Read more information*
> *about logging and diagnostics in Chapter 29, "Tracing, Logging, and Analytics."*

USING DEPENDENCY INJECTION

EF Core has built-in support for dependency injection, and there's also great support for using EF Core with a dependency injection container. Instead of defining the connection and the use of SQL Server with the `DbContext` derived class, the connection and SQL Server selection can be injected by using a dependency injection framework.

To see this in action, the previous sample has been modified with the `BooksSampleWithDI` sample project.

The `BooksContext` class now looks a lot simpler in just defining the `Books` property (code file `UsingDependencyInjection/BooksContext.cs`):

```
public class BooksContext : DbContext
{
  public BooksContext(DbContextOptions<BooksContext> options)
    : base(options) { }

  public DbSet<Book> Books { get; set; }
}
```

The `BooksService` is the new class that makes use of the `BooksContext`. Here, the `BooksContext` is injected via constructor injection. The methods `AddBooksAsync` and `ReadBooks` are very similar to these methods from the previous sample, but they use the context member of the `BooksService` class instead of creating a new one (code file `UsingDependencyInjection/BooksService.cs`):

```
public class BooksService
{
  private readonly BooksContext _booksContext;
  public BooksService(BooksContext context) => _booksContext = context;

  public async Task AddBooksAsync()
  {
    var b1 = new Book
    {
      Title = "Professional C# 6 and .NET Core 1.0",
      Publisher = "Wrox Press"
    };
    var b2 = new Book
    {
      Title = "Professional C# 5.0 and .NET 4.5.1",
      Publisher = "Wrox Press"
    };
    var b3 = new Book
    {
      Title = "JavaScript for Kids",
      Publisher = "Wrox Press"
    };
    var b4 = new Book
    {
      Title = "Web Design with HTML and CSS",
```

```
        Publisher = "For Dummies"
    };

    _booksContext.AddRange(b1, b2, b3, b4);
    int records = await _booksContext.SaveChangesAsync();
    Console.WriteLine($"{records} records added");
}

public async Task ReadBooksAsync()
{
    List<Book> books = await _booksContext.Books.ToListAsync();
    foreach (var b in books)
    {
        Console.WriteLine($"{b.Title} {b.Publisher}");
    }
    Console.WriteLine();
}
}
```

The container of the dependency injection framework is initialized in the `InitializeServices` method. Here, a `ServiceCollection` instance is created, and the `BooksService` class is added to this collection with a transient lifetime management. With this, the `BooksService` is instantiated every time this service is requested. For registering Entity Framework and SQL Server, the extension methods `AddEntityFrameworkSqlServer`, and `AddDbContext` are available. The `AddDbContext` method requires an Action delegate as parameter where a `DbContextOptionsBuilder` parameter is received. With this options parameter, the context can be configured using the `UseSqlServer` extension method. This is the similar functionality to register SQL Server with Entity Framework in the previous sample (code file `UsingDependencyInjection/Program.cs`):

```
private void InitializeServices()
{
  const string ConnectionString =
    @"server=(localdb)\MSSQLLocalDb;database=Books;trusted_connection=true";
  var services = new ServiceCollection();
  services.AddTransient<BooksService>()
    .AddEntityFrameworkSqlServer()
    .AddDbContext<BooksContext>(options =>
      options.UseSqlServer(ConnectionString));
  //...

  Container = services.BuildServiceProvider();
}

public ServiceProvider Container { get; private set; }
```

The initialization of the services as well as the use of the `BooksService` is done from the `Main` method. The `BooksService` is retrieved invoking the `GetService` method of the `IServiceProvider` (code file `UsingDependencyInjection/Program.cs`):

```
static async Task Main()
{
  var p = new Program();
  p.InitializeServices();
  p.ConfigureLogging();
  var service = p.Container.GetService<BooksService>();
  await service.AddBooksAsync();
  service.ReadBooks();
}
```

When you run the application, you can see that records are added and read from the `Books` database.

To configure logging with this application setup, you can add the `ILoggerFactory` interface with the help of the `AddLogging` extension method to the DI container:

```
private void InitializeServices()
{
  const string ConnectionString =
    @"server=(localdb)\MSSQLLocalDb;database=Books;trusted_connection=true";
  var services = new ServiceCollection();
  services.AddTransient<BooksService>()
    .AddEntityFrameworkSqlServer()
    .AddDbContext<BooksContext>(options =>
      options.UseSqlServer(ConnectionString));
  services.AddLogging();

  Container = services.BuildServiceProvider();
}
```

Next, you configure logging. With the implementation of the `ConfigureLogging` method, the `ILoggerFactory` is retrieved from the DI container. Using this factory, the console is added to write information logs:

```
private void ConfigureLogging()
{
  ILoggerFactory loggerFactory = Container.GetService<ILoggerFactory>();
  loggerFactory.AddConsole(LogLevel.Information);
}
```

EF Core itself uses the `ILoggerFactory` interface by injecting the service, and thus EF Core logging is now written to the console like the previous sample.

CREATING A MODEL

The first examples of this chapter mapped a single table. Now, let's get into a more complex example with a relationship between tables. The new database will be created programmatically, but of course you also can create a database first and use the code to access the existing database.

Creating a Relation

Let's start creating a model. The sample project defines a one-to-many relation using the `MenuCard` and `Menu` types. The `MenuCard` contains a list of `Menu` objects. This relation is simply defined by the `Menu` property of type `List<Menu>` (code file `MenusSample/MenuCard.cs`):

```
public class MenuCard
{
  public int MenuCardId { get; set; }
  public string Title { get; set; }
  public List<Menu> Menus { get; } = new List<Menu>();
  public override string ToString() => Title;
}
```

The relation can also be accessed in the other direction; a `Menu` can access the `MenuCard` using the `MenuCard` property. The `MenuCardId` property is specified to define a foreign key relationship (code file `MenusSample/Menu.cs`):

```
public class Menu
{
  public int MenuId { get; set; }
  public string Text { get; set; }
  public decimal Price { get; set; }
```

```
      public int MenuCardId { get; set; }
      public MenuCard MenuCard { get; set; }
      public override string ToString() => Text;
  }
```

The mapping to the database is done by the MenusContext class. This class is defined similarly to the previous context type; it just contains two properties to map the two object types: the properties Menus and MenuCards (code file MenusSamples/MenusContext.cs):

```
  public class MenusContext: DbContext
  {
      private const string ConnectionString = @"server=(localdb)\MSSQLLocalDb;" +
        "Database=MenuCards;Trusted_Connection=True";

      public DbSet<Menu> Menus { get; set; }
      public DbSet<MenuCard> MenuCards { get; set; }

      protected override void OnConfiguring(DbContextOptionsBuilder optionsBuilder)
      {
        base.OnConfiguring(optionsBuilder);
        optionsBuilder.UseSqlServer(ConnectionString);
      }
  }
```

There are some parts in the creation code that would be useful to change. For example, the size of the Text and Title column could be reduced in size from NVARCHAR(MAX). In addition to that, SQL Server defines a Money type that could be used for the Price column, and the schema name could be changed from dbo. Entity Framework gives you two options to make these changes from code: data annotations and the Fluent API, which are both discussed next.

Data Annotations

One way to influence the generated database is to add data annotations to the entity types. By default, the name of the table comes from the property of the context. Thus, to map the Menu class, the Menus table is used because the DbSet property mapping Menu has the name Menus. With data annotations, the tables can be changed by using the Table attribute. To change the schema name, the Table attribute defines the Schema property. To specify a different length for a string type, you can apply the MaxLength attribute (code file MenusWithDataAnnotations/MenuCard.cs):

```
  [Table("MenuCards", Schema = "mc")]
  public class MenuCard
  {
      public int MenuCardId { get; set; }

      [MaxLength(120)]
      public string Title { get; set; }
      public List<Menu> Menus { get; } = new List<Menu>();
  }
```

> **NOTE** *Using the property name in the context to map it to the table is different from Entity Framework. Entity Framework used a dictionary to find plural and singular names.*

With the Menu class, the Table and MaxLength attributes are applied as well. To change the SQL type, the Column attribute can be used (code file MenusWithDataAnnotations/Menu.cs):

```
  [Table("Menus", Schema = "mc")]
  public class Menu
```

```
    {
      public int MenuId { get; set; }
      [MaxLength(50)]
      public string Text { get; set; }
      [Column(TypeName ="Money")]
      public decimal Price { get; set; }
      public int MenuCardId { get; set; }
      public MenuCard MenuCard { get; set; }
    }
```

After applying the migrations and creating the database, you can see the new names of the tables with the schema name, as well as the changed data types on the Title, Text, and Price columns:

```
CREATE TABLE [mc].[MenuCards] (
  [MenuCardId] INT IDENTITY (1, 1) NOT NULL,
  [Title] NVARCHAR (120) NULL,
  CONSTRAINT [PK_MenuCard] PRIMARY KEY CLUSTERED ([MenuCardId] ASC)
);

CREATE TABLE [mc].[Menus] (
  [MenuId] INT IDENTITY (1, 1) NOT NULL,
  [MenuCardId] INT NOT NULL,
  [Price] MONEY NOT NULL,
  [Text] NVARCHAR (50) NULL,
  CONSTRAINT [PK_Menu] PRIMARY KEY CLUSTERED ([MenuId] ASC),
  CONSTRAINT [FK_Menu_MenuCard_MenuCardId] FOREIGN KEY ([MenuCardId])
  REFERENCES [mc].[MenuCards] ([MenuCardId]) ON DELETE CASCADE
);
```

Fluent API

Another way to influence the tables created is to use the Fluent API with the OnModelCreating method of the DbContext derived class. Using this has the advantage that you can keep the entity types simple without adding any attributes, and the fluent API also gives you more options than you have with applying attributes.

The following code snippet shows the override of the OnModelCreating method of the BooksContext class. The ModelBuilder class that is received as parameter offers a few methods, and several extension methods are defined. The HasDefaultSchema is an extension method that applies a default schema to the model that is now used with all types. The Entity method returns an EntityTypeBuilder that enables you to customize the entity, such as mapping it to a specific table name and defining keys and indexes:

```
protected override void OnModelCreating(ModelBuilder modelBuilder)
{
  base.OnModelCreating(modelBuilder);
  modelBuilder.HasDefaultSchema("mc");
  modelBuilder.Entity<MenuCard>()
    .ToTable("MenuCards")
    .HasKey(c => c.MenuCardId);
  //...
  modelBuilder.Entity<Menu>()
    .ToTable("Menus")
    .HasKey(m => m.MenuId);
  //...
}
```

The EntityTypeBuilder defines a Property method to configure a property. The Property method returns a PropertyBuilder that in turn enables you to configure the property with max length values, required settings, and SQL types and to specify whether values should be automatically generated (such as identity columns):

```
protected override void OnModelCreating(ModelBuilder modelBuilder)
{
```

```
    //...
    modelBuilder.Entity<MenuCard>()
      .Property(c => c.MenuCardId)
      .ValueGeneratedOnAdd();

    modelBuilder.Entity<MenuCard>()
      .Property(c => c.Title)
      .HasMaxLength(50);
    //...

    modelBuilder.Entity<Menu>()
      .Property(m => m.MenuId)
      .ValueGeneratedOnAdd();

    modelBuilder.Entity<Menu>()
      .Property(m => m.Text)
      .HasMaxLength(120);

    modelBuilder.Entity<Menu>()
      .Property(m => m.Price)
      .HasColumnType("Money");
    //...
}
```

To define one-to-many mappings, the `EntityTypeBuilder` defines mapping methods. The method `HasMany` combined with `WithOne` defines a mapping of many menus with one menu card. `HasMany` needs to be chained with `WithOne`. The method `HasOne` needs a chain with `WithMany` or `WithOne`. Chaining `HasOne` with `WithMany` defines a one-to-many relationship; chaining `HasOne` with `WithOne` defines a one-to-one relationship:

```
protected override void OnModelCreating(ModelBuilder modelBuilder)
{
    //...
    modelBuilder.Entity<MenuCard>()
      .HasMany(c => c.Menus)
      .WithOne(m => m.MenuCard);

    modelBuilder.Entity<Menu>()
      .HasOne(m => m.MenuCard)
      .WithMany(c => c.Menus)
      .HasForeignKey(m => m.MenuCardId);
}
```

Self-Contained Type Configuration

Having a more complex `DbContext`, the `OnModelCreating` method can become quite long. EF Core 2.0 gives a new option to define configuration classes for every type. To create a configuration class, the class needs to implement the interface `IEntityTypeConfiguration` with the method `Configure`. Creating `MenuCardConfiguration` for the `MenuCard` type, the configuration can be simplified as shown in the following code snippet (code file `MenusSample/MenuCardConfiguration.cs`):

```
public class MenuCardConfiguration : IEntityTypeConfiguration<MenuCard>
{
    public void Configure(EntityTypeBuilder<MenuCard> builder)
    {
      builder.ToTable("MenuCards")
        .HasKey(c => c.MenuCardId);
      builder.Property(c => c.MenuCardId)
        .ValueGeneratedOnAdd();
      builder.Property(c => c.Title)
        .HasMaxLength(50);
```

```
      builder.HasMany(c => c.Menus)
        .WithOne(m => m.MenuCard);
    }
  }
```

The configuration for the class `Menu` is defined in the `MenuConfiguration` class. The methods used by the `EntityTypeBuilder` are the same as used previously. The code is just simpler because the entity type does not need to be selected because with `IEntityTypeConfiguration`, the entity type is already specified:

```
public class MenuConfiguration : IEntityTypeConfiguration<Menu>
{
  public void Configure(EntityTypeBuilder<Menu> builder)
  {
    builder.ToTable("Menus")
      .HasKey(m => m.MenuId);

    builder.Property(m => m.MenuId)
      .ValueGeneratedOnAdd();

    builder.Property(m => m.Text)
      .HasMaxLength(120);

    builder.Property(m => m.Price)
      .HasColumnType("Money");

    builder.HasOne(m => m.MenuCard)
      .WithMany(m => m.Menus)
      .HasForeignKey(m => m.MenuCardId);
  }
}
```

The `OnModelCreating` method of the `MenusContext` class can now be simplified. To apply the configuration from the `IEntityTypeConfiguration` types, the `ApplyConfiguration` method of the `ModelBuilder` needs to be invoked (code file `MenusSample/MenusContext.cs`):

```
protected override void OnModelCreating(ModelBuilder modelBuilder)
{
  base.OnModelCreating(modelBuilder);
  modelBuilder.HasDefaultSchema("mc");

  modelBuilder.ApplyConfiguration(new MenuCardConfiguration());
  modelBuilder.ApplyConfiguration(new MenuConfiguration());
}
```

Scaffolding a Model from the Database

Instead of creating the database from the model, you can also create the model from the database.

To do this, you need to add the NuGet package `Microsoft.EntityFrameworkCore.Design` to the packages list of the project and add `Microsoft.EntityFrameworkCore.Tools.Dotnet` within a `DotnetCliToolReference` element. As the `Microsoft.EntityFrameworkCore.Design` package is only needed for the project itself and not for other projects referencing this package, the attribute `PrivateAssets` can be specified (project file `ScaffoldSample/ScaffoldSample.csproj`):

```
<Project Sdk="Microsoft.NET.Sdk">
  <PropertyGroup>
    <OutputType>Exe</OutputType>
    <TargetFramework>netcoreapp2.0</TargetFramework>
  </PropertyGroup>
  <ItemGroup>
    <PackageReference Include="Microsoft.EntityFrameworkCore"
```

```
            Version="2.0.0" />
          <PackageReference Include="Microsoft.EntityFrameworkCore.SqlServer"
            Version="2.0.0" />
          <PackageReference Include="Microsoft.EntityFrameworkCore.Design"
            Version="2.0.0" PrivateAssets="All" />
      </ItemGroup>
      <ItemGroup>
        <DotNetCliToolReference
          Include="Microsoft.EntityFrameworkCore.Tools.Dotnet"
          Version="2.0.0" />
      </ItemGroup>
    </Project>
```

After the tools are installed, you can start the `dotnet ef` command from the Developer Command Prompt:

```
> dotnet ef dbcontext scaffold
"server=(localdb)\MSSQLLocalDb;database=MenuCards;
trusted_connection=true" "Microsoft.EntityFrameworkCore.SqlServer"
```

The `dbcontext` command enables you to list `DbContext` objects from the project, as well as create `DBContext` objects. The command `scaffold` creates `DbContext`-derived classes as well as model classes. `dotnet ef dbcontext scaffold` needs two required arguments: the connection string to the database and the provider that should be used. With the statement shown earlier, the database `MenuCards` was accessed on the `SQL Server (localdb)\MSSQLLocalDb`. The provider used was `Microsoft.EntityFrameworkCore.SqlServer`. This NuGet package needs to be added to the project.

After running this command, you can see the `DbContext` derived classes as well as the model types generated. The configuration of the model by default is done using the fluent API. However, you can change that to using the data annotations supplying the `--data-annotations` option. You can also influence the generated context class name as well as the output directory. Just check the different available options using the option `--help`.

Mapping to Fields

EF Core not only allows mapping table columns to properties, but also to private fields. This makes it possible to create read-only properties and use private fields that are not accessible outside of the class.

Let's have a look at the class `Book` in the following code snippet. This class contains a private field `_bookId` that is only accessible within the class (and it's used from the `ToString` method). `Title` is a read/write property, and `Publisher` a read-only property. The publisher uses the field `_publisher`. What's needed by EF Core in the class is a default constructor, but this one can be declared with the private access modifier (code file `BooksSample/Book.cs`):

```
public class Book
{
  // parameterless constructor neeeded for EF Core
  private Book() { }

  public Book(string title, string publisher)
  {
    _title = title;
    _publisher = publisher;
  }

  private int _bookId = 0;
  public string Title { get; set; }
  private string _publisher;
  public string Publisher => _publisher;

  public override string ToString() =>
    $"id: {_bookId}, title: {Title}, publisher: {Publisher}";
}
```

To avoid typos, for the column names, the class `ColumnNames` with strongly typed names of the columns is defined. Also, the `using static` declaration accesses the `const` values without the class name (code file `BooksSample/BooksContext.cs`):

```
using static BooksSample.ColumnNames;

namespace BooksSample
{
  internal class ColumnNames
  {
    public const string LastUpdated = nameof(LastUpdated);
    public const string IsDeleted = nameof(IsDeleted);
    public const string BookId = nameof(BookId);
    public const string AuthorId = nameof(AuthorId);
  }
  //...
}
```

The property `Publisher` can now be configured to map to the corresponding field with the `HasField` method. The `_bookId` doesn't have a corresponding property, thus it is configured with an overload of the `Property` method where the name is assigned as string. This maps the `BookId` column in the database table to the field `_bookId` (code file `BooksSample/BooksContext.cs`):

```
protected override void OnModelCreating(ModelBuilder modelBuilder)
{
  base.OnModelCreating(modelBuilder);
  //...

  modelBuilder.Entity<Book>().Property(b => b.Title)
    .IsRequired()
    .HasMaxLength(50);

  modelBuilder.Entity<Book>().Property(b => b.Publisher)
    .HasField("_publisher")
    .IsRequired(false)
    .HasMaxLength(30);

  modelBuilder.Entity<Book>().Property<int>(BookId)
    .HasField("_bookId")
    .IsRequired();

  modelBuilder.Entity<Book>()
    .HasKey(BookId);
}
```

When you're creating `Book` objects, you need to use the constructor. The properties don't have a set accessor. After the `Book` objects are initialized, they are added to `BooksContext` with the `AddRangeAsync` method (code file `BooksSample/Program.cs`):

```
private async Task AddBooksAsync()
{
  using (var context = new BooksContext())
  {
    var b1 = new Book("Professional C# 6 and .NET Core 1.0", "Wrox Press");
    var b2 = new Book("Professional C# 5 and .NET 4.5.1", "Wrox Press");
    var b3 = new Book("JavaScript for Kids", "Wrox Press");
    var b4 = new Book("Web Design with HTML and CSS", "For Dummies");
    await context.Books.AddRangeAsync(b1, b2, b3, b4);
    int records = await context.SaveChangesAsync();

    Console.WriteLine($"{records} records added");
  }
  Console.WriteLine();
}
```

Shadow Properties

EF Core not only allows mapping database columns to private fields, you can also define a mapping that doesn't show up in the model at all. You can use shadow properties that can be retrieved with the entity in the context but are not available with the model.

Shadow properties are defined as strings. To avoid typos when using these strings multiple times, a class defining const strings is defined (code file `BooksSample/BooksContext.cs`):

```
public class ColumnNames
{
  public const string LastUpdated = nameof(LastUpdated);
  public const string IsDeleted = nameof(IsDeleted);
  public const string BookId = nameof(BookId);
}
```

To access the members of the class without the class name, the using static declaration is used:

```
using static MappingToFields.ColumnNames;
```

The following code snippet defines the shadow properties `IsDeleted` and `LastUpdated` using the strongly typed strings defined earlier:

```
protected override void OnModelCreating(ModelBuilder modelBuilder)
{
  base.OnModelCreating(modelBuilder);
  //...

  // shadow properties
  modelBuilder.Entity<Book>().Property<bool>(IsDeleted);
  modelBuilder.Entity<Book>().Property<DateTime>(LastUpdated);
}
```

The shadow property `LastUpdated` is used to write the actual time when the entity was updated last. The `IsDeleted` property is used to define a state that the entity is deleted instead of deleting it. Sometimes it can be useful not to delete the data on the request of the user, but mark it as deleted instead. This allows making an undo to recover the entity and offers history information.

To update the shadow property `LastUpdated` automatically, the method `SaveChangesAsync` is overridden. In case you're using the synchronous `SaveChanges` method to write changes to the database, you need to override this method as well. With the implementation, the actual state of the entities is checked. If the state is `Added`, `Modified`, or `Deleted`, the shadow property is updated with the current time. To manage the shadow property `IsDeleted`, deleted entities are changed to the `Modified` state, and the `IsDeleted` shadow property is set to `true`. Shadow properties don't have a property in the model that allows for accessing it; instead you can use the `CurrentValues` indexer of the `EntityEntry` (code file `BooksSample/BooksContext.cs`):

```
public override Task<int> SaveChangesAsync(CancellationToken cancellationToken
  = default)
{
  ChangeTracker.DetectChanges();

  foreach (var item in ChangeTracker.Entries<Book>()
    .Where(e => e.State == EntityState.Added ||
                e.State == EntityState.Modified ||
                e.State == EntityState.Deleted))
  {
    item.CurrentValues[LastUpdated] = DateTime.Now;

    if (item.State == EntityState.Deleted)
```

```
        {
          item.State = EntityState.Modified;
          item.CurrentValues[IsDeleted] = true;
        }
      }

    return base.SaveChangesAsync(cancellationToken);
}
```

> **NOTE** *The change tracker that is used with the sample code is shown in detail later in the section "Object Tracking."*

> **NOTE** *Having an* IsDeleted *property, it would be a good idea to not return entities where* IsDeleted *is set to true when using normal queries. You can do this with the EF Core 2.0 feature global query filters that is discussed later in the section with this name.*

To show deleted entities, the `DeleteBookAsync` method is defined to delete the entity with the ID that is passed to this method. Here, the `Remove` method is invoked by passing the entity object, and `SaveChanges` is invoked (code file `BooksSample/Program.cs`):

```
private async Task DeleteBookAsync(int id)
{
  using (var context = new BooksContext())
  {
    Book b = await context.Books.FindAsync(id);
    if (b == null) return;

    context.Books.Remove(b);
    int records = await context.SaveChangesAsync();
    Console.WriteLine($"{records} books deleted");
  }
  Console.WriteLine();
}
```

Behind the scenes, the `IsDeleted` shadow property is set because of the change to the `SaveChangesAsync` method. To verify this, you can access the shadow property using the method `EF.Property` by passing the `IsDeleted` string. All the Book entities with this flag are shown in the `QueryDeletedBooksAsync` method:

```
private async Task QueryDeletedBooksAsync()
{
  using (var context = new BooksContext())
  {
    IEnumerable<Book> deletedBooks =
      await context.Books
        .Where(b => EF.Property<bool>(b, IsDeleted))
        .ToListAsync();

    foreach (var book in deletedBooks)
    {
      Console.WriteLine($"deleted: {book}");
    }
  }
}
```

> **NOTE** EF *is a static class in the namespace* Microsoft.EntityFrameworkCore *that offers static methods that are useful when EF types are not available. In this section you've seen the* Property *method that can be used to access shadow state. Later in this chapter, the* EF *class is used with compiled queries and* EF.Functions.

QUERIES

Now that we've defined the model, let's get into more details of queries. This section covers

➤ Basic queries

➤ Evaluation on the server and on the client

➤ Raw SQL queries

➤ Compiled queries for better performance

➤ Global query filters

➤ EF.Functions

Basic Queries

You've already seen that accessing a context-property of DbSet returns a list of all entities of the specified table. Let's look at this in more detail.

Accessing the Books property retrieves all the Book records from the database (code file BooksSample/QuerySamples.cs):

```
private async Task QueryAllBooksAsync()
{
  Console.WriteLine(nameof(QueryAllBooksAsync));
  using (var context = new BooksContext())
  {
    List<Book> books = await context.Books.ToListAsync();
    foreach (var b in books)
    {
      Console.WriteLine(b);
    }
  }
  Console.WriteLine();
}
```

With the asynchronous API it's also possible to use an IAsyncEnumerable that is returned from the ToAsyncEnumerable method and use the ForEachAsync method instead of the foreach loop:

```
await context.Books.ToAsyncEnumerable()
  .ForEachAsync(b =>
  {
    Console.WriteLine(b);
  });
```

Accessing the Books property results in this SQL statement sent to the database:

```
SELECT [b].[BookId], [b].[IsDeleted], [b].[LastUpdated], [b].[Publisher],
       [b].[Title]
FROM [Books] AS [b]
```

You can query for an object with a specific key with the `Find` and the `FindAsync` methods. In case the record is not found, this method returns `null`:

```
Book b = await context.Books.FindAsync(id);
if (b != null)
{
  //...
```

This results in a `SELECT` SQL statement with `TOP(1)` and a `WHERE` clause:

```
SELECT TOP(1) [e].[BookId], [e].[IsDeleted], [e].[LastUpdated],
              [e].[Publisher], [e].[Title]
FROM [Books] AS [e]
WHERE [e].[BookId] = @__get_Item_0
```

Instead of using a `Find` method, you can also use the synchronous `Single` or `SingleOrDefault` methods, or the asynchronous variants `SingleAsync` or `SingleOrDefaultAsync`. The difference between `Single` and `SingleOrDefault` is that `Single` throws an exception when no records are found, whereas `SingleOrDefault` returns null when no records are found. These methods also throw an exception of more than one record is found.

The following code snippet uses the method `SingleOrDefaultAsync` to ask for a book title:

```
Book book = await context.Books.SingleOrDefaultAsync(b => b.Title == title);
```

The generated SQL statement asks for the `TOP(2)` records, which allows throwing an exception if two records are found:

```
SELECT TOP(2) [b].[BookId], [b].[IsDeleted], [b].[LastUpdated],
              [b].[Publisher], [b].[Title]
FROM [Books] AS [b]
WHERE [b].[Title] = @__title_0
```

The `Where` method allows for simple filtering based on a condition. You can also use the `Contains` method within the `Where` expression. An asynchronous variant of the `Where` method is not available, as the `Where` method uses lazy evaluation. You can use a `foreach` statement to iterate all the results from the query. However, `foreach` triggers the execution of the query and blocks the thread until the result is retrieved. Instead of using `foreach` with the result of the `Where` method, you can use `ToListAsync` to immediately trigger the execution but in a task:

```
List<Book> wroxBooks = await context.Books
  .Where(b => b.Title.Contains(title))
  .ToListAsync();
```

The resulting SQL statement makes use of a simple `WHERE` in the SQL clause:

```
SELECT [b].[BookId], [b].[IsDeleted], [b].[LastUpdated], [b].[Publisher],
       [b].[Title]
FROM [Books] AS [b]
WHERE (CHARINDEX(@__title_0, [b].[Title]) > 0) OR (@__title_0 = N'')
```

In Chapter 12, you can read about many more LINQ methods and LINQ clauses which you can also use with EF Core. Just bear in mind that the implementation is different between LINQ to Objects and LINQ to EF Core. With LINQ to EF Core, expression trees are used that allow creating a SQL query with the complete LINQ expression at runtime. With LINQ to objects, most of the LINQ queries are defined in the `Enumerable` class. LINQ with expression trees is implemented in the `Queryable` class, and many enhancements for EF Core such as the `Async` variants are implemented in the `EntityFrameworkQueryableExtensions` class. For more information about the expression tree, also check Chapter 12.

Client and Server Evaluation

Not every part of a query can be converted to a SQL statement and thus run on the server. Some parts need to run on the client. EF Core allows for transparent client and server evaluation. If a query cannot be resolved, it automatically runs on the client. This has a big advantage for using different providers. For example, with one provider the query can be completely evaluated on the server. Using a different provider that doesn't translate all queries, the program still runs, but some parts are now evaluated on the client.

Let's get into one example with a n-to-n relationship. The Book type is related to the Author type with a relation entity. One book can be written by multiple authors, and one author can write multiple books.

The following code snippet accesses the Book objects via the Books property. The Where method is used for filtering, and the OrderBy method defines the order. With the Select method, the result is defined—including a relation to the authors using the BookAuthors property:

```
var books = context.Books
  .Where(b => b.Title.StartsWith("Pro"))
  .OrderBy(b => b.Title)
  .Select(b => new
  {
    b.Title,
    Authors = b.BookAuthors
  });
```

All this is translated using EF Core 2.0 to a SQL statement. The evaluation happens completely on the server, translating Where, OrderBy, and Select with the relation, using SELECT, INNER JOIN, WHERE, and ORDER BY:

```
SELECT [b.BookAuthors].[BookId], [b.BookAuthors].[AuthorId]
FROM [BookAuthors] AS [b.BookAuthors]
INNER JOIN (
  SELECT [b0].[BookId], [b0].[Title]
  FROM [Books] AS [b0]
  WHERE [b0].[Title] LIKE N'Pro' + N'%' AND (LEFT([b0].[Title], LEN(N'Pro')) =
  N'Pro')
) AS [t] ON [b.BookAuthors].[BookId] = [t].[BookId]
ORDER BY [t].[Title], [t].[BookId]
```

If the Select statement is modified to return a comma-separated string containing the authors, the result is very different. This is done in the following code snippet: a string is assigned to the Authors property. Using the relation BookAuthors, just the FirstName and LastName properties of the authors are selected, and string.Join joins the list to a single string (code file BooksSample/QuerySamples.cs):

```
var books = context.Books
  .Where(b => b.Title.StartsWith("Pro"))
  .OrderBy(b => b.Title)
  .Select(b => new
  {
    b.Title,
    Authors = string.Join(", ", b.BookAuthors.Select(a =>
      $"{a.Author.FirstName} {a.Author.LastName}").ToArray())
  });
```

EF Core 2.0 cannot translate this query to a SQL statement. Logging information from EF Core shows this warning:

```
warn: Microsoft.EntityFrameworkCore.Query[200500]
  The LINQ expression 'join Author a.Author in value(
    Microsoft.EntityFrameworkCore.Query.Internal.EntityQueryable`1[
      BooksSample.Author]) on Property([a], "AuthorId") equals
      Property([a.Author], "AuthorId")'
  could not be translated and will be evaluated locally.
```

Three queries are now executed. The result of these queries is joined on the client. The application still works, but the queries are not that efficient. Three statements are executed in SQL Server instead of one, and as you analyze the queries you can see that all authors are retrieved from the server before the evaluation happens on the client. This might result in a large transfer to the client:

```
SELECT [b].[Title], [b].[BookId]
FROM [Books] AS [b]
WHERE [b].[Title] LIKE N'Pro' + N'%' AND (LEFT([b].[Title], LEN(N'Pro')) =
    N'Pro')
ORDER BY [b].[Title]

SELECT [b0].[BookId], [b0].[AuthorId]
FROM [BookAuthors] AS [b0]
WHERE @_outer_BookId = [b0].[BookId]

SELECT [a.Author].[AuthorId], [a.Author].[FirstName], [a.Author].[LastName]
FROM [Authors] AS [a.Author]
```

It's practical to automatically have client and server evaluation. Unlike EF Core 1.0, the SQL Server provider for EF Core 2.0 can do more evaluation on the server, and future versions will even support more evaluations on the server. Using other providers can have different results. The efficiency is not the same, but at least the program works.

To avoid evaluation on the server, you can configure the context to throw exceptions when evaluation should be done only on the server. You can do this by invoking the `ConfigureWarnings` method on the `optionsBuilder` when configuring the context:

```
optionsBuilder.UseSqlServer(ConnectionString)
    .ConfigureWarnings(warnings =>
    warnings.Throw(RelationalEventId.QueryClientEvaluationWarning));
```

> **WARNING** *Client and server evaluation is a great feature to make your program work across different providers. However, this can lead to a performance penalty. To define queries for best performance, you can easily find out when evaluation happens on the client by configuring to throw exceptions. Then you can change your queries accordingly.*

Raw SQL Queries

EF Core 2.0 also enables you to define raw SQL queries, which in turn returns entity objects and tracks these objects. You just need to invoke the `FromSql` method of the `DbSet` object as shown in the following code snippet (code file BooksSample/QuerySamples.cs):

```
private async Task RawSqlQuery(string publisher)
{
  Console.WriteLine(nameof(RawSqlQuery));
  using (var context = new BooksContext())
  {
    IList<Book> books = await context.Books.FromSql(
      $"SELECT * FROM Books WHERE Publisher = {publisher}")
      .ToListAsync();

    foreach (var b in books)
    {
      Console.WriteLine($"{b.Title} {b.Publisher}");
    }
  }
  Console.WriteLine();
}
```

The SQL query assigned to the `RawSql` method needs to return entity types that are part of the model, and data for all the properties of the model needs to be returned.

The SQL string assigned to the `FromSql` method might look like SQL injection can happen as the string is defined. However, this is not the case. `FromSql` requires that a `FormattableString` type be assigned. For this `FormattableString`, EF Core extracts the parameters and creates SQL parameters.

> **NOTE** *For more information about string interpolation and the* `FormattableString` *type, read Chapter 9, "Strings and Regular Expressions."*

Compiled Queries

For queries that need to be done again and again, you can create a compiled query that only needs to be executed. A compiled query can be created using `EF.CompileQuery`. This method offers different generic overloads where you can pass a different number of arguments. In the following code snippet, one query is created that defines one string parameter. This method needs a delegate parameter where the first parameter is of type `BooksContext`, the second parameter is the string parameter—here the publisher is used. After defining the compiled query, you can use it passing a context and the parameter (code file `BooksSample/QuerySamples.cs`):

```
private void CompiledQuery()
{
  Console.WriteLine(nameof(CompiledQuery));
  Func<BooksContext, string, IEnumerable<Book>> query =
    EF.CompileQuery<BooksContext, string, Book>((context, publisher) =>
      context.Books.Where(b => b.Publisher == publisher));

  using (var context = new BooksContext())
  {
    IEnumerable<Book> books = query(context, "Wrox Press");

    foreach (var b in books)
    {
      Console.WriteLine($"{b.Title} {b.Publisher}");
    }
  }
  Console.WriteLine();
}
```

You can create a compiled query to a member field for having it available later when it's needed, and you can invoke the query passing different contexts as needed.

Global Query Filters

Earlier in this chapter, you saw shadow state used with the `IsDeleted` column. You do not need to define a WHERE clause with every query not to return the records where `IsDeleted` is true; instead you can define a global query filter when creating the mode. This is what the next code snippet does—globally checking for `IsDeleted`. Because `IsDeleted` is not mapped to the model and just via shadow state, the value can be retrieved using `EF.Property` (code file `BooksSample/BooksContext.cs`):

```
protected override void OnModelCreating(ModelBuilder modelBuilder)
{
  base.OnModelCreating(modelBuilder);

  modelBuilder.Entity<Book>().HasQueryFilter(
    b => !EF.Property<bool>(b, IsDeleted));
  //...
}
```

With this query filter defined, the WHERE check for IsDeleted is added to every query used with this context.

> **NOTE** *Global query filters are also of practical use with multi-tenancy requirements. You can filter all queries for a context for a specific tenant-id. You just need to pass the tenant-id when constructing the context. Without using dependency injection, you can pass a tenant-id to the constructor. With dependency injection, you just need to specify a service that is injected with the constructor where the tenant-id can be retrieved in the query filter.*

> **NOTE** *Global query filters can be ignored. For example, to get all the deleted entities, you can apply the method* IgnoreQueryFilters *with LINQ expressions.*

EF.Functions

EF Core allows custom extension methods that can be implemented by providers. For this, the EF class defines the Functions property of type DbFunctions that can be extended using extension methods. At the time of this writing, the Like method is such an extension for relational data providers.

The following code snippet enhances the query of the Where method by using EF.Functions.Like and supplying an expression containing the parameter titleSegment. The parameter titleSegment is embedded within two % characters (code file BooksSample/QuerySample.cs):

```
public static async Task UseEFCunctions(string titleSegment)
{
    Console.WriteLine(nameof(UseEFCunctions));
    using (var context = new BooksContext())
    {
        string likeExpression = $"%{titleSegment}%";

        IList<Book> books = await context.Books.Where(
          b => EF.Functions.Like(b.Title, likeExpression)).ToListAsync();
        foreach (var b in books)
        {
            Console.WriteLine($"{b.Title} {b.Publisher}");
        }
    }
    Console.WriteLine();
}
```

When you run the application, the method Where that contains EF.Functions.Like is translated to the SQL clause WHERE with LIKE:

```
SELECT [b].[BookId], [b].[IsDeleted], [b].[LastUpdated], [b].[Publisher],
  [b].[Title]
FROM [Books] AS [b]
WHERE ([b].[IsDeleted] = 0) AND [b].[Title] LIKE @__likeExpression_1
```

RELATIONSHIPS

Relationships can be defined as one-to-one or one-to-many. For many-to-many relationships, with EF Core 2.0 you need to specify an intermediate class inside the relation, thus you split this relation to one-to-many and many-to-one.

Relationships can be specified by using conventions, using annotations, and with the fluent API. All the three variants are discussed in the next sections.

Relationships Using Conventions

The first way to define relationships is simply by conventions. Let's have a look using an example with `Book` and `Chapter` types. A book can have multiple chapters; thus, this is a one-to-many relationship. The `Book` type also defines a relationship to an author. Here, the author is represented by the `User` class. Later, when you define relationships using annotations, you'll see the reasoning for this name. Book and author defines a one-to-one relation. (With multi-author books, the author specified with the book is the lead author.)

The book is defined with the `Book` class. This class has a primary key `BookId` that is created because of its name. The relationship is defined by the `Chapters` property. The `Chapters` property is of type `List<Chapter>`; this is all that's needed for the `Book` type to define the one-to-many relationship. The relationship of the book to the author is specified by the `Author` property of type `User`. It would also be possible to define an `AuthorId` property of the same type as the key in the `User` class to specify the foreign key. Without this definition, a shadow property gets created (code file `RelationUsingConventions/Book.cs`):

```
public class Book
{
    public int BookId { get; set; }
    public string Title { get; set; }
    public List<Chapter> Chapters { get; } = new List<Chapter>();
    public User Author { get; set; }
}
```

> **NOTE** *Another possible implementation of the* `Chapters` *property is to define a read/write property of type* `List<Chapter>` *without creating an instance beforehand. With such an implementation, an instance would be created automatically from the EF Core context.*

The chapter is defined with the `Chapter` class. The relationship is defined using the `Book` property. A one-to-many relationship defines a collection on one side (the `Book` defines a collection of `Chapter` objects), and a simple relationship on the other side (the `Chapter` defines a simple property `Book`). Using the `Book` property from a chapter, the related book can be directly accessed. With this type, the `BookId` property specifies a foreign key to the `Book`. As already mentioned with the `Book` type, in case the `BookId` is not specified as a member of the class, a shadow property is created by convention (code file `RelationUsingConventions/Chapter.cs`):

```
public class Chapter
{
    public int ChapterId { get; set; }
    public int Number { get; set; }
    public string Title { get; set; }
    public int BookId { get; set; }
    public Book Book { get; set; }
}
```

The `User` class defines the `UserId` property for the primary key, the `Name` property, and the `AuthoredBooks` property for the relationship (code file `RelationUsingConventions/User.cs`):

```
public class User
{
    public int UserId { get; set; }
    public string Name { get; set; }
    public List<Book> AuthoredBooks { get; set; }
}
```

All that's needed with the context is to specify properties for the `Book`, `Chapter` and `User` types using properties of type `DbSet<T>` (code file `RelationUsingConventions/BooksContext.cs`):

```
public class BooksContext : DbContext
{
  private const string ConnectionString =
    @"server=(localdb)\MSSQLLocalDb;database=Books;trusted_connection=true";

  protected override void OnConfiguring(DbContextOptionsBuilder optionsBuilder)
  {
    base.OnConfiguring(optionsBuilder);

    optionsBuilder.UseSqlServer(ConnectionString);
  }
  public DbSet<Book> Books { get; set; }
  public DbSet<Chapter> Chapters { get; set; }
  public DbSet<User> Users { get; set; }
}
```

> **NOTE** *The downloadable sample code contains database-generation code and code to generate sample data. Because this code is very similar to what you've already seen in this chapter, it's not specifically covered with the samples going forward. Just consult the downloadable code samples for more information.*

Creating the database when you start the application creates the database using the mapping as defined by convention. Figure 26-2 shows the `Books`, `Chapters`, and `Users` table with their relationships. The `Book` class does not define a foreign key property to the `User` type, but one is created that fills a shadow property: `AuthorUserId`.

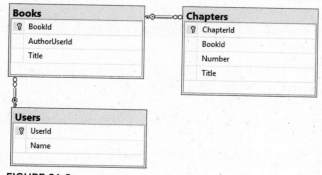

FIGURE 26-2

Before I get into different ways of defining relationships (using annotations and the fluent API), let's have a look at accessing related data with queries.

Explicit Loading Related Data

If you query for books and want to display related properties—for example, the related chapters and the related author—you can use explicit loading of relations.

Have a look at the following code snippet. The query requests all books with a specified title and only needs a single record. If you try to access the `Chapters` and the `Author` properties of the resulting book after starting the query, the values for these properties is null. Relations are not loaded implicitly. EF Core supports explicit loading by using `Entry` methods of the context that return `EntityEntry` objects by passing an entity. The `EntityEntry` class defines `Collection` and `Reference` methods that allow explicit loading of relations. With a one-to-many relationship, you can use the `Collection` method to specify the collection, whereas a one-to-one relation needs the `Reference` method to specify the relation. Explicit loading then happens with the `Load` method (code file `RelationUsingConventions/Program.cs`):

```csharp
private static void ExplicitLoading()
{
  Console.WriteLine(nameof(ExplicitLoading));
  using (var context = new BooksContext())
  {
    var book = context.Books
      .Where(b => b.Title.StartsWith("Professional C# 7"))
      .FirstOrDefault();
    if (book != null)
    {
      Console.WriteLine(book.Title);
      context.Entry(book).Collection(b => b.Chapters).Load();
      context.Entry(book).Reference(b => b.Author).Load();
      Console.WriteLine(book.Author.Name);
      foreach (var chapter in book.Chapters)
      {
        Console.WriteLine($"{chapter.Number}. {chapter.Title}");
      }
    }
  }
  Console.WriteLine();
}
```

The `NavigationEntry` class that implements the `Load` method also implements an `IsLoaded` property where you can check whether the relation is already loaded. You do not need to check for a loaded relation before invoking the `Load` method; in cases when the relation is already loaded when you invoke the `Load` method, the query to the database doesn't happen a second time.

When you run the application with the query for the books, the following `SELECT` statement is executed on SQL Server. This query only accesses the `Books` table:

```sql
SELECT TOP(1) [b].[BookId], [b].[AuthorUserId], [b].[Title]
FROM [Books] AS [b]
WHERE [b].[Title] LIKE N'Professional C# 7' + N'%' AND (LEFT([b].[Title],
LEN(N'Professional C# 7')) = N'Professional C# 7')
```

With the following `Load` method to retrieve the chapters for the book, the `SELECT` statement retrieves the chapters based on the book ID:

```sql
SELECT [e].[ChapterId], [e].[BookId], [e].[Number], [e].[Title]
FROM [Chapters] AS [e]
WHERE [e].[BookId] = @__get_Item_0
```

With a third query, user information is retrieved from the `Users` table:

```sql
SELECT [e].[UserId], [e].[Name]
FROM [Users] AS [e]
WHERE [e].[UserId] = @__get_Item_0
```

Instead of explicitly loading related data that results in multiple queries sent to SQL server, EF Core also supports *eager loading* as shown next.

Eager Loading Related Data

Loading of related data immediately when a query is executed can be done by invoking the `Include` method and specifying the relation. The following code snippet includes the chapters of the books and the author for books that successfully apply the `Where` expression (code file `RelationUsingConventions/Program.cs`):

```
private static void EagerLoading()
{
  Console.WriteLine(nameof(EagerLoading));
  using (var context = new BooksContext())
  {
    var book = context.Books
      .Include(b => b.Chapters)
      .Include(b => b.Author)
      .Where(b => b.Title.StartsWith("Professional C# 7"))
      .FirstOrDefault();
    if (book != null)
    {
      Console.WriteLine(book.Title);

      foreach (var chapter in book.Chapters)
      {
        Console.WriteLine($"{chapter.Number}. {chapter.Title}");
      }
    }
  }
  Console.WriteLine();
}
```

Using `Include`, just a single SQL statement is executed to access the `Books` table and join the `Chapters` and `Users` table:

```
SELECT [b.Chapters].[ChapterId], [b.Chapters].[BookId], [b.Chapters].[Number],
  [b.Chapters].[Title]
FROM [Chapters] AS [b.Chapters]
INNER JOIN (
  SELECT DISTINCT [t].*
  FROM (
    SELECT TOP(1) [b0].[BookId]
    FROM [Books] AS [b0]
    LEFT JOIN [Users] AS [b.Author0] ON [b0].[AuthorUserId] =
      [b.Author0].[UserId]
    WHERE [b0].[Title] LIKE N'Professional C# 7' + N'%' AND (LEFT([b0].[Title],
      LEN(N'Professional C# 7')) = N'Professional C# 7')
    ORDER BY [b0].[BookId]
  ) AS [t]
) AS [t0] ON [b.Chapters].[BookId] = [t0].[BookId]
ORDER BY [t0].[BookId]
```

In case multiple levels of relationships need to be included, the method `ThenInclude` can be used on the result of the `Include` method.

Relationships Using Annotations

Instead of using conventions, entity types can be annotated by applying relation information. Let's modify the previously created `Book` type by adding `ForeignKey` attributes to the relation properties and specify the property that represents the foreign key. Here, the `Book` is not only associated with the author of the book but also the reviewer and the project editor. These relations map to the `User` type. The foreign key properties are defined of type `int?` to make them optional. With mandatory relations, EF Core creates a cascading delete; when the `Book` is deleted, the related author, editor, and reviewer are deleted as well (code file `RelationUsingAnnotations/Book.cs`):

```
public class Book
{
  public int BookId { get; set; }
  public string Title { get; set; }
  public List<Chapter> Chapters { get; } = new List<Chapter>();

  public int? AuthorId { get; set; }
  [ForeignKey(nameof(AuthorId))]
  public User Author { get; set; }
  public int? ReviewerId { get; set; }
  [ForeignKey(nameof(ReviewerId))]
  public User Reviewer { get; set; }
  public int? ProjectEditorId { get; set; }
  [ForeignKey(nameof(ProjectEditorId))]
  public User ProjectEditor { get; set; }
}
```

The `User` class now has multiple associations with the `Book` type. The `WrittenBooks` property lists all books for the user where the user is added as author. Similarly, the `ReviewedBooks` and `EditedBooks` properties are related with the `Book` type just on the `Reviewer` and the `ProjectEditor` properties. The properties need to be annotated with the `InverseProperty` attribute if more than one relation between the same types exists. With this attribute, the related property on the other side of the relation is specified (code file `RelationUsingAnnotations/User.cs`):

```
public class User
{
  public int UserId { get; set; }
  public string Name { get; set; }
  [InverseProperty("Author")]
  public List<Book> WrittenBooks { get; set; }
  [InverseProperty("Reviewer")]
  public List<Book> ReviewedBooks { get; set; }
  [InverseProperty("ProjectEditor")]
  public List<Book> EditedBooks { get; set; }
}
```

Figure 26-3 shows the relations of the generated tables in SQL Server. The `Books` table is associated with the `Chapters` table as in the previous sample. Now, the `Users` table has three associations with the `Books` table.

Relationships Using Fluent API

The most powerful way to specify relations is by using the fluent API. Using the fluent API, one-to-one relationships are defined with the methods `HasOne` and `WithOne`, whereas one-to-many relationships are defined by the methods `HasOne` and `WithMany`, and many-to-one relationships are defined by `HasMany` and `WithOne`.

With the following code sample, the model types do not include any annotations on the database schema. The `Book` class is a simple POCO type that defines properties for a book information including relation properties (code file `RelationUsingFluentAPI/Book.cs`):

```
public class Book
{
  public int BookId { get; set; }
  public string Title { get; set; }
  public List<Chapter> Chapters { get; } = new List<Chapter>();

  public User Author { get; set; }
  public User Reviewer { get; set; }
  public User Editor { get; set; }
}
```

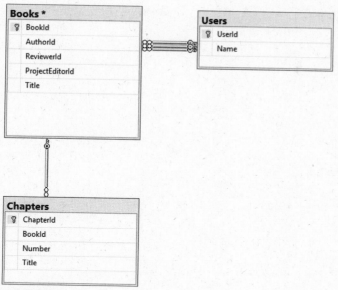

FIGURE 26-3

The `User` type is similarly defined. Besides having a `Name` property, the `User` type defines three different relationships to the `Book` type (code file `RelationUsingFluentAPI/User.cs`):

```
public class User
{
  public int UserId { get; set; }
  public string Name { get; set; }
  public List<Book> WrittenBooks { get; set; }
  public List<Book> ReviewedBooks { get; set; }
  public List<Book> EditedBooks { get; set; }
}
```

The `Chapter` class has a relation to the `Book` class. However, the `Chapter` class is different from the `Book` class because the `Chapter` class also defines a property to associate a foreign key: `BookId` (code file `RelationUsingFluentAPI/Chapter.cs`):

```
public class Chapter
{
  public int ChapterId { get; set; }
  public int Number { get; set; }
  public string Title { get; set; }
  public int BookId { get; set; }
  public Book Book { get; set; }
}
```

The mapping between the model types is now defined in the `OnModelCreating` method of the `BooksContext`. The `Book` class is associated with multiple `Chapter` objects; this is defined using `HasMany` and `WithOne`. The `Chapter` class is associated with one `Book` object; this is defined using `HasOne` and `WithMany`. Because there's also a foreign key property in the `Chapter` class, the method `HasForeignKey` is used to specify this key (code file `RelationUsingFluentAPI/BooksContext.cs`):

```
protected override void OnModelCreating(ModelBuilder modelBuilder)
{
  modelBuilder.Entity<Book>()
    .HasMany(b => b.Chapters)
    .WithOne(c => c.Book);
```

```
    modelBuilder.Entity<Book>()
      .HasOne(b => b.Author)
      .WithMany(a => a.WrittenBooks);
    modelBuilder.Entity<Book>()
      .HasOne(b => b.Reviewer)
      .WithMany(r => r.ReviewedBooks);
    modelBuilder.Entity<Book>()
      .HasOne(b => b.Editor)
      .WithMany(e => e.EditedBooks);

    modelBuilder.Entity<Chapter>()
      .HasOne(c => c.Book)
      .WithMany(b => b.Chapters)
      .HasForeignKey(c => c.BookId);

    modelBuilder.Entity<User>()
      .HasMany(a => a.WrittenBooks)
      .WithOne(b => b.Author);
    modelBuilder.Entity<User>()
      .HasMany(r => r.ReviewedBooks)
      .WithOne(b => b.Reviewer);
    modelBuilder.Entity<User>()
      .HasMany(e => e.EditedBooks)
      .WithOne(b => b.Editor);
  }
```

Table per Hierarchy with Conventions

EF Core also supports the relationship type of table per hierarchy (TPH). With this relationship, multiple model classes that form a hierarchy are used to map to a single table. This relationship can be specified by using conventions and by using the fluent API.

Let's start using conventions and the types `Payment`, `CashPayment`, and `CreditcardPayment` that form a hierarchy as shown in Figure 26-4. `Payment` is a base class; `CashPayment` and `CreditcardPayment` derive from it.

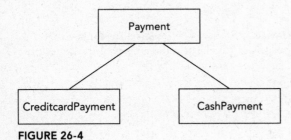

FIGURE 26-4

With the implementation, the `Payment` class defines the primary key with the `PaymentId` property, a required `Name`, and an `Amount` property. The `Amount` property maps to a database column type `Money` (code file `TPHWithConventions/Payment.cs`):

```
public class Payment
{
  public int PaymentId { get; set; }

  [Required]
  public string Name { get; set; }
  [Column(TypeName = "Money")]
  public decimal Amount { get; set; }
}
```

The class `CreditcardPayment` derives from `Payment` and adds a `CreditcardNumber` property (code file `TPHWithConventions/CreditcardPayment.cs`):

```
public class CreditcardPayment : Payment
{
  public string CreditcardNumber { get; set; }
}
```

Finally, the `CashPayment` class derives from `Payment` but doesn't declare any additional members (code file `TPHWithConventions/CashPayment.cs`):

```
public class CashPayment : Payment
{
}
```

The EF Core context class, the `BankContext`, defines `DbSet` properties for every class in the hierarchy (code file `TPHWithConventions/BankContext.cs`):

```
public class BankContext : DbContext
{
  private const string ConnectionString = @"server=(localdb)\MSSQLLocalDb;" +
    "Database=LocalBank;Trusted_Connection=True";

  protected override void OnConfiguring(DbContextOptionsBuilder optionsBuilder)
  {
    base.OnConfiguring(optionsBuilder);

    optionsBuilder.UseSqlServer(ConnectionString);
  }

  public DbSet<Payment> Payments { get; set; }
  public DbSet<CreditcardPayment> CreditcardPayments { get; set; }
  public DbSet<CashPayment> CashPayments { get; set; }
}
```

The sample data created defines two `CashPayment` and one `CreditcardPayment` payments (code file `TPHWithConventions/Program.cs`):

```
private static void AddSampleData()
{
  using (var context = new BankContext())
  {
    context.CashPayments.Add(
      new CashPayment { Name = "Donald", Amount = 0.5M });
    context.CashPayments.Add(
      new CashPayment { Name = "Scrooge", Amount = 20000M });
    context.CreditcardPayments.Add(
      new CreditcardPayment
      {
        Name = "Gus Goose",
        Amount = 300M,
        CreditcardNumber = "987654321"
      });
    context.SaveChanges();
  }
}
```

When you run the application to create the database, just a single table—Payments—gets created (as shown in Figure 26-5). This table defines a `Discriminator` column that maps a record from the table to the corresponding model type.

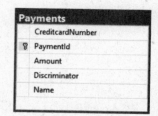

FIGURE 26-5

To query only specific types from the hierarchy, you can use the `OfType` extension method. In the following code snippet, you can see a query to return only payments of type `CreditcardPayment` (code file `TPHWithConventions/Program.cs`):

```
private static void QuerySample()
{
  using (var context = new BankContext())
  {
    var creditcardPayments = context.Payments.OfType<CreditcardPayment>();
    foreach (var payment in creditcardPayments)
    {
      Console.WriteLine($"{payment.Name}, {payment.Amount}");
    }
  }
}
```

Using `OfType`, EF Core creates a query with a `WHERE` clause to distinguish records only with a value of `CreditcardPayment`:

```
SELECT [p].[PaymentId], [p].[Amount], [p].[Discriminator], [p].[Name],
  [p].[CreditcardNumber]
FROM [Payments] AS [p]
WHERE [p].[Discriminator] = N'CreditcardPayment'
```

Of course, with this scenario it also would be possible to invoke the context property `CreditcardPayments`, which results in the same query.

Table per Hierarchy with Fluent API

Using the fluent API, you have more control to define the hierarchy. With this, the `Payment` class has been stripped off the annotations, and it's now an abstract type (code file `TPHWithFluentAPI/Payment.cs`):

```
public abstract class Payment
{
  public int PaymentId { get; set; }
  public string Name { get; set; }
  public decimal Amount { get; set; }
}
```

The `CreditcardPayment` and `Payment` classes look the same as in the previous sample, so they aren't repeated here. The context is different. The new name of the discriminator is `Type`. This just should be a column in the `Payments` table, but it should not show up in the `Payment` type. The strings `Cash` and `Creditcard` should be used to differentiate the model types. For all the strings, the `ColumnNames` and `ColumnValues` classes are defined (code file `TPHWithFluentAPI/BankContext.cs`):

```
public static class ColumnNames
{
  public const string Type = nameof(Type);
}

public static class ColumnValues
{
  public const string Cash = nameof(Cash);
  public const string Creditcard = nameof(Creditcard);
}
```

This time the context defines just a single property `Payments` for all the different `Payment` types. Of course, it would be possible to have specialized properties as well, but in the previous sample this was a necessity. The required schema information for the `Name` property as well as the `Money` type for the `Amount` property is now specified in the method `OnModelCreating` instead of using annotations. The TPH hierarchy is specified with the `HasDiscriminator` method. The name of the discriminator is `Type`, which is also specified as a shadow property. The differentiation for the derived types is specified with the `HasValue` method. `HasValue` is a method of the `DiscriminatorBuilder` that is returned from the `HasDiscriminator` method.

```
public class BankContext : DbContext
{
  //...
  protected override void OnModelCreating(ModelBuilder modelBuilder)
  {
    modelBuilder.Entity<Payment>().Property(p => p.Name).IsRequired();
    modelBuilder.Entity<Payment>().Property(p => p.Amount)
      .HasColumnType("Money");

    // shadow property for the discriminator
    modelBuilder.Entity<Payment>().Property<string>(ColumnNames.Type);
    modelBuilder.Entity<Payment>()
      .HasDiscriminator<string>(ColumnNames.Type)
      .HasValue<CashPayment>(ColumnValues.Cash)
      .HasValue<CreditcardPayment>(ColumnValues.Creditcard);
  }

  public DbSet<Payment> Payments { get; set; }
}
```

The database created looks similar like before, just instead of the `Discriminator` column the table `Payments` now defines the `Type` column—as specified with the creation of the model. The new query asking for credit card numbers filters the `Type` column:

```
SELECT [p].[PaymentId], [p].[Amount], [p].[Name], [p].[Type],
  [p].[CreditcardNumber]
FROM [Payments] AS [p]
WHERE [p].[Type] = N'Creditcard'
```

Table Splitting

Table splitting is another new feature of EF Core 2.0. With *table splitting*, a database table can be split into multiple entity types. Using table splitting, each class that belongs to the same table needs a one-to-one relationship and defines its own primary key. However, because they share the same table, also the same primary key is shared.

Let's get into an example with the `Menu` class that represents information about a lunch menu, and `MenuDetails` contains information for the kitchen. The `Menu` class defines some properties for the menu including the `Details` property. The `Details` property maps the relation to the `MenuDetails` class (code file `TableSplitting/Menu.cs`):

```
public class Menu
{
  public int MenuId { get; set; }
  public string Title { get; set; }
  public string Subtitle { get; set; }
  public decimal Price { get; set; }
  public MenuDetails Details { get; set; }
}
```

The `MenuDetails` class looks like it would map to its own table—with a primary key—and map to the `Menu` class with the `Menu` property (code file `TableSplitting/MenuDetails.cs`):

```
public class MenuDetails
{
  public int MenuDetailsId { get; set; }
  public string KitchenInfo { get; set; }
  public int MenusSold { get; set; }
  public Menu Menu { get; set; }
}
```

Within the context, Menus and MenuDetails are two DbSet properties. In the OnModelCreating method, the Menu class is configured to a one-to-one relationship with MenuDetails using HasOne and WithOne. These APIs already have been discussed in the section "Relationships Using Fluent API." Now you should put your attention to the invocation of the ToTable methods. Without these code lines, by default, the classes Menu and MenuDetails would map to two different tables. Here, the argument passed to the ToTable methods specify the same table name. Both Menu and MenuDetails map to the same table Menus. This makes the difference for table splitting (code file TableSplitting/MenusContext.cs):

```
public static class SchemaNames
{
  public const string Menus = nameof(Menus);
}

public class MenusContext : DbContext
{
  //...
  protected override void OnModelCreating(ModelBuilder modelBuilder)
  {
    modelBuilder.Entity<Menu>()
      .HasOne<MenuDetails>(m => m.Details)
      .WithOne(d => d.Menu)
      .HasForeignKey<MenuDetails>(d => d.MenuDetailsId);
    modelBuilder.Entity<Menu>().ToTable(SchemaNames.Menus);
    modelBuilder.Entity<MenuDetails>().ToTable(SchemaNames.Menus);
  }

  public DbSet<Menu> Menus { get; set; }
  public DbSet<MenuDetails> MenuDetails { get; set; }
}
```

When you verify how the table was generated in the database, you can see with the following SQL statement that the Menus table includes the columns for both the Menu and MenuDetails classes, and only the primary key from the Menu class:

```
CREATE TABLE [dbo].[Menus] (
  [MenuId] [int] IDENTITY(1,1) NOT NULL,
  [Price] [decimal](18, 2) NOT NULL,
  [Subtitle] [nvarchar](max) NULL,
  [Title] [nvarchar](max) NULL,
  [KitchenInfo] [nvarchar](max) NULL,
  [MenusSold] [int] NOT NULL,
CONSTRAINT [PK_Menus] PRIMARY KEY CLUSTERED
(
  [MenuId] ASC
)WITH (PAD_INDEX = OFF, STATISTICS_NORECOMPUTE = OFF, IGNORE_DUP_KEY = OFF,
  ALLOW_ROW_LOCKS = ON, ALLOW_PAGE_LOCKS = ON) ON [PRIMARY]
) ON [PRIMARY] TEXTIMAGE_ON [PRIMARY]
GO
```

> **NOTE** Entity splitting *is the reverse of table splitting where an entity is split into multiple tables. This feature is not yet available with EF Core 2.0, but it's planned with a later version of EF Core.*

Owned Entities

A different way to split a table into multiple entity types is with the feature known as *owned entities*. The owned entities don't need a primary key; they simply can be types owned within a normal entity. Entity classes from owned entities can map to a single table—using the table splitting feature—but also to different tables. When different tables are used, they share the same primary key.

Let's get into an example that shows both scenarios: using owned entities with a single table and mapping it to another table.

The following code snippet shows the main entity type, `Person`. This is the owner of owned entities with the primary key `PersonId`. This type contains two addresses: a `PrivateAddress` and a `CompanyAddress` (code file OwnedEntities/Person.cs):

```
public class Person
{
    public int PersonId { get; set; }
    public string Name { get; set; }
    public Address PrivateAddress { get; set; }
    public Address CompanyAddress { get; set; }
}
```

The `Address` is an owned entity—a type without its own primary key. This type has two string properties, and a relation named `Location` of type `Location`. `Location` is another owned entity (code file OwnedEntities/Address.cs):

```
public class Address
{
    public string LineOne { get; set; }
    public string LineTwo { get; set; }
    public Location Location { get; set; }
}
```

`Location` just contains `Country` and `City` properties, and as an owned entity, it also doesn't define a key (code file OwnedEntities/Location.cs):

```
public class Location
{
    public string Country { get; set; }
    public string City { get; set; }
}
```

The most interesting part now comes with the context, where owned entities are defined in the `OnModelCreating` method. Customizing the model for the `Person` class, the first invocation of `OwnsOne` specifies that the Person entity owns the entity referenced from the `CompanyAddress` property, which is an `Address` type. The second invocation to `OwnsOne` now invokes `OwnsOne` with the return type of the first `OwnsOne` invocation, a `ReferenceOwnershipBuilder`. This way, the `Address` is defined to own a `Location`. With the second invocation a different overload of `OwnsOne` is used that allows some customization. With this customization shown, the column names for the `City` and `Country` properties are specified to be different from the default names. The result of the `CompanyAddress` customization is having columns for `CompanyAddress` and `Location` all contained within the `People` table with customized column names for the `City` and `Country` properties. The customization using the next `OwnsOne` invocation defines the ownership for the `PrivateAddress` property. This time, the `Address` type is mapped to a different table: to the table named `Addr`. This table also contains the columns from the `Location` class with default column names (code file OwnedEntities/OwnedEntitiesContext.cs):

```
public class OwnedEntitiesContext : DbContext
{
    //...
    protected override void OnModelCreating(ModelBuilder modelBuilder)
    {
        modelBuilder.Entity<Person>()
            .OwnsOne(p => p.CompanyAddress)
            .OwnsOne<Location>(a => a.Location, builder =>
            {
                builder.Property(p => p.City).HasColumnName("BusinessCity");
```

```
          builder.Property(p => p.Country).HasColumnName("BusinessCountry");
        });
      modelBuilder.Entity<Person>()
        .OwnsOne(p => p.PrivateAddress)
        .ToTable("Addr")
        .OwnsOne(a => a.Location);
    }

    public DbSet<Person> People { get; set; }
  }
```

When you run the sample application, it creates the database with two tables. The first table is the `People` table as shown here. This table has all the columns from the `Person` class, and the `Address` and `Location` classes as mapped from the `CompanyAddress` property. `LineOne` and `LineTwo` have the default naming where the property names are concatenated, and underscores are used between the hierarchical property names:

```
CREATE TABLE [dbo].[People](
    [PersonId] [int] IDENTITY(1,1) NOT NULL,
    [Name] [nvarchar](max) NULL,
    [CompanyAddress_LineOne] [nvarchar](max) NULL,
    [CompanyAddress_LineTwo] [nvarchar](max) NULL,
    [BusinessCity] [nvarchar](max) NULL,
    [BusinessCountry] [nvarchar](max) NULL,
CONSTRAINT [PK_People] PRIMARY KEY CLUSTERED
(
    [PersonId] ASC
)WITH (PAD_INDEX = OFF, STATISTICS_NORECOMPUTE = OFF, IGNORE_DUP_KEY = OFF,
    ALLOW_ROW_LOCKS = ON, ALLOW_PAGE_LOCKS = ON) ON [PRIMARY]
) ON [PRIMARY] TEXTIMAGE_ON [PRIMARY]
GO
```

The second table created (`Addr`) is created because of the `ToTable` mapping on the `PrivateAddress` property. The columns have default naming because nothing else was defined. The key for this table is the same as the `People` table (`PersonId`):

```
CREATE TABLE [dbo].[Addr](
    [PersonId] [int] NOT NULL,
    [LineOne] [nvarchar](max) NULL,
    [LineTwo] [nvarchar](max) NULL,
    [Location_City] [nvarchar](max) NULL,
    [Location_Country] [nvarchar](max) NULL,
CONSTRAINT [PK_Addr] PRIMARY KEY CLUSTERED
(
    [PersonId] ASC
)WITH (PAD_INDEX = OFF, STATISTICS_NORECOMPUTE = OFF, IGNORE_DUP_KEY = OFF,
    ALLOW_ROW_LOCKS = ON, ALLOW_PAGE_LOCKS = ON) ON [PRIMARY]
) ON [PRIMARY] TEXTIMAGE_ON [PRIMARY]
GO
```

SAVING DATA

After creating the database with models and relations, you can write to it. The section "Introducing EF Core" showed you how to add, update, and delete records, but now let's get into more details about how this can be influenced and can include relations.

Adding Objects with Relations

The following code snippet writes a relationship, a `MenuCard` containing `Menu` objects. Here, the `MenuCard` and Menu objects are instantiated. The bidirectional associations are assigned. With the Menu, the `MenuCard` property is assigned to the `MenuCard`, and with the `MenuCard`, the `Menus` property is filled with

Menu objects. The `MenuCard` instance is added to the context invoking the `Add` method of the `MenuCards` property. When you add an object to the context, by default all objects are added to the tree with the state added. Not only the `MenuCard` but also the `Menu` objects are saved. Invoking `SaveChanged` on the context now creates four records (code file `MenusSample/Program.cs`):

```
private static void AddRecords()
{
  //...
  using (var context = new MenusContext())
  {
    var soupCard = new MenuCard();
    Menu[] soups =
    {
      new Menu
      {
        Text = "Consommé Célestine (with shredded pancake)",
        Price = 4.8m,
        MenuCard = soupCard
      },
      new Menu
      {
        Text = "Baked Potato Soup",
        Price = 4.8m,
        MenuCard = soupCard
      },
      new Menu
      {
        Text = "Cheddar Broccoli Soup",
        Price = 4.8m,
        MenuCard = soupCard
      },
    };
    soupCard.Title = "Soups";
    soupCard.Menus.AddRange(soups);
    context.MenuCards.Add(soupCard);
    ShowState(context);
    int records = context.SaveChanges();
    Console.WriteLine($"{records} added");
    //...
  }
}
```

The method `ShowState` that is invoked after adding the four objects to the context shows the state of all objects that are associated with the context. The `DbContext` class has a `ChangeTracker` associated that can be accessed using the `ChangeTracker` property. The `Entries` method of the `ChangeTracker` returns all the objects the change tracker knows about. With the `foreach` loop, every object including its state is written to the console (code file `MenusSample/Program.cs`):

```
public static void ShowState(MenusContext context)
{
  foreach (EntityEntry entry in context.ChangeTracker.Entries())
  {
    Console.WriteLine($"type: {entry.Entity.GetType().Name}, " +
      $"state: {entry.State}, {entry.Entity}");
  }
  Console.WriteLine();
}
```

Run the application to see the `Added` state with these four objects:

```
type: MenuCard, state: Added, Soups
type: Menu, state: Added, Consommé Célestine (with shredded pancake)
type: Menu, state: Added, Baked Potato Soup
type: Menu, state: Added, Cheddar Broccoli Soup
```

Because of this state, the SaveChanges method creates SQL Insert statements to write every object to the database.

Object Tracking

You've seen the context knows about added objects. However, the context also needs to know about changes. To know about changes, every object retrieved needs its state in the context. For seeing this in action let's create two different queries that return the same object. The following code snippet defines two different queries where each query returns the same object with the menus as they are stored in the database. Indeed, only one object gets materialized, as with the second query result it is detected that the record returned has the same primary key value as an object already referenced from the context. Verifying whether the references of the variables m1 and m2 are the same results in returning the same object (code file MenusSample/Program.cs):

```
private static void ObjectTracking()
{
  using (var context = new MenusContext())
  {
    var m1 = (from m in context.Menus
              where m.Text.StartsWith("Con")
              select m).FirstOrDefault();
    var m2 = (from m in context.Menus
              where m.Text.Contains("(")
              select m).FirstOrDefault();
    if (object.ReferenceEquals(m1, m2))
    {
      Console.WriteLine("the same object");
    }
    else
    {
      Console.WriteLine("not the same");
    }
    ShowState(context);
  }
}
```

The first LINQ query results in a SQL SELECT statement with a LIKE comparison to compare for the string to start with the value Con:

```
SELECT TOP(1) [m].[MenuId], [m].[MenuCardId], [m].[Price], [m].[Text]
FROM [mc].[Menus] AS [m]
WHERE [m].[Text] LIKE 'Con' + '%'
```

With the second LINQ query, the database needs to be consulted as well. Here, a LIKE comparison is done to compare for a (in the middle of the text:

```
SELECT TOP(1) [m].[MenuId], [m].[MenuCardId], [m].[Price], [m].[Text]
FROM [mc].[Menus] AS [m]
WHERE [m].[Text] LIKE ('%' + '(') + '%'
```

When you run the application, the same object is written to the console, and only one object is kept with the ChangeTracker. The state is Unchanged:

```
the same object
type: Menu, state: Unchanged, Consommé Célestine (with shredded pancake)
```

To not track the objects running queries from the database, you can invoke the AsNoTracking method with the DbSet:

```
var m1 = (from m in context.Menus.AsNoTracking()
          where m.Text.StartsWith("Con")
          select m).FirstOrDefault();
```

You can also configure the default tracking behavior of the `ChangeTracker` to `QueryTrackingBehavior`.`NoTracking`:

```
using (var context = new MenusContext())
{
  context.ChangeTracker.QueryTrackingBehavior =
    QueryTrackingBehavior.NoTracking;
  //...
}
```

For a more global configuration, the tracking behavior also can be configured with the SQL Server configuration:

```
protected override void OnConfiguring(DbContextOptionsBuilder optionsBuilder)
{
  base.OnConfiguring(optionsBuilder);
  optionsBuilder.UseSqlServer(ConnectionString)
    .UseQueryTrackingBehavior(QueryTrackingBehavior.NoTracking);
}
```

With such a configuration, two queries are made to the database, two objects are materialized, and the state information is empty.

> **NOTE** *Using the* `NoTracking` *configuration is useful when the context is used to only read records, but changes are not made. This reduces the overhead of the context as state information is not kept.*

Updating Objects

As objects are tracked, they can be updated easily, as shown in the following code snippet. First, a `Menu` object is retrieved. With this tracked object, the price is modified before the change is written to the database. In between all changes, state information is written to the console (code file `MenusSample/Program`.`cs`):

```
private static void UpdateRecords()
{
  using (var context = new MenusContext())
  {
    Menu menu = context.Menus
      .Skip(1)
      .FirstOrDefault();
    ShowState(context);
    menu.Price += 0.2m;
    ShowState(context);
    int records = context.SaveChanges();
    Console.WriteLine($"{records} updated");
    ShowState(context);
  }
}
```

When you run the application, you can see that the state of the object is `Unchanged` after loading the record, `Modified` after the property value is changed, and `Unchanged` after saving is completed:

```
type: Menu, state: Unchanged, Baked Potato Soup
type: Menu, state: Modified, Baked Potato Soup
1 updated
type: Menu, state: Unchanged, Baked Potato Soup
```

When you access the entries from the change tracker, by default changes are automatically detected. You configure this by setting the `AutoDetectChangesEnabled` property of the `ChangeTracker`. For checking manually to see whether changes have been done, you invoke the method `DetectChanges`. With the invocation of `SaveChangesAsync`, the state is changed back to `Unchanged`. You can do this manually by invoking the method `AcceptAllChanges`.

Updating Untracked Objects

DB contexts are usually very short-lived. Using EF Core with ASP.NET Core MVC, with one HTTP request one object context is created to retrieve objects. When you receive an update from the client, the object must again be created on the server. This object is not associated with the object context. To update it in the database, the object needs to be associated with the DB context, and the state changed to create an `INSERT`, `UPDATE`, or `DELETE` statement.

Such a scenario is simulated with the next code snippet. The local function `GetMenu` method returns a `Menu` object that is disconnected from the context; the context is disposed at the end of the local function. `GetMenu` is invoked by the method `ChangeUntracked`. This method changes the `Menu` object that is not associated with any context. After the change, the `Menu` object is passed to the method `UpdateUntracked` to save it in the database (code file `MenusSample/Program.cs`):

```
private static void ChangeUntracked()
{
  Menu GetMenu()
  {
    using (var context = new MenusContext())
    {
      Menu menu = context.Menus
        .Skip(2)
        .FirstOrDefault();
      return menu;
    }
  }
  Menu m = GetMenu();
  m.Price += 0.7m;
  UpdateUntracked(m);
}
```

The method `UpdateUntracked` receives the updated object and needs to attach it with the context. One way to attach an object with the context is by invoking the `Attach` method of the `DbSet`, and set the state as needed. The `Update` method does both with one call: attaching the object and setting the state to `Modified` (code file `MenusSample/Program.cs`):

```
private static void UpdateUntracked(Menu m)
{
  using (var context = new MenusContext())
  {
    ShowState(context);
    // EntityEntry<Menu> entry = context.Menus.Attach(m);
    // entry.State = EntityState.Modified;
    context.Menus.Update(m);
    ShowState(context);
    context.SaveChanges();
  }
}
```

When you run the application with the `ChangeUntracked` method, you can see that the state is modified. The object was untracked at first, but because the state was explicitly updated, you can see the `Modified` state:

```
type: Menu, state: Modified, Cheddar Broccoli Soup
```

Batching

An object mapping tool is not geared to support all scenarios. For example, if the ZIP Code of a city changed to a new code, and you want to update all customers with the old ZIP Code to the new one, it would be best to invoke a single SQL UPDATE statement to update all these records. Using EF Core, update statements are generated for every customer.

However, EF Core is not that bad for sending a bunch of separate SQL statements with a single call to SaveChanges. EF Core supports batching. SaveChanges sends one command to SQL Server where multiple inserts or updates just happen with one statement. You can control the batch size—for example, deactivate batching by invoking MaxBatchSize with a value of 1 when configuring SQL Server:

```
protected override void OnConfiguring(DbContextOptionsBuilder optionsBuilder)
{
  base.OnConfiguring(optionsBuilder);
  optionsBuilder.UseSqlServer(ConnectionString,
    options => options.MaxBatchSize(1));
}
```

The following code snippet creates hundred menu objects, and adds these as added objects to the context, to write it to the database with the SaveChanges method (code file MenusSample/Program.cs):

```
private static void AddHundredRecords()
{
  Console.WriteLine(nameof(AddHundredRecords));
  using (var context = new MenusContext())
  {
    var card = context.MenuCards.FirstOrDefault();
    if (card != null)
    {
      var menus = Enumerable.Range(1, 100).Select(x => new Menu
      {
        MenuCard = card,
        Text = $"menu {x}",
        Price = 9.9m
      });
      context.Menus.AddRange(menus);
      Stopwatch stopwatch = Stopwatch.StartNew();
      int records = context.SaveChanges();
      stopwatch.Stop();
      Console.WriteLine($"{records} records added after " +
        $"{stopwatch.EllapsedMilliseconds} milliseconds");
    }
  }
  Console.WriteLine();
}
```

Running the application with batching enabled, the EF Core provider creates a TABLE MERGE statement where 100 new menu records are written with one statement. Changing the batch size to 1, 100 INSERT statements are sent to the database. On my system the time difference is 56 milliseconds with batching compared to 105 milliseconds without batching—when the database is running on the same system. With a database on a different system, the difference will be larger.

CONFLICT HANDLING

What if multiple users change the same record and then save the state? Who will win with the changes?

If multiple users accessing the same database work on different records, there's no conflict. All users can save their data without interfering with data edited by other users. If multiple users work on the same record, though, you need to give some thought to conflict resolution. You have different ways to deal with this. The easiest one is that *the last one wins.* The user saving the data last overwrites changes from the user that did the changes previously.

EF Core also offers a way for letting the *first one win.* With this option, when saving a record, a verification is needed if the data originally read is still in the database. If this is the case, saving data can continue as no changes occurred between reading and writing. However, if the data changed, a conflict resolution needs to be done.

Let's get into these different options.

The Last One Wins

The default scenario is that the last one saving changes wins. To see multiple accesses to the database, the `BooksSample` application is extended.

For an easy simulation of two users, the method `ConflictHandling` invokes the method `PrepareUpdate` two times, makes different changes to two `Book` objects within two contexts that reference the same record, and invokes the `Update` method two times. Last, the book ID is passed to the `CheckUpdate` method, which shows the actual state of the book from the database (code file `BooksSample/Program.cs`):

```
public static void ConflictHandling()
{
  // user 1
  var tuple1 = await PrepareUpdate();
  tuple1.book.Title = "updated from user 1";

  // user 2
  var tuple2 = await PrepareUpdate();
  tuple2.book.Title = "updated from user 2";

  // user 1
  Update(tuple1.context, tuple1.book, "user 1");

  // user 2
  UpdateAsync(tuple2.context, tuple2.book, "user 2");

  tuple1.context.Dispose();
  tuple2.context.Dispose();

  CheckUpdate(tuple1.book.BookId);
}
```

The `PrepareUpdate` method opens a `BookContext` and returns both the context and the book within a tuple. Remember, this method is invoked two times, and different `Book` objects associated with different context objects are returned (code file `ConflictHandlingSample/Program.cs`):

```
private static (BooksContext context, Book book) PrepareUpdate()
{
  var context = new BooksContext();
  Book book = await context.Books
    .Where(b => b.Title == BookTitle)
    .FirstOrDefault();
  return (context, book);
}
```

> **NOTE** *Tuples are explained in Chapter 13, "Functional Programming with C#."*

The Update method receives the opened BooksContext with the updated Book object to save the book to the database. Remember, this method is invoked two times as well (code file BooksSample/Program.cs):

```
private static void Update(BooksContext context, Book book, string user)
{
  int records = context.SaveChanges();
  Console.WriteLine($"{user}: {records} record updated from {user}");
}
```

The CheckUpdate method writes the book with the specified id to the console (code file BooksSample/Program.cs):

```
private static void CheckUpdate(int id)
{
  using (var context = new BooksContext())
  {
    Book book = context.Books.Find(id);
    Console.WriteLine($"updated: {book.Title}");
  }
}
```

What happens when you run the application? You see the first update is successful, and so is the second update. When updating a record, it is not verified whether any changes happened after reading the record, which is the case with this sample application. The second update just overwrites the data from the first update, as you can see with the application output:

```
user 1: 1 record updated from user 1
user 2: 1 record updated from user 2
this is the updated state: updated from user 2
```

The First One Wins

In case you need a different behavior, such as the first user's changes being saved to the record, you need to do some changes. The sample project ConflictHandlingSample uses the Book and BookContext objects like before, but it deals with the first-one-wins scenario.

For conflict resolution, you need to specify the properties that should be verified if any change happened between reading and updating with a *concurrency token*. Based on the property you specify, the SQL UPDATE statement is modified to verify not only for the primary key, but also all properties that are marked with the concurrency token. Adding many concurrency tokens to the entity type creates a huge WHERE clause with the UPDATE statement, which is not very efficient. Instead you can add a property that is updated from SQL Server with every UPDATE statement—and this is what's done with the Book class. The property TimeStamp is defined as timeStamp in SQL Server (code file ConflictHandlingSample/Book.cs):

```
public class Book
{
  public int BookId { get; set; }
  public string Title { get; set; }
  public string Publisher { get; set; }
  public byte[] TimeStamp { get; set; }
}
```

To define the TimeStamp property as a timestamp type in SQL Server, you use the Fluent API. The SQL data type is defined using the HasColumnType method. The method ValueGeneratedOnAddOrUpdate informs the context that with every SQL INSERT or UPDATE statement the TimeStamp property can change, and it needs to be set with the context after these operations. The IsConcurrencyToken method marks this property as required to check whether it didn't change after reading it (code file ConflictHandlingSample/BooksContext.cs):

```
protected override void OnModelCreating(ModelBuilder modelBuilder)
{
  base.OnModelCreating(modelBuilder);
```

```
var book = modelBuilder.Entity<Book>();
book.HasKey(p => p.BookId);
book.Property(p => p.Title).HasMaxLength(120).IsRequired();
book.Property(p => p.Publisher).HasMaxLength(50);
book.Property(p => p.TimeStamp)
  .HasColumnType("timestamp")
  .ValueGeneratedOnAddOrUpdate()
  .IsConcurrencyToken();
}
```

> **NOTE** *Instead of using the* `IsConcurrencyToken` *method with the Fluent API, you can also apply the attribute* `ConcurrencyCheck` *to the property where concurrency should be checked.*

The process of the conflict-handling check is like what was done before. Both user 1 and user 2 invoke the `PrepareUpdateAsync` method, change the book title, and call the `UpdateAsync` method to make the change in the database (code file `ConflictHandlingSample/Program.cs`):

```
public static void ConflictHandling()
{
  // user 1
  var tuple1 = PrepareUpdate();
  tuple1.book.Title = "user 1 wins";

  // user 2
  var tuple2 = await PrepareUpdate();
  tuple2.book.Title = "user 2 wins";

  // user 1
  Update(tuple1.context, tuple1.book);
  // user 2
  Update(tuple2.context, tuple2.book);
  tuple1.context.Dispose();
  tuple2.context.Dispose();
  CheckUpdate(context1.book.BookId);
}
```

The `PrepareUpdate` method is not repeated here, as this method is implemented in the same way as with the previous sample. What's quite different is the `Update` method. To see the different timestamps, before and after the update, a custom extension method `StringOutput` for the byte array is implemented that writes the byte array in a readable form to the console. Next, the changes of the `Book` object are shown calling the `ShowChanges` helper method. The `SaveChanges` method is invoked to write all updates to the database. In case the update fails with a `DbUpdateConcurrencyException`, information is written to the console about the failure (code file `ConflictHandlingSample/Program.cs`):

```
private static Update(BooksContext context, Book book, string user)
{
  try
  {
    Console.WriteLine($"{user}: updating id {book.BookId}, " +
      $"timestamp: {book.TimeStamp.StringOutput()}");
    ShowChanges(book.BookId, context.Entry(book));
    int records = await context.SaveChangesAsync();
    Console.WriteLine($»{user}: updated {book.TimeStamp.StringOutput()}»);
    Console.WriteLine($"{user}: {records} record(s) updated while updating " +
      $"{book.Title}");
  }
  catch (DbUpdateConcurrencyException ex)
```

```
    {
      Console.WriteLine($"{user}: update failed with {book.Title}");
      Console.WriteLine($"error: {ex.Message}");
      foreach (var entry in ex.Entries)
      {
        if (entry.Entity is Book b)
        {
          Console.WriteLine($"{b.Title} {b.TimeStamp.StringOutput()}");
          ShowChanges(book.BookId, context.Entry(book));
        }
      }
    }
  }
}
```

With objects that are associated with the context, you can access the original values and the current values with a `PropertyEntry` object. The original values that were retrieved when reading the object from the database can be accessed with the `OriginalValue` property, the current values with the `CurrentValue` property. The `PropertyEntry` object can be accessed with the Property method of an `EntityEntry` as shown in the `ShowChanges` and `ShowChange` methods (code file `ConflictHandlingSample/Program.cs`):

```
private static void ShowChanges(int id, EntityEntry entity)
{
  void ShowChange(PropertyEntry propertyEntry) =>
    Console.WriteLine($"id: {id}, current: {propertyEntry.CurrentValue}, " +
      $"original: {propertyEntry.OriginalValue}, " +
      $"modified: {propertyEntry.IsModified}");

  ShowChange(entity.Property("Title"));
  ShowChange(entity.Property("Publisher"));
}
```

To convert the byte array of the `TimeStamp` property that is updated from SQL Server for visual output, the extension method `StringOutput` is defined (code file `ConflictHandlingSample/ByteArrayExtensions.cs`):

```
static class ByteArrayExtension
{
  public static string StringOutput(this byte[] data)
  {
    var sb = new StringBuilder();
    foreach (byte b in data)
    {
      sb.Append($"{b}.");
    }
    return sb.ToString();
  }
}
```

When you run the application, you can see output such as the following. The timestamp values and book IDs differ with every run. The first user updates the book with the original title *sample book* to the new title *user 1 wins*. The `IsModified` property returns true for the `Title` property but false for the `Publisher` property, as only the title changed. The original timestamp ends with 1.1.209; after the update to the database the timestamp is changed to 1.17.114. In the meantime, user 2 opened the same record; this book still has a timestamp of 1.1.209. User 2 updates this book, but here the update failed because the timestamp of this book does not match the timestamp from the database. Here, a `DbUpdateConcurrencyException` exception is thrown. In the exception handler, the reason of the exception is written to the console as you can see in the program output:

```
user 1: updating id 1, timestamp 0.0.0.0.0.0.7.209.
id: 1, current: user 1 wins, original: sample book, modified: True
id: 1, current: Sample, original: Sample, modified: False
user 1: updated 0.0.0.0.0.0.7.210.
user 1: 1 record(s) updated while updating user 1 wins
```

```
user 2: updating id 1, timestamp 0.0.0.0.0.0.7.209.
id: 1, current: user 2 wins, original: sample book, modified: True
id: 1, current: Sample, original: Sample, modified: False
user 2 update failed with user 2 wins
user 2 error: Database operation expected to affect 1 row(s) but actually
affected 0 row(s). Data may have been modified or deleted since entities were loaded.
See http://go.microsoft.com/fwlink/?LinkId=527962 for information on
understanding and handling optimistic concurrency exceptions.
user 2 wins 0.0.0.0.0.0.7.209.
id: 1, current: user 2 wins, original: sample book, modified: True
id: 1, current: Sample, original: Sample, modified: False
this is the updated state: user 1 wins
```

When using concurrency tokens and handling the DbConcurrencyException, you can deal with concurrency conflicts as needed. You can, for example, automatically resolve concurrency issues. If different properties are changed, you can retrieve the changed record and merge the changes. If the property changed is a number where you do some calculations—for example, a point system—you can increment or decrement the values from both updates and just throw an exception if a limit is reached. You can also ask the user to resolve the concurrency issue by giving the user the information that's currently in the database and ask what changes he or she would like to do. Just don't ask too much from the user. It's likely that the only thing the user wants is to get rid of this rarely shown dialog, which means he or she might click OK or Cancel without reading the content. For rare conflicts, you can also write logs and inform the system administrator that an issue needs to be resolved.

CONTEXT POOLING

With EF Core 2.0 you can increase performance by pooling the context. Connections are already pooled for a long time. You should open connections just before they are needed and close them immediately after use. With EF Core, this behavior is already implemented in the framework. On closing a connection, the connection to the database server is not really closed. Instead, the connection returns to the pool and can be reused when the next connection is opened. Connection pools are configured with the connection string.

DB contexts have similar usage guidelines to connections. They should be created just before they are needed and closed (disposed) immediately after use. The overhead of this is not as significant as you might expect. The model is not newly initialized with every new invocation of the context; instead the model is reused. With Entity Framework and the XML file mapping, the overhead on creating the context was a lot larger than it is now with EF Core. However, when you have big contexts, the overhead of creating the context might be still significant in your scenario. Here, you can increase performance by using context pooling.

To use context pooling, dependency injection must be used. All you need to do to activate context pooling is to change the EF Core registration from AddDbContext to AddDbContextPool. This way, the context injected (in the sample code the BooksContext) is retrieved from the context pool.

```
var services = new ServiceCollection();
services.AddTransient<BooksController>();
services.AddTransient<BooksService>();
services.AddEntityFrameworkSqlServer();
services.AddDbContextPool<BooksContext>(options =>
  options.UseSqlServer(ConnectionString));
services.AddLogging();

Container = services.BuildServiceProvider();
```

USING TRANSACTIONS

Chapter 25 introduces programming with transactions. With every access of the database using the Entity Framework, a transaction is involved, too. You can use transactions implicitly or create them explicitly with configurations as needed. The sample project used with this section demonstrates transactions in both ways. Here, the `Menu`, `MenuCard`, and `MenuContext` classes are used as shown earlier with the `MenusSample` project.

Using Implicit Transactions

An invocation of the `SaveChanges` method automatically resolves to one transaction. If one part of the changes that need to be done fails—for example, because of a database constraint—all the changes already done are rolled back. This is demonstrated with the following code snippet. Here, the first `Menu` (`m1`) is created with valid data. A reference to an existing `MenuCard` is done by supplying the `MenuCardId`. After the update succeeds, the `MenuCard` property of the `Menu` `m1` is filled automatically. However, the second `Menu` created, `mInvalid`, references an invalid menu card by supplying a `MenuCardId` that is one value higher than the highest ID available in the database. Because of the defined foreign key relation between `MenuCard` and `Menu`, adding this object will fail (code file `TransactionsSample/Program.cs`):

```
private static void AddTwoRecordsWithOneTx()
{
  Console.WriteLine(nameof(AddTwoRecordsWithOneTx));
  try
  {
    using (var context = new MenusContext())
    {
      var card = context.MenuCards.First();
      var m1 = new Menu
      {
        MenuCardId = card.MenuCardId,
        Text = "added",
        Price = 99.99m
      };

      int hightestCardId = context.MenuCards.Max(c => c.MenuCardId);
      var mInvalid = new Menu
      {
        MenuCardId = ++hightestCardId,
        Text = "invalid",
        Price = 999.99m
      };
      context.Menus.AddRange(m1, mInvalid);
      int records = context.SaveChanges();
      Console.WriteLine($"{records} records added");
    }
  }
  catch (DbUpdateException ex)
  {
    Console.WriteLine($"{ex.Message}");
    Console.WriteLine($"{ex?.InnerException.Message}");
  }
  Console.WriteLine();
}
```

After running the application invoking the method `AddTwoRecordsWithOneTx`, you can verify the content of the database to see that not a single record was added. The exception message as well as the message of the inner exception gives the details:

```
AddTwoRecordsWithOneTx
  trying to add one invalid record to the database, this should fail...
```

```
An error occurred while updating the entries. See the inner exception for details.
The MERGE statement conflicted with the FOREIGN KEY constraint
"FK_Menus_MenuCards_MenuCardId".
The conflict occurred in database "ProCSharpMenuCards",
table "mc.MenuCards", column 'MenuCardId'.
The statement has been terminated.
```

In case writing the first record to the database should be successful even if the second record write fails, you must invoke the SaveChanges method multiple times as shown in the following code snippet. In the method AddTwoRecordsWithTwoTx, the first invocation of SaveChanges inserts the m1 Menu object, whereas the second invocation tries to insert the mInvalid Menu object (code file TransactionsSample/Program.cs):

```
private static void AddTwoRecordsWithTwoTx()
{
  Console.WriteLine(nameof(AddTwoRecordsWithTwoTx));
  try
  {
    using (var context = new MenusContext())
    {
      var card = context.MenuCards.First();
      var m1 = new Menu
      {
        MenuCardId = card.MenuCardId,
        Text = "added",
        Price = 99.99m
      };
      context.Menus.Add(m1);
      int records = context.SaveChanges();
      Console.WriteLine($"{records} records added");

      int hightestCardId = context.MenuCards.Max(c => c.MenuCardId);
      var mInvalid = new Menu
      {
        MenuCardId = ++hightestCardId,
        Text = "invalid",
        Price = 999.99m
      };
      context.Menus.Add(mInvalid);
      records = context.SaveChanges();
      Console.WriteLine($"{records} records added");
    }
  }
  catch (DbUpdateException ex)
  {
    Console.WriteLine($"{ex.Message}");
    Console.WriteLine($"{ex?.InnerException.Message}");
  }
  Console.WriteLine();
}
```

When you run the application, adding the first INSERT statement succeeds, but of course the second one results in a DbUpdateException. You can verify the database to see that one record was added this time:

```
AddTwoRecordsWithTwoTx
adding two records with two transactions to the database.
One record should be written, the other not....
1 records added
An error occurred while updating the entries. See the inner exception for details.
The INSERT statement conflicted with the FOREIGN KEY constraint "FK_Menus_MenuCards_MenuCardId".
The conflict occurred in database "ProCSharpMenuCards",
table "mc.MenuCards", column 'MenuCardId'.
The statement has been terminated.
```

Creating Explicit Transactions

Instead of using implicitly created transactions, you can also create them explicitly. This gives you the advantage of also having the option to roll back in case some of your business logic fails, and you can combine multiple invocations of SaveChanges within one transaction. To start a transaction that is associated with the DbContext derived class, you need to invoke the BeginTransaction method of the DatabaseFacade class that is returned from the Database property. The transaction returned implements the interface IDbContextTransaction. The SQL statements done with the associated DbContext are enlisted with the transaction. To commit or roll back, you must explicitly invoke the methods Commit or Rollback. In the sample code, Commit is done when the end of the DbContext scope is reached; Rollback is done in cases where an exception occurs (code file TransactionsSample/Program.cs):

```
private static void TwoSaveChangesWithOneTx()
{
    Console.WriteLine(nameof(TwoSaveChangesWithOneTxAsync));
    IDbContextTransaction tx = null;
    try
    {
        using (var context = new MenusContext())
        using (tx = await context.Database.BeginTransaction())
        {
            var card = context.MenuCards.First();
            var m1 = new Menu
            {
                MenuCardId = card.MenuCardId,
                Text = "added with explicit tx",
                Price = 99.99m
            };
            context.Menus.Add(m1);
            int records = await context.SaveChanges();
            Console.WriteLine($"{records} records added");

            int hightestCardId = context.MenuCards.Max(c => c.MenuCardId);
            var mInvalid = new Menu
            {
                MenuCardId = ++hightestCardId,
                Text = "invalid",
                Price = 999.99m
            };
            context.Menus.Add(mInvalid);
            records = await context.SaveChanges();

            Console.WriteLine($"{records} records added");
            tx.Commit();
        }
    }
    catch (DbUpdateException ex)
    {
        Console.WriteLine($"{ex.Message}");
        Console.WriteLine($"{ex?.InnerException.Message}");
        Console.WriteLine("rolling back…");
        tx.Rollback();
    }
    Console.WriteLine();
}
```

When you run the application, you can see that no records have been added, although the SaveChanges method was invoked multiple times. The first return of SaveChanges lists one record as being added, but this record is removed based on the Rollback later. Depending on the setting of the isolation level, the updated record can only be seen before the rollback was done within the transaction, but not outside the transaction.

```
TwoSaveChangesWithOneTx
using one explicit transaction, writing should roll back...
1 records added
An error occurred while updating the entries. See the inner exception for details.
The INSERT statement conflicted with the FOREIGN KEY constraint
"FK_Menus_MenuCards_MenuCardId".
The conflict occurred in database "ProCSharpMenuCards",
table "mc.MenuCards", column 'MenuCardId'.
The statement has been terminated.
rolling back...
```

> **NOTE** *With the* BeginTransaction *method, you can also supply a value for the isolation level to specify the isolation requirements and locks needed in the database. Isolation levels are discussed in Chapter 25.*

MIGRATIONS

You can use EF Core with an existing database (known as "database first"). In many scenarios where EF Core is used, the database already exists. Updates to the database happen independently of the applications, and the application is updated after database changes are done. In such a scenario, EF Core migrations do not help much.

If you create the database with the application, EF Core migrations can be very helpful. As you change your code models, the database can be updated automatically. If your customers each have their own database, and you change the database schema with newer versions of the application, updating customers with older application versions can be a challenge. EF Core migrations can solve this: With migrations you can easily upgrade from version x to version y. The current version of the database is read from the database, and migration has the information that's needed with every step to upgrade to the newest version. You also can upgrade or downgrade to a specific version.

You have different options to upgrade the database. Migration can happen directly from the application with upgrade commands. You can also update the database from the command line using a dotnet command. Another option is to create an SQL server script that can be used by the database administrator to update the database.

The sample application to show migrations exists from a .NET Standard library and a .NET Core Web application. Typically, data access code is implemented within a library, and there are some additional command-line options needed to deal with this, that's why migrations are demonstrated in such a scenario.

Preparing the Project File

Let's start with a .NET Standard 2.0 Library. This library contains Menu and MenuCard classes to define the model, MenuConfiguration and MenuCardConfiguration classes to configure the mapping for the corresponding model types by implementing the interface IEntityTypeConfiguration, and the context class MenusContext.

The project file needs to be prepared to not only reference the NuGet packages Microsoft .EntityFrameworkCore and Microsoft.EntityFrameworkCore.SqlServer but also for having the EF

Core tools extension with the dotnet command line, a tool reference to `Microsoft.EntityFrameworkCore`
`.Tools.Dotnet` (project file `MigrationsLib/MigrationsLib.csproj`):

```
<Project Sdk="Microsoft.NET.Sdk">

  <PropertyGroup>
    <TargetFramework>netstandard2.0</TargetFramework>
  </PropertyGroup>

  <ItemGroup>
    <PackageReference Include="Microsoft.EntityFrameworkCore"
      Version="2.0.0" />
    <PackageReference Include="Microsoft.EntityFrameworkCore.SqlServer"
      Version="2.0.0" />
  </ItemGroup>

  <ItemGroup>
    <DotNetCliToolReference
      Include="Microsoft.EntityFrameworkCore.Tools.Dotnet"
      Version="2.0.0" />
  </ItemGroup>

</Project>
```

For using the context class from a web application, the `MenusContext` is implemented to use dependency
injection with the constructor requiring `DbContextOptions` (code file `MigrationsLib/MenusContext.cs`):

```
public class MenusContext : DbContext
{
  public MenusContext(DbContextOptions<MenusContext> options):
    base(options) { }

  public DbSet<Menu> Menus { get; set; }
  public DbSet<MenuCard> MenuCards { get; set; }

  protected override void OnModelCreating(ModelBuilder modelBuilder)
  {
    base.OnModelCreating(modelBuilder);
    modelBuilder.HasDefaultSchema("mc");

    modelBuilder.ApplyConfiguration(new MenuCardConfiguration());
    modelBuilder.ApplyConfiguration(new MenuConfiguration());
  }
}
```

Hosting Applications with ASP.NET Core MVC

With a new ASP.NET Core MVC web application, dependency injection using `Microsoft.Extensions`
`.DependencyInjection` is already built in to the template. All you need to do to enable migrations is to
add the EF Core DB context using the extension method `AddDbContext` and configure SQL Server with
`UseSqlServer`. The connection string to the database needs to be configured in the configuration file. With
this, you are ready for using the command line for migrations (code file `MigrationsWebApp/Startup.cs`):

```
public void ConfigureServices(IServiceCollection services)
{
  services.AddMvc();
  services.AddDbContext<MenusContext>(options =>
    options.UseSqlServer(
      Configuration.GetConnectionString("MenusConnection")));
}
```

> **NOTE** *ASP.NET Core MVC is covered in Chapter 31, "ASP.NET Core MVC."*
> *Before that you should read Chapter 20, "Dependency Injection," and Chapter 30,*
> *"ASP.NET Core."*

Hosting .NET Core Console App

If your EF Core DB context is not using dependency injection, you are ready to go and use the context class with the tools configured. In that case, the connections string can be retrieved with the `OnConfiguring` method of the context. Using dependency injection, the connection string is injected from the outside. ASP .NET Core has special support from the tools in accessing the `Main` method of the web application to get the connection string via the dependency injection container. Your `Main` method in console applications (and with UWP, WPF, and Xamarin applications) looks different. Here, you need to implement a factory class that returns the DB context by implementing the interface `IDesignTimeDbContextFactory`. A class implementing this interface is automatically detected from the .NET Core tools when accessing the assembly. The method `CreateDbContext` defined by this interface needs to return a configured context (code file `MigrationsConsoleApp/MenusContextFactory.cs`):

```
public class MenusContextFactory : IDesignTimeDbContextFactory<MenusContext>
{
  private const string ConnectionString =
  @"server=(localdb)\mssqllocaldb;database=ProCSharpMigrations;" +
    "trusted_connection=true";

  public MenusContext CreateDbContext(string[] args)
  {
    var optionsBuilder = new DbContextOptionsBuilder<MenusContext>();
    optionsBuilder.UseSqlServer(ConnectionString);
    return new MenusContext(optionsBuilder.Options);
  }
}
```

The project file of the console application that is used by the .NET Core tools needs to reference the NuGet package `Microsoft.EntityFrameworkCore.Design`. The Design-Library is only needed for the tools and does not need to be referenced from calling apps, that's why the `PrivateAssets` attribute can be set (project file `MigrationsConsoleApp/MigrationsConsoleApp.csproj`):

```
<Project Sdk="Microsoft.NET.Sdk">

  <PropertyGroup>
    <OutputType>Exe</OutputType>
    <TargetFramework>netcoreapp2.0</TargetFramework>
  </PropertyGroup>

  <ItemGroup>
    <PackageReference Include="Microsoft.EntityFrameworkCore"
      Version="2.0.0" />
    <PackageReference Include="Microsoft.EntityFrameworkCore.SqlServer"
      Version="2.0.0" />
    <PackageReference Include="Microsoft.EntityFrameworkCore.Design"
      Version="2.0.0" PrivateAssets="All" />
  </ItemGroup>

  <ItemGroup>
    <ProjectReference Include="..\MigrationsLib\MigrationsLib.csproj" />
  </ItemGroup>

</Project>
```

Creating Migrations

With all this in place, you can create an initial migration. Using the following command, the current directory needs to be the directory of the library—the directory where the tool reference is defined. The following command creates the initial migration named `InitMenus`. The startup project referenced with the option `--startup-project` contains the initial code that contains the connection string to the server—either with the `Main` method generated from the default project template of the ASP.NET Core web application or an object implementing `IDesignTimeContextFactory` as shown in the previous section:

```
> dotnet ef migrations add InitMenus --startup-project ../MigrationsConsoleApp
```

In case your project contains multiple DB contexts, you need to supply the additional option `--context` and supply the name of the DB context class.

Running this command creates a `Migrations` folder with a snapshot to create the complete database schema based on the model (code file `MigrationsLib/Migration/MenusContextModelSnapshot.cs`):

```csharp
[DbContext(typeof(MenusContext))]
partial class MenusContextModelSnapshot : ModelSnapshot
{
    protected override void BuildModel(ModelBuilder modelBuilder)
    {
#pragma warning disable 612, 618
        modelBuilder
            .HasDefaultSchema("mc")
            .HasAnnotation("ProductVersion", "2.0.0-rtm-26452")
            .HasAnnotation("SqlServer:ValueGenerationStrategy",
                SqlServerValueGenerationStrategy.IdentityColumn);

        modelBuilder.Entity("MigrationsLib.Menu", b =>
        {
            b.Property<int>("MenuId")
                .ValueGeneratedOnAdd();

            b.Property<int>("MenuCardId");

            b.Property<decimal>("Price")
                .HasColumnType("Money");

            b.Property<string>("Text")
                .HasMaxLength(120);

            b.HasKey("MenuId");

            b.HasIndex("MenuCardId");

            b.ToTable("Menus");
        });

        modelBuilder.Entity("MigrationsLib.MenuCard", b =>
        {
            b.Property<int>("MenuCardId")
                .ValueGeneratedOnAdd();

            b.Property<bool>("IsDeleted");

            b.Property<DateTime>("LastUpdated");

            b.Property<string>("Title")
                .HasMaxLength(50);

            b.HasKey("MenuCardId");
```

```
        b.ToTable("MenuCards");
      });

    modelBuilder.Entity("MigrationsLib.Menu", b =>
    {
      b.HasOne("MigrationsLib.MenuCard", "MenuCard")
        .WithMany("Menus")
        .HasForeignKey("MenuCardId")
        .OnDelete(DeleteBehavior.Cascade);
    });
#pragma warning restore 612, 618
  }
}
```

For every migration, a migration class deriving from the base class Migration is created. This base class defines the Up and Down methods that allow applying the migration to this migration version or to step a level back (code file MigrationsLib/<version>_InitialMenus.cs):

```
public partial class InitialMenus : Migration
{
  protected override void Up(MigrationBuilder migrationBuilder)
  {
    migrationBuilder.EnsureSchema(name: "mc");

    migrationBuilder.CreateTable(
      name: "MenuCards",
      schema: "mc",
      columns: table => new
      {
        MenuCardId = table.Column<int>(type: "int", nullable: false)
          .Annotation("SqlServer:ValueGenerationStrategy",
            SqlServerValueGenerationStrategy.IdentityColumn),
        IsDeleted = table.Column<bool>(type: "bit", nullable: false),
        LastUpdated = table.Column<DateTime>(type: "datetime2",
          nullable: false),
        Title = table.Column<string>(type: "nvarchar(50)", maxLength: 50,
          nullable: true)
      },
      constraints: table =>
      {
        table.PrimaryKey("PK_MenuCards", x => x.MenuCardId);
      });

    migrationBuilder.CreateTable(
      name: "Menus",
      schema: "mc",
      columns: table => new
      {
        MenuId = table.Column<int>(type: "int", nullable: false)
          .Annotation("SqlServer:ValueGenerationStrategy",
            SqlServerValueGenerationStrategy.IdentityColumn),
        MenuCardId = table.Column<int>(type: "int", nullable: false),
        Price = table.Column<decimal>(type: "Money", nullable: false),
        Text = table.Column<string>(type: "nvarchar(120)", maxLength: 120,
          nullable: true)
      },
      constraints: table =>
      {
        table.PrimaryKey("PK_Menus", x => x.MenuId);
        table.ForeignKey(
          name: "FK_Menus_MenuCards_MenuCardId",
          column: x => x.MenuCardId,
          principalSchema: "mc",
```

```
          principalTable: "MenuCards",
          principalColumn: "MenuCardId",
          onDelete: ReferentialAction.Cascade);
      });

    migrationBuilder.CreateIndex(
      name: "IX_Menus_MenuCardId",
      schema: "mc",
      table: "Menus",
      column: "MenuCardId");
  }

  protected override void Down(MigrationBuilder migrationBuilder)
  {
    migrationBuilder.DropTable(
    name: "Menus",
    schema: "mc");

    migrationBuilder.DropTable(
    name: "MenuCards",
    schema: "mc");
  }
}
```

After making a change to a model, such as adding `Allergens` to the `Menu` class (code file `MigrationsLib/ Menu.cs`):

```
public class Menu
{
  public int MenuId { get; set; }
  public string Text { get; set; }
  public decimal Price { get; set; }
  public string Allergens { get; set; }
  public int MenuCardId { get; set; }
  public MenuCard MenuCard { get; set; }
  public override string ToString() => Text;
}
```

Requires a new migration:

```
> dotnet ef migrations add AddAllergens --startup-project ..\MigrationsConsoleApp
```

With the new migration, that snapshot class is updated to show the current state, and a new `Migration` type is added to add and remove the allergen column with the `Up` and `Down` methods (code file `MigrationsLib/<version>_AddAllergens.cs`)

```
public partial class AddAllergens : Migration
{
  protected override void Up(MigrationBuilder migrationBuilder)
  {
    migrationBuilder.AddColumn<string>(
      name: "Allergens",
      schema: "mc",
      table: "Menus",
      type: "nvarchar(max)",
      nullable: true);
  }

  protected override void Down(MigrationBuilder migrationBuilder)
  {
    migrationBuilder.DropColumn(
      name: "Allergens",
      schema: "mc",
      table: "Menus");
  }
}
```

Pay attention to build the library before applying a new migration. Otherwise, the new migration can be empty.

> **NOTE** *With every change you're doing, you can create another migration. The new migration defines only the changes needed to get from the previous version to the new version. In case a customer's database needs to be updated from any earlier version, the necessary migrations are invoked when migrating the database.*
>
> *During the development process, you might end up with many migrations that are not needed in production. You just need to keep the migrations for all the versions that might be running on the customer sites. To remove the migrations from development time, you can invoke* dotnet ef migrations remove *to remove the latest migration code. Then add new larger migrations that contain all the changes since the previous migration.*

Applying Migrations Programmatically

After you've configured the migrations, you can start the migration process of the database directly from the application. To do this, the console application is configured to use the dependency injection container to retrieve the DB context and then to invoke the `Migrate` method of the `Database` property (code file `MigrationsConsoleApp/Program.cs`):

```
class Program
{
  private const string ConnectionString =
    @"server=(localdb)\mssqllocaldb;database=ProCSharpMigrations;" +
    @"trusted_connection=true";

  static void Main(string[] args)
  {
    RegisterServices();
    var context = Container.GetService<MenusContext>();
    context.Database.Migrate();
  }

  private static void RegisterServices()
  {
    var services = new ServiceCollection();
    services.AddDbContext<MenusContext>(options =>
      options.UseSqlServer(ConnectionString));
    Container = services.BuildServiceProvider();
  }
  public static IServiceProvider Container { get; private set; }
}
```

In case the database does not exist yet, the `Migrate` method creates the database—with the schemas defined by the model—as well as a `__EFMigrationsHistory` table that lists all the migrations that have been applied to the database. You cannot use the `EnsureCreated` method to create the database as was used earlier because this method does not apply the migration information to the database.

With an existing database, the database gets updated to the current version of the migration. Programmatically you can get all the migrations available in the application with the `GetMigrations` method. To see all applied migrations, you can use the `GetAppliedMigrations` method. For all migrations that are missing in the database, use the `GetPendingMigrations` method.

Other Ways to Apply Migrations

Instead of applying migrations programmatically, you can apply migrations using the command line:

```
> dotnet ef database update --startup-project ../MigrationsConsoleApp
```

This command applies the latest migration to the database. You can also supply the name of the migration to this command to put the database into a specific version of the migration.

In case you have a database administrator who needs to keep full control over the database and doesn't allow programmatic changes, and no changes from a tool such as the .NET Core CLI command line, you can create a SQL script and hand this over or use it by yourself.

The following command line creates the SQL script `migrationsscript.sql` from the initial database creation up to the latest migration. You can also supply specific from/to values for the range of the migrations that should be applied in the script:

```
> dotnet ef migrations script --output migrationsscript.sql
--startup-project ..\MigrationsConsoleApp
```

SUMMARY

This chapter introduced you to the features of the EF Core. You've learned how the object context keeps knowledge about entities retrieved and updated, and how changes can be written to the database. You've also seen how migrations can be used to create and change the database schema from C# code. To define the schema, you've seen how the database mapping can be done using data annotations, and you've also seen the fluent API that offers more features compared to the annotations.

You've seen possibilities for reacting to conflicts when multiple users work on the same record, as well as using transactions implicitly or explicitly for more transactional control.

New features of EF Core 2.0, such as compiled queries, global query filters, table splitting, and owned entities, have been covered with great information to get you started.

The next chapter gets into globalization and localization features of .NET, using culture specific date, time, and number formats, as well as resources to define text for different languages.

27

Localization

WROX.COM CODE DOWNLOADS FOR THIS CHAPTER

The Wrox.com code downloads for this chapter are found at www.wrox.com on the Download Code tab. The source code is also available in the GitHub repository https://github.com/ProfessionalCSharp/ProfessionalCSharp7 in the folder Localization.

The code for this chapter is divided into the following major examples:

- ➤ NumberAndDateFormatting
- ➤ SortingDemo
- ➤ CreateResource
- ➤ UWPCultureDemo
- ➤ ResourcesDemo
- ➤ WebApplicationSample
- ➤ ASPNETCoreMVCSample
- ➤ UWPLocalization

GLOBAL MARKETS

NASA's Mars Climate Orbiter was lost on September 23, 1999, at a cost of $125 million, because one engineering team used metric units while another one used inches for a key spacecraft operation. When writing applications for international distribution, different cultures and regions must be kept in mind.

Different cultures have diverging calendars and use different number and date formats; and sorting strings may lead to various results because the order of A–Z is defined differently based on the culture. To make usable applications for global markets, you must globalize and localize them.

This chapter covers the globalization and localization of .NET applications. *Globalization* is about internationalizing applications: preparing applications for international markets. With globalization, the application supports number and date formats that vary according to culture, calendars, and so on. *Localization* is about translating applications for specific cultures. For translations of strings, you can use resources such as .NET resources or WPF resource dictionaries.

.NET supports the globalization and localization of Windows and web applications. To globalize an application, you can use classes from the namespace System.Globalization; to localize an application, you can use resources supported by the namespace System.Resources.

NAMESPACE SYSTEM.GLOBALIZATION

The System.Globalization namespace holds all the culture and region classes necessary to support different date formats, different number formats, and even different calendars that are represented in classes such as GregorianCalendar, HebrewCalendar, JapaneseCalendar, and so on. By using these classes, you can display different representations according to the user's locale.

This section looks at the following issues and considerations when using the System.Globalization namespace:

➤ Unicode issues

➤ Cultures and regions

➤ An example showing all cultures and their characteristics

➤ Sorting

Unicode Issues

A Unicode character has 16 bits, so there is room for 65,536 characters. Is this enough for all languages currently used in information technology? In the case of the Chinese language, for example, more than 80,000 characters are needed. Fortunately, Unicode has been designed to deal with this issue. With Unicode you must differentiate between base characters and combining characters. You can add multiple combining characters to a base character to build a single display character or a text element.

Take, for example, the Icelandic character Ogonek. Ogonek can be combined by using the base character 0x006F (Latin small letter o), and the combining characters 0x0328 (combining Ogonek), and 0x0304 (combining Macron), as shown in Figure 27-1. Combining characters are defined within ranges from 0x0300 to 0x0345. For American and European markets, predefined characters exist to facilitate dealing with special characters. The character Ogonek is also defined by the predefined character 0x01ED.

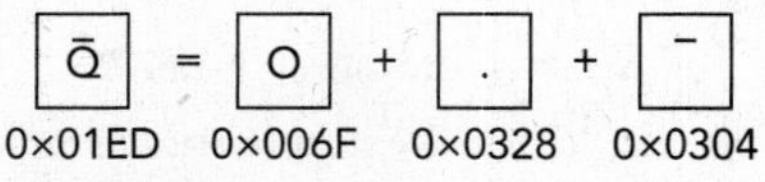

FIGURE 27-1

For Asian markets, where more than 80,000 characters are necessary for Chinese alone, such predefined characters do not exist. In Asian languages, you always have to deal with combining characters. The problem is getting the right number of display characters or text elements and getting to the base characters instead of the combined characters. The namespace System.Globalization offers the class StringInfo, which you can use to deal with this issue.

The following table lists the static methods of the class StringInfo that help in dealing with combined characters.

METHOD	DESCRIPTION
GetNextTextElement	Returns the first text element (base character and all combining characters) of a specified string
GetTextElementEnumerator	Returns a TextElementEnumerator object that allows iterating all text elements of a string
ParseCombiningCharacters	Returns an integer array referencing all base characters of a string

> **NOTE** *A single display character can contain multiple Unicode characters. To address this issue, when you write applications that support international markets, don't use the data type* char; *use* string *instead. A* string *can hold a text element that contains both base characters and combining characters, whereas a* char *cannot.*

Cultures and Regions

The world is divided into multiple cultures and regions, and applications must be aware of these cultural and regional differences. A culture is a set of preferences based on a user's language and cultural habits. RFC 4646 (http://www.ietf.org/rfc/rfc4646.txt) defines culture names that are used worldwide, depending on a language and a country or region. Some examples are en-AU, en-CA, en-GB, and en-US for the English language in Australia, Canada, the United Kingdom, and the United States, respectively.

Possibly the most important class in the System.Globalization namespace is CultureInfo. CultureInfo represents a culture and defines calendars, formatting of numbers and dates, and sorting strings used with the culture.

The class RegionInfo represents regional settings (such as the currency) and indicates whether the region uses the metric system. Some regions can use multiple languages. One example is the region of Spain, which has Basque (eu-ES), Catalan (ca-ES), Spanish (es-ES), and Galician (gl-ES) cultures. Like one region can have multiple languages, one language can be spoken in different regions; for example, Spanish is spoken in Mexico, Spain, Guatemala, Argentina, and Peru, to name only a few countries.

Later in this chapter is a sample application that demonstrates these characteristics of cultures and regions.

Specific, Neutral, and Invariant Cultures

When using cultures in the .NET Framework, you must differentiate between three types: *specific, neutral,* and *invariant* cultures. A specific culture is associated with a real, existing culture defined with RFC 4646, as described in the preceding section. A specific culture can be mapped to a neutral culture. For example, de is the neutral culture of the specific cultures de-AT, de-DE, de-CH, and others. de is shorthand for the German language (Deutsch); AT, DE, and CH are shorthand for the countries Austria, Germany, and Switzerland, respectively.

When translating applications, it is typically not necessary to do translations for every region; not much difference exists between the German language in the countries Austria and Germany. Instead of using specific cultures, you can use a neutral culture to localize applications.

The invariant culture is independent of a real culture. When storing formatted numbers or dates in files, or sending them across a network to a server, using a culture that is independent of any user settings is the best option.

Figure 27-2 shows how the culture types relate to each other.

Current Culture and CurrentUICulture

When you set cultures, you need to differentiate between a culture for the user interface and a culture for the number and date formats. Cultures are associated with a thread, and with these two culture types, two culture settings can be applied to a thread. The `CultureInfo` class has the static properties `CurrentCulture` and `CurrentUICulture`. The property `CurrentCulture` is for setting the culture that is used with formatting and sort options, whereas the property `CurrentUICulture` is used for the language of the user interface.

Users can install additional languages to Windows 10 by selecting Time & Language in the Windows settings, and from there Region & Language (see Figure 27-3). The language configured as default is the current UI culture.

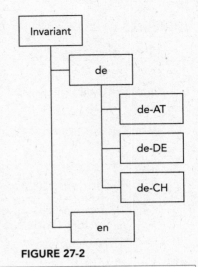

FIGURE 27-2

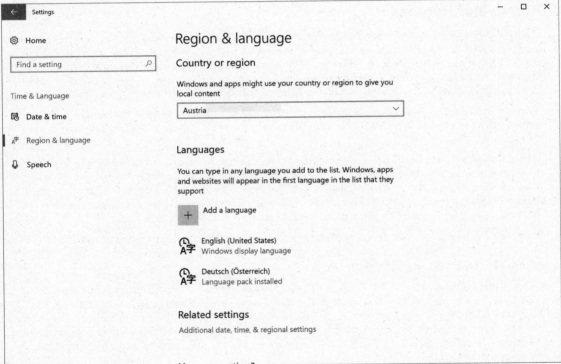

FIGURE 27-3

To change the current culture, you use the Additional Date, Time, & Regional Settings link in the dialog shown in Figure 27-3. From there, you click the Change Date, Time, or Number Formats option to see the dialog shown in Figure 27-4. The language setting for the format influences the current culture. It is also possible to change the defaults for the number format, the time format, and the date format independent of the culture.

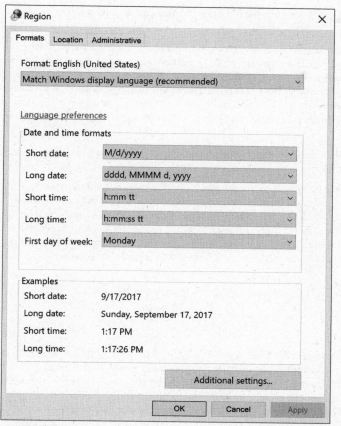

FIGURE 27-4

These settings provide a very good default, and in many cases, you won't need to change the default behavior. If the culture should be changed, you can easily do this programmatically by changing both cultures to, say, the Spanish culture, as shown in this code snippet (using the namespace System.Globalization):

```
var ci = new CultureInfo("es-ES");
CultureInfo.CurrentCulture = ci;
CultureInfo.CurrentUICulture = ci;
```

Now that you know how to set the culture, the following sections discuss number and date formatting, which are influenced by the CurrentCulture setting.

Number Formatting

The number structures Int16, Int32, Int64, and so on in the System namespace have an overloaded ToString method. You can use this method to create a different representation of the number, depending on the locale. For the Int32 structure, ToString is overloaded with the following four versions:

```
public string ToString();
public string ToString(IFormatProvider);
public string ToString(string);
public string ToString(string, IFormatProvider);
```

`ToString` without arguments returns a string without format options. You can also pass a string and a class that implements `IFormatProvider`.

The string specifies the format of the representation. The format can be a standard numeric formatting string or a picture numeric formatting string. For standard numeric formatting, strings are predefined where C specifies the currency notation, D creates a decimal output, E creates scientific output, F creates fixed-point output, G creates general output, N creates number output, and X creates hexadecimal output. With a picture numeric formatting string, it is possible to specify the number of digits, section and group separators, percent notation, and so on. The picture numeric format string `###,###` means two three-digit blocks separated by a group separator.

The `IFormatProvider` interface is implemented by the `NumberFormatInfo`, `DateTimeFormatInfo`, and `CultureInfo` classes. This interface defines a single method, `GetFormat`, that returns a format object.

You can use `NumberFormatInfo` to define custom formats for numbers. With the default constructor of `NumberFormatInfo`, a culture-independent or invariant object is created. Using the properties of `NumberFormatInfo`, it is possible to change all the formatting options, such as a positive sign, a percent symbol, a number group separator, a currency symbol, and a lot more. A read-only, culture-independent `NumberFormatInfo` object is returned from the static property `InvariantInfo`. A `NumberFormatInfo` object in which the format values are based on the `CultureInfo` of the current thread is returned from the static property `CurrentInfo`.

The sample code `NumberAndDateFormatting` makes use of the following namespaces:

```
System

System.Globalization
```

To create the next example, you can start with a Console App (.NET Core) project. In this code, the first example shows a number displayed in the format of the current culture (here: English-US, the setting of the operating system). The second example uses the `ToString` method with the `IFormatProvider` argument. `CultureInfo` implements `IFormatProvider`, so create a `CultureInfo` object using the French culture. The third example changes the current culture. The culture is changed to German by using the property `CurrentCulture` of the `CultureInfo` instance (code file `NumberAndDateFormatting\Program.cs`):

```csharp
public static void NumberFormatDemo()
{
    int val = 1234567890;
    // culture of the current thread
    Console.WriteLine(val.ToString("N"));
    // use IFormatProvider
    Console.WriteLine(val.ToString("N", new CultureInfo("fr-FR")));
    // change the current culture
    CultureInfo.CurrentCulture = new CultureInfo("de-DE");
    Console.WriteLine(val.ToString("N"));
}
```

You can compare the following different output for U.S. English, French, and German, respectively, shown here:

```
1,234,567,890.00
1 234 567 890,00
1.234.567.890,00
```

Date Formatting

The same support for numbers is available for dates. The `DateTime` structure has some overloads of the `ToString` method for date-to-string conversions. You can pass a string format and assign a different culture:

```csharp
public string ToString();
public string ToString(IFormatProvider);
```

```
public string ToString(string);
public string ToString(string, IFormatProvider);
```

With the string argument of the ToString method, you can specify a predefined format character or a custom format string for converting the date to a string. The class DateTimeFormatInfo specifies the possible values. With DateTimeFormatInfo, the case of the format strings has a different meaning. D defines a long date format; d defines a short date format. Other examples of possible formats are ddd for the abbreviated day of the week, dddd for the full day of the week, yyyy for the year, T for a long time, and t for a short time. With the IFormatProvider argument, you can specify the culture. Using an overloaded method without the IFormatProvider argument implies that the current culture is used (code file NumberAndDateFormatting/Program.cs):

```
public static void DateFormatDemo()
{
  var d = new DateTime(2017, 09, 17);
  // current culture
  Console.WriteLine(d.ToLongDateString());
  // use IFormatProvider
  Console.WriteLine(d.ToString("D", new CultureInfo("fr-FR")));
  // use current culture
  Console.WriteLine($"{CultureInfo.CurrentCulture}: {d:D}");
  CultureInfo.CurrentCulture = new CultureInfo("es-ES");
  Console.WriteLine($"{CultureInfo.CurrentCulture}: {d:D}");
}
```

The output of this example program shows ToLongDateString with the current culture of the thread, a French version where a CultureInfo instance is passed to the ToString method, and a Spanish version where the CurrentCulture property of the thread is changed to es-ES:

```
Sunday, September 17, 2017
dimanche 17 septembre 2017
en-US: Sunday, September 17, 2017
es-ES: domingo, 17 de septiembre de 2017
```

Cultures in Action

To see all cultures in action, you can use a sample UWP app that lists all cultures and demonstrates different characteristics of culture properties. On the left side of the UI, a tree view is used to display all the cultures. On the right side is a user control that displays relevant information about the selected culture and region. Figure 27-5 shows the user interface of the user control in the Visual Studio 2017 Designer.

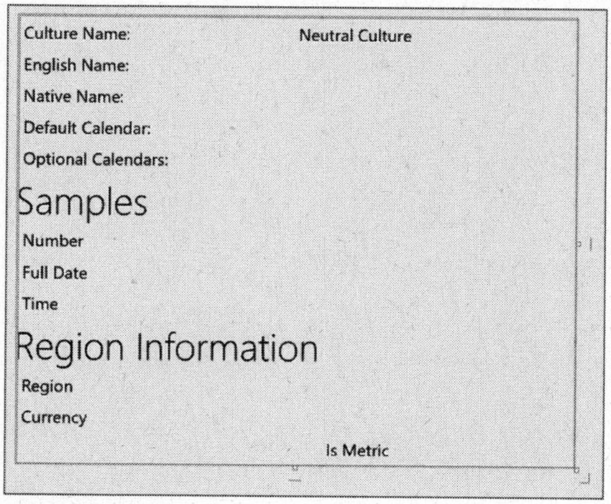

FIGURE 27-5

> **NOTE** *The sample code makes use of a tree control. The Windows 10 Runtime does not include a tree view control with the Fall Creators Update 2017, but one is expected later. Several third-party tree controls are available for UWP that you could use. Microsoft's Windows Universal Samples at* https://github.com/Microsoft/ Windows-universal-samples *also include a tree view control. This control is used with this UWP sample. Because this control is written with C++ code, you need to install the C++ component with the Universal Windows Platform development workload.*

During initialization of the application, all available cultures are added to the `TreeView` control that is placed on the left side of the application. This initialization happens in a view-model in the method `SetupCultures`, which is called in the constructor of the `CulturesViewModel` class (code file `UWPCultureDemo/CulturesViewModel.cs`):

```
public CulturesViewModel()
{
    SetupCultures();
}
```

For the data that is shown in the user interface, the custom class `CultureData` is created. This class can be bound to a `TreeView` control, as it has a property `SubCultures` that contains a list of `CultureData`. Therefore, the `TreeView` control enables walking through this tree. Other than the subcultures, `CultureData` contains the `CultureInfo` type and sample values for a number, a date, and a time. The number returns a string in the number format for the specific culture, and the date and time return strings in the specific culture formats as well. `CultureData` contains a `RegionInfo` class to display regions. With some neutral cultures (for example, English), creating a `RegionInfo` throws an exception, as there are regions only with specific cultures. However, with other neutral cultures (for example, German), creating a `RegionInfo` succeeds and is mapped to a default region. The exception thrown here is handled (code file `UWPCultureDemo/CultureData.cs`):

```
public class CultureData
{
    public CultureInfo CultureInfo { get; set; }
    public List<CultureData> SubCultures { get; set; }
    double numberSample = 9876543.21;
    public string NumberSample => numberSample.ToString("N", CultureInfo);
    public string DateSample => DateTime.Today.ToString("D", CultureInfo);
    public string TimeSample => DateTime.Now.ToString("T", CultureInfo);

    public RegionInfo RegionInfo
    {
        get
        {
            RegionInfo ri;
            try
            {
                ri = new RegionInfo(CultureInfo.Name);
            }
            catch (ArgumentException)
            {
                // with some neutral cultures regions are not available
                return null;
            }
            return ri;
        }
    }
}
```

In the method `SetupCultures`, you get all cultures from the static method `CultureInfo.GetCultures`. Passing `CultureTypes.AllCultures` to this method returns an unsorted array of all available cultures. The result is sorted by the name of the culture. With the result of the sorted cultures, a collection of `CultureData` objects is created and the `CultureInfo` and `SubCultures` properties are assigned. With the result of this, a dictionary is created to enable fast access to the culture name.

For the data that should be shown in the UI, a list of `CultureData` objects is created that contains all the root cultures for the tree view after the `foreach` statement is completed. Root cultures can be verified to determine whether they have the invariant culture as their parent. The invariant culture has the Locale Identifier (LCID) 127. Every culture has its own unique identifier that can be used for a fast verification. In the code snippet, root cultures are added to the `rootCultures` collection within the block of the `if` statement. If a culture has the invariant culture as its parent, it is a root culture.

If the culture does not have a parent culture, it is added to the root nodes of the tree. To find parent cultures, all cultures are remembered inside a dictionary. (See Chapter 10, "Collections," for more information about dictionaries, and Chapter 8, "Delegates, Lambdas, and Events," for details about lambda expressions.) If the culture iterated is not a root culture, it is added to the `SubCultures` collection of the parent culture. The parent culture can be quickly found by using the dictionary. In the last step, the root cultures are made available to the UI by assigning them to the `RootCultures` property (code file `UWPCultureDemo/CulturesViewModel.cs`):

```csharp
private void SetupCultures()
{
  var cultureDataDict = CultureInfo.GetCultures(CultureTypes.AllCultures)
    .OrderBy(c => c.Name)
    .Select(c => new CultureData
    {
      CultureInfo = c,
      SubCultures = new List<CultureData>()
    })
    .ToDictionary(c => c.CultureInfo.Name);

  var rootCultures = new List<CultureData>();
  foreach (var cd in cultureDataDict.Values)
  {
    if (cd.CultureInfo.Parent.LCID == 127)
    {
      rootCultures.Add(cd);
    }
    else
    {
      if (cultureDataDict.TryGetValue(cd.CultureInfo.Parent.Name,
        out CultureData parentCultureData))
      {
        parentCultureData.SubCultures.Add(cd);
      }
      else
      {
        throw new InvalidOperationException(
          "parent culture not found");
      }
    }
  }

  foreach (var rootCulture in rootCultures.OrderBy(
    cd => cd.CultureInfo.EnglishName))
  {
    RootCultures.Add(rootCulture);
  }
}

public IList<CultureData> RootCultures { get; } = new List<CultureData>();
```

Now let's get into the XAML code for the display. A TreeView is used to display all the cultures. For the display of items inside the TreeView, an item template is used. This template uses a TextBlock that is bound to the EnglishName property of the CultureInfo class (code file UWPCultureDemo/MainPage .xaml):

```xaml
<tvc:TreeView x:Name="treeView1"
  IsMultiSelectCheckBoxEnabled="False"
  IsItemClickEnabled="True"
  SelectionChanged="{x:Bind OnSelectionChanged, Mode=OneTime}">
  <tvc:TreeView.ItemTemplate>
    <DataTemplate>
      <StackPanel Orientation="Horizontal" Height="40"
        Margin="{Binding Depth,
          Converter={StaticResource IntegerToIndConverter}}">
        <FontIcon x:Name="expandCollapseChevron"
          Glyph="{Binding IsExpanded,
            Converter={StaticResource ExpandCollapseGlyphConverter}}"
          Visibility="{Binding Data.SubCultures,
            Converter={StaticResource EmptyConverter}}"
          FontSize="12"
          Margin="12,8,12,8"
          FontFamily="Segoe MDL2 Assets" />
        <TextBlock Text="{Binding Data.CultureInfo.EnglishName}" />
      </StackPanel>
    </DataTemplate>
  </tvc:TreeView.ItemTemplate>
  <tvc:TreeView.ItemContainerTransitions>
    <TransitionCollection>
      <ContentThemeTransition />
      <ReorderThemeTransition />
      <EntranceThemeTransition IsStaggeringEnabled="False" />
    </TransitionCollection>
  </tvc:TreeView.ItemContainerTransitions>
</tvc:TreeView>
```

In the code-behind file, the TreeView is initialized by accessing the CultureData objects from the view-model. Using the CultureData objects, TreeNode objects are created for the TreeView. The TreeNode class defines a Data property where the CultureData object is assigned. The Add method of the TreeNode allows adding child objects. Child objects are added by recursively invoking the local function AddSubNodes (code file UWPCultureDemo/MainPage.xaml.cs):

```csharp
protected override void OnNavigatedTo(NavigationEventArgs e)
{
  void AddSubNodes(TreeNode parent)
  {
    if (parent.Data is CultureData cd && cd.SubCultures != null)
    {
      foreach (var culture in cd.SubCultures)
      {
        var node = new TreeNode
        {
          Data = culture,
          ParentNode = parent
        };
        parent.Add(node);

        foreach (var subCulture in culture.SubCultures)
        {
          AddSubNodes(node);
        }
      }
    }
  }
}
```

```
    base.OnNavigatedTo(e);
    var rootNodes = ViewModel.RootCultures.Select(cd => new TreeNode
    {
      Data = cd
    });

    foreach (var node in rootNodes)
    {
      treeView1.RootNode.Add(node);
      AddSubNodes(node);
    }
}
```

When the user selects a node inside the tree, the handler of the `SelectedItemChanged` event of the `TreeView` is called. In the following code snippet, the handler is implemented in the method `OnSelectionChanged`. With the implementation, the `SelectedCulture` property of the associated `ViewModel` is set to the selected `CultureData` object (code file `UWPCultureDemo/MainPage.xaml.cs`):

```
private void OnSelectionChanged(object sender, SelectionChangedEventArgs e)
{
  ViewModel.SelectedCulture =
    (treeView1.SelectedItems?.FirstOrDefault() as TreeNode)?.Data
      as CultureData;
}
```

To display the values of the selected item, you use several `TextBlock` controls. These bind to the `CultureInfo` property of the `CultureData` class and in turn to properties of the `CultureInfo` type that is returned from `CultureInfo`, such as `Name`, `IsNeutralCulture`, `EnglishName`, `NativeName`, and so on. To convert a Boolean value, as returned from the `IsNeutralCulture` property, to a `Visibility` enumeration value, and to display calendar names, you use converters (XAML file `UWPCultureDemo/CultureDetailUC.xaml`):

```
<TextBlock Grid.Row="0" Grid.Column="0" Text="Culture Name:" />
<TextBlock Grid.Row="0" Grid.Column="1"
  Text="{x:Bind CultureData.CultureInfo.Name, Mode=OneWay}"
  Width="100" />
<TextBlock Grid.Row="0" Grid.Column="2" Text="Neutral Culture"
  Visibility="{x:Bind CultureData.CultureInfo.IsNeutralCulture, Mode=OneWay}" />

<TextBlock Grid.Row="1" Grid.Column="0" Text="English Name:" />
<TextBlock Grid.Row="1" Grid.Column="1" Grid.ColumnSpan="2"
  Text="{x:Bind CultureData.CultureInfo.EnglishName, Mode=OneWay}" />

<TextBlock Grid.Row="2" Grid.Column="0" Text="Native Name:" />
<TextBlock Grid.Row="2" Grid.Column="1" Grid.ColumnSpan="2"
  Text="{x:Bind CultureData.CultureInfo.NativeName}" />

<TextBlock Grid.Row="3" Grid.Column="0" Text="Default Calendar:" />
<TextBlock Grid.Row="3" Grid.Column="1" Grid.ColumnSpan="2"
  Text="{x:Bind CultureData.CultureInfo.Calendar, Mode=OneWay
  Converter={StaticResource calendarConverter}}" />

<TextBlock Grid.Row="4" Grid.Column="0" Text="Optional Calendars:" />
<ListBox Grid.Row="4" Grid.Column="1" Grid.ColumnSpan="2"
  ItemsSource="{x:Bind CultureData.CultureInfo.OptionalCalendars}">
  <ListBox.ItemTemplate>
    <DataTemplate>
      <TextBlock Text="{Binding
        Converter={StaticResource calendarConverter}}" />
    </DataTemplate>
  </ListBox.ItemTemplate>
</ListBox>
```

To display the calendar text, you use an object that implements IValueConverter. Here is the implementation of the Convert method in the class CalendarTypeToCalendarInformationConverter. The implementation uses the class name and calendar type name to return a useful value for the calendar (code file UWPCultureDemo/Converters/CalendarTypeToCalendarInformationConverter.cs):

```
public object Convert(object value, Type targetType, object parameter,
  string language)
{
  if (value is Calendar cal)
  {
    var calText = new StringBuilder(50);
    calText.Append(cal.ToString());
    calText.Remove(0, 21); // remove the namespace
    calText.Replace("Calendar", "");

    if (cal is GregorianCalendar gregCal)
    {
      calText.Append($" {gregCal.CalendarType}");
    }

    return calText.ToString();
  }
  else
  {
    return null;
  }
}
```

The CultureData class contains properties to display sample information for number, date, and time formats. These properties are bound with the following TextBlock elements (XAML file UWPCultureDemo/CultureDetailUC.xaml):

```
<TextBlock Grid.Row="0" Grid.Column="0" Text="Number" />
<TextBlock Grid.Row="0" Grid.Column="1"
  Text="{x:Bind CultureData.NumberSample, Mode=OneWay}" />
<TextBlock Grid.Row="1" Grid.Column="0" Text="Full Date" />
<TextBlock Grid.Row="1" Grid.Column="1"
  Text="{x:Bind CultureData.DateSample, Mode=OneWay}" />
<TextBlock Grid.Row="2" Grid.Column="0" Text="Time" />
<TextBlock Grid.Row="2" Grid.Column="1"
  Text="{x:Bind CultureData.TimeSample, Mode=OneWay}" />
```

The information about the region is shown with the last part of the XAML code. The complete area hidden if the RegionInfo is not available. The TextBlock elements bind the DisplayName, CurrencySymbol, ISOCurrencySymbol, and IsMetric properties of the RegionInfo type:

```
<Grid Grid.Row="6" Grid.Column="0" Grid.ColumnSpan="3"
  Visibility="{x:Bind CultureData.RegionInfo, Mode=OneWay,
  Converter={StaticResource NullConverter}}">
  <!-- ... -->
  <TextBlock Grid.Row="0" Grid.Column="0" Text="Region Information"
    Style="{StaticResource SubheaderTextBlockStyle" />
  <TextBlock Grid.Row="0" Grid.Column="1" Grid.ColumnSpan="2"
    Text="{x:Bind CultureData.RegionInfo.DisplayName, Mode=OneWay}" />

  <TextBlock Grid.Row="1" Grid.Column="0" Text="Currency" />
  <TextBlock Grid.Row="1" Grid.Column="1"
    Text="{x:Bind CultureData.RegionInfo.CurrencySymbol, Mode=OneWay}" />
```

```
<TextBlock Grid.Row="1" Grid.Column="2"
    Text="{x:Bind CultureData.RegionInfo.ISOCurrencySymbol, Mode=OneWay}" />

<TextBlock Grid.Row="2" Grid.Column="1" Text="Is Metric"
    Visibility="{x:Bind CultureData.RegionInfo.IsMetric, Mode=OneWay}" />
</Grid>
```

When you start the application, you can see all available cultures in the tree view, and selecting a culture lists its characteristics, as shown in Figure 27-6.

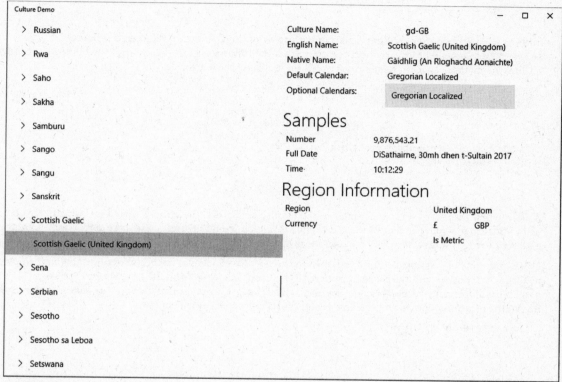

FIGURE 27-6

Sorting

The sample `SortingDemo` makes use of the following namespaces:

```
System

System.Collections

System.Collections.Generic

System.Globalization
```

Sorting strings varies according to the culture. The algorithms that compare strings for sorting by default are culture-specific. For example, in Finnish the characters V and W are treated the same. To demonstrate this behavior with a Finnish sort, the following code creates a small sample console application in which some U.S. states are stored unsorted inside an array.

The method `DisplayNames` shown here is used to display all elements of an array or a collection on the console (code file `SortingDemo/Program.cs`):

```
public static void DisplayNames(string title, IEnumerable<string> names)
{
  Console.WriteLine(title);
  Console.WriteLine(string.Join("-", names));
  Console.WriteLine();
}
```

In the `Main` method, after creating the array with some of the U.S. states, the thread property `CurrentCulture` is set to the Finnish culture so that the following `Array.Sort` uses the Finnish sort order. Calling the method `DisplayNames` displays all the states on the console:

```
public static void Main()
{
  string[] names = {"Alabama", "Texas", "Washington", "Virginia",
    "Wisconsin", "Wyoming", "Kentucky", "Missouri", "Utah",
    "Hawaii","Kansas", "Louisiana", "Alaska", "Arizona"};
  CultureInfo.CurrentCulture = new CultureInfo("fi-FI");
  Array.Sort(names);
  DisplayNames("Sorted using the Finnish culture", names);
  //...
}
```

After the first display of some U.S. states in the Finnish sort order, the array is sorted once again. If you want a sort that is independent of the users' culture, which would be useful when the sorted array is sent to a server or stored somewhere, you can use the invariant culture.

You can do this by passing a second argument to `Array.Sort`. The `Sort` method expects an object implementing `IComparer` with the second argument. The `Comparer` class from the `System.Collections` namespace implements `IComparer`. `Comparer.DefaultInvariant` returns a `Comparer` object that uses the invariant culture for comparing the array values for a culture-independent sort:

```
public static void Main()
{
  //...
  // sort using the invariant culture
  Array.Sort(names, System.Collections.Comparer.DefaultInvariant);
  DisplayNames("Sorted using the invariant culture", names);
}
```

The program output shows different sort results with the Finnish and culture-independent cultures— Virginia is before Washington when using the invariant sort order, and vice versa when using Finnish:

```
Sorted using the Finnish culture
Alabama-Alaska-Arizona-Hawaii-Kansas-Kentucky-Louisiana-Missouri-Texas-Utah-
Washington-Virginia-Wisconsin-Wyoming
Sorted using the invariant culture
Alabama-Alaska-Arizona-Hawaii-Kansas-Kentucky-Louisiana-Missouri-Texas-Utah-
Virginia-Washington-Wisconsin-Wyoming
```

> **NOTE** *If sorting a collection should be independent of a culture, the collection must be sorted with the invariant culture. This can be particularly useful when sending the sort result to a server or storing it inside a file. To display a sorted collection to the user, it's best to sort it with the user's culture.*

In addition to a locale-dependent formatting and measurement system, text and pictures may differ depending on the culture. This is where resources come into play.

RESOURCES

You can put resources such as pictures or string tables into resource files or satellite assemblies. Such resources can be very helpful when localizing applications, and .NET has built-in support to search for localized resources. Before you see how to use resources to localize applications, the following sections explain how you can create and read resources without looking at language aspects.

Resource Readers and Writers

With .NET Core, the resource readers and writers are limited compared to the full .NET version (at the time of this writing). However, for many scenarios—including multiplatform support—what is needed is available.

The `CreateResource` sample application creates a resource file dynamically and reads resources from the file. This sample makes use of the following namespaces:

> System
>
> System.Collections
>
> System.IO
>
> System.Resources

`ResourceWriter` enables you to create binary resource files. The constructor of the writer requires a `Stream` that is created using the `File` class. You add resources by using the `AddResource` method (code file `CreateResource/Program.cs`):

```
private const string ResourceFile = "Demo.resources";
public static void CreateResource()
{
  FileStream stream = File.OpenWrite(ResourceFile);
  using (var writer = new ResourceWriter(stream))
  {
    writer.AddResource("Title", "Professional C#");
    writer.AddResource("Author", "Christian Nagel");
    writer.AddResource("Publisher", "Wrox Press");
  }
}
```

To read the resources of a binary resource file, you can use `ResourceReader`. The `GetEnumerator` method of the reader returns an `IDictionaryEnumerator` that is used within the following `foreach` statement to access the key and value of the resource:

```
public static void ReadResource()
{
  FileStream stream = File.OpenRead(ResourceFile);
  using (var reader = new ResourceReader(stream))
  {
    foreach (DictionaryEntry resource in reader)
    {
      Console.WriteLine($"{resource.Key} {resource.Value}");
    }
  }
}
```

Running the application returns the keys and values that have been written to the binary resource file. As shown in the next section, you can also use a command-line tool—the Resource File Generator (resgen)—to create and convert resource files.

Using the Resource File Generator

Resource files can contain items such as pictures and string tables. A resource file is created by using either a normal text file or a `.resX` file that uses XML. This section starts with a simple text file.

You can create a resource that embeds a string table by using a normal text file. The text file assigns strings to keys. The key is the name that can be used from a program to get the value. Spaces are allowed in both keys and values.

This example shows a simple string table in the file `Wrox.ProCSharp.Localization.MyResources.txt`:

```
Title = Professional C#
Chapter = Localization
Author = Christian Nagel
Publisher = Wrox Press
```

> **NOTE** *When saving text files with Unicode characters, you must save the file with the proper encoding. To select the UTF8 encoding, use the Save As dialog.*

You can use the Resource File Generator (`Resgen.exe`) utility to create a resource file out of `Wrox .ProCSharp.Localization.MyResources.txt`. Typing the line

resgen Wrox.ProCSharp.Localization.MyResources.txt

creates the file `Wrox.ProCSharp.Localization.MyResources.resources`. The resulting resource file can be either added to an assembly as an external file or embedded into the DLL or EXE. Resgen also supports the creation of XML-based `.resX` resource files. One easy way to build an XML file is by using Resgen itself:

```
resgen Wrox.ProCSharp.Localization.MyResources.txt
Wrox.ProCSharp.Localization.MyResources.resX
```

This command creates the XML resource file `Wrox.ProCSharp.LocalizationMyResources.resX`. Resgen supports strongly typed resources. A strongly typed resource is represented by a class that accesses the resource. You can create the class with the `/str` option of the Resgen utility:

```
resgen /str:C#,Wrox.ProCSharp.Localization,MyResources,MyResources.cs
Wrox.ProCSharp.Localization.MyResources.resX
```

With the `/str` option, the language, namespace, class name, and filename for the source code are defined, in that order.

Using Resource Files with ResourceManager

By default, resource files are embedded in the assembly. You can customize this—for example, by removing resources from the assembly by adding an `EmbeddedResource` element with the `Remove` attribute to an `ItemGroup` in the project file as shown:

```
<ItemGroup>
  <EmbeddedResource Remove="Resources\Messages.de.resx" />
</ItemGroup>
```

To see how resource files can be loaded with the `ResourceManager` class, create a Console App (.NET Core) and name it `ResourcesDemo`. This sample makes use of the following namespaces:

```
System

System.Globalization

System.Reflection

System.Resources
```

Create a `Resources` folder and add a `Messages.resx` file to this folder. The `Messages.resx` file is filled with a key and value for English-US content—for example, the key `GoodMorning` and the value `Good Morning!` This will be the default language. You can add other language resource files with the naming convention to add the culture to the resource file, for example, `Messages.de.resx` for German languages and `Messages.de-AT.resx` for Austrian differences.

To access the embedded resource, use the `ResourceManager` class from the `System.Resources` namespace and the `System.Resources.ResourceManager` NuGet package. When you're instantiating the `ResourceManager`, one overload of the constructor needs the name of the resource and the assembly. The namespace of the application is `ResourcesDemo`; the resource file is in the folder `Resources`, which defines the sub-namespace Resources, and it has the name `Messages.resx`. This defines the name `ResourcesDemo.Resources.Messages`. You can retrieve the assembly of the resource using the `GetTypeInfo` method of the `Program` type, which defines an `Assembly` property. Using the resources instance, the `GetString` method returns the value of the key passed from the resource file. Passing a culture such as de-AT for the second argument looks for resources in the de-AT resource file. If it's not found there, the neutral language for de is taken, the de resource file. If it's not found there, the default resource file without culture naming succeeds to return the value (code file `ResourcesDemo/Program.cs`):

```
var resources = new ResourceManager("ResourcesDemo.Resources.Messages",
  typeof(Program).GetTypeInfo().Assembly);
string goodMorning = resources.GetString("GoodMorning",
  new CultureInfo("de-AT"));
Console.WriteLine(goodMorning);
```

Another overload of the `ResourceManager` constructor just requires the type of the class. This `ResourceManager` looks for a resource file named `Program.resx`:

```
var programResources = new ResourceManager(typeof(Program));
Console.WriteLine(programResources.GetString("Resource1"));
```

The System.Resources Namespace

Before moving on to the next example, this section provides a review of the classes contained in the `System.Resources` namespace that deal with resources:

➤ `ResourceManager`—Can be used to get resources for the current culture from assemblies or resource files. Using the `ResourceManager`, you can also get a `ResourceSet` for a culture.

➤ `ResourceSet`—Represents the resources for a culture. When a `ResourceSet` instance is created, it enumerates over a class, implementing the interface `IResourceReader`, and it stores all resources in a Hashtable.

➤ `IResourceReader`—Used from the `ResourceSet` to enumerate resources. The class `ResourceReader` implements this interface.

➤ `ResourceWriter`—Used to create a resource file. `ResourceWriter` implements the interface `IResourceWriter`.

LOCALIZATION WITH ASP.NET CORE

> **NOTE** *For using localization with ASP.NET Core, you need to know about both cultures and resources that are discussed in this chapter as well as creating ASP.NET Core applications. In case you didn't create ASP.NET Core web applications with .NET Core before, you should read Chapter 30, "ASP.NET Core," before continuing with this part of the chapter.*

For localization of ASP.NET Core web applications, you can use the `CultureInfo` class and resources like what you've seen earlier in this chapter, but there are some additional issues that you need to resolve. Setting the culture for the complete application doesn't fulfill usual needs because users are coming from different cultures. So, it's necessary to set the culture with every request to the server.

How do you know about the culture of the user? There are different options. The browser sends preferred languages within the HTTP header with every request. This information from the browser can come from browser settings or when the browser itself checks the installed languages. Another option is to define URL parameters or use different domain names for different languages. You can use different domain names in some scenarios, such as www.cninnovation.com for an English version of the site and www.cninnovation .de for a German version. But what about www.cninnovation.ch? This should be offered both in German and French and probably Italian. URL parameters such as www.cninnovation.com/culture=de could help here. Using www.cninnovation.com/de works like the URL parameter by defining a specific route. Another option is to allow the user to select the language and define a cookie to remember this option.

All these scenarios are supported out of the box by ASP.NET Core.

Registering Localization Services

To start seeing this in action, create a new ASP.NET Core Web Application using an Empty ASP.NET Core project template. This sample project makes use of the following dependency and namespaces:

Dependency

```
Microsoft.AspNetCore.All
```

Namespaces

```
Microsoft.AspNetCore
```

```
Microsoft.AspNetCore.Builder
```

```
Microsoft.AspNetCore.Hosting
```

```
Microsoft.AspNetCore.Http
```

```
Microsoft.AspNetCore.Localization
```

```
Microsoft.Extensions.DependencyInjection
```

```
Microsoft.Extensions.Localization
```

```
System
```

```
System.Globalization
```

```
System.Text.Encodings.Web
```

Within the `Startup` class, you need to invoke the `AddLocalization` extension method to register services for localization (code file `WebApplicationSample/Startup.cs`):

```
public void ConfigureServices(IServiceCollection services)
{
    services.AddLocalization(options => options.ResourcesPath =
        "CustomResources");
}
```

The `AddLocalization` method registers services for the interfaces `IStringLocalizerFactory` and `IStringLocalizer`. With the registration code, the type `ResourceManagerStringLocalizerFactory` is registered as a singleton, and `StringLocalizer` is registered with transient lifetime. The class `ResourceManagerStringLocalizerFactory` is a factory for `ResourceManagerStringLocalizer`. This class in turn makes use of the `ResourceManager` class shown earlier for retrieving strings from resource files.

Injecting Localization Services

After localization is added to the service collection, you can request localization in the `Configure` method of the `Startup` class. The `UseRequestLocalization` method defines an overload where you can pass `RequestLocalizationOptions`. The `RequestLocalizationOptions` enables you to customize what cultures should be supported and to set the default culture. Here, the `DefaultRequestCulture` is set to en-US. The class `RequestCulture` is just a small wrapper around the culture for formatting—which is accessible via the `Culture` property—and the culture for using the resources (`UICulture` property). The sample code accepts en-US, en, de-AT, and de cultures for `SupportedCultures` and `SupportedUICultures` (code file `WebApplicationSample/Startup.cs`):

```
public void Configure(IApplicationBuilder app, IHostingEnvironment env,
    IStringLocalizer<Startup> sr)
{
    //...
    var supportedCultures = new[]
    {
        new CultureInfo("en-US"),
        new CultureInfo("en"),
        new CultureInfo("de-AT"),
        new CultureInfo("de")
    };

    var options = new RequestLocalizationOptions
    {
        DefaultRequestCulture = new RequestCulture(new CultureInfo("en-US")),
        SupportedCultures = supportedCultures,
        SupportedUICultures = supportedCultures
    };
    app.UseRequestLocalization(options);
    //...
}
```

With the `RequestLocalizationOptions` settings, the property `RequestCultureProviders` is also set. By default, three providers are configured: `QueryStringRequestCultureProvider`, `CookieRequestCultureProvider`, and `AcceptLanguageHeaderRequestCultureProvider`.

Culture Providers

Let's get into more details on these culture providers. The `QueryStringRequestCultureProvider` uses the query string to retrieve the culture. By default, the query parameters `culture` and `ui-culture` are used with this provider, as shown with this URL:

```
http://localhost:5000/?culture=de&ui-culture=en-US
http://localhost:5000/?culture=de&ui-culture=en-US
```

You can also change the query parameters by setting the `QueryStringKey` and `UIQueryStringKey` properties of the `QueryStringRequestCultureProvider`.

The `CookieRequestCultureProvider` defines the cookie named `ASPNET_CULTURE` (which can be set using the `CookieName` property). The values from this cookie are retrieved to set the culture. To create a cookie and send it to the client, you can use the static method `MakeCookieValue` to create a cookie from a `RequestCulture` and send it to the client. The `CookieRequestCultureProvider` uses the static method `ParseCookieValue` to get a `RequestCulture`.

With the third option for culture settings, you can use the HTTP header information that is sent by the browser. The HTTP header that is sent looks like this:

```
Accept-Language: en-us, de-at;q=0.8, it;q=0.7
```

The `AcceptLanguageHeaderRequestCultureProvider` uses this information to set the culture. You use up to three language values in the order as defined by the quality value to find a first match with the supported cultures.

The following code snippet now uses the request culture to generate HTML output. First, you access the requested culture using the `IRequestCultureFeature` contract. The `RequestCultureFeature` that implements the interface `IRequestCultureFeature` uses the first culture provider that matches the culture setting. If a URL defines a query string that matches the culture parameter, the `QueryStringRequestCultureProvider` is used to return the requested culture. If the URL does not match, but a cookie with the name `ASPNET_CULTURE` is received, the `CookieRequestCultureProvider` is used, and otherwise the `AcceptLanguageRequestCultureProvider`. The resulting culture that is used by the user is written to the response stream using properties of the returned `RequestCulture`. Then, today's date is written to the stream using the current culture. The variable of type `IStringLocalizer` used here needs some more examination that is discussed next (code file `WebApplicationSample/Startup.cs`):

```csharp
public void Configure(IApplicationBuilder app, IHostingEnvironment env,
    IStringLocalizer<Startup> sr)
{
  //...
  app.Run(async context =>
  {
    IRequestCultureFeature requestCultureFeature =
      context.Features.Get<IRequestCultureFeature>();
    RequestCulture requestCulture = requestCultureFeature.RequestCulture;
    var today = DateTime.Today;
    await context.Response.WriteAsync("<h1>Sample Localization</h1>");
    await context.Response.WriteAsync(
      $"<div>{requestCulture.Culture} {requestCulture.UICulture}</div>");
    await context.Response.WriteAsync($"<div>{today:D}</div>");

    //...
  });
}
```

Using Resources from ASP.NET Core

Resource files, as you've seen in the Resources section in this chapter, can be used with ASP.NET Core. The sample project adds the `CustomResources` folder and the file `Startup.resx` within. Localized versions for the resources are offered with `Startup.de.resx` and `Startup.de-AT.resx`.

The folder name where the resources are found is defined with the options when injecting the localization service (code file `WebApplicationSample/Startup.cs`):

```
public void ConfigureServices(IServiceCollection services)
{
  services.AddLocalization(
    options => options.ResourcesPath = "CustomResources");
}
```

With dependency injection, `IStringLocalizer<Startup>` is injected as a parameter of the `Configure` method. The generic type `Startup` parameter is used to find a resource file with the same name in the resources directory; this matches with `Startup.resx`.

```
public void Configure(IApplicationBuilder app, IHostingEnvironment env,
  IStringLocalizer<Startup> sr)
{
  //...
}
```

> **NOTE** *Read more about dependency injection in Chapter 20, "Dependency Injection."*

The following code snippet makes use of the `sr` variable of type `IStringLocalizer<Startup>` to access a resource named `message1` using an indexer and with the `GetString` method. The resource `message2` uses string format placeholders, which are injected with an overload of the `GetString` method where any number of parameters can be passed to:

```
public void Configure(IApplicationBuilder app, IHostingEnvironment env,
  IStringLocalizer<Startup> sr)
{
  //...
  app.Run(async context =>
  {
    //...
    await context.Response.WriteAsync(
      $"<div>{HtmlEncoder.Default.Encode(sr["message1"])}</div>");
    await context.Response.WriteAsync(
      $"<div>{HtmlEncoder.Default.Encode(sr.GetString("message1"))}</div>");
    await context.Response.WriteAsync(
      $"<div>{HtmlEncoder.Default.Encode(sr.GetString("message2",
        requestCulture.Culture, requestCulture.UICulture))}</div>");
  });
}
```

> **NOTE** *With the sample code, the `HtmlEncoder` is used to change the output from the resources before passing it to the `WriteAsync` method of the `HttpResponse`. With this encoder, the resource values are converted to the HTML format to correctly display special characters such as the German ü and ß. With HTML encoding, these characters are translated to the HTML format ü and ß.*

The resource for `message1` is a simple string; the resource for `message2` is defined with string format placeholders:

```
Using culture {0} and UI culture {1}
```

> **NOTE** *Using formatted strings in resources, the new syntax with interpolated strings cannot be used in this case. The variables or expressions used with interpolated strings in the placeholders are not available from resources.*

Running the web application results in the view shown in Figure 27-7.

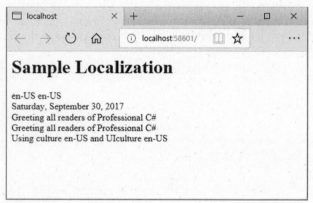

FIGURE 27-7

Adding `?culture=de-AT` to the URL request (which uses the `QueryStringRequestCultureProvider`), you can see output as shown in Figure 27-8. When you pass cultures that aren't supported with the URL request, you can see an output of the default culture.

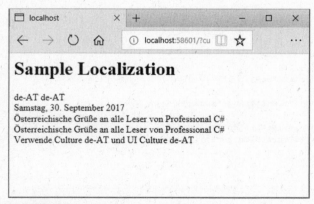

FIGURE 27-8

Localizing with Controllers and Views

Using ASP.NET Core MVC, there's special support for localization. You can create specific resource files for controllers and views, you can add annotations to model data that are used to retrieve values from resources.

> **NOTE** *ASP.NET Core MVC is discussed in detail in Chapter 31, "ASP.NET Core MVC." Annotations are discussed in Chapter 16, "Reflection, Metadata, and Dynamic Programming."*

The ASP.NET Core Web Application named `ASPNETCoreMVCSample` used in this section is based on the Web Application (Model View Controller) template, and it uses the following dependency and namespaces:

Dependency

`Microsoft.AspNetCore.All`

Namespaces

`Microsoft.AspNetCore`

`Microsoft.AspNetCore.Builder`

`Microsoft.AspNetCore.Hosting`

`Microsoft.AspNetCore.Localization`

`Microsoft.AspNetCore.Mvc.Localization`

`Microsoft.AspNetCore.Mvc.Razor`

`Microsoft.Extensions.Configuration`

`Microsoft.Extensions.DependencyInjection`

`Microsoft.Extensions.Localization`

`System`

`System.ComponentModel`

`System.Diagnostics`

`System.Globalization`

Let's start with creating resources. The resources are now stored in the folder `Resources`. The folder name is specified with the options of the `AddLocalization` helper method (code file `ASPNETCoreMVCSample/Startup.cs`):

```
public void ConfigureServices(IServiceCollection services)
{
  services.AddLocalization(options => options.ResourcesPath = "Resources");
  //...
}
```

You can put resources for controllers, views, and models into subfolders, or you can use a dot notation with the filename. For example, you can put resources for the `HomeController` into the subdirectory `Resources\Controllers`—for example, the resource file named `HomeController.resx` with the default language, as well as language specific resource files— such as `HomeController.de.resx`. Instead of using the directory structure, you can use the dot notation for the filename. Here you store the resource file directly within the `Resources` folder. With this convention, the resource file for the `HomeController` needs to be named `Controllers.HomeController.resx`.

For the view named `Hello` that is activated from the `HomeController`, you can use directory notation for the resource file `Hello.resx` to put it into the directory structure `Resources/Views/Home`. Using dot notation, the resource file `Views.Home.Hello.resx` needs to be saved in the folder `Resources`.

The version of resource files that is used is specified with the `AddViewLocalization` method, an extension method for the `IMvcBuilder` interface. An object implementing this interface is returned from the `AddMvc` method, thus `AddViewLocalization` can be invoked using fluent API syntax. When you pass the option `LanguageViewLocationExpanderFormat.SubFolder`, it defines that the subfolder resources are used. The other option would be `LanguageViewLocationExpanderFormat.Suffix`. In the following code snippet, the extension method `AddDataAnnotationsLocalization` also is invoked to enable localization with data annotations (code file `ASPNETCoreMVCSample/Startup.cs`):

```
public void ConfigureServices(IServiceCollection services)
{
    services.AddLocalization(options => options.ResourcesPath = "Resources");
    services.AddMvc()
        .AddViewLocalization(LanguageViewLocationExpanderFormat.SubFolder)
        .AddDataAnnotationsLocalization();
}
```

With the `HomeController`, the `IStringLocalizer` can be injected and used like what you've seen with the `Configure` method of the `WebSampleApp` sample where an `IStringLocalizer` was injected as well. In the following code snippet, the `IStringLocalizer<HomeController>` is injected in the constructor of the `HomeController`, and used with the `Hello` action method (code file `ASPNETCoreMVCSample/Controllers/HomeController.cs`):

```
private readonly IStringLocalizer<HomeController> _localizer;
public HomeController(IStringLocalizer<HomeController> localizer)
{
    _localizer = localizer;
}

public IActionResult Hello()
{
    ViewBag.Message1 = _localizer.GetString("Message1");
    return View();
}
```

In the view, the `Message1` passed from the controller is directly accessed (code file `ASPNETCoreMVCSample/Views/Home/Hello.cshtml`):

```
<h3>@ViewBag.Message1</h3>
```

To access a resource directly from the resource in the view, the `IViewLocalizer` can be injected using the `@inject` declaration. Here, a local variable `Localizer` is defined that is then used to access the resource named Message2; the resource just needs to be saved in the resource file `Resources/Views/Home/Hello.resx` (code file `ASPNETCoreMVCSample/Views/Home/Hello.cshtml`):

```
@using Microsoft.AspNetCore.Mvc.Localization

@inject IViewLocalizer Localizer

@{
    ViewData["Title"] = "Hello";
}
```

```
<h2>Hello</h2>

<h3>@ViewBag.Message1</h3>

<h3>@Localizer["Message2"]</h3>
```

Running the application and accessing the link `/Home/Hello`, resources are retrieved both from the controller and the view as shown in Figure 27-9.

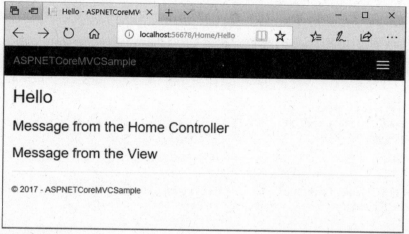

FIGURE 27-9

Another way to retrieve resource values with ASP.NET Core MVC is via applying annotations. To see the annotations in action, the `Book` type is defined in the `Models` directory. This type has `DisplayName` attributes added to the properties `Booktitle` and `Publisher` (code file `ASPNETCoreMVCSample/Models/Book.cs`):

```
public class Book
{
  [DisplayName("Booktitle")]
  public string Booktitle { get; set; }
  [DisplayName("Publisher")]
  public string Publisher { get; set; }
}
```

> **NOTE** *Don't forget to enable annotations for localization by invoking the method* `AddDataAnnotationsLocalization` *in the* `Startup` *class.*

The resource file `Book.resx` is now added to the directory `Resources/Models` (resource file `ASPNETCoreMVCSample/Resources/Models/Book.resx`):

```
<!-- ... -->
<data name="Publisher" xml:space="preserve">
  <value>Publisher</value>
</data>
<data name="Booktitle" xml:space="preserve">
  <value>Title</value>
</data>
<!-- ... -->
```

A German language representation is added as well (resource file `ASPNETCoreMVCSample/Resources/Models/Book.de.resx`):

```xml
<!-- ... -->
<data name="Publisher" xml:space="preserve">
  <value>Verlag</value>
</data>
<data name="Booktitle" xml:space="preserve">
  <value>Titel</value>
</data>
<!-- ... -->
```

The `Book` action method from the `HomeController` passes a `Book` model to the view (code file `ASPNETCoreMVCSample/Controllers/HomeController.cs`):

```csharp
public IActionResult Book()
{
  var b = new Book
  {
    Booktitle = "Professional C# 7 and .NET Core 2",
    Publisher = "Wrox Press"
  };
  return View(b);
}
```

To display the book, the HTML Helper method `EditorForModel` is used to display all the properties of the model with input fields (code file `ASPNETCoreMVCSample/Views/Home/Book.cshtml`):

```
@{
    ViewData["Title"] = "Book";
}

<h2>Book</h2>

@Html.EditorForModel()
```

Figure 27-10 shows the running application accessing Home/Book with the German culture.

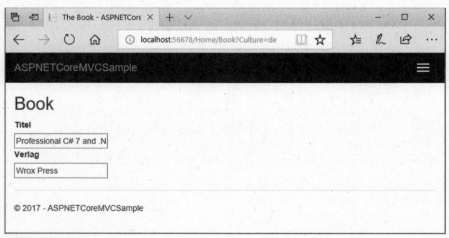

FIGURE 27-10

> **NOTE** *For more information about controllers, views, and HTML Helper, read Chapter 31.*

LOCALIZATION WITH THE UNIVERSAL WINDOWS PLATFORM

Localization with the Universal Windows Platform (UWP) is based on the concepts you've learned so far, but it brings some fresh ideas, as described in this section. For the best experience, you need to install the Multilingual App Toolkit that is available via Visual Studio Extensions and Updates.

The concepts of cultures, regions, and resources are the same, but because Windows apps can be written with C# and XAML, C++ and XAML, and JavaScript and HTML, these concepts need to be available with all languages. Only Windows Runtime is available with all these programming languages and UWP apps. Therefore, new namespaces for globalization and resources are available with Windows Runtime: `Windows .Globalization` and `Windows.ApplicationModel.Resources`. With the globalization namespaces you can find `Calendar`, `GeographicRegion` (this can be compared to the .NET `RegionInfo`), and `Language` classes. With sub-namespaces, there are also classes for number and date formatting that vary according to the language. With C# and Windows apps, you can still use the .NET classes for cultures and regions.

Let's get into an example so you can see localization with a Universal Windows app in action. Create a small application using the Blank App (Universal Windows) Visual Studio project template. Add two `TextBlock` controls and one `TextBox` control to the page.

Within the `OnNavigatedTo` method of the code file you can assign a date with the current format to the `Text` property of the `text1` control. You can use the `DateTime` structure in the same way you've done it with the console application earlier in this chapter (code file `UWPLocalization/MainPage.xaml.cs`):

```
protected override void OnNavigatedTo(NavigationEventArgs e)
{
  base.OnNavigatedTo(e);
  text1.Text = DateTime.Today.ToString("D");
  //...
}
```

Using Resources with UWP

With UWP, you can create resource files with the file extension `resw` instead of `resx`. Behind the scenes, the same XML format is used with `resw` files, and you can use the same Visual Studio resource editor to create and modify these files. The following example uses the structure shown in Figure 27-11. The subfolder `Messages` contains a subdirectory, `en-us`, in which two resource files `Errors.resw` and `Messages.resw` are created. In the folder `Strings\en-us`, the resource file `Resources.resw` is created.

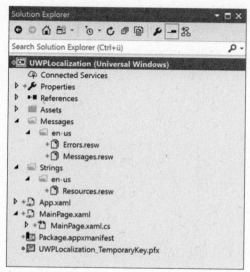

FIGURE 27-11

The `Messages.resw` file contains some English text resources, `Hello` with a value of `Hello World`, and resources named `GoodDay`, `GoodEvening`, and `GoodMorning`. The file `Resources.resw` contains the resources `Text3.Text` and `Text3.Width`, with the values `"This is a sample message for Text 4"` and a value of `"300"`.

With the code, you can access resources with the help of the `ResourceLoader` class from the namespace `Windows.ApplicationModel.Resources`. Here you use the string `"Messages"` with the method `GetForCurrentView`. Thus, you're using the resource file `Messages.resw`. Invoking the method `GetString` retrieves the resource with the key `"Hello"` (code file `UWPLocalization/MainPage.xaml.cs`):

```
protected override void OnNavigatedTo(NavigationEventArgs e)
{
    //...
    var resourceLoader = ResourceLoader.GetForCurrentView("Messages");
    text2.Text = resourceLoader.GetString("Hello");
}
```

With UWP Windows apps it is also easy to use the resources directly from XAML code. With the following `TextBox`, the `x:Uid` attribute is assigned the value `Text3`. This way, a resource named `Text3` with extensions is searched for in the resource file `Resources.resw`. This resource file contains value for the keys `Text3.Text` and `Text3.Width`. The values are retrieved, and both the `Text` and `Width` properties are set (code file `UWPLocalization/MainPage.xaml`):

```
<TextBox x:Uid="FileName_Text3" HorizontalAlignment="Left" Margin="40"
    TextWrapping="Wrap" Text="TextBox" VerticalAlignment="Top"/>
```

When you run the application at this stage, you can see the English text accessed from the resource files as shown in Figure 27-12.

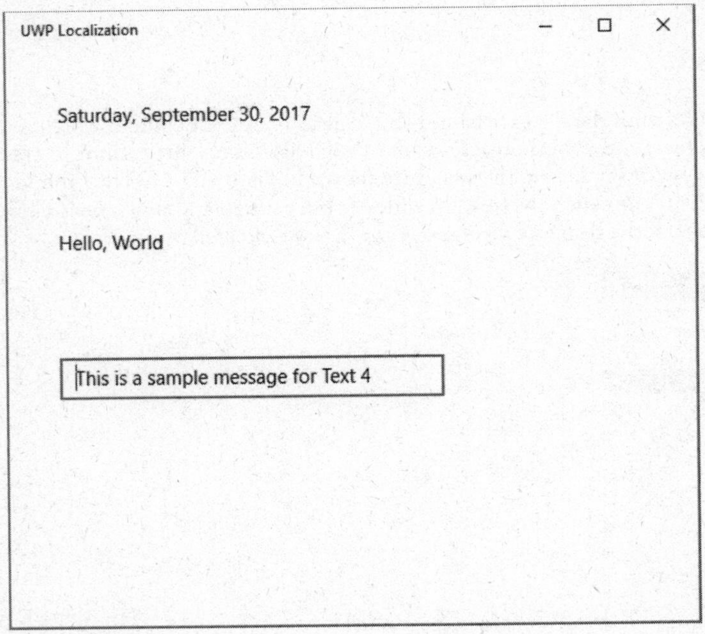

FIGURE 27-12

Localization with the Multilingual App Toolkit

To localize UWP apps you can download the previously mentioned Multilingual App Toolkit. This toolkit integrates with Visual Studio 2017. After installing the toolkit, you can enable it within Visual Studio using the menu Tools ⇨ Multilingual App Toolkit ⇨ Enable Selection. This adds a build command to the project file and adds one more option to the context menu in Solution Explorer. Open the context menu in Solution Explorer and select Multilingual App Toolkit ⇨ Add Translation Languages to invoke the dialog shown in Figure 27-13, where you can choose which languages should be translated. The sample uses Pseudo Language, French, German, and Spanish. For these languages, a Microsoft Translator is available. This tool now creates a `MultilingualResources` subdirectory that contains `.xlf` files for the selected languages. The `.xlf` files are defined with the XLIFF (XML Localisation Interchange File Format) standard. This is a standard of the Open Architecture for XML Authoring and Localization (OAXAL) reference architecture.

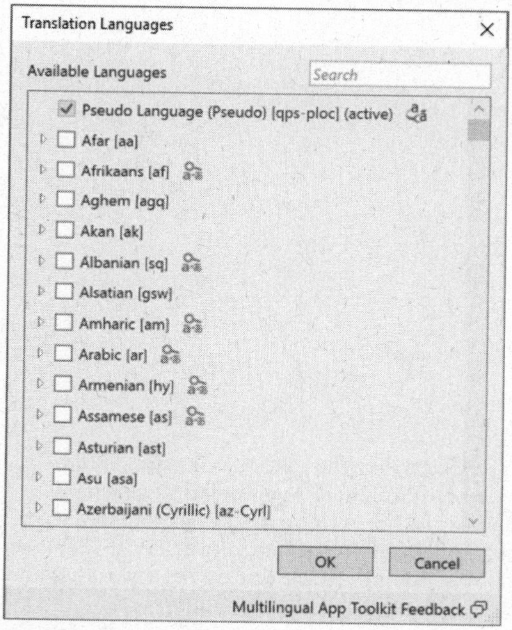

FIGURE 27-13

> **NOTE** *The Multilingual App Toolkit can also be installed from* `http://aka.ms/matinstallv4` *without using Visual Studio. Download the Multilingual App Toolkit.*

The next time you start the build process for the project, the XLIFF files are filled with content from all the resources. When you select the XLIFF files in Solution Explorer, you can send it to translation. To do so, open the context menu in Solution Explorer while selecting the `.xlf` files, and select Multilingual App Toolkit ⇨ Export Translations, which opens the dialog shown in Figure 27-14. With this dialog you can configure the information that should be sent, and you can send an email with the XLIFF files attached.

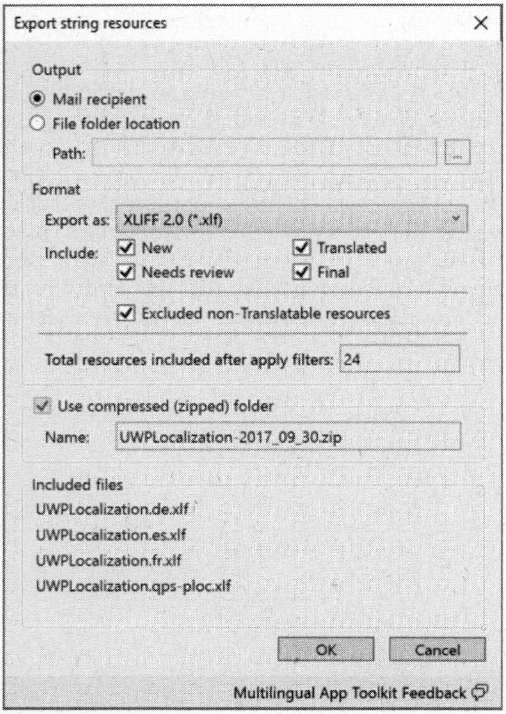

FIGURE 27-14

For translation, you can also use Microsoft's translation service. Select the `.xlf` files in Visual Studio Solution Explorer, and after opening the context menu, select Multilingual App Toolkit ➪ Generate Machine Translations. To make this work with the version used while writing this book, you need to create an Microsoft Azure account and add the Translator Speech API of Microsoft Cognitive Services. This service is used by the translation services of the Multilingual App Toolkit. A free pricing tier exists that allows up to 2,000,000 characters to be translated each month.

When you open the `.xlf` files, the Multilingual Editor (see Figure 27-15) is opened. With this tool you can verify the automatic translations and make necessary changes.

> **WARNING** *Don't use the machine translation without a manual review. The tool shows a status for every resource that is translated. After the automatic translation, the status is set to Needs Review. You have probably seen applications with machine translations that are incorrect—and sometimes really funny.*

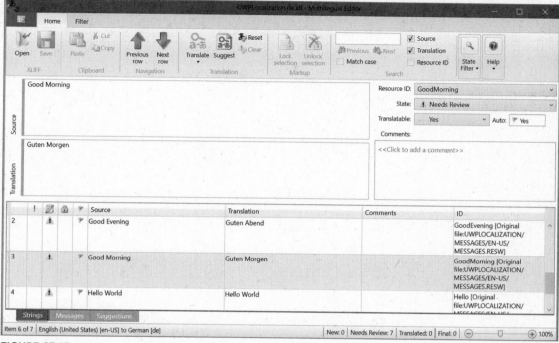

FIGURE 27-15

SUMMARY

This chapter demonstrated how to globalize and localize .NET applications. For the globalization of applications, you learned about using the namespace `System.Globalization` to format culture-dependent numbers and dates. Furthermore, you learned that sorting strings by default varies according to the culture, and you looked at using the invariant culture for a culture-independent sort.

Localizing an application is accomplished by using resources, which you can pack into files or satellite assemblies. The classes used with localization are in the namespace `System.Resources`.

You also learned how to localize ASP.NET Core, used special features for ASP.NET Core MVC, and localized apps using the Universal Windows Platform.

The next chapter provides information about testing. You learn how to create unit tests, as well as UI tests for Windows and web applications.

28

Testing

WHAT'S IN THIS CHAPTER?

➤ Unit tests with MSTest and xUnit

➤ Unit tests with xUnit with .NET Core

➤ Unit tests with EF Core

➤ Coded UI testing

➤ Web testing

WROX.COM CODE DOWNLOADS FOR THIS CHAPTER

The Wrox.com code downloads for this chapter are found at www.wrox.com on the Download Code tab. The source code is also available at https://github.com/ProfessionalCSharp/ProfessionalCSharp7 in the directory tests.

The code for this chapter is divided into the following major examples:

➤ Unit Testing Sample

➤ Mocking Sample

➤ EF Core Sample

➤ Windows App Sample

➤ ASPNETCore Integration Test Sample

➤ Web Application Load Test Sample

> **NOTE** *Unit testing is available with all editions of Visual Studio. All other testing features—such as Live Unit Testing, Web Load & Performance Testing, Coded UI Testing, Code Coverage, Microsoft Fakes, and IntelliTest—require Visual Studio Enterprise 2017.*

OVERVIEW

Application development is becoming agile. When using waterfall process models to analyze the requirements, it's not unusual that you design the application architecture, do the implementation, and then find out two or three years later that you built an application that is not needed by the user. Instead, software development becomes agile with faster release cycles, and early participation of the end users. Just have a look at Windows 10: With millions of Windows insiders who give feedback to early builds, updates happen every few months or even weeks. There was one special week during the Beta program of Windows 10 when Windows insiders received three builds of Windows 10 within one week. Windows 10 is a huge program, but Microsoft managed to change development in a big way. Also, if you participate in the open-source project of .NET Core, you can get nightly builds of NuGet packages. If you're adventurous, you might even write a book about an upcoming technology.

With such fast and continuous changes—and nightly builds that you are creating—you can't wait for insiders or end users to find all the issues. Windows 10 insiders wouldn't have been happy with Windows 10 crashing every few minutes. How often have you done a change in the implementation of a method to find out something that doesn't seem related is not working anymore? You might have tried to avoid such issues by not changing the method and creating a new one by copying the code and doing the necessary changes there, which in turn creates a maintenance nightmare. It happens too easily that you fix a method in one place but miss the other ones with code duplicates.

You can avoid issues like these. Create tests for your methods, and let the tests run automatically on checking in the source code or during nightly builds. Creating tests from the start increases the cost for the project from the beginning, but as the project processes and during maintenance, creating tests has advantages and reduces the overall project cost.

This chapter explains different kinds of tests, starting with *unit tests*, which are tests for small functionality. These tests should verify the functionality of the smallest testable parts of an application—for example, methods. When you pass different input values, a unit test should check all possible paths through a method.

MSTest is a testing framework from Microsoft for creating unit tests. When .NET Core was built, MSTest did not support creating tests for .NET Core libraries and applications. That's why Microsoft itself is using xUnit to create unit tests for .NET Core. Now, you can use both MSTest and XUnit to create unit tests for .NET Core. This chapter covers both Microsoft's test framework MSTest and xUnit.

With *web testing* you can test web applications, send HTTP requests, and simulate a load of users. Creating these kinds of tests enables you to simulate different user loads and allow stress testing. You can use test controllers to create higher loads to simulate thousands of users and thus also know what infrastructure you need and whether your application is scalable.

The final testing feature covered in this chapter is UI testing. You can create automated tests of your XAML-based applications. Of course, it is a lot easier to create unit tests for your view models and the view components with ASP.NET Core, but it's not possible to cover every aspect of testing in this chapter. You can automate *UI testing*. Just imagine the hundreds of different Android mobile devices that are available. Would you buy one of every model to test your app manually on every device? It's better to use a cloud service and send the app to be tested where the app is indeed installed on hundreds of devices. Don't assume humans will start the app in the cloud on hundreds of devices and click through the possible interactions of the app. This needs to be automated using UI tests.

First, let's start creating unit tests.

UNIT TESTING WITH MSTEST

Writing unit tests helps with code maintenance. For example, when you're performing a code update, you want to be confident that the update isn't going to break something else. Having automatic unit tests in place helps to ensure that all functionality is retained after code changes are made. Visual Studio 2017 offers a unit testing framework, and you can also use other testing frameworks from within Visual Studio.

Creating Unit Tests with MSTest

The following example tests a very simple method in a class library named `UnitTestingSamples`. This is a .NET Standard 2.0 class library. Of course, you can create any other MSBuild-based project. The class `DeepThought` contains the `TheAnswerToTheUltimateQuestionOfLifeTheUniverseAndEverything` method, which returns 42 as a result (code file `UnitTestingSamples/DeepThought.cs`):

```
public class DeepThought
{
    public int TheAnswerOfTheUltimateQuestionOfLifeTheUniverseAndEverything() =>
        42;
}
```

To ensure that nobody changes the method to return a wrong result (maybe someone who didn't read *The Hitchhiker's Guide to the Galaxy*), a unit test is created. To create a unit test, you can use the dotnet command

```
> dotnet new mstest
```

or you can add the project template Unit Test Project (.NET Core) from Visual Studio.

Before creating the first tests, it's a good idea to think about naming tests and test projects. Of course, you can use names as you like, but you can find a good guideline from the .NET Core team at

```
https://github.com/aspnet/Home/wiki/Engineering-guidelines#unit-tests-and-
functional-tests
```

Here's a summary of the guidelines:

➤ A test project has the name `Tests` appended to the name of the project—for example, for the project `UnitTestingSamples`, the test project has the name `UnitTestingSamples.Tests`.

➤ Test class names have the same class name as the class under being tested, and the word `Test` is appended to the name—for example, the test class for `UnitTestingSamples.DeepThought` is `UnitTestingSamples.DeepThoughtTest`.

➤ Unit test method names have a descriptive name—for example the name `AddOrUpdateBookAsync_ThrowsForNull` indicates a unit test to invoke the `AddOrUpdateBookAsync` method to check if it throws an exception passing `null`.

The MSTest project contains references to the NuGet packages `Microsoft.NET.Test.Sdk`, `MSTest.TestAdapter`, and `MSTest.TestFramework` (project file `UnitTestingSamples.MSTests/UnitTestingSamples.MSTests.csproj`):

```xml
<Project Sdk="Microsoft.NET.Sdk">
  <PropertyGroup>
    <TargetFramework>netcoreapp2.0</TargetFramework>
    <IsPackable>false</IsPackable>
  </PropertyGroup>

  <ItemGroup>
    <PackageReference Include="Microsoft.NET.Test.Sdk" Version="15.5.0" />
    <PackageReference Include="MSTest.TestAdapter" Version="1.2.0" />
    <PackageReference Include="MSTest.TestFramework" Version="1.2.0" />
  </ItemGroup>

  <ItemGroup>
    <ProjectReference Include="..\UnitTestingSamples\UnitTestingSamples.csproj" />
  </ItemGroup>

</Project>
```

A unit test class is marked with the `TestClass` attribute, and a test method is marked with the `TestMethod` attribute. The implementation creates an instance of `DeepThought` and invokes the method that is to be tested: `TheAnswerToTheUltimateQuestionOfLifeTheUniverseAndEverything`. The return value is compared with the value 42 using `Assert.AreEqual`. In case `Assert.AreEqual` fails, the test fails (code file `UnitTestingSamples.MSTests/DeepThoughtTest.cs`):

```
[TestClass]
public class TestProgram
{
  [TestMethod]
  public void
    ResultOfTheAnswerToTheUltimateQuestionOfLifeTheUniverseAndEverything()
  {
    // arrange
    int expected = 42;
    var dt = new DeepThought();

    // act
    int actual =
      dt.TheAnswerToTheUltimateQuestionOfLifeTheUniverseAndEverything();

    // assert
    Assert.AreEqual(expected, actual);
  }
}
```

Unit tests are defined by three A's: arrange, act, and assert. First, everything is *arranged* for the unit test to start. In the first test, with the arrange phase, a variable `expected` is assigned the value that is expected from calling the method to test, and an instance of the `DeepThought` class is invoked. Now everything is ready to test the functionality. This happens with the *act* phase—the method is invoked. After completing the act phase, you need to verify whether the result is as expected. This is done in the *assert* phase using a method of the `Assert` class.

The `Assert` class is part of the MSTest framework in the `Microsoft.VisualStudio.TestTools.UnitTesting` namespace. This class offers several static methods that you can use with unit tests. The `Assert.Fail` method can be used to mark a unit test to give the information that the test is not yet implemented. Some of the other methods are `AreNotEqual`, which verifies whether two objects are not the same; `IsFalse` and `IsTrue`, which verify Boolean results; `IsNull` and `IsNotNull`, which verify null results; and `IsInstanceOfType` and `IsNotInstanceOfType`, which verify the passed type.

Running Unit Tests

Using the Test Explorer (which you open via Test ➪ Windows ➪ Test Explorer), you can run the tests from the solution (see Figure 28-1).

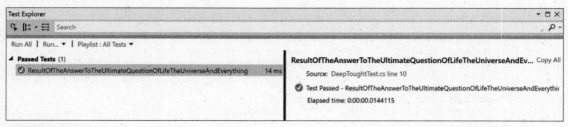

FIGURE 28-1

Figure 28-2 shows a failed test, which includes all details about the failure.

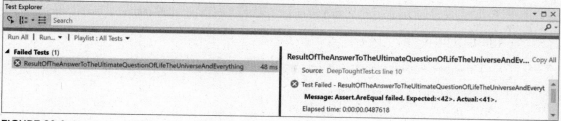

FIGURE 28-2

To run the test from the command line, you can invoke `dotnet test`:

```
> dotnet test
```

With the sample application, this results in this successful output:

```
Build started, please wait...
Build completed.

Test run for
C:\procsharp\Tests\UnitTestingSamples\UnitTestingSamples.MSTests\bin\Debug\
netcoreapp2.0\UnitTestingSamples.MSTests.dll(.NETCoreApp,Version=v2.0)
Microsoft (R) Test Execution Command Line Tool Version 15.5.0
Copyright (c) Microsoft Corporation.  All rights reserved.

Starting test execution, please wait...

Total tests: 1. Passed: 1. Failed: 0. Skipped: 0.
Test Run Successful.
Test execution time: 1.2312 Seconds
```

Of course, this was a very simple scenario; the tests are not usually that simple. For example, methods can throw exceptions; they can have different routes for returning other values; and they can make use of other code (for example, database access code, or services that are invoked) that shouldn't be tested with the single unit. Now let's look at a more involved scenario for unit testing.

The following class, `StringSample`, defines a constructor with a string parameter, the method `GetStringDemo`, and a field. The method `GetStringDemo` uses different paths depending on the `first` and `second` parameters and returns a string that results from these parameters (code file `UnitTestingSamples/StringSample.cs`):

```csharp
public class StringSample
{
  public StringSample(string init)
  {
    if (init is null)
      throw new ArgumentNullException(nameof(init));

    _init = init;
  }

  private string _init;

  public string GetStringDemo(string first, string second)
  {
    if (first is null)
    {
      throw new ArgumentNullException(nameof(first));
    }
    if (string.IsNullOrEmpty(first))
```

```
    {
      throw new ArgumentException("empty string is not allowed", first);
    }
    if (second is null)
    {
      throw new ArgumentNullException(nameof(second));
    }
    if (second.Length > first.Length)
    {
      throw new ArgumentOutOfRangeException(nameof(second),
        "must be shorter than first");
    }
    int startIndex = first.IndexOf(second);
    if (startIndex < 0)
    {
      return $"{second} not found in {first}";
    }
    else if (startIndex < 5)
    {
      string result = first.Remove(startIndex, second.Length);
      return $"removed {second} from {first}: {result}";
    }
    else
    {
      return _init.ToUpperInvariant();
    }
  }
}
```

> **NOTE** *When you're writing unit tests for complex methods, the unit test also some-times gets complex. Here it is helpful to debug into the unit test to find out what's going on. Debugging unit tests is straightforward: Just add breakpoints to the unit test code, and from the context menu of the Test Explorer select Debug Selected Tests (see Figure 28-3).*

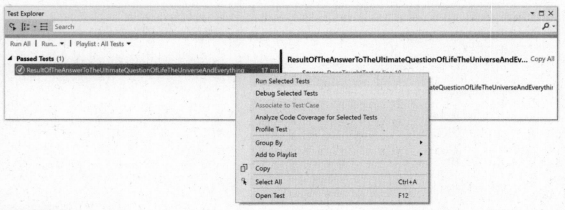

FIGURE 28-3

Every possible execution route and check for exceptions should be covered by unit tests, as discussed next.

Expecting Exceptions with MSTest

When invoking the constructor of the `StringSample` class and calling the method `GetStringDemo` with null, an `ArgumentNullException` is expected. You can easily check exceptions with testing code: apply the `ExpectedException` attribute to the test method as shown in the following example. This way, the test method succeeds with the exception (code file `UnitTestingSamples.MSTests/StringSampleTest.cs`):

```
[TestMethod]
[ExpectedException(typeof(ArgumentNullException))]
public void ConstructorShouldThrowOnNull()
{
    var sample = new StringSample(null);
}
```

You can deal with the exception thrown by the `GetStringDemo` method in a similar way.

Testing All Code Paths

To test all code paths, you can create multiple tests, with each one taking a different route. The following test sample passes the strings a and b to the `GetStringDemo` method. Because the second string is not contained within the first string, the first path of the `if` statement applies. The result is checked accordingly (code file `UnitTestingSamples.MSTests/StringSampleTest.cs`):

```
[TestMethod]
public void GetStringDemoBNotInA()
{
    string expected = "b not found in a";
    var sample = new StringSample(String.Empty);
    string actual = sample.GetStringDemo("a", "b");
    Assert.AreEqual(expected, actual);
}
```

The next test method verifies another path of the `GetStringDemo` method. Here, the second string is found in the first one, and the index is lower than 5; therefore, it results in the second code block of the `if` statement:

```
[TestMethod]
public void GetStringDemoRemoveBCFromABCD()
{
    string expected = "removed bc from abcd: ad";
    var sample = new StringSample(String.Empty);
    string actual = sample.GetStringDemo("abcd", "bc");
    Assert.AreEqual(expected, actual);
}
```

All other code paths can be tested similarly. To see what code is covered by unit tests, and what code is still missing, you can start Code Coverage in Visual Studio and use the `--collect` option of the `dotnet test` command. In the Visual Studio 2017 Code Coverage Results window (Test ⇨ Windows ⇨ Code Coverage Results), you can see the percentage of code covered by unit tests.

External Dependencies

Many methods are dependent on some functionality outside the application's control, for example, calling a web service or accessing a database. Maybe the service or database is not available during some test runs, which tests the availability of these external resources. Or worse, maybe the database or service returns different data over time, and it's hard to compare this with expected data. Such functionality outside the scope of what should be tested must be excluded from the unit test.

The following example is dependent on some outside functionality. The method `ChampionsByCountry` accesses an XML file from a web server that contains a list of Formula-1 world champions with `Firstname`, `Lastname`, `Wins`, and `Country` elements. This list is filtered by country, and it's numerically ordered using the value from the `Wins` element. The returned data is an `XElement` that contains converted XML code:

```
public XElement ChampionsByCountry(string country)
{
  XElement champions = XElement.Load(F1Addresses.RacersUrl);
  var q = from r in champions.Elements("Racer")
          where r.Element("Country").Value == country
          orderby int.Parse(r.Element("Wins").Value) descending
          select new XElement("Racer",
            new XAttribute("Name", r.Element("Firstname").Value + " " +
              r.Element("Lastname").Value),
            new XAttribute("Country", r.Element("Country").Value),
            new XAttribute("Wins", r.Element("Wins").Value));
  return new XElement("Racers", q.ToArray());
}
```

> **NOTE** *For more information on LINQ to XML, read Bonus Chapter 2, "XML and JSON," which you can find online.*

The link to the XML file is defined by the `F1Addresses` class (code file `UnitTestingSamples/F1Addresses.cs`):

```
public class F1Addresses
{
  public const string RacersUrl =
    "http://www.cninnovation.com/downloads/Racers.xml";
}
```

For the method `ChampionsByCountry`, you should do a unit test. The test should not be dependent on the source from the server. Server unavailability is one issue, but it can also be expected that the data on the server changes over time to return new champions, and other values. The current test should ensure that filtering is done as expected, returning a correctly filtered list, and in the correct order.

One way to create a unit test that is independent of the data source is to refactor the implementation of the `ChampionsByCountry` method by using the dependency injection pattern. Here, a factory that returns an `XElement` is created to replace the `XElement.Load` method. The interface `IChampionsLoader` is the only outside requirement used from the `ChampionsByCountry` method. The interface `IChampionsLoader` defines the method `LoadChampions` that can replace the aforementioned method (code file `UnitTestingSamples/IChampionsLoader.cs`):

```
public interface IChampionsLoader
{
  XElement LoadChampions();
}
```

The class `ChampionsLoader` implements the interface `IChampionsLoader` by using the `XElement.Load` method—the method that was used beforehand by the `ChampionsByCountry` method (code file `UnitTestingSamples/ChampionsLoader.cs`):

```
public class ChampionsLoader: IChampionsLoader
{
  public XElement LoadChampions() => XElement.Load(F1Addresses.RacersUrl);
}
```

> **NOTE** *The dependency injection pattern is explained with more detail in Chapter 20, "Dependency Injection."*

Now it's possible to change the implementation of the `ChampionsByCountry` method by using an interface to load the champions instead of directly using `XElement.Load`. The `IChampionsLoader` is passed with the constructor of the class `Formula1`, and this loader is then used by `ChampionsByCountry`: (code file `UnitTestingSamples/Formula1.cs`):

```
public class Formula1
{
  private IChampionsLoader _loader;
  public Formula1(IChampionsLoader loader)
  {
    _loader = loader;
  }

  public XElement ChampionsByCountry(string country)
  {
    var q = from r in _loader.LoadChampions().Elements("Racer")
            where r.Element("Country").Value == country
            orderby int.Parse(r.Element("Wins").Value) descending
            select new XElement("Racer",
              new XAttribute("Name", r.Element("Firstname").Value + " " +
                r.Element("Lastname").Value),
              new XAttribute("Country", r.Element("Country").Value),
              new XAttribute("Wins", r.Element("Wins").Value));
    return new XElement("Racers", q.ToArray());
  }
}
```

With a typical implementation, a `ChampionsLoader` instance would be passed to the `Formula1` constructor to retrieve the racers from the server.

When you're creating the unit test, you can implement a custom method that returns sample Formula-1 champions, as shown in the method `Formula1SampleData` (code file `UnitTestingSamples.MSTests/Formula1Test.cs`):

```
internal static string Formula1SampleData()
{
  return @"
<Racers>
  <Racer>
    <Firstname>Nelson</Firstname>
    <Lastname>Piquet</Lastname>
    <Country>Brazil</Country>
    <Starts>204</Starts>
    <Wins>23</Wins>
  </Racer>
  <Racer>
    <Firstname>Ayrton</Firstname>
    <Lastname>Senna</Lastname>
    <Country>Brazil</Country>
    <Starts>161</Starts>
    <Wins>41</Wins>
  </Racer>
  <Racer>
```

```
      <Firstname>Nigel</Firstname>
      <Lastname>Mansell</Lastname>
      <Country>England</Country>
      <Starts>187</Starts>
      <Wins>31</Wins>
    </Racer>
    //... more sample data
```

The method `Formula1VerificationData` returns sample test data that matches the expected result (code file `UnitTestingSamples.MSTests/Formula1Test.cs`):

```
internal static XElement Formula1VerificationData()
{
  return XElement.Parse(@"
<Racers>
  <Racer Name=""Mika Hakkinen"" Country=""Finland"" Wins=""20"" />
  <Racer Name=""Kimi Raikkonen"" Country=""Finland"" Wins=""18"" />
</Racers>");
}
```

The loader of the test data implements the same interface—`IChampionsLoader`—as the `ChampionsLoader` class. This loader makes use of the sample data; it doesn't access the web server (code file `UnitTestingSamples.MSTests/Formula1Test.cs`):

```
public class F1TestLoader: IChampionsLoader
{
  public XElement LoadChampions() => XElement.Parse(Formula1SampleData());
}
```

Now it's easy to create a unit test that makes use of the sample data (code file `UnitTestingSamples.MSTests/Formula1Test.cs`):

```
[TestMethod]
public void ChampionsByCountryFilterFinland()
{
  Formula1 f1 = new Formula1(new F1TestLoader());
  XElement actual = f1.ChampionsByCountry("Finland");
  Assert.AreEqual(Formula1VerificationData().ToString(), actual.ToString());
}
```

Of course, a real test should do more than cover a case that passes `Finland` as a string and two champions are returned with the test data. You should write other tests to pass a string with no matching result, to return more than two champions, and to result in a number sort order that is different from the alphanumeric sort order.

> **NOTE** *To test methods that don't use dependency injection, to replace the internally used dependencies with test classes, you can use the Fakes Framework. This is available only for .NET Framework projects with Visual Studio Enterprise.*

UNIT TESTING WITH XUNIT

When .NET Core was implemented, xUnit was available to create unit tests, and the .NET Core team used this product. xUnit is an open-source implementation from the same developer who created NUnit 2.0. Nowadays, both MSTest and xUnit are supported by the .NET Core command-line interface.

TIP *See* https://xunit.github.io/ *for documentation on xUnit.*

With the Visual Studio Test environment, several testing frameworks can be used. Test adapters such as NUnit, xUnit, Boost (for C++), Chutzpah (for JavaScript), and Jasmine (for JavaScript) are available via Extensions and Updates; these test adapters integrate with the Visual Studio Test Explorer.

Because xUnit is a great testing framework for .NET Core, and it's also used by Microsoft with the open-source code of .NET Core and ASP.NET Core, xUnit is the focus of this section.

Using xUnit with .NET Core

You can create xUnit tests in a similar manner to MSTest tests with .NET Core applications. From the command line, you can use

```
> dotnet new xunit
```

to create an xUnit test project. With Visual Studio 2017, you can select the project type xUnit Test Project (.NET Core).

With this sample project, the same .NET Standard library as before—UnitTestingSamples—is tested. This library includes the same types for testing that were shown earlier: DeepThought and StringSample. The test project has the name UnitTestingSamples.xUnit.Tests.

This project needs references to xunit (for the unit tests, xunit.runner.visualstudio [to run the tests within Visual Studio]) and to the UnitTestingSamples project (the code that should be tested). For integration with the .NET Core command line, the DotNetCliToolReference for dotnet-xunit is added (project file UnitTestingSamples.xUnit.Tests/UnitTestingSamples.xUnit.Tests.csproj):

```xml
<Project Sdk="Microsoft.NET.Sdk">

  <PropertyGroup>
    <TargetFramework>netcoreapp2.0</TargetFramework>
    <IsPackable>false</IsPackable>
  </PropertyGroup>

  <ItemGroup>
    <PackageReference Include="Microsoft.NET.Test.Sdk" Version="15.5.0" />
    <PackageReference Include="xunit" Version="2.3.1" />
    <PackageReference Include="xunit.runner.visualstudio" Version="2.3.1" />
    <DotNetCliToolReference Include="dotnet-xunit" Version="2.3.1" />
  </ItemGroup>

  <ItemGroup>
    <ProjectReference Include="..\UnitTestingSamples\UnitTestingSamples.csproj" />
  </ItemGroup>

</Project>
```

Creating Facts

The way you create the test is very similar to what you did before. With MSTest you had to add an attribute to the testing class. This is not necessary with xUnit because all public classes are searched for test methods. The differences on testing the method

TheAnswerToTheUltimateQuestionOfLifeTheUniverseAndEverything between MSTest and xUnit are just the annotated test method with the `Fact` attribute and the different `Assert.Equal` method (code file `UnitTestingSamples.xUnit.Tests/DeepThoughtTest.cs`):

```
public class DeepThoughtTest
{
  [Fact]
  public void
    ResultOfTheAnswerToTheUltimateQuestionOfLifeTheUniverseAndEverythingTest()
  {
    int expected = 42;
    var dt = new DeepThought();
    int actual =
    dt.TheAnswerToTheUltimateQuestionOfLifeTheUniverseAndEverything();
    Assert.Equal(expected, actual);
  }
}
```

The `Assert` class used now is defined in the `XUnit` namespace. This class defines a lot more methods for validation compared to the `Assert` method from MSTest. For example, instead of adding an attribute to specify an expected exception, use the `Assert.Throws` method, which allows multiple checks for exceptions within a single test method (code file `UnitTestingSamples.xUnit.Tests/StringSampleTest.cs`):

```
[Fact]
public void GetStringDemoExceptions()
{
  var sample = new StringSample(string.Empty);
  Assert.Throws<ArgumentNullException>(() => sample.GetStringDemo(null, "a"));
  Assert.Throws<ArgumentNullException>(() => sample.GetStringDemo("a", null));
  Assert.Throws<ArgumentException>(() =>
    sample.GetStringDemo(string.Empty, "a"));
}
```

Creating Theories

xUnit defines the `Fact` attribute for test methods that don't require parameters. With xUnit you can also invoke unit test methods that require parameters; you use the `Theory` attribute and supply data to add an attribute that derives from `Data`. This makes it possible to define multiple unit tests by a single method.

In the following code snippet, the `Theory` attribute is applied to the `GetStringDemoInlineData` unit test method. The method `StringSample.GetStringDemo` defines different paths that depend on the input data. The first path is reached if the string passed with the second parameter is not contained within the first parameter. The second path is reached if the second string is contained within the first five characters of the first string. The third path is reached with the `else` clause. To reach all the different paths, three `InlineData` attributes are applied to the testing method. Every one of these attributes defines four parameters that are directly sent to the invocation of the unit testing method, in the same order. The attributes also define the values that should be returned by the method under test (code file `UnitTestingSamples.xUnit.Tests/StringSampleTest.cs`):

```
[Theory]
[InlineData("", "longer string", "nger",
  "removed nger from longer string: lo string")]
[InlineData("init", "longer string", "string", "INIT")]
public void GetStringDemoInlineData(string init, string a, string b,
  string expected)
{
  var sample = new StringSample(init);
  string actual = sample.GetStringDemo(a, b);
  Assert.Equal(expected, actual);
}
```

The attribute `InlineData` derives from the attribute `Data`. Instead of directly supplying the values for the test method with the attribute, the values can also come from a property, method, or a class. The following example defines a static method that returns the same values with an `IEnumerable<object>` object (code file `UnitTestingSamples.xUnit.Tests/StringSampleTest.cs`):

```
public static IEnumerable<object[]> GetStringSampleData() =>
  new[]
  {
    new object[] { "", "a", "b", "b not found in a" },
    new object[] { "", "longer string", "nger",
    "removed nger from longer string: lo string" },
    new object[] { "init", "longer string", "string", "INIT" }
};
```

The unit test method is now changed with the `MemberData` attribute. This attribute allows using static properties or methods that return `IEnumerable<object>` to fill in the parameters of the unit test method (code file `UnitTestingSamples.xUnit.Tests/StringSampleTest.cs`):

```
[Theory]
[MemberData("GetStringSampleData")]
public void GetStringDemoMemberData(string init, string a, string b,
  string expected)
{
  var sample = new StringSample(init);
  string actual = sample.GetStringDemo(a, b);
  Assert.Equal(expected, actual);
}
```

Using a Mocking Library

Let's get into a more complex example: creating a unit test for a client-side service library from an app using the MVVM pattern. Read Chapter 34, "Patterns with XAML Apps," for a complete picture from this app. The sample code for this chapter only includes a library used by this app. This service uses dependency injection to inject the repository defined by the interface `IBooksRepository`. The unit tests for testing the method `AddOrUpdateBookAsync` shouldn't test the repository; they test only the functionality within the method. For the repository, another unit test should be done: The following code snippet shows the implementation of the `BooksService` class (code file `MockingSamples/BooksLib/Services/BooksService.cs`):

```
public class BooksService: IBooksService
{
  private ObservableCollection<Book> _books = new ObservableCollection<Book>();
  private IBooksRepository _booksRepository;
  public BooksService(IBooksRepository repository)
  {
    _booksRepository = repository;
  }

  public async Task LoadBooksAsync()
  {
    if (_books.Count > 0) return;
    IEnumerable<Book> books = await _booksRepository.GetItemsAsync();
    _books.Clear();
    foreach (var b in books)
    {
      _books.Add(b);
    }
  }

  public Book GetBook(int bookId) =>
    _books.Where(b => b.BookId == bookId).SingleOrDefault();
```

```
public async Task<Book> AddOrUpdateBookAsync(Book book)
{
  if (book == null) throw new ArgumentNullException(nameof(book));

  Book updated = null;
  if (book.BookId == 0)
  {
    updated = await _booksRepository.AddAsync(book);
    if (updated == null) throw new InvalidOperationException();

    _books.Add(updated);
  }
  else
  {
    updated = await _booksRepository.UpdateAsync(book);
    if (updated == null) throw new InvalidOperationException();

    Book old = _books.Where(b => b.BookId == updated.BookId).Single();
    int ix = _books.IndexOf(old);
    _books.RemoveAt(ix);
    _books.Insert(ix, updated);
  }
  return updated;
}

public IEnumerable<Book> Books => _books;
}
```

Because the unit test for `AddOrUpdateBookAsync` shouldn't test the repository used for `IBooksRepository`, you need to implement a repository used for testing. To make this easy, you can use a mocking library that automatically fills in the blanks. A commonly used mocking library is Moq. With the unit testing project, the NuGet package `Moq` is added.

> **NOTE** *Instead of using the Moq framework, you also can implement an in-memory repository with sample data. You probably do this anyway to have sample data for the app during design time of the user interface.*

When you use xUnit, a new instance of the test class is created for every test run. In case you need common functionality for multiple tests, you can move this functionality to the constructor. In case resources need to be released after each test run, you can implement the interface `IDisposable`.

Within the constructor of the `BooksServiceTest` class, a `Mock` object is instantiated with the generic parameter `IBooksRepository`. The `Mock` constructor creates an implementation for the interface. Because you need some results from the repository other than null to create useful tests, the `Setup` method defines which parameters can be passed, and the `ReturnsAsync` method defines the result that's returned from the method stub. You access the mock object by using the `Object` property of the `Mock` class, and it is passed on to create an instance of the `BooksService` class. With these settings in place, you can implement the unit tests (code file `MockingSamples/BooksLib.Tests/Services/BooksServiceTest.cs`):

```
public class BooksServiceTest : IDisposable
{
  private const string TestTitle = "Test Title";
  private const string UpdatedTestTitle = "Updated Test Title";
  public const string APublisher = "A Publisher";
  private BooksService _booksService;
  private Book _newBook = new Book
  {
    BookId = 0,
```

```
      Title = TestTitle,
      Publisher = APublisher
    };
    private Book _expectedBook = new Book
    {
      BookId = 1,
      Title = TestTitle,
      Publisher = APublisher
    };
    private Book _notInRepositoryBook = new Book
    {
      BookId = 42,
      Title = TestTitle,
      Publisher = APublisher
    };
    private Book _updatedBook = new Book
    {
      BookId = 1,
      Title = UpdatedTestTitle,
      Publisher = APublisher
    };

    public BooksServiceTest()
    {
      var mock = new Mock<IBooksRepository>();
      mock.Setup(repository =>
        repository.AddAsync(_newBook)).ReturnsAsync(_expectedBook);
      mock.Setup(repository =>
        repository.UpdateAsync(_notInRepositoryBook)).ReturnsAsync(null as Book);
      mock.Setup(repository =>
        repository.UpdateAsync(_updatedBook)).ReturnsAsync(_updatedBook);

      _booksService = new BooksService(mock.Object);
    }
    //...
```

> **NOTE** *The* IDisposable *interface is explained in detail in Chapter 17, "Managed and Unmanaged Memory."*

The first unit test implemented—AddOrUpdateBookAsync_ThrowsForNull—verifies that an ArgumentNullException is thrown in case null is passed to the AddOrUpdateBookAsync method. The implementation just needs the _booksService member variable that is instantiated within the constructor, but it doesn't need the mocking setup. This code sample also shows that unit test methods can be implemented as asynchronous methods that return a Task (code file MockingSamples/BooksLib.Tests/Services/BooksServiceTest.cs):

```
[Fact]
public async Task AddOrUpdateBookAsync_ThrowsForNull()
{
  // arrange
  Book nullBook = null;
  // act and assert
  await Assert.ThrowsAsync<ArgumentNullException>(() =>
    _booksService.AddOrUpdateBookAsync(nullBook));
}
```

The unit test method AddOrUpdateBook_AddedBookReturnsFromRepository adds a new book (variable _newBook) to the service and expects the book _expectedBook to be returned. Within the implementation of the `AddOrUpdateBookAsync` method, the `AddAsync` method of the `IBooksRepository` is invoked; thus, the previously defined mock setup for this method applies. The result of this method should be that the `Book` returned is equal to the `_expectedBook`, and the `_expectedBook` also needs to be added to the books collection of the `BooksService` (code file `MockingSamples/BooksLib.Tests/Services/BooksServiceTest.cs`):

```
[Fact]
public async Task AddOrUpdateBook_AddedBookReturnsFromRepository()
{
    // arrange in constructor
    // act
    Book actualAdded = await _booksService.AddOrUpdateBookAsync(_newBook);

    // assert
    Assert.Equal(_expectedBook, actualAdded);
    Assert.Contains(_expectedBook, _booksService.Books);
}
```

The unit test `AddOrUpdateBook_UpdateNotExistingBookThrows` verifies that trying to update a book that does not exist in the service needs to result in an `InvalidOperationException` (code file `MockingSamples/BooksLib.Tests/Services/BooksServiceTest.cs`):

```
[Fact]
public async Task AddOrUpdateBook_UpdateNotExistingBookThrows()
{
    // arrange in constructor
    // act and assert
    await Assert.ThrowsAsync<InvalidOperationException>(() =>
        _booksService.AddOrUpdateBookAsync(_notInRepositoryBook));
}
```

The usual case to update a book is dealt with the unit test `AddOrUpdateBook_UpdateBook`. Here, extra preparation is needed to first add the book to the service before updating it (code file `MockingSamples/BooksLib.Tests/Services/BooksServiceTest.cs`):

```
[Fact]
public async Task AddOrUpdateBook_UpdateBook()
{
    // arrange
    await _booksService.AddOrUpdateBookAsync(_newBook);

    // act
    Book updatedBook = await _booksService.AddOrUpdateBookAsync(_updatedBook);

    // assert
    Assert.Equal(_updatedBook, updatedBook);
    Assert.Contains(_updatedBook, _booksService.Books);
}
```

When you use the MVVM pattern with XAML-based applications and the MVC pattern with web-based applications, you reduce the complexity of the user interface and reduce the need for complex UI testing. However, there are still some scenarios that should be tested with the UI—for example, navigating through pages, drag and drop of elements, and more. This is where Visual Studio's functionality of UI testing comes into place.

Testing user interfaces is covered in the section "UI Testing." Testing web applications is covered in the section "Web Integration, Load, and Performance Testing."

LIVE UNIT TESTING

A great feature for unit testing is available with the Enterprise edition of Visual Studio 2017: Live Unit Testing. It's best to see errors as early as possible, and the first place you can see them is in the Visual

Studio editor. From the Test menu, you can start Live Unit Testing. With Live Unit Testing turned on, you can directly see in the editor what code lines are covered by tests and where the test runs successful (see Figure 28-4).

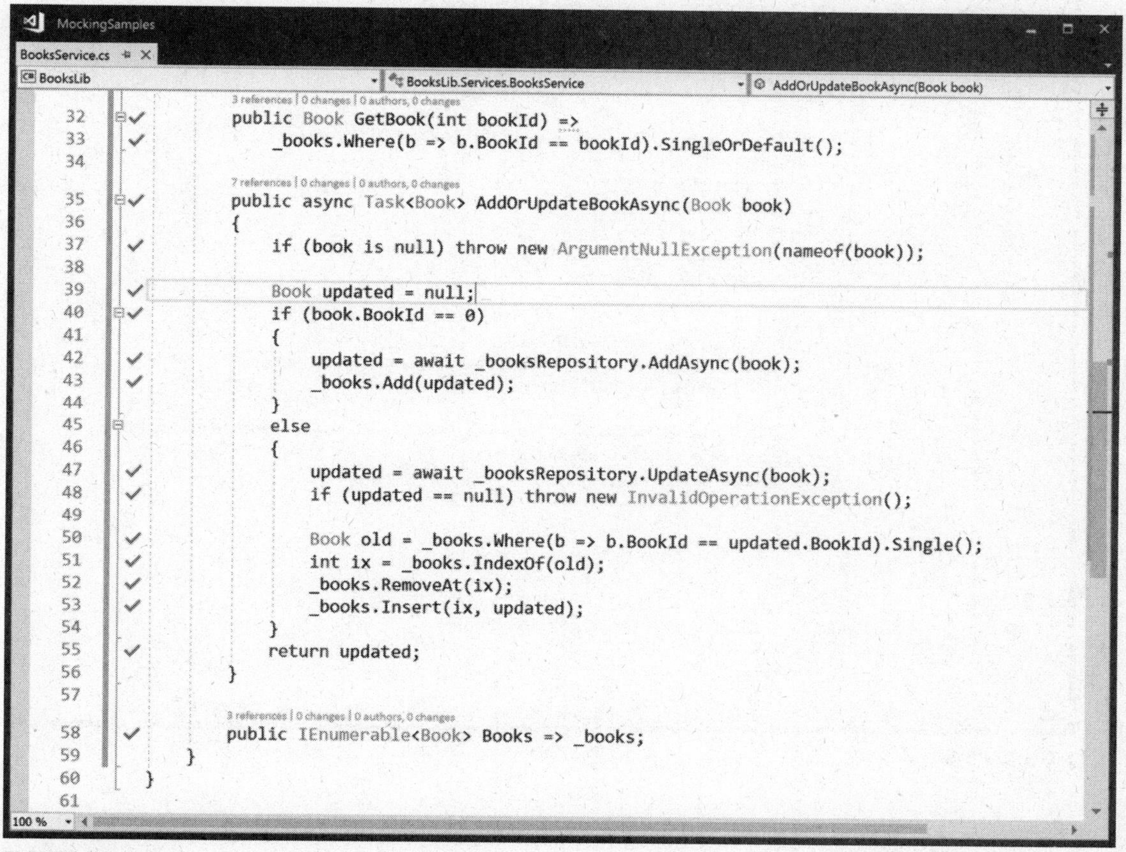

FIGURE 28-4

In case you introduce some error in the code editor, you can see the issue immediately—even without saving the file. If the compiler runs successfully while you're editing, the unit tests associated with the method you just edited runs, and you can see the results (as shown in Figure 28-5) and can react accordingly.

All tests running while editing should run fast. You shouldn't run integration tests with Live Unit Testing. In the Solution Explorer, you can select test projects and test classes to be excluded or included from Live Unit Testing.

You also can exclude specific test methods using annotations—with xUnit using the `Trait` attribute:

```
[Trait("Category", "SkipWhenLiveUnitTesting")]
```

and with MSTest using the `TestCategory` attribute:

```
[TestCategory("SkipWhenLiveUnitTesting")]
```

Live Unit Tests also don't run when the battery is less than 30 percent. You can configure this setting and other Live Unit Test settings with Visual Studio by selecting Tools ⇨ Options.

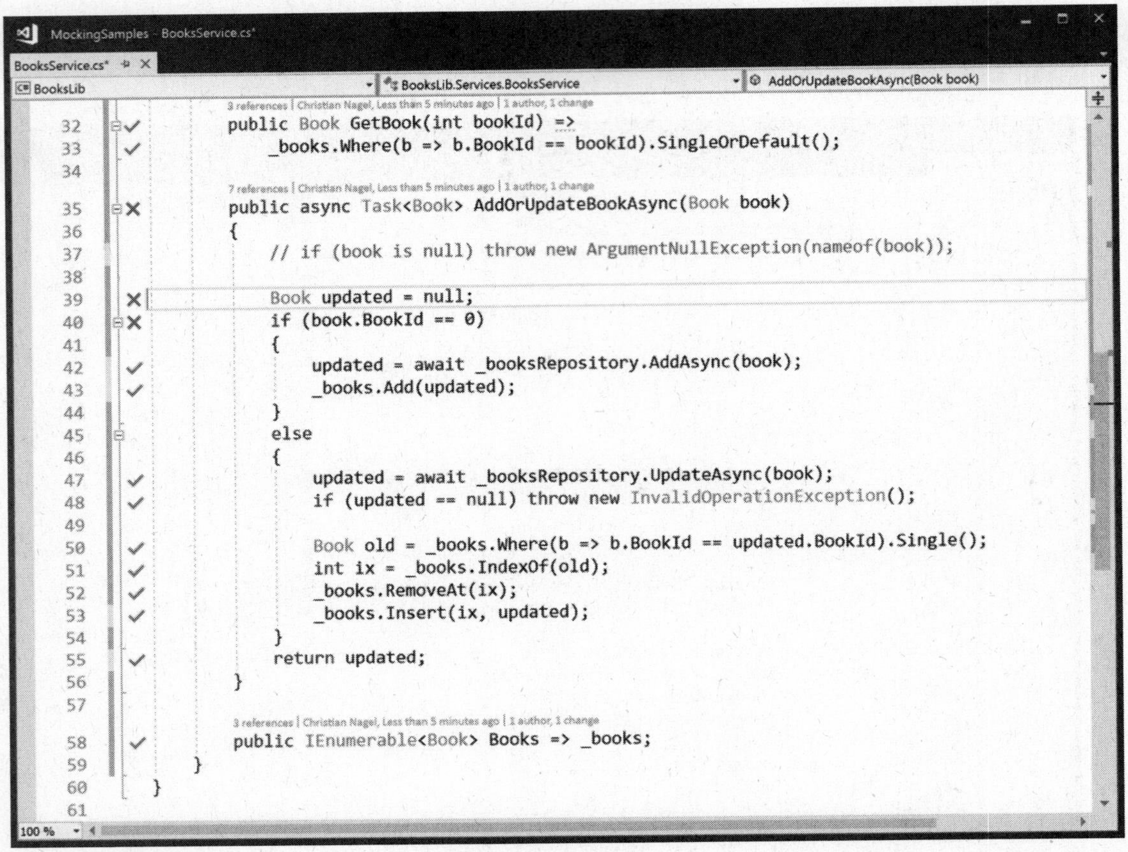

```
32      public Book GetBook(int bookId) =>
33          _books.Where(b => b.BookId == bookId).SingleOrDefault();
34
35      public async Task<Book> AddOrUpdateBookAsync(Book book)
36      {
37          // if (book is null) throw new ArgumentNullException(nameof(book));
38
39          Book updated = null;
40          if (book.BookId == 0)
41          {
42              updated = await _booksRepository.AddAsync(book);
43              _books.Add(updated);
44          }
45          else
46          {
47              updated = await _booksRepository.UpdateAsync(book);
48              if (updated == null) throw new InvalidOperationException();
49
50              Book old = _books.Where(b => b.BookId == updated.BookId).Single();
51              int ix = _books.IndexOf(old);
52              _books.RemoveAt(ix);
53              _books.Insert(ix, updated);
54          }
55          return updated;
56      }
57
58      public IEnumerable<Book> Books => _books;
59      }
60  }
61
```

FIGURE 28-5

UNIT TESTING WITH EF CORE

When you create unit tests, you need to replace dependencies with test classes that offer test data. What about dependencies on the Entity Framework Core (EF Core) context? Usually there's not an interface that is implemented by the context, but the context (for example, the BooksContext) is injected itself. EF Core offers a solution with a memory-based provider that can be used as a mocking class instead of using the EF Core SQL Server provider.

> **NOTE** *EF Core is discussed in detail in Chapter 26, "Entity Framework Core."*

Let's start with a simple Book type, a BooksContext, and a BooksService. The BooksService class should be tested from unit tests.

The Book class is a simple class that keeps a few properties (code file EFCoreSample/EFCoreSample/Book.cs):

```
public class Book
{
```

```
      public int BookId { get; set; }
      public string Title { get; set; }
      public string Publisher { get; set; }
}
```

The class `BooksContext` manages the connection to the database and maps the `Book` type to the `Books` table (code file `EFCoreSample/EFCoreSample/BooksContext.cs`):

```
public class BooksContext : DbContext
{
  public BooksContext(DbContextOptions<BooksContext> options)
    : base(options) { }

  public DbSet<Book> Books { get; set; }
}
```

And finally, the class `BooksService` uses the `BooksContext` via dependency injection and defines the method `GetTopBooksByPublisher`. This method should be tested to only return 10 books (code file `EFCoreSample/EFCoreSample/BooksService.cs`):

```
public class BooksService
{
  private readonly BooksContext _booksContext;

  public BooksService(BooksContext booksContext)
  {
    _booksContext = booksContext;
  }

  public IEnumerable<Book> GetTopBooksByPublisher(string publisher)
  {
    if (publisher == null) throw new ArgumentNullException(nameof(publisher));

    return _booksContext.Books
      .Where(b => b.Publisher == publisher)
      .Take(10)
      .ToList();
  }
}
```

For unit testing, an xUnit project is created. For using the EF Core in-memory provider, the NuGet package `Microsoft.EntityFrameworkCore.InMemory` is added in addition to the `EFCoreSample` project.

Now, you can use the `DbContextOptionsBuilder` to create the options with the in-memory database. `UseInMemoryDatabase` is an extension method from the package `Microsoft.EntityFrameworkCore.InMemory` to add the EF Core in-memory provider. In the `InitContext` method, 1000 book objects are created and saved into the object list of the context to be ready to be used by the unit test (code file `EFCoreSample/EFCoreSample.Tests/BooksServiceTest.cs`):

```
public class BooksServiceTest : IDisposable
{
  private BooksContext _booksContext;
  private const string PublisherName = "A Publisher";
  public BooksServiceTest()
  {
    InitContext();
  }

  private void InitContext()
  {
    var builder = new DbContextOptionsBuilder<BooksContext>()
      .UseInMemoryDatabase("BooksDB");
    _booksContext = new BooksContext(builder.Options);
```

```
              // init with 1000 books
              var books = Enumerable.Range(1, 1000)
                .Select(i =>
                  new Book
                  {
                    BookId = i,
                    Title = $"Sample {i}",
                    Publisher = PublisherName })
                .ToList();
              _booksContext.Books.AddRange(books);
              _booksContext.SaveChanges();
          }

          //...

          public void Dispose()
          {
              _booksContext?.Dispose();
          }
      }
```

> **NOTE** *The* Enumerable *class and the* Range *method are discussed in Chapter 12,* *"Language Integrated Query."*

The unit test method GetTopBooksByPublisherCount now instantiates the BooksService in the *arrange* section, invokes the GetTopBooksByPublisher method in the *act* section, and finally checks the number of books returned in the *assert* section (code file EFCoreSample/EFCoreSample.Tests/ BooksServiceTest.cs):

```
[Fact]
public void GetTopBooksByPublisherCount()
{
  // arrange
  var booksService = new BooksService(_booksContext);
  // act
  var topbooks = booksService.GetTopBooksByPublisher(PublisherName);
  // assert
  Assert.Equal(10, topbooks.Count());
}
```

UI TESTING WITH WINDOWS APPS

For testing the user interface, Visual Studio offers Coded UI Test Project templates for Universal Windows apps, WPF applications, and Windows Forms. When you create a new project, you can find the project template for WPF and Windows Forms in the Test group. However, this template doesn't work for Windows apps. The project template for Universal Windows apps is in the Windows Universal group. Be aware that automatic recording is not supported for Windows apps.

> **NOTE** *Read chapters 33 to 36 for more detailed information on creating Windows Apps.*

In this chapter you create a UI test for a simple Windows app. This application is part of the downloadable files for this chapter, so you can use it for testing. The app just contains a TextBox control to enter some text, a `Button` control, and a `TextBlock` control where the text entered should show up when the user clicks the button as shown in Figure 28-6.

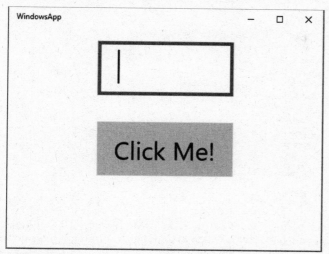

FIGURE 28-6

When you create a new Coded UI Test Project (Universal Windows), you see the dialog shown in Figure 28-7. When you select the Edit UI Map or Add Assertions option, you can select controls from a running app that adds automation peers of the controls to a map, so you can easily access it programmatically.

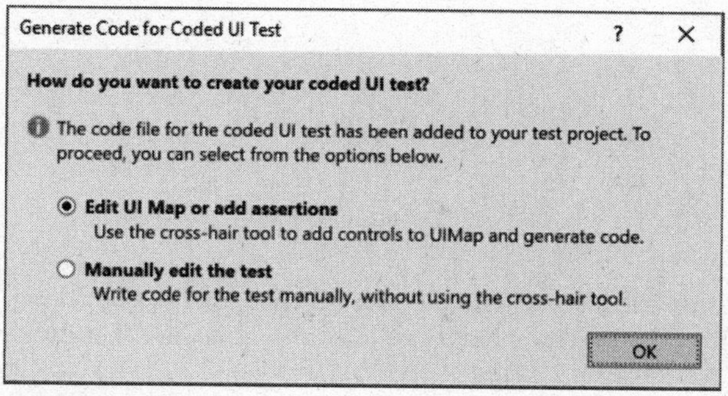

FIGURE 28-7

After you click OK to create a new project, the Coded UI Test Builder opens (see Figure 28-8). Recording of actions is not supported for Windows apps, so this option is grayed out, but you can add controls to the UI map by dragging the crosshair over controls of the running app.

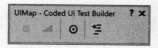

FIGURE 28-8

As you select controls, the list of them shows up in the left part of the tool, and the right part shows the properties of the selected controls (see Figure 28-9). You need to click the leftmost button (Add Control to UI Control Map) to finally add the control to the map.

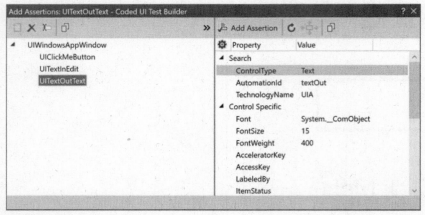

FIGURE 28-9

As the last step you need to click the Generate button (Figure 28-10) in the UIMap - Coded UI Test Builder window. A dialog with a method name shows up, but as with Windows apps only controls are generated, a method name is not needed, and you just need to click the Generate button.

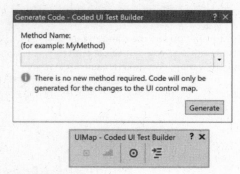

FIGURE 28-10

You can find the generated code in a partial class in the file UIMap.Designer.cs. You can extend this class in the file UIMap.cs. The designer-generated file will be overwritten if you start the Coded UI Test Builder again.

The designer-generated code defines the UIMap class that contains a property for the UIWindowsAppWindow. This class represents the window with the contained controls (code file WindowsApp/WindowsApp.UITest/UIMap.Designer.cs):

```
[GeneratedCode("Coded UITest Builder", "15.0.26621.2")]
public partial class UIMap
{
    public UIWindowsAppWindow UIWindowsAppWindow
    {
        get
        {
            if ((this.mUIWindowsAppWindow == null))
            {
                this.mUIWindowsAppWindow = new UIWindowsAppWindow();
            }
```

```
            return this.mUIWindowsAppWindow;
        }
    }
    private UIWindowsAppWindow mUIWindowsAppWindow;
}
```

The class `UIWindowsAppWindow` derives from the base class `XamlWindow` and defines `SearchProperties` that are used when the app is launched. If the app is already running, you can find the app by using the name of the window. With the sample app it is set to `WindowsApp` and the class name `Windows.UI.Core` `.CoreWindow` (code file WindowsApp/WindowsApp.UITest/UIMap.Designer.cs):

```
[GeneratedCode("Coded UITest Builder", "15.0.26621.2")]
public class UIWindowsAppWindow : XamlWindow
{
    public UIWindowsAppWindow()
    {
        this.SearchProperties[XamlControl.PropertyNames.Name] = "WindowsApp";
        this.SearchProperties[XamlControl.PropertyNames.ClassName] =
            "Windows.UI.Core.CoreWindow";
        this.WindowTitles.Add("WindowsApp");
    }
    //...
```

For every control that is selected using the Coded UI Test Builder, a field and a property are created. In the following code snippet, you can see the generated code for the `TextBox` control. Every UWP control has an automation peer. For the `TextBox` control it is the `XamlEdit` class. To map the `UITextInEdit` property to the corresponding `TextBox` control, you use an `AutomationId`. The `AutomationId` can be set with the control definition using the attached property `AutomationProperties.AutomationId`. The sample code of the Windows app defines this attached property in the XAML code in the file `MainPage.xaml`. In case the `AutomationId` is not directly set, it is generated with the same name as the `Name` property of the control. The get accessor of the property implements the creation of the `XamlEdit` control the first time the property is accessed. After the initial creation, the value of the field is returned (code file WindowsApp/WindowsApp .UITest/UIMap.Designer.cs):

```
public XamlEdit UITextInEdit
{
    get
    {
        if ((this.mUITextInEdit == null))
        {
            this.mUITextInEdit = new XamlEdit(this);
            this.mUITextInEdit
                .SearchProperties[XamlEdit.PropertyNames.AutomationId] = "textIn";
            this.mUITextInEdit.WindowTitles.Add("WindowsApp");
        }
        return this.mUITextInEdit;
    }
}
private XamlEdit mUITextInEdit;
```

> **NOTE** *Attached properties are covered in Chapter 33, "Windows Apps."*

The test class `MainPageTest` is annotated with the attribute `CodedUITest`. This attribute derives from the base class `TestClassExtensionAttribute` and identifies the kind of the UI test. To start the application, you need the automation ID of the application. You can get this ID either by using the crosshair from the Coded UI Test Builder and selecting the tile of the application, or by opening the Packaging tab in the `Package.appxmanifest` editor. In the Packaging tab (see Figure 28-11), you can copy the package family name and add !App as postfix. To access the generated UIMap, the test class defines a property (code file WindowsApp/WindowsApp.UITest/MainPageTest.cs):

```
[CodedUITest(CodedUITestType.WindowsStore)]
public class MainPageTest
{
  private string TileAutomationId =
    "0e07ecab-af0f-4129-965b-eed7a5beef75_p2wxv0ry6mv8g!App";

  //...

  public TestContext TestContext
  {
    get => testContextInstance;
    set => testContextInstance = value;
  }
  private TestContext testContextInstance;

  public UIMap UIMap
  {
    get
    {
      if (this.map == null)
      {
        this.map = new UIMap();
      }
      return this.map;
    }
  }
  private UIMap map;
}
```

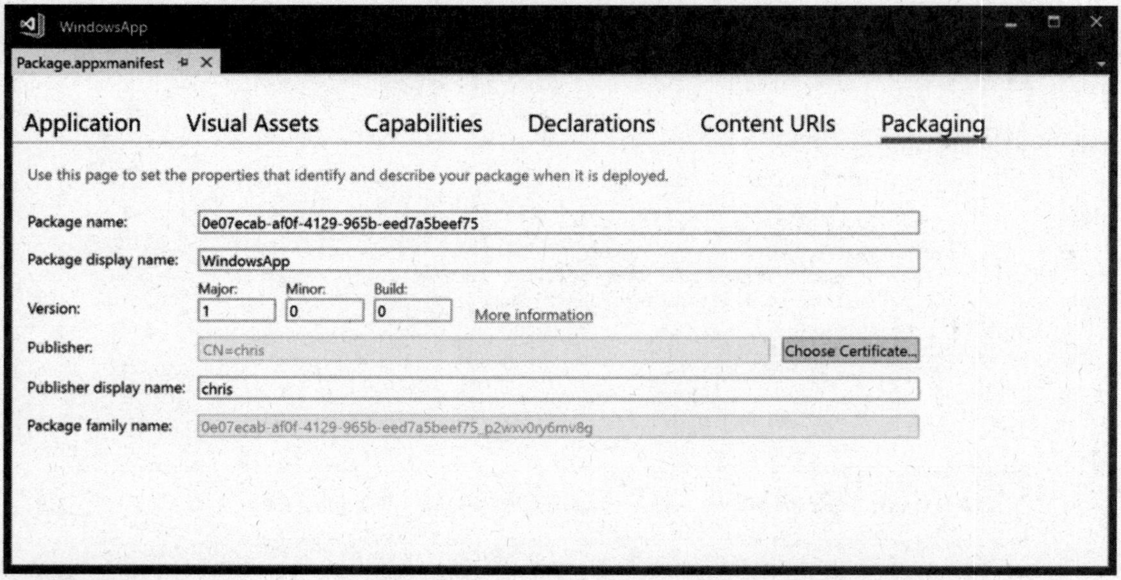

FIGURE 28-11

The test is defined in the test method EnterTextAndButtonClick. First, you launch the application using the previously defined automation ID of the app. Next, the Text property of the TextBox control is filled by setting the `Text` property of the automation peer `XamlEdit` control. Gestures such as button clicks are done with the `Gesture` class. `Gesture.Tap` taps or clicks into a control; with the code snippet the control that is clicked into is selected by using the `UIClickMeButton`, which is the associated `XamlButton` peer control. Finally, the text is read from the `TextBlock` associated `XamlText` control (code file `WindowsApp/WindowsApp.UITest/MainPageTest.cs`):

```
[TestMethod]
public void EnterTextAndButtonClick()
{
  string inText = "Hello, Windows!";
  XamlWindow xamlWindow = XamlWindow.Launch(TileAutomationId);
  UIMap.UIWindowsAppWindow.UITextInEdit.Text = inText;
  Gesture.Tap(UIMap.UIWindowsAppWindow.UIClickMeButton);
  string outText = UIMap.UIWindowsAppWindow.UITextOutText.DisplayText;
  xamlWindow.Close();
  Assert.AreEqual(inText, outText);
}
```

Now you can run the UI test in the same way you run the unit tests, as shown earlier in this chapter.

WEB INTEGRATION, LOAD, AND PERFORMANCE TESTING

To test web applications, you can create unit tests that invoke methods of the controllers, repository, and utility classes. Tag helpers are simple methods in which the test can be covered by unit tests. Unit tests are used to test the functionality of the algorithms of the methods—in other words, the logic inside the methods. With web applications, it is also a good practice to create integration, performance, and load tests. Does everything work together? Does the application scale? How many users can the application support with one server? How many servers are needed to support a specific number of users? Which bottleneck is not that easy to scale? To answer these questions, Web tests can help.

ASP.NET Core offers a hosting class to create integration tests. Visual Studio Enterprise 2017 offers the Web Load and Performance Tests with a recorder to record HTTP requests. The recorder needs an add-in within Internet Explorer.

ASP.NET Core Integration Tests

With integration tests, you test everything about the web app from the HTTP request to the back end. You should have a lot more unit tests than integration tests. You probably have thousands of unit tests, but only a few integration tests. If the same functionality could be covered either by unit or integration tests, you should choose unit tests. The Visual Studio feature Live Unit Testing is useful to run with unit tests, but you shouldn't use this with integration tests. Integration tests are needed to have the complete picture, to see how everything runs from the front end to the back end.

To create an ASP.NET Core integration test, create an ASP.NET Core Web Application named `ASPNETCoreSample` with the Empty template. Running the application from the generated code returns the string "`Hello World!`", and this will be tested from an integration test using xUnit.

> **NOTE** *ASP.NET Core is covered in detail in the Chapters 30 to 32 and Bonus Chapter 3, which you can find online.*

The xUnit project `ASPNETCoreSample.IntegrationTest` needs a package reference to `Microsoft.AspNetCore.TestHost`. This package contains the `TestServer` class to host and start the web application and to send requests. A reference to the web project `ASPNETCoreSample` is needed as well.

A common arrangement of the integration tests is handled in the constructor. Here the `TestServer` is instantiated, passing an `IWebHostBuilder` to the constructor of the `TestServer` class. You need to do a

similar setup as in your `Program.cs` file from the ASP.NET Core web application to enable the same configuration files, and the same middleware (code file `ASPNETCoreSample/ASPNETCoreSample`
`.IntegrationTest/AspNetCoreSampleTest.cs`):

```
public class ASPNETCoreSampleTest : IDisposable
{
  private TestServer _testServer;

  public ASPNETCoreSampleTest()
  {
    _testServer = new TestServer(
      WebHost.CreateDefaultBuilder().UseStartup<Startup>());
  }

  public void Dispose() => _testServer?.Dispose();

  //...
}
```

In the integration test, using the `_testServer` variable you can create a request to the Home page, and invoke the `GetAsync` method of the returned `RequestBuilder`. The returned `HttpResponseMessage` is checked for a successful status code before the content is read using `ReadAsStringAsync` from the `Content` property. In the assert section, the result is compared with the expected string (code file `ASPNETCoreSample/ASPNETCoreSample.IntegrationTest/AspNetCoreSampleTest.cs`):

```
[Fact]
public async Task ReturnHelloWorld()
{
  // act
  RequestBuilder requestBuilder = _testServer.CreateRequest("/");
  HttpResponseMessage response = await requestBuilder.GetAsync();
  response.EnsureSuccessStatusCode();

  var responseString = await response.Content.ReadAsStringAsync();

  // assert
  Assert.Equal("Hello World!", responseString);
}
```

With the `RequestBuilder` class you can create HTTP GET, POST, PUT... requests, and add HTTP header information. The result of the `GetAsync` method looks like the results from the `HttpClient` class in Chapter 23, "Networking." Indeed, you can directly access the `HttpClient` class from the `TestServer` by invoking the `CreateClient` method. The method `CreateWebSocketClient` returns a `WebSocketClient` instance, thus you can also create WebSocket requests. WebSockets are covered in Bonus Chapter 3, "WebHooks and SignalR," which you can find online.

Creating the Web Test

Now that you've created an integration test for ASP.NET Core, let's move into a feature of Visual Studio Enterprise 2017, Web Performance and Load Tests.

For creating a web test, you can create a new ASP.NET Core Web Application by selecting Web Application (Model-View-Controller), and making sure Authentication is set to Individual User Accounts. This template has functionality built in that allows for creating tests. Before creating the web tests, start the application and register a user with the application.

To create web tests, you add a Web Performance and Load Test Project named `WebAndLoadTest` to the solution. Click the generated file `WebTest1.webtest` file to open the Web Test Editor. Then start a web recording by clicking the Add Recording button. For this recording, you must have the Web Test Recorder add-in with Internet Explorer that's installed with the installation of Visual Studio. The recorder records all HTTP requests sent to the server. Click some links on the `WebApplicationSample` web application such as About and Contact and register a new user. Then click the Stop button to stop the recording.

After the recording is finished, you can edit the recording with the Web Test Editor. A recording is shown in Figure 28-12. With all the requests, you can see header information as well as form POST data that you can influence and change.

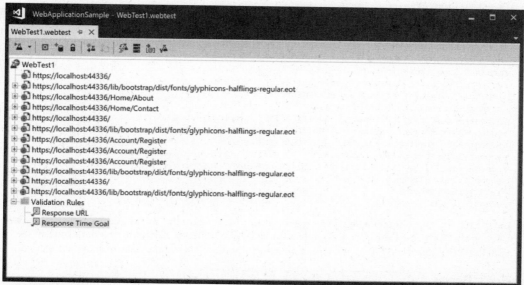

FIGURE 28-12

Delete the recordings you don't need, and then click the Generate Code button with the test name `NavigateAndRegisterTest` to generate source code to send all the requests programmatically. With web tests, the test class derives from the base class `WebTest` and overrides the `GetRequestEnumerator` method. This method returns one request after the other (code file `WebApplicationSample/WebAndLoadTest/NavigateAndRegisterTest.cs`):

```
public class NavigateAndRegisterTest: WebTest
{
  public NavigateAndRegister()
  {
    this.PreAuthenticate = true;
    this.Proxy = "default";
  }

  public override IEnumerator<WebTestRequest> GetRequestEnumerator()
  {
    //...
  }
}
```

The method `GetRequestEnumerator` defines requests to the website—for example, a request to the About page. With this request, an HTTP header is added to define that the request originates from the home page:

```
public override IEnumerator<WebTestRequest> GetRequestEnumerator()
{
  //...
  WebTestRequest request2 =
    new WebTestRequest("http://localhost:44336/Home/About");
```

```
    request2.ThinkTime = 1;
    request2.Headers.Add(new WebTestRequestHeader("Referer",
      "http://localhost:44336/"));
    yield return request2;
    request2 = null;
    //...
  }
```

And this is the request to send an HTTP POST request to the `Register` page that is passing form data:

```
WebTestRequest request6 =
  new WebTestRequest("http://localhost:44336/Account/Register");
  request6.Method = "POST";
  request6.ExpectedResponseUrl = "http://localhost:44336/";
  request6.Headers.Add(new WebTestRequestHeader("Referer",
    "http://localhost:44336/Account/Register"));
  FormPostHttpBody request6Body = new FormPostHttpBody();
  request6Body.FormPostParameters.Add("Email", "sample1@test.com");
  request6Body.FormPostParameters.Add("Password", "Pa$$w0rd");
  request6Body.FormPostParameters.Add("ConfirmPassword", "Pa$$w0rd");
  request6Body.FormPostParameters.Add("__RequestVerificationToken",
  this.Context["$HIDDEN1.__RequestVerificationToken"].ToString());
  request6.Body = request6Body;
  yield return request6;
  request6 = null;
```

With some data you enter in forms, it can be a good idea to add flexibility by taking the data from a data source. Using the Web Test Editor, you can add a database, CSV file, or XML file as a data source (see Figure 28-13). With this dialog box, you can change form parameters to take data from a data source.

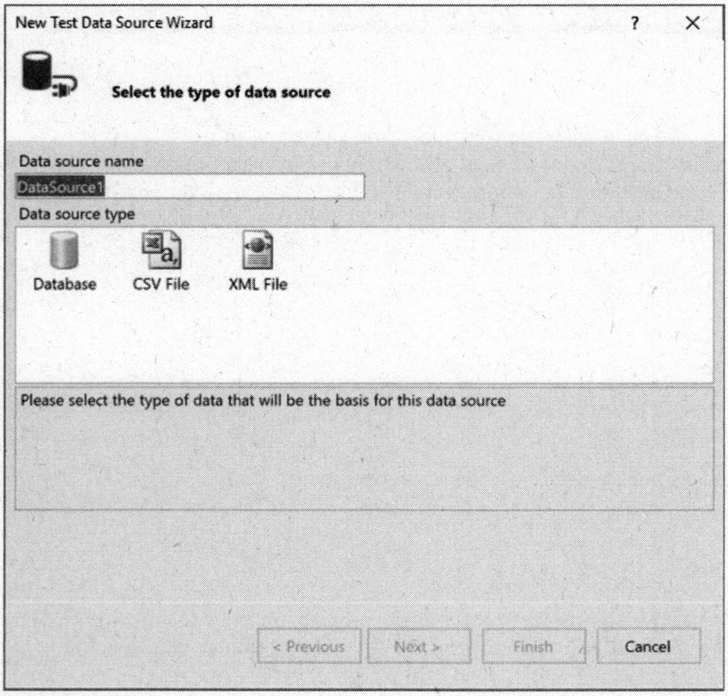

FIGURE 28-13

Adding a data source modifies the testing code. With a data source, the test class is annotated with the `DeploymentItem` attribute (if a CSV or XML file is used), and with `DataSource` and `DataBinding` attributes:

```
[DeploymentItem("webandloadtestproject\\EmailTests.csv",
  "webandloadtestproject")]
[DataSource("EmailDataSource",
  "Microsoft.VisualStudio.TestTools.DataSource.CSV",
  "|DataDirectory|\\webandloadtestproject\\EmailTests.csv",
  Microsoft.VisualStudio.TestTools.WebTesting.DataBindingAccessMethod
    .Sequential,
  Microsoft.VisualStudio.TestTools.WebTesting.DataBindingSelectColumns
    .SelectOnlyBoundColumns, "EmailTests#csv")]
[DataBinding("EmailDataSource", "EmailTests#csv", "sample1@test#com",
  "EmailDataSource.EmailTests#csv.sample1@test#com")]
public class NavigateAndRegister1: WebTest
{
  //...
}
```

Now, in the code the data source can be accessed using the `Context` property of the `WebTest` that returns a `WebTestContext` to access the required data source via an index:

```
request6Body.FormPostParameters.Add("Email",
  this.Context["EmailDataSource.EmailTests#csv.sample1@test#com"].ToString());
```

Running the Web Test

With the tests in place, the testing can start. You can run—and debug—the test directly from the Web Test Editor. Remember to start the web application before you start the test. When you run the test from the Web Test Editor, you can see the resulting web pages as well as the detail information about requests and responses, as shown in Figure 28-14.

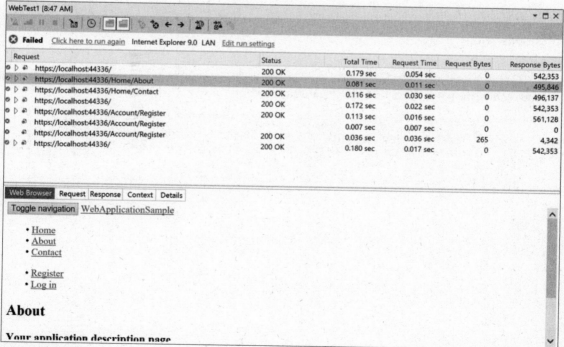

FIGURE 28-14

Using Web Load Tests, you can simulate a high load on the web application. Clicking on the solution item `Local.testsettings`, you can select to run the tests on Visual Studio Team Services for running the tests on multiple servers (see Figure 28-15). For the sample, we'll stay on the local machine.

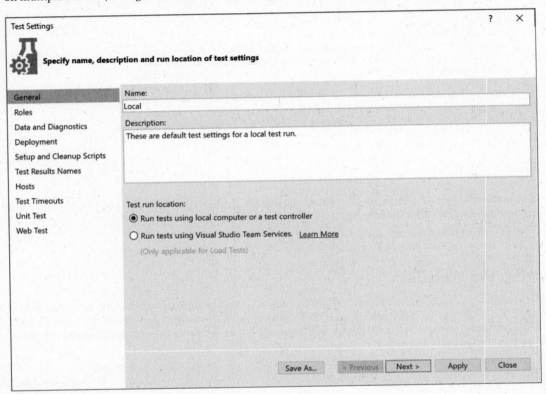

FIGURE 28-15

In the Web Test dialog, you can influence the test runs by specifying a browser type, simulating think times, and running the test multiple times (see Figure 28-16).

> **NOTE** *Load testing of web apps with Visual Studio requires the Enterprise edition of Visual Studio. If you don't have the Enterprise edition, you can check an alternative: Selenium—*`http://www.seleniumhq.org/`.

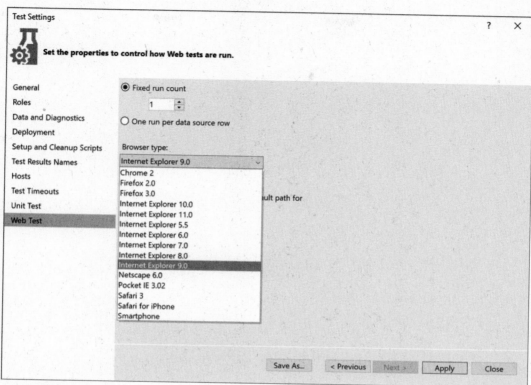

FIGURE 28-16

SUMMARY

In this chapter, you've seen the most important aspects about testing applications: creating unit tests, coded UI tests, and Web tests.

Visual Studio offers a Test Explorer to run unit tests, no matter whether they have been created using MSTest or xUnit. This chapter also showed you triple A in action: Arrange, Act, and Assert.

With coded UI tests, you've seen how to create recordings and adapt the recordings to modify the UI testing code as needed.

With ASP.NET Core Web applications, you've seen how the TestHost class can be used for integration tests, and this chapter gave you an introduction to the web load and performance tests from Visual Studio.

Although testing helps with fixing issues with applications before they are deployed, Chapter 29, "Tracing, Logging, and Analytics," helps you fix applications that are running.

29

Tracing, Logging, and Analytics

WHAT'S IN THIS CHAPTER?

➤ Simple tracing with EventSource

➤ Advanced tracing with EventSource

➤ Creating a custom trace listener

➤ Using the ILogger interface

➤ Using Visual Studio App Center with Windows apps

WROX.COM CODE DOWNLOADS FOR THIS CHAPTER

The Wrox.com code downloads for this chapter are found at www.wrox.com on the Download Code tab. The source code is also available at https://github.com/ProfessionalCSharp/ProfessionalCSharp7 in the directory Diagnostics.

The code for this chapter is divided into the following major examples:

➤ SimpleEventSourceSample

➤ EventSourceSampleInheritance

➤ EventSourceSampleAnnotations

➤ ClientApp/MyApplicationEvents

➤ LoggingSample

➤ WinAppAnalytics

DIAGNOSTICS OVERVIEW

As release cycles for applications become faster and faster, it's becoming more and more important to learn how the application behaves while it's running in production. What exceptions are occurring? Knowing what features are used is also of interest. Do users find the new feature of the app? How long do they stay in the page? To answer these questions, you need real-time information on the application.

When you're getting information about the application, you need to differ logging, tracing, and analytics. With logging, error information is recorded in centralized places. This information is used by system administrators to find out issues with applications. Tracing helps to find out which method is called by which method. This information is useful for development, and you should turn it off when the application runs in production. With .NET, the same technology can be used for logging and tracing using classes from the `System.Diagnostics` namespace. Analytics gives information about the users, where they reside, what operating system version they use, and what features they use in the application. This helps to know if there are some issues with the application based on a location, hardware, or an operating system, and it also helps to understand what the users are doing. Users might not find a new feature of the application if it's hard to find out about this feature.

This chapter explains how to get real-time information about your running application to identify any issues that it might have during production or to monitor resource usage to ensure that higher user loads can be accommodated. This is where the namespace `System.Diagnostics.Tracing` comes into play. This namespace offers classes for tracing using Event Tracing for Windows (ETW).

One way to deal with errors in your application, of course, is by throwing exceptions. However, an application might not fail with an exception, but it still doesn't behave as expected. The application might be running well on most systems but have a problem on a few. On the live system, you can change the log by starting a trace collector and get detailed live information about what's going on in the application. You can do this using ETW.

If there are problems with applications, the system administrator needs to be informed. The *Event Viewer* is a commonly used tool that not only the system administrator should be aware of but also the software developer. With the Event Viewer, you can both interactively monitor problems with applications and can add subscriptions to be informed about specific events that happen. ETW enables you to write information about the application.

Application Insights is a Microsoft Azure cloud service that enables you to monitor apps in the cloud. With just a few lines of code, you can get detailed information about how a web application or service is used.

Visual Studio App Center allows monitoring of Windows and Xamarin apps. After you've registered the app, you just need a few lines of code to receive useful information about the app.

This chapter explains these facilities and demonstrates how you can use them for your applications.

TRACING WITH EVENTSOURCE

Tracing enables you to see informational messages about the running application. To get information about a running application, you can start the application in the debugger. During debugging, you can walk through the application step by step and set breakpoints at specific lines and when you reach specific conditions. The problem with debugging is that a program with release code can behave differently from a program with debug code. For example, while the program is stopping at a breakpoint, other threads of the application are suspended as well. Also, with a release build, the compiler-generated output is optimized and, thus, different effects can occur. With optimized release code, garbage collection is much more aggressive than with debug code. The order of calls within a method can be changed, and some methods can be removed completely and be called in place. There is a need to have runtime information from the release build of a program as well. Trace messages are written with both debug and release code.

A scenario showing how tracing helps is described here. After an application is deployed, it runs on one system without problems, whereas on another system intermittent problems occur. When you enable verbose tracing, the system with the problems gives you detailed information about what's happening inside the application. The system that is running without problems has tracing configured just for error messages redirected to the Windows event log system. Critical errors are seen by the system administrator. The overhead of tracing is very small because you configure a trace level only when needed.

Tracing has quite a history with .NET. After a simple tracing functionality with the first version of .NET and the `Trace` class, .NET 2.0 made huge improvements on tracing and introduced the `TraceSource` class. The architecture behind `TraceSource` is very flexible in separating the source, the listener, and a switch to turn tracing on and off based on a list of trace levels.

Starting with .NET 4.5, again a new tracing class was introduced and enhanced with .NET 4.6: the `EventSource` class. This class is defined in the `System.Diagnostics.Tracing` namespace in the NuGet package `Sytem.Diagnostics`.

The new tracing architecture is based on Event Tracing for Windows (ETW), which was introduced with Windows Vista. It allows for fast system-wide messaging that is also used by the Windows event-logging and performance-monitoring facilities.

Let's get into the concepts of ETW tracing and the `EventSource` class.

> An **ETW provider** is a library that fires ETW events. The applications created with this chapter are ETW providers.

> An **ETW manifest** describes the events that can be fired from ETW providers. Using a predefined manifest has the advantage that the system administrator already knows what events an application can fire as soon as the application is installed. This way the administrator can already configure listening for specific events. The new version of the `EventSource` allows both self-describing events and events described by a manifest.

> **ETW keywords** can be used to create categories for events. They are defined as bit-flags.

> **ETW tasks** are another way to group events. Tasks can be created to define events based on different scenarios of the program. Tasks are usually used with opcodes.

> **ETW opcodes** identify operations within a task. Both tasks and opcodes are defined with integer values.

> An **event source** is the class that fires events. You can either use the `EventSource` class directly or create a class that derives from the base class `EventSource`.

> An **event method** is a method of the event source that fires events. Deriving from the class `EventSource`, every void method is an event method if it is not annotated with the `NonEvent` attribute. Event methods can be annotated with the `Event` attribute.

> The **event level** defines the severity or verbosity of an event. This can be used to differ between critical, error, warning, informational, and verbose events.

> **ETW channels** are sinks for events. Events can be written to channels and log files. Admin, Operational, Analytic, and Debug are predefined channels.

Using the `EventSource` class, you will see the ETW concepts in action.

Examining a Simple Use of EventSource

The sample code using the `EventSource` class makes use of these namespaces:

```
System

System.Collections.Generic

System.Diagnostics.Tracing

System.IO

System.Net.Http

System.Threading.Tasks
```

The `EventSource` class offers various ways to use it. There's a simple way when instantiating this class and invoking methods for logging, and a more advanced way when using it as a base class. There's also a way of adding annotations.

The first example for using `EventSource` shows a simple case that is useful in small projects. `EventSource` is instantiated as a static member of the `Program` class with a Console App (.NET Core) project. With the constructor, the name of the event source is specified (code file `SimpleEventSourceSample/Program.cs`):

```
private static EventSource sampleEventSource =
    new EventSource("Wrox-EventSourceSample1");
```

With the `Main` method of the `Program` class, the unique identifier of the event source is retrieved using the `Guid` property. This identifier is created based on the name of the event source. After this, the first event is written to invoke the `Write` method of `EventSource`. The parameter required is the event name that needs to be passed. Other parameters are available with overloads of the object. The second parameter that is passed is an anonymous object defining the `Info` property. This can be used to pass any information about the event to the event log (code file `SimpleEventSourceSample/Program.cs`):

```
static async Task Main()
{
    Console.WriteLine($"Log Guid: {sampleEventSource.Guid}");
    Console.WriteLine($"Name: {sampleEventSource.Name}");
    sampleEventSource.Write("Startup", new { Info = "started app" });
    await NetworkRequestSampleAsync();
    Console.ReadLine();
    sampleEventSource?.Dispose();
}
```

> **NOTE** *Instead of passing an anonymous object with custom data to the* `EventSource.Write` *method, you can create a class that derives from the base class* `EventSource` *and mark it with the attribute* `EventData`. *This attribute is shown later in this chapter.*

The method `NetworkRequestSampleAsync` that is invoked from the `Main` method makes a network request and writes a trace log passing the URL that is requested to the trace information. On completion of the network call, trace information is written again. The exception-handling code shows another method overload on writing trace information. Different overloads allow passing specific information that is shown in the next sections. The following code snippet shows `EventSourceOptions` setting a trace level. The `Error` event level is set by writing error information. This level can be used to filter specific trace information. With filtering you can decide to read just error information—for example, information with the error level and information that is more critical than the error level. During another tracing session you can decide to read all trace information using the verbose level. The `EventLevel` enumeration defines the values `LogAlways`, `Critical`, `Error`, `Warning`, `Informational`, and `Verbose` (code file `SimpleEventSourceSample/Program.cs`):

```
private static async Task NetworkRequestSample()
{
    try
    {
        using (var client = new HttpClient())
        {
            string url = "http://www.cninnovation.com";
            sampleEventSource.Write("Network", new { Info = $"requesting {url}" });
            string result = await client.GetStringAsync(url);
            sampleEventSource.Write("Network",
                new
                {
                    Info =
                        $"completed call to {url}, result string length: {result.Length}"
```

```
            });
        }
        Console.WriteLine("Complete................");
    }
    catch (Exception ex)
    {
        sampleEventSource.Write("Network Error",
            new EventSourceOptions { Level = EventLevel.Error },
            new { Message = ex.Message, Result = ex.HResult });
        Console.WriteLine(ex.Message);
    }
}}
```

Before you run the application, you need to do some preparation: download and configure tools you use for reading the traces. The next section explains how to do this.

Understanding Tools for Tracing

For analyzing trace information, several tools are available. *logman* is a tool that is part of Windows. With logman you can create and manage event trace sessions and write ETW traces to a binary log file. *tracerpt* is also available with Windows. This tool enables you to convert the binary information written from logman to a CSV, XML, or EVTX file format. PerfView is a tool that offers graphical information for ETW traces.

Logman

Let's begin using logman to create a trace session from the previously created application. You need to first start the application to copy the GUID that's created for the application. You need this GUID to start a log session with `logman`. The `start` option starts a new session to log. The `-p` option defines the name of the provider; here the GUID is used to identify the provider. The `-o` option defines the output file, and the `-ets` option sends the command directly to the event trace system without scheduling. Be sure to start `logman` in a directory where you have write access; otherwise it fails to write the output file `mytrace.etl`:

```
logman start mysession -p {3b0e7fa6-0346-5781-db55-49d84d7103de}
-o mytrace.etl -ets
```

After running the application, you can stop the trace session with the `stop` command:

```
logman stop mysession -ets
```

> **NOTE** *logman has a lot more commands that are not covered here. Using logman, you can see all the installed ETW trace providers and their names and identifiers, create data collectors to start and stop at specified times, define maximum log file sizes, and more. You can see the different options of logman with* `logman -h`.

Tracerpt

The log file is in a binary format. To get a readable representation, you can use the utility `tracerpt`. With this tool, it's possible to extract CSV, XML, and EVTX formats, as specified with the `-of` option:

```
tracerpt mytrace.etl -o mytrace.xml -of XML
```

Now the information is available in a readable format. With the information that is logged by the application, you can see the event name passed to the `EventSource.Write` method manifests within the `Task` element, and you can find the anonymous object within the `EventData` element:

```
<Event xmlns="http://schemas.microsoft.com/win/2004/08/events/event">
  <System>
    <Provider Name="Wrox-SimpleEventSourceSample"
      Guid="{3b0e7fa6-0346-5781-db55-49d84d7103de}" />
```

```
    <EventID>2</EventID>
    <Version>0</Version>
    <Level>5</Level>
    <Task>0</Task>
    <Opcode>0</Opcode>
    <Keywords>0x0</Keywords>
    <TimeCreated SystemTime="2017-12-23T10:42:07.960330900+00:59" />
    <Correlation ActivityID="{00000000-0000-0000-0000-000000000000}" />
    <Execution ProcessID="12700" ThreadID="19340" ProcessorID="1"
      KernelTime="30" UserTime="15" />
    <Channel />
    <Computer />
  </System>
  <EventData>
    <Data Name="Info">started app</Data>
  </EventData>
  <RenderingInfo Culture="en-US">
    <Task>Startup</Task>
  </RenderingInfo>
</Event>
```

The error information is shown with the trace as shown here:

```
<EventData>
  <Data Name="Message">An error occurred while sending the request.</Data>
  <Data Name="Result">-2146233088</Data>
</EventData>
```

PerfView

Another tool to read trace information is PerfView. You can download this tool from the Microsoft downloads page https://www.microsoft.com/download/details.aspx?id=28567). Version 1.9 of this tool has great enhancements for using it with Visual Studio and the self-describing ETW format from EventSource. This tool doesn't need to be installed; just copy the tool where you need it. After you start this tool, it makes use of the subdirectories where it is located and allows directly opening the binary ETL file. Figure 29-1 shows PerfView opening the file mytrace.etl created by logman.

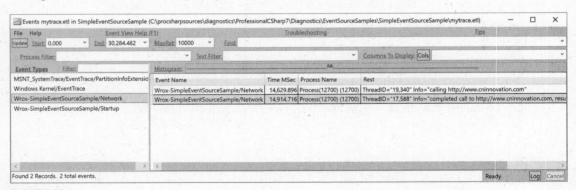

FIGURE 29-1

Deriving from EventSource

Instead of directly using an instance of EventSource, all the information that could be traced can be defined in a single place. For many applications, it's enough to define just one event source. This event source can be defined in a separate logging assembly. The event source class needs to derive from the base class EventSource. With this custom class, all the trace information that should be written can be defined by separate methods that invoke the WriteEvent method of the base class. The class is implemented with the Singleton pattern, which offers a static Log property that returns an instance. Naming this property Log is a convention used with event sources. The private constructor calls the constructor of the base class to set the event source name (code file EventSourceSampleInheritance/SampleEventSource .cs):

```csharp
public class SampleEventSource : EventSource
{
  private SampleEventSource()
    : base("Wrox-SampleEventSource2") { }

  public static SampleEventSource Log = new SampleEventSource();

  public void Startup() => WriteEvent(1);

  public void CallService(string url) => WriteEvent(2, url);

  public void CalledService(string url, int length) =>
    WriteEvent(3, url, length);


  public void ServiceError(string message, int error) =>
    WriteEvent(4, message, error);
}
```

All the void methods of an event source class are used to write event information. In case you're defining a helper method, it needs to be annotated with the NonEvent attribute.

In a simple scenario where only information messages should be written, nothing more is necessary. Besides passing an event ID to the trace log, the WriteEvent method has 18 overloads that allow passing message strings, int, and long values, and any number of objects.

With this implementation, you can use the members of the SampleEventSource type to write trace messages as shown in the Program class. The Main method makes a trace log calling the Startup method, invokes the NetworkRequestSample method to create a trace log via the CallService method, and makes a trace log in case of an error (code file EventSourceSampleInheritance/Program.cs):

```csharp
public class Program
{
  Static async Task Main()
  {
    SampleEventSource.Log.Startup();
    Console.WriteLine($"Log Guid: {SampleEventSource.Log.Guid}");
    Console.WriteLine($"Name: {SampleEventSource.Log.Name}");
    await NetworkRequestSampleAsync();
    Console.ReadLine();
  }

  private static async Task NetworkRequestSampleAsync()
  {
    try
    {
      var client = new HttpClient();
      string url = "http://www.cninnovation.com";
      SampleEventSource.Log.CallService(url);
      string result = await client.GetStringAsync(url);
      SampleEventSource.Log.CalledService(url, result.Length);
      Console.WriteLine("Complete................");
    }
    catch (Exception ex)
```

```
    {
        SampleEventSource.Log.ServiceError(ex.Message, ex.HResult);
        Console.WriteLine(ex.Message);
    }
  }
}
```

When you run the app with these commands with a developer command prompt from the directory of the project, you produce an XML file that contains information about the traces:

```
> logman start mysession -p "{1cedea2a-a420-5660-1ff0-f718b8ea5138}"
  -o log2.etl -ets
> dotnet run
> logman stop mysession -ets
> tracerpt log2.etl -o log2.xml -of XML
```

The event information about the service call is shown here:

```
<Event xmlns="http://schemas.microsoft.com/win/2004/08/events/event">
  <System>
    <Provider Name="Wrox-SampleEventSource2"
      Guid="{1cedea2a-a420-5660-1ff0-f718b8ea5138}" />
    <EventID>7</EventID>
    <Version>0</Version>
    <Level>4</Level>
    <Task>0</Task>
    <Opcode>0</Opcode>
    <Keywords>0xF00000000000</Keywords>
    <TimeCreated SystemTime="2017-12-23T13:32:59.015066500+00:59" />
    <Correlation ActivityID="{00000000-0000-0000-0000-000000000000}" />
    <Execution ProcessID="6196" ThreadID="36392" ProcessorID="0"
      KernelTime="30" UserTime="45" />
    <Channel />
    <Computer />
  </System>
  <EventData>
    <Data Name="url">http://www.cninnovation.com</Data>
  </EventData>
  <RenderingInfo Culture="en-US">
    <Task>CallService</Task>
  </RenderingInfo>
</Event>
```

Using Annotations with EventSource

Creating an event source class that derives from EventSource, you have more control on defining the trace information. You can add annotations to the methods by using attributes.

By default, the name of the event source is the same as the name of the class, but you can change the name and the unique identifier by applying the EventSource attribute. Every event trace method can be accompanied by the Event attribute. Here you can define the ID of the event, an opcode, the trace level, custom keywords, and tasks. This information is used to create manifest information for Windows to define what information is logged. The base methods WriteEvent that are called within the methods using the EventSource need to match the event ID defined by the Event attribute, and the variable names passed to the WriteEvent methods need to match the argument names of the declared method.

With the sample class SampleEventSource, custom keywords are defined by the inner class Keywords. The members of this class are cast to the enumeration type EventKeywords. EventKeywords is a flag-based enum of type long that defines only values with upper bits starting with bit 42. You can use all the lower bits to define custom keywords. The Keywords class defines values for the lowest four bits set to Network, Database, Diagnostics, and Performance. The enum EventTask is a similar flags-based enumeration.

Contrary to `EventKeywords`, an int is enough for its backing store, and `EventTask` doesn't have predefined values (only the enumeration value `None = 0` is predefined). Like the `Keywords` class, the `Task` class defines custom tasks for the `EventTask` enumeration (code file `EventSourceSampleAnnotations/SampleEventSource.cs`):

```csharp
class SampleEventSource : EventSource
{
  public class Keywords
  {
    public const EventKeywords Network = (EventKeywords)1;
    public const EventKeywords Database = (EventKeywords)2;
    public const EventKeywords Diagnostics = (EventKeywords)4;
    public const EventKeywords Performance = (EventKeywords)8;
  }

  public class Tasks
  {
    public const EventTask CreateMenus = (EventTask)1;
    public const EventTask QueryMenus = (EventTask)2;
  }

  private SampleEventSource()
  {
  }

  public static SampleEventSource Log = new SampleEventSource ();

  [Event(1, Opcode=EventOpcode.Start, Level=EventLevel.Verbose)]
  public void Startup() => WriteEvent(1);

  [Event(2, Opcode=EventOpcode.Info, Keywords=Keywords.Network,
    Level=EventLevel.Verbose, Message="{0}")]
  public void CallService(string url) => WriteEvent(2, url);

  [Event(3, Opcode=EventOpcode.Info, Keywords=Keywords.Network,
    Level=EventLevel.Verbose, Message="{0}, length: {1}")]
  public void CalledService(string url, int length) =>
    WriteEvent(3, url, length);

  [Event(4, Opcode=EventOpcode.Info, Keywords=Keywords.Network,
    Level=EventLevel.Error, Message="{0} error: {1}")]
  public void ServiceError(string message, int error) =>
    WriteEvent(4, message, error);

  [Event(5, Opcode=EventOpcode.Info, Task=Tasks.CreateMenus,
    Level=EventLevel.Verbose, Keywords=Keywords.Network)]
  public void SomeTask() => WriteEvent(5);
}
```

The `Program` class to write these events is unchanged. The information from these events can now be used on using a listener and filtering only events for specific keywords, for specific log levels, or for specific tasks. You see how to create listeners later in this chapter in the "Creating Custom Listeners" section.

Creating Event Manifest Schema

Creating a custom event source class has the advantage that you can create a manifest that describes all the trace information. Using the `EventSource` class without inheritance, the `Settings` property is set to the value `EtwSelfDescribingEventFormat` of the enumeration `EventSourceSettings`. The events are directly described by the methods invoked. When you use a class that inherits from `EventSource`, the `Settings` property has the value `EtwManifestEventFormat`. The event information is described by a manifest.

You can create the manifest file by using the static method `GenerateManifest` of the `EventSource` class. The first parameter defines the class of the event source; the second parameter describes the path of the assembly that contains the event source type (code file `EventSourceSampleAnnotations/Program.cs`):

```
public static void GenerateManifest()
{
  string schema = SampleEventSource.GenerateManifest(
    typeof(SampleEventSource), ".");
  File.WriteAllText("sampleeventsource.xml", schema);
}
```

This is the manifest information containing tasks, keywords, events, and templates for the event messages (code file `EventSourceSampleAnnotations/sampleeventsource.xml`):

```
<instrumentationManifest
  xmlns="http://schemas.microsoft.com/win/2004/08/events">
  <instrumentation xmlns:xs="http://www.w3.org/2001/XMLSchema"
    xmlns:xsi="http://www.w3.org/2001/XMLSchema-instance"
    xmlns:win="http://manifests.microsoft.com/win/2004/08/windows/events">
    <events xmlns="http://schemas.microsoft.com/win/2004/08/events">
      <provider name="EventSourceSample"
        guid="{45fff0e2-7198-4e4f-9fc3-df6934680096}" resourceFileName="."
        messageFileName="." symbol="EventSourceSample">
        <tasks>
          <task name="CreateMenus" message="$(string.task_CreateMenus)"
            value="1"/>
          <task name="QueryMenus" message="$(string.task_QueryMenus)"
            value="2"/>
          <task name="ServiceError" message="$(string.task_ServiceError)"
            value="65530"/>
          <task name="CalledService" message="$(string.task_CalledService)"
            value="65531"/>
          <task name="CallService" message="$(string.task_CallService)"
            value="65532"/>
          <task name="EventSourceMessage"
            message="$(string.task_EventSourceMessage)" value="65534"/>
        </tasks>
        <opcodes>
        </opcodes>
        <keywords>
          <keyword name="Network" message="$(string.keyword_Network)"
            mask="0x1"/>
          <keyword name="Database" message="$(string.keyword_Database)"
            mask="0x2"/>
          <keyword name="Diagnostics" message="$(string.keyword_Diagnostics)"
            mask="0x4"/>
          <keyword name="Performance" message="$(string.keyword_Performance)"
            mask="0x8"/>
          <keyword name="Session3" message="$(string.keyword_Session3)"
            mask="0x100000000000"/>
          <keyword name="Session2" message="$(string.keyword_Session2)"
            mask="0x200000000000"/>
          <keyword name="Session1" message="$(string.keyword_Session1)"
            mask="0x400000000000"/>
          <keyword name="Session0" message="$(string.keyword_Session0)"
            mask="0x800000000000"/>
        </keywords>
        <events>
          <event value="0" version="0" level="win:LogAlways"
            symbol="EventSourceMessage" task="EventSourceMessage"
            template="EventSourceMessageArgs"/>
          <event value="1" version="0" level="win:Verbose" symbol="Startup"
```

```
                opcode="win:Start"/>
            <event value="2" version="0" level="win:Verbose" symbol="CallService"
              message="$(string.event_CallService)" keywords="Network"
              task="CallService" template="CallServiceArgs"/>
            <event value="3" version="0" level="win:Verbose"
              symbol="CalledService" message="$(string.event_CalledService)"
              keywords="Network" task="CalledService"
              template="CalledServiceArgs"/>
            <event value="4" version="0" level="win:Error" symbol="ServiceError"
              message="$(string.event_ServiceError)" keywords="Network"
              task="ServiceError" template="ServiceErrorArgs"/>
            <event value="5" version="0" level="win:Verbose" symbol="SomeTask"
              keywords="Network" task="CreateMenus"/>
          </events>
          <templates>
            <template tid="EventSourceMessageArgs">
              <data name="message" inType="win:UnicodeString"/>
            </template>
            <template tid="CallServiceArgs">
              <data name="url" inType="win:UnicodeString"/>
            </template>
            <template tid="CalledServiceArgs">
              <data name="url" inType="win:UnicodeString"/>
              <data name="length" inType="win:Int32"/>
            </template>
            <template tid="ServiceErrorArgs">
              <data name="message" inType="win:UnicodeString"/>
              <data name="error" inType="win:Int32"/>
            </template>
          </templates>
        </provider>
      </events>
    </instrumentation>
    <localization>
      <resources culture="en-US">
        <stringTable>
          <string id="event_CalledService" value="%1 length: %2"/>
          <string id="event_CallService" value="%1"/>
          <string id="event_ServiceError" value="%1 error: %2"/>
          <string id="keyword_Database" value="Database"/>
          <string id="keyword_Diagnostics" value="Diagnostics"/>
          <string id="keyword_Network" value="Network"/>
          <string id="keyword_Performance" value="Performance"/>
          <string id="keyword_Session0" value="Session0"/>
          <string id="keyword_Session1" value="Session1"/>
          <string id="keyword_Session2" value="Session2"/>
          <string id="keyword_Session3" value="Session3"/>
          <string id="task_CalledService" value="CalledService"/>
          <string id="task_CallService" value="CallService"/>
          <string id="task_CreateMenus" value="CreateMenus"/>
          <string id="task_EventSourceMessage" value="EventSourceMessage"/>
          <string id="task_QueryMenus" value="QueryMenus"/>
          <string id="task_ServiceError" value="ServiceError"/>
        </stringTable>
      </resources>
    </localization>
  </instrumentationManifest>
```

Having this metadata and registering it with the system allows the system administrator to filter for specific events and get notifications when something happens. You can handle registration in two ways: static and dynamic. Static registration requires administrative privileges, and a registration via the wevtutil.exe command-line tool, which passes the DLL that contains the manifest. The EventSource class also offers the preferred dynamic registration. This happens during runtime without the need for administrative privileges returning the manifest in an event stream, or in a response to a standard ETW command.

Using Activity IDs

A new feature of the new version of `TraceSource` makes it possible to easily write activity IDs. As soon as you have multiple tasks running, it helps to know which trace messages belong to each other and not have the trace message based only on time. For example, when you're using tracing with a web application, multiple requests from clients are dealt concurrently when it is good to know which trace messages belong to one request. Such issues don't occur only on the server; the problem is also in the client application as soon as you're running multiple tasks, or when you're using the C# `async` and `await` keywords on calling asynchronous methods. Different tasks come into play.

When you create a class that derives from `TraceSource`, all you have to do to create activity IDs is define methods that are post-fixed with `Start` and `Stop`.

For the sample showing activity IDs in action, a Class Library (.NET Standard) is created. You can use this library from both .NET Framework and .NET Core applications.

Previous versions of .NET don't support the new `TraceSource` features for activity IDs. The `ProcessingStart` and `RequestStart` methods are used to start activities; `ProcessingStop` and `RequestStop` stop activities (code file `MyApplicationEvents/SampleEventSource`):

```
public class SampleEventSource : EventSource
{
  private SampleEventSource()
    : base("Wrox-SampleEventSource") { }

  public static SampleEventSource Log = new SampleEventSource();

  public void ProcessingStart(int x) => WriteEvent(1, x);

  public void Processing(int x) => WriteEvent(2, x);

  public void ProcessingStop(int x) => WriteEvent(3, x);

  public void RequestStart() => WriteEvent(4);

  public void RequestStop() => WriteEvent(5);
}
```

The client application that's writing the events makes use of the following dependency and namespaces:

Dependency

`MyApplicatonEvents`

Namespaces

`System`

`System.Collections.Generic`

`System.Diagnostics.Tracing`

`System.Net.Http`

`System.Threading.Tasks`

The `ParallelRequestSample` method invokes the `RequestStart` and `RequestStop` methods to start and stop the activity. Between these calls, a parallel loop is created using `Parallel.For`. The `Parallel` class uses multiple tasks to run concurrently by calling the delegate of the third parameter. This parameter is implemented as a lambda expression to invoke the `ProcessTaskAsync` method (code file `ClientApp/Program.cs`):

```
private static void ParallelRequestSample()
{
  SampleEventSource.Log.RequestStart();
  Parallel.For(0, 20, async x =>
  {
    await ProcessTaskAsync(x);
  });

  SampleEventSource.Log.RequestStop();
  Console.WriteLine("Activity complete");
}
```

> **NOTE** *The* `Parallel` *class is explained in detail in Chapter 21, "Tasks and Parallel Programming."*

The method `ProcessTaskAsync` writes traces using `ProcessingStart` and `ProcessingStop`. Here, an activity is started within another activity. As you can see from the output analyzing the logs, activities can be hierarchical (code file `ClientApp/Program.cs`):

```
private static async Task ProcessTaskAsync(int x)
{
  SampleEventSource.Log.ProcessingStart(x);
  var r = new Random();
  await Task.Delay(r.Next(500));
  using (var client = new HttpClient())
  {
    var response = await client.GetAsync("http://www.bing.com");
  }
  SampleEventSource.Log.ProcessingStop(x);
}
```

Previously, you have used the PerfView tool to open an ETL log file. PerfView can also analyze running applications. You can run PerfView with the following option:

```
> PerfView /onlyproviders=*Wrox-SampleEventSource collect
```

The option `collect` starts the data collection. Using the qualifier `/onlyproviders` turns off the Kernel and CLR providers and only logs messages from the providers listed. Use the qualifier `-h` to see possible options and qualifiers of PerfView. When you start PerfView this way, data collection starts immediately and continues until you click the Stop Collection button (see Figure 29-2).

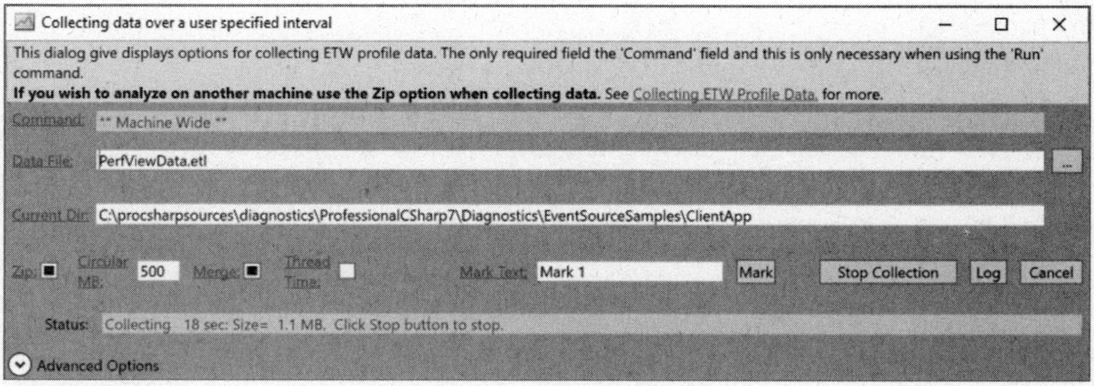

FIGURE 29-2

When you run the application after you've started the trace collection, and then have stopped the collection afterward, you can see activity IDs generated with the event type `Wrox-SampleEventSource/ProcessingStart/Start`. The IDs allow a hierarchy, such as `//1/2` with one parent activity and a child activity. For every loop iteration, you see a different activity ID (see Figure 29-3). With the event type `Wrox-SampleEventSource/ProcessingStop/Stop`, you can see the same activity IDs as they relate to the same activity.

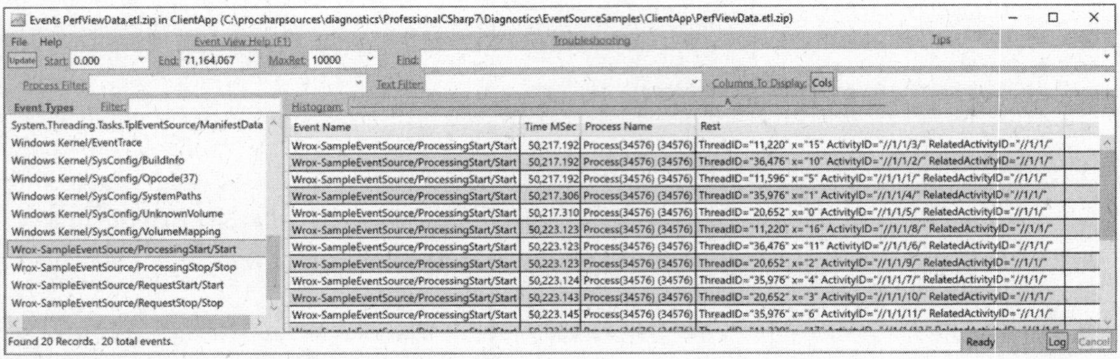

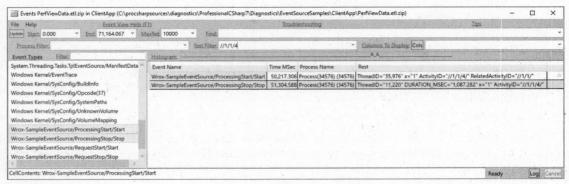

FIGURE 29-3

Using PerfView, you can select multiple event types on the left, and add a filter—for example, `//1/1/4`—so you see all the events that belong to this activity (see Figure 29-4). Here you can see that an activity ID can span multiple threads. The start and stop events from the same activity use different threads.

FIGURE 29-4

CREATING CUSTOM LISTENERS

As you've written trace messages, you've seen how to read them using tools such as logman, tracerpt, and PerfView. You can also create a custom in-process event listener to write the events where you want.

You create custom event listeners by creating a class that derives from the base class `EventListener`. All you need to do is to override the `OnEventWritten` method. With this method, trace messages are passed to the parameter of type `EventWrittenEventArgs`. The sample implementation sends information about the event, including the payload, which is the additional data passed to the `WriteEvent` method of the `EventSource` (code file `ClientApp/MyEventListener.cs`):

```
public class MyEventListener : EventListener
{
  protected override void OnEventSourceCreated(EventSource eventSource)
  {
    Console.WriteLine($"created {eventSource.Name} {eventSource.Guid}");
  }

  protected override void OnEventWritten(EventWrittenEventArgs eventData)
  {
    Console.WriteLine($"event id: {eventData.EventId} source: " +
      $" {eventData.EventSource.Name}");
    foreach (var payload in eventData.Payload)
    {
      Console.WriteLine($"\t{payload}");
    }
  }
}
```

The listener is activated in the `Main` method of the `Program` class. You can access event sources by calling the static method `GetSources` of the `EventSource` class (code file `ClientApp/Program.cs`):

The `InitListener` method invokes the `EnableEvents` method of the custom listener and passes every event source. The sample code registers the setting `EventLevel.LogAlways` to listen to every log message written. You can also specify to just write information messages—which also include errors—or to write errors only.

```
private static void InitListener(IEnumerable<EventSource> sources)
{
  listener = new MyEventListener();
  foreach (var source in sources)
  {
    listener.EnableEvents(source, EventLevel.LogAlways);
  }
}
```

When you run the application, you see events of the `FrameworkEventSource` and the `Wrox-SampleEventSource` written to the console. Using a custom event listener like this, you can easily write events to Application Insights, which is a cloud-based telemetry service that's explained in the next section.

WRITING LOGS WITH THE ILOGGER INTERFACE

Over the years several different logging and tracing facilities in .NET, and there also are many different third-party loggers. Trying to change an application from one logging technology to another one is not an easy task because the use of the logging API is spread throughout the source code. To make logging independent of any logging technology, interfaces can be used.

.NET Core defines the generic `ILogger` interface in the NuGet package `Microsoft.Extensions.Logging`. This interface defines a `Log` method. The `Log` method defines parameters to specify a `LogLevel` (an enumeration value), an event ID (using the struct `EventId`), generic state information, an `Exception` type to log exception information, and a formatter to define how the output should look with a string:

```
void Log<TState>(LogLevel logLevel, EventId eventide, TState state,
  Exception exception, Func<TState, Exception, string> formatter);
```

Other than the `Log` method, the `ILogger` interface also defines the `IsEnabled` method to check whether logging is currently enabled based on a `LogLevel`, and the method `BeginScope` that returns a disposable scope for logging. The members from the `ILogger` interface are really all that's needed for logging. The `Log` method just has many parameters that need to be filled. To make logging easier, extension methods for the `ILogger` interface are defined in the `LoggerExtensions` class. You will see extension methods such as `LogDebug`, `LogTrace`, `LogInformation`, `LogWarning`, `LogError`, `LogCritical`, and `BeginScope` with several overloads and easier-to-use parameters.

Let's make use of dependency injection and inject the `ILogger` interface using the contained class `SampleController` as a generic parameter. The generic parameter defines the category of the logger. With the generic parameter, the category is made of the class name, including the namespace (code file `LoggingSample/SampleController.cs`):

```
class SampleController
{
  private readonly ILogger<SampleController> _logger;
  public SampleController(ILogger<SampleController> logger)
  {
    _logger = logger;
  }
  //...
}
```

In the section "Filtering" you can read how the category name can be used to filter the logs.

> **NOTE** *Dependency injection is discussed in detail in Chapter 20, "Dependency Injection."*

The logging samples make use of the following dependencies and namespaces:

Dependencies

`Microsoft.Extensions.DependencyInjection`

`Microsoft.Extensions.Logging`

`Microsoft.Extensions.Logging.Configuration`

`Microsoft.Extensions.Logging.Console`

`Microsoft.Extensions.Logging.Debug`

`Microsoft.Extensions.Logging.EventSource`

`Microsoft.Extensions.Logging.Filter`

Namespaces

`Microsoft.Extensions.DependencyInjection`

`Microsoft.Extensions.Logging`

`Microsoft.Extensions.Logging.Console`

`System`

`System.Net.Http`

`System.Threading.Tasks`

The `ILogger` interface can simply be used to invoke an extension method such as `LogInformation`:

```
_logger.LogInformation("NetworkRequestSample started");
```

The extension methods offer overloads to pass additional parameters, exception information, and an event ID. For using the event ID, a list of constant values is defined with the application (code file `LoggingSample/LoggingEvents.cs`):

```
class LoggingEvents
{
  public const int Injection = 2000;
  public const int Networking = 2002;
}
```

Next, `LogInformation` and `LogError` extension methods are used to show the start of the `NetworkRequestSampleAsync` method, when it finishes, and error information when an exception is thrown (code file `LoggingSample/SampleController.cs`):

```
public async Task NetworkRequestSampleAsync(string url)
{
  try
  {
    _logger.LogInformation(LoggingEvents.Networking,
      "NetworkRequestSampleAsync started with url {0}", url);
    var client = new HttpClient();

    string result = await client.GetStringAsync(url);
    _logger.LogInformation(LoggingEvents.Networking,
      "NetworkRequestSampleAsync completed, received {0} characters",
      result.Length);
  }
  catch (Exception ex)
  {
    _logger.LogError(LoggingEvents.Networking, ex,
      "Error in NetworkRequestSampleAsync, error message: {0}, HResult: {1}",
      ex.Message, ex.HResult);
  }
}
```

> **NOTE** *One of the overloaded* `ILogger` *extension methods requires* `EventId` *with the first parameter. With the sample code, an* `int` *is passed. This is possible because the* `EventId` *struct implements an implicit operator to convert* `int` *to* `EventId`*. Operator overloading is discussed in Chapter 6, "Operators and Casts."*
>
> *When you pass the message to the* `LogXX` *methods, any number of objects can be supplied that are put into the format message string. This format string uses positional arguments to pass in the following objects. Formattable strings are not used because format strings often are coming from resources that allow for localization of these messages. Localization is discussed in Chapter 27, "Localization."*

Next, logging providers need to be configured to make the log information available.

Configuring Providers

The location where logs are configured needs to be defined with the `ILoggingBuilder`. The `ILoggingBuilder` can be configured when you invoke the `AddLogging` extension method for the

IServiceCollection—one overload of this method accepts an Action<ILoggingBuilder> parameter. When you use ILoggingBuilder, you can add providers. The sample code adds providers for the console, debugs (which shows up in the Output window with Visual Studio), and adds the event source (code file LoggingSample/Program.cs):

```
static void RegisterServices()
{
  var services = new ServiceCollection();
  services.AddLogging(builder =>
  {
    builder.AddEventSourceLogger();
    builder.AddConsole();
#if DEBUG
    builder.AddDebug();
#endif
    //...
  });
  services.AddScoped<SampleController>();
  AppServices = services.BuildServiceProvider();
}

public static IServiceProvider AppServices { get; private set; }
```

The Main method of the sample application invokes the RegisterServices method to register the services in the dependency injection container, and then it invokes the RunSampleAsync method (code file LoggingSample/Program.cs):

```
private static string s_url = "https://csharp.christiannagel.com";
static async Task Main(string[] args)
{
  if (args.Length == 1)
  {
    s_url = args[0];
  }
  RegisterServices();
  await RunSampleAsync();
  Console.ReadLine();
}

static async Task RunSampleAsync()
{
  var controller = AppServices.GetService<SampleController>();
  await controller.NetworkRequestSampleAsync(s_url);
}
```

When you run the application successfully, you can see these informational logs on the console output:

```
info: LoggingSample.SampleController[2002]
    NetworkRequestSampleAsync started with url https://csharp.christiannagel.com
info: LoggingSample.SampleController[2002]
    NetworkRequestSampleAsync completed, received 76318 characters
```

Passing an invalid hostname results in the error information shown here:

```
info: LoggingSample.SampleController[2002]
    NetworkRequestSampleAsync started with url https://csharp.christiannagel1.com
fail: LoggingSample.SampleController[2002]
    Error in NetworkRequestSampleAsync, error message: An error occurred
    while sending the request., HResult: -2147012889
```

Using Scopes

With scopes, you can combine log information that belongs with the output.

A scope can be defined by invoking the `BeginScope` method and passing a message to the scope. The message will be shown in the output with every log message defined within the scope. `BeginScope` returns an `IDisposable` object. Invoking the `Dispose` method (which is done in the code sample with the `using` statement) ends the scope (code file `LoggingScopeSample/SampleController.cs`):

```
public async Task NetworkRequestSampleAsync(string url)
{
  using (_logger.BeginScope("NetworkRequestSampleAsync, url: {0}", url))
  {
    try
    {
      _logger.LogInformation(LoggingEvents.Networking, "Started");
      var client = new HttpClient();

      string result = await client.GetStringAsync(url);
      _logger.LogInformation(LoggingEvents.Networking,
        "Completed with characters {0} received", result.Length);
    }
    catch (Exception ex)
    {
      _logger.LogError(LoggingEvents.Networking, ex,
        "Error, error message: {0}, HResult: {1}", ex.Message, ex.HResult);
    }
  }
}
```

With the providers, the scope needs to be enabled to show it. You can change the configuration of the `AddConsole` method to set the `IncludeScopes` property (code file `LoggingScopeSample/Program.cs`):

```
static void RegisterServices()
{
  var services = new ServiceCollection();
  services.AddLogging(builder =>
  {
    builder.AddEventSourceLogger();
    builder.AddConsole(options => options.IncludeScopes = true);
    builder.AddDebug();
  });
  services.AddScoped<SampleController>();
  AppServices = services.BuildServiceProvider();
}
```

When you run the application now, you can see the information you passed to the scope after the `=>`, as shown in the following code snippet:

```
info: LoggingScopeSample.SampleController[2002]
   => NetworkRequestSampleAsync, url: https://csharp.christiannagel.com
   Started
info: LoggingScopeSample.SampleController[2002]
   => NetworkRequestSampleAsync, url: https://csharp.christiannagel.com
   Completed with characters 76395 received
```

Filtering

You don't need all log messages at all times. While the application is running in the production environment, error and critical information are of interest. As you're debugging the application, you might change the configuration to show trace messages for specific trace sources to learn all the things going on in the application. You can define filters for the logging needs you have.

Filtering is possible based on the logger provider and based on the log categories.

The following code snippet defines a filter for the `ConsoleLoggerProvider` and the category name `LoggingSample` to filter only errors with the log level `Error` and higher (code file `LoggingSample/Program.cs`):

```
static void RegisterServices()
{
  var services = new ServiceCollection();
  services.AddLogging(builder =>
  {
    builder.AddEventSourceLogger();
    builder.AddConsole();
#if DEBUG
    builder.AddDebug();
#endif
    builder.AddFilter<ConsoleLoggerProvider>("LoggingSample", LogLevel.Error);
    //...
```

Instead of just specifying the name of the category and the `LogLevel`, you can also pass a delegate with category and `LogLevel` parameters. The following code snippet returns a filter value true if the category name includes `SampleController`, and the received `LogLevel` is at least `Information`. For all other categories, the filter returns true if the `LogLevel` has at least the value `Error`:

```
builder.AddFilter<ConsoleLoggerProvider>((category, logLevel) =>
{
  if (category.Contains("SampleController") &&
    logLevel >= LogLevel.Information) return true;
  else if (logLevel >= LogLevel.Error) return true;
  else return false;
});
```

Configure Logging

Filtering can also be defined by using a configuration file.

With .NET Core, you can use providers for configuration files, such as reading configuration from JSON or XML files, environment variables, or command-line arguments. You just need to create a `ConfigurationBuilder` from the NuGet package `Microsoft.Extensions.Configuration` and add providers to this builder. To add the JSON provider, you need to invoke the extension method `AddJsonFile`. The `Build` method of the builder returns an object that implements `IConfiguration`. You can use this interface to access configured values with any of the configured providers. With the sample code, the section `Logging` is retrieved from the configuration and passed to the `RegisterServices` method (code file `LoggingConfigurationSample/Program.cs`):

```
var configurationBuilder = new ConfigurationBuilder();
configurationBuilder.AddJsonFile("appsettings.json");
IConfiguration configuration = configurationBuilder.Build();
RegisterServices(configuration);
```

The configuration file of the sample application configures different configuration values based on providers and categories. For the Debug provider, the `LogLevel` is set to Information. With this, for all categories, `Information` and up is logged to the Output window of Visual Studio. With the Console provider, the `LogLevel` differs based on categories. Below the configuration of the Console provider, the default configuration for all other providers is defined with specific log levels based on categories (configuration file `LoggingConfigurationSample/appsettings.json`):

```
{
  "Logging": {
    "Debug": {
      "LogLevel": "Information"
    },
```

```
      "Console": {
        "LogLevel": {
          "LoggingConfigurationSample.SampleController": "Information",
          "Default": "Warning"
        }
      },
      "LogLevel": {
        "Default": "Warning",
        "System": "Information",
        "LoggingConfigurationSample.SampleController": "Warning"
      }
    }
  }
}
```

With the logging configuration in place, now the `AddConfiguration` method is invoked to pass a reference to the `IConfiguration` object. The `AddConfiguration` method expects the content of the `Logging` section from the configuration file (code file `LoggingConfigurationSample/Program.cs`):

```
static void RegisterServices(IConfiguration configuration)
{
  var services = new ServiceCollection();
  services.AddLogging(builder =>
  {
    builder.AddConfiguration(configuration.GetSection("Logging"))
      .AddConsole();
#if DEBUG
    builder.AddDebug();
#endif
  });
  services.AddScoped<SampleController>();
  AppServices = services.BuildServiceProvider();
}
```

Without changing any code, you now have flexibility in defining the logging configuration.

> **NOTE** *Read more about the architecture of* `Microsoft.Extensions.Configuration` *and using different configuration providers in Chapter 30, "ASP.NET Core."*

Using ILogger Without Dependency Injection

Dependency injection has big advantages. However, you can use the logging API without DI as well. All you need to do is to create a `LoggerFactory` and create a logger using the `CreateLogger` method. Configuration providers can be added to the logger factory—similar as they provide extension methods for the `ILoggingBuilder` interface, extension methods for the `ILoggerFactory` are provided as well (code file `LoggingWithoutDI/Program.cs`):

```
var loggerFactory = new LoggerFactory();
loggerFactory.AddConsole().AddDebug();
ILogger<Program> logger = loggerFactory.CreateLogger<Program>();
logger.LogInformation("Info Message");
```

ANALYTICS WITH VISUAL STUDIO APP CENTER

Visual Studio App Center (`https://appcenter.ms`) is Microsoft's entry point to build Windows and mobile apps, distribute apps to beta testers, test apps, extend apps with push notifications, and get user analytics for apps.

You can get reports of users having issues with your apps—for example, you can find out about exceptions—and you can also find out the features users are using from your apps. For example, let's say you have added a new feature to your app. Are users finding the button to activate the feature?

When you use Application Insights, it's easy to identify issues that users are having with the app. There's a good reason Microsoft makes it easy to integrate Application Insights with all kinds of apps.

> **NOTE** *Here are some examples of features that users had trouble finding from Microsoft's own products. The Xbox was the first device to offer a user interface with large tiles. The search feature was available directly below the tiles. Although this button was available directly in front of the user, users didn't see it. Microsoft moved the search functionality within a tile, and now users can find it.*
>
> *Another example is the physical Search button on the Windows Phone. This button was meant to be used to search within apps. Users complained about not having an option to search within email because they didn't think to press this physical button to search for emails. Microsoft changed the functionality. Now the physical Search button is used only to search content from the web, and the mail app has its own Search button.*
>
> *Windows 8 had a similar issue with search; users didn't use the search functionality from the Charms bar to search within apps. Windows 8.1 changed the guideline to use search from the Charms bar, and now the app contains its own Search box; in Windows 10 there's also an auto suggest box. Does it look like some commonalities?*

To enable app analytics, you first need to register with the Visual Studio App Center. Don't be afraid of costs that are too high—crash reporting and analytics are available for free (at the time of this writing). Next, you need to create an app, and copy the App Secret from the web portal. Then you can create a new Blank App (Universal Windows) with Visual Studio. To enable analytics, add the NuGet package `Microsoft.AppCenter.Analytics` to the project.

With just a few API calls, you're can find out issues your users have. In the constructor of the `App` class, add `AppCenter.Start`, and add your previously copied App Secret. To enable Analytics, you need to pass the type of the `Analytics` object as the second argument to the `Start` method (code file `WinAppAnalytics/App.xaml.cs`):

```
public App()
{
  this.InitializeComponent();
  this.Suspending += OnSuspending;

  AppCenter.Start("84df09c4-d560-4c46-a44f-a5524c3abb7f", typeof(Analytics));
}
```

> **NOTE** *Remember to add your App Secret from your app configuration in the Visual Studio App Center to the* `Application.Start` *method.*

Running the application now, you'll see user information, when users start the application, and locations as well as devices from users.

To get some more information from users, you need to create calls to `Analytics.TrackEvent`. All the possible events from the app are defined within the class `EventNames` (code file `WinAppAnalytics/EventNames.cs`):

```
public class EventNames
{
```

```
public const string ButtonClicked = nameof(ButtonClicked);
public const string PageNavigation = nameof(PageNavigation);
public const string CreateMenu = nameof(CreateMenu);
}
```

The sample application contains controls to enable/disable analytics, to enter some text, and to click a button (see Figure 29-5). Events are collected when the `MainPage` is activated. The `TrackEvent` method requires a string for the event name, which is taken from the `EventNames` class. The name of the event is not prefixed by the class name because a `using static` declaration is used to import the members of this class. The second argument of the `TrackEvent` method is optional. Here you can pass a dictionary of strings to track additional information. In the sample code, when the page is navigated to, the `PageNavigation` event contains information about the type of the page navigated to (code file `WinAppAnalytics/MainPage.xaml.cs`):

```
protected override void OnNavigatedTo(NavigationEventArgs e)
{
  base.OnNavigatedTo(e);
  Analytics.TrackEvent(PageNavigation,
    new Dictionary<string, string> { ["Page"] = nameof(MainPage) });
}
```

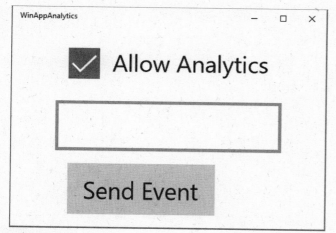

FIGURE 29-5

With the click of the button, `TrackEvent` tracks the `ButtonClick` event, with the information the user entered in the `TextBox` control:

```
private void OnButtonClick(object sender, RoutedEventArgs e)
{
  Analytics.TrackEvent(ButtonClicked,
    new Dictionary<string, string> { ["State"] = textState.Text });
}
```

Users might not agree to allow you to collect information as they wander around your app, so you can create a setting the user can use to enable and disable this functionality. If you set `Analytics .SetEnabledAsync(false)`, the Analytics APIs no longer report data:

```
private async void OnAnalyticsChanged(object sender, RoutedEventArgs e)
{
  if (sender is CheckBox checkbox)
  {
    bool isChecked = checkbox?.IsChecked ?? true;
    await Analytics.SetEnabledAsync(isChecked);
  }
}
```

Visual Studio App Center has some limits regarding analytics, as shown in this list:

➤ You can have only 200 or fewer event names.

➤ The event name is limited to 256 characters.

➤ The dictionary can contain only 5 or fewer properties.

➤ Event property names and event property values are limited to 64 characters.

> **NOTE** *These are the limits at the time of this writing. They might change with future versions.*

When you run the application and monitor the Visual Studio App Center portal, you can see the events that occurred and the number of users that were affected (see Figure 29-6). When you click into the events, you can see event count by user, events per session, and the details of the dictionary properties passed. You can also see the live event log flow, as shown in Figure 29-7.

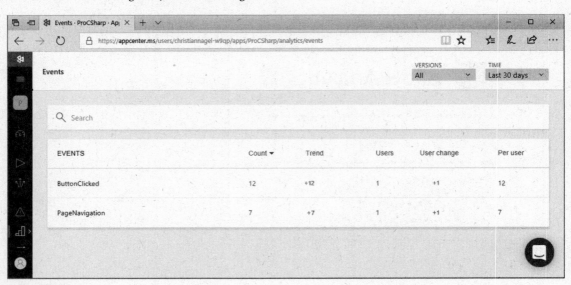

FIGURE 29-6

Apart from this information, Visual Studio App Center Analytics also gives you information about the following:

➤ The number of active users

➤ Daily sessions per user

➤ Session duration

➤ Top devices

➤ OS versions used

➤ Languages

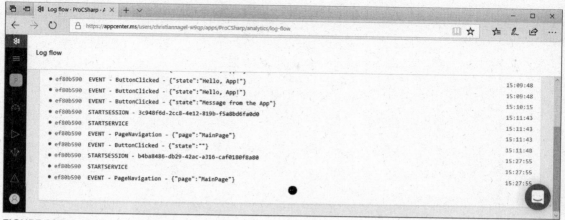

FIGURE 29-7

SUMMARY

In this chapter, you have looked at tracing and logging facilities that can help you find intermittent problems in your applications. You should plan early and build these features into your applications; doing so will help you avoid many troubleshooting problems later.

With tracing, you can write debugging messages to an application that you can also use for the final product delivered. If there are problems, you can turn tracing on by changing configuration values and find the issues.

With Visual Studio App Center Analytics, you've seen that many features come out of the box when you use this cloud service. You can easily get information from your users with just a few lines of code. If you add some more lines, you can find out if users don't use some features of the app because they are having trouble finding them.

This was the last chapter of the second part of this book, ".NET Core and Windows Runtime." The next part, "Web Applications and Services," is based on a lot of features you were introduced to in this part. The next chapter, "ASP.NET Core," is where you begin to dig into web applications and services.

PART III
Web Applications and Services

30

ASP.NET Core

WHAT'S IN THIS CHAPTER?

- ➤ Understanding ASP.NET Core and web technologies
- ➤ Using static content
- ➤ Working with HTTP request and response
- ➤ Using dependency injection with ASP.NET
- ➤ Defining custom simple routing
- ➤ Creating middleware components
- ➤ Using sessions for state management
- ➤ Reading configuration settings

WROX.COM CODE DOWNLOADS FOR THIS CHAPTER

The Wrox.com code downloads for this chapter are found at http://www.wrox.com on the Download Code tab. The source code is also available at https://github.com/ProfessionalCSharp/ProfessionalCSharp7 in the directory aspnetcore.

The code for this chapter contains this example project:

- ➤ Simple Host
- ➤ WebSampleApp
- ➤ CustomConfiguration

ASP.NET CORE

After more than 15 years of ASP.NET, ASP.NET Core was a complete rewrite of ASP.NET. ASP.NET Core features modular programming, makes use of modern patterns, is fully open sourced, is lightweight for best use in the cloud, and is available to non-Microsoft platforms.

A full rewrite of ASP.NET gives a lot of advantages, but this also means reworking existing web applications based on older versions of ASP.NET. Is it necessary to rewrite existing web applications to ASP.NET Core? Let's try to answer this question.

ASP.NET Web Forms is no longer part of ASP.NET Core. However, having web applications that include this technology does not mean you have to rewrite them. It's still possible to maintain legacy applications written with ASP.NET Web Forms with the full framework. ASP.NET Web Forms even received some enhancements with the latest versions of the .NET Framework, such as asynchronous model binding.

The ASP.NET MVC variant of ASP.NET is still part of ASP.NET Core, but it's different from the previous framework with the .NET Framework. When doing a high-level comparison of ASP.NET MVC and ASP.NET Core MVC, the two technologies look very much alike. However, behind the scenes everything is different. When you transfer ASP.NET MVC applications to ASP.NET Core MVC, you need to make some changes to the source code to bring it to the new application stack. For some applications this might mean making minor changes to namespaces, types, and some methods. If the application makes use of more advanced features from ASP.NET MVC, you must do more work to move the application to the new technology.

Converting ASP.NET Web Forms to ASP.NET Core MVC might be a lot of work. ASP.NET Web Forms abstracts HTML and JavaScript from the developer. Using ASP.NET Web Forms, it's not necessary to know HTML and JavaScript. Instead you use server-side controls with C# code. The server-side controls themselves return HTML and JavaScript. This programming model is like the old Windows Forms programming model. With ASP.NET MVC, developers need to know HTML and JavaScript. ASP.NET MVC is based on the *Model-View-Controller* (MVC) pattern, which makes unit testing easy. Because ASP.NET Web Forms and ASP.NET MVC are based on very different architecture patterns, it can be a huge undertaking to migrate ASP.NET Web Forms applications to ASP.NET MVC. Before taking on this task, you should create a checklist of the advantages and the disadvantages of keeping the old technology with your solution and compare this with the advantages and disadvantages of going to the new technology. You will still be able to work with ASP.NET Web Forms for many years to come.

> **NOTE** *My website at* `http://www.cninnoation.com` *was originally created with ASP.NET Web Forms. I've converted this website with an early version of ASP.NET MVC to this new technology stack. Because my original site already made use of a lot of separate components to abstract the database and service code, it was not really a huge undertaking and was done very fast. I was able to use the database and service code directly from ASP.NET MVC. On the other hand, if I had used Web Forms controls to access the database instead of using my own controls, it would have been a lot more work. Nowadays, this web application is implemented with ASP.NET Core.*

> **NOTE** *This book does not cover the legacy technology ASP.NET Web Forms. ASP.NET MVC also is not covered. This book has a focus on new technologies; consequently, the material about web applications is based on ASP.NET Core and ASP.NET Core MVC. You should use these technologies for new web applications. In case you need to maintain older applications, you should read older editions of this book, such as* Professional C# 5.0 and .NET 4.5.1, *which covers ASP.NET 4.5, ASP.NET Web Forms 4.5, and ASP.NET MVC 5.*

This chapter covers the foundation of ASP.NET Core 2.0. Chapter 31 covers ASP.NET Core MVC, a framework that is built on top of ASP.NET Core. Chapter 32 covers creating a web API with ASP.NET Core MVC.

WEB TECHNOLOGIES

Before getting into the foundations of ASP.NET Core later in this chapter, this section describes core web technologies that are important to know when creating web applications: HTML, CSS, JavaScript, scripting libraries.

HTML

HTML is the markup language that is interpreted by web browsers. It defines elements to display various headings, tables, lists, and input elements such as text and combo boxes.

HTML5 has been a W3C recommendation since October 2014 (`http://w3.org/TR/html5`), and it is offered by all the major browsers. You can find lists of work in progress at `http://w3.org/TR/html`. At the time of this writing, HTML 5.2 has been a W3C recommendation since December 2017. With the features of HTML 5, several browser add-ins (such as Flash and Silverlight) are not required anymore because the things the add-ins do can now be done directly with HTML and JavaScript. Of course, you might still need Flash and Silverlight because not all websites have moved to the new technologies or your users might still be using older browser versions that don't support HTML 5.

HTML 5 adds new semantic elements that search engines are better able to use for analyzing the site. A `canvas` element enables the dynamic use of 2D shapes and images, and `video` and `audio` elements make the `object` element obsolete. With recent additions to the media source (`http://w3c.github.io/media-source`), adaptive streaming is also offered by HTML; previously this had been an advantage of Silverlight.

HTML 5 also defines JavaScript APIs for drag-and-drop, storage, web sockets, and much more.

CSS

Whereas HTML defines the content of web pages, CSS defines the look. In the earlier days of HTML, for example, the list item tag `<li>` defined whether list elements should be displayed with a circle, a disc, or a square. Nowadays such information is completely removed from HTML and is instead put into a cascading style sheet (CSS).

With CSS styles, you can use flexible selectors to select HTML elements, and you can define styles for these elements. You can select an element via its ID or its name, and you can define CSS classes that can be referenced from within the HTML code. With newer versions of CSS, you can define quite complex rules for selecting specific HTML elements.

As of Visual Studio 2017, some web project templates make use of Twitter Bootstrap. This is a collection of CSS and HTML conventions, and you can easily adapt different looks and download ready-to-use templates. Visit `www.getbootstrap.com` for documentation and basic templates.

JavaScript and TypeScript

Not all platforms and browsers can use .NET code, but nearly every browser understands *JavaScript*. One common misconception about JavaScript is that it has something to do with Java. In fact, only the name is similar because Netscape (the originator of JavaScript) made an agreement with Sun (Sun invented Java) to be allowed to use Java in the name. Nowadays, neither of these companies exist. Sun was bought by Oracle, and now Oracle holds the trademark for Java.

Both Java and JavaScript (and C#) have the same roots—the C programming language. JavaScript is a functional programming language that is not object-oriented, although object-oriented capabilities have been added to it.

JavaScript enables accessing the *document object model* (DOM) from the HTML page, which makes it possible to change elements dynamically on the client.

ECMAScript is the standard that defines the current and upcoming features of the JavaScript language. Because other companies are not allowed to use the term Java with their language implementations, the standard has the name ECMAScript. Microsoft's implementation of JavaScript had the name JScript. Check `https://tc39.github.io/ecma262/` for the current state and future changes of the JavaScript language.

Even though many browsers don't support the newest ECMAScript version, you can still write ECMAScript 2018 code. Instead of writing JavaScript code, you can use *TypeScript*. The TypeScript syntax is based on ECMAScript, but it has some enhancements, such as strongly typed code and annotations. You'll find many similarities between C# and TypeScript. Because the TypeScript compiler compiles to JavaScript, TypeScript can be used in every place where JavaScript is needed. For more information on TypeScript, check `http://www.typescriptlang.org`.

Scripting Libraries

Beside the JavaScript programming language, you also need scripting libraries to make life easier. Scripting libraries can be used with the server-side functionality of ASP.NET Core.

➤ jQuery (`http://www.jquery.org`) is a library that abstracts browser differences when accessing DOM elements and reacting to events. A few years ago, this library was used with nearly every website. Nowadays, more options are available, and you can't expect to have jQuery available everywhere.

➤ Angular (`https://angular.io`) is a library from Google based on the MVC pattern for simplifying development and testing with single-page web applications. (Unlike ASP.NET MVC, Angular offers the MVC pattern with client-side code.)

➤ React (`https://reactjs.org`) is a library from Facebook that offers functionality to easily update user interfaces as data changes in the background.

ASP.NET Core 2.0 templates for Visual Studio include templates for Angular and React. Visual Studio 2017 supports IntelliSense and debugging JavaScript code.

> **NOTE** *Styling web applications and writing JavaScript code is not covered in this book. You can read more about HTML and styles in* HTML and CSS: Design and Build Websites *by John Duckett (John Wiley & Sons, 2011); and get up to speed with* Beginning JavaScript, *Fifth Edition by Jeremy McPeak (Wrox, 2015).*

ASP.NET WEB PROJECT

Start by creating an empty ASP.NET Core 2.0 web application. The first application is a simple host that does nothing more than answer requests. You start with a new ASP.NET Core web application and select the Empty template (see Figure 30-1). However, for the first sample, empty is not empty enough. Delete the file `Startup.cs` and the directory `wwwroot` from the template.

The `Main` method is simplified to invoke the `Start` method of the `WebHost` class. This method has a parameter of `RequestDelegate`. `RequestDelegate` is a delegate that receives an `HttpContext` as parameter and returns a `Task`. The `HttpContext` can be used to read the request from the client and send a return. With the sample code, a response containing an HTML string is returned (code file `SimpleHost/Program.cs`):

```
using Microsoft.AspNetCore;
using Microsoft.AspNetCore.Hosting;
using Microsoft.AspNetCore.Http;

namespace SimpleHost
{
```

```
public class Program
{
  public static void Main()
  {
    WebHost.Start(async context =>
    {
      await context.Response.WriteAsync("<h1>A Simple Host!</h1>");
    }).WaitForShutdown();
  }
}
```

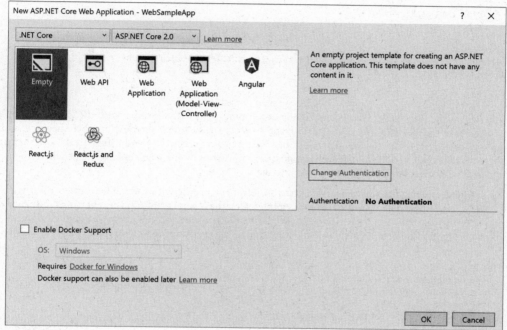

FIGURE 30-1

When you run the application, you can see the HTML content in the browser.

Creating a web host with ASP.NET Core is extremely simple, but now we get into a more complex scenario to see the features. The next application is named `WebSampleApp` and is created with the same Empty template.

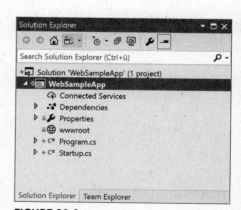

After you've created the project, you see a solution and a project file named `WebSampleApp`, which includes a few files and folders (see Figure 30-2).

Within the project structure, you can see a Dependencies folder. This contains a `NuGet` subfolder that includes NuGet packages. With ASP.NET Core 2.0, the package list has been simplified, and you see only the reference package `Microsoft`
`.AspNetCore.All`. This is a reference package that includes a whole bunch of ASP.NET Core packages. You can see the list

FIGURE 30-2

of packages that are referenced by opening `Microsoft.AspNetCore.All` in Solution Explorer.

In the project file you also can see the reference to this package. The project file lists the project SDK (Software Development Kit) with `Microsoft.NET.Sdk.Web`. This makes use of the SDK installed on the system. This entry is different from console applications where the SDK is `Microsoft.NET.Sdk`. With the Web SDK, additional tools for web development are available (project file `WebSampleApp.cspoj`):

```xml
<Project Sdk="Microsoft.NET.Sdk.Web">

  <PropertyGroup>
    <TargetFramework>netcoreapp2.0</TargetFramework>
  </PropertyGroup>

  <ItemGroup>
    <Folder Include="wwwroot\" />
  </ItemGroup>

  <ItemGroup>
    <PackageReference Include="Microsoft.AspNetCore.All" Version="2.0.0" />
  </ItemGroup>

</Project>
```

You can configure the web server that is used while developing with Visual Studio with the Debug option in Project settings (see Figure 30-3). By default, IIS Express is configured with the port number specified with the Debug settings. IIS Express derives from Internet Information Server (IIS) and offers all the core features of IIS. This makes it easy to develop the web application in practically the same environment where the application will be hosted later (if IIS is used for hosting).

To run the application with the Kestrel server, you can select the profile with the name of the project with the Debug Project settings. The settings that you change with the Visual Studio project settings influence the configuration of the `launchSettings.json` file. With this file you can define some additional configurations such as command line arguments (code file `WebSampleApp/Properties/launchsettings.json`):

```json
{
  "iisSettings": {
    "windowsAuthentication": false,
    "anonymousAuthentication": true,
    "iisExpress": {
      "applicationUrl": "http://localhost:19879/",
      "sslPort": 0
    }
  },
  "profiles": {
    "IIS Express": {
      "commandName": "IISExpress",
      "launchBrowser": true,
      "environmentVariables": {
        "Hosting:Environment": "Development"
      }
    },
    "web": {
      "commandName": "web",
      "launchBrowser": true,
      "launchUrl": "http://localhost:5000/",
      "commandLineArgs": "Environment=Development",
      "environmentVariables": {
        "Hosting:Environment": "Development"
      }
    }
  }
}
```

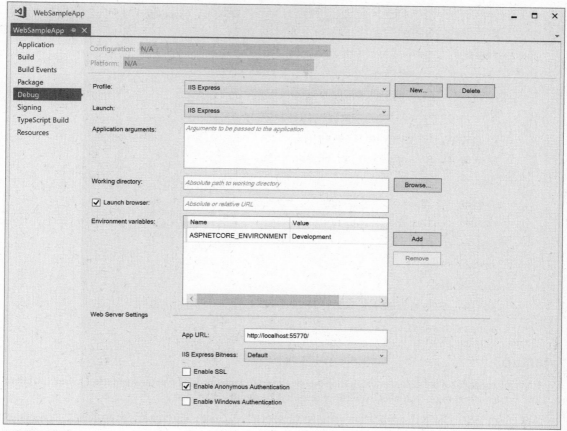

FIGURE 30-3

> **NOTE** *The Kestrel server was developed by the ASP.NET Core team to provide simple hosting with ASP.NET Core. When hosting the web application with IIS, IIS forwards requests to the Kestrel server. This is like web applications that are hosted with the Apache server on Linux—the request is forwarded to the Kestrel server. Starting with ASP.NET Core 2.0, the Kestrel server is supported for public-facing use, so you can directly host the web application in the Kestrel server and have it reachable from port 80.*

The `Dependencies` folder in the project structure in Solution Explorer shows the dependencies on the JavaScript libraries. When you create an empty project, this folder is empty. You add dependencies later in this chapter in the section "Adding Static Content."

The `wwwroot` folder is the folder for static files that need to be published to the server. Currently, this folder is empty, but as you work through this chapter you add HTML and CSS files and JavaScript libraries.

A C# source file—`Startup.cs`—is included with an empty project as well. This file is discussed next.

During the creation of the project, these namespaces are needed:

```
Microsoft.AspNetCore.Builder;

Microsoft.AspNetCore.Hosting;

Microsoft.AspNetCore.Http;

Microsoft.Extensions.Configuration

Microsoft.Extensions.DependencyInjection

Microsoft.Extensions.Logging

Microsoft.Extensions.PlatformAbstractions

Newtonsoft.Json

System

System.Collections.Generic

System.Globalization

System.Linq

System.Text

System.Text.Encodings.Web

System.Threading.Tasks
```

Startup

It's time to start to get some functionality out of the web application. To get information about the client and return a response, you need to write a response to the HttpContext.

The empty ASP.NET web application template creates a Main method in the Program class that contains the following code (code file WebSampleApp/Program.cs):

```
public class Program
{
  public static void Main(string[] args)
  {
    BuildWebHost(args).Run();
  }

  public static IWebHost BuildWebHost(string[] args) =>
    WebHost.CreateDefaultBuilder(args)
      .UseStartup<Startup>()
      .Build();
}
```

The CreateDefaultBuilder returns an object that implements IWebHostBuilder, which set up the following functionality:

➤   It configures Kestrel as the web server to be used.

➤   The root path for the content is set to the current directory.

➤   Configurations are defined to load configuration from the file appsettings.json.

➤   An additional JSON configuration file is added with different names based on the environment: appsettings.{environmentname}.json

➤   The configuration from *user secrets* is read when the environment name is Development.

➤ The configuration settings providers are configured to load settings from environment variables and the command line.

➤ The logger factory is configured to log to the console and the debug output window.

➤ IIS integration is enabled.

> **NOTE** *User secrets are discussed in Chapter 24, "Security."*

When you use the `IWebHostBuilder` returned from `CreateDefaultBuilder`, the `UseStartup` method is invoked. This method defines the `Startup` class that will be instantiated and the methods that will be invoked when you run the web host.

The `UseStartup` method is implemented as a fluent API and returns `IWebHostBuilder` again. `IWebHostBuilder` can be used to configure additional services that are needed before the `Startup` class, and to define additional configuration providers.

The `Build` method is the final method in the chain to set up the web host. This method builds the host to run the application and returns the `IWebHost` interface. You can use this interface to access the dependency injection container using the `Services` property, and you can access hosting server features from the `ServerFeatures` property. `IServerAddressesFeature` is one server feature that you can use to retrieve the addresses of the host. Calling the `Start` method starts the listening on the socket for the configured ports.

> **NOTE** *Dependency injection and the .NET Core dependency injection container* `Microsoft.Extensions.DependencyInjection` *are discussed in Chapter 20, "Dependency Injection."*

The empty ASP.NET web application template creates a `Startup` class that contains the following code:

```
//...
using Microsoft.AspNetCore.Builder;
using Microsoft.AspNetCore.Hosting;
using Microsoft.AspNetCore.Http;
using Microsoft.Extensions.DependencyInjection;

namespace WebSampleApp
{
  public class Startup
  {
    public void ConfigureServices(IServiceCollection services)
    {
    }

    public void Configure(IApplicationBuilder app, IHostingEnvironment env)
    {
      if (env.IsDevelopment())
      {
        app.UseDeveloperExceptionPage();
      }

      app.Run(async (context) =>
      {
        await context.Response.WriteAsync("Hello World!");
      });
    }
  }
}
```

Because the `Startup` class is passed to the `UseStartup` method with a generic template parameter, in turn the methods `ConfigureServices` and `Configure` are invoked.

You can use the `ConfigureServices` method to configure services in the dependency injection container. This method has a `IServiceCollection` property that contains all the services already registered in the `Main` method, and it allows you to add additional services. `IServiceCollection` derives from the base interface `IList<T>` with a `ServiceDescriptor` as generic parameter and thus allows not only read services but also add services.

The `Configure` method receives parameters via dependency injection. The parameters defined in the template are of type `IApplicationBuilder` and `IHostingEnvironment`.

The interface `IHostingEnvironment` allows you to access the name of the environment (`EnvironmentName`), the root path for the content (the directory of the sources), and the root path for the web content files (the subdirectory `wwwroot`). The default provider that accesses these directories is the `PhysicalFileProvider`. With a different provider, the content can be served from other sources—for example, from a database. Within the implementation of the `Configure` method, the `IHostingEnvironment` is used to check whether the current environment is `Development` by invoking the extension method `IsDevelopment`. Only in this environment are exceptions shown. Because of security issues, in the production environment the user doesn't see detail information on the exception.

The `IApplicationBuilder` interface is used to add middleware to the HTTP request pipeline. When you invoke the `Use` method of this interface, you can build the HTTP request pipeline to define what should be done in answer to a request. The `Use` method is implemented using fluent API, and it again returns an `IApplicationBuilder`. With this, multiple middleware objects can easily be added to the pipeline. Several extension methods exist that make it easier to add middleware. Later in this chapter, in the section "Using Middleware," you can create custom middleware and add it to the pipeline.

The `Run` method is an extension method for the interface `IApplicationBuilder` and returns `void`. Thus, it registers the last middleware in the request pipeline. The parameter of the `Run` method is a delegate of type `RequestDelegate`. This type receives an `HttpContext` as a parameter, and it returns a `Task`. With the `HttpContext` (the `context` variable in the code snippet), you have access to the request information from the browser (HTTP headers, cookies, and form data) and can send a response. The generated code returns a simple string—Hello, World!—to the client, as shown in Figure 30-4.

FIGURE 30-4

NOTE *If you're using Microsoft Edge for testing the web application, you need to enable localhost. Type **about:flags** in the URL box and enable the Allow Localhost Loopback option (see Figure 30-5). Instead of using the built-in user interface of Microsoft Edge to set this option, you can also use a command line option: the utility* `CheckNetIsolation`. *The command* `CheckNetIsolation LoopbackExempt -a -n=Microsoft.MicrosoftEdge_8wekyb3d8bbwe` *enables localhost similarly to using the friendlier user interface for Microsoft Edge. The utility* `CheckNetIsolation` *is useful if you want to configure other Windows apps to allow localhost.*

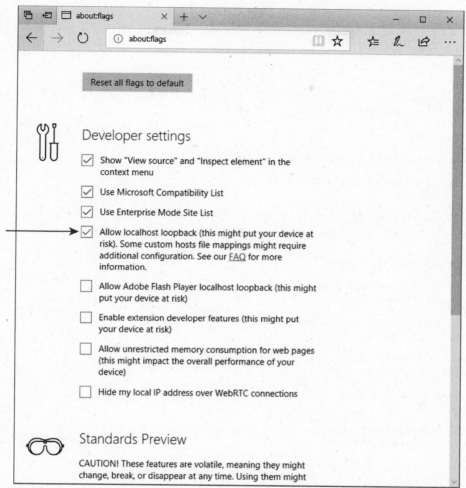

FIGURE 30-5

Sample Application

The sample application contains an entry page where all the features shown by the application can easily be accessed using HTML links:

```
app.Run(async (context) =>
{
    string[] lines = new[]
    {
        @"<ul>",
            @"<li><a href=""/hello.html"">Static Files</a> - requires " +
                @"UseStaticFiles</li>",
            @"<li>Request and Response",
                @"<ul>",
                    @"<li><a href=""/RequestAndResponse"">Request and Response</a></li>",
                    @"<li><a href=""/RequestAndResponse/header"">Header</a></li>",
                    @"<li><a href=""/RequestAndResponse/add?x=38&y=4"">Add</a></li>",
```

```
        //...

        @"</ul>",
      @"</li>",
    @"</ul>"
};

    var sb = new StringBuilder();
    foreach (var line in lines)
    {
      sb.Append(line);
    }
    string html = sb.ToString().HtmlDocument("Web Sample App");

    await context.Response.WriteAsync(html);
  });
```

The HTMLExtensions class is defined to create some specific HTML and reduce the HTML code needed to write. This class defines extension methods to create div, span, and li elements (code file WebSampleApp/HtmlExtensions.cs):

```
public static class HtmlExtensions
{
  public static string Div(this string value) =>
    $"<div>{value}</div>";

  public static string Span(this string value) =>
    $"<span>{value}</span>";

  public static string Div(this string key, string value) =>
    $"{key.Span()}: {value.Span()}".Div();

  public static string Li(this string value) =>
    $@"<li>{value}</li>";

  public static string Li(this string value, string url) =>
    $@"<li><a href=""{url}"">{value}</a></li>";

  public static string Ul(this string value) =>
    $"<ul>{value}</ul>";

  public static string HtmlDocument(this string content, string title)
  {
    var sb = new StringBuilder();
    sb.Append("<!DOCTYPE HTML>");
    sb.Append("<head><meta charset=\"utf-8\"><title>{title}</title></head>");
    sb.Append("<body>");
    sb.Append(content);
    sb.Append("</body>");
    return sb.ToString();
  }
}
```

ADDING CLIENT-SIDE CONTENT

Usually you don't want to just send simple strings to the client. By default, simple HTML files and other static content can't be sent. ASP.NET Core reduces the overhead as much as possible. Even static files are not returned from the server if you do not enable them.

To enable static files served from the web server, you can add the extension method `UseStaticFiles` to add the required middleware (code file `WebSampleApp/Startup.cs`):

```
public void Configure(IApplicationBuilder app, IHostingEnvironment env)
{
    //...
    app.UseStaticFiles();

    app.Run(async (context) =>
    {
        await context.Response.WriteAsync("Hello World!");
    });
}
```

The folder where you add static files is the `wwwroot` folder within the project. Let's add static content by adding a simple HTML file to the `wwwroot` folder (code file `WebSampleApp/wwwroot/Hello.html`), as shown here:

```
<!DOCTYPE html>
<html>
  <head>
    <meta charset="utf-8" />
    <title>ASP.NET Core Sample</title>
  </head>
  <body>
    <h1>Hello, ASP.NET with Static Files</h1>
  </body>
</html>
```

Now you make a request to the HTML file from the browser after starting the server—for example, `http://localhost:32146/Hello.html`. Depending on the configuration you are using, the port number might differ for your project. If you uncomment the extension method `UseStaticFiles`, the HTML file is not returned from the request.

> **NOTE** *When creating web applications with ASP.NET Core, you also need to know HTML, CSS, JavaScript, and some JavaScript libraries. As this book's focus is C# and .NET Core, the content for these topics is kept to a minimum. I just cover the most important tasks you need to know with ASP.NET Core.*

Using Tools for Client Content

To create content for the client, you also need some tools. With the older version of ASP.NET, everything was integrated within Visual Studio. JavaScript libraries could be downloaded and installed in the project using NuGet packages. However, because communities around script libraries typically don't use the NuGet server, they also don't create NuGet packages for JavaScript libraries. Instead of NuGet, communities around JavaScript libraries use servers with functionality like NuGet.

Microsoft and the community around NuGet were building NuGet packages for JavaScript libraries to have them available with Visual Studio. This always generated some delay, and often the experience of using Visual Studio was not the best in the web world.

Many tools and libraries to develop web applications offer command-line interfaces. This is now also true for the .NET Core CLI. You've already seen the `dotnet` command for creating applications, and you also used some extensions, such as `dotnet user-secrets` (Chapter 24, "Security") and `dotnet ef` (Chapter 26, "Entity Framework Core"). This experience fits now a lot better with the tools used to create web applications. On the other hand, Visual Studio offers a great integration of some web tools.

What tools are needed to develop the client part of the web application?

➤ Tools to download packages

➤ Tools to process compile or transpile source files (for example, TypeScript to JavaScript)

➤ Tools to analyze source files

➤ Tools for bundling script files

➤ Tools for unit testing

Depending on the templates you use, different tools are integrated to use the source code. For example, if you create an ASP.NET Core MVC web application using the template from the dotnet CLI, these tools are integrated in the project:

➤ **Bower** is for downloading JavaScript libraries (`https://www.bower.io`).

➤ **Bundler and Minifier** is a Visual Studio extension from Mads Kristensen to bundle and minify JavaScript and CSS files, see more at `https://github.com/madskristensen/BundlerMinifier`.

When you create a new Angular project with Visual Studio or the dotnet CLI, you see these tools and libraries to be used:

➤ **npm** to download JavaScript packages (`https://www.npmjs.com`)

➤ **tsc** (the TypeScript compiler) to transpile TypeScript files to JavaScript (`https://www.typescriptlang.org`)

➤ **Jasmine**, a JavaScript testing framework (`https://jasmine.github.io/`)

➤ **Karma**, a test runner to test JavaScript code (`http://karma-runner.github.io/1.0/index.html`)

➤ **Chai**, which is an assertion library for unit tests (`http://chaijs.com/`)

➤ **webpack**, a module bundler to package, bundle, and load JavaScript libraries (`https://webpack.js.org/`)

You are not restricted to using the tools from the templates. You can customize the code and project configuration to use the tools that best fit your way of work.

Using Client-Side Libraries with Bower

.NET packages are available from the NuGet server. With .NET Core, JavaScript libraries are no longer available on this server. The JavaScript community uses other servers and is more agile on changing the server. When Visual Studio 2015 was released, nearly all client-side JavaScript libraries had been available on the Bower server. That's why Microsoft built integration with Bower like NuGet into Visual Studio. At that time, scripting libraries for use on the server usually have been available on the npm (Node Package Manager) server (`https://www.npmjs.com`). Today, not only the scripting libraries used on the server but also the scripting libraries used on the client are available on the npm server.

With .NET projects, NuGet packages are managed in the `csproj` project file. When using packages from the Bower server, the Visual Studio item template *Bower Configuration File* adds the file `bower.json` to the project.

When you select the bower configuration file in Solution Explorer, you can manage bower packages and open the package manager that looks like the NuGet package manager (see Figure 30-6). You can browse and search for packages, install specific versions, and update packages in a way that's like using the NuGet package manager.

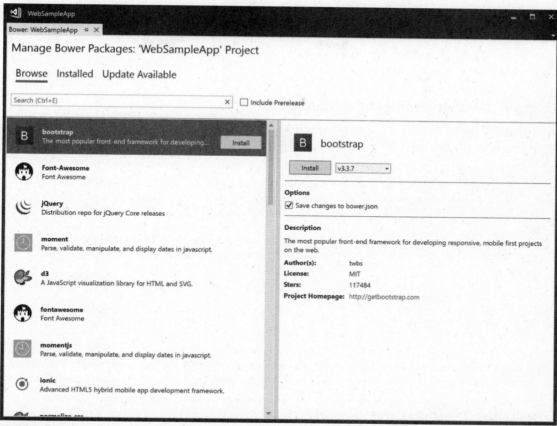

FIGURE 30-6

Installing Bootstrap via the Bower package manager adds a reference to bootstrap to the bower configuration file (configuration file WebSampleApp/bower.json):

```
{
    "name": "asp.net",
    "private": true,
    "dependencies": {
        "bootstrap": "v3.3.7"
    }
}
```

Bower dependencies show up within the Dependencies list in the Solution Explorer as well. The package is automatically downloaded to wwwroot/lib. The location where the package is downloaded is specified by the .bowerrc file:

```
{
    "directory": "wwwroot/lib"
}
```

When you use bower from the command line, you can install the bower command-line utility with npm:

```
> npm install -g bower
```

You also can install packages, which writes the packages to the bower.json file:

```
> bower install jquery
```

Using a JavaScript Package Manager: npm

Today, the host of the Node Package Manager (*npm*) not only serves server-side JavaScript libraries but most of the client-side JavaScript libraries also are available from the npm server.

> **NOTE** *With the Visual Studio Installer, you can install the Node Package Manager as optional component. You can also get it directly from* https://nodejs.org/.

Using Visual Studio 2017, you can add npm to the project by adding the *NPM Configuration File* from the item templates. When you add the item template, the following package.json file is added to the project:

```
{
  "version": "1.0.0",
  "name": "ASP.NET",
  "private": "true",
  "devDependencies": {
  }
}
```

devDependencies is the section for the libraries that are needed only during development. The section dependencies is for libraries needed during runtime; these need to be deployed on the production server.

You can add libraries with their version to the corresponding section within package.json. Visual Studio offers IntelliSense and contacts the package server to get package names and available versions. Alternatively, you can use the npm command line to add packages—for example, as shown with the following command-line statement in which the option --save writes the dependency to the package.json file:

```
> npm install @angular/core --save
```

When you select the version number in the Visual Studio editor, you can select between ^ and ~ prefixes. Without a prefix, the version of the library with the exact name you typed is retrieved from the server. With the ^ prefix, the latest library with the same major version number is retrieved; with the ~ prefix, the latest library with the same minor version number is retrieved.

After the packages are added, you can easily update or uninstall the package using the npm node within the Dependencies section in Solution Explorer.

Bundling

Returning JavaScript and CSS files to the browser should be different in a production environment than in the development environment. Comments and whitespaces can be removed—a process known as *minifying*—and multiple files can be combined to one—which is known as *bundling*. Both minifying and bunding increases the performance. Minifying reduces the file size. Bundling reduces the number of network transfers.

One option for bunding is the Visual Studio 2017 integrated Bundler and Minifier. All you need to do is add a bundleconfig.json file (which is automatically added from the ASP.NET Core MVC project template) as shown in the following snippet. This file contains sections with outputFileName and inputFiles directives. The input files are minified and bundled to create one output file. You can add all your CSS files to bundle into one CSS file, and the JavaScript files of your project to bundle into one JavaScript file:

```
[
  {
    "outputFileName": "wwwroot/css/site.min.css",
    // An array of relative input file paths. Globbing patterns supported
    "inputFiles": [
      "wwwroot/css/site.css"
    ]
  },
  {
    "outputFileName": "wwwroot/js/site.min.js",
    "inputFiles": [
      "wwwroot/js/site.js"
    ],
    // Optionally specify minification options
    "minify": {
      "enabled": true,
      "renameLocals": true
    },
    // Optionally generate .map file
    "sourceMap": false
  }
]
```

Packaging with webpack

As previously mentioned, webpack is a modern (at the time of this writing) way to package web projects. Using the ASP.NET Core template for Angular makes use of webpack and creates the file `webpack.config` `.js` to configure webpack for the web application. In this file you can find bundle configuration to bundle JavaScript and CSS files.

For starting webpack also check the .NET project file `csproj`. With the Angular project `AngularWithDotnetCore`, this file contains the `DebugRunWebpack` task that runs before a build and executes the `webpack` JavaScript file:

```
<Target Name="DebugRunWebpack" BeforeTargets="Build"
  Condition=" '$(Configuration)' == 'Debug' And !Exists('wwwroot\dist') ">
  <!-- Ensure Node.js is installed -->
  <Exec Command="node --version" ContinueOnError="true">
    <Output TaskParameter="ExitCode" PropertyName="ErrorCode" />
  </Exec>
  <Error Condition="'$(ErrorCode)' != '0'"
    Text="Node.js is required to build and run this project. To continue,
please install Node.js from https://nodejs.org/, and then restart your command
prompt or IDE." />

  <!-- In development, the dist files won't exist on the first run or when
    cloning to a different machine, so rebuild them if not already present. -->
  <Message Importance="high" Text="Performing first-run Webpack build..." />
  <Exec Command="node node_modules/webpack/bin/webpack.js
    --config webpack.config.vendor.js" />
  <Exec Command="node node_modules/webpack/bin/webpack.js" />
</Target>
```

You use the task `PublishRunWebpack` where npm modules are installed, and webpack is started with minifying and bundling:

```
<Target Name="PublishRunWebpack" AfterTargets="ComputeFilesToPublish">
  <!-- As part of publishing, ensure the JS resources are freshly built in
    production mode -->
  <Exec Command="npm install" />
  <Exec Command="node node_modules/webpack/bin/webpack.js --config
    webpack.config.vendor.js --env.prod" />
```

```
<Exec Command="node node_modules/webpack/bin/webpack.js --env.prod" />

<!-- Include the newly-built files in the publish output -->
<ItemGroup>
  <DistFiles Include="wwwroot\dist\**; ClientApp\dist\**" />
  <ResolvedFileToPublish Include="@(DistFiles->'%(FullPath)')"
    Exclude="@(ResolvedFileToPublish)">
    <RelativePath>%(DistFiles.Identity)</RelativePath>
    <CopyToPublishDirectory>PreserveNewest</CopyToPublishDirectory>
  </ResolvedFileToPublish>
</ItemGroup>
</Target>
```

REQUEST AND RESPONSE

With the HTTP protocol, the client sends an HTTP request to the server. This request is answered with an HTTP response.

The request consists of a header and, in many cases, body information to the server. The server uses the header information to know about the needs of the client and can send different results based on this information. Let's have a look at what information is sent by the client.

To return an HTML-formatted output to the client, the Span and Div methods create an HTML div element that contains HTML span elements with the passed arguments key and value (code file WebSampleApp/HtmlExtensions.cs):

```
public static string Span(this string value) =>
  $"<span>{value}</span>";

public static string Div(this string key, string value) =>
  $"{key.Span()}: {value.Span()}".Div();
```

The method GetRequestInformation uses an HttpRequest object to access Scheme, Host, Path, QueryString, Method, and Protocol properties (code file WebSampleApp/RequestAndResponseSamples .cs):

```
public static string GetRequestInformation(HttpRequest request)
{
  var sb = new StringBuilder();
  sb.Append("scheme".Div(request.Scheme));
  sb.Append("host".Div(request.Host.HasValue ? request.Host.Value :
    "no host"));
  sb.Append("path".Div(request.Path));
  sb.Append("query string".Div(request.QueryString.HasValue ?
    request.QueryString.Value : "no query string"));
  sb.Append("method".Div(request.Method));
  sb.Append("protocol".Div(request.Protocol));
  return sb.ToString();
}
```

All the requests to demonstrate the sample code of this section are served passing the path /RequestAndResponse to the server. That's why the Map method is defined in the Configure method of the Startup class:

```
app.Map("/RequestAndResponse", app1 =>
{
  app1.Run(async context =>
  {
    //...
  }
}
```

> **NOTE** *Routing using the* Map *method is explained later in this chapter in the section* "*Simple Routing.*"

The implementation of the `Run` method invokes the `GetRequestInformation` method and pass the `HttpRequest` via the `Request` property of the `HttpContext`. The result is written to the `Response` object (code file `WebSampleApp/Startup.cs`):

```
app1.Run(async context =>
{
  await context.Response.WriteAsync(
    RequestAndResponseSample.GetRequestInformation(context.Request));
});
```

Starting the program and accessing `http://localhost:32146/RequestAndResponse/` results in the following information:

```
scheme: http
host: localhost:32146
path: /
query string: no query string
method: GET
protocol: HTTP/1.1
```

Adding a path, such as `http://localhost:32146/RequestAndResponse/Index`, to the request results in the path value set:

```
scheme:http
host:localhost:32146
path: /Index
query string: no query string
method: GET
protocol: HTTP/1.1
```

When you add a query string, such as `http://localhost:32146/RequestAndResponse/Sub?x=3&y=5`, the query string accessing the property `QueryString` shows up:

```
query string: ?x=3&y=5
```

In the next code snippet, you use the `Path` property of the `HttpRequest` to create a lightweight custom routing. Depending on the path that is set by the client, different methods are invoked (code file `WebSampleApp/Startup.cs`):

```
app.Run(async (context) =>
{
  context.Response.ContentType = "text/html";
  string result = string.Empty;
  switch (context.Request.Path.Value.ToLower())
  {
    case "/header":
      result = RequestAndResponseSamples.GetHeaderInformation(context.Request);
      break;
    case "/add":
      result = RequestAndResponseSamples.QueryString(context.Request);
      break;
    case "/content":
      result = RequestAndResponseSamples.Content(context.Request);
      break;
    case "/encoded":
      result = RequestAndResponseSamples.ContentEncoded(context.Request);
      break;
    case "/form":
```

```
            result = RequestAndResponseSamples.GetForm(context.Request);
            break;
          case "/writecookie":
            result = RequestAndResponseSamples.WriteCookie(context.Response);
            break;
          case "/readcookie":
            result = RequestAndResponseSamples.ReadCookie(context.Request);
            break;
          case "/json":
            result = RequestAndResponseSamples.GetJson(context.Response);
            break;
          default:
            result =
              RequestAndResponseSamples.GetRequestInformation(context.Request);
            break;
        }
      await context.Response.WriteAsync(result);
    });
```

The following sections implement the different methods to show request headers, query strings, and more.

Request Headers

Let's have a look at what information the client sends within the HTTP header. To access the HTTP header information, the `HttpRequest` object defines the `Headers` property. This is of type `IHeaderDictionary`, and it contains a dictionary with the name of the header and a string array for the values. Using this information, the `GetDiv` method created earlier is used to write `div` elements for the client (code file `WebSampleApp/RequestAndResponseSamples.cs`):

```
public static string GetHeaderInformation(HttpRequest request)
{
  var sb = new StringBuilder();
  foreach (var header in request.Headers)
  {
    sb.Append(header.Key.Div(string.Join("; ", header.Value)));
  }
  return sb.ToString();
}
```

The results you see depend on the browser you're using. Let's compare a few of them. The following is from Internet Explorer 11 on a Windows 10 touch device:

```
Connection: Keep-Alive
Accept: text/html,application/xhtml+xml,image/jxr,*.*
Accept-Encoding: gzip, deflate
Accept-Language: en-Us,en;q=0.8,de-AT;q=0.5,de;q=0.3
Host: localhost:32146
User-Agent: Mozilla/5.0 (Windows NT 10.0; WOW64; Trident/7.0; Touch; rv:11.0)
like Gecko
MS-ASPNETCORE-TOKEN: f7fd3899-4436-40a2-b736-1118f43cbef3
X-Original-Proto: http
X-Original-For: 127.0.0.1:8639
```

Google Chrome version 61.0 shows this information, including version numbers from AppleWebKit, Chrome, and Safari:

```
Connection: Keep-Alive
Accept: text/html,application/xhtml+xml,application/xml;q=0.9,image/webp,
  image/apng,*/*;q=0.8
Accept-Encoding: gzip, deflate, br
Accept-Language: en-US,en;q=0.9
Host: localhost:32146
```

```
User-Agent: Mozilla/5.0 (Windows NT 10.0; Win64; x64)
   AppleWebKit/537.36 (KHTML, like Gecko) Chrome/62.0.3202.62 Safari/537.36
Upgrade-Insecure-Requests: 1
MS-ASPNETCORE-TOKEN: f7fd3899-4436-40a2-b736-1118f43cbef3
X-Original-Proto: http
X-Original-For: 127.0.0.1:8693
```

And Microsoft Edge comes with this information, including version numbers from AppleWebKit, Chrome, Safari, and Edge:

```
Connection: Keep-Alive
Accept: text/html, application/xhtml+xml, image/jxr, */*
Accept-Encoding: gzip, deflate
Accept-Language: en-US,en;q=0.8,de-AT;q=0.5,de;q=0.3
Cookie: color=red
Host: localhost:32146
Referer: http://localhost:32146/
User-Agent: Mozilla/5.0 (Windows NT 10.0; Win64; x64)
   AppleWebKit/537.36 (KHTML, like Gecko) Chrome/58.0.3029.110
   Safari/537.36 Edge/16.16299
MS-ASPNETCORE-TOKEN: f7fd3899-4436-40a2-b736-1118f43cbef3
X-Original-Proto: http
X-Original-For: 127.0.0.1:8639
```

What can you get out of this header information?

The `Connection` header was an enhancement of the HTTP 1.1 protocol. With this header the client can request to keep connections open. Usually with HTML, the client makes multiple requests, e.g. to get the images, CSS, and JavaScript files. The server might honor the request, or it might ignore the request in case the load is too high and it's better to close the connection.

The `Accept` header defines the mime formats the browser accepts. The list is in order by the preferred formats. Depending on this information, you might decide to return data with different formats based on the client's needs. IE prefers HTML followed by XHTML and JXR. Google Chrome has a different list. It prefers these formats: HTML, XHTML, XML, and WEBP. With some of this information, a quantifier is also defined. The browsers used for the output all have *.* at the end of this list to accept all data returned.

The `Accept-Language` header information shows the languages the user has configured. Using this information, you can return localized information. Localization is discussed in Chapter 29, "Localization."

> **NOTE** *In ancient times, the server kept long lists of browser capabilities. These lists have been used to know what feature is available with which browser. To identify a browser, the agent string from the browser was used to map the capabilities. Over time, browsers lied by giving wrong information, or they even allowed the user to configure the browser name that should be used so that they could get some more features (because browser lists often were not updated on the server). In the past, Internet Explorer (IE) often required different programming than all the other browsers. Microsoft Edge is very different from IE and has more features in common with other vendors' browsers. That's why Microsoft Edge shows Mozilla, AppleWebKit, Chrome, Safari, and Edge in the* `User-Agent` *string. It's best not to use this* `User-Agent` *string at all for getting a list of features available. Instead, check for specific features you need programmatically.*

The header information that you've seen so far that was sent with the browser is what is sent for very simple sites. Usually, there will be more detail, such as cookies, authentication information, and custom information. To see all the information that is sent to and from a server, including the header information, you can use the browser's developer tools and start a Network session; you'll see not only all the requests that are sent to the server but also header, body, parameters, cookies, and timing information as shown in Figure 30-7.

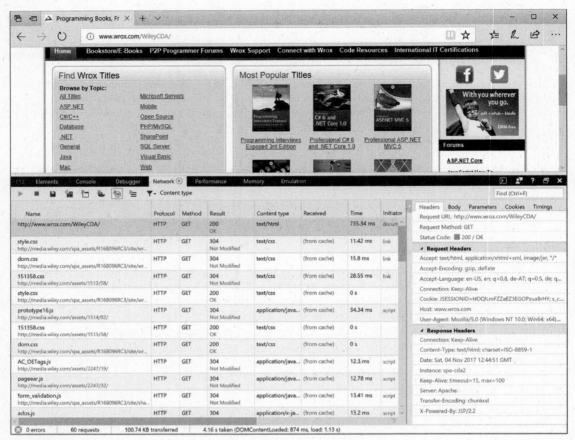

FIGURE 30-7

Query String

You can use the Add method to analyze the query string. This method requires x and y parameters, makes an addition if these parameters are numbers, and returns the calculation within a div tag. The method GetRequestInformation shown in the previous section demonstrated how to access the complete query string using the QueryString property of the HttpRequest object. To access the parts of the query string, you can use the Query property. The following code snippet accesses the values of x and y by using the Get method. This method returns null if the corresponding key is not found in the query string (code file WebSampleApp/RequestAndResponseSamples.cs):

```
public static string QueryString(HttpRequest request)
{
    string xtext = request.Query["x"];
    string ytext = request.Query["y"];

    if (xtext == null || ytext == null)
    {
        return "x and y must be set".Div();
```

```
      }

      if (!int.TryParse(xtext, out int x))
      {
        return $"Error parsing {xtext}".Div();
      }

      if (!int.TryParse(ytext, out int y))
      {
        return $"Error parsing {ytext}".Div();
      }
      return $"{x} + {y} = {x + y}".Div();
    }
```

The `IQueryCollection` returned from the `Query` string also enables you to access all the keys using the `Keys` property, and it offers a `ContainsKey` method to check whether a specified key is available.

Using the URL `http://localhost:32146/RequestAndResponse/add?x=39&y=3` shows this result in the browser:

```
39 + 3 = 42
```

Encoding

Returning data that has been entered by a user can be dangerous. Let's do this with the `Content` method. The following method directly returns the data that is passed with the query data string (code file `WebSampleApp/RequestAndResponseSamples.cs`):

```
public static string Content(HttpRequest request) =>
    request.Query["data"];
```

Invoking this method using the URL `http://localhost:32146/RequestAndResponse/content?data=sample`, just the string sample is returned. Using the same method, users can also pass HTML content such as `http://localhost:32146/RequestAndResponse/content?data=<h1>Heading 1</h1>` What's the result of this? Figure 30-8 shows that the `h1` element is interpreted by the browser, and the text is shown with the heading format. There are cases where you want to allow this—for example, when users (maybe not anonymous users) are writing articles for a site.

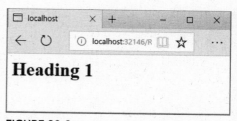

FIGURE 30-8

Without checking the user input, it is also possible for the users to pass JavaScript such as `http://localhost:32146/RequestAndResponse/content?data=<script>alert("hacker");</script>`. You can use the JavaScript alert function to make a message box pop up. It's similarly easy to redirect the user to a different site. When this user input is stored in the site, one user can enter such a script, and all other users who open this page are redirected accordingly.

Returning user-entered data should always be encoded. Let's have a look at how the result looks with and without encoding. You can do HTML encoding using the `HtmlEncoder` class as shown in the following code snippet (code file `WebSampleApp/RequestResponseSamples.cs`):

```
public static string ContentEncoded(HttpRequest request) =>
    HtmlEncoder.Default.Encode(request.Query["data"]);
```

When the application is run, the same JavaScript code with encoding is passed using `http://localhost:32146/RequestAndResponse/encoded?data=<script>alert("hacker");</script>`, and the client just sees the JavaScript code in the browser; it is not interpreted (see Figure 30-9).

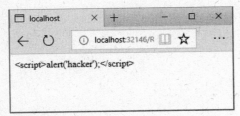

FIGURE 30-9

The encoded string that is sent looks like the following example—with the character reference less-than sign (<), greater-than sign (>), and quotation mark ("):

```
<script>alert("hacker");</script>
```

Form Data

Instead of passing data from the user to the server with a query string, you can use the form HTML element. This example uses an HTTP POST request instead of GET. With a POST request the user data are passed with the body of the request instead of within the query string.

Using form data is defined with two requests. First, the form is sent to the client with a GET request and then the user fills in the form and submits the data with a POST request. The method that is invoked passing the /form path in turn invokes the GetForm or ShowForm method, depending on the HTTP method type (code file WebSampleApp/RequestResponseSamples.cs):

```
public static string GetForm(HttpRequest request)
{
  string result = string.Empty;
  switch (request.Method)
  {
    case "GET":
      result = GetForm();
      break;
    case "POST":
      result = ShowForm(request);
      break;
    default:
      break;
  }
  return result;
}
```

The form is created with an input element named text1 and a Submit button. Clicking the Submit button invokes the form's action method with an HTTP method as defined with the method argument:

```
private static string GetForm() =>
  "<form method=\"post\" action=\"form\">" +
  "<input type=\"text\" name=\"text1\" />" +
  "<input type=\"submit\" value=\"Submit\" />" +
  "</form>";
```

For reading the form data, the HttpRequest class defines a Form property. This property returns an IFormCollection object that contains all the data from the form that is sent to the server:

```
private static string ShowForm(HttpRequest request)
{
  var sb = new StringBuilder();
  if (request.HasFormContentType)
  {
```

```
        IFormCollection coll = request.Form;
        foreach (var key in coll.Keys)
        {
          sb.Append(key.Div(HtmlEncoder.Default.Encode(coll[key])));
        }
        return sb.ToString();
    }
    else return "no form".Div();
}
```

Using the /form link, the form is received with the GET request (see Figure 30-10). When you click the Submit button, the form is sent with the POST request, and you can see the text1 key of the form data (see Figure 30-11).

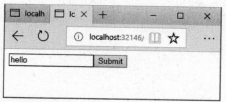

FIGURE 30-10

FIGURE 30-11

Cookies

To remember user data between multiple requests, you can use cookies. Adding a cookie to the HttpResponse object sends the cookie within the HTTP header from the server to the client. By default, a cookie is temporary (not stored on the client), and the browser sends it back to the server if the URL is the same domain where the cookie was coming from. You can set the Path to restrict when the browser returns the cookie. In this case, the cookie is only returned when it comes from the same domain and the path /cookies is used. When you set the Expires property, the cookie is a persistent cookie and thus is stored on the client. When the expiration time passes, the cookie will be removed. However, there's no guarantee that the cookie isn't removed earlier (code file WebSampleApp/RequestResponseSamples.cs):

```
public static string WriteCookie(HttpResponse response)
{
    response.Cookies.Append("color", "red", new CookieOptions
    {
      Path = "/cookies",
      Expires = DateTime.Now.AddDays(1)
    });
    return "cookie written".Div();
}
```

The cookie can be read again by reading the HttpRequest object. The Cookies property contains all the cookies that are returned by the browser:

```
public static string ReadCookie(HttpRequest request)
{
    var sb = new StringBuilder();
    IRequestCookieCollection cookies = request.Cookies;
    foreach (var key in cookies.Keys)
    {
      sb.Append(key.Div(cookies[key]));
    }
    return sb.ToString();
}
```

For testing cookies, you can also use the browser's developer tools. The tools show all the information about the cookies that are sent and received.

Sending JSON

The server returns more than HTML code; it also returns many different kind of data formats, such as CSS files, images, and videos. The client knows what kind of data it receives with the help of a mime type in the response header.

The method GetJson creates a JSON string from an anonymous object with Title, Publisher, and Author properties. To serialize this object with JSON, the NuGet package NewtonSoft.Json is added, and the namespace NewtonSoft.Json imported. The mime type for the JSON format is application/json. This is set via the ContentType property of the HttpResponse (code file WebSampleApp/RequestResponseSample.cs):

```
public static string GetJson(HttpResponse response)
{
  var b = new
  {
    Title = "Professional C# 7",
    Publisher = "Wrox Press",
    Author = "Christian Nagel"
  };
  string json = JsonConvert.SerializeObject(b);
  response.ContentType = "application/json";
  return json;
}
```

> **NOTE** *The* JsonConvert *class is part of the NuGet package* Newtonsoft.Json. *This third-party package is automatically referenced from the reference package* Microsoft.AspNetCore.All.

This is the data returned to the client.

```
{"Title":"Professional C# 7","Publisher":"Wrox Press",
  "Author":"Christian Nagel"}
```

> **NOTE** *Sending and receiving JSON is covered in Chapter 32, "ASP.NET Core Web API."*

DEPENDENCY INJECTION

Dependency injection is deeply integrated within ASP.NET Core. This design pattern gives loose coupling as a service is used only with an interface. The concrete type that implements the interface is injected. With the ASP.NET Core built-in dependency injection mechanism, injection happens via constructors that have arguments of the injected interface type.

> **NOTE** *For more details on dependency injection, read Chapter 20.*

Dependency injection separates the service contract and the service implementation. The service can be used without knowing the concrete implementation—just a contract is needed. This allows replacing the service (for example, logging) in a single place for all using the service.

Let's have a more detailed look at dependency injection by creating a custom service.

Defining a Service

First, a contract for a sample service is declared. Defining a contract via an interface enables you to separate the service implementation from its use—for example, to use a different implementation for unit testing (code file `WebSampleApp/Services/ISampleService.cs`):

```
public interface ISampleService
{
   IEnumerable<string> GetSampleStrings();
}
```

You implement the interface `ISampleService` with the class `DefaultSampleService` (code file `WebSampleApp/Services/DefaultSampleService.cs`):

```
public class DefaultSampleService : ISampleService
{
   private List<string> _strings = new List<string> { "one", "two", "three" };
   public IEnumerable<string> GetSampleStrings() => _strings;
}
```

Registering the Service

Using the `AddTransient` method (which is an extension method for `IServiceCollection` defined in the assembly `Microsoft.Extensions.DependencyInjection.Abstractions` in the namespace `Microsoft.Extensions.DependencyInjection`), the type `DefaultSampleService` is mapped to `ISampleService`. When you use the `ISampleService` interface, the `DefaultSampleService` type is instantiated (code file `WebSampleApp/Startup.cs`):

```
public void ConfigureServices(IServiceCollection services)
{
   services.AddTransient<ISampleService, DefaultSampleService>();
   //...
}
```

The built-in dependency injection service defines several lifetime options. Using the `AddTransient` method, the service is newly instantiated every time the service is injected.

Using the `AddSingleton` method, the service is instantiated only once. Every injection makes use of the same instance:

```
services.AddSingleton<ISampleService, DefaultSampleService>();
```

The `AddInstance` method requires you to instantiate a service and pass the instance to this method. This way you're defining the lifetime of the service:

```
var sampleService = new DefaultSampleService();
services.AddInstance<ISampleService>(sampleService);
```

With the fourth option, the lifetime of the service is based on the current context. With ASP.NET MVC, the current context is based on the HTTP request. As long as actions for the same request are invoked, the same instance is used with different injections. With a new request, a new instance is created. For defining a context-based lifetime, the `AddScoped` method maps the service contract to the service:

```
services.AddScoped<ISampleService>();
```

Injecting the Service

After the service is registered, you can inject it. A controller type named `HomeController` is created in the directory `Controllers`. The built-in dependency injection framework makes use of constructor injection; thus, a constructor is defined that receives an `ISampleService` interface. The method `Index` receives an `HttpContext` and can use this to read request information. Within the implementation, the `ISampleService` is used to get the strings from the service. The controller adds some HTML elements to put the strings in a list and sets the status code (code file `WebSampleApp/Controllers/HomeController.cs`):

```
public class HomeController
{
  private readonly ISampleService _service;
  public HomeController(ISampleService service) =>
    _service = service;

  public async Task Index(HttpContext context)
  {
    var sb = new StringBuilder();
    sb.Append("<ul>");
    sb.Append(string.Join(string.Empty,
      _service.GetSampleStrings().Select(s => s.Li()).ToArray()));
    sb.Append("</ul>");
    context.Response.StatusCode = 200;
    await context.Response.WriteAsync(sb.ToString());
  }
}
```

> **NOTE** *This sample controller directly returns HTML code. It's better to separate the functionality from the user interface and to create the HTML code from a different class—a view. For this separation it's best to use a framework: ASP.NET MVC. This framework is explained in Chapter 31.*

Calling the Controller

To instantiate the controller via dependency injection, the `HomeController` class is registered with the `IServiceCollection` services. This time you do not use an interface; thus, you need only the concrete implementation of the service type with the `AddTransient` method call (code file `WebSampleApp/Startup.cs`):

```
public void ConfigureServices(IServiceCollection services)
{
  services.AddTransient<ISampleService, DefaultSampleService>();
  services.AddTransient<HomeController>();
  //...
}
```

The `Configure` method that contains the route information is now changed to add a map for the `/Home` path. If this expression returns `true`, the `HomeController` is instantiated via dependency injection by calling the `GetService` method on the registered application services. The `IApplicationBuilder` interface defines an `ApplicationServices` property that returns an object implementing `IServiceProvider`. Here, you can access all the services that have been registered. Using this controller, the `Index` method is invoked by passing the `HttpContext`:

```
public void Configure(IApplicationBuilder app, ILoggerFactory loggerFactory)
{
  //...
```

```
    app.Map("/Home", homeApp =>
    {
      homeApp.Run(async (context) =>
      {
        HomeController controller =
          homeApp.ApplicationServices.GetService<HomeController>();
        await controller.Index(context);
      }
    });
    //...
  }
```

Figure 30-12 shows the output of the unordered list when you run the application with a URL to the home address.

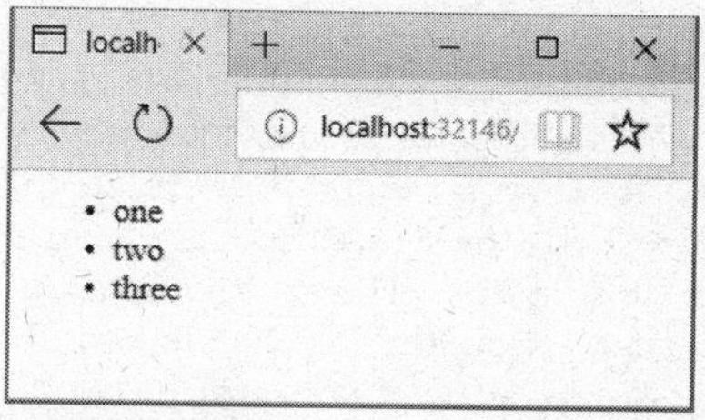

FIGURE 30-12

SIMPLE ROUTING

The Map method— an extension method of the IApplicationBuilder interface to create a simple routing—was used in the previous code samples. The Map method offers a simple routing facility with ASP.NET Core. With each map defined, ASP .NET Core specifies a new middleware pipeline that ends with the Run method based on an URL path.

If the request is received, and the path of a Map succeeds, the method assigned to the Action parameter defines the remaining pipeline that is active with the request. The Run method in the implementation of the code block specifies the last step of the pipeline.

The following code snippet defines a map to the /Home path and runs the Invoke method of the HomeController when a request is received (code file WebSampleApp/Startup.cs):

```
public void Configure(IApplicationBuilder app, ILoggerFactory loggerFactory)
{
  //...
  app.Map("/Home", homeApp =>
  {
    homeApp.Run(async context =>
    {
      HomeController controller =
        app.ApplicationServices.GetService<HomeController>();
      await controller.Index(context);
    });
  });
  //...
}
```

Instead of using the Map method, you can also use MapWhen. With the following code snippet, the map managed by MapWhen applies when the path contains the string hello. It doesn't matter if hello is at the begin or at the end, or if it is prefixed or postfixed (code file WebSampleApp/Startup.cs):

```
public void Configure(IApplicationBuilder app, IHostingEnvironment env)
{
  //...
  app.MapWhen(context => context.Request.Path.Value.Contains("hello"),
    helloApp =>
    {
      helloApp.Run(async context =>
      {
        await context.Response.WriteAsync("hello in the path".Div());
      });
    });
  //...
}
```

Instead of just using the path, you can also access any other information of the `HttpContext`, such as the host information of the client (`context.Request.Host`) or authenticated users (`context.User.Identity.IsAuthenticated`).

CREATING CUSTOM MIDDLEWARE

ASP.NET Core makes it easy to create modules that are invoked before the Run method is invoked. This can be used to add header information, verify tokens, build a cache, create log traces, and so on. One middleware module is chained after the other until all connected middleware types have been invoked.

You can create a middleware class by using the Visual Studio item template *Middleware Class*. With this middleware type, you create a constructor that receives a reference to the next middleware type. `RequestDelegate` is a delegate that receives an `HttpContext` as parameter and returns a `Task`. This is exactly the signature of the `Invoke` method. Within this method, you have access to request and response information. The type `HeaderMiddleware` adds a sample header to the response of the `HttpContext`. As the last action, the `Invoke` method invokes the next middleware module (code file `WebSampleApp/Middleware/HeaderMiddleware.cs`):

```
public class HeaderMiddleware
{
  private readonly RequestDelegate _next;

  public HeaderMiddleware(RequestDelegate next) =>
    _next = next;

  public Task Invoke(HttpContext httpContext)
  {
    httpContext.Response.Headers.Add("sampleheader",
      new[] { "addheadermiddleware"});
    return _next(httpContext);
  }
}
```

For making it easy to configure the middleware type, the extension method `UseHeaderMiddleware` extends the interface `IApplicationBuilder` where the method `UseMiddleware` is called:

```
public static class HeaderMiddlewareExtensions
{
  public static IApplicationBuilder UseHeaderMiddleware(
    this IApplicationBuilder builder) =>
      builder.UseMiddleware<HeaderMiddleware>();
}
```

Now it's the job of the `Startup` class and the `Configure` method to configure all the middleware types. The extension methods are already prepared for invocation (code file `WebSampleApp/Startup.cs`):

```
public void Configure(IApplicationBuilder app, ILoggerFactory loggerFactory)
{
  //...
  app.UseHeaderMiddleware();
  //...
}
```

When you run the application, you see the header returned to the client (using the browser's developer tools), and the heading shows up in every page, no matter which of the previously created links you use (see Figure 30-13).

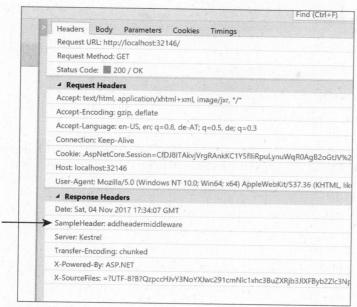

Find (Ctrl+F)

Headers Body Parameters Cookies Timings

Request URL: http://localhost:32146/

Request Method: GET

Status Code: ▇ 200 / OK

◢ **Request Headers**

Accept: text/html, application/xhtml+xml, image/jxr, */*

Accept-Encoding: gzip, deflate

Accept-Language: en-US, en; q=0.8, de-AT; q=0.5, de; q=0.3

Connection: Keep-Alive

Cookie: .AspNetCore.Session=CfDJ8ITAkvjVrgRAnkKC1Y5fIliRpuLynuWqR0AgB2oGtJV%2

Host: localhost:32146

User-Agent: Mozilla/5.0 (Windows NT 10.0; Win64; x64) AppleWebKit/537.36 (KHTML, lik

◢ **Response Headers**

Date: Sat, 04 Nov 2017 17:34:07 GMT

SampleHeader: addheadermiddleware

Server: Kestrel

Transfer-Encoding: chunked

X-Powered-By: ASP.NET

X-SourceFiles: =?UTF-8?B?QzpcHJvY3NoYwc291cmNlNlc1xhc3BuZXRcQXJjb3b3JlXFByb2Zlc3Np

FIGURE 30-13

SESSION STATE

A service that is implemented using middleware is *session state*. Session state enables temporarily remembering data from the client on the server. Session state itself is implemented as middleware.

Session state is initiated when a user first requests a page from a server. While the user keeps opening pages on the server, the session continues until a timeout (typically 10 minutes) occurs. To keep state on the server while the user navigates to a new page, state can be written to a session. When a timeout is reached, the session data is removed.

To identify a session, on the first request a temporary cookie with a session identifier is created. This cookie is returned from the client with every request to the server until the browser is closed, and then the cookie is deleted. Session identifiers can also be sent in the URL string as an alternative to using cookies.

On the server side, session information can be stored in memory. In a web farm, session state that is stored in memory doesn't propagate between different systems. With a sticky session configuration, the user always returns to the same physical server. Using sticky sessions, it doesn't matter that the same state is not available on other systems (with the exception when one server fails). Without sticky sessions, and to also deal with failing servers, options exist to store session state within distributed memory of a SQL server database. Storing session state in distributed memory also helps with process recycling of the server process; recycling kills session state also if you're using just a single server process.

For using session state with ASP.NET, you need to add the NuGet package `Microsoft.AspNet.Session`. This package gives the `AddSession` extension method that can be called within the `ConfigureServices` method in the `Startup` class. The parameter enables you to configure the idle timeout and the cookie options. The cookie is used to identify the session. The session also makes use of a service that implements the interface `IDistributedCache`. A simple implementation is the cache for in-process session state. The method `AddCaching` adds the following cache service (code file `WebSampleApp/Startup.cs`):

```
public void ConfigureServices(IServiceCollection services)
{
  services.AddTransient<ISampleService, DefaultSampleService>();
  services.AddTransient<HomeController>();
  services.AddDistributedMemoryCache();
  services.AddSession(options =>
    options.IdleTimeout = TimeSpan.FromMinutes(10));
}
```

For using the session, you need to configure the middleware in the pipeline by calling the `UseSession` extension method. You need to invoke this method before any response is written to the response—such as is done with the `UseHeaderMiddleware`—thus `UseSession` is called before the other methods. The code that uses session information is mapped to the `/Session` path (code file `WebSampleApp/Startup.cs`):

```
public void Configure(IApplicationBuilder app, ILoggerFactory loggerFactory)
{
  //...
  app.UseSession();
  app.UseHeaderMiddleware();
  app.Map("/Session", sessionApp =>
  {
    sessionApp.Run(async context =>
    {
      await SessionSample.SessionAsync(context);
    });
  });
  //...
}
```

You can write session state using `Setxxx` methods, such as `SetString` and `SetInt32`. These methods are defined with the `ISession` interface that is returned from the `Session` property of the `HttpContext`. Session data is retrieved using `Getxxx` methods (code file `WebSampleApp/SessionSample.cs`):

```
public static class SessionSample
{
  private const string SessionVisits = nameof(SessionVisits);
  private const string SessionTimeCreated = nameof(SessionTimeCreated);
  public static async Task SessionAsync(HttpContext context)
  {
    int visits = context.Session.GetInt32(SessionVisits) ?? 0;
    string timeCreated = context.Session.GetString(SessionTimeCreated) ??
      string.Empty;
    if (string.IsNullOrEmpty(timeCreated))
    {
      timeCreated = DateTime.Now.ToString("t", CultureInfo.InvariantCulture);
      context.Session.SetString(SessionTimeCreated, timeCreated);
    }
    DateTime timeCreated2 = DateTime.Parse(timeCreated);
    context.Session.SetInt32(SessionVisits, ++visits);
    await context.Response.WriteAsync(
      $"Number of visits within this session: {visits} " +
      $"that was created at {timeCreated2:T}; " +
      $"current time: {DateTime.Now:T}");
  }
}
```

> **NOTE** *The sample code uses an invariant culture to store the time when the session was created. The time shown to the user is using a specific culture. It's a good practice to use invariant cultures storing culture-specific data on the server. Information about invariant cultures and how to set cultures is explained in Chapter 26, "Localization."*

CONFIGURING WITH ASP.NET CORE

With web applications, it's necessary to store configuration information that can be changed by system administrators—for example, connection strings. In the next chapter you create a data-driven application where a connection string is needed.

Configuration of ASP.NET Core is no longer based on the XML configuration files `web.config` and `machine.config` as was the case with previous versions of ASP.NET. With the old configuration file, assembly references and assembly redirects were mixed with database connection strings and application settings. This is no longer the case. Application settings are typically stored within `appsettings.json`, but the configuration is a lot more flexible and you can choose to make your configuration with several JSON or XML files and with environment variables.

When you use the `WebHost` with the default builder as created with the default template, several configuration providers are configured (code file `WebSampleApp/Program.cs`):

```
public static IWebHost BuildWebHost(string[] args) =>
    WebHost.CreateDefaultBuilder(args)
        .UseStartup<Startup>()
        .Build();
```

In detail, these five providers are configured by default:

➤ `MemoryConfigurationProvider`

➤ `JsonConfigurationProvider` (`appsetttings.json`)

➤ `JsonConfigurationProvider` (`appsettings.{environment}.json`)

➤ `EnvironmentVariablesConfigurationProvider`

➤ `CommandLineConfigurationProvider`

One way to access configuration values from the `Startup` class is to inject the `IConfiguration` interface in the constructor and assign a property to the received configuration (code file `WebSampleApp/Startup.cs`):

```
public Startup(IConfiguration configuration)
{
    Configuration = configuration;
}

public IConfiguration Configuration { get; }
```

Create an Application Configuration file with this content (configuration file `WebSampleApp/appsettings.json`):

```
{
    "SampleSettings": {
        "Setting1": "Value1"
    },
    "AppSettings": {
        "setting2": "Value2",
        "Setting3": "Value3",
```

```
      "SubSection1": {
        "Setting4": "Value4"
      }
    },
    "ConnectionStrings": {
      "DefaultConnection":
        "Server=(localdb)\\MSSQLLocalDB;Database=_CHANGE_ME;
         Trusted_Connection=True;MultipleActiveResultSets=true"
    }
  }
```

This setting will be accessed in the next section.

Reading the Configuration

To read the configuration, you can use the IConfiguration interface and access the sections. The ConfigurationSample class accesses this interface via dependency injection (code file WebSampleApp/ConfigurationSample.cs):

```
public class ConfigurationSample
{
  private readonly IConfiguration _configuration;
  public ConfigurationSample(IConfiguration configuration) =>
    _configuration = configuration;
  //...
}
```

The settings can be retrieved using an indexer, and the sections within the configuration file can be accessed using GetSection. GetSection("SampleSettings") retrieves the SampleSettings section, followed by accessing the indexer passing the string Setting1. With this, the value Value1 is retrieved:

```
public async Task ShowApplicationSettingsAsync(HttpContext context)
{
  string settings = _configuration.GetSection("SampleSettings")["Setting1"];
  await context.Response.WriteAsync(settings.Div());
}
```

Instead of using the GetSection method to access hierarchical configuration, the colon syntax can be used with the indexer to separate all the hierarchies. The following code snippet retrieves the same values from the configuration file as the previous one:

```
public async Task ShowApplicationSettingsUsingColonsAsync(HttpContext context)
{
  string settings = _configuration["SampleSettings:Setting1"];
  await context.Response.WriteAsync(settings.Div());
}
```

For the section named ConnectionStrings an extension method exists to easily access connection strings. Instead of using GetSection and the indexer, you can use just the method GetConnectionString, retrieving the settings in this section:

```
public async Task ShowConnectionStringSettingAsync(HttpContext context)
{
  string connectionString = _configuration
    .GetConnectionString("DefaultConnection");
  await context.Response.WriteAsync(connectionString.Div());
}
```

You can also create a class for strongly typed access to configuration values. To use this feature, you can create the classes AppSettings and SubSection1 with property names that map directly to keys in the configuration file (code file WebSampleApp/ConfigurationSample.cs):

```
public class SubSection1
{
```

```
    public string Setting4 { get; set; }
  }

  public class AppSettings
  {
    public string Setting2 { get; set; }
    public string Setting3 { get; set; }
    public SubSection1 SubSection1 { get; set; }
  }
```

The custom classes to map the custom configuration types are filled by invoking the generic `Get` method and passing the `AppSettings` class as a generic parameter.

```
public async Task ShowApplicationSettingsStronglyTyped(HttpContext context)
{
  AppSettings settings = _configuration.GetSection("AppSettings")
    .Get<AppSettings>();
  await context.Response.WriteAsync($"setting 2: {settings.Setting2}, " +
    $"setting3: {settings.Setting3}, " +
    $"setting4: {settings.SubSection1.Setting4}".Div());
}
```

For running the application and calling the different methods of the `ConfigurationSample` class, the `MapWhen` defines a map to the `/Configuration` link and passes the remaining path to the `remainingPath` variable. Depending on the remaining part, different methods from the `ConfigurationSample` class are invoked (code file `WebSampleApp/Startup.cs`):

```
PathString remainingPath;
// out var not possible with lambda following in next parameter
app.MapWhen(context =>
  context.Request.Path.StartsWithSegments("/Configuration", out remainingPath),
  configurationApp =>
  {
    configurationApp.Run(async context =>
    {
      var configSample = app.ApplicationServices
        .GetService<ConfigurationSample>();
      if (remainingPath.StartsWithSegments("/appsettings"))
      {
        await configSample.ShowApplicationSettingsAsync(context);
      }
      else if (remainingPath.StartsWithSegments("/colons"))
      {
        await configSample.ShowApplicationSettingsUsingColonsAsync(context);
      }
      else if (remainingPath.StartsWithSegments("/database"))
      {
        await configSample.ShowConnectionStringSettingAsync(context);
      }
      else if (remainingPath.StartsWithSegments("/stronglytyped"))
      {
        await configSample.ShowApplicationSettingsStronglyTyped(context);
      }
    });
  });
```

Changing Configuration Providers

You've seen that five configuration providers are configured with the default host builder. The order of these providers is important. If different values for the same key are specified multiple times, the last configured value is returned. For example, when you pass values from the command line, these values are taken rather than configured in a JSON file. Make a complete custom configuration with a .NET Core console application and add the following NuGet packages to this application:

```
Microsoft.Extensions.Configuration

Microsoft.Extensions.Configuration.CommandLine

Microsoft.Extensions.Configuration.EnvironmentVariables

Microsoft.Extensions.Configuration.Json
```

The configuration of the console application is done using a `ConfigurationBuilder`. The `ConfigurationBuilder` class implements the interface `IConfigurationBuilder`. For this interface, various extension methods are defined in the NuGet packages `Microsoft.Extensions.Configuration.*`. The method `SetupConfiguration` adds providers for JSON, environmental variables, and the command line (code file `CustomConfiguration/Program.cs`):

```
static void SetupConfiguration(string[] args)
{
  var builder = new ConfigurationBuilder()
    .SetBasePath(Directory.GetCurrentDirectory())
    .AddJsonFile("appsettings.json")
    .AddEnvironmentVariables()
    .AddCommandLine(args);
  Configuration = builder.Build();
}


public static IConfigurationRoot Configuration { get; private set; }
```

The configuration is read using the `GetSection` method and the indexer of the `IConfiguration` interface, as discussed in earlier sections:

```
private static void ReadConfiguration()
{
  string val1 = Configuration.GetSection("section1")["key1"];
  Console.WriteLine(val1);
  string val2 = Configuration.GetSection("section1")["key2"];
  Console.WriteLine(val2);
}
```

The JSON configuration file defines these settings (configuration file `CustomConfiguration/appsettings.json`):

```
{
  "section1": {
    "key1": "value 1",
    "key2": "value 2"
  }
}
```

Because the environment variables and the command-line providers are added after the JSON provider, settings defined by these providers override the other settings. When you use the command line with the `dotnet` command, arguments to the application are assigned after a -- to separate the arguments from the application from the arguments of the `dotnet` command. Hierarchical configuration sections are separated with a colon:

```
> dotnet run -- section1:key1="settings from command line"
```

Command-line arguments and environment variables can be configured from within Visual Studio in the Debug settings as shown in Figure 30-14.

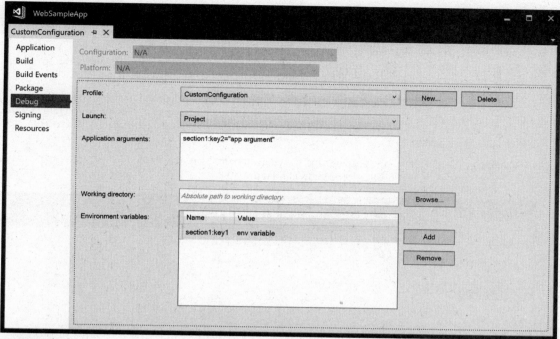

FIGURE 30-14

The debug settings are written to the file `LaunchSettings.json`:

```
{
  "profiles": {
    "CustomConfiguration": {
      "commandName": "Project",
      "commandLineArgs": "section1:key2=\"app argument\"",
      "environmentVariables": {
        "section1:key1": "env variable"
      }
    }
  }
}
```

With an ASP.NET Core web application, you can define the configuration providers, as you've seen previously with the console application. However, ASP.NET Core 2 offers a simpler way to add extra configuration with extension methods of the `IWebHostBuilder`, such as the `ConfigureAppConfiguration` method. The following code snippet adds the XML file `appsettings.xml` by using the `AddXmlFile` extension method. A runtime exception should not occur when the file does not exist, thus the file is marked as optional (code file `WebSampleApp/Program.cs`):

```csharp
public static IWebHost BuildWebHost(string[] args) =>
  WebHost.CreateDefaultBuilder(args)
    .UseStartup<Startup>()
    .ConfigureAppConfiguration(configure =>
    {
      configure.AddXmlFile("appsettings.xml", optional: true);
    })
    .Build();
```

Different Configurations Based on the Environment

When running your web application with different environments—for example, during development, testing, and production—you might also use a staging server because it's likely you are using some different configurations. You don't want to add test data to the production database. For the configuration values that should be different, you can use different configuration files.

The default builder of the `WebHost` adds two JSON configuration files, `appsettings.json` and `appsettings.{env.EnvironmentName}.json`. The second file is configured to be optional, just like the XML file configuration from the previous section. The environment name is configured differently based on debug and release builds.

You can configure the environment by setting the environmental variable named `ASPNETCORE_ENVIRONMENT` in the Visual Studio project properties as shown in Figure 30-15.

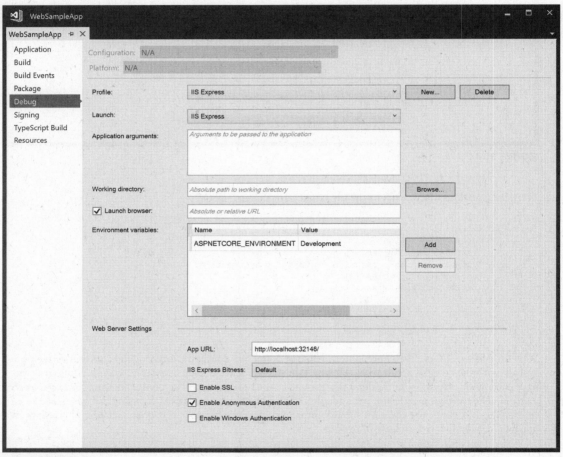

FIGURE 30-15

To verify the hosting environment programmatically, extension methods are defined for the interface `IHostingEnvironment`, such as `IsDevelopment`, `IsStaging`, and `IsProduction`. You can use these methods, or to test for any environmental name, you can pass a verification string to `IsEnvironment`:

```
if (env.IsDevelopment())
{
  //...
}
```

SUMMARY

In this chapter, you explored the foundation of ASP.NET Core and web applications. You've seen requests from a browser and returning simple responses after reading request information. You've seen the foundation of ASP.NET Core with dependency injection and services, and you've seen a concrete implementation using dependency injection such as session state. You've also seen how configuration information can be stored in different ways, such as JSON configuration for different environments such as development and production.

The next chapter shows how ASP.NET Core MVC, which uses the foundation discussed in this chapter, can be used to create web applications.

31

ASP.NET Core MVC

WHAT'S IN THIS CHAPTER?

➤ Features of ASP.NET Core MVC
➤ Routing
➤ Creating controllers
➤ Creating views
➤ Validating user inputs
➤ Using filters
➤ Working with HTML and Tag Helpers
➤ Creating data-driven web applications
➤ Implementing authentication and authorization
➤ Working with Razor Pages

WROX.COM CODE DOWNLOADS FOR THIS CHAPTER

The Wrox.com code downloads for this chapter are found at http://www.wrox.com on the Download Code tab. The source code is also available at https://github.com/ProfessionalCSharp/ProfessionalCSharp7 in the directory MVC.

The code for this chapter is divided into the following major examples:

➤ MVC Sample App
➤ Menu Planner
➤ AzureB2C Sample
➤ Razor Pages Sample

SETTING UP SERVICES FOR ASP.NET CORE MVC

Chapter 30, "ASP.NET Core," showed you the foundation of ASP.NET Core with dependency injection and middleware. This chapter makes use of dependency injection by injecting ASP.NET Core MVC services.

ASP.NET Core MVC is based on the MVC (Model-View-Controller) pattern. As shown in Figure 31-1, this standard pattern (a pattern documented in *Design Patterns: Elements of Reusable Object-Oriented Software* book by the Gang of Four [Addison-Wesley Professional, 1994]) defines a model that implements data entities and data access, a view that represents the information shown to the user, and a controller that makes use of the model and sends data to the view. The controller receives a request from the browser and returns a response. To build the response, the controller can make use of a model to provide some data, and a view to define the HTML that is returned.

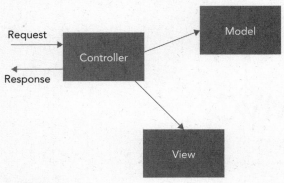

FIGURE 31-1

With ASP.NET Core MVC, the controller and model are typically created with C# and .NET code that is run server-side. The view is HTML code with JavaScript and just a little C# code for accessing server-side information.

The big advantage of this separation in the MVC pattern is that you can use unit tests to easily test the functionality. The controller just contains methods with parameters and return values that can be covered easily with unit tests.

Let's start setting up services for ASP.NET Core MVC. With ASP.NET Core dependency injection is deeply integrated as you've seen in Chapter 30. You can create an ASP.NET Core MVC project selecting the ASP .NET Core template *Web Application (Model-View-Controller)*. This template already includes NuGet packages required with ASP.NET Core MVC, and a directory structure that helps with organizing the application. However, here we'll start with the Empty template (as in Chapter 30), so you can see what's all needed to build up an ASP.NET Core MVC project, without the extra stuff you might not need with your project.

The first project created is named MVCSampleApp. The Empty template already includes a reference to the NuGet package Microsoft.AspNetCore.All, so the packages needed for ASP.NET Core MVC are already included. You add the MVC services by invoking the extension method AddMvc within the ConfigureServices method (code file MVCSampleApp/Startup.cs):

```
using Microsoft.AspNetCore.Builder;
using Microsoft.AspNetCore.Hosting;
using Microsoft.AspNetCore.Http;
using Microsoft.Extensions.DependencyInjection;

namespace MVCSampleApp
{
  public class Startup
  {
    //...
    public void ConfigureServices(IServiceCollection services)
    {
```

```
            services.AddMvc();
        }
    }
}
```

The `AddMvc` extension method adds and configures several ASP.NET Core MVC core services, such as configuration features (`IConfigureOptions` with `MvcOptions` and `RouteOptions`); controller factories and controller activators (`IControllerFactory`, `IControllerActivator`); action method selectors, invocators, and constraint providers (`IActionSelector`, `IActionInvokerFactory`, `IActionConstraintProvider`); argument binders and model validators (`IControllerActionArgumentBinder`, `IObjectModelValidator`); and filter providers (`IFilterProvider`).

In addition to the core services it adds, the `AddMvc` method adds ASP.NET Core MVC services to support authorization, CORS, data annotations, views, the Razor view engine, and more.

DEFINING ROUTES

Chapter 30 explains how the `Map` extension method of the `IApplicationBuilder` defines a simple route. This chapter shows how the ASP.NET Core MVC routes are based on this mapping to offer a flexible routing mechanism for mapping URLs to controllers and action methods.

The controller is selected based on a route. A simple way to create the default route is to invoke the method `UseMvcWithDefaultRoute` in the `Startup` class (code file `MVCSampleApp/Startup.cs`):

```
public void Configure(IApplicationBuilder app)
{
    //...
    app.UseStaticFiles();
    app.UseMvcWithDefaultRoute();
    //...
}
```

> **NOTE** *The extension method* `UseStaticFiles` *is discussed in Chapter 30.*

With this default route, the name of the controller type (without the `Controller` suffix) and the method name make up the route, such as `http://server[:port]/controller/action`. You can also use an optional parameter named `id`, like so: `http://server[:port]/controller/action/id`. The default name of the controller is `Home`; the default name of the action method is `Index`.

The following code snippet shows another way to specify the same default route. The `UseMvc` method can receive a parameter of type `Action<IRouteBuilder>`. This `IRouteBuilder` interface contains a list of routes that are mapped. You define routes using the `MapRoute` extension method:

```
app.UseMvc(routes => routes.MapRoute(
  name: "default",
  template: "{controller}/{action}/{id?}",
  defaults: new {controller = "Home", action = "Index"}
));
```

This route definition is the same as the default one. The `template` parameter defines the URL; the `?` with the `id` defines that this parameter is optional; the `defaults` parameter defines the default values for the `controller` and `action` part of the URL.

Let's have a look at this URL:

```
http://localhost:[port]/UseAService/GetSampleStrings
```

With this URL, UseAService maps to the name of the controller, because the Controller suffix is automatically added; the type name is UseAServiceController; and GetSampleStrings is the action, which represents a method in the UseAServiceController type.

Adding Routes

There are several reasons to add or change routes. For example, you can modify routes to use actions with the link, to define Home as the default controller, to add entries to the link, or to use multiple parameters.

You can define a route where the user can use links—such as http://<server>/About to address the About action method in the Home controller without passing a controller name—as shown in the following snippet. Notice that the controller name is left out from the URL. The controller keyword is mandatory with the route, but you can supply it with the defaults:

```
app.UseMvc(routes => routes.MapRoute(
  name: "default",
  template: "{action}/{id?}",
  defaults: new {controller = "Home", action = "Index"}
));
```

Another scenario for changing the route is shown in the following code snippet. In this snippet, you are adding the variable language to the route. This variable is set to the section within the URL that follows the server name and is placed before the controller—for example, http://server/en/Home/About. You can use this to specify a language:

```
app.UseMvc(routes => routes.MapRoute(
  name: "default",
  template: "{controller}/{action}/{id?}",
  defaults: new {controller = "Home", action = "Index"}
).MapRoute(
  name: "language",
  template: "{language}/{controller}/{action}/{id?}",
  defaults: new {controller = "Home", action = "Index"}
);
```

If one route matches and the controller and action method are found, the route is taken; otherwise the next route is selected until one route matches.

Using Route Constraints

When you map the route, you can specify constraints. This way, URLs other than those defined by the constraint are not possible. The following constraint defines that the language parameter can be only en or de by using the regular expression (en)|(de). URLs such as http://<server>/en/Home/About or http://<server>/de/Home/About are valid:

```
app.UseMvc(routes => routes.MapRoute(
  name: "language",
  template: "{language}/{controller}/{action}/{id?}",
  defaults: new {controller = "Home", action = "Index"},
  constraints: new {language = @"(en)|(de)"}
));
```

Constraints can be specified within the template definition, or with the constraints definition. With the id parameter in the previous sample, the ? followed by the parameter name specifies that this parameter is optional. You can also specify a specific data type in the template, such as using int parameter type for the product ID:

```
routes.MapRoute(
  name: "products",
  template: "{controller}/{action}/{productId:int}",
  defaults: new {controller = "Home", action = "Index"});
```

Besides the data types, you also can specify constraints for minimum values, maximum values, a range, and strings with minimum and maximum length. If a link should enable only numbers (for example, to access products with a product number), the regular expression \d+ matches any number of numerical digits, but it must match at least one:

```
app.UseMvc(routes => routes.MapRoute(
  name: "products",
  template: "{controller}/{action}/{productId?}",
  defaults: new {controller = "Home", action = "Index"},
  constraints: new {productId = @"\d+"}
));
```

> **NOTE** *With all these constraints available, you shouldn't use constraints for input validation. Constraints can be used to select a route, and this is what they should be used for. If a constraint doesn't match, the next routes are checked for matches. In case there's no route that matches, the HTTP status code 404 (not found) is returned. Input validation is discussed later in this chapter in the section "Receiving Data from the Client."*

Now you've seen how routing specifies the controller that is used and the action of the controller. The next section, "Creating Controllers," covers the details of controllers.

CREATING CONTROLLERS

A *controller* reacts to requests from the user and sends a response. As described in this section, a view is not required.

There are some conventions for using ASP.NET Core MVC. Conventions are preferred over configuration. With controllers you'll also see some conventions. You can find controllers in the directory Controllers, and the name of the controller class must be suffixed with the name Controller.

Before creating the first controller, create the Controllers directory. Then you can create a controller by selecting this directory in Solution Explorer, select Add ⇨ New Item from the context menu, and select the MVC Controller Class item template. The HomeController is created for the route that is specified.

The generated code contains a HomeController class that derives from the base class Controller. This class also contains an Index method that corresponds to the Index action. When you request an action as defined by the route, a method within the controller is invoked (code file MVCSampleApp/Controllers/HomeController.cs):

```
public class HomeController : Controller
{
  public IActionResult Index() => View();
}
```

Understanding Action Methods

A controller contains action methods. A simple action method is the Hello method from the following code snippet (code file MVCSampleApp/Controllers/HomeController.cs):

```
public string Hello() => "Hello, ASP.NET Core MVC";
```

You can invoke the Hello action in the Home controller with the link http://localhost:4944/Home/Hello. Of course, the port number depends on your settings, and you can configure it with the web properties in the project settings. When you open this link from the browser, the controller returns just the string Hello, ASP.NET Core MVC; no HTML—just a string. The browser displays the string.

An action can return anything—for example, the bytes of an image, a video, XML or JSON data, or, of course, HTML. Views are of great help for returning HTML.

Using Parameters

You can declare action methods with parameters, as in the following code snippet (code file `MVCSampleApp/Controllers/HomeController.cs`):

```
public string Greeting(string name) =>
    HtmlEncoder.Default.Encode($"Hello, {name}");
```

With this declaration, the `Greeting` action method can be invoked to request this URL to pass a value with the `name` parameter in the URL: `http://localhost:4944/Home/Greeting?name=Stephanie`.

To use links that can be better remembered, you can use route information to specify the parameters. The `Greeting2` action method specifies the parameter named `id`.

```
public string Greeting2(string id) =>
    HtmlEncoder.Default.Encode($"Hello, {id}");
```

This matches the default route `{controller}/{action}/{id?}` where `id` is specified as an optional parameter. Now you can use this link, and the `id` parameter contains the string `Matthias`: `http://localhost:4944/Home/Greeting2/Matthias`.

You can also declare action methods with any number of parameters. For example, you can add the `Add` action method to the Home controller with two parameters, like so:

```
public int Add(int x, int y) => x + y;
```

You can invoke this action with the URL `http://localhost:4944/Home/Add?x=4&y=5` to fill the x and y parameters.

With multiple parameters, you can also define a route to pass the values with a different link. The following code snippet shows an additional route defined in the route table to specify multiple parameters that fill the variables x and y and only allows numbers with up to three digits (code file `MVCSampleApp/Startup.cs`):

```
app.UseMvc(routes => routes.MapRoute(
  name: "default",
  template: "{controller}/{action}/{id?}",
  defaults: new {controller = "Home", action = "Index"}
).MapRoute(
  name: "multipleparameters",
  template: "{controller}/{action}/{x:int}/{y:int}",
  defaults: new {controller = "Home", action = "Add"},
  constraints: new {x = @"\d{1,3}", y = @"\d{1,3}"}
));
```

Now you can invoke the same action as before using this URL: `http://localhost:4994/Home/Add/7/2`.

> **NOTE** *Later in this chapter, in the section "Passing Data to Views," you see how parameters of custom types can be used and how data from the client can map to properties.*

Returning Data

So far, you have returned only string values from the controller. Usually, an object implementing the interface `IActionResult` is returned.

Following are several examples with the `ResultController` class. The first code snippet uses the `ContentResult` class to return simple text content. Instead of creating an instance of the `ContentResult` class and returning the instance, you can use methods from the base class `Controller` to return `ActionResults`. In the following example, the method `Content` is used to return text content. The `Content` method enables specifying the content, the MIME type, and encoding (code file `MVCSampleApp/Controllers/ResultController.cs`):

```
public IActionResult ContentDemo() =>
    Content("Hello World", "text/plain");
```

To return JSON-formatted data, you can use the `Json` method. The following sample code creates a `Menu` object:

```
public IActionResult JsonDemo()
{
  var m = new Menu
  {
    Id = 3,
    Text = "Grilled sausage with sauerkraut and potatoes",
    Price = 12.90,
    Date = new DateTime(2018, 3, 31),
    Category = "Main"
  };
  return Json(m);
}
```

The `Menu` class is defined within the `Models` directory and defines a simple POCO class with a few properties (code file `MVCSampleApp/Models/Menu.cs`):

```
public class Menu
{
  public int Id {get; set;}
  public string Text {get; set;}
  public double Price {get; set;}
  public DateTime Date {get; set;}
  public string Category {get; set;}
}
```

The client sees this JSON data in the response body. JSON data can easily be consumed as a JavaScript object:

```
{"id":3,"text":"Grilled sausage with sauerkraut and potatoes",
"price":12.9,"date":"2018-03-31T00:00:00","category":"Main"}
```

Using the `Redirect` method of the `Controller` class, the client receives an HTTP redirect request. After receiving the redirect request, the browser requests the link it received. The `Redirect` method returns a `RedirectResult` (code file `MVCSampleApp/Controllers/ResultController.cs`):

```
public IActionResult RedirectDemo() =>
    Redirect("https://www.cninnovation.com");
```

You can also build a redirect request to the client by specifying a redirect to another controller and action. `RedirectToRoute` returns a `RedirectToRouteResult` that enables specifying route names, controllers, actions, and parameters. This builds a link that is returned to the client with an HTTP redirect request:

```
public IActionResult RedirectRouteDemo() =>
    RedirectToRoute(new {controller = "Home", action="Hello"});
```

The `File` method of the `Controller` base class defines different overloads that return different types. This method can return `FileContentResult`, `FileStreamResult`, and `VirtualFileResult`. The different return types depend on the parameters used—for example, a string for a `VirtualFileResult`, a `Stream` for a `FileStreamResult`, and a byte array for a `FileContentResult`.

The next code snippet returns an image. Create an Images folder and add a JPG file. For the next code snippet to work, create an `Images` folder in the `wwwroot` directory and add the file `Matthias.jpg`. The sample code returns a `VirtualFileResult` that specifies a filename with the first parameter. The second parameter specifies the `contentType` argument with the MIME type `image/jpeg`:

```
public IActionResult FileDemo() =>
   File("~/images/Matthias.jpg", "image/jpeg");
```

The next section shows how to return different `ViewResult` variants.

Working with the Controller Base Class and POCO Controllers

So far, all the controllers created have been derived from the base class `Controller`. ASP.NET Core MVC also supports controllers—known as known as POCO (Plain Old CLR Objects) controllers—that do not derive from this base class. This way you can use your own base class to define your own type hierarchy with controllers.

What do you get out of the `Controller` base class? With this base class, the controller can directly access properties of the base class. The following table describes these properties and their functionality.

PROPERTY	DESCRIPTION
ControllerContext	This property wraps some other properties. Here you can get information about the action descriptor, which contains the name of the action, controller, filters, and method information; the `HttpContext`, which is directly accessible from the `HttpContext` property; the state of the model that is directly accessible from the `ModelState` property, and route information that is directly accessible from the `RouteData` property.
HttpContext	This property returns the `HttpContext`. With this context you can access the `ServiceProvider` to access services registered with dependency injection (`ApplicationServices` property), authentication and user information, request and response information that is also directly accessible from the `Request` and `Response` properties, and web sockets (if they are in use).
ModelBinderFactory	With this property you can create a binder that binds the received data to the parameters of the action method. Binding request information to custom types is discussed later in this chapter in the section "Submitting Data from the Client."
MetadataProvider	You use a binder to bind parameters. The binder can make use of metadata that is associated with the model. Using the `MetadataProvider` property, you can access information about what providers are configured to deal with metadata information.
ModelState	The `ModelState` property lets you know whether model binding was successful or had errors. In case of errors, you can read the information about what properties resulted in errors.
Request	With this property you can access all information about the HTTP request: header and body information, the query string, form data, and cookies. The header information contains a `User-Agent` string that gives information about the browser and client platform.

PROPERTY	DESCRIPTION
Response	This property holds information that is returned to the client. Here, you can send cookies, change header information, and write directly to the body. Earlier in this chapter, in the section Startup, you've seen how a simple string can be returned to the client by using the Response property.
RouteData	The RouteData property gives information about the complete route table that is registered in the startup code.
ViewBag ViewData	You use these properties to send information to the view. This is explained later in the section "Passing Data to Views."
TempData	This property is written to the user state that is shared between multiple requests (whereas data written to ViewBag and ViewData can be written to share information between views and controllers within a single request). By default, TempData writes information to the session state.
User	The User property returns information, including identity and claims, about an authenticated user.

A POCO controller doesn't have the Controller base class, but it's still important to access such information. The following code snippet defines a POCO controller that derives from the object base class (you can use your own custom type as a base class). To create an ActionContext with the POCO class, you can create a property of this type. The POCOController class uses ActionContext as the name of this property, like the way the Controller class does. However, just having a property doesn't set it automatically. You need to apply the ActionContext attribute. Using this attribute injects the actual ActionContext. The Context property directly accesses the HttpContext property from the ActionContext. The HttpContext property is used from the UserAgentInfo action method to access and return the User-Agent header information from the request (code file MVCSampleApp/Controllers/POCOController.cs):

```csharp
public class POCOController
{
  public string Index() =>
    "this is a POCO controller";

  [ActionContext]
  public ActionContext ActionContext {get; set;}

  public HttpContext HttpContext => ActionContext.HttpContext;

  public ModelStateDictionary ModelState => ActionContext.ModelState;

  public string UserAgentInfo()
  {
    if (HttpContext.Request.Headers.ContainsKey("User-Agent"))
    {
      return HttpContext.Request.Headers["User-Agent"];
    }
    return "No user-agent information";
  }
}
```

CREATING VIEWS

The HTML code that is returned to the client is best specified with a view. For the samples in this section, the `ViewsDemoController` is created. The views are all defined within the `Views` folder. The views for the `ViewsDemo` controller need a `ViewsDemo` subdirectory. This is a convention for the views (code file `MVCSampleApp/Controllers/ViewsDemoController.cs`):

```
public ActionResult Index() => View();
```

> **NOTE** *Another place where views are searched is the* `Shared` *directory. You can put views that should be used by multiple controllers (and special partial views used by multiple views) into the* `Shared` *directory.*

After creating the `ViewsDemo` directory within the `Views` directory, the view can be created using Add ⇨ New Item and selecting the MVC View Page item template. Because the action method has the name `Index`, the view file is named `Index.cshtml`.

The action method `Index` uses the `View` method without parameters, and thus the view engine searches for a view file with the same name as the action name in the `ViewsDemo` directory. The `View` method used in the controller has overloads that enable passing a different view name. In that case, the view engine looks for a view with the name passed to the `View` method.

A view contains HTML code mixed with a little server-side code, as shown in the following snippet (code file `MVCSampleApp/Views/ViewsDemo/Index.cshtml`):

```
@{
  Layout = null;
}
<!DOCTYPE html>
<html>
<head>
  <meta charset="utf-8" />
  <meta name="viewport" content="width=device-width" />
  <title>Index</title>
</head>
<body>
</body>
</html>
```

Server-side code is written using the @ sign, which starts the Razor syntax, which is discussed later in this chapter. Before getting into the details of the Razor syntax, the next section shows how to pass data from a controller to a view.

Passing Data to Views

The controller and view run in the same process. The view is directly created from within the controller. This makes it easy to pass data from the controller to the view. To pass data, you can use a `ViewDataDictionary`. This dictionary stores keys as strings and enables object values. You can use the `ViewDataDictionary` with the `ViewData` property of the `Controller` class—for example, you can pass a string to the dictionary where the key value `MyData` is used: `ViewData["MyData"] = "Hello"`. An easier syntax uses the `ViewBag` property. `ViewBag` is a dynamic type that enables assigning any property name to pass data to the view (code file `MVCSampleApp/Controllers/SubmitDataController.cs`):

```
public IActionResult PassingData()
{
  ViewBag.MyData = "Hello from the controller";
  return View();
}
```

> **NOTE** *Using dynamic types has the advantage that there is no direct dependency from the view to the controller. Dynamic types are explained in detail in Chapter 16, "Reflection, Metadata, and Dynamic Programming."*

From within the view, you can access the data passed from the controller in a similar way as in the controller. The base class of the view (`WebViewPage`) defines a `ViewBag` property (code file `MVCSampleApp/Views/ViewsDemo/PassingData.cshtml`):

```
<div>
  <div>@ViewBag.MyData</div>
</div>
```

Understanding Razor Syntax

As discussed earlier when you were introduced to views, the view contains both HTML and server-side code. With ASP.NET Core MVC you can use Razor syntax to write C# code in the view. Razor uses the @ character as a transition character. Starting with @, C# code begins.

With Razor you need to differentiate statements that return a value and methods that don't. A value that is returned can be used directly. For example, `ViewBag.MyData` returns a string. The string is put directly between the HTML div tags as shown here:

```
<div>@ViewBag.MyData</div>
```

When you're invoking methods that return void or specifying some other statements that don't return a value, you need a Razor code block. The following code block defines a string variable:

```
@{
    string name = "Angela";
}
```

You can now use the variable with the simple syntax; you just use the transition character @ to access the variable:

```
<div>@name</div>
```

With the Razor syntax, the engine automatically detects the end of the C# code when it finds an HTML element. There are some cases in which the end of the C# code cannot be detected automatically. You can resolve this by using parentheses as shown in the following example to mark a variable, and then the normal text continues:

```
<div>@(name), Stephanie</div>
```

Another way to start a Razor code block is with the `foreach` statement:

```
@foreach(var item in list)
{
    <li>The item name is @item.</li>
}
```

> **NOTE** *Usually text content is automatically detected with Razor—for example, Razor detects an opening angle bracket or parentheses with a variable. There are a few cases in which this does not work. Here, you can explicitly use @: to define the start of text.*

Creating Strongly Typed Views

Passing data to views, you've seen the `ViewBag` in action. There's another way to pass data to a view—pass a *model* to the view. Using models allows you to create *strongly typed views*.

The `ViewsDemoController` is now extended with the action method `PassingAModel`. The following example creates a new list of `Menu` items, and this list is passed as the model to the `View` method of the `Controller` base class (code file `MVCSampleApp/Controllers/ViewsDemoController.cs`):

```
private IEnumerable<Menu> GetSampleData() =>
  new List<Menu>
  {
    new Menu
    {
      Id=1,
      Text="Schweinsbraten mit Knödel und Sauerkraut",
      Price=6.9,
      Category="Main"
    },
    new Menu
    {
      Id=2,
      Text="Erdäpfelgulasch mit Tofu und Gebäck",
      Price=6.9,
      Category="Vegetarian"
    },
    new Menu
    {
      Id=3,
      Text="Tiroler Bauerngröst'l mit Spiegelei und Krautsalat",
      Price=6.9,
      Category="Main"
    }
  };

public IActionResult PassingAModel() =>
  View(GetSampleData());
```

When model information is passed from the action method to the view, you can create a strongly typed view. A strongly typed view is declared using the `model` keyword. The type of the model passed to the view must match the declaration of the `model` directive. In the following code snippet, the strongly typed view declares the type `IEnumerable<Menu>`, which matches the model type. Because the `Menu` class is defined within the namespace `MVCSampleApp.Models`, this namespace is opened with the `using` keyword.

The base class of the view that is created from the `.cshtml` file derives from the base class `RazorPage`. With a model in place, the base class is of type `RazorPage<TModel>`; with the following code snippet the base class is `RazorPage<IEnumerable<Menu>>`. This generic parameter in turn defines a `Model` property of type `IEnumerable<Menu>`. With the code snippet, the `Model` property of the base class is used to iterate through the `Menu` items with `@foreach` and displays a list item for every menu (code file `MVCSampleApp/ViewsDemo/PassingAModel.cshtml`):

```
@using MVCSampleApp.Models
@model IEnumerable<Menu>
@{
  Layout = null;
}
```

```
<!DOCTYPE html>
<html>
<head>
  <meta name="viewport" content="width=device-width" />
  <title>PassingAModel</title>
</head>
<body>
  <div>
    <ul>
      @foreach (var item in Model)
      {
        <li>@item.Text</li>
      }
    </ul>
  </div>
</body>
</html>
```

You can pass any object as the model—whatever you need with the view. For example, when you're editing a single Menu object, you'd use a model of type Menu. When you're showing or editing a list, you can use IEnumerable<Menu>.

When you run the application showing the defined view, you see a list of menus in the browser, as shown in Figure 31-2.

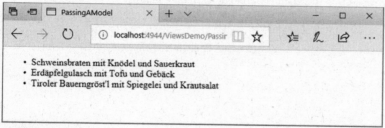

FIGURE 31-2

Defining the Layout

Usually many pages of web applications share some of the same content—for example, copyright information, a logo, and a main navigation structure. Until now, all your views have contained complete HTML content, but there's an easier way to manage the shared content. This is where layout pages come into play.

To define a layout, you set the Layout property of the view. For defining default properties for all views, you can create a view start page. You need to put this file into the Views folder, and you can create it using the item template MVC View Start Page. This creates the file _ViewStart.cshtml (code file MVCSampleApp/Views/_ViewStart.cshtml):

```
@{
  Layout = "_Layout";
}
```

For all views that don't need a layout, you can set the Layout property to null:

```
@{
  Layout = null;
}
```

Using a Default Layout Page

You can create the default layout page using the item template MVC View Layout Page. You can create this page in the `Shared` folder so that it is available for all views from different controllers. The Visual Studio item template MVC View Layout Page creates the following code:

```
<!DOCTYPE html>
<html>
<head>
  <meta name="viewport" content="width=device-width" />
  <title>@ViewBag.Title</title>
</head>
<body>
  <div>
    @RenderBody()
  </div>
</body>
</html>
```

The layout page contains the HTML content that is common to all pages (for example, header, footer, and navigation) that use this layout page. You've already seen how views and controllers can communicate with the `ViewBag`. The same mechanism can be used with the layout page. You can define the value for `ViewBag`
`.Title` within a content page; from the layout page, it is shown in the preceding code snippet within the HTML `title` element. The `RenderBody` method of the base class `RazorPage` renders the content of the content page and thus defines the position in which the content should be placed.

With the following code snippet, the generated layout page is updated to reference a style sheet and to add header, footer, and navigation sections to every page. `environment`, `asp-controller`, and `asp-action` are Tag Helpers that create HTML elements. Tag Helpers are discussed later in this chapter in the "Helpers" section (code file `MVCSampleApp/Views/Shared/_Layout.cshtml`):

```
<!DOCTYPE html>
<html>
<head>
<head>
  <meta charset="utf-8" />
  <meta name="viewport" content="width=device-width, initial-scale=1.0" />
  <title>@ViewBag.Title</title>

  <environment include="Development">
    <link rel="stylesheet" href="~/lib/bootstrap/dist/css/bootstrap.css" />
    <link rel="stylesheet" href="~/css/site.css" />
  </environment>
  <environment exclude="Development">
    <link rel="stylesheet"
      href="https://ajax.aspnetcdn.com/ajax/bootstrap/3.3.7/css/bootstrap.min.css"
      asp-fallback-href="~/lib/bootstrap/dist/css/bootstrap.min.css"
      asp-fallback-test-class="sr-only" asp-fallback-test-property="position"
      asp-fallback-test-value="absolute" />
    <link rel="stylesheet" href="~/css/site.min.css" asp-append-version="true" />
  </environment>

  <title>@ViewBag.Title - My ASP.NET Application</title>
</head>
<body>
  <div class="container body-content">
    <header>
      <h1>ASP.NET Core MVC Sample App</h1>
    </header>
    <nav>
      <ul>
      <li><a asp-controller="ViewsDemo" asp-action="LayoutSample">
```

```
         Layout Sample</a></li>
      <li><a asp-controller="ViewsDemo" asp-action="LayoutUsingSections">
         Layout Using Sections</a></li>
      </ul>
   </nav>
   <div>
      @RenderBody()
   </div>
   <hr />
   <footer>
      <p>
         <div>Sample Code for Professional C#</div>
         &copy; @DateTime.Now.Year - My ASP.NET Application
      </p>
   </footer>
   </div>
</body>
</html>
```

A view is created for the action `LayoutSample` (code file `MVCSampleApp/Views/ViewsDemo/`
`LayoutSample.cshtml`). This view doesn't set the `Layout` property and thus uses the default layout. The
following code snippet sets `ViewBag.Title`, which is used within the HTML `title` element in the layout:

```
@{
   ViewBag.Title = "Layout Sample";
}
<h2>Layout Sample</h2>
<p>
   This content is merged with the layout page
</p>
```

When you run the application now, the content from the layout and the view is merged, as shown in
Figure 31-3.

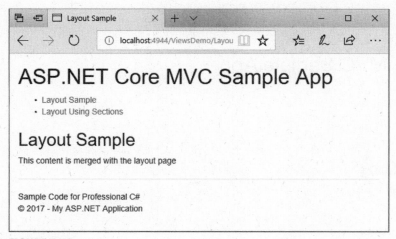

FIGURE 31-3

Using Sections

Rendering the body and using the `ViewBag` is not the only way to exchange data between the layout and the
view. With section areas you can define where the named content should be placed within a view. The following code snippet makes use of a section named `PageNavigation`. Such sections are required by default,

and loading the view fails if the section is not defined. When the `required` parameter is set to `false`, the section becomes optional (code file `MVCSampleApp/Views/Shared/_Layout.cshtml`):

```
<!-- ... -->
<div>
  @RenderSection("PageNavigation", required: false)
</div>
<div>
@RenderBody()
</div>
<!-- ... -->
```

Within the view page, the `section` keyword defines the section. The position where the section is placed is completely independent from the other content. The view doesn't define the position within the page; this is defined by the layout (code file `MVCSampleApp/Views/ViewsDemo/LayoutUsingSections.cshtml`):

```
@{
ViewBag.Title = "Layout Using Sections";
}
<h2>Layout Using Sections</h2>
<div>Main content here</div>
@section PageNavigation
{
  <div>Navigation defined from the view</div>
  <ul>
    <li>Nav1</li>
    <li>Nav2</li>
  </ul>
}
```

When you run the application, the content from the view and the layout are merged according to the positions defined by the layout, as shown in Figure 31-4.

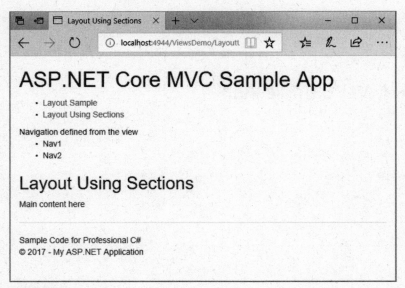

FIGURE 31-4

> **NOTE** *Sections aren't used only to place some content within the body of an HTML page; they are also useful for allowing the view to place something in the head—for example, metadata from the page.*

Defining Content with Partial Views

Whereas layouts give an overall definition for multiple pages from the web application, you can use partial views to define content within views. A partial view doesn't have a layout.

Other than that, partial views are like normal views. Partial views use the same base class as normal views, and they have a model.

Following is an example of partial views. Here you start with a model that contains properties for independent collections, events, and menus as defined by the class `EventsAndMenusContext` (code file `MVCSampleApp/Models/EventsAndMenusContext.cs`):

```
public class EventsAndMenusContext
{
  private IEnumerable<Event> GetEvents() =>
    new List<Event>
    {
      new Event(1, "Formula 1 G.P. Australia, Melbourne", new DateTime(2018, 3, 25)),
      new Event(2, "Formula 1 G.P. Bahrain, Sakhir", new DateTime(2018, 4, 8)),
      new Event(3, "Formula 1 G.P. China, Shanghai", new DateTime(2018, 4, 15)),
      new Event(4, "Formula 1 G.P. Aserbaidschan, Baku", new DateTime(2018, 4, 29))
    };

    //...

  private IEnumerable<Event> _events = null;
  public IEnumerable<Event> Events
  {
    get => _events ?? (_events = GetEvents());
  }
  private IEnumerable<Menu> _menus = null;
  public IEnumerable<Menu> Menus
  {
    get => _menus ?? (_menus = GetMenus());
  }
}
```

The context class is registered with the dependency injection startup code to have the type injected with the controller constructor (code file `MVCSampleApp/Startup.cs`):

```
public void ConfigureServices(IServiceCollection services)
{
  services.AddMvc();
  services.AddScoped<EventsAndMenusContext>();
}
```

This model will now be used with partial view samples in the following sections, a partial view that is loaded from server-side code, as well as a view that is requested using JavaScript code on the client.

Using Partial Views from Server-Side Code

In the `ViewsDemoController` class, the constructor is modified to inject the `EventsAndMenusContext` type (code file `MVCSampleApp/Controllers/ViewsDemoController.cs`):

```
public class ViewsDemoController : Controller
{
  private EventsAndMenusContext _context;
  public ViewsDemoController(EventsAndMenusContext context)
  {
    _context = context;
  }
  //...
```

The action method `UseAPartialView1` passes an instance of `EventsAndMenus` to the view (code file `MVCSampleApp/Controllers/ViewsDemoController.cs`):

```
public IActionResult UseAPartialView1() => View(_context);
```

The view page is defined to use the model of type `EventsAndMenusContext`. You can show a partial view by using the HTML Helper method `Html.PartialAsync`. This method returns a `Task<HtmlString>`. With the sample code that follows, the string is written as content of the `div` element using the Razor syntax. The first parameter of the `PartialAsync` method accepts the name of the partial view. With the second parameter, the `PartialAsync` method enables passing a model. If no model is passed, the partial view has access to the same model as the view. Here, the view uses the model of type `EventsAndMenusContext`, and the partial view just uses a part of it with the type `IEnumerable<Event>` (code file `MVCSampleApp/Views/ViewsDemo/UseAPartialView1.cshtml`):

```
@using MVCSampleApp.Models
@model EventsAndMenusContext
@{
  ViewBag.Title = "Use a Partial View";
  ViewBag.EventsTitle = "Live Events";
}
<h2>Use a Partial View</h2>
<div>this is the main view</div>
<div>
  @await Html.PartialAsync("ShowEvents", Model.Events)
</div>
```

Instead of using an async method, you can use the synchronous variant `Html.Partial`. This is an extension method that returns an object implementing the interface `IHtmlContent`.

Another way to render a partial view within the view is to use the HTML Helper method `Html.RenderPartialAsync`, which is defined to return a `Task`. This method directly writes the partial view content to the response stream. This way, you can use `RenderPartialAsync` within a Razor code block.

You create the partial view the same way you create a normal view. You have access to the model and to the dictionary that is accessed by using the `ViewBag` property. A partial view receives a copy of the dictionary to receive the same dictionary data that can be used (code file `MVCSampleApp/Views/ViewsDemo/ShowEvents.cshtml`):

```
@using MVCSampleApp.Models
@model IEnumerable<Event>
<h2>
  @ViewBag.EventsTitle
</h2>
<table>
  @foreach (var item in Model)
  {
    <tr>
```

```
      <td>@item.Day.ToShortDateString()</td>
      <td>@item.Text</td>
    </tr>
  }
</table>
```

When you run the application, the view, partial view, and layout are rendered, as shown in Figure 31-5.

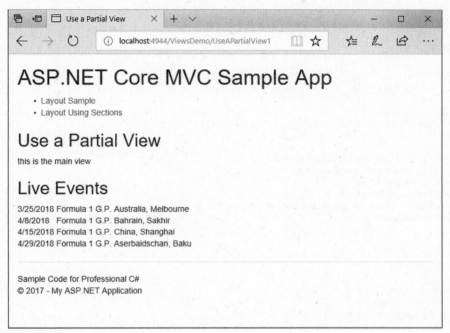

FIGURE 31-5

Returning Partial Views from the Controller

So far, the partial view has been loaded directly without the interaction with a controller, but you can also use controllers to return a partial view.

In the following code snippet, two action methods are defined within the class `ViewsDemoController`. The first action method `UsePartialView2` returns a normal view; the second action method `ShowEvents` returns a partial view using the base class method `PartialView`. The partial view `ShowEvents` was already created and used previously, and it is used here. With the method `PartialView` a model containing the event list is passed to the partial view (code file `MVCSampleApp/Controllers/ViewDemoController.cs`):

```
public ActionResult UseAPartialView2() => View();
public ActionResult ShowEvents()
{
  ViewBag.EventsTitle = "Live Events";
  return PartialView(_context.Events);
}
```

When the partial view is offered from the controller, the partial view can be called directly from client-side code. The following code snippet makes use of the fetch API for the download from the server. jQuery: An event handler is linked to the `click` event of a button. Inside the event handler, a GET request is made to the server with the jQuery `load` function to request `/ViewsDemo/ShowEvents`. This request returns a partial view, and the result from the partial view is placed within the `div` element named `events` (code file `MVCSampleApp/Views/ViewsDemo/UseAPartialView2.cshtml`):

```
@using MVCSampleApp.Models
@model EventsAndMenusContext
@{
    ViewBag.Title = "Use a Partial View";
}
<script src="~/lib/jquery/dist/jquery.js"></script>
<script>
  (function () {
    window.onload = function () {
      var buttonEvents = document.getElementById("getEvents");
      buttonEvents.onclick = function () {
        if (window.fetch == null) {
          output.innerHTML =
            "<div>window.fetch not supported. Use another browser</div>";
          return;
        }
        var result = fetch("/ViewsDemo/ShowEvents");
        result.then(function (response) {
          return response.text();
        }).then(function (text) {
          var output = document.getElementById("output");
          output.innerHTML = text;
        });
      };
    };
  })();
</script>
<h2>Use a Partial View</h2>
<div>this is the main view</div>
<button id="getEvents">Get Events</button>
<div id="output">
</div>
```

> **NOTE** *The fetch API is a modern replacement of the XmlHttpRequest API. This API is not supported by IE11, but is supported in modern browsers like Microsoft Edge, Firefox, Safari, Chrome, and Opera. See* `https://fetch.spec.whatwg.org/` *for more information of this new API.*

Working with View Components

ASP.NET Core MVC offers an alternative to partial views: view components. View components are very similar to partial views; the main difference is that view components are not related to a controller. This makes it easy to use them with multiple controllers. Examples of where view components are really useful are dynamic navigation of menus, a login panel, or sidebar content in a blog. These scenarios are useful independent of a single controller.

Like controllers and views, view components have two parts. With view components the controller functionality is taken over by a class that derives from `ViewComponent` (or a POCO class with the attribute `ViewComponent`). The user interface is defined similarly to a view, but the method to invoke the view component is different.

The following code snippet defines a view component that derives from the base class `ViewComponent`. This class makes use of the `EventsAndMenusContext` type that was earlier registered in the `Startup` class to be available with dependency injection. This works similarly to the controllers with constructor injection. The

`InvokeAsync` method is defined to be called from the view that shows the view component. This method can have any number and type of parameters, as the method defined by the `IViewComponentHelper` interface defines a flexible number of parameters using the `params` keyword. Instead of using an async method implementation, you can synchronously implement this method returning `IViewComponentResult` instead of `Task<IViewComponentResult>`. However, typically the async variant is the best to use—for example, for accessing a database. The view component needs to be stored in a `ViewComponents` directory. This directory itself can be placed anywhere within the project (code file MVCSampleApp/ViewComponents/EventListViewComponent.cs):

```
public class EventListViewComponent : ViewComponent
{
  private readonly EventsAndMenusContext _context;
  public EventListViewComponent(EventsAndMenusContext context) =>
    _context = context;

  public Task<IViewComponentResult> InvokeAsync(DateTime from, DateTime to) =>
    Task.FromResult<IViewComponentResult>(
      View(EventsByDateRange(from, to)));

  private IEnumerable<Event> EventsByDateRange(DateTime from, DateTime to) =>
    _context.Events.Where(e => e.Day >= from && e.Day <= to);
}
```

The user interface for the view component is defined within the following code snippet. The view for the view component can be created with the item template MVC View Page; it uses the same Razor syntax. Specifically, it must be put into the `Components/[viewcomponent]` folder—for example, `Components/EventList`. For the view component to be available with all the controls, you need to create the `Components` folder in the `Shared` folder for the views. When you're using a view component only from one specific controller, you can put it into the views controller folder instead. What's different with this view, though, is that it needs to be named `default.cshtml`. You can create other view names as well; you need to specify these views using a parameter for the View method returned from the `InvokeAsync` method (code file MVCSampleApp/Views/Shared/Components/EventList/default.cshtml):

```
@using MVCSampleApp.Models;
@model IEnumerable<Event>
<h3>Formula 1 Calendar</h3>
<ul>
  @foreach (var ev in Model)
  {
    <li><div>@ev.Day.ToString("D")</div><div>@ev.Text</div></li>
  }
</ul>
```

Now as the view component is completed, you can show it by invoking the `InvokeAsync` method. `Component` is a dynamically created property of the view that returns an object implementing `IViewComponentHelper`. `IViewComponentHelper` allows you to invoke synchronous or asynchronous methods such as `Invoke`, `InvokeAsync`, `RenderInvoke`, and `RenderInvokeAsync`. Of course, you can only invoke these methods that are implemented by the view component. The parameters need to be passed using a `Dictionary<string, object>`, where the key matches the parameter name (code file MVCSampleApp/Views/ViewsDemo/UseViewComponent1.cshtml):

```
@{
ViewBag.Title = "View Components Sample";
}
<h2>@ViewBag.Title</h2>
<p>
  @await Component.InvokeAsync("EventList", new Dictionary<string, object>()
  {
    ["from"] = new DateTime(2018, 4, 1),
    ["to"] = new DateTime(2018, 4, 20)
  })
</p>
```

Since ASP.NET Core 1.1, you have been able to invoke view components using Tag Helpers. Tag Helpers are written with HTML-like code that simplifies the code for the view. Creating another view to invoke the same view component as before, to use Tag Helpers for view components, the `@addTagHelper` directive needs to be added with the name of the assembly where the view component resides—in this example, the name of the web application. After adding Tag Helpers for the view component, view components can be referenced with the `vc` tag. After the colon of the `vc` tag, the name of the view component follows. While the class is defined with Pascal naming convention, the Tag Helper changes the name by switching to lowercase letters; instead of an uppercase letter, a hyphen is added, thus `EventList` becomes `event-list` (code file `MVCSampleApp/Views/ViewsDemo/UseViewComponent2.cshtml`):

```
@addTagHelper *, MVCSampleApp
@{
  ViewBag.Title = "View Components Sample";
}
<h2>@ViewBag.Title</h2>
<vc:event-list from="@new DateTime(2018, 4, 1)" to="@new DateTime(2018, 4, 20)" />
```

> **NOTE** *The naming of Tag Helpers with lowercase and hyphens is known as* lower kebab casing.

> **NOTE** *Tag helpers are explained later in this chapter in the section "Getting to Know Tag Helpers".*

When you run the application, you can see the view component rendered as shown in Figure 31-6.

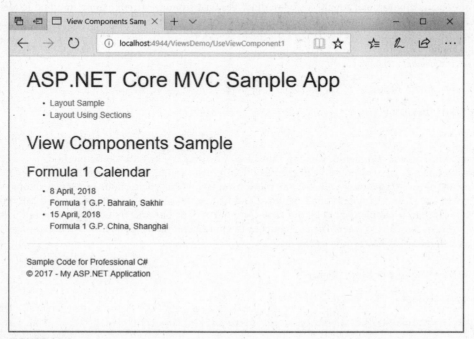

FIGURE 31-6

Using Dependency Injection in Views

In case a service is needed directly from within a view, you can inject it using the `inject` keyword (code file `MVCSampleApp/Views/ViewsDemo/InjectServiceInView.cshtml`):

```
@using MVCSampleApp.Services
@inject ISampleService sampleService
<p>
  @string.Join(" * ", sampleService.GetSampleStrings())
</p>
```

When you do this, it's a good idea to register services using the `AddScoped` method. As previously mentioned, registering a service that way means it's only instantiated once for one HTTP request. Using `AddScoped`, injecting the same service within a controller and the view, it is only instantiated once for a request.

Importing Namespaces with Multiple Views

All the previous samples for views have used the `using` keyword to open all the namespaces needed. Instead of opening the namespaces with every view, you can use the Visual Studio item template MVC View Imports Page to create a file (`_ViewImports.cshtml`) that defines all using declarations (code file `MVCSampleApp/Views/_ViewImports.cshtml`):

```
@using MVCSampleApp.Models
@using MVCSampleApp.Services
```

With this file in place, there's no need to add all the `using` keywords to all the views.

RECEIVING DATA FROM THE CLIENT

Until now you used only HTTP GET requests from the client to retrieve HTML code from the server. What about sending form data from the client?

To submit form data, you create the view `CreateMenu` for the controller `SubmitData`. This view contains an HTML form element that defines what data should be sent to the server. The form method is declared as an HTTP POST request. The `input` elements that define the input fields all have names that correspond to the properties of the `Menu` type. With the input elements, types are used that correspond to the types of the properties. This allows for input validation on the client without writing JavaScript code (code file `MVCSampleApp/Views/SubmitData/CreateMenu.cshtml`):

```
@{
  ViewBag.Title = "Create Menu";
}
<h2>Create Menu</h2>
<form action="/SubmitData/CreateMenu" method="post">
  <fieldset>
    <legend>Menu</legend>
    <label for="id">Id</label><br />
    <input name="id" id="id" type="number" /><br />

    <label for="text">Text</label><br />
    <input name="text" id="text" type="text" /><br />

    <label for="price">Price</label><br />
    <input name="price" id="price" type="number" step="0.01" /><br />

    <label for="date">Date</label><br />
    <input name="date" id="date" type="date" /><br />
```

```
        <label for="category">Category</label><br />
        <input name="category" id="category" type="text" /><br />

        <button type="submit">Submit</button>
    </fieldset>
</form>
```

Figure 31-7 shows the opened page within the browser.

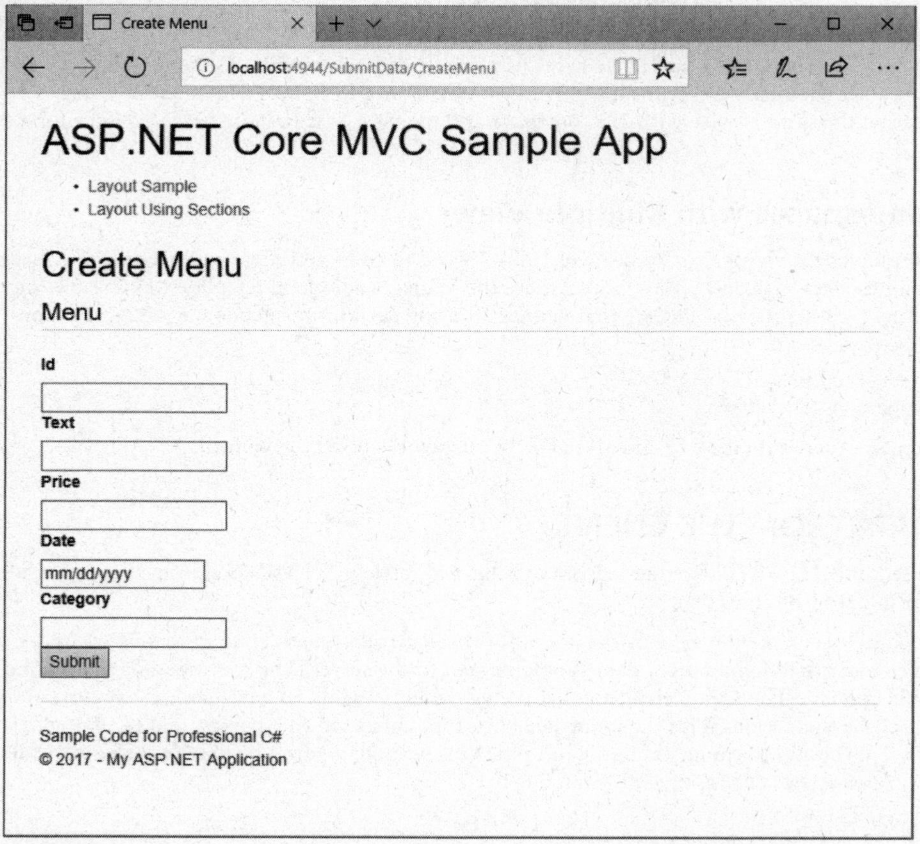

FIGURE 31-7

Within the SubmitData controller, two CreateMenu action methods are created: one for an HTTP GET request and another for an HTTP POST request. Because C# has different methods with the same name, it's required that the parameter numbers or types are different. Of course, this requirement is the same with action methods. Action methods also need to differ with the HTTP request method. By default, the request method is GET; when you apply the attribute HttpPost, the request method is POST. For reading HTTP POST data, you could use information from the Request object. However, it's much simpler to define the CreateMenu method with parameters. The parameters are matched with the name of the form fields (code file MVCSampleApp/Controllers/SubmitDataController.cs):

```
public IActionResult Index() => View();

public IActionResult CreateMenu() => View();
```

```
[HttpPost]
public IActionResult CreateMenu(int id, string text, double price,
  DateTime date, string category)
{
  var m = new Menu
          {
            Id = id,
            Text = text,
            Price = price,
            Date = date,
            Category = category
          };
  ViewBag.Info = $"menu created: {m.Text}, Price: {m.Price}, " +
    $"date: {m.Date}, category: {m.Category}";
  return View("Index");
}
```

To display the result, just the value of the `ViewBag.Info` is shown (code file `MVCSampleApp/Views/SubmitData/Index.cshtml`):

```
@ViewBag.Info
```

Model Binder

Instead of using multiple parameters with the action method, you can also use a type that contains properties that match the incoming field names (code file `MVCSampleApp/Controllers/SubmitDataController.cs`):

```
[HttpPost]
public IActionResult CreateMenu2(Menu menu)
{
  ViewBag.Info = $"menu created: {menu.Text}, Price: {menu.Price}, " +
    $"date: {menu.Date}, category: {menu.Category}";
  return View("Index");
}
```

When the user submits the data with the form, a `CreateMenu` method is invoked that shows the `Index` view with the submitted menu data, as shown in Figure 31-8.

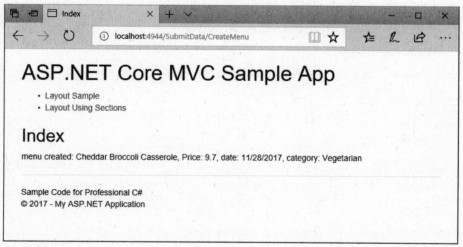

FIGURE 31-8

A model binder is responsible for transferring the data from the HTTP POST request. A model binder implements the interface `IModelBinder`. By default, the `FormCollectionModelBinder` class is used to bind the input fields to the model. This binder supports primitive types, model classes (such as the `Menu` type), and collections implementing `ICollection<T>`, `IList<T>`, and `IDictionary<TKey, TValue>`.

In case not all the properties of the parameter type should be filled from the model binder, you can use the `Bind` attribute. With this attribute you can specify a list of property names that should be included with the binding.

You can also pass the input data to the model using an action method without parameters, as demonstrated by the next code snippet. Here, a new instance of the `Menu` class is created, and this instance is passed to the `TryUpdateModelAsync` method of the `Controller` base class. `TryUpdateModelAsync` returns false if the updated model is not in a valid state after the update:

```
[HttpPost]
public async Task<IActionResult> CreateMenu3Result()
{
    var m = new Menu();
    bool updated = await TryUpdateModelAsync<Menu>(m);
    if (updated)
    {
        ViewBag.Info = $"menu created: {m.Text}, Price: {m.Price}, " +
            $"date: {m.Date}, category: {m.Category}";
        return View("Index");
    }
    else
    {
        return View("Error");
    }
}
```

Annotations and Validation

You can add some annotations to the model type; the annotations are used when updating the data for validation. The namespace `System.ComponentModel.DataAnnotations` contains attribute types that can be used to specify some information for data on the client and can be used for validation.

With the following code snippet, the `Menu` type is changed with these added attributes:

```
public class Menu
{
    public int Id { get; set; }
    [Required, StringLength(50)]
    public string Text { get; set; }
    [Display(Name="Price"), DisplayFormat(DataFormatString="{0:C}")]
    public double Price { get; set; }
    [DataType(DataType.Date)]
    public DateTime Date { get; set; }
    [StringLength(10)]
    public string Category { get; set; }
}
```

Possible attribute types you can use for validation are `CompareAttribute` to compare different properties, `CreditCardAttribute` to verify a valid credit card number, `EmailAddressAttribute` to verify an e-mail address, `EnumDataTypeAttribute` to compare the input to enumeration values, and `PhoneAttribute` to verify a phone number.

You can also use other attributes to get values for display and error messages—for example, `DataTypeAttribute` and `DisplayFormatAttribute`.

To use the validation attributes, you can verify the state of the model using `ModelState.IsValid` within an action method as shown here (code file `MVCSampleApp/Controllers/SubmitDataController.cs`):

```
[HttpPost]
public IActionResult CreateMenu4(Menu menu)
{
  if (ModelState.IsValid)
  {
    ViewBag.Info = $"menu created: {menu.Text}, Price: {menu.Price}, " +
      $"date: {menu.Date}, category: {menu.Category}";
  }
  else
  {
    ViewBag.Info = "not valid";
  }
  return View("Index");
}
```

If you use tool-generated model classes, you might think it's hard to add attributes to properties. As the tool-generated classes are defined as partial classes, you can extend the class by adding properties and methods, by implementing additional interfaces, and by implementing partial methods that are used by the tool-generated classes. You cannot add attributes to existing properties and methods if you can't change the source code of the type, but there's help for such scenarios! Assume the `Menu` class is a tool-generated partial class. Then a new class with a different name (for example, `MenuMetadata`) can define the same properties as the entity class and add the annotations, as shown here (code file `MVCSampleApp/Models/MenuMetadata.cs`):

```
public class MenuMetadata
{
  public int Id { get; set; }
  [Required, StringLength(25)]
  public string Text { get; set; }
  [Display(Name="Price"), DisplayFormat(DataFormatString="{0:C}")]
  public double Price { get; set; }
  [DataType(DataType.Date)]
  public DateTime Date { get; set; }
  [StringLength(10)]
  public string Category { get; set; }
}
```

The `MenuMetadata` class must be linked to the `Menu` class. With tool-generated partial classes, you can create another partial type in the same namespace to add the `ModelMetadataType` attribute to the type definition that creates the connection:

```
[ModelMetadataType(typeof(MenuMetadata))]
public partial class Menu
{
}
```

HTML Helper methods can also make use of annotations to add information to the client.

WORKING WITH HTML HELPERS

HTML Helpers are helpers that create HTML code. You can use them directly within the view using Razor syntax.

`Html` is a property of the view base class `RazorPage` and is of type `IHtmlHelper`. HTML Helper methods are implemented as extension methods to extend the `IHtmlHelper` interface.

The class `InputExtensions` defines HTML Helper methods to create check boxes, password controls, radio buttons, and text box controls. The `Action` and `RenderAction` helpers are defined by the class

ChildActionExtensions. Helper methods for display are defined by the class DisplayExtensions. Helper methods for HTML forms are defined by the class FormExtensions.

The following sections get into some examples using HTML Helpers.

Using Simple Helpers

The following code snippet uses the HTML Helper methods BeginForm, Label, and CheckBox. BeginForm starts a form element. There's also an EndForm for ending the form element. The sample makes use of the IDisposable interface implemented by the MvcForm returned from the BeginForm method. On disposing of the MvcForm, EndForm is invoked. This way the BeginForm method can be surrounded by a using statement to end the form at the closing curly brackets. The method DisplayName directly returns the content from the argument; the method CheckBox is an input element with the type attribute set to checkbox (code file MVCSampleApp/Views/HtmlHelpers/SimpleHelper.cshtml):

```
@using (Html.BeginForm()) {
  @Html.DisplayName("Check this (or not)")
  @Html.CheckBox("check1")
}
```

The resulting HTML code is shown in the next code snippet. The CheckBox method creates two input elements with the same name; one is set to hidden. There's a good reason for this behavior: If a check box has a value of false, the browser does not pass this information to the server with the forms content. Only check box values of selected check boxes are passed to the server. This HTML characteristic creates a problem with automatic binding to the parameters of action methods. A simple solution is performed by the CheckBox helper method. This method creates a hidden input element with the same name that is set to false. If the check box is not selected, the hidden input element is passed to the server, and the false value can be bound. If the check box is selected, two input elements with the same name are sent to the server. The first input element is set to true; the second one is set to false. With automatic binding, only the first input element is selected to bind:

```
<form action="/HtmlHelpers/SimpleHelper" method="post">
  Check this (or not)
  <input id="check1" name="check1" type="checkbox" value="true" />
  <input name="check1" type="hidden" value="false" />
</form>
```

Using Model Data

You can use helper methods with model data. This example creates a Menu object. This type was declared earlier in this chapter within the Models directory and passes a sample menu as a model to the view (code file MVCSampleApp/Controllers/HTMLHelpersController.cs):

```
public IActionResult HelperWithMenu() => View(GetSampleMenu());
private Menu GetSampleMenu() =>
  new Menu
  {
    Id = 1,
    Text = "Schweinsbraten mit Knödel und Sauerkraut",
    Price = 6.9,
    Date = new DateTime(2017, 11, 14),
    Category = "Main"
  };
```

The view has the model defined to be of type Menu. The DisplayName HTML Helper returns the text from the parameter, as shown with the previous sample. The Display method uses an expression as the parameter where a property name can be passed in the string format. This way this property tries to find a property with this name and accesses the property accessor to return the value of the property (code file `MVCSampleApp/Views/HTMLHelpers/HelperWithMenu.cshtml`):

```
@model MVCSampleApp.Models.Menu
@{
  ViewBag.Title = "HelperWithMenu";
}
<h2>Helper with Menu</h2>
@Html.DisplayName("Text:")
@Html.Display("Text")
<br />
@Html.DisplayName("Category:")
@Html.Display("Category")
```

With the resulting HTML code, you can see this as output from calling the `DisplayName` and `Display` methods:

```
Text:
Schweinsbraten mit Kn&#246;del und Sauerkraut
<br />
Category:
Main
```

> **NOTE** *Helper methods also offer strongly typed variants to access members of the model. See the "Using Strongly Typed Helpers" section for more information.*

Defining HTML Attributes

Most HTML Helper methods have overloads in which you can pass any HTML attributes. For example, the following `TextBox` method creates an `input` element of type text. The first parameter defines the name; the second parameter defines the value that is set with the text box. The third parameter of the `TextBox` method is of type object that enables passing an anonymous type where every property is changed to an attribute of the HTML element. Here, the result of the input element has the `required` attribute set to `required`, the `maxlength` attribute to `15`, and the `class` attribute to `CSSDemo`. Because `class` is a C# keyword, it cannot be directly set as a property. Instead it is prefixed with `@` to generate the `class` attribute for CSS styling:

```
@Html.TextBox("text1", "input text here",
  new { required="required", maxlength=15, @class="CSSDemo" });
```

The resulting HTML output is shown here:

```
<input name="text1" class="CSSDemo" id="text1" maxlength="15"
  required="required" type="text" value="input text here" />
```

Creating Lists

For displaying lists, helper methods such as `DropDownList` and `ListBox` exist. These methods create the HTML select element.

Within the controller, first a dictionary is created that contains keys and values. The dictionary is then converted to a list of `SelectListItem` with the custom extension method `ToSelectListItems`. The `DropDownList` and `ListBox` methods make use of `SelectListItem` collections (code file `MVCSampleApp/Controllers/HTMLHelpersController.cs`):

```
public IActionResult HelperList()
{
  var cars = new Dictionary<int, string>();
```

```
        cars.Add(1, "Red Bull Racing");
        cars.Add(2, "McLaren");
        cars.Add(3, "Mercedes");
        cars.Add(4, "Ferrari");
        return View(cars.ToSelectListItems(4));
    }
```

The custom extension method `ToSelectListItems` is defined within the class `SelectListItemsExtensions` that extends `IDictionary<int, string>`, the type from the cars collection. Within the implementation, a new `SelectListItem` object is returned for every item in the dictionary (code file `MVCSampleApp/Extensions/SelectListItemsExtensions.cs`):

```
    public static class SelectListItemsExtensions
    {
      public static IEnumerable<SelectListItem> ToSelectListItems(
        this IDictionary<int, string> dict, int selectedId) =>
          dict.Select(item =>
            new SelectListItem
            {
              Selected = item.Key == selectedId,
              Text = item.Value,
              Value = item.Key.ToString()
            });
    }
```

With the view, the helper method `DropDownList` directly accesses the Model that is returned from the controller (code file `MVCSampleApp/Views/HTMLHelpers/HelperList.cshtml`):

```
    @{
      ViewBag.Title = "Helper List";
    }
    @model IEnumerable<SelectListItem>
    <h2>Helper2</h2>
    @Html.DropDownList("carslist", Model)
```

The resulting HTML creates a `select` element with `option` child elements as created from the `SelectListItem` and defines the selected item as returned from the controller:

```
    <select id="carslist" name="carslist">
      <option value="1">Red Bull Racing</option>
      <option value="2">McLaren</option>
      <option value="3">Mercedes</option>
      <option selected="selected" value="4">Ferrari</option>
    </select>
```

Using Strongly Typed Helpers

The HTML Helper methods offer strongly typed methods to access the model passed from the controller. These methods are all suffixed with the name `For`. For example, instead of the `TextBox` method, here the `TextBoxFor` method can be used.

The next sample again makes use of a controller that returns a single entity (code file `MVCSampleApp/Controllers/HTMLHelpersController.cs`):

```
    public IActionResult StronglyTypedMenu() => View(GetSampleMenu());
```

The view uses the `Menu` type as a model; thus, the methods `DisplayNameFor` and `DisplayFor` can directly access the `Menu` properties. By default, `DisplayNameFor` returns the name of the property (in this example, it's the `Text` property), and `DisplayFor` returns the value of the property (code file `MVCSampleApp/Views/HTMLHelpers/StronglyTypedMenu.cshtml`):

```
    @using MVCSampleApp.Models
    @model Menu
```

```
@Html.DisplayNameFor(m => m.Text)
<br />
@Html.DisplayFor(m => m.Text)
```

Similarly, you can use `Html.TextBoxFor(m => m.Text)`, which returns an input element that enables setting the `Text` property of the model. This method also makes use of the annotations added to the `Text` property of the `Menu` type. The `Text` property has the `Required` and `MaxStringLength` attributes added, which is why the `data-val-length`, `data-val-length-max`, and `data-val-required` attributes are returned from the `TextBoxFor` method:

```
<input data-val="true"
   data-val-length="The field Text must be a string with a maximum length of 50."
   data-val-length-max="50"
   data-val-required="The Text field is required."
   id="FileName_Text" name="Text"
   type="text"
   value="Schweinsbraten mit Knödel und Sauerkraut" />
```

Working with Editor Extensions

Instead of using at least one helper method for every property, helper methods from the class `EditorExtensions` offer an editor for all the properties of a type.

Using the same `Menu` model as before, with the method `Html.EditorFor(m => m)` the complete user interface (UI) for editing the menu is built. The result from this method invocation is shown in Figure 31-9.

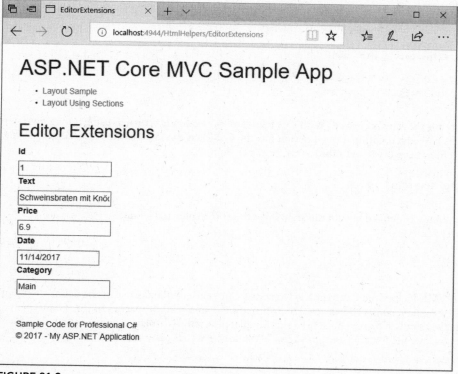

FIGURE 31-9

Instead of using `Html.EditorFor(m => m)`, you can use `Html.EditorForModel`. The method `EditorForModel` makes use of the model of the view without the need to specify it explicitly. `EditorFor` has more flexibility in using other data sources (for example, properties offered by the model), and `EditorForModel` needs fewer parameters to specify.

Implementing Templates

A great way to extend the outcome from HTML Helpers is by using templates. A *template* is a simple view used—either implicitly or explicitly—by the HTML Helper methods. Templates are stored within special folders. Display templates are stored within the `DisplayTemplates` folder that is in the view folder (for example, `Views/HtmlHelpers/DisplayTemplates`) or in a shared folder (`Shared/DisplayTemplates`). The shared folder is used by all views; the specific view folder is used only by views within this folder. Editor templates are stored in the folder `EditorTemplates`.

Now have a look at an example. With the `Menu` type, the `Date` property has the annotation `DataType` with a value of `DataType.Date`. When you specify this attribute, the `DateTime` type by default does not show as date and time; it shows only with the short date format (code file `MVCSampleApp/Models/Menu.cs`):

```
public class Menu
{
  public int Id { get; set; }

  [Required, StringLength(50)]
  public string Text { get; set; }

  [Display(Name="Price"), DisplayFormat(DataFormatString="{0:c}")]
  public double Price { get; set; }

  [DataType(DataType.Date)]
  public DateTime Date { get; set; }

  [StringLength(10)]
  public string Category { get; set; }
}
```

Now the template for the date is created. With this template, the `Model` is returned using a long date string format `D`, which is embedded within a `div` tag that has the CSS class `markRed` (code file `MVCSampleApp/Views/HTMLHelpers/DisplayTemplates/Date.cshtml`):

```
<div class="markRed">
  @string.Format("{0:D}", Model)
</div>
```

The CSS class `markRed` is defined within the style sheet to set the color red (code file `MVCSampleApp/wwwroot/css/site.css`):

```
.markRed {
  color: #f00;
}
```

Now a display HTML Helper such as `DisplayForModel` can be used to make use of the defined template. The model is of type `Menu`, so the `DisplayForModel` method displays all properties of the `Menu` type. For the `Date` it finds the template `Date.cshtml`, so this template is used to display the date in long date format with the CSS style (code file `MVCSampleApp/Views/HTMLHelpers/Display.cshtml`):

```
@model MVCSampleApp.Models.Menu
@{
  ViewBag.Title = "Display";
}
```

```
<h2>@ViewBag.Title</h2>
@Html.DisplayForModel()
```

If a single type should have different presentations in the same view, you can use other names for the template file. Then you can use the attribute UIHint to specify the template name, or you can specify the template with the template parameter of the helper method.

GETTING TO KNOW TAG HELPERS

ASP.NET Core MVC offers a new technology that can be used instead of HTML Helpers: *Tag Helpers*. With Tag Helpers you don't write C# code mixed with HTML; instead you use HTML attributes and elements that are resolved on the server. Nowadays many JavaScript libraries extend HTML with their own attributes (such as Angular), so it's very convenient to be able to do use custom HTML attributes with server-side technology. Many of the ASP.NET Core MVC Tag Helpers have the prefix asp-, so you can easily see what's resolved on the server. These attributes are not sent to the client but instead are resolved on the server to generate HTML code.

Activating Tag Helpers

To use the ASP.NET Core MVC Tag Helpers, you need to activate the tags by calling addTagHelper. The first parameter defines the types to use (a * opens all Tag Helpers of the assembly); the second parameter defines the assembly of the Tag Helpers. With removeTagHelper, the Tag Helpers are deactivated again. Deactivating Tag Helpers might be important—for example, to not get into naming conflicts with scripting libraries. You're most likely not getting into a conflict using the built-in Tag Helpers with the asp- prefix, but conflicts can easily happen with other Tag Helpers that can have the same names as other Tag Helpers or HTML attributes used with scripting libraries.

To have the Tag Helpers available with all views, add the addTagHelper statement to the shared file _ViewImports.cshtml (code file MVCSampleApp/Views/_ViewImports.cshtml):

```
@addTagHelper *, Microsoft.AspNetCore.Mvc.TagHelpers
```

Using Anchor Tag Helpers

Let's start with Tag Helpers that extend the anchor a element. The sample controller for the Tag Helpers is TagHelpersController. The Index action method returns a view for showing the anchor Tag Helpers (code file MVCSampleApp/Controllers/TagHelpersController.cs):

```
public class TagHelpersController : Controller
{
    public IActionResult Index() => View();
    //...
}
```

The anchor Tag Helper defines the asp-controller and asp-action attributes. With these, the controller and action methods are used to build up the URL for the anchor element. With the second and third examples, the controller is not needed because it's the same controller the view is coming from (code file MVCSampleApp/Views/TagHelpers/Index.cshtml):

```
<a asp-controller="Home" asp-action="Index">Home</a>
<br />
<a asp-action="LabelHelper">Label Tag Helper</a>
<br />
<a asp-action="InputTypeHelper">Input Type Tag Helper</a>
```

The following snippet shows the resulting HTML code. The asp-controller and asp-action attributes generate an href attribute for the a element. With the first sample to access the Index action method in the

Home controller, as both are defaults as defined by the route, an href to / is all that's needed in the result. When you specify the asp-action LabelHelper, the href directs to /TagHelpers/LabelHelper, the action method LabelHelper in the current controller:

```
<a href="/">Home</a>
<br />
<a href="/TagHelpers/LabelHelper">Label Tag Helper</a>
<br />
<a href="/TagHelpers/InputTypeHelper">Input Type Tag Helper</a>
```

Using Label Tag Helpers

In the following code snippet, which demonstrates the features of the label Tag Helper, the action method LabelHelper passes a Menu object to the view (code file MVCSampleApp/Controllers/TagHelpersController.cs):

```
public IActionResult LabelHelper() => View(GetSampleMenu());
private Menu GetSampleMenu() =>
  new Menu
  {
    Id = 1,
    Text = "Schweinsbraten mit Knödel und Sauerkraut",
    Price = 6.9,
    Date = new DateTime(2018, 10, 5),
    Category = "Main"
  };
}
```

The Menu class has some data annotations applied to influence the outcome of the Tag Helpers. Have a look at the Display attribute for the Text property. It sets the Name property of the Display attribute to "Menu" (code file MVCSampleApp/Models/Menu.cs):

```
public class Menu
{
  public int Id { get; set; }

  [Required, StringLength(50)]
  [Display(Name = "Menu")]
  public string Text { get; set; }

  [Display(Name = "Price"), DisplayFormat(DataFormatString = "{0:C}")]
  public double Price { get; set; }

  [DataType(DataType.Date)]
  public DateTime Date { get; set; }

  [StringLength(10)]
  public string Category { get; set; }
}
```

The view makes use of asp-for attributes applied to label controls. The value that is used for this attribute is a property of the model of the view. With Visual Studio 2017, you can use IntelliSense for accessing the Text, Price, and Date properties (code file MVCSampleApp/Views/TagHelpers/LabelHelper.cshtml):

```
@model MVCSampleApp.Models.Menu
@{
  ViewBag.Title = "Label Tag Helper";
}
<h2>@ViewBag.Title</h2>
<label asp-for="Text"></label>
<br/>
<label asp-for="Price"></label>
<br />
<label asp-for="Date"></label>
```

With the generated HTML code, you can see the `for` attribute, which references elements with the same name as the property names and the content that is either the name of the property or the value of the `Display` attribute. You can use this attribute also to localize values:

```
<label for="Text">Menu</label>
<br/>
<label for="Price">Price</label>
<br />
<label for="Date">Date</label>
```

Using Input Tag Helpers

An HTML `label` typically is associated with an `input` element. The following code snippet gives you a look at what's generated using `input` elements with Tag Helpers (code file `MVCSampleApp/Views/TagHelpers/InputHelper.cshtml`):

```
<div>
  <label asp-for="Text"></label>
  <input asp-for="Text"/>
</div>
<div>
  <label asp-for="Price"></label>
  <input asp-for="Price" />
</div>
<div>
  <label asp-for="Date"></label>
  <input asp-for="Date" />
</div>
```

Checking the result of the generated HTML code reveals that the `input` type Tag Helpers create a `type` attribute depending on the type of the property, and they also apply the `DateType` attribute. The property `Price` is of type double, which results in a number input type. Because the `Date` property has the `DataType` with a value of `DataType.Date` applied, the input type is a date. In addition to that you can see `data-val-length`, `data-val-length-max`, and `data-val-required` attributes that are created because of annotations:

```
<div>
  <label for="Text">Text</label>
  <input type="text" data-val="true"
    data-val-length="The field Text must be a string with a maximum length of 50."
    data-val-length-max="50" data-val-required="The Text field is required."
    id="Text" name="Text"
    value="Schweinsbraten mit Kn&#xF6;del und Sauerkraut" />
</div>
<div>
  <label for="Price">Price</label>
  <input type="text" data-val="true"
    data-val-number="The field Price must be a number."
    data-val-required="The Price field is required." id="Price"
    name="Price" value="6.9" />
</div>
<div>
  <label for="Date">Date</label>
  <input type="date" data-val="true"
    data-val-required="The Date field is required." id="Date" name="Date"
    value="2018-10-05" />
</div>
```

Modern browsers have a special look for HTML 5 input controls such as date control. The input date control of Microsoft Edge is shown in Figure 31-10. It looks different with other browsers.

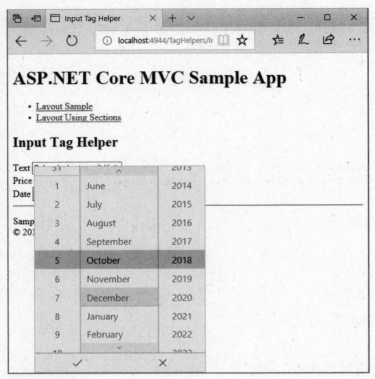

FIGURE 31-10

Using a Form with Validation

For sending data to the server, the input fields need to be surrounded by a form. A Tag Helper for the form defines the `action` attribute by using `asp-method` and `asp-controller`. With `input` controls, you've seen that validation information is defined by these controls. The validation errors need to be displayed. For display, the validation message Tag Helper extends the span element with `asp-validation-for` (code file `MVCSampleApp/Views/TagHelpers/FormHelper.cshtml`):

```
<form method="post" asp-method="FormHelper">
  <input asp-for="Id" hidden="hidden" />
  <hr />
  <label asp-for="Text"></label>
  <div>
    <input asp-for="Text" />
    <span asp-validation-for="Text"></span>
  </div>
  <br />
    <label asp-for="Price"></label>
    <div>
    <input asp-for="Price" />
    <span asp-validation-for="Price"></span>
</div>
<br />
<label asp-for="Date"></label>
<div>
<input asp-for="Date" />
<span asp-validation-for="Date"></span>
```

```
</div>
<label asp-for="Category"></label>
<div>
<input asp-for="Category" />
<span asp-validation-for="Category"></span>
</div>
<input type="submit" value="Submit" />
</form>
```

The controller verifies whether the receive data is correct by checking the ModelState. In case it's not correct, the same view is displayed again (code file MVCSampleApp/Controllers/TagHelpersController.cs):

```
public IActionResult FormHelper() => View(GetSampleMenu());

[HttpPost]
public IActionResult FormHelper(Menu m)
{
  if (!ModelState.IsValid)
  {
    return View(m);
  }
  return View("ValidationHelperResult", m);
}
```

When you run the application, you can see error information like that shown in Figure 31-11.

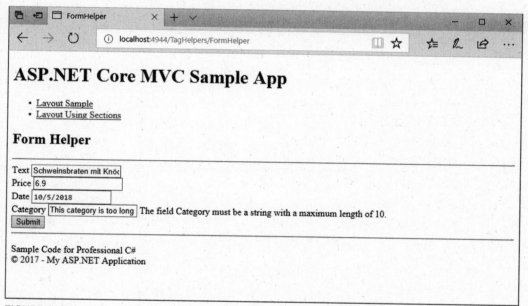

FIGURE 31-11

Environment Tag Helper

The environment Tag Helper allows specified parts of the UI to be available only from specified environments. Chapter 30 shows you how to distinguish between different environments using the IHostingEnvironment interface with the EnvironmentName property, and extension methods IsDevelopment, IsStaging, and IsProduction. The environment Tag Helper allows for similar functionality.

In the following code snippet, the first environment tag is used to show the containing content only when running in `Development` and `Staging` environments using the `include` attribute. The second environment tag excludes the `Production` environment; thus, the containing content is shown in `Development`, `Staging`, and other environments that can be configured (code file `MVCSampleApp/Views/TagHelpers/EnvironmentHelper.cshtml`):

```
<environment include="Development, Staging">
  <div>This shows up for the <strong>Development</strong>
    and <strong>Staging</strong> environments</div>
</environment>
<environment exclude="Production">
  <div>Not visible in the <strong>Production</strong> environment</div>
</environment>
```

You can configure the active environment by setting the environmental variable ASPNETCORE_ENVIRONMENT, which can be done with the project settings in Visual Studio (see Figure 31-12), or by configuring the `launchsettings.json` file.

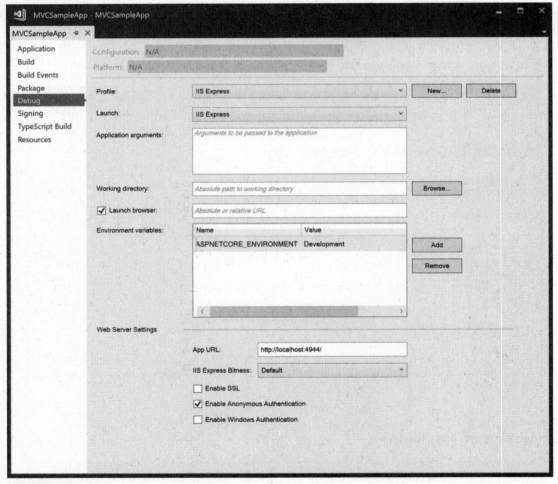

FIGURE 31-12

Creating Custom Tag Helpers

Aside from using the predefined Tag Helpers, you can create a custom Tag Helper. The first custom Tag Helper converts Markdown code to HTML with the help of the NuGet package Markdig.

> **NOTE** *Markdown is a markup language that can be easily created with a text editor. Markdown is designed to be easily converted to HTML. Read my blog article "Using Markdown" for information about using Markdown with .NET at* https://csharp .christiannagel.com/2016/07/03/markdown/.

The Tag Helper MarkdownTagHelper is implemented in a .NET Core library named TagHelperSamples referencing the NuGet packages Microsoft.AspNetCore.All and Markdig.

The following code snippet shows the class declaration of the MarkdownTagHelper. A Tag Helper derives from the base class TagHelper. The attribute HtmlTargetElement specifies the element or attribute names that are used to specify the Tag Helper. This Tag Helper can be used either with the markdown element, or the markdownfile attribute that can be used within a div element. The TagStructure attribute allows configuration if the element needs self-closing (enumeration value WithoutEndTag, or allows an end tag or self-closing with NormalOrSelfClosing) (code file TagHelperSamples/MarkdownTagHelper.cs):

```
[HtmlTargetElement("markdown",
    TagStructure = TagStructure.NormalOrSelfClosing)]
[HtmlTargetElement(Attributes = "markdownfile")]
public class MarkdownTagHelper : TagHelper
{
    //...
}
```

Tag helpers can make use of dependency injection. Because the MarkdownTagHelper needs the directory of the wwwroot files, and this directory is returned from the IHostingEnvironment interface, this interface is injected in the constructor:

```
private readonly IHostingEnvironment _env;
public MarkdownTagHelper(IHostingEnvironment env) => _env = env;
```

Properties of a Tag Helper are automatically applied by the infrastructure when they are annotated with the HtmlAttributeName attribute. Here, the property MarkdownFile gets its value from the markdownfile attribute:

```
[HtmlAttributeName("markdownfile")]
public string MarkdownFile { get; set; }
```

Next, let's get into the main functionality of this Tag Helper. Tag Helpers need to override one of the methods Process or ProcessAsync. The ProcessAsync method is used when async functionality is needed, whereas you can use the Process method if you only invoke synchronous methods. The following code snippet overrides the ProcessAsync method because the asynchronous method GetChildContentAsync is used within the implementation. With the implementation, the two different uses of the MarkdownTagHelper are considered. One use is to specify the markdown element where the content comes as child of the element, and the other is the markdownfile attribute that references a Markdown file.

If the attribute markdownfile is used, the MarkdownFile property is set, and thus the file specified with this property is read, and the content is written to the markdown variable. The directory of the file is retrieved via the _env variable of type IHostingEnvironment. This interface defines the WebRootPath property that returns the root path for the web files.

If the `MarkdownFile` property is not set, but instead the `markdown` element is used, the content of this element is read. The content of the element that is specified within markdown can be accessed using the `TagHelperOutput`. To retrieve the content, the method `GetChildContentAsync` needs to be invoked, and after this method returns, the `GetContent` method needs to be invoked that finally returns the content as specified in the HTML page. Using the `Markdown` class of the Markdig library, the Markdown content is converted to HTML. This HTML code is then put into the content of the `TagHelperOutput` invoking the `SetHtmlContent` method (code file TagHelperSamples/MarkdownTagHelper.cs):

```
public override async Task ProcessAsync(TagHelperContext context,
  TagHelperOutput output)
{
  if (context == null) throw new ArgumentNullException(nameof(context));
  if (output == null) throw new ArgumentNullException(nameof(output));

  string markdown = string.Empty;
  if (MarkdownFile != null)
  {
    string filename = Path.Combine(_env.WebRootPath, MarkdownFile);
    markdown = File.ReadAllText(filename);
  }
  else
  {
    markdown = (await output.GetChildContentAsync()).GetContent();
  }
  output.Content.SetHtmlContent(Markdown.ToHtml(markdown));
}
```

After creating the `MarkdownTagHelper` Tag Helper, it can be used from a CSHTML file. First, `@addTagHelper` adds all Tag Helpers from the library `TagHelperSamples`. In the HTML code, the markdown element is used. This element contains a small segment of Markdown syntax with heading 2, a link, and a list (code file MVCSampleApp/Views/TagHelpers/Markdown.cshtml):

```
@addTagHelper *, TagHelperSamples

<h2>Markdown Sample</h2>

<markdown>
## This is simple Markdown

[C# Blog](https://csharp.christiannagel.com)

* one
* two
* three
</markdown>
```

When you run the application, the markdown syntax gets converted to HTML, as shown in Figure 31-13.

Now, the same functionality can be achieved by creating the file `Sample.md` (which contains the same Markdown content as shown earlier), and referencing the file from the `markdownfile` attribute (code file MVCSampleApp/Views/TagHelpers/MarkdownAttribute.cshtml):

```
<div markdownfile="Sample.md"></div>
```

With this in place, the property `MarkdownFile` of the `MarkdownTagHelper` is set, and thus the markdown file is read.

Creating Elements with Tag Helpers

The next custom Tag Helper you build in this section extends the HTML `table` element to show a row for every item in a list and a column for every property. A model of data information is passed to the Tag

Helper, and the Tag Helper creates `table`, `tr`, `th`, and `td` elements dynamically. Information what should be created is done using reflection. Similar functionality like this can be implemented in view components as well, and the view helpers can be used with a Tag Helper. This section goes into detail about creating more complex Tag Helpers and using the `TagBuilder` class to dynamically create HTML elements.

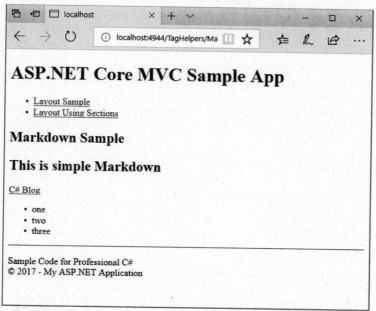

FIGURE 31-13

> **NOTE** *Reflection is explained in Chapter 16.*

For this sample, the controller implements the method `CustomTable` to return a view with a list of `Menu` objects (code file `MVCSampleApp/Controllers/TagHelpersController.cs`):

```
public IActionResult CustomTable() => View(GetSampleMenus());

private IList<Menu> GetSampleMenus() =>
  new List<Menu>()
  {
    new Menu
    {
      Id = 1,
      Text = "Schweinsbraten mit Knödel und Sauerkraut",
      Price = 8.5,
      Date = new DateTime(2018, 10, 5),
      Category = "Main"
    },
    new Menu
    {
      Id = 2,
      Text = "Erdäpfelgulasch mit Tofu und Gebäck",
      Price = 8.5,
      Date = new DateTime(2018, 10, 6),
```

```
        Category = "Vegetarian"
      },
      new Menu
      {
        Id = 3,
        Text = „Tiroler Bauerngröst'l mit Spiegelei und Krautsalat",
        Price = 8.5,
        Date = new DateTime(2018, 10, 7),
        Category = "Vegetarian"
      }
    };
```

The Tag Helper class `TableTagHelper` is activated with the HTML `table` element. Contrary to the previous helper with the `markup` element, this helper is used with a valid HTML element. The `HtmlTargetElement` specifies `table` to apply this helper, and the attribute `items`. This attribute is used to set the `Items` property as specified by the `HtmlAttributeName` attribute (code file `TagHelperSamples/TableTagHelper.cs`):

```csharp
[HtmlTargetElement("table", Attributes = ItemsAttributeName)]
public class TableTagHelper : TagHelper
{
  private const string ItemsAttributeName = "items";

  [HtmlAttributeName(ItemsAttributeName)]
  public IEnumerable<object> Items { get; set; }
  //...
}
```

The heart of the Tag Helper is in the method `Process`. This time the synchronous variant of this method can be used because no async method is used in the implementation. With the parameters of the `Process` method you receive a `TagHelperContext` This context contains both the attributes of the HTML element where the Tag Helper is applied and all child elements. With the `table` element specified when using the Tag Helper, rows and columns could already have been defined, and you could merge the result with the existing content. In the sample, this is ignored, and just the attributes are taken to put them in the result. The result needs to be written to the second parameter: the `TagHelperOutput` object. For creating HTML code, the `TagBuilder` type is used. The `TagBuilder` helps create HTML elements with attributes, and it deals with closing of elements. To add attributes to the `TagBuilder`, you use the method `MergeAttributes`. This method requires a dictionary of all attribute names and their values. This dictionary is created by using the LINQ extension method `ToDictionary`. With the `Where` method, all of the existing attributes—with the exception of the items attribute—of the table element are taken. The `items` attribute is used for defining items with the Tag Helper but is not needed later on by the client:

```csharp
public override void Process(TagHelperContext context, TagHelperOutput output)
{
  if (context == null) throw new ArgumentNullException(nameof(context));
  if (output == null) throw new ArgumentNullException(nameof(output));

  var table = new TagBuilder("table");
  table.GenerateId(context.UniqueId, "id");
  var attributes = context.AllAttributes
    .Where(a => a.Name != ItemsAttributeName)
    .ToDictionary(a => a.Name);
  table.MergeAttributes(attributes);

  PropertyInfo[] properties = CreateHeading(table);
  //...
}
```

> **NOTE** *LINQ is explained in Chapter 12, "Language Integrated Query."*

Next create the first row in the table by using the `CreateHeading` method. This first row contains a `tr` element as a child of the `table` element, and it contains `th` (table heading) elements for every property. To get all the property names, you invoke the `First` method to retrieve the first object of the collection. You access the properties of this instance using reflection, invoking the `GetProperties` method on the `Type` object, and writing the name of the property to the inner text of the `th` HTML element:

```
private PropertyInfo[] CreateHeading(TagBuilder table)
{
  var tr = new TagBuilder("tr");
  var heading = Items.First();
  PropertyInfo[] properties = heading.GetType().GetProperties();
  foreach (var prop in properties)
  {
    var th = new TagBuilder("th");
    th.InnerHtml.Append(prop.Name);
    tr.InnerHtml.AppendHtml(th);
  }
  table.InnerHtml.AppendHtml(tr);
  return properties;
}
```

The final part of the `Process` method iterates through all items of the collection and creates more rows (`tr`) for every item. With every property, a `td` element is added, and the value of the property is written as inner text. Last, the inner HTML code of the created `table` element is written to the output:

```
foreach (var item in Items)
{
  tr = new TagBuilder("tr");
  foreach (var prop in properties)
  {
    var td = new TagBuilder("td");
    td.InnerHtml.Append(prop.GetValue(item).ToString());
    tr.InnerHtml.AppendHtml(td);
  }
  table.InnerHtml.AppendHtml(tr);
}
output.Content.Append(table.InnerHtml);
}
```

After you've created the Tag Helper, creating the view becomes very simple. After you've defined the model, you reference the Tag Helper with `addTagHelper` passing the assembly name. The Tag Helper itself is instantiated when you define an HTML `table` with the attribute `items` (code file `MVCSampleApp/Views/TagHelpers/CustomHelper.cshtml`):

```
@model IEnumerable<Menu>
@addTagHelper *, MVCSampleApp
<table items="Model" class="sample"></table>
```

When you run the application, the table you see should look like the one shown in Figure 31-14. After you've created the Tag Helper, it is really easy to use. All the formatting that is defined using CSS still applies as all the attributes of the defined HTML table are still in the resulting HTML output.

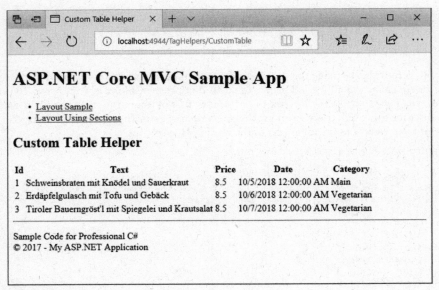

FIGURE 31-14

IMPLEMENTING ACTION FILTERS

ASP.NET Core MVC is extensible in many areas. For example, you can implement a controller factory to search and instantiate a controller (interface `IControllerFactory`). Controllers implement the `IController` interface. Finding action methods in a controller is resolved by using the `IActionInvoker` interface. You can use attribute classes derived from `ActionMethodSelectorAttribute` to define the HTTP methods allowed. The model binder that maps the HTTP request to parameters can be customized by implementing the `IModelBinder` interface. The section "Model Binder" uses the `FormCollectionModelBinder` type. You can use different view engines that implement the interface `IViewEngine`. This chapter uses the Razor view engine. You can also customize by using HTML Helpers, Tag Helpers, and action filters. Most of the extension points are out of the scope of this book, but action filters are likely ones that you will implement or use, and thus these are covered here.

Action filters are called before and after an action is executed. They are assigned to controllers or action methods of controllers using attributes. Action filters are implemented by creating a class that derives from the base class `ActionFilterAttribute`. With this class, the base class members `OnActionExecuting`, `OnActionExecuted`, `OnResultExecuting`, and `OnResultExecuted` can be overridden. `OnActionExecuting` is called before the action method is invoked, and `OnActionExecuted` is called when the action method is completed. After that, before the result is returned, the method `OnResultExecuting` is invoked, and finally `OnResultExecuted` is invoked.

Within these methods, you can access the `Request` object to retrieve information of the caller. Using the `Request` object, you can decide some actions depending on the browser, you can access routing information, you can change the view result dynamically, and so on. The code snippet accesses the variable language from routing information. To add this variable to the route, you can change the route as described earlier in this chapter in the section "Defining Routes." By adding a `language` variable with the route information, you can access the value supplied with the URL using `RouteData.Values` as shown in the following code snippet. You can use the retrieved value to change the culture for the user:

```
public class LanguageAttribute : ActionFilterAttribute
{
    private string _language = null;
```

```
public override void OnActionExecuting(ActionExecutingContext filterContext)
{
  _language = filterContext.RouteData.Values["language"] == null ?
    null : filterContext.RouteData.Values["language"].ToString();
  //...
}

public override void OnResultExecuting(ResultExecutingContext filterContext)
{
}
}
```

> **NOTE** *Globalization and localization, setting cultures, and other regional specifics are explained in Chapter 27, "Localization."*

With the created action filter attribute class, you can apply the attribute to a controller as shown in the following code snippet. Using the attribute with the class, the members of the attribute class are invoked with every action method. Instead, you can also apply the attribute to an action method, so the members are invoked only when the action method is called:

```
[Language]
public class HomeController : Controller
{
```

The `ActionFilterAttribute` implements several interfaces: `IActionFilter`, `IAsyncActionFilter`, `IResultFilter`, `IAsyncResultFilter`, `IFilter`, and `IOrderedFilter`.

ASP.NET Core MVC includes some predefined action filters, such as a filter to require HTTPS, authorize callers, handle errors, or cache data.

Using the attribute `Authorize` is covered later in this chapter in the section "Authentication and Authorization."

CREATING A DATA-DRIVEN APPLICATION

Now that you've read about all the foundations of ASP.NET Core MVC, it's time to look into a data-driven application that uses Entity Framework Core. Here you can see features offered by ASP.NET Core MVC in combination with data access.

> **NOTE** *Entity Framework Core (EF Core) is covered in detail in Chapter 26, "Entity Framework Core."*

The sample application `MenuPlanner` is used to maintain restaurant menu entries in a database. Only an authenticated account may perform maintenance of the database entries. Browsing menus should be possible for non-authenticated users.

This project is started by using the ASP.NET Core Web Application template. For the authentication, you use the default selection of Individual User Accounts with the selection Store User Accounts In-App. This project template adds several folders for ASP.NET Core MVC and controllers, including a `HomeController` and `AccountController`. It also adds several script libraries.

Defining a Model

Start by defining a model within the `Models` directory. You create the model using the Entity Framework Core (EF Core). The `MenuCard` type defines some properties and a relation to a list of menus (code file `MenuPlanner/Models/MenuCard.cs`):

```
public class MenuCard
{
  public int Id { get; set; }

  [MaxLength(50)]
  public string Name { get; set; }
  public bool Active { get; set; }
  public int Order { get; set; }
  public virtual List<Menu> Menus { get; set; }
}
```

The menu types that are referenced from the `MenuCard` are defined by the `Menu` class (code file `MenuPlanner/Models/Menu.cs`):

```
public class Menu
{
  public int Id { get; set; }
  public string Text { get; set; }
  public decimal Price { get; set; }
  public bool Active { get; set; }
  public int Order { get; set; }
  public string Type { get; set; }
  public DateTime Day { get; set; }
  public int MenuCardId { get; set; }
  public virtual MenuCard MenuCard { get; set; }
}
```

The connection to the database, and the sets of both `Menu` and `MenuCard` types, are managed by `MenuCardsContext`. Using `ModelBuilder`, the context specifies that the `Text` property of the `Menu` type may not be null, and it has a maximum length of 50 (code file `MenuPlanner/Models/MenuCardsContext.cs`):

```
public class MenuCardsContext : DbContext
{
  public MenuCardsContext(DbContextOptions<MenuCardsContext> options)
    : base(options)
  {
  }

  public DbSet<Menu> Menus { get; set; }
  public DbSet<MenuCard> MenuCards { get; set; }

  protected override void OnModelCreating(ModelBuilder modelBuilder)
  {
    modelBuilder.Entity<Menu>().Property(p => p.Text)
      .HasMaxLength(50).IsRequired();
    base.OnModelCreating(modelBuilder);
  }
}
```

The startup code for the web application defines `MenuCardsContext` to be used as data context, and reads the connection string from the configuration file (code file `MenuPlanner/Startup.cs`):

```
public void ConfigureServices(IServiceCollection services)
{
  services.AddDbContext<ApplicationDbContext>(options =>
    options.UseSqlServer(
      Configuration.GetConnectionString("DefaultConnection")));
```

```
services.AddDbContext<MenuCardsContext>(options =>
  options.UseSqlServer(
    Configuration.GetConnectionString("DefaultConnection")));

//...
}
```

With the configuration file, the `DefaultConnection` connection string references the local SQL Server instance that comes with Visual Studio 2017. Of course, you can change this and also add a connection string to SQL Azure (code file `MenuPlanner/appsettings.json`):

```
{
  "ConnectionStrings": {
    "DefaultConnection":  "Server=(localdb)\\mssqllocaldb;Database=MenuPlanner;
    Trusted_Connection=True;MultipleActiveResultSets=true"
  },
  //...
}
```

Creating a Database

You can use EF Core commands to create the code to create the database. With a command-line prompt, you use the .NET Core Command Line (CLI) with the `ef` command to create code to create the database automatically. Using the command prompt, you must set the current folder to the directory where the project file is located:

```
>dotnet ef migrations add InitMenuCards --context MenuCardsContext
```

> **NOTE** *The dotnet ef tool extensions are discussed in Chapter 26.*

Because multiple data contexts (the `MenuCardsContext` and the `ApplicationDbContext`) are defined with the project, you need to specify the data context with the `--context` option. The `ef` command creates a `Migrations` folder within the project structure and the `InitMenuCards` class with an `Up` method to create the database tables, and the `Down` method to delete the changes again (code file `MenuPlanner/Migrations/[date]InitMenuCards.cs`):

```
public partial class InitMenuCards : Migration
{
  public override void Up(MigrationBuilder migrationBuilder)
  {
    migrationBuilder.CreateTable(
      name: "MenuCards",
      columns: table => new
      {
        Id = table.Column<int>(nullable: false)
          .Annotation("SqlServer:ValueGenerationStrategy",
            SqlServerValueGenerationStrategy.IdentityColumn),
        Active = table.Column<bool>(nullable: false),
        Name = table.Column<string>(maxLength: 50, nullable: true),
        Order = table.Column<int>(nullable: false)
      },
      constraints: table =>
      {
        table.PrimaryKey("PK_MenuCards", x => x.Id);
      });
```

```
    migrationBuilder.CreateTable(
      name: "Menus",
      columns: table => new
      {
        Id = table.Column<int>(nullable: false)
          .Annotation("SqlServer:ValueGenerationStrategy",
            SqlServerValueGenerationStrategy.IdentityColumn),
        Active = table.Column<bool>(nullable: false),
        Day = table.Column<DateTime>(nullable: false),
        MenuCardId = table.Column<int>(nullable: false),
        Order = table.Column<int>(nullable: false),
        Price = table.Column<decimal>(nullable: false),
        Text = table.Column<string>(maxLength: 50, nullable: false),
        Type = table.Column<string>(nullable: true)
      },
      constraints: table =>
      {
        table.PrimaryKey("PK_Menus", x => x.Id);
        table.ForeignKey(
          name: "FK_Menus_MenuCards_MenuCardId",
          column: x => x.MenuCardId,
          principalTable: "MenuCards",
          principalColumn: "Id",
          onDelete: RefeerentialAction.Cascade);
      });
  }

  public override void Down(MigrationBuilder migration)
  {
    migration.DropTable("Menus");
    migration.DropTable("MenuCards");
  }
}
```

Now you just need some code to start the migration process, filling the database with initial sample data. The `MenuCardDatabaseInitializer` applies the migration process by invoking the extension method `MigrateAsync` on the `DatabaseFacade` object that is returned from the `Database` property. This in turn checks whether the database associated with the connection string already has the same version as the database specified with the migrations. If it doesn't have the same version, required `Up` methods are invoked to get to the same version. In addition to that, a few `MenuCard` objects are created to have them stored in the database (code file MenuPlanner/Models/MenuCardDatabaseInitializer.cs):

```
using Microsoft.EntityFrameworkCore;
using System.Threading.Tasks;

namespace MenuPlanner.Models
{
  public class MenuCardDatabaseInitializer
  {
    private static bool s_databaseChecked = false;
    private readonly MenuCardsContext _context;

    public MenuCardDatabaseInitializer(MenuCardsContext context) =>
      _context = context;

    public async Task CreateAndSeedDatabaseAsync()
    {
      if (!s_databaseChecked)
      {
        s_databaseChecked = true;
        await _context.Database.MigrateAsync();
        if (await _context.MenuCards.CountAsync() == 0)
```

```
        {
          _context.MenuCards.Add(
            new MenuCard { Name = "Breakfast", Active = true, Order = 1 });
          _context.MenuCards.Add(
            new MenuCard { Name = "Vegetarian", Active = true, Order = 2 });
          _context.MenuCards.Add(
            new MenuCard { Name = "Steaks", Active = true, Order = 3 });
        }
        await _context.SaveChangesAsync();
      }
    }
  }
}
```

With the database and model in place, you can create a service.

Creating a Service

Before creating the service, you create the interface `IMenuCardsService` that defines all the methods that are needed by the service (code file `MenuPlanner/Services/IMenuCardsService.cs`):

```
using MenuPlanner.Models;
using System.Collections.Generic;
using System.Threading.Tasks;

namespace MenuPlanner.Services
{
  public interface IMenuCardsService
  {
    Task AddMenuAsync(Menu menu);
    Task DeleteMenuAsync(int id);
    Task<Menu> GetMenuByIdAsync(int id);
    Task<IEnumerable<Menu>> GetMenusAsync();
    Task<IEnumerable<MenuCard>> GetMenuCardsAsync();
    Task UpdateMenuAsync(Menu menu);
  }
}
```

The service class `MenuCardsService` implements the methods to return menus and menu cards, and it creates, updates, and deletes menus (code file `MenuPlanner/Services/MenuCardsService.cs`):

```
using MenuPlanner.Models;
using Microsoft.EntityFrameworkCore;
using System.Collections.Generic;
using System.Linq;
using System.Threading.Tasks;

namespace MenuPlanner.Services
{
  public class MenuCardsService : IMenuCardsService
  {
    private readonly MenuCardsContext _menuCardsContext;
    public MenuCardsService(MenuCardsContext menuCardsContext) =>
      _menuCardsContext = menuCardsContext;

    public async Task<IEnumerable<Menu>> GetMenusAsync()
    {
      await EnsureDatabaseCreatedAsync();
      var menus = _menuCardsContext.Menus.Include(m => m.MenuCard);
      return await menus.ToArrayAsync();
    }
```

```
public async Task<IEnumerable<MenuCard>> GetMenuCardsAsync()
{
  await EnsureDatabaseCreatedAsync();
  var menuCards = _menuCardsContext.MenuCards;
  return await menuCards.ToArrayAsync();
}

public async Task<Menu> GetMenuByIdAsync(int id) =>
  await _menuCardsContext.Menus.SingleOrDefaultAsync(m => m.Id == id);

public async Task AddMenuAsync(Menu menu)
{
  await _menuCardsContext.Menus.AddAsync(menu);
  await _menuCardsContext.SaveChangesAsync();
}

public async Task UpdateMenuAsync(Menu menu)
{
  _menuCardsContext.Menus.Update(menu);
  await _menuCardsContext.SaveChangesAsync();
}

public async Task DeleteMenuAsync(int id)
{
  Menu menu = await _menuCardsContext.Menus.SingleAsync(m => m.Id == id);
  _menuCardsContext.Menus.Remove(menu);
  await _menuCardsContext.SaveChangesAsync();
}

private async Task EnsureDatabaseCreatedAsync()
{
  var init = new MenuCardDatabaseInitializer(_menuCardsContext);
  await init.CreateAndSeedDatabaseAsync();
}
  }
}
```

To have the service available via dependency injection, the service is registered in the service collection using the `AddScoped` method (code file `MenuPlanner/Startup.cs`):

```
public void ConfigureServices(IServiceCollection services)
{
  //...
  services.AddScoped<IMenuCardsService, MenuCardsService>();
  //...
}
```

Creating a Controller

ASP.NET Core MVC offers scaffolding to create controllers for directly accessing the database. You can do this by selecting the Controllers folder in Solution Explorer, and from the context menu select Add ⇨ Controller. The Add Scaffold dialog opens. From the Add Scaffold dialog, you can select MVC Controller views, using Entity Framework. Clicking the Add button opens the Add MVC Controller dialog shown in Figure 31-15. With this dialog, you can select the Menu model class and the Entity Framework data context MenuCardsContext, configure to generate views, and give the controller a name. Create the controller with the views to look at the generated code including the views.

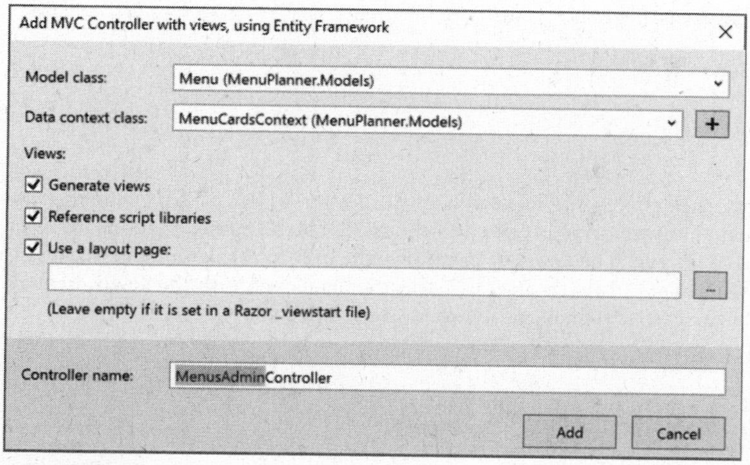

FIGURE 31-15

The book sample doesn't use the data context directly from the controller but puts a service in between. Doing it this way offers more flexibility. You can use the service from different controllers and also use the service from a service such as ASP.NET Core Web API.

> **NOTE** *ASP.NET Core Web API is discussed in Chapter 32, "ASP.NET Web API."*

With the following sample code, the ASP.NET Core MVC controller injects the menu card service via constructor injection (code file `MenuPlanner/Controllers/MenusAdminController.cs`):

```
public class MenusAdminController : Controller
{
  private readonly IMenuCardsService _service;
  public MenusAdminController(IMenuCardsService service) =>
    _service = service;
  //...
}
```

The `Index` method is the default method that is invoked when only the controller is referenced with the URL without passing an action method. Here, all `Menu` items from the database are created and passed to the `Index` view. The `Details` method returns the `Details` view passing the menu found from the service. Pay attention to the error handling. When no ID is passed to the `Details` method, and when the menu is not found in the database, an HTTP Not Found (404 error response) is returned using the `NotFound` method. This method is defined in a base class of the controller, `ControllerBase` (code file `MenuPlanner/Controllers/MenusAdminController.cs`):

```
public async Task<IActionResult> Index() =>
  View(await _service.GetMenusAsync());

public async Task<IActionResult> Details(int? id = 0)
{
  if (id == null)
  {
    return NotFound();
  }
```

```
    Menu menu = await _service.GetMenuByIdAsync(id.Value);
    if (menu == null)
    {
        return NotFound();
    }
    return View(menu);
}
```

When the user creates a new menu, the first `Create` method is invoked after an HTTP GET request from the client. With this method, `ViewBag` information is passed to the view. This `ViewBag` contains information about the menu cards in a `SelectList`. The `SelectList` allows the user to select an item. Because the `MenuCard` collection is passed to the `SelectList`, the user can select a menu card with the newly created menu (code file `MenuPlanner/Controllers/MenusAdminController.cs`):

```
public async Task<IActionResult> Create()
{
    IEnumerable<MenuCard> cards = await _service.GetMenuCardsAsync();
    ViewBag.MenuCardId = new SelectList(cards, "Id", "Name");
    return View();
}
```

After the user fills out the form and submits the form with the new menu to the server, the second `Create` method is invoked from an HTTP POST request. This method uses model binding to pass the form data to the `Menu` object and adds the `Menu` object to the data context to write the newly created menu to the database (code file `MenuPlanner/Controllers/MenusAdminController.cs`):

```
[HttpPost]
[ValidateAntiForgeryToken]
public async Task<ActionResult> Create(
    [Bind("Id","MenuCardId", "Text", "Price", "Active", "Order", "Type", "Day")]
    Menu menu)
{
    if (ModelState.IsValid)
    {
        await _service.AddMenuAsync(menu);
        return RedirectToAction("Index");
    }
    IEnumerable<MenuCard> cards = await _service.GetMenuCardsAsync();
    ViewBag.MenuCards = new SelectList(cards, "Id", "Name", menu.MenuCardId);
    return View(menu);
}
```

> **NOTE** *Anti-forgery tokens the attribute* `ValidateAntiForgeryToken` *are explained in Chapter 24, "Security."*

To edit a menu card, two action methods named `Edit` are defined—one for a GET request, and one for a POST request. The first `Edit` method returns a single menu item; the second one invokes the `UpdateMenuAsync` method of the service after the model binding is done successfully:

```
public async Task<IActionResult> Edit(int? id)
{
    if (id == null)
    {
        return NotFound();
    }
    Menu menu = await _service.GetMenuByIdAsync(id.Value);
    if (menu == null)
    {
        return NotFound();
    }
}
```

```
    IEnumerable<MenuCard> cards = await _service.GetMenuCardsAsync();
    ViewBag.MenuCardId = new SelectList(cards, "Id", "Name", menu.MenuCardId);
    return View(menu);
}


[HttpPost]
[ValidateAntiForgeryToken]
public async Task<IActionResult> Edit(int id,
    [Bind("Id", "MenuCardId", "Text", "Price", "Order", "Type", "Day")]
      Menu menu)
{
  if (id != menu.Id)
  {
    return NotFound();
  }

  if (ModelState.IsValid)
  {
    await _service.UpdateMenuAsync(menu);
    return RedirectToAction("Index");
  }
  IEnumerable<MenuCard> cards = await _service.GetMenuCardsAsync();
  ViewBag.MenuCardId = new SelectList(cards, "Id", "Name", menu.MenuCardId);
  return View(menu);
}
```

The last part of the implementation of the controller includes the Delete methods. Because both methods have the same parameter—which is not possible with C#—the second method has the name DeleteConfirmed. However, the second method can be accessed from the same URL Link as the first Delete method, but the second method is accessed with HTTP POST instead of GET using the ActionName attribute. This method invokes the DeleteMenuAsync method of the service:

```
public async Task<IActionResult> Delete(int? id)
{
  if (id == null)
  {
    return NotFound();
  }
  Menu menu = await _service.GetMenuByIdAsync(id.Value);
  if (menu == null)
  {
    return NotFound();
  }
  return View(menu);
}


[HttpPost, ActionName("Delete")]
[ValidateAntiForgeryToken]
public async Task<IActionResult> DeleteConfirmed(int id)
{
  Menu menu = await _service.GetMenuByIdAsync(id);
  await _service.DeleteMenuAsync(menu.Id);
  return RedirectToAction("Index");
}
```

> **NOTE** *When you're using a Web API, deleting a resource is usually done with a HTTP DELETE verb. Read Chapter 32, "Web API," for information about the Web API. This is not the case with a browser that's accessing a page. The* DeleteConfirmed *method is requested using a HTTP POST verb (as defined by the* HttpPost *attribute).*

Creating Views

Now it's time to create views. The views are created within the folder `Views/MenuAdmin`. You can create the view by selecting the `MenuAdmin` folder in Solution Explorer and select Add ⇨ View from the context menu. This opens the Add MVC View dialog as shown in Figure 31-16. With this dialog you can choose List, Details, Create, Edit, Delete templates, which arrange HTML elements accordingly. The Model class you select with this dialog defines the model that the view is based on.

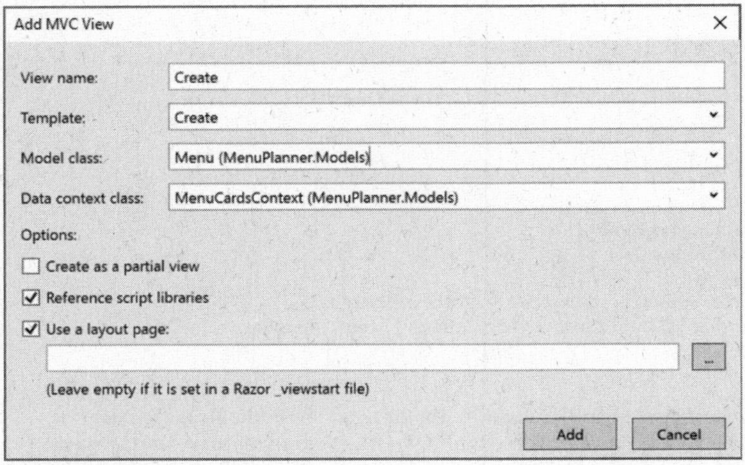

FIGURE 31-16

The `Index` view, which defines an HTML table, has a `Menu` collection as its model. For the header elements of the table, the HTML element label with a HTML Helper `DisplayNameFor` is used to access property names for display. For displaying the items, the menu collection is iterated using `@foreach`, and every property value is accessed with a HTML Helper for the input element. A Tag Helper for the anchor element creates links for the `Edit`, `Details`, and `Delete` pages (code file `MenuPlanner/Views/MenuAdmin/Index.cshtml`):

```
@model IEnumerable<MenuPlanner.Models.Menu>
@{
    ViewData["Title"] = "Index";
}
<h2>Index</h2>
<p>
  <a asp-action="Create">Create New</a>
</p>
<table class="table">
  <thead>
    <tr>
      <th>
        @Html.DisplayNameFor(model => model.Text)
      </th>
      <th>
        @Html.DisplayNameFor(model => model.Price)
      </th>
      <th>
        @Html.DisplayNameFor(model => model.Active)
      </th>
      <th>
        @Html.DisplayNameFor(model => model.Order)
      </th>
```

```
        <th>
          @Html.DisplayNameFor(model => model.Type)
        </th>
        <th>
          @Html.DisplayNameFor(model => model.Day)
        </th>
        <th>
          @Html.DisplayNameFor(model => model.MenuCard)
        </th>
        <th></th>
      </tr>
    </thead>
    <tbody>
    @foreach (var item in Model) {
      <tr>
        <td>
          @Html.DisplayFor(modelItem => item.Text)
        </td>
        <td>
          @Html.DisplayFor(modelItem => item.Price)
        </td>
        <td>
          @Html.DisplayFor(modelItem => item.Active)
        </td>
        <td>
          @Html.DisplayFor(modelItem => item.Order)
        </td>
        <td>
          @Html.DisplayFor(modelItem => item.Type)
        </td>
        <td>
          @Html.DisplayFor(modelItem => item.Day)
        </td>
        <td>
          @Html.DisplayFor(modelItem => item.MenuCard.Id)
        </td>
        <td>
          <a asp-action="Edit" asp-route-id="@item.Id">Edit</a> |
          <a asp-action="Details" asp-route-id="@item.Id">Details</a> |
          <a asp-action="Delete" asp-route-id="@item.Id">Delete</a>
        </td>
      </tr>
    }
    </tbody>
</table>
```

In the `MenuPlanner` project, the second view for the `MenuAdmin` controller is the `Create` view. The HTML form uses the `asp-action` Tag Helper to reference the `Create` action method of the controller. It's not necessary to reference the controller with the `asp-controller` helper, as the action method is in the same controller where the view was coming from. The form content is built up using the Tag Helpers for label and input elements. The `asp-for` helper for the label returns the name of the property; the `asp-for` helper for the input element returns the value (code file `MenuPlanner/Views/MenuAdmin/Create.cshtml`):

```
@model MenuPlanner.Models.Menu
@{
    ViewData["Title"] = "Create";
}
<h2>Create</h2>
<h4>Menu</h4>
<hr />
<div class="row">
  <div class="col-md-4">
```

```
<form asp-action="Create">
  <div asp-validation-summary="ModelOnly" class="text-danger"></div>
  <div class="form-group">
    <label asp-for="Text" class="control-label"></label>
    <input asp-for="Text" class="form-control" />
    <span asp-validation-for="Text" class="text-danger"></span>
  </div>
  <div class="form-group">
    <label asp-for="Price" class="control-label"></label>
    <input asp-for="Price" class="form-control" />
    <span asp-validation-for="Price" class="text-danger"></span>
  </div>
  <div class="form-group">
    <div class="checkbox">
      <label>
        <input asp-for="Active" />
        @Html.DisplayNameFor(model => model.Active)
      </label>
    </div>
  </div>
  <div class="form-group">
    <label asp-for="Order" class="control-label"></label>
    <input asp-for="Order" class="form-control" />
    <span asp-validation-for="Order" class="text-danger"></span>
  </div>
  <div class="form-group">
    <label asp-for="Type" class="control-label"></label>
    <input asp-for="Type" class="form-control" />
    <span asp-validation-for="Type" class="text-danger"></span>
  </div>
  <div class="form-group">
    <label asp-for="Day" class="control-label"></label>
    <input asp-for="Day" class="form-control" />
    <span asp-validation-for="Day" class="text-danger"></span>
  </div>
  <div class="form-group">
    <label asp-for="MenuCardId" class="control-label"></label>
    <select asp-for="MenuCardId" class ="form-control"
      asp-items="ViewBag.MenuCardId"></select>
  </div>
  <div class="form-group">
    <input type="submit" value="Create" class="btn btn-default" />
  </div>
</form>
  </div>
</div>

<div>
  <a asp-action="Index">Back to List</a>
</div>

@section Scripts {
  @{await Html.RenderPartialAsync("_ValidationScriptsPartial");}
}
```

The other views are created similarly to the views shown here, so they are not covered in this book.

You can now use the application to add and edit menus to existing menu cards.

IMPLEMENTING AUTHENTICATION AND AUTHORIZATION

Authentication and authorization are important aspects of web applications. If a website or parts of it should not be public, users must be authorized. For authentication of users, different options are available when you create an ASP.NET Core Web Application (see Figure 31-17): No Authentication, Individual User Accounts, Work and School Accounts, and Windows Authentication.

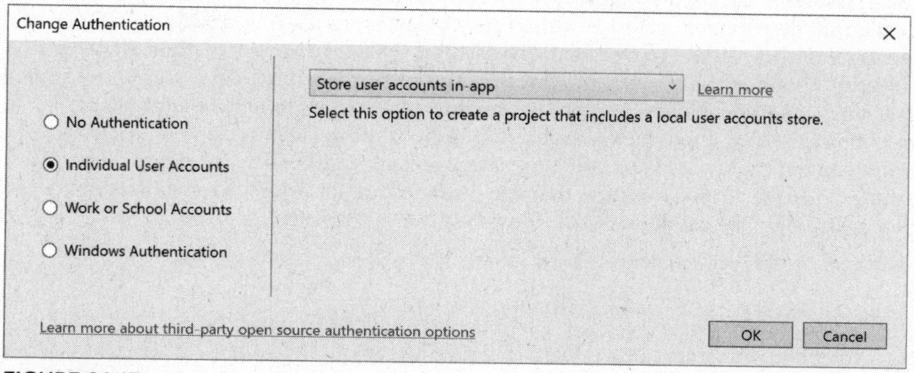

FIGURE 31-17

With Individual User Accounts, you can select to store the users in a SQL Server database or use Azure Active Directory B2C. Both options are discussed in this chapter. Users can register and log in, and they can also use existing accounts from Facebook, Twitter, Google, or Microsoft.

Storing and Retrieving User Information

For user management, user information needs to be added to a store. The type `IdentityUser` (namespace `Microsoft.AspNet.Identity.EntityFramework`) defines a name and lists roles, logins, and claims. The Visual Studio template that you've used to create the `MenuPlanner` application created some noticeable code to save the user: the class `ApplicationUser` that is part of the project derives from the base class `IdentityUser` (namespace `Microsoft.AspNet.Identity.EntityFramework`). The `ApplicationUser` is empty by default, but you can add information you need from the user, and the information will be stored in the database (code file `MenuPlanner/Models/IdentityModels.cs`):

```
public class ApplicationUser : IdentityUser
{
}
```

The connection to the database is made via the `IdentityDbContext<TUser>` type. This is a generic class that derives from `DbContext` and thus makes use of Entity Framework Core. The `IdentityDbContext<TUser>` type defines properties `Roles` and `Users` of type `IDbSet<TEntity>`. The `IDbSet<TEntity>` type defines the mapping to the database tables. For convenience, the `ApplicationDbContext` is created to define the `ApplicationUser` type as the generic type for the `IdentityDbContext` class (code file `MenuPlanner/Data/ApplicationDbContext.cs`):

```
public class ApplicationDbContext : IdentityDbContext<ApplicationUser>
{
  protected override void OnModelCreating(ModelBuilder builder)
  {
    base.OnModelCreating(builder);
  }
}
```

Starting Up the Identity System

The connection to the database is registered with the dependency injection service collection in the startup code. Similar to the `MenuCardsContext` that you created earlier, the `ApplicationDbContext` is configured to use SQL Server with a connection string from the `config` file. The identity service itself is registered using the extension method `AddIdentity`. The `AddIdentity` method maps the type of the user and role classes that are used by the identity service. The class `ApplicationUser` is the previously mentioned class that derives from `IdentityUser`; `IdentityRole` is a string-based role class that derives from `IdentityRole<string>`. An overloaded method of the `AddIdentity` method allows you to configure the identity system with two-factor authentication; email token providers; user options, such as requiring unique emails; or a regular expression that requires a username to match. `AddIdentity` returns an `IdentityBuilder` that allows additional configurations for the identity system, such as the entity framework context that is used (`AddEntityFrameworkStores`), and the token providers (`AddDefaultTokenProviders`). Other providers that can be added are for errors, password validators, role managers, user managers, and user validators (code file `MenuPlanner/Startup.cs`):

```
public void ConfigureServices(IServiceCollection services)
{
  services.AddDbContext<ApplicationDbContext>(options =>
    options.UseSqlServer(
      Configuration.GetConnectionString("DefaultConnection")));

  services.AddDbContext<MenuCardsContext>(options =>
    options.UseSqlServer(
      Configuration.GetConnectionString("DefaultConnection")));
  services.AddScoped<IMenuCardsService, MenuCardsService>();

  services.AddIdentity<ApplicationUser, IdentityRole>()
    .AddEntityFrameworkStores<ApplicationDbContext>()
    .AddDefaultTokenProviders();

  services.AddTransient<IEmailSender, EmailSender>();

  services.AddMvc();
}
```

Performing User Registration

Now let's step into the generated code for registering and logging in the user. The heart of the functionality is within the `AccountController` class. The controller class has the `Authorize` attribute applied, which restricts all action methods to authenticated users. The constructor receives a user manager, sign-in manager, and database context via dependency injection. Email and SMS can be used for two-factor authentication. In case you don't implement the empty `AuthMessageSender` class that is part of the generated code, you can remove the injection for `IEmailSender` (code file `MenuPlanner/Controllers/AccountController.cs`):

```
  [Authorize]
[Route("[controller]/[action]")]
public class AccountController : Controller
{
  private readonly UserManager<ApplicationUser> _userManager;
  private readonly SignInManager<ApplicationUser> _signInManager;
  private readonly IEmailSender _emailSender;
  private readonly ILogger _logger;

  public AccountController(
    UserManager<ApplicationUser> userManager,
    SignInManager<ApplicationUser> signInManager,
    IEmailSender emailSender,
    ILogger<AccountController> logger)
```

```
    {
        _userManager = userManager;
        _signInManager = signInManager;
        _emailSender = emailSender;
        _logger = logger;
    }
```

To register a user, you define `RegisterViewModel`. This model defines what data the user needs to enter on registration. From the generated code, this model only requires email, password, and confirmation password (which must be the same as the password). In case you would like to get more information from the user, you can add properties as needed (code file `MenuPlanner/Models/AccountViewModels.cs`):

```
public class RegisterViewModel
{
    [Required]
    [EmailAddress]
    [Display(Name = "Email")]
    public string Email { get; set; }

    [Required]
    [StringLength(100, ErrorMessage =
        "The {0} must be at least {2} characters long.", MinimumLength = 6)]
    [DataType(DataType.Password)]
    [Display(Name = "Password")]
    public string Password { get; set; }

    [DataType(DataType.Password)]
    [Display(Name = "Confirm password")]
    [Compare("Password", ErrorMessage =
        "The password and confirmation password do not match.")]
    public string ConfirmPassword { get; set; }
}
```

User registration must be possible for non-authenticated users. That's why the `AllowAnonymous` attribute is applied to the `Register` methods of the `AccountController`. This overrules the `Authorize` attribute for these methods. The HTTP POST variant of the `Register` method receives the `RegisterViewModel` object and writes an `ApplicationUser` to the database by calling the method `_userManager.CreateAsync`. After the user is created successfully, an email is sent to the user using the email provider, and sign-in is done via `_signInManager.SignInAsync` (code file `MenuPlanner/Controllers/AccountController.cs`):

```
[HttpGet]
[AllowAnonymous]
public IActionResult Register(string returnUrl = null)
{
    ViewData["ReturnUrl"] = returnUrl;
    return View();
}

[HttpPost]
[AllowAnonymous]
[ValidateAntiForgeryToken]
public async Task<IActionResult> Register(RegisterViewModel model,
    string returnUrl = null)
{
    ViewData["ReturnUrl"] = returnUrl;
    if (ModelState.IsValid)
    {
        var user = new ApplicationUser
        {
            UserName = model.Email,
            Email = model.Email
        };
```

```
        var result = await _userManager.CreateAsync(user, model.Password);
        if (result.Succeeded)
        {
          _logger.LogInformation("User created a new account with password.");

          var code = await _userManager.GenerateEmailConfirmationTokenAsync(user);
          var callbackUrl = Url.EmailConfirmationLink(user.Id, code,
            Request.Scheme);
          await _emailSender.SendEmailConfirmationAsync(model.Email, callbackUrl);

          await _signInManager.SignInAsync(user, isPersistent: false);
          _logger.LogInformation("User created a new account with password.");
          return RedirectToLocal(returnUrl);
        }
        AddErrors(result);
      }
      // If we got this far, something failed, redisplay form
      return View(model);
    }
```

Now the view (code file `MenuPlanner/Views/Account/Register.cshtml`) just needs information from the user. Figure 31-18 shows the dialog that asks the user for information.

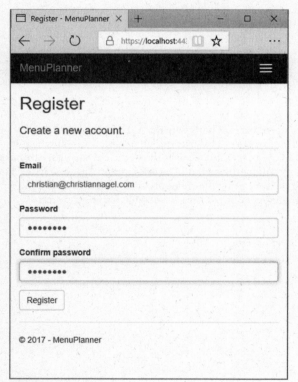

FIGURE 31-18

Setting Up User Login

When the user registers, a login occurs directly after the successful registration is completed. The `LoginViewModel` model defines `UserName`, `Password`, and `RememberMe` properties—all the information the user is asked with the login. This model has some annotations used with HTML Helpers (code file `MenuPlanner/Models/AccountViewModels.cs`):

```
public class LoginViewModel
{
  [Required]
  [EmailAddress]
  public string Email { get; set; }

  [Required]
  [DataType(DataType.Password)]
  public string Password { get; set; }

  [Display(Name = "Remember me?")]
  public bool RememberMe { get; set; }
}
```

To log in a user that is already registered, you need to call the `Login` method of the `AccountController`. After the user enters login information, the sign-in manager is used to validate login information with `PasswordSignInAsync`. If login is successful, the user is redirected to the original requested page. If login fails, the same view is returned to give the user one more option to enter the username and password correctly (code file `MenuPlanner/Controllers/AccountController.cs`):

```
[HttpGet]
[AllowAnonymous]
public IActionResult Login(string returnUrl = null)
{
  Await HttpContext.SignOutAsync(IdentityConstants.ExternalScheme);

  ViewData["ReturnUrl"] = returnUrl;
  return View();
}


[HttpPost]
[AllowAnonymous]
[ValidateAntiForgeryToken]
public async Task<IActionResult> Login(LoginViewModel model,
  string returnUrl = null)
{
  ViewData["ReturnUrl"] = returnUrl;
  if (ModelState.IsValid)
  {
    var result = await _signInManager.PasswordSignInAsync(
      model.Email, model.Password, model.RememberMe, lockoutOnFailure: false);
    if (result.Succeeded)
    {
      _logger.LogInformation("User logged in.");
      return RedirectToLocal(returnUrl);
    }
    if (result.RequiresTwoFactor)
    {
      return RedirectToAction(nameof(LoginWith2fa),
        new { returnUrl, model.RememberMe });
    }
```

```
        if (result.IsLockedOut)
        {
          _logger.LogWarning("User account locked out.");
          return RedirectToAction(nameof(Lockout));
        }
        else
        {
          ModelState.AddModelError(string.Empty, "Invalid login attempt.");
          return View(model);
        }
      }
    }
    return View(model);
  }
```

Authenticating Users

With the authentication infrastructure in place, it's easy to require user authentication by annotating the controller or action methods with the Authorize attribute. Applying this attribute to the class requires the role for every action method of the class. If there are different authorization requirements on different action methods, the Authorize attribute can also be applied to the action methods. With this attribute, it is verified if the caller is already authorized (by checking the authorization cookie). If the caller is not yet authorized, a 401 HTTP status code is returned with a redirect to the login action.

Applying the attribute Authorize without setting parameters requires users to be authenticated. To have more control you can define that only specific user roles are allowed to access the action methods by assigning roles to the Roles property as shown in the following code snippet:

```
[Authorize(Roles="Menu Admins")]
public class MenuAdminController : Controller
{
```

You can also access user information by using the User property of the Controller base class, which allows a more dynamic approval or denial of the user. For example, depending on parameter values passed, different roles are required.

> **NOTE** *You can read more information about user authentication and other information about security in Chapter 24.*

Authenticating Users with Azure Active Directory

Nowadays it's best not to keep usernames and passwords in your own database. Users don't like to remember another password. I'm just guessing you are using some password manager tool because it's just impossible otherwise to deal with many passwords. This is not the only issue. To fulfill security requirements, with the ASP.NET Core identity system you've worked with in the previous sections in this chapter, passwords are hashed so they can't be read from the database. This is only a one-way process from the password to the hash, but not the other way around. You still need to make sure to keep the user information safe.

> **NOTE** *It's a good practice to separate the user management from your application into separate services.*

For usernames and passwords, you can use accounts that users already have, such as Microsoft, Google, Facebook, and Twitter accounts, and use the tokens from these providers. This way users don't need to deal with additional passwords, and all the password management is not part of your application. For making this happen, you need to create applications with the providers you select and configure ASP.NET Core identity accordingly. Using one or more of these providers, you just need to add additional information about the user, and the identifier of the user from the provider in your database.

For managing this additional user information, the best practice is to keep this separate from the application. You can write a service application for this functionality and use it from several of your web applications. You can use a service out of the box, such as the Identity Server (`https://identityserver.io/`), and host it in your own web application, or you can use a PaaS service such as Azure Active Directory. This section demonstrates the use of the Azure AD B2C (Active Directory Business to Consumer) with ASP.NET Core MVC. Contrary to Azure AD, Azure AD B2C allows registration of users, and allows adding other providers such as Microsoft, Google, Facebook, Twitter, and others.

Creating the Azure Active Directory B2C Tenant

For using Azure Active Directory B2C from ASP.NET Core, first you need to create the Azure Active Directory. This can be done from the portal site `https://portal.azure.com`. I've created one with the domain name `procsharp.onmicrosoft.com`. You need to create a different domain name, as this one is not available anymore.

For a web application to access this Azure AD B2C, you need to create an application as shown in Figure 31-19. Besides entering the name of the application, you need to select the Web App option and configure the Reply URI. You'll get the Reply URI when creating the ASP.NET Core Web Application—for example, `https://localhost:44359/signin-oidc`. The port will differ on your system. Just for testing purposes, `localhost` can be used. For production you need to change this to the URL of the production server.

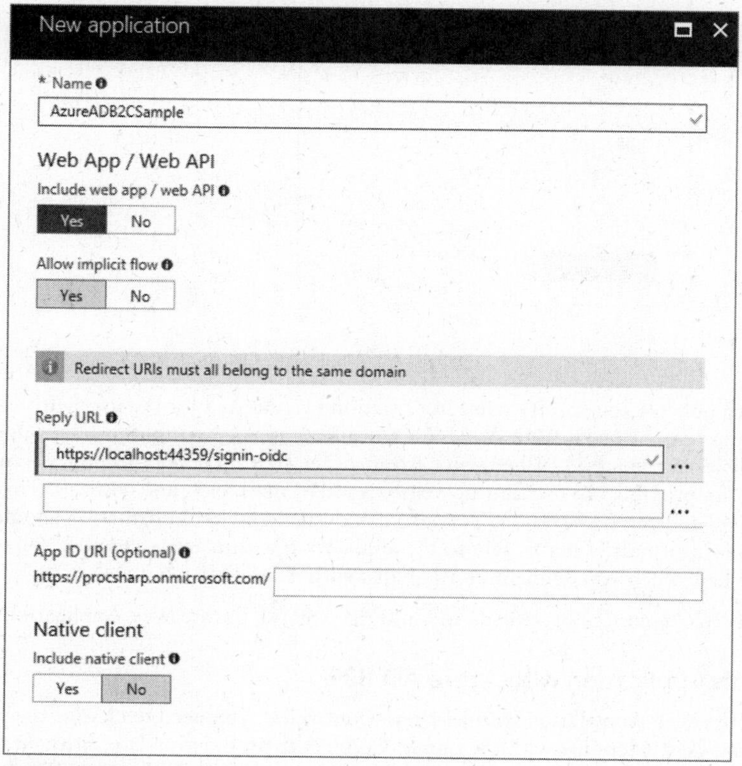

FIGURE 31-19

To enable users to enter a new username and password from another provider, you can add identity providers as shown in Figure 31-20. With each identity provider you select, you need to configure a client ID and client secret. For using a Microsoft Account, you can register an application to retrieve the ID and secret at https://apps.dev.microsoft.com/.

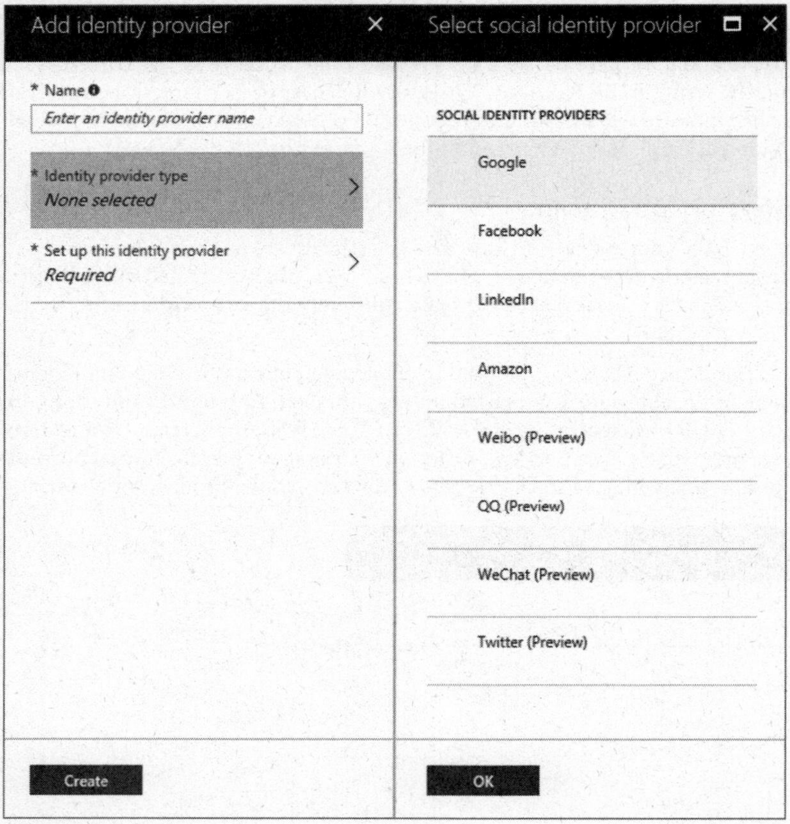

FIGURE 31-20

Next you need some policies. With policies you specify what information is requested for the user with the registration, and which providers can be used. With ASP.NET Core Web apps, at a minimum sign-up or sign-in and password reset policies are required. When you customize the sign-up or sign-in policy (see Figure 31-21), you define the identity providers to use sign-up attributes like email, city, and country. This information needs to be given by the user on registration. You also can designate what information should be put into the application claims—information that is sent to the application within access tokens. You can define custom fields that show up here when you define user attributes with Azure AD B2C.

After you configure the Azure AD B2C tenant, you're ready to build the ASP.NET Core Web Application.

Creating the ASP.NET Core Web Application with Azure AD B2C

When you create the ASP.NET Core Web Application (Model-View-Controller), you need to change the authentication setting to Individual User Accounts with the option Connect to an Existing User Store in the Cloud (see Figure 31-22). In this dialog you also need to specify the domain name, the Application ID, the Callback Path, and the policies you specified with the Azure AD B2C configuration. All these settings are saved to the configuration file appsettings.json, so you can change it there later.

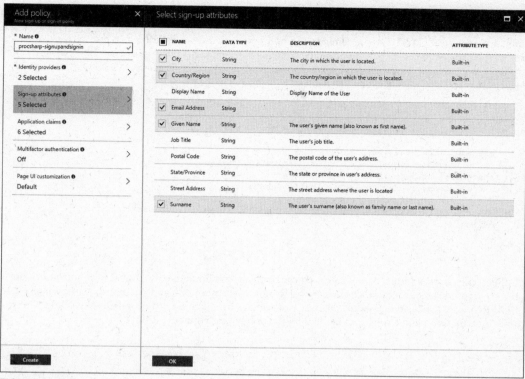

FIGURE 31-21

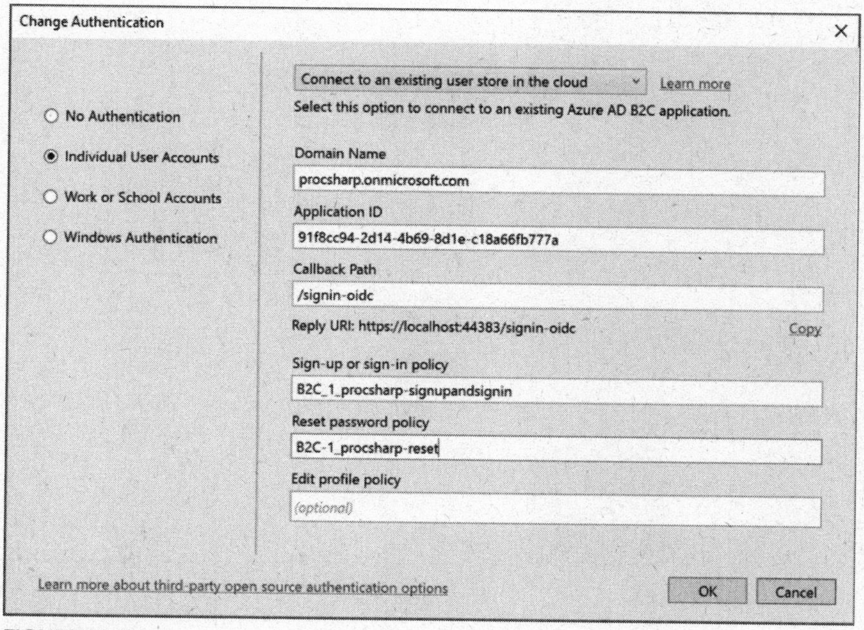

Change Authentication   ×

○ No Authentication

◉ Individual User Accounts

○ Work or School Accounts

○ Windows Authentication

Connect to an existing user store in the cloud ▾   Learn more
Select this option to connect to an existing Azure AD B2C application.

Domain Name

procsharp.onmicrosoft.com

Application ID

91f8cc94-2d14-4b69-8d1e-c18a66fb777a

Callback Path

/signin-oidc

Reply URI: https://localhost:44383/signin-oidc   Copy

Sign-up or sign-in policy

B2C_1_procsharp-signupandsignin

Reset password policy

B2C_1_procsharp-reset

Edit profile policy

(optional)

Learn more about third-party open source authentication options   OK   Cancel

FIGURE 31-22

The Startup code that gets generated registers needed services for the authentication in the Startup class. The AddAuthentication extension method is invoked to configure cookies and the OpenID standard. For Azure AD B2C, the extension method AddAzureAdB2C is defined in the Extensions folder of the project in the class AzureAdB2CAuthenticationBuilderExtensions. This method takes the AzureAdB2C section from the settings to configure authentication (code file AzureADB2CSample/Startup.cs):

```
public void ConfigureServices(IServiceCollection services)
{
  services.AddAuthentication(sharedOptions =>
  {
    sharedOptions.DefaultScheme =
      CookieAuthenticationDefaults.AuthenticationScheme;
    sharedOptions.DefaultChallengeScheme =
      OpenIdConnectDefaults.AuthenticationScheme;
  })
  .AddAzureAdB2C(options => Configuration.Bind("AzureAdB2C", options))
  .AddCookie();

  services.AddMvc();
}
```

With this configuration in place, you can start the application and then click the Sign-In button to sign-in via the configured social account identity providers or with a username and password, as shown in Figure 31-23. If the user is not yet registered, the user can register by clicking on the Sign Up Now link. This dialog requests information from the user as defined by the policy (see Figure 31-24).

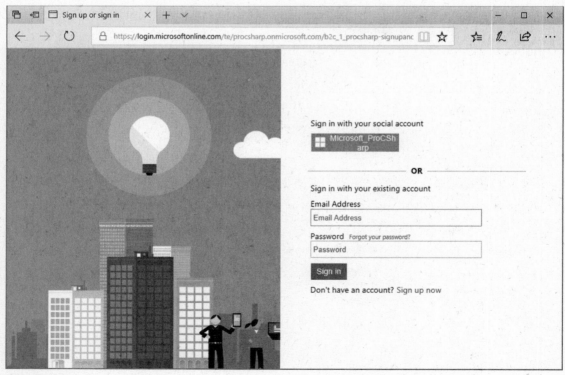

FIGURE 31-23

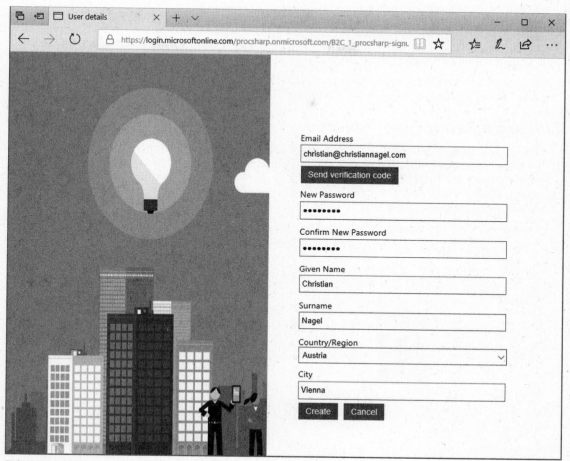

FIGURE 31-24

With Azure AD B2C, you mainly have to do configuration and you write less code to integrate your application. This allows for a better focus on your business code.

RAZOR PAGES

ASP.NET Core 2.0 offers a new technology to create web applications: Razor Pages. This technology is easier to understand than the MVC pattern, and sometimes your controller has nothing else to do than to forward the request to a view. With previous samples, you've seen several action methods that do nothing more than invoke the View method. If you're creating a Single Page Application (SPA) with a scripting library such as Angular, Razor Pages can be all that's needed to start the Angular page.

With Razor Pages you don't need model-view-controller separation. You still write CSHTML pages as you do with MVC with the views. With Razor Pages, you can add C# code directly within the CSHTML page—more than just the Razor syntax you've already done with views. You can also use code-behind files that are directly related to the CSHTML file, and you can do some separation with the C# code. Code-behind files are like what you already know from other technologies, such as WPF, UWP, and ASP.NET Web Forms.

Razor Pages are based on ASP.NET Core MVC. The NuGet package `Microsoft.AspNetCore.All` includes support for Razor Pages. You can use the same features shown for the views, such as Razor syntax, HTML helpers, Tag Helpers, dependency injection in views, and more. You just don't need the controllers. The CSHTML files have an `@Page` directive, and you can add C# code to the code-behind files of the pages.

Because Razor Pages are using the same features as the views from ASP.NET Core MVC, this section just looks into the differences between ASP.NET Core MVC and Razor Pages.

Creating a Razor Pages Project

When you're using Visual Studio, you can create a Razor Page application by using the project template Web Application with ASP.NET Core 2.0. The sample project `RazorPagesSample` is using this project template (see Figure 31-25). You can also start with the Web Application (Model-View-Controller) template and add Razor Pages to this project. You just need to add the Razor Page files to the Pages folder. It's easy to mix Razor Pages with MVC.

If you're using the command line, a Razor Pages project is created with

```
>dotnet new razor
```

FIGURE 31-25

The `ConfigureServices` method of the `Startup` class looks like what you've seen with the ASP.NET Core MVC projects and contains an invocation to `AddMvc` to register all the services needed by ASP.NET Core MVC (code file `RazorPagesSample/Startup.cs`):

```
public void ConfigureServices(IServiceCollection services)
{
    services.AddMvc();
}
```

The invocation of `AddMvc` includes services needed for Razor Pages. Razor can also be configured by using the `AddRazorOptions` and `AddRazorPageOptions` methods. By default, Razor Pages are searched for in the `Pages` folder and subfolders. For example, if you're accessing the URL `/Hello`, the page `Pages/Hello.cshtml` is searched. With the URL `/Admin/User`, the page `Pages/Admin/User.cshtml` is expected. If these pages are not found, search continues in the `Views/Shared` folder. When you set the property `PageViewLocationFormats` with the method `AddRazorOptions`, this behavior can be changed. Just by changing the folder `Pages` to a different folder, the `AddRazorPagesOptions` method can be used to set the `RootDirectory` property of the `RazorPagesOptions`.

Implementing Data Access

The sample application will read and write from a database using EF Core. This is similar to what you've already seen before, thus it doesn't need specific explanations. The `Book` and `BooksContext` classes are created in the `Model` directory to demonstrate you can use the same service-based code from ASP.NET Core MVC and Razor Pages.

The `Book` class from the following code snippet defines the model for the data to read and write (code file `RazorPagesSample/Models/Book.cs`):

```
public class Book
{
  public int BookId { get; set; }

  [StringLength(50)]
  public string Title { get; set; }

  [StringLength(20)]
  public string Publisher { get; set; }
}
```

The `BooksContext` class maps the `Book` type to the `Books` table and is implemented to be used with dependency injection (code file `RazorPagesSample/Models/BooksContext.cs`):

```
public class BooksContext : DbContext
{
  public BooksContext(DbContextOptions<BooksContext> options)
    : base(options) { }

  public DbSet<Book> Books { get; set; }
}
```

The `BooksContext` class is now registered with the dependency injection container using the `AddDbContext` extension method (code file `RazorPagesSample/Startup.cs`):

```
public void ConfigureServices(IServiceCollection services)
{
  services.AddMvc();
  services.AddDbContext<BooksContext>(options =>
    options.UseSqlServer(
      Configuration.GetConnectionString("BooksConnection")));
}
```

What's left for the database management is to define the connection string (configuration file `RazorPagesSample/appsettings.json`):

```
{
  "ConnectionStrings": {
    "BooksConnection":   "server=(localdb)\\mssqllocaldb;database=RazorBooks;trusted_connection=true"
  }
}
```

So far, the code for the Razor Pages was not different from using the controllers from ASP.NET Core MVC. The most interesting part for Razor Pages follow in the next sections.

Using Inline Code

After you create the project and add code to access the database, Razor Pages can be added using the Visual Studio Item Template Razor Pages. With this template, you can select between a simple Razor Page, a Razor Page using Entity Framework, and multiple Razor Pages using Entity Framework (see Figure 31-26). While the dialog lists Entity Framework, EF Core can be used to create these pages. Let's begin with a simple Razor Page.

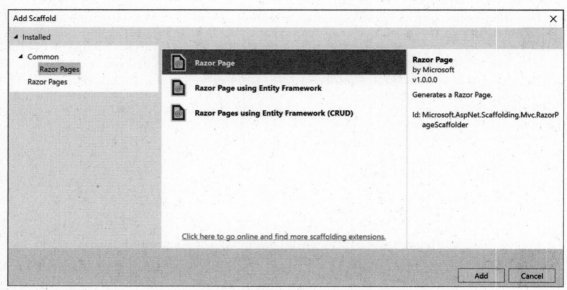

FIGURE 31-26

After selecting Razor Pages, you can select the options Generate a PageModel class, Create as a Partial View, and Use a Layout Page (see Figure 31-27). While you already know *partial views* and *layout pages* from this chapter with ASP.NET Core MVC, the selection for the PageModel is new with Razor Pages. When you selecting the option Generate a PageModel class, a code-behind file gets generated; without PageModel, all the C# code needs to go within the CSHTML file. With the sample code, the first created page will be inline, without code-behind.

When you request the page from the browser, all the books from the database should be shown in a table. On top of the CSHTML file you can see a `page` directive. This directive marks the file as Razor Page. Because the `BooksContext` class is registered in the dependency injection container, you can inject it directly into the page by using `@inject`. This uses the same functionality as you've seen in this chapter in the section "Using Dependency Injection in Views" (code file `RazorPagesSample/Pages/Inline.cshtml`):

```
@page
@using RazorPagesSample.Models
@inject BooksContext _context
@{
    ViewData["Title"] = "Inline";
}
```

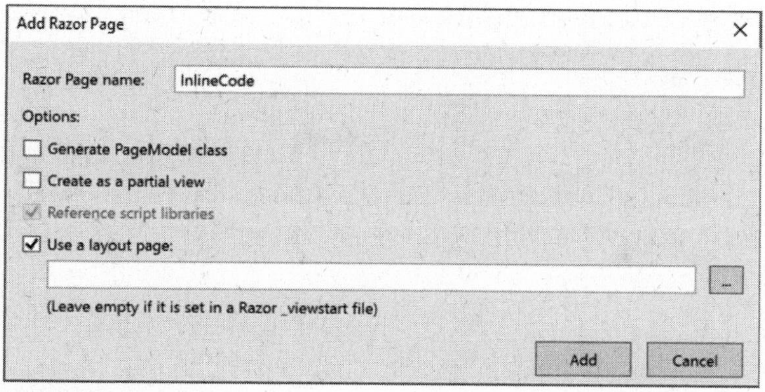

FIGURE 31-27

Writing inline C# code in the Razor Page, you can use the @functions directive. The OnGet method is invoked on every GET request of the page. With the implementation, the database is created if it doesn't exist yet, and the SeedBooks method is invoked to write two Book objects to the database. After a successfully created database, the books are retrieved and written to the Books property (code file RazorPagesSample/Pages/Inline.cshtml):

```
@functions
{
  public void OnGet()
  {
    bool created = _context.Database.EnsureCreated();
    if (created) SeedBooks();

    Books = _context.Books.ToList();
  }

  public IEnumerable<Book> Books { get; set; }

  private void SeedBooks()
  {
    _context.Books.Add(new Book
    { Title = "Professional C# 6 and .NET Core 1", Publisher = "Wrox Press" });
    _context.Books.Add(new Book
    { Title = "Professional C# 7 and .NET Core 2", Publisher = "Wrox Press" });
    _context.SaveChanges();
  }
  //...
}
```

> **NOTE** *With Razor Pages,* On ... *methods are invoked depending on the HTTP method of the request. A GET request invokes the* OnGet *method, a POST request the* OnPost *method, the PUT request the* OnPut *method, and so on. You can also add postfixes to the method names and implement asynchronous variants returning a* Task.

To display the books, in the same page after the `@function` declaration, HTML code with added Razor code follows. Using `@foreach`, the books from the `Books` property are iterated and displayed (code file `RazorPagesSample/Pages/Inline.cshtml`):

```
@* ... *@

<h2>Inline Razor Page Sample</h2>

@if (Books != null)
{
  <table>
    <thead>
      <tr>
        <th>Title</th>
        <th>Publisher</th>
      </tr>
    </thead>
    <tbody>
      @foreach (var book in Books)
      {
        <tr>
          <td>@book.Title</td>
          <td>@book.Publisher</td>
        </tr>
      }
    </tbody>
  </table>
}
```

Let's extend this functionality by creating a form and sending a POST request. In the same page, a form element is defined to allow the user to enter book title and publisher. When you click the Submit button, a POST request is made to the same page (code file `RazorPagesSample/Inline.cshtml`):

```
<div>@Message</div>

<form method="post">
  Enter a new book
  <br />
  <input type="text" name="Title" id="Title" />
  <br />
  <input type="text" name="Publisher" id="Publisher" />
  <br />
  <button type="submit">Submit</button>
</form>
```

Within the `@functions` declaration, the `OnPost` method is defined to act on POST requests. Here, the book referenced from the `Book` property is written to the database, and the books are once more retrieved. The `Book` property has the `BindProperty` annotation. This attribute takes the body from the POST request (which is the values of the input fields in the form) to create a `Book` object; thus, this is a new way for a model binding (code file `RazorPagesSample/Pages/Inline.cshtml`):

```
@functions
{
  //...

  public void OnPost()
  {
    _context.Books.Add(Book);
    _context.SaveChanges();
    Message = "Book saved";
    Books = _context.Books.ToList();
  }
```

```
[BindProperty()]
public Book Book { get; set; }

public string Message { get; set; } = string.Empty;
}
```

Marking properties with the `BindProperty` attribute by default doesn't make the property available with GET requests, which is useful most times, as the binding should just happen on a POST request from a form. However, you can also set the property `SupportGet` to `true`, which binds the property also with GET requests.

Running the application and entering the `/Inline` link in the browser opens the Razor Page, creates a database, lists the books from the database, and allows the user to enter a new book, as shown in Figure 31-28—all defined within a single code file. Of course, it's also possible to define the `Book` and `BooksContext` in the same CSHTML file, so you really can have all in a single file.

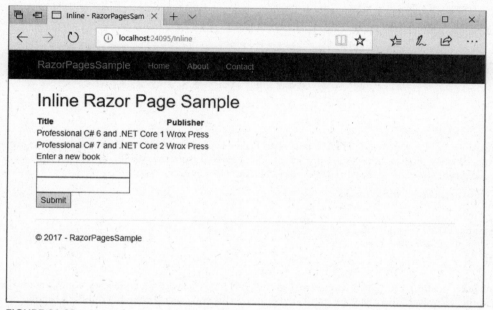

FIGURE 31-28

Having all the code to read and write books in a single file can be useful as long as there are not too many code lines. Everything in a single file can be good for beginners in .NET Core, but it can become confusing with large files because it can become hard to find the lines you want to update.

Using Inline Code with a Page Model

The first change after creating the Razor Page with inline code is to change the inline C# code to a model class. Now, within the `@functions` declaration the class `InlinePageModel` that derives from the class `PageModel` is defined. The base class `PageModel` is defined in the namespace `Microsoft.AspNetCore.Mvc.RazorPages`. This class is assigned to the page with the `@model` directive—the same directive you used when passing information from a controller to the view. In this scenario, `@inject` can be removed from the page to inject the `BooksContext` with the constructor of the `InlinePageModel` class. Except for the constructor, the code you've seen within `@function` in the earlier example is now defined in the class (code file `RazorPagesSample/Pages/InlineWithClasses.cshtml`):

```
@page
@model InlinePageModel
@using Microsoft.AspNetCore.Mvc.RazorPages
```

```
@using RazorPagesSample.Models

@{
  ViewData["Title"] = "Inline";
}

@functions
{
  public class InlinePageModel : PageModel
  {
    private readonly BooksContext _context;
    public InlinePageModel(BooksContext context) => _context = context;

    public void OnGet()
    {
      bool created = _context.Database.EnsureCreated();
      if (created) SeedBooks();

      Books = _context.Books.ToList();
    }

    public IEnumerable<Book> Books { get; set; }

    //...
  }
}
@* ... *@
```

Small changes need to be done to the HTML part with Razor code. Because the Books and Message properties cannot be directly accessed, the Model property (that is created from the @model directive) needs to be used (code file RazorPagesSample/Pages/InlineWithClasses.cshtml):

```
@foreach (var book in Model.Books)
{
  <tr>
    <td>@book.Title</td>
    <td>@book.Publisher</td>
  </tr>
}
```

With this change, defining the InlinePageModel in the CSHTML file, the C# code grew compared to the previous sample. However, now there's a small step to move this code to the code-behind file as shown in the next section.

Using Code-Behind

When you create a Razor Page you can select the option Generate PageModel class. This creates the code-behind file CodeBehind.cshtml.cs together with CodeBehind.cshtml. The CSHTML file references the type in the code-behind file using the @model directive. There's no @functions declaration in this file (code file RazorPagesSample/Pages/CodeBehind.cshtml):

```
@page
@model RazorPagesSample.Pages.CodeBehindModel
@{
  ViewData["Title"] = "Code Behind";
}
<h2>Code Behind Razor Page Sample</h2>
@* ... *@
```

The code-behind file contains the same code as the inline class did; code changes apart from the class name are not needed (code file RazorPagesSample/Pages/CodeBehind.cshtml.cs):

```
public class CodeBehindModel : PageModel
{
  private readonly BooksContext _context;
  public CodeBehindModel(BooksContext context) => _context = context;

  public void OnGet()
  {
    bool created = _context.Database.EnsureCreated();
    if (created) SeedBooks();

    Books = _context.Books.ToList();
  }
  //...
}
```

With this splitting into two files, C# code and HTML code are separated. Instead of having a controller that invokes multiple views, now you have the functionality for the page nearby.

Page Parameters

With the simple routing functionality of Razor Pages, you need a way to pass parameters. This is what the @page directive offers: You can add parameters as the optional id parameter of type int in the following code snippet (code file RazorPagesSample/Pages/PageWithParameter.cshtml):

```
@page "{id:int?}"
```

To retrieve the parameter, you can modify the OnGet method to receive this number value (code file RazorPagesSample/Pages/PageWithParameter.cshtml.cs):

```
public class PageWithParameterModel : PageModel
{
  public void OnGet(int id = 0)
  {
    Id = id;
  }
  public int Id { get; set; }
}
```

With the route defined in the page directive, the page can be accessed either by passing the value directly in the route:

```
http://localhost:24095/PageWithParameter/42
```

or by passing it as a URL parameter:

```
http://localhost:24095/PageWithParameter/?id=42
```

Instead of changing the OnGet method to receive the parameter, you can also bind it directly to a property applying the BindProperty attribute. Remember to set the SupportsGet property of this attribute (code file RazorPagesSample/Pages/PageWithParameterAndBinding.cshtml.cs):

```
public class PageWithParameterAndBindingModel : PageModel
{
  public void OnGet()
  {
  }

  [BindProperty(SupportsGet = true)]
  public int Id { get; set; }
}
```

After learning the foundation of Razor Pages, you can easily use the Razor Pages item template in Visual Studio to create pages to list, create, edit, or delete objects including with code-behind using the `BooksContext` class created earlier. Check the downloadable source code within the folder `RazorPagesSample/Pages/Books` for generated source files that include HTML Helpers, Tag Helpers, and access code to EF Core.

SUMMARY

In this chapter, you explored the latest web technology to make use of the ASP.NET Core MVC framework. You saw how this provides a robust structure for you to work with, which is ideal for large-scale applications that require proper unit testing. You saw how easy it is to provide advanced capabilities with minimum effort, and how the logical structure and separation of functionality that this framework provides makes code easy to understand and easy to maintain.

You also learned about Razor Pages, a new technology with ASP.NET Core 2.0, and its differences with ASP.NET Core MVC. Razor Pages not only offers an easy way to begin with ASP.NET Core; it also might be exactly what's needed to create web pages with mainly HTML and JavaScript.

Here it's important that Razor Pages can easily mix with ASP.NET Core MVC because it's is used for developing web APIs—APIs used to communicate between clients and servers—whereas the clients can be web pages or WPF, UWP, and Xamarin clients. Creating Web APIs is the topic of the next chapter.

32

Web API

WROX.COM CODE DOWNLOADS FOR THIS CHAPTER

The Wrox.com code downloads for this chapter are found at www.wrox.com on the Download Code tab. The source code is also available at https://github.com/ProfessionalCSharp/ProfessionalCSharp7 in the directory API.

The code for this chapter is divided into the following major examples:

➤ Book Service Sample

➤ Book Service Async Sample

➤ Book Service Client App

➤ Book Service OData

➤ Book Service Azure Functions

OVERVIEW

When Windows Communication Foundation (WCF) was announced with .NET 3.0, it was *the* technology for communication and replaced several other technologies in the .NET stack (a few mentioned here are .NET Remoting and ASP.NET Web Services). The goal was to have one communication technology that is very flexible and fulfills all needs. However, WCF was initially based on SOAP (Simple Object Access Protocol). Nowadays we have many scenarios where the powerful SOAP enhancements are not needed. For simpler scenarios such as HTTP requests returning JSON, WCF is too complex. That's why another technology was introduced in 2012: ASP.NET Web API. With the release of ASP.NET Core, the third major version of a Web API using an ASP.NET technology was released.

ASP.NET MVC and ASP.NET Web API previously had different types and configurations (the previous versions were ASP.NET MVC 5 and ASP.NET Web API 2), but the Web API from ASP.NET Core is the same as the one from ASP.NET Core MVC.

The Web API offers a simple communication technology based on Representational State Transfer (REST). REST is an architecture style based on some constraints. Let's compare a service that is based on the REST architectural style with a service that makes use of SOAP to see these constraints.

Both REST services and services making use of the SOAP protocol make use of a client-server technology. SOAP services can be stateful or stateless; REST services are always stateless. SOAP defines its own message format with a header and body to select a method of the service. With REST, HTTP verbs such as GET, POST, PUT, and DELETE are used. GET is used to retrieve resources, POST to add new resources, PUT to update resources, and DELETE to delete resources.

This chapter takes you through a journey that covers various important aspects of the Web API using ASP. NET Core MVC—creating a service, using different routing methods, creating a client, using OData, securing the service, and using custom hosts. The chapter shows you how you can take the same services created for hosting with ASP.NET Core and use them from Microsoft Azure Functions, which is another option to create a Web API with C# and .NET.

CREATING SERVICES

Let's start with creating a service. Using .NET Core, you need to start with an ASP.NET Core Web Application and select the Web API in the following dialog (see Figure 32-1). This template adds folders and references needed with the Web API. You can also use the template Web Application (Model-View-Controller) in case you need both web pages and services. With the sample code, this project is named `BooksServiceSampleHost` in the solution `BooksServiceSample`.

> **NOTE** *ASP.NET Core MVC is discussed in Chapter 31, "ASP.NET Core MVC," and the core technology that is the foundation of ASP.NET Core MVC is covered in Chapter 30, "ASP.NET Core."*

The directory structure that is created with this template contains folders that are needed for creating the services. The `Controllers` directory contains the Web API controllers. You've seen such controllers already in Chapter 31, and indeed, Web API and ASP.NET Core MVC make use of the same infrastructure. This was not the case with the .NET Framework version of ASP.NET. With the default template, the `ValuesController` is created with a simple sample implementation. In larger applications, it's a good idea for separation into multiple libraries. If you create a library containing services and models, it's an easy task to use the same types from different technologies—for example, from Web API projects, as well as from Azure Functions. The implementation of the Web API (the controller) can also be in a library separate from the hosting application. From the web application you can use controllers implemented in the application's own library. The libraries both for the services (`BookServices`) and the Web API (`APIBookServices`) are implemented as .NET Standard 2.0 libraries. With the library `APIBookServices`, the NuGet packages `Microsoft.AspNetCore.Mvc.Core` and `Microsoft.AspNetCore.Mvc.ViewFeatures` need to be added to implement the controller. Using the metadata package `Microsoft.AspNetCore.All`, which you've used in previous chapters, is not possible with a .NET Standard 2.0 library. This would need a .NET Core 2.0 library.

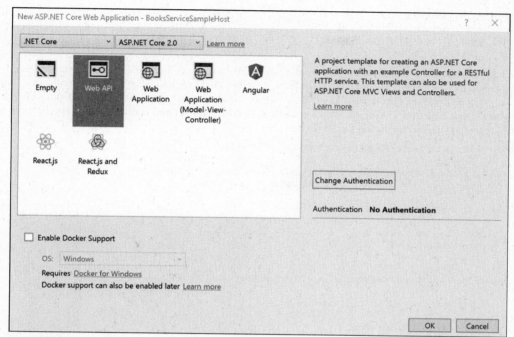

FIGURE 32-1

Now, let's start with the model. In the project BooksService, the Models directory is for the data model. You can add your entity types to this directory, as well as repositories that return model types.

The service that is created returns a list of book chapters and allows adding and deleting chapters dynamically.

Defining a Model

First you need a type that represents the data to return and change. The class defined in the Models directory has the name BookChapter and includes simple properties to represent a chapter (code file Sync/BookServices/Models/BookChapter.cs):

```
public class BookChapter
{
  public Guid Id { get; set; }
  public int Number { get; set; }
  public string Title { get; set; }
  public int Pages { get; set; }
}
```

Creating a Service

Next, you create a service. The methods offered by the service are defined with the interface IBookChaptersService—methods to retrieve, add, and update book chapters (code file Sync/BookServices/Services/IBookChaptersService.cs):

```
public interface IBookChaptersService
{
  void Add(BookChapter bookChapter);
  void AddRange(IEnumerable<BookChapter> chapters);
  IEnumerable<BookChapter> GetAll();
```

```
    BookChapter Find(Guid id);
    BookChapter Remove(Guid id);
    void Update(BookChapter bookChapter);
}
```

The implementation of the service is defined by the class `BookChaptersService`. The book chapters are kept in a collection class. Because multiple tasks from different client requests can access the collection concurrently, the type `ConcurrentDictionary` is used for the book chapters. This class is thread safe. The `Add`, `Remove`, and `Update` methods make use of the collection to add, remove, and update book chapters (code file `BookServices/Services/BookChaptersService.cs`):

```csharp
public class BookChaptersService : IBookChaptersService
{
  private readonly ConcurrentDictionary<Guid, BookChapter> _chapters =
    new ConcurrentDictionary<Guid, BookChapter>();

  public void Add(BookChapter chapter)
  {
    chapter.Id = Guid.NewGuid();
    _chapters[chapter.Id] = chapter;
  }

  public void AddRange(IEnumerable<BookChapter> chapters)
  {
    foreach (var chapter in chapters)
    {
      chapter.Id = Guid.NewGuid();
      _chapters[chapter.Id] = chapter;
    }
  }

  public BookChapter Find(Guid id)
  {
    _chapters.TryGetValue(id, out BookChapter chapter);
    return chapter;
  }

  public IEnumerable<BookChapter> GetAll() => _chapters.Values;

  public BookChapter Remove(Guid id)
  {
    BookChapter removed;
    _chapters.TryRemove(id, out removed);
    return removed;
  }

  public void Update(BookChapter chapter) =>
    _chapters[chapter.Id] = chapter;
}
```

> **NOTE** *With the sample code, the* `Remove` *method makes sure that the* `BookChapter` *passed with the* `id` *parameter is not in the dictionary. If the dictionary already does not contain the book chapter, that's okay.*
>
> *An alternative implementation of the* `Remove` *method can throw an exception if the book chapter passed cannot be found. The controller can change this error to return an HTTP not found status code (404).*
>
> *The Microsoft REST API guidelines (*`https://github.com/Microsoft/api-guidelines/blob/master/Guidelines.md`*) specifies the DELETE request to be idempotent,* thus it should return the same result with multiple requests.

> **NOTE** *Concurrent collections are discussed in Chapter 11, "Special Collections."*

So that some sample chapters are available when you first access of the service, the class `SampleChapters` fills the book chapter service with chapter information (code file `Sync/BookServices/Services/SampleChapter.cs`):

```
public class SampleChapters
{
  private readonly IBookChaptersService _bookChaptersService;
  public SampleChapters(IBookChaptersService bookChapterService)
  {
    _bookChaptersService = bookChapterService;
  }

  private string[] sampleTitles = new[]
  {
    ".NET Application Architectures",
    "Core C#",
    "Objects and Types",
    "Object-Oriented Programming with C#",
    "Generics",
    "Operators and Casts",
    "Arrays",
    "Delegates, Lambdas, and Events",
    "Windows Communication Foundation"
  };

  private int[] chapterNumbers = { 1, 2, 3, 4, 5, 6, 7, 8, 44 };

  private int[] numberPages = { 35, 42, 33, 20, 24, 38, 20, 32, 44 };

  public void CreateSampleChapters()
  {
    var chapters = new List<BookChapter>();
    for (int i = 0; i < 8; i++)
    {
      chapters.Add(new BookChapter
      {
        Number = chapterNumbers[i],
        Title = sampleTitles[i],
        Pages = numberPages[i]
      });
    }
    _bookChaptersService.AddRange(chapters);
  }
}
```

In the hosting application, the libraries are referenced. To have the services available, they need to be registered with the dependency injection (DI) container. This is done in the Startup class.

With the startup, the `BookChaptersService` service and the `SampleChapters` service are registered with the `AddSingleton` method of the DI container to create just one instance for all clients requesting the service. Because the `BookChaptersService` is registered as a singleton, it can be accessed from multiple threads concurrently; that's why the `ConcurrentDictionary` is needed in its implementation (code file `Sync/BookServiceSampleHost/Startup.cs`):

```
public void ConfigureServices(IServiceCollection services)
{
  services.AddMvc();
  //...
```

```
  services.AddSingleton<IBookChaptersService, BookChaptersService>();
  services.AddSingleton<SampleChapters>();
}
```

The invocation to create the sample chapters is done in the Configure method. Here, the SampleChapters object is injected, and within the implementation of the method, sample chapters are created invoking CreateSampleChapters (code file Sync/BookServiceSampleHost/Startup.cs):

```
public void Configure(IApplicationBuilder app, IHostingEnvironment env,
  SampleChapters sampleChapters)
{
  if (env.IsDevelopment())
  {
    app.UseDeveloperExceptionPage();
  }

  app.UseMvc();
  sampleChapters.CreateSampleChapters();
}
```

Creating a Controller

The Web API controller uses the book chapter service. The controller can be created from the Solution Explorer context menu Add New Item ⇨ Web API Controller Class. The controller class to manage book chapters is named BookChaptersController. This class derives from the base class Controller. The route to the controller is defined with the Route attribute. The route starts with api followed by the name of the controller—which is the name of the controller class without the Controller postfix. The constructor of the BookChaptersController requires an object implementing the interface IBookChaptersService. This object is injected via DI (code file Sync/APIBookServices/Controllers/BookChaptersController.cs):

```
[Produces("application/json", "application/xml")]
[Route("api/[controller]")]
public class BookChaptersController : Controller
{
  private readonly IBookChaptersService _bookChaptersService;
  public BookChaptersController(IBookChaptersService bookChaptersService)
  {
    _bookChaptersService = bookChaptersService;
  }
```

The Get method that is created from the template is renamed and modified to return the complete collection of type IEnumerable<BookChapter> (code file Sync/APIBookServices/Controllers/BookChaptersController.cs):

```
// GET api/bookchapters
[HttpGet]
public IEnumerable<BookChapter> GetBookChapters() =>
  _bookChaptersService.GetAll();
```

The Get method with a parameter is renamed to GetBookChapterById and filters the dictionary of the repository with the Find method. The parameter of the filter, id, is retrieved from the URL. The repository's Find method returns null if the chapter was not found. In this case, NotFound is returned. NotFound returns a 404 (not found) response. When the object is found, it is returned creating a new ObjectResult: The ObjectResult returns a status code 200 with the book chapter in the body (code file Sync/APIBookServices/Controllers/BookChaptersController.cs):

```
// GET api/bookchapters/guid
[HttpGet("{id}", Name = nameof(GetBookChapterById))]
public IActionResult GetBookChapterById(Guid id)
{
  BookChapter chapter = _bookChaptersService.Find(id);
```

```
      if (chapter == null)
      {
        return NotFound();
      }
      else
      {
        return new ObjectResult(chapter);
      }
    }
```

> **NOTE** *Read Chapter 31 for information on defining routes.*

On adding a new book chapter, the method `PostBookChapter` is added. This method receives a `BookChapter` as part of the HTTP body that is assigned to the method parameter after deserialization. In case the parameter chapter is null, an `BadRequest` (HTTP error 400) is returned. Adding the `BookChapter`, this method returns `CreatedAtRoute`. `CreatedAtRoute` returns the HTTP status 201 (Created) with the object serialized. The returned header information contains a link to the resource—that is, a link to the `GetBookChapterById` with the `id` set to the identifier of the newly created object (code file `Sync/APIBookServices/Controllers/BookChaptersController.cs`):

```
// POST api/bookchapters
[HttpPost]
public IActionResult PostBookChapter([FromBody]BookChapter chapter)
{
  if (chapter == null)
  {
    return BadRequest();
  }
  _bookChaptersService.Add(chapter);
  return CreatedAtRoute(nameof(GetBookChapterById), new { id = chapter.Id },
    chapter);
}
```

Updating items is based on the HTTP PUT request. The `PutBookChapter` method updates an existing item from the collection. In case the object is not yet in the collection, `NotFound` is returned. If the object is found, it is updated, and a success result 204—no content with an empty body—is returned (code file `Sync/APIBookServices/Controllers/BookChaptersController.cs`):

```
// PUT api/bookchapters/guid
[HttpPut("{id}")]
public IActionResult PutBookChapter(Guid id, [FromBody]BookChapter chapter)
{
  if (chapter == null || id != chapter.Id)
  {
    return BadRequest();
  }
  if (_bookChaptersService.Find(id) == null)
  {
    return NotFound();
  }
  _bookChaptersService.Update(chapter);
  return new NoContentResult();
}
```

With the HTTP DELETE request, book chapters are simply removed from the dictionary (code file `Sync/APIBookServices/Controllers/BookChaptersController.cs`):

```
// DELETE api/bookchapters/5
[HttpDelete("{id}")]
public void Delete(Guid id) => _bookChaptersService.Remove(id);
```

With this controller in place, it is already possible to do first tests from the browser. Opening the link (your port number might differ) `http://localhost:1079/api/BookChapters` returns JSON as shown:

```
[{"id":"015b0fb6-1a0f-44ac-ba0d-3d6d743bf4df","number":2,"title":"Objects and Types","pages":
33},{"id":"33cc122a-6be2-48b6-83b1-e913fc10da77","number":0,"title":".NET Application Archite
ctures","pages":35},{"id":"47bcfa1e-085e-4d11-9a63-ed2421cad912","number":6,"title":"Arrays",
"pages":20},{"id":"069a1755-05da-40d7-96d4-a1422eddfcd1","number":3,"title":"Object-Oriented
Programming with C#","pages":20},{"id":"a11cdc6b-087b-4c69-a4c7-cc48f472c1b0","number":5,"title
":"Operators and Casts","pages":38},{"id":"1b638e90-f553-4635-8b54-b6c5a938ad5d","number":1,"ti
tle":"Core C#","pages":42},{"id":"3871a10e-ca1a-4d63-944e-984d869b9416","number":7,"title":"Del
egates, Lambdas, and Events","pages":32},{"id":"311d1c72-844c-4b0b-a674-6af7b24d7530","number":
4,"title":"Generics","pages":24}]
```

Changing the Response Format

The .NET Framework version of the ASP.NET Web API returned JSON or XML, depending on the requested format by the client. With ASP.NET Core MVC, when returning an `ObjectResult`, by default JSON is returned. In case you need to return XML as well, you can add a call to `AddXmlSerializerFormatters` to the `Startup` class. `AddXmlSerializerFormatters` is an extension method for the `IMvcBuilder` interface and can be added using fluent API to the `AddMvc` method (code file `Sync/BooksServiceSampleHost/Startup.cs`):

```
public void ConfigureServices(IServiceCollection services)
{
    services.AddMvc().AddXmlSerializerFormatters();
    services.AddSingleton<IBookChaptersService, BookChaptersService>();
    services.AddSingleton<SampleChapters>();
}
```

With the controllers, the allowed content type(s) and selectable result can be specified with the `Produces` attribute (`Sync/APIBookServices/Controllers/BookChaptersController.cs`):

```
[Produces("application/json", "application/xml")]
[Route("api/[controller]")]
public class BookChaptersController: Controller
{
    //...
}
```

> **NOTE** *Later in this chapter, in the section "Receiving XML from the Service," you see how to receive XML-formatted responses.*

REST Results and Status Codes

The following table summarizes the results a service returns based on the HTTP methods:

HTTP METHOD	DESCRIPTION	REQUEST BODY	RESPONSE BODY
GET	Returns a resource	Empty	The resource
POST	Adds a resource	The resource to add	The resource
PUT	Updates a resource	The resource to update	None
DELETE	Deletes a resource	Empty	Empty

The following table shows important HTTP status codes as well as the `Controller` method with the instantiated object that returns the status code. To return any HTTP status code, you can return an `HttpStatusCodeResult` object that can be initialized with the status code you need:

HTTP STATUS CODE	CONTROLLER METHOD	TYPE
200 OK	Ok	OkResult
201 Created	CreatedAtRoute	CreatedAtRouteResult
204 No Content	NoContent	NoContentResult
400 Bad Request	BadRequest	BadRequestResult
401 Unauthorized	Unauthorized	UnauthorizedResult
404 Not Found	NotFound	NotFoundResult
Any status code		StatusCodeResult

All success status codes start with 2; error status codes start with 4. You can find a list of status codes in RFC 7231:

```
https://tools.ietf.org/html/rfc7231#section-6.3
```

CREATING AN ASYNC SERVICE

The previous sample code made use of a synchronous service. Using Entity Framework Core (EF Core) with your repository, you can use either synchronous or asynchronous methods. EF Core supports both. However, many technologies, for example calling other services with the `HttpClient` class, offer only asynchronous methods. This can lead to an asynchronous service as shown in the project `BooksServiceSample` in the `Async` folder.

With the asynchronous project, the `IBookChaptersService` has been changed to an asynchronous version. This interface is defined to use it with services accessing asynchronous methods, such as network or database clients. All the methods return a `Task` (code file `Async/BooksServiceSample/Services/IBookChaptersService.cs`):

```
public interface IBookChaptersRepository
{
    Task AddAsync(BookChapter chapter);
    Task AddRangeAsync(IEnumerable<BookChapter> chapters);
    Task<BookChapter> RemoveAsync(Guid id);
    Task<IEnumerable<BookChapter>> GetAllAsync();
    Task<BookChapter> FindAsync(Guid id);
    Task UpdateAsync(BookChapter chapter);
}
```

The class `BookChaptersService` implements the asynchronous methods. When reading and writing from the dictionary, asynchronous functionality is not needed, so the `Task` to return is created using the `FromResult` method (code file `Async/BooksServiceSample/Services/BookChaptersService.cs`):

```
public class BookChaptersService: IBookChaptersService
{
    private readonly ConcurrentDictionary<string, BookChapter> _chapters =
      new ConcurrentDictionary<string, BookChapter>();

    public Task AddAsync(BookChapter chapter)
    {
```

```
            chapter.Id = Guid.NewGuid();
            _chapters[chapter.Id] = chapter;
            return Task.CompletedTask;
        }

        public Task AddRangeAsync(IEnumerable<BookChapter> chapters)
        {
            foreach (var chapter in chapters)
            {
                chapter.Id = Guid.NewGuid();
                _chapters[chapter.Id] = chapter;
            }
            return Task.CompletedTask;
        }

        public Task<BookChapter> RemoveAsync(Guid id)
        {
            BookChapter removed;
            _chapters.TryRemove(id, out removed);
            return Task.FromResult(removed);
        }

        public Task<IEnumerable<BookChapter>> GetAllAsync() =>
            Task.FromResult<IEnumerable<BookChapter>>(_chapters.Values);

        public Task<BookChapter> FindAsync(Guid id)
        {
            _chapters.TryGetValue(id, out BookChapter chapter);
            return Task.FromResult(chapter);
        }

        public Task UpdateAsync(BookChapter chapter)
        {
            _chapters[chapter.Id] = chapter;
            return Task.CompletedTask;
        }
    }
}
```

The API controller BookChaptersController just needs a few changes to be implemented as asynchronous. The controller methods return a Task as well. With this it is easy to invoke the asynchronous methods of the repository (code file Async/BooksServiceAsyncSample/Controllers/BookChaptersController.cs):

```
[Produces("application/json", "application/xml")]
[Route("api/[controller]")]
public class BookChaptersController: Controller
{
    private readonly IBookChaptersService _bookChaptersService;
    public BookChaptersController(IBookChaptersService bookChaptersService)
    {
        _bookChaptersService = bookChaptersService;
    }

    // GET: api/bookchapters
    [HttpGet()]
    public Task<IEnumerable<BookChapter>> GetBookChaptersAsync() =>
        _bookChaptersService.GetAllAsync();

    // GET api/bookchapters/guid
    [HttpGet("{id}", Name = nameof(GetBookChapterByIdAsync))]
    public async Task<IActionResult> GetBookChapterByIdAsync(Guid id)
    {
        BookChapter chapter = await _bookChaptersService.FindAsync(id);
```

```
        if (chapter == null)
        {
          return NotFound();
        }
        else
        {
          return new ObjectResult(chapter);
        }
      }

      // POST api/bookchapters
      [HttpPost]
      public async Task<IActionResult> PostBookChapterAsync(
        [FromBody]BookChapter chapter)
      {
        if (chapter == null)
        {
          return BadRequest();
        }
        await _ bookChaptersService.AddAsync(chapter);
        return CreatedAtRoute(nameof(GetBookChapterByIdAsync),
          new { id = chapter.Id }, chapter);
      }

      // PUT api/bookchapters/guid
      [HttpPut("{id}")]
      public async Task<IActionResult> PutBookChapterAsync(
        Guid id, [FromBody]BookChapter chapter)
      {
        if (chapter == null || id != chapter.Id)
        {
          return BadRequest();
        }
        if (await _ bookChaptersService.FindAsync(id) == null)
        {
          return NotFound();
        }
        await _ bookChaptersService.UpdateAsync(chapter);
        return new NoContentResult();
      }

      // DELETE api/bookchapters/guid
      [HttpDelete("{id}")]
      public async Task DeleteAsync(Guid id) =>
        await _ bookChaptersService.RemoveAsync(id);
    }
```

For the client, it doesn't matter if the controller is implemented as synchronous or asynchronous, the API calls are the same. The client creates the same HTTP requests for both kinds.

CREATING A .NET CLIENT

Using the browser to call the service is a simple way to handle testing. The clients more typically make use of JavaScript—this is where JSON shines—and .NET clients. In this book, a Console App (.NET Core) project is created to call the service.

The sample code for BookServiceClientApp makes use of the following dependencies and namespaces:

Dependencies

```
Microsoft.Extensions.DependencyInjection
```

```
Microsoft.Extensions.Logging.Console

Newtonsoft.Json
```

Namespaces

```
Microsoft.Extensions.Logging

Newtonsoft.Json

System

System.Collections.Generic

System.Linq

System.Net.Http

System.Net.Http.Headers

System.Runtime.CompilerServices

System.Text

System.Threading.Tasks

System.Xml.Linq
```

Sending GET Requests

For sending HTTP requests, you use the HttpClient class. This class is introduced in Chapter 23, "Networking." In this chapter, this class is used to send different kinds of HTTP requests. To use the HttpClient class, you need to add the NuGet package System.Net.Http and open the namespace System .Net.Http. To convert JSON data to a .NET type, the NuGet package Newtonsoft.Json is added.

> **NOTE** *JSON serialization and using Json.NET is discussed in Bonus Chapter 2, "XML and JSON," which you can find online.*

To have all the URLs needed in one place, the UrlService class defines properties for the URLs needed (code file Async/BookServiceClientApp/Services/UrlService.cs):

```
public class UrlService
{
  public string BaseAddress => "http://localhost:1079/";
  public string BooksApi => "api/BookChapters/";
}
```

> **NOTE** *You need to change the* BaseAddress *in the* UrlService *class to the host and port number of your service. You can see the port number in the browser when you start the service host.*

With the sample project, the generic class HttpClientService is created to have just one implementation for different data types. The constructor expects the UrlService via DI and creates the HttpClient using the base address retrieved from the UrlService (code file Async/BookServiceClientApp/Services/ HttpClientService.cs):

```
public abstract class HttpClientService<T> : IDisposable
    where T: class
```

```
{
  private HttpClient _httpClient;
  private readonly UrlService _urlService;
  private readonly ILogger<HttpClientService<T>> _logger;

  public HttpClientService(UrlService urlService,
    ILogger<HttpClientService<T>> logger)
  {
    _urlService = urlService ??
      throw new ArgumentNullException(nameof(urlService));
    _logger = logger ?? throw new ArgumentNullException(nameof(logger));

    _httpClient = new HttpClient();
    _httpClient.BaseAddress = new Uri(_urlService.BaseAddress);
  }
  //...
}
```

> **NOTE** *In the sample code, the* ILogger *interface is used to write log information to the console. Logging is discussed in detail in Chapter 29, "Tracing, Logging, and Analytics."*

The method GetInternalAsync makes a GET request to receive a list of items. This method invokes the GetAsync method of the HttpClient to send a GET request. The HttpResponseMessage contains the information received. The status code of the response is written to the console to show the result. In case the server returns an error, the GetAsync method doesn't throw an exception. An exception is thrown from the method EnsureSuccessStatusCode that is invoked with the HttpResponseMessage instance that is returned. This method throws an exception in case the HTTP status code is of an error type. The body of the response contains the JSON data returned. This JSON information is read as string and returned (code file Async/BookServiceClientApp/Services/HttpClientService.cs):

```
private async Task<string> GetInternalAsync(string requestUri)
{
  if (requestUri == null) throw new ArgumentNullException(nameof(requestUri));
  if (_objectDisposed) throw new ObjectDisposedException(nameof(_httpClient));

  HttpResponseMessage resp = await _httpClient.GetAsync(requestUri);
  LogInformation($"status from GET {resp.StatusCode}");
  resp.EnsureSuccessStatusCode();
  return await resp.Content.ReadAsStringAsync();
}

private void LogInformation(string message,
  [CallerMemberName] string callerName = null) =>
  _logger.LogInformation(
    $"{nameof(HttpClientService<T>)}.{callerName}: {message}");
```

The server controller defines two methods with GET requests: one method that returns all chapters and the other one returns just a single chapter but requires the chapter's identifier with the URI. The method GetAllAsync invokes the GetInternalAsync method to convert the returned JSON information to a collection, while the method GetAsync converts the result to a single item. These methods are declared virtual to allow overriding them from a derived class (code file Async/BookServiceClientApp/Services/HttpClientService.cs):

```
public async virtual Task<T> GetAsync(string requestUri)
{
  if (requestUri == null) throw new ArgumentNullException(nameof(requestUri));
```

```
    string json = await GetInternalAsync(requestUri);
    return JsonConvert.DeserializeObject<T>(json);
}

public async virtual Task<IEnumerable<T>> GetAllAsync(string requestUri)
{
    if (requestUri == null) throw new ArgumentNullException(nameof(requestUri));

    string json = await GetInternalAsync(requestUri);
    return JsonConvert.DeserializeObject<IEnumerable<T>>(json);
}
```

Instead of using the generic `HttpClientService` class from the client code, a specialization is done with the `BookChapterClientService` class. This class derives from `HttpClientService` passing a `BookChapter` for the generic parameter. This class also overrides the `GetAllAsync` method from the base class to have the returned chapters sorted by the chapter number (code file `Async/BookServiceClientApp/Services/BookChapterClientService.cs`):

```
public class BookChapterClientService : HttpClientService<BookChapter>
{
    public BookChapterClientService(UrlService urlService,
        ILogger<BookChapterClientService> logger)
        : base(urlService, logger) { }

    public override async Task<IEnumerable<BookChapter>> GetAllAsync(
        string requestUri)
    {
        IEnumerable<BookChapter> chapters = await base.GetAllAsync(requestUri);
        return chapters.OrderBy(c => c.Number);
    }
}
```

The `BookChapter` class contains the properties that are received with the JSON content (code file `Async/BookServiceClientApp/Models/BookChapter.cs`):

```
public class BookChapter
{
    public Guid Id { get; set; }
    public int Number { get; set; }
    public string Title { get; set; }
    public int Pages { get; set; }
}
```

The `Main` method of the client application invokes the different methods to show GET, POST, PUT, and DELETE requests that use methods from the `SampleRequest` class. Before that, services to be used for DI are registered by calling the `ConfigureServices` method (code file `Async/BookServiceClientApp/Program.cs`):

```
static async Task Main()
{
    Console.WriteLine("Client app, wait for service");
    Console.ReadLine();
    ConfigureServices();
    var test = ApplicationServices.GetRequiredService<SampleRequest>();

    await test.ReadChaptersAsync();
    await test.ReadChapterAsync();
    await test.ReadNotExistingChapterAsync();
    await test.ReadXmlAsync();
    await test.AddChapterAsync();
    await test.UpdateChapterAsync();
    await test.RemoveChapterAsync();
    Console.ReadLine();
}
```

The method `ConfigureServices` registers the needed services in the `Microsoft.Extensions` `.DependencyInjection` container and configures logging to write to the console (code file `Async/` `BookServiceClientApp/Program.cs`):

```
public static void ConfigureServices()
{
  var services = new ServiceCollection();
  services.AddSingleton<UrlService>();
  services.AddSingleton<BookChapterClientService>();
  services.AddTransient<SampleRequest>();
  services.AddLogging(logger =>
  {
    logger.AddConsole();
  });

  ApplicationServices = services.BuildServiceProvider();
}

public static IServiceProvider ApplicationServices { get; private set; }
```

The class `SampleRequest` implements all the sample methods to invoke the methods of the `BookChapterClientService`. In the constructor, the `UrlService` and the `BookChapterClientService` are injected (code file `Async/BookServiceClientApp/SampleRequest.cs`):

```
public class SampleRequest
{
  private readonly UrlService _urlService;
  private readonly BookChapterClientService _client;
  public SampleRequest(UrlService urlService,
    BookChapterClientService client)
  {
    _urlService = urlService ??
      throw new ArgumentNullException(nameof(urlService));
    _client = client ?? throw new ArgumentNullException(nameof(client));
  }
  //...
}
```

The method `ReadChaptersAsync` invokes the `GetAllAsync` method from the `BookChapterClient` to retrieve all chapters and shows the titles of the chapters on the console (code file `Async/` `BookServiceClientApp/SampleRequest.cs`):

```
public async Task ReadChaptersAsync()
{
  Console.WriteLine(nameof(ReadChaptersAsync));
  IEnumerable<BookChapter> chapters =
    await _client.GetAllAsync(_urlService.BooksApi);
  foreach (BookChapter chapter in chapters)
  {
    Console.WriteLine(chapter.Title);
  }
  Console.WriteLine();
}
```

When you run the application (starting both the service and the client app), the `ReadChaptersAsync` method shows the OK status code and the titles from the chapters:

```
ReadChaptersAsync
info: BookServiceClientApp.Services.BookChapterClientService[0]
      HttpClientService.GetInternalAsync: status from GET OK
.NET Application Architectures
Core C#
Objects and Types
Object-Oriented Programming with C#
```

```
Generics
Operators and Casts
Arrays
Delegates, Lambdas, and Events
```

The method `ReadChapterAsync` shows the GET request to retrieve a single chapter. With this, the identifier of a chapter is added to the URI string (code file `Async/BookServiceClientApp/SampleRequest.cs`):

```
public async Task ReadChapterAsync()
{
  Console.WriteLine(nameof(ReadChapterAsync));
  var chapters = await _client.GetAllAsync(_urlService.BooksApi);
  Guid id = chapters.First().Id;
  BookChapter chapter = await _client.GetAsync(Addresses.BooksApi + id);
  Console.WriteLine($" {chapter.Number} {chapter.Title}");
  Console.WriteLine();
}
```

The result of the `ReadChapterAsync` method is shown here. It shows the OK status two times because the first time this method retrieves all the chapters before sending a request for a single chapter:

```
ReadChapterAsync
info: BookServiceClientApp.Services.BookChapterClientService[0]
      HttpClientService.GetInternalAsync: status from GET OK
Info 0 .NET Application Architectures
: BookServiceClientApp.Services.BookChapterClientService[0]
      HttpClientService.GetInternalAsync: status from GET OK
```

What if a GET request is sent with a nonexistent chapter identifier? How to deal with this is shown in the method `ReadNotExistingChapterAsync`. Calling the `GetAsync` method is like the previous code snippet, but an identifier that does not exist is added to the URI. Remember from the implementation of the `HttpClientHelper` class, the `GetAsync` method of the `HttpClient` class does not throw an exception. However, the `EnsureSuccessStatusCode` does. This exception is caught with a catch to the `HttpRequestException` type. Here, an exception filter is also used to only handle exception code 404 (not found) (code file `Async/BookServiceClientApp/SampleRequest.cs`):

```
private async Task ReadNotExistingChapterAsync()
{
  Console.WriteLine(nameof(ReadNotExistingChapterAsync));
  string requestedIdentifier = Guid.NewGuid().ToString();
  try
  {
    BookChapter chapter = await _client.GetAsync(
      Addresses.BooksApi + requestedIdentifier.ToString());
    Console.WriteLine($" {chapter.Number} {chapter.Title}");
  }
  catch (HttpRequestException ex) when (ex.Message.Contains("404"))
  {
    Console.WriteLine($"book chapter with the identifier " +
      $"{requestedIdentifier} not found");
  }
  Console.WriteLine();
}
```

> **NOTE** *Handling exceptions and using exception filters is discussed in Chapter 14, "Errors and Exceptions."*

The result of the method shows the `NotFound` result from the service:

```
ReadNotExistingChapterAsync
info: BookServiceClientApp.Services.BookChapterClientService[0]
      HttpClientService.GetInternalAsync: status from GET NotFound
book chapter with the identifier a0f629f4-8c46-4d66-8543-74592dba5d5b not found
```

Receiving XML from the Service

In the section "Changing the Response Format," the XML format was added to the service. With a service that is enabled to return XML beside JSON, XML content can be explicitly requested by adding the accept header value to accept application/xml content.

How this can be done is shown in the following code snippet. Here, the `MediaTypeWithQualityHeaderValue` specifying application/xml is added to the `Accept` headers collection. Then, the result is parsed as XML using the `XElement` class (code file `BookServiceClientApp/Services/HttpClientService.cs`):

```
public async Task<XElement> GetAllXmlAsync(string requestUri)
{
  if (requestUri is null) throw new ArgumentNullException(nameof(requestUri));

  using (var client = new HttpClient())
  {
    client.BaseAddress = _baseAddress;
    client.DefaultRequestHeaders.Accept.Add(
      new MediaTypeWithQualityHeaderValue("application/xml"));
    HttpResponseMessage resp = await client.GetAsync(requestUri);
    Console.WriteLine($"status from GET {resp.StatusCode}");
    resp.EnsureSuccessStatusCode();
    string xml = await resp.Content.ReadAsStringAsync();
    XElement chapters = XElement.Parse(xml);
    return chapters;
  }
}
```

> **NOTE** The `XElement` class and XML serialization are discussed in Bonus Chapter 2.

From the `SampleRequest` class, the `GetAllXmlAsync` method is invoked to directly write the XML result to the console (code file `Async/BookServiceClientApp/SampleRequest.cs`):

```
private static async Task ReadXmlAsync()
{
  Console.WriteLine(nameof(ReadXmlAsync));
  XElement chapters = await _client.GetAllXmlAsync(_urlService.BooksApi);
  Console.WriteLine(chapters);
  Console.WriteLine();
}
```

When you run this method, you can see that now XML is returned from the service:

```
ReadXmlAsync
info: BookServiceClientApp.Services.BookChapterClientService[0]
      HttpClientService.GetAllXmlAsync: status from GET OK
<ArrayOfBookChapter xmlns:xsi="http://www.w3.org/2001/XMLSchema-instance"
  xmlns:xsd="http://www.w3.org/2001/XMLSchema">
```

```xml
  <BookChapter>
    <Id>015b0fb6-1a0f-44ac-ba0d-3d6d743bf4df</Id>
    <Number>2</Number>
    <Title>Objects and Types</Title>
    <Pages>33</Pages>
  </BookChapter>
  <BookChapter>
    <Id>33cc122a-6be2-48b6-83b1-e913fc10da77</Id>
    <Number>0</Number>
    <Title>.NET Application Architectures</Title>
    <Pages>35</Pages>
  </BookChapter>
  <BookChapter>
    <Id>47bcfa1e-085e-4d11-9a63-ed2421cad912</Id>
    <Number>6</Number>
    <Title>Arrays</Title>
    <Pages>20</Pages>
  </BookChapter>
  <!--... more chapters ...-->
</ArrayOfBookChapter>
```

Sending POST Requests

Let's send new objects to the service using the HTTP POST request. The HTTP POST request works similarly to the GET request. This request creates a new object server side. The `PostAsync` method of the `HttpClient` class requires the object that is added with the second parameter. You use Json.NET's `JsonConvert` class to serialize the object to JSON. With a successful return, the `Headers.Location` property contains a link where the object can be retrieved again from the service. The response also contains a body with the object returned. When the object changed from the service, the `Id` property was filled in the service code on creating the object. This new information is returned by the `PostAsync` method after deserialization of the JSON code (code file `Async/BookServiceClientApp/Services/HttpClientService.cs`):

```csharp
public async Task<T> PostAsync(string requestUri, T item)
{
    if (requestUri is null) throw new ArgumentNullException(nameof(requestUri));
    if (item is null) throw new ArgumentNullException(nameof(item));
    if (_objectDisposed) throw new ObjectDisposedException(nameof(_httpClient));

    string json = JsonConvert.SerializeObject(item);
    HttpContent content = new StringContent(json, Encoding.UTF8,
        "application/json");
    HttpResponseMessage resp = await _httpClient.PostAsync(requestUri, content);
    LogInformation($"status from POST {resp.StatusCode}");
    resp.EnsureSuccessStatusCode();
    LogInformation($"added resource at {resp.Headers.Location}");
    json = await resp.Content.ReadAsStringAsync();
    return JsonConvert.DeserializeObject<T>(json);
}
```

With the `SampleRequest` class, you can see the chapter that is added to the service. After invoking the `PostAsync` method of the `BookChapterClient`, the returned `Chapter` contains the new identifier (code file `Async/BookServiceClientApp/SampleRequest.cs`):

```csharp
private static async Task AddChapterAsync()
{
    Console.WriteLine(nameof(AddChapterAsync));
    var client = new BookChapterClient(Addresses.BaseAddress);
    BookChapter chapter = new BookChapter
    {
        Number = 34,
        Title = "ASP.NET Core Web API",
```

```
    Pages = 35
  };
  chapter = await client.PostAsync(Addresses.BooksApi, chapter);
  Console.WriteLine($"added chapter {chapter.Title} with id {chapter.Id}");
  Console.WriteLine();
}
```

The result of the `AddChapterAsync` method shows a successful run to create the object:

```
AddChapterAsync
info added chapter ASP.NET Web API with id b490c5c3-ff30-4ad4-8ca4-7436edfb04c0

: BookServiceClientApp.Services.BookChapterClientService[0]
      HttpClientService.PostAsync: status from POST Created
info: BookServiceClientApp.Services.BookChapterClientService[0]
      HttpClientService.PostAsync: added resource at
        http://localhost:1079/api/BookChapters/b490c5c3-ff30-4ad4-8ca4-7436edfb04c0
```

Sending PUT Requests

The HTTP PUT request—used for updating a record—is sent with the help of the `HttpClient` method `PutAsync`. `PutAsync` requires the updated content with the second parameter, and the URL to the service including the identifier in the first (code file `Async/BookServiceClientApp/Services/HttpClientService.cs`):

```
public async Task PutAsync(string requestUri, T item)
{
  if (requestUri is null) throw new ArgumentNullException(nameof(requestUri));
  if (item is null) throw new ArgumentNullException(nameof(item));
  if (_objectDisposed) throw new ObjectDisposedException(nameof(_httpClient));

  string json = JsonConvert.SerializeObject(item);
  HttpContent content = new StringContent(json, Encoding.UTF8,
    "application/json");
  HttpResponseMessage resp = await _httpClient.PutAsync(requestUri, content);
  LogInformation($"status from PUT {resp.StatusCode}");
  resp.EnsureSuccessStatusCode();
}
```

In the `SampleRequest` class, the chapter .NET Application Architectures is updated to a different title .NET Applications and Tools (code file `Async/BookServiceClientApp/SampleRequest.cs`):

```
public async Task UpdateChapterAsync()
{
  Console.WriteLine(nameof(UpdateChapterAsync));
  var chapters = await _client.GetAllAsync(_urlService.BooksApi);
  var chapter = chapters.SingleOrDefault(
    c => c.Title == ".NET Application Architectures");
  if (chapter != null)
  {
    chapter.Title = ".NET Applications and Tools";
    await _client.PutAsync(_urlService.BooksApi + chapter.Id, chapter);
    Console.WriteLine($"updated chapter {chapter.Title}");
  }
  Console.WriteLine();
}
```

The console output of the `UpdateChapterAsync` method shows an HTTP NoContent result and the updated chapter title:

```
UpdateChapterAsync
info: BookServiceClientApp.Services.BookChapterClientService[0]
      HttpClientService.GetInternalAsync: status from GET OK
```

```
info: BookServiceClientApp.Services.BookChapterClientService[0]
      HttpClientService.PutAsync: status from PUT NoContent
updated chapter .NET Applications and Tools
```

Sending DELETE Requests

The last request shown with the sample client is the HTTP DELETE request. After invoking `GetAsync`, `PostAsync`, and `PutAsync` of the `HttpClient` class, it should be obvious that the format is `DeleteAsync`. What's shown in this code snippet is that the `DeleteAsync` method just needs a URI parameter to identify the object to delete (code file `Async/BookServiceClientApp/Services/HttpClientService.cs`):

```
public async Task DeleteAsync(string requestUri)
{
  if (requestUri is null) throw new ArgumentNullException(nameof(requestUri));
  if (_objectDisposed) throw new ObjectDisposedException(nameof(_httpClient));

  HttpResponseMessage resp = await _httpClient.DeleteAsync(requestUri);
  LogInformation($"status from DELETE {resp.StatusCode}");
  resp.EnsureSuccessStatusCode();
}
```

The `SampleRequest` class defines the `RemoveChapterAsync` method (code file `Async/BookServiceClientApp/SampleRequest.cs`):

```
public async Task RemoveChapterAsync()
{
  Console.WriteLine(nameof(RemoveChapterAsync));
  var chapters = await _client.GetAllAsync(_urlService.BooksApi);
  var chapter = chapters.SingleOrDefault(
    c => c.Title == "Windows Communication Foundation");
  if (chapter != null)
  {
    await _client.DeleteAsync(_urlService.BooksApi + chapter.Id);
    Console.WriteLine($"removed chapter {chapter.Title}");
  }
  Console.WriteLine();
}
```

When you run the application, the `RemoveChapterAsync` method first shows the status of the HTTP GET method as a GET request is done first to retrieve all chapters, and then the successful DELETE request on deleting the Windows Communication Foundation chapter:

```
RemoveChapterAsync
info: BookServiceClientApp.Services.BookChapterClientService[0]
      HttpClientService.GetInternalAsync: status from GET OK
info: BookServiceClientApp.Services.BookChapterClientService[0]
      HttpClientService.DeleteAsync: status from DELETE OK
removed chapter Windows Communication Foundation
```

WRITING TO THE DATABASE

Chapter 26, "Entity Framework Core," introduced you to mapping objects to relations with Entity Framework Core (EF Core). A Web API controller can easily use a `DbContext`. In the sample app, you don't need to change the controller at all; you just need to create and register a different repository for using EF Core. All the steps needed are described in this section.

Using EF Core

Let's start with the code accessing the database. For using EF Core with SQL Server, the NuGet package `Microsoft.EntityFrameworkCore.SqlServer` need to be added to the library project that contains the services.

The `BookChapter` class was already defined earlier. This class stays unchanged for filling instances from the database. Mapping to properties is defined in the `BooksContext` class. With this class, the `OnModelCreating` method is overridden to map the `BookChapter` type to the `Chapters` table and to define a unique identifier for the `Id` column with a default unique identifier created from the database. The `Title` column is restricted to a maximum of 120 characters (code file `Async/BookServiceSample/Models/BooksContext.cs`):

```
public class BooksContext: DbContext
{
  public BooksContext(DbContextOptions<BooksContext> options)
    : base(options) { }

  public DbSet<BookChapter> Chapters { get; set; }

  protected override void OnModelCreating(ModelBuilder modelBuilder)
  {
    modelBuilder.Entity<BookChapter>()
      .ToTable("Chapters")
      .HasKey(c => c.Id);
    modelBuilder.Entity<BookChapter>()
      .Property(c => c.Id)
      .HasColumnType("UniqueIdentifier")
      .HasDefaultValueSql("newid()");
    modelBuilder.Entity<BookChapter>()
      .Property(c => c.Title)
      .HasMaxLength(120);
  }
}
```

With the DI container, EF Core and SQL Server need to be added to invoke the extension methods `AddEntityFramework` and `AddSqlServer`. The just-created `BooksContext` needs to be registered as well. The `BooksContext` is added with the method `AddDbContext`. With the options of this method, the connection string is passed (code file `Async/BookServiceSampleHost/Startup.cs`):

```
public async void ConfigureServices(IServiceCollection services)
{
  services.AddMvc().AddXmlSerializerFormatters();
  //...
  services.AddDbContext<BooksContext>(optons =>
    options.UseSqlServer(
      Configuration.GetConnectionString("BooksConnection")));
  //...
}
```

The connection string itself is defined with the application settings in the host application project (configuration file `Async/BookServiceSampleHost/appsettings.json`):

```
"ConnectionStrings": {
  "BooksConnection": "server=(localdb)\\mssqllocaldb;database=APIBooksSample;
  trusted_connection=true;MultipleActiveResultSets=true"
}
```

With the sample application, the database will be automatically created from the C# code. This is done by injecting the `BooksContext` with the `Configure` method of the `Startup` class and invoking the `EnsureCreated` method of the `Database` property. `EnsureCreated` creates the database if it doesn't exist. If the database was created, the `CreateSampleChaptersAsync` method is invoked to feed sample chapters into the database. `SampleChapters` is the same service that was used previously with the in-memory chapter list (code file `Async/BooksServiceSampleHost/Startup.cs`):

```
public async void Configure(IApplicationBuilder app, IHostingEnvironment env,
    SampleChapters sampleChapters, BooksContext booksContext)
{
  if (env.IsDevelopment())
  {
    app.UseDeveloperExceptionPage();
  }

  app.UseMvc();
  //...

  bool created = booksContext.Database.EnsureCreated();
  if (created)
  {
    await sampleChapters.CreateSampleChaptersAsync();
  }
}
```

> **NOTE** *EF Core also allows creating databases using Migration. Read Chapter 26 for information about how to implement* Migration *in the application.*

Creating the Data Access Service

For using the `BooksContext`, you need to create a service implementing the interface `IBookChaptersService`. The class `DBBookChaptersService` makes use of the `BooksContext` instead of using an in-memory dictionary as was done with the `BookChaptersService` (code file `Async/BookServiceSample/Models/DBBookChaptersService.cs`):

```
public class DBBookChaptersService, IBookChaptersService
{
  Private readonly BooksContext _booksContext;
  public BookChaptersRepository(BooksContext booksContext)
  {
    _booksContext = booksContext;
  }

  public async Task AddAsync(BookChapter chapter)
  {
    await _booksContext.Chapters.AddAsync(chapter);
    await _booksContext.SaveChangesAsync();
  }

  public Task<BookChapter> FindAsync(Guid id) =>
    _booksContext.Chapters.FindAsyncDefaultAsync(c => c.Id == id);

  public async Task<IEnumerable<BookChapter>> GetAllAsync() =>
    await _booksContext.Chapters.ToListAsync();
```

```csharp
public async Task<BookChapter> RemoveAsync(Guid id)
{
  BookChapter chapter = await _booksContext.Chapters
    .SingleOrDefaultAsync(c => c.Id == id);
  if (chapter == null) return null;

  _booksContext.Chapters.Remove(chapter);
  await _booksContext.SaveChangesAsync();
  return chapter;
}

public async Task UpdateAsync(BookChapter chapter)
{
  _booksContext.Chapters.Update(chapter);
  await _booksContext.SaveChangesAsync();
}
}
```

If you are wondering about the use of the context, read Chapter 26, which covers more information about the EF Core.

To use this service, you have to remove the `BookChaptersService` from the registration in the container (or comment it out), and add the `DBBookChaptersService` to let the DI container create an instance of this class when asked for the interface `IBookChaptersService` (code file `Async/BookServiceSampleHost/Startup.cs`):

```csharp
public void ConfigureServices(IServiceCollection services)
{
  services.AddMvc().AddXmlSerializerFormatters();
  // services.AddScoped<IBookChaptersService, BookChaptersService>();
  services.AddScoped<IBookChaptersService, DBBookChaptersService>();
  services.AddScoped<SampleChapters>();

  services.AddDbContext<BooksContext>(options =>
    options.UseSqlServer(
      Configuration.GetConnectionString("BooksConnection")));
  //...
}
```

Now—without changing the controller or the client—you can run the service and client again. Depending on the data you enter initially in the database, you see results for the GET/POST/PUT/DELETE requests.

CREATING METADATA WITH THE OPENAPI OR SWAGGER

Creating metadata for a service allows getting a description on the service, and also allows you to create the client by using this metadata. With web services using SOAP, metadata have been around since the early days of SOAP—with the Web Services Description Language (WSDL). Nowadays, metadata for REST services is here as well. Currently it's not a standard as with WSDL, but the most popular framework for describing APIs is Swagger (http://www.swagger.io). As of January 2016, the Swagger specification has been renamed to OpenAPI, and the standard is already available in version 3.0 as of this writing (http://www.openapis.org). The specification is available as a GitHub repository at https://github.com/OAI/OpenAPI-Specification/blob/OpenAPI.next/versions/3.0.0.md.

To add Swagger or OpenAPI to an ASP.NET Web API service, you can use Swashbuckle. The NuGet package `Swashbuckle.AspNetCore` is the library for ASP.NET Core.

After you add the NuGet package, you need to add Swagger to the DI container. `AddSwaggerGen` is an extension method to add swagger services to the collection. To configure Swagger, you invoke the method `SwaggerDoc`. Passing an Info object, you can define title, description, contact information, and more (code file `Async/BooksServiceSampleHost/Startup.cs`):

```
public void ConfigureServices(IServiceCollection services)
{
  services.AddMvc().AddXmlSerializerFormatters();
  // services.AddScoped<IBookChaptersService, BookChaptersService>();
  services.AddScoped<IBookChaptersService, DBBookChaptersService>();
  services.AddScoped<SampleChapters>();

  services.AddDbContext<BooksContext>(options =>
    options.UseSqlServer(
      Configuration.GetConnectionString("BooksConnection")));

  services.AddSwaggerGen(options =>
  {
    options.SwaggerDoc("v2", new Info
    {
      Title = "Books Service API",
      Version = "v2",
      Description = "Sample service for Professional C# 7",
      Contact = new Contact { Name = "Christian Nagel",
        Url = "https://csharp.christiannagel.com" },
      License = new License { Name = "MIT License" }
    });
  });
}
```

What's left is the Swagger configuration in the `Configure` method of the `Startup` class. The extension method `UseSwagger` adds Swagger middleware and specifies that a JSON schema file should be generated.

The default URI that you can configure with `UseSwagger` is `/swagger/{version}/swagger.json`. With the document configured in the previous code snippet, the URL is `/swagger/v1/swagger.json`. The method `UseSwaggerUi` enables the graphical user interface for Swagger and defines the URL (code file `Async/BooksServiceSampleHost/Startup.cs`):

```
public async void Configure(IApplicationBuilder app, IHostingEnvironment env,
    SampleChapters sampleChapters, BooksContext booksContext)
{
  if (env.IsDevelopment())
  {
    app.UseDeveloperExceptionPage();
  }

  app.UseMvc();
  app.UseSwagger();
  app.UseSwaggerUI(options =>
    options.SwaggerEndpoint("/swagger/v2/swagger.json",
      "Book Chapter Services"));
  //...
}
```

When you run the application with Swagger configured, you can see nice information about the APIs offered by the service. Figure 32-2 shows the APIs offered by the `BooksServiceSample`, the template generated by `Values` service, and the `BooksService` sample. You can also see the title and description as configured with the Swagger document.

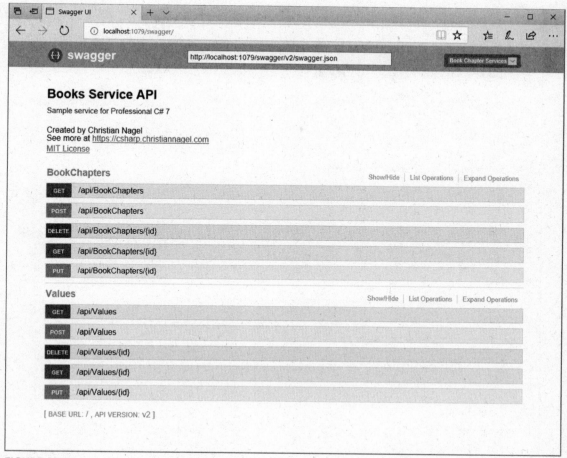

FIGURE 32-2

Figure 32-3 shows some details of the GET request of the BookChapters service with the UI to test the API call. You can see details of every API including the model.

Swagger allows for easy customization of the output by using .NET features. Adding annotations to the model types, such as Required and DefaultValue, makes it into the JSON metadata definition, and is shown in the help pages (code file Async/BooksServiceSample/Models/BookChapter.cs):

```
public class BookChapter
{
  public Guid Id { get; set; }
  [Required]
  public int Number { get; set; }
  [Required]
  [MaxLength(40)]
  public string Title { get; set; }
  [DefaultValue(0)]
  public int Pages { get; set; }
}
```

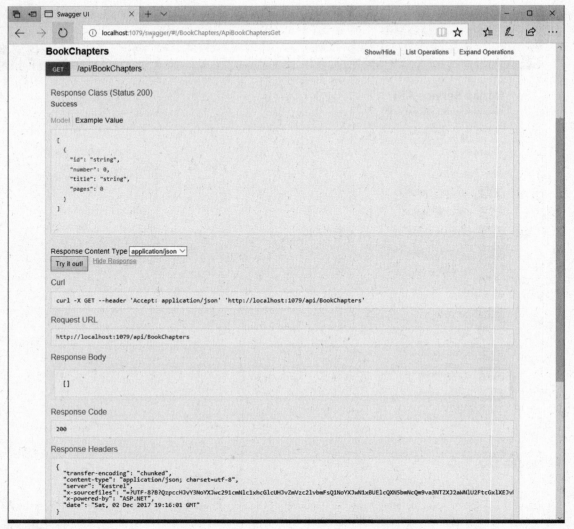

FIGURE 32-3

With the action methods of the controllers, you can specify the different options for the response types, and the model information that is returned in specific cases with the ProducesResponseType attribute (code file Async/BooksServiceSample/Controllers/BookChaptersController.cs):

```
[HttpPost]
[ProducesResponseType(typeof(BookChapter), 201)]
[ProducesResponseType(400)]
public async Task<IActionResult> PostBookChapterAsync(
```

```
    [FromBody]BookChapter chapter)
    {
      //...
    }
```

You can also write XML comments to the action methods of the controllers, and this will show up with the help pages. Of special interest is the response element that is used by Swagger to give more information about the possible outcome of the method (code file `Async/BooksServiceSample/Controllers/BookChaptersController.cs`):

```
/// <summary>
/// Creates a BookChapter
/// </summary>
/// <remarks>
/// Sample request:
///     POST api/bookchapters
///     {
///        Number: 42,
///        Title: "Sample Title",
///        Pages: 98
///     }
/// </remarks>
/// <param name="chapter"></param>
/// <returns>A newly created book chapter</returns>
/// <response code="201">Returns the newly created book chapter</response>
/// <response code="400">If the chapter is null</response>
[HttpPost]
[ProducesResponseType(typeof(BookChapter), 201)]
[ProducesResponseType(400)]
public async Task<IActionResult> PostBookChapterAsync(
[FromBody]BookChapter chapter)
{
    //...
}
```

To generate XML documentation from the XML comments, you need to enable the Build configuration of the Project Settings and select the XML Documentation File check box as shown in Figure 32-4. This setting specifies the `DocumentationFile` setting in the project configuration file (project file `Async/BooksServiceSample/BooksServiceSample.csproj`):

```
<PropertyGroup>
  <DocumentationFile>..\docs\BooksServiceSample.xml</DocumentationFile>
</PropertyGroup>
```

Swagger now also needs to be configured to use this generated XML documentation file when invoking the `AddSwaggerGen` method (code file `Async/BooksServiceSampleHost/Startup.cs`):

```
services.AddSwaggerGen(options =>
{
  options.IncludeXmlComments("../docs/BooksServiceSample.xml");
  options.SwaggerDoc("v2", new Info
  {
    Title = "Books Service API",
    Version = "v2",
    Description = "Sample service for Professional C# 7",
```

```
    Contact = new Contact { Name = "Christian Nagel",
      Url = "https://csharp.christiannagel.com" },
    License = new License { Name = "MIT License" }
  });
});
//...
```

With all this information added, Swagger shows the model containing annotations, the information from the XML documentation, and special information for the response codes, as shown in Figure 32-5.

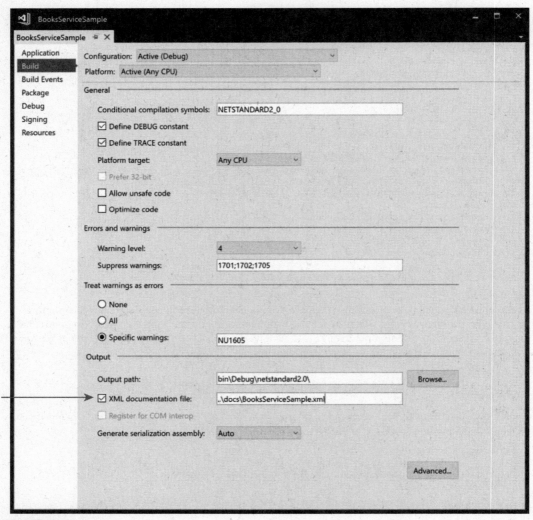

FIGURE 32-4

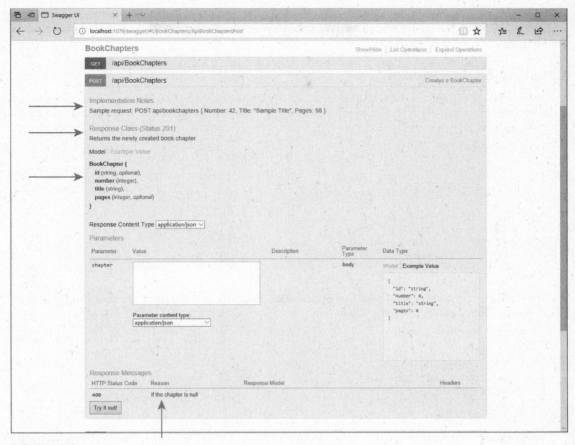

FIGURE 32-5

CREATING AND USING ODATA SERVICES

ASP.NET Core offers support for the Open Data Protocol (OData) with version 2.1. At the time of this writing, a Beta version of Web API OData exists. Please check the book's GitHub page for late updates.

OData offers CRUD access to a data source via the HTTP protocol. Sending a GET request retrieves a collection of entity data; a POST request creates a new entity; a PUT request updates existing entities; and a DELETE request removes an entity. In this chapter you've already seen the HTTP methods mapped to action methods in the controller. OData is built on JSON and AtomPub (an XML format) for the data serialization. You've seen direct support of JSON and XML with the ASP.NET Core as well. What OData offers more of is that every resource can be accessed with simple URI queries. For having a look into that, and how this is solved with ASP.NET Web API, let's get into a sample and start with a database.

With the service application `BooksODataService`, for offering OData, the NuGet package `Microsoft` `.AspNetCore.OData` needs to be added. The sample service enables you to query `Book` and `BookChapter` objects and the relation between.

Creating a Data Model

The sample service defines the `Book` and `BookChapter` classes for the model. The `Book` class defines simple properties and a one-to-many relationship with the `BookChapter` type (code file `BooksODataService/` `Models/Book.cs`):

```
public class Book
{
  public Book()
  {
    Chapters = new List<BookChapter>();
  }
  public int Id { get; set; }
  public string Isbn { get; set; }
  public string Title { get; set; }
  public string Publisher { get; set; }
  public List<BookChapter> Chapters { get; set; }
}
```

The `BookChapter` class defines simple properties and a many-to-one relation to the `Book` type (code file `BooksODataService/Models/BookChapter.cs`):

```
public class BookChapter
{
  public int Id { get; set; }
  public int BookId { get; set; }
  public Book Book { get; set; }
  public string Title { get; set; }
  public int Number { get; set; }
}
```

The `BooksContext` class defines the `Books` and `Chapters` properties as well as the definition of the SQL database relations (code file `BooksODataService/Models/BooksContext.cs`):

```
public class BooksContext: DbContext
{
  public DbSet<Book> Books { get; set; }
  public DbSet<BookChapter> Chapters { get; set; }
  protected override void OnModelCreating(ModelBuilder modelBuilder)
  {
    base.OnModelCreating(modelBuilder);
    var bookBuilder = modelBuilder.Entity<Book>();
    bookBuilder.HasMany(b => b.Chapters)
      .WithOne(c => c.Book)
      .HasForeignKey(c => c.BookId);
    bookBuilder.Property(b => b.Title)
      .HasMaxLength(120)
      .IsRequired();
    bookBuilder.Property(b => b.Publisher)
      .HasMaxLength(40)
      .IsRequired(false);
    bookBuilder.Property(b => b.Isbn)
      .HasMaxLength(20)
      .IsRequired(false);
    var chapterBuilder = modelBuilder.Entity<Chapter>();
    chapterBuilder.Property(c => c.Title)
      .HasMaxLength(120);
    chaptersBuilder.HasOne(c => c.Book)
```

```
            .WithMany(b => b.Chapters)
            .HasForeignKey(c => c.BookId);
    }
}
```

Creating the Database

To create the database on the fly with sample data, with the class `CreateBooksService` a `BooksContext` is injected, and the database is created if it doesn't exist yet. The `EnsureCreated` method on the `DatabaseFacade` class returned from the `Database` property of the `BooksContext` makes sure the database exists. The `EnsureCreated` method returns `true` if the database was created, and then the database is filled with some books by invoking the `CreateSampleBooks` method (code file `BooksODataService/Services/CreateBooksService.cs`):

```
public class CreateBooksService
{
    private readonly BooksContext _booksContext;
    public SampleBooks(BooksContext booksContext)
    {
        _booksContext = booksContext;
    }

    public void CreateDatabase()
    {
        bool created = _booksContext.Database.EnsureCreated();
        if (created)
        {
            CreateSampleBooks();
        }
    }
    //...
}
```

Sample data for the books and chapters is defined in the fields `_bookTitles`, `_bookIsbns`, and `_chapterTitles` (code file `BooksODataService/Services/CreateBooksService.cs`):

```
private string[] _bookTitles = new[]
{
    "Professional C# 7 and .NET Core 2",
    "Professional C# 6 and .NET Core 1.0",
    "Professional C# 5 and .NET 4.5.1"
};

private string[] _bookIsbns = new[]
{
    "978-1-119-44927-0",
    "978-1-119-09660-3",
    "978-1-118-83303-2"
};

private string[][] chapterTitles = new[]
{
    new []
    {
        ".NET Applications and Tools",
        "Core C#",
        "Objects and Types",
        "Object-Oriented Programming with C#",
        "Generics",
        //...
    }
}
```

The `CreateSampleBooks` method uses the data defined with the private fields to write this information to the database (code file `BooksODataService/Services/CreateBooksService.cs`):

```
private void CreateSampleBooks()
{
  for (int i = 0; i < _bookTitles.Length; i++)
  {
    var b = new Book
    {
      Title = _bookTitles[i],
      Isbn = _bookIsbns[i],
      Publisher = "Wrox Press"
    };
    var chapters = GetChapters(i, b);
    _booksContext.Chapters.AddRange(chapters);
    _booksContext.Books.Add(b);
  }
  int recordsChanged = _booksContext.SaveChanges();
}
```

OData Startup Code

With ASP.NET Core, you can easily add OData Services. Services need to be added to the dependency injection container, and middleware needs to be added, as you've already seen in the previous ASP.NET Core chapters.

In the `ConfigureServices` method of the `Startup` class, the `CreateBooksService` class is registered with the DI container, which allows for creating the database. When you use the `AddDbContext` method, the EF Core context is registered with the DI container, and it's configured to use SQL Server. For OData, the extension method `AddOData` method is invoked. This extension method registers multiple services needed by OData (code file `BooksODataService/Startup.cs`):

```
public void ConfigureServices(IServiceCollection services)
{
  services.AddMvc();
  services.AddTransient<CreateBooksService>();
  services.AddDbContext(options =>
  {
    options.UseSqlServer(Configuration.GetConnectionString("BooksConnection"));
  });
  services.AddOData();
}
```

The middleware is configured with the `Configure` method. The parameters of this method are changed to inject the `CreateBooksService`. The first line in the implementation creates the database if it doesn't exist yet. The OData relevant code follows with the creation of the `ODataConventionModelBuilder`. The `ODataConventionModelBuilder` maps .NET classes to an Entity Data Model (EDM). EDM models are used by OData to define what data is exposed by the service. The OData routes are configured by passing a `routeBuilder` parameter to the `UseMvc` extension method. The OData route is specified by invoking the `MapODataServiceRoute` extension method. The first parameter of this method specifies the name of the route; the second parameter specifies the route prefix, and the third parameter specifies the `IEdmModel` that is returned after creating the model using the previously created `ODataConventionModelBuilder` (code file `BooksODataService/Startup.cs`):

```
public void Configure(IApplicationBuilder app, IHostingEnvironment env,
  CreateBooksService sampleBooks)
{
  sampleBooks.CreateDatabase();

  if (env.IsDevelopment())
```

```
    {
        app.UseDeveloperExceptionPage();
    }

    var builder = new ODataConventionModelBuilder(app.ApplicationServices);
    builder.EntitySet<Book>("Books");
    builder.EntitySet<BookChapter>("BookChapters");

    app.UseMvc(routeBuilder =>
        routeBuilder.MapODataServiceRoute("ODataRoute", "odata",
            builder.GetEdmModel()));
}
```

Creating the OData Controller

The `BooksController` class needs to derive from the base class `ODataController`. In the following code snippet, the `Get` method returns a list of `Book` objects including the contained `BookChapter` objects. Instead of returning the `IEnumerable` interface, `IQueryable` is returned to enable OData queries. This interface is implemented by the `DbSet` class from EF Core. Returning a `List<T>` from in-memory data, you can convert this to `IQueryable` using the `AsQueryable` extension method. Returning a single result, for using OData functionality, you need to return a result of type `SingleResult`. The method `SingleResult.Create` creates a `SingleResult`, but needs `IQueryable` as parameter (code file `BooksODataService/Controllers/BooksController.cs`):

```
public class BooksController: ODataController
{
    private readonly BooksContext _booksContext;
    public BooksController(BooksContext booksContext)
    {
        _booksContext = booksContext;
    }

    public IQueryable<Book> Get() =>
        _booksContext.Books.Include(b => b.Chapters);

    [EnableQuery()]
    public SingleResult<Book> Get([FromODataUri] int id) =>
        SingleResult.Create(_booksContext.Books.Where(b => b.Id == key);
}
```

The `ChaptersController` is implemented similarly—returning a list of `BookChapter` objects and a single `BookChapter` (code file `BooksODataService/Controllers/ChaptersController.cs`):

```
public class ChaptersController : ODataController
{
    private readonly BooksContext _booksContext;
    public ChaptersController(BooksContext booksContext)
    {
        _booksContext = booksContext;
    }

    public IQueryable<BookChapter> Get() =>
        _booksContext.Chapters.Include(c => c.Book);

    [EnableQuery]
    public SingleResult<BookChapter> Get([FromODataUri] int key) =>
        SingleResult.Create(_booksContext.Chapters.Where(c => c.Id == key));
}
```

Other than the change with the `EnableQuery` attribute, no other special actions are needed for the controller.

OData Query

Now it's an easy task to get all the books from the database using this URL (the port number might differ on your system) with the `odata` route prefix as specified by the OData route in the `Startup` class and the name of the controller using conventions:

```
http://localhost:50000/odata/Books
```

The data returned consists of JSON data with the `Book` objects:

```
{"@odata.context":"http://localhost:6614/odata/$metadata#Books",
  "value":
    [{"Id":1,"Isbn":"978-1-119-44927-0",
      "Title":"Professional C# 7 and .NET Core 2"},
      "Publisher":"Wrox Press"}
    {"Id":2,"Isbn":"978-1-119-09660-3",
      "Title":"Professional C# 6 and .NET Core 1.0"},
      "Publisher":"Wrox Press"}
    {"Id":3,"Isbn":"978-1-118-83303-2",
      "Title":"Professional C# 5 and .NET 4.5.1"},
      "Publisher":"Wrox Press"}]}
```

Similarly, the `BookChapter` objects are returned with this URL:

```
http://localhost:50000/odata/Chapters
```

For getting just a single book, the identifier of the book can be passed with the URL. This request calls the `Get` action method passing the key that returns a single result:

```
http://localhost:50000/odata/Books(2)
```

You can access generated EDM information passing the `$metadata` string following the `odata` prefix:

```
http://localhost:50000/odata/$metadata
```

This returns EDM information generated from the model using the `ODataConventionModelBuilder`:

```xml
<?xml version="1.0" encoding="UTF-8"?>
<edmx:Edmx xmlns:edmx="http://docs.oasis-open.org/odata/ns/edmx" Version="4.0">
  <edmx:DataServices>
    <Schema xmlns="http://docs.oasis-open.org/odata/ns/edm"
      Namespace="BooksODataService.Models">
      <EntityType Name="Book">
        <Key>
          <PropertyRef Name="Id"/>
        </Key>
        <Property Name="Id" Nullable="false" Type="Edm.Int32"/>
        <Property Name="Isbn" Type="Edm.String"/>
        <Property Name="Title" Type="Edm.String"/>
        <NavigationProperty Name="Chapters"
          Type="Collection(BooksODataService.Models.BookChapter)"/>
      </EntityType>
      <EntityType Name="BookChapter">
        <Key>
          <PropertyRef Name="Id"/>
        </Key>
        <Property Name="Id" Nullable="false" Type="Edm.Int32"/>
        <Property Name="BookId" Type="Edm.Int32"/>
        <Property Name="Title" Type="Edm.String"/>
        <Property Name="Number" Nullable="false" Type="Edm.Int32"/>
        <NavigationProperty Name="Book" Type="BooksODataService.Models.Book">
          <ReferentialConstraint ReferencedProperty="Id" Property="BookId"/>
        </NavigationProperty>
      </EntityType>
    </Schema>
```

```xml
<Schema xmlns="http://docs.oasis-open.org/odata/ns/edm"
  Namespace="Default">
  <EntityContainer Name="Container">
    <EntitySet Name="Books" EntityType="BooksODataService.Models.Book">
      <NavigationPropertyBinding Target="Chapters" Path="Chapters"/>
    </EntitySet>
    <EntitySet Name="Chapters"
      EntityType="BooksODataService.Models.BookChapter">
      <NavigationPropertyBinding Target="Books" Path="Book"/>
    </EntitySet>
  </EntityContainer>
</Schema>
</edmx:DataServices>
</edmx:Edmx>
```

OData offers powerful query options that are supported by ASP.NET Core Web API. The OData specification allows passing parameters to the server for paging, filtering, and sorting. Let's get into these.

Each book has multiple results. With a URL query, it's also possible to just get the `Title` of the book:

```
http://localhost:50000/odata/Books(1)/Title
```

You can also use a relation to retrieve the book chapters:

```
http://localhost:50000/odata/Books(1)/Chapters
```

To return the number of book chapters in the database, you can use the `$count` function:

```
http://localhost:50000/odata/Chapters/$count
```

To return only a limited number of entities to the client, the client can limit the count using the `$top` parameter. This also allows paging by using `$skip`; for example, you can skip 3 and take 3:

```
http://localhost:50000/odata/Books?$top=3&$skip=3
```

There are many more named parameters for the `Queryable` attribute to restrict the query—for example, the maximum skip and top values, the maximum expansion depth, and restrictions for sorting.

To filter the requests based on properties of the `Book` type, the `$filter` option can be applied to properties of the `Book`. To filter only the books that are from the publisher Wrox Press, you can use the `eq` operator (equals) with `$filter`:

```
http://localhost:50000/odata/Books?$filter=Publisher eq 'Wrox Press'
```

You can use `lt` (less than) and `gt` (greater than) logical operators with `$filter` as well. This request returns only chapters with an id larger than 40:

```
http://localhost:50000/odata/Chapters?$filter=Id gt 40
```

To request a sorted result, the `$orderby` option defines the sorting order. Adding the `desc` keyword makes the sorting in descending order:

```
http://localhost:50000/odata/Book(2)/Chapters?$orderby=Title desc
```

All these query functions need to be explicitly enabled. You can enable OData functions and limits by applying the `EnableQuery` attribute on an action method, or globally by using `IRouteBuilder` extension methods. With the following code snippet, the `EnableQuery` attribute is applied to an action method. Here, the `AllowedQueryOptions` property is set to the enum value `AllowedQueryOptions.All`. You can also define a parameter of type `ODataQueryOptions` that you can check for the query options sent via the URL request and validate it programmatically:

```csharp
[EnableQuery(AllowedQueryOptions = AllowedQueryOptions.All)]
public IQueryable<Book> Get(ODataQueryOptions options)
{
  ODataValidationSettings settings = new ODataValidationSettings()
  {
```

```
        MaxExpansionDepth = 4
    };
    options.Validate(settings);
    var books = _booksContext.Books.Include(b => b.Chapters);
    return books;
}
```

The `EnableQuery` attribute allows you to specify the maximum number of nodes returned, the maximum top and skip values, the maximum page size, whether ordering is allowed based on which properties, as well as allowed logical and arithmetic operators, allowed functions, and allowed query options.

To configure the options globally with the `Startup` class, you can use the `SetDefaultQuerySettings` method to set the default values, and the `GetDefaultQuerySettings` method to retrieve the default values.

USING AZURE FUNCTIONS

When you create a Web API with ASP.NET Core, you can host it either with your own Windows server running IIS, a Linux server running Apache, or even the Kestrel server without another web server front end. You can use a Platform as a Service (PaaS) offering like Azure App Services to host your Web APIs. When you use Azure App Services, you pay for a server instance based on the number of CPU cores, the size of the RAM, and the storage size. These resources are reserved for your web apps (you can run multiple Web Apps in one App Service instance).

Based on your loads, there's another option for hosting a Web API: *Consumption plan* or an *App Service plan*. With the App Service plan, you can run the Azure Function in the same App Service you might already have. The other variant, the Consumption plan, is also known as *serverless* or *Function as a Service* (FaaS). With this option you pay for the number of requests and the memory needed for the seconds the Azure Function runs. Depending on the resources needed, this option can be a lot cheaper than using App Services, but it also can be more expensive. You also can run Azure Functions within an App Service instance, which changes this to the same payment plan as App Services.

When you use Azure Functions serverless, there's still a server behind it. The technology of Azure Functions is always based on App Services. However, when you use it serverless, you don't have control on this server, and you don't have CPU and memory reserved. That's why the pricing is different. For more information on the pricing model for Microsoft Azure, see `https://azure.microsoft.com/pricing/`.

Hosting the Azure Functions with FaaS, some limits apply. An Azure Function can run for a maximum of 10 minutes. The default timeout is 5 minutes, but this can be extended to 10 minutes. In case your Function needs to run for a longer time, you should host the Azure Function within an App Service plan.

Azure Functions are implemented with static methods. Static state is shared between multiple invocations. However, your Azure Function will be unloaded when it's not needed, and it's freshly loaded and instantiated when the HTTP request arrives again. A first request might need a longer time to return the result. An option like "always on" as with App Services is not available with the Consumption plan. Based on the load, additional machines can automatically be started with Azure Functions, which is another feature of the Consumption plan. Just make sure to not share state between invocations in static class members. State sharing can be done using external storage features, such as Azure Storage or SQL database.

Creating Azure Functions

If you created your Web API using services that are used via DI, and the services are defined in a .NET Standard library, you can easily use the same services from Azure Functions. When you use Visual Studio 2017, you can create an Azure Functions project by selecting the Cloud category in Add New Project and select the Azure Functions template. The Visual Studio Extension "Azure Functions and Web Jobs Tools" need to be installed for having this option available. After selecting this option, you can see the first configuration options shown in Figure 32-6.

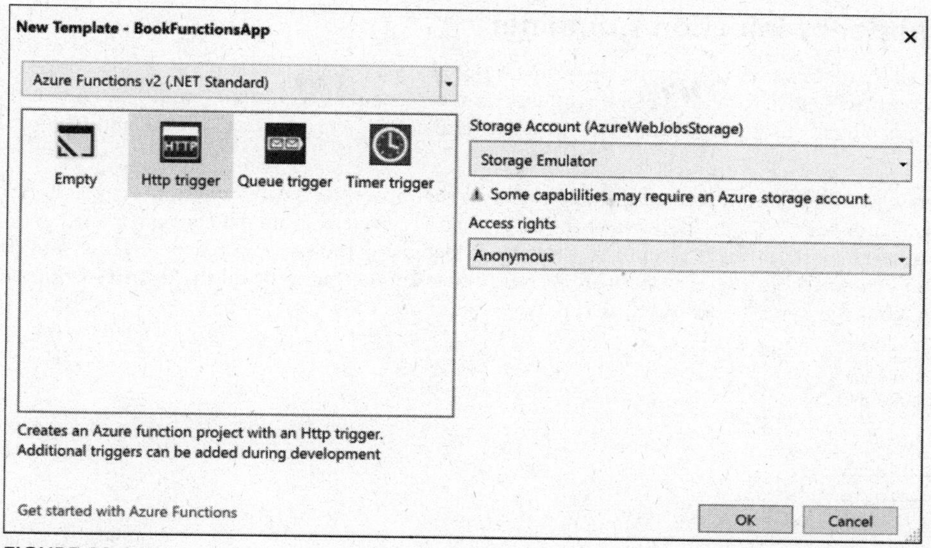

FIGURE 32-6

With these options, you can select the type of the trigger when the Function should be invoked. Many different triggers are available. Examples for these triggers are when some data is written to Azure Cosmos DB, a WebHook is activated, events happen on Microsoft Graph, an SMS arrives, events arrive at Event Hubs, events occur in Blob Storage, and many more. The most commonly used triggers show up in this dialog; these are HTTP requests, items in the Azure Storage Queue, and timing events. With Storage queues, a Function can start when a message arrives in a queue. With the Timer trigger, you can specify a time interval, or start the Function at specific times, such as every Saturday or on every 1st Monday of a month. Azure Functions are a good practice to run background functionality needed on a time interval—for example, a stored procedure to clean up or analyze data. As this chapter is about Web APIs, here the HTTP trigger will be used—a trigger that fires on receiving HTTP requests.

Other options to select are the version of Azure Functions. With Azure Functions 1.0, a .NET Framework library is created. Azure Functions 2.0 makes use of .NET Standard 2.0, which is typically the best option. You just need to pay attention to what triggers are available with which version you select. At the time of this writing, Webhooks are not available for Azure Functions 2.0, but they are available with Azure Functions 1.0.

You also need a Storage Account with Azure Functions. To create and test Azure Functions on your local system, a Storage Emulator is available. The Storage Account is needed to write log information from Azure Functions.

With Access rights you specify for whom the functions should be available. You can choose to invoke the Function to be accessible only from other Functions but not from the public. Here we select Anonymous for the access rights to access the Azure Function from the outside.

When you create the project, a .NET Standard 2.0 library that references the NuGet package `Microsoft .NET.Sdk.Functions` is created. The library contains the source file `Function1.cs` with a simple `Hello, name` implementation for a GET request. This will be changed in the next section to invoke the `BookChapterService` on GET, POST, and PUT requests.

Using a Dependency Injection Container

Although the `BookChaptersService` can be easily instantiated via a default constructor, this is not possible with many other services, such as with the `DbBookChaptersService` that requires a `BooksContext` in the constructor. That's why it's useful to add the DI container `Microsoft.Extensions.DependencyInjection` NuGet package.

The static constructor of the `BookFunction` class—the class that hosts the Azure Function— invokes the `ConfigureServices` method where the services are registered in the DI container, the `FeedSampleChapters` method where sample chapters are added using the `SampleChapters` class, and the `GetRequiredService` method where services are retrieved that are used later by all the features from the Azure Function (code file `Sync/BookFunctionApp/BookFunction.cs`):

```
public static class BookFunction
{
  static BookFunction()
  {
    ConfigureServices();
    FeedSampleChapters();
    GetRequiredServices();
  }
  //...
}
```

The `ConfigureServices` method configures services into the DI container, which is functionality you've already seen several times as you've used ASP.NET Core:

```
private static void ConfigureServices()
{
  var services = new ServiceCollection();
  services.AddSingleton<IBookChaptersService, BookChaptersService>();
  services.AddSingleton<SampleChapters>();
  ApplicationServices = services.BuildServiceProvider();
}

public static IServiceProvider ApplicationServices { get; private set; }
```

To have some sample chapters available without needing to create a database, the `CreateSampleChapters` method creates some in-memory chapters using the `BookChaptersService`. Remember to not share state in memory when using Azure Functions in production. I'm using it here, though, because it's easier to demonstrate for the example. For a short time, this data survives, but when the function is idle for a long enough time, or because of a higher load multiple instances are created simultaneously, you might get unexpected results. To use the database for a stable outcome, you just need to change the service registration from the `BookChaptersService` to the `DbBookChaptersService` and add the EF Core context as well:

```
private static void FeedSampleChapters()
{
  var sampleChapters =
    ApplicationServices.GetRequiredService<SampleChapters>();
  sampleChapters.CreateSampleChapters();
}
```

The `IBookChaptersService` is needed from GET, POST, and PUT requests to the Azure Function; that's why this service is retrieved and stored within a static variable. When you use the static constructor to invoke `GetRequiredServices`, this method is invoked every time the host is started again:

```
private static void GetRequiredServices()
{
  s_bookChaptersService =
    ApplicationServices.GetRequiredService<IBookChaptersService>();
}

private static IBookChaptersService s_bookChaptersService;
```

After the setup of the Azure Function is complete, you can step into implementing the main functionality in the next section.

Implementing GET, POST, and PUT Requests

The heart of an Azure Function is defined with the static `Run` method. The name of the function is defined by the `FunctionName` attribute. The parameters differ on the trigger type. The sample code specifies a trigger on an HTTP request using the `HttpTrigger` attribute. Because of this attribute, the first parameter of the `Run` method is of type `HttpRequest`. This type contains information on the HTTP request and allows sending an HTTP response. The `HttpTrigger` attribute specifies the `AuthorizationLevel` that you specified when creating the application and follows it with a variable parameter list of the HTTP verbs when the Azure Function should be activated. You also can specify route information to this Azure Function with parameters. Parameters you define with the route can also be added as parameters to the `Run` method. The last parameter of the `Run` method is the `TraceWriter`. This writer is used to log information into the Azure Storage account that was specified when you created the application. With the implementation of the `Run` method, a switch is done to invoke `DoGet`, `DoPost`, and `DoPut` methods based on the HTTP method received (code file `Sync/BookFunctionApp/BookFunction.cs`):

```
[FunctionName("BookFunction")]
public static IActionResult Run([HttpTrigger(AuthorizationLevel.Anonymous,
   "get", "post", "put", Route = "null")]HttpRequest req, TraceWriter log)
{
    log.Info("C# HTTP trigger function processed a request.");

    IActionResult result = null;
    switch (req.Method)
    {
      case "GET":
        result = DoGet(req);
        break;
      case "POST":
        result = DoPost(req);
        break;
      case "PUT":
        result = DoPut(req);
        break;
      default:
        result = new BadRequestResult();
        break;
    }
    return result;
}
```

With a GET request, the client can retrieve all book chapters or just a single one. If the HTTP URL contains a query with `Id` (`/?Id=Guid`), the identifier is parsed, and the `Find` method of the `IBookChaptersService` is invoked. Based on the result of the `Find` method, either a `NotFoundResult` is returned or an `OkObjectResult` that includes the book chapter in the HTTP body is returned. If `Id` is not part of the query, all book chapters are retrieved using the `GetAll` method, and the result list is put into the constructor of the `OkObjectResult` (code file `Sync/BookFunctionApp/BookFunction.cs`):

```
private static IActionResult DoGet(HttpRequest req)
{
    string id = req.Query["Id"];
    if (id != null)
    {
      Guid guid = Guid.Parse(id);
      var chapter = s_bookChaptersService.Find(guid);
      if (chapter == null)
      {
```

```
          return new NotFoundResult();
      }
      return new OkObjectResult(chapter);
    }
    else
    {
      var chapters = s_bookChaptersService.GetAll();
      return new OkObjectResult(chapters);
    }
}
```

With a HTTP POST request, the `DoPost` method is invoked. A POST request includes the new book chapter in the HTTP body of the request. The HTTP body can be retrieved by accessing the `Body` property of the `HttpRequest`. The `Body` property is of type `Stream`, which can be put into the constructor of the `StreamReader` class. With the `StreamReader`, the complete JSON string is retrieved by invoking `ReadToEnd`. This JSON string is then converted to a `BookChapter` with the help of `Newtonsoft.Json`. This converted `BookChapter` is then passed to the `Add` method of the `IBookChaptersService` (code file `Sync/BookFunctionApp/BookFunction.cs`):

```
private static IActionResult DoPost(HttpRequest req)
{
    string json = new StreamReader(req.Body).ReadToEnd();
    BookChapter chapter = JsonConvert.DeserializeObject<BookChapter>(json);
    s_bookChaptersService.Add(chapter);
    return new OkResult();
}
```

> **NOTE** *Streams are covered in detail in Chapter 22, "Files and Streams."*

The HTTP PUT request to update a `BookChapter` object is very similar to the previous HTTP POST request. This time just the `Update` method of the `IBookChaptersService` is invoked (code file `Sync/BookFunctionApp/BookFunction.cs`):

```
private static IActionResult DoPut(HttpRequest req)
{
    string json = new StreamReader(req.Body).ReadToEnd();
    BookChapter chapter = JsonConvert.DeserializeObject<BookChapter>(json);
    s_bookChaptersService.Update(chapter);
    return new OkResult();
}
```

With this in place, it's possible to use all the functionality you've already implemented when offering the service using ASP.NET Core. Using a small façade to the services, the services didn't require any changes. Let's run and publish the Azure Function next.

Running the Azure Function

When you run the application from Visual Studio, a console window shows the Azure Function logo (see Figure 32-7) and shows the output of the listener with the URL to access the HTTP service. Now you can use a browser to do GET requests and test the Azure Function. For testing POST and PUT requests, you can adapt the previously created client to invoke the Azure Function, or you can use a tool such as Postman (https://www.getpostman.com) to create POST and PUT requests. This is also a great tool for creating integration and running integration tests.

FIGURE 32-7

When you run the application, you'll find the file `function.json` in the `bin/Debug/netstandard2.0/BookFunction` directory. This file describes the Azure Function as it is deployed when you publish on Microsoft Azure. When you use the .NET Standard library, the information for `function.json` comes from the annotations you specify with the `Run` method; as you can see it lists the type of the trigger, configuration of the trigger, such as the HTTP methods, and the entry-point of the Azure Function:

```
{
    "generatedBy": "Microsoft.NET.Sdk.Functions.Generator-1.0.6",
    "configurationSource": "attributes",
    "bindings": [
      {
        "type": "httpTrigger",
        "methods": [
          "GET",
          "POST",
          "PUT"
        ],
        "authLevel": "anonymous",
        "name": "req"
      }
    ],
    "disabled": false,
    "scriptFile": "../bin/BookFunctionApp.dll",
    "entryPoint": "BookFunctionApp.BookFunction.Run"
}
```

When you successfully run the application locally, you can publish it to Microsoft Azure either in a Consumption or an App Service plan.

SUMMARY

This chapter described the features of the Web API using ASP.NET Core. This technology offers an easy way to create services that can be called from any client—be it JavaScript or a .NET client—with the help of the `HttpClient` class. Either JSON or XML can be returned, but nowadays JSON is the preferred format.

Dependency injection was already used in several chapters of this book, particularly in Chapter 20, "Dependency Injection." In this chapter you've seen how easy it is to replace a memory-based repository using a dictionary with a repository by making use of EF Core.

This chapter also introduced you to OData, with which it's easy to reference data in a tree using resource identifiers.

Besides using ASP.NET Core to host the Web API, you've also used the same services created earlier with Azure Functions. Services have been implemented independent of a hosting technology, and thus it was an easy task to create a small façade and host the services from Azure Functions, which offer a different cost model when hosting a Web API on Microsoft Azure.

The next chapter is the start of Part IV of the book and is the first chapter of several that cover how to use XAML to create Windows apps.

PART IV
Apps

33

Windows Apps

WHAT'S IN THIS CHAPTER?

- ➤ Introduction to XAML
- ➤ Controls
- ➤ Compiled data binding
- ➤ Navigation
- ➤ Layout panels

WROX.COM CODE DOWNLOADS FOR THIS CHAPTER

The wrox.com code downloads for this chapter are found at www.wrox.com on the Download Code tab. The source code is also available at https://github.com/ProfessionalCSharp/ProfessionalCSharp7 in the directory Windows.

The code for this chapter is divided into the following major examples:

- ➤ IntroXAML
- ➤ ControlsSample
- ➤ ParallaxViewSample
- ➤ PageLayouts
- ➤ NavigationSample
- ➤ LayoutPanels

INTRODUCING WINDOWS APPS

Windows Apps make use of .NET Core, but there's a big difference with web apps and ASP.NET Core. Windows apps run only on the Windows platform, on Windows 10. You can use these apps not only for the desktop, but also for Xbox, HoloLens, and Raspberry PI.

> **NOTE** *For creating apps using XAML on iPhone and Android, you should read Chapter 37, "Xamarin.Forms." However, be sure to read this chapter first, because the Xamarin.Forms chapter only explains the differences.*

Windows Runtime

Windows apps also make use of the Windows Runtime (WinRT). The Windows Runtime is a platform created using C++ with a new generation of COM objects. With this, the Windows Runtime is not only available for .NET applications but also for C++ and applications created with JavaScript. For accessing the Windows Runtime from these different platforms, a compatibility layer was created: the *language projection*. With language projection, the API offered by the Windows Runtime looks like a .NET API.

That the runtime looks like .NET is because of the language projection. Metadata of the Windows Runtime is created in the same form as with .NET. You can use the same tools (for example, ildasm) to read metadata information from the Windows Runtime. Dynamically reading metadata already has a history with COM. There, metadata was accessible from type libraries. This metadata technology was not as powerful as metadata was when it was implemented with .NET. With .NET, metadata is extensible with custom attributes and can be accessed using reflection. (Read more about this in Chapter 16, "Reflection, Metadata, and Dynamic Programming.") The Windows Runtime is now using the same format for its metadata as .NET. Thus, you can open the `.winmd` files (metadata files for the Windows Runtime) using the ildasm command line to see the API calls with their parameters. You can find the Windows Metadata files in the directory `%ProgramFiles(x86)\Windows Kits\10\References\`.

Language projection maps Windows Runtime types to .NET types. For example, in the file `Windows.Foundation.FoundationContract.winmd` you'll find the `IIterable` and `IIterator` interfaces in the namespace `Windows.Foundation.Collections`. These interfaces look very similar to the .NET interfaces `IEnumerable` and `IEnumerator`. Indeed, they are automatically mapped with language projection.

The Windows Runtime doesn't contain any collections. Instead, collections are implemented by the different platforms that use the Windows Runtime—for example, C++, JavaScript, and .NET.

Not all the interfaces of the contracts can be directly mapped. Chapter 22, "Files and Streams," showed files and streams with the Windows Runtime from the namespace `Windows.Storage.Streams`. To use the Windows streams together with .NET streams, you can use extension methods such as `AsStream`, `AsStreamForRead`, and `AsStreamForWrite`.

> **NOTE** *Creating Windows apps, your app uses .NET Core APIs and Windows Runtime APIs.*

Hello, Windows

Let's start creating a new Windows App with Visual Studio 2017. Select the Universal Windows Platform project. The first question asked is the target and minimum platform to support (see Figure 33-1). With every newer platform version, you get more features. However, you need to pay attention what version of Windows 10 your users have. They can't install and run your Windows 10 app if the platform version is not supported.

With the target version you select, you specify the API version that can be used by the app. With the minimum version you specify the build version where the app can be installed to and run. If you set the target and minimum version to different values, you need to write adaptive code. Before invoking an API, you need to make sure the API is available on the supported builds. Without the newer API available, you can reduce the features from the app, or you can offer different features based on the build the user is running.

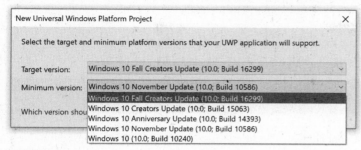

FIGURE 33-1

The following table lists the Windows 10 versions, the build numbers, their release dates, and features from the build. From the API documentation you sometimes need the version, and sometimes the build number to know if an API is available for your support requirements. This table will help.

VERSION	BUILD	BUILD NAME	RELEASE DATE	FEATURES
1507	10240		July 2015	Better adaptive layouts, compiled data binding, declarative incremental rendering of lists (phases), deferred UI loading, `RelativePanel`, `SplitPanel`, `CalendarDatePicker`, Cortana, and app-to-app communication
1511	10586	November Update	November 2015	Windows Hello, Storage APIs updated, and ORTC (Object Real-Time Communication) for real-time audio/video calls
1607	14393	Anniversary Update	July 2016	New ink controls, Cortana APIs, animated GIF with XAML images, composition interactions, and connected animations
1703	15063	Creators Update	March 2017	New composition APIs, ink support for protractor and ruler, images on a map, and `RadialController` (Surface Dial)
1709	16299	Fall Creators Update	October 2017	.NET Standard 2.0, Fluent Design, conditional XAML, User Activities, My People, and new UI controls (`ColorPicker`, `NavigationView`, `PersonPicture`, `RatingControl`)

> **NOTE** *To use .NET Standard 2.0 libraries, the app needs to have build version 16299 as minimum build number. Most sample apps of the book have both the target and minimum version set to 16299.*

Application Manifest

You can change the build target and minimum version numbers with the project properties. Windows apps have another important configuration for the packaging. The file `Package.appxmanifest` can be configured using the Package Manifest Editor.

With the Application settings (see Figure 33-2), you can configure the display name of the application, the default language, supported rotations of the device, and automatic periodic tile updates.

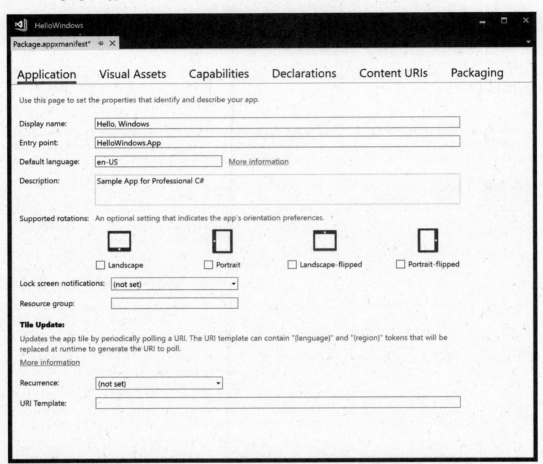

FIGURE 33-2

In the Visual Assets tab, you can configure all the different icons of the application—tile images for different tile sizes, different device resolutions, a splash screen, and a package logo for the Windows Store.

Settings in the Capabilities tab (see Figure 33-3) allow you to select the capabilities needed by the app. A capability that is by default selected is the Internet (Client) capability. In case you need to do network requests to a server, this capability needs to be turned on. Other capabilities enable you to access location information, access the microphone and the webcam, access different folders on the file system such as the Music Library, the Pictures Library, or the Videos Library.

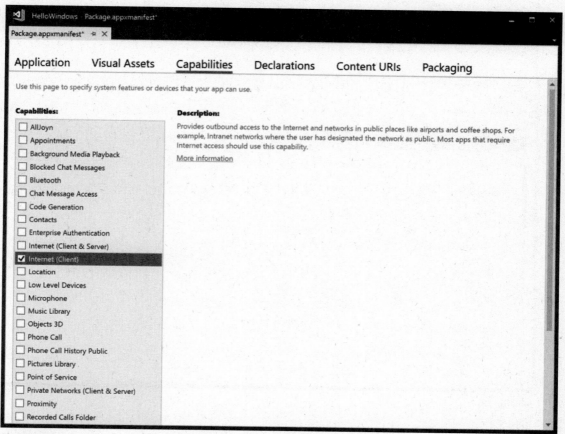

FIGURE 33-3

With the Declarations settings (see Figure 33-4), you can add features of the application Windows needs to know about. For example, when sharing data from one app, Windows shows the apps that accept the shared data. For this, the app needs to be registered as Share Target. Registering apps as a share target, to be activatable via a protocol or a file type extension, to communicate between app services, and more, settings in declarations are available.

The Content URIs tab allow for deep linking within the app. Here, you can specify URLs to open pages in the app. Finally, with the Packaging tab, you can configure the package name, version, and information about the publisher.

> **NOTE** *Several of the capabilities and declarations are discussed in this book. Read Chapter 36, "Advanced Windows Apps," for more information about such features.*

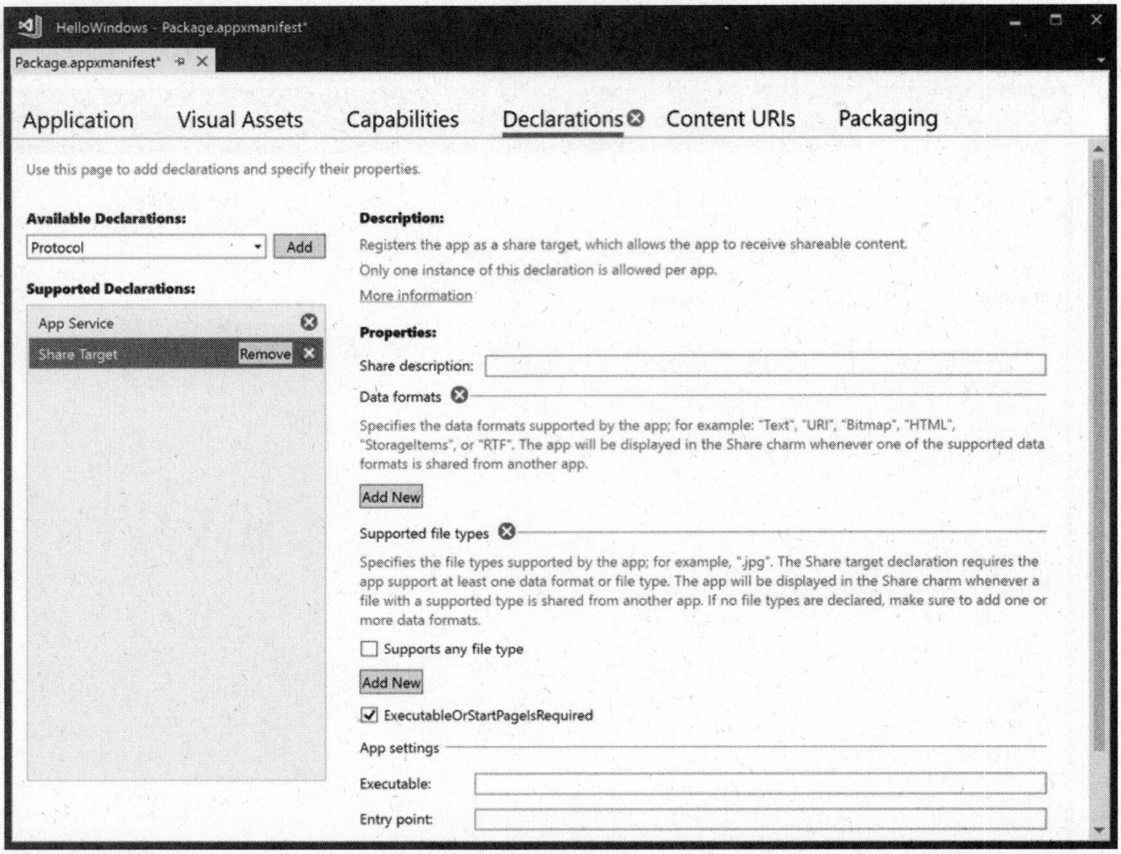

FIGURE 33-4

Application Startup

The entry point into the application, HelloWindows.App, is defined in the application manifest, as shown in the previous section. The App class derives from the Application base class and contains an implementation to handle the Suspending event (code file HelloWindows/App.xaml.cs):

```
sealed partial class App : Application
{
  public App()
  {
    this.InitializeComponent();
    this.Suspending += OnSuspending;
  }
  //...
```

The OnLaunched method is overridden. This method is invoked when the application is started by the user. As you learned from the application manifest, there are different ways to start the application. The application can be started directly from the user, but also started when the user shares data from another application. Different activation methods can be overridden for such scenarios.

When the user launches the application, different scenarios exist as well. The application can be started fresh, or, if the application was previously suspended, it can be started again. When the application is launched and there's no current `Frame`, a new `Frame` is created. Frames can be used for navigation between pages. Pages contain the UI controls, and frames offer navigation between pages. After the frame is instantiated, navigation happens by invoking the `Navigate` method to the `MainPage` (code file `HelloWindows/App.xaml.cs`):

```
protected override void OnLaunched(LaunchActivatedEventArgs e)
{
  Frame rootFrame = Window.Current.Content as Frame;

  if (rootFrame == null)
  {
    rootFrame = new Frame();

    rootFrame.NavigationFailed += OnNavigationFailed;

    if (e.PreviousExecutionState == ApplicationExecutionState.Terminated)
    {
      //TODO: Load state from previously suspended application
    }

    Window.Current.Content = rootFrame;
  }

  if (e.PrelaunchActivated == false)
  {
    if (rootFrame.Content == null)
    {
      rootFrame.Navigate(typeof(MainPage), e.Arguments);
    }
    Window.Current.Activate();
  }
}
```

Main Page

Let's add a `Button` with a message to the `MainPage`. The user interface is defined using XAML (eXtensible Application Markup Language), a language that extends XML with some functionality. With the `Button` control, the `Content` is set to show a simple string, the `Click` event is assigned to the `OnButtonClicked` event handler, and the properties `HorizontalAlignment`, `VerticalAlignment`, and `Margin` are used to let the button take the complete space of the grid except for a margin outside of the button (code file `HelloWindows/MainPage.xaml`):

```
<Grid Background="{ThemeResource ApplicationPageBackgroundThemeBrush}">
  <Button
    Content="Hello, Windows!"
    Click="OnButtonClicked"
    HorizontalAlignment="Stretch"
    VerticalAlignment="Stretch"
    Margin="20" />
</Grid>
```

In the code-behind file, a `MessageDialog` is shown with the `OnButtonClicked` event handler. To not block the user interface, the `ShowAsync` method is only available as an asynchronous method.

```
private async void OnButtonClicked(object sender, RoutedEventArgs e)
{
  await new MessageDialog("Hello, Windows!").ShowAsync();
}
```

When you build, deploy, and run the application, the user interface looks as shown in Figure 33-5. Windows apps not only need to be built before running but they also need to be deployed. Deployment is automatically done from Visual Studio on a build when the Deploy configuration is set in the Configuration Manager (Build ⇨ Configuration Manager) (see Figure 33-6). If you don't deploy the app on build, you need to deploy it after build by using the Deploy option in the context menu when you select the project in Solution Explorer, or you can deploy all the projects in the solution with the Visual Studio by selecting Build ⇨ Deploy Solution.

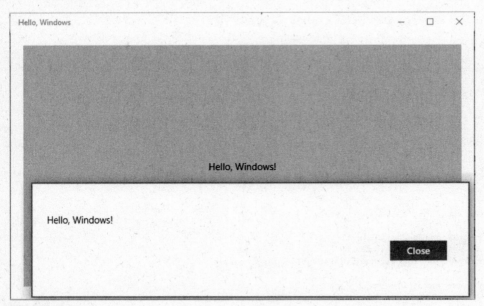

FIGURE 33-5

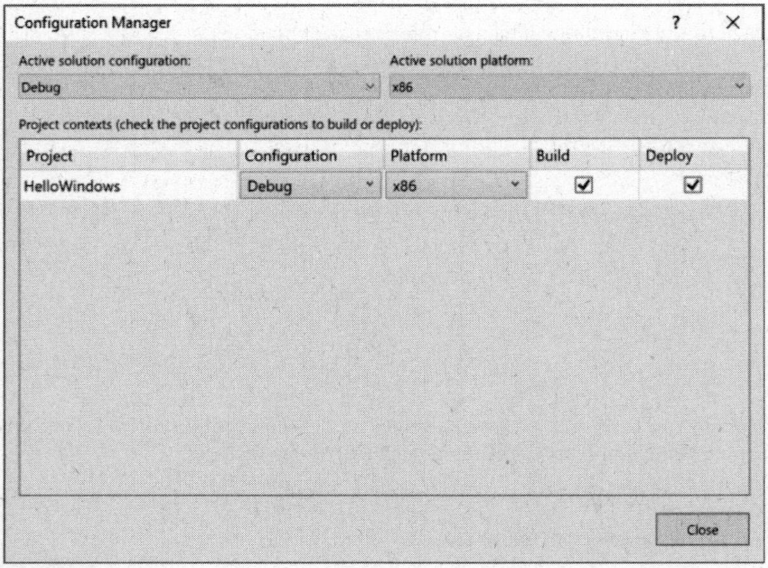

Configuration Manager			? ×

Active solution configuration:

Debug

Active solution platform:

x86

Project contexts (check the project configurations to build or deploy):

Project	Configuration	Platform	Build	Deploy
HelloWindows	Debug	x86	☑	☑

Close

FIGURE 33-6

INTRO TO XAML

When creating web applications with ASP.NET Core, you need to know HTML, CSS, and JavaScript in addition to knowing C#. When you create Windows apps, you need to know XAML besides C#. XAML is not only used to create Windows apps but it's also used with Windows Presentation Foundation (WPF), Windows Workflow Foundation (WF), and cross-platform apps with Xamarin.

Anything that can be done with XAML can also be done with C#. Every XAML element is represented with a class, and thus can be accessed from C#. Why is there a need for XAML? XAML is typically used to describe objects and their properties, and this is possible in a deep hierarchy. For example, a `Page` contains a `Grid` control; the `Grid` control contains a `StackPanel` and other controls; and the `StackPanel` contains `Button` and `TextBox` controls. XAML makes it easy to describe such a hierarchy and assign properties of objects via XML attributes or elements.

XAML allows writing code in a declarative manner. Whereas C# is mainly an imperative programming language, XAML allows for declarative definitions. With an imperative programming language (like C#), the compiler compiles a C# for loop to a `for` loop with the Intermediate Language (IL) code. With a declarative programming language, you declaratively declare what should be done, but not how it should be done.

> **NOTE** *C# is not a pure imperative programming language. When using LINQ, you can write syntax in a declarative way. The LINQ provider for Entity Framework Core (EF Core) translates a LINQ query to a SQL statement. This is covered in Chapter 26, "Entity Framework Core."*

XAML is an XML syntax, but it defines several enhancements to XML. With these enhancements, XAML is still valid XML. The enhancements just have special meaning and special functionality. Examples for the enhancements are curly brackets within XML attributes. For XML, this is still just a string and thus valid XML. For XAML, this is a markup extension.

Before you can use XAML efficiently, you need to understand some important features of this programming language. Let's step into an introduction for these features in the next sections:

➤ **Dependency properties**—From the outside, dependency properties look like normal properties. However, they need less storage and implement change notification.

➤ **Routed events**—From the outside, routed events look like normal .NET events. However, you use custom event implementation with add and remove accessors to allow bubbling and tunneling. Events can tunnel from outer controls to inner controls, and bubble from inner controls to outer controls.

➤ **Attached properties**—With attached properties it is possible to add properties to other controls. For example, the `Button` control doesn't have a property to position it within a `Grid` control in a specific row and column. With XAML, it looks like it has such a property.

➤ **Markup extensions**—Writing XML attributes requires less coding compared to XML elements. However, XML attributes can only be strings; you can write much more powerful syntax with XML elements. To reduce the amount of code that needs to be written, markup extensions allow writing powerful syntax within attributes.

> **NOTE** *.NET properties are explained in Chapter 3, "Objects and Types." Events, including writing custom events with add and remove accessors, are explained in Chapter 8, "Delegates, Lambdas, and Events." The power of XML is explained in Bonus Chapter 2, "XML and JSON," which you can find online.*

XAML Standard

WPF, UWP, and Xamarin used (partly still uses) a different syntax for XAML elements. For example, with WPF and UWP a Button has a Content property, while the Button from Xamarin has a Text property. With WPF and UWP a StackPanel can be used to arrange multiple elements. A similar control with Xamarin is the StackLayout.

For making it easier to switch between different UI technology stacks, the XAML Standard is defined. See https://github.com/Microsoft/xaml-standard/ for the actual state of the standard.

Mapping Elements to Classes

Behind every XAML element there's a class with properties, methods, and events. As previously mentioned, you can create UI elements either with C# code or using XAML. Let's get into an example. With the following code snippet, a StackPanel is defined that contains a Button control. Using XML attributes, the Button has the Content property and the Click event assigned. The Content property just contains a simple string, whereas the Click event references the address of the method OnButtonClick. The XML attribute x:Name is used to declare a name to the Button control that can be used both from XAML as well as from the C# code-behind file (code file XAMLIntro/MainPage.xaml):

```
<StackPanel x:Name="stackPanel1">
  <Button Content="Click Me!" x:Name="button1" Click="OnButtonClick" />
  <!-- ... -->
</StackPanel>
```

On top of the page, you can see the Page element with the XML attribute x:Class. This defines the name of the class where the XAML compiler generates partial code. With the code-behind file in Visual Studio you can see the part of this class that you can modify (code file XAMLIntro/MainPage.xaml):

```
<Page
    x:Class="XAMLIntro.MainPage"
    <!-- ... -->
```

The code-behind file contains part of the class MainPage (the part that is not generated by the XAML compiler). In the constructor, the method InitializeComponent is invoked. The implementation of InitializeComponent is created by the XAML compiler. This method loads the XAML file and converts it to an object as specified with the root element in the XAML file. The OnButtonClick method is a handler for the Click event of the Button that was previously created in XAML code. The implementation just opens up a MessageDialog (code file XAMLIntro/MainPage.xaml.cs):

```
public sealed partial class MainPage : Page
{
  public MainPage()
  {
    this.InitializeComponent();
  }

  private async void OnButtonClick(object sender, RoutedEventArgs e)
  {
    await new MessageDialog("button 1 clicked").ShowAsync();
  }
}
```

Now let's create a new object from the Button class from C# code, and add it to the existing StackPanel. In the following code snippet, the constructor of the MainPage was modified to create a new Button, set the Content property, and assign a Lambda expression to the Click event. Finally, the newly created button is added to the Children of the StackPanel (code file XAMLIntro/MainPage.xaml.cs):

```
public MainPage()
{
  this.InitializeComponent();
```

```
        var button2 = new Button
        {
            Content = "created dynamically"
        };
        button2.Click += async (sender, e) =>
            await new MessageDialog("button 2 clicked").ShowAsync();
        stackPanel1.Children.Add(button2);
    }
```

As you've seen, XAML is just another way to deal with objects, properties, and events. The next sections show you the advantages of XAML for user interfaces.

Using Custom .NET Classes with XAML

To use custom .NET classes within XAML code, you can use a simple POCO class, there are no special requirements on the class definition. You just have to add the .NET namespace to the XAML declaration. To demonstrate this, a simple `Person` class with the `FirstName` and `LastName` properties is defined as shown here (code file `DataLib/Person.cs`):

```
public class Person
{
    public string FirstName { get; set; }
    public string LastName { get; set; }
    public override string ToString() => $"{FirstName} {LastName}";
}
```

In XAML, an XML namespace alias named `datalib` is defined that maps to the .NET namespace `DataLib` in the assembly `DataLib`. With this alias in place, it's now possible to use all classes from this namespace by using the alias as a prefix for the elements.

In the XAML code, you add a `ListBox` that contains items of type `Person`. Using XAML attributes, you set the values of the properties `FirstName` and `LastName`. When you run the application, the output of the `ToString` method is shown inside the `ListBox` (code file `XAMLIntro/MainPage.xaml`):

```
<Page x:Class="XamlIntro.MainPage"
    xmlns="http://schemas.microsoft.com/winfx/2006/xaml/presentation"
    xmlns:x="http://schemas.microsoft.com/winfx/2006/xaml"
    xmlns:local="using:XAMLIntro"
    xmlns:datalib="using:DataLib"
    xmlns:d="http://schemas.microsoft.com/expression/blend/2008"
      xmlns:mc="http://schemas.openxmlformats.org/markup-compatibility/2006"
      mc:Ignorable="d">
    <StackPanel x:Name="stackPanel1" >
        <Button Content="Click Me!" x:Name="button1" Click="OnButtonClick">
        <ListBox>
            <datalib:Person FirstName="Stephanie" LastName="Nagel" />
            <datalib:Person FirstName="Matthias" LastName="Nagel" />
            <datalib:Person FirstName="Katharina" LastName="Nagel" />
        </ListBox>
    </StackPanel>
</Window>
```

> **NOTE** *WPF and Xamarin use* `clr-namespace` *within the alias declaration instead of using. The reason is that XAML with UWP is neither based on nor restricted to .NET. You can use native C++ with XAML as well, and thus* `clr` *(Common Language Runtime) would not be a good fit.*

Setting Properties as Attributes

With the previous XAML samples, properties of classes have been set by using XML attributes. To set properties from XAML, you can use XML attributes as long as the property type can be represented as a string or there is a conversion from a string to the property type. The following code snippet sets the `Content` and `Background` properties of the `Button` element with XML attributes:

```
<Button Content="Click Me!" Background="LightGoldenrodYellow" />
```

With the previous code snippet, the `Content` property is of type `object` and thus accepts a string. The `Background` property is of type `Brush`. A string is converted to a `SolidColorBrush` type that derives from `Brush`.

Using Properties as Elements

It's also always possible to use the element syntax to supply the value for properties. You can set the `Background` property of the `Button` class with the child element `Button.Background`. The following code snippet defines the `Button` with the same result as shown earlier with attributes:

```
<Button>
  Click Me!
  <Button.Background>
    <SolidColorBrush Color="LightGoldenrodYellow" />
  </Button.Background>
</Button>
```

Using elements instead of attributes allows you to apply more complex brushes to the `Background` property, such as a `LinearGradientBrush`, as shown in the following example (code file `XAMLIntro/MainWindow .xaml`):

```
<Button x:Name="button1" Click="OnButtonClick">
  Click Me!
  <Button.Background>
    <LinearGradientBrush StartPoint="0.5,0.0" EndPoint="0.5, 1.0">
      <GradientStop Offset="0" Color="Yellow" />
      <GradientStop Offset="0.3" Color="Orange" />
      <GradientStop Offset="0.7" Color="Red" />
      <GradientStop Offset="1" Color="DarkRed" />
    </LinearGradientBrush>
  </Button.Background>
</Button>
```

> **NOTE** *When setting the content in the sample, neither the* `Content` *attribute nor a* `Button.Content` *element is used to write the content; instead, the content is written directly as a child value to the* `Button` *element. That's possible because with a base class of the* `Button` *class* (`ContentControl`)*, the* `ContentProperty` *attribute is applied with* `[ContentProperty("Content")]`*. This attribute marks the* `Content` *property as a* `ContentProperty`*. This way the direct child of the XAML element is applied to the* `Content` *property.*

Dependency Properties

XAML uses dependency properties for data binding, animations, property change notification, styling, and so forth. What's the reason for dependency properties? Let's assume you create a class with 100 properties of type `int`, and this class is instantiated 100 times on a single form. How much memory is needed?

Because an int has a size of 4 bytes, the result is 4 × 100 × 100 = 40,000 bytes. Did you already have a look at the properties of an XAML element? Because of the huge inheritance hierarchy, a XAML element defines hundreds of properties. The property types are not simple int types, but a lot more complex types instead. I think you can imagine that such properties could consume a huge amount of memory. However, usually you change only the values of a few of these properties, and most of the properties keep their default values that are common for all instances. This dilemma is solved with dependency properties. With dependency properties, an object memory is not allocated for every property and every instance. Instead, the dependency property system manages a dictionary of all properties and allocates memory only if a value is changed. Otherwise, the default value is shared between all instances.

Dependency properties also have built-in support for change notification. With normal properties, you need to implement the interface INotifyPropertyChanged for change notification. How the interface INotifyPropertyChanged can be implemented is explained later in this chapter in the section "Data Binding." Such a change mechanism is built-in with dependency properties. For data binding, the property of the UI element that is bound to the source of a .NET property must be a dependency property. Now, let's get into the details of dependency properties.

From the outside, a dependency property looks like a normal .NET property. However, with a normal .NET property you usually also define the data member that is accessed by the get and set accessors of the property:

```
private int _value;
public int Value
{
  get => _value;
  Set => _value = value;
}
```

That's not the case with dependency properties. A dependency property usually has a get and set accessor of a property as well. This is common with normal properties. However, with the implementation of the get and set accessors, the methods GetValue and SetValue are invoked. GetValue and SetValue are members of the base class DependencyObject, which also stipulates a requirement for dependency objects—that they must be implemented in a class that derives from DependencyObject.

With a dependency property, the data member is kept inside an internal collection that is managed by the base class and only allocates data if the value changes. With unchanged values the data can be shared between different instances or base classes. The GetValue and SetValue methods require a DependencyProperty argument. This argument is defined by a static member of the class that has the same name as the property appended to the term Property. With the property Value, the static member has the name ValueProperty. DependencyProperty.Register is a helper method that registers the property in the dependency property system. The following code snippet uses the Register method with four arguments to define the name of the property, the type of the property, the type of the owner—that is, the class MyDependencyObject—and the default value with the help of PropertyMetadata (code file DependencyObjectSample/MyDependencyObject.cs):

```
public class MyDependencyObject: DependencyObject
{
  public int Value
  {
    get => (int)GetValue(ValueProperty);
    set => SetValue(ValueProperty, value);
  }

  public static readonly DependencyProperty ValueProperty =
    DependencyProperty.Register("Value", typeof(int),
      typeof(MyDependencyObject), new PropertyMetadata(0));
}
```

Creating a Dependency Property

This section looks at an example that defines not one but three dependency properties. The class `MyDependencyObject` defines the dependency properties `Value`, `Minimum`, and `Maximum`. All of these properties are dependency properties that are registered with the method `DependencyProperty.Register`. The methods `GetValue` and `SetValue` are members of the base class `DependencyObject`. For the `Minimum` and `Maximum` properties, default values are defined that can be set with the `DependencyProperty.Register` method and a fourth argument to set the `PropertyMetadata`. Using a constructor with one parameter, `PropertyMetadata`, the `Minimum` property is set to `0`, and the `Maximum` property is set to `100` (code file `DependencyObjectSample/MyDependencyObject.cs`):

```
public class MyDependencyObject: DependencyObject
{
  public int Value
  {
    get => (int)GetValue(ValueProperty);
    set => SetValue(ValueProperty, value);
  }

  public static readonly DependencyProperty ValueProperty =
    DependencyProperty.Register(nameof(Value), typeof(int),
      typeof(MyDependencyObject));

  public int Minimum
  {
    get => (int)GetValue(MinimumProperty);
    set => SetValue(MinimumProperty, value);
  }

  public static readonly DependencyProperty MinimumProperty =
    DependencyProperty.Register(nameof(Minimum), typeof(int),
      typeof(MyDependencyObject), new PropertyMetadata(0));

  public int Maximum
  {
    get => (int)GetValue(MaximumProperty);
    set => SetValue(MaximumProperty, value);
  }

  public static readonly DependencyProperty MaximumProperty =
    DependencyProperty.Register(nameof(Maximum), typeof(int),
      typeof(MyDependencyObject), new PropertyMetadata(100));
}
```

> **NOTE** *Within the implementation of the* `get` *and* `set` *property accessors, you should not do anything other than invoke the* `GetValue` *and* `SetValue` *methods. Using the dependency properties, the property values can be accessed from the outside with the* `GetValue` *and* `SetValue` *methods, which is also done from UWP; therefore, the strongly typed property accessors might not be invoked at all. They are just here for convenience, so you can use the normal property syntax from your custom code.*

Value Changed Callbacks and Events

To get some information on value changes, dependency properties also support value changed callbacks. You can add a `DependencyPropertyChanged` event handler to the `DependencyProperty.Register` method that is invoked when the property value changes. In the sample code, the handler method `OnValueChanged` is assigned to the `PropertyChangedCallback` of the `PropertyMetadata` object. In the `OnValueChanged` method, you can access the old and new values of the property with the `DependencyPropertyChangedEventArgs` argument (code file `DependencyObjectSample/MyDependencyObject.cs`):

```
public class MyDependencyObject: DependencyObject
{
  public int Value
  {
    get => (int)GetValue(ValueProperty);
    set => SetValue(ValueProperty, value);
  }

  public static readonly DependencyProperty ValueProperty =
    DependencyProperty.Register(nameof(Value), typeof(int),
      typeof(MyDependencyObject),
        new PropertyMetadata(0, OnValueChanged, CoerceValue));

  private static void OnValueChanged(DependencyObject obj,
    DependencyPropertyChangedEventArgs e)
  {
    int oldValue = (int)e.OldValue;
    int newValue = (int)e.NewValue;
    //...
  }
}
```

Routed Events

Chapter 8 covers the .NET event model. With default implemented events, when an event is fired, the handler directly connected to the event is invoked. When you use UI technologies, there are different requirements for event handling. With some events it should be possible to create a handler with a container control and react to events coming from children controls. Such an implementation is possible by creating a custom implementation for .NET events, as shown in Chapter 8 with `add` and `remove` accessors.

UWP offers routed events. The sample app defines a UI consisting of a `CheckBox` that, if selected, stops the routing; a `Button` control with the `Tapped` event set to the `OnTappedButton` handler method; and a `Grid` with the `Tapped` event set to the `OnTappedGrid` handler. The `Tapped` event is one of the routed events of Universal Windows apps. This event can be fired with the mouse, touch, and pen devices (code file `RoutedEvents/MainPage.xaml`):

```
<Grid Tapped="OnTappedGrid">
  <Grid.RowDefinitions>
    <RowDefinition Height="auto" />
    <RowDefinition Height="auto" />
    <RowDefinition />
  </Grid.RowDefinitions>
  <StackPanel Grid.Row="0" Orientation="Horizontal">
    <CheckBox x:Name="CheckStopRouting">Stop Routing</CheckBox>
    <Button Click="OnCleanStatus">Clean Status</Button>
  </StackPanel>
  <Button Grid.Row="1" Tapped="OnTappedButton">Tap me!</Button>
  <TextBlock Grid.Row="2" Margin="20" x:Name="textStatus" />
</Grid>
```

The `OnTappedXX` handler methods write status information to a `TextBlock` to show the handler method as well as the control that was the original source of the event (code file `RoutedEventsUWP/MainPage.xaml.cs`):

```
private void OnTappedButton(object sender, TappedRoutedEventArgs e)
{
  ShowStatus(nameof(OnTappedButton), e);
  e.Handled = CheckStopRouting.IsChecked == true;
}
```

```
private void OnTappedGrid(object sender, TappedRoutedEventArgs e)
{
  ShowStatus(nameof(OnTappedGrid), e);
  e.Handled = CheckStopRouting.IsChecked == true;
}

private void ShowStatus(string status, RoutedEventArgs e)
{
  textStatus.Text += $"{status} {e.OriginalSource.GetType().Name}";
  textStatus.Text += "\r\n";
}

private void OnCleanStatus(object sender, RoutedEventArgs e)
{
  textStatus.Text = string.Empty;
}
```

When you run the application, and click outside the button but within the grid, you see the `OnTappedGrid` event handled with the `Grid` control as the originating source:

```
OnTappedGrid Grid
```

Click in the middle of the button to see that the event is routed. The first handler that is invoked is `OnTappedButton` followed by `OnTappedGrid`:

```
OnTappedButton TextBlock
OnTappedGrid TextBlock
```

What's also interesting is that the event source is not the `Button`, but a `TextBlock`. The reason is that the button is styled using a `TextBlock` to contain the button text. If you click to other positions within the button, you can also see `Grid` or `ContentPresenter` as the originating event source. The `Grid` and `ContentPresenter` are other controls the button is created from.

If you check the check box `CheckStopRouting` before clicking on the button, you can see that the event is no longer routed because the `Handled` property of the event arguments is set to `true`:

```
OnTappedButton TextBlock
```

Within the Microsoft API documentation of the events, you can see whether an event type is routing within the remarks section of the documentation. With Universal Windows apps, tapped, drag and drop, key up and key down, pointer, focus, and manipulation events are routed events.

Attached Properties

Whereas dependency properties are properties available with a specific type, with an attached property you can define properties for other types. Some container controls define attached properties for their children; for example, if the `DockPanel` control is used, a `Dock` property is available for its children. The `Grid` control defines `Row` and `Column` properties.

The following code snippet demonstrates how this looks in XAML. The `Button` class doesn't have the property `Grid.Row`, but it's attached from the `Grid`:

```
<Grid>
  <Grid.RowDefinitions>
    <RowDefinition />
    <RowDefinition />
  </Grid.RowDefinitions>
  <Button Content="First" Grid.Row="0" Background="Yellow" />
  <Button Content="Second" Grid.Row="1" Background="Blue" />
</Grid>
```

Attached properties are defined very similarly to dependency properties, as shown in the next example. The class that defines the attached properties must derive from the base class `DependencyObject` and defines a normal property, where the `get` and `set` accessors invoke the methods `GetValue` and `SetValue` of the base class. This is where the similarities end. Instead of invoking the method `Register` with the `DependencyProperty` class, now `RegisterAttached` is invoked, which registers an attached property that is available with every element (code file `AttachedProperty/MyAttachedProperyProvider.cs`):

```
public class MyAttachedPropertyProvider: DependencyObject
{
  public static readonly DependencyProperty MySampleProperty =
    DependencyProperty.RegisterAttached
      "MySample",
      typeof(string),
      typeof(MyAttachedPropertyProvider),
      new PropertyMetadata(string.Empty));

  public static void SetMySample(UIElement element, string value) =>
    element.SetValue(MySampleProperty, value);

  public static int GetMyProperty(UIElement element) =>
    (string)element.GetValue(MySampleProperty);
}
```

> **NOTE** *You might assume that `Grid.Row` can be added only to elements within a `Grid`. That's not the case. Attached properties can be added to any element. However, no one would use this property value. The `Grid` is aware of this property and reads it from its children elements to arrange them. It doesn't read it from children of children.*

In the XAML code, the attached property can now be attached to any elements. The second `Button` control, named button2, has the property `MyAttachedPropertyProvider.MySample` attached to it and the value 42 assigned (code file `AttachedProperty/MainPage.xaml`):

```
<Grid x:Name="grid1">
  <Grid.RowDefinitions>
    <RowDefinition Height="Auto" />
    <RowDefinition Height="Auto" />
    <RowDefinition Height="*" />
  </Grid.RowDefinitions>
  <Button Grid.Row="0" x:Name="button1" Content="Button 1" />
  <Button Grid.Row="1" x:Name="button2" Content="Button 2"
    local:MyAttachedPropertyProvider.MySample="42" />
  <ListBox Grid.Row="2" x:Name="list1" />
</Grid>
```

Doing the same in code-behind it is necessary to invoke the static method `SetMyProperty` of the class `MyAttachedPropertyProvider`. It's not possible to extend the class `Button` with a property. The method `SetProperty` gets a `UIElement` instance that should be extended by the property and the value. In the following code snippet, the property is attached to button1 and the value is set to `sample value` (code file `AttachedProperty/MainPage.xaml.cs`):

```
public MainPage()
{
  InitializeComponent();
  MyAttachedPropertyProvider.SetMySample(button1, "sample value");
  //...
}
```

To read attached properties that are assigned to elements, you can use the VisualTreeHelper to iterate every element in the hierarchy and try to read its attached properties. The VisualTreeHelper is used to read the visual tree of the elements during runtime. The method GetChildrenCount returns the count of the child elements. To access a child, you can use the method GetChild and pass the index for an element with the second argument. This method then returns the element. The implementation of the GetChildren method returns elements only if they are of type FrameworkElement (or derived thereof), and if the predicate passed with the Func argument returns true (code file AttachedProperty/MainPage.xaml.cs):

```
private IEnumerable<FrameworkElement> GetChildren(FrameworkElement element,
  Func<FrameworkElement, bool> pred)
{
  int childrenCount = VisualTreeHelper.GetChildrenCount(rootElement);
  for (int i = 0; i < childrenCount; i++)
  {
    var child = VisualTreeHelper.GetChild(rootElement, i) as FrameworkElement;
    if (child != null && pred(child))
    {
      yield return child;
    }
  }
}
```

The method GetChildren is now used from within the constructor of the page to add all elements with an attached property to the ListBox control (code file AttachedProperty/MainPage.xaml.cs):

```
public MainPage()
{
  InitializeComponent();
  MyAttachedPropertyProvider.SetMySample(button1, "sample value");
  foreach (var item in GetChildren(grid1, e =>
    MyAttachedPropertyProvider.GetMySample(e) != string.Empty))
  {
    list1.Items.Add(
      $"{item.Name}: {MyAttachedPropertyProvider.GetMySample(item)}");
  }
}
```

When you run the application, you see the two button controls in the ListBox with these values:

```
button1: sample value
button2: 42
```

> **NOTE** *Later in this chapter in the section "Layout Panels," you can see attached properties with many container controls such as* Canvas, Grid, *and* RelativePanel.

Markup Extensions

With markup extensions you can extend XAML with either element or attribute syntax. If an XML attribute contains curly brackets, that's a sign of a markup extension. Often markup extensions with attributes are used as shorthand notation instead of using elements.

One example of such a markup extension is StaticResourceExtension, which finds resources. Here's a resource of a linear gradient brush with the key gradientBrush1 (code file MarkupExtensions/MainPage .xaml):

```
<Page.Resources>
  <LinearGradientBrush x:Key="gradientBrush1" StartPoint="0.5,0.0"
    EndPoint="0.5, 1.0">
```

```
        <GradientStop Offset="0" Color="Yellow" />
        <GradientStop Offset="0.3" Color="Orange" />
        <GradientStop Offset="0.7" Color="Red" />
        <GradientStop Offset="1" Color="DarkRed" />
      </LinearGradientBrush>
    </Page.Resources>
```

This resource can be referenced by using the `StaticResourceExtension` with attribute syntax to set the `Background` property of a `Button`. Attribute syntax is defined by curly brackets and the name of the extension class without the `Extension` suffix:

```
    <Button Content="Test" Background="{StaticResource gradientBrush1}" />
```

Windows apps do not support all the markup extensions that have been available with WPF, but there are some. `StaticResource` and `ThemeResource` are discussed in Chapter 35, "Styling XAML Apps," and the binding markup extensions `Binding` and `x:Bind` are discussed later in this chapter in the section "Data Binding." Starting with the Fall Creators Update (Windows 10 build 16299), creating custom markup extensions is also supported, as shown next.

Custom Markup Extensions

Custom markup extensions allow you to add your own features within the curly brackets in XAML code. You can create custom binding, condition-based evaluation, or a simple calculator, as shown in the next sample.

The Calculator markup extension enables you to calculate two values using add, subtract, multiply, and divide operations. A markup extension is really simple: The class name contains the `Extension` postfix, and it derives from the base class `MarkupExtension` and overrides the method `ProvideValue`. With `ProvideValue`, the markup extension returns the value or object that is assigned to the property where the markup is defined. The type of the returned value is defined by the `MarkupExtensionReturnType` attribute. The following code snippet shows the implementation of the Calculator markup extension. This extension defines three properties that can be set: properties for `X`, `Y`, and the `Operation` that should be applied to `X` and `Y`. The operation is defined using an enum. In the implementation of the `ProvideValue` method, an operation is applied to `X` and `Y`, and the result is returned (code file `CustomMarkupExtension/CalculatorExtension.cs`):

```csharp
public enum Operation
{
  Add,
  Subtract,
  Multiply,
  Divide
}

[MarkupExtensionReturnType(ReturnType = typeof(string))]
public class CalculatorExtension : MarkupExtension
{
  public double X { get; set; }
  public double Y { get; set; }
  public Operation Operation { get; set; }

  protected override object ProvideValue()
  {
    double result = 0;
    switch (Operation)
    {
      case Operation.Add:
        result = X + Y;
        break;
      case Operation.Subtract:
```

```
            result = X - Y;
            break;
        case Operation.Multiply:
            result = X * Y;
            break;
        case Operation.Divide:
            result = X / Y;
            break;
        default:
            break;
        }
        return result.ToString();
    }
}
```

Now, the Calculator markup extension can be used with the XML attribute syntax. Here, the markup extension is initialized for setting the properties. The return string is applied to the Text property of a TextBlock (code file CustomMarkupExtension/MainPage.xaml):

```
<TextBlock Text="{local:Calculator Operation=Add, X=38, Y=4}" />
```

Using the markup extension syntax, the name Extension is not used. This postfix is automatically applied. This is, of course, different if the CalculatorExtension class is just used to instantiate it as child of the Text property, and set the properties of the extension (code file CustomMarkupExtension/MainPage.xaml):

```
<TextBlock>
  <TextBlock.Text>
    <local:CalculatorExtension Operation="Multiply" X="7" Y="6" />
  </TextBlock.Text>
</TextBlock>
```

When you run the application, the value 42 is returned from both operations used.

Conditional XAML

In case you need to support multiple builds of Windows 10, but still use newer features, such as custom markup extensions, you need to write adaptive code that doesn't crash the application when you invoke a newer API on an older version of Windows. With adaptive code, you first verify whether an API is available before it is invoked, and you offer alternatives for older versions of Windows. Such conditional code is possible with XAML as well, as long as your minimum build version to support is build 15063. Older versions are not supported by conditional XAML.

Conditional XAML is done by specifying XAML namespaces that are only available based on specific conditions. For example, the namespace alias contract5 is only available when the IsApiContractPresent passing the Windows.Foundation.UniversalApiContract with version 5 returns true. Otherwise, the XAML compiler ignores this namespace alias and does not create elements or attributes with this alias. The ? after the namespace defines the condition when the alias is valid (XAML file ConditionalXAML/MainPage.xaml):

```
xmlns:contract5=
    "http://schemas.microsoft.com/winfx/2006/xaml/presentation?
     IsApiContractPresent(Windows.Foundation.UniversalApiContract, 5)"
```

The APIs defined in the following table can be used with conditional XAML. With the method IsApiContractPresent, you can check whether a specific API from a specific version number is available. The IsTypePresent returns true if the specified type of a control is available, and IsPropertyPresent returns true if a specific property of a control is available. Inverse methods also are implemented with all these methods. The inverse methods return the inverse Boolean value. For example, if IsApiContractPresent returns true, the method IsApiContractNotPresent returns false. You might wonder why inverse methods are necessary, and you can't just use the C# ! operator. The reason is that XAML doesn't have such an operator.

METHOD	INVERSE METHOD
IsApiContractPresent(contract, version)	IsApiContractNotPresent(contract, version)
IsTypePresent(type)	IsTypeNotPresent(type)
IsPropertyPresent(type, property)	IsPropertyNotPresent(type, property)

The namespace alias can now be used with elements and attributes from the http://schemas .microsoft.com/winfx/2006/xaml/presentation namespace—for example, with the Text property of the TextBlock:

```
<TextBlock x:Name=text1 contract5:Text="contract 5 present" />
```

With the C# code, you can do the similar functionality using the IsApiContractPresent method defined in the ApiInformation class from the namespace Windows.Foundation.Metadata (code file ConditionalXAML/MainPage.xaml.cs):

```
if (ApiInformation.IsApiContractPresent(
  "Windows.Foundation.UniversalApiContract", 5))
{
  text1.Text = "contract 5 present";
}
```

In XAML code, you can't set the Text property multiple times without making sure that the property is only set once with a specific version. Otherwise you'll get the error that the Text property is defined multiple times. That's why inverse methods are defined that can be used to set alias namespaces.

What you can do is set multiple namespaces, depending on the contract that's available (XAML file ConditionalXAML/MainPage.xaml):

```
xmlns:contract5=
"http://schemas.microsoft.com/winfx/2006/xaml/presentation?
  IsApiContractPresent(Windows.Foundation.UniversalApiContract, 5)"
xmlns:notcontract5="http://schemas.microsoft.com/winfx/2006/xaml/presentation?
  IsApiContractNotPresent(Windows.Foundation.UniversalApiContract, 5)"
```

The different namespace aliases are now used to set the Text property of the TextBlock. With these alias definitions, it's sure that only one of these is defined (XAML file ConditionalXAML/MainPage.xaml):

```
<TextBlock
  x:Name="text1"
  contract5:Text="contract 5 present"
  notcontract5:Text="contract 5 not present" />
```

Where can you find the names of the API contracts? With every Windows Runtime API documented at https://docs.microsoft.com/uwp/api, the documentation lists the API contract with the version number when the API was introduced. Windows.Foundation.UniversalApiContract itself is a reference contract that references other contracts. You can find all the contracts in the folder %ProgramFiles(x86)%\ Windows Kits\10\References. You can use the ildasm tool to read the .md files that contain the contract information.

CONTROLS

Because of the many controls available for Windows Apps, it's good to know about the hierarchy of controls and UI classes some specific base classes. Knowing these makes it easier to work with the UWP controls, where you also know what you can do with these types.

Let's get into the hierarchy of the UI classes with Windows Apps.

➤ **DependencyObject**—This class is on top of the hierarchy for the Windows Runtime XAML elements. Every class that derives from `DependencyObject` can have dependency properties. You've already seen dependency properties with the introduction to XAML in this chapter.

➤ **UIElement**—This is the base class for elements with visual appearance. This class offers functionality for user interaction, such as pointer events (`PointerPressed`, `PointerMoved`, and so on), key handling events (`KeyDown`, `KeyUp`), focus events (`GotFocus`, `LostFocus`), pointer captures (`CapturePointer`, `PointerCanceled`, and so on), drag and drop (`DragOver`, `Drop`, and so on). This class also offers the new `Lights` property that's been available since build 15063 for highlighting via light.

➤ **FrameworkElement**—The class `FrameworkElement` derives from `UIElement` and adds more features. Classes deriving from `FrameworkElement` can participate in the layout system. The properties `MinWidth`, `MinHeight`, `Height`, and `Width` are defined by the `FrameworkElement` class. Lifetime events are defined by `FrameworkElement` as well: `Loaded`, `SizeChanged`, `Unloaded`, are some of these events. Data binding features are another group of functionalities defined by the `FrameworkElement` class. This class defines the `DataContext`, `DataContextChanged`, `SetBinding`, and `GetBindingExpression` APIs.

➤ **Control**—The class `Control` derives from `FrameworkElement` and is the base class for UI controls—for example, `TextBox`, `Hub`, `DatePicker`, `SearchBox`, `UserControl`, and others. Controls typically have a default style with a `ControlTemplate` that is assigned to the `Template` property. The `Control` class defines overridable `On*` methods for the events defined by the base class `UIElement`. Controls define a `TabIndex`; properties for the foreground, background, and the border (`Foreground`, `Background`, `BorderBrush`, `BorderThickness`); and properties to enable it and use keyboard tabs to access it (`IsTabStop`, `TabIndex`).

➤ **ContentControl**—The class `ContentControl` derives from `Control` and enables you to have any content as child of the control. Examples of `ContentControl` are `AppBar`, `Frame`, `ButtonBase`, `GroupItem`, and `ToolTip` controls. The `ContentControl` defines the `Content` property where any content can be assigned, a `ContentTemplate` property to assign a `DataTemplate`, a `ContentTemplateSelector` to dynamically assign a data template, and the `ContentTransitions` property for simple animations.

➤ **ItemsControl**—Contrary to the `ContentControl`, which can only have one content, the `ItemsControl` can view a content list. While the `ContentControl` defines the `Content` property to list its child items, the `ItemsControl` defines this with the `Items` property. Both `ContentControl` and `ItemsControl` derive from the base class `Control`. The `ItemsControl` can display a fixed number of items or items that are bound through a list. Controls that derive from `ItemsControl` are `ListView`, `GridView`, `ListBox`, `Pivot`, and `Selector`.

➤ **Panel**—Another class that can serve as a container of items is the `Panel` class. This class derives from the base class `FrameworkElement`. Panels are used to position and arrange child objects. Examples of classes that derive from `Panel` are `Canvas`, `Grid`, `StackPanel`, `VariableSizedWrapGrid`, `VirtualizingPanel`, `ItemsStackPanel`, `ItemsWrapGrid`, and `RelativePanel`. Panel controls are discussed later in the section "Layout Panels."

➤ **RangeBase**—This class derives from the `Control` class and is the base class for `ProgressBar`, `ScrollBar`, and `Slider`. `RangeBase` defines the `Value` property for the current value, `Minimum` and `Maximum` properties, and a `ValueChanged` event handler.

➤ **FlyoutBase**—This class directly derives from `DependencyObject` and enables you to show user interfaces on top of other elements—in other words, they "fly out."

> **NOTE** *Control templates are covered in detail in Chapter 35.*

After going through the main categories and the hierarchy of the types, let's get into the details.

Framework-Derived UI Elements

Some elements aren't really controls, but they're still UI elements that are classes that derive from `FrameworkElement`. These classes don't allow a custom look by specifying a template. The following categories of UI elements have this base class: presenters, media elements, and text display elements.

CLASS	DESCRIPTION
Border Viewbox ContentPresenter ItemsPresenter	Presenters are classes that are not interactive, but they still offer a visual appearance. The `Border` class defines a border around a single control (which can be a `Grid` containing several other controls). The `Viewbox` enables you to stretch and scale the child element. The `ContentPresenter` is used within a `ControlTemplate`. It defines where the content of the control will be displayed. An `ItemsPresenter` is used to define the position of items within an `ItemsControl`. Control and item templates are discussed in Chapter 35.
TextBlock RichTextBlock	The `TextBlock` and `RichTextBlock` controls are used to display text. Text input is not possible with these controls; they are just used for display. The `TextBlock` control not only allows assigning simple text, but also allows more complex text elements such as paragraphs and inline elements. The `RichTextBlock` supports overflow as well. Be aware that the `RichTextBlock` doesn't support working with RTF (rich text files). You need to use the `RichEditBox` instead. Using these controls to display flow text is shown in Chapter 36.
Ellipse Polygon Polyline Path Rectangle	The `Shape` class derives from `FrameworkElement`. `Shape` itself is a base class for `Ellipse`, `Polygon`, `Polyline`, `Path`, `Rectangle`, and others. These classes are used to draw vectors to the screen. These classes are shown in Chapter 35.
Panel	The `Panel` class derives from `FrameworkElement`. Panels are used to organize the UI elements on the screen. The different panels available that derive from the `Panel` class are discussed later in this chapter in the section "Layout Panels."
CaptureElement	`CaptureElement` is a class that renders a stream from a capture device, such as a camera or a webcam. This class is used in Chapter 36.
InkCanvas	The `InkCanvas` control is the drawing area to draw with a pen and ink. Read Chapter 36 for more information on using ink.
Image	The `Image` control is used to display images. This control supports displaying images of these formats: JPEG, PNG, BMP, GIF, TIFF, JPEG XR, ICO, and SVG. Support for Scalable Vector Graphics (SVG) has been available since Windows version 1703; support for animated GIF has been available since Windows version 1607.
ParallaxView	The `ParallaxView` is a new control with build 16299 to create a parallax effect while scrolling.

Presenters

With the `PresentersPage`, some of the presenters controls are used—`Border` and `Viewbox`. The border is used to group two `TextBox` elements. Because the `Border` element can contain only one child, a `StackPanel` is used within the `Border` element. The `Border` specifies a `Background`, a `BorderBrush`, and a `BorderThickness`.

The two `Viewbox` controls in the following code snippet are used to stretch a `Button` control. The first `Viewbox` makes a stretch of mode `Fill` to completely fill the `Button` within the `Viewbox`, whereas the second `Viewbox` makes a stretch of mode `Uniform`. With `Uniform`, the aspect ratio is maintained (code file `ControlsSamples/Views/PresentersPage.xaml`):

```xml
<Border Background="LightSeaGreen" BorderBrush="DarkGreen" BorderThickness="12"
  Margin="12" Padding="8">
  <StackPanel Orientation="Vertical">
    <TextBox Header="Title" x:Name="Title" FontSize="34" />
    <TextBox Header="Publisher" x:Name="Publisher" FontSize="34" />
  </StackPanel>
</Border>
<Viewbox Grid.Row="1" Stretch="Fill" StretchDirection="Both">
  <Button Margin="4" FontSize="14">Button with fill stretch</Button>
</Viewbox>
<Viewbox Grid.Row="2" Stretch="Uniform" StretchDirection="Both">
  <Button Margin="4" FontSize="14">Button with uniform stretch</Button>
</Viewbox>
```

Figure 33-7 shows the presenters page from the running app. Here you can see how the `TextBox` controls are surrounded, and the buttons are shown in the two different `Viewbox` configurations.

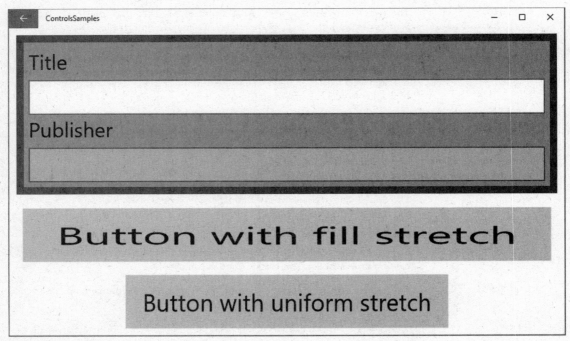

FIGURE 33-7

> **NOTE** Control-*derived classes have an implicit border that you can customize with the* BorderThickness *and* BorderBrush *properties.*

Parallax

The ParallaxView gives a parallax effect. With a parallax effect you can display a list in the foreground, and a picture in the background. The picture in the background moves slower than the foreground to give a three-dimensional effect, known as the *parallax effect*.

The sample application ParallaxViewSample demonstrates this effect while you can use a slider to increase or decrease the effect.

What's shown in the sample app is a simple model of LunchMenu objects (code file ParallaxViewSample/Models/LunchMenu.cs):

```csharp
public class LunchMenu
{
  public int MenuId { get; set; }
  public string Text { get; set; }
  public string ImageUrl { get; set; }
}
```

The ParallaxView control defines an Image as child element. You can create other shapes for the background, as well. The Source property of the ParallaxView is bound to a ListView control. The ListView control displays a list of items and is bound to a list of LunchMenu objects. To define the effect with the ParallaxView, you need to set the HorizontalShift and VerticalShift properties. With the source code as shown, the ListView scrolls vertically, so let's discuss the vertical movement. With a VerticalShift set to 0, there's no parallax effect. Setting the value to 100 means that the ParallaxView is configured to be 100 pixels smaller than the ListView, thus the ListView scrolls faster. The following code snippet binds the HorizontalShift and VerticalShift properties to a Slider, thus you can configure the effect while the app runs (code file ParallaxViewSample/MainPage.xaml):

```xml
<StackPanel Orientation="Vertical">
  <Slider x:Name="HorizontalSlider" Header="Horizontal Shift" Minimum="0"
    Maximum="1000" Value="0" />
  <Slider x:Name="VerticalSlider" Header="Vertical Shift" Minimum="0"
    Maximum="1000" Value="0" />
</StackPanel>

<ParallaxView Source="{x:Bind MenuItems}" Grid.Row="1"
            HorizontalShift="{x:Bind HorizontalSlider.Value, Mode=OneWay}"
            VerticalShift="{x:Bind VerticalSlider.Value, Mode=OneWay}">
  <Image Source="https://kantinem101.blob.core.windows.net/menuimages/" +
    "Hirschragout_1024">
  </Image>
</ParallaxView>

<ListView HorizontalAlignment="Center" x:Name="MenuItems"
  ItemsSource="{x:Bind Menus, Mode=OneWay}" SelectionMode="None"  Grid.Row="1">
  <ListView.ItemTemplate>
    <DataTemplate x:DataType="model:LunchMenu">
      <Grid Margin="12">
        <Image Width="300" Source="{x:Bind ImageUrl, Mode=OneWay}" />
        <TextBlock Margin="8" VerticalAlignment="Bottom"
          HorizontalTextAlignment="Center" Text="{x:Bind Text, Mode=OneWay}"
          Style="{StaticResource SubtitleTextBlockStyle}" FontWeight="Bold" />
      </Grid>
    </DataTemplate>
  </ListView.ItemTemplate>
</ListView>
```

> **NOTE** *Data binding is explained in detail later in this chapter in the section "Data Binding."*

When you run the app, you can see how the background image moves with different speeds compared to the foreground as shown in Figure 33-8.

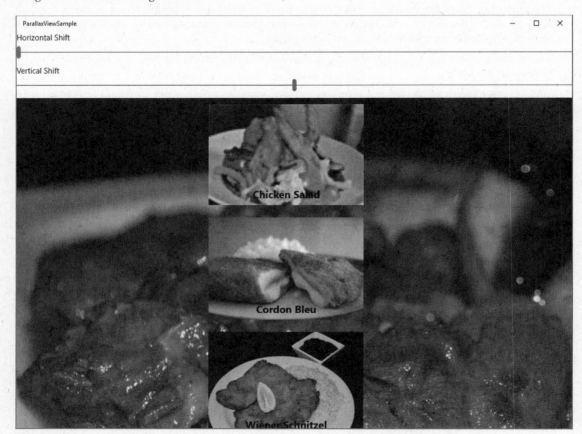

FIGURE 33-8

To see the parallax effect in horizontal mode, you can change the ListView to scroll horizontally. To do this, you can change the ItemsPanel of the ListView as shown in the following code snippet. In the downloadable code sample, you need to uncomment this ListView configuration to make it active (code file ParallaxViewSample/MainPage.xaml):

```
<ListView HorizontalAlignment="Center" x:Name="MenuItems"
   ItemsSource="{x:Bind Menus, Mode=OneWay}" SelectionMode="None"
   ScrollViewer.VerticalScrollBarVisibility="Disabled"
   ScrollViewer.VerticalScrollMode="Disabled" Grid.Row="1"
   ScrollViewer.HorizontalScrollBarVisibility="auto"
   ScrollViewer.HorizontalScrollMode="Enabled">
   <ListView.ItemsPanel>
     <ItemsPanelTemplate>
```

```
        <ItemsStackPanel Orientation="Horizontal" />
      </ItemsPanelTemplate>
    </ListView.ItemsPanel>
    <ListView.ItemTemplate>
      <DataTemplate x:DataType="model:LunchMenu">
        <Grid Margin="12">
          <Image Width="300" Source="{x:Bind ImageUrl, Mode=OneWay}" />
          <TextBlock Margin="8" VerticalAlignment="Bottom"
            HorizontalTextAlignment="Center" Text="{x:Bind Text, Mode=OneWay}"
            Style="{StaticResource SubtitleTextBlockStyle}" FontWeight="Bold" />
        </Grid>
      </DataTemplate>
    </ListView.ItemTemplate>
  </ListView>
```

Figure 33-9 shows the horizontal version of the `ParallaxViewSample`.

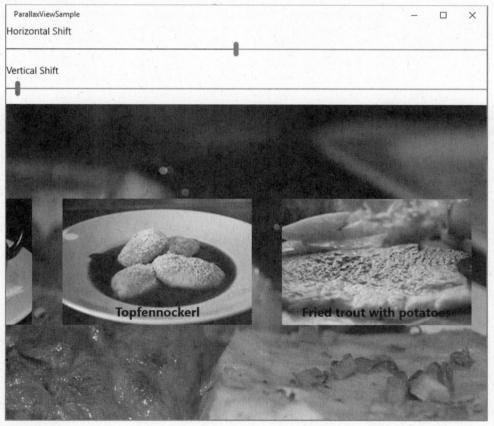

FIGURE 33-9

Control-Derived Controls

Controls that directly derive from the base class `Control` belong to this category. The following table describes some of these controls.

CONTROL	DESCRIPTION
TextBox	This control is used to display simple, unformatted text. This control can be used for user input. The Text property contains the user input. PlaceholderText allows to give information to the user what to enter in the input field. Usually some information what's the input text about is shown nearby. This can be done directly using the Header property.
RichEditBox	Contrary to the TextBox control, the RichEditBox allows formatted text, hyperlinks, and images. The Text Object Model (TOM) is used from the Document property. Chapter 36 goes into details on using this control. You can use Microsoft Word to create RTF files that can be read into the RichEditBox.
PasswordBox	This control is used to enter a password. It has specific properties for password input, such as PasswordChar to define the character that should be displayed as the user enters the password. The password entered can be retrieved using the Password property. This control also has Header and PlaceholderText properties similar to the TextBox control.
ProgressRing	This control indicates that an operation is ongoing. It's displayed as a ring-shaped "spinner." Another control to display an ongoing operation is the ProgressBar, but this one belongs to the range controls.
DatePicker CalendarDatePicker CalendarView	The DatePicker and CalendarDatePicker controls are used to allow the user to select a date. The DatePicker is useful for date selection where the user knows the date, and showing a calendar is not helpful. The CalendarDatePicker uses the CalendarView internally. If a calendar should be visible all the times, or you need to select multiple dates, you can use the CalendarView. Be aware there's also a DatePickerFlyout (a control that derives from Flyout) that allows the user to select a date in a new opened window.
TimePicker	The TimePicker allows the user to enter a time. Similar to the DatePicker, with the TimePicker you can also use a TimePickerFlyout.
AppBarSeparator	AppBarSeparator controls can be used as separator within a CommandBar.
ColorPicker	The ColorPicker allows the user to select a color.
Hub HubSection	The Hub control allows grouping content in a panning view. The content within this control is defined in multiple HubSection controls. The Hub control is used with many apps to layout the main view of the app with "Hero" images. This control is discussed later in the section "Navigation."
UserControl	The UserControl is a control that can be used for reuse, and to simplify the XAML code with pages. User controls can be added to pages, and you'll use user controls in this and the next chapters.
Page	The Page class itself derives from UserControl, thus it is also a UserControl. Pages are used to navigate to from within a Frame. Navigation is discussed later in the section "Navigation," and in Chapter 34, "Patterns with XAML Apps," with the MVVM pattern.

CONTROL	DESCRIPTION
PersonPicture	PersonPicture is a new control with build 16929. It's used to show the avatar image of a person. This control is used with the ContactManager and Contact APIs.
RatingControl	RatingControl is another new control with build 16929. Using this control, the user can enter a star rating.
SemanticZoom	The SemanticZoom control defines two views: one zoom-out view and one zoom-in view. This allows the user to fast navigate into a large data set—for example, to just display first characters in the zoom-out view. In the zoom-in view, the user is positioned at the data objects with the selected letter.
SplitView	The SplitView control has a pane and a content. The pane can be opened and closed. When opening the pane, the content can be either partially behind the pane, or move to the right. The opened pane can be small (compact) or wide. The SplitView is used within the new NavigationPane.

Using a TextBox

The first sample with Control derived controls shows several TextBox controls. With the TextBox class, you can specify the InputScope property to values of a large list of values such as EmailNameOrAddress, CurrencyAmountAndSymbol, or Formula. In case the app is used in tablet mode with an on-screen keyboard, the keyboard is adjusted a different layout and shows keys as needed by the input field. The last TextBox in the sample code shows a multiline TextBox. To allow the user to press the Return key, the AcceptsReturn property is set. Also, the TextWrapping property is set to wrap the text if it doesn't fit into one line. The height of the TextBox is set to 150. In case the entered text doesn't fit with this size, a scrollbar is shown by using the attached property ScrollViewer.VerticalScrollBarVisibility (code file ControlsSamples/Views/TextPage.xaml):

```xml
<TextBox Header="Email" InputScope="EmailNameOrAddress"></TextBox>
<TextBox Header="Currency" InputScope="CurrencyAmountAndSymbol"></TextBox>
<TextBox Header="Alpha Numeric" InputScope="AlphanumericFullWidth"></TextBox>
<TextBox Header="Formula" InputScope="Formula"></TextBox>
<TextBox Header="Month" InputScope="DateMonthNumber"></TextBox>
<TextBox Header="Multiline" AcceptsReturn="True" TextWrapping="Wrap"
  Height="150" ScrollViewer.VerticalScrollBarVisibility="Auto"  />
```

The result of the multiline TextBox with multiple lines that wrap and a scrollbar is shown in Figure 33-10.

Selecting a Date

For selecting a date, multiple options are available. Let's look at the different options, and special features of the CalendarView control.

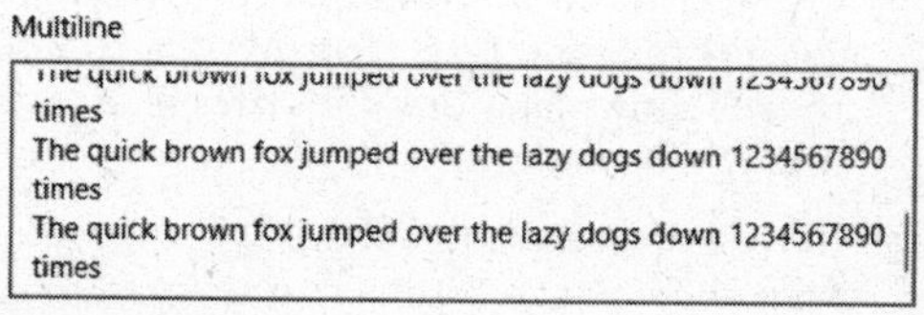

With the following code snippet, the CalendarView is configured to allow multiple days selected. The first day of the week is set to Monday, the minimum day is set to the

Multiline

The quick brown fox jumped over the lazy dogs down 1234567890 times
The quick brown fox jumped over the lazy dogs down 1234567890 times
The quick brown fox jumped over the lazy dogs down 1234567890 times

FIGURE 33-10

bound property `MinDate`, and the events `CalendarViewDayItemChanging` and `SelectedDatesChanged` are assigned to event handlers (code file `DateSelectionSample/MainPage.xaml`):

```
<CalendarView x:Name="CalendarView1" Margin="12" HorizontalAlignment="Center"
    SelectionMode="Multiple"
    FirstDayOfWeek="Monday"
    MinDate="{x:Bind MinDate, Mode=OneTime}"
    CalendarViewDayItemChanging="OnDayItemChanging"
    SelectedDatesChanged="OnDatesChanged" />
```

With the code-behind, the `MinDate` property is just set to a predefined day. The user cannot use the calendar to go to a day before that (code file `DateSelectionSample/MainPage.xaml.cs`):

```
public DateTimeOffset MinDate { get; } =
    DateTimeOffset.Parse("1/1/1965, new CultureInfo("en-US"));
```

With the `OnDayItemChanging` event handler, some days should be marked special. Days before today should be blocked out from a selection, and based on actual bookings, the day should be marked with colored lines.

To get the bookings, the method `GetBookings` is defined to return sample data. With a real app, you could get the data from a Web API or a database. The `GetBookings` method just returns bookings for a number of days from now (`2`, `3`, `5...`), and the number of bookings in a day (`1`, `4`, `3...`) by returning a tuple (code file `DateSelectionSample/MainPage.xaml.cs`):

```
private IEnumerable<(DateTimeOffset day, int bookings)> GetBookings()
{
    int[] bookingDays = { 2, 3, 5, 8, 12, 13, 18, 21, 23, 27 };
    int[] bookingsPerDay = { 1, 4, 3, 6, 4, 5, 1, 3, 1, 1 };

    for (int i = 0; i < 10; i++)
    {
        yield return (DateTimeOffset.Now.Date.AddDays(bookingDays[i]),
            bookingsPerDay[i]);
    }
}
```

> **NOTE** *Tuples and local functions are explained in Chapter 13, "Functional Programming." The yield statement is covered in Chapter 12, "Language Integrated Query."*

The `OnDayItemChanging` method is invoked when the items of the `CalendarView` are displayed. Every displayed day invokes this method. The method `OnDayItemChanging` is implemented using local functions. The main block of this method contains a switch statement to switch based on data binding phases. The `CalendarView` control supports multiple phases to allow adapting the user interface in different iterations. The first phase is fast; after this phase, already some information can be displayed to the user. Every next phase follows later on. With later phases, information might be retrieved from a Web API, and this information will be updated.

In the implementation of `OnDayItemChanging`, in the first phase, the local function `RegisterUpdateCallback` is invoked to register the next call to the `OnDayItemChanging` event handler. In the second phase the dates are blocked out with the local function `SetBlackoutDates`. In the third phase, the bookings are retrieved (code file `DateSelectionSample/MainPage.xaml.cs`):

```
private void OnDayItemChanging(CalendarView sender,
    CalendarViewDayItemChangingEventArgs args)
{
    switch (args.Phase)
    {
```

```
      case 0:
        RegisterUpdateCallback();
        break;
      case 1:
        SetBlackoutDates();
        break;
      case 2:
        SetBookings();
        break;
      default:
        break;
    }

    // local functions...
  }
```

The local function `RegisterUpdateCallback` just invokes the `RegisterUpdateCallback` of the `CalendarViewDayItemChangingEventArgs` argument passing the event handler method, so this method is invoked again (code file `DateSelectionSample/MainPage.xaml.cs`):

```
private void OnDayItemChanging(CalendarView sender,
  CalendarViewDayItemChangingEventArgs args)
{
  //...
  void RegisterUpdateCallback() =>
    args.RegisterUpdateCallback(OnDayItemChanging);
  //...
}
```

The local function `SetBlackoutDates` blacks out the dates before today, as well as all Saturdays and Sundays. The `CalendarViewDayItem` that is returned from the `args.Item` property defines a `IsBlackout` property (code file `DateSelectionSample/MainPage.xaml.cs`):

```
private void OnDayItemChanging(CalendarView sender,
  CalendarViewDayItemChangingEventArgs args)
{
  //...
  void SetBlackoutDates()
  {
    if (args.Item.Date < DateTimeOffset.Now || args.Item.Date.DayOfWeek ==
      DayOfWeek.Saturday || args.Item.Date.DayOfWeek == DayOfWeek.Sunday)
    {
      args.Item.IsBlackout = true;
    }
    RegisterUpdateCallback();
  }
  //...
}
```

Finally, the `SetBookings` method retrieves the information about the bookings. The received date found in the `CalendarViewDayItem` is checked if it is also found in the bookings. If it is, a list of red or green colors (depending on the weekday) is added to the day item by invoking `SetDensityColors`. Finally, the `RegisterUpdateCallback` local function is invoked once again; otherwise, only the first day shown would be invoked with the third phase (code file `DateSelectionSample/MainPage.xaml.cs`):

```
private void OnDayItemChanging(CalendarView sender,
  CalendarViewDayItemChangingEventArgs args)
{
  //...

  void SetBookings()
  {
    var bookings = GetBookings().ToList();
```

```
      var booking = bookings.SingleOrDefault(
        b => b.day.Date == args.Item.Date.Date);
    if (booking.bookings > 0)
    {
      var colors = new List<Color>();
      for (int i = 0; i < booking.bookings; i++)
      {
        if (args.Item.Date.DayOfWeek == DayOfWeek.Saturday ||
          args.Item.Date.DayOfWeek == DayOfWeek.Sunday)
        {
          colors.Add(Colors.Red);
        }
        else
        {
          colors.Add(Colors.Green);
        }
      }

      args.Item.SetDensityColors(colors);
    }
    RegisterUpdateCallback();
  }
}
```

When a user selects a date, the OnDatesChanged method is invoked. With this method, all the dates selected are received in the CalendarViewSelectedDatesChangedEventArgs. The selected dates are written to the currentDatesSelected list, and the deselected dates are removed from the list again. Using a string.Join, all the selected dates are shown with the MessageDialog (code file DateSelectionSample/MainPage.xaml.cs):

```
private List<DateTimeOffset> currentDatesSelected = new List<DateTimeOffset>();

private async void OnDatesChanged(CalendarView sender,
  CalendarViewSelectedDatesChangedEventArgs args)
{
  currentDatesSelected.AddRange(args.AddedDates);
  args.RemovedDates.ToList().ForEach(date =>
    currentDatesSelected.Remove(date));

  string selectedDates = string.Join(", ",
    currentDatesSelected.Select(d => d.ToString("d")));

  await new MessageDialog($"dates selected: {selectedDates}").ShowAsync();
}
```

When you run the app, you can see the calendar as shown in Figure 33-11, the previous days as well as Saturday/Sunday blocked, and the information about bookings is shown with color lines.

FIGURE 33-11

When you click the month of the calendar, a complete year is shown, as you can see in Figure 33-12. When you click on the year on top, an epoch is visible (see Figure 33-13). This makes it easy to select dates far away.

FIGURE 33-12

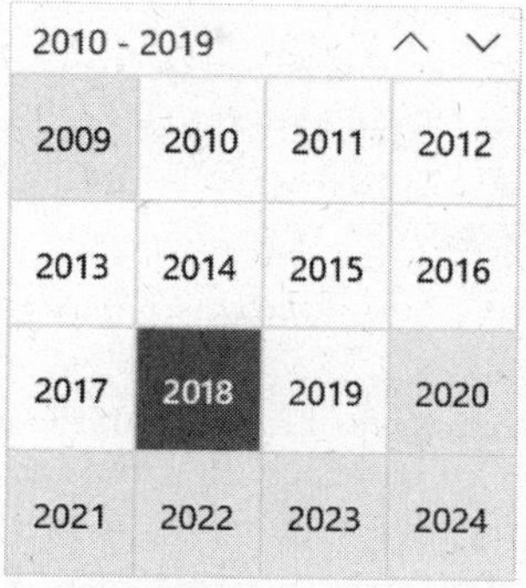

2010 - 2019			∧ ∨
2009	2010	2011	2012
2013	2014	2015	2016
2017	2018	2019	2020
2021	2022	2023	2024

FIGURE 33-13

When using a `CalendarDatePicker`, you don't have as many features as with the `CalendarView`, but it doesn't occupy the space of the screen unless the user opens it to select a date. A `CalendarDatePicker` defines the `DateChanged` event; you can only select a single day (code file `DateSelectionSample/MainPage.xaml`):

```
<CalendarDatePicker x:Name="CalendarDatePicker1" Grid.Row="0" Grid.Column="1"
  DateChanged="OnDateChanged" Margin="12" />
```

With the `OnDateChanged` event handler, `CalendarDatePickerDateChangedEventArgs` are received that contains `NewDate` property (code file `DateSelectionSample/MainPage.xaml.cs`):

```
private async void OnDateChanged(CalendarDatePicker sender,
  CalendarDatePickerDateChangedEventArgs args)
{
  await new MessageDialog($"date changed to {args.NewDate}").ShowAsync();
}
```

Figure 33-14 shows the user interface when the calendar is opened.

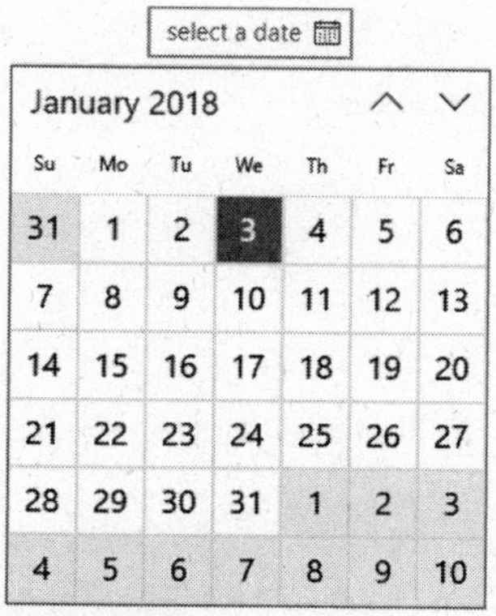

select a date 📅						
January 2018					∧	∨
Su	Mo	Tu	We	Th	Fr	Sa
31	1	2	3	4	5	6
7	8	9	10	11	12	13
14	15	16	17	18	19	20
21	22	23	24	25	26	27
28	29	30	31	1	2	3
4	5	6	7	8	9	10

FIGURE 33-14

The XAML code for the `DatePicker` is very similar. It just doesn't show a calendar to select the date, but has a completely different view (code file `DateSelectionSample/MainPage.xaml`):

```
<DatePicker DateChanged="OnDateChanged1" x:Name="DatePicker1" Grid.Row="1"
  Margin="12" />
```

The event handler for the `DatePicker` receives object and `DatePickerValueChangedEventArgs` arguments (code file `DateSelectionSample/MainPage.xaml`):

```
private async void OnDateChanged1(object sender,
  DatePickerValueChangedEventArgs e)
{
  await new MessageDialog($"date changed to {e.NewDate}").ShowAsync();
}
```

Figure 33-15 shows the `DatePicker` when it's open. If the user knows the date without checking a calendar (for example, a birthday), it is a lot faster scrolling through the years, the months, and the days.

30	September	2014
31	October	2015
1	November	2016
2	December	2017
3	January	2018
4	February	2019
5	March	2020
6	April	2021
7	May	2022

FIGURE 33-15

The last option for selecting a date is a flyout. Flyouts can be used with other controls. Here, a `Button` control is used, and the `Flyout` property of the button defines to use the `DatePickerFlyout`.

```
<Button Content="Select a Date" Grid.Row="1" Grid.Column="1" Margin="12">
  <Button.Flyout>
    <DatePickerFlyout x:Name="DatePickerFlyout1" DatePicked="OnDatePicked" />
  </Button.Flyout>
</Button>
```

Clicking the button opens the flyout as shown in Figure 33-16.

Range Controls

Range controls such as `ScrollBar`, `ProgressBar`, and `Slider` derive from the common class `RangeBase`.

CONTROL	DESCRIPTION
ScrollBar	This control contains a Thumb that enables the user to select a value. A scrollbar can be used, for example, if a document doesn't fit on the screen. Some controls contain scrollbars that are displayed if the content is too big.
ProgressBar	This control indicates the progress of a lengthy operation.
Slider	This control enables users to select a range of values by moving a Thumb.

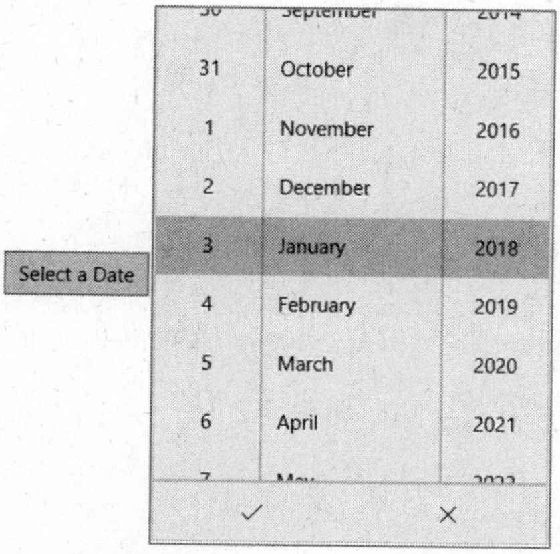

FIGURE 33-16

Progress Bar

The sample application shows two ProgressBar controls. The second control has the IsIndeterminate property set to true. In case you don't know how long an activity takes, it's a good idea to use this property. If you think to know how long the action takes, you can set the current status value in the ProgressBar without setting the IsIndeterminate mode; the default is False (code file ControlsSamples/Views/RangeControlsPage.xaml):

```xml
<ProgressBar x:Name="progressBar1" Grid.Row="0" Margin="12" />
<ProgressBar IsIndeterminate="True" Grid.Row="1" Margin="12" />
```

On loading of the page, the ShowProgress method is invoked. Here, the current value of the first ProgressBar is set using a DispatcherTimer. The DispatcherTimer is configured to fire every second, and every second the Value property of the ProgressBar gets incremented (code file ControlsSamples/Views/RangeControlsPage.xaml.cs):

```csharp
private void ShowProgress()
{
  var timer = new DispatcherTimer();
  timer.Interval = TimeSpan.FromSeconds(1);
  int i = 0;
  timer.Tick += (sender, e) =>
  {
    progressBar1.Value = i++;
    if (i >= 100)
    {
      i = 0;
    }
  };
  timer.Start();
}
```

> **NOTE** The DispatcherTimer class is explained in Chapter 21, "Tasks and Parallel Programming."

When you run the application, you can see two ProgressBar controls active. With the first one you can see the status, whereas the second one shows dots floating horizontally (see Figure 33-17).

FIGURE 33-17

Slider

With the Slider control, you can specify `Minimum` and `Maximum` values, and use the `Value` property to assign the current value. The code sample uses a `TextBox` to display the current value of the slider (code file `ControlsSamples/Views/RangeControlsPage.xaml`):

```
<Slider x:Name="slider" Minimum="10" Maximum="140" Value="60"
  Grid.Row="2" Margin="12" />
<TextBox Header="Slider Value" IsReadOnly="True"
  Text="{x:Bind slider.Value, Mode=OneWay}" Grid.Row="3" Margin="12" />
```

In Figure 33-18 you can see the `Slider` and the `TextBox`; notice how they correlate other as the `TextBox` shows the actual value of the `Slider`.

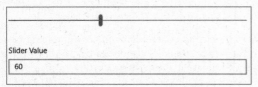

FIGURE 33-18

Content Controls

A `ContentControl` has a `Content` property and allows adding any single content. Multiple content objects are not allowed as a direct child of the `Content` property, but you can add, for example, a `StackPanel` which itself can than have multiple controls as children.

CONTROL	DESCRIPTION	
ScrollViewer	ScrollViewer is a ContentControl that can contain a single item and offers horizontal and vertical scrollbars. You can also use ScrollViewer with attached properties as has been shown previously with the ParallaxViewSample.	
Frame	The Frame control is used for navigation between pages. This control is discussed later in the section "Navigation."	
SelectorItem ComboBoxItem FlipViewItem GridViewItem ListBoxItem ListViewItem GroupItem PivotItem	These controls are ContentControl objects that belong as items to an ItemsControl. For example, The ComboBox control contains ComboBoxItem objects, the ListBox control contains ListBoxItem objects, and the Pivot control contains PivotItem objects. GroupItem objects are typically not used directly; they're used when you use an ItemsControl-derived control with a grouping configuration.	

CONTROL	DESCRIPTION
ToolTip	The ToolTip gives a pop-up window when the user hovers over the information to show a tooltip. Tooltips can be configured using the ToolTipService.ToolTip attached property. The tooltip cannot be more than text; it is a ContentControl.
CommandBar	With the CommandBar you can arrange AppBarButton controls and controls that belong to the command elements (such as AppBarSeparator). The CommandBar offers some layout features for these controls. With Windows 8, the AppBar was used instead of the CommandBar—that's why the buttons have these names. Now the CommandBar derives from the AppBar. However, you can also use other controls to lay out your commands if the layout from the CommandBar doesn't fit your requirements.
ContentDialog	Using the ContentDialog opens a dialog box. You can customize this control with any XAML controls you need for your dialog.
SwipeControl	The SwipeControl allows contextual commands through touch interactions—for example, to open specific actions for items as the user swipes to the left or to the right.

> **NOTE** *See the next section, which includes a sample to fill the content of a* ContentControl—*with a* Button, *which itself is a* ContentControl.

Buttons

Buttons form a hierarchy. The ButtonBase class derives from ContentControl, thus a button has a Content property and can contain any single content. The ButtonBase class also defines a Command property; thus, all buttons can have a command associated. Let's compare the different buttons.

CONTROL	DESCRIPTION
Button	The Button class is the most commonly used button. This class derives from ButtonBase (as all the other buttons do as well). ButtonBase is the base class of all buttons.
HyperlinkButton	The HyperlinkButton appears as a link. You can open web pages in the browser, open other apps, or navigate to other pages.
RepeatButton	The RepeatButton is a button where the Click event continuously fires while the user presses the button. With the normal Button, the Click event only fires once.
AppBarButton	The AppBarButton is used to activate commands in the app. You can add this button to the CommandBar and use an icon and a label to display information for the user.
AppBarToggleButton CheckBox RadioButton	CheckBox, RadioButton, and AppBarToggleButton derive from the base class ToggleButton. A ToggleButton can have three states: Checked, Unchecked, and Indeterminate represented by bool?. The AppBarToggleButton is a toggle button for the CommandBar.

Replacing the Content of the Button

A button is a `ContentControl` and can have any content. The following sample adds a `Grid` control to the button that contains an `Ellipse` and a `TextBlock`. The button also defines a `Click` event, to demonstrate it looks different, but it acts the same (code file `ControlsSample/Views/ButtonsPage.xaml`):

```xml
<Button Margin="12" Click="OnButtonClick">
  <Grid>
    <Ellipse Width="200" Height="90" Fill="red" />
    <TextBlock HorizontalAlignment="Center" VerticalAlignment="Center"
      Text="Click Me!" FontSize="24" />
  </Grid>
</Button>
```

In Figure 33-19 you can see the new look of the button. The `Content` property replaces the foreground, but the button still has the default background.

FIGURE 33-19

> **NOTE** *To replace the complete look of the button, including the background, and to make the button non-rectangular, you need to create a* `ControlTemplate` *for the button. How this can be done is explained in Chapter 35.*

Linking with the HyperlinkButton

With the `HyperlinkButton` control you can easily activate other apps. The `NavigateUri` property can be set to a URL, and clicking the button opens the default browser to open the web page.

```xml
<HyperlinkButton NavigateUri="https://csharp.christiannagel.com"
  Content="C# Infos" Grid.Column="1"
  Style="{StaticResource TextBlockButtonStyle}" FontSize="24" />
```

The `HyperlinkButton` by default looks like a link in the browser. With the `HyperlinkButton`, you can either set the `NavigateUri` or define a `Click` event, but you can't do both. As an action to a `Click` event, you can, for example, programmatically navigate to another page. Navigation is explained in the section "Navigation."

You can not only assign `http://` or `https://` values to the `NavigateUri` property but also use `ms-appx://` to activate other apps.

Items Controls

Contrary to a `ContentControl`, an `ItemsControl` can contain a list of items. With an `ItemsControl` you can either define items with the `Items` property or fill it using data binding and the `ItemsSource` property. You cannot use both.

CONTROL	DESCRIPTION
ItemsControl	The `ItemsControl` is the base class for all other items controls and can also be used directly to display a list of items.
Pivot	The `Pivot` control is a control for creating a tab-like behavior for the application. Read the section "Navigation" for more information on this control.
AutoSuggestBox	The `AutoSuggestBox` replaces the previous `SearchBox`. With the `AutoSuggestBox`, the user can enter text, and the control offers auto-completion. Read Chapter 36, "Advanced Windows Apps," for more information using this control.

CONTROL	DESCRIPTION
ListBox ComboBox FlipView	ListBox, ComboBox, and FlipView are three items controls that derive from the base class Selector. Selector derives from ItemsControl and adds the SelectedItem and SelectedValue properties to make it possible to select an item from the collection. The ListBox shows a list the user can select from. The ComboBox combines a TextBox and a drop-down list to allow the selection of a list while using less screen space. The FlipView control allows using touch interaction to flip through a list of items while only one item is shown.
ListView GridView	ListView and GridView derive from the base class ListViewBase, which derives from Selector—so these are the most powerful selectors. ListViewBase offers additional drag and drop of items, reordering of items, adds a header and a footer, and allows selecting multiple items. The ListView displays items vertically (but you can also create a template to have the list horizontally). The GridView displays items with rows and columns.

Flyouts

Flyouts are used to open a window above other UI elements—for example, a context menu. All flyouts derive from the base class FlyoutBase. The FlyoutBase class defines a Placement property that allows defining where the flyout should be positioned. It can be centered in the screen or positioned around the target element.

CONTROL	DESCRIPTION
MenuFlyout	The MenuFlyout control is used to display a list of menu items.
Flyout	The Flyout control can contain one item that you can customize with XAML elements.

DATA BINDING

Data binding is an extremely important concept with XAML-based apps. Data binding gets data from .NET objects to the UI or the other way around. Simple objects can be bound to UI elements, a list of objects, and XAML elements themselves. With data binding, the target can be any dependency property of a XAML element, and every property of a CLR object can be the source. Because XAML elements also offer .NET properties, every XAML element can be the source as well. Figure 33-20 shows the connection between the source and the target. The binding defines the connection.

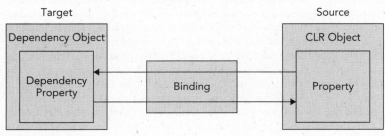

FIGURE 33-20

Binding supports several binding modes between the target and source. With *one-way* binding, the source information goes to the target, but if the user changes information in the user interface, the source is not updated. For updates to the source, *two-way* binding is required.

The following table shows the binding modes and their requirements.

BINDING MODE	DESCRIPTION
One-time	Binding goes from the source to the target and occurs only once when the application is started or the data context changes. Here, you get a snapshot of the data.
One-way	Binding goes from the source to the target. This is useful for read-only data, because it is not possible to change the data from the user interface. To get updates to the user interface, the source must implement the interface `INotifyPropertyChanged`.
Two-way	With two-way binding, the user can make changes to the data from the UI. Binding occurs in both directions—from the source to the target and from the target to the source. The source needs to implement read/write properties so that changes can be updated from the UI to the source.
One-way-to-source	With one-way-to-source binding, if the target property changes, the source object is updated. This binding is not available with UWP, but with WPF and Xamarin.

> **NOTE** *UWP supports two binding types. Traditional binding using the* `Binding` *markup extension, and the new compiled binding using the* `x:Bind` *markup extension. Be aware that the defaults with the binding modes differ between these binding types, so it's best to always specify the binding mode. This section has the main focus on the new compiled binding. Later in the section "Traditional Binding," the older binding type is compared.*

Data binding involves many facets besides the binding modes. This section provides binding to simple .NET objects, and binding to lists. Using change notifications, the UI is updated with changes in the bound objects. This section also describes dynamically selecting data templates.

Let's start with the `DataBindingSamples` sample application. The app shows a list of books and allows the user to select a book to see the book details.

Change Notification with INotifyPropertyChanged

First, the model is created. To get updates to the user interface when property values change, the interface `INotifyPropertyChanged` needs to be implemented. For reusing this implementation, the `BindableBase` class is created that implements this interface. The interface defines the `PropertyChanged` event handler. This event is fired from the method `OnPropertyChanged`. The method `Set` is used to change a property value and to fire the `PropertyChanged` event. If the value to be set is not different to the current value, no event is fired, and the method just returns `false`. Only with different values, the property is set to the new value, and the `PropertyChanged` event is fired. This method makes use of the caller information feature from C# using the attribute `CallerMemberName`. Defining the parameter `propertyName` as an optional parameter with this attribute, the C# compiler passes the name of the property with this parameter, so it's not necessary to add a hard-coded string to the code (code file `DataBindingSamples/Models/BindableBase.cs`):

```
public abstract class BindableBase : INotifyPropertyChanged
{
```

```
public event PropertyChangedEventHandler PropertyChanged;

public virtual bool Set<T>(ref T item, T value,
   [CallerMemberName] string propertyName = null)
{
  if (EqualityComparer<T>.Default.Equals(item, value)) return false;
  item = value;
  OnPropertyChanged(propertyName);
  return true;
}

protected virtual void OnPropertyChanged(string propertyName) =>
   PropertyChanged?.Invoke(this, new PropertyChangedEventArgs(propertyName));
}
```

> **NOTE** *Caller information is covered in Chapter 14, "Errors and Exceptions." The implementation of* INotifyPropertyChanged *is covered with more detail in Chapter 34, "Patterns with XAML Apps."*

The Book class derives from the base class BindableBase and implements the properties BookId, Title, Publisher, and Authors. The BookId property is read-only; Title and Publisher make use of the change notification implementation from the base class; and the Authors property is a read-only property to return a list of authors (code file DataBindingSamples/Models/Book.cs):

```
public class Book : BindableBase
{
  public Book(int id, string title, string publisher, params string[] authors)
  {
    BookId = id;
    Title = title;
    Publisher = publisher;
    Authors = authors;
  }

  public int BookId { get; }

  private string _title;
  public string Title
  {
    get => _title;
    set => Set(ref _title, value);
  }

  private string __publisher;
  public string Publisher
  {
    get => _publisher;
    set => Set(ref _publisher, value);
  }

  public IEnumerable<string> Authors { get; }

  public override string ToString() => Title;
}
```

Creating a List of Books

The method GetSampleBooks returns a list of books that should be shown using the constructor of the Book class (code file DataBindingSamples/Services/SampleBooksService.cs):

```
public class SampleBooksService
{
  public IEnumerable<Book> GetSampleBooks() =>
    new List<Book>()
    {
      new Book(1, "Professional C# 7 and .NET Core 2", "Wrox Press",
        "Christian Nagel"),
      new Book(2, "Professional C# 6 and .NET Core 1.0", "Wrox Press",
        "Christian Nagel"),
      new Book(3, "Professional C# 5.0 and .NET 4.5.1", "Wrox Press",
        "Christian Nagel", "Jay Glynn", "Morgan Skinner"),
      new Book(4, "Enterprise Services with the .NET Framework", "AWL",
        "Christian Nagel")
    };
}
```

Now, the BooksService class offers the methods RefreshBooks, GetBook, and AddBook, and the property Books. Books returns an ObservableCollection<Book> object. ObservableCollection is a generic class offering change notification by implementing the interface INotifyCollectionChanged. (code file DataBindingSamples/Services/BooksService.cs):

```
public class BooksService
{
  private ObservableCollection<Book> _books = new ObservableCollection<Book>();

  public void RefreshBooks()
  {
    _books.Clear();
    var sampleBooksService = new SampleBooksService();
    var books = sampleBooksService.GetSampleBooks();
    foreach (var book in books)
    {
      _books.Add(book);
    }
  }

  public Book GetBook(int bookId) =>
    _books.Where(b => b.BookId == bookId).SingleOrDefault();

  public void AddBook(Book book) => _books.Add(book);

  public IEnumerable<Book> Books => _books;
}
```

> **NOTE** *The generic class* ObservableCollection *is covered in detail in Chapter 11, "Special Collections."*

List Binding

Now you're ready to display a list of books. Any ItemsSource-derived control can be used to assign the ItemsSource property to binding to a list. The following code snippet uses the ListView control to bind the `ItemsSource` to the `Books` property. With the markup extension `x:Bind`, this first name specified is the source for the binding, The `Mode` parameter defines the binding mode. With `OneWay`, UWP makes use of change notification to update the user interface when the source changes:

```
<ListView ItemsSource="{x:Bind Books, Mode=OneWay}" Grid.Row="1" />
```

With the code-behind file, the `Books` property is specified to reference the `Books` property of the `BooksService` (code file `DataBindingSamples/MainPage.xaml.cs`):

```
public sealed partial class MainPage : Page
{
  private BooksService _booksService = new BooksService();
  public MainPage()
  {
    this.InitializeComponent();
  }

  public IEnumerable<Book> Books => _booksService.Books;
}
```

Binding Events to Methods

Without invoking the `RefreshBooks` method from the `BooksService`, the list stays empty. With the XAML file, a `CommandBar` is created that lists two `AppBarButton` controls. With the `AppBarButton` controls, the `Click` event again is bound—to the methods `OnRefreshBooks` and `OnRefresh` (code file `DataBindingSamples/MainPage.xaml`):

```
<CommandBar Grid.Row="0" Grid.Column="0" Grid.ColumnSpan="2">
  <AppBarButton Icon="Refresh" Label="Refresh"
    Click="{x:Bind OnRefreshBooks}" />
  <AppBarButton Icon="Add" Label="Add Book" Click="{x:Bind OnAddBook}" />
</CommandBar>
```

Binding events to methods is possible if the method either has no arguments or has arguments as specified by the delegate type of the event. With the following code snippet, the methods `OnRefreshBooks` and `OnAddBook` are declared void without arguments (code file `DataBindingSamples/MainPage.xaml.cs`):

```
public void OnRefreshBooks()
{
  _booksService.RefreshBooks();
}

public void OnAddBook() =>
  _booksService.AddBook(new Book(GetNextBookId(),
    $"Professional C# {GetNextBookId() + 3}", "Wrox Press"));

private int GetNextBookId() => Books.Select(b => b.BookId).Max() + 1;
```

> **NOTE** *Binding to methods is only possible with the* `x:Bind` *markup extension, not with the traditional* `Binding` *markup extension.*

You can see the running app with the two `AppBar` buttons as shown in Figure 33-21. Clicking the `Refresh` button loads the books and displays the book titles because the `ToString` method of the `Book` class returns the title. Clicking the `Add` button creates a new book object that shows up in the list because the list is of type `ObservableCollection`. The `ObservableCollection` implements change notification with the interface `INotifyCollectionChanged`.

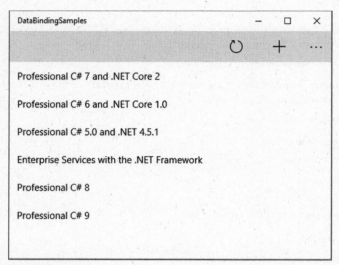

FIGURE 33-21

Using Data Templates and the Data Template Selector

For creating a different look of the items, you can create a DataTemplate. The DataTemplate can be referenced using the key that is specified with the x:Key attribute. When you use the x:DataType attribute, you can use compiled binding within the data template. Compiled binding requires the type it binds to at compile time. To bind to the Title property, the type is defined with the Book class (code file DataBindingSamples/MainPage.xaml):

```xml
<Page.Resources>
  <DataTemplate x:DataType="models:Book" x:Key="WroxTemplate">
   <Border Background="Red" Margin="4" Padding="4" BorderThickness="2"
     BorderBrush="DarkRed">
     <TextBlock Text="{x:Bind Title, Mode=OneWay}" Foreground="White"
       Width="300" />
    </Border>
  </DataTemplate>
  <!-- ... -->
</Page.Resources>
```

Data templates that should be used for items in an ItemsControl can be referenced using the ItemTemplate property of an ItemsControl. Instead of fixed specifying the DataTemplate, now a DataTemplateSelector will be used to dynamically chose the DataTemplate based on the name of the publisher.

The BookDataTemplateSelector derives from the base class DataTemplateSelector. A data template selector needs to override the method SelectTemplateCore and return the selected DataTemplate. With the implementation of the BookTemplateSelector, two properties are specified: the WroxTemplate and the DefaultTemplate. In the SelectTemplateCore method, Book objects are received. You can use pattern matching with the switch statement so that if the publisher is Wrox Press, the WroxTemplate is returned. In other cases, the DefaultTemplate is returned. You can extend the switch statement with more publishers (code file DataBindingSamples/Utilities/BookTemplateSelector.cs):

```csharp
public class BookTemplateSelector : DataTemplateSelector
{
```

```
public DataTemplate WroxTemplate { get; set; }
public DataTemplate DefaultTemplate { get; set; }

protected override DataTemplate SelectTemplateCore(object item)
{
  DataTemplate selectedTemplate = null;

  switch (item)
  {
    case Book b when b.Publisher == "Wrox Press":
      selectedTemplate = WroxTemplate;
      break;
    default:
      selectedTemplate = DefaultTemplate;
      break;
  }
  return selectedTemplate;
}
}
```

> **NOTE** *Pattern matching is explained in Chapter 13.*

Next, the data template selector needs to be instantiated and initialized. You do this in the XAML code. Here, the properties `WroxTemplate` and `DefaultTemplate` are assigned to reference the previously created `DataTemplate` templates (code file `DataBindingSamples/MainPage.xaml`):

```xml
<Page.Resources>
  <DataTemplate x:DataType="models:Book" x:Key="WroxTemplate">
    <Border Background="Red" Margin="4" Padding="4" BorderThickness="2"
      BorderBrush="DarkRed">
      <TextBlock Text="{x:Bind Title, Mode=OneWay}" Foreground="White"
        Width="300" />
    </Border>
  </DataTemplate>
  <DataTemplate x:DataType="models:Book" x:Key="DefaultTemplate">
    <Border Background="LightBlue" Margin="4" Padding="4" BorderThickness="2"
      BorderBrush="DarkBlue">
      <TextBlock Text="{x:Bind Title, Mode=OneWay}" Foreground="Black"
        Width="300" />
    </Border>
  </DataTemplate>
  <utils:BookTemplateSelector x:Key="BookTemplateSelector"
    WroxTemplate="{StaticResource WroxTemplate}"
    DefaultTemplate="{StaticResource DefaultTemplate}" />
</Page.Resources>
```

For using the `BookTemplateSelector` with the items in the `ListView`, the `ItemTemplateSelector` property references the template using the key and the `StaticResource` markup extension:

```xml
<ListView ItemsSource="{x:Bind Books, Mode=OneWay}"
  ItemTemplateSelector="{StaticResource BookTemplateSelector}"
  Grid.Row="1" />
```

When you run the app at this stage, Figure 33-22 shows the new output with the different views based on the publisher.

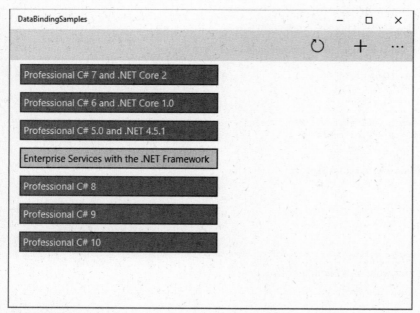

FIGURE 33-22

Binding Simple Objects

Instead of just binding a list, the single book should be displayed on the right side of the app. Compiled binding is used to bind to the `BookId`, `Title`, and `Publisher` properties of the `Book` property (code file `DataBindingSamples/Views/BookUserControl.xaml`):

```xml
<UserControl
    x:Class="DataBindingSamples.Views.BookUserControl"
    xmlns="http://schemas.microsoft.com/winfx/2006/xaml/presentation"
    xmlns:x="http://schemas.microsoft.com/winfx/2006/xaml"
    xmlns:local="using:DataBindingSamples.Views"
    xmlns:conv="using:DataBindingSamples.Converters"
    xmlns:d="http://schemas.microsoft.com/expression/blend/2008"
    xmlns:mc="http://schemas.openxmlformats.org/markup-compatibility/2006"
    mc:Ignorable="d"
    d:DesignHeight="300"
    d:DesignWidth="400">
    <!-- ... -->
    <StackPanel Orientation="Vertical" Grid.Row="1">
        <TextBox Header="BookId" IsReadOnly="True"
            Text="{x:Bind Book.BookId, Mode=OneWay}" />
        <TextBox Header="Title" Text="{x:Bind Book.Title, Mode=TwoWay}" />
        <TextBox Header="Publisher"
            Text="{x:Bind Book.Publisher, Mode=TwoWay}"  />
        <!-- ... -->
    </StackPanel>
    </Grid>
</UserControl>
```

In the code-behind file, the `Book` property is defined as a dependency property. Change notification is needed for making updates when the values change, that's why a dependency property is used. It would also be possible to implement `INotifyPropertyChanged`, but because dependency properties are already available from the base class `DependencyObject`, dependency properties can be used easily (code file `DataBindingSamples/Views/BookUserControl.xaml.cs`):

```
public Book Book
{
  get => (Book)GetValue(BookProperty);
  set => SetValue(BookProperty, value);
}

public static readonly DependencyProperty BookProperty =
  DependencyProperty.Register("Book", typeof(Book), typeof(BookUserControl),
    new PropertyMetadata(null));
```

Now the user control needs to be displayed in the `MainPage`, and the currently selected book should be assigned to the `Book` property of the user control. You do this using XAML code. The `BookUserControl` is added within the `Grid` in the `MainPage`, and with the `ListView`, the `SelectedItem` property binds to the `Book` property. This time, `TwoWay` binding is needed to update the `UserControl` from the `ListView` (code file `DataBindingSamples/MainPage.xaml`):

```
<ListView x:Name="BooksList" ItemsSource="{x:Bind Books, Mode=OneWay}"
  ItemTemplateSelector="{StaticResource BookTemplateSelector}"
  SelectedItem="{x:Bind CurrentBook.Book, Mode=TwoWay}" Grid.Row="1" />
<views:BookUserControl x:Name="CurrentBook" Grid.Row="1" Grid.Column="1"
  Margin="4" />
```

> **NOTE** *It would be also possible to create the binding in the other way around—to bind the* `BookUserControl` *to the* `ListView`*. This way,* `OneWay` *binding would be enough—to just take the updated values from the* `ListView` *to the* `BookUserControl`*. However, here the XAML compiler complains because it can't assign an* `object` *(coming from the* `ListView`*) to the strongly typed* `Book` *property of the* `BookUserControl`*. You could resolve this by creating a value converter as discussed next. The problem does not exist with the* `SelectedItem` *property, because Microsoft changed the implementation to not complain with a recent Windows 10 release. In earlier versions, you need to use an object-to-object converter in that scenario as well.*

As you run the app, you can see the books, and as you select a book in the list, the details show up in the user control as shown in Figure 33-23.

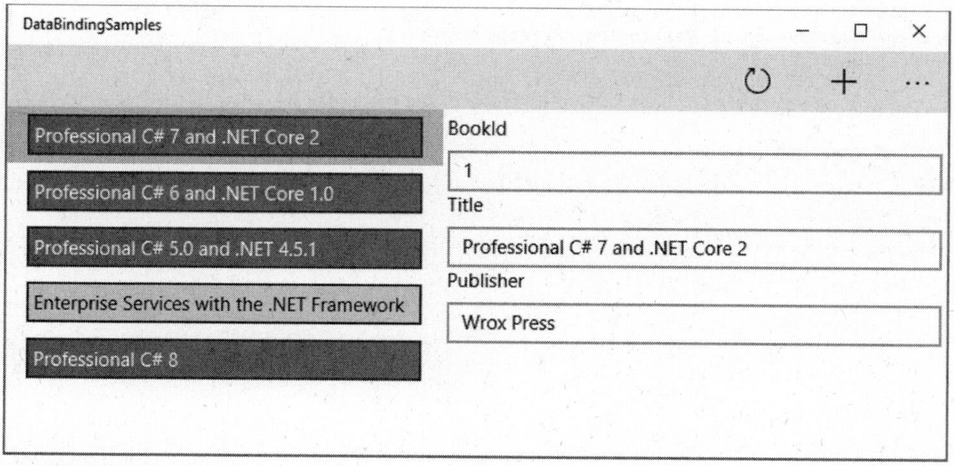

FIGURE 33-23

Value Conversion

The authors haven't been displayed yet in the user control. The reason is that the Authors property is a list. You can define an ItemsControl in the user control to display the Authors property. However, just to display a simple comma-separated list of authors, it would be okay to use the TextBlock. You just need a converter to convert IEnumerable<string>—the type of the Authors property to a string.

A value converter is an implementation of the IValueConverter interface. This interface defines the methods Convert and ConvertBack. With two-way binding, both methods need to be implemented. Using one-way binding, the Convert method is enough. The class CollectionToStringConverter implements the Convert method by using the string.Join method to create a single string. A value converter also receives an object parameter that you can specify when using the value converter. Here, this parameter is used as a string separator (code file DataBindingSamples/Converters/CollectionToStringConverter.cs):

```
public class CollectionToStringConverter : IValueConverter
{
  public object Convert(object value, Type targetType, object parameter,
    string language)
  {
    IEnumerable<string> names = (IEnumerable<string>)value;
    return string.Join(parameter?.ToString() ?? ", ", names);
  }

  public object ConvertBack(object value, Type targetType, object parameter,
    string language)
  {
    throw new NotImplementedException();
  }
}
```

With the user control, the CollectionToStringConverter is instantiated in the resources section (code file DataBindingSamples/Views/BookUserControl.xaml):

```
<UserControl.Resources>
  <conv:CollectionToStringConverter x:Key="CollectionToStringConverter" />
</UserControl.Resources>
```

The converter can now be referenced from within the x:Bind markup extension using the Converter property. The ConverterParameter property specifies the string separator that is used within the string.Join method earlier (code file DataBindingSamples/Views/BookUserControl.xaml):

```
<TextBox Header="Authors" IsReadOnly="True"
  Text="{x:Bind Book.Authors, Mode=OneWay,
    Converter={StaticResource CollectionToStringConverter},
    ConverterParameter='; '}" />
```

When you run the app, the authors are now shown as you can see in Figure 33-24.

> **NOTE** *Chapter 36 covers more features with compiled data binding, such as using the binding lifetime, compiled binding in resource files, and phased binding.*

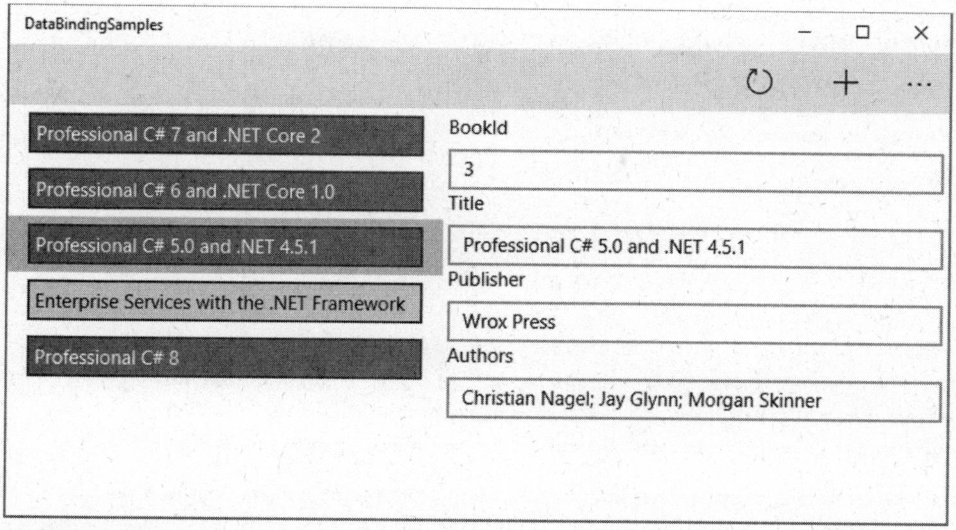

FIGURE 33-24

NAVIGATION

If your application is composed of multiple pages, you need the ability to navigate between these pages. There are different application structures to navigate, such as using a hamburger button to navigate to different root pages, or to use different tabs and replace tab items.

If you need to provide a way for the user to navigate, the heart of the navigation is the Frame class. The Frame class enables the user to navigate to specific pages using the Navigate method and optionally pass parameters. The Frame class keeps a stack of the pages to which the user has navigated, which makes it possible to go back, go forward, limit the number of pages in the stack, and more.

An important aspect of navigation is having the ability to navigate back. The following sections show you the Windows 10 way of using back navigation.

Navigating to the Initial Page

Let's start creating a Windows app with multiple pages to navigate. The template-generated code contains the OnLaunched method within the App class where a Frame object gets instantiated and then used to navigate to the MainPage by calling the Navigate method (code file PageNavigation/App.xaml.cs):

```
protected override void OnLaunched(LaunchActivatedEventArgs e)
{
  Frame rootFrame = Window.Current.Content as Frame;
  if (rootFrame == null)
  {
    rootFrame = new Frame();
```

```
      rootFrame.NavigationFailed += OnNavigationFailed;
      if (e.PreviousExecutionState == ApplicationExecutionState.Terminated)
      {
        //TODO: Load state from previously suspended application
      }
      Window.Current.Content = rootFrame;
    }
    if (rootFrame.Content == null)
    {
      rootFrame.Navigate(typeof(MainPage), e.Arguments);
    }
    Window.Current.Activate();
}
```

> **NOTE** *The source code has a* TODO *comment to load the state from the previously sus-*
> *pended application. How you can deal with suspension is explained in Chapter 36.*

The Frame class keeps a stack of pages that have been visited. The GoBack method makes it possible to navigate back within this stack (if the CanGoBack property returns true), and the GoForward method enables you to go forward one page after a back navigation. The Frame class also offers several events for navigation, such as Navigating, Navigated, NavigationFailed, and NavigationStopped.

To see navigation in action, besides the MainPage, the SecondPage and ThirdPage pages are created to navigate between these pages. From the MainPage, you can navigate to the SecondPage, and from the SecondPage to the ThirdPage, by passing some data.

Because there's common functionality between these pages, the base class NavigationPage is created from which all these pages derive. The NavigationPage class derives from the base class Page and implements the interface INotifyPropertyChanged for user interface updates (code file PageNavigation/NavigationPage.cs):

```
public abstract class NavigationPage : Page, INotifyPropertyChanged
{
  public event PropertyChangedEventHandler PropertyChanged;

  protected virtual void OnPropertyChanged(
    [CallerMemberName] string propertyName = null) =>
      PropertyChanged?.Invoke(this, new PropertyChangedEventArgs(propertyName));

  protected bool SetProperty<T>(ref T item, T value,
    [CallerMemberName] string propertyName = null)
  {
    if (EqualityComparer<T>.Default.Equals(item, value)) return false;
    item = value;
    OnPropertyChanged(propertyName);
    return true;
  }

  private string _navigationMode;
  public string NavigationMode
  {
    get => _navigationMode;
    set => SetProperty(ref _navigationMode, value);
  }

  //...
}
```

Overriding Page Class Navigation

The Page class that is the base class of NavigationPage (and the base class of XAML pages) defines methods that are used on navigation. The method OnNavigatedTo is invoked when the page is navigated to. Within this page you can read how the navigation was done (NavigationMode property) and parameters for the navigation. The method OnNavigatingFrom is the first method that is invoked when you navigate away from the page. Here, the navigation can be cancelled. The method OnNavigatedFrom is finally invoked when you navigate away from this page. Here, you should do some cleanup of resources that have been allocated with the OnNavigatedTo method (code file PageNavigation/App.xaml.cs):

```
public abstract class NavigationPage : Page, INotifyPropertyChanged
{
  //...
  protected override void OnNavigatedTo(NavigationEventArgs e)
  {
    base.OnNavigatedTo(e);
    NavigationMode = $"Navigation Mode: {e.NavigationMode}";
    //...
  }

  protected override void OnNavigatingFrom(NavigatingCancelEventArgs e)
  {
    base.OnNavigatingFrom(e);
  }

  protected override void OnNavigatedFrom(NavigationEventArgs e)
  {
    base.OnNavigatedFrom(e);
  }
}
```

Navigating Between Pages

Let's implement the three pages. For using the NavigationPage class, the code-behind file needs to be modified to use the NavigationPage as a base class (code file PageNavigation/MainPage.xaml.cs):

```
public sealed partial class MainPage : NavigationPage
{
  //...
}
```

The change of the base class also needs to be reflected in the XAML file using the NavigationPage element instead of the Page (code file PageNavigation/MainPage.xaml):

```
<local:NavigationPage
  x:Class="PageNavigation.MainPage"
  xmlns="http://schemas.microsoft.com/winfx/2006/xaml/presentation"
  xmlns:x="http://schemas.microsoft.com/winfx/2006/xaml"
  xmlns:local="using:PageNavigation"
  xmlns:d="http://schemas.microsoft.com/expression/blend/2008"
  xmlns:mc="http://schemas.openxmlformats.org/markup-compatibility/2006"
  mc:Ignorable="d">
```

The MainPage contains a TextBlock element that binds to the NavigationMode property declared in the BasePage, and a Button control with a Click event binding to the method OnNavigateToSecondPage (code file PageNavigation/MainPage.xaml):

```
<StackPanel Orientation="Vertical">
  <TextBlock Style="{StaticResource TitleTextBlockStyle}" Margin="8">
    Main Page</TextBlock>
```

```
<TextBlock Text="{x:Bind NavigationMode, Mode=OneWay}" Margin="8" />
<Button Content="Navigate to SecondPage" Click="OnNavigateToSecondPage"
    Margin="8" />
</StackPanel>
```

The handler method OnNavigateToSecondPage navigates to the SecondPage using Frame.Navigate. Frame is a property of the Page class that returns the Frame instance (code file PageNavigation/MainPage.xaml.cs):

```
public void OnNavigateToSecondPage()
{
    Frame.Navigate(typeof(SecondPage));
}
```

When you navigate from the SecondPage to the ThirdPage, a parameter is passed to the target page. The parameter can be entered in the TextBox that is bound to the Data property (code file PageNavigation/SecondPage.xaml):

```
<StackPanel Orientation="Vertical">
  <TextBlock Style="{StaticResource TitleTextBlockStyle}" Margin="8">
    Second Page</TextBlock>
  <TextBlock Text="{x:Bind NavigationMode, Mode=OneWay}" Margin="8" />
  <TextBox Header="Data" Text="{x:Bind Data, Mode=TwoWay}" Margin="8" />
  <Button Content="Navigate to Third Page"
    Click="{x:Bind OnNavigateToThirdPage, Mode=OneTime}" Margin="8" />
</StackPanel>
```

With the code-behind file, the Data property is passed to the Navigate method (code file PageNavigation/SecondPage.xaml.cs):

```
public string Data { get; set; }

public void OnNavigateToThirdPage()
{
    Frame.Navigate(typeof(ThirdPage), Data);
}
```

The parameter received is retrieved in the ThirdPage. In the OnNavigatedTo method, the NavigationEventArgs receives the parameter with the Parameter property. The Parameter property is of type object as you can pass any data with the page navigation (code file PageNavigation/ThirdPage.xaml.cs):

```
protected override void OnNavigatedTo(NavigationEventArgs e)
{
    base.OnNavigatedTo(e);
    Data = e.Parameter as string;
}

private string _data;
public string Data
{
    get => _data;
    set => SetProperty(ref _data, value);
}
```

Back Button

When you have navigation in the app, it's necessary to include a way to go back. With Windows 8, a custom Back button was located in the upper-left corner of the page. You can still do this with Windows 10. Indeed, some Microsoft apps include such a button; Microsoft Edge puts a Back and Forward button at the top-left position. It makes sense to have a Back button nearby when there is also a Forward button. With Windows 10, you can make use of the system Back button.

Depending on whether the app is running in desktop mode or tablet mode, the Back button is located in different positions. To enable this Back button, you need to set the `AppViewBackButtonVisibility` of the `SystemNavigationManager` to `AppViewBackButtonVisiblitity`, which is the case in the following code when the property `Frame.CanGoBack` returns true (code file `PageNavigation/NavigationPage.cs`):

```
protected override void OnNavigatedTo(NavigationEventArgs e)
{
  NavigationMode = $"Navigation Mode: {e.NavigationMode}";
  SystemNavigationManager.GetForCurrentView().AppViewBackButtonVisibility =
    Frame.CanGoBack ? AppViewBackButtonVisibility.Visible :
    AppViewBackButtonVisibility.Collapsed;
  base.OnNavigatedTo(e);
}
```

Next, you use the `BackRequested` event of the `SystemNavigationManager` class. Reacting to the `BackRequestedEvent` can be done globally for the app, as is shown here. In case you need this functionality only in a few pages, you can also put this code within the `OnNavigatedTo` method of the page (code file `PageNavigation/App.xaml.cs`):

```
protected override void OnLaunched(LaunchActivatedEventArgs e)
{
  //...
  SystemNavigationManager.GetForCurrentView().BackRequested +=
    App_BackRequested;
  Window.Current.Activate();
}
```

The handler method `App_BackRequested` invokes the `GoBack` method on the frame object (code file `PageNavigation/App.xaml.cs`):

```
private void App_BackRequested(object sender, BackRequestedEventArgs e)
{
  Frame rootFrame = Window.Current.Content as Frame;
  if (rootFrame == null) return;
  if (rootFrame.CanGoBack && e.Handled == false)
  {
    e.Handled = true;
    rootFrame.GoBack();
  }
}
```

When you run the app in desktop mode, you can see the Back button in the left corner of the top border (see Figure 33-25). In cases where the app is running in tablet mode, the border is not visible, but the Back button is shown in the bottom border beside the Windows button (see Figure 33-26). This is the new Back button of the app. In cases where navigation in the app is not possible, the user navigates back to the previous app when he or she taps the Back button.

Hub

You can also allow the user to navigate between content within a single page using the `Hub` control. An example of when you might use this is if you want to show an image as an entry point for the app and more information is shown as the user scrolls (see Figure 33-27, the Picture Search app from the Microsoft Store).

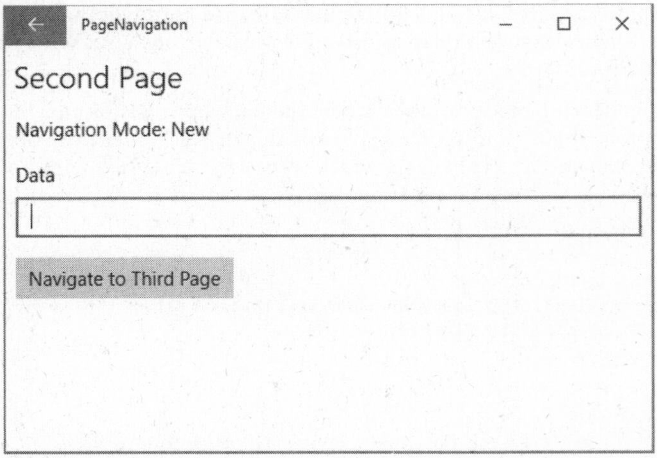

FIGURE 33-25

FIGURE 33-26

FIGURE 33-27

With the Hub control you can define multiple sections. Each section has a header and content. You can also make the header clickable—for example, to navigate to a detail page. The following code sample defines a Hub control where you can click the headers of sections 2 and 3. When you click the section header, the method assigned with the SectionHeaderClick event of the Hub control is invoked. Each section consists of a header and some content. The content of the section is defined by a DataTemplate (code file NavigationControls/HubPage.xaml):

```xaml
<Hub Background="{ThemeResource ApplicationPageBackgroundThemeBrush}"
  SectionHeaderClick="{x:Bind OnHeaderClick}">
  <Hub.Header>
    <StackPanel Orientation="Horizontal">
      <TextBlock>Hub Header</TextBlock>
      <TextBlock Text="{x:Bind Info, Mode=TwoWay}" />
    </StackPanel>
  </Hub.Header>
  <HubSection Width="400" Background="LightBlue" Tag="Section 1">
    <HubSection.Header>
      <TextBlock>Section 1 Header</TextBlock>
    </HubSection.Header>
    <DataTemplate>
      <TextBlock>Section 1</TextBlock>
    </DataTemplate>
  </HubSection>
  <HubSection Width="300" Background="LightGreen" IsHeaderInteractive="True"
    Tag="Section 2">
    <HubSection.Header>
      <TextBlock>Section 2 Header</TextBlock>
    </HubSection.Header>
    <DataTemplate>
      <TextBlock>Section 2</TextBlock>
    </DataTemplate>
  </HubSection>
  <HubSection Width="300" Background="LightGoldenrodYellow"
    IsHeaderInteractive="True" Tag="Section 3">
    <HubSection.Header>
      <TextBlock>Section 3 Header</TextBlock>
    </HubSection.Header>
    <DataTemplate>
      <TextBlock>Section 3</TextBlock>
    </DataTemplate>
  </HubSection>
</Hub>
```

When you click the header section, the Info dependency property is assigned the value of the Tag property. The Info property in turn is bound within the header of the Hub control (code file NavigationControls/HubPage.xaml.cs):

```csharp
public void OnHeaderClick(object sender, HubSectionHeaderClickEventArgs e)
{
  Info = e.Section.Tag as string;
}

public string Info
{
  get => (string)GetValue(InfoProperty);
  set => SetValue(InfoProperty, value);
}

public static readonly DependencyProperty InfoProperty =
  DependencyProperty.Register("Info", typeof(string), typeof(HubPage),
    new PropertyMetadata(string.Empty));
```

When you run the app, you can see multiple hub sections (see Figure 33-28) with a See More link in sections 2 and 3 because with these sections `IsHeaderInteractive` is set to `true`. Of course, you can create a custom header template to have a different look for the header.

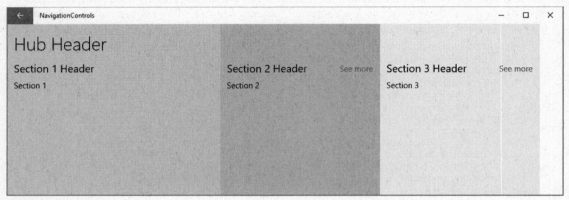

FIGURE 33-28

> **NOTE** *Creating custom templates is explained in Chapter 35.*

Pivot

You can create a pivot-like look for the navigation using the `Pivot` control. The `Pivot` control can contain multiple `PivotItem` controls. Each of these item controls has a header and content. The `Pivot` itself contains left and right headers. The sample code fills the right header (code file `NavigationControls/PivotPage.xaml`):

```
<Pivot Title="Pivot Sample"
  Background="{ThemeResource ApplicationPageBackgroundThemeBrush}">
  <Pivot.RightHeader>
    <StackPanel>
      <TextBlock>Right Header</TextBlock>
    </StackPanel>
  </Pivot.RightHeader>
  <PivotItem>
    <PivotItem.Header>Header Pivot 1</PivotItem.Header>
    <TextBlock>Pivot 1 Content</TextBlock>
  </PivotItem>
  <PivotItem>
    <PivotItem.Header>Header Pivot 2</PivotItem.Header>
    <TextBlock>Pivot 2 Content</TextBlock>
  </PivotItem>
  <PivotItem>
    <PivotItem.Header>Header Pivot 3</PivotItem.Header>
    <TextBlock>Pivot 3 Content</TextBlock>
  </PivotItem>
  <PivotItem>
    <PivotItem.Header>Header Pivot 4</PivotItem.Header>
    <TextBlock>Pivot 4 Content</TextBlock>
  </PivotItem>
</Pivot>
```

When you run the application, you can see the `Pivot` control (see Figure 33-29). The right header is always visible on the right. Click one of the headers to see the content of the item.

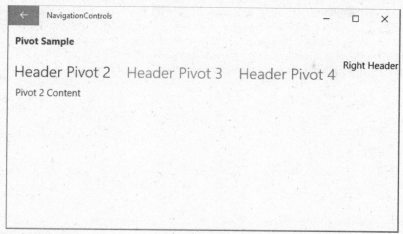

FIGURE 33-29

In case all headers do not fit the screen, the user can scroll. Using the mouse for navigation, you can see arrows on the left and right as shown in Figure 33-30.

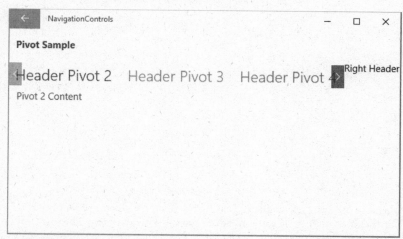

FIGURE 33-30

NavigationView

Windows 10 apps often use the `SplitView` control together with a hamburger button. The hamburger button is used to open a list of menus. The menus are shown either just with an icon, or with icon and text if more space is available. For arranging the space for the content and the menus, the `SplitView` control comes into play. The `SplitView` offers space for a pane and a content where the pane usually contains menu items. The pane can have a small and a large size, which can be configured depending on the available screen sizes.

Before Windows 10 build 16299, you had to manually construct user interfaces with the `SplitView`, a hamburger button, and a menu list that shows up within the pane. You can get a sample for this in the code download from the previous edition of the book, *Professional C# 6 and .NET Core 1.0*, which is necessary to do in case you need to support editions of Windows 10 previous to build 16299. With build 16299, the `NavigationView` control is available. The `NavigationView` integrates all this behavior into one control. Figure 33-31 shows the pane of the `NavigationView` opened. Clicking on the hamburger button or making the app smaller changes the pane to the compact mode as shown in Figure 33-32. Reducing the size of the app even more reduces the left part of the `NavigationView` to a hamburger button, as shown with Figure 33-33.

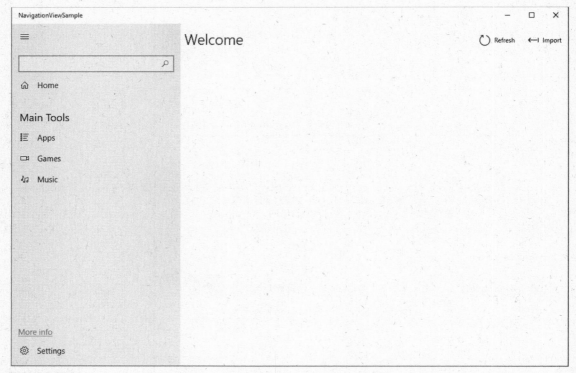

FIGURE 33-31

Let's get into the features of the `NavigationView`. Figure 33-34 highlights the different parts of the `NavigationView`. The first part defined in the `NavigationView` is the list of `MenuItems`. This list contains `NavigationViewItem` objects. Each of these items contains an `Icon`, `Content`, and a `Tag`. The `Tag` can be used programmatically to use this information for navigation. With some of these items, a predefined icon is used. The `NavigationViewItem` tagged with `home` makes use of a `FontIcon` with the Unicode number E10F. To separate menu items, you can use the `NavigationViewItemSeparator`. With the `NavigationViewItemHeader`, you can specify a header content for a group of items. Pay attention not to cut this content when the pane is in compact mode. With the code snippet, the `NavigationViewItemHeader` is hidden if the pane is not fully opened (code file `NavigationViewSample/MainPage.xaml`):

```
<NavigationView x:Name="NavigationView1"
  Background="{ThemeResource ApplicationPageBackgroundThemeBrush}">
  <NavigationView.MenuItems>
    <NavigationViewItem Content="Home" Tag="home">
      <NavigationViewItem.Icon>
        <FontIcon Glyph="&#xE10F;"/>
      </NavigationViewItem.Icon>
    </NavigationViewItem>
    <NavigationViewItemSeparator/>
    <NavigationViewItemHeader Content="Main Tools"
      Visibility="{x:Bind NavigationView1.IsPaneOpen, Mode=OneWay}"/>
    <NavigationViewItem Icon="AllApps" Content="Apps" Tag="apps"/>
    <NavigationViewItem Icon="Video" Content="Games" Tag="games"/>
    <NavigationViewItem Icon="Audio" Content="Music" Tag="music"/>
  </NavigationView.MenuItems>

  <!-- ... -->

</NavigationView>
```

FIGURE 33-32

FIGURE 33-33

The `AutoSuggestBox` property of the `NavigationView` allows adding an `AutoSuggestsBox` control to the navigation. This is shown on top of the menu items. The `AutoSuggestBox` is covered in Chapter 36 (code file `NavigationViewSample/MainPage.xaml`):

```
<NavigationView.AutoSuggestBox>
  <AutoSuggestBox x:Name="autoSuggest" QueryIcon="Find"/>
</NavigationView.AutoSuggestBox>
```

With the `HeaderTemplate`, the top of the app can be customized. The code snippet defines a header template with a `Grid`, a `TextBlock`, and a `CommandBar` (code file `NavigationViewSample/MainPage.xaml`):

```
<NavigationView.HeaderTemplate>
  <DataTemplate>
    <Grid Margin="8,8,0,0">
      <Grid.ColumnDefinitions>
        <ColumnDefinition Width="Auto"/>
        <ColumnDefinition/>
      </Grid.ColumnDefinitions>
      <TextBlock Style="{StaticResource TitleTextBlockStyle}"
        FontSize="28"
        VerticalAlignment="Center"
        Text="Welcome"/>
      <CommandBar Grid.Column="1"
        DefaultLabelPosition="Right"
```

```
                Background="{ThemeResource SystemControlBackgroundAltHighBrush}">
              <AppBarButton Label="Refresh" Icon="Refresh"/>
              <AppBarButton Label="Import" Icon="Import"/>
            </CommandBar>
          </Grid>
        </DataTemplate>
    </NavigationView.HeaderTemplate>
```

The `PaneFooter` defines the lower part in the pane. Below the footer, by default a menu item for the Settings is shown; this menu, which is used by many apps, is included by default (code file `NavigationViewSample/ MainPage.xaml`):

```
<NavigationView.PaneFooter>
  <HyperlinkButton x:Name="MoreInfoBtn"
    Content="More info"
    Margin="12,0"/>
</NavigationView.PaneFooter>
```

Finally, the content of the `NavigationPane` is covered by a `Frame` control. This control is used to navigate to pages. The `NavigationPane` surrounds the page content (code file `NavigationViewSample/MainPage .xaml`):

```
<Frame x:Name="ContentFrame" Margin="24">
  <Frame.ContentTransitions>
    <TransitionCollection>
      <NavigationThemeTransition/>
    </TransitionCollection>
  </Frame.ContentTransitions>
</Frame>
```

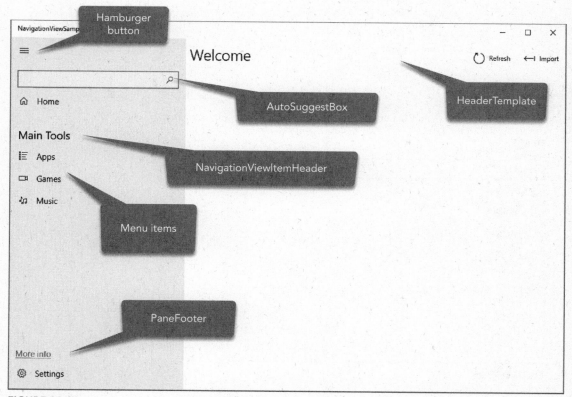

FIGURE 33-34

LAYOUT PANELS

The `NavigationView` control discussed in the previous section is an important control to organize the layout of the user interface. With many new Windows 10 apps you can see this control used for the main layout. There are several other controls to define a layout. This section demonstrates the `VariableSizedWrapGrid` for arranging multiple items in a grid that automatically wraps, the `RelativePanel` for arranging items relative to each other or relative to a parent, and adaptive triggers for rearranging the layout depending on the window size.

StackPanel

If you need to add multiple elements to a control that supports only one control, the easiest way is to use a `StackPanel`. The `StackPanel` is a simple panel that shows one element after the other. The orientation of the `StackPanel` can be horizontal or vertical.

In the following code snippet, the page contains a `StackPanel` with various controls organized vertical. In the `ListBox` within the first `ListBoxItem` contains a `StackPanel` organized horizontally (code file `LayoutSamples/Views/StackPanelPage.xaml`):

```xml
<Grid Background="{ThemeResource ApplicationPageBackgroundThemeBrush}">
  <StackPanel Orientation="Vertical">
    <TextBox Text="TextBox" />
    <CheckBox Content="Checkbox" />
    <CheckBox Content="Checkbox" />
    <ListBox>
      <ListBoxItem>
        <StackPanel Orientation="Horizontal">
          <TextBlock Text="One A" />
          <TextBlock Text="One B" />
        </StackPanel>
      </ListBoxItem>
      <ListBoxItem Content="Two" />
    </ListBox>
    <Button Content="Button" />
  </StackPanel>
</Grid>
```

Figure 33-35 shows the child controls of the `StackPanel` organized vertically.

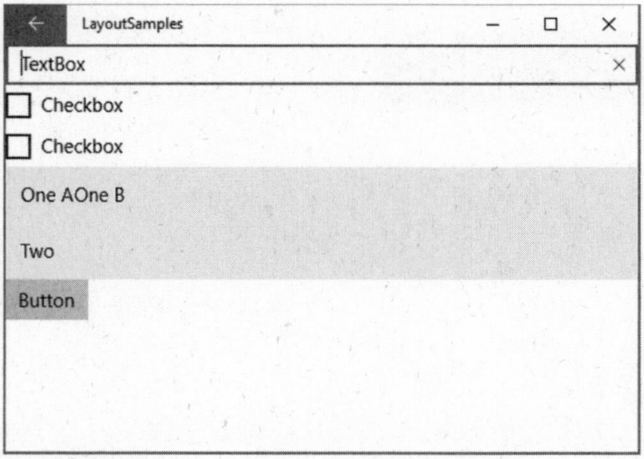

FIGURE 33-35

Canvas

Canvas is a panel that enables you to explicitly position controls. Canvas defines the attached properties Left, Right, Top, and Bottom that can be used by the children for positioning within the panel (code file LayoutSamples/Views/CanvasPage.xaml):

Figure 33-36 shows the output of the Canvas panel with the positioned children TextBlock, TextBox, and Button.

```xaml
<Canvas Background="LightBlue">
  <TextBlock Canvas.Top="30" Canvas.Left="20">Enter here:</TextBlock>
  <TextBox Canvas.Top="30" Canvas.Left="120" Width="100" />
  <Button Canvas.Top="70" Canvas.Left="120" Content="Click Me!" Padding="4" />
</Canvas>
```

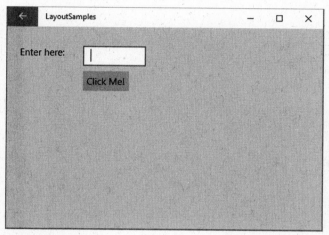

FIGURE 33-36

> **NOTE** *The* Canvas *control is best used for the layout of graphic elements, like* Shape *controls shown in Chapter 35.*

Grid

The Grid is an important panel. Using the Grid, you can arrange your controls with rows and columns. For every column, you can specify a ColumnDefinition. For every row, you can specify a RowDefinition. The following example code lists two columns and three rows. With each column and row, you can specify the width or height. ColumnDefinition has a Width dependency property; RowDefinition has a Height dependency property. You can define the height and width in device-independent pixels, or you can set it to Auto to base the size on the content. The grid also allows *star sizing*, which means the space for the rows and columns is calculated according to the available space and relative to other rows and columns. When providing the available space for a column, you can set the Width property to *. To have the size doubled for another column, you specify 2*. The sample code, which defines two columns and three rows, uses star sizing for the columns (this is the default), the first row has a fixed size, and the second and third row use star sizing again. With the height calculation, the available height is reduced by the 200 pixels from the first row. The remaining area is divided between rows 2 and 3 in the relation 1.5:1.

The grid contains several `Rectangle` controls with different colors to make the cell sizes visible. Because the parent of these controls is a grid, you can set the attached properties `Column`, `ColumnSpan`, `Row`, and `RowSpan` (code file `LayoutSamples/Views/GridPage.xaml`):

```xml
<Grid Background="{ThemeResource ApplicationPageBackgroundThemeBrush}">
  <Grid.ColumnDefinitions>
    <ColumnDefinition />
    <ColumnDefinition />
  </Grid.ColumnDefinitions>
  <Grid.RowDefinitions>
    <RowDefinition Height="200" />
    <RowDefinition Height="1.5*" />
    <RowDefinition Height="*" />
  </Grid.RowDefinitions>
  <Rectangle Fill="Blue" />
  <Rectangle Grid.Row="0" Grid.Column="1" Fill="Red" />
  <Rectangle Grid.Row="1" Grid.Column="0" Grid.ColumnSpan="2" Fill="Green" />
  <Rectangle Grid.Row="2" Grid.Column="0" Grid.ColumnSpan="2" Fill="Yellow" />
</Grid>
```

The outcome of arranging rectangles in a grid is shown in Figure 33-37.

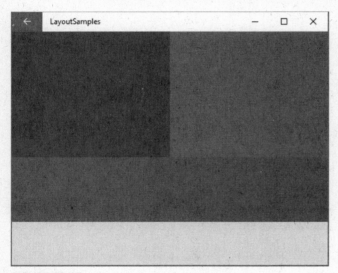

FIGURE 33-37

VariableSizedWrapGrid

`VariableSizedWrapGrid` is a wrap grid that automatically wraps to the next row or column if the size available for the grid is not large enough. The second feature of this grid is an allowance for items with multiple rows or columns; that's why it's called variable.

The following code snippet creates a `VariableSizedWrappedGrid` with orientation `Horizontal`, a maximum number of 20 items in the row, and rows and columns that have a size of 50 (code file `LayoutSamples/Views/VariableSizedWrapGridSample.xaml`):

```xml
<VariableSizedWrapGrid x:Name="grid1" MaximumRowsOrColumns="20" ItemHeight="50"
  ItemWidth="50" Orientation="Horizontal" />
```

The VariableSizedWrapGrid is filled with 30 Rectangle and TextBlock elements that have random sizes and colors. Depending on the size, 1 to 3 rows or columns can be used within the grid. The size of the items is set using the attached properties VariableSizedWrapGrid.ColumnSpan and VariableSizedWrapGrid .RowSpan (code file LayoutSamples/Views/VariableSizedWrapGridSample.xaml.cs):

```
protected override void OnNavigatedTo(NavigationEventArgs e)
{
  base.OnNavigatedTo(e);
  Random r = new Random();
  Grid[] items =
    Enumerable.Range(0, 30).Select(i =>
    {
      byte[] colorBytes = new byte[3];
      r.NextBytes(colorBytes);
      var rect = new Rectangle
      {
        Height = r.Next(40, 150),
        Width = r.Next(40, 150),
        Fill = new SolidColorBrush(new Color
        {
          R = colorBytes[0],
          G = colorBytes[1],
          B = colorBytes[2],
          A = 255
        })
      };

      var textBlock = new TextBlock
      {
        Text = (i + 1).ToString(),
        HorizontalAlignment = HorizontalAlignment.Center,
        VerticalAlignment = VerticalAlignment.Center
      };
      var grid = new Grid();
      grid.Children.Add(rect);
      grid.Children.Add(textBlock);
      return grid;
    }).ToArray();

  foreach (var item in items)
  {
    grid1.Children.Add(item);
    Rectangle rect = item.Children.First() as Rectangle;
    if (rect.Width > 50)
    {
      int columnSpan = ((int)rect.Width / 50) + 1;
      VariableSizedWrapGrid.SetColumnSpan(item, columnSpan);
      int rowSpan = ((int)rect.Height / 50) + 1;
      VariableSizedWrapGrid.SetRowSpan(item, rowSpan);
    }
  }
}
```

When you run the application, you can see the rectangles and how they wrap for different window sizes in Figures 33-38 and 33-39.

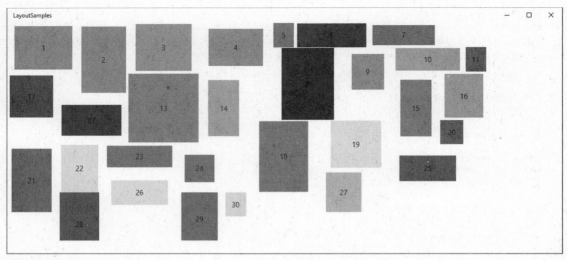

FIGURE 33-38

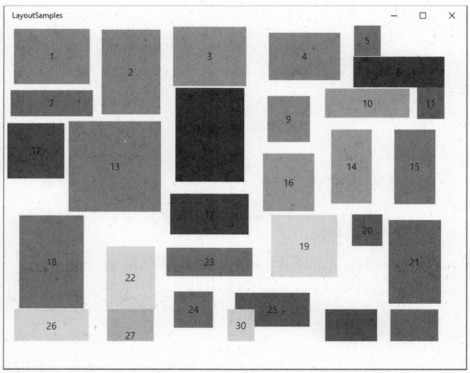

FIGURE 33-39

RelativePanel

`RelativePanel` is a panel that allows one element to be positioned in relation to another element. If you've used the `Grid` control with definitions for rows and columns and you had to insert a row, you had to change all elements that were below the row that was inserted. The reason is that all rows and columns are indexed by numbers. This is not an issue with the `RelativePanel`, which enables you to place elements in relation to each other.

> **NOTE** *Compared to the* `RelativePanel`, *the* `Grid` *control still has its advantages with auto, star, and fixed sizing.*

The following code snippet aligns several `TextBlock` and `TextBox` controls, a `Button`, and a `Rectangle` within a `RelativePanel`. The `TextBox` elements are positioned to the right of the corresponding `TextBlock` elements; the `Button` is positioned relative to the bottom of the panel; and the `Rectangle` is aligned with the top with the first `TextBlock` and to the right of the first `TextBox` (code file `LayoutSamples/Views/RelativePanelPage.xaml`):

```
<RelativePanel>
  <TextBlock x:Name="FirstNameLabel" Text="First Name" Margin="8" />
  <TextBox x:Name="FirstNameText" RelativePanel.RightOf="FirstNameLabel"
    Margin="8" Width="150" />
  <TextBlock x:Name="LastNameLabel" Text="Last Name"
    RelativePanel.Below="FirstNameLabel" Margin="8" />
  <TextBox x:Name="LastNameText" RelativePanel.RightOf="LastNameLabel"
    Margin="8" RelativePanel.Below="FirstNameText" Width="150" />
  <Button Content="Save" RelativePanel.AlignHorizontalCenterWith="LastNameText"
    RelativePanel.AlignBottomWithPanel="True" Margin="8" />
  <Rectangle x:Name="Image" Fill="Violet" Width="150" Height="250"
    RelativePanel.AlignTopWith="FirstNameLabel"
    RelativePanel.RightOf="FirstNameText" Margin="8" />
</RelativePanel>
```

Figure 33-40 shows the alignment of the controls when you run the application.

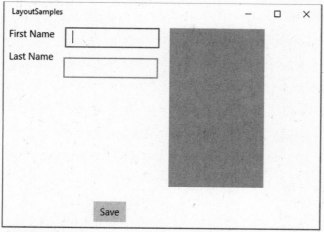

FIGURE 33-40

Adaptive Triggers

The RelativePanel is a great control for alignment. However, to support multiple screen sizes and rearrange the controls depending on the screen size, you can use adaptive triggers with the RelativePanel control. For example, on a small screen the TextBox controls should be arranged below the TextBlock controls, but on a larger screen the TextBox controls should be right of the TextBlock controls.

In the following code, the RelativePanel from before is changed to remove all RelativePanel attached properties that should not apply to all screen sizes, and an optional image is added (code file LayoutSamples/Views/AdaptiveRelativePanelPage.xaml):

```xml
<RelativePanel ScrollViewer.VerticalScrollBarVisibility="Auto" Margin="16">
  <TextBlock x:Name="FirstNameLabel" Text="First Name" Margin="8" />
  <TextBox x:Name="FirstNameText" Margin="8" Width="150" />
  <TextBlock x:Name="LastNameLabel" Text="Last Name" Margin="8" />
  <TextBox x:Name="LastNameText" Margin="8" Width="150" />
  <Button Content="Save" RelativePanel.AlignBottomWithPanel="True"
    Margin="8" />
  <Rectangle x:Name="Image" Fill="Violet" Width="150" Height="250"
    Margin="8" />
  <Rectangle x:Name="OptionalImage" RelativePanel.AlignRightWithPanel="True"
    Fill="Red" Width="350" Height="350" Margin="8" />
</RelativePanel>
```

Using an adaptive trigger—with which the MinWindowWidth can be set to define when the trigger is fired—values for different properties are set to arrange the elements depending on the space available for the app. As the screen size gets smaller, the width needed by the app gets smaller as well. Moving elements below instead of beside reduces the width needed. Instead, the user can scroll down. With the smallest window width, the optional image is set to collapsed (code file LayoutSamples/Views/AdaptiveRelativePanelPage.xaml):

```xml
<VisualStateManager.VisualStateGroups>
  <VisualStateGroup>
    <VisualState x:Name="WideState">
      <VisualState.StateTriggers>
        <AdaptiveTrigger MinWindowWidth="1024" />
      </VisualState.StateTriggers>
      <VisualState.Setters>
        <Setter Target="FirstNameText.(RelativePanel.RightOf)"
          Value="FirstNameLabel" />
        <Setter Target="LastNameLabel.(RelativePanel.Below)"
          Value="FirstNameLabel" />
        <Setter Target="LastNameText.(RelativePanel.Below)"
          Value="FirstNameText" />
        <Setter Target="LastNameText.(RelativePanel.RightOf)"
          Value="LastNameLabel" />
        <Setter Target="Image.(RelativePanel.AlignTopWith)"
          Value="FirstNameLabel" />
        <Setter Target="Image.(RelativePanel.RightOf)" Value="FirstNameText" />
      </VisualState.Setters>
    </VisualState>
    <VisualState x:Name="MediumState">
      <VisualState.StateTriggers>
        <AdaptiveTrigger MinWindowWidth="720" />
      </VisualState.StateTriggers>
      <VisualState.Setters>
        <Setter Target="FirstNameText.(RelativePanel.RightOf)"
          Value="FirstNameLabel" />
        <Setter Target="LastNameLabel.(RelativePanel.Below)"
          Value="FirstNameLabel" />
        <Setter Target="LastNameText.(RelativePanel.Below)"
          Value="FirstNameText" />
        <Setter Target="LastNameText.(RelativePanel.RightOf)"
```

```
              Value="LastNameLabel" />
         <Setter Target="Image.(RelativePanel.Below)" Value="LastNameText" />
         <Setter Target="Image.(RelativePanel.AlignHorizontalCenterWith)"
            Value="LastNameText" />
      </VisualState.Setters>
    </VisualState>
    <VisualState x:Name="NarrowState">
      <VisualState.StateTriggers>
        <AdaptiveTrigger MinWindowWidth="320" />
      </VisualState.StateTriggers>
      <VisualState.Setters>
        <Setter Target="FirstNameText.(RelativePanel.Below)"
          Value="FirstNameLabel" />
        <Setter Target="LastNameLabel.(RelativePanel.Below)"
          Value="FirstNameText" />
        <Setter Target="LastNameText.(RelativePanel.Below)"
          Value="LastNameLabel" />
        <Setter Target="Image.(RelativePanel.Below)" Value="LastNameText" />
        <Setter Target="OptionalImage.Visibility" Value="Collapsed" />
      </VisualState.Setters>
    </VisualState>
  </VisualStateGroup>
</VisualStateManager.VisualStateGroups>
```

You can establish the minimum window width needed by the application by setting the
`SetPreferredMinSize` with the `ApplicationView` class (code file `LayoutSamples/App.xaml.cs`):

```
protected override void OnLaunched(LaunchActivatedEventArgs e)
{
  ApplicationView.GetForCurrentView().SetPreferredMinSize(
  new Size { Width = 320, Height = 300 });
  //...
}
```

When you run the application, you can see different layout arrangements with the smallest width (see
Figure 33-41), a medium width (see Figure 33-42), and the maximum width (see Figure 33-43).

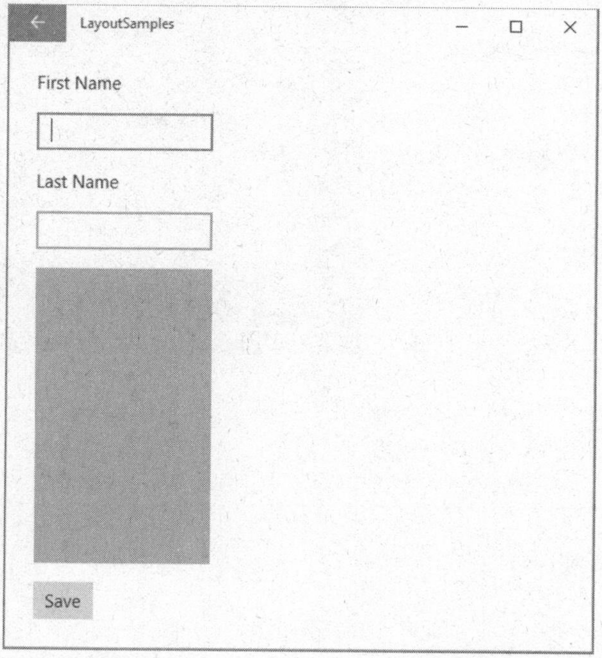

FIGURE 33-41

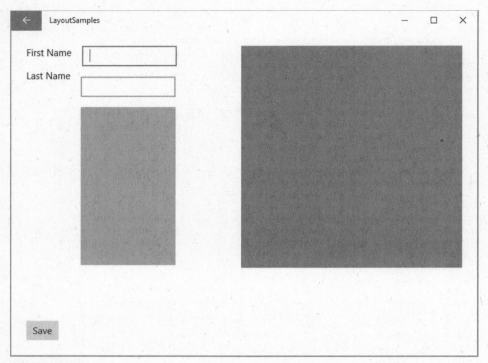

FIGURE 33-42

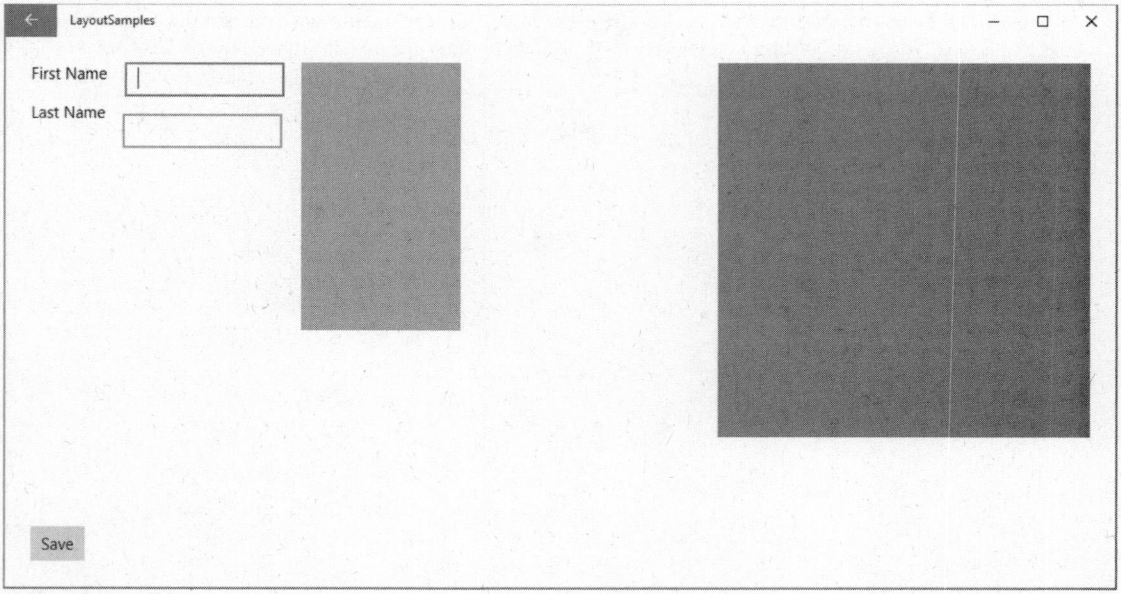

FIGURE 33-43

XAML Views

Adaptive triggers can help support a lot of different window sizes as well as support layouts of the app for running it on the Xbox, the HoloLens, and on the desktop with different resolutions. If the user interface for your app should have more differences than can be solved by using the `RelativePanel`, the best option can be to use different XAML views. An XAML view contains just XAML code and uses the same code-behind as the corresponding page. You can create different XAML views for the same page for every device family.

You can define XAML views for mobile devices by creating a folder `DeviceFamily-Mobile`. The device-specific folder always starts with the name `DeviceFamily`. Examples of other device families supported are `Team`, `Desktop`, and `IoT`. You can use this device family name as postfix to specify XAML views for the corresponding device family. You create a XAML view using the XAML View Visual Studio item template. This template creates the XAML code but no code-behind file. This view needs to have the same name as the page where the view should be replaced.

Instead of creating a different folder for the mobile XAML views, you can also create the views in the same folder as the page, but the view file is named using `DeviceFamily-Mobile`.

Deferred Loading

For a faster UI, you can delay creation of controls until they are needed. On small devices, some controls might not be needed at all, but with larger screens and faster systems they are needed. With previous versions of XAML applications, elements that have been added to the XAML code also have been instantiated. This is no longer the case with Windows 10. Here you can defer loading of controls as they are needed.

You can use deferred loading with adaptive triggers to load only some controls at a later time. One sample scenario where this is useful is when you have a smaller window that the user can resize to be larger. With the smaller window, some controls should not be visible, but they should be visible with the bigger size of the window. Another scenario where deferred loading can be useful is when some parts of the layout may take more time to load. Instead of letting the user wait until he sees the complete loaded layout, you can use deferred loading.

To use deferred loading, you need to add the `x:Load` attribute with a value `False` to a control, as shown in the following code snippet with a `Grid` control. This control also needs to have a name assigned to it (code file `LayoutSamples/Views/DelayLoadingPage.xaml`):

```
<Grid x:Load="False" x:Name="deferGrid">
  <Grid.ColumnDefinitions>
    <ColumnDefinition />
    <ColumnDefinition />
  </Grid.ColumnDefinitions>
  <Grid.RowDefinitions>
    <RowDefinition />
    <RowDefinition />
  </Grid.RowDefinitions>
  <Rectangle Fill="Red" Grid.Row="0" Grid.Column="0" />
  <Rectangle Fill="Green" Grid.Row="0" Grid.Column="1" />
  <Rectangle Fill="Blue" Grid.Row="1" Grid.Column="0" />
  <Rectangle Fill="Yellow" Grid.Row="1" Grid.Column="1" />
</Grid>
```

To make this deferred control visible, all you need to do is invoke the `FindName` method to access the identifier of the control. This not only makes the control visible but also loads the XAML tree of the control before the control is made visible (code file `LayoutSamples/Views/DelayLoadingPage.xaml.cs`):

```
private void OnDeferLoad(object sender, RoutedEventArgs e)
{
  FindName(nameof(deferGrid));
}
```

> **NOTE** *The* x:Load *attribute is new with build 15063. Previous to build 15063, you could use the* x:DeferLoadingStrategy *attribute.* x:Load *has the advantage that the element can also be unloaded after it was loaded.*

When you run the application, you can verify with the Live Visual Tree window that the tree containing the deferGrid element is not available (see Figure 33-44), but after the FindName method is invoked to find the deferGrid element, the deferGrid element is added to the tree (see Figure 33-45).

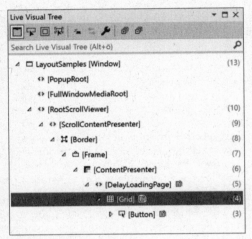

FIGURE 33-44

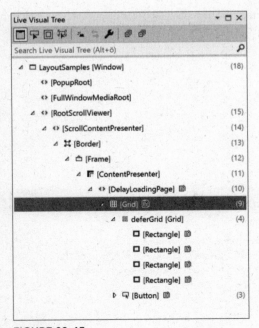

FIGURE 33-45

> **NOTE** *The attribute* x:Load *has an overhead of about 600 bytes, so you should use it only on elements that need to be hidden. If this attribute is used on a container element, you only pay the overhead once with the element where the attribute is applied to.*

SUMMARY

This chapter introduced many different aspects of programming Windows apps. You've seen the foundation on XAML and how it extends XML with attached properties and markup extensions. You've seen how to deal with XAML differences in different Windows 10 versions using conditional XAML.

You've seen how different screen sizes can be dealt with, options for laying out controls with different panels, and the categories and features of different controls.

The next chapter continues with XAML-based apps, the MVVM pattern, commands, and creating shareable view-models.

34

Patterns with XAML Apps

WHAT'S IN THIS CHAPTER?

➤ Sharing code
➤ Creating models
➤ Creating repositories
➤ Creating ViewModels
➤ Navigation between pages
➤ Adaptive user interfaces
➤ Using an event aggregator
➤ List Items with view models

WROX.COM CODE DOWNLOADS FOR THIS CHAPTER

The Wrox.com code downloads for this chapter are found at www.wrox.com on the Download Code tab. The source code is also available at https://github.com/ProfessionalCSharp/ProfessionalCSharp7 in the directories Patterns and PatternsXamarinShared. The libraries are shared between Chapter 34 and Chapter 37, "Xamarin.Forms."

The code for this chapter contains the project BooksApp.

WHY MVVM?

Technologies and frameworks change. I created the first version of my company website (http://www.cninnovation.com) with ASP.NET Web Forms. When ASP.NET MVC came along, I tried it out to migrate a feature of my site to MVC. The progress was a lot faster than I expected. Within one day I transformed the complete site to MVC. The site uses SQL Server, integrates RSS feeds, and shows trainings and books. Information about the trainings and books is coming from the SQL Server database. The fast migration to ASP.NET MVC was only possible because I had separation of concerns from the beginning; I had created separate layers for the data access and business logic. With ASP.NET Web Forms it would have been possible to directly use data source and data controls within the ASPX page. Separating the data access and business logic took more time in the beginning, but it turned out to be a huge advantage, as it allows for unit tests and reuse. Because I had separated things this way, moving to another technology was a breeze. Nowadays this site is running with ASP.NET Core.

With regard to Windows apps, technology changes fast as well. For many years, Windows Forms was the technology of choice for wrapping native Windows controls to create desktop applications. Next followed Windows Presentation Foundation (WPF), in which the user interface is defined using eXtensible Application Markup Language (XAML). Silverlight offered a lightweight framework for XAML-based applications that run within the browser. Windows Store apps followed with Windows 8, changing to Universal Windows apps with Windows 8.1 for apps running both on the PC and the Windows phone. With Windows 8.1 and Visual Studio 2013, three projects with shared code have been created to support both the PC and the phone. This changed with Visual Studio 2015, Windows 10, and the Universal Windows Platform (UWP). You can have one project that can support the PC, the phone, Xbox One, Windows IoT, large screens with the Surface Hub, and even Microsoft's HoloLens.

One project to support all Windows 10 platforms might not fit your needs. Can you write a program that supports Windows 10 only? Some of your customers might still be running Windows 7. In this case, WPF is the answer, but it doesn't support other Windows 10 devices like HoloLens and Xbox. What about supporting Android and iOS? You can use Xamarin to create C# and .NET code here as well, but it's different.

The goal should be to reuse as much code as possible, to support the platforms needed, and to have an easy switch from one technology to another. These goals—with many organizations where administration and development joins as DevOps to bring new features and bug fixes in a fast pace to the user—require automated tests. Unit testing is a must that needs to be supported by the application architecture.

> **NOTE** *Unit testing is covered in Chapter 28, "Testing."*

With XAML-based applications, the *Model-View-ViewModel* (MVVM) design pattern is favored for separating the view from functionality. This design pattern was invented by John Gossman of the Expression Blend team as a better fit to XAML with advancements to the Model-View-Controller (MVC) and Model-View-Presenter (MVP) patterns because it uses data binding, a number-one feature of XAML.

With XAML-based applications, the XAML file and code-behind file are tightly coupled to each other. This makes it hard to reuse the code-behind and also hard to do unit testing. To solve this issue, the MVVM pattern allows for a better separation of the code from the user interface.

In principle, the MVVM pattern is not that hard to understand. However, when you're creating applications based on the MVVM pattern, you need to pay attention to a lot more needs: several patterns come into play for making applications work and making reuse possible, including dependency injection mechanisms for being independent of the implementation and communication between view models.

All this is covered in this chapter, and with this information you can not only use the same code with Windows apps and Windows desktop applications, but you can also use it for iOS and Android with the help of Xamarin. This chapter gives you a sample app that covers all the different aspects and patterns needed for a good separation to support different technologies.

DEFINING THE MVVM PATTERN

First, let's have a look at the MVC design pattern that is one of the origins of the MVVM pattern. The *Model-View-Controller* (MVC) pattern separates the model, the view, and the controller (see Figure 34-1). The model defines the data that is shown in the view as well as business rules about how the data can be changed and manipulated. The controller is the manager between the model and the view, updates the model, and sends data for display to the view. When a user request comes in, the controller takes action, uses the model, and updates the view.

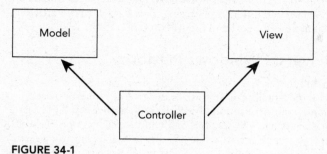

FIGURE 34-1

> **NOTE** *The MVC pattern is heavily used with ASP.NET MVC, which is covered in Chapter 31, "ASP.NET Core MVC."*

With the *Model-View-Presenter* (MVP) pattern (see Figure 34-2), the user interacts with the view. The presenter contains all the business logic for the view. The presenter can be decoupled from the view by using an interface to the view as contract. This allows easily changing the view implementation for unit tests. With MVP, the view and model are completely shielded from each other.

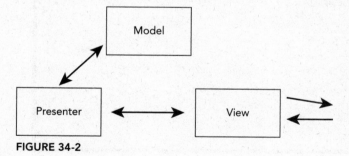

FIGURE 34-2

The main pattern used with XAML-based applications is the *Model-View-ViewModel* pattern (MVVM) (see Figure 34-3). This pattern takes advantage of the data-binding capabilities with XAML. With MVVM, the user interacts with the view. The view uses data binding to access information from the view model and invokes commands in the view model that are bound in the view as well. The view model doesn't have a direct dependency to the view. The view model itself uses the model to access data and gets change information from the model as well.

In the following sections of this chapter you see how to use this architecture with the application to create views, view models, models, and other patterns that are needed.

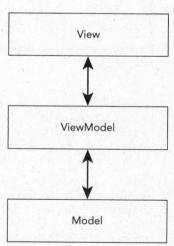

FIGURE 34-3

SHARING CODE

Before creating the sample solution and starting to create a model, we need to take a step back and have a look at different options for how to share code between different platforms. This section covers different options to address the different platforms you need to support and the APIs you need.

Using API Contracts with the Universal Windows Platform

The Universal Windows Platform defines an API that is available with all Windows 10 devices. However, this API changes from version to version. With the Application settings in the Project Properties (see Figure 34-4) you can define the *target version* of your application (this is the version that you build for) and the *minimum version* that is required on the system. The versions of all Software Developer Kits (SDKs) you select need to be installed on your system, so you can verify what APIs are available. For using features of the target version that are not available within the minimum version, you need to programmatically check whether the device supports the specific feature you need, before using that API.

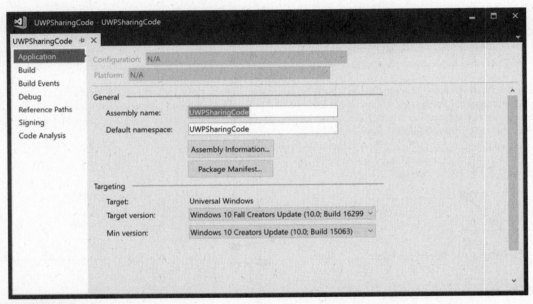

FIGURE 34-4

With the UWP, you can support different device families. The UWP defines several device families: Universal, Desktop (PC), Mobile, IoT (Raspberry Pi), Surface Hub, Holographic (HoloLens), and Xbox. Over time, more device families will follow. Each of these device families offers APIs that are available only for this family of devices. The APIs of device families are specified via an API contract. Each device family can offer multiple API contracts.

You can use features specific to device families, but you can still create one binary image that runs on all. Typically, your application will not support all the device families, but it might support a few of them. To support specific device families and use those families' APIs, you can add an *Extension SDK* from Solution Explorer; select References ⇨ Add Reference and then select Universal Windows ⇨ Extensions (see Figure 34-5). There you can see your installed SDKs and select the ones you need.

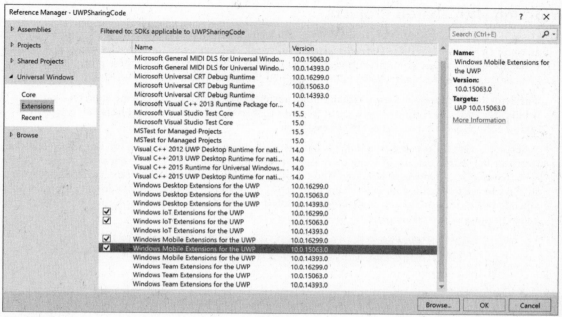

FIGURE 34-5

After selecting the Extension SDK, you can use the API from the code after verifying whether the API contract is available. The `ApiInformation` class (namespace `Windows.Foundation.Metadata`) defines the `IsApiContractPresent` method where you can check whether a specific API contract with a specific major and minor version is available. The following code snippet asks for the `Windows.Phone.PhoneContract`, major version 1. If this contract is available, the `VibrationDevice` can be used:

```
if (ApiInformation.IsApiContractPresent("Windows.Phone.PhoneContract", 1))
{
  VibrationDevice vibration = VibrationDevice.GetDefault();
  vibration.Vibrate(TimeSpan.FromSeconds(1));
}
```

> **NOTE** *You also can check for available API contracts with XAML code. Read about Conditional XAML in Chapter 33, "Windows Apps."*

You might be afraid to get convoluted code that checks all over the place using the checks for the API contracts. In a case where you're targeting just a single device family, it's not necessary to check to see whether the API is present. In the previous sample, if the application is only targeted for the phone, the API check is not necessary. In a case where you're targeting multiple device platforms, you only have to check for the device-specific APIs you're calling. You can write useful apps spanning multiple device families just by using the Universal API. In a case where you're supporting multiple device families with a lot of device-specific API calls, I propose you avoid using the `ApiInformation` and instead use dependency injection.

> **NOTE** *Read Chapter 20, "Dependency Injection," for more information about dependency injection (DI) and using DI containers.*

Working with Shared Projects

Using the same binary with API contracts is possible only with the Universal Windows Platform. This is not an option if you need to share code, for example, between Windows desktop applications with WPF and UWP apps, or between Xamarin.Forms apps and UWP apps. When you create these project types where you can't use the same binary, you can use the Shared Project template with Visual Studio 2017.

The *Shared Project* template with Visual Studio creates a project that doesn't create a binary—no assembly is built. Instead, code is shared between all projects that reference this shared project. You compile the code within each project that references the shared project.

When you create a class as shown in the following code snippet, this class can be used in all projects that reference the shared project. You can even use platform-specific code using preprocessor directives. The Visual Studio 2017 Universal Windows App template sets the conditional compilation symbol WINDOWS_UWP, so you can use this symbol for code that should only compile for the Universal Windows Platform. For WPF, you add WPF to the conditional compilation symbols with a WPF project, and for Xamarin, XAMARIN can be added to the conditional compilation symbols.

```
public partial class Demo
{
  public int Id { get; set; }
  public string Title { get; set; }
#if WPF
  public string WPFOnly { get; set; }
#endif
#if WINDOWS_UWP
  public string WindowsAppOnly {get; set; }
#endif
#if XAMARIN
  public string XamarinAppOnly {get; set; }
#endif
}
```

Editing shared code with the Visual Studio editor, you can select the project name in the upper-left bar, and the parts of the code that are not active for the actual project are dimmed (see Figure 34-6). When you're editing the file, IntelliSense also offers the API for the corresponding selected project.

Instead of using the preprocessor directives, you can also maintain differing parts of the class in the WPF, UWP, or Xamarin projects. This is a good reason to declare the class partial.

> **NOTE** *The C# partial keyword is explained in Chapter 3, "Objects and Types."*

When you define the same class name with the same namespace in the WPF project, you can extend the shared class. It is also possible to use a base class (if the shared project doesn't define a base class):

```
public class MyBase
{
  //...
}

public partial class Demo: MyBase
{
  public string WPFTitle => $"WPF{Title}";
}
```

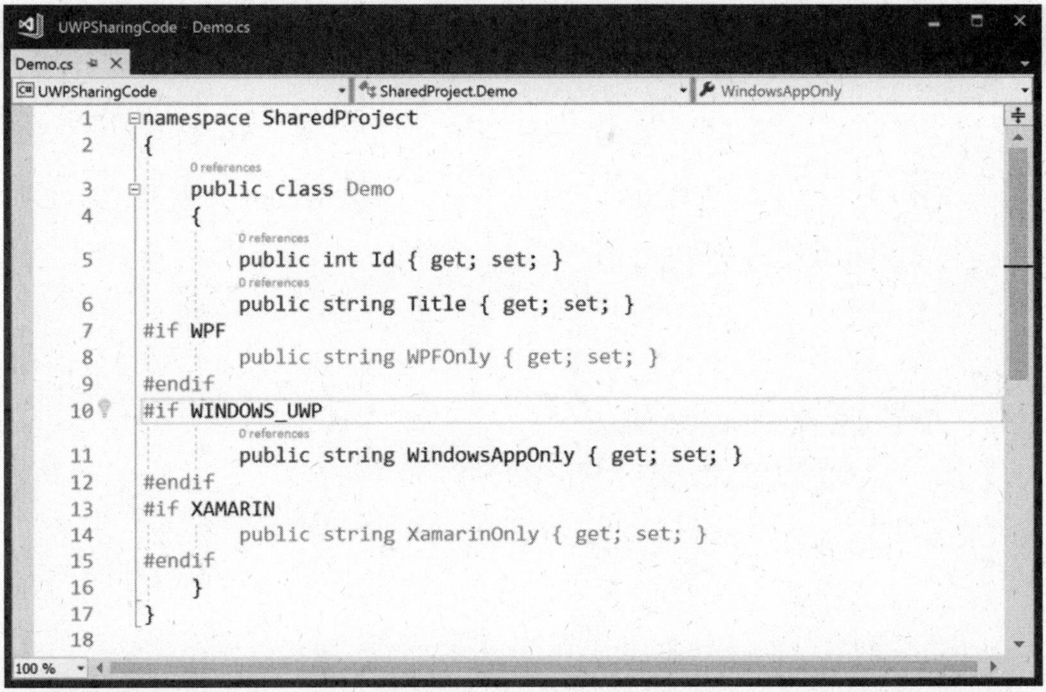

```
    UWPSharingCode - Demo.cs

Demo.cs  ✕
UWPSharingCode                    SharedProject.Demo              WindowsAppOnly

     1    ⊟namespace SharedProject
     2     {
              0 references
     3    ⊟      public class Demo
     4         {
                  0 references
     5              public int Id { get; set; }
                  0 references
     6              public string Title { get; set; }
     7    #if WPF
     8              public string WPFOnly { get; set; }
     9    #endif
    10    #if WINDOWS_UWP
                  0 references
    11              public string WindowsAppOnly { get; set; }
    12    #endif
    13    #if XAMARIN
    14              public string XamarinOnly { get; set; }
    15    #endif
    16         }
    17     }
    18

100 %
```

FIGURE 34-6

Working with .NET Standard Libraries

There's another option for sharing code: *.NET Standard Libraries.* All the actual technologies can use .NET Standard nowadays, so this is an easy task: Just create a .NET Standard Library, and you can share it between different platforms. You just need to pay attention to the version for the .NET Standard to use. The sample application is using a .NET Standard 2.0 library; this can be used from Windows Apps starting with build 16299, Xamarin.iOS 10.14, Xamarin.Android 8.0, Xamarin.Mac 3.8, and the .NET Framework 4.6.1.

> **NOTE** *Standard Libraries are the replacement for the Portable Class Library (PCL) and are a lot easier to use. Creating .NET Standard Libraries is discussed in detail in Chapter 19, "Libraries, Assemblies, Packages, and NuGet."*

With .NET Standard Libraries, every new version gets additional APIs. APIs are never removed. After creating a .NET Standard Library, with the Project Properties you can select the version of the standard (see Figure 34-7) that should be supported. With the selection, you're limited to the APIs that are available with this version.

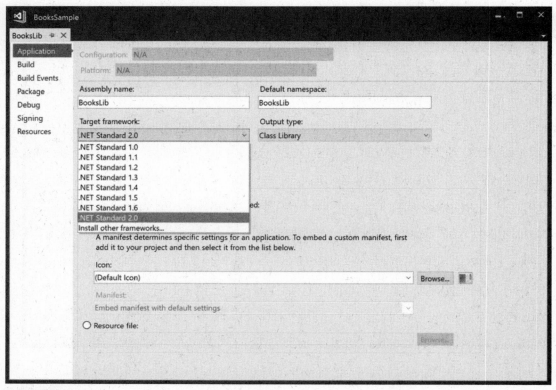

FIGURE 34-7

When you're using shared projects, you can write code that is only available from one platform. To differentiate the code from other platforms, you can use preprocessor statements to compile the code only when compiling it for this one platform. You can't do this with .NET Standard Libraries. As a practical way around this, you can use standard libraries to define code for contracts and implement the contracts with platform-specific libraries where needed. To use the code from the platform-specific libraries with libraries that are not platform specific, you can use dependency injection. How to do this is part of the bigger sample in this chapter, which is covered in the "View Models" section.

> **NOTE** *With .NET Standard Libraries, it's possible to add references to non-standard .NET libraries. As long as you don't use APIs that are not available on all your target platforms, you are fine. As soon as you use APIs specific to one target platform, the other ones will break. You can add runtime checks before using the specific APIs to avoid this issue. A cleaner solution on using platform-specific code is with dependency injection, as is shown in the sample application.*

SAMPLE SOLUTION

The sample solution consists of a Universal Windows Platform app for showing and editing a list of books. In Chapter 37, the app will be extended for use on iPhone and Android. The solution uses these projects:

➤ **BooksApp**—A UWP app project for the UI of a modern app. This application contains the views for the app with XAML code, and platform-specific implementation of services.

➤ **BooksLib**—A .NET Standard Library 2.0 with models, view models, and services to create, read, and update books; common for all platforms supporting .NET Standard 2.0.

➤ **Framework**—A .NET Standard Library 2.0 containing classes that are useful for all XAML-based applications. Here you can find base classes for view models, implementation of `INotifyPropertyChanged`, `ICommand`, and other useful features.

The user interface of the application will have two views: one view to show as a list of books and one view to show book details. When you select a book from the list, the detail is shown. It's also possible to add and edit books.

The `BooksLib` and `Framework` library can be used by multiple applications with XAML code—for example, with UWP, WPF, and Xamarin. The `Framework` library is built in a way that it can be used by different apps, not only apps for working with books. Book-specific functionality is implemented in the `BooksLib`. The sample application demonstrates sharing view models not only between UWP and Xamarin, but also between different apps having the need for master/detail functionality. Base classes for the view models are implemented in the `Framework` library.

MODELS

Let's start defining the models, particularly the `Book` type. This is the type that will be shown and edited in the UI. To support data binding, the properties where values are updated from the user interface need a change notification implementation. The `BookId` property is only shown but not changed, so change notification is not needed with this property. The method `SetProperty` is defined by the base class `BindableBase` (code file `BooksLib/Models/Book.cs`):

```
public class Book: BindableBase
{
  public int BookId { get; set; }

  private string _title;
  public string Title
  {
    get => _title;
    set => Set(ref _title, value);
  }

  private string _publisher;
  public string Publisher
  {
    get => _publisher;
    set => Set(ref _publisher, value);
  }

  public override string ToString() => Title;
}
```

Implementing Change Notification

The object source of XAML elements needs either dependency properties or INotifyPropertyChanged to allow change notification with data binding. With model types, it makes sense to implement INotifyPropertyChanged. For having an implementation available with different projects, the implementation is done within the Framework library project in the class BindableBase. The INotifyPropertyChanged interface defines the event PropertyChanged. To fire the change notification, the method Set is implemented as a generic function for supporting any property type. Before the notification is fired, a check is done to see whether the new value is different from the current value (code file Framework/BindableBase.cs):

```
public abstract class BindableBase: INotifyPropertyChanged
{
  public event PropertyChangedEventHandler PropertyChanged;

  protected virtual void OnPropertyChanged(
    [CallerMemberName] string propertyName = null) =>
      PropertyChanged?.Invoke(this,
        new PropertyChangedEventArgs(propertyName));

  protected virtual bool SetProperty<T>(ref T item, T value,
    [CallerMemberName] string propertyName = null)
  {
    if (EqualityComparer<T>.Default.Equals(item, value)) return false;
    item = value;
    OnPropertyChanged(propertyName);
    return true;
  }
}
```

> **NOTE** *Dependency properties are explained in Chapter 33.*

Using the Repository Pattern

Next you need a way to retrieve, update, and delete Book objects. You can read and write books from a database with EF Core. Although EF Core can be accessed from the Universal Windows Platform, usually this is a task from the back end and is consequently not covered in this chapter. To make the back end accessible from a client app, Web API is the technology of choice on the server side. These topics are covered in Chapter 26, "Entity Framework Core," and Chapter 32, "Web API." With the client application it's best to be independent of the data store. For this, the Repository design pattern was defined. The *Repository* pattern is a mediator between the model and the data access layer; it can act as an in-memory collection of objects. It gives an abstraction of the data access layer and allows for easier unit tests.

The generic interface IQueryRepository defines methods for retrieving one item by ID or a list of items (code file BooksLib/Services/IQueryRepository.cs):

```
public interface IQueryRepository<T, in TKey>
  where T: class
{
  Task<T> GetItemAsync(TKey id);
  Task<IEnumerable<T>> GetItemsAsync();
}
```

The generic interface `IUpdateRepository` defines methods to add, update, and delete items (code file `BooksLib/Services/IUpdateRepository.cs`):

```
public interface IUpdateRepository<T, in TKey>
  where T: class
{
  Task<T> AddAsync(T item);
  Task<T> UpdateAsync(T item);
  Task<bool> DeleteAsync(TKey id);
}
```

The `IBooksRepository` interface makes the previous two generic interfaces concrete by defining the type `Book` for the generic type `T` (code file `BooksLib/Services/IBooksRepository.cs`):

```
public interface IBooksRepository: IQueryRepository<Book, int>,
  IUpdateRepository<Book, int>
{
}
```

By using these interfaces, it's possible to change the repository. Create a sample repository `BooksSampleRepository` that implements the members of the interface `IBooksRepository` and contains a list of initial books (code file `BooksLib/Services/BooksSampleRepository.cs`):

```
public class BooksSampleRepository: IBooksRepository
{
  private List<Book> _books;
  public BooksRepository()
  {
    InitSampleBooks();
  }

  private void InitSampleBooks()
  {
    _books = new List<Book>()
    {
      new Book
      {
        BookId = 1,
        Title = "Professional C# 7 and .NET Core 2",
        Publisher = "Wrox Press"
      },
      new Book
      {
        BookId = 2,
        Title = "Professional C# 6 and .NET Core 1.0",
        Publisher = "Wrox Press"
      },
      new Book
      {
        BookId = 3,
        Title = "Professional C# 5.0 and .NET 4.5.1",
        Publisher = "Wrox Press"
      },
      new Book
      {
        BookId = 4,
        Title = "Enterprise Services with the .NET Framework",
        Publisher = "AWL"
      }
    };
  }
```

```
    public Task<bool> DeleteAsync(int id)
    {
      Book bookToDelete = _books.Find(b => b.BookId == id);
      if (bookToDelete != null)
      {
        return Task.FromResult<bool>(_books.Remove(bookToDelete));
      }
      return Task.FromResult<bool>(false);
    }

    public Task<Book> GetItemAsync(int id) =>
      Task.FromResult(_books.Find(b => b.BookId == id));

    public Task<IEnumerable<Book>> GetItemsAsync() =>
      Task.FromResult<IEnumerable<Book>>(_books);

    public Task<Book> UpdateAsync(Book item)
    {
      Book bookToUpdate = _books.Find(b => b.BookId == item.BookId);
      int ix = _books.IndexOf(bookToUpdate);
      _books[ix] = item;
      return Task.FromResult(_books[ix]);
    }

    public Task<Book> AddAsync(Book item)
    {
      item.BookId = _books.Select(b => b.BookId).Max() + 1;
      _books.Add(item);
      return Task.FromResult(item);
    }
  }
```

> **NOTE** *The repository defines asynchronous methods, although they are not needed in this case because books are retrieved and updated only within memory. The methods are defined asynchronously because repositories for accessing the ASP.NET Core Web API are asynchronous in nature.*

SERVICES

To get the books from the repository, you use a service, and you can use it across multiple view models that access the same data. Thus, the service is a good place to share data between view models.

The sample service for the books implements the generic interface IItemsService. This interface defines the Items property of a type ObservableCollection. ObservableCollection implements the interface INotifyCollectionChanged for notifications when the collection changes. The interface IItemsService also defines the SelectedItem property and change notification with the event SelectedItemChanged. Aside from that, the methods RefreshAsync, AddOrUpdateAsync, and DeleteAsync are methods that need to be implemented by the service class (code file Framework/Services/IItemsService.cs):

```
    public interface IItemsService<T>
    {
      Task RefreshAsync();

      Task<T> AddOrUpdateAsync(T item);

      Task DeleteAsync(T item);
```

```
    ObservableCollection<T> Items { get; }

    T SelectedItem { get; set; }
    event EventHandler<T> SelectedItemChanged;
}
```

The class `BooksService` derives from the base class `BindableBase` and implements the generic interface `IItemsService`. The `BooksService` uses the previously created `SampleBooksRepository`, but just requires the functionality of this class offered by the `IBooksRepository` interface. The class is injected via the constructor, and used on refreshing the books list, adding or updating books, and deleting books (code file `BooksLib/Services/BooksService.cs`):

```csharp
public class BooksService : BindableBase, IItemsService<Book>
{
  private ObservableCollection<Book> _books = new ObservableCollection<Book>();
  private readonly IBooksRepository _booksRepository;

  public event EventHandler<Book> SelectedItemChanged;

  public BooksService(IBooksRepository repository)
  {
    _booksRepository = repository;
  }

  public ObservableCollection<Book> Items => _books;

  private Book _selectedItem;
  public Book SelectedItem
  {
    get => _selectedItem;
    set
    {
      if (Set(ref _selectedItem, value))
      {
        SelectedItemChanged?.Invoke(this, _selectedItem);
      }
    }
  }

  public async Task<Book> AddOrUpdateAsync(Book book)
  {
    Book updated = null;
    if (book.BookId == 0)
    {
      updated = await _booksRepository.AddAsync(book);
    }
    else
    {
      updated = await _booksRepository.UpdateAsync(book);
    }
    return updated;
  }

  public Task DeleteAsync(Book book) =>
    _booksRepository.DeleteAsync(book.BookId);

  public async Task RefreshAsync()
  {
    IEnumerable<Book> books = await _booksRepository.GetItemsAsync();
    _books.Clear();
    foreach (var book in books)
    {
```

```
        _books.Add(book);
      }
      SelectedItem = Items.FirstOrDefault();
    }
  }
```

Now that the service-functionality is in place, let's move on to the view models.

VIEW MODELS

Every view or page has a view model. With the sample app, the BooksPage has the BooksViewModel associated. Later in the sample you'll see that user controls can have their specific view models as well, but this is not always necessary. The BookDetailPage has the BookDetailViewModel associated. It's a UI design decision if the list of the books and the details can be implemented in the same page. That's a matter of the available screen size of the app: What can fit on the screen? With the sample application, a flexible approach was taken. In case the size available for the app is large enough, the BooksPage shows the list and the details; if the size is not large enough, data will be shown in separate pages with navigation between.

There's a one-to-one mapping between page view and view model. In reality, there's a many-to-one mapping between view and view model because the same view is implemented multiple times with different technologies—UWP, WPF, and Xamarin. This makes it important that the view model doesn't know anything about the view, but the view knows the view model. The view model is implemented in a .NET Standard Library, which allows using it from many technologies.

For common functionality of view models, it makes sense to create base classes. The Framework library contains a ViewModelBase class that implements features for progress information and for errors (code file Framework/ViewModels/ViewModelBase.cs):

```
public abstract class ViewModelBase : BindableBase
{
  // functionality for progress information and
  // error information
}
```

The sample application shows a list of books and allows the user to select a book. Here it is useful to define a generic base class for the view models with the properties Items and SelectedItem. The implementation of these properties makes use of the previously created service that implements the interface IItemsService (code file Framework/ViewModels/MasterDetailViewModel.cs):

```
public abstract class MasterDetailViewModel<TItemViewModel, TItem> :
  ViewModelBase
  where TItemViewModel : IItemViewModel<TItem>
  where IItem: class
{
  private readonly IItemsService<TItem> _itemsService;

  public MasterDetailViewModel(IItemsService<TItem> itemsService)
  {
    _itemsService = itemsService;

    //...
  }


  public ObservableCollection<TItem> Items => _itemsService.Items;

  protected TItem _selectedItem;
  public virtual TItem SelectedItem
  {
    get => _itemsService.SelectedItem;
```

```
    set
    {
      if (!EqualityComparer<TItem>.Default.Equals(
        _itemsService.SelectedItem, value))
      {
        _itemsService.SelectedItem = value;
        OnPropertyChanged();
      }
    }
  }

  //...

}
```

> **NOTE** *Generics are discussed in Chapter 5, "Generics."*

To display a single item in detail, the base class `ItemViewModel` defines an `Item` property (code file `Framework/ViewModels/ItemViewModel.cs`):

```
public abstract class ItemViewModel<T> : ViewModelBase, IItemViewModel<T>
{
    private T _item;
    public virtual T Item
    {
        get => _item;
        set => Set(ref _item, value);
    }
}
```

More complex than the simple class `ItemViewModel` is the view model class `EditableItemViewModel`. This class extends `ItemViewModel` by allowing editing, and thus it defines a read or edit mode. The property `IsReadMode` is just the inverse of `IsEditMode`. The `EditableItemViewModel` makes use of the same service as the `MasterDetailViewModel` class, the service that implements the interface `IItemsService`. This way, the `EditableItemViewModel` and the `MasterDetailViewModel` classes can share the same items and the same selection. The view model class allows the user to cancel the input. For this, the item has a copied version with the `EditItem` property (code file `Framework/ViewModels/EditableItemViewModel.cs`):

```
public abstract class EditableItemViewModel<TItem> : ItemViewModel<TItem>,
  IEditableObject
  where TItem : class
{
  private readonly IItemsService<TItem> _itemsService;

  public EditableItemViewModel(IItemsService<TItem> itemsService)
  {
    _itemsService = itemsService;
    Item = _itemsService.SelectedItem;

    PropertyChanged += (sender, e) =>
    {
      if (e.PropertyName == nameof(Item))
      {
        OnPropertyChanged(nameof(EditItem));
      }
    };
    //...
  }
```

```
//...
private bool _isEditMode;
public bool IsReadMode => !IsEditMode;
public bool IsEditMode
{
  get => _isEditMode;
  set
  {
    if (Set(ref _isEditMode, value))
    {
      OnPropertyChanged(nameof(IsReadMode));
      //...
    }
  }
}

private TItem _editItem;
public TItem EditItem
{
  get => _editItem ?? Item;
  set => Set(ref _editItem, value);
}
//...
}
```

Using IEditableObject

An interface that defines methods to change an object between different edit states is the interface `IEditableObject`. This interface is defined in the namespace `System.ComponentModel`. `IEditableObject` defines the methods `BeginEdit`, `CancelEdit`, and `EndEdit`. `BeginEdit` is invoked to change the item from the read mode to the edit mode. `CancelEdit` cancels the edit and switches back to read mode. `EndEdit` is for a successful end of the edit mode, and thus needs to save the data. The `EditableItemViewModel` class implements the methods of this interface by switching the edit mode, creating a copy of the item, and saving the state. This view model class is a generic one and doesn't know what should be done for copying and saving the item. Copying would be possible by using binary serialization. However, not all objects support binary serialization. Instead, the implementation is forwarded to the class that derives from `EditableItemViewModel`, similar to the save method `OnSaveAsync`. `OnSaveAsync` and `CreateCopy` are defined as abstract methods, and thus need to be implemented by the derived class. Another method is defined to be invoked at the end of `CancelEdit` and `EndEdit`: `OnEndEditAsync`. This method can be implemented by a derived class, but it's not necessary to do. That's why the method is declared virtual with an empty body (code file `Framework/ViewModels/EditableItemViewModel.cs`):

```
public virtual void BeginEdit()
{
  IsEditMode = true;
  TItem itemCopy = CreateCopy(Item);
  if (itemCopy != null)
  {
    EditItem = itemCopy;
  }
}

public async virtual void CancelEdit()
{
  IsEditMode = false;
  EditItem = default(TItem);
  await _itemsService.RefreshAsync();
  await OnEndEditAsync();
}

public async virtual void EndEdit()
```

```
{
  using (StartInProgress())
  {
    await OnSaveAsync();
    EditItem = default(TItem);
    IsEditMode = false;
    await _itemsService.RefreshAsync();
    await OnEndEditAsync();
  }
}

public abstract Task OnSaveAsync();
public abstract TItem CreateCopy(TItem item);
public virtual Task OnEndEditAsync() => Task.CompletedTask;
```

Concrete View Model Implementations

Let's move on to the concrete implementations of the view models. BookDetailViewModel derives
from EditableItemViewModel and specifies Book as the generic parameter. With the base class
already implementing the major functionality, this class can be simple. It injects the services for the
interfaces IItemsService and INavigationSerivce. In the method OnSaveAsync, the request is forwarded to the IItemsService. The OnSaveAsync method also makes use of the interfaces ILogger
and IMessageService. In the view model class, the CreateCopy method implements the creation
of a copy of the book. This method is invoked by the base class (code file BooksLib/ViewModels/
BookDetailViewModel.cs):

```
public class BookDetailViewModel : EditableItemViewModel<Book>
{
  private readonly IItemsService<Book> _itemsService;
  private readonly INavigationService _navigationService;
  private readonly IMessageService _messageService;
  private readonly ILogger _logger;

  public BookDetailViewModel(IItemsService<Book> itemsService,
    INavigationService navigationService, IMessageService messageService,
    ILogger<BookDetailViewModel> logger)
    : base(itemsService)
  {
    _itemsService = itemsService;
    _navigationService = navigationService;
    _messageService = messageService;
    _logger = logger;

    itemsService.SelectedItemChanged += (sender, book) =>
    {
      Item = book;
    };
  }

  public bool UseNavigation { get; set; }

  public override Book CreateCopy(Book item) =>
    new Book
    {
      BookId = item?.BookId ?? -1,
      Title = item?.Title ?? "enter a title",
      Publisher = item?.Publisher ?? "enter a publisher"
    };

  public override async Task OnSaveAsync()
```

```
    {
      try
      {
        await _itemsService.AddOrUpdateAsync(EditItem);
      }
      catch (Exception ex)
      {
        _logger.LogError("error {0} in {1}", ex.Message, nameof(OnSaveAsync));
        await _messageService.ShowMessageAsync("Error saving the data");
      }
    }
    //...
  }
```

> **NOTE** *The* `ILogger` *interface is explained in Chapter 29, "Tracing, Logging, and Analytics." The interface* `IMessageService` *is discussed later in this chapter in the section "Opening Dialogs from View Models." The definition and use of the navigation service is discussed later in this chapter in the section "Navigation Between Pages."*

The class `BooksViewModel` can be kept simple by inheriting the main functionality from `MasterDetailViewModel`. This class just injects the `INavigationService` interface that will be discussed later, forwards the `IItemsService` interface to the base class, and overrides the `OnAdd` method that is invoked by the base class (code file `BooksLib/ViewModels/BooksViewModel.cs`):

```
public class BooksViewModel : MasterDetailViewModel<BookItemViewModel, Book>
{
  private readonly IItemsService<Book> _booksService;
  private readonly INavigationService _navigationService;

  public BooksViewModel(IItemsService<Book> booksService,
    INavigationService navigationService)
    : base(booksService)
  {
    _booksService = booksService ??
      throw new ArgumentNullException(nameof(booksService));
    _navigationService = navigationService ??
      throw new ArgumentNullException(nameof(navigationService));
    //...
  }

  public override void OnAdd()
  {
    var newBook = new Book();
    Items.Add(newBook);
    SelectedItem = newBook;
  }

  //...
}
```

Commands

The view models offer commands that implement the interface `ICommand`. Commands allow a separation between the view and the command handler method via data binding. Commands also offer the functionality to enable or disable the command. The `ICommand` interface defines the methods `Execute` and `CanExecute`, and the event `CanExecuteChanged`.

To map the commands to methods, the `RelayCommand` class is defined in the `Framework` library.

`RelayCommand` defines two constructors, where a delegate can be passed for the method that should be invoked via the command, and another delegate defines whether the command is available (code file `Framework/RelayCommand.cs`):

```
public class RelayCommand: ICommand
{
  private readyonly Action _execute;
  private readonly Func<bool> _canExecute;

  public RelayCommand(Action execute, Func<bool> canExecute)
  {
    _execute = execute ?? throw new ArgumentNullException(nameof(execute));
    _canExecute = canExecute;
  }

  public RelayCommand(Action execute)
    : this(execute, null)
  { }

  public event EventHandler CanExecuteChanged;

  public bool CanExecute(object parameter) => _canExecute?.Invoke() ?? true;

  public void Execute(object parameter) => _execute();
}
```

The constructor of the `EditableItemViewModel` creates new `RelayCommand` objects and assigns the previously shown methods `BeginEdit`, `CancelEdit`, and `EndEdit` on execution of the commands. All these commands also specify a check whether the command is available by using the `IsReadMode` and `IsEditMode` properties. When the `IsEditMode` property changes, the `CanExecuteChanged` event of the command is fired to update the command accordingly (code file `Framework/ViewModels/EditableItemViewModel.cs`):

```
public abstract class EditableItemViewModel<TItem> : ItemViewModel<TItem>,
  IEditableObject
  where TItem : class
{
  private readonly IItemsService<TItem> _itemsService;

  public EditableItemViewModel(IItemsService<TItem> itemsService)
  {
    _itemsService = itemsService;
    Item = _itemsService.SelectedItem;

    EditCommand = new RelayCommand(BeginEdit, () => IsReadMode);
    CancelCommand = new RelayCommand(CancelEdit, () => IsEditMode);
    SaveCommand = new RelayCommand(EndEdit, () => IsEditMode);
  }

  public RelayCommand EditCommand { get; }
  public RelayCommand CancelCommand { get; }
  public RelayCommand SaveCommand { get; }

  //...

  public bool IsEditMode
  {
    get => _isEditMode;
    set
    {
      if (Set(ref _isEditMode, value))
```

```
        {
          OnPropertyChanged(nameof(IsReadMode));
          CancelCommand.OnCanExecuteChanged();
          SaveCommand.OnCanExecuteChanged();
          EditCommand.OnCanExecuteChanged();
        }
      }
    }
    //...
  }
```

From the XAML code, the commands are bound to the Command property of a Button. This is discussed when creating the views in more detail (code file `BooksApp/Views/BookDetailUserControl.xaml`):

```xml
<AppBarButton Content="Edit" Icon="Edit"
  Command="{x:Bind ViewModel.EditCommand, Mode=OneTime}" />
<AppBarButton Content="Save" Icon="Save"
  Command="{x:Bind ViewModel.SaveCommand, Mode=OneTime}" />
<AppBarButton Content="Cancel" Icon="Cancel"
  Command="{x:Bind ViewModel.CancelCommand, Mode=OneTime}" />
```

Services, ViewModels, and Dependency Injection

View models and services inject services, and view models need to be created. For this, you can use a dependency injection container. The sample application makes use of `Microsoft.Extensions .DependencyInjection`. The container is configured in the `ApplicationServices` class. This class is implemented with the Singleton pattern. In the constructor, the DI container is configured. The property `ServiceProvider` returns the container where the services can be retrieved (code file `BooksApp/App .xaml.cs`):

```csharp
public class ApplicationServices
{
  private ApplicationServices()
  {
    var services = new ServiceCollection();
    services.AddSingleton<IBooksRepository, BooksSampleRepository>();
    services.AddSingleton<IItemsService<Book>, BooksService>();
    services.AddTransient<BooksViewModel>();
    services.AddTransient<BookDetailViewModel>();
    services.AddTransient<MainPageViewModel>();
    services.AddSingleton<IMessageService, UWPMessageService>();
    services.AddSingleton<INavigationService, UWPNavigationService>();
    services.AddSingleton<UWPInitializeNavigationService>();
    services.AddLogging(builder =>
    {
#if DEBUG
      builder.AddDebug();
#endif
    });
    ServiceProvider = services.BuildServiceProvider();
  }

  private static ApplicationServices _instance;
  private static object _instanceLock = new object();
  private static ApplicationServices GetInstance()
  {
    lock (_instanceLock)
    {
      return _instance ?? (_instance = new ApplicationServices());
    }
```

```
    }

    public static ApplicationServices Instance => _instance ?? GetInstance();

    public IServiceProvider ServiceProvider { get; }
}
```

Now the view model needs to be associated with the view, which is done in the BooksPage by accessing the AppServices property of the App class and invoking the GetService method from the DI container. The container then instantiates the view model class with the required services as defined in the constructor of the view model class. The BooksPage contains a user control for the detail information of the book that needs a different view model. This view model is assigned by setting the property ViewModel of the BookDetailUC user control (code file BooksApp/Views/BooksPage.xaml.cs):

```
public sealed partial class BooksPage : Page
{
    public BooksPage()
    {
        this.InitializeComponent();
        ViewModel.UseNavigation = false;
        BookDetailUC.ViewModel =
            ApplicationServices.Instance.ServiceProvider
              .GetService<BookDetailViewModel>();
    }

    public BooksViewModel ViewModel { get; } =
        (Application.Current as App).AppServices.GetService<BooksViewModel>();
```

With the BookDetailPage, the association to the view model happens similarly (code file BooksApp/Views/BookDetailPage.xaml.cs):

```
public sealed partial class BookDetailPage : Page
{
    public BookDetailPage()
    {
        this.InitializeComponent();
        ViewModel.UseNavigation = true; // if the Page is used, enable navigation
    }

    public BookDetailViewModel ViewModel { get; } =
        ApplicationServices.Instance.ServiceProvider
          .GetService<BookDetailViewModel>();
}
```

VIEWS

Now that you've been introduced to creating the view models and to connecting the views to the view models it's time to get into the views.

The main view of the application is defined by the MainPage. This page makes use of the NavigationView control that is new with the Windows 10 update 16299 (Fall Creators Update). Usually if you only have a small list of items for navigation, you shouldn't use this UI control. However, with the sample application uses the control because it is assumed the application will grow to more than eight items.

The NavigationView control assigns the SelectionChanged event to the OnNavigationSelectionChanged method of the MainPageViewModel. This view model is very different from the other ones and will be discussed later in the section "Navigation Between Pages." One NavigationViewItem is defined to navigate to the BooksPage (code file BooksApp/MainPage.xaml):

```
<NavigationView Background=
  "{ThemeResource ApplicationPageBackgroundThemeBrush}"
```

```
  SelectionChanged="{x:Bind ViewModel.OnNavigationSelectionChanged,
    Mode=OneTime}">
  <NavigationView.MenuItems>
    <NavigationViewItem Content="Books" Tag="books">
      <NavigationViewItem.Icon>
        <FontIcon FontFamily="Segoe MDL2 Assets" Glyph="&#xE82D;" />
      </NavigationViewItem.Icon>
    </NavigationViewItem>
  </NavigationView.MenuItems>

  <Frame x:Name="ContentFrame" Margin="24">
    <Frame.ContentTransitions>
      <TransitionCollection>
        <NavigationThemeTransition/>
      </TransitionCollection>
    </Frame.ContentTransitions>
  </Frame>
</NavigationView>
```

> **NOTE** *The* `NavigationView` *control is discussed in Chapter 33.*

Figure 34-8 shows the `NavigationView` of the running app with the navigation item to the `BooksPage`.

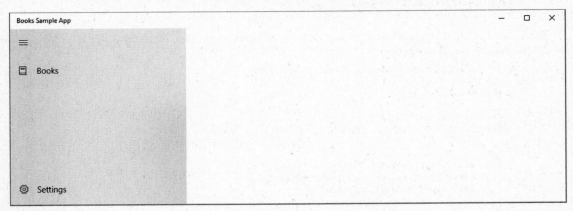

FIGURE 34-8

The `BooksPage` contains a `ListView` and binds the `ItemsSource` to the `ItemsViewModel` property of the `BooksViewModel`. Usually you would bind it to the `Items` property of the `BooksViewModel`. However, the display of a single list item is not only used to show the value of the `Book` objects, but also contains buttons that are bound to commands. To implement such functionality, another view model is used for the items. How this can be done is discussed in the section "Using Actions in List Items" (code file `BooksApp/Views/BooksPage.xaml`):

```
<StackPanel Orientation="Horizontal" Grid.Row="1">
  <AppBarButton Icon="Refresh" IsCompact="True"
    Command="{x:Bind ViewModel.RefreshCommand}"
    Label="Get Books" />
  <AppBarButton Icon="Add" IsCompact="True"
    Command="{x:Bind ViewModel.AddCommand}"
    Label="Add Book" />
</StackPanel>
```

```
<ListView ItemTemplate="{StaticResource BookItemTemplate}" Grid.Row="2"
    ItemsSource="{x:Bind ViewModel.ItemsViewModels, Mode=OneWay}"
    SelectedItem="{x:Bind ViewModel.SelectedItemViewModel, Mode=TwoWay}" >
</ListView>
<views:BookDetailUserControl x:Name="BookDetailUC" Visibility="Collapsed"
    Grid.Column="1" Grid.Row="1" Grid.RowSpan="2" />
```

The `BookDetailPage` just contains a user control: the `BookDetailUserControl`. The `BookDetailPage` has the `BookDetailViewModel` associated, as you've seen previously. This view model is forwarded to the `BookDetailUserControl` by assigning the `ViewModel` property of the `BookDetailPage` to the `ViewModel` property of the `BookDetailUserControl` (code file `BooksApp/Views/BookDetailPage.xaml`):

```
<Grid Background="{ThemeResource ApplicationPageBackgroundThemeBrush}">
    <views:BookDetailUserControl ViewModel="{x:Bind ViewModel, Mode=OneTime}" />
</Grid>
```

The dependency property of the `BookDetailUserControl` is shown in the following code snippet. This mapping to the view model is then used for data binding in the XAML code (code file `BooksApp/Views/BookDetailUserControl.xaml.cs`):

```
public BookDetailViewModel ViewModel
{
    get => (BookDetailViewModel)GetValue(ViewModelProperty);
    set => SetValue(ViewModelProperty, value);
}

public static readonly DependencyProperty ViewModelProperty =
    DependencyProperty.Register("ViewModel", typeof(BookDetailViewModel),
    typeof(BookDetailUserControl), new PropertyMetadata(null));
```

The user interface of the `BookDetailUserControl` makes use of two `StackPanel` elements. With the first `StackPanel`, the `Command` property of the `AppBarButton` controls is bound to the `EditCommand`, `SaveCommand`, and `CancelCommand` commands defined in the view model. The buttons will be automatically enabled or disabled depending on the state of the commands. With the second `StackPanel`, `TextBox` elements are used to display the `Title` and `Publisher` properties of the `Book`. For a read-only display, the `IsReadOnly` property is assigned to the `IsReadMode` property of the view model. When the view model is set to edit mode, the `TextBox` controls allow entering data (code file `BooksApp/Views/BookDetailUserControl.xaml`):

```
<StackPanel Orientation="Horizontal">
    <AppBarButton Content="Edit" Icon="Edit"
        Command="{x:Bind ViewModel.EditCommand, Mode=OneTime}" />
    <AppBarButton Content="Save" Icon="Save"
        Command="{x:Bind ViewModel.SaveCommand, Mode=OneTime}" />
    <AppBarButton Content="Cancel" Icon="Cancel"
        Command="{x:Bind ViewModel.CancelCommand, Mode=OneTime}" />
</StackPanel>
<StackPanel Orientation="Vertical" Grid.Row="1">
    <TextBox Header="Title"
            IsReadOnly="{x:Bind ViewModel.IsReadMode, Mode=OneWay}"
            Text="{x:Bind ViewModel.EditItem.Title, Mode=TwoWay,
                UpdateSourceTrigger=PropertyChanged}" />
    <TextBox Header="Publisher"
            IsReadOnly="{x:Bind ViewModel.IsReadMode, Mode=OneWay}"
            Text="{x:Bind ViewModel.EditItem.Publisher, Mode=TwoWay,
                UpdateSourceTrigger=PropertyChanged}" />
</StackPanel>
```

Figure 34-9 shows the running application with the books in the `ListView`. In the `BookDetailUserControl`, the Edit command is enabled while the Save and Cancel commands are currently disabled.

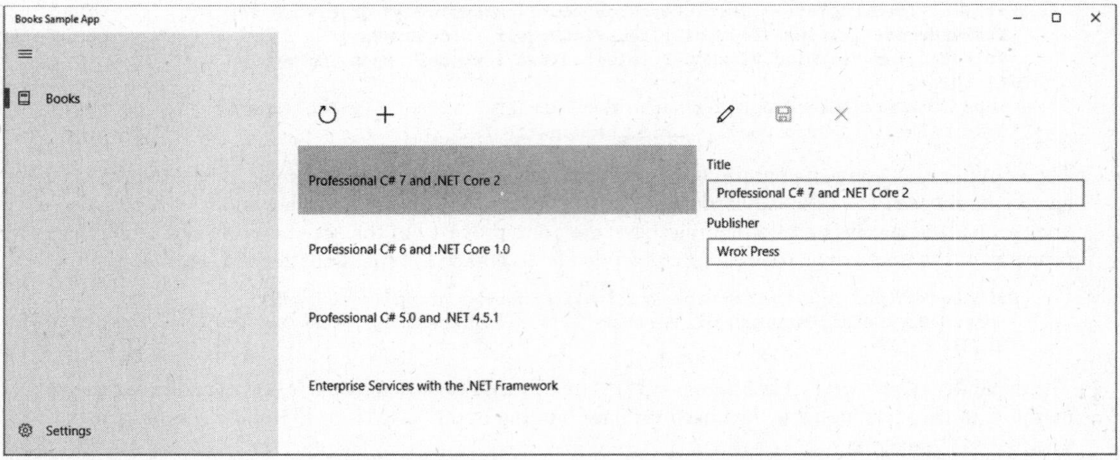

FIGURE 34-9

Opening Dialogs from View Models

Sometimes it's necessary to show dialogs from actions within view models. As the view model is implemented in a .NET Standard Library, access to the `MessageDialog` class from UWP is not possible. You should avoid this situation, anyway, because the `MessageDialog` is UWP specific. With WPF you use the `MessageBox` class instead. With `Xamarin.Forms`, you use `Page.DisplayAlert`.

What needs to be done is to define a contract that can be used by the view models and services. This contract is defined in the `BooksLib` library with the `IMessageService` interface (code file `BooksLib/Services/IMessageService.cs`):

```
public interface IMessageService
{
    Task ShowMessageAsync(string message);
}
```

In the `BookDetailViewModel`, the `IMessageService` is injected in the constructor, and used on the `OnSaveAsync` method. The `ShowMessageAsync` method is invoked in the case of an exception (code file `BooksLib/ViewModels/BookDetailViewModel.cs`):

```
public override async Task OnSaveAsync()
{
    try
    {
        await _itemsService.AddOrUpdateAsync(EditItem);
    }
    catch (Exception ex)
    {
        _logger.LogError("error {0} in {1}", ex.Message, nameof(OnSaveAsync));
        await _messageService.ShowMessageAsync("Error saving the data");
    }
}
```

Now just a specific implementation for the Universal Windows Platform is needed. The `ShowMessageAsync` method is implemented using the `MessageDialog` class. The `UWPMessageService` is implemented in the Universal Windows Platform app; that's why access to `MessageDialog` is now possible (code file `BooksApp/Services/UWPMessageService.cs`):

```
public class UWPMessageService : IMessageService
{
```

```
    public async Task ShowMessageAsync(string message) =>
      await new MessageDialog(message).ShowAsync();
  }
```

In the `ApplicationServices` constructor, where the services are registered with the dependency injection container, the `UWPMessageService` class is registered as the implementation class for the `IMessageService` contract. That's why the view model will receive the UWP implementation (code file `BooksApp/ApplicationServices.cs`):

```
  private ApplicationServices()
  {
    var services = new ServiceCollection();
    services.AddSingleton<IBooksRepository, BooksSampleRepository>();
    services.AddSingleton<IItemsService<Book>, BooksService>();
    services.AddTransient<BooksViewModel>();
    services.AddTransient<BookDetailViewModel>();
    services.AddTransient<MainPageViewModel>();
    services.AddSingleton<IMessageService, UWPMessageService>();
    services.AddSingleton<INavigationService, UWPNavigationService>();
    services.AddSingleton<UPInitializeNavigationService>();
    services.AddLogging(builder =>
    {
#if DEBUG
      builder.AddDebug();
#endif
    });
    ServiceProvider = services.BuildServiceProvider();
  }
```

With an error you can now see a dialog as shown in Figure 34-10.

FIGURE 34-10

Navigation Between Pages

As with opening dialogs, navigation between pages is different between different technologies. With UWP, the `Frame` class is used to navigate pages within the app. With WPF, it's again a `Frame` class, but it's a different one. With Xamarin.Forms, the `NavigationPage` is used for navigation. How the navigation is implemented with these technologies also differs. With UWP, you need a `Type` object to navigate to. With Xamarin.Forms, you need an object instance of the page. With Xamarin.Forms, the navigation methods are asynchronous, whereas they are synchronous with UWP. For this, a common contract is needed again.

With the sample application, navigation to a page is needed, and navigation back needs to be done. Also, the current page needs to be accessed to know whether navigation needs to be done. For this, the interface `INavigationService` is defined. This interface is based on strings for navigation, which makes it possible to create implementations for the different platforms (code file `Framework/Services/INavigationService.cs`):

```
  public interface INavigationService
  {
    bool UseNavigation { get; set; }
```

```
    Task NavigateToAsync(string page);
    Task GoBackAsync();
    string CurrentPage { get; }
}
```

The `UWPNavigationService` needs a `Frame` assigned, so it can navigate for UWP. When you define a property of a `Frame`, it's not possible to access it because from the outside just the `INavigationService` interface is used. With the `INavigationService` interface, the `Frame` cannot be used because this interface is in the .NET Standard Library. When you use the `INavigationService` from UWP, it would be possible to cast it to an `UWPNavigationService` to access a specific UWP property. Requiring casts is not a good design. Instead, what you can do easily is specify a UWP specific service such as the `UWPInitializeNavigationService` and inject this in the constructor of the `UWPNavigationService`. Internally, when the `Pages` and `Frame` properties are accessed, this information is taken from the initialization service, as shown in the following code snippet (code file `BooksApp/Services/UWPNavigationService.cs`):

```
public class UWPNavigationService : INavigationService
{
  private readonly UWPInitializeNavigationService _initializeNavigation;

  public UWPNavigationService(
    UWPInitializeNavigationService initializeNavigation)
  {
    _initializeNavigation = initializeNavigation ??
      throw new ArgumentNullException(nameof(initializeNavigation));
  }

  private Dictionary<string, Type> _pages;
  private Dictionary<string, Type> Pages => _pages ??
    (_pages = _initializeNavigation.Pages);

  private Frame _frame;
  private Frame Frame => _frame ?? (_frame = _initializeNavigation.Frame);
  //...
}
```

The implementation of the `CurrentPage` property, the `GoBackAsync` method, and the `NavigateToAsync` method are now making use of the `Frame.GoBack` and `Frame.Navigate` methods (code file `BooksApp/Services/UWPNavigationService.cs`):

```
public class UWPNavigationService : INavigationService
{
  //...
  private string _currentPage;
  public string CurrentPage => _currentPage;

  public Task GoBackAsync()
  {
    PageStackEntry stackEntry = Frame.BackStack.Last();
    Type backPageType = stackEntry.SourcePageType;
    KeyValuePair<string, Type> pageEntry =
      Pages.FirstOrDefault(pair => pair.Value == backPageType);
    _currentPage = pageEntry.Key;

    Frame.GoBack();
    return Task.CompletedTask;
  }

  public Task NavigateToAsync(string pageName)
  {
    _currentPage = pageName;
```

```
          Frame.Navigate(Pages[pageName]);
          return Task.CompletedTask;
      }
  }
```

The only functionality the `UWPInitializeNavigationService` offers is to initialize it with a `Frame` and a dictionary of pages, and to retrieve this information (code file `BooksApp/Services/ UWPInitializeNavigationService.cs`):

```
public class UWPInitializeNavigationService
{
    public void Initialize(Frame frame, Dictionary<string, Type> pages)
    {
        Frame = frame ?? throw new ArgumentNullException(nameof(frame));
        Pages = pages ?? throw new ArgumentNullException(nameof(pages));
    }
    public Frame Frame { get; private set; }
    public Dictionary<string, Type> Pages { get; private set; }
}
```

The `UWPInitializeNavigationService` can now be initialized on a place where the `Frame` is available. With the UWP sample application, this is in the `MainPage`. Within the `NavigationView` control specified earlier, the `Frame` with the name `ContentFrame` is specified. Now it would be possible to define the initialization within the code-behind file of the `MainPage`, or in a UWP-specific `MainPageViewModel`. For the sample application, the second option was chosen.

In the following code-snippet, the `MainPageViewModel` keeps a list of pages for the navigation and initializes the navigation service when the `SetNavigationFrame` is invoked (code file `BooksApp/ViewModels/ MainPageViewModel.cs`):

```
public class MainPageViewModel : ViewModelBase
{
    private Dictionary<string, Type> _pages = new Dictionary<string, Type>
    {
        [PageNames.BooksPage] = typeof(BooksPage),
        [PageNames.BookDetailPage] = typeof(BookDetailPage)
    };

    private readonly INavigationService _navigationService;
    private readonly UWPInitializeNavigationService _initializeNavigationService;
    public MainPageViewModel(INavigationService navigationService,
        UWPInitializeNavigationService initializeNavigationService)
    {
        _navigationService = navigationService;
        _initializeNavigationService = initializeNavigationService;
    }

    public void SetNavigationFrame(Frame frame) =>
        _initializeNavigationService.Initialize(frame, _pages);

    //...
}
```

With this view model in place, all that needs to be in the code-behind file of the `MainPage` is the `ViewModel` property and the passing of the `ContentFrame` to the navigation service via invocation of the method `SetNavigationFrame` (code file `BooksApp/MainPage.xaml.cs`):

```
public sealed partial class MainPage : Page
{
    public MainPage()
    {
        this.InitializeComponent();
        ViewModel =
```

```
          (Application.Current as App).AppServices.GetService<MainPageViewModel>();
        ViewModel.SetNavigationFrame(ContentFrame);
      }

      public MainPageViewModel ViewModel { get; }
    }
```

The first navigation to the `BooksPage` happens in the `MainPageViewModel`. The method `OnNavigationSelectionChanged` is the handler for the `NavigationSelectionChanged` event of the `NavigationView` control. With the `Tag` set to `books`, navigation to the `BooksPage` is done using the `INavigationService` (code file `BooksApp/ViewModels/MainPageViewModel.cs`):

```
    public class MainPageViewModel : ViewModelBase
    {
      //...
      public void OnNavigationSelectionChanged(NavigationView sender,
        NavigationViewSelectionChangedEventArgs args)
      {
        if (args.SelectedItem is NavigationViewItem navigationItem)
        {
          switch (navigationItem.Tag)
          {
            case "books":
              _navigationService.NavigateToAsync(PageNames.BooksPage);
              break;
            default:
              break;
          }
        }
      }
    }
```

Following on navigation from the `BooksPage` is directly done from a shared view model. The navigation from the `BooksPage` to the `BooksDetailPage` happens when a list item is selected, and thus the `PropertyChanged` event fires. Navigation is also only done when the property `UseNavigation` is set to `true`. As previously mentioned, with UWP when the UI is large enough, navigation is not needed at this place because the detail information is then shown side by side with the list (code file `BooksLib/ViewModels/BooksViewModel.cs`):

```
    public class BooksViewModel : MasterDetailViewModel<BookItemViewModel, Book>
    {
      private readonly IItemsService<Book> _booksService;
      private readonly INavigationService _navigationService;

      public BooksViewModel(IItemsService<Book> booksService,
        INavigationService navigationService)
        : base(booksService)
      {
        _booksService = booksService ??
          throw new ArgumentNullException(nameof(booksService));
        _navigationService = navigationService ??
          throw new ArgumentNullException(nameof(navigationService));

        PropertyChanged += async (sender, e) =>
        {
          if (UseNavigation && e.PropertyName == nameof(SelectedItem) &&
            _navigationService.CurrentPage == PageNames.BooksPage)
```

```
            {
                await _navigationService.NavigateToAsync(PageNames.BookDetailPage);
            }
        };
    }

    public bool UseNavigation { get; set; }
    //...
}
```

For making the user interface small enough to require navigation between pages, the next section explains adaptive user interfaces.

Adaptive User Interfaces

Depending on the available size on the screen, either a user control should show up side by side to the list control or within a separate page. To make this possible, with the `BookDetailUserControl` used within the `BooksPage`, the `Visibility` property is by default set to `Collapsed` (code file `BooksApp/Views/BooksPage.xaml`):

```
<views:BookDetailUserControl x:Name="BookDetailUC" Visibility="Collapsed"
  Grid.Column="1" Grid.Row="1" Grid.RowSpan="2" />
```

Now an `AdaptiveTrigger` can be used to make the control visible with a window width larger than `1023`. When the `AdaptiveTrigger` triggers, the `Setter` sets the `Visibility` property of the user control to `Visible` (code file `BooksApp/Views/BooksPage.xaml`):

```
<Grid>
  <!-- ... -->
  <views:BookDetailUserControl x:Name="BookDetailUC" Visibility="Collapsed"
    Grid.Column="1" Grid.Row="1" Grid.RowSpan="2" />

  <VisualStateManager.VisualStateGroups>
    <VisualStateGroup x:Name="WindowStates">
      <VisualState x:Name="WideState">
        <VisualState.StateTriggers>
          <AdaptiveTrigger MinWindowWidth="1024"/>
        </VisualState.StateTriggers>
        <VisualState.Setters>
          <Setter Target="BookDetailUC.Visibility" Value="Visible" />
        </VisualState.Setters>
      </VisualState>
      <VisualState x:Name="MediumState">
        <VisualState.StateTriggers>
          <AdaptiveTrigger MinWindowWidth="720"/>
        </VisualState.StateTriggers>
      </VisualState>
      <!-- ... -->
    </VisualStateGroup>
  </VisualStateManager.VisualStateGroups>
</Grid>
```

When you run the app, you can see the `BooksPage` with the user control visible (see Figure 34-11). Figure 34-12 shows the smaller state where the user control is hidden. Here, the `NavigationView` also triggers to make a smaller view. Making the app even smaller to the `NarrowState` (see Figure 34-13), an `AdaptiveTrigger` with the `NavigationView` triggers again to only show the hamburger button. The pane of the `NavigationView` is then only shown when the hamburger button is clicked.

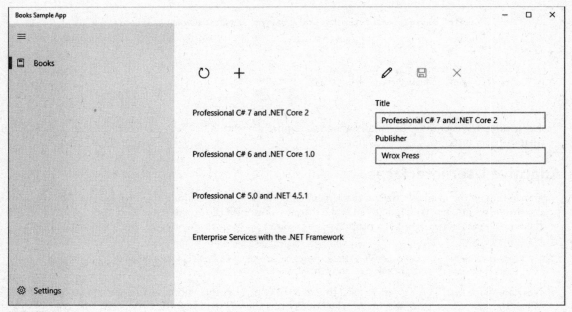

FIGURE 34-11

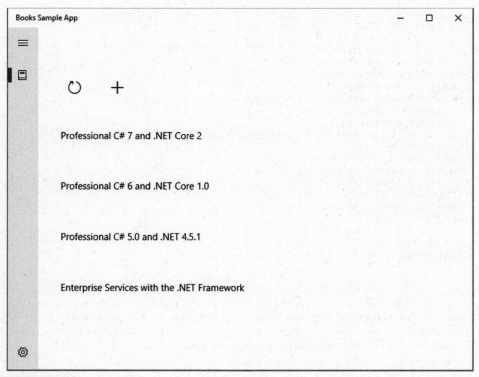

FIGURE 34-12

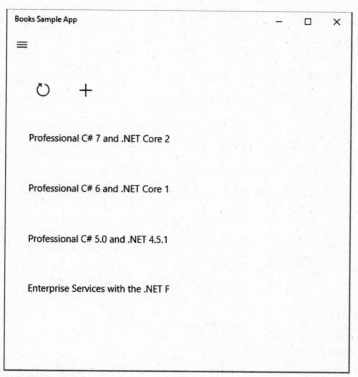

FIGURE 34-13

NOTE *For more information on adaptive triggers read Chapter 33.*

NOTE *What's missing is to change the* UseNavigation *property of the view model to use or not use navigation. One way is to set the property of the view model directly or via a service. Another way is by using an event aggregator, which is demonstrated later in this chapter in the section "Messaging Using Events."*

Showing Progress Information

Showing progress information is necessary in many apps, and in many view models. That's why with the sample app, showing progress has been implemented in the ViewModelBase class.

Showing progress information in the view model can be something simple like a Boolean ShowProgress property. For a more complex scenario where multiple parallel actions can be started, it can be useful to create an implementation with a counter. After invoking the SetInProgress method, to not forget to decrement the count again, the StartInProgress method returns an IDisposable that automatically decrements on Dispose (code file Framework/ViewModels/ViewModelBase.cs):

```
public abstract class ViewModelBase : BindableBase
{
    private class StateSetter : IDisposable
```

```
  {
    private Action _end;
    public StateSetter(Action start, Action end)
    {
      start?.Invoke();
      _end = end;
    }
    public void Dispose() => _end?.Invoke();
  }

  private int _inProgressCounter = 0;
  protected void SetInProgress(bool set = true)
  {
    if (set)
    {
      Interlocked.Increment(ref _inProgressCounter);
      OnPropertyChanged(nameof(InProgress));
    }
    else
    {
      Interlocked.Decrement(ref _inProgressCounter);
      OnPropertyChanged(nameof(InProgress));
    }
  }

  public IDisposable StartInProgress() =>
    new StateSetter(() => SetInProgress(), () => SetInProgress(false));

  public bool InProgress => _inProgressCounter != 0;
  //...
}
```

With every action that might take longer, as, for example, the EndEdit method where saving occurs, the StartInProgress method is invoked where the return of this method is passed to a using statement. Thus, at the end of the using statement, the Dispose method is invoked to decrement the progress count again (code file Framework/ViewModels/EditableViewModel.cs):

```
public async virtual void EndEdit()
{
  using (StartInProgress())
  {
    await OnSaveAsync();
    EditItem = default(TItem);
    IsEditMode = false;
    await _itemsService.RefreshAsync();
    await OnEndEditAsync();
  }
}
```

Now, you can use a ProgressBar that binds the Visibility property to the InProgress property of the view model, and the progress bar is shown automatically (code file BooksApp/Views/BooksPage.xaml):

```
<ProgressBar Margin="8" HorizontalAlignment="Stretch"
    Visibility="{x:Bind ViewModel.InProgress, Mode=OneWay}"
    IsIndeterminate="True" Grid.ColumnSpan="2" />
```

Using Actions in List Items

With modern user interfaces, when a list is shown, the list items also offer some additional information or allow some actions when hovering over the items. For example, Microsoft's Mail program allows the user to flag/delete/archive an email without selecting it first. How is this done?

Instead of binding the Book items directly to the list, you can bind BookItemViewModel objects. With BookItemViewModel items, you can define commands in addition to the information about the book.

With the sample code, the BookItemViewModel is a view model that wraps a Book object. Contrary to the other view models, it will not be created via the DI container, and thus it is possible to have a Book object in the constructor. The book instance is assigned to the Item property of the ItemViewModel base class. In addition to the base class, the BookItemViewModel defines the DeleteBookCommand and the OnDeleteBook method that invokes the DeleteAsync method of the IItemsService (code file BooksLib/ViewModels/BookItemViewModel.cs):

```
public class BookItemViewModel : ItemViewModel<Book>
{
  private readonly IItemsService<Book> _booksService;

  public BookItemViewModel(Book book, IItemsService<Book> booksService)
  {
    Item = book;
    _booksService = booksService;
    DeleteBookCommand = new RelayCommand(OnDeleteBook);
  }

  public RelayCommand DeleteBookCommand { get; set; }

  private async void OnDeleteBook()
  {
    await _booksService.DeleteAsync(Item);
  }
}
```

When the BookItemViewModel is not created via the DI container, how is it created? The MasterDetailViewModel not only defines the Items property that can be bound to a list control; it also defines the ItemsViewModels property. This property just takes the Items and converts them to a TItemViewModel by using the abstract method ToViewModel (code file Framework/ViewModels/MasterDetailViewModel.cs):

```
public abstract class MasterDetailViewModel<TItemViewModel, TItem> :
  ViewModelBase
  where TItemViewModel : IItemViewModel<TItem>
  where TItem: class
{
  //...
  public ObservableCollection<TItem> Items => _itemsService.Items;

  protected abstract TItemViewModel ToViewModel(TItem item);

  public virtual IEnumerable<TItemViewModel> ItemsViewModels =>
    Items.Select(item => ToViewModel(item));
  //...
}
```

The derived class BooksViewModel just needs to override the ToViewModel method to convert the Book objects to the BookItemViewModel objects. You do this by a simple creation of BookItemViewModel objects passing the Book and the services needed (code file BooksLib/ViewModels/BooksViewModel.cs):

```
protected override BookItemViewModel ToViewModel(Book item) =>
  new BookItemViewModel(item, _booksService);
```

Now the view model types can be bound to the ListView. A user control is defined to be shown with the list items. How is it possible to display a button only when the mouse hovers over the item? A technique you've already used with the adaptive user interface is that one element—in this case a Grid control—has the visibility set to Collapsed. Now you define custom Visual State elements with the names HoverButtonsShown and `HoverButtonsHidden`. With the state `HoverButtonsShown`, the `Visibility` of the `Grid` is set to `Visible` (code file `BooksApp/Views/BookItemUserControl.xaml`):

```xml
<Grid>
  <VisualStateManager.VisualStateGroups>
    <VisualStateGroup x:Name="HoveringStates">
      <VisualState x:Name="HoverButtonsShown">
        <VisualState.Setters>
          <Setter Target="hoverArea.Visibility" Value="Visible" />
        </VisualState.Setters>
      </VisualState>
      <VisualState x:Name="HoverButtonsHidden">
      </VisualState>
    </VisualStateGroup>
  </VisualStateManager.VisualStateGroups>

  <Grid.ColumnDefinitions>
    <ColumnDefinition Width="*" />
    <ColumnDefinition Width="auto" />
  </Grid.ColumnDefinitions>
  <StackPanel VerticalAlignment="Center">
    <TextBlock
      Text="{x:Bind Mode=OneWay, Path=BookItemViewModel.Item.Title}" />
  </StackPanel>
  <Grid Grid.Column="1" x:Name="hoverArea" Visibility="Collapsed"
    VerticalAlignment="Center">
    <AppBarButton
      Command="{x:Bind Mode=OneWay, Path=BookItemViewModel.DeleteBookCommand}"
      Icon="Delete" Label="Delete" IsTabStop="False"
      VerticalAlignment="Stretch"/>
  </Grid>
</Grid>
```

With the code-behind, with the overridden methods `OnPointerEntered` and `OnPointerExited`, the state is set using the `VisualStateManager`. The state is only set when the user uses the mouse or the pen (code file `BooksApp/Views/BookItemUserControl.xaml.cs`):

```csharp
public sealed partial class BookItemUserControl : UserControl
{
  public BookItemUserControl()
  {
    this.InitializeComponent();
  }

  public BookItemViewModel BookItemViewModel
  {
    get => (BookItemViewModel)GetValue(BookItemViewModelProperty);
    set => SetValue(BookItemViewModelProperty, value);
  }

  public static readonly DependencyProperty BookItemViewModelProperty =
    DependencyProperty.Register("BookViewModel", typeof(BookItemViewModel),
    typeof(BookItemUserControl), new PropertyMetadata(null));

  protected override void OnPointerEntered(PointerRoutedEventArgs e)
  {
    base.OnPointerEntered(e);

    if (e.Pointer.PointerDeviceType == PointerDeviceType.Mouse ||
        e.Pointer.PointerDeviceType == PointerDeviceType.Pen)
```

```
        {
            VisualStateManager.GoToState(this, "HoverButtonsShown", true);
        }
    }

    protected override void OnPointerExited(PointerRoutedEventArgs e)
    {
        base.OnPointerExited(e);

        VisualStateManager.GoToState(this, "HoverButtonsHidden", true);
    }
}
```

When you run the application, you can see the state changes as the mouse hovers over the item, as shown in Figure 34-14.

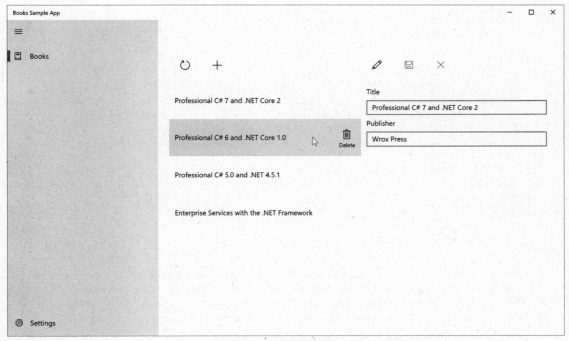

FIGURE 34-14

MESSAGING USING EVENTS

With the current state of the application there's the issue of whether the state of the view models need to be set to use navigation depending on the size of the app window. One way to deal with this is to create a singleton service with an event, use this service from the view models to subscribe to the event, and the main window fires the event. Such a service can also be defined globally—a service for events. With many MVVM frameworks, this is also known as event-aggregator.

A generic `EventAggregator` is defined with the `Framework` project. This aggregator defines an event named `Event` where a handler of type `Action<object, TEvent>` can subscribe and unsubscribe, and a method

`Publish` fires the event. This aggregator is implemented as a singleton to make it easily accessible without needing to create an instance (code file `Framework/EventAggregator.cs`):

```
public class EventAggregator<TEvent>
  where TEvent: EventArgs
{
  private static EventAggregator<TEvent> s_eventAggregator;

  public static EventAggregator<TEvent> Instance =>
    s_eventAggregator ?? (s_eventAggregator = new EventAggregator<TEvent>());

  private EventAggregator()
  {
  }

  public event Action<object, TEvent> Event;

  public void Publish(object source, TEvent ev) =>
    Event?.Invoke(source, ev);
}
```

> **NOTE** *With a generic Singleton class, there's not only one instance created; there's one instance for every generic parameter type used. That's fine for the* `EventAggregator`, *as different event types don't need to share some data, and it allows for better scalability.*

For passing the information about the navigation from the main window to the view model, the `NavigationInfoEvent` is needed. This event information class uses a Boolean property to define whether navigation should be used (code file `BooksLib/Events/NavigationInfoEvent.cs`):

```
public class NavigationInfoEvent : EventArgs
{
  public bool UseNavigation { get; set; }
}
```

The `BooksViewModel` can now subscribe to the event. With the constructor of the `BooksViewModel`, the static member `Instance` is accessed to get the singleton object of the `NavigationInfoEvent` type, and the `UseNavigation` property method is assigned to the event information `e.UseNavigation` (code file `BooksLib/ViewModels/BooksViewModel.cs`):

```
public BooksViewModel(IItemsService<Book> booksService,
  INavigationService navigationService)
  : base(booksService)
{
  _booksService = booksService ??
    throw new ArgumentNullException(nameof(booksService));
  _navigationService = navigationService ??
    throw new ArgumentNullException(nameof(navigationService));

  EventAggregator<NavigationInfoEvent>.Instance.Event += (sender, e) =>
  {
    UseNavigation = e.UseNavigation;
  };
  //...
}
```

The event is published when the size of the main page changes. With the `MainPage` class, the `OnSizeChanged` event handler is registered to the `SizeChanged` event of the page. In the event handler, the `EventAggregator` can be accessed similar to subscription using the static `Instance` property, by invoking the `Publish` method, which passes a `NavigationInfoEvent` object. The `NavigationInfoEvent` object is initialized depending on the size of the window (code file `ViewModels/BooksViewModel.cs`):

```
public sealed partial class MainPage : Page
{
  //...
  private void OnSizeChanged(object sender, SizeChangedEventArgs e)
  {
    EventAggregator<NavigationInfoEvent>.Instance.Publish(this,
      new NavigationInfoEvent { UseNavigation = e.NewSize.Width < 1024 });
  }
}
```

USING A FRAMEWORK

With the sample application, you've seen classes defined in a Framework project such as `BindableBase`, `DelegateCommand`, and `EventAggregator`. These classes are needed with all MVVM-based applications, and you don't need to implement them on your own. They are not a big deal to do, but you can instead use an existing MVVM framework.

MVVM Light (`http://mvvmlight.net`), from Laurent Bugnion, is a small framework that exactly fits the purpose of MVVM applications and is available for many different platforms.

Another framework that originally was created by the Microsoft Patterns and Practices team and has now moved to the community is Prism.Core (`https://github.com/PrismLibrary`). Although the Prism framework is a full-blown framework that supports add-ins and regions in which to position the controls, Prism.Core is very light and contains only a few types such as `BindableBase`, `DelegateCommand`, and `ErrorsContainer`.

SUMMARY

This chapter gave you an architectural guideline for creating XAML-based applications around the MVVM pattern. You've seen a separation of concerns with the model, view, and view model. Besides that, you've seen implementing change notification with the interface `INotifyPropertyChanged`, the repository pattern to separate the data access code, messaging between view models (that can also be used to communicate with views) by using events, and dependency injection with an IoC container.

The chapter also showed you a library of view models that can be used across applications. All this allows for code sharing while still using features of specific platforms. You can use platform-specific features with repository and service implementations, and contracts are available with all platforms. Chapter 37 makes use of the same library to create an app with Xamarin.

The next chapter continues the discussion of XAML and is about styles and resources.

35

Styling Windows Apps

WHAT'S IN THIS CHAPTER?

- ➤ Styling Windows Apps
- ➤ Creating the base drawing with shapes and geometry
- ➤ Scaling, rotating, and skewing with transformations
- ➤ Using brushes to fill backgrounds
- ➤ Working with styles, templates, and resources
- ➤ Creating animations
- ➤ Visual State Manager

WROX.COM CODE DOWNLOADS FOR THIS CHAPTER

The Wrox.com code downloads for this chapter are found at www.wrox.com on the Download Code tab. The source code is also available at https://github.com/ProfessionalCSharp/ProfessionalCSharp7 in the directory Styles.

The code for this chapter is divided into the following major examples:

- ➤ Shapes
- ➤ Geometry
- ➤ Transformation
- ➤ Brushes
- ➤ Styles and Resources
- ➤ Templates
- ➤ Animation
- ➤ Transitions
- ➤ Visual State

STYLING

In recent years, developers have become a lot more concerned with having good-looking apps. When Windows Forms was the technology for creating desktop applications, the user interface didn't offer many options for styling the applications. Controls had a standard look that varied slightly based on the operating system version on which the application was running, but it was not easy to define a complete custom look.

This changed with Windows Presentation Foundation (WPF). WPF is based on DirectX and thus offers vector graphics that allow easy resizing of Windows and controls. Controls are completely customizable and can have different looks. Styling of applications has become extremely important. An application can have any look. With a good design, the user can work with the application without the need to know how to use a Windows application. Instead, the user just needs to have his domain knowledge. For example, the airport in Zurich created a WPF application where buttons look like airplanes. With the button, the user can get information of the position of the plane (the complete application looks like the airport). Colors of the buttons can have different meanings based on the configuration: they can show the either the airline, or on-time/delay information of the plane. This way, the user of the app easily sees what planes that are currently at the airport have small or big delays.

Having different looks of the app is even more important with modern Windows apps. With these apps, the device can be used by users who haven't used Windows applications before. With users who are knowledgeable of Windows applications, you should think about helping these users be more productive by having the typical process for how the user works easily accessible.

Microsoft has not provided a lot of guidance for styling WPF applications. How an application looks mainly depends on your (or the designer's) imagination. With UWP apps, Microsoft has provided a lot more guidance and predefined styles, but you're still able to change anything you like.

This chapter starts with the core elements of XAML—*shapes* that enable you to draw lines, ellipses, and path elements. After that you're introduced to the foundation of shapes—*geometry* elements. You can use geometry elements to create fast vector-based drawings.

With *transformations*, you can scale and rotate any XAML element. With *brushes* you can create solid color, gradient, or more advanced backgrounds. You see how to use brushes within *styles* and place styles within XAML *resources*.

Finally, with *templates* you can completely customize the look of controls, and you also learn how to create animations in this chapter.

SHAPES

Shapes are the core elements of XAML. With shapes you can draw two-dimensional graphics using rectangles, lines, ellipses, paths, polygons, and polylines that are represented by classes derived from the abstract base class `Shape`. Shapes are defined in the namespace `Windows.UI.Xaml.Shapes`.

The following XAML example draws a yellow face consisting of an ellipse for the face, two ellipses for the eyes, two ellipses for the pupils in the eyes, and a path for the mouth (code file `Shapes/MainPage.xaml`):

```xaml
<Canvas>
  <Ellipse Canvas.Left="10" Canvas.Top="10" Width="100" Height="100"
    Stroke="Blue" StrokeThickness="4" Fill="Yellow" />
  <Ellipse Canvas.Left="30" Canvas.Top="12" Width="60" Height="30">
    <Ellipse.Fill>
      <LinearGradientBrush StartPoint="0.5,0" EndPoint="0.5, 1">
        <GradientStop Offset="0.1" Color="DarkGreen" />
        <GradientStop Offset="0.7" Color="Transparent" />
      </LinearGradientBrush>
    </Ellipse.Fill>
  </Ellipse>
```

```
    <Ellipse Canvas.Left="30" Canvas.Top="35" Width="25" Height="20"
      Stroke="Blue" StrokeThickness="3" Fill="White" />
    <Ellipse Canvas.Left="40" Canvas.Top="43" Width="6" Height="5"
      Fill="Black" />
    <Ellipse Canvas.Left="65" Canvas.Top="35" Width="25" Height="20"
      Stroke="Blue" StrokeThickness="3" Fill="White" />
    <Ellipse Canvas.Left="75" Canvas.Top="43" Width="6" Height="5"
      Fill="Black" />
    <Path Stroke="Blue" StrokeThickness="4"
      Data="M 40,74 Q 57,95 80,74" />
  </Canvas>
```

Figure 35-1 shows the result of the XAML code.

All these XAML elements can be accessed programmatically—even if they are buttons or shapes, such as lines or rectangles. Setting the Name or x:Name property with the Path element to mouth enables you to access this element programmatically with the variable name mouth:

```
<Path Name="mouth" Stroke="Blue" StrokeThickness="4"
  Data="M 40,74 Q 57,95 80,74 " />
```

With the next code changes, the mouth of the face is changed dynamically from code-behind. A button with a click handler is added where the SetMouth method is invoked (code file Shapes/MainPage.xaml.cs):

```
private void OnChangeShape(object sender, RoutedEventArgs e)
{
  SetMouth();
}
```

Using code-behind, a geometrical shape can be created using figures and segments. First, you create a two-dimensional array of six points to define three points for the happy and three points for the sad state (code file Shapes/MainPage.xaml.cs):

```
private readonly Point[,] _mouthPoints = new Point[2, 3]
{
  {
    new Point(40, 74), new Point(57, 95), new Point(80, 74),
  },
  {
    new Point(40, 82), new Point(57, 65), new Point(80, 82),
  }
};
```

Next, you assign a new PathGeometry object to the Data property of the Path. The PathGeometry contains a PathFigure with the start point defined (setting the StartPoint property is the same as the letter M with path markup syntax). The PathFigure contains a QuadraticBezierSegment with two Point objects assigned to the properties Point1 and Point2 (the same as the letter Q with two points):

```
private bool _laugh = false;
public void SetMouth()
{
  int index = _laugh ? 0: 1;

  var figure = new PathFigure() { StartPoint = _mouthPoints[index, 0] };
  figure.Segments = new PathSegmentCollection();
  var segment1 = new QuadraticBezierSegment
  {
    Point1 = _mouthPoints[index, 1];
    Point2 = _mouthPoints[index, 2];
  }

  figure.Segments.Add(segment1);
```

```
        var geometry = new PathGeometry();
        geometry.Figures = new PathFigureCollection();
        geometry.Figures.Add(figure);

        mouth.Data = geometry;
        _laugh = !_laugh;
    }
```

Using segments and figures is explained in more detail in the next section. When you run the app, Figure 35-2 shows the sad face.

The following table describes the shapes available in the namespaces `System.Windows` `.Shapes` and `Windows.Ui.Xaml.Shapes`.

FIGURE 35-2

SHAPE CLASS	DESCRIPTION
Line	You can draw a line from the coordinates X1,Y1 to X2,Y2.
Rectangle	You draw a rectangle by specifying Width and Height for this class.
Ellipse	You can draw an ellipse.
Path	You can draw a series of lines and curves. The `Data` property is a `Geometry` type. You can do the drawing by using classes that derive from the base class `Geometry`, or you can use the path markup syntax to define geometry.
Polygon	You can draw a closed shape formed by connected lines. The polygon is defined by a series of `Point` objects assigned to the `Points` property.
Polyline	Like the `Polygon` class, you can draw connected lines with `Polyline`. The difference is that the polyline does not need to be a closed shape.

GEOMETRY

The previous sample showed that one of the shapes, `Path`, uses `Geometry` for its drawing. You can also use `Geometry` elements in other places, such as with a `DrawingBrush`.

In some ways, geometry elements are very similar to shapes. Just as there are `Line`, `Ellipse`, and `Rectangle` shapes, there are also geometry elements for these drawings: `LineGeometry`, `EllipseGeometry`, and `RectangleGeometry`. There are also big differences between shapes and geometries. A `Shape` is a `FrameworkElement` that you can use with any class that supports `UIElement` as its children. `FrameworkElement` derives from `UIElement`. Shapes participate with the layout system and render themselves. The `Geometry` class can't render itself and has fewer features and less overhead than `Shape`. The `Geometry` class directly derives from `DependencyObject`.

The `Path` class uses `Geometry` for its drawing. The geometry can be set with the `Data` property of the `Path`. Simple geometry elements that can be set are `EllipseGeometry` for drawing an ellipse, `LineGeometry` for drawing a line, and `RectangleGeometry` for drawing a rectangle.

Geometries Using Segments

You can also create geometries by using segments. The geometry class `PathGeometry` uses segments for its drawing. The following code segment uses the `BezierSegment` and `LineSegment` elements to build one red and one green figure, as shown in Figure 35-3. The first `BezierSegment` draws a Bézier curve between the points 70,40, which is the starting point of the figure, and 150,63 with control points 90,37

FIGURE 35-3

and 130,46. The following LineSegment uses the ending point of the Bézier curve and draws a line to 120,110 (code file Geometries/MainPage.xaml):

```xaml
<Path Canvas.Left="0" Canvas.Top="0" Fill="Red" Stroke="Blue"
  StrokeThickness="2.5">
  <Path.Data>
    <GeometryGroup>
      <PathGeometry>
        <PathGeometry.Figures>
          <PathFigure StartPoint="70,40" IsClosed="True">
            <PathFigure.Segments>
              <BezierSegment Point1="90,37" Point2="130,46"
                Point3="150,63" />
              <LineSegment Point="120,110" />
              <BezierSegment Point1="100,95" Point2="70,90"
                Point3="45,91" />
            </PathFigure.Segments>
          </PathFigure>
        </PathGeometry.Figures>
      </PathGeometry>
    </GeometryGroup>
  </Path.Data>
</Path>

<Path Canvas.Left="0" Canvas.Top="0" Fill="Green" Stroke="Blue"
  StrokeThickness="2.5">
  <Path.Data>
    <GeometryGroup>
      <PathGeometry>
        <PathGeometry.Figures>
          <PathFigure StartPoint="160,70">
            <PathFigure.Segments>
              <BezierSegment Point1="175,85" Point2="200,99"
                Point3="215,100" />
              <LineSegment Point="195,148" />
              <BezierSegment Point1="174,150" Point2="142,140"
                Point3="129,115" />
              <LineSegment Point="160,70" />
            </PathFigure.Segments>
          </PathFigure>
        </PathGeometry.Figures>
      </PathGeometry>
    </GeometryGroup>
  </Path.Data>
</Path>
```

Other than the BezierSegment and LineSegment elements, you can use ArcSegment to draw an elliptical arc between two points. With PolyLineSegment you can define a set of lines: PolyBezierSegment consists of multiple Bézier curves, QuadraticBezierSegment creates a quadratic Bézier curve, and PolyQuadraticBezierSegment consists of multiple quadratic Bézier curves.

Geometries Using Path Markup

Earlier in this chapter you saw a use of path markup with the Path shape. Using path markup, behind the scenes a speedy drawing with StreamGeometry gets created. XAML for UWP apps creates figures and segments. Programmatically, you can define the figure by creating lines, Bézier curves, and arcs. With XAML, you can use path markup syntax. You can use path markup with the Data property of the Path class. Special characters define how the points are connected. In the following example, M marks the start point, L is a line command to the point specified, and Z is the Close command

FIGURE 35-4

to close the figure. Figure 35-4 shows the result. The path markup syntax allows more commands such as horizontal lines (H), vertical lines (V), cubic Bézier curves (C), quadratic Bézier curves (Q), smooth cubic Bézier curves (S), smooth quadratic Bézier curves (T), and elliptical arcs (A) (code file Geometries/MainPage.xaml):

```
<Path Canvas.Left="0" Canvas.Top="200" Fill="Yellow" Stroke="Blue"
  StrokeThickness="2.5"
  Data="M 120,5 L 128,80 L 220,50 L 160,130 L 190,220 L 100,150
    L 80,230 L 60,140 L0,110 L70,80 Z" StrokeLineJoin="Round">
</Path>
```

TRANSFORMATION

Because XAML is vector based, you can resize every element. In the next example, the vector-based graphics are now scaled, rotated, and skewed. Hit testing (for example, with mouse moves and mouse clicks) still works but without the need for manual position calculation.

Figure 35-5 shows a rectangle in several different forms. All the rectangles are positioned within a StackPanel element with horizontal orientation to have the rectangles one beside the other. The first rectangle has its original size and layout. The second one is resized, the third moved, the forth rotated, the fifth skewed, the sixth transformed using a transformation group, and the seventh transformed using a matrix. The following sections get into the code samples of all these options.

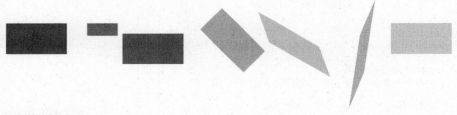

FIGURE 35-5

Scaling

Adding the ScaleTransform element to the RenderTransform property of the Rectangle element, as shown here, resizes the content of the complete rectangle by 0.5 in the x axis and 0.4 in the y axis (code file Transformations/MainPage.xaml):

```
<Rectangle Width="120" Height="60" Fill="Red" Margin="20">
  <Rectangle.RenderTransform>
    <ScaleTransform ScaleX="0.5" ScaleY="0.4" />
  </Rectangle.RenderTransform>
</Rectangle>
```

You can do more than transform simple shapes like rectangles; you can transform any XAML element as XAML defines vector graphics. In the following code, the Canvas element with the face shown earlier is put into a user control named SmilingFace, and this user control is shown first without transformation and then resized. You can see the result in Figure 35-6.

FIGURE 35-6

```
<local:SmilingFace />
<local:SmilingFace>
  <local:SmilingFace.RenderTransform>
    <ScaleTransform ScaleX="1.6" ScaleY="0.8" CenterY="180" />
  </local:SmilingFace.RenderTransform>
</local:SmilingFace>
```

Translating

For moving an element in x or y direction, you can use `TranslateTransform`. In the following snippet, the element moves to the left by assigning `-90` to `X`, and in the direction to the bottom by assigning `20` to `Y` (code file `Transformations/MainPage.xaml`):

```
<Rectangle Width="120" Height="60" Fill="Green" Margin="20">
  <Rectangle.RenderTransform>
    <TranslateTransform X="-90" Y="20" />
  </Rectangle.RenderTransform>
</Rectangle>
```

Rotating

You can rotate an element by using `RotateTransform`. With `RotateTransform`, you set the angle of the rotation and the center of the rotation with `CenterX` and `CenterY` (code file `Transformations/MainPage.xaml`):

```
<Rectangle Width="120" Height="60" Fill="Orange" Margin="20">
  <Rectangle.RenderTransform>
    <RotateTransform Angle="45" CenterX="10" CenterY="-80" />
  </Rectangle.RenderTransform>
</Rectangle>
```

Skewing

For skewing, you can use the `SkewTransform` element. With skewing you can assign angles for the x and y axes (code file `Transformations/MainPage.xaml`):

```
<Rectangle Width="120" Height="60" Fill="LightBlue" Margin="20">
  <Rectangle.RenderTransform>
    <SkewTransform AngleX="20" AngleY="30" CenterX="40" CenterY="390" />
  </Rectangle.RenderTransform>
</Rectangle>
```

Transforming with Groups and Composite Transforms

An easy way to do multiple transformations at once is by using the `CompositeTransform` and `TransformationGroup` elements. The `TransformationGroup` element can have `SkewTransform`, `RotateTransform`, `TranslateTransform`, and `ScaleTransform` as its children (code file `Transformations/MainPage.xaml`):

```
<Rectangle Width="120" Height="60" Fill="LightGreen" Margin="20">
  <Rectangle.RenderTransform>
    <TransformGroup>
      <SkewTransform AngleX="45" AngleY="20" CenterX="-390" CenterY="40" />
      <RotateTransform Angle="90" />
      <ScaleTransform ScaleX="0.5" ScaleY="1.2" />
    </TransformGroup>
  </Rectangle.RenderTransform>
</Rectangle>
```

To rotate and skew together, it is possible to define a `TransformGroup` that contains both `RotateTransform` and `SkewTransform`. The class `CompositeTransform` defines properties to do multiple transformations at once—for example, `ScaleX` and `ScaleY` for scaling as well as `TranslateX` and `TranslateY` for moving an element. You can also define a `MatrixTransform` whereby the `Matrix` element specifies the properties `M11` and `M22` for stretching and `M12` and `M21` for skewing, as shown in the next section.

Transforming Using a Matrix

Another option for defining multiple transformations at once is to specify a matrix. Here, you use `MatrixTransform`. `MatrixTransform` defines a `Matrix` property that has six values. Setting the values 1, 0, 0, 1, 0, 0 doesn't change the element. With the values 0.5, 1.4, 0.4, 0.5, –200, and 0, the element is resized, skewed, and translated (code file `Transformations/MainPage.xaml`):

```
<Rectangle Width="120" Height="60" Fill="Gold" Margin="20">
  <Rectangle.RenderTransform>
    <MatrixTransform Matrix="0.5, 1.4, 0.4, 0.5, -200, 0" />
  </Rectangle.RenderTransform>
</Rectangle>
```

The class `MatrixTransform` defines the public fields `M11`, `M12`, `M21`, `M22`, `OffsetX`, and `OffsetY` that are set in that order if a string is assigned to the `Matrix` property. `MatrixTransform` implements an affine transformation, so only six of the nine matrix members need to be specified. The remaining matrix members have fixed values 0, 0, and 1. The `M11` and `M22` fields have a default value 1 and are used to scale in x and y direction. `M12` and `M21` have a default value 0 and are used to skew the control. `OffsetX` and `OffsetY` have a default value 0 and are used to move the control.

BRUSHES

This section demonstrates how to use XAML's brushes for drawing backgrounds and foregrounds. In this section, you learn about using solid color and linear gradient colors with brushes, you draw images with brushes, and you use the new `AcrylicBrush` and `RevealBrush`.

SolidColorBrush

The first button shown in Figure 35-7 uses the `SolidColorBrush`, which, as the name suggests, uses a solid color. The complete area is drawn with the same color.

You can define a solid color just by setting the `Background` attribute to a string that defines a solid color. The string is converted to a `SolidColorBrush` element with the help of the `BrushValueSerializer` (code file `Brushes/MainPage.xaml`):

FIGURE 35-7

```
<Button Background="#FFC9659C">Solid Color</Button>
```

Of course, you will get the same effect by setting the `Background` child element and adding a `SolidColorBrush` element as its content. The first button in the application uses a hexadecimal value for the solid background color (code file `Brushes/MainPage.xaml`):

```
<Button Content="Solid Color 2">
  <Button.Background>
    <SolidColorBrush Color="#FFC9659C" />
  </Button.Background>
</Button>
```

LinearGradientBrush

For a smooth color change, you can use the `LinearGradientBrush`, as the button in Figure 35-8 shows. This brush defines the `StartPoint` and `EndPoint` properties. With this, you can assign two-dimensional coordinates for the linear gradient. The default gradient is diagonal linear

FIGURE 35-8

from 0,0 to 1,1. By defining different values, the gradient can take different directions. For example, with a StartPoint of 0,0 and an EndPoint of 0,1, you get a vertical gradient. The StartPoint and EndPoint value of 1,0 creates a horizontal gradient.

With the content of this brush, you can define the color values at the specified offsets with the GradientStop element. Between the stops, the colors are smoothed (code file Brushes/MainPage.xaml):

```
<Button Content="Linear Gradient Brush">
  <Button.Background>
    <LinearGradientBrush StartPoint="0,0" EndPoint="0,1">
      <GradientStop Offset="0" Color="LightGreen" />
      <GradientStop Offset="0.4" Color="Green" />
      <GradientStop Offset="1" Color="DarkGreen" />
    </LinearGradientBrush>
  </Button.Background>
</Button>
```

ImageBrush

To load an image into a brush, you can use the ImageBrush element. With this element, the image defined by the ImageSource property is displayed. The image can be accessed from the file system or from a resource within the assembly. In the code example, the image is added from the file system (code file Brushes/MainPage.xaml):

```
<Button Content="Image Brush" FontWeight="ExtraBold" FontSize="28"
  RenderTransformOrigin="0.5,0.5" >
  <Button.Background>
    <ImageBrush ImageSource="msbuild.png" Opacity="0.5" />
  </Button.Background>
</Button>
```

When you run the application, you can see a button as shown in Figure 35-9.

AcrylicBrush

A new brush available with Windows 10 build 16299 is the AcrylicBrush. This brush is part of the new Fluent Design. The AcrylicBrush allows a transparency effect that lets other elements of the app or the host shine through.

FIGURE 35-9

An application that ships as part of Windows 10 is the Calculator. The Calculator has some slight transparency that lets other applications or the wallpaper image shine through to the app (see Figure 35-10). This effect isn't applied to the main number buttons in the calculator, but the other elements of the calculator let the light of the background shine through.

You assign AcrylicBrush to the Background property of the Button. The value for the TintOpacity is taken from the value of a slider. This allows to see the different effects of this brush based on the opacity when you move the slider in the app. The TintColor property specifies the main color of the brush. With the BackgroundSource property, you can select between HostBackdrop or Backdrop. When you use Backdrop, the colors from the app itself shines through. This is known as *in-app acrylic*. Elements that are overlaid from the controls using the brush shine through. With HostBackdrop, the colors from below the application are taken; this is *background acrylic*. Because acrylic UI effects require GPU power, this feature can shorten battery life. AcrylicBrush uses the solid color defined by the FallbackColor property when the system runs low on power. You also can configure the property AlwaysUseFallback to always use the

fallback color. This setting can be triggered by user configuration to enhance the battery lifetime (code file
Brushes/MainPage.xaml):

```
<Button Content="Acrylic Brush Host Backdrop">
  <Button.Background>
    <AcrylicBrush BackgroundSource="HostBackdrop" TintColor="#FFFF0000"
      TintOpacity="{x:Bind slider1.Value, Mode=OneWay}"
      FallbackColor="Orange" />
  </Button.Background>
</Button>
```

FIGURE 35-10

Figure 35-11 shows AcrylicBrush with a current TintOpacity setting of 0.2. The button on the top
is configured with HostBackdrop. Here, you can see the background underneath the application shines
through. The button on the bottom is configured with Backdrop. Here, you can see an orange rectangle that
is positioned underneath the button shines through.

Acrylic Brush Backdrop

FIGURE 35-11

Reveal Brushes

Another new brush with the Windows 10 build 16299 is the `RevealBrush`. This brush highlights the area where the user moves the mouse using a light effect. One simple way to style a button using this brush is to use the `ButtonRevealStyle` as the following code snippet demonstrates (code file `Brushes/MainPage.xaml`):

```
<Button Content="Button with Reveal Style" Padding="12" Margin="12"
  Style="{StaticResource ButtonRevealStyle}" />
```

When you use `ButtonRevealStyle`, you need to look carefully when the application is running to see the effect. The following button defines a thicker border that uses the `BorderBrush` defined in the theme resource `SystemColorControlHighlightAccentRevealBorderBrush`, which helps you see the effect more clearly. As you move the mouse around the button, the border of the button lights up near to the mouse.

```
<Button Margin="4" BorderThickness="8"
  Background="{ThemeResource SystemControlHighlightAccentRevealBackgroundBrush}"
  BorderBrush="{ThemeResource SystemControlHighlightAccentRevealBorderBrush}">
  With Reveal Border</Button>
```

Now as you've used predefined styles, let's get into defining custom styles within resources.

STYLES AND RESOURCES

You can define the look and feel of the XAML elements by setting properties, such as `FontSize` and `Background`, with the `Button` element (code file StylesAndResources/MainPage.xaml):

```
<Button Width="150" FontSize="12" Background="AliceBlue" Content="Click Me!" />
```

Instead of defining the look and feel with every element, you can define styles that are stored with resources. To completely customize the look of controls, you can use templates and add them to resources.

Styles

You can assign the `Style` property of a control to a `Style` element that has setters associated with it. A `Setter` element defines the `Property` and `Value` properties to set the specific properties and values for the target element. In the following example, the `Background`, `FontSize`, `FontWeight`, and `Margin` properties are set. The `Style` is set to the `TargetType` `Button`, so that the properties of the `Button` can be directly accessed (code file StylesAndResources/MainPage.xaml):

```
<Button Width="150" Content="Click Me!">
  <Button.Style>
    <Style TargetType="Button">
      <Setter Property="Background" Value="Yellow" />
      <Setter Property="FontSize" Value="14" />
      <Setter Property="FontWeight" Value="Bold" />
      <Setter Property="Margin" Value="5" />
    </Style>
  </Button.Style>
</Button>
```

Setting the `Style` directly with the `Button` element doesn't really help a lot with style sharing. Styles can be put into resources. Within the resources you can assign styles to specific elements, assign a style to all elements of a type, or use a key for the style. To assign a style to all elements of a type, use the `TargetType` property of the `Style` and assign it to a `Button`. To define a style that needs to be referenced, `x:Key` must be set:

```
<Page.Resources>
  <Style TargetType="Button">
    <Setter Property="Background" Value="LemonChiffon" />
    <Setter Property="FontSize" Value="18" />
    <Setter Property="Margin" Value="5" />
  </Style>
  <Style x:Key="ButtonStyle1" TargetType="Button">
    <Setter Property="Background" Value="Red" />
    <Setter Property="Foreground" Value="White" />
    <Setter Property="FontSize" Value="18" />
    <Setter Property="Margin" Value="5" />
  </Style>
</Page.Resources>
```

In the sample application, the styles that are defined globally within the page are defined within the `Resources` property of the `Page` element.

In the following XAML code the first button—which doesn't have a style defined with the element properties—gets the style that is defined for the `Button` type. With the next button, the `Style` property is set with the `StaticResource` markup extension to `{StaticResource ButtonStyle}`, whereas `ButtonStyle` specifies the key value of the style resource defined earlier, so this button has a red background and a white foreground:

```
<Button Width="200" Content="Default Button style" Margin="3" />
<Button Width="200" Content="Named style"
    Style="{StaticResource ButtonStyle1}" Margin="3" />
```

Rather than set the `Background` of a button to just a single value, you can do more. You can set the `Background` property to a `LinearGradientBrush` with a gradient color definition:

```
<Style x:Key="FancyButtonStyle" TargetType="Button">
  <Setter Property="FontSize" Value="22" />
  <Setter Property="Foreground" Value="White" />
  <Setter Property="Margin" Value="5" />
  <Setter Property="Background">
    <Setter.Value>
      <LinearGradientBrush StartPoint="0,0" EndPoint="0,1">
        <GradientStop Offset="0.0" Color="LightCyan" />
        <GradientStop Offset="0.14" Color="Cyan" />
        <GradientStop Offset="0.7" Color="DarkCyan" />
      </LinearGradientBrush>
    </Setter.Value>
  </Setter>
</Style>
```

The next button in this example has a fancy style with cyan applied as the linear gradient:

```
<Button Width="200" Content="Fancy button style"
    Style="{StaticResource FancyButtonStyle}" Margin="3" />
```

Styles offer a kind of inheritance. One style can be based on another one. The style `AnotherButtonStyle` is based on the style `FancyButtonStyle`. It uses all the settings defined by the base style (referenced by the `BasedOn` property), except the `Foreground` property—which is set to `LinearGradientBrush`:

```
<Style x:Key="AnotherButtonStyle" BasedOn="{StaticResource FancyButtonStyle}"
    TargetType="Button">
  <Setter Property="Foreground">
    <Setter.Value>
      <LinearGradientBrush>
        <GradientStop Offset="0.2" Color="White" />
        <GradientStop Offset="0.5" Color="LightYellow" />
        <GradientStop Offset="0.9" Color="Orange" />
      </LinearGradientBrush>
    </Setter.Value>
  </Setter>
</Style>
```

The last button has `AnotherButtonStyle` applied:

```
<Button Width="200" Content="Style inheritance"
    Style="{StaticResource AnotherButtonStyle}" Margin="3" />
```

The result of all these buttons after styling is shown in Figure 35-12.

Resources

As you have seen with the styles sample, usually styles are stored within resources. You can define any sharable element within a resource. For example, the brush created

FIGURE 35-12

earlier for the background style of the button can be defined as a resource, so you can use it everywhere a brush is required.

The following example defines a `LinearGradientBrush` with the key name `MyGradientBrush` inside the `StackPanel` resources. `button1` assigns the `Background` property by using a `StaticResource` markup extension to the resource `MyGradientBrush` (code file StylesAndResources/ResourceDemoPage.xaml):

```
<StackPanel x:Name="myContainer">
  <StackPanel.Resources>
    <LinearGradientBrush x:Key="MyGradientBrush" StartPoint="0,0"
      EndPoint="0.3,1">
      <GradientStop Offset="0.0" Color="LightCyan" />
      <GradientStop Offset="0.14" Color="Cyan" />
      <GradientStop Offset="0.7" Color="DarkCyan" />
    </LinearGradientBrush>
  </StackPanel.Resources>
  <Button Width="200" Height="50" Foreground="White" Margin="5"
    Background="{StaticResource MyGradientBrush}" Content="Click Me!" />
</StackPanel>
```

Here, the resources have been defined with the `StackPanel`. In the previous example, the resources were defined with the `Page` or `Window` element. The base class `FrameworkElement` defines the property `Resources` of type `ResourceDictionary`. That's why resources can be defined with every class that is derived from the `FrameworkElement`—any XAML element.

Resources are searched hierarchically. If you define the resource with the root element, it applies to every child element. If the root element contains a `Grid`, and the `Grid` contains a `StackPanel`, and you define the resource with the `StackPanel`, then the resource applies to every control within the `StackPanel`. If the `StackPanel` contains a `Button`, and you define the resource just with the `Button`, then this style is valid only for the `Button`.

> **NOTE** *With hierarchies, you need to pay attention if you use the* `TargetType` *without a* `Key` *for styles. If you define a resource with the* `Canvas` *element and set the* `TargetType` *for the style to apply to* `TextBox` *elements, then the style applies to all* `TextBox` *elements within the* `Canvas`. *The style even applies to* `TextBox` *elements that are contained in a* `ListBox` *when the* `ListBox` *is in the* `Canvas`.

If you need the same style for more than one window, then you can define the style with the application. Creating a Windows app using Visual Studio, the file App.xaml is created for defining global resources of the application. The application styles are valid for every page or window of the application. Every element can access resources that are defined with the application. If resources are not found with the parent window, then the search for resources continues with the `Application` (code file StylesAndResources/App .xaml):

```
<Application x:Class="StylesAndResources.App"
  xmlns="http://schemas.microsoft.com/winfx/2006/xaml/presentation"
  xmlns:x="http://schemas.microsoft.com/winfx/2006/xaml"
  RequestedTheme="Light">
  <Application.Resources>
  </Application.Resources>
</Application>
```

Accessing Resources from Code

To access resources from code-behind, the `Resources` property of the base class `FrameworkElement` returns a `ResourceDictionary`. This dictionary offers access to the resources using an indexer with the name of the resource. You can use the `ContainsKey` method to check whether the resource is available.

Let's see that in action. The `Button` control `button1` doesn't have a background specified, but the `Click` event is assigned to the method `OnApplyResources` to change this dynamically (code file `StylesAndResources/ResourceDemoPage.xaml`):

```
<Button Name="button1" Width="220" Height="50" Margin="5"
  Click="OnApplyResources" Content="Apply Resource Programmatically" />
```

When you use WPF, you would have a `TryFindResource` method to iterate all the resources. When you use UWP, you can use a similar method, but you need to implement it yourself. The method `OnApplyResources` invokes the extension method `TryFindResource` to find the resource named `MyGradientBrush` and assigns it to the `Background` property of the control (code file `StylesAndResources/ResourceDemo.xaml.cs`):

```
private void OnApplyResources(object sender, RoutedEventArgs e)
{
  if (sender is Control ctrl)
  {
    ctrl.Background = ctrl.TryFindResource("MyGradientBrush") as Brush;
  }
}
```

The implementation of the method `TryFindResource` checks whether the resource requested is available using `ContainsKey`, and it recursively invokes the method in case the resource is not yet found (code file `StylesAndResources/FrameworkElementExtensions.cs`):

```
public static class FrameworkElementExtensions
{
  public static object TryFindResource(this FrameworkElement e, string key)
  {
    if (e == null) throw new ArgumentNullException(nameof(e));
    if (key == null) throw new ArgumentNullException(nameof(key));

    if (e.Resources.ContainsKey(key))
    {
      return e.Resources[key];
    }
    else if (e.Parent is FrameworkElement parent)
    {
      return TryFindResource(parent, key);
    }
    else
    {
      return null;
    }
  }
}
```

Resource Dictionaries

If you use the same resources with different pages or even different apps, it's useful to put the resource in a resource dictionary. When you use resource dictionaries, you can share the files between multiple apps, or you can put the resource dictionary into an assembly that is shared.

To share a resource dictionary in an assembly, create a library. You can add a resource dictionary file—here `Dictionary1.xaml`—to the assembly.

`Dictionary1.xaml` defines two resources: `LinearGradientBrush` with the `CyanGradientBrush` key, and a style for a `Button` that can be referenced with the `PinkButtonStyle` key (code file download `ResourcesLib/Dictionary1.xaml`):

```
<ResourceDictionary
  xmlns="http://schemas.microsoft.com/winfx/2006/xaml/presentation"
  xmlns:x="http://schemas.microsoft.com/winfx/2006/xaml">
```

```
<LinearGradientBrush x:Key="CyanGradientBrush" StartPoint="0,0"
  EndPoint="0.3,1">
  <LinearGradientBrush.GradientStops>
    <GradientStop Offset="0.0" Color="LightCyan" />
    <GradientStop Offset="0.14" Color="Cyan" />
    <GradientStop Offset="0.7" Color="DarkCyan" />
  </LinearGradientBrush.GradientStops>
</LinearGradientBrush>

<Style x:Key="PinkButtonStyle" TargetType="Button">
  <Setter Property="FontSize" Value="22" />
  <Setter Property="Foreground" Value="White" />
  <Setter Property="Background">
    <Setter.Value>
      <LinearGradientBrush StartPoint="0,0" EndPoint="0,1">
        <LinearGradientBrush.GradientStops>
          <GradientStop Offset="0.0" Color="Pink" />
          <GradientStop Offset="0.3" Color="DeepPink" />
          <GradientStop Offset="0.9" Color="DarkOrchid" />
        </LinearGradientBrush.GradientStops>
      </LinearGradientBrush>
    </Setter.Value>
  </Setter>
</Style>
</ResourceDictionary>
```

With the target project, the library needs to be referenced, and the resource dictionary needs to be added to the dictionaries. You can use multiple resource dictionary files that you can add by using the `MergedDictionaries` property of the `ResourceDictionary`. You can add a list of resource dictionaries to the merged dictionaries. With UWP apps, the referenced resource dictionary must be prefixed with the `ms-appx:///` scheme (code file StylesAndResources/App.xaml):

```
<Application x:Class="StylesAndResources.App"
xmlns="http://schemas.microsoft.com/winfx/2006/xaml/presentation"
xmlns:x="http://schemas.microsoft.com/winfx/2006/xaml"
xmlns:local="using:StylesAndResources"
RequestedTheme="Light">
  <Application.Resources>
    <ResourceDictionary>
      <ResourceDictionary.MergedDictionaries>
        <ResourceDictionary
          Source="ms-appx:///ResourcesLibUWP/Dictionary1.xaml" />
      </ResourceDictionary.MergedDictionaries>
    </ResourceDictionary>
  </Application.Resources>
</Application>
```

Now it is possible to use the resources from the referenced assembly in the same way as local resources (code file StylesAndResources/ResourceDemoPage.xaml):

```
<Button Width="300" Height="50" Style="{StaticResource PinkButtonStyle}"
  Content="Referenced Resource" />
```

Theme Resources

WPF supports the `DynamicResource` markup extension to dynamically update the user interface when resources change while the app runs. UWP apps don't support this markup extension, but you have a different way to change styles dynamically. The feature is based on themes, with which you can allow the user to switch between a light and a dark theme (this is like the themes you can change with Visual Studio).

Defining Theme Resources

Theme resources can be defined in a resource dictionary within the `ThemeDictionaries` collection. The `ResourceDictionary` objects that are defined within the `ThemeDictionaries` collection need to have a key assigned that has the name of a theme—either `Light` or `Dark`. The sample code defines a button for the light theme that has a light background and dark foreground, and for the dark theme a dark background and light foreground. The key for the style is the same within both dictionaries: `SampleButtonStyle` (code file `StylesAndResources/Styles/SampleThemes.xaml`):

```
<ResourceDictionary
    xmlns="http://schemas.microsoft.com/winfx/2006/xaml/presentation"
    xmlns:x="http://schemas.microsoft.com/winfx/2006/xaml"
    xmlns:local="using:StylesAndResourcesUWP">
  <ResourceDictionary.ThemeDictionaries>
    <ResourceDictionary x:Key="Light">
      <Style TargetType="Button" x:Key="SampleButtonStyle">
        <Setter Property="Background" Value="LightGray" />
        <Setter Property="Foreground" Value="Black" />
      </Style>
    </ResourceDictionary>

    <ResourceDictionary x:Key="Dark">
      <Style TargetType="Button" x:Key="SampleButtonStyle">
        <Setter Property="Background" Value="Black" />
        <Setter Property="Foreground" Value="White" />
      </Style>
    </ResourceDictionary>
  </ResourceDictionary.ThemeDictionaries>
</ResourceDictionary>
```

You can assign the style using the `ThemeResource` markup extension. Other than using a different markup extension, everything else is the same as with the `StaticResource` markup extension (code file `StylesAndResourcesUWP/ThemeDemoPage.xaml`):

```
<Button Style="{ThemeResource SampleButtonStyle}" Click="OnChangeTheme"
    Content="Change Theme" />
```

Depending on the theme that is selected, the corresponding style will be used.

Selecting a Theme

There are different ways to select a theme. First, there's a default for the app itself. The `RequestedTheme` property of the `Application` class defines the default theme of the app. This is defined within `App.xaml`, which is the place where the themes dictionary file is referenced as well (code file `StylesAndResources/App.xaml`):

```
<Application
    x:Class="StylesAndResourcesUWP.App"
    xmlns="http://schemas.microsoft.com/winfx/2006/xaml/presentation"
    xmlns:x="http://schemas.microsoft.com/winfx/2006/xaml"
    xmlns:local="using:StylesAndResourcesUWP"
    RequestedTheme="Light">
  <Application.Resources>
    <ResourceDictionary>
      <ResourceDictionary.MergedDictionaries>
        <ResourceDictionary Source="ms-appx:///StylesLib/Dictionary1.xaml" />
        <ResourceDictionary Source="Styles/SampleThemes.xaml" />
      </ResourceDictionary.MergedDictionaries>
    </ResourceDictionary>
  </Application.Resources>
</Application>
```

The `RequestedTheme` property is defined in the XAML element hierarchy. Every element can override the theme to be used for itself and its children. The following `Grid` element changes the default theme for the `Dark` theme. This is now the theme used for the `Grid` and all its children elements (code file `StylesAndResources/ThemeDemoPage.xaml`):

```
<Grid x:Name="grid1"
  Background="{ThemeResource ApplicationPageBackgroundThemeBrush}"
  RequestedTheme="Dark">
  <Button Style="{ThemeResource SampleButtonStyle}" Click="OnChangeTheme"
    Content="Change Theme" />
</Grid>
```

You can also dynamically change the theme by setting the `RequestedTheme` property from code (code file `StylesAndResources/ThemeDemoPage.xaml.cs`):

```
private void OnChangeTheme(object sender, RoutedEventArgs e)
{
  grid1.RequestedTheme = grid1.RequestedTheme == ElementTheme.Dark ?
  ElementTheme.Light: ElementTheme.Dark;
}
```

> **NOTE** *Using the `ThemeResource` markup extension is useful only in cases where the resource should look different based on the theme. If the resource should look the same, with all themes, keep using the `StaticResource` markup extension.*

TEMPLATES

An XAML `Button` control can contain any content. The content can be simple text, but you can also add a `Canvas` element, which can contain shapes; a `Grid`; or a video. In fact, you can do even more than that with a button! With template-based XAML controls, the functionality of controls is completely separate from their look and feel. A button has a default look, but you can completely customize that look.

Windows apps offer several template types that derive from the base class `FrameworkTemplate`.

TEMPLATE TYPE	DESCRIPTION
ControlTemplate	Enables you to specify the visual structure of a control and override its look.
ItemsPanelTemplate	For an `ItemsControl` you can specify the layout of its items by assigning an `ItemsPanelTemplate`. Each `ItemsControl` has a default `ItemsPanelTemplate`. For the `MenuItem`, it is a `WrapPanel`. The `StatusBar` uses a `DockPanel`, and the `ListBox` uses a `VirtualizingStackPanel`.
DataTemplate	These are very useful for graphical representations of objects. When styling a `ListBox`, by default the items of the `ListBox` are shown according to the output of the `ToString` method. By applying a `DataTemplate` you can override this behavior and define a custom presentation of the items.

Control Templates

Previously in this chapter you've seen how you can style the properties of a control. If setting simple properties of the controls doesn't give you the look you want, you can change the `Template` property. With the `Template` property, you can customize the complete look of the control. The next example demonstrates customizing buttons, and later in the chapter list views are customized step by step so you can see the intermediate results of the changes.

You customize the Button type in a separate resource dictionary file: ControlTemplates.xaml. Here, a style with the key name RoundedGelButton is defined. The style RoundedGelButton sets the properties Background, Height, Foreground, and Margin, and the Template. The Template is the most interesting aspect with this style. The Template specifies a Grid with just one row and one column.

Inside this cell, you can find an ellipse with the name GelBackground. This ellipse has a linear gradient brush for the stroke. The stroke that surrounds the rectangle is very thin because the StrokeThickness is set to 0.5.

The second ellipse, GelShine, is a small ellipse whose size is defined by the Margin property and so is visible within the first ellipse. The stroke is transparent, so there is no line surrounding the ellipse. This ellipse uses a linear gradient fill brush, which transitions from a light, partly transparent color to full transparency. This gives the ellipse a shimmering effect (code file Templates/Styles/ControlTemplates.xaml):

```xml
<ResourceDictionary
  xmlns="http://schemas.microsoft.com/winfx/2006/xaml/presentation"
  xmlns:x="http://schemas.microsoft.com/winfx/2006/xaml">

  <Style x:Key="RoundedGelButton" TargetType="Button">
    <Setter Property="Width" Value="100" />
    <Setter Property="Height" Value="100" />
    <Setter Property="Foreground" Value="White" />
    <Setter Property="Template">
      <Setter.Value>
        <ControlTemplate TargetType="Button">
          <Grid>
            <Ellipse Name="GelBackground" StrokeThickness="0.5" Fill="Black">
              <Ellipse.Stroke>
                <LinearGradientBrush StartPoint="0,0" EndPoint="0,1">
                  <GradientStop Offset="0" Color="#ff7e7e7e" />
                  <GradientStop Offset="1" Color="Black" />
                </LinearGradientBrush>
              </Ellipse.Stroke>
            </Ellipse>
            <Ellipse Margin="15,5,15,50">
              <Ellipse.Fill>
                <LinearGradientBrush StartPoint="0,0" EndPoint="0,1">
                  <GradientStop Offset="0" Color="#aaffffff" />
                  <GradientStop Offset="1" Color="Transparent" />
                </LinearGradientBrush>
              </Ellipse.Fill>
            </Ellipse>
          </Grid>
        </ControlTemplate>
      </Setter.Value>
    </Setter>
  </Style>
</ResourceDictionary>
```

From the app.xaml file, the resource dictionary is referenced as shown here (code file Templates/App.xaml):

```xml
<Application x:Class="TemplateDemo.App"
  xmlns="http://schemas.microsoft.com/winfx/2006/xaml/presentation"
  xmlns:x="http://schemas.microsoft.com/winfx/2006/xaml"
  StartupUri="MainWindow.xaml">
  <Application.Resources>
    <ResourceDictionary Source="Styles/ControlTemplates.xaml" />
  </Application.Resources>
</Application>
```

Now a `Button` control can be associated with the style. The new look of the button is shown in Figure 35-13 and uses code file `Templates/StyledButtons.xaml`:

```
<Button Style="{StaticResource RoundedGelButton}" Content="Click Me!" />
```

FIGURE 35-13

The button now has a completely different look. However, the content that is defined with the button itself is missing. The template created previously must be extended to get the content of the `Button` into the new look. What needs to be added is a `ContentPresenter`. The `ContentPresenter` is the placeholder for the control's content, and it defines the place where the content should be positioned. In the code that follows, the content is placed in the first row of the `Grid`, as are the `Ellipse` elements. The `Content` property of the `ContentPresenter` defines what the content should be. The content is set to a `TemplateBinding` markup expression. `TemplateBinding` binds the template parent, which is the `Button` element in this case. `{TemplateBinding Content}` specifies that the value of the `Content` property of the `Button` control should be placed inside the placeholder as content. Figure 35-14 shows the result with the content shown in the here (code file `Templates/Styles/ControlTemplates.xaml`):

FIGURE 35-14

```xml
<Setter Property="Template">
  <Setter.Value>
    <ControlTemplate TargetType="Button">
      <Grid>
        <Ellipse Name="GelBackground" StrokeThickness="0.5" Fill="Black">
          <Ellipse.Stroke>
            <LinearGradientBrush StartPoint="0,0" EndPoint="0,1">
              <GradientStop Offset="0" Color="#ff7e7e7e" />
              <GradientStop Offset="1" Color="Black" />
            </LinearGradientBrush>
          </Ellipse.Stroke>
        </Ellipse>
        <Ellipse Margin="15,5,15,50">
          <Ellipse.Fill>
            <LinearGradientBrush StartPoint="0,0" EndPoint="0,1">
              <GradientStop Offset="0" Color="#aaffffff" />
              <GradientStop Offset="1" Color="Transparent" />
            </LinearGradientBrush>
          </Ellipse.Fill>
        </Ellipse>
        <ContentPresenter Name="GelButtonContent"
          VerticalAlignment="Center"
          HorizontalAlignment="Center"
          Content="{TemplateBinding Content}" />
      </Grid>
    </ControlTemplate>
  </Setter.Value>
</Setter>
```

> **NOTE** The `TemplateBinding` *allows talking values to the template that are defined by the control. This can not only be used for the content but also can be used for colors and stroke styles and much more.*

Such a styled button now looks very fancy on the screen, but there's still a problem: There is no action if the button is clicked or touched, or the mouse moves over the button. This isn't the typical experience a user has with a button. However, there is a solution. With a template-styled button, you must have visual states or triggers that enable the button to have different looks in response to mouse moves and mouse clicks. Visual states also make use of animations; thus, I'm delaying this change to later in this chapter.

However, for getting an advance glimpse into this, you can use Visual Studio to create a button template. Instead of creating such a template fully from scratch, you can select a Button control either in the XAML designer or in the Document Explorer and select Edit Template from the context menu. Here, you can create an empty template or copy the predefined template. You use a copy of the template to have a look at how the predefined template looks. You see the dialog to create a style resource (see Figure 35-15). Here you can define whether the resource containing the template should be created in the document, the application (when used for multiple pages and windows), or a resource dictionary. For the previously styled button, the resource dictionary `ControlTemplates.xaml` already exists; with the sample code the resource is created there.

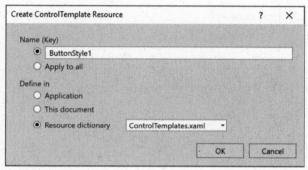

FIGURE 35-15

Some highlights of the template for the default button template for Windows apps are shown in the following code snippets. Several of the button settings, such as `Background`, `Foreground`, and `BorderBrush`, are taken from theme resources. They are different based on the light or dark theme. Some values, such as `Padding` and `HorizontalAlignment`, are fixed. You can change these by creating a custom style (code file `Templates/Styles/ControlTemplates.xaml`):

```
<Style x:Key="ButtonStyle1" TargetType="Button">
  <Setter Property="Background" Value="{ThemeResource ButtonBackground}"/>
  <Setter Property="Foreground" Value="{ThemeResource ButtonForeground}"/>
  <Setter Property="BorderBrush" Value="{ThemeResource ButtonBorderBrush}"/>
  <Setter Property="BorderThickness"
    Value="{ThemeResource ButtonBorderThemeThickness}"/>
  <Setter Property="Padding" Value="8,4,8,4"/>
  <Setter Property="HorizontalAlignment" Value="Left"/>
  <Setter Property="VerticalAlignment" Value="Center"/>
  <Setter Property="FontFamily"
    Value="{ThemeResource ContentControlThemeFontFamily}"/>
  <Setter Property="FontWeight" Value="Normal"/>
  <Setter Property="FontSize"
    Value="{ThemeResource ControlContentThemeFontSize}"/>
  <Setter Property="UseSystemFocusVisuals" Value="True"/>
  <Setter Property="FocusVisualMargin" Value="-3"/>
```

The template of the control consists of a `Grid` and a `ContentPresenter` where values for brushes and borders are bound using `TemplateBinding`. This way it is possible to define these values directly with the `Button` control to influence the look.

```
<Setter Property="Template">
  <Setter.Value>
    <ControlTemplate TargetType="Button">
      <Grid x:Name="RootGrid" Background="{TemplateBinding Background}">
```

```
        <!—Visual State Manager settings removed—>
        <ContentPresenter x:Name="ContentPresenter"
          AutomationProperties.AccessibilityView="Raw"
          BorderBrush="{TemplateBinding BorderBrush}"
          BorderThickness="{TemplateBinding BorderThickness}"
          ContentTemplate="{TemplateBinding ContentTemplate}"
          ContentTransitions="{TemplateBinding ContentTransitions}"
          Content="{TemplateBinding Content}"
          HorizontalContentAlignment=
            "{TemplateBinding HorizontalContentAlignment}"
          Padding="{TemplateBinding Padding}"
          VerticalContentAlignment=
            "{TemplateBinding VerticalContentAlignment}"/>
      </Grid>
    </ControlTemplate>
  </Setter.Value>
</Setter>
```

For dynamic button changes, if the mouse moves over the button, or the button is pressed, the app template for the button makes use of the VisualStateManager. Here, key-frame animations are defined when the button changes to the states PointerOver, Pressed, and Disabled:

```
<VisualStateManager.VisualStateGroups>
  <VisualStateGroup x:Name="CommonStates">
    <VisualState x:Name="Normal">
      <Storyboard>
        <PointerUpThemeAnimation Storyboard.TargetName="RootGrid"/>
      </Storyboard>
    </VisualState>
    <VisualState x:Name="PointerOver">
      <Storyboard>
        <ObjectAnimationUsingKeyFrames
          Storyboard.TargetProperty="BorderBrush"
          Storyboard.TargetName="ContentPresenter">
          <DiscreteObjectKeyFrame KeyTime="0"
            Value="{ThemeResource SystemControlHighlightBaseMediumLowBrush}"/>
        </ObjectAnimationUsingKeyFrames>
        <ObjectAnimationUsingKeyFrames
          Storyboard.TargetProperty="Foreground"
          Storyboard.TargetName="ContentPresenter">
          <DiscreteObjectKeyFrame KeyTime="0"
            Value="{ThemeResource SystemControlHighlightBaseHighBrush}"/>
        </ObjectAnimationUsingKeyFrames>
      </Storyboard>
    </VisualState>
    <VisualState x:Name="Pressed">
      <Storyboard>
        <!—animations removed—>
      </Storyboard>
    </VisualState>
    <VisualState x:Name="Disabled">
      <Storyboard>
        <!—animations removed—>
      </Storyboard>
    </VisualState>
  </VisualStateGroup>
</VisualStateManager.VisualStateGroups>
```

Data Templates

The content of `ContentControl` elements can be any content—not only XAML elements but also .NET objects. For example, an object of the `Country` type can be assigned to the content of a `Button` class. In the following example, the `Country` class is created to represent the name and flag with a path to an image. This class defines the `Name` and `ImagePath` properties, and it has an overridden `ToString` method for a default string representation (code file `Models/Country.cs`):

```
public class Country
{
    public string Name { get; set; }
    public string ImagePath { get; set; }
    public override string ToString() => Name;
}
```

How does this content look within a `Button` or any other `ContentControl`? By default, the `ToString` method is invoked, and the string representation of the object is shown.

For a custom look, you can create a `DataTemplate` for the `Country` type. The sample code defines the key `CountryDataTemplate`. You can use this key to reference the template. Within the `DataTemplate` the main elements are a `TextBlock` with the `Text` property bound to the `Name` property of the `Country`, and an `Image` with the `Source` property bound to the `ImagePath` property of the `Country`. The `Grid` and `Border` elements define the layout and visual appearance (code file `Templates/Styles/DataTemplates.xaml`):

```xml
<DataTemplate x:Key="CountryDataTemplate">
  <Border Margin="4" BorderThickness="2" CornerRadius="6">
    <Border.BorderBrush>
      <LinearGradientBrush StartPoint="0,0" EndPoint="0,1">
        <GradientStop Offset="0" Color="#aaa" />
        <GradientStop Offset="1" Color="#222" />
      </LinearGradientBrush>
    </Border.BorderBrush>
    <Border.Background>
      <LinearGradientBrush StartPoint="0,0" EndPoint="0,1">
        <GradientStop Offset="0" Color="#444" />
        <GradientStop Offset="1" Color="#fff" />
      </LinearGradientBrush>
    </Border.Background>
    <Grid Margin="4">
      <Grid.RowDefinitions>
        <RowDefinition Height="auto" />
        <RowDefinition Height="auto" />
      </Grid.RowDefinitions>
      <Image Width="120" Source="{Binding ImagePath}" />
      <TextBlock Grid.Row="1" Opacity="0.6" FontSize="16"
        VerticalAlignment="Bottom" HorizontalAlignment="Right" Margin="15"
        FontWeight="Bold" Text="{Binding Name}" />
    </Grid>
  </Border>
</DataTemplate>
```

With the XAML code in the `Page`, a simple `Button` element with the name `button1` is defined:

```xml
<Button x:Name="countryButton" Grid.Row="2" Margin="20"
  ContentTemplate="{StaticResource CountryDataTemplate}" />
```

In the code-behind a new `Country` object is instantiated that is assigned to the `Content` property (code file `Templates/StyledButtons.xaml.cs`):

```
this.countryButton.Content = new Country
{
  Name = "Austria",
  ImagePath = "images/Austria.bmp"
};
```

After running the application, you can see that the `DataTemplate` is applied to the `Button` because the `Country` data type has a default template, shown in Figure 35-16.

Of course, you can also create a control template and use a data template from within.

FIGURE 35-16

Styling a ListView

Changing a style of a button or a label is a simple task, such as changing the style of an element that contains a list of elements. For example, how about changing a `ListView`? Again, this list control has behavior and a look. It can display a list of elements, and you can select one or more elements from the list. For the behavior, the `ListView` class defines methods, properties, and events. The look of the `ListView` is separate from its behavior. It has a default look, but you can change this look by creating a template.

To fill a `ListView` with some items, the class `CountryRepository` returns a list of a few countries that will be displayed (code file `Models/CountryRepository.cs`):

```
public sealed class CountryRepository
{
  private static IEnumerable<Country> s_countries;
  public IEnumerable<Country> GetCountries() =>
    s_countries ?? (s_countries = new List<Country>
    {
      new Country { Name="Austria", ImagePath = "Images/Austria.bmp" },
      new Country { Name="Germany", ImagePath = "Images/Germany.bmp" },
      new Country { Name="Norway", ImagePath = "Images/Norway.bmp" },
      new Country { Name="USA", ImagePath = "Images/USA.bmp" }
    });
}
```

Inside the code-behind file in the constructor of the `StyledList` class, a read-only property `Countries` is created and filled with the help of the `GetCountries` method of the `CountryRepository` (code file `Templates/StyledList.xaml.cs`):

```
public ObservableCollection<Country> Countries { get; } =
  new ObservableCollection<Country>();

public StyledListBox()
{
  this.InitializeComponent();
  this.DataContext = this;
  var countries = new CountryRepository().GetCountries();
  foreach (var country in countries)
  {
    Countries.Add(country);
  }
}
```

Within the XAML code, the `ListView` named `countryList1` is defined. `countryList1` just uses the default style. The property `ItemsSource` is set to the `Binding` markup extension, which is used by data binding. From the code-behind, you have seen that the binding is done to an array of `Country` objects.

Figure 35-17 shows the default look of the ListView. By default, only the names of the countries returned by the ToString method are displayed in a simple list (code file Templates/StyledList.xaml):

```
<Grid>
  <ListView ItemsSource="{Binding Countries}" Margin="10"
    x:Name="countryList1" />
</Grid>
```

DataTemplate for ListView Items

Next, you use the DataTemplate created earlier for the ListView control. The DataTemplate can be directly assigned to the ItemTemplate property (code file Templates/StyledList.xaml):

```
<ListView ItemsSource="{Binding Countries}" Margin="10"
  ItemTemplate="{StaticResource CountryDataTemplate}" />
```

| Austria |
| Germany |
| Norway |
| USA |

FIGURE 35-17

With this XAML in place, the items are displayed as shown in Figure 35-18.

Of course, it's also possible to define a style that references the data template (code file Templates/Styles/ListTemplates.xaml):

```
<Style x:Key="ListViewStyle1" TargetType="ListView">
  <Setter Property="ItemTemplate"
    Value="{StaticResource CountryDataTemplate}" />
</Style>
```

And use this style from the ListView control (code file Templates/StyledList.xaml):

```
<ListView ItemsSource="{Binding Countries}" Margin="10"
  Style="{StaticResource ListViewStyle1}" />
```

Item Container Style

The data template defines the look for every item, and there's also a container for every item. The ItemContainerStyle can define how the container for every item looks—for example, what foreground and background brushes should be used when the item is selected, pressed, and so on. For an easy view of the boundaries of the container, the Margin and Background properties are set (code file Templates/Styles/ListTemplates.xaml):

```
<Style x:Key="ListViewItemStyle1" TargetType="ListViewItem">
  <Setter Property="Background" Value="Orange"/>
  <Setter Property="Margin" Value="5" />
  <Setter Property="Template">
    <Setter.Value>
      <ControlTemplate TargetType="ListViewItem">
        <ListViewItemPresenter ContentMargin="{TemplateBinding Padding}"
          FocusBorderBrush=
            "{ThemeResource SystemControlForegroundAltHighBrush}"
          HorizontalContentAlignment=
            "{TemplateBinding HorizontalContentAlignment}"
          PlaceholderBackground=
            "{ThemeResource ListViewItemPlaceholderBackgroundThemeBrush}"
          SelectedPressedBackground=
            "{ThemeResource SystemControlHighlightListAccentHighBrush}"
          SelectedForeground=
            "{ThemeResource SystemControlHighlightAltBaseHighBrush}"
          SelectedBackground=
            "{ThemeResource SystemControlHighlightListAccentLowBrush}"
          VerticalContentAlignment=
```

```
                    "{TemplateBinding VerticalContentAlignment}"/>
            </ControlTemplate>
        </Setter.Value>
    </Setter>
</Style>
```

The style is associated with the `ItemContainerStyle` property of the `ListView`. The result of this style is shown in Figure 35-19. This figure gives a good view of the boundaries of the items container (code file `Templates/StyledList.xaml`):

```
<ListView ItemsSource="{Binding Countries}" Margin="10"
    ItemContainerStyle="{StaticResource ListViewItemStyle1}"
    Style="{StaticResource ListViewStyle1}" MaxWidth="180" />
```

FIGURE 35-18

FIGURE 35-19

Items Panel

By default, the `ListView` arranges the items vertically. This is not the only way to arrange the items with this view; you can arrange them in other ways as well, such as horizontally. Arranging the items in an items control is the responsibility of the items panel.

The following code snippet defines a resource for an `ItemsPanelTemplate` and arranges the `ItemsStackPanel` horizontally instead of vertically (code file `Templates/Styles/ListTemplates.xaml`):

```
<ItemsPanelTemplate x:Key="ItemsPanelTemplate1">
    <ItemsStackPanel Orientation="Horizontal" Background="Yellow" />
</ItemsPanelTemplate>
```

The following `ListView` declaration uses the same `Style` and `ItemContainerStyle` as before but adds the resource for the `ItemsPanel`. Figure 35-20 shows the items now arranged horizontally (code file `Templates/StyledList.xaml`):

```
<ItemsPanelTemplate x:Key="ItemsPanelTemplate1">
    <VirtualizingStackPanel IsItemsHost="True" Orientation="Horizontal"
```

```
      Background="Yellow"/>
   </ItemsPanelTemplate>
   <ListView ItemsSource="{Binding Countries}" Margin="10"
      ItemContainerStyle="{StaticResource ListViewItemStyle1}"
      Style="{StaticResource ListViewStyle1}"
      ItemsPanel="{StaticResource ItemsPanelTemplate1}" />
```

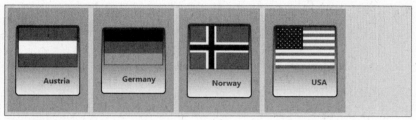

FIGURE 35-20

List View Control Template

What's still missing with the control is the scroll functionality in case the items do not fit on the screen. This behavior can be changed by defining the template for the ListView control.

The style ListViewStyle2 defines horizontal and vertical scroll bar behaviors as required with a horizontal items alignment. This style also includes a resource reference to the date templates and container item templates defined earlier. By setting the Template property, you can now also change the UI of the complete ListView control (code file Templates/Styles/ListTemplates.xaml):

```
<Style x:Key="ListViewStyle2" TargetType="ListView">
  <Setter Property="ScrollViewer.HorizontalScrollBarVisibility" Value="Auto"/>
  <Setter Property="ScrollViewer.VerticalScrollBarVisibility"
    Value="Disabled"/>
  <Setter Property="ScrollViewer.HorizontalScrollMode" Value="Auto"/>
  <Setter Property="ScrollViewer.IsHorizontalRailEnabled" Value="False"/>
  <Setter Property="ScrollViewer.VerticalScrollMode" Value="Disabled"/>
  <Setter Property="ScrollViewer.IsVerticalRailEnabled" Value="False"/>
  <Setter Property="ScrollViewer.ZoomMode" Value="Disabled"/>
  <Setter Property="ScrollViewer.IsDeferredScrollingEnabled" Value="False"/>
  <Setter Property="ScrollViewer.BringIntoViewOnFocusChange" Value="True"/>
  <Setter Property="ItemTemplate"
    Value="{StaticResource CountryDataTemplate}" />
  <Setter Property="ItemContainerStyle"
    Value="{StaticResource ListViewItemStyle1}" />
  <Setter Property="ItemsPanel">
    <Setter.Value>
      <ItemsPanelTemplate>
        <ItemsStackPanel Orientation="Horizontal" Background="Yellow"/>
      </ItemsPanelTemplate>
    </Setter.Value>
  </Setter>
  <Setter Property="Template">
    <Setter.Value>
      <ControlTemplate TargetType="ListView">
        <Border BorderBrush="{TemplateBinding BorderBrush}"
          BorderThickness="{TemplateBinding BorderThickness}"
          Background="{TemplateBinding Background}">
          <ScrollViewer x:Name="ScrollViewer">
            <!--ScrollViewer definitions removed for clarity-->
            <ItemsPresenter FooterTransitions=
```

```
                            "{TemplateBinding FooterTransitions}"
                            FooterTemplate="{TemplateBinding FooterTemplate}"
                            Footer="{TemplateBinding Footer}"
                            HeaderTemplate="{TemplateBinding HeaderTemplate}"
                            Header="{TemplateBinding Header}"
                            HeaderTransitions="{TemplateBinding HeaderTransitions}"
                            Padding="{TemplateBinding Padding}"/>
                    </ScrollViewer>
                </Border>
            </ControlTemplate>
        </Setter.Value>
    </Setter>
</Style>
```

With this resource available, the definition of the `ListView` becomes simple as just the `ListViewStyle2` needs to be referenced in addition to the `ItemsSource` to retrieve the data (code file `Templates/ StyledList.xaml`):

```
<ListView ItemsSource="{Binding Countries}" Margin="10"
    Style="{StaticResource ListViewStyle2}" />
```

The new view is shown in Figure 35-21. Now a scrollbar is available.

FIGURE 35-21

ANIMATIONS

Using animations, you can make a smooth transition between images by using moving elements, color changes, transforms, and so on. XAML makes it easy to create animations. You can animate the value of any dependency property. Different animation classes exist to animate the values of different properties, depending on their type.

The most important element of an animation is the timeline. This element defines how a value changes over time. Different kinds of timelines are available for changing different types of values. The base class for all timelines is `Timeline`. To animate a property of type `double`, you can use the class `DoubleAnimation`. The `Int32Animation` is the animation class for `int` values. You use `PointAnimation` to animate points and `ColorAnimation` to animate colors.

You can combine multiple timelines by using the `Storyboard` class. The `Storyboard` class itself is derived from the base class `TimelineGroup`, which derives from `Timeline`.

Timeline

A `Timeline` defines how a value changes over time. The following example animates the size of an ellipse. In the code that follows, `DoubleAnimation` timelines change scaling and translation of an ellipse; `ColorAnimation` changes the color of the fill brush. The `Triggers` property of the `Ellipse` class is set to an `EventTrigger`. The event trigger is fired when the ellipse is loaded. `BeginStoryboard` is a trigger action that begins the storyboard. With the storyboard, a `DoubleAnimation` element is used to animate the `ScaleX`, `ScaleY`, `TranslateX`, and `TranslateY` properties of the `CompositeTransform` class. The animation changes the horizontal scale to 5 and the vertical scale to 3 within ten seconds (code file `Animation/SimpleAnimation.xaml`):

```xml
<Ellipse x:Name="ellipse1" Width="100" Height="40"
  HorizontalAlignment="Left" VerticalAlignment="Top">
  <Ellipse.Fill>
    <SolidColorBrush Color="Green" />
  </Ellipse.Fill>
  <Ellipse.RenderTransform>
    <CompositeTransform ScaleX="1" ScaleY="1" TranslateX="0" TranslateY="0" />
  </Ellipse.RenderTransform>
  <Ellipse.Triggers>
    <EventTrigger>
      <BeginStoryboard>
        <Storyboard x:Name="MoveResizeStoryboard">
          <DoubleAnimation Duration="0:0:10" To="5"
            Storyboard.TargetName="ellipse1"
            Storyboard.TargetProperty=
            "(UIElement.RenderTransform).(CompositeTransform.ScaleX)" />
          <DoubleAnimation Duration="0:0:10" To="3"
            Storyboard.TargetName="ellipse1"
            Storyboard.TargetProperty=
            "(UIElement.RenderTransform).(CompositeTransform.ScaleY)" />
          <DoubleAnimation Duration="0:0:10" To="400"
            Storyboard.TargetName="ellipse1"
            Storyboard.TargetProperty=
            "(UIElement.RenderTransform).(CompositeTransform.TranslateX)" />
          <DoubleAnimation Duration="0:0:10" To="200"
            Storyboard.TargetName="ellipse1"
            Storyboard.TargetProperty=
            "(UIElement.RenderTransform).(CompositeTransform.TranslateY)" />
          <ColorAnimation Duration="0:0:10" To="Red"
            Storyboard.TargetName="ellipse1"
            Storyboard.TargetProperty=
            "(Ellipse.Fill).(SolidColorBrush.Color)" />
        </Storyboard>
      </BeginStoryboard>
    </EventTrigger>
  </Ellipse.Triggers>
</Ellipse>
```

Using `ScaleTransform` and `TranslateTransform` results in animations accessing the collection of the `TransformGroup` and accessing the `ScaleX`, `ScaleY`, `X`, and `Y` properties by using an indexer:

```xml
<DoubleAnimation Duration="0:0:10" To="5" Storyboard.TargetName="ellipse1"
  Storyboard.TargetProperty=
  "(UIElement.RenderTransform).Children[0].(ScaleTransform.ScaleX)" />
<DoubleAnimation Duration="0:0:10" To="3" Storyboard.TargetName="ellipse1"
  Storyboard.TargetProperty=
  "(UIElement.RenderTransform).Children[0].(ScaleTransform.ScaleY)" />
<DoubleAnimation Duration="0:0:10" To="400" Storyboard.TargetName="ellipse1"
  Storyboard.TargetProperty=
  "(UIElement.RenderTransform).Children[1].(TranslateTransform.X)" />
<DoubleAnimation Duration="0:0:10" To="200" Storyboard.TargetName="ellipse1"
  Storyboard.TargetProperty=
  "(UIElement.RenderTransform).Children[1].(TranslateTransform.Y)" />
```

Instead of using the indexer within the transformation group it would also be possible to access the `ScaleTransform` element by its name. The following code simplifies the name of the property:

```
<DoubleAnimation Duration="0:0:10" To="5" Storyboard.TargetName="scale1"
  Storyboard.TargetProperty="(ScaleX)" />
```

Figures 35-22 and 35-23 show two states from the animated ellipse.

FIGURE 35-22

FIGURE 35-23

Animations are far more than typical window-dressing animation that appears onscreen constantly and immediately. You can add animation to business applications that make the user interface feel more responsive. The look when a cursor moves over a button, or a button is clicked, is defined by animations.

The following table describes what you can do with a timeline.

TIMELINE PROPERTIES	DESCRIPTION
AutoReverse	Use this property to specify whether the value that is animated should return to its original value after the animation.
SpeedRatio	Use this property to transform the speed at which an animation moves. You can define the relation to the parent. The default value is 1; setting the ratio to a smaller value makes the animation move slower; setting the value greater than 1 makes it move faster.
BeginTime	Use this to specify the time span from the start of the trigger event until the moment the animation starts. You can specify days, hours, minutes, seconds, and fractions of seconds. This might not be real time, depending on the speed ratio. For example, if the speed ratio is set to 2, and the beginning time is set to six seconds, the animation will start after three seconds.
Duration	Use this property to specify the length of time for one iteration of the animation.
RepeatBehavior	Assigning a RepeatBehavior struct to the RepeatBehavior property enables you to define how many times or for how long the animation should be repeated.
FillBehavior	This property is important if the parent timeline has a different duration. For example, if the parent timeline is shorter than the duration of the actual animation, setting FillBehavior to Stop means that the actual animation stops. If the parent timeline is longer than the duration of the actual animation, HoldEnd keeps the actual animation active before resetting it to its original value (if AutoReverse is set).

Depending on the type of the Timeline class, more properties may be available. For example, with DoubleAnimation you can specify From and To properties for the start and end of the animation. An alternative is to specify the By property, whereby the animation starts with the current value of the Bound property and is incremented by the value specified by By.

Easing Functions

With the animations you've seen so far, the value changes in a linear way. In real life, a move never happens in a linear way. The move could start slowly and progressively get faster until reaching the highest speed, and then it slows down before reaching the end. When you let a ball fall against the ground, the ball bounces a few times before staying on the ground. Such nonlinear behavior can be created by using easing functions.

Animation classes have an `EasingFunction` property. This property accepts an object that derives from the base class `EasingFunctionBase`. With this type, an easing function object can define how the value should be animated over time. Several easing functions are available to create a nonlinear animation. Examples include `ExponentialEase`, which uses an exponential formula for animations; `QuadraticEase`, `CubicEase`, `QuarticEase`, and `QuinticEase`, with powers of 2, 3, 4, or 5; and `PowerEase`, with a power level that is configurable. Of special interest are `SineEase`, which uses a sinusoid curve; `BounceEase`, which creates a bouncing effect; and `ElasticEase`, which resembles animation values of a spring oscillating back and forth.

The following code snippet adds the `BounceEase` function to the `DoubleAnimation`. Adding different ease functions results in very interesting animation effects:

```
<DoubleAnimation Storyboard.TargetProperty="(Ellipse.Width)"
  Duration="0:0:3" AutoReverse="True"
  FillBehavior=" RepeatBehavior="Forever"
  From="100" To="300">
  <DoubleAnimation.EasingFunction>
    <BounceEase EasingMode="EaseInOut" />
  </DoubleAnimation.EasingFunction>
</DoubleAnimation>
```

To see different easing animations in action, the next sample lets an ellipse move between two small rectangles. The `Rectangle` and `Ellipse` elements are defined within a `Canvas`, and the ellipse defines a `TranslateTransform` transformation to move the ellipse (code file `Animation/EasingFunctions.xaml`):

```
<Canvas Grid.Row="1">
  <Rectangle Fill="Blue" Width="10" Height="200" Canvas.Left="50"
    Canvas.Top="100" />
  <Rectangle Fill="Blue" Width="10" Height="200" Canvas.Left="550"
    Canvas.Top="100" />
  <Ellipse Fill="Red" Width="30" Height="30" Canvas.Left="60" Canvas.Top="185">
    <Ellipse.RenderTransform>
      <TranslateTransform x:Name="translate1" X="0" Y="0" />
    </Ellipse.RenderTransform>
  </Ellipse>
</Canvas>
```

Figure 35-24 shows the rectangles and ellipse.

FIGURE 35-24

The user starts the animation by clicking a button. Before clicking the button, the user can select the easing function from the `ComboBox` `comboEasingFunctions` and an `EasingMode` enumeration value using radio buttons.

```
<StackPanel Orientation="Horizontal">
  <ComboBox x:Name="comboEasingFunctions" Margin="10" />
  <Button Click="OnStartAnimation" Margin="10">Start</Button>
```

```
    <Border BorderThickness="1" BorderBrush="Black" Margin="3">
      <StackPanel Orientation="Horizontal">
        <RadioButton x:Name="easingModeIn" GroupName="EasingMode" Content="In" />
        <RadioButton x:Name="easingModeOut" GroupName="EasingMode"
          Content="Out" IsChecked="True" />
        <RadioButton x:Name="easingModeInOut" GroupName="EasingMode"
          Content="InOut" />
      </StackPanel>
    </Border>
  </StackPanel>
```

The list of easing functions that are shown in the `ComboBox` and activated with the animation is returned from the `EasingFunctionModels` property of the `EasingFunctionManager`. This manager converts the easing function to an `EasingFunctionModel` for display (code file `Animation/EasingFunctionsManager.cs`):

```
public class EasingFunctionsManager
{
  private static IEnumerable<EasingFunctionBase> s_easingFunctions =
    new List<EasingFunctionBase>()
    {
      new BackEase(),
      new SineEase(),
      new BounceEase(),
      new CircleEase(),
      new CubicEase(),
      new ElasticEase(),
      new ExponentialEase(),
      new PowerEase(),
      new QuadraticEase(),
      new QuinticEase()
    };

  public IEnumerable<EasingFunctionModel> EasingFunctionModels =>
    s_easingFunctions.Select(f => new EasingFunctionModel(f));
}
```

The class `EasingFunctionModel` defines a `ToString` method that returns the name of the class that defines the easing function. This name is shown in the combo box (code file `Animation/EasingFunctionModel.cs`):

```
public class EasingFunctionModel
{
  public EasingFunctionModel(EasingFunctionBase easingFunction) =>
    EasingFunction = easingFunction;

  public EasingFunctionBase EasingFunction { get; }

  public override string ToString() => EasingFunction.GetType().Name;
}
```

The `ComboBox` is filled in the constructor of the code-behind file (code file `Animation/EasingFunctions.xaml.cs`):

```
private EasingFunctionsManager _easingFunctions = new EasingFunctionsManager();
private const int AnimationTimeSeconds = 6;

public EasingFunctions()
{
  this.InitializeComponent();
```

```
foreach (var easingFunctionModel in _easingFunctions.EasingFunctionModels)
{
  comboEasingFunctions.Items.Add(easingFunctionModel);
}
}
```

From the user interface you can not only select the type of easing function that should be used for the animation, but you also can select the easing mode. The base class of all easing functions (EasingFunctionBase) defines the EasingMode property that can be a value of the EasingMode enumeration.

Clicking the button to start the animation invokes the OnStartAnimation method. This in turn invokes the StartAnimation method. With this method a Storyboard containing a DoubleAnimation is created programmatically. You've seen similar code earlier using XAML. The animation animates the X property of the translate1 element (code file Animation/EasingFunctionsPage.xaml.cs):

```
private void OnStartAnimation(object sender, RoutedEventArgs e)
{
  var easingFunctionModel =
    comboEasingFunctions.SelectedItem as EasingFunctionModel;
  if (easingFunctionModel != null)
  {
    EasingFunctionBase easingFunction = easingFunctionModel.EasingFunction;
    easingFunction.EasingMode = GetEasingMode();
    StartAnimation(easingFunction);
  }
}

private void StartAnimation(EasingFunctionBase easingFunction)
{
  var storyboard = new Storyboard();
  var ellipseMove = new DoubleAnimation();
  ellipseMove.EasingFunction = easingFunction;
  ellipseMove.Duration = new
    Duration(TimeSpan.FromSeconds(AnimationTimeSeconds));
  ellipseMove.From = 0;
  ellipseMove.To = 460;
  Storyboard.SetTarget(ellipseMove, translate1);
  Storyboard.SetTargetProperty(ellipseMove, "X");

  // start the animation in 0.5 seconds
  ellipseMove.BeginTime = TimeSpan.FromSeconds(0.5);

  // keep the position after the animation
  ellipseMove.FillBehavior = FillBehavior.HoldEnd;
  storyboard.Children.Add(ellipseMove);
  storyBoard.Begin();
}
```

Now you can run the application and see the ellipse move from the left to the right rectangle in different ways—with different easing functions. With some of the easing functions, such as BackEase, BounceEase, or ElasticEase, the difference is obvious. The difference is not as noticeable with some of the other easing functions. To better understand how the easing values behave, a line chart is created that shows a line with the value that is returned by the easing function based on time.

To display the line chart, you create a user control that defines a Canvas element. By default, the x direction goes from left to right and the y direction from top to bottom. To change the y direction to go from bottom to top, you define a transformation (code file Animation/EasingChartControl.xaml):

```
<Canvas x:Name="canvas1" Width="500" Height="500" Background="Yellow">
  <Canvas.RenderTransform>
    <TransformGroup>
```

```
                <ScaleTransform ScaleX="1" ScaleY="-1" />
                <TranslateTransform X="0" Y="500" />
            </TransformGroup>
        </Canvas.RenderTransform>
    </Canvas>
```

In the code-behind file, the line chart is drawn using line segments. Line segments were previously discussed using XAML code in this chapter in the section "Geometries Using Segments." Here you see how they can be used from code. The Ease method of the easing function returns a value that is shown in the y axis passing a normalized time value that is shown in the x axis (code file Animation/EasingChartControl.xaml.cs):

```
private const double SamplingInterval = 0.01;

public void Draw(EasingFunctionBase easingFunction)
{
    canvas1.Children.Clear();
    var pathSegments = new PathSegmentCollection();
    for (double i = 0; i < 1; i += _samplingInterval)
    {
        double x = i * canvas1.Width;
        double y = easingFunction.Ease(i) * canvas1.Height;
        var segment = new LineSegment();
        segment.Point = new Point(x, y);
        pathSegments.Add(segment);
    }

    var p = new Path();
    p.Stroke = new SolidColorBrush(Colors.Black);
    p.StrokeThickness = 3;
    var figures = new PathFigureCollection();
    figures.Add(new PathFigure { Segments = pathSegments });
    p.Data = new PathGeometry { Figures = figures };
    canvas1.Children.Add(p);
}
```

The Draw method of the EasingChartControl is invoked on the start of the animation (code file Animation/EasingFunctions.xaml.cs):

```
private void StartAnimation(EasingFunctionBase easingFunction)
{
    // show the chart
    chartControl.Draw(easingFunction);
    //...
```

When you run the application, you can see in Figure 35-25 what it looks like to use CubicEase and EaseOut. When you select EaseIn, the value changes slower in the beginning of the animation and faster in the end, as shown in Figure 35-26. Figure 35-27 shows what it looks like to use CubicEase with EaseInOut. The chart for BounceEase, BackEase, and ElasticEase is shown in Figures 35-28, 35-29, and 35-30.

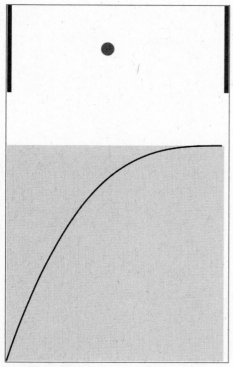

FIGURE 35-25

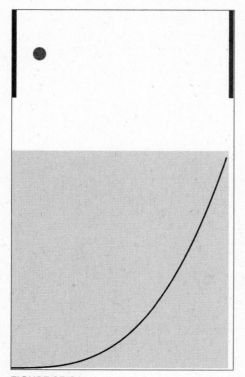

FIGURE 35-26

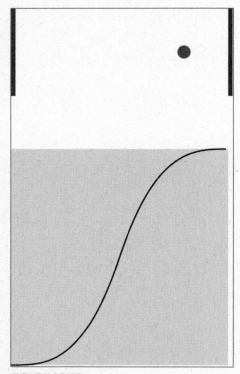

FIGURE 35-27

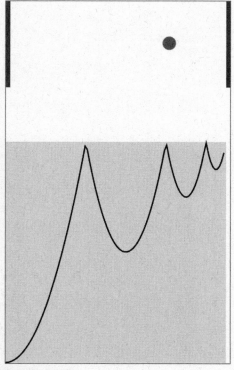

FIGURE 35-28

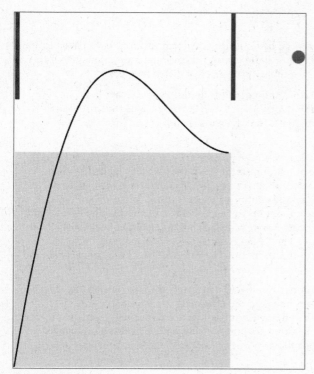

FIGURE 35-29

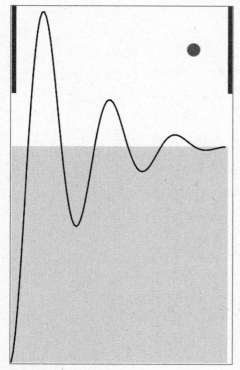

FIGURE 35-30

Keyframe Animations

With ease functions, you've seen how animations can be built in a nonlinear fashion. If you need to specify several values for an animation, you can use *keyframe animations*. Like normal animations, keyframe animations are various animation types that exist to animate properties of different types.

DoubleAnimationUsingKeyFrames is the keyframe animation for double types. Other keyframe animation types are Int32AnimationUsingKeyFrames, PointAnimationUsingKeyFrames, ColorAnimationUsingKeyFrames, SizeAnimationUsingKeyFrames, and ObjectAnimationUsingKeyFrames.

The following example XAML code animates the position of an ellipse by animating the X and Y values of a TranslateTransform element. The animation starts when the ellipse is loaded by defining an EventTrigger to RoutedEvent Ellipse.Loaded. The event trigger starts a Storyboard with the BeginStoryboard element. The Storyboard contains two keyframe animations of type DoubleAnimationUsingKeyFrame. A keyframe animation consists of frame elements. The first keyframe animation uses a LinearKeyFrame, a DiscreteDoubleKeyFrame, and a SplineDoubleKeyFrame; the second animation is an EasingDoubleKeyFrame. The LinearDoubleKeyFrame makes a linear change of the value. The KeyTime property defines when in the animation the value of the Value property should be reached.

Here, the LinearDoubleKeyFrame has three seconds to move the property X to the value 30. DiscreteDoubleKeyFrame makes an immediate change to the new value after four seconds. SplineDoubleKeyFrame uses a Bézier curve whereby two control points are specified by the KeySpline property. EasingDoubleKeyFrame is a frame class that supports setting an easing function such as BounceEase to control the animation value (code file Animation/KeyFrameAnimationPage.xaml):

```xaml
<Canvas>
  <Ellipse Fill="Red" Canvas.Left="20" Canvas.Top="20" Width="25" Height="25">
    <Ellipse.RenderTransform>
      <TranslateTransform X="50" Y="50" x:Name="ellipseMove" />
    </Ellipse.RenderTransform>
    <Ellipse.Triggers>
      <EventTrigger>
        <BeginStoryboard>
          <Storyboard>
            <DoubleAnimationUsingKeyFrames Storyboard.TargetProperty="X"
              Storyboard.TargetName="ellipseMove">
              <LinearDoubleKeyFrame KeyTime="0:0:2" Value="30" />
              <DiscreteDoubleKeyFrame KeyTime="0:0:4" Value="80" />
              <SplineDoubleKeyFrame KeySpline="0.5,0.0 0.9,0.0"
                KeyTime="0:0:10" Value="300" />
              <LinearDoubleKeyFrame KeyTime="0:0:20" Value="150" />
            </DoubleAnimationUsingKeyFrames>
            <DoubleAnimationUsingKeyFrames Storyboard.TargetProperty="Y"
              Storyboard.TargetName="ellipseMove">
              <SplineDoubleKeyFrame KeySpline="0.5,0.0 0.9,0.0"
                KeyTime="0:0:2" Value="50" />
              <EasingDoubleKeyFrame KeyTime="0:0:20" Value="300">
                <EasingDoubleKeyFrame.EasingFunction>
                  <BounceEase />
                </EasingDoubleKeyFrame.EasingFunction>
              </EasingDoubleKeyFrame>
            </DoubleAnimationUsingKeyFrames>
          </Storyboard>
        </BeginStoryboard>
      </EventTrigger>
    </Ellipse.Triggers>
  </Ellipse>
</Canvas>
```

Transitions

For making it easier for you to create animated user interfaces, UWP apps define transitions. Transitions make it easier to create compelling apps without the need to think about what makes a cool animation. Transitions predefine animations for adding, removing, and rearranging items in a list; opening panels; changing the content of content controls; and more.

The following sample demonstrates several transitions to show them in the left side of a user control versus the right side, and it shows similar elements without transitions, which helps you see the differences. Of course, you need to start the application to see the difference, as it is hard to demonstrate this in a printed book.

Reposition Transition

The first example makes use of the `RepositionThemeTransition` within the `Transitions` property of a `Button` element. A transition always needs to be defined within a `TransitionCollection` because such collections are never created automatically, and there's a misleading runtime error in case you don't use the `TransitionCollection`. The second button doesn't use a transition (code file Transitions/RepositionUserControl.xaml):

```xml
<Button Grid.Row="1" Click="OnReposition" Content="Reposition"
  x:Name="buttonReposition" Margin="10">
  <Button.Transitions>
    <TransitionCollection>
      <RepositionThemeTransition />
    </TransitionCollection>
  </Button.Transitions>
</Button>
<Button Grid.Row="1" Grid.Column="1" Click="OnReset" Content="Reset"
  x:Name="button2" Margin="10" />
```

The `RepositionThemeTransition` is a transition when a control changes its position. In the code-behind file, when the user clicks the button, the `Margin` property is changed, which also changes the position of the button.

```csharp
private void OnReposition(object sender, RoutedEventArgs e)
{
  buttonReposition.Margin = new Thickness(100);
  button2.Margin = new Thickness(100);
}

private void OnReset(object sender, RoutedEventArgs e)
{
  buttonReposition.Margin = new Thickness(10);
  button2.Margin = new Thickness(10);
}
```

Pane Transition

The `PopupThemeTransition` and `PaneThemeTransition` are shown in the next user control. Here, the transitions are defined with the `ChildTransitions` property of the `Popup` control (code file Transitions/PaneTransitionUserControl.xaml):

```xml
<StackPanel Orientation="Horizontal" Grid.Row="2">
  <Popup x:Name="popup1" Width="200" Height="90" Margin="60">
    <Border Background="Red" Width="100" Height="60">
    </Border>
    <Popup.ChildTransitions>
      <TransitionCollection>
        <PopupThemeTransition />
      </TransitionCollection>
```

```
        </Popup.ChildTransitions>
      </Popup>
      <Popup x:Name="popup2" Width="200" Height="90" Margin="60">
        <Border Background="Red" Width="100" Height="60">
        </Border>
        <Popup.ChildTransitions>
          <TransitionCollection>
            <PaneThemeTransition />
          </TransitionCollection>
        </Popup.ChildTransitions>
      </Popup>
      <Popup x:Name="popup3" Margin="60" Width="200" Height="90">
        <Border Background="Green" Width="100" Height="60">
        </Border>
      </Popup>
    </StackPanel>
```

The code-behind file opens and closes the Popup controls by setting the IsOpen property. This in turn starts the transition (code file Transitions\PaneTransitionUserControl.xaml):

```
private void OnShow(object sender, RoutedEventArgs e)
{
  popup1.IsOpen = true;
  popup2.IsOpen = true;
  popup3.IsOpen = true;
}

private void OnHide(object sender, RoutedEventArgs e)
{
  popup1.IsOpen = false;
  popup2.IsOpen = false;
  popup3.IsOpen = false;
}
```

When you run the application, you can see that the PopupThemeTransition looks good for opening Popup and Flyout controls. The PaneThemeTransition opens the popup slowly from the right side. This transition can also be configured to open from other sides by setting properties, and thus is best for panels, such as the settings bar, that move in from a side.

Transitions for Items

Adding and removing items from an item's control also defines a transition. The following ItemsControl makes use of the EntranceThemeTransition and RepositionThemeTransition. The EntranceThemeTransition is used when an item is added to the collection; the RepositionThemeTransition is used when items are re-arranged—for example, by removing an item from the list (code file Transitions/ListItemsUserControl.xaml):

```
<ItemsControl Grid.Row="1" x:Name="list1">
  <ItemsControl.ItemContainerTransitions>
    <TransitionCollection>
      <EntranceThemeTransition />
      <RepositionThemeTransition />
    </TransitionCollection>
  </ItemsControl.ItemContainerTransitions>
</ItemsControl>
<ItemsControl Grid.Row="1" Grid.Column="1" x:Name="list2" />
```

In the code-behind file, `Rectangle` objects are added and removed from the list control. As one of the `ItemsControl` objects doesn't have a transition associated, you can easily the difference in behavior when you run the application (code file `Transitions/ListItemsUserControl.xaml.cs`):

```
private void OnAdd(object sender, RoutedEventArgs e)
{
  list1.Items.Add(CreateRectangle());
  list2.Items.Add(CreateRectangle());
}

private Rectangle CreateRectangle() =>
  new Rectangle
  {
    Width = 90,
    Height = 40,
    Margin = new Thickness(5),
    Fill = new SolidColorBrush { Color = Colors.Blue }
  };

private void OnRemove(object sender, RoutedEventArgs e)
{
  if (list1.Items.Count > 0)
  {
    list1.Items.RemoveAt(0);
    list2.Items.RemoveAt(0);
  }
}
```

> **NOTE** *With these transitions, you get an idea of how they reduce the work needed to animate the user interface. Be sure to check out more transitions available with UWP apps. You can see all the transitions by checking the derived classes from Transition in the Microsoft documentation.*

VISUAL STATE MANAGER

Earlier in this chapter in the section "Control Templates," you saw how to create control templates to customize the look of controls. Something was missing there. With the default template of a button, the button reacts to mouse moves and clicks and looks differently when the mouse moves over the button or the button is clicked. This look change is handled with the help of visual states and animations, controlled by the visual state manager.

This section looks at changing the button style to react to mouse moves and clicks, but it also describes how to create custom states to deal with changes of a complete page when several controls should switch to the disabled state—for example, when some background processing occurs.

With an XAML element, visual states, state groups, and states can be defined that specify specific animations for a state. State groups exist to allow having multiple states at once. For one group, only one state is allowed at one time. However, another state of another group can be active at the same time. Examples for this are the states and state groups with a button. The `Button` control defines the state groups `CommonStates` and `FocusStates`. States defined with `FocusStates` are `Focused`, `Unfocused`, and `PointerFocused`. The `CommonStates` group defines the states `Normal`, `Pressed`, `Disabled`, and `PointerOver`. With these options, multiple states can be active at the same time, but there is always only one state active within a state group. For example, a button can be in focus and in the normal state. It can also be in focus and pressed. You can also define custom states and state groups.

Let's get into concrete examples.

Predefined States with Control Templates

Let's take the custom control template created earlier to style the Button control and enhance it by using visual states. An easy way to do this is by using Microsoft Blend for Visual Studio. Figure 35-31 shows the States Window that is shown when you are selecting the control template. Here you can see available states of the control and record changes based on these states.

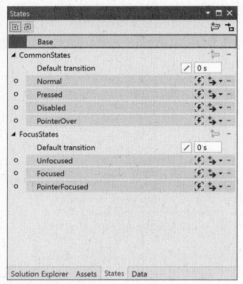

FIGURE 35-31

The button template from before is changed to define visual states for the states Pressed, Disabled, and PointerOver. Within the states, a Storyboard defines a ColorAnimation to change the color of the Fill property of an ellipse (code file VisualStates/MainPage.xaml):

```xml
<Style x:Key="RoundedGelButton" TargetType="Button">
  <Setter Property="Width" Value="100" />
  <Setter Property="Height" Value="100" />
  <Setter Property="Foreground" Value="White" />
  <Setter Property="Template">
    <Setter.Value>
      <ControlTemplate TargetType="Button">
        <Grid>
          <VisualStateManager.VisualStateGroups>
            <VisualStateGroup x:Name="CommonStates">
              <VisualState x:Name="Normal"/>
              <VisualState x:Name="Pressed">
                <Storyboard>
                  <ColorAnimation Duration="0" To="#FFC8CE11"
                    Storyboard.TargetProperty=
                      "(Shape.Fill).(SolidColorBrush.Color)"
                    Storyboard.TargetName=
                      "GelBackground" />
```

```
              </Storyboard>
            </VisualState>
            <VisualState x:Name="Disabled">
              <Storyboard>
                <ColorAnimation Duration="0" To="#FF606066"
                  Storyboard.TargetProperty=
                    "(Shape.Fill).(SolidColorBrush.Color)"
                  Storyboard.TargetName="GelBackground" />
              </Storyboard>
            </VisualState>
            <VisualState x:Name="PointerOver">
              <Storyboard>
                <ColorAnimation Duration="0" To="#FF0F9D3A"
                  Storyboard.TargetProperty=
                    "(Shape.Fill).(SolidColorBrush.Color)"
                  Storyboard.TargetName="GelBackground" />
              </Storyboard>
            </VisualState>
          </VisualStateGroup>
        </VisualStateManager.VisualStateGroups>
        <Ellipse x:Name="GelBackground" StrokeThickness="0.5" Fill="Black">
          <Ellipse.Stroke>
            <LinearGradientBrush StartPoint="0,0" EndPoint="0,1">
              <GradientStop Offset="0" Color="#ff7e7e7e" />
              <GradientStop Offset="1" Color="Black" />
            </LinearGradientBrush>
          </Ellipse.Stroke>
        </Ellipse>
        <Ellipse Margin="15,5,15,50">
          <Ellipse.Fill>
            <LinearGradientBrush StartPoint="0,0" EndPoint="0,1">
              <GradientStop Offset="0" Color="#aaffffff" />
              <GradientStop Offset="1" Color="Transparent" />
            </LinearGradientBrush>
          </Ellipse.Fill>
        </Ellipse>
        <ContentPresenter x:Name="GelButtonContent"
          VerticalAlignment="Center"
          HorizontalAlignment="Center"
          Content="{TemplateBinding Content}" />
      </Grid>
    </ControlTemplate>
  </Setter.Value>
</Setter>
</Style>
```

Now when you run the application, you can see the color changes based on moving and clicking the mouse.

Defining Custom States

You can define custom states by using the `VisualStateManager`, defining custom state groups using `VisualStateGroup` and states with `VisualState`. The following code snippet creates the `Enabled` and `Disabled` states within the `CustomStates` group. The visual states are defined within the `Grid` of the main window. On changing the state, the `IsEnabled` property of a `Button` element is changed using a `DiscreteObjectKeyFrame` animation in no time (code file `VisualStates/MainPage.xaml`):

```
<VisualStateManager.VisualStateGroups>
  <VisualStateGroup x:Name="CustomStates">
    <VisualState x:Name="Enabled"/>
    <VisualState x:Name="Disabled">
      <Storyboard>
```

```
            <ObjectAnimationUsingKeyFrames
              Storyboard.TargetProperty="(Control.IsEnabled)"
              Storyboard.TargetName="button1">
              <DiscreteObjectKeyFrame KeyTime="0">
                <DiscreteObjectKeyFrame.Value>
                  <x:Boolean>False</x:Boolean>
                </DiscreteObjectKeyFrame.Value>
              </DiscreteObjectKeyFrame>
            </ObjectAnimationUsingKeyFrames>
            <ObjectAnimationUsingKeyFrames
              Storyboard.TargetProperty="(Control.IsEnabled)"
              Storyboard.TargetName="button2">
              <DiscreteObjectKeyFrame KeyTime="0">
                <DiscreteObjectKeyFrame.Value>
                  <x:Boolean>False</x:Boolean>
                </DiscreteObjectKeyFrame.Value>
              </DiscreteObjectKeyFrame>
            </ObjectAnimationUsingKeyFrames>
          </Storyboard>
        </VisualState>
      </VisualStateGroup>
    </VisualStateManager.VisualStateGroups>
```

Setting Custom States

Now the states need to be set. You can do this easily by invoking the GoToState method of the VisualStateManager class. In the code-behind file, the OnEnable and OnDisable methods are Click event handlers for two buttons in the page (code file VisualStates/MainPage.xaml.cs):

```
private void OnEnable(object sender, RoutedEventArgs e)
{
  VisualStateManager.GoToState(this, "Enabled", useTransitions: true);
}

private void OnDisable(object sender, RoutedEventArgs e)
{
  VisualStateManager.GoToState(this, "Disabled", useTransitions: true);
}
```

In a real application, you can change the state in a similar manner—for example, when a network call is invoked, and the user should not act on some of the controls within the page. The user should still be allowed to click a cancellation button. By changing the state, you can also show progress information.

SUMMARY

In this chapter you have taken a tour through many of the features of styling Windows apps. With XAML it is easy to separate the work of developers and designers. All UI features can be created with XAML, and the functionality can be created by using code-behind.

You have seen many shapes and geometry elements, which are the basis for all other controls that you'll see in the next chapters. Vector-based graphics enable XAML elements to be scaled, sheared, and rotated.

Different kinds of brushes are available for painting the background and foreground of elements. You can use not only solid brushes and linear or radial gradient brushes but also visual brushes that enable you to include reflections or show videos.

Styling and templates enable you to customize the look of controls; with the visual state manager you can change properties of XAML elements dynamically. You can easily create animations by animating a property value from an XAML control. The next chapter continues with Windows Apps and dives into advanced features of the Universal Windows Platform.

36

Advanced Windows Apps

WHAT'S IN THIS CHAPTER?

➤ Sharing data

➤ Using app services

➤ Compiled binding features

➤ Rich text displays

➤ Using ink

➤ AutoSuggest

WROX.COM CODE DOWNLOADS FOR THIS CHAPTER

The Wrox.com code downloads for this chapter are found at `http://www.wrox.com` on the Download Code tab. The source code is also available at `https://github.com/ProfessionalCSharp/ProfessionalCSharp7` in the directory `AdvancedWindows`.

The code for this chapter is divided into these major samples:

➤ AppLifetime

➤ Sharing Samples

➤ AppServices

➤ CompiledBindingLifetime

➤ CompiledBindingMethods

➤ PhasedBinding

➤ TextSample

➤ Text Overflow

➤ InkSample

➤ AutoSuggestSample

OVERVIEW

The previous chapters introduced you to user interface (UI) elements for Windows apps, patterns to share code, and styling apps with XAML. This chapter continues from there to show you several aspects specific to Windows apps. You see how Windows apps have a lifetime management that is different from traditional desktop applications. You use the share contract to create share source and target apps to share data between apps. You use advanced binding features with compiled binding, create text flow, and use the `AutoSuggestBox` to auto-complete user input.

Let's start with the app lifetime of Windows apps, which is very different from the lifetime of traditional desktop applications.

APP LIFETIME

Windows 8 introduced a new life cycle for apps that is completely different from the life cycle of traditional desktop applications. This changed a little with Windows 8.1, and again with Windows 10. If you're using Windows 10 and *tablet mode*, the life cycle of the app is different compared to *desktop mode*. With tablet mode, apps are typically full-screen. You can either switch to tablet mode automatically by detaching the keyboard (with tablet devices such as the Microsoft Surface), or by using the Tablet Mode button in the Action Center. When you run an application in tablet mode, the app gets suspended if it moves to the background (the user switches to another app), and it doesn't get any more CPU utilization. This way the app doesn't consume any battery. The app just uses memory while it's in the background and gets activated again as soon as the user switches to this app.

In case memory resources are low, Windows can terminate suspended applications. To terminate an app, the process is killed. No information is sent to the application, so it cannot react to this event. That's why an application should act on the suspended event and save its state there. Upon termination it is too late to save the state.

When receiving the suspended event, an app should store its state on disk. If the app is started again, the app can present itself to the user as if it was never terminated. You just need to store information about the page stack to navigate the user to the page where he or she left off, allow the user to go back by restoring the page back stack, and initialize the fields to the data the user entered.

The sample app for this section—`ApplicationLifetime`—does exactly this. With this app, multiple pages allow navigation between the pages, and the state can be entered. The page stack and state are stored when the app is suspended, and both are restored when the app is started.

Application Execution States

States of the application are defined with the `ApplicationExecutionState` enumeration. This enumeration defines the states `NotRunning`, `Running`, `Suspended`, `Terminated`, and `ClosedByUser`. The application needs to be aware of and store its state, as users returning to the application expect to continue where they left it previously.

With the `OnLaunched` method in the `App` class, you can get the previous execution state of the application with the `PreviousExecutionState` property of the `LaunchActivatedEventArgs` argument. The previous execution state is `NotRunning` if the application is being started for the first time after installing it, or after a reboot, or when the user stopped the process from the Task Manager. The application is in the `Running` state if it was already running when the user activated it from a second tile or it's activated by one of the activation contracts. The `PreviousExecutionState` property returns `Suspended` when the application was suspended previously. Usually there's no need to do anything special in that case as the state is still available in memory. While in a suspended state, the app doesn't use any CPU cycles, and there's no disk access.

> **NOTE** *The application can implement one or more activation contracts and then can be activated with one of these. An example of such a contract is share. With this contract, the user can share some data from another application and start a Windows app by using it as a share target. Implementing the share contract is shown later in this chapter in the "Sharing Data" section.*

Navigation Between Pages

The sample application for demonstrating the life cycle of Windows apps (`ApplicationLifetime`) is started with the Blank App template. After creating the project, you add the pages `Page1` and `Page2` to implement navigation between the pages.

To the `MainPage`, you add two `Button` controls for navigation to `Page1` and `Page2` and two `TextBox` controls to allow passing data with the navigation (code file ApplicationLifetime/MainPage .xaml):

```
<Button Content="Page 1" Click="{x:Bind GotoPage1, Mode=OneTime}"
   Grid.Row="1" />
<TextBox Header="Parameter 1" Text="{x:Bind ParameterPage1, Mode=TwoWay}"
   Grid.Row="1" Grid.Column="1" />
<Button Content="Page 2" Click="{x:Bind GotoPage2, Mode=OneTime}"
   Grid.Row="2" />
<TextBox Header="Parameter 2" Text="{x:Bind Parameter2, Mode=TwoWay}"
   Grid.Row="2" Grid.Column="1" />
```

The code-behind file contains the event handler with navigation code to `Page1` and `Page2` and properties for the parameters (code file ApplicationLifetime/MainPage.xaml.cs):

```
public void GotoPage1() =>
   Frame.Navigate(typeof(Page1), ParameterPage1);

public string ParameterPage1 { get; set; }

public void GotoPage2() =>
   Frame.Navigate(typeof(Page2), ParameterPage2);

public string ParameterPage2 { get; set; }
```

The UI elements for `Page1` show the data that is received on navigating to this page, a `Button` to allow the user to navigate to `Page2`, and a `TextBox` to allow the user to enter some state information that should be saved when the app is terminated (code file ApplicationLifetime/Page1.xaml) :

```
<TextBlock Text="Page 1" Style="{StaticResource HeaderTextBlockStyle}" />
<TextBlock Grid.Row="1" Text="{x:Bind ReceivedContent, Mode=OneTime}"
   Style="{StaticResource BodyTextBlockStyle}" Margin=12 />
<TextBox Grid.Row="2" Text="{x:Bind Parameter1, Mode=TwoWay}" />
<Button Grid.Row="3" Content="Navigate to Page 2"
   Click="{x:Bind GotoPage2, Mode=OneTime}" />
<TextBox Header="Session State 1" Grid.Row="4"
   Text="{x:Bind Data.Session1, Mode=TwoWay}" />
<TextBox Header="Session State 2" Grid.Row="5"
   Text="{x:Bind Data.Session2, Mode=TwoWay}" />
```

Like the `MainPage`, the navigation code for `Page1` defines an auto-implemented property for the data that is passed with the navigation and an event handler implementation for navigating to `Page2` (code file ApplicationLifetime/Page1.xaml.cs) :

```
public void GotoPage2() => Frame.Navigate(typeof(Page2), Parameter1);

public string Parameter1 { get; set; }
```

With the code-behind file, the navigation parameter is received in the `OnNavigatedTo` method override. The received parameter is assigned to the auto-implemented property `ReceivedContent` (code file `ApplicationLifetime/Page1.xaml.cs`):

```
protected override void OnNavigatedTo(NavigationEventArgs e)
{
  base.OnNavigatedTo(e);
  //...
  ReceivedContent = e.Parameter?.ToString() ?? string.Empty;
  Bindings.Update();
}

public string ReceivedContent { get; private set; }
```

With the implementation of the navigation, `Page2` is very similar to `Page1`, so I'm not repeating its implementation here.

Using the system back button is covered in Chapter 33, "Windows Apps." Here, the visibility and handler of the back button is defined in the class `BackButtonManager`. The implementation of the constructor makes the back button visible if the `CanGoBack` property of the frame instance returns true. The method `OnBackRequested` is implemented to go back in the page stack if the stack is available (code file `ApplicationLifetime/Utilities/BackButtonManager.cs`):

```
public class BackButtonManager: IDisposable
{
  private SystemNavigationManager _navigationManager;
  private Frame _frame;

  public BackButtonManager(Frame frame)
  {
    _frame = frame ?? throw new ArgumentNullException(nameof(frame));
    _navigationManager = SystemNavigationManager.GetForCurrentView();
    _navigationManager.AppViewBackButtonVisibility = frame.CanGoBack ?
      AppViewBackButtonVisibility.Visible:
        AppViewBackButtonVisibility.Collapsed;
    _navigationManager.BackRequested += OnBackRequested;
  }

  private void OnBackRequested(object sender, BackRequestedEventArgs e)
  {
    if (_frame.CanGoBack) _frame.GoBack();
    e.Handled = true;
  }

  public void Dispose()
  {
    _navigationManager.BackRequested -= OnBackRequested;
  }
}
```

With all the pages, the `BackButtonManager` is instantiated by passing the `Frame` in the `OnNavigatedTo` method, and it's disposed in the `OnNavigatedFrom` method (code file `ApplicationLifetime/MainPage.xaml.cs`):

```
private BackButtonManager _backButtonManager;
protected override void OnNavigatedTo(NavigationEventArgs e)
{
  base.OnNavigatedTo(e);
  _backButtonManager = new BackButtonManager(Frame);
}

protected override void OnNavigatingFrom(NavigatingCancelEventArgs e)
```

```
    {
      base.OnNavigatingFrom(e);
      _backButtonManager.Dispose();
    }
```

With all this code in place, the user can navigate back and forward between the three different pages. What needs to be done next is to remember the page and the page stack to navigate the app to the page the user accessed most recently.

NAVIGATION STATE

To store and load the navigation state, the class `NavigationSuspensionManager` defines the methods `SetNavigationStateAsync` and `GetNavigationStateAsync`. The page stack for the navigation can be represented in a single string. This string is written to a local cache file named as defined by a constant. In case the file already exists from a previous app run, it is just overwritten. You don't need to remember page navigations between multiple app runs (code file `ApplicationLifetime/Utilities/NavigationSuspensionManager.cs`):

```
public class NavigationSuspensionManager
{
  private const string NavigationStateFile = "NavigationState.txt";
  public async Task SetNavigationStateAsync(string navigationState)
  {
    StorageFile file = await
      ApplicationData.Current.LocalCacheFolder.CreateFileAsync(
        NavigationStateFile, CreationCollisionOption.ReplaceExisting);
    Stream stream = await file.OpenStreamForWriteAsync();
    using (var writer = new StreamWriter(stream))
    {
      await writer.WriteLineAsync(navigationState);
    }
  }

  public async Task<string> GetNavigationStateAsync()
  {
    Stream stream = await
      ApplicationData.Current.LocalCacheFolder.OpenStreamForReadAsync(
        NavigationStateFile);
    using (var reader = new StreamReader(stream))
    {
      return await reader.ReadLineAsync();
    }
  }
}
```

> **NOTE** *The* `NavigationSuspensionManager` *class makes use of the Windows Runtime API with the .NET* `Stream` *class to read and write contents to a file. Both features are shown in detail in Chapter 22, "Files and Streams."*

Suspending the App

To save state on suspension of the application, the Suspending event of the App class is set in the `OnSuspending` event handler. The event is fired when the application moves into suspended mode (code file `ApplicationLifetime/App.xaml.cs`):

```
public App()
{
```

```
        this.InitializeComponent();
        this.Suspending += OnSuspending;
    }
```

The method OnSuspending is an event handler method, and thus is declared to return void. There's an issue with that. As soon as the method is finished, the app can be terminated. However, as the method is declared void it is not possible to wait for the method until it is finished. Because of this, the received SuspendingEventArgs parameter defines a SuspendingDeferral that can be retrieved by calling the method GetDeferral. As soon as the async functionality of your code is completed, you need to invoke the Complete method on the deferral. This way, the caller knows the method is finished, and the app can be terminated (code file ApplicationLifetime/App.xaml.cs):

```
    private async void OnSuspending(object sender, SuspendingEventArgs e)
    {
        var deferral = e.SuspendingOperation.GetDeferral();
        //...
        deferral.Complete();
    }
```

> **NOTE** *You can read details about asynchronous methods in Chapter 15, "Asynchronous Programming."*

Within the implementation of the OnSuspending method, the page stack is written to the temporary cache. You can retrieve the pages on the page stack using the BackStack property of the Frame. This property returns a list of PageStackEntry objects where every instance represents the type, navigation parameter, and navigation transition information. For storing the page track with the SetNavigationStateAsync method, just a string is needed that contains the complete page stack information. This string can be retrieved by calling the GetNavigationState method of the Frame (code file ApplicationLifetime/App.xaml.cs):

```
    private async void OnSuspending(object sender, SuspendingEventArgs e)
    {
        var deferral = e.SuspendingOperation.GetDeferral();
        var frame = Window.Current.Content as Frame;
        if (frame?.BackStackDepth >= 1)
        {
            var suspensionManager = new NavigationSuspensionManager();
            string navigationState = frame.GetNavigationState();
            if (navigationState != null)
            {
                await suspensionManager.SetNavigationStateAsync(navigationState);
            }
        }
        //...
        deferral.Complete();
    }
```

By default, you have only a few seconds for suspending the app before it can be terminated. However, you can extend this time for making network calls, retrieving data from a service or uploading data to a service, or doing location tracking. All you have to do for this is to create an ExtendedExecutionSession within the OnSuspending method, set a reason, such as ExtendedExecutionReason.SavingData, and request the extension by calling RequestExecutionAsync. If the extended execution is not denied, you can go on with the extended task.

Activating the App from Suspension

The string returned from `GetNavigationState` is comma-separated and lists the complete information of the page stack including type information and parameters. You shouldn't parse the string to get the different parts because this can be changed with newer implementations of the Windows Runtime. Just using this string to restore the state later to recover the page stack with `SetNavigationState` is okay. In case the string format changes with a future version, both these methods will be changed as well.

To set the page stack when the app is started, you need to change the `OnLaunched` method. This method is overridden from the `Application` base class, and it's invoked when the app is started. The argument `LaunchActivatedEventArgs` gives information on how the app is started. The `Kind` property returns an `ActivationKind` enumeration value where you can read whether the app was started by the user clicking on the tile stating a voice command, or from Windows, such as by launching it as a share target. The `PreviousExecutionState`—which is needed in this scenario—returns an `ApplicationExecutionState` enumeration value that provides the information of how the app ended previously. If the app ended with the `ClosedByUser` value, no special action is needed; the app should start fresh. However, if the app was previously terminated, the `PreviousExecutionState` contains the value `Terminated`. With this state, it's useful to arrange the app to a state where the user previously left it. Here, the page stack is retrieved from the `NavigationSuspensionManager` and set to the root frame by passing the previously saved string to the method `SetNavigationState` (code file `ApplicationLifetime/App.xaml.cs`):

```
protected override async void OnLaunched(LaunchActivatedEventArgs e)
{
  Frame rootFrame = Window.Current.Content as Frame;
  if (rootFrame == null)
  {
    rootFrame = new Frame();
    rootFrame.NavigationFailed += OnNavigationFailed;
    if (e.PreviousExecutionState == ApplicationExecutionState.Terminated)
    {
      var suspensionManager = new NavigationSuspensionManager();
      string navigationState =
        await suspensionManager.GetNavigationStateAsync();
      rootFrame.SetNavigationState(navigationState);
      //...
    }

    // Place the frame in the current Window
    Window.Current.Content = rootFrame;
  }
  if (rootFrame.Content == null)
  {
    rootFrame.Navigate(typeof(MainPage), e.Arguments);
  }
  Window.Current.Activate();
}
```

Testing Suspension

Now you can start the application (see Figure 36-1), navigate to another page, and then open other applications to wait until the application is terminated. With the Task Manager, you can see the suspended applications with the Details view if the Status Values option is set to Show Suspended Status. This is not an easy way to test suspension (because it can take a long time before the termination happens), however, and it would be nice to debug the different states.

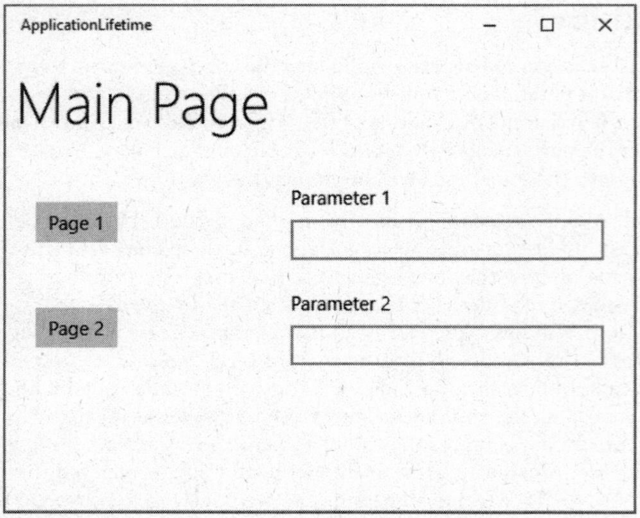

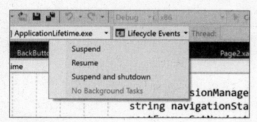

FIGURE 36-1

When you use the debugger, everything works differently. If the application would be suspended as soon as it doesn't have a focus, it would be suspended every time a breakpoint is reached. That's why suspension is disabled while running under the debugger—the normal suspension mechanism doesn't apply. However, it's easy to simulate. If you open the Debug Location toolbar, there are three buttons for Suspend, Resume, and Suspend and Shutdown (see Figure 36-2). If you click Suspend and shutdown and then start the application again, the application continues from the previous state of `ApplicationExecutionState.Terminated` and thus opens the page the user opened previously.

FIGURE 36-2

Page State

Any data that was input by the user should be restored as well. For this demonstration, on `Page1` two input fields are created (code file `ApplicationLifetime/Page1.xaml`):

```
<TextBox Header="Session State 1" Grid.Row="4"
  Text="{x:Bind Data.Session1, Mode=TwoWay}" />
<TextBox Header="Session State 2" Grid.Row="5"
  Text="{x:Bind Data.Session2, Mode=TwoWay}" />
```

The data representation of this input field is defined by the `DataManager` class that is returned from the `Data` property, as shown in the following code snippet (code file `ApplicationLifetime/Page1.xaml.cs`):

```
public DataManager Data => DataManager.Instance;
```

The `DataManager` class defines the properties `Session1` and `Session2` where the values are stored within a Dictionary (code file `ApplicationLifetime/Services/DataManager.cs`):

```
public class DataManager: INotifyPropertyChanged
{
  private const string SessionStateFile = "TempSessionState.json";
  private Dictionary<string, string> _state = new Dictionary<string, string>()
  {
    [nameof(Session1)] = string.Empty,
    [nameof(Session2)] = string.Empty
  };

  private DataManager()
  {
  }

  public event PropertyChangedEventHandler PropertyChanged;
  protected void OnPropertyChanged(
    [CallerMemberName] string propertyName = null) =>
    PropertyChanged?.Invoke(this, new PropertyChangedEventArgs(propertyName));

  public static DataManager Instance { get; } = new DataManager();

  public string Session1
  {
    get => _state[nameof(Session1)];
    set
    {
      _state[nameof(Session1)] = value;
      OnPropertyChanged();
    }
  }

  public string Session2
  {
    get => _state[nameof(Session2)];
    set
    {
      _state[nameof(Session2)] = value;
      OnPropertyChanged();
    }
  }
  //...
}
```

For loading and storing the session state, the methods `SaveTempSessionAsync` and `LoadTempSessionAsync` are defined. The implementation makes use of Json.Net to serialize the dictionary in JSON format. However, you can use any serialization you like (code file `ApplicationLifetime/Services/DataManager.cs`):

```
public async Task SaveTempSessionAsync()
{
  StorageFile file =
    await ApplicationData.Current.LocalCacheFolder.CreateFileAsync(
      SessionStateFile, CreationCollisionOption.ReplaceExisting);
  Stream stream = await file.OpenStreamForWriteAsync();
  var serializer = new JsonSerializer();
  using (var writer = new StreamWriter(stream))
  {
    serializer.Serialize(writer, _state);
  }
}
```

```
public async Task LoadTempSessionAsync()
{
  Stream stream = await
    ApplicationData.Current.LocalCacheFolder.OpenStreamForReadAsync(
      SessionStateFile);
  var serializer = new JsonSerializer();
  using (var reader = new StreamReader(stream))
  {
    string json = await reader.ReadLineAsync();
    Dictionary<string, string> state =
      JsonConvert.DeserializeObject<Dictionary<string, string>>(json);
    _state = state;
    foreach (var item in state)
    {
      OnPropertyChanged(item.Key);
    }
  }
}
```

> **NOTE** *Serialization with XML and JSON is discussed in Bonus Chapter 2, "XML and JSON," which you can find online.*

What's left is to invoke the `SaveTempSessionAsync` and `LoadTempSessionAsync` methods on suspending and activating of the app. These methods are added to the same places where the page stack is written and read, to the `OnSuspending` and `OnLaunched` methods (code file `ApplicationLifetime/App.xaml.cs`):

```
private async void OnSuspending(object sender, SuspendingEventArgs e)
{
  var deferral = e.SuspendingOperation.GetDeferral();
  //...
  await DataManager.Instance.SaveTempSessionAsync();
  deferral.Complete();
}

protected override async void OnLaunched(LaunchActivatedEventArgs e)
{
  Frame rootFrame = Window.Current.Content as Frame;
  if (rootFrame == null)
  {
    rootFrame = new Frame();
    rootFrame.NavigationFailed += OnNavigationFailed;
    if (e.PreviousExecutionState == ApplicationExecutionState.Terminated)
    {
      //...
      await DataManager.Instance.LoadTempSessionAsync();
    }
    // Place the frame in the current Window
    Window.Current.Content = rootFrame;
  }
  if (rootFrame.Content == null)
  {
    rootFrame.Navigate(typeof(MainPage), e.Arguments);
  }
  Window.Current.Activate();
}
```

Now you can run the app, enter state in `Page2`, suspend and terminate the app, start it again, and the state shows up again.

With the app lifetime you've seen how special programming is needed for Windows apps to consider battery consumption. The next session discusses sharing data between apps, which is also available on the phone platform.

SHARING DATA

Your app becomes a lot more useful when it can interact with other apps. With Windows 10, apps can share data using drag and drop, even with desktop applications. Between Windows apps, it's also possible to share data using a sharing contract.

When you use a sharing contract, one app (the sharing source) can share data in many different formats—for example, text, HTML, image, or custom data—and the user can select an app that accepts the data format as a sharing target. Windows finds the apps that support the corresponding data format by using a contract that's registered with the app at installation time.

Sharing Source

The first consideration in terms of sharing is determining what data should be shared in what format. It's possible to share simple text, rich text, HTML, and images, but also a custom type. Of course, all these types must be known and used from other applications—the sharing targets. Sharing custom types can only be done with other applications that know the type and are a share target for the type. The sample application offers shared data in text format and a book list in HTML format.

To offer book information in HTML format, you define a simple `Book` class (code file `SharingData/ShareSource/Models/Book.cs`):

```
public class Book
{
  public string Title { get; set; }
  public string Publisher { get; set; }
}
```

A list of `Book` objects is returned from the `GetSampleBooks` method of the `BooksRepository` class (code file `SharingData/ShareSource/Models/BooksRepository.cs`):

```
public class BooksRepository
{
  public IEnumerable<Book> GetSampleBooks() =>
    new List<Book>()
    {
      new Book
      {
        Title = "Professional C# 7 and .NET Core 2",
       Publisher = "Wrox Press"
      },
      new Book
      {
        Title = "Professional C# 6 and .NET Core 1.0",
        Publisher = "Wrox Press"
      }
    };
}
```

To convert a list of `Book` objects to HTML, the extension method `ToHtml` returns an HTML table with the help of LINQ to XML (code file `SharingData/ShareSource/Utilities/BookExtensions.cs`):

```
public static class BookExtensions
{
  public static string ToHtml(this IEnumerable<Book> books) =>
    new XElement("table",
      new XElement("thead",
```

```
        new XElement("tr",
          new XElement("td", "Title"),
          new XElement("td", "Publisher"))),
      books.Select(b =>
        new XElement("tr",
          new XElement("td", b.Title),
          new XElement("td", b.Publisher)))).ToString();
}
```

> **NOTE** *LINQ to XML is covered in Bonus Chapter 2.*

With the `MainPage`, you define a `Button`, where the user can initiate the sharing, and a `TextBox` control for the user to enter textual data to share (code file `SharingData/ShareSource/MainPage.xaml`):

```xml
<RelativePanel Margin="24">
  <Button x:Name="shareDataButton" Content="Share Data"
    Click="{x:Bind DataSharing.ShowShareUI, Mode=OneTime}" Margin="12" />
  <TextBox RelativePanel.RightOf="shareDataButton"
    Text="{x:Bind DataSharing.SimpleText, Mode=TwoWay}" Margin="12" />
</RelativePanel>
```

In the code-behind file, the `DataSharing` property returns the `ShareDataViewModel` where all the important features for sharing are implemented (code file `SharingData/ShareSource/MainPage.xaml.cs`):

```csharp
public ShareDataViewModel DataSharing { get; set; } = new ShareDataViewModel();
```

The `ShareDataViewModel` defines the property `SimpleText` that is bound by the XAML file to enter the simple text to be shared. For sharing, the event handler method `ShareDataRequested` is assigned to the event `DataRequested` of the `DataTransferManager`. This event is fired when the user requests sharing data (code file `SharingData/ShareSource/ViewModels/ShareDataViewModel.cs`):

```csharp
public class ShareDataViewModel
{
  public ShareDataViewModel()
  {
    DataTransferManager.GetForCurrentView().DataRequested +=
      ShareDataRequested;
  }

  public string SimpleText { get; set; } = string.Empty;
  //...
}
```

When the event is fired, the `OnShareDataRequested` method is invoked. This method receives the `DataTransferManager` as the first argument, and `DataRequestedEventArgs` as the second. On sharing data, the `DataPackage` referenced by `args.Request.Data` needs to be filled. You can use the `Title`, `Description`, and `Thumbnail` properties to give information to the user interface. The data that should be shared must be passed with one of the `SetXXX` methods. The sample code shares a simple text and HTML code, thus the methods `SetText` and `SetHtmlFormat` are used. The `HtmlFormatHelper` class helps create the surrounding HTML code that's needed for sharing. The HTML code for the books is created with the extension method `ToHtml` that was shown earlier (code file `SharingData/ShareSource/ViewModels/ShareDataViewModel.cs`):

```csharp
private void ShareDataRequested(DataTransferManager sender,
  DataRequestedEventArgs args)
{
  var books = new BooksRepository().GetSampleBooks();
  Uri baseUri = new Uri("ms-appx:///");
  DataPackage package = args.Request.Data;
  package.Properties.Title = "Sharing Sample";
  package.Properties.Description = "Sample for sharing data";
  package.Properties.Thumbnail = RandomAccessStreamReference.CreateFromUri(
```

```
        new Uri(baseUri, "Assets/Square44x44Logo.png"));
    package.SetText(SimpleText);
    package.SetHtmlFormat(HtmlFormatHelper.CreateHtmlFormat(books.ToHtml()));
}
```

In case you need the information when the sharing operation is completed—for example, to remove the data from the source application—the `DataPackage` class fires `OperationCompleted` and `Destroyed` events.

> **NOTE** *Instead of offering text or HTML code, other methods, such as* `SetBitmap`, `SetRtf`, *and* `SetUri`, *make it possible to offer other data formats.*

> **NOTE** *In case you need to build the data for sharing using async methods within the* `ShareDataRequested` *method, you need to use a deferral to give the information when the data is available. This is like the page suspension mechanism shown earlier in this chapter. Using the* `Request` *property of the* `DataRequestedEventArgs` *type, you can invoke the* `GetDeferral` *method. This method returns a deferral of type* `DataRequestedDeferral`. *With this object, you can invoke the* `Complete` *method when the data is readily available.*

Finally, the user interface for sharing needs to be shown. This enables the user to select the target app:

```
public void ShowShareUI()
{
    DataTransferManager.ShowShareUI();
}
```

Figure 36-3 shows the user interface after calling the `ShowShareUI` method of the `DataTransferManager`. Depending on what data format is offered and the apps that are installed, the corresponding apps are shown for selection. Starting with the Fall Creators Update of Windows 10 (build 16299), you not only see apps but also some of your contacts. When you select a contact, you can share the data directly with your contact, using apps that are used both by you and your contact to communicate.

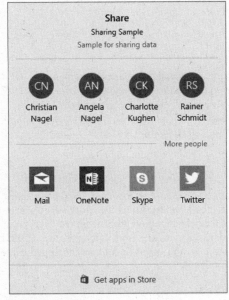

FIGURE 36-3

If you select the Mail app, HTML information is passed. Figure 36-4 shows the received data within this app.

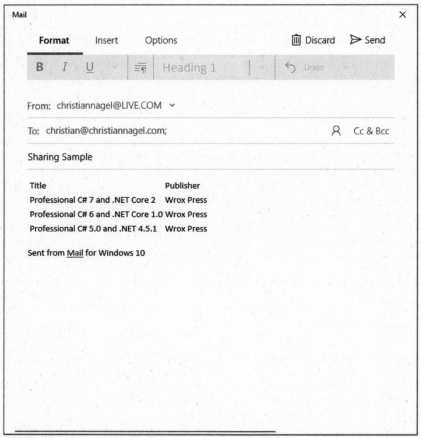

FIGURE 36-4

Sharing Target

Now let's have a look at the recipient of sharing. If an application should receive information from a sharing source, it needs to be declared as a share target. Figure 36-5 shows the Manifest Designer's Declarations page within Visual Studio, where you can define share targets. Here is where you add the Share Target declaration, which must include at least one data format. Possible data formats are Text, URI, Bitmap, HTML, StorageItems, or RTF. You can also specify which file types should be supported by adding the appropriate file extensions.

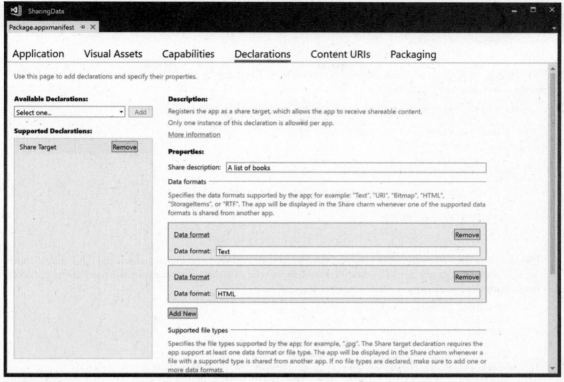

FIGURE 36-5

The information in the package manifest is used upon registration of the application. This tells Windows which applications are available as a share target. The sample app `SharingTarget` defines share targets for `Text` and `HTML`.

When the user launches the app as a share target, the `OnShareTargetActivated` method is called in the `App` class instead of the `OnLaunched` method. Here, a different page (`ShareTargetPage`) gets created that shows the screen when the user selects this app as a share target (code file `SharingData/ShareTarget/App.xaml.cs`):

```
protected override void OnShareTargetActivated(
    ShareTargetActivatedEventArgs args)
{
    Frame rootFrame = CreateRootFrame();
    rootFrame.Navigate(typeof(ShareTargetPage), args.ShareOperation);
    Window.Current.Activate();
}
```

To not create the root frame in two different places, the `OnLaunched` method has been refactored to put the frame creation code in a separate method: `CreateRootFrame`. This method is now called from both `OnShareTargetActivated` as well as `OnLaunched`:

```
private Frame CreateRootFrame()
{
    Frame rootFrame = Window.Current.Content as Frame;
    if (rootFrame == null)
    {
        rootFrame = new Frame();
```

```
    rootFrame.NavigationFailed += OnNavigationFailed;
    Window.Current.Content = rootFrame;
  }
  return rootFrame;
}
```

The change of the `OnLaunched` method is shown here. Contrary to the `OnShareTargetActivated`, this method navigates to the `MainPage`:

```
protected override void OnLaunched(LaunchActivatedEventArgs e)
{
  Frame rootFrame = CreateRootFrame();
  if (!e.PreLaunchActivated)
  {
    if (rootFrame.Content == null)
    {
      rootFrame.Navigate(typeof(MainPage), e.Arguments);
    }
    Window.Current.Activate();
  }
}
```

The `ShareTargetPage` contains controls where the user can see information about the data shared, such as the title and description, and a combo box that shows the available data formats the user can select (code file `SharingData/ShareTarget/ShareTargetPage.xaml`):

```
<StackPanel Orientation="Vertical">
  <TextBlock Text="Share Target Page" />
  <TextBox Header="Title" IsReadOnly="True"
    Text="{x:Bind ViewModel.Title, Mode=OneWay}" Margin="12" />
  <TextBox Header="Description" IsReadOnly="True"
    Text="{x:Bind ViewModel.Description, Mode=OneWay}" Margin="12" />
  <ComboBox ItemsSource="{x:Bind ViewModel.ShareFormats, Mode=OneTime}"
    SelectedItem="{x:Bind ViewModel.SelectedFormat, Mode=TwoWay}"
    Margin="12" />
  <Button Content="Retrieve Data"
    Click="{x:Bind ViewModel.RetrieveData, Mode=OneTime}" Margin="12" />
  <Button Content="Report Complete"
    Click="{x:Bind ViewModel.ReportCompleted, Mode=OneTime}" Margin="12" />
  <TextBox Header="Text" IsReadOnly="True"
    Text="{x:Bind ViewModel.Text, Mode=OneWay}" Margin="12" />
  <TextBox AcceptsReturn="True" IsReadOnly="True"
    Text="{x:Bind ViewModel.Html, Mode=OneWay}" Margin="12" />
</StackPanel>
```

In the code-behind file, a `ShareTargetPageViewModel` is assigned to the `ViewModel` property. In the XAML code earlier, this property is used with compiled binding. Also, with the `OnNavigatedTo` method, the `SharedTargetPageViewModel` is activated passing a `ShareOperation` object to the `Activate` method (code file `SharingTarget/ShareTargetPage.xaml.cs`):

```
public sealed partial class ShareTargetPage: Page
{
  public ShareTargetPage() => InitializeComponent();

  public ShareTargetPageViewModel ViewModel { get; } =
    new ShareTargetPageViewModel();

  protected override void OnNavigatedTo(NavigationEventArgs e)
  {
    ViewModel.Activate(e.Parameter as ShareOperation);
    base.OnNavigatedTo(e);
  }
}
```

The class `ShareTargetPageViewModel` defines properties for values that should be displayed in the page, as well as change notification by implementing the interface `INotifyPropertyChanged` (code file `SharingTarget/ViewModels/ShareTargetViewModel.cs`):

```csharp
public class ShareTargetPageViewModel: INotifyPropertyChanged
{
  public event PropertyChangedEventHandler PropertyChanged;

  public void OnPropertyChanged(
    [CallerMemberName] string propertyName = null) =>
    PropertyChanged?.Invoke(this, new PropertyChangedEventArgs(propertyName));

  public void Set<T>(ref T item, T value,
    [CallerMemberName] string propertyName = null)
  {
    if (!EqualityComparer<T>.Default.Equals(item, value))
    {
      item = value;
      OnPropertyChanged(propertyName);
    }
  }
  //...

  private string _text;
  public string Text
  {
    get => _text;
    set => Set(ref _text, value);
  }

  private string _html;
  public string Html
  {
    get => _html;
    set => Set(ref _html, value);
  }

  private string _title;
  public string Title
  {
    get => _title;
    set => Set(ref _title, value);
  }

  private string _description;
  public string Description
  {
    get => _description;
    set => Set(ref _description, value);
  }
}
```

The `Activate` method is an important part of the `ShareTargetPageViewModel`. Here, the `ShareOperation` object is used to access information about the share data and get some metadata available to display it to the user, such as `Title`, `Description`, and the list of available data formats. In case of an error, error information is shown to the user by invoking the `ReportError` method of the `ShareOperation` (code file `SharingTarget/ViewModels/ShareTargetViewModel.cs`):

```csharp
public class ShareTargetPageViewModel: INotifyPropertyChanged
{
  //...
  private ShareOperation _shareOperation;
```

```csharp
private readonly ObservableCollection<string> _shareFormats =
  new ObservableCollection<string>();
public string SelectedFormat { get; set; }
public IEnumerable<string> ShareFormats => _shareFormats;

public void Activate(ShareOperation shareOperation)
{
  if (shareOperation == null)
    throw new ArgumentNullException(nameof(shareOperation));

  string title = null;
  string description = null;
  try
  {
    _shareOperation = shareOperation;
    title = _shareOperation.Data.Properties.Title;
    description = _shareOperation.Data.Properties.Description;
    foreach (var format in _shareOperation.Data.AvailableFormats)
    {
      _shareFormats.Add(format);
    }
    Title = title;
    Description = description;
  }
  catch (Exception ex)
  {
    _shareOperation.ReportError(ex.Message);
  }
}
//...
}
```

As soon as the user chooses the data format, he or she can click the button to retrieve the data. This in turn invokes the method RetrieveData. Depending on the user's selection, either GetTextAsync or GetHtmlFormatAsync is invoked on the DataPackageView instance that is returned from the Data property. Before retrieving the data, the method ReportStarted is invoked; after the data is retrieved, the method ReportDataRetrieved is invoked (code file SharingTarget/ViewModels/ShareTargetViewModel.cs):

```csharp
public class ShareTargetPageViewModel: INotifyPropertyChanged
{
  //...
  private bool dataRetrieved = false;
  public async void RetrieveData()
  {
    try
    {
      if (dataRetrieved)
      {
        await new MessageDialog("data already retrieved").ShowAsync();
      }
      _shareOperation.ReportStarted();
      switch (SelectedFormat)
      {
```

```
        case "Text":
          Text = await _shareOperation.Data.GetTextAsync();
          break;
        case "HTML Format":
          Html = await _shareOperation.Data.GetHtmlFormatAsync();
          break;
        default:
          break;
      }
      _shareOperation.ReportDataRetrieved();
      dataRetrieved = true;
    }
    catch (Exception ex)
    {
      _shareOperation.ReportError(ex.Message);
    }
  }
  //...
}
```

With the sample app, the retrieved data is shown in the user interface. With a real app, you can use the data in any form—for example, store it locally on the client or call your own web service and pass the data there.

Finally, the user can click the Report Completed button in the UI. Using the `Click` handler, this invokes the `ReportCompleted` method in the view model, which in turn invokes the `ReportCompleted` method on the `ShareOperation` instance. This method closes the dialog (code file `SharingTarget/ViewModels/ShareTargetViewModel.cs`):

```
public class ShareTargetPageViewModel: INotifyPropertyChanged
{
  //...
  public void ReportCompleted()
  {
    _shareOperation.ReportCompleted();
  }
  //...
}
```

With your app, you can invoke the `ReportCompleted` method earlier after retrieving the data. Just remember that the dialog of the app is closed when this method is called.

To activate the `ShareTarget` app, first you need to run the `ShareTarget` app once to have it registered as a share source. After that, start the `ShareSource` app again. Now, as you share data, the `ShareTarget` is listed as an app to choose from. Selecting this app, you'll see the running `ShareTarget` app as shown in Figure 36-6.

> **NOTE** *The best way to test sharing with all the formats you would like to support is by using the sample app's Sharing Content Source app sample and Sharing Content Target app sample. Both sample apps are available at* https://github.com/Microsoft/Windows-universal-samples. *In case you have an app as sharing source, use the sample target app, and vice versa.*

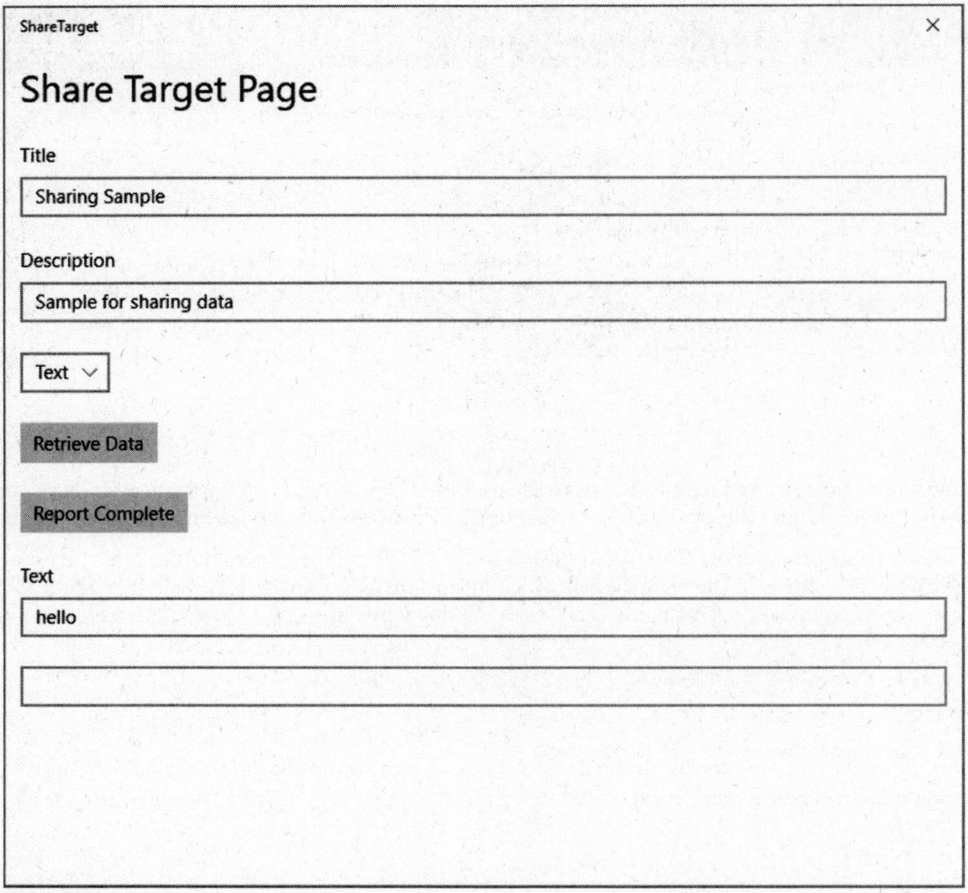

FIGURE 36-6

> **NOTE** *An easy way to debug share targets is to set the Debug option Do Not Launch, but Debug My Code When It Starts. This setting is in the Project Properties, Debug tab (see Figure 36-7). With this setting you can start the debugger, and the app starts as soon as you share data with this app from a data source app. When you set both the share and target app to start with the debugger, the target app launches as soon as it is activated as share target.*

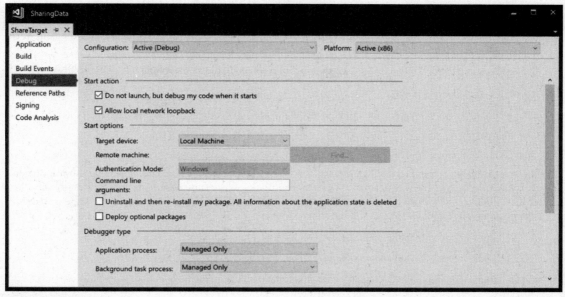

FIGURE 36-7

APP SERVICES

Another way to share data between your apps is by using app services. You can compare *app services* to calling into web services, but the service is local on the user's system. Multiple apps can access the same service, which is how you can share information between apps. An important difference between app services and web services is that the user doesn't need to interact using this feature; it all can be done from the app.

The sample app `AppServices` uses a service to cache `Book` objects. Calling the service, the list of `Book` objects can be retrieved, and new `Book` objects can be added to the service.

The app consists of multiple projects:

➤ One .NET Standard Library (`BooksCacheModel`) defines the model of this app—the `Book` class. For an easy transfer of data, extension methods are offered to convert `Book` objects to JSON and the other way around. This library is used from all the other projects.

➤ The second project (`BooksCacheService`) is a Windows Runtime component that defines the book service itself. Such a service needs to run in the background; thus, a background task is implemented.

➤ The background task needs to be registered with the system. This project is a Windows app: `BooksCacheProvider`.

➤ The client application calling the app service is a Windows app: `BooksCacheClient`.

Let's get into these parts.

Creating the Model

The portable library `BooksCacheModel` contains the `Book` class, a converter to JSON with the help of the NuGet package `Newtonsoft.Json`, and a repository.

The `Book` class defines `Title` and `Publisher` properties (code file `AppServices/BooksCacheModel/Book.cs`):

```
public class Book
{
  public string Title { get; set; }
  public string Publisher { get; set; }
}
```

The `BooksRepository` class holds a memory cache of `Book` objects, allows the user to add book objects via the `AddBook` method, and returns all the cached books with the `Books` property. To already see a book without adding a new book, one book is added to the list at initialization time (code file `AppServices/BooksCacheModel/BooksRepository.cs`):

```
public class BooksRepository
{
  private readonly List<Book> _books = new List<Book>()
  {
    new Book
    {
      Title = "Professional C# 7 and .NET Core 2",
      Publisher = "Wrox Press"
    }
  };

  public IEnumerable<Book> Books => _books;

  private BooksRepository() { }

  public static BooksRepository Instance = new BooksRepository();

  public void AddBook(Book book) => _books.Add(book);

}
```

Because the data that is sent across an app service needs to be serializable, the extension class `BookExtensions` defines a few extension methods that convert a `Book` and a `Book` list to a JSON string, and the other way around. Passing a string across the App service is a simple task. The extension methods make use of the class `JsonConvert` that is available with the NuGet package `Newtonsoft.Json` (code file `AppServices/BooksCacheModel(BookExtensions.cs`):

```
public static class BookExtensions
{
  public static string ToJson(this Book book) =>
    JsonConvert.SerializeObject(book);

  public static string ToJson(this IEnumerable<Book> books) =>
    JsonConvert.SerializeObject(books);

  public static Book ToBook(this string json) =>
    JsonConvert.DeserializeObject<Book>(json);

  public static IEnumerable<Book> ToBooks(this string json) =>
    JsonConvert.DeserializeObject<IEnumerable<Book>>(json);
}
```

Creating a Background Task for App Service Connections

Now let's get into the heart of this sample app: the app service. You need to implement the app service as a Windows Runtime component library and as a background task by implementing the interface `IBackgroundTask`. Windows background tasks can run in the background without user interaction.

Different kinds of background tasks are available. Background tasks can be started based on a timer interval, Windows push notifications, location information, Bluetooth device connections, or other events.

The class `BooksCacheTask` is a background task for the app service. The interface `IBackgroundTask` defines the `Run` method that needs to be implemented. Within the implementation, a request handler is defined on receiving an app service connection (code file `AppServices/BooksCacheService/BooksCacheTask.cs`):

```
public sealed class BooksCacheTask: IBackgroundTask
{
  private BackgroundTaskDeferral _taskDeferral;
  public void Run(IBackgroundTaskInstance taskInstance)
  {
    _taskDeferral = taskInstance.GetDeferral();
    taskInstance.Canceled += OnTaskCanceled;

    var trigger = taskInstance.TriggerDetails as AppServiceTriggerDetails;
    AppServiceConnection connection = trigger.AppServiceConnection;
    connection.RequestReceived += OnRequestReceived;
  }

  private void OnTaskCanceled(IBackgroundTaskInstance sender,
    BackgroundTaskCancellationReason reason)
  {
    _taskDeferral?.Complete();
  }
  //...
}
```

With the implementation of the `OnRequestReceived` handler, the service can read the request and needs to supply an answer. The request received is contained in the `Request.Message` property of the `AppServiceRequestReceivedEventArgs`. The `Message` property returns a `ValueSet` object. `ValueSet` is a dictionary of keys with their corresponding values. The service here requires a `command` key with either the value `GET` or `POST`. The `GET` command returns a list of all books, whereas the `POST` command requires the additional key `book` with a JSON string as the value for the `Book` object representation. Depending on the message received, either the `GetBooks` or `AddBook` helper method is invoked. The result returned from these messages is returned to the caller by invoking `SendResponseAsync`:

```
private async void OnRequestReceived(AppServiceConnection sender,
  AppServiceRequestReceivedEventArgs args)
{
  AppServiceDeferral deferral = args.GetDeferral();
  try
  {
    ValueSet message = args.Request.Message;
    ValueSet result = null;
    switch (message["command"].ToString())
    {
      case "GET":
        result = GetBooks();
        break;
      case "POST":
        result = AddBook(message["book"].ToString());
      break;
        default:
```

```
            break;
        }
        await args.Request.SendResponseAsync(result);
    }
    finally
    {
        deferral.Complete();
    }
}
```

The `GetBooks` method uses the `BooksRepository` to get all the books in JSON format, and it creates a `ValueSet` with the result key:

```
private ValueSet GetBooks()
{
    var result = new ValueSet();
    result.Add("result", BooksRepository.Instance.Books.ToJson());
    return result;
}
```

The `AddBook` method uses the repository to add a book, and returns a `ValueSet` with a `result` key and the value ok:

```
private ValueSet AddBook(string book)
{
    BooksRepository.Instance.AddBook(book.ToBook());
    var result = new ValueSet();
    result.Add("result", "ok");
    return result;
}
```

Registering the App Service

You now need to register the app service with the operating system. This is done by creating a normal UWP app that has a reference to the `BooksCacheService`. With this app, you must define a declaration in the `package.appxmanifest` (see Figure 36-8). Add an app service to the app declaration list and give it a name. You need to set the entry point to the background task, including the namespace and the class name.

For the client app, you need the name of the app that you defined with the `package.appxmanifest` as well as the package name. To see the package name, see the Packaging tab of the Package Manifest Editor. Programmatically, you can invoke `Package.Current.Id.FamilyName`. To see this name easily when starting the app, it is written to the property `PackageFamilyName` that is bound within a control in the user interface (code file `AppServices/BooksCacheProvider/MainPage.xaml.cs`):

```
public sealed partial class MainPage: Page
{
    public MainPage()
    {
        this.InitializeComponent();
        PackageFamilyName = Package.Current.Id.FamilyName;
    }

    public string PackageFamilyName
    {
        get => (string)GetValue(PackageFamilyNameProperty);
        set => SetValue(PackageFamilyNameProperty, value);
    }

    public static readonly DependencyProperty PackageFamilyNameProperty =
        DependencyProperty.Register("PackageFamilyName", typeof(string),
            typeof(MainPage), new PropertyMetadata(string.Empty));
}
```

When you run this app, it registers the background task and shows the package name that you need for the client app.

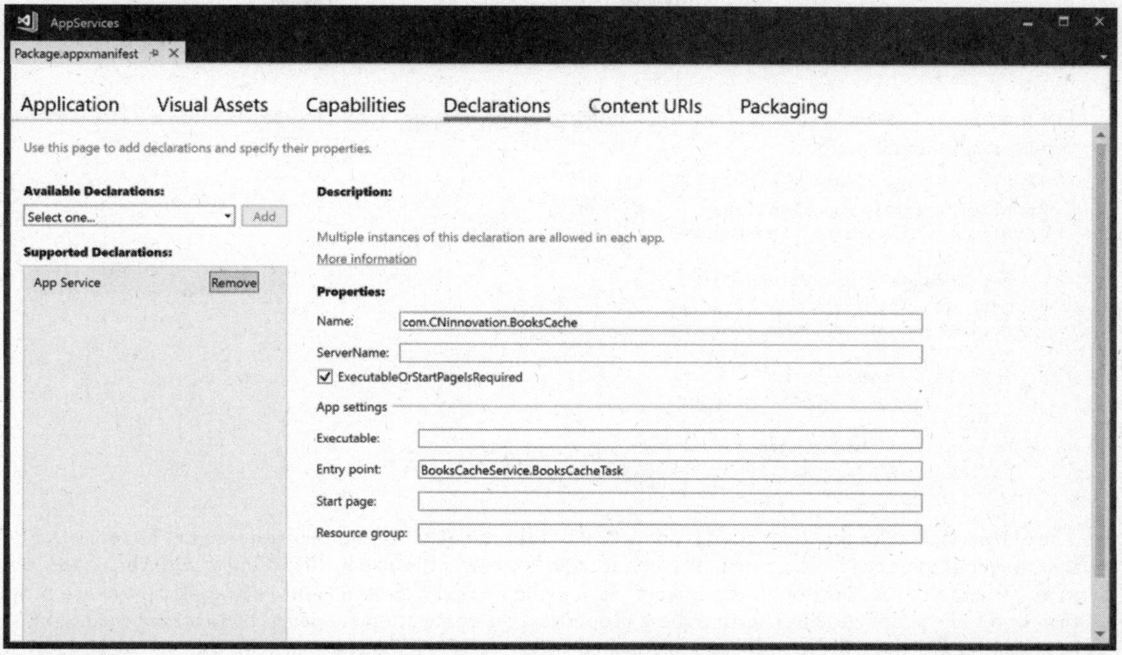

FIGURE 36-8

Calling the App Service

With the client app, the app service can now be called. The main parts of the client app `BooksCacheClient` are implemented with the view model. The `Books` property is bound in the UI to show all books returned from the service. This collection is filled by the `GetBooksAsync` method. `GetBooksAsync` creates a `ValueSet` with the `GET` command that is sent to the app service with the helper method `SendMessageAsync`. This helper method returns a JSON string, which in turn is converted to a `Book` collection that is used to fill the `ObservableCollection` for the `Books` property (code file `AppServices/BooksCacheClient/ViewModels/BooksViewModel.cs`):

```
public class BooksViewModel
{
  private const string BookServiceName = "com.CNinnovation.BooksCache";
  private const string BooksPackageName =
    "085f62ed-e72b-4c07-9970-b4d01c066dd6_p2wxv0ry6mv8g";

  public ObservableCollection<Book> Books { get; } =
    new ObservableCollection<Book>();

  public async void GetBooksAsync()
  {
    var message = new ValueSet();
    message.Add("command", "GET");
    string json = await SendMessageAsync(message);
    IEnumerable<Book> books = json.ToBooks();
```

```
      foreach (var book in books)
      {
        Books.Add(book);
      }
    }
    //...
  }
```

The method `PostBookAsync` creates a `Book` object, serializes it to JSON, and sends it via a `ValueSet` to the `SendMessageAsync` method:

```
public string NewBookTitle { get; set; }
public string NewBookPublisher { get; set; }
public async void PostBookAsync()
{
  var message = new ValueSet();
  message.Add("command", "POST");
  string json = new Book
  {
    Title = NewBookTitle,
    Publisher = NewBookPublisher
  }.ToJson();
  message.Add("book", json);
  string result = await SendMessageAsync(message);
}
```

The app service–relevant client code is contained within the method `SendMessageAsync`. Here, an `AppServiceConnection` is created. The connection is closed after use by disposing it with the `using` statement. To map the connection to the correct service, the `AppServiceName` and `PackageFamilyName` properties need to be supplied. After setting these properties, the connection is opened by invoking the method `OpenAsync`. Only when the connection is opened successfully is a request sent with the `ValueSet` received from the calling method. The `AppServiceConnection` method `SendMessageAsync` makes the request to the service and returns an `AppServiceResponse` object. The response contains the result from the service, which is dealt with accordingly:

```
private async Task<string> SendMessageAsync(ValueSet message)
{
  using (var connection = new AppServiceConnection())
  {
    connection.AppServiceName = BookServiceName;
    connection.PackageFamilyName = BooksPackageName;
    AppServiceConnectionStatus status = await connection.OpenAsync();
    if (status == AppServiceConnectionStatus.Success)
    {
      AppServiceResponse response =
        await connection.SendMessageAsync(message);
      if (response.Status == AppServiceResponseStatus.Success &&
        response.Message.ContainsKey("result"))
      {
        string result = response.Message["result"].ToString();
        return result;
      }
      else
      {
        await ShowServiceErrorAsync(response.Status);
      }
    }
    else
    {
      await ShowConnectionErrorAsync(status);
    }
    return string.Empty;
  }
}
```

After building the solution and deploying both the provider and the client app, you can start the client app and invoke the service. You can also create multiple client apps calling the same service.

After you register the background task by running the provider app, you can run the client app, get the books, and add new books, as shown in Figure 36-9.

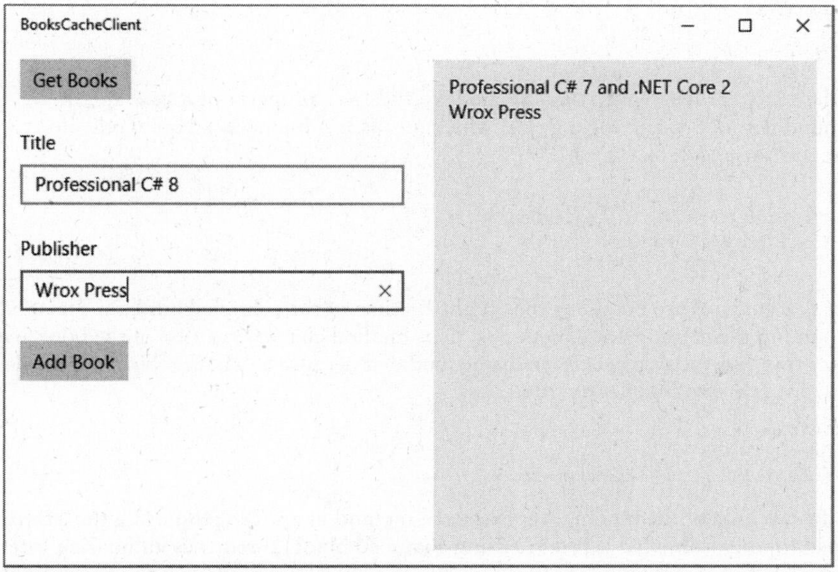

FIGURE 36-9

ADVANCED COMPILED BINDING

Chapter 33 covers compiled binding with Windows apps, but there are some other interesting features with compiled binding. This section looks at the binding lifetime, binding to methods, and phased binding.

Compiled Data Binding Lifetime

With compiled data binding, C# code gets generated from the binding in the XAML file. You can also programmatically influence the lifetime of the binding.

Let's start with a simple Book type that is bound from the user interface (code file CompiledBindingLifetime/Models/Book.cs):

```
public class Book : BindableBase
{
  public int BookId { get; set; }

  private string _title;
  public string Title
  {
    get => _title;
    set => Set(ref _title, value);
  }

  public string Publisher { get; set; }

  public override string ToString() => Title;
}
```

With the page class, a read-only property `Book` is created that returns a `Book` instance. The values of the Book instance can be changed, whereas the `Book` instance itself is read only (code file `CompiledBindingLifetime/MainPage.xaml.cs`):

```
public Book Book { get; } = new Book
{
  Title = "Professional C# 7",
  Publisher = "Wrox Press"
};
```

With the XAML code, the `Title` property is in `OneWay` mode to the `Text` property of a `TextBlock`, and the `Publisher` is bound without specifying a mode, which means it is bound `OneTime` (code file `CompiledBindingLifetime/MainPage.xaml`):

```
<StackPanel>
  <TextBlock Text="{x:Bind Book.Title, Mode=OneWay}" />
  <TextBlock Text="{x:Bind Book.Publisher}" />
</StackPanel>
```

Next, several `AppBarButton` controls are bound to change the lifetime of the compiled binding. The `Click` event of one button is bound to the method `OnChangeBook`. This method changes the title of the book with very invocation. If you try this out, the title gets immediately updated because a `OneTime` binding was done (code file `CompiledBindingLifetime/MainPage.xaml.cs`):

```
private int csharpversion = 7;
public void OnChangeBook() =>
  Book.Title = $"Professional C# {++csharpversion}";
```

However, you can stop the tracking of the binding. Invoking the method `StopTracking` using the `Bindings` property of the page (this property is created if you are using compiled binding) removes all binding listeners. When you call this method before invoking the method `OnChangeBook`, the update of the book is not reflected in the user interface (code file `CompiledBindingLifetime/MainPage.xaml.cs`):

```
private void OnStopTracking() =>
  Bindings.StopTracking();
```

To explicitly update the user interface from bound sources, you can invoke the `Update` method. Calling this method reflects changes not only from `OneWay` or `TwoWay` bindings, but also `OneTime` bindings (code file `CompiledBindingLifetime/MainPage.xaml.cs`):

```
private void OnUpdateBinding() =>
  Bindings.Update();
```

On loading of the window, the `Initialize` method is invoked. This method invokes `Update` once. When `Initialize` is called again, `Update` is not invoked again. You directly need to call the method `Update` for an explicit update. `Update` and `StopTracking` are the two important methods for controlling the lifetime with compiled binding after its initialization. You can also use the `Update` method to update properties that don't implement `INotifyPropertyChanged`.

When you run the app (Figure 36-10), you can click the Stop button in the lower area, followed by the Edit button to change the book. Updates happen only if you click the Refresh button explicitly. If the Stop button is not clicked, updates to the UI happen immediately as you click the Edit button.

Binding to Methods

With compiled binding you've already used *event binding*—binding events to methods. Compiled binding also supports binding properties to methods. This can be used, for example to replace the multi-binding feature that's supported by WPF to bind multiple properties of a model to one property of a XAML element. With binding to methods, you can also replace value converters.

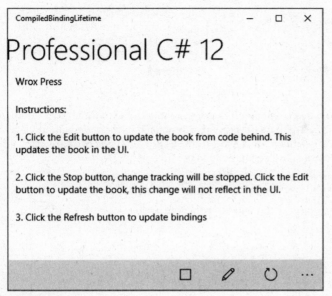

FIGURE 36-10

The next sample app makes use of binding to methods. The model used in the sample app is the `Person` class. This class doesn't implement change notification, so it's necessary to invoke the `Update` method in the bindings to see updated changes in the UI (code file `CompiledBindingMethods/Models/Person.cs`):

```
public class Person
{
  public string GivenName { get; set; }
  public string Surname { get; set; }
}
```

Two `Person` objects are instantiated in the `MainPage`, and assigned to the properties `Person1` and `Person2` (code file `CompiledBindingMethods/MainPage.xaml.cs`):

```
public MainPage()
{
  Person1 = new Person { GivenName = "Katharina", Surname = "Nagel" };
  Person2 = new Person { GivenName = "Stephanie", Surname = "Nagel" };
  this.InitializeComponent();
}

public Person Person1 { get; }
public Person Person2 { get; set; }
```

Within the code-behind file, the method `ToName` converts a `Person` object to a string. Two different variants to convert a person object to a string are implemented: The first variant returns the given name before the surname; the second variant returns the surname before the given name with a comma in between. To choose between the variants, the second parameter of the `ToName` method accepts a Boolean input value to select one of the options (code file `CompiledBindingMethods/MainPage.xaml.cs`):

```
public string ToName(Person p, bool firstLast)
{
  if (p == null) throw new ArgumentNullException(nameof(p));

  if (firstLast)
```

```
      {
        return $"{p.FirstName} {p.LastName}";
      }
      else
      {
        return $"{p.LastName}, {p.FirstName}";
      }
    }
```

To invoke the `ToName` method, the method name is used with the `x:Bind` markup extension. Two values are passed to the `ToName` method: the value of the `Person1` property that is defined in the code-behind file and a Boolean parameter. `x:True` and `x:False` is defined for XAML in the `http://schemas.microsoft.com/winfx/2006/xaml` namespace (code file `CompiledBindingMethods/MainPage.xaml`):

```
<TextBlock Text="{x:Bind ToName(Person1, x:False)}" />
<TextBlock Text="{x:Bind ToName(Person1, x:True)}" />
```

With these bindings in action, the `Person1` object is shown with either variant:

➤   FirstName LastName

➤   LastName, FirstName

How about changing values back? You can also define a method that is invoked with a two-way binding from the XAML code. The value from the property is passed to the method; you need to define a method to receive this parameter. When you bind a `Text` property of a `TextBlock`, a string is received. The `ToPerson2` method declares a parameter of type string. This value is split to assign its values to the `GivenName` and `Surname` properties of `Person2`. Because the `GivenName` and `Surname` properties don't implement change notification, the `Update` method is called explicitly to update the user interface (code file `CompiledBindingMethods/MainPage.xaml.cs`):

```
public void ToPerson2(string name)
{
  string[] names = name.Split(' ');
  if (names.Length != 2) return, // don't do anything with wrong inputs
  Person2.GivenName = names[0];
  Person2.Surname = names[1];
  Bindings.Update();
}
```

The method to invoke the method to receive the value of the `Text` property makes use of the `BindBack` property of the `x:Bind` markup extension. `BindBack` requires the name of the method. Also, the compiled binding needs to be declared `TwoWay` (code file `CompiledBindingMethods/MainPage.xaml`):

```
<TextBox
    Text="{x:Bind ToName(Person2, x:True), BindBack=ToPerson2, Mode=TwoWay}" />
<TextBlock Text="{x:Bind ToName(Person2, x:True)}" />
```

When you rung the app, you can see the bound values and change the value in the `TextBox` by using *binding to methods*.

Phasing with x:Bind

Users don't want to wait. Sometimes getting information takes some time. Using *phasing* can improve the user experience because you can offer some data earlier and update the user interface as more data is available.

> **NOTE** *If you're familiar with Priority Binding from WPF, compiled binding with phasing offers similar functionality with a different implementation.*

With phasing, you can define different phases with binding by using the `ListView` and `GridView` controls. Only these controls support phasing.

The example app implements a typical scenario: Data is retrieved from an API service that can take some time. In the meantime, other information should be displayed. Data is retrieved phase by phase. With every phase, the type of data returned can be different. The sample app just shows static information at first, but similar local cached information can be used for display.

The information retrieved from a service is defined by the `LunchMenu` class (code file `PhasedBinding/Models/LunchMenu.cs`):

```
public class LunchMenu
{
  public int MenuId { get; set; }
  public string Text { get; set; }
  public string ImageUrl { get; set; }
}
```

The `LunchMenuService` class simulates getting a list of menus from a service. Here it's just a memory list. Returning a simple list from the network depends on your network speed and the distance to the server, and you might not see a big difference between the phases. However, as more server-side processing is needed, the effects become easily visible. To simulate a longer process, a delay of ten seconds is done before returning the menu data from the method `GetLunchMenusAsync` (code file `PhasedBinding/Services/LunchMenuService.cs`):

```
public class LunchMenuService
{
  private IEnumerable<LunchMenu> _menusList = new List<LunchMenu>()
  {
    new LunchMenu { MenuId = 1, Text = "Chicken Salad", ImageUrl =
      "https://kantinem101.blob.core.windows.net/menuimages/Backhendelsalat"},
    new LunchMenu { MenuId = 2, Text = "Cordon Bleu", ImageUrl =
      "https://kantinem101.blob.core.windows.net/menuimages/CordonBleu_250"},
    new LunchMenu { MenuId = 3, Text = "Wiener Schnitzel", ImageUrl =
      "https://kantinem101.blob.core.windows.net/menuimages/" +
      "WienerSchnitzel_250"},
    new LunchMenu { MenuId = 4, Text = "Lasagne", ImageUrl =
      "https://kantinem101.blob.core.windows.net/menuimages/Lasagne_250"},
    new LunchMenu { MenuId = 5, Text = "Lentils with bacon and dumplings",
      ImageUrl =
        "https://kantinem101.blob.core.windows.net/menuimages/Linsen_250"},
    new LunchMenu { MenuId = 6, Text = "Schweinslungenbraten", ImageUrl =
      "https://kantinem101.blob.core.windows.net/menuimages/" +
      "Schweinslungenbraten_250"},
    new LunchMenu { MenuId = 7, Text = "Spätzle", ImageUrl =
      "https://kantinem101.blob.core.windows.net/menuimages/" +
      "Spinatspaetzle_250"},
    new LunchMenu { MenuId = 8, Text = "Topfennockerl", ImageUrl =
      "https://kantinem101.blob.core.windows.net/menuimages/" +
      "Topfennockerl_250"},
    new LunchMenu { MenuId = 9, Text = "Fried trout with potatoes", ImageUrl =
      "https://kantinem101.blob.core.windows.net/menuimages/forelle_250"},
  };

  public async Task<IEnumerable<LunchMenu>> GetLunchMenusAsync()
  {
    await Task.Delay(10000); // simulate a delay
    return _menusList;
  }
}
```

The list in the user interface is bound to a `LunchMenuViewModel`. This view-model class defines a property `LunchMenu` that returns one object of the same type as its name. In addition to that, the `IntroText` property is offered. This read-only property just returns static text. The intro text will be shown first before the result from the `LunchMenu` becomes available (code file `PhasedBinding/ViewModels/LunchMenuViewModel.cs`):

```
public class LunchMenuViewModel : BindableBase
{
  private LunchMenuService _service = new LunchMenuService();

  public LunchMenuViewModel()
  {
  }

  public string IntroText { get; } = "A Lunch";

  private LunchMenu _lunchMenu;
  public LunchMenu LunchMenu
  {
    get => _lunchMenu;
    set => Set(ref _lunchMenu, value);
  }
}
```

In the code-behind file, a list of `LunchViewModel` objects is created and assigned to the `LunchViewModels` property. At the start of the page, the property `IntroText` of this view-model is already initialized and can be displayed. After the page has been loaded, the `OnLoaded` method is invoked. In this method, the lunch menus are retrieved from the service, and the returned result is used to update the existing `LunchMenuViewModel` objects in the `ObservableCollection` (code file `PhasedBinding/MainPage.xaml.cs`):

```
public sealed partial class MainPage : Page
{
  private ObservableCollection<LunchMenuViewModel> _lunchViewModels =
    new ObservableCollection<LunchMenuViewModel>(
      Enumerable.Range(0, 8).Select(x => new LunchMenuViewModel()));

  private LunchMenuService _service = new LunchMenuService();
  public ObservableCollection<LunchMenuViewModel> LunchViewModels =>
    _lunchViewModels;

  public MainPage()
  {
    this.InitializeComponent();
    this.Loaded += OnLoaded;
  }

  private async void OnLoaded(object sender, RoutedEventArgs e)
  {
    try
    {
```

```
        List<LunchMenu> lunchMenus =
          (await _service.GetLunchMenusAsync()).ToList();
        for (int i = 0; i < 8; i++)
        {
          lunchViewModels[i].LunchMenu = lunchMenus[i];
        }
      }
      catch (Exception ex)
      {
        // TODO: log the exception
        throw;
      }
    }
  }
```

The important code now follows with the XAML syntax The `ListView` control binds to the `LunchViewModels` defined in the code behind. To define what should be displayed of the view-models, a `DataTemplate` is used. In this data template you can see in addition to the `x:Bind` markup expression, `x:Phase` attributes. The numbers defined with the `x:Phase` attribute specifies the phase ordering. The binding is done in the order of the binding phases. In the example code, in the first phase, just the value of the `IntroText` property is shown. You can also add local images. Phase 2 displays the text information from the `LunchMenu` property of the view-model, and phase 3 displays the image. Verify the different orders between phase 2 and phase 3 in the XAML code. To display the text over the image, the image is declared first. The `TextBox` in the first line is just to demonstrate that the UI is responsive while the data is loaded. You can enter some text and work with the UI while the different phases are processed (code file `PhasedBinding/MainPage.xaml`):

```xml
<TextBox Header="Enter Some Text" PlaceholderText=
  "UI is responsive - enter some text while the actual data is retrieved"
  Grid.Row="1" />
<ListView HorizontalAlignment="Center" x:Name="MenuItems"
  ItemsSource="{x:Bind LunchViewModels, Mode=OneWay}"
  SelectionMode="None" Grid.Row="2">
  <ListView.ItemTemplate>
    <DataTemplate x:DataType="vm:LunchMenuViewModel">
      <Grid Margin="12">
        <TextBlock Text="{x:Bind IntroText}" x:Phase="1" />
        <Image Width="300" Source="{x:Bind LunchMenu.ImageUrl, Mode=OneWay}"
          x:Phase="3" />
        <TextBlock Margin="8" VerticalAlignment="Bottom"
          HorizontalTextAlignment="Center"
          Text="{x:Bind LunchMenu.Text, Mode=OneWay}"
          Style="{StaticResource SubtitleTextBlockStyle}" FontWeight="Bold"
          x:Phase="2" />
      </Grid>
    </DataTemplate>
  </ListView.ItemTemplate>
</ListView>
```

When you run the app, you see the initial data first in Figure 36-11 and then you see the data updated with the menu information and the images as in Figure 36-12.

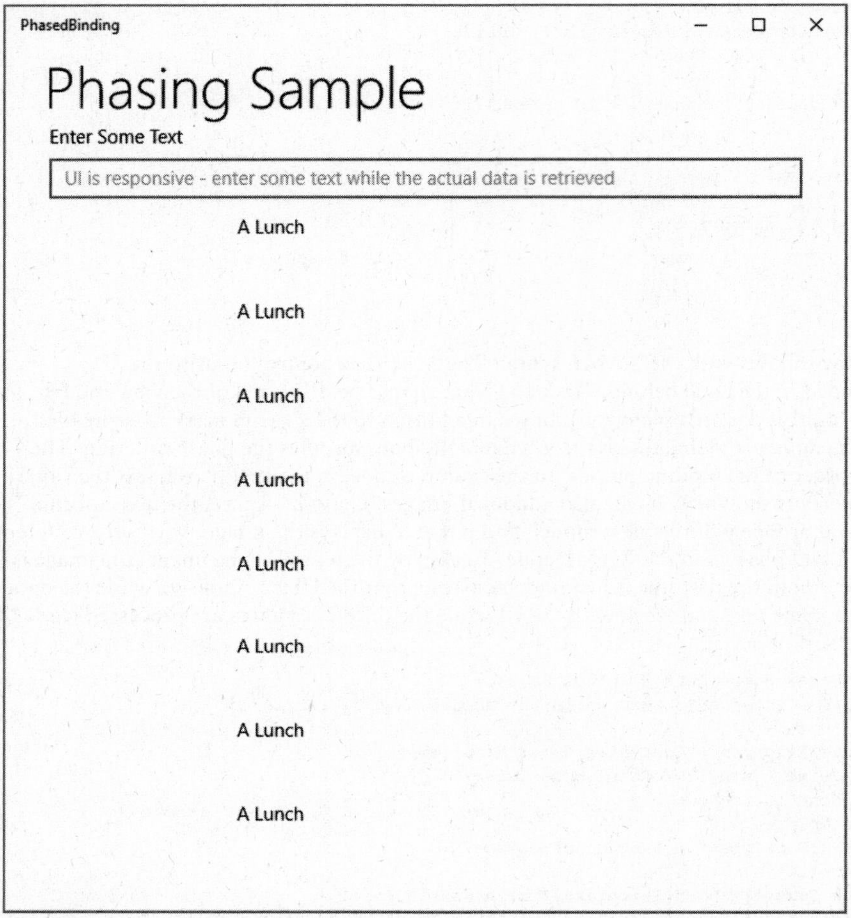

FIGURE 36-11

> **NOTE** *Chapter 33 shows how phases are implemented with the* `CalendarView` *control.*

FIGURE 36-12

USING TEXT

Windows apps have rich support for text. The `TextBlock` control not only supports displaying a simple string but it also supports more complex text elements such as using different styles, weight, inline elements, and block elements. The `RichTextBlock` control extends this functionality to allow overflow text; if one column is not enough, you can easily flow the information to overflow areas. With the `RichTextBox` control, working with RTF (rich text files) is supported.

Using Fonts

An important aspect of text is how it looks, and which makes the font important. With the `TextBlock` control, you can specify font with the properties `FontWeight`, `FontStyle`, `FontStretch`, `FontSize`, and `FontFamily`:

➤ `FontWeight`—Predefined values are specified by the `FontWeights` class, which offers values such as `ExtraLight`, `Light`, `Medium`, `Normal`, `Bold`, and `ExtraBold`.

➤ `FontStyle`—Values are defined by the `FontStyles` class, which offers `Normal`, `Italic`, and `Oblique`.

➤ `FontStretch`—Use this to specify the degrees to stretch the font compared to the normal aspect ratio. `FrontStretch` defines predefined stretches that range from 50% (`UltraCondensed`) to 200% (`UltraExpanded`). Predefined values in between the range are `ExtraCondensed` (62.5%), `Condensed` (75%), `SemiCondensed` (87.5%), `Normal` (100%), `SemiExpanded` (112.5%), `Expanded` (125%), and `ExtraExpanded` (150%).

➤ `FontSize`—This is of type `double` and enables you to specify the size of the font in device-independent units.

➤ `FontFamily`—Use this to define the name of the preferred font family—for example, Arial or Times New Roman. With this property you can specify a list of font family names, so if one font is not available, the next one in the list is used.

To give you a feel for the look of different fonts, the following sample app includes a `ListView`. The `ListView` shows the name of a font in the list displayed in that font. When you select the font, more information of the font is shown, such as the font with bold font weight, font style italic, font stretch expanded and condensed, and some text using the font (code file `FontsSample/MainPage.xaml`):

```xml
<ListView x:Name="listFonts" ItemsSource="{x:Bind FontNames, Mode=OneTime}"
  SelectedItem="{x:Bind SelectedFont, Mode=TwoWay}" Margin="12">
  <ListView.ItemTemplate>
    <DataTemplate x:DataType="x:String">
      <StackPanel Orientation="Horizontal">
        <TextBlock Text="{x:Bind Mode=OneTime}" FontFamily="{x:Bind }" />
      </StackPanel>
    </DataTemplate>
  </ListView.ItemTemplate>
</ListView>
<StackPanel Grid.Column="1" Margin="12" Padding="8">
  <TextBlock Text="{x:Bind SelectedFont, Mode=OneWay}"
    FontFamily="{x:Bind SelectedFont, Mode=OneWay}" />
  <TextBlock Text="Bold" FontFamily="{x:Bind SelectedFont, Mode=OneWay}"
    FontWeight="Bold" />
  <TextBlock Text="Italic" FontFamily="{x:Bind SelectedFont, Mode=OneWay}"
    FontStyle="Italic" />
  <TextBlock Text="Expanded" FontFamily="{x:Bind SelectedFont, Mode=OneWay}"
    FontStretch="Expanded" />
  <TextBlock Text="Condensed" FontFamily="{x:Bind SelectedFont, Mode=OneWay}"
    FontStretch="Condensed" />
  <TextBlock Text="The quick brown fox jumped over the lazy dogs"
    FontFamily="{x:Bind SelectedFont, Mode=OneWay}" />
  <TextBlock Text="&#xE700;&#xE701;&#xE702;"
    FontFamily="{x:Bind SelectedFont, Mode=OneWay}" />
  <TextBlock Text="&#x2467;&#x2468;&#x2469;"
    FontFamily="{x:Bind SelectedFont, Mode=OneWay}" />
</StackPanel>
```

In the code-behind, the fonts that are guaranteed available on a Windows 10 system are combined in a collection—fonts that are good for headings and UI elements such as Calibri, Consolas, and Segoe UI; fonts that are good for large amounts of text such as Cambria and Courier New; fonts for symbols and icons such as Segoe UI Emoji and Segoe MDL2 Assets; and non-latin fonts. The combined fonts are assigned to the

`FontNames` property. This property is bound from the UI. A dependency property is used for selecting the font (code file `FontsSample/MainPage.xaml.cs`):

```
public sealed partial class MainPage : Page
{
  public MainPage()
  {
    this.InitializeComponent();
    SelectedFont = FontNames.First();
  }

  // good for headings and UI elements
  private readonly string[] _sansSerifFontNames = { "Arial", "Calibri",
    "Consolas", "Segoe UI", "Segoe UI Historic", "Selawik", "Verdana" };

  // good for large amounts of text
  private readonly string[] _serifFontNames = { "Cambria", "Courier New",
    "Georgia", "Times New Roman" };

  // symbols and icons
  private readonly string[] _symbolsAndIconFontNames = { "Segoe MDL2 Assets",
    "Segoe UI Emoji", "Segoe UI Symbol" };

  // non-latin
  private readonly string[] _nonLatinFontNames = { "Ebrima", "Gadugi",
    "Javanese", "Leelawadee UI", "Malgun Gothic", "Microsoft Himalaya",
    "Microsoft JhengHei UI", "Microsoft PhagsPa", "Microsoft Tai Le",
    "Microsoft YaHei UI", "Microsoft Yi Baiti", "Mongolian Baiti", "MV Boli",
    "Myanmar Text", "Nirmala UI", "SimSun", "Yu Gothic", "Yu Gothic UI" };

  private string[] allFonts;
  public string[] FontNames => allFonts ?? (allFonts =
    _sansSerifFontNames.Concat(_serifFontNames)
      .Concat(_symbolsAndIconFontNames).Concat(_nonLatinFontNames).ToArray());

  public string SelectedFont
  {
    get => (string)GetValue(SelectedFontProperty);
    set => SetValue(SelectedFontProperty, value);
  }

  public static readonly DependencyProperty SelectedFontProperty =
    DependencyProperty.Register("SelectedFont", typeof(string),
      typeof(MainPage), new PropertyMetadata(string.Empty));
}
```

When you run the application, you get a list of these fonts with different characteristics, as shown in Figure 36-13.

> **NOTE** *Not all fonts have all characters defined. Some text might not be shown with the font Segoe MDL2 Assets, while this font shows icons at Unicode characters where other fonts don't have elements defined. Special characters shown or not shown can differ on what font extensions are installed on a system.*

Inline and Block Elements

When you define text elements, you need to differentiate elements that derive from the `Inline` class, and elements that derive from the `Block` class. `Inline` derives from the base class `TextElement`: all `Inline` elements are `TextElements` and represent a text. A `Block` element allows you to define a paragraph. The `Paragraph` class derives from `Block`. Blocks can contain `Inline` elements.

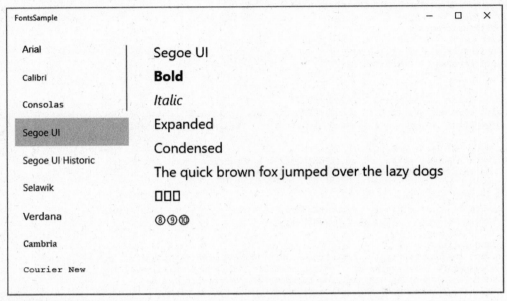

FIGURE 36-13

Let's have a look at the following `TextBlock` element containing `Bold`, `LineBreak`, `Hyperlink`, `Italic`, `Underline`, `Run`, and `Span` elements (code file `TextSample/MainPage.xaml`):

```
<TextBlock Margin="12" x:Name="text1" IsTextSelectionEnabled="True"
  SelectionHighlightColor="Green" FontFamily="Segoe UI" Foreground="Black">
  <Bold>This is bold.</Bold><LineBreak />
  <Hyperlink NavigateUri="https://csharp.christiannagel.com">
    C# Blog</Hyperlink><LineBreak />
  <Italic>This is italic.</Italic><LineBreak />
  <Underline>This is underlined.</Underline><LineBreak />
  <Run>Run element</Run><LineBreak />
  <Span>Span element</Span><LineBreak />
  <Span FontFamily="Calibri">
    <Run FontSize="24">A span can contain inlines</Run>
    <Italic>Italic is a span<LineBreak />
      and thus <Underline>underlines</Underline> can contain inlines as well
  </Span>
</TextBlock>
```

All the elements defined as the children of the `TextBlock` are added to the `Inlines` property. The class `TextBlock` defines the property `Inlines` as a `ContentProperty`, much as the `ButtonBase` class defines the property `Content` as a `ContentProperty`.

The classes `LineBreak`, `Run`, and `Span` derive from `Inline` and can be used in an `Inline` collection. The `Run` class defines a `Text` property that you can fill with text content, and you set font information with properties of the `Run` element. The `Span` element itself can be a container for further inline elements. `Bold`, `Italic`, and `Hyperlink` derive from `Span`; thus, they can be used as `Inline` elements as well, and they can contain other `Inline` elements.

Figure 36-14 shows the `TextBlock` element that contains all those `Inline` elements.

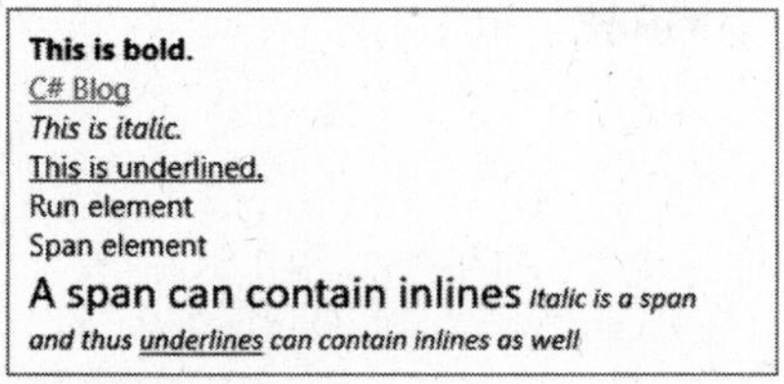

FIGURE 36-14

The RichTextBlock uses the Blocks property for its content. The Block class defines the text formatting properties LineHeight, LineStackingStrategy, Margin, and TextAlignment. Paragraph is the only concrete class that derives from Block, and it can be used with the Blocks property. The Block class is not abstract, but the constructor is declared with the protected access modifier.

The following code snippet uses multiple Paragraph elements within the RichTextBlock. The Paragraph itself contains a list of Inline elements (code file TextSample/MainPage.xaml):

```xml
<RichTextBlock>
  <Paragraph FontSize="18">Paragraph 1</Paragraph>
  <Paragraph LineStackingStrategy="BaselineToBaseline" LineHeight="16"
    TextAlignment="Justify">
    <Run FontStretch="ExtraExpanded" FontWeight="Black" Text="Paragraph 2" />
    <LineBreak />
    <Run>
      The quick brown fox jumped over the lazy dogs down 1234567890 times.
    </Run>
    <Run>
      The quick brown fox jumped over the lazy dogs down 1234567890 times.
    </Run>
  </Paragraph>
  <Paragraph>
    <Bold>Paragraph 3</Bold>
    <LineBreak />
    <InlineUIContainer>
      <Ellipse Width="30" Height="20" Fill="Red" />
    </InlineUIContainer>
    <LineBreak />
    <Run>More Text</Run>
  </Paragraph>
  <Paragraph LineStackingStrategy="BaselineToBaseline" LineHeight="16"
    TextAlignment="Left">
    <Run FontWeight="Bold" Text="Paragraph 4" />
    <LineBreak />
    <Run>
      The quick brown fox jumped over the lazy dogs down 1234567890 times.
    </Run>
    <Run>
      The quick brown fox jumped over the lazy dogs down 1234567890 times.
    </Run>
  </Paragraph>
</RichTextBlock>
```

When you run the app, you can see the RichTextBlock in Figure 36-15. If you compare paragraphs 2 and 4, you can see how the text aligns differently. Paragraph 2 is justified, and paragraph 4 is left aligned. Paragraph 3 contains an InlineUIContainer. InlineUIContainer is another Inline element; just be aware that this Inline element cannot be used with a TextBlock. It's displayed successfully in a RichTextBlock. InlineUIContainer elements can display other XAML elements. The sample code displays an Ellipse—a Shape class—within the RichTextBlock.

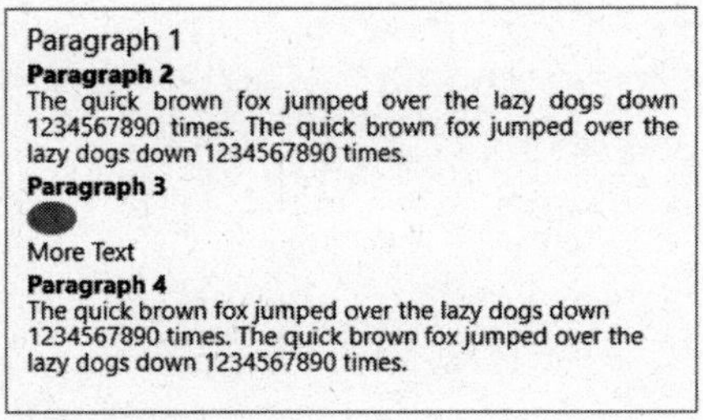

Paragraph 1
Paragraph 2
The quick brown fox jumped over the lazy dogs down
1234567890 times. The quick brown fox jumped over the
lazy dogs down 1234567890 times.
Paragraph 3

More Text
Paragraph 4
The quick brown fox jumped over the lazy dogs down
1234567890 times. The quick brown fox jumped over the
lazy dogs down 1234567890 times.

FIGURE 36-15

Using Overflow Areas

Compared to the `TextBlock`, the `RichTextBlock` can display multiple paragraphs. Another thing that's possible is to allow a `RichTextBlock` to overflow the text to another area if it doesn't fit. This time, the text is created programmatically. The `GetInlineElements` method returns a list of inline elements (code file `TextOverflow/MainPage.xaml.cs`):

```
public IEnumerable<Inline> GetInlineElements()
{
  var inlines = new List<Inline>();
  var header = new Bold();
  header.Inlines.Add(new Run { Text = "Lorem ipsum" });
  inlines.Add(header);
  inlines.Add(new LineBreak());
  inlines.Add(new Run { Text = "Lorem ipsum dolor sit amet, con... " });
  inlines.Add(new LineBreak());
  return inlines;
}
```

The `GetBlock` method returns a `Paragraph` that contains the inline elements (code file `TextOverflow/MainPage.xaml.cs`):

```
public Block GetBlock()
{
  var paragraph = new Paragraph { TextAlignment = TextAlignment.Justify };
  foreach (var inline in GetInlineElements())
  {
    paragraph.Inlines.Add(inline);
  }
  return paragraph;
}
```

When the page is loaded, the `Block` retrieved from the `GetBlock` method is added repeatedly to the `RichTextBlock` (code file `TextOverflow/MainPage.xaml.cs`):

```
public MainPage()
{
  InitializeComponent();
  Loaded += OnLoadData;
}

private void OnLoadData(object sender, RoutedEventArgs e)
{
  for (int i = 0; i < 8; i++)
  {
    textBlock.Blocks.Add(GetBlock());
  }
}
```

With the user interface, two `RichTextBlockOverflow` controls are adjacent to the `RichTextBlock`. From the `RichTextBlock`, overflow goes into the first `RichTextBlockOverflow`. This is defined by the `OverflowContentTarget` property. The same property is used to overflow the content from the first `RichContentBlockOverflow` control to the second (code file `TextOverflow/MainPage.xaml`):

```xml
<RichTextBlock x:Name="textBlock" TextWrapping="Wrap" Margin="20,0"
  OverflowContentTarget="{x:Bind overflowContainer1}"
  TextLineBounds="Full"></RichTextBlock>
<RichTextBlockOverflow Visibility="Collapsed" x:Name="overflowContainer1"
  Grid.Column="1" Margin="20,0"
  OverflowContentTarget="{x:Bind overflowContainer2}"></RichTextBlockOverflow>
<RichTextBlockOverflow Visibility="Collapsed" x:Name="overflowContainer2"
  Grid.Column="2" Margin="20,0"></RichTextBlockOverflow>
```

To automatically hide the overflow controls when the page is too small, the `RichTextBlockOverflow` controls are positioned within columns of a grid (code file `TextOverflow/MainPage.xaml`):

```xml
<Grid>
  <Grid.ColumnDefinitions>
    <ColumnDefinition />
    <ColumnDefinition x:Name="Column2" />
    <ColumnDefinition x:Name="Column3" />
  </Grid.ColumnDefinitions>

  <!-- RichTextBlock and overflow controls -->
</Grid>
```

With the help of an `AdaptiveTrigger`, the overflow containers are set to visible or collapsed. The `AdaptiveTrigger` also defines the size of the columns of the grid—to a size of 0 or to star sizing. With star sizing, the `RichTextBlock` and the `RichTextBlockOverflow` have the same width (code file `TextOverflow/MainPage.xaml`):

```xml
<VisualStateManager.VisualStateGroups>
  <VisualStateGroup>
    <VisualState x:Name="WideState">
      <VisualState.StateTriggers>
        <AdaptiveTrigger MinWindowWidth="1024" />
      </VisualState.StateTriggers>

      <VisualState.Setters>
        <Setter Target="overflowContainer1.Visibility" Value="Visible" />
        <Setter Target="overflowContainer2.Visibility" Value="Visible" />
        <Setter Target="Column3.Width" Value="*" />
        <Setter Target="Column2.Width" Value="*" />
      </VisualState.Setters>
    </VisualState>

    <VisualState x:Name="MediumState">
      <VisualState.StateTriggers>
        <AdaptiveTrigger MinWindowWidth="720" />
      </VisualState.StateTriggers>

      <VisualState.Setters>
        <Setter Target="overflowContainer1.Visibility" Value="Visible" />
        <Setter Target="overflowContainer2.Visibility" Value="Collapsed" />
        <Setter Target="Column3.Width" Value="0" />
        <Setter Target="Column2.Width" Value="*" />
      </VisualState.Setters>
    </VisualState>

    <VisualState x:Name="NarrowState">
      <VisualState.StateTriggers>
```

```
        <AdaptiveTrigger MinWindowWidth="320" />
    </VisualState.StateTriggers>

    <VisualState.Setters>
      <Setter Target="overflowContainer1.Visibility" Value="Collapsed" />
      <Setter Target="overflowContainer2.Visibility" Value="Collapsed" />
      <Setter Target="Column3.Width" Value="0" />
      <Setter Target="Column2.Width" Value="0" />
    </VisualState.Setters>
  </VisualState>
  </VisualStateGroup>
</VisualStateManager.VisualStateGroups>
```

> **NOTE** *Adaptive triggers are discussed in Chapter 33.*

When you run the application, you can see the overflow with a wide screen size and two overflow controls (see Figure 36-16), a medium screen size and one overflow control (see Figure 36-17), or a narrow screen without overflow controls (see Figure 36-18).

FIGURE 36-16

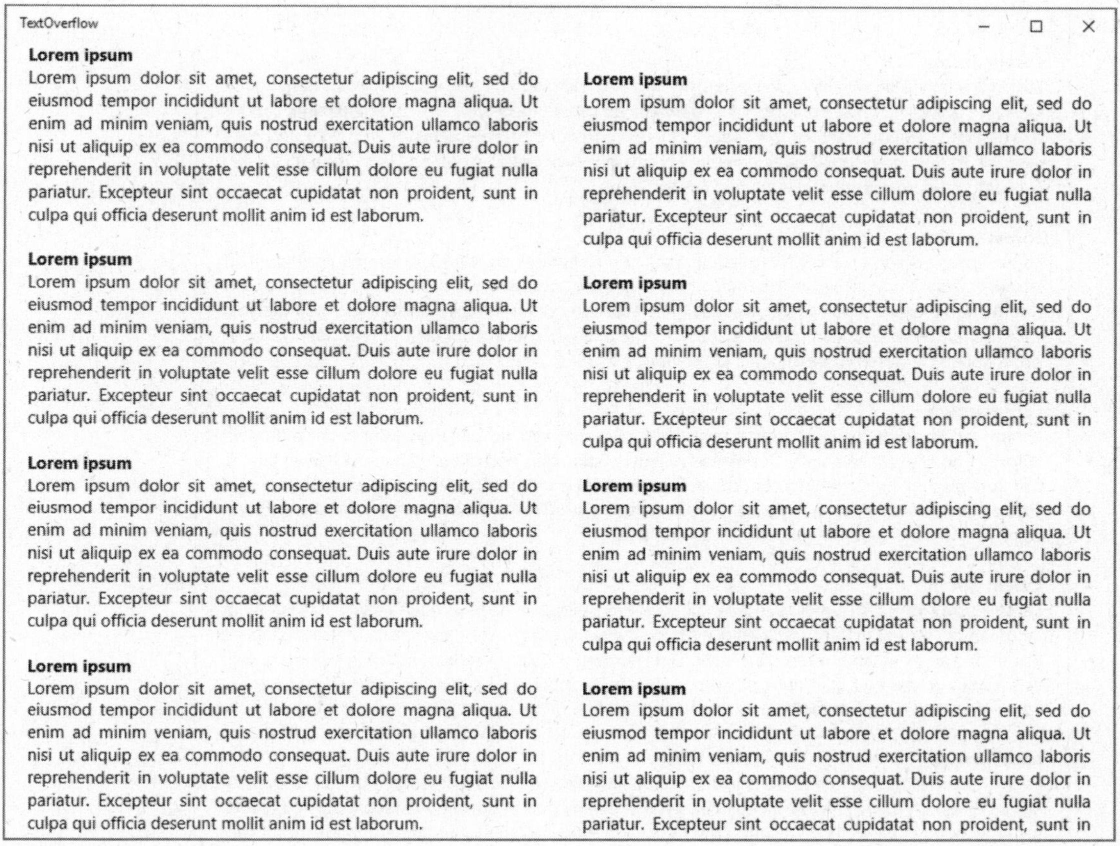

TextOverflow — □ ✕

Lorem ipsum

Lorem ipsum dolor sit amet, consectetur adipiscing elit, sed do eiusmod tempor incididunt ut labore et dolore magna aliqua. Ut enim ad minim veniam, quis nostrud exercitation ullamco laboris nisi ut aliquip ex ea commodo consequat. Duis aute irure dolor in reprehenderit in voluptate velit esse cillum dolore eu fugiat nulla pariatur. Excepteur sint occaecat cupidatat non proident, sunt in culpa qui officia deserunt mollit anim id est laborum.

Lorem ipsum

Lorem ipsum dolor sit amet, consectetur adipiscing elit, sed do eiusmod tempor incididunt ut labore et dolore magna aliqua. Ut enim ad minim veniam, quis nostrud exercitation ullamco laboris nisi ut aliquip ex ea commodo consequat. Duis aute irure dolor in reprehenderit in voluptate velit esse cillum dolore eu fugiat nulla pariatur. Excepteur sint occaecat cupidatat non proident, sunt in culpa qui officia deserunt mollit anim id est laborum.

Lorem ipsum

Lorem ipsum dolor sit amet, consectetur adipiscing elit, sed do eiusmod tempor incididunt ut labore et dolore magna aliqua. Ut enim ad minim veniam, quis nostrud exercitation ullamco laboris nisi ut aliquip ex ea commodo consequat. Duis aute irure dolor in reprehenderit in voluptate velit esse cillum dolore eu fugiat nulla pariatur. Excepteur sint occaecat cupidatat non proident, sunt in culpa qui officia deserunt mollit anim id est laborum.

Lorem ipsum

Lorem ipsum dolor sit amet, consectetur adipiscing elit, sed do eiusmod tempor incididunt ut labore et dolore magna aliqua. Ut enim ad minim veniam, quis nostrud exercitation ullamco laboris nisi ut aliquip ex ea commodo consequat. Duis aute irure dolor in reprehenderit in voluptate velit esse cillum dolore eu fugiat nulla pariatur. Excepteur sint occaecat cupidatat non proident, sunt in culpa qui officia deserunt mollit anim id est laborum.

Lorem ipsum

Lorem ipsum dolor sit amet, consectetur adipiscing elit, sed do eiusmod tempor incididunt ut labore et dolore magna aliqua. Ut enim ad minim veniam, quis nostrud exercitation ullamco laboris nisi ut aliquip ex ea commodo consequat. Duis aute irure dolor in reprehenderit in voluptate velit esse cillum dolore eu fugiat nulla pariatur. Excepteur sint occaecat cupidatat non proident, sunt in culpa qui officia deserunt mollit anim id est laborum.

Lorem ipsum

Lorem ipsum dolor sit amet, consectetur adipiscing elit, sed do eiusmod tempor incididunt ut labore et dolore magna aliqua. Ut enim ad minim veniam, quis nostrud exercitation ullamco laboris nisi ut aliquip ex ea commodo consequat. Duis aute irure dolor in reprehenderit in voluptate velit esse cillum dolore eu fugiat nulla pariatur. Excepteur sint occaecat cupidatat non proident, sunt in culpa qui officia deserunt mollit anim id est laborum.

Lorem ipsum

Lorem ipsum dolor sit amet, consectetur adipiscing elit, sed do eiusmod tempor incididunt ut labore et dolore magna aliqua. Ut enim ad minim veniam, quis nostrud exercitation ullamco laboris nisi ut aliquip ex ea commodo consequat. Duis aute irure dolor in reprehenderit in voluptate velit esse cillum dolore eu fugiat nulla pariatur. Excepteur sint occaecat cupidatat non proident, sunt in culpa qui officia deserunt mollit anim id est laborum.

Lorem ipsum

Lorem ipsum dolor sit amet, consectetur adipiscing elit, sed do eiusmod tempor incididunt ut labore et dolore magna aliqua. Ut enim ad minim veniam, quis nostrud exercitation ullamco laboris nisi ut aliquip ex ea commodo consequat. Duis aute irure dolor in reprehenderit in voluptate velit esse cillum dolore eu fugiat nulla pariatur. Excepteur sint occaecat cupidatat non proident, sunt in

FIGURE 36-17

INKING

More and more Windows 10 devices make use of a pen. With the pen, inking is an important concept, and it's easily supported by Windows apps. All you need to do is to use the `InkCanvas` control to do some drawing. This control supports inking using the pen, touchscreen, and mouse, and it also supports retrieving all the created strokes, which makes it possible to save this information (code file `InkSample/MainPage.xaml`):

```
<Grid Background="{ThemeResource ApplicationPageBackgroundThemeBrush}">
  <InkCanvas x:Name="inkCanvas" Margin="8,32,8,8" />
  <!-- ... -->
```

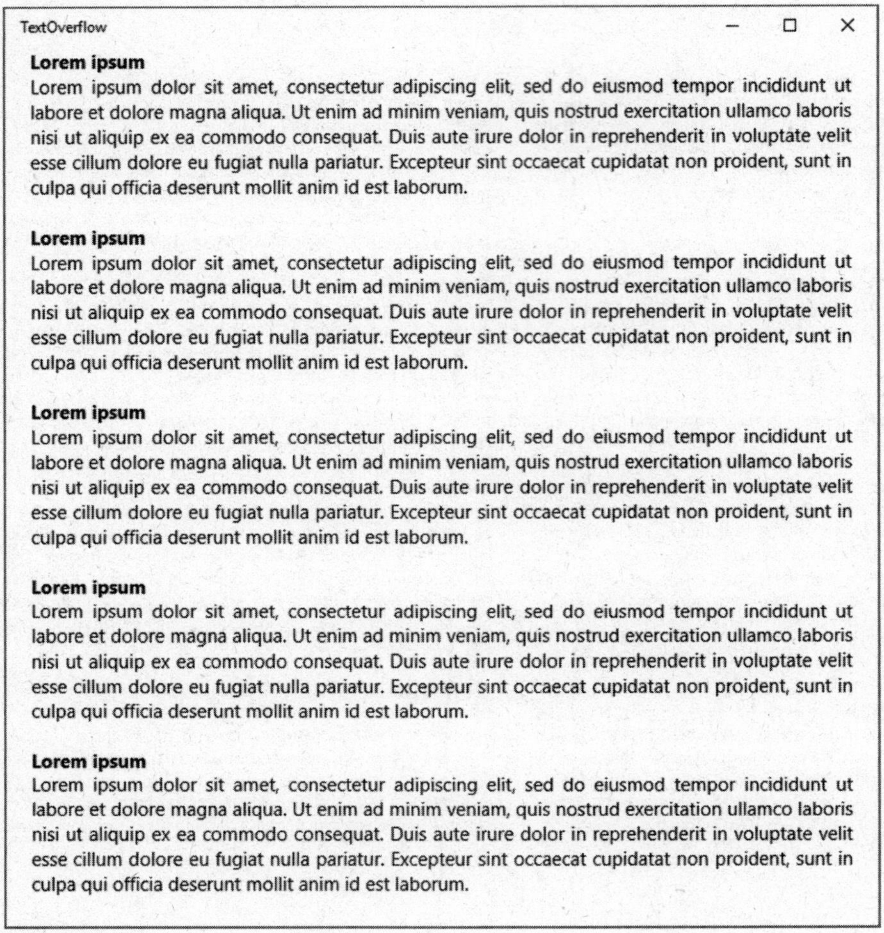

FIGURE 36-18

By default, the `InkCanvas` control is configured to support the pen. You can also define it to support the mouse and touchscreen by setting the `InputDevicesType` property of the `InkPresenter` (code file `InkSample/MainPage.xaml.cs`):

```
public MainPage()
{
  this.InitializeComponent();
  inkCanvas.InkPresenter.InputDeviceTypes = CoreInputDeviceTypes.Mouse |
    CoreInputDeviceTypes.Touch | CoreInputDeviceTypes.Pen;
    ColorSelection = new ColorSelection(inkCanvas);
}
```

With the `InkCanvas` in place, you already can use an input device and create the same drawings with a black pen. To change the pen configuration, there's also a `InkToolBar`. This toolbar needs to be associated with the `InkCanvas` using the `TargetInkCanvas` property. With the example app, another toolbar that is positioned right of the `InkToolBar` is used to open and save a file with the ink strokes (code file `InkSample/MainPage.xaml`):

```
<RelativePanel VerticalAlignment="Top">
  <InkToolbar x:Name="inkToolbar" RelativePanel.AlignLeftWithPanel="True"
```

```
       RelativePanel.AlignTopWithPanel="True"
       TargetInkCanvas="{x:Bind inkCanvas}" />
    <CommandBar RelativePanel.RightOf="inkToolbar"
      Template="{StaticResource CommandBarControlTemplate1}">
      <AppBarButton Icon="OpenFile" IsCompact="True" Click="{x:Bind OnLoad}"
        ToolTipService.ToolTip="Open File" />
      <AppBarButton Icon="Save" IsCompact="True" Click="{x:Bind OnSave}"
        ToolTipService.ToolTip="Save" />
      <AppBarButton Icon="Clear" IsCompact="True" Click="{x:Bind OnClear}"
        ToolTipService.ToolTip="Clear" />
    </CommandBar>
  </RelativePanel>
```

The `InkToolBar` offers buttons to customize the colors and the size of the pen as shown in Figure 36-19.
You can also to select a ruler (see Figure 36-20) and a protractor (see Figure 36-21).

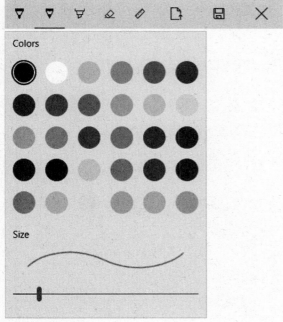

FIGURE 36-19

As previously mentioned, the `InkCanvas` control also supports accessing the created strokes. These strokes
are used with the following sample to store it in a file. The file is selected using the `FileSavePicker`. The
method `OnSave` is invoked when the user clicks the `Save AppBarButton` that was created previously. First,
the `FileSavePicker` is configured by assigning a start location, a file type extension, and a filename. At
least one file type choice needs to be added to allow the user to select a file type. When you invoke the
method `PickSaveFileAsync`, the user is asked to select a file. This file is opened for transactional write
access by invoking the method `OpenTransactedWriteAsync`. The strokes of the `InkCanvas` are stored
in the `StrokeContainer` of the `InkPresenter`. The strokes can be directly saved to a stream with the
`SaveAsync` method (code file `InkSample/MainPage.xaml.cs`):

```
    private const string FileTypeExtension = ".strokes";
    public async void OnSave()
    {
      var picker = new FileSavePicker
      {
```

```
    SuggestedStartLocation = PickerLocationId.PicturesLibrary,
    DefaultFileExtension = FileTypeExtension,
    SuggestedFileName = "sample"
};

picker.FileTypeChoices.Add("Stroke File", new List<string>()
{ FileTypeExtension });

StorageFile file = await picker.PickSaveFileAsync();
if (file != null)
{
  using (StorageStreamTransaction tx = await file.OpenTransactedWriteAsync())
  {
    await inkCanvas.InkPresenter.StrokeContainer.SaveAsync(tx.Stream);
    await tx.CommitAsync();
  }
}
}
```

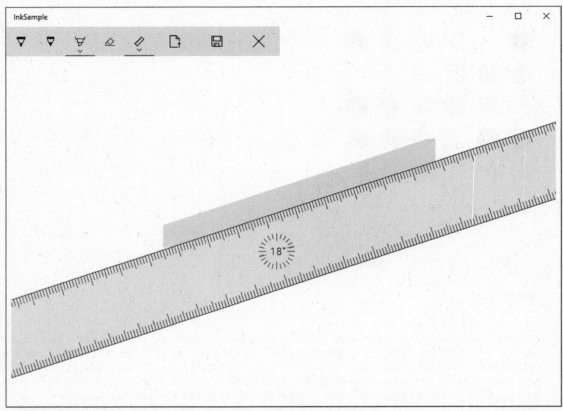

FIGURE 36-20

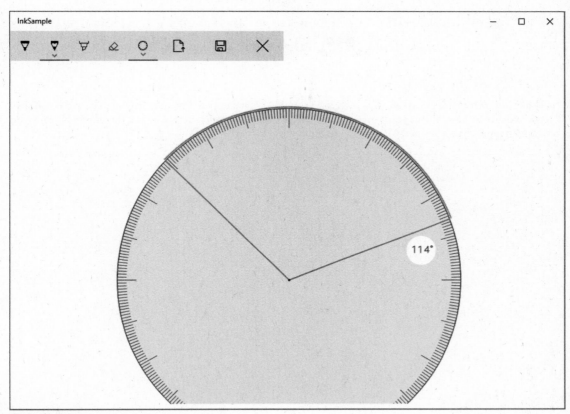

FIGURE 36-21

> **NOTE** *Using the* `FileOpenPicker` *and* `FileSavePicker` *to read and write streams is discussed in more detail in Chapter 22, "Files and Streams."*

To load a file, you use `FileOpenPicker` and `StrokeContainer` with the `LoadAsync` method (code file `InkSample/MainPage.xaml.cs`):

```
public async void OnLoad()
{
  var picker = new FileOpenPicker
  {
    SuggestedStartLocation = PickerLocationId.PicturesLibrary
  };

  picker.FileTypeFilter.Add(FileTypeExtension);
  StorageFile file = await picker.PickSingleFileAsync();
  if (file != null)
```

```
          {
            using (var stream = await file.OpenReadAsync())
            {
              await inkCanvas.InkPresenter.StrokeContainer.LoadAsync(stream);
            }
          }
        }
```

When you run the application, as shown in Figure 36-22, it's easy to create a drawing using the pen. In case you don't have a pen, you can also use a finger with your touch device or use the mouse because the `InputDeviceTypes` property has been configured accordingly.

FIGURE 36-22

AUTOSUGGEST

The search functionality has some history with Windows. In Windows 8, search functionality was on a charms bar that the user needed to swipe to open . With Windows 10, this was replaced by the `SearchBox` control. Now, the `SearchBox` is replaced by the `AutoSuggestBox` control. This control allows offering suggestions to the user as the user types into the control.

Three events are important with this control. As soon as the user types into the control, the `TextChanged` event is fired. With the sample code, the `OnTextChanged` handler method is invoked. In cases where suggestions are offered to the user and the user selects a suggestion, the `SuggestionChosen` event is fired. After the text—which might be a suggestion or other words typed—is entered by the user, the `QuerySubmitted` event is fired (code file `AutoSuggestSample/MainPage.xaml`):

```
<AutoSuggestBox Header="Formula 1 Champion"
  TextChanged="{x:Bind OnTextChanged}"
  SuggestionChosen="{x:Bind OnSuggestionChosen}"
  QuerySubmitted="{x:Bind OnQuerySubmitted}" />
```

To have some example code to create a suggestion, load the XML file containing Formula 1 champions from `http://www.cninnovation.com/downloads/Racers.xml` using the `HttpClient` class. When you navigate to the page, the XML file is retrieved, and the content is converted to a list of `Racer` objects (code file `AutoSuggestSample/MainPage.xaml.cs`):

```
private const string RacersUri =
  "http://www.cninnovation.com/downloads/Racers.xml";
private IEnumerable<Racer> _racers;

protected async override void OnNavigatedTo(NavigationEventArgs e)
{
  base.OnNavigatedTo(e);
  XElement xmlRacers = null;
  using (var client = new HttpClient())
  using (Stream stream = await client.GetStreamAsync(RacersUri))
  {
    xmlRacers = XElement.Load(stream);
  }

  _racers = xmlRacers.Elements("Racer").Select(r => new Racer
  {
    FirstName = r.Element("Firstname").Value,
    LastName = r.Element("Lastname").Value,
    Country = r.Element("Country").Value
  }).ToList();
}
```

The `Racer` class contains `FirstName`, `LastName`, and `Country` properties and an overload of the `ToString` method (code file `AutoSuggestSample/Models/Racer.cs`):

```
public class Racer
{
  public string FirstName { get; set; }
  public string LastName { get; set; }
  public string Country { get; set; }
  public override string ToString() => $"{FirstName} {LastName}, {Country}";
}
```

The `OnTextChanged` event is invoked as soon as the text of the `AutoSuggestBox` changes. Arguments received are the `AutoSuggestBox` itself—the sender—and `AutoSuggestBoxTextChangedEventArgs`. With the `AutoSuggestBoxTextChangedEventArgs`, the reason for the change is shown in the `Reason` property. Possible reasons are `UserInput`, `ProgrammaticChange`, and `SuggestionChosen`. Only if the reason is `UserInput` is there a need to offer suggestions to the user. Here, a check is also done to see whether the user entered at least two characters. The user input is retrieved by accessing the `Text` property of the `AutoSuggestBox`. This text is used to query the first names, last names, and countries based on the input string. The result from the query is assigned to the `ItemsSource` property of the `AutoSuggestBox` (code file `AutoSuggestSample/MainPage.xaml.cs`):

```
private void OnTextChanged(AutoSuggestBox sender,
  AutoSuggestBoxTextChangedEventArgs args)
{
  if (args.Reason == AutoSuggestionBoxTextChangeReason.UserInput &&
    sender.Text.Length >= 2)
```

```
    {
      string input = sender.Text;
      var racers = _racers.Where(
        r => r.FirstName.StartsWith(input,
          StringComparison.CurrentCultureIgnoreCase))
          .OrderBy(r => r.FirstName).ThenBy(r => r.LastName)
          .ThenBy(r => r.Country).ToArray();

      if (racers.Length == 0)
      {
        racers = _racers.Where(r => r.LastName.StartsWith(input,
          StringComparison.CurrentCultureIgnoreCase))
          .OrderBy(r => r.LastName).ThenBy(r => r.FirstName)
          .ThenBy(r => r.Country).ToArray();

        if (racers.Length == 0)
        {
          racers = _racers.Where(r => r.Country.StartsWith(input,
            StringComparison.CurrentCultureIgnoreCase))
            .OrderBy(r => r.Country).ThenBy(r => r.LastName)
            .ThenBy(r => r.FirstName).ToArray();
        }
      }

    sender.ItemsSource = racers;
    }
}
```

When you run the app and enter Aus in the `AutoSuggestBox`, the query can't find first or last names start-ing with this text, but it does find countries. Formula 1 champions from countries starting with Aus are shown in the suggestion list, as shown in Figure 36-23.

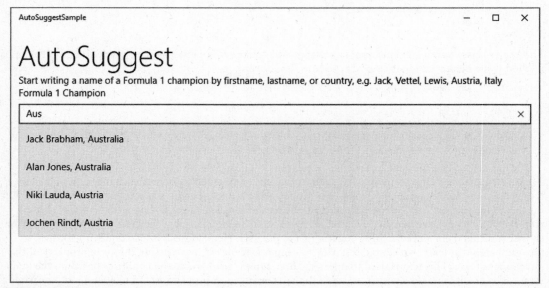

FIGURE 36-23

In cases where the user selects one of the suggestions, the `OnSuggestionChosen` handler is invoked. The sugges-tion can be retrieved from the `SelectedItem` property of the `AutoSuggestBoxSuggestionChosenEventArgs`:

```
private async void OnSuggestionChosen(AutoSuggestBox sender,
  AutoSuggestBoxSuggestionChosenEventArgs args)
```

```
  {
    var dlg = new MessageDialog($"suggestion: {args.SelectedItem}");
    await dlg.ShowAsync();
  }
```

No matter whether the user selects a suggestion, the OnQuerySubmitted method gets invoked to show the result. The result is shown in the QueryText property of the AutoSuggestBoxQuerySubmittedEventArgs argument. In case a suggestion was selected, this is found in the ChosenSuggestion property:

```
private async void OnQuerySubmitted(AutoSuggestBox sender,
AutoSuggestBoxQuerySubmittedEventArgs args)
{
  string message = $"query: {args.QueryText}";
  if (args.ChosenSuggestion != null)
  {
    message += $" suggestion: {args.ChosenSuggestion}";
  }
  var dlg = new MessageDialog(message);
  await dlg.ShowAsync();
}
```

SUMMARY

This chapter provided more information on writing Windows apps. You've seen how the life cycle is different compared to Window desktop applications, and how you need to take action on the Suspending event.

Interaction with other apps was covered by using share contracts. The DataTransferManager was used to offer HTML data for other apps. Implementing a share target contract enables the app to receive data from other apps.

This chapter showed you some features with compiled binding, such as binding properties to methods and phasing.

The next chapter continues with XAML for mobile devices using Xamarin for iPhone and Android.

37

Xamarin.Forms

WHAT'S IN THIS CHAPTER?

- ➤ Tools for Xamarin development
- ➤ Application architectures with Android and iOS
- ➤ Using Xamarin.Forms
- ➤ Pages
- ➤ Navigation
- ➤ Layout
- ➤ Views
- ➤ Data binding and commands

WROX.COM CODE DOWNLOADS FOR THIS CHAPTER

The wrox.com code downloads for this chapter are found at www.wrox.com on the Download Code tab. The source code is also available at `https://github.com/ProfessionalCSharp/ProfessionalCSharp7` in the directories `Xamarin` and `PatternsXamarinShared`.

The code for this chapter is divided into the following major examples:

- ➤ AndroidSample
- ➤ iPhoneSample
- ➤ BooksAppX (Xamarin.Forms)

STARTING WITH XAMARIN DEVELOPMENT

Mobile app development is shared mainly between two products: iOS from Apple and Android from Google. Native development on iOS is done using the programming languages Objective-C or Swift and Cocoa and Cocoa Touch frameworks. Cocoa is the name of Apple's API. When developing for Android, you use the Android Software Development Kit from Google, and Java is the main programming language.

Instead of rewriting the code using different programming languages, you can use C# and XAML. Xamarin offers cross-platform development, and you can still use the native APIs.

As Xamarin was bought by Microsoft, and because the Xamarin tools integration in Visual Studio is becoming better and better, productivity can be increased with many apps using cross-platform technologies.

This chapter gives you an introduction to start creating Xamarin apps. Using the foundation you learned from other chapters about C#, .NET Core, and XAML, you can start your app development with Xamarin after reading this chapter. There is a lot more that is covered in other books that cover only Xamarin, but this is a good start.

> **NOTE** *To create and compile the samples from this chapter, you need to have the Mobile Development with .NET workload installed on your Windows system. As an alternative, you can use Visual Studio for Mac. Having an Android phone helps to run the Android apps. To create and compile the iOS samples, you need a Mac for compilation, and an iPhone is useful as well.*

Architecture Xamarin with Android

When you're creating Xamarin apps for Android phones, it's good to know what happens behind the scenes. Figure 37-1 gives you an overview architecture. Android is running on the Linux kernel. From Google you can see the Android SDK running on top of the Android Runtime (ART). The left side of this figure shows the .NET part—the .NET APIs that make use of the .NET Mono runtime. The Mono runtime and the ART run parallel in the process of your app. A Mono Callable Wrapper (MCW) is used to invoke the Android SDKs from .NET. It's also possible the other way around: To get into .NET from Android, use an Android Callable Wrapper (ACW). Probably you have used .NET with COM (the Component Object Model from Microsoft) sometime in the past. Here, the architecture is very similar with Runtime Callable Wrappers (RCW) and COM Callable Wrappers (CCW). To make it easy to get into the Android SDK from .NET, Xamarin created Android Bindings.

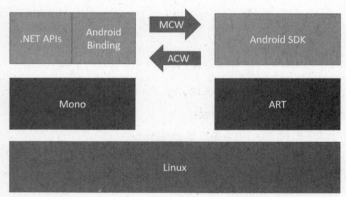

FIGURE 37-1

In case you want to use an existing Java library that is not part of the Android SDK to be called from .NET, you can create an MCW.

Xamarin.Android makes the Java APIs from Android available for .NET, and it's huge. You can find the APIs at https://developer.xamarin.com/api/root/MonoAndroid-lib/. I mention just a few important namespaces here: The `Android.App` namespace with the `Activity` class, the `Service` class for long-running background operations, and the `Android.Widget` namespace with UI elements. The documentation on the Xamarin site misses a lot of information that you can directly read at the source: `https://developer.android.com/reference/packages.html`. As the types are mapped, the information from `https://developer.android.com` applies.

Architecture Xamarin with iOS

The architecture of Xamarin apps on iOS is different. Because of security restrictions on iOS, it's not allowed to execute dynamic generated code on the device. That's why Xamarin uses an ahead-of-time (AOT) compiler to compile the IL code that is created from the C# compiler to native code. This gives a great runtime performance and better startup times, but it also has some restrictions. C# compiles generics to generic IL types. Using generic types with a just-in-time (JIT) compiler, the generics are resolved when the IL code is compiled at runtime. Using an AOT compiler, the IL code needs to be compiled before it is deployed on the device. That's why generics can't be used in some scenarios. For example, it's not possible to create generic methods in classes that derive from NSObject. Generics also cannot be used with P/Invoke. With Android. iOS, P/Invoke is used to define a method with C#, but it uses its implementation from Objective-C. Also, reflection is limited. You can't emit code with reflection; dynamic code generation is not allowed. Some more features from the Mono iOS Runtime are disabled—for example, the metadata verifier and the JIT engine— because the IL code is already precompiled.

Figure 37-2 gives an overview picture of the iOS architecture with Xamarin. iOS uses a UNIX-like kernel with the Objective-C runtime and iOS APIs on top. The .NET APIs bind to the iOS APIs to offer the same functionality and use the AOT compiler with a reduced Mono runtime.

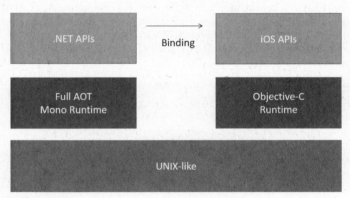

FIGURE 37-2

You can find the documentation for Xamarin.iOS at `https://developer.xamarin.com/api/root/ios-unified/`. Many SDKs are available from Xamarin for iOS. The main section for the user interface is the UIKit namespace. You can find information from Apple at `https://developer.apple.com/documentation/uikit`.

Luckily, you can use C# and XAML to develop for these platforms. Xamarin offers cross-platform development, but it still uses all the features from the platforms.

> **NOTE** *You might wonder why the iOS classes for the user interface have the* `UI` *prefix. The reason is that Objective-C—the programming language used to implement native iOS apps—doesn't support namespaces. For avoiding conflicts with other classes, classes for the user interface have the* `UI` *prefix, and classes from other areas have other prefixes. Classes from the* `Xamarin.iOS.Contacts` *namespace have the prefix* `CN`—*for example,* `CNContact`.

> **NOTE** *You'll also find Xamarin.iOS (classic) is different from Xamarin.iOS, which is also marked as "unified." Xamarin.iOS (classic) was only for the iPhone, whereas the newer version Xamarin.iOS uses a unified API for the iPhone, iPad, and the Mac. The classic API is also limited to 32-bit, which can no longer be used anymore in the App Store.*

Xamarin.Forms

Using Xamarin, you can use Xamarin.Android to create Android apps, Xamarin.iOS to create iOS apps, or Xamarin.Forms to create apps for Android, iOS, Windows, and more platforms.

With Xamarin.Android, you have the complete API and all controls of the Android SDK available. With Xamarin.iOS, you see the full range of the iOS SDKs that are accessible from C#. When you use either Xamarin.Android or Xamarin.iOS, you create separate user interfaces and use platform-specific code, but you can share your business logic and services.

With Xamarin.Forms, you can share the user interface code, and you can create the user interface with XAML code. However, contrary to the Universal Windows Platform where vector graphics are used to draw the elements, Xamarin.Forms renders the user interface using the native controls of every platform. Using the native controls has a big advantage as you get the look and performance of the native controls of every platform. There's also a disadvantage, though. With Xamarin.Forms, you only get controls that can map to every platform. You don't have controls that are available only on Android. You can implement a custom, platform-specific renderer to use platform-specific controls or features from platform controls that are not directly accessible from Xamarin.Forms.

> **NOTE** *Do you remember Windows Forms? Windows Forms is a wrapper of the native Windows controls. Maybe the name Xamarin.Forms was chosen because it's also a wrapper to native controls. Xamarin.Forms wraps the native controls on iOS, Android, and Windows.*

TOOLS FOR XAMARIN DEVELOPMENT

When you're create apps for Android and iOS, you need to know the versions of the platforms to support and the tools you need.

Android

When developing for Windows, you learned to specify the minimum and target version to develop your application for. This is very similar with Android. With Android, you have a version of Android with a code name that corresponds to a numbered API level.

You need to decide what version of the platform you want to support. A reason for support probably is the distribution on the market. The following table lists the latest versions of Android versions with their code names, API levels, and a percentage how many Android phones access the Google Playground. At the time of this writing (January 2018), Lollipop (5.0), API level 21 is the oldest version supported by Google, but KitKat 4.4 still has a market share of 12.8%. Marshmallow has the biggest market share with 28.6%. You can use this information to decide what Android version you need to support. Oreo was released in August 2017, but it is still way behind in market share. Many newly sold devices don't come with the newest Android versions installed, and not all phones can be updated to the newest versions. See https://developer.android.com/about/dashboards/index.html for actual distributions.

VERSION	CODENAME	API LEVEL	DISTRIBUTION	FEATURES
4.4	KitKat	19	12.8%	Printing using cloud services, a new storage access framework, NFC-based transactions, hardware sensor batching, step detector and step counter
5.0 5.1	Lollipop	21 22	25.1%	Material design, new widgets, JobScheduler
6.0	Marshmallow	23	28.6%	Permission architecture changed, voice interactions
7.0 7.1	Nougat	24 25	26.3%	Split-screen, enhanced notifications, app shortcuts (secondary tiles)
8.0 8.1	Oreo	26 27	0.7%	Adaptive icons, downloadable fonts, WebView APIs

> **NOTE** *The Android code names are alphabetical by their release times. Cupcake (1.5) was followed by Donut (1.6), Eclair (2.0), Froyo (2.2), Gingerbread (2.3), Honeycomb (3.0), Ice Cream Sandwich (4.0), Jelly Bean (4.1), KitKat (4.4), Lollipop (5.0), Marshmallow (6.0), Nougat (7.0), and Oreo (8.0).*

When you develop for Android, you need to install the Android SDKs you need for the versions you support as well as the simulators. Microsoft recently created its own Android and SDK Tools extension that makes it easier to install Android platforms and tools (see Figure 37-3). You can access it from Visual Studio Tools ➪ Android ➪ Android SDK Manager.

You can also use emulators that you can configure with the Android Emulator Manager. It helps if you can use real devices; they are usually faster than emulators. You should test on multiple devices. Different devices from the same hardware vendor can behave differently. It's not likely that you'll not go buy hundreds of devices from different vendors that use different platform versions, so there's an option. With Visual Studio App Center, you can use the Test Cloud to test your apps on thousands of physical devices. You just need to create a UI test and—after a 30-day free period—pay a monthly fee, which is probably cheaper than buying all those phones.

FIGURE 37-3

To use your Android device, you need to enable it for debugging. Then just connect it to the USB port of your computer. Although a Windows device can be enabled for developers by selecting Developer Mode in the Update settings, with Android you need to open the Settings page and tap the build number seven times.

iOS

For developing iOS applications, you need a Mac to build the XCode. If you're using Visual Studio 2016 version 15.6, pairing has been made easy. From Visual Studio Tools ➪ iOS ➪ Pair to Mac, you can pair to your Mac and remotely install the Android SDKs you need. During this process, you also get the information to register with the Apple portal and to provision your physical device, so it can be used for debugging.

When you're creating an app for iOS, you also need to decide what iOS version you support. The versions of iOS are numbered, and there are not too many device types you need to support. To see the what iPhone and iPad devices support which iOS versions, check `http://iossupportmatrix.com/`.

iOS users are faster at updating to the newer iOS versions than Android users are. You can see the number of devices using the App Store at `https://developer.apple.com/support/app-store/`. As of December 2017, iOS 11 is used by 59% of users, iOS 10 by 33%, and earlier versions by just 8%.

Visual Studio 2017

Other than for compiling XCode (which is restricted by licensing from Apple), Visual Studio 2017 has all you need to create Xamarin apps for the Android, iOS, and for Windows. You get project templates for Android apps, for iOS apps, and for cross-platform apps if you installed the Mobile Development with .NET workload. Visual Studio offers to install the Android SDKs, you can use Android and iPhone emulators, and you can have designers for Android XML (AXML) files and iOS storyboards.

Visual Studio for Mac

Visual Studio for Mac originated in Xamarin Studio that was used on the Mac to create Xamarin apps. Nowadays not only has the name changed but Visual Studio for Mac is a lot more. The editor from Visual Studio is now integrated, and you can also create ASP.NET Core web apps.

Visual Studio for Mac includes project templates to create iOS and Android apps. You cannot use Visual Studio for Mac to create Windows apps. Here, a Windows 10 system is needed with Visual Studio.

Visual Studio for Mac is like Visual Studio for managing the Android SDK versions and offers designers AXML files, as well as iOS storyboards.

Visual Studio App Center

Visual Studio App Center (`https://appcenter.ms`) was already mentioned with the Test Cloud for Android devices. The test cloud also supports iPhone and iPad devices. Using UI tests, you can automatically test your app on thousands of devices.

Testing is not the only feature of Visual Studio App Center. You can create an *automatic build* and run unit tests as the source code is checked into Visual Studio Team Services, GitHub, or several other code repositories.

You can use Visual Studio App Center as a distribution vehicle to distribute your apps to beta testers and get information about issues with the app.

Finally, you can get nice reports for the apps in production with app analytics, find out what your users are doing, discover where the app is crashing, and automatically file issues in your source code repository.

> **NOTE** *Analytics with Visual Studio App Center is covered in Chapter 29, "Tracing, Logging, and Analytics."*

ANDROID FOUNDATION

Before getting into Xamarin.Forms, it's good to know some foundation information about a platform. The first app is a Hello Android! App, which is created using the template Blank App (Android).

The first setting you should check is the Android Manifest, which you can access from the Project Properties on the Android Manifest tab (see Figure 37-4). Here, you need to define the minimum and target Android versions; this is like the Windows Runtime configurations in Chapter 33, "Windows Apps." Here you need to select the API level your app supports. Depending on the devices you want to support, you can use the available features.

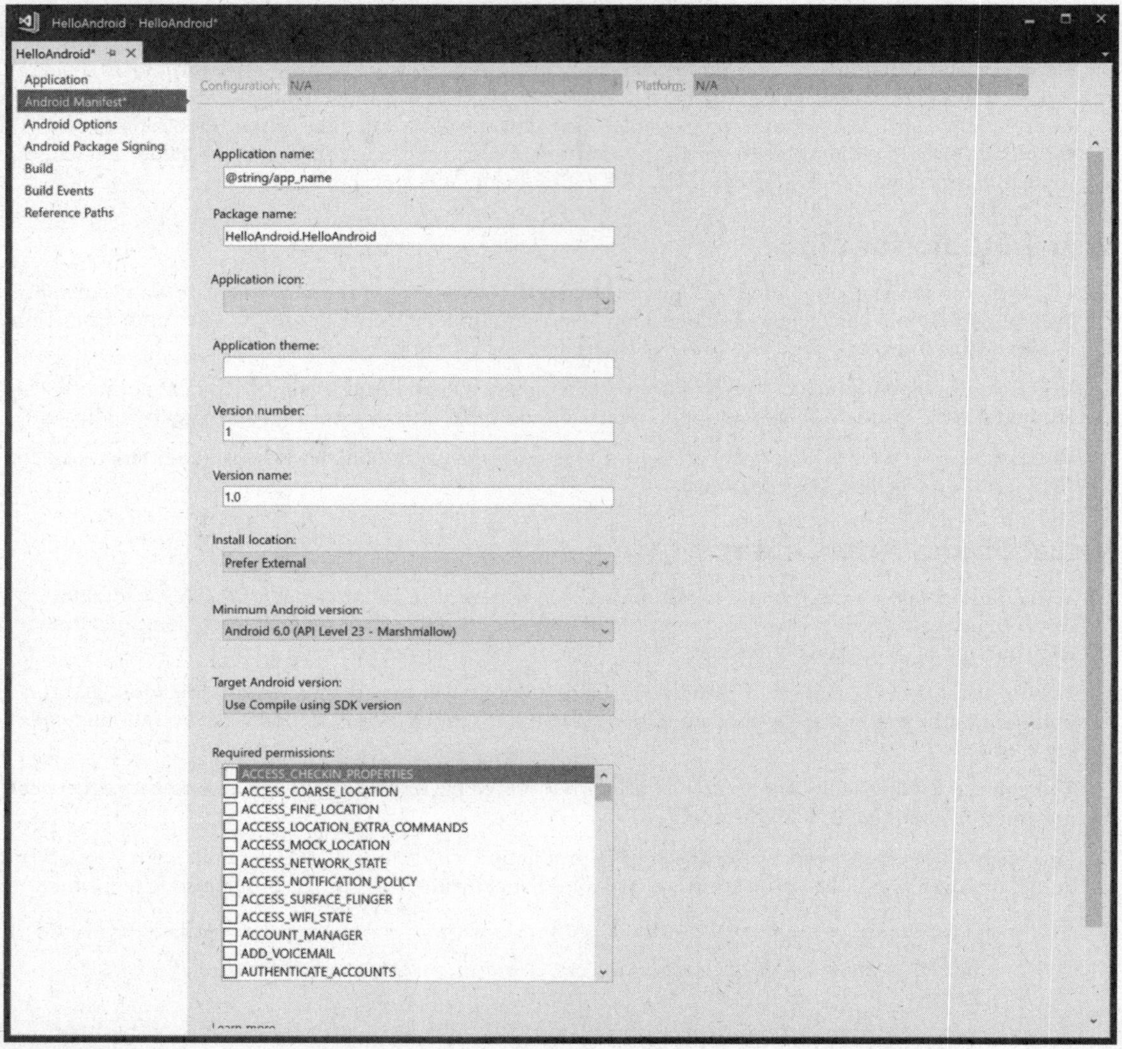

FIGURE 37-4

Activity

With Android, a user interface screen maps to an activity. Create an activity for every view. Android development makes use of the MVC (Model-View-Controller) pattern. The activity class is the *controller*. The code sample shows the MainActivity—the activity for the main view. Every activity derives from the Activity class or a class that itself derives from Activity. With this class, you can override lifecycle methods offered by the Activity base class. The OnCreate method is invoked when the activity is created. Invoking the method SetContentView defines the user interface that is defined for this activity. The UI is defined within resources, as covered in the next section (code file HelloAndroid/MainActivity.cs):

```
[Activity(Label = "HelloAndroid", MainLauncher = true)]
public class MainActivity : Activity
{
```

```
protected override void OnCreate(Bundle savedInstanceState)
{
    base.OnCreate(savedInstanceState);
    //...
    // Set our view from the "main" layout resource
    SetContentView(Resource.Layout.Main);
}
}
```

The activity defines the lifecycle of the Android app. Lifecycle methods of an activity are listed in the following table.

METHOD	DESCRIPTION
OnCreate	This method is invoked when an activity is created, with the main activity when the user starts the app. Views are created at this stage.
	The lifetime of the activity is defined between OnCreate and OnDestroy.
	This method receives a Bundle with the parameter. Bundles can be used to pass data between activities, and it's used to recover data after a restart. The method OnSaveInstanceState is invoked before the activity is put into the background state, so you can write the data with this method before recovering it in OnCreate.
	Create views, initialize variables, and bind data to lists at this stage.
OnStart	After OnCreate, OnStart is invoked. This method also is invoked when the activity is restarted after it was stopped. With a restart, first OnRestart is invoked before OnStart.
	The visible lifetime of the activity is defined between OnStart and OnStop.
	Set data you need before the activity becomes visible.
OnResume	The next method after OnStart is OnResume. After OnResume, the activity is in the running state.
	The foreground lifetime of the activity is defined between OnResume and OnPause.
	Here you can start animations, display alerts, listen for GPS updates, add event handlers to external events, which are tasks needed before the activity goes into the foreground.
OnPause	When another activity comes into the foreground, OnPause is invoked. If the user returns to the activity, and it is in the foreground again, the next method is OnResume.
	Release resources you allocated with OnResume. The implementation of this method should be fast, as the next activity for the user starts only when the OnPause method is completed.
OnStop	If the activity is completely hidden, OnStop is invoked. If the user navigates to the activity again, the next methods called are OnRestart and OnStart.
	Release resources you allocated with OnStart.
OnDestroy	The activity is destroyed by the system and no longer can use resources. Many apps don't override this method as cleaning up resources is already done in OnStop and OnPause.
	If you have a long-running resource, such as a background thread started in OnCreate, you should reset state here.
	This method is not guaranteed to be called. The activity can be killed by the user or the OS, and OnDestroy is not invoked.

Resources

In the Solution Explorer, you can see the Resources folder with several subfolders. The drawable folder is used to store images. The views are defined in the layout folder, and the values folder contains simple strings.

In the sample code, the strings resources are updated to contain a string for a button text, the app name, and a string that's identified by the name hello (code file HelloAndroid/Resources/values/Strings .xml):

```xml
<?xml version="1.0" encoding="utf-8"?>
<resources>
  <string name="main_button1_text">Click Me!</string>
  <string name="app_name">Hello Android</string>
  <string name="hello">Hello Android!</string>
  <string name="somedata_clickeditem_title">Clicked Item</string>
</resources>
```

Views are defined using AXML files, which have similarities to XAML files. The LinearLayout is a layout control that arranges its child elements. You can compare the LinearLayout to the StackPanel class; it has the same functionality. With the sample app, inside the layout a Button control is added. You can drag the Button control from the toolbox to the designer. The android prefix with the attributes is the alias for the namespace http://schemas.android.com/apk/res/android. With the Button, the text is set to the resource string main_button_text from the string resources, the width is set to match the width of the parent, and the height to wrap to a new line in case it doesn't fit in one line. Assigning the id to @+id/button1 creates a new ID with the name button1. @+id is the shortcut notation to create a new ID in the designer generated file Resource.Designer.cs to access the button (code file HelloAndroid/Resources/layout/Main.axml):

```xml
<?xml version="1.0" encoding="utf-8"?>
<LinearLayout xmlns:android="http://schemas.android.com/apk/res/android"
  android:orientation="vertical"
  android:layout_width="match_parent"
  android:layout_height="match_parent"
  android:minWidth="25px"
  android:minHeight="25px">
  <Button
    android:text="@string/main_button_text"
    android:layout_width="match_parent"
    android:layout_height="wrap_content"
    android:id="@+id/button1" />
</LinearLayout>
```

Within the activity, you can access the button control using the FindFyById method from the base class Activity, passing the ID that is referenced via Resource.Id.button1. With the code snippet, the button is retrieved for adding a Click event handler. The implementation of the handler shows a notification to the user (code file HelloAndroid/MainActivity.cs):

```csharp
protected override void OnCreate(Bundle savedInstanceState)
{
  base.OnCreate(savedInstanceState);

  SetContentView(Resource.Layout.Main);

  Button button1 = FindViewById<Button>(Resource.Id.button1);
  button1.Click += (sender, e) =>
    Toast.MakeText(ApplicationContext, "Hello Android!",
      ToastLength.Long).Show();
}
```

When you run the app in the simulator or on your physical device, the button displays, and you can click it to see a toast as shown in Figure 37-5.

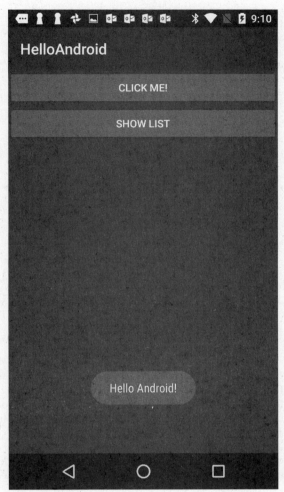

FIGURE 37-5

Displaying Lists

A common scenario is to navigate to pages, and to display lists. This is shown with the next enhancement of the app. For doing this, let's first create a model.

Defining a Model

The model is a simple class defining a few properties and overriding the `ToString` method (code file `HelloAndroid/Models/SomeData.cs`):

```
public class SomeData
{
  public int Number { get; set; }
  public string Text { get; set; }
  public override string ToString() => $"{Number} {Text}";
}
```

Using the ListActivity

Next, you create an activity. Instead of deriving the activity from the `Activity` base class, now you use the `ListActivity` base class. `ListActivity` defines virtual properties and methods useful to select items in lists. When the `SomeDataListActivity` is created, a collection with sample data is created and stored within the `_items` field. In the `OnCreate` method, also the `ListAdapter` property of the base class is assigned to a new instance of the `SomeDataListAdapter`. In the `MainActivity`, the user interface for the activity was defined by a resource using `SetContentView`. Here, instead an adapter is used to supply the user interface. The activity also defines the overridden method `OnListItemClick` to display the selected item (code file `HelloAndroid/SomeDataListActivity.cs`):

```
[Activity(Label = "SomeDataListActivity")]
public class SomeDataListActivity : ListActivity
{
  private IList<SomeData> _items;
  protected override void OnCreate(Bundle savedInstanceState)
  {
    base.OnCreate(savedInstanceState);

    _items = Enumerable.Range(0, 100)
      .Select(i => new SomeData { Number = i, Text = $"sample {i}" })
      .ToList();
    ListAdapter = new SomeDataListAdapter(this, _items);
  }

  protected override void OnListItemClick(ListView l, View v, int position,
    long id)
  {
    //... implementation of the OnListItemClick event handler
  }
}
```

Implementing an Adapter

The `SomeDataListAdapter` is used to define the UI for the `SomeDataListActivity`. The heart of this class is the overridden method `GetView` that needs to return the view for every item in the list. This method receives the parent `ViewGroup` where the view for the item will be displayed. The `LayoutInflater` inflates an AXML file into a view. You can create the view for the items within the resources. The code sample makes use of a predefined AXML file for Android. `Android.Resource.Layout.SimpleListItem1` returns an ID for a predefined AXML file. This layout defines a simple item using a `TextView` element. The `TextView` element is accessed by using the `FindViewById` where the `Text` property is assigned to information from the item (code file `HelloAndroid/SomeDataListAdapter.cs`):

```
public class SomeDataListAdapter : BaseAdapter
{
  private readonly Activity _activity;
  private readonly IList<SomeData> _items;

  public SomeDataListAdapter(Activity activity, IList<SomeData> items)
  {
    _activity = activity;
    _items = items;
  }

  public override Java.Lang.Object GetItem(int position) => position;
```

```
public override long GetItemId(int position) => position;

public override View GetView(int position, View convertView,
  ViewGroup parent)
{
  var view = convertView;
  if (view == null)
  {
    view = _activity.LayoutInflater
      .Inflate(Android.Resource.Layout.SimpleListItem1, null);
  }
  view.FindViewById<TextView>(Android.Resource.Id.Text1).Text =
    $"{_items[position].Number}: {_items[position].Text}";
  return view;
}

public override int Count => _items.Count;
}
```

> **NOTE** *To know how the* `SimpleListItem1` *and other predefined layouts are defined, check* `https://github.com/aosp-mirror/platform_frameworks_base/tree/master/core/res/res/layout.`

Navigation with Android

To navigate to the `SomeDataList` activity, with Android you need to start the activity passing the activity type. This is done from the `showlistButton` in the `MainActivity` (code file `HelloAndroid/MainActivity.cs`):

```
showlistButton.Click += (sender, e) =>
  StartActivity(typeof(SomeDataListActivity));
```

When you run the app, you can see the item list returned from the `SomeDataListAdapter` with the predefined `SimpleListItem1` in Figure 37-6.

Showing a Message

With the first button in the Android app, a Toast was shown after the button had been clicked. How can you display something like a `MessageDialog` from UWP? With Android, you have the `AlertDialog`. This dialog is used when you click on an item in the list.

Before you can use the dialog, you need to create it. For creation of the `AlertDialog`, the inner `Builder` class needs to be instantiated. Using `AlertDialog.Builder`, you can define the message to display using `SetMessage` and the title using `SetTitle`. To define what buttons should be shown, the `Builder` class defines methods such as `SetNeutralButton`, `SetPositiveButton`, and `SetNegativeButton`. You can even create a multiple-choice selection `SetMultiChoiceItems`. In the code snippet, the `SetNeutralButton` is set by using the predefined resource string `Android.Resource.String.Ok`. After the builder is configured, the `AlertDialog` is created from the `Create` method of the `Builder`. Finally, just the `Show` method needs to be invoked to display the dialog (code file `HelloAndroid/SomeDataListActivity.cs`):

```
protected override void OnListItemClick(ListView l, View v, int position,
  long id)
{
```

```
AlertDialog.Builder builder = new AlertDialog.Builder(this);
builder.SetMessage($"clicked {_items[position]}")
  .SetTitle(Resource.String.somedata_clickeditem_title);

builder.SetNeutralButton(Android.Resource.String.Ok, (sender, e) =>
{
  // user clicked the ok button
});
AlertDialog dialog = builder.Create();

dialog.Show();
}
```

When you run the app, you can see the AlertDialog as shown in Figure 37-7.

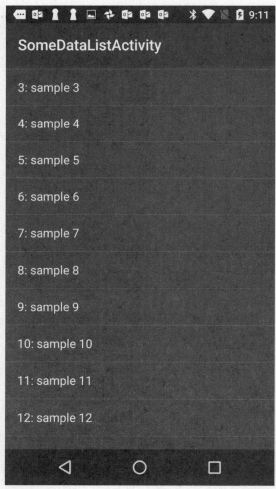

FIGURE 37-6

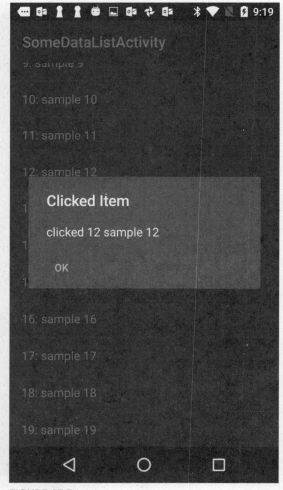

FIGURE 37-7

Building apps with Android offers some interesting aspects, but the development is very different to creating Windows apps. How does a similar scenario look like with the iPhone?

iOS FOUNDATION

Using Android.iOS, the app `HelloiOS` is created. To create and build this app, you need to have a Mac in place with Xcode installed, so the build process can use the Xcode engine. The app created is started with using the Single View App (iPhone) project template.

The generated file `Info.plist` contains information about the app that is like the `package.manifest` file you've seen with Windows apps (see Figure 37-8). Here, you can configure the deployment target to support—the iOS version you support with your app, add visual assets for icons, configure capabilities (e.g. when background functionality is needed), and configure document types that are used to start the app.

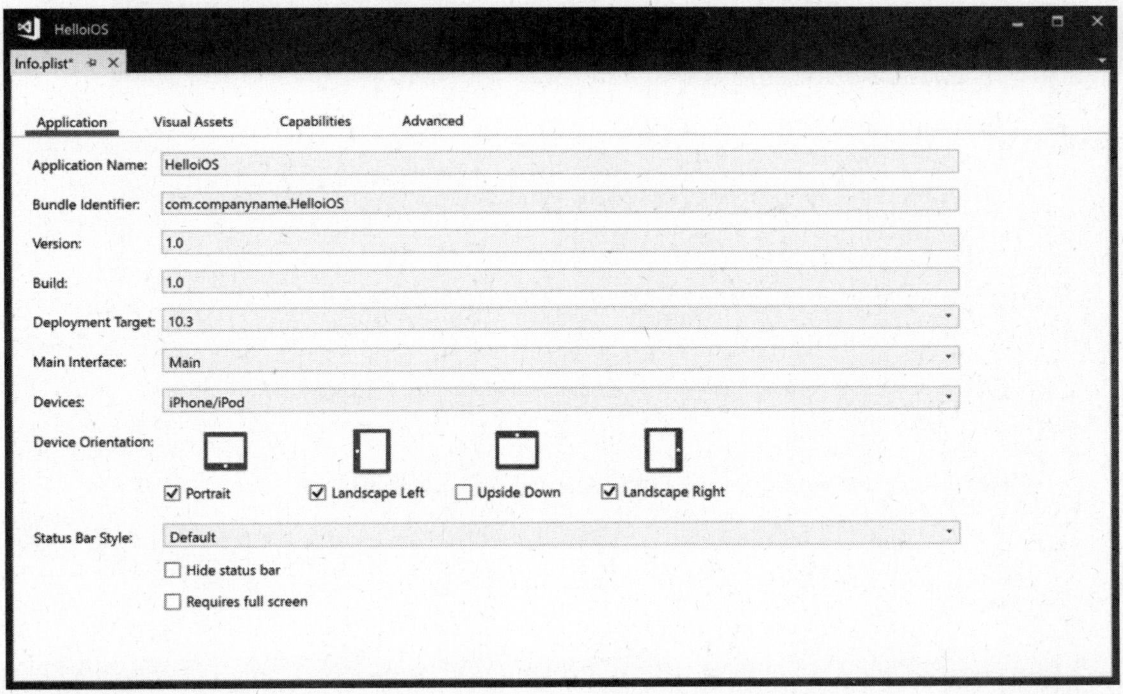

FIGURE 37-8

iOS App Structure

With the generated code you'll see a `Main` method as the entry point of the app. Invoking the static `Main` method of the `UIApplication` class, the message look is started to react to events. This requires the name of the application delegate that handles the events (code file `HelloiOS/Main.cs`):

```
public class Application
{
  static void Main(string[] args)
  {
    UIApplication.Main(args, null, "AppDelegate");
  }
}
```

The `AppDelegate` class defines the lifecycle of the app. You can implement functionality for initialization when the app starts before it can be used (`FinishedLaunching`), the app will be informed when it moves from the active to the inactive state (for example, a phone call arriving) with `OnResignActivation`, when the user moves another app to the front (`DidEnterBackground`) to save user data, when the app moves back to the foreground (`WillEnterForeground`), when the app gets activated (`OnActivated`) to restart paused tasks and refresh the user interface, and when the app will be terminated (`WillTerminate`) to save data (code file `HelloiOS/AppDelegate.cs`):

```
[Register("AppDelegate")]
public class AppDelegate : UIApplicationDelegate
{
  public override UIWindow Window
  {
    get;
    set;
  }

  public override bool FinishedLaunching(UIApplication application,
    NSDictionary launchOptions)
  {
    return true;
  }

  public override void OnResignActivation(UIApplication application)
  {
  }

  public override void DidEnterBackground(UIApplication application)
  {
  }

  public override void WillEnterForeground(UIApplication application)
  {
  }

  public override void OnActivated(UIApplication application)
  {
  }

  public override void WillTerminate(UIApplication application)
  {
  }
}
```

Storyboard

iOS apps are based on the MVC pattern as well. However, with iOS the user interface is organized around Storyboards. A Storyboard defines the flow of the user interaction with the views. With the Storyboard designer (see Figure 37-9), you can use the Toolbox to add controllers and controls to the storyboard (see Figure 37-10).

When you add controls to a view—for example, a `Button`—you can specify the properties (see Figure 37-11), the layout, and events (see Figure 37-12). Instead of assigning a `Click` event to a button, you can use Touch Down or Touch Up Inside. Touch Up Inside is fired when a touch event in the button ends within the button. Touch Up Outside is fired when a touch event inside the button ends outside of the button (for example, the user moves the finger to outside of the button). Touch Down is fired before the Touch In events and is always fired on a touch. For a typical click event, use Touch Up Inside.

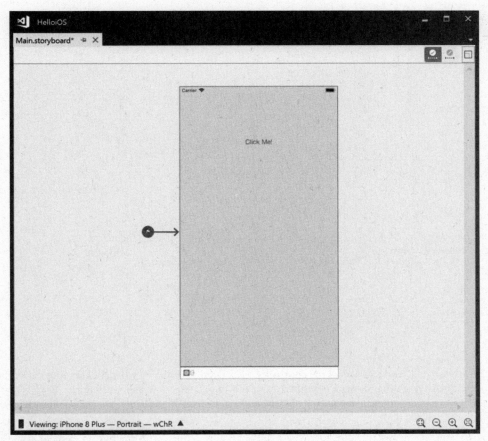

FIGURE 37-9

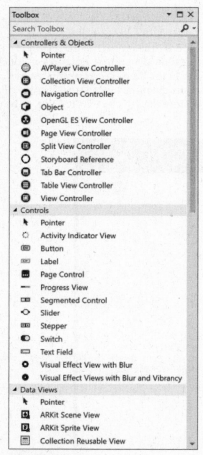

FIGURE 37-10

In the Storyboard designer, you can access the controller associated with the view by clicking an icon in the lower-left corner of the view; this shows the properties of the associated controller (see Figure 37-13). As you select the `ViewController`, you can see that the Is Initial View Controller setting is enabled. This setting makes this view the initial UI.

The Storyboard designer creates an XML file, where the `Button` is defined with the button element, and the click event with a connection and an action. The selector defined with the action defines a partial method in the designer-generated code file of the associated controller:

```
<connections>
  <action selector="OnButtonClick:" destination="BYZ-38-t0r" id="1110"
    eventType="touchUpInside"/>
</connections>
```

Controller

The controller class associated with the view of the storyboard derives from the base class `UIViewController`. The controller manages the interaction between the model and the views of the app.

The base class `UIViewController` manages the layout of the views, including sizing and responding to orientation changes. In this file you also implement the handlers to react on events from the UI elements as shown next (code file `HelloiOS/ViewController.cs`):

```
public partial class ViewController : UIViewController
{
    public ViewController(IntPtr handle) : base(handle)
    {
    }

    public override void ViewDidLoad()
    {
        base.ViewDidLoad();
    }

    public override void DidReceiveMemoryWarning()
    {
        base.DidReceiveMemoryWarning();
    }
    //...
}
```

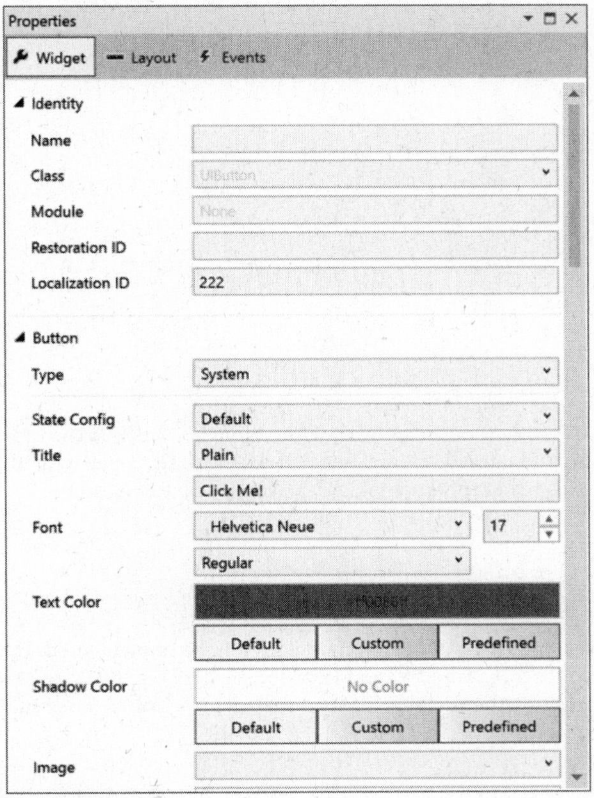

FIGURE 37-11

FIGURE 37-12

Showing a Message

With the button declaration in the Storyboard, the `OnButtonClick` was defined for the `touchUpInside` event. This defines the declaration of a partial method named `OnButtonClick` in the designer-generated file of the controller. The `Action` attribute maps this to the event (code file `HelloiOS/ViewController` `.designer.cs`):

```
[Action ("OnButtonClick:")]
[GeneratedCode ("iOS Designer", "1.0")]
partial void OnButtonClick (UIKit.UIButton sender);
```

In the custom controller implementation class, the `OnButtonClick` method can now be implemented. In the sample app, a new `UIAlertView` is created where the `Title` and `Message` properties are set. A Close button is added using the `AddButton` method. Finally, to show the dialog, the `Show` method is invoked (code file `HelloiOS/ViewController.cs`):

```
public partial class ViewController : UIViewController
{
  //...
```

```
partial void OnButtonClick(UIButton sender)
{
  var alert = new UIAlertView
  {
    Title = "Hello",
    Message = "Hello iOS!",
  };
  alert.AddButton("Close");
  alert.Clicked += (sender1, e) =>
  {
    // dialog closed
  };
  alert.Show();
}
}
```

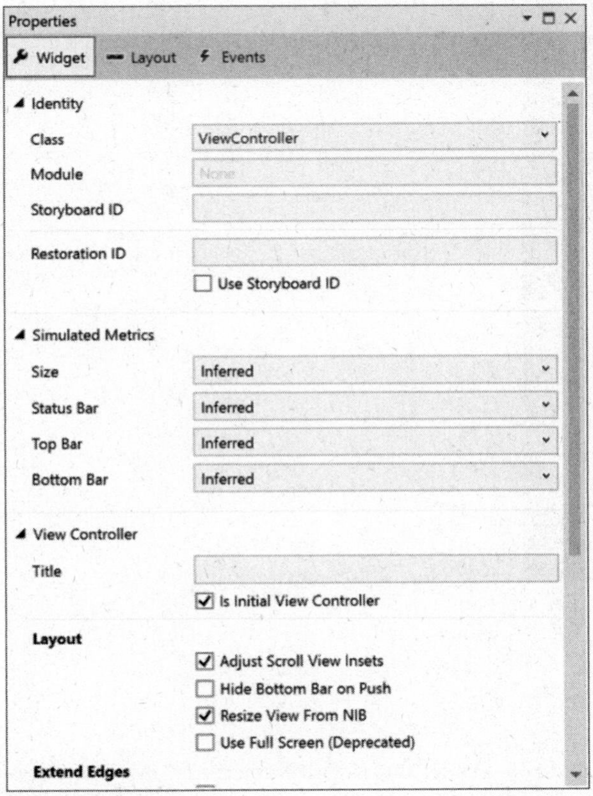

FIGURE 37-13

When you run the app in the simulator, you can see the button with the UIAlertView, as shown in Figure 37-14.

FIGURE 37-14

XAMARIN.FORMS APPLICATION

Now that you know some principles about Android and iOS, let's start with Xamarin.Forms. This project is named BooksAppX and uses the libraries for view-models and core features from Chapter 34, "Patterns with XAML Apps." The projects for these libraries is in the folder PatternsXamarinShared.

The Windows app project from Chapter 34 shows a list of books and detail information about a book. The same functionality will now be implemented—using the same libraries—using Xamarin.Forms.

To create the Xamarin.Forms project, the template Cross-Platform App (Xamarin.Forms) is a good starter. Using this project template, on Windows you can select three platforms, the UI technology, and the code sharing strategy, as shown in Figure 37-15.

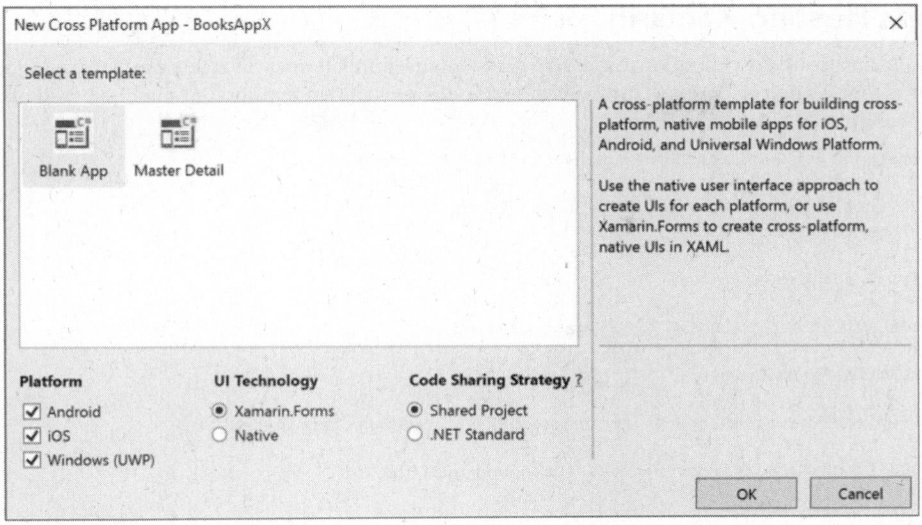

FIGURE 37-15

Cross-platform apps using Xamarin.Forms can be created for Android, iOS, and the Windows platform. At the time of this writing, already a preview of Xamarin.Forms for WPF is available, so Xamarin.Forms won't stop with these three platforms. The UI technology to select is either Xamarin.Forms or Native. When you select Native, native apps are created, and the implementations are like what you've seen before in the sections "Android Foundation" and "iOS Foundation." The user interfaces are not shared in this scenario. However, you can use common view-models and common services. Using Xamarin.Forms, the user interface is created using XAML—for all these platforms. This is the option that is from now on used in this chapter. With the Code Sharing Strategy, you can choose between a Shared Project and .NET Standard. With .NET Standard, a library containing the UI code is created that is shared between the platforms you select. When you select Shared Project, the source code is built into every platform app you select; a library isn't shared, but the source code is. With the sample project, two projects that are shared between the Patterns and the Xamarin chapter share a .NET Standard library, but the XAML code is shared with a shared project.

> **NOTE** *For more information on shared projects and .NET Standard, read Chapter 19, "Libraries, Assemblies, Packages, and NuGet."*

Templates you can choose when you're using the new Cross Platform App are Blank App and Master Detail app. Although the app will have some master-detail functionality, let's start with the blank, and implement the master-detail functionality with the help of the libraries created earlier.

When you create the project BooksAppX, four projects are created: three hosting projects for the Universal Windows Platform, iOS, and Android, and a shared project that contains the XAML files. As you've already created projects with these three platforms, the hosting code will be familiar. Let's get through the startup with these three technologies.

Windows Apps Hosting Xamarin

The generated `App` class looks very similar to the `App` class you used in Chapter 33 to create Windows apps. What's different is that Xamarin.Forms is now initialized in the overridden method `OnLaunched` (code file `BooksAppX/BooksAppX/UWP/App.xaml.cs`):

```
protected override void OnLaunched(LaunchActivatedEventArgs e)
{
  Frame rootFrame = Window.Current.Content as Frame;
  if (rootFrame == null)
  {
    rootFrame = new Frame();

    rootFrame.NavigationFailed += OnNavigationFailed;

    Xamarin.Forms.Forms.Init(e);

    if (e.PreviousExecutionState == ApplicationExecutionState.Terminated)
    {
      //TODO: Load state from previously suspended application
    }

    Window.Current.Content = rootFrame;
  }

  if (rootFrame.Content == null)
  {
    rootFrame.Navigate(typeof(MainPage), e.Arguments);
  }
  Window.Current.Activate();
}
```

The `MainPage` created from the `OnLaunched` method now is a class that derives from `Xamarin.Forms .Platform.UWP.WindowsPage`. This class hosts the Xamarin.Forms pages. The common code is loaded in the constructor of the `MainPage` class. `LoadApplication` is the start for Xamarin.Forms; it creates a new `App` class from the shared project, and it passes the instance to the `LoadApplication` method (code file `BooksAppX/BooksAppX/UWP/MainPage.xaml.cs`):

```
public MainPage()
{
  this.InitializeComponent();

  LoadApplication(new BooksAppX.App());
}
```

> **NOTE** *Don't be confused by two* `MainPage` *and two* `App` *classes in the UWP scenario. One* `App` *and* `MainPage` *class is in the UWP project. These classes are used only by the Windows app. The other* `App` *and* `MainPage` *classes are in the shared project. These classes are used by UWP, Android, and iOS apps. The namespace of these classes differs.*

Android Hosting Xamarin

With the Android project, you'll find the `MainActivity`. This activity now derives from the base class `Xamarin.Forms.Platform.Android.FormsAppCompatActivity`. The initialization of Xamarin.Forms and the instantiation of the common `App` class happens in the `OnCreate` method (code file `BooksAppX/ BooksAppX.Android/MainActivity.cs`):

```
[Activity(Label = "BooksAppX", Icon = "@drawable/icon",
  Theme = "@style/MainTheme", MainLauncher = true,
```

```
      ConfigurationChanges = ConfigChanges.ScreenSize | ConfigChanges.Orientation)]
  public class MainActivity :
    global::Xamarin.Forms.Platform.Android.FormsAppCompatActivity
  {
    protected override void OnCreate(Bundle bundle)
    {
      TabLayoutResource = Resource.Layout.Tabbar;
      ToolbarResource = Resource.Layout.Toolbar;

      base.OnCreate(bundle);

      global::Xamarin.Forms.Forms.Init(this, bundle);
      LoadApplication(new App());
    }
  }
}
```

iOS Hosting Xamarin

The iOS project hosting Xamarin.Forms contains the `Main` method with the invocation of `UIApplication` `.Main` passing the `AppDelegate` string, which is like what you've seen before with iOS. The implementation of the `AppDelegate` class is different. The class now derives from the base class `Xamarin.Forms.Platform` `.iOS.FormsApplicationDelegate`, and the implementation of the `FinishedLaunching` method initializes Xamarin.Forms and loads the app (code file `BooksAppX/BooksAppX.iOS/AppDelegate.cs`):

```
[Register("AppDelegate")]
public partial class AppDelegate :
  global::Xamarin.Forms.Platform.iOS.FormsApplicationDelegate
{
  public override bool FinishedLaunching(UIApplication app,
    NSDictionary options)
  {
    global::Xamarin.Forms.Forms.Init();
    LoadApplication(new App());

    return base.FinishedLaunching(app, options);
  }
}
```

Starting from here, the common coding of the UI can begin.

Shared Project

The shared project contains the common `App` class with overridable methods `OnStart`, `OnSleep`, and `OnResume`. This maps to the lifecycle with Android, iOS, and Windows systems. In the constructor, the `MainPage` is created (code file `BooksAppX/BooksAppX/App.xaml.cs`):

```
public partial class App : Application
{
  public App()
  {
    InitializeComponent();
    MainPage = new BooksAppX.MainPage();
  }

  protected override void OnStart()
  {
  }
  protected override void OnSleep()
  {
  }
  protected override void OnResume()
  {
  }
}
```

The XAML content of the `MainPage` looks something like you know it from Windows apps, but it's also different. There are different XAML elements used, such as the `ContentPage` and the `Label`. These are defined with Xamarin.Forms and are available on all the Xamarin.Forms platforms:

```
<?xml version="1.0" encoding="utf-8" ?>
<ContentPage xmlns="http://xamarin.com/schemas/2014/forms"
  xmlns:x="http://schemas.microsoft.com/winfx/2009/xaml"
  xmlns:local="clr-namespace:BooksAppX"
  x:Class="BooksAppX.MainPage">
  <Label Text="Welcome to Xamarin.Forms!"
    VerticalOptions="Center"
    HorizontalOptions="Center" />
</ContentPage>
```

> **NOTE** *The* `MainPage.xaml` *shown here that contains a* `ContentPage` *is created when a new* `Xamarin.Forms` *project is created. With the downloadable source code, the* `MainPage.xaml` *contains a* `TabbedPage` *as explained later in the section "Pages."*

USING THE COMMON LIBRARIES

To use the .NET Standard libraries `BooksLib` and `Framework` that you created in Chapter 34, the projects from the folder `PatternsXamarinShared` are added to the Xamarin.Forms solution. These projects need to be referenced from each of the Xamarin projects.

The NuGet packages `Microsoft.Extensions.DependencyInjection` and `Microsoft.Extensions.Configuration` need to be added as well. The `ILogger` interface is used by services and view-models.

Xamarin includes a dependency injection container as well; it's accessible from the `DependencyService` class. `DependencyService.Register` registers a service, whereas `DependencyService.Get` returns a service from the container. However, because the UWP project as well as many other chapters make use of the .NET Core DI container `Microsoft.Extensions.DependencyInjection`, it is used with the `BooksAppX` as well.

The dependency injection container can be instantiated, and services can be registered in the shared `App` class. For the services that had UWP-specific implementations, now Xamarin-specific implementations need to be done. The platform-specific services that need a Xamarin implementation are `IMessageService` to display a message dialog and `INavigationService` to navigate between pages (code file `BooksAppX/BooksAppX/App.xaml.cs`):

```
public partial class App : Application
{
  public App()
  {
    InitializeComponent();
    RegisterServices();

    MainPage = new BooksAppX.Views.MainPage();
  }
  //...

  private void RegisterServices()
  {
    var services = new ServiceCollection();
    services.AddSingleton<IBooksRepository, BooksSampleRepository>();
    services.AddSingleton<IItemsService<Book>, BooksService>();
```

```
        services.AddTransient<BooksViewModel>();
        services.AddTransient<BookDetailViewModel>();
        services.AddSingleton<IMessageService, XamarinMessageService>();
        services.AddSingleton<INavigationService, XamarinNavigationService>();
        services.AddSingleton<XamarinInitializeNavigationService>();
        services.AddLogging();
        AppServices = services.BuildServiceProvider();
    }

    public IServiceProvider AppServices { get; private set; }
}
```

The implementations for the `IMessageService` and the `INavigationService` will be discussed later in the section "Navigation."

CONTROL HIERARCHY

Chapter 33 covers the main hierarchy of Windows app controls. Xamarin.Forms has a similar hierarchy, but it's different enough to merit discussion here. Also, the controls have different names.

Let's get into the most important classes in the hierarchy with Xamarin.Forms.

➤ **BindableObject**—This is the base class for the Xamarin.Forms controls. This class implements the interface `INotifyPropertyChanged`. You can't find this class with UWP, but you've seen a custom implementation with the `BindableBase` class. `BindableObject` also implements the interface `IDynamicResourceHandler`. This interface is used by platform renderers.

➤ **Element**—The `Element` class is used as base class for all elements in the Forms hierarchy. This class defines methods and properties to iterate through the tree, and it implements functionality for platform renderers.

➤ **Cell**—The `Cell` class derives from `Element`. Cells can be added into the `ListView` and `TableView` classes. Unlike what you can do with UWP, you can't add any XAML element into a `ListView`. With Xamarin.Forms only classes that derive from `Cell` can be added.

➤ **VisualElement**—`VisualElement` derives from `Element` and is the base class for all elements that have a visual appearance. With UWP you have `Height` and `Width` properties that define the desired size and is arranged based on the container arrangements. With Xamarin.Forms, the `Height` and `Width` properties are read-only and are used like `ActualHeight` and `ActualWidth` with UWP. `HeightRequest` and `WidthRequest` with Xamarin.Forms are the `Height` and `Width` variants of UWP. With the `VisualElement` class you also have a `Style` property, you can define scale, rotation, and opacity, and you can set the element to be enabled and visible with `IsEnabled` and `IsVisible`.

➤ **Page**—The `Page` class derives from `VisualElement` and is the base class for all pages. This class defines a title (`Title` property), toolbars (`ToolbarItems`), an icon (`Icon`). With the method `DisplayAlert` you can show a dialog with accept and cancel buttons.

➤ **View**—The `View` class derives from `VisualElement` and is the base class for nearly all controls. This class defines horizontal and vertical options to define how the element should be used in the layout as well as a `Margin` property to define the margin of the view, and gesture recognizers.

➤ **ItemsView**—`ItemsView` derives from `View` and can be compared to the UWP `ItemsControl` class. `ItemsView` is the base class for `ListView` and defines `ItemsSource` and `ItemTemplate` properties.

➤ **InputView**—`InputView` derives from `View` and is the base class to allow keyboard input. This class has a `Keyboard` property.

➤ **Layout**—The `Layout` class derives from `View` as well and allows the `Layout`-derived classes to position its child elements. With UWP, this is the `Panel` class.

Throughout the next sections, I discuss many of these controls and categories.

PAGES

To create the user interface, let's start with `MainPage`. The Windows app uses the `NavigationView` for the main page. This control is not available with Xamarin.Forms. Remember, Xamarin.Forms only offers controls that can be mapped to all platforms.

One page type available is the `TabbedPage`. With UWP, the `TabbedPage` becomes a `Pivot` control, and with iOS it's a `UiTabBarController`. The `TabbedPage` contains the `AboutPage`, which itself is a `ContentPage`, and a `NavigationPage`. The `NavigationPage` is the equivalent of a `Frame` with Windows apps. The content of the `NavigationPage` will be replaced when navigating (code file `BooksAppX/BooksAppX/Views/MainPage.xaml`):

```xml
<?xml version="1.0" encoding="utf-8" ?>
<TabbedPage xmlns="http://xamarin.com/schemas/2014/forms"
  xmlns:x="http://schemas.microsoft.com/winfx/2009/xaml"
  x:Class="BooksAppX.Views.MainPage">
  <TabbedPage.Children>
    <NavigationPage Title="Books">
      <NavigationPage.Icon>
        <OnPlatform x:TypeArguments="FileImageSource">
          <On Platform="iOS" Value="tab_feed.png"/>
        </OnPlatform>
      </NavigationPage.Icon>
      <x:Arguments>
        <views:BooksPage x:Name="booksPage" />
      </x:Arguments>
    </NavigationPage>
    <views:AboutPage Title="About" />
  </TabbedPage.Children>
</TabbedPage>
```

The other pages of the app—the `BooksPage` and `BooksDetailPage`—use the simple `ContentPage` page. The `ContentPage` can include one content.

The pages available with Xamarin.Forms are described in the following table.

XAMARIN.FORMS PAGE CLASS	UWP CLASS	DESCRIPTION
TabbedPage	Pivot	The `TabbedPage` offers multiple tabs to navigate between pages. This is a commonly used user interface.
NavigationPage	Frame	The `NavigationPage` offers navigation functionality like the UWP `Frame` class. The Xamarin.Forms `Frame` class can be compared to the UWP `Border` class.
ContentPage	N/A	The `ContentPage` derives from `TemplatedPage`, which itself derives from `Page`. With a `TemplatedPage`, you can assign the `ControlTemplate` property to define the content. The `ContentPage` can have only one content.
MasterDetailPage	N/A	The `MasterDetailPage` shows a list and details. Different pages can be used for the master and the detail part.
CarouselPage	FlipView	`CarouselPage` derives from `MultiPage`. This page allows the user to swipe through multiple pages. This functionality is common with UWP, but not so with Android and iOS.

NAVIGATION

The root page of the app includes the TabbedPage, and this itself includes the NavigationPage. The NavigationPage defines the Navigation property that returns an object that initializes the INavigation interface. With this, you can use the method PushAsync to navigate to another page, and the method PopAsync to go back.

With the .NET Standard Library "Framework," the INavigationService was defined with these methods:

```
public interface INavigationService
{
  Task NavigateToAsync(string page);
  Task GoBackAsync();
  string CurrentPage { get; }
}
```

Now a specific implementation for Xamarin.Forms is needed. This initialization uses the INavigation interface for the navigation (code file BooksAppx/Services/XamarinNavigationService.cs):

```
public class XamarinNavigationService : INavigationService
{
  private Dictionary<string, Func<Page>> _pages =
    new Dictionary<string, Func<Page>>
  {
    [PageNames.BookDetailPage] = () => new BookDetailPage()
  };

  private INavigation _navigation;
  private INavigation Navigation
  {
    get => _navigation ?? (_navigation = _initializeNavigation.Navigation);
  }

  public string CurrentPage => throw new NotImplementedException();

  private readonly XamarinInitializeNavigationService _initializeNavigation;

  public XamarinNavigationService(
    XamarinInitializeNavigationService initializeNavigation)
  {
    _initializeNavigation = initializeNavigation;
  }

  public Task GoBackAsync() => Navigation.PopAsync();

  public Task NavigateToAsync(string pagename) =>
    Navigation.PushAsync(_pages[pagename]());
}
```

Now you need XamarinInitializeNavigationService for the initialization. This class just defines the SetNavigation method and the Navigation property that's used by the XamarinNavigationService class (code file BooksAppX/Services/XamarinInitializeNavigationService.cs):

```
public class XamarinInitializeNavigationService
{
  public void SetNavigation(INavigation navigation) =>
    _navigation = navigation;

  private INavigation _navigation;
  public INavigation Navigation => _navigation ??
    throw new ArgumentException("navigation not initialized");
}
```

Now you need to set the `Navigation` property from a page where the `NavigationPage` is available—the code-behind file of the `MainPage` (code file `BooksAppX/Views/MainPage.xaml.cs`):

```
[XamlCompilation(XamlCompilationOptions.Compile)]
public partial class MainPage : TabbedPage
{
  public MainPage ()
  {
    InitializeComponent();

    (Application.Current as App).AppServices
      .GetService<XamarinInitializeNavigationService>()
      .SetNavigation(navigationPage.Navigation);
  }
}
```

LAYOUT

The About page uses the `Grid` and `StackLayout` controls to arrange its children. The `Grid` control allows defining rows and columns—as you do with the UWP Grid control—with auto, star, and fixed sizing (code file `BooksAppX/Views/AboutPage.xaml`):

```
<?xml version="1.0" encoding="utf-8" ?>
<ContentPage xmlns="http://xamarin.com/schemas/2014/forms"
  xmlns:x="http://schemas.microsoft.com/winfx/2009/xaml"
  x:Class="BooksAppX.Views.AboutPage">
  <Grid>
    <Grid.RowDefinitions>
      <RowDefinition Height="Auto" />
      <RowDefinition Height="*" />
    </Grid.RowDefinitions>
    <StackLayout BackgroundColor="{StaticResource Accent}"
      VerticalOptions="FillAndExpand" HorizontalOptions="Fill">
      <StackLayout Orientation="Horizontal" HorizontalOptions="Center"
        VerticalOptions="Center">
        <ContentView Padding="0,40,0,40" VerticalOptions="FillAndExpand">
          <Image Source="xamarin_logo.png" VerticalOptions="Center"
            HeightRequest="64">
            <Image.Source>
              <OnPlatform x:TypeArguments="ImageSource">
                <On Platform="UWP" Value="Assets/xamarin_logo.png" />
              </OnPlatform>
            </Image.Source>
          </Image>
        </ContentView>
      </StackLayout>
    </StackLayout>
    <ScrollView Grid.Row="1">
      <StackLayout Orientation="Vertical" Padding="16,40,16,40" Spacing="10">
        <Label FontSize="22">
          <Label.FormattedText>
            <FormattedString>
              <FormattedString.Spans>
                <Span Text="AppName" FontAttributes="Bold" FontSize="22" />
                <Span Text=" " />
                <Span Text="1.0"
                  ForegroundColor="{StaticResource LightTextColor}" />
              </FormattedString.Spans>
            </FormattedString>
          </Label.FormattedText>
        </Label>
```

```
<Label>
  <Label.FormattedText>
    <FormattedString>
      <FormattedString.Spans>
        <Span Text="This is a sample app for " />
        <Span Text="Professional C# 7 and .NET Core 2.0"
          FontAttributes="Bold" />
        <Span Text="." />
      </FormattedString.Spans>
    </FormattedString>
  </Label.FormattedText>
</Label>
<Label>
  <Label.FormattedText>
    <FormattedString>
      <FormattedString.Spans>
        <Span Text="It shares code with" />
        <Span Text=" " />
        <Span Text="iOS, Android, and Windows" FontAttributes="Bold" />
        <Span Text="." />
      </FormattedString.Spans>
    </FormattedString>
  </Label.FormattedText>
</Label>
<Button Margin="0,10,0,0" Text="Learn more" Command="{Binding
  ViewModel.OpenWebCommand, Mode=OneWay}"
  BackgroundColor="{StaticResource Primary}" TextColor="White" />
        </StackLayout>
      </ScrollView>
    </Grid>
  </ContentPage>
```

The following table lists the layout controls from Xamarin.Forms, and how they compare to the Windows panel controls.

XAMARIN.FORMS CONTROL	UWP CONTROL	DESCRIPTION
Grid	Grid	Organizes the content in rows and columns, using star, auto, and fixed sizing
StackLayout	StackPanel	Organizes children one after the other—horizontally or vertically
AbsoluteLayout	Canvas	Positions child elements with absolute coordinates using the attached properties AbsoluteLayout.LayoutBounds and AbsoluteLayout.LayoutFlags
RelativeLayout	RelativePanel	Arranges controls in relation to other controls

The About page has some other interesting aspects. Using the OnPlatform element, you can define different XAML elements and properties based on platforms. With the Image element, the Source property is set to a PNG file. The file is valid for Android and iOS, but with Windows the file is stored in the Assets folder. Setting the Source property differently just for UWP is defined by the OnPlatform element:

```
<Image Source="xamarin_logo.png" VerticalOptions="Center"
  HeightRequest="64">
  <Image.Source>
    <OnPlatform x:TypeArguments="ImageSource">
      <On Platform="UWP" Value="Assets/xamarin_logo.png" />
```

```
      </OnPlatform>
    </Image.Source>
  </Image>
```

Another interesting part is the `Label` element. Like the `TextBlock` from UWP, the `Label` can not only contain simple text but also text formatted with different fonts and colors. See Chapter 36, "Advanced Windows," for more information about text formats with the `TextBlock`. Using different text formats with the `Label`, the `FormattedText` property needs to be set to a `FormattedString`:

```
<Label>
  <Label.FormattedText>
    <FormattedString>
      <FormattedString.Spans>
        <Span Text="This is a sample app for " />
        <Span Text="Professional C# 7 and .NET Core 2.0"
          FontAttributes="Bold" />
        <Span Text="." />
      </FormattedString.Spans>
    </FormattedString>
  </Label.FormattedText>
</Label>
```

VIEWS

Let's get into some of the view types and compare them to controls you already know, as shown in the following table.

XAMARIN.FORMS CONTROL	UWP CONTROL	DESCRIPTION
Button	Button	The `Button` reacts to touch events and is like the UWP `Button`. However, the `Button` can't contain any content—only text.
Label	TextBlock	The `Label` can not only contain text like the `TextBlock`, but also formatted text as you've already seen in the previous section.
Editor Entry	TextBox	Unlike to UWP, Xamarin.Forms has different controls for multiline editing and single-line editing. To edit only one line, you use the `Entry` class. Multiple lines are supported with `Editor`.
SearchBar	AutoSuggestBox	The `SearchBar` is rendered with UWP using the `AutoSuggestBox`.
Stepper	N/A	With UWP, there's no `Stepper` control equivalent. With Xamarin.Forms, this is implemented using a user control and two buttons.
ListView	ListView	Xamarin.Forms defines a `ListView` with similar functionality as the UWP `ListView` to display a list of items using an `ItemTemplate`.
ProgressBar	ProgressBar	Xamarin.Forms defines the `ProgressBar` to show progress information, which is; this is like UWP.
Switch	ToggleSwitch	The `Switch` class is like the `ToggleSwitch` you know from UWP.

> **NOTE** *Xamarin.Forms and UWP have many similarities, but also many differences with the names of the classes and the property and method names. As there is the .NET Standard, now a XAML Standard is in the works:* `https://github.com/Microsoft/xaml-standard`. *You need to check the issues to see actual progress. At the time of this writing, for Xamarin.Forms a preview package is available that allows using the XAML Standard with the XAML files. With this, XAML code is translated from the XAML Standard to the Xamarin.Forms controls. The Xamarin controls themselves don't change with the XAML Standard, but you'll get the same XAML syntax.*

DATA BINDING

Data binding with Xamarin.Forms is done using a markup extension. The `x:Bind` markup extension is not available, but you can use the `Binding` markup extension that can also be used with UWP. Be aware that the default modes are different, and the modes you can use. Xamarin.Forms doesn't support `OneTime`, but `OneWay`, `TwoWay`, and `OneWayToSource`. `OneWayToSource` is not available with UWP. This mode binds the data from the source to the target (the UI element) but doesn't work the other way around. The following code snippet binds the `Text` and `IsEnabled` properties of the `Entry` control (code file `BooksAppX/Views/BookDetailPage.xaml`):

```xml
<ContentPage.Content>
  <StackLayout Spacing="20" Padding="15">
    <Label Text="Id:" FontSize="Medium" />
    <Entry IsEnabled="False"
      Text="{Binding ViewModel.EditItem.BookId, Mode=OneWay}" />
    <Label Text="Title:" FontSize="Medium" />
    <Entry IsEnabled="{Binding ViewModel.IsEditMode, Mode=OneWay}"
      Text="{Binding ViewModel.EditItem.Title, Mode=TwoWay}"
      FontSize="Small" />
    <Label Text="Publisher:" FontSize="Medium" />
    <Entry IsEnabled="{Binding ViewModel.IsEditMode, Mode=OneWay}"
      Text="{Binding ViewModel.EditItem.Publisher, Mode=TwoWay}"
      FontSize="Small" />
  </StackLayout>
</ContentPage.Content>
```

Instead of assigning the `DataContext` to activate the binding, the property has the name `BindingContext` (code file `BooksAppX/Views/BookDetailPage.xaml.cs`):

```csharp
[XamlCompilation(XamlCompilationOptions.Compile)]
public partial class BookDetailPage : ContentPage
{
  public BookDetailPage()
  {
    InitializeComponent();
    BindingContext = this;
  }

  public BookDetailViewModel ViewModel { get; } =
    (Application.Current as App).AppServices.GetService<BookDetailViewModel>();
}
```

COMMANDS

Like UWP, commands with Xamarin.Forms implement the `ICommand` interface. Xamarin.Forms already includes an implementation with the `Command` class. The `Command` class has an implementation like the `RelayCommand` implemented in the Framework library. The `Command` is used in the `AboutViewModel` (code file `BooksAppX/ViewModels/AboutViewModel.cs`):

```
public class AboutViewModel
{
  public AboutViewModel()
  {
    OpenWebCommand = new Command(() =>
      Device.OpenUri(new Uri("https://csharp.christiannagel.com")));
  }

  public ICommand OpenWebCommand { get; }
}
```

The `Command` property of the `Button` class is assigned via data binding (code file `BooksAppX/Views/AboutPage.xaml`):

```
<Button Margin="0,10,0,0" Text="Learn more"
  Command="{Binding ViewModel.OpenWebCommand, Mode=OneWay}"
  BackgroundColor="{StaticResource Primary}" TextColor="White" />
```

Xamarin.Forms also supports `ToolBarItem` controls that can be assigned to the `ToolBarItems` property of the `ContentPage` . These commands are bound to the commands defined in the view-models of the `BooksLib` library (code file `BooksAppX/Views/BooksPage.xaml`):

```
<ContentPage.ToolbarItems>
  <ToolbarItem Text="Refresh"
    Command="{Binding ViewModel.RefreshCommand, Mode=OneWay}" />
  <ToolbarItem Text="Add Book"
    Command="{Binding ViewModel.AddCommand, Mode=OneWay}" />
</ContentPage.ToolbarItems>
```

LISTVIEW AND VIEWCELL

The `ListView` control is used to display a list of items. With the sample app, the `ItemsSource` property is bound to the `Items` property of the view-model. For a display, a `DataTemplate` is assigned to the `ItemTemplate` property. This looks very similar to UWP, just with the difference that the `DataTemplate` for the items in the `ListView` can only contain `Cell`-derived classes. Here, a `ViewCell` is used, which allows using other elements such as the `StackLayout` and the `Label` controls (code file `BooksAppX/Views/BooksPage.xaml`):

```
<ListView x:Name="BooksListView"
  ItemsSource="{Binding ViewModel.Items}"
  VerticalOptions="FillAndExpand"
  HasUnevenRows="true"
  RefreshCommand="{Binding ViewModel.RefreshCommand}"
  IsPullToRefreshEnabled="true"
  IsRefreshing="{Binding IsBusy, Mode=OneWay}"
  CachingStrategy="RecycleElement"
  SelectedItem="{Binding ViewModel.SelectedItem, Mode=TwoWay}">
```

```
<ListView.ItemTemplate>
  <DataTemplate>
    <ViewCell>
      <StackLayout Padding="10">
        <Label Text="{Binding Title}"
          LineBreakMode="NoWrap"
          Style="{DynamicResource ListItemTextStyle}"
          FontSize="16" />
      </StackLayout>
    </ViewCell>
  </DataTemplate>
</ListView.ItemTemplate>
</ListView>
```

Other `Cell`-derived classes already contain predefined functionality where you don't need to add `Entry` or `Label` controls. The following table lists the `Cell`-derived classes.

CELL	DESCRIPTION
EntryCell	A cell that allows editing one line like the `Entry` control
SwitchCell	A switch with a label and a switch
TextCell	Primary and secondary text
ImageCell	A cell with an image
ViewCell	Developer-defined view as shown with the `BooksPage` sample

> **NOTE** *You can see what the running app looks like in screen shots from Windows, iOS, and Android devices, which are on the book's GitHub site at https://github.com/ ProfessionalCSharp/ProfessionalCSharp7/blob/master/Xamarin/Readme.md.*

SUMMARY

This chapter gave you an introduction to developing mobile apps with Xamarin. You've seen the different aspects of Android and iPhone, and how to start developing apps with Xamarin.Android and Xamarin.iOS.

The focus of this chapter was on Xamarin.Forms, and how it offers the same functionality as UWP, and what's different. While the element names and properties are different to UWP, the functionality is not that different—and you can implement XAML code just once and get apps for Windows, iOS, and Android.

The complete functionality of the app implemented in view-models and services is shared between a native UWP app and Xamarin.Forms. With Xamarin.Forms it was just necessary to define the small layer on top for the user interface.

INDEX

T